CARSON CITY LIBRARY
3 1472 70037 3180
S0-AVV-447

AN

Ref 493.1 BUD 1978 v.1

EGYPTIAN HIEROGLYPHIC DICTIONARY.

WITH AN INDEX OF ENGLISH WORDS, KING LIST AND GEOGRAPHICAL LIST WITH INDEXES, LIST OF HIEROGLYPHIC CHARACTERS, COPTIC AND SEMITIC ALPHABETS, ETC.

IN TWO VOLUMES
VOL. I

By Sir E. A. WALLIS BUDGE, Knt., F.S.A.,

M.A. and Litt.D., Cambridge; M.A. and D.Litt., Oxford; D.Lit., Durham;
sometime scholar of Christ's College, Cambridge, and Tyrwhitt Hebrew Scholar;
keeper of the Egyptian and Assyrian antiquities, British Museum.

DOVER PUBLICATIONS, INC.
NEW YORK

CARSON CITY LIBRARY
900 N. ROOP STREET
CARSON CITY, NV 89701

Published in Canada by General Publishing Company, Ltd., 30 Lesmill Road, Don Mills, Toronto, Ontario.

Published in the United Kingdom by Constable and Company, Ltd.

This Dover edition, first published in 1978, is a republication of the work originally published in two volumes by John Murray, London, in 1920. The present edition differs in the following ways: the volumes are divided differently; the originally appended List of Egyptian Hieroglyphic Characters in the Fount of Messrs. Harrison and Sons (a printer's catalogue) is here omitted; the dedication page is reproduced in black and white rather than in color; and a specially prepared new text, "On the Arrangement of Words in This Dictionary," has been added.

International Standard Book Number: 0-486-23615-3
Library of Congress Catalog Card Number: 77-90344

Manufactured in the United States of America
Dover Publications, Inc.
180 Varick Street
New York, N.Y. 10014

ON THE ARRANGEMENT OF WORDS IN THIS DICTIONARY

Dr. Budge's transliterations of Egyptian words are arranged basically according to the following values assigned to the Egyptian letters or phonetic symbols:

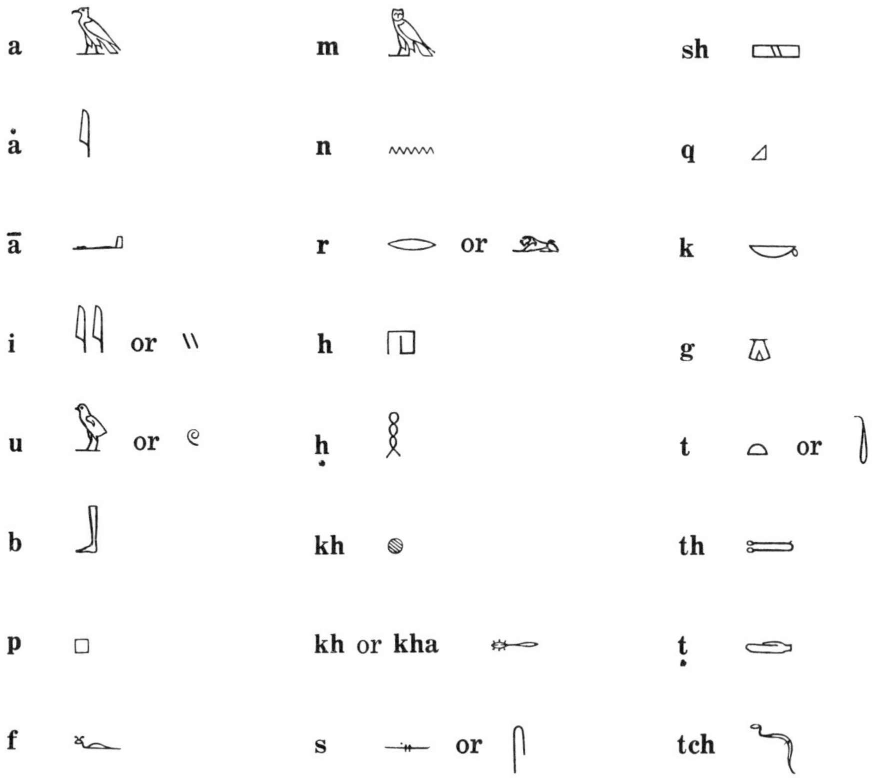

It should be noted, however, that this is not a complete explanation for the order of words. The following other factors should be noted: (1) In many words hieroglyphic symbols appear. These are transliterated according to the tables given on pages xcvii through cxlvii, and are then alphabetized along with renderings from the phonetic symbols. (2) The helping vowel "e" (often of indeterminate phonetic value) usually is not indicated in the Egyptian writing system and does not affect alphabetization in such cases. Thus **temi** will be placed as if spelled **tmi**, **seb** as if **sb**. In other instances, however, particularly in the **kha** series, words containing the letter "e" are considered to form a separate alphabetic series. (3) In accordance with the older system of forming language dictionaries, words that are related by derivation or original spelling or other factors are often grouped together, after the base word, with the result that a perfect alphabetic sequence may be broken. (4) It should be remembered that Ancient Egyptian was neither perfectly alphabetical nor completely consistent in writing.

For these reasons the reader is recommended to browse through each major section until he becomes familiar with Dr. Budge's practice.

DOVER PUBLICATIONS, INC.

CONTENTS.

THIS BOOK

IS

DEDICATED TO

THE MEMORY OF

SAMUEL BIRCH,

AUTHOR OF THE

FIRST EGYPTIAN DICTIONARY

ARRANGED ALPHABETICALLY.

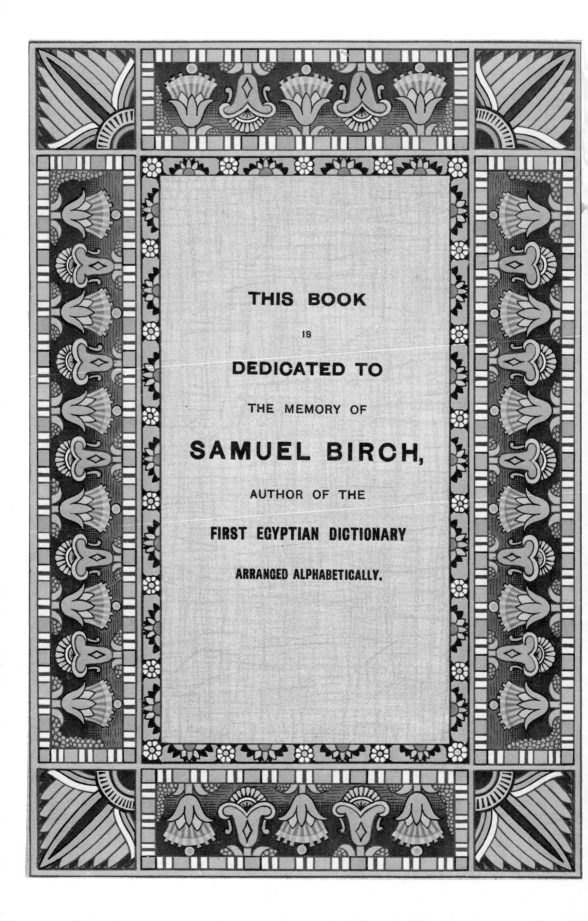

INTRODUCTION.

It may be taken for granted that, from the time when Åkerblad, Young and Champollion le Jeune laid the foundation of the science of Egyptology in the first quarter of the nineteenth century down to the present day, every serious student of Egyptian texts, whether hieroglyphic, hieratic or demotic, has found it necessary to compile in one form or another his own Egyptian Dictionary. In these days when we have at our disposal the knowledge which has been acquired during the last hundred years by the unceasing toil of the above-mentioned pioneers and their immediate followers—Birch, Lepsius, Brugsch, Chabas, Goodwin, E. de Rougé and others—we are apt to underrate the difficulties which they met and overcame, as well as to forget how great is the debt which we owe to them. I therefore propose, before passing on to describe the circumstances under which the present Egyptian Hieroglyphic Dictionary has been produced, to recall briefly the labours of the "famous men" who have preceded me in the field of Egyptian lexicography, and "who were honoured in their generations, and were the glory of their times."

Labours of pioneer Egyptian lexicographers.

The Abbé J. J. Barthélemy (1716–1795) as far back as 1761 showed satisfactorily that the ovals in Egyptian inscriptions which we call "cartouches" contained royal names. Zoega (1756–1809) accepted this view, and, developing it, stated that the hieroglyphs in them were alphabetic letters.[1] Had Åkerblad (1760–1819) and S. de Sacy (1758–1838) accepted these facts, and worked to develop them, the progress of Egyptological science would have been materially hastened. They failed, however, to pay much attention to the hieroglyphic inscriptions of which copies were available, and devoted all their time and labour to the elucidation of the enchorial, or demotic, text on the Rosetta Stone, the discovery of which had roused such profound interest among the learned men of the day. Their labours in connection with this text were crowned with considerable success. To Åkerblad belongs the credit of being the first European to formulate a "Demotic Alphabet," and to give the values of its characters in Coptic letters, but neither he nor S. de Sacy seems to have suspected the existence of a hieroglyphic alphabet. Both these eminent scholars produced lists, or small vocabularies, of demotic

Åkerblad and Zoega's discoveries.

Silvestre de Sacy.

[1] See my *Rosetta Stone*, vol. I, p. 40.

Demotic vocabularies of Åkerblad and de Sacy.

words, and added translations of them which are surprisingly correct considering the period when they were compiled. And both were able to read correctly the demotic equivalents of several Greek royal names, *e.g.*, Alexander, Ptolemy and Berenice. Their failure to apply the method by which they achieved such success to the hieroglyphic inscriptions is inexplicable. It has been suggested that their scholarly minds revolted at the absurd views, theories and statements about the Egyptian hieroglyphs made by Athanasius Kircher (1601–1680), Jablonski (1673–1757), J. de Guignes (1721–1800), Tychsen (1734–1815) and others, and the suggestion is probably correct. After the publication of his famous "Letter" to S. de Sacy,[1] Akerblad seems to have dropped his Egyptological studies. At all events, he published nothing about them. De Sacy, though he did not consider that he had wasted the time that he had spent on the demotic text on the Rosetta Stone, refrained from further research in Egyptology, and nothing of importance was effected in the decipherment of the Egyptian hieroglyphs until Dr. Thomas Young (June 13th, 1773–May 10th, 1830) turned his attention to them.

Kircher, Jablonski, de Guignes and Tychsen.

YOUNG'S HIEROGLYPHIC ALPHABET AND VOCABULARY.

Thomas Young and the Rosetta Stone.

In 1814 Young began to study the inscriptions on the Rosetta Stone, and, according to his own statement, succeeded in a few months in translating both the demotic and the hieroglyphic texts. His translations, together with notes and some remarks on Åkerblad's Demotic Alphabet, were printed in *Archæologia* for 1815, under the title "Remarks on Egyptian Papyri and on the Inscription of Rosetta." With respect to the Egyptian Alphabet he says, "I had hoped to find an alphabet which would enable me to read the enchorial inscription. . . . But . . . I had gradually been compelled to abandon this expectation, and to admit the conviction that no such alphabet would ever be discovered, because it had never been in existence." During the next three or four years he made striking progress in the decipherment of both demotic and hieroglyphic characters. The results of his studies at this period were published in his article EGYPT, which appeared in Part I of the fourth volume of the *Encyclopædia Britannica* in 1819. It was accompanied by five plates, containing *inter alia* a hieroglyphic vocabulary of 218 words, a

[1] *Lettre sur l'Inscription Égyptienne de Rosette, adressée au citoyen Silvestre de Sacy,* Paris (Imprimerie de la République Française) and Strasbourg, an X (1802), 8vo. With a plate containing the Demotic Alphabet.

"supposed enchorial, *i.e.*, demotic alphabet," and "specimens of phrases." The VIIth Section of the letterpress contained the "Rudiments of a Hieroglyphic Vocabulary," and thus Young became the "father" of English compilers of Egyptian Vocabularies. In this article, which formed a most important and epoch-making contribution to Egyptology, Young gave a list containing a number of alphabetic Egyptian characters, to which, in most cases, he assigned correct phonetic values, *i.e.*, values which are accepted by Egyptologists at the present day. In fact, he showed that he had rightly grasped the idea of a phonetic principle in the reading of Egyptian hieroglyphs, the existence of which had been assumed and practically proved by Barthélemy and Zoega, and applied it FOR THE FIRST TIME in the decipherment of Egyptian hieroglyphs. This seems to me to be an indisputable fact, which can easily be verified by any one who will take the trouble to read Young's article, EGYPT, in the "Supplement" to the *Encyclopædia Britannica* and study his correspondence and papers which John Leitch reprinted in the third volume of the *Miscellaneous Works of the late Thomas Young, M.D., F.R.S.*, London, 1855. Those whom such evidence will not satisfy may consult the five volumes of his papers that are preserved in the British Museum (Additional MSS. 27,281–27,285). In the first volume (Add. 27,281) are all the principal documents dealing with his work on the Rosetta Stone, and in the second (Add. 27,282) will be found his copies of a series of short vocabularies of Egyptian words. Without wishing in any way to reopen the dispute as to the merits and value of Young's work in comparison with that of Champollion, it may be pointed out that scholars who were contemporaries of both and who had competent knowledge of Egyptology couple together the names of Young and Champollion, and place Young's name first. Thus Kosegarten groups Young, Champollion and Peyron[1]; Birch speaks of the "discoveries of Dr. Young and M. Champollion"[2]; and Tattam says that the sculptured monuments and papyri of Egypt have long "engaged the attention of the Learned, who have in vain endeavoured to decipher them, till our indefatigable and erudite countryman, Dr. Young, and, after him, M. Champollion, undertook the task."[3]

Young's Hieroglyphic Vocabulary.

His application of the Phonetic Principle.

Young's correspondence with Champollion and others.

Contemporary opinions on the merits of Young's discovery.

[1] Debitas vero gratias refero Youngio, Champolliono, Peyronio, viris praeclarissimis, quo quoties aliquid ad hoc studiorum genus pertinens ab iis sciscitarem, toties benevole semper et promte quae desiderarem mecum communicaverunt. *De Prisca Aegyptiorum Litteratura Commentatio prima.* Weimar, 1828, p. iv.

[2] *Sketch of a Hieroglyphical Dictionary.* London, 1838, p. 3.

[3] *Coptic Grammar.* London, 1830, p. ix.

The great value and importance of Young's application of the phonetic principle to Egyptian hieroglyphs has been summed up with characteristic French terseness and accuracy by Chabas, the distinguished Egyptologist, who wrote, "Cette idée fut, dans la réalité, le FIAT LUX de la science."[1]

Curiously enough Young did not follow up his discovery by a continued application of his phonetic principle to Egyptian inscriptions other than those on the Rosetta Stone, but seems to have been content to leave its further application and development to Champollion le Jeune.[2] And for some reason he made no attempt to add to the Egyptian Vocabulary containing 218 words which he published in his article EGYPT in the *Encyclopædia Britannica*, or if he did, his additions were never printed. On the other hand, he devoted himself to the preparation of a Demotic Dictionary and this work occupied the last ten years of his life. The "Advertisement" is of considerable interest, for it shows that it was only his inability to decide upon the system of arrangement that ought to be employed in an Egyptian Dictionary, that prevented him from publishing the work during his lifetime. His difficulty is described by him thus:

Young's Demotic Dictionary.

"From the mixed nature of the characters employed in the written language or rather languages of the Egyptians, it is difficult to determine what would be the best arrangement for a dictionary, even if they were all perfectly clear in their forms, and perfectly well understood: at present, however, so many of them remain unknown, and those which are better known assume so diversified an appearance, that the original difficulty is greatly increased. Every methodical arrangement, however arbitrary, has the advantage of bringing together such words as nearly resemble each other: and it appears most likely to be subservient to the purposes of future investigation, to employ an imitation of an alphabetical order, or an artificial alphabet, founded upon the resemblance of the characters to those of which the phonetic value was clearly and correctly determined by the late Mr. Åkerblad; and to arrange the words that are to be interpreted according to their places in this artificial order; choosing, however, in each instance, not always the first character that enters into the composition of the word, but that which appears to be the most radical, or the most essential in its signification, or

Alphabetic arrangement of the Dictionary.

[1] *Inscription de Rosette*, p. 5.

[2] See *Advertisement to Dr. Young's Egyptian Dictionary* printed in *Rudiments of an Egyptian Dictionary*, which formed an Appendix to Tattam's *Coptic Grammar*. London, 1830, 8vo, and was reprinted by Leitch, *op. cit.*, p. 472 ff.

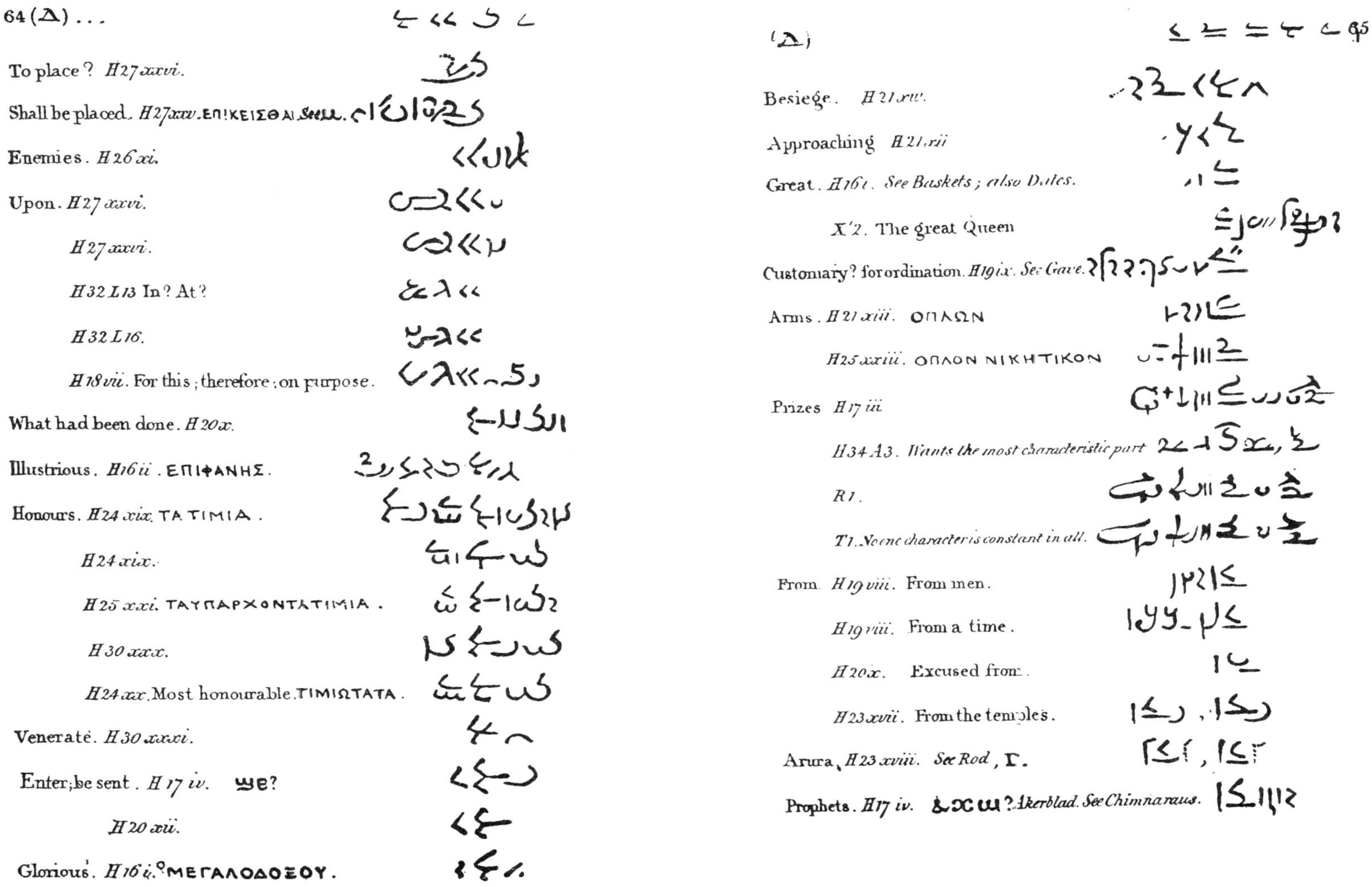
64 (Δ) . . .
To place? H27 xxvi.
Shall be placed. H27 xxv. ΕΠΙΚΕΙΣΘΑΙ
Enemies. H26 xi.
Upon. H27 xxvi.
H27 xxvi.
H32 L13 In? At?
H32 L16.
H18 vii. For this; therefore; on purpose.
What had been done. H20 x.
Illustrious. H16 ii. ΕΠΙΦΑΝΗΣ.
Honours. H24 xix. ΤΑ ΤΙΜΙΑ.
H24 xix.
H25 xxi. ΤΑΥΠΑΡΧΟΝΤΑΤΙΜΙΑ.
H30 xxx.
H24 xx. Most honourable. ΤΙΜΙΩΤΑΤΑ.
Venerate. H30 xxxi.
Enter; be sent. H17 iv. ϣe?
H20 xii.
Glorious. H16 ii. ΜΕΓΑΛΟΔΟΞΟΥ.
(Δ)
Besiege. H21 xiv.
Approaching H21 xii
Great. H16 i. See Baskets; also Dates.
X'2. The great Queen
Customary? for ordination. H19 ix. See Gave.
Arms. H21 xiii. ΟΠΛΩΝ
H25 xxiii. ΟΠΛΟΝ ΝΙΚΗΤΙΚΟΝ
Prizes H17 iii.
H34 A3. Wants the most characteristic part
R1.
T1. No one character is constant in all.
From. H19 viii. From men.
H19 viii. From a time.
H20 x. Excused from.
H23 xvii. From the temples.
Arura. H23 xviii. See Rod, Γ.
Prophets. H17 iv. ϩⲟⲩⲱ? Akerblad. See Chimnaraus.

Two pages of Young's *Rudiments of an Egyptian Dictionary in the Ancient Enchorial Character.* London, 1830.

sometimes that which is merely the most readily ascertained or distinguished."[1]

Now although Young was the first to apply the phonetic, or alphabetic, principle to Egyptian hieroglyphs, it is quite clear from the above that he failed to see its value in arranging Egyptian words in a dictionary. Speaking of Champollion's alphabet, which was in reality his own with modifications and considerable additions, he says: "His SYSTEM of phonetic characters may often be of use in assisting the memory, but it can only be applied with confidence to particular cases when supported in each case by the same kind of evidence that had been employed before its invention. His communications have furnished many valuable additions to this work, all of which have been acknowledged in their proper places." So then rejecting his own system of phonetic, *i.e.* alphabetic, characters, and Champollion's development of it, he drew up his "Rudiments of the Egyptian Dictionary in the ancient Enchorial Character," intending the work to appear as an Appendix to the "Coptic Grammar," which Henry Tattam was then writing. Whilst the printing of the "Rudiments" was in progress he fell ill, but his interest in the work was so great that in spite of his illness he continued to prepare its pages for the lithographer and to correct the proofs. When he had passed for press six sheets, *i.e.* 96 pages, death overtook him, and Tattam corrected the last 14 pages (pp. 97–110) of proof, saw them through the press, and compiled an Index to the work, which appeared with Tattam's "Coptic Grammar" in

Champollion's Hieroglyphic Alphabet.

Kosegarten's testimony.

[1] Writing to M. Arago on July 4th, 1828, Young says, "Now of the nine letters which I insist that I had discovered, M. Champollion himself allows me five, and I maintain that a single one would have been sufficient for all that I wished to prove; the method by which that one was obtained being allowed to be correct, and to be capable of further application. The true foundation of the analysis of the Egyptian system, I insist, is the great fact of the original identity of the enchorial with the sacred characters, which I discovered and printed in 1816 [in the *Museum Criticum* No. VI, pp. 155–204], and which M. Champollion probably rediscovered, and certainly republished in 1821; besides the reading of the name of Ptolemy, which I had completely ascertained and published in 1814, and the name of Cleopatra, which Mr. Bankes had afterwards discovered by means of the information that I had sent him out to Egypt, and which he asserts that he communicated indirectly to M. Champollion [see H. Salt, *Essay on Dr. Young's and M. Champollion's Phonetic System of Hieroglyphics*, London, 1825, p. 7]; and whatever deficiencies there might have been in my original alphabet, supposing it to have contained but one letter correctly determined, they would and must have been gradually supplied by a continued application of the same method to other monuments which have been progressively discovered and made public since the date of my first paper." Leitch, Miscellaneous Works of the late Thomas Young, M.D., F.R.S., Vol. III, p. 464 ff.

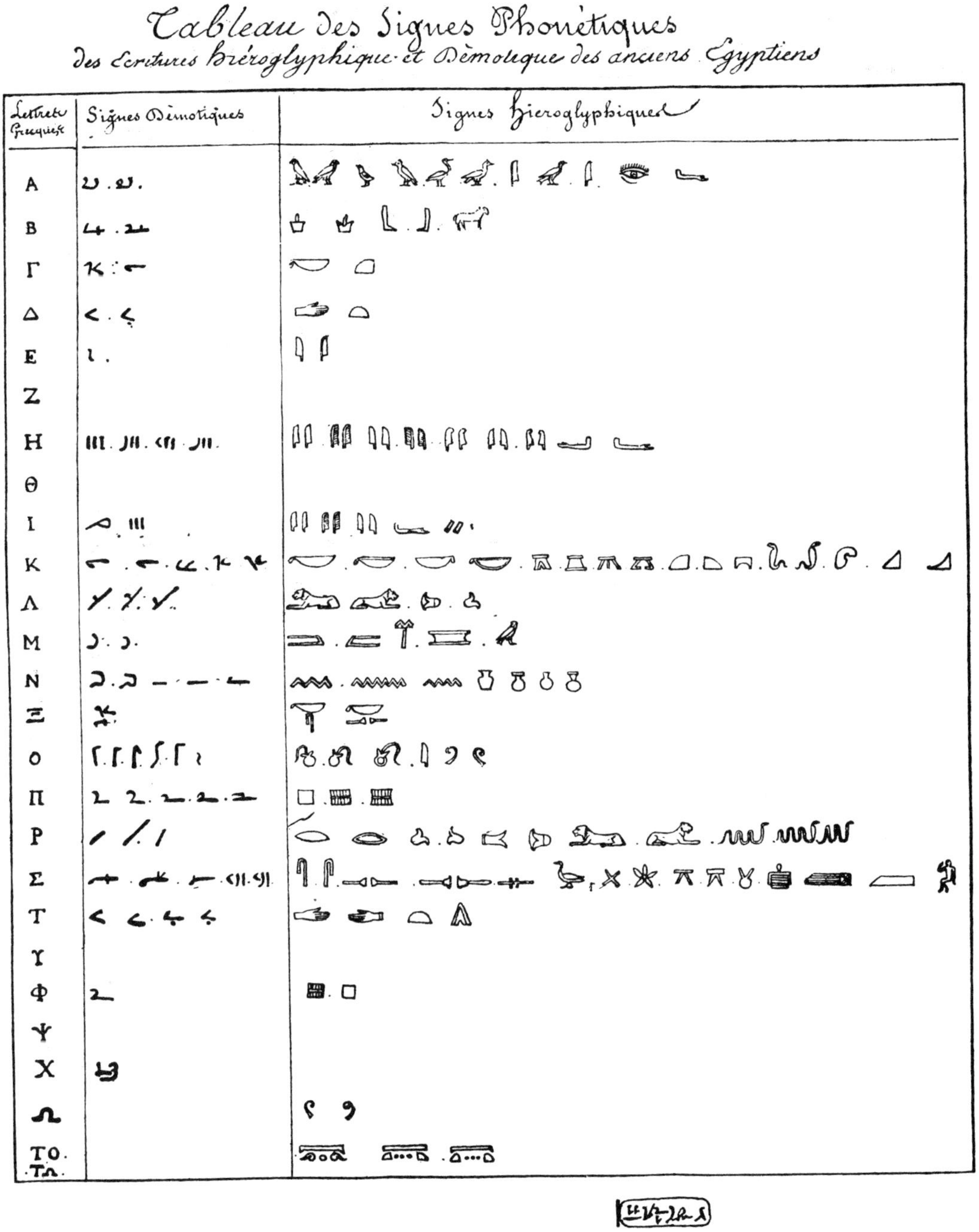

Champollion's Table of Hieroglyphic and Demotic phonetic signs. From his *Lettre à M. Dacier relative à l'Alphabet des Hiéroglyphes Phonétiques.* Paris, 1822. Plate IV.

1830.[1] The "Rudiments," to paraphrase Kosegarten's words, contains a valuable and well-arranged collection of all the most important groups of enchorial characters hitherto deciphered. These Young selected from enchorial texts which had been published by himself, and by Champollion and Kosegarten, and from letters which he had received from Champollion describing the contents of unpublished papyri at Paris.[2]

Progress of Egyptology retarded by the death of Young and Champollion.

The progress of Egyptology suffered a severe set-back by the death of Young on May 10th, 1830, and by the death of Champollion on March 4th, 1832, and there was no scholar sufficiently advanced in the science to continue their work. With the exception of books and papers of a polemical character, some authors championing Young's system of phonetics, and others loudly proclaiming the superior merits of that of Champollion, and others advocating the extraordinary views of Spohn and Seyffarth (1796–1885), no important work on Egyptological decipherment appeared for several years. Soon after the death of Champollion a rumour circulated freely among the learned of Europe to the effect that the great Frenchman had left in manuscript, almost complete, many works which he was preparing for press when death overtook him, and that these were to appear shortly under the editorship of his brother, Champollion-Figeac (1778–1867). It was widely known that Champollion had been engaged for

[1] In his Observations on the Hieroglyphic and Enchorial Alphabets (*Coptic Grammar*, p. ix ff.) Tattam describes briefly and accurately the various steps in the early history of Egyptian decipherment. He shows that Young was the first to read correctly the names of Ptolemy and Berenice, that Bankes, with the help of Young, discovered the name of Cleopatra, and says that the system of letters thus discovered was "taken up, and extended, by M. Champollion, and afterwards by Mr. Salt, our late Consul-General in Egypt." He then gives the Hieroglyphic Alphabet as constructed from the researches of Young, Bankes, Champollion and Salt.

[2] Das Werk (Nro. 2), mit welchem der treffliche Young seine literarische Laufbahn und zugleich sein Leben beschlossen hat, enthält eine schätzbare, wohlgeordnete Sammlung aller wichtigsten bisher erklärten enchorischen Schriftgruppen. Er hat diese Sammlung aus den von ihm selbst, von Champollion, und von mir bekannt gemachten enchorischen Texten ausgewählt, aber auch briefliche Mittheilungen Champollion's aus noch nicht herausgegebenen Pariser Papyrusrollen benutzt. Er leitete den Druck und die Correktur dieser Schrift, welche ihm sehr am Herzen lag, und die gleichsam sein Vermächtniss über die Aegyptischen Untersuchungen liefert, noch auf seinem letzten Krankenbette, so schwer ihm auch zuletzt das Schreiben schon ward. Als er bis zur 96sten Seite mit der Correktur gelangt war, ereilte ihn der Tod; die Correktur der letzten Seiten, und die *Indices* besorgte daher Hy. Tattam. See *Jahrbücher für wissenschaftliche Kritik*, Jahrgang 1831, Bd. II, Stuttgart und Tübingen, 4to, Col. 771.

PHONETICK ALPHABET

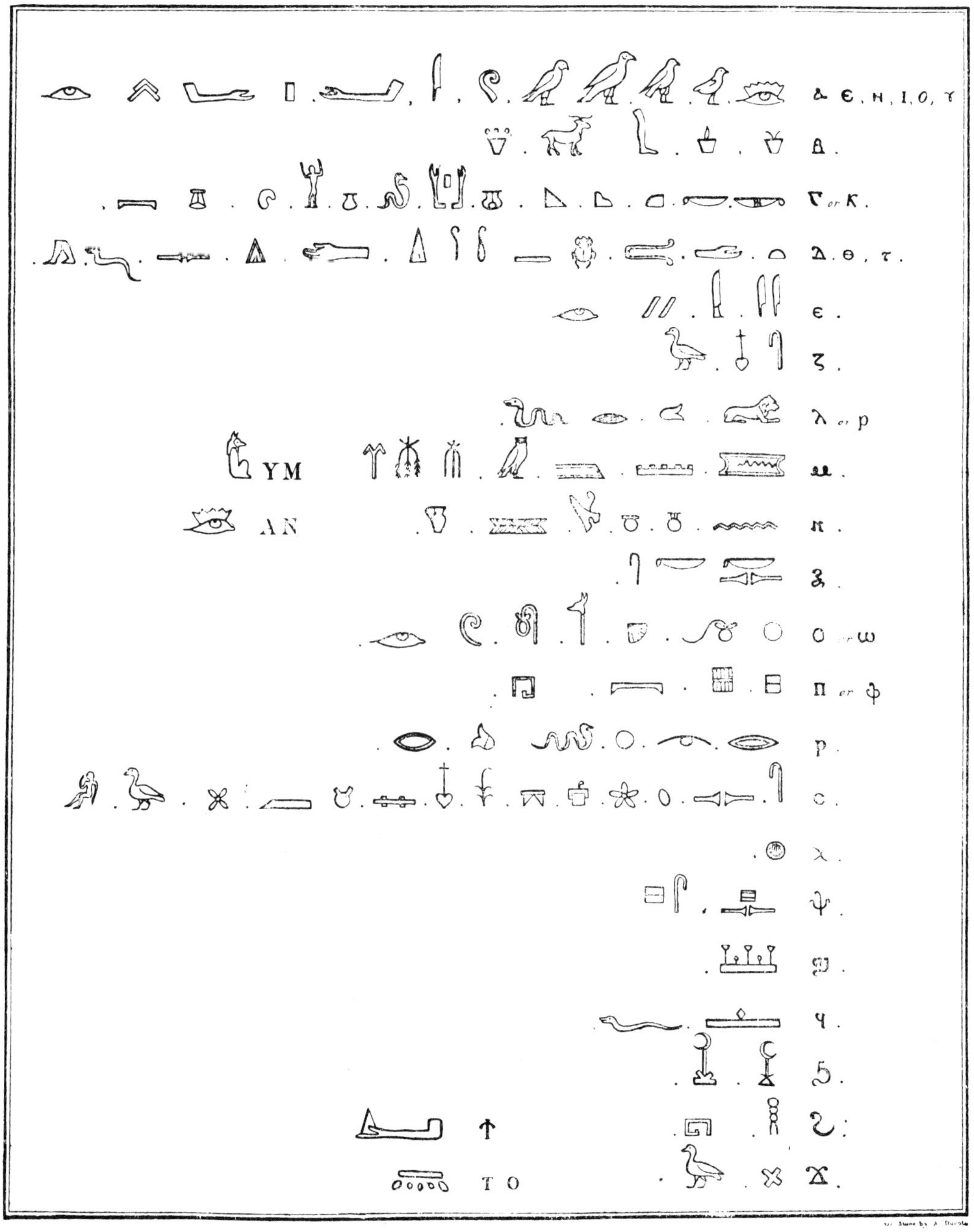

The "Phonetick Alphabet." From Tattam's *Compendious Grammar of the Egyptian Language, as contained in the Coptic and Sahidic Dialects.* London, 1830.

Champollion's manuscripts.

many years in compiling a Hieroglyphic Dictionary; that he had been assisted by his friend, Salvador Cherubini (1760–1842); that Charles Lenormant (1802–1859) had helped him in transcribing the slips; and that Ippolito Rosellini (1800–1843?) had made a copy of this Dictionary before Champollion set out on his last journey to Egypt. But when year after year passed and Champollion-Figeac failed to issue any of his brother's works, many scholars came to the conclusion that the manuscripts did not exist.

Richard Lepsius and Samuel Birch.

Meanwhile two young men, C. R. Lepsius (1810–1884) and Samuel Birch (1813–1885), had turned their attention to the study of Egyptian hieroglyphs, and succeeded in completing Champollion's system of decipherment and establishing it. Lepsius first studied in Berlin under Bopp (1791–1867), and having received his doctor's degree in philosophy in 1833, departed to Paris, where he won the Volney prize in 1834. In 1835 he published the two Dissertations[1] which established his reputation as a comparative philologist. He went to Rome, where he became an intimate friend of Ippolito Rosellini, the Egyptologist and friend and travelling companion of Champollion. Here he wrote and published in the "Annali dell' Instituto Archeologico di Roma" (Vol. IX, 1837) his famous "Lettre à M. le Professeur Rosellini sur l'Alphabet Hiéroglyphique." In this letter, which created widespread interest, he succeeded in removing many of the defects of Champollion's development of Young's system of phonetics, and treated the whole question of Egyptian decipherment in such a masterly manner that all adverse criticism of a serious character was silenced once and for all. It is unnecessary to refer here to the great works to the publication of which he devoted the remaining forty-eight years of his life, for they do not concern the question under discussion.

Lepsius completes Champollion's system of decipherment.

The Phonetic Alphabet of Lepsius.

Whilst Lepsius was perfecting Champollion's system, Birch was studying the whole question of Egyptian decipherment from an entirely different point of view, namely, that of a Chinese scholar. It will be remembered that so far back as 1764 Joseph

[1] Zwei Sprachvergleichende Abhandlungen. *I. Ueber die Anordnung und Verwandtschaft des Semitischen, Indischen, Aethiopischen, Alt-Persischen und Alt-Aegyptischen Alphabets. II. Ueber den Ursprung und die Verwandtschaft der Zahlwörter in der Indo-Germanischen, Semitischen, und der Koptischen Sprache.* Berlin 1835–6. 8vo.

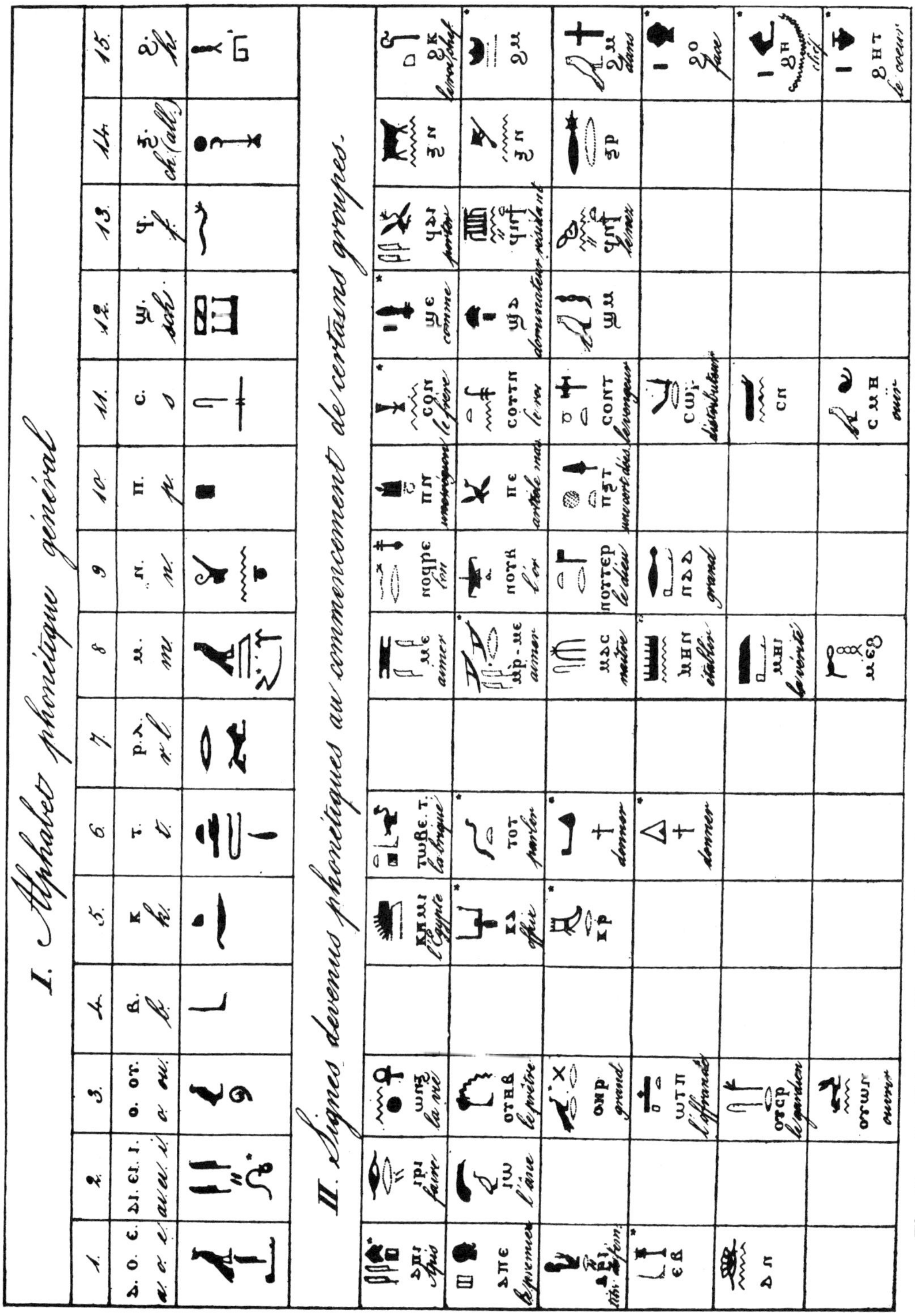

The Phonetic Alphabet of Lepsius. From *Lettre à M. le Professeur H. Rosellini sur l'Alphabet Hiéroglyphique.* Rome, 1837.

Theories of de Guignes the Sinologist and Palin.

de Guignes (1721–1800), an eminent Sinologist, tried to prove that the epistolographic and symbolic characters of the Egyptians were to be found in the Chinese characters, and that the Chinese nation was nothing but an Egyptian colony. Following in his steps, M. le Comte de Palin (or Pahlin) held that the Chinese and Egyptian characters were identical in origin and meaning;[1] he believed that if either the ancient forms of Chinese characters, or those which their values indicate, were given to them, true hieroglyphs similar to those that exist on the Rosetta Stone would very often be found. And he thought that if the Psalms of David were translated into Chinese, and they were then written in the ancient characters of that language, the inscriptions in Egyptian papyri would be reproduced.[2] Now whatever may have been the opinions held by Young and Champollion about the relationship of the Chinese language to the ancient Egyptian language, or the similarity of the principles on which Chinese and Egyptian writing had been developed, these scholars could neither affirm nor deny effectively the statements of de Guignes and de Palin, for both of them were ignorant of the Chinese language. With Birch the case was very different, for he studied Chinese under a competent master when still at the Merchant Taylors' School, with the direct object of obtaining an appointment in the Consular Service in China. The friend of the family who had promised to obtain this appointment for him died unexpectedly in 1831, with the result that Birch remained in England. He continued his Chinese studies, and began to read the works of Young and Champollion, thinking that his knowledge of Chinese would enable him to read the Egyptian texts easily. In 1834 he became an assistant in the Public Record Office, and worked in the Tower until January, 1836, when he entered the service of the Trustees of the British Museum. There he was able to make use of his knowledge of Chinese and Egyptian, and his first official task was to arrange and describe the Chinese coins.[3] When this work was completed he was directed to describe

Birch's Chinese studies.

[1] See his *Essai sur le moyen de parvenir à la lecture et à l'intelligence des Hiéroglyphes Égyptiens* in *Mémoires de l'Académie.* tom. XXIX, 1764; tom. XXXIV, 1770.

[2] See De Palin, N. G., *Lettres sur les Hiéroglyphes*, Weimar, 1802; *Essai sur les Hiéroglyphes,* Weimar, 1804; *Analyse de l'Inscription en Hiéroglyphes du Monument trouvé à Rosette*, Dresden, 1804; *Nouvelles Recherches,* Florence, 1830.

[3] Some of the descriptions which he wrote at this time are still in the coin trays of the Department of Coins and Medals, and by the courtesy of my colleague, the Keeper of the Department, Mr. G. F. Hill, I have been able to examine them.

the Collections of Egyptian monuments and papyri for the official Guide to the British Museum, and his account of them was published in the "Synopsis" for 1838. Long before he entered the Museum he conceived the idea of compiling a Hieroglyphic Dictionary, and began to write down, each on a separate slip of paper, the hieroglyphic words which he found in the texts published by James Burton,[1] Gardner Wilkinson,[2] Champollion,[3] Rosellini[4] and Salvolini.[5]

Birch's idea of a Hieroglyphic Dictionary.

BIRCH'S "SKETCH OF A HIEROGLYPHICAL DICTIONARY."

This work of word-collecting had been somewhat interrupted by his duties in the Public Record Office in 1834–5, but soon after he entered the Museum he took it up with redoubled zeal, and he copied every hieroglyphic text and transcribed every hieratic papyrus which the Museum possessed. In 1837, the year in which Lepsius published his famous Letter to Rosellini, Birch revised his slips carefully, and decided to attempt to publish a "Hieroglyphical Dictionary." In those days no fount of hieroglyphic type existed, and lithography was expensive, and publishers were not eager to spend their money on a dictionary of a language of which scarcely a dozen people in the whole world had any real knowledge. At length Messrs. William Allen & Co., of Leadenhall Street, London, were induced to consider the publication of a hieroglyphic dictionary, but they decided to issue first of all a few specimen pages, with a short Preface by Birch, with the view of finding out how far the work would be supported by the learned and the general public. Thereupon Birch prepared for the lithographer twelve small quarto pages containing ninety-three words, and having written a Preface of two pages to explain his system of arrangement of the words, they were published in the autumn of 1838 under the title of "Sketch of a Hieroglyphical Dictionary. Part I. Hieroglyphs and English. Division I. Phonetical Symbols. Vowels."

Publication of Birch's "Sketch of a Hieroglyphical Dictionary."

In his Preface Birch says that he has drawn up his work to help the student of hieroglyphs in his researches, and that he intends it to be used as a manual which "all who appreciate the value of the phonetic system may use, and by which, at one glance, may be seen the extent of the discoveries of Dr. Young and

Birch's Phonetic system.

1 *Excerpta Hieroglyphica.* Cairo, 1825–1837, fol. (privately printed).

2 *Materia Hieroglyphica.* Malta, 1824–1830 (privately printed).

3 *Lettres écrites d'Égypte et de Nubie en* 1828 *et* 1829. Paris, 1833.

4 *I Monumenti dell' Egitto e della Nubia.* Pisa, 1832 ff.

5 *Campagne de Rhamsès le Grand contre les Shéta et leurs alliés.* Paris, 1835.

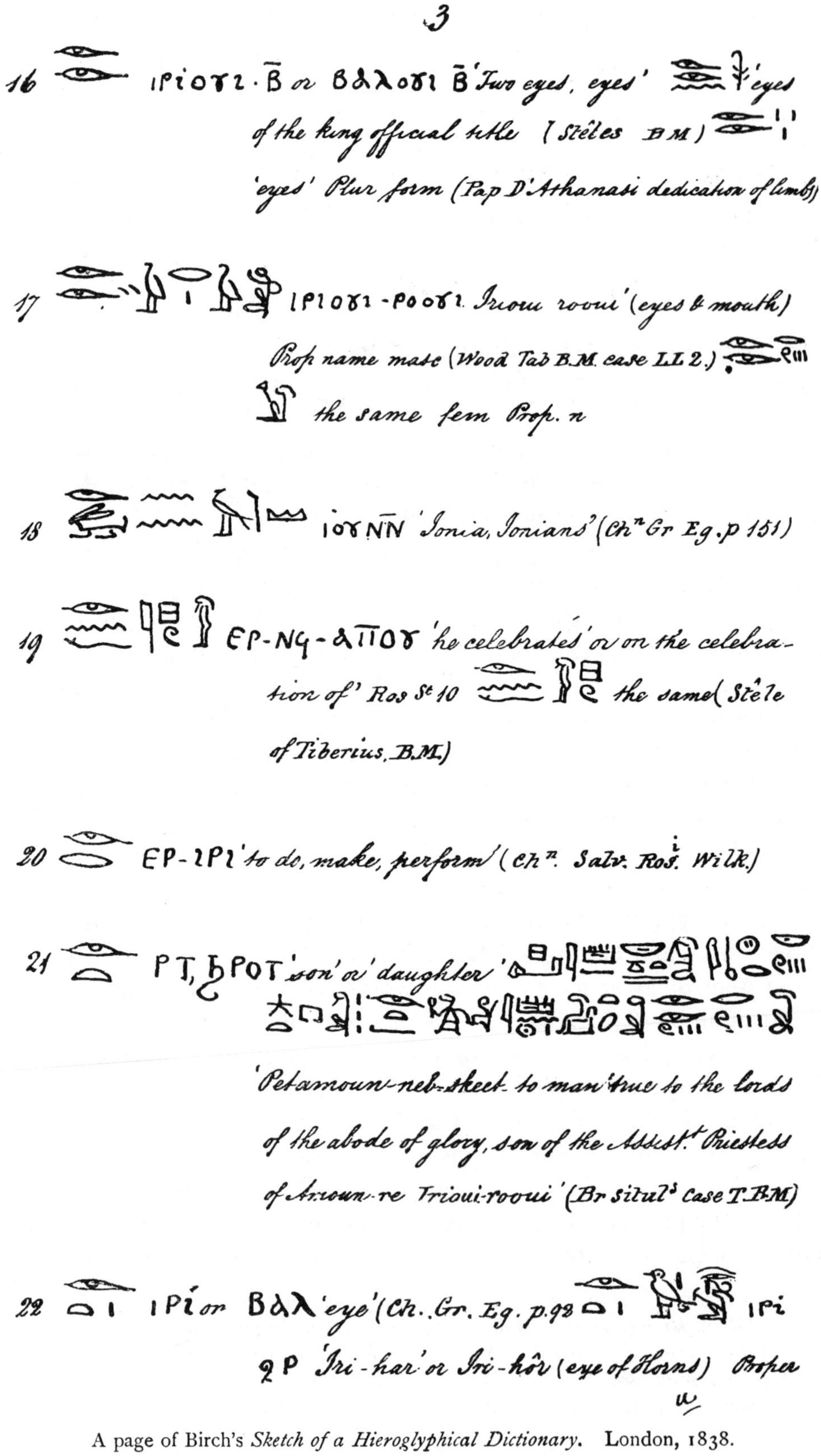
3

16 ιριουι · Β̄ or βαλουι Β̄ 'Two eyes, eyes' 'eyes of the king official title (Stèles B M) 'eyes' Plur form (Pap D'Athanasi dedication of limbs)

17 ιριουι - ροουι. Iriou rooui' (eyes & mouth) Prop name masc (Wood Tab B.M. case LL 2.) the same fem Prop. n

18 ιουΝΝ 'Ionia, Ionians' (Ch^{n} Gr Eg. p 151)

19 ερ-νϥ-αποτ 'he celebrates' or on the celebration of' Ros S^{t} 10 the same (Stèle of Tiberius, B.M.)

20 ερ-ϩρι 'to do, make, perform' (Ch^{n}. Salv. Ros. Wilk.)

21 ρτ, ϣρωτ 'son' or 'daughter' 'Petamoun-neb-skeet- to man' true to the lords of the abode of glory, son of the Assist^{t} Priestess of Amoun-re Trioui-rooui' (Br situl^{s} case T.B.M)

22 ιρι or βαλ 'eye' (Ch. Gr. Eg. p.92 ιρι ϩρ 'Iri-har' or Iri-hôr (eye of Horus) Proper n

A page of Birch's *Sketch of a Hieroglyphical Dictionary.* London, 1838.

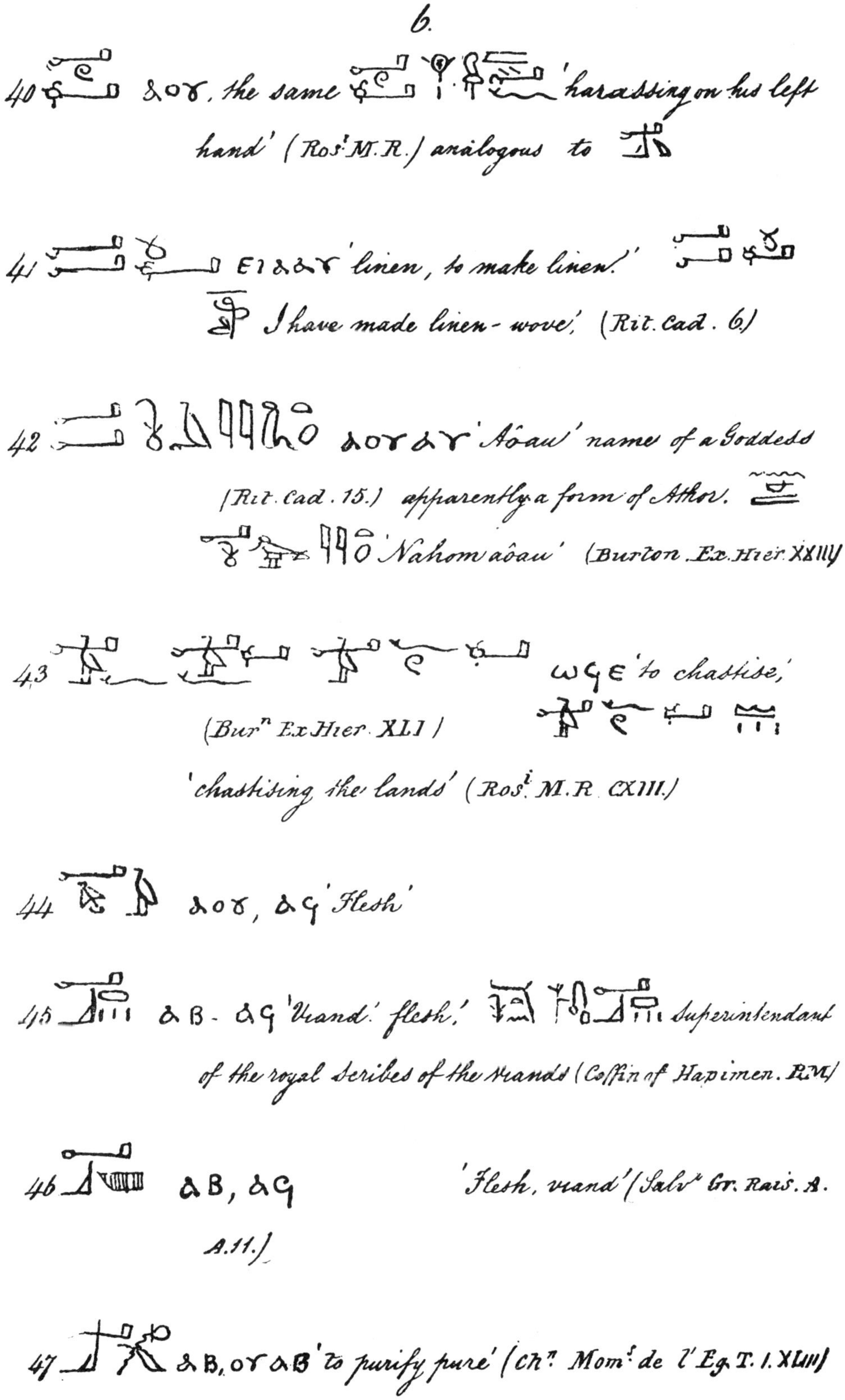
6.

40 ⲁⲟⲩ, the same 'harassing on his left hand' (Ros. M.R.) analogous to

41 ⲉⲓⲁⲁⲩ 'linen, to make linen.' 'I have made linen-wove.' (Rit. Cad. 6)

42 ⲁⲟⲩⲁⲩ 'Aôau' name of a Goddess (Rit. Cad. 15.) apparently a form of Athor. 'Nahom aôau' (Burton. Ex. Hier. XXIII)

43 ⲱϥⲉ 'to chastise,' (Bur^n Ex Hier. XLI) 'chastising the lands' (Ros^i. M.R. CXIII.)

44 ⲁⲟⲩ, ⲁϥ 'Flesh'

45 ⲁⲃ - ⲁϥ 'Viand.' 'flesh.' Superintendant of the royal scribes of the viands (Coffin of Hapimen. B.M.)

46 ⲁⲃ, ⲁϥ 'Flesh, viand' (Salv^r Gr. Rais. A. A. 11.)

47 ⲁⲃ, ⲟⲩⲁⲃ 'to purify pure' (Ch^n Mom^s de l'Eg. T. I. XLIII)

A page of Birch's *Sketch of a Hieroglyphical Dictionary*. London, 1838.

M. Champollion, and of their application to the monuments of the Egyptians." The dictionary does not claim even comparative perfection, "but it has been judged that the publication of such a work might be of slight service to those who are desirous of possessing, in a compendious form, the results of much labour, comparison and instruction." The matter contained in the work is not entirely original, but the arrangement is, and "if not

His ideophonetic arrangement.

scientific, [it is] perhaps the only one by which tyros could at once find the particular group or word which they seek. It may be termed ideophonetic, as it embraces both principles of ideal and phonetic classification, and its arrangement has been borrowed from a language very cognate in its construction—the Chinese."

The hieroglyphical and English part of the Dictionary was to be divided into two parts. Part I was to contain words "commencing with symbols, representatives of sounds, or phonetic," and Part II words "whose initial character is the equivalent of

Arrangement of the proposed Dictionary.

an idea, or ideographic." Part I was to be "subdivided into symbols, having the power of vowels or consonants, the vowels forming (on account of one symbol frequently having the force of many) one large class, and the consonants, according to their position in the Coptic alphabet." That is to say, Division I of

Polyphonous symbols.

Part I was to contain symbols or characters some of which Birch held to be polyphonous, and Division II symbols to which he had given consonantal values, and these were to be arranged in the order

Natural classification of symbols.

of the letters of the Coptic Alphabet. The internal classification of the characters or symbols was to be strictly ideographical, "taking the symbols in their arrangement, according to the rank they hold in natural and other sciences, as the human form, limbs, animals, inanimate objects, etc." At the end of the

The tabulated symbols to form the key.

Dictionary Birch intended to give "all the symbols in a similar classification, and in a tabular view," and this section was to form the key to the whole work. With the view of illustrating the way in which he intended his Dictionary to be used, he says, "Suppose, for example, it were required to find the meaning of a group beginning with a human eye [𓁹]—as the eye is a component part of the human body, it will be found in that division in the table, and there will be affixed to the depicted eye, v[ide Nos] 13–43." In this group of words will be found all those words in which an eye [𓁹] is the first character; and the eye generally represents a vowel. These remarks will be clear to the reader after examining the two pages from Birch's "Sketch of a Hieroglyphical Dictionary," which are reproduced on pp. xviii and xix. The twelve-paged specimen which he published only illustrates the plan and arrangement of what he called the "Phonetic Division" of his Dictionary, and it is much to be regretted that he did not issue specimens of the other Divisions.

First application of the phonetic principle to an Egyptian Dictionary.

The above extracts from Birch's Preface and the specimen pages which are here given prove beyond all doubt that he had grasped the importance of the "phonetic principle" for lexicographical purposes, and that he was the first to apply it to the arrangement of the words of the Egyptian language. He says that he borrowed [the idea of] his "ideophonetic arrangement" from the Chinese, a statement which should be noted. My colleague, Mr. L. Giles, the Sinologist, informs me that though the Chinese had no alphabet they developed a phonetic principle. Some eighty per cent. of the characters of the language are made up of two parts, one part serving as a phonetic and giving a clue to the SOUND of the word, and the other as a "classifier," which gives a clue as to its MEANING;[1] the "classifiers"[2] are in number about 214, and the phonetic symbols between 1,600 and 1,700. In the case of Egyptian the signs which are now called "determinatives" are the equivalents of the "classifiers," and the alphabetic characters are the equivalents of the phonetic symbols in Chinese texts.

Classifiers and determinatives.

Sad to relate, Birch's "Sketch" did not meet with sufficient encouragement to induce the publisher to continue the publication of the "Hieroglyphical Dictionary," and no more parts appeared.

CHAMPOLLION'S "DICTIONNAIRE ÉGYPTIEN EN ÉCRITURE HIÉROGLYPHIQUE."

Champollion's "Dictionnaire Égyptien."

Nothing more was done in the field of Egyptian lexicography until 1841, when the "Dictionnaire Égyptien en écriture hiéroglyphique" of Champollion appeared at Paris under the careful editorship of Champollion-Figeac. In a lengthy "Préface" the editor describes the history of the Dictionary and the plan on which it is arranged, and the untoward events which delayed its publication; and from it the following summary has been made. Even before 1822, the year in which Champollion published his

[1] See his article on the Chinese Language in the *Encyclopædia Britannica*, last edition.

[2] A list of them is given in Dr. J. Marshman's *Elements of Chinese Grammar*. Serampore, 1814. 4to, pp. 9–14. The "phonetic stage" in Chinese writing is described and discussed in W. Hillier, *The Chinese Language and how to learn it*, 2nd edit., London, 1910, p. 3 ff.; and in Dr. H. Allen Giles' *China and the Chinese*, New York, 1902, p. 29 ff., and 35.

Lettre à M. Dacier[1] *relative à l' Alphabet des Hiéroglyphes Phonétiques employés par les Égyptiens pour inscrire sur leurs Monuments les titres, les noms et les surnoms des souverains Grecs et Romains,* he had made one list containing all the hieroglyphic characters he had found, and another list containing all the characters the meaning of which appeared to be manifest. He wrote each character on a separate card, and afterwards tabulated them systematically. Already in 1818–19 he had made a manuscript list of hieroglyphic words entitled, *Premier essai d'un Dictionnaire des Hiéroglyphes Égyptiens,* adding the legend, *Davus sum, non Œdipus.* When later he learned to distinguish three classes of characters, figurative, symbolic and phonetic, and was able to prove that they were employed simultaneously in the texts of all periods, he began to compile an Egyptian Dictionary. He first wrote each word on a separate slip of paper, or card, and then copied each on to a separate sheet of small folio paper, ruled in five columns. Col. 1 gave the character in outline and its hieratic form, Col. 2 its name, Col. 3 its graphic character (symbolic, figurative or phonetic), Col. 4 its actual meaning or value, and Col. 5 a reference to the text in which it had that value. Thus the Dictionary existed in duplicate, in slips and in sheets, and it had assumed very large proportions before Champollion went to Egypt in 1838. At this time Rosellini, who was a great friend of Champollion long before he became his fellow traveller, was allowed to make a copy of the Dictionary, presumably for his own use. It must be this copy which he bequeathed to the Biblioteca dell' Imperiale e Reale Università of Pisa, and which is thus described in the Inventory of the bequest by Dr. Giuseppe Dei :[2] " No. 4 casette, divise in caselle contenenti il non ultimato ma molto avanzato Dizionario dei Geroglifici, eseguito in parecchie migliaia di cartelle fatte per ordine alfabetico pei caratteri *fonetici,* e metodico per i *figurativi* e ideografici simbolici."

Champollion's classification of hieroglyphic characters.

Rosellini's copy of Champollion's Egyptian Dictionary.

When Champollion went to Egypt he took with him both copies of his Dictionary, and while in that country he added to both very considerably ; MM. Salvador Cherubini and Lenormant wrote many slips for him, and their contributions formed part of the original manuscript. On his return from Egypt he continued his labours on the Dictionary and added largely to it.

[1] Born 1742, died 1833. He was the Permanent Secretary to the Académie des Inscriptions et Belles Lettres, and was well known as a classic and historian.

[2] *Biographia del Cav. Prof. Ippolito Rosellini.* Florence, 1843, p. 15.

Champollion died on March 4th, 1832, and when his brother wished to take steps to publish the Dictionary he found that as a result of "funestes conseils des plus funestes passions," one half of each copy of the *Dictionnaire* had been carried off, but by whom Champollion-Figeac does not say in his edition of the *Dictionnaire.* All that he says on the subject there is that in spite of all opposition he succeeded in 1840 in regaining possession of 329 folios of the copy of the *Dictionnaire,* which was written out fairly on sheets of paper, and a large number of the slips belonging to the copy, which was kept purposely in slip form. And that having these in his hands he felt justified in thinking that he was in possession of both manuscript copies of the *Dictionnaire* in a nearly complete state. In a footnote he refers to a pamphlet in which he tell us how he regained possession of the parts of the two manuscript copies of the *Dictionnaire* which had disappeared, and as the pamphlet is now very rare, and his story is not generally known, I summarise it here.

Disapearance of portions of Champollion's MSS.

Their recovery by Champollion-Figeac in 1840.

Champollion-Figeac's pamphlet is entitled, *Notice sur les Manuscrits Autographes de Champollion le Jeune perdus en l'Année 1832, et retrouvés en* 1840. Paris, March, 1842. He says that when in April, 1832, he set to work to arrange his brother's literary effects with the view of offering the MSS. to the Government, he found at once that several of the most important of them were missing. He devoted himself to the task of making enquiries for them among his brother's friends, but they could give him no information about them, and the only result of his labour was to make widely known the fact that they were lost. The savants of the day, remembering how freely Champollion lent his writings to his intimate friends, hoped that they were not lost but only mislaid by some friend who had forgotten all about them. A year passed, and nothing was heard of the lost manuscripts. Meanwhile Champollion-Figeac began to suspect that one of his brother's friends, a man who was peculiarly indebted to him, had them in his possession. This friend was a young Italian called Salvolini, a native of Faenza, who came to Paris to study Egyptology in 1831, and who became a close friend of Champollion and his family. Champollion-Figeac's suspicions were aroused by the fact that a few months after the death of his brother, Salvolini sent him a prospectus of a work on the inscriptions on the Rosetta Stone, the Book of the Dead, etc., which he intended to publish in three volumes quarto. That a young man, 22 years of age,

Portions of Champollion's manuscripts missing.

Champollion-Figeac's search for the same.

Suspicion falls on Salvolini.

who had only studied Egyptian for a year could produce an elaborate work on difficult Egyptian texts in three volumes quarto was absurd on the face of it, and as Champollion-Figeac knew that his brother had written monographs on the very texts that were mentioned in the prospectus, he came to the conclusion that Salvolini had stolen the missing manuscripts. This was quite possible, for Salvolini had had free access to the study of Champollion, and was constantly in his house during his last illness. In August, 1833, at a public meeting of the Académie des Inscriptions Silvestre de Sacy solemnly called upon the man or men who had the missing manuscripts in their possession to restore them to their author's family, and Salvolini had the audacity to join him in mourning the loss of them, and with tears in his eyes he implored the man who had them to give them up. And at that moment he was announcing the publication of them under his own name! Still nothing was heard of the missing manuscripts. In February, 1838, Salvolini died, aged 28. Champollion-Figeac tried to find out what papers he had left behind, and was told that they had been claimed by a foreign messenger, and that they had been sent beyond the Alps. As a matter of fact, they had never left Paris, where they remained forgotten in some rooms. When Salvolini died his relatives commissioned an artist, Luigi Verardi, to wind up his affairs, and when this gentleman examined the effects the manuscripts on which was inscribed the name of François Salvolini seemed to be the most valuable parts of them. Verardi really believed that the manuscripts were the work of Salvolini, and wishing to do the best he could for his friend's family, tried to sell them, but no one would buy them. Finally, not knowing what else to do with the manuscripts, he wished to show them to Charles Lenormant, the friend and fellow traveller of Champollion, and to take his advice on the subject. At first Lenormant refused to look at them, but after a time, to oblige his friend Verardi, he agreed to do so. As soon as Lenormant began to turn over the leaves of the bundles of manuscripts which bore on them Salvolini's name, he recognised at once two of the works of Champollion, the loss of which had been publicly deplored by Silvestre de Sacy at the meeting of the Académie mentioned above. There was no longer any doubt about the matter. Salvolini had stolen the manuscripts of his friend and master, and as he made no response to de Sacy's appeal for their restoration, it was quite clear that he had intended to keep them. With the manuscripts of Champollion were several

Effrontery of Salvolini.

Salvolini's publications—and death.

Verardi the artist offers Salvolini's MSS. to Lenormant.

Lenormant recognises the Champollion MSS. stolen by Salvolini.

papers that were the work of Salvolini, but when Lenormant showed Verardi a whole volume which Champollion had written in French with his own hand, and pointed out to him the title, " Storia d'Egitto par F. Salvolini," which Salvolini had written on the title sheet, Verardi was convinced that he had been deceived by his dead friend. He realised quickly that Champollion's manuscripts must be given up to his heirs, and showed himself amenable to Lenormant's representations. Lenormant agreed to give him 600 francs for the documents, and with this sum Salvolini's family had to be content. Lenormant took possession of all Champollion's stolen manuscripts, and handed them over to the Government, who, by a special resolution passed on the 24th of April, 1833, had ordered their acqusition in the interests of science. Salvolini published the first volume of the " Analyse Grammaticale " in 1836; the second and third volumes did not appear. His papers fill five volumes. See Catalogue des Papyrus Égyptiens de la Bibliothèque Nationale, Paris, No. 331, MS. 4to. See also the two letters to M. C. Gazzera in *Des principales expressions qui servent à la Notation des Dates sur les Monuments de l'Ancienne Égypte.* Paris, 1832–3. 8vo.

Lenormant purchases the MSS. from Verardi.

Champollion's manuscripts, however, needed a great deal of alteration and arrangement before they could be printed. And their editor describes in detail how he was himself obliged to make a copy of the Dictionary in which he incorporated the contents of both the slips and the folios, as well as very many important particulars from his brother's *Grammaire Égyptienne.* Having written out all his material, he had to decide how to arrange the words. This was no easy matter, and finally he adopted the system which was foreshadowed in his brother's " Mémoire sur l'Écriture Hiératique," and was printed in 1821. At that time Champollion was endeavouring to classify and arrange the Egyptian hieroglyphs, and found great difficulty in doing so. He believed that the ancient Egyptians must have had some system of arrangement for them, though he had no support for this view, and no evidence on the subject was forthcoming from native sources, and none from the works of classical writers. Finally he adopted a " methodical, or so to say, natural classification," that is, he grouped into sections the figures of men, human members, animals, birds, fish, reptiles, plants, etc. This method was a modification of the system of arrangement of words in their Vocabularies by the Copts, for Champollion argued that if the Copts, who are racially the descendants of the ancient

Champollion-Figeac edits his brother's MSS.

Champollion's natural classification of hieroglyphs based on the Coptic " Scala."

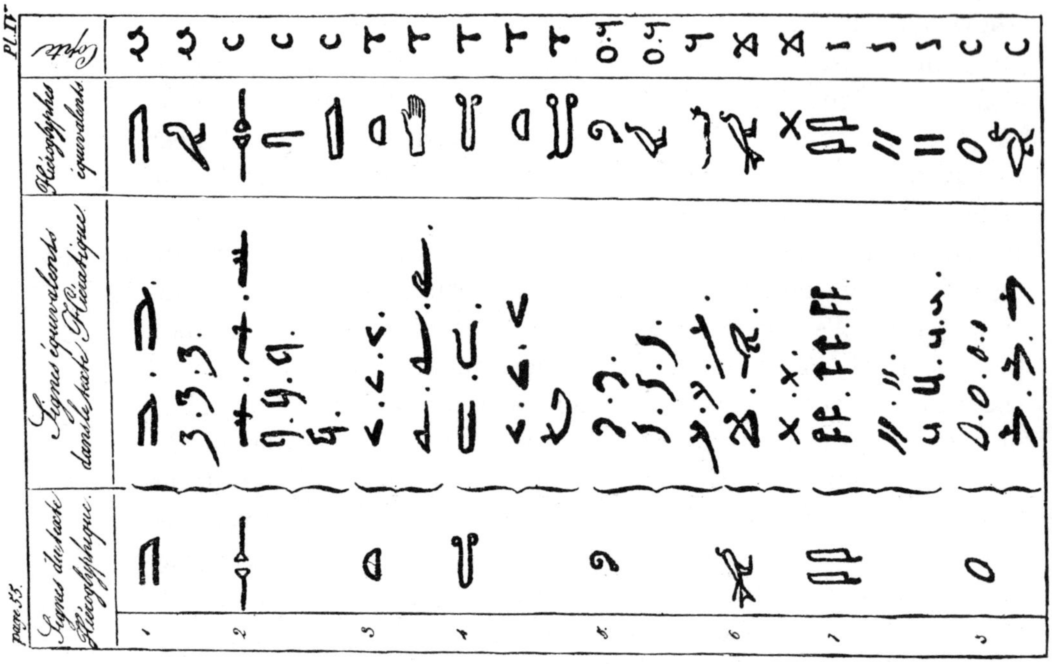

Hieroglyphic and Hieratic signs compared by Champollion.
From *Précis du Système Hiéroglyphique.* Paris, 1824.

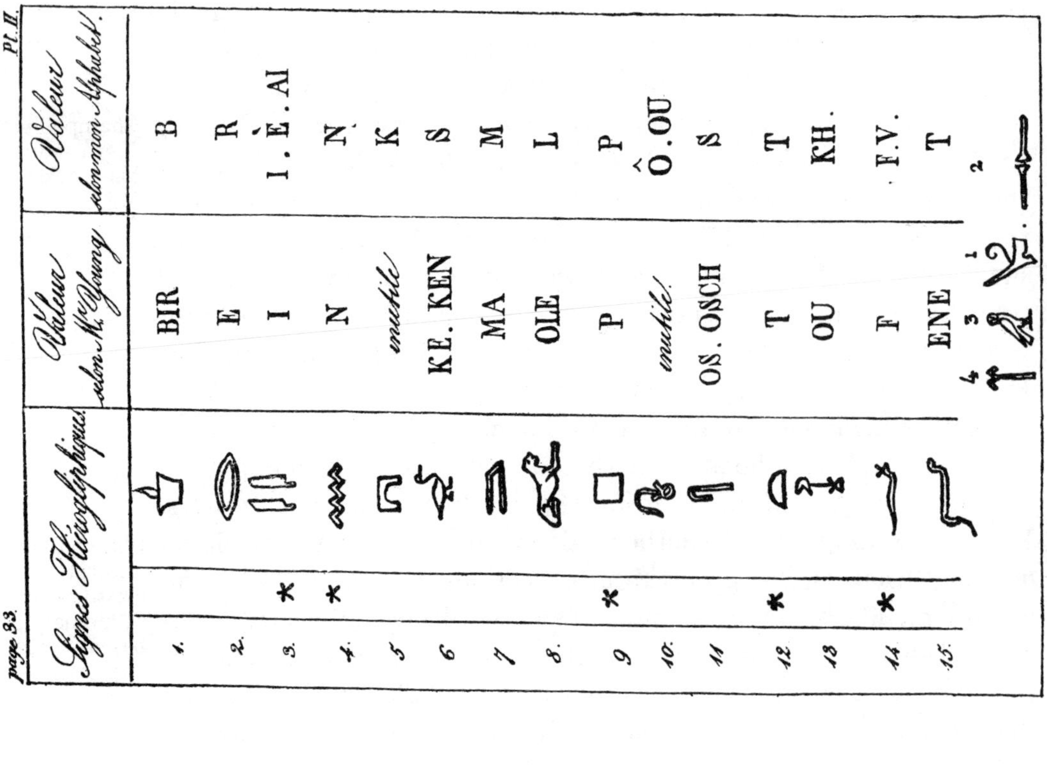
page 33.
Pl. II.
Signes Hiéroglyphiques.
Valeur selon Mr. Young
Valeur selon mon Alphabet.
1. BIR B
2. E R
3. I I. È. E. AI
4. N N
5. inutile K
6. KE. KEN S
7. MA M
8. OLE L
9. P P
10. inutile Ô. OU
11. OS. OSCH S
12. T T
13. OU KH.
14. F F.V.
15. ENE T
4 3 1 2

Champollion's comparison of the values given to certain hieroglyphic signs by Young and himself. From *Précis du Système Hiéroglyphique.* Paris, 1824.

Egyptians, and whose language is substantially the same as that of the ancient Egyptians, arranged their Vocabularies in this way, they must be reproducing a system that had been in use among their remote ancestors thousands of years earlier. Champollion-Figeac accepted his brother's arguments, and arranged the words of the Dictionary according to the order of the Sign-list composed by him, and printed in his earlier work.

The Coptic "Scala."

The following paragraph will explain the general system of arranging words in a Coptic Vocabulary, the common native names for which are ⲙⲟⲩⲕⲓ or ⲙⲟⲕⲓ, and ϭⲗⲟϭ or ϭⲗⲟⲟϭⲉ, *i.e.* Scala, "steps" or "stair." A typical example of such a Scala is given in the bilingual Coptic and Arabic MS. in Brit. Mus. Orient 1325, fol. 90 ff,[1] where we find the Scala Magna (Copt. ϯⲛⲓϣϯ ⲙ̅ⲙ̅ ⲙⲟⲕⲓ, Arab. سُلَّم الكَبِير) of Ibn Kabr.[2] It is divided into ten Gates or Doors (ⲣⲟ = ), and each gate contains several Chapters (ⲕⲉⲫⲁⲗⲉⲟⲛ). The First Gate (fol. 90A) contains four Chapters. The First Chapter gives the names of the Creator, ⲛⲓⲣⲁⲛ ⲛ̅ⲧⲉ ⲡⲣⲉϥⲥⲱⲛⲧ, the names of the Son from the Holy Scriptures, and the names of the Holy Spirit. The Second Chapter gives the names of the world which is above, ⲡⲕⲟⲥⲙⲟⲥ ⲉⲧⲥⲁ ⲡϣⲱⲓ, and of its orders and ranks, ⲛⲉⲙ ⲛⲉϥⲧⲁⲝⲓⲥ ⲛⲉⲙ ⲛⲉϥⲧⲁⲅⲙⲁ. The Third Chapter gives the names of the Firmament, and its towers, and its stars, ⲡⲓⲥⲧⲉⲣⲁⲱⲙⲁ ⲛⲉⲙ ⲛⲉϥⲡⲩⲣⲅⲟⲥ ⲛⲉⲙ ⲛⲉϥⲑⲱⲃϣ, and towers of the second station and the stations of the moon, ⲛⲓⲡⲩⲣⲅⲟⲥ ⲙ̅ⲙⲁϩⲓ ⲃ̅ ⲛⲓⲙⲟⲛⲏ ⲛ̅ⲧⲉ ϯⲙⲉⲧⲓⲟϩ. The Fourth Chapter deals with the world as it exists and its physical constitution and its Elements, ⲡⲓⲕⲟⲥⲙⲟⲥ ⲉⲧ̀ ϣⲟⲡ ⲛⲉⲙ ⲛⲉϥⲫⲩⲥⲓⲥ ⲛⲉⲙ ⲛⲉϥⲥⲧⲟⲓⲭⲓⲟⲛ.. The Second Gate (fol. 97A) contains seven Chapters, and deals with men, their worship, their qualities, occupations, grades, clothing, etc. Then follows a series of Chapters giving the names of beasts and animals (fol. 118A), birds (fol. 119A), the monsters and fish of the sea (fol 120A), trees and fruits (fol. 121A), scents and unguents (fol. 122A), seeds and grain (fol. 125A), precious metals, stones, etc. (fol. 127A), colours, names of countries (fol. 128A), rivers (130A), churches (Gate VII, fol. 130B), persons mentioned in Holy Scripture (fol. 132A), foreign words in Holy Scripture (Gate IX, fol. 135B), miscellaneous series of words (Gate X, fol. 138B).

The Ten Gates of the "Scala."

Summary of their contents.

[1] For a full description of the MS. see Rieu, *Catalogue of Arabic MSS., Supplement*, No. 47, and Crum, *Catalogue of the Coptic Manuscripts in the British Museum*, No. 920.

[2] See also Kircher, *Lingua Ægyptiaca restituta*, p. 41.

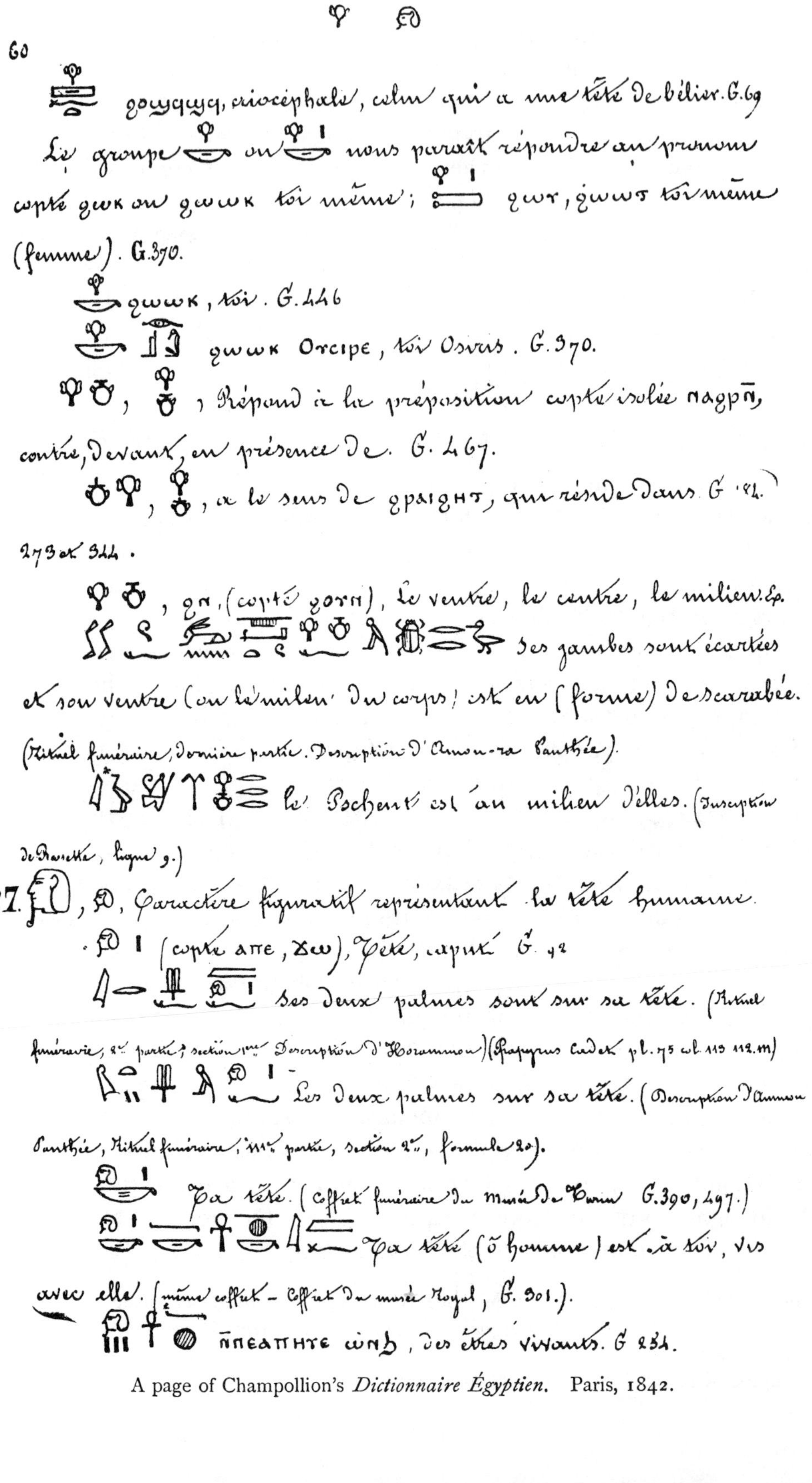
60
ϩⲟⲩϣϥⲱϥ, criocéphale, celui qui a une tête de bélier. G.69
Le groupe ou nous paraît répondre au pronom copte ϩⲱⲕ ou ϩⲱⲱⲕ toi même; ϩⲱⲧ, ϩⲱⲱⲧ toi même (femme). G.370.
ϩⲱⲱⲕ, toi. G.446
ϩⲱⲱⲕ Ⲟⲩⲥⲓⲣⲉ, toi Osiris. G.370.
, , Répond à la préposition copte isolée ⲛⲁϩⲣⲛ̄, contre, devant, en présence de. G.467.
, , a le sens de ϩⲣⲁⲓϩⲏⲧ, qui réside dans. G. 82, 273 et 344.
, ϩⲛ, (copte ϩⲟⲧⲛ), le ventre, le centre, le milieu. Ex.
ses jambes sont écartées et son ventre (ou le milieu du corps) est en (forme) de scarabée. (Rituel funéraire, dernière partie. Description d'Amon-ra Panthée).
le Pschent est au milieu d'elles. (Inscription de Rosette, ligne 9.)
27. , , Caractère figuratif représentant la tête humaine.
(copte ⲁⲡⲉ, ϫⲱ), Tête, caput. G. 42
Ses deux palmes sont sur sa tête. (Rituel funéraire, 2e partie, section 1re. Description d'Horammon) (Papyrus Cadet pl. 75 col. 113 112.111)
Les deux palmes sur sa tête. (Description d'Amon Panthée, Rituel funéraire, IIIe partie, section 2e, formule 20).
Ta tête. (Coffret funéraire du Musée de Turin G.390, 497.)
Ta tête (ô homme) est à toi, vis avec elle. (même coffret — Coffret du musée Royal, G. 301.)
ⲛⲁⲡⲉⲁⲡⲏⲧⲉ ⲱⲛϩ, des êtres vivants. G. 234.

A page of Champollion's *Dictionnaire Égyptien.* Paris, 1842.

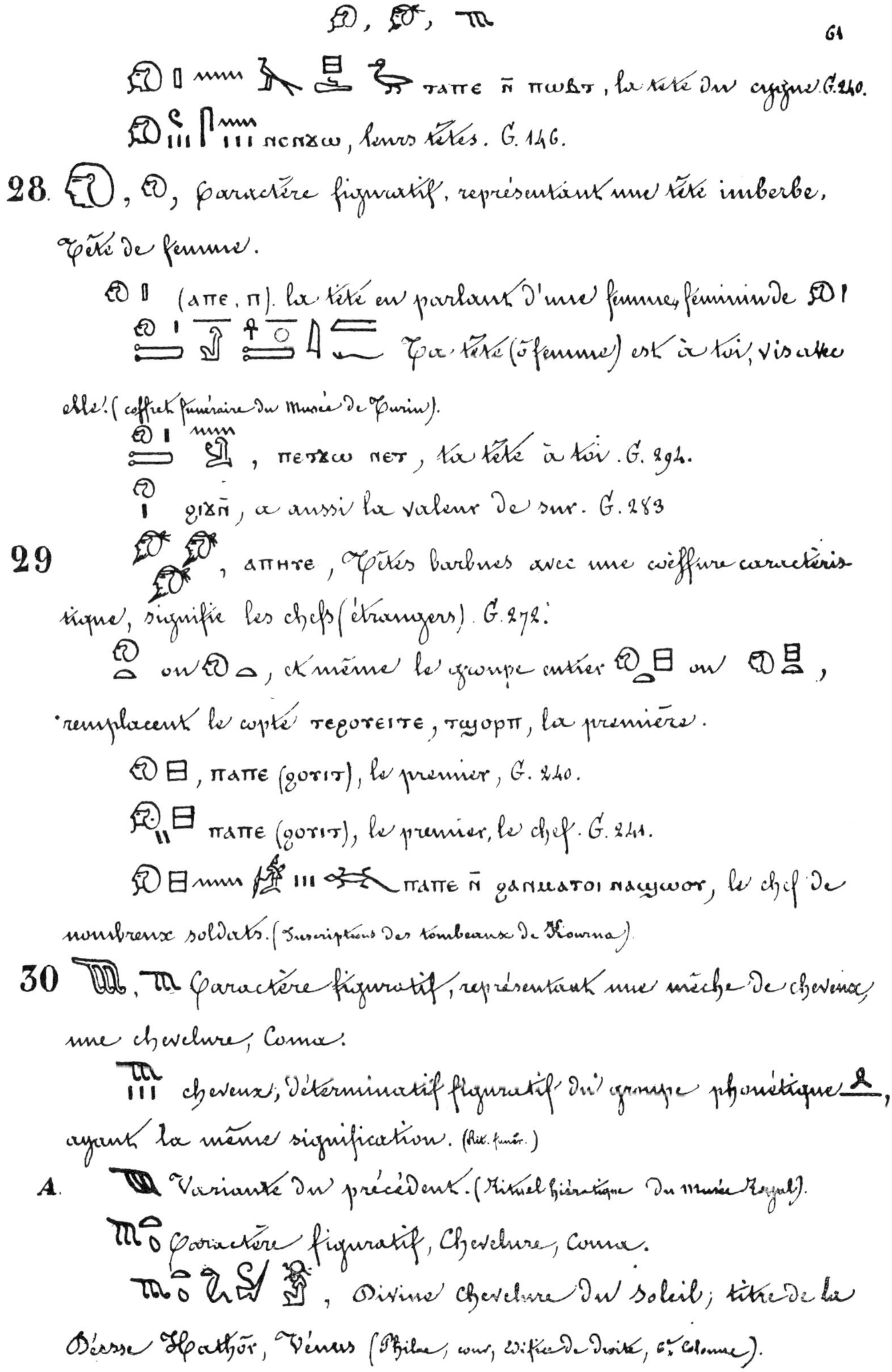

61

ⲧⲁⲡⲉ ⲛ̄ ⲡϣⲱⲃⲧ, la tête du cygne. G. 240.

ⲛⲉⲛϫⲱ, leurs têtes. G. 146.

28. , , Caractère figuratif, représentant une tête imberbe, Tête de femme.

(ⲁⲡⲉ, ⲡ). la tête en parlant d'une femme, féminin de

Ta tête (ô femme) est à toi, vis avec elle! (coffret funéraire du Musée de Turin).

, ⲡⲉⲧϫⲱ ⲛⲉⲧ, ta tête à toi. G. 294.

ϩⲓϫⲛ̄, a aussi la valeur de sur. G. 283

29 , ⲁⲡⲏⲩⲉ, Têtes barbues avec une coiffure caractéristique, signifie les chefs (étrangers). G. 272.

ou , et même le groupe entier ou , remplacent le copte ⲧⲉϩⲟⲩⲉⲓⲧⲉ, ⲧϣⲟⲣⲡ, la première.

, ⲡⲁⲡⲉ (ϩⲟⲩⲓⲧ), le premier, G. 240.

ⲡⲁⲡⲉ (ϩⲟⲩⲓⲧ), le premier, le chef. G. 241.

ⲡⲁⲡⲉ ⲛ̄ ϩⲁⲙⲙⲁⲧⲟⲓ ⲛⲁϣⲱⲟⲩ, le chef de nombreux soldats. (Inscriptions des tombeaux de Kourna).

30 , Caractère figuratif, représentant une mèche de cheveux, une chevelure, Coma.

cheveux, déterminatif figuratif du groupe phonétique , ayant la même signification. (Rit. funér.)

A. Variante du précédent. (Rituel hiératique du Musée Royal).

Caractère figuratif, Chevelure, Coma.

, Divine Chevelure du Soleil; titre de la Déesse Hathôr, Vénus (Philae, cour, édifice de droite, 6e colonne).

A page of Champollion's *Dictionnaire Égyptien*. Paris, 1842.

Champollion-Figeac accepts the arrangement of the "Scala."

Such was the arrangement of words in the model which Champollion-Figeac took as a guide for the arrangement of words in his brother's Egyptian Dictionary, and he asks the question "L'expérience ou le raisonnement indiquaient ils une autre méthode?" Experience, he says, suggests a single example only, namely the Chinese, but having described at some length the differences that exist between the Chinese and Egyptian languages, he decides that even if analogies and a similitude between these

He rejects the Chinese arrangement of characters.

two languages did exist originally they do so no longer. The Chinese Dictionary must not be employed as the model for a Hieroglyphic Dictionary, only the Coptic *Scala* is any use for this purpose. Champollion-Figeac then goes on to mention that another system has been proposed and even tried, namely that advocated by Samuel Birch in his "Sketch of a Hieroglyphical Dictionary." Having examined the Preface to this work he says, "Though the specimen, which I owe to the courtesy of Mr. Birch, is brief, it seems to me to be sufficient to make clear the defect in the general plan adopted by this scholar. The phonetic characters are divided into vowel characters and consonantal characters; the symbolic or ideographic characters are separated and form a section by themselves. He who would search for

He discusses Birch's plan and rejects it

the value of one of the eight hundred Egyptian characters would then be obliged to know first of all whether it is a symbolic or phonetic character, and when the character forms one of this second series, to know also whether its value is that of a vowel or a consonant, that is to say, to know beforehand all that he seeks to learn in the Dictionary. The general table proposed by Mr. Birch will undoubtedly facilitate his searchings, but would it not be more advantageous to spare students (1) the labour of searching; (2) the trouble of finding the *human eye* belonging to the vowel I, the *arms* belonging to the vowel A, the *leg* belonging to the consonant B, the *two arms raised* belonging to the consonant K, the *hand* belonging to the consonant T, the *mouth* belonging to the consonant R, the *head full-faced* belonging to the aspirated consonant ϩ; and (3) the inextricable confusion of forms and expressions that results from the mixing-up of the members of the human body with quadrupeds, and fish and flowers? On the other hand, would not all the analogous characters which the natural or rational system would write in the same series, or the members of the human body, or animals, or vegetables, placed together and each species grouped in a single chapter, characterise more clearly a system which is truly natural and, in consequence, preferable to any other? This is the actual system which was adopted by the author of our *Dictionnaire Hiéroglyphique*, and it is necessary to hope that Mr. Birch will not deny to it his suffrage.[1] . . . In the general order of the divisions [of the *Dictionnaire*] the characters are placed according to the order of merit of the object which they represent; heaven before the stars which appear therein; man before all other animated creatures; the products of the divine creation before the products of human invention; plants before objects of art and fantastic emblems. Finally, the whole before its parts, and these even in a certain order of relative pre-eminence, which is regulated by the customs or opinions of the world. . . . Each hieroglyphic character is followed by the groups of which it is the primitive character, the key-character, and in the arrangement of these groups, the order of priority adopted for the general classification of the characters has been followed. . . . Moreover, this order for the second character is followed equally for the third, the fourth, etc., just as is done for the second, third and fourth letter of the words of our dictionaries arranged in the order of the alphabet."[2]

He pleads for Birch's suffrage for his brother's system.

Champollion-Figeac describes his "natural and rational" system.

However "natural" and "rational" this system may have been from Champollion's point of view, there is no doubt that the beginner and student with only a limited knowledge of hieroglyphs would find it very difficult to get from his Dictionary much help in reading even an ordinary historical inscription, or a formula from the Book of the Dead. This will be apparent to the reader if he will examine the extract from it which is printed on pp. xxviii, xxix, even after making due allowance for the imperfect knowledge of the interpretation of hieroglyphs which Egyptologists possessed in 1832. At all events Champollion's system was not adopted by the Egyptologists of the day, though all admitted his *Dictionnaire* to be a fine monument of research and learning.

The "natural and rational" system of arrangement of hieroglyphs rejected by contemporary Egyptologists.

In the Preface to his "Sketch of a Hieroglyphical Dictionary," Birch stated that he did not intend to proceed with the publication of his work until the second part of Champollion's *Grammaire Égyptienne* had appeared. This decision is easily understood and it is only natural that he should wait to see what further details of Champollion's incomplete works might be contained in manuscripts which Champollion-Figeac was publishing as fast as possible. The last fascicule of the *Grammaire Égyptienne* appeared in 1841, and Champollion's *Dictionnaire Égyptien* in

Birch finds the "natural and rational" system unpractical.

[1] Préface of Champollion-Figeac, pp. xxviii and xxix. [2] *Ibid.*, p. xxxii.

1842, and Birch and his great contemporary Lepsius spent some years in digesting these works. Birch told me more than forty years ago that the more he studied the monuments, and the more he copied hieroglyphic and hieratic papyri, the more he became convinced that Champollion's "natural and rational" system of arranging words in the Egyptian Dictionary was hopelessly unpractical. He had profound respect for Champollion's learning and ability, but he could not give his "suffrage" to the *Dictionnaire* as Champollion-Figeac hoped he would. In the end he decided once and for all that in continuing his lexicographical labours he must adopt a purely phonetic, *i.e.*, alphabetic arrangement, even though it implied the rejection of the "ideophonetic" arrangement which he himself had proposed in 1838. Moreover, his own study of the Sallier and Anastasi Papyri, which the British Museum acquired about that time, convinced him of the fact that the time for the publication of a really useful Egyptian Dictionary had not yet come. Material out of which a dictionary might be compiled existed in abundance, but it was unpublished. What was most wanted was good copies of texts on which scholars in every country could work, and the Trustees of the British Museum rendered Egyptology great service when they published the wonderfully good copies of the Sallier and Anastasi Papyri, made by Mr. Netherclift under the superintendence of Birch.[1] Dr. Leemans urged the Government of the Netherlands to publish the monuments and papyri at Leyden, and they wisely did so,[2] and Lepsius put an end to vague talk about the Book of the Dead when he published a facsimile of the famous Turin Codex, containing the Saïte Recension of this important work. Further, the last-named scholar, having persuaded the Prussian Government of the importance of collecting the fast-perishing inscriptions in Egypt, was despatched to that country in 1842 to carry out the work, and so was able to place at the disposal of Egyptologists throughout the world his great *Corpus* of Egyptian texts and papyri, Nubian inscriptions, etc., called the "Denkmäler."[3]

He finally adopts a phonetic alphabetic arrangement and rejects his own ideophonetic system.

Birch, Leemans and Lepsius begin to publish the Egyptian texts.

The Leyden Papyri.

The Turin Book of the Dead.

The "Denkmäler."

[1] (1) *Papyri in Hieroglyphic and Hieratic Characters, etc., in the British Museum.* London, 1844, fol.; (2) *Select Papyri in the Hieratic Character with prefatory remarks* [by S. Birch]. London, 1844, fol. A mass of valuable material was published by Sharpe in his *Egyptian Inscriptions from the British Museum and other sources.* London, 1837–41.

[2] *Monuments Égyptiens du Musée d'Antiquités des Pays-Bas à Leide* [Parts 1 and 2 contain facsimiles of Monuments and Papyri]. Leyden, 1841–2.

[3] *Denkmäler aus Aegypten und Aethiopien,* 12 Bände, large folio, 1849–59.

Birch's Dictionary of Hieroglyphics.

Birch's decision to adopt a purely alphabetic arrangement in his Egyptian Dictionary was induced largely by the results of the careful study of the alphabetic hieroglyphs which Edward Hincks carried out after the appearance of Champollion's *Dictionnaire Égyptien.* Whilst making this study he was in frequent communication with Birch, who was greatly impressed with his clearness of thought and the ease with which he recognised the difficulties of the problem, and found their true solution. Birch was at that time engaged in preparing a list of Egyptian characters[1] for the first volume of Bunsen's "Aegyptens Stelle," and the matter for the last three Sections in it,[2] and, judging from Bunsen's remark,[3] Birch's official duties left him very little leisure for the compilation of his Dictionary. Hincks published the results of his investigation in 1847,[4] and in that year Birch, as he himself told me, began to write the slips for his Egyptian Dictionary, and to arrange them alphabetically in boxes. The work of publishing and reading new texts occupied him for several years, but at length the large mass of material which he had collected justified him in considering the publication of his work. Thereupon arose the two difficult questions: Was the Dictionary to be printed or lithographed? Who would undertake the expense of publication? To print it was impossible, for there was no fount of Egyptian type in existence. It might, of course, be lithographed, but that pre-supposed the writing out of the whole Dictionary on transfer paper by Birch himself, a work that would require a vast amount of time and labour. As no immediate solution of the difficulty seemed possible, Birch continued to write slips and revise his manuscript.

Hincks's researches.

Birch begins to write his Dictionary of Hieroglyphics.

Typographical difficulties.

Meanwhile Bunsen had published further additions to his voluminous "Historical Investigation into Egypt's Place in

[1] This list contained about 830 characters, and was printed on eight plates in the first volume of Bunsen's work (Hamburg and Gotha, 1845. 8vo).

[2] Bunsen thanks his friends for their help (Vorredé, p. xxvi, Vol. I) "und Samuel Birch am Britischen Museum (in welchem ein grosser Theil der drei letzten Abschnitte des ersten Buches geschrieben ist), sagen wir Dank mit freudigen Wünschen."

[3] Ein vollständiges Wörterbuch des Hieroglyphenschatzes, mit allen Mannigfaltigkeiten der Darstellung und mit Anführung des Textes der entscheidenden Stellen, darf die gelehrte Welt von Herr Birch erwarten, sobald seine amtlichen Beschäftigungen ihm die Musse dazu gewähren (Vol. I, p. 646).

[4] See his paper, *An attempt to ascertain the number, names and powers of the letters of the Hieroglyphic ancient Egyptian Alphabet, grounded on the establishment of a new principle in the use of phonetic characters* in the *Transactions of the Royal Irish Academy.* Dublin, 1847. 4to.

An English edition of Bunsen's "Aegyptens Stelle" called for.

Universal History," which excited general interest not only on the Continent, but in England, and an English edition was called for. Negotiations with Messrs. Longman were entered into, presumably by Bunsen himself, and the outcome of them was that, at a very heavy cost, they undertook to cast a fount of hieroglyphic type in order to print Birch's Egyptian Sign-List, Grammar, Dictionary and Chrestomathy as essential portions of the English edition of the first and fifth volumes of Bunsen's work.[1] Thus a firm of publishers undertook to perform, at their own private expense, a task which abroad would have been heavily subsidised by the Government. The designs for the bold, handsome type (see a specimen page of the Dictionary on p. xxxvii) were drawn by Mr. Joseph Bonomi, the matrices were cut by Mr. L. Martin, and the casting was carried out by Mr. Branston, all under Birch's direction. When the printing of Birch's Egyptian Dictionary began I have been unable to find out, but I remember his saying that it took nearly three years to pass the sheets through the press, even after the greater number of the types were cast and ready for use. The English translation of the fifth volume of "Egypt's Place in Universal History" appeared in the first half of the year 1867, and the official date stamp of the copy in the British Museum reads "11 Ju[ly] 67." It was seen through the press by Birch after the death of Bunsen and Cottrell, the English translator, and in the Preface Birch says that "a few words are required to indicate the additional labours which have been bestowed upon it, and the introduction of certain portions which are not to be found in the German Edition." The first 122 pages were revised by Bunsen, who was enabled to use the English translation of the Turin Codex of the Book of the Dead which Birch had made and placed in his hands. The Hieroglyphic Grammar, Chrestomathy and Dictionary, which according to the original plan of the work

A fount of hieroglyphic type cast in London.

Birch edits the fifth volume of Bunsen's work.

[1] Writing at Highwood on September 27th, 1847, Bunsen says in the Postscript to the first English edition of Vol. I, "This English edition owes many valuable remarks and additions to my learned friend, Mr. Samuel Birch, particularly in the grammatical, lexicographic, and mythological part. That I have been able to make out of the collection of Egyptian roots, printed in the German edition, a complete hieroglyphical dictionary, is owing to him. To him also belong the references to the monumental evidence for the signification of an Egyptian word, wherever the proof exhibited in Champollion's dictionary or grammar is not clear or satisfactory. Without any addition to the bulk of the volume, and without any incumbrance to the text, the work may now be said to contain the only complete Egyptian grammar and dictionary, as well as the only existing collection and interpretation of all the hieroglyphical signs; in short, all that a general scholar wants to make himself master of the hieroglyphic system by studying the monuments."

were to form parts of the fifth volume, were not completed when Bunsen died on November 28th, 1860. The unfinished translation of the comparative vocabularies was completed by Birch and Dr. Rieu, Assistant Keeper of Oriental Manuscripts in the British Museum, who also inserted Bunsen's additions and corrections. Birch's translation of the Book of the Dead, together with his Introduction, fills 209 pages (pp. 125–333), the Egyptian Dictionary fills 250 pages (pp. 337–586), and the Hieroglyphic Grammar and Chrestomathy fill 153 pages (pp. 589–741). Thus the original matter supplied by him to the fifth volume fills 612 pages, or nearly three-quarters of the whole volume. The number of entries on a page of the Egyptian Dictionary averages eighteen, and the total number of entries is therefore about 4,500.

The comparative vocabularies completed by Birch and Rieu.

Birch's contributions to the fifth volume.

"The Dictionary," Birch says in his Preface, "is phonetic in its arrangement, the words being placed under the phonetic value[s] of the signs at the time of compilation. It is important to remember this, as Egyptologists give a different power to a few signs, or regard others as polyphone[s]. The ideographic and determinative hieroglyphics, having been already given in the first volume,[1] have not been repeated in this, and the student must seek them in their appropriate places. It is also to be borne in mind that the meaning of all Egyptian words has not yet been determined, and that the researches of Egyptologists continue to enrich the number of interpreted words. A reference to the place where it is found is given with each word, but it was not possible, without exceeding the limits of this work, to give in every instance the name of the scholar who discovered its meaning [here follows

[1] Bunsen says ("Egypt's Place," Vol. I, p. 503), "I have, together with Mr. Birch, submitted to the test of accurate criticism all the hieroglyphical signs hitherto collected and explained, and have classified each of them in its proper place, according to that arrangement. [The general arrangement is laid down in the text.] At the same time I have requested that gentleman to add his own valuable remarks to this collection, so as to complete and correct it. . . . Through his assistance I am enabled to give, not only a more critical, but also a more complete exposition of the hieroglyphical signs, than has hitherto been embodied in previous works, all of which are very expensive, and some very rare. Where the Grammar or Dictionary of Champollion is not quoted, the signs and interpretations are supplied by Mr. Birch from other authorities or his own researches. . . . The arrangement is the natural one, proposed and adopted by Champollion, in the early stages of the study of hieroglyphics: viz., signs of astronomical or geographical objects; human forms, animals—from the quadruped down to the worm—plants, stones, instruments, etc., and signs as yet undeciphered." The List contains: A. IDEOGRAPHICS, 890 characters. B. DETERMINATIVES, 201 characters. C. PHONETICS, C. I, 153 characters; C. II, 135 characters. D. MIXED CHARACTERS, 70 characters.

Contemporary Egyptologists.

mention of Hincks, Goodwin and Le Page Renouf in England, Chabas, E. de Rougé, Devéria in France, H. Brugsch, Dümichen, Lauth, Lepsius and Pleyte in Germany, as being the men to whom the advance of the study of Egyptology is principally due]. The advantage of [Messrs. Longmans'] hieroglyphic type to the present volume cannot be too highly appreciated, as it has rendered it practicable to print the Egyptian Dictionary, the Grammar, and the Chrestomathy in a form which renders the study of the hieroglyphs accessible both to the student and general enquirer. The Dictionary is the only one hitherto printed in this country, nor has any hieroglyphical dictionary appeared elsewhere, except that of Champollion, published in 1841 [read 1842], which contained only a few of the principal words. Its phonetic arrangement will, it is hoped, render it particularly easy of consultation. It has been a great labour to compile and print it, and the execution of it has been a task of many years. Other Egyptologists, indeed, have attached vocabularies to their labours on particular inscriptions, but no dictionary on a large scale has as yet been attempted, although the absolute want of one has been long felt." This Preface is dated April 13th, 1867. The publication of the first Egyptian Dictionary arranged on phonetic, *i.e.*, alphabetic, principles, and printed in hieroglyphic type, was a great triumph for English Egyptology and the craft of the typographer, and to Birch the compiler and Spottiswoode the printer, and Longmans the publishers, every Egyptologist owes a debt of gratitude.

Birch's opinion of his Dictionary of Hieroglyphics.

But it is quite impossible to hide the fact that the inclusion of Birch's Egyptian Dictionary in the fifth volume of the English translation was a great misfortune for the Dictionary itself and for the beginner in Egyptology for whom the work was primarily intended. There was an interval of seven years between the publication of the fourth and fifth volumes of the English translation of *Aegyptens Stelle in der Weltgeschichte*, and there seems to be no doubt that public interest in Bunsen's scheme of chronology drooped when its author died in 1860, the year which saw the appearance of the fourth volume, and was practically dead when the fifth volume was published in 1867. According to Birch, the volume fell "flat," and its editor and publishers were greatly disappointed. Whether the edition was a small one or not I have no evidence to show, but it was certainly the fact that for some reason or other copies of the volume were difficult to get in the early "seventies." It was said at the time that the publishers, being dissatisfied with the sales, had "disposed" of the sheets

Birch's Egyptian Dictionary falls "flat."

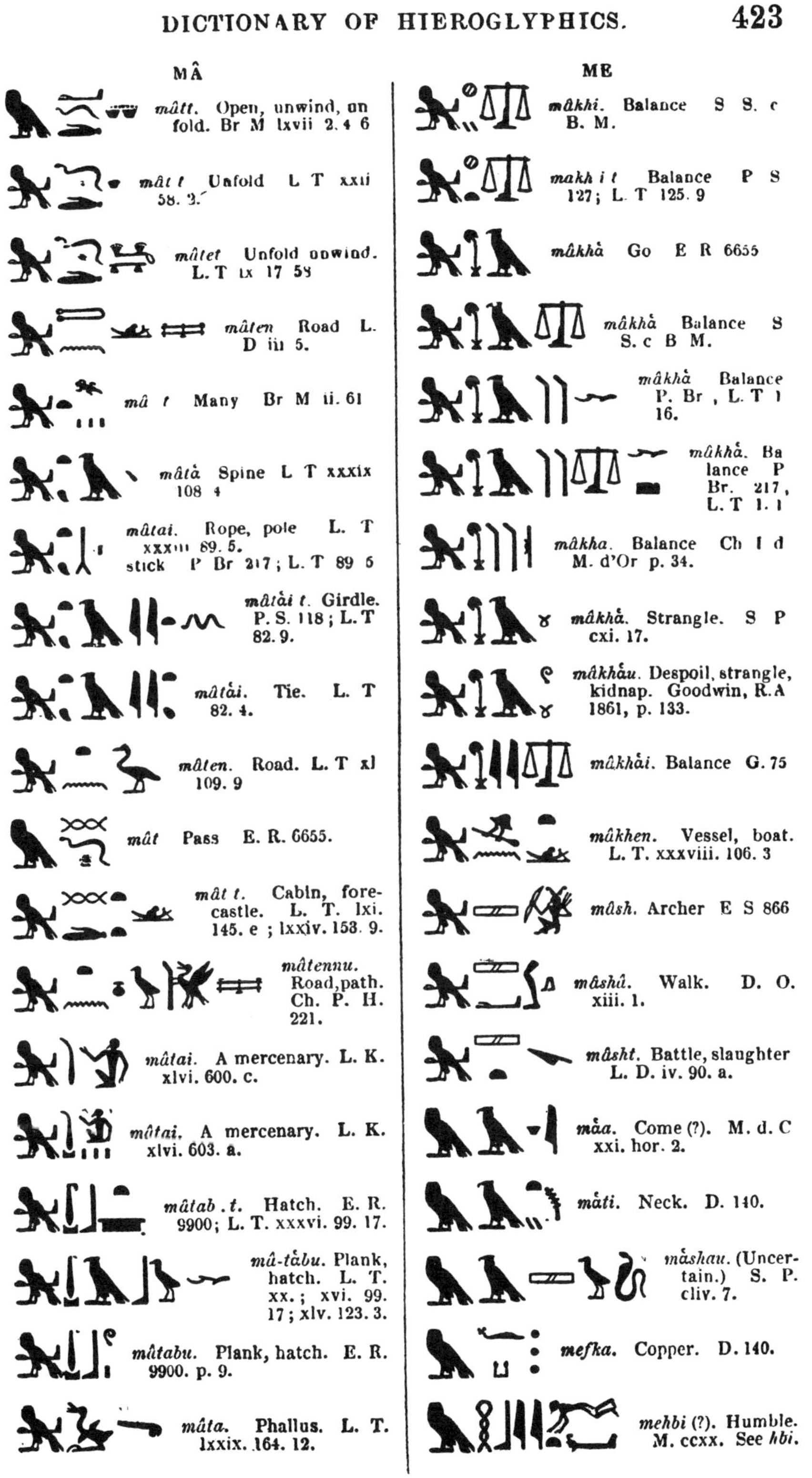
DICTIONARY OF HIEROGLYPHICS. 423

MÂ

mâtt. Open, unwind, unfold. Br M lxvii 2. 4 6

mât t Unfold L T xxii 58. 3.

mâtet Unfold unwind. L. T lx 17 58

mâten Road L. D iii 5.

mâ t Many Br M ii. 61

mâtà Spine L T xxxix 108 4

mâtai. Rope, pole L. T xxxiii 89. 5. stick P Br 217 ; L. T 89 5

mâtâi t. Girdle. P. S. 118 ; L. T 82. 9.

mâtâi. Tie. L. T 82. 4.

mâten. Road. L. T xl 109. 9

mât Pass E. R. 6655.

mât t. Cabin, fore-castle. L. T. lxi. 145. e ; lxxiv. 153. 9.

mâtennu. Road, path. Ch. P. H. 221.

mâtai. A mercenary. L. K. xlvi. 600. c.

mâtai. A mercenary. L. K. xlvi. 603. a.

mâtab . t. Hatch. E. R. 9900; L. T. xxxvi. 99. 17.

mâ-tâbu. Plank, hatch. L. T. xx. ; xvi. 99. 17 ; xlv. 123. 3.

mâtabu. Plank, hatch. E. R. 9900. p. 9.

mâta. Phallus. L. T. lxxix. 164. 12.

ME

mâkhi. Balance S S. c B. M.

makh i t Balance P S 127 ; L. T 125. 9

mâkhà Go E R 6655

mâkhà Balance S S. c B M.

mâkhà Balance P. Br , L. T 1 16.

mâkhà. Balance P Br. 217, L. T 1. 1

mâkha. Balance Ch I d M. d'Or p. 34.

mâkhà. Strangle. S P cxi. 17.

mâkhâu. Despoil, strangle, kidnap. Goodwin, R. A 1861, p. 133.

mâkhâi. Balance G. 75

mâkhen. Vessel, boat. L. T. xxxviii. 106. 3

mâsh. Archer E S 866

mâshâ. Walk. D. O. xiii. 1.

mâsht. Battle, slaughter L. D. iv. 90. a.

mâa. Come (?). M. d. C xxi. hor. 2.

mâti. Neck. D. 140.

mâshau. (Uncertain.) S. P. cliv. 7.

mefka. Copper. D. 140.

mehbi (?). Humble. M. ccxx. See *hbi*.

A page of Birch's *Dictionary of Hieroglyphics*. London, 1867.

of a large number of copies. The natural result was that when people found out that the volume contained Birch's Dictionary and Grammar and Chrestomathy the copies that found their way into the market fetched relatively very high prices, or at all events prices which effectively placed the book beyond the reach of the ordinary student. When I attended Birch's Egyptian classes in 1875–76 and needed the book urgently, I was obliged to trace each page of it on a separate sheet of tracing paper, omitting the references, and when these sheets were bound I used them for some years with great benefit. Moreover, the fifth volume of the English translation of Bunsen's work formed a veritable tomb for Birch's Dictionary. The title-page of it sets forth quite clearly that the "Historical Investigation" was by Bunsen, and that it was translated from the German by Charles H. Cottrell, Esq., M.A., and that it contains "Additions by Samuel Birch, LL.D." But who could possibly imagine from this last remark that Birch's contribution was 594 pages, *i.e.*, nearly three-quarters of the whole volume, or that his contribution included an Egyptian Dictionary, the first ever published arranged on phonetic principles (!), and containing about 4,500 entries of Egyptian words, and names of gods and places, with references and translations, and an Egyptian Grammar and Chrestomathy? Or, again, take the case of the student who wants to consult these works and who, hearing that copies of them are to be seen in the British Museum Library, goes to the Reading Room to see them. He turns up the entry Birch, Samuel, LL.D., of the British Museum, in the Great Catalogue, but fails to find any mention of the Dictionary of Hieroglyphics or Grammar and Chrestomathy, because they are not mentioned in any one of the columns of names of the other books and papers which Birch wrote. All that he will find connecting Birch with an Egyptian Dictionary is the entry, "Sketch of a Hieroglyphical Dictionary, London, 1838," and unless he receives further instruction he will conclude that the "Sketch" published in 1838 is useless to him, and that Birch's Egyptian Dictionary never appeared. The same is the case with Birch's translation of the Book of the Dead, the first ever made and published, which also appeared in the fifth volume of "Egypt's Place," and his List of Hieroglyphic Characters which appeared in the first volume, first with plates of characters, and secondly with the hieroglyphic characters printed in the new type. The only mention of Birch in the Great Catalogue in connection with the Book of the Dead is contained in the title of the Trustees' publication of the texts

Bunsen's fifth volume the tomb of Birch's Dictionary of Hieroglyphics.

Birch's translation of the Book of the Dead and his List of Hieroglyphics.

on the coffin of Amamu. The fault lies not with any of the generations of the learned and devoted men who have spent their lives in compiling that wonderful Great Catalogue, with its millions of entries of books in every printed language of the world, but with those who buried in their own books Birch's greatest works so effectually that they have no mention under his name in the authors' great Book of Life, the British Museum Catalogue. In his admirable Bibliography, *The Literature of Egypt and the Soudan*, 2 vols., London, 1886, 4to, Prince Ibrâhîm Hilmy rightly mentioned the translation of the Book of the Dead, and the Dictionary of Hieroglyphics and the Hieroglyphic Grammar under the entry Birch, Samuel, LL.D., etc. But even so, he refers the reader for particulars of these works to the entry Bunsen, C. C. J.

HEINRICH BRUGSCH AND HIS "HIEROGLYPHISCH-DEMOTISCHES WÖRTERBUCH."

The publication of Bunsen's *Aegyptens Stelle in der Weltgeschichte* in 1845 fired the imagination of a young German called Heinrich Brugsch,[1] who was at that time a pupil in the Real Gymnasium at Cologne, and he devoted himself ardently to the study of the Egyptian inscriptions in the demotic character. In 1849 he published the paper, *Die demotische Schrift der alten Aegypter und ihre Monumente*, in the *Zeitschrift* of the German Oriental Society (Bd. III, pp. 262–272), and in 1850 he received his Doctorate from the University of Berlin for his Thesis *De Natura et Indole Linguae Popularis Aegyptiorum*, Berlin (Dümmler, 1850, 8vo). In the same year he published *Die Inschrift von Rosette, nach ihrem Aegyptisch-demotischen Texte sprachlich und sachlich erklärt*, with an Appendix containing a series of hitherto unpublished demotic texts. In 1851 he published the hieroglyphic text of the Rosetta Stone,[2] with a Hieroglyphic-Coptic-Latin vocabulary and a list of hieroglyphic characters, and after a Mission to Egypt in 1853–54 he published his famous *Grammaire Démotique*.[3] Ten years later he published his epoch-making work on the Rhind Papyri,[4] and proved himself to be an expert in translating very difficult hieratic and demotic texts. Brugsch did not confine his studies to demotic, and between 1855 and 1865 he was engaged in drawing up a

Brugsch's studies in demotic.

His editions of demotic texts

His Grammar of demotic.

[1] Born and died in Berlin (February 18th, 1827—September 9th, 1894).

[2] *Inscriptio Rosettana Hieroglyphica.* Berlin, 1851. 4to.

[3] *Grammaire Démotique, contenant les Principes Généraux de la Langue et de l'Écriture Populaire des Anciens Égyptiens.* Berlin, 1855. 4to.

[4] *Henry Rhind's Zwei Bilingue Papyri, hieratisch und demotisch, übersetzt und herausgegeben.* Leipzig, 1865. 4to.

His mission to Persia.

History of Ancient Egypt under its native kings,[1] and in publishing a series of geographical texts,[2] etc. He was attached to the Mission to Persia of the Baron Minutoli in 1850–51, and served as Prussian Vice-Consul in Cairo from 1864 to 1866, but in spite of the official duties attached to these posts he managed to find time to undertake the compilation of a Hieroglyphic Dictionary. It is more than probable that he knew that Birch was engaged on a similar task, but if he had this knowledge, it did not prevent him from making arrangements for the publication of his work. That Birch knew of these arrangements is quite certain, for his name appears in the list of subscribers issued by the publisher.

Race for priority between Brugsch and Birch.

Each scholar naturally wished to be the first in the field with his Egyptian Dictionary, so that he might claim the credit of being the first to publish a really large collection of ancient Egyptian words arranged alphabetically. In this race for priority Birch was the winner, for he dated his short Preface to the fifth volume of "Egypt's Place" on April 13th, 1867, and his whole Dictionary was then printed off. In the other case only the *first volume* of Brugsch's Hieroglyphic-Demotic Dictionary, containing the letters 𓄿, 𓇋, 𓂝, 𓅱 and 𓃀, was printed off at that time, and the publisher's advertisement on the cover is dated "Ende April 1867," though Brugsch's Preface is dated März 1867.

Brugsch's Hieroglyphic Demotic Dictionary.

The Hieroglyphic-Demotic Dictionary[3] of Brugsch is, with the exception of the Introduction, lithographed throughout. The first four volumes form the Dictionary proper and contain 1,707 pages, and the last three form the Supplement, and contain 1,418 pages. The number of words treated in the Dictionary proper is 4,637, not counting the additions in the Supplement, which were derived from newly published texts. Whilst writing out his Dictionary for the lithographer, Brugsch's object seems to have been to make the work as large as possible. He states his views on points of Egyptian Grammar at great but unequal length, and many of his paragraphs are filled with

[1] *Histoire d'Égypte sous les Rois indigènes.* Paris, 1859.

[2] *Geographische Inschriften Altägyptischer Denkmäler,* Bände I–III, Leipzig, 1857–60; *Die Geographie der Aegypter nach den Denkmälern.* Leipzig, 1860. 4to.

[3] The full title reads: *Hieroglyphisch-Demotisches Wörterbuch enthaltend in wissenschaftlicher Anordnung die Gebräuchlichsten Wörter und Gruppen der heiligen und der Volks-Sprache und Schrift der alten Aegypter nebst deren Erklärung in Französischer, Deutscher und Arabischer Sprache und Angabe ihrer Verwandschaft mit den entsprechenden Wörtern des Koptischen und der Semitische Idiome,* 7 Bände, Leipzig, 1867–1882, 4to, Vol. I, 1867; Vols. II–IV, 1868; supplement. Vol. V, 1880; Vol. VI, 1881; Vol. VII, 1882.

extracts from Egyptian texts followed by translations and wordy comments. In some respects his work resembles an Encyclopædia of Egyptology rather than a Dictionary, and contains a great deal of information which, it seems to me, should have been given elsewhere. As no publisher could afford to defray the cost of printing the Dictionary, even on the Continent, where great scholarly works are often subsidized by the Government, it was decided to reproduce Brugsch's manuscript by lithography, which in those days was a tolerably inexpensive method of publication; and Brugsch undertook to write the transfers for the lithographer with his own hand. Thus he was given practically a free hand by his publisher, and a Dictionary containing 3,125 pages is the result. The amount of Egyptological knowledge which he displays in this truly great work is marvellous, and his familiarity with the contents of the most difficult texts, whether hieroglyphic, hieratic or demotic, is phenomenal. He was the greatest Egyptologist that Germany had produced, and his energy and zeal and devotion and power of work must ever command our warmest admiration. Brugsch, like Birch, arranged the words in his Hieroglyphic Dictionary alphabetically, and it is an interesting fact that both scholars, apparently independently, came to the conclusion that Champollion's "natural and rational" system of arrangement must be rejected. Birch, as we know from his Preface to the fifth volume of "Egypt's Place," had no high opinion of Champollion's *Dictionnaire Égyptien* as a Dictionary, for he says that it "contained only a few of the principal words." Brugsch dedicated his Dictionary to the Manes of Champollion, and in his Introduction says that Champollion's Dictionary, which was published five and twenty years ago, after its author's death, under the name of *Dictionnaire Égyptien*, could and can lay claim to-day at the very least to this name. He goes on to say that it was published without the will and intention of the immortal French scholar, and that it consists of little more than an epitome of the words and groups in his *Grammaire Égyptienne*, and that it contains mistakes of which the master, had he been alive, would never have allowed himself to be guilty.[1]

Brugsch's encyclopædic knowledge of Egyptology.

He rejects Champollion's "natural and rational" arrangement.

Brugsch's opinion of Champollion's Egyptian Dictionary.

[1] "Das unter dem Namen eines *Dictionnaire Égyptien* vor fünf und zwanzig Jahren nach dem Tode Champollion's veröffentliche Wörterbuch konnte, und kann am allerwenigsten heut zu Tage, Anspruch auf diesen Namen machen. Ohne Absicht und Willen des unsterblichen französischen Gelehrten publicir , enthält es beinahe nur einen Auszug der Wörter und Gruppen der *Grammaire Égyptienne*, dazu mit Irrthümern, deren sich niemals der lebende Meister schuldig gemacht haben würde." Einleitung, p. III.

Whilst Birch was preparing the manuscript of his Dictionary for the printer, and seeing the sheets through the press, other Egyptologists, *e.g.*, Goodwin, E. de Rougé, Chabas, Devéria, Dümichen, Lepsius and Pleyte were actively engaged in publishing and translating hieroglyphic, hieratic and demotic texts. And long before he had finished printing his Dictionary, Birch had come to the conclusion that he must prepare a second edition in which he could give all the new words and forms that appeared in the newly published texts. As he read these texts he noted every word and form that ought to be in the new edition, and he continued to write slips for many years. Those who have visited him in his room in the British Museum may remember the glass box containing slips for this new edition ; this always stood in front of his inkstand and was added to daily. More than one publisher was ready to publish the new edition of his Dictionary, but his multitudinous duties and advancing years prevented him from reading all the texts that were published. And he did not see that if ever he was to publish the new edition he must at some time or other cease from the writing of slips and adding to his manuscript, and so he rejected the advice both of his publisher and his friends, and continued to write ever more and more slips.

Birch contemplates a second edition of his Dictionary of Hieroglyphics.

In 1882 Maspero began to publish the hieroglyphic inscriptions from the Pyramids of Ṣaḳḳârah in the *Recueil de Travaux*, and in them Birch found whole paragraphs of Egyptian text similar to passages in the funerary texts on the coffin of Amamu, which he was preparing for publication by the Trustees. Naturally he was anxious to include in his new edition as many as possible of the words and forms from these very ancient texts, and he set to work to read them and to extract from them additional matter for his Dictionary. He found his task more difficult than he imagined it would be, for though he doubted the accuracy of many of the readings of Maspero's text, he had no means in the shape of photographs or paper " squeezes " whereby to control them. Moreover, he was seventy years of age and his health was failing. But he struggled on gallantly and continued to write slips for the new edition of his Dictionary (which he was certain he would live to see) until death overtook him on December 26th, 1885. When his books and literary effects were being sold several boxes containing many thousands of slips were put up to be bid for as a separate lot, and a bidder bought them for ten shillings. Thus the labour of twenty years was wasted.

Maspero's edition of the Pyramid Texts.

Birch dies and leaves his manuscript for the second edition unfinished.

PIERRET'S "VOCABULAIRE HIÉROGLYPHIQUE."

The difficulty of obtaining copies of Birch's Dictionary of Hieroglyphics, and the expense of both that work and Brugsch's *Wörterbuch* practically left the students of the ancient Egyptian language without a dictionary. The first scholar who made any serious attempt to help the beginner and the advanced student out of their difficulty was Paul Pierret, Conservateur adjoint des Antiquités Égyptiennes au Musée du Louvre, and he set to work to compile the handy and comparatively inexpensive *Vocabulaire Hiéroglyphique*,[1] which so many students have found to be a useful book of reference. It consists of 759 lithographed pages in which the words are arranged alphabetically, and an index to all the French words by which the hieroglyphic words are translated in the volume, which fills forty-eight double-columned pages. It contains, in a condensed form, the substance of the Dictionaries of Birch and Brugsch, and most of the 987 royal names which Lepsius published in his *Königsbuch der alten Aegypter*, Berlin, 1858, fol., and most of the 2,000 geographical names given by Brugsch in his *Dictionnaire Géographique*, Leipzig, 1877, fol.[2] In his Preface Pierret calls attention to the fact that Brugsch's Dictionary cost 600 francs, and this was without the *Supplement*, which cost about 500 francs more when it was completed in 1882. He justifies his inclusion of geographical names in his *Vocabulaire* by pointing out what every one has found who has tried to use the *Dictionnaire Géographique*, how difficult it is to find a given name in that "merveille d'érudition." He claims no special merit for his *Vocabulaire*, and says, "Mon but est de fournir aux commençants un moyen d'aborder directement les textes, et à tous un *manuel* commode et pratique." There is no doubt that he succeeded in his aim.

Pierret's Hieroglyphic Vocabulary.

Inclusion of royal and geographical names.

SIMEONE LEVI'S "VOCABOLARIO GEROGLIFICO COPTO-EBRAICO."

For a few years after the appearance of the last volume of Brugsch's *Wörterbuch* in 1882 no attempt was made to publish in a collected form the lexicographical material that could be collected from the editions of hitherto unpublished texts, which were appearing frequently in England, France, Germany, Russia and Italy. But meanwhile this material was being diligently

[1] *Vocabulaire Hiéroglyphique comprenant les mots de la Langue, les Noms géographiques, divins, royaux et historiques, classés alphabétiquement.* Paris, 1875. 8vo.

[2] His *Supplement* to this work, containing 1,420 pages, appeared in 1879–80.

collected by one scholar at least who was dissatisfied with the existing Egyptian Dictionaries, and was determined to publish a new one. This was Simeone Levi, an Italian Egyptologist, who was well known for the very useful list of hieratic characters which he published[1] in 1880. Under the title of *Pa Uatch-ur en Metchut* 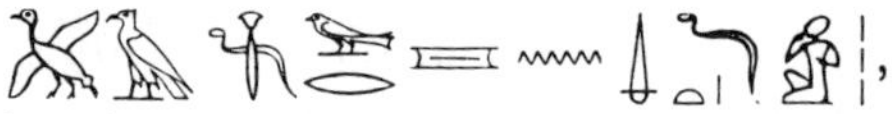, i.e., *The Great Sea of Words,* he began to publish a *Coptic-Hebrew Hieroglyphic Vocabulary* with translations of the hieroglyphic words in Italian and numerous quotations of Coptic and Hebrew words which he held to be cognate to the ancient Egyptian words.[2]

Levi's Egyptian-Italian Dictionary.

The *Vocabolario* proper consists of six parts folio, which were published in 1887–88 and contain 1,705 lithographed double-columned pages; the Supplement consists of two parts, and contains 696 pages; Part I was published in 1889, and Part II in 1894. In a very closely written Preface, which fills 30 pages, Signor Levi discusses the grammar and the structure of the ancient Egyptian language, which he treats as though the speech that is revealed to us by the hieroglyphic, hieratic and demotic texts belonged to the Semitic family of languages. It was a mistake on his part to do this, for he assumed to be a fact that which has never been proved; to him Egyptian, Coptic and Hebrew are substantially forms of one and the same language. He adopted an unusual arrangement of the alphabet, placing h  and ḥ  after tch , and t , or , and ṭ  after sh , and kh (χ)  and 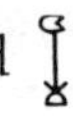 at the end of the alphabet, etc. Thus the arrangement and the values of the letters of his alphabet are as follows:—

Levi holds Egyptian to be a Semitic language.

 a = אָ.  ȧ = אֶ or אֱ.  ā = אָ.  ī = אִי.  i = אִ.  u = וּ, אֻ or ֻ.  o = א or אֹ or אָ.  ua = הוּא.  ur הוּר.  b = ב,  p = פּ.  f = פ. 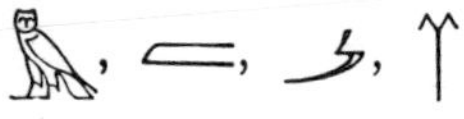 m = מ. 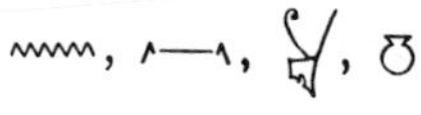 n = נ.  r = ר.  r, l = ר, ל. 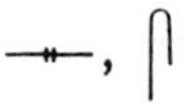 s = ס, שׂ. 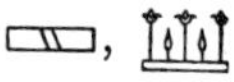 sh = שׁ.  t = ת, ס.  d = ד.  z = צ, ז.  h = ה.  ḥ = ח. 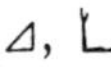 q = ק.  k = כּ.  g = ג. 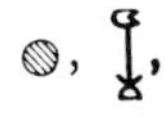 χ = ח, כ.

His Egyptian-Hebrew alphabet.

[1] *Raccolta dei Segni Ieratici Egizi nelle diverse Epoche, con i correspondenti Geroglifici ed i loro differenti valori fonetici.* Turin, 1880. 4to.

[2] *Vocabolario Geroglifico Copto-Ebraico: opera che vinse il grande premio reale di linguistica conferito nell' anno* 1886 *dalla R. Accademia dei Lincei, e pubblicato dopo incorraggiamento della giunta del consiglio superiore della istruzione pubblica.* Turin, 1887–1894.

This system seems to represent an attempt to show that the ancient Egyptians adopted the Hebrew alphabet. By some curious oversight Levi failed to find an equivalent for the Hebrew letter ע.

Hagemans "Lexique Français-Hiéroglyphique."

The list of published Egyptian Dictionaries ends with the *Lexique Français-Hiéroglyphique* that was compiled by M. G. Hagemans and was published at Brussels in 1896. It is an octavo volume of 923 lithographed, double-columned pages, which contain a French-Egyptian Dictionary and Supplement, a hieroglyphic, hieratic-demotic alphabet, and a list of determinatives.

Hagemans French-Egyptian Lexicon.

The Present Egyptian Dictionary.

It will probably be admitted by all that the compiler of an Egyptian Hieroglyphic Dictionary should know at first hand every collection of Egyptian monuments and papyri in the world, that he should have visited every great Museum on the Continent and in Egypt, England and America, and copied, or collated with printed editions, every hieroglyphic, hieratic and demotic text of importance, that he should know well the histories of Egypt written by classical writers, and the works of the Arab geographers, and Coptic in all its dialects, and that he should have had at his disposal unlimited time, in short that he should have been able to devote his whole life to the making of his Egyptian Dictionary. That he should also have one or more assistants to help him in his laborious task also goes without saying. I am conscious that, unfortunately, I possess none of the qualifications necessary for such a great work except in a very limited degree. Nevertheless I have written this Dictionary and how I came to do so the following paragraphs will show.

Qualifications necessary for writing an Egyptian Dictionary.

Between the years 1880 and 1883 the Natural History Collections were removed from the British Museum, Bloomsbury, to the new buildings which were specially constructed to receive them at South Kensington. Thereupon several of the rooms of the First and Second Northern Galleries, and the long room that ran parallel to the fourth room of the First Northern Gallery and had contained the studies and workrooms of the Natural History Staff, were allotted to the Department of Oriental Antiquities. When Dr. Birch, Keeper of the Department, had removed the Collections of Egyptian and Semitic Antiquities into them, and rearranged the Egyptian Collections, he took

Rearrangement of the Egyptian Collections in the British Museum.

in hand a task which he had contemplated for many years, namely, the compilation of a detailed description of the Egyptian hieroglyphic and hieratic funerary papyri. The English translation of the Saite Recension of the Book of the Dead according to the Turin Papyrus,[1] which he published in 1867,[2] had aroused universal interest, and he was urged to supplement it with a version of the older Theban Recension translated from the rich collection of XVIIIth dynasty papyri in the British Museum. The smaller papyri had been cut up into sections and mounted under sheets of glass, and were at that time arranged in drawers in the Table-Cases in the public rooms. The longer papyri, *i.e.*, those which measured from 5 to 30 feet in length, had been mounted in black glazed wooden frames and hung upon the walls of the North-West Staircase. But as in this position it was well-nigh impossible to consult them, and as it was feared that they might suffer injury through damp, they were taken down and, where possible, were cut up into sections, mounted under sheets of glass and stored with the shorter papyri. During the general rearrangement of the papyri which followed these alterations Birch seized the opportunity of re-examining and describing with minute care the papyri which Professor Naville had selected as authorities for the text of his edition of the Theban Recension of the Book of the Dead, and he directed me to assist him in this work. He was chiefly anxious to collect variant readings, and unusual forms of words, and new words, and to make lists of the papyri in which particular Chapters appeared. The work was long and difficult, chiefly because we possessed no concordance of the words of the Theban Recensions, and therefore could not easily identify the Chapters in which they occurred in mutilated papyri. So long as we were dealing with papyri containing the Saite Recension we found Lieblein's little " Index "[3] very useful, but for identifying Chapters and passages in the Theban Recension it afforded no help. Having grouped the funerary papyri chronologically, *i.e.*, according to dynasties, Birch began to write his descriptions of the papyri, and he directed me to make a concordance to them, and intended to incorporate the slips that I wrote with those which he was heaping up as material for the new edition of his " Dictionary

The Theban Recension of the Book of the Dead.

Naville's edition of the Book of the Dead.

Birch's proposed concordance to the funerary papyri.

[1] For the Egyptian text see Lepsius, *Das Todtenbuch.* Leipzig, 1842.

[2] In the fifth volume of *Egypt's Place in Universal History.* London, 1867, pp. 161–326.

[3] Lieblein, J., *Index Alphabétique de tous les Mots contenus dans le Livre des Morts publié par R. Lepsius d'après le Papyrus de Turin.* Lithographed. Paris, 1875. 8vo.

of Hieroglyphics," which he fully believed he would one day publish (see p. xlii).

When I had been engaged on this work, officially and unofficially, for nearly two years, Birch died, but I continued to write slips for the concordance to the Theban Recension, and began to collect words from the Bremner (Rhind) Papyrus (Brit. Mus. No. 10,188), and other funerary works. It was now quite certain that the new edition of Birch's "Dictionary of Hieroglyphics" could never appear, and my friends advised me to go on collecting Egyptian words with the view of publishing a "Vocabulary" on much the same lines as Pierret's "Vocabulaire." By that time the slips which I had written amounted to many thousands, and I soon found that the work of arranging them and of incorporating the new ones consumed a vast amount of time. It was impossible to continue the work on the scale on which I had begun, and I foresaw that the task of making a concordance to Egyptian literature could not be carried out by any man who could not devote his whole time to the work.

I abandon the idea of making a concordance to the funerary papyri.

Between 1888 and 1892 the British Museum acquired the Papyrus of Ani, the Papyrus of Nu, the Papyrus of Nekht and other remarkable Codices of the Theban Recension of the Book of the Dead. The first edition (500 copies) of the Facsimile of the Papyrus of Ani was sold in less than two years, and it became a part of my official work to prepare a second and more correct edition of the Facsimile and to write the volume of English text which was published with it in 1894. I made a Vocabulary to the Egyptian text, but want of space prevented its inclusion in the volume of English translations. I then began to make a Vocabulary to the Papyrus of Nu, and in working through it I was so much impressed with the importance of this Codex that I decided to publish an edition of the Theban Recension, and to make it and the Papyrus of Nebseni the principal authorities for the Egyptian text. I have described the Papyrus of Nu at length elsewhere,[1] and it is only necessary to say here that it contains 131 Chapters, *i.e.*, more than any other copy[2] of the Book of the Dead now known. The whole papyrus is carefully written, Nu himself probably having been the scribe. The father of Nu was called Amen-ḥetep and his mother Senseneb, and it is probable that she was no other than the lady Senseneb, the wife of Nebseni the scribe, whose copy of the Book

Vocabulary to the Papyrus of Ani.

The Papyrus of Nu.

[1] See my *The Chapters of Coming Forth by Day*, Vol. I, p. xii. London, 1898.

[2] The Papyrus of Nebseni contains 77 Chapters.

of the Dead in the British Museum (No. 9900) has so much in common with that of Nu. Taking 115 Chapters from the Papyrus of Nu, 25 from the Papyrus of Nebseni, 27 from the Papyrus of Ani, and some half-dozen hymns, etc., from the Papyri of Hunefer, Mut-hetep and Nekht, I prepared an edition of the Egyptian texts and translated them. When I ventured to suggest to Messrs. Kegan Paul, who undertook to publish the edition, that text and translation should be accompanied by a Concordance they demurred, saying that no one would buy the Concordance, or Vocabulary, for no one wanted such a thing. Finally they decided to print 750 copies of the Egyptian text and Vocabulary, and 1,000 copies of the Translation, thinking there would be a larger demand for it than for the first two volumes of the work. Two years later they wrote to me saying that the whole edition of the Egyptian text and Vocabulary was sold, and that as about 230 copies of the Translation were unsold they had decided to sell them as a " remainder," and they did so. Thus it was proved that there was a considerable demand for an Egyptian Vocabulary to the Theban Recension of the Book of the Dead, and that there were students who would not buy the Translation unless they could have the Vocabulary with it. In printing the Vocabulary I adopted a plan hitherto untried. I placed the transliteration of the Egyptian words in the first instead of in the second column as was usual, for it seemed to me that it would enable the beginner to find the word he wanted more easily and quickly. This plan has been much approved of in England, and as it has been adopted in an " Aegyptisches Glossar " published in Berlin in 1904 it has evidently seemed useful to the practical Teutonic mind.

My edition of the Theban Recension of the Book of the Dead.

My Vocabulary of the Theban Recension.

The success of the Vocabulary to the Book of the Dead and the encouragement of many friends emboldened me to write an Egyptian Hieroglyphic Dictionary,[1] and with this object in view I began to collect words from Egyptian literature generally. I first laid under contribution the Dictionaries of Birch, Brugsch and Pierret and verified, as far as possible, all doubtful readings. From the Vocabularies published with editions of special texts I obtained much material, and from my own reading of texts, both published and unpublished, I obtained a

The collection of material for this Dictionary.

[1] As Brugsch died in 1894, all hope of a new edition of his *Wörterbuch* had to be abandoned. His private copy of this work was purchased by the British Museum, and is now in the Library of the Department of Egyptian and Assyrian Antiquities. It is interleaved and in several volumes, and the extensive notes and additions in his own handwriting suggest that he contemplated the issue of a new edition.

great deal more. The result of all this work was that I filled many boxes and drawers with slips on each of which a word was written, with its certain or problematical meaning, and a reference to the text or monument where it was to be found. In 1908 I had written over three hundred thousand slips, and in spite of the constant help of my wife in arranging them and in making incorporations, I realised that the publication of such a mass of material was impossible. No one man could write the fair copy of it for press, and no publisher could afford to undertake its publication. I therefore set to work to revise the slips, and to destroy all that had redundant references, and references to words the meanings of which were commonly accepted. In this revision I got rid of more than one-half of the slips, but even then the compilation was far too large, and further revision was necessary. I then cut out all the numerous quotations from texts, and nearly all comments, abbreviated the references to published works, and, at the risk of making a somewhat bald Egyptian Vocabulary, eschewed, except in very rare cases, any attempt to discuss theoretical renderings of words. This second revision was completed in 1913, and the slips which I proposed to print numbered nearly 28,500.

Revisions of the slips.

The question of publication then arose. During the early stages of the writing of this Dictionary an understanding existed between Mr. Blackett, Manager of Messrs. Kegan, Paul, Trench, Trübner & Co., and myself that his firm would endeavour to include it among their publications, but by the time the manuscript was ready for the printer, he had left their service, and they were not in a position to fulfil his wish. I talked the matter over with Mr. Horace Hart, Printer to the Oxford University Press, and showed him the manuscript of the Dictionary, and, having made a rough calculation of the probable cost of printing it, he came to the conclusion that no publisher ought to undertake the work without a subsidy. He thought that the cost of production might be lowered by printing it in Vienna, and spoke highly of the Austrian firm of Messrs. Adolf Holzhausen, who had already printed several books of mine, and with whose excellent typography I was well acquainted. Further enquiry made by me among printers and publishers showed the correctness of Mr. Hart's opinion, and I accepted it as final. I decided that it was unwise to attempt to reproduce my manuscript by lithography, because works of reference printed by lithography are often very unsatisfactory and difficult

Difficulty of finding a publisher.

Printing in Vienna recommended.

to use, and I lacked the skill of Brugsch in writing the transfers.

A friend offers to defray the cost of printing the Dictionary.

Soon after my conversation with Mr. Hart I had the opportunity of placing my difficulty before a friend—an English gentleman who has been all his life intensely interested in the ancient languages of the Near East, and has proved himself to be a generous patron and supporter of English archæological enterprise in Egypt and Western Asia for many years past. This gentleman, who persists in his determination to remain anonymous, gave me a sympathetic hearing, and a few days later wrote and offered to defray the cost of printing the Dictionary in Vienna. With heartfelt gratitude I accepted this munificent offer, and made preparations to take the manuscript, which filled seven large tray-boxes, each about two feet three inches in length, to Vienna in May, 1914. The completing of a piece of work on which I was then engaged made it necessary for me to postpone my journey from the spring till the early autumn, when I hoped to conclude my negotiations with Messrs. Holzhausen speedily, and to begin to print before the end of the year. The delay was providential for the Dictionary, for the Great War broke out early in August, and my manuscript was safe in England; had it been in Vienna it would have been impossible to regain possession of it for a very considerable time, and even if I had eventually succeeded in recovering it, its publication must have been delayed for some years. As things were, I was able, with the consent of my friend and benefactor, to open negotiations with Messrs. Harrison and Sons for the printing of the book, and very soon after their completion the printing began.

The printing of the Dictionary begun in England.

Contents of this Dictionary.

The present Dictionary of Egyptian Hieroglyphs contains nearly twenty-three thousand forms of Egyptian words collected from texts of all periods between the time of the IIIrd Dynasty and the Roman Period. Strictly speaking, the words belonging to each of the great periods of Egyptian literature should have been printed in separate sections, but the time for making such a series of Egyptian Dictionaries has not yet arrived, it seems to me. Birch excluded from his Dictionary the names of deities and the names of places, and printed lists of them as Appendices to his Dictionary of words. Pierret included in his "Vocabulaire" the names of deities, kings and places, and made it to contain practically all the essential parts of the Hieroglyphic Dictionaries of Birch and Brugsch, Champollion's "Panthéon

Égyptien,"[1] Lepsius' "Book of Kings,"[2] and Brugsch's "Geographical Dictionary."[3] And Brugsch, expecting the student to refer at first hand to these works, devoted all the space in his *Wörterbuch* to registering and explaining Egyptian words. Though there is much to be said in favour of following this plan strictly, I have nevertheless included in the Dictionary of Egyptian words the names of all the gods and goddesses, and other mythological beings that I have been able to collect, and thus the total number of entries in this section of the book amounts to 23,889. Names of gods and goddesses included.

Pierret's instinct, which told him that a "Vocabulaire Hiéroglyphique" that was intended to help beginners in the study of Egyptology, ought to contain the names of kings, was undoubtedly correct, but it seems to me that he made a mistake in scattering them throughout his work. As the "Königsbuch" of Lepsius, and the "Livre des Rois" of Brugsch and Bouriant[4] are out of print and scarce, and the edition of my own "Book of Kings"[5] is rapidly becoming exhausted, I have printed a full list of the names of Egyptian kings as Part II of this work. This was necessary, for of *Das Handbuch der Aegyptischen Königsnamen* by Pieper and Burchardt only one part has appeared (Berlin, 1912, 8vo), and few students can ever hope to possess the splendid but expensive *Le Livre des Rois de l'Égypte,* which Gauthier has published in the *Mémoires* of the French Archæological Institute of Cairo, in five parts, folio (Cairo, 1902–16). My List contains 439 entries, which give the names of all the known kings, from Menȧ, the first king of all Egypt, to the Roman Emperor Decius. It includes all their principal Ka and Nebti names, and their names and titles as the Horus of Gold, the King of the South and North, and the Son of Rā. It illustrates at a glance the development of the use of these names and titles, which in many cases resemble the "strong names" that were adopted by the kings Names of kings included.

[1] *Collection des personnages mythologiques de l'ancienne Égypte, d'après les Monumens; avec un texte explicatif par J. F. C. et les figures d'après les dessins de L. J. J. Dubois. Avec 90 planches en couleur.* Paris, 1823–25. 4to.

[2] *Königsbuch der alten Aegypter.* Berlin, 1858. Fol.

[3] *Dictionnaire Géographique de l'Ancienne Égypte.* Leipzig, 1877. Fol. *Supplement.* Leipzig, 1879–80. Fol.

[4] É. Brugsch-Bey et Urbain Bouriant, *Le Livre des Rois, contenant la Liste Chronologique des Rois, Reines, Princes, Princesses, et Personnages Importants de l'Égypte depuis Ménes jusqu'à Nectanebo II.* Cairo, 1887.

[5] *The Book of the Kings of Egypt or the Ka, Nebti, Horus, Suten Bȧt and Rā names of the Pharaohs with transliterations, from Menes, the first dynastic king of Egypt, to the Emperor Decius, with Chapters on the Royal Names, Chronology, etc.* London, 2 Vols., 1908. 8vo.

of Dahomey. Some of the abnormally long strings of bombastic epithets which the later Pharaohs loved to see prefixed to their names as Kings of the South and North I have omitted, for they only contain quite ordinary titles.

Geographical names included.

The importance to the beginner of having a list of geographical names available for handy reference is so obvious that no apology is needed for devoting a section of this work to a register of the names of countries, districts, localities, cities, towns, etc., in Egypt, the Egyptian Sûdân and Western Asia. Brugsch's *Dictionnaire Géographique*, Leipzig, 1887–80, and the three volumes of his *Geographische Inschriften Altägyptischer Denkmäler*, Leipzig, 1857–60, contain a vast amount of information, but the facts needed re-stating and supplementing in the light of the studies of modern Egyptologists. In drawing up the Geographical List, which forms Part III of this Dictionary, and contains nearly 3,500 entries, I have derived much help from Müller's *Asien und Europa nach Altägyptischen Denkmälern*, Leipzig, 1893, and Burchardt's *Die Altkanaanäischen Fremdworte und Eigennamen im Aegyptischen*, Leipzig, 1909–10. In the first of these the writer has treated the geography of Egypt and her colonies historically and chronologically, and has grouped, in a clear and systematic manner, all the facts that were available at the time when he wrote the book. In the second, the author collected a mass of material of the utmost importance for the student of Egyptian Geography and Philology. His work is of peculiar value because he possessed a good working knowledge of Hebrew and other Semitic dialects, and was able to use it authoritatively in dealing with Egyptian forms of Semitic words and place-names. Every Egyptologist must lament the untimely death of this sound scholar. I have also obtained much help in identifying the original names of Syrian and Palestinian places mentioned in Egyptian texts from Knudtzon's *Die El-Amarna Tafeln*, Leipzig, 1907, and Winckler's complete edition of the texts from the Tall al-ʻAmârnah Tablets (*Der Thontafelfund von El Amarna*, Berlin, 1889). Wherever possible I have added the cuneiform originals in the Egyptian Geographical Lists from the Tall al-ʻAmârnah Tablets and from the historical inscriptions of the kings of the later Assyrian Empires which flourished between 1350 and 620 B.C. The exact positions of scores of places must always remain unknown because their conquerors, whether Egyptian or Assyrian, often destroyed cities and towns utterly, and in a generation or two their sites would be forgotten.

Geography of Egypt, Syria and Palestine.

The Tall al-'Amârnah Tablets.

The English Index.

The last section of this Dictionary contains a series of Indexes. The First Index contains a complete alphabetical list of all the English words, with references, which are used to translate the Egyptian words, and it forms a kind of English-Egyptian Dictionary. I have found the French Index in Pierret's *Vocabulaire Hiéroglyphique* very useful in reading Egyptian texts, and I hope that mine, which is much larger and fuller, and contains over sixty thousand references, will be acceptable to the beginner.

The Index of Kings' names.

The Second Index ought to assist in the identification of royal names when they occur in mutilated texts. In it many of the prenomens, which begin with Rā or some other god's name, are given under two forms; thus 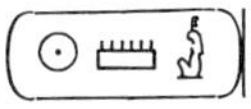, the prenomen of Seti I, will be found both under Rā-men-Maāt and Men-Maāt-Rā. The Hebrew and Greek forms of Egyptian royal names, the identifications of which are tolerably certain, are also given.

The Geographical Index.

The Third Index contains a list of geographical names, with references, under the ordinary forms in which they are found in English books. These are followed by lists of the forms in which they occur in Coptic Literature, in the works of Greek writers, in the Hebrew Bible, in Semitic texts, and in the cuneiform inscriptions, both Assyrian and Persian.

Coptic Index. **Index of Semitic words.**

The Fourth Index contains a list of all the Coptic words, with references, that occur in the Dictionary, and the Fifth Index consists of lists of all the non-Egyptian words, Hebrew, Syriac, Arabic, Ethiopic, Amharic and Greek, that are quoted or referred to in it.

The arrangement of the words.

The system on which the words are arranged in the Dictionary is alphabetical, like that followed by Birch in his "Dictionary of Hieroglyphics," and by Brugsch in his "Wörterbuch," and by the makers of Vocabularies to editions of special texts, *e.g.*, by Stern[1] and Erman[2] in Germany, Lieblein[3] in Norway, Piehl[4] in Sweden, Schiaparelli[5] in Italy, Maspero[6] and Moret[7] in

[1] See the "Vollständiges Hieroglyphisch-Lateinisches Glossar," by L. Stern in Vol. II of Ebers, *Papyros Ebers, das hermetische Buch conservirt in der Universitäts-Bibliothek zu Leipzig.* Leipzig, 1875. Fol.

[2] *Die Märchen des Papyrus Westcar*, 2 vols. Berlin, 1890.

[3] *Index alphabétique de tous les Mots contenus dans le Livre des Morts.* Paris, 1875. 8vo.

[4] *Dictionnaire du Papyrus Harris*, No. 1. Upsala, 1882. 8vo.

[5] *Il Libro dei Funerali.* Turin, 1880–83. Fol.

[6] *Les Mémoires de Sinouhit.* Paris, 1908. 4to.

[7] *Le Rituel du Culte Divin Journalier.* Paris, 1902.

France, by Griffith,[1] and by Griffith and Thompson[2] in their Demotic Glossaries, and by myself in England.[3] In the case of several words belonging to the late period here and there inconsistency will be found, but this is due chiefly to the fact that many signs which had syllabic values under the Middle and New Empires were used as mere letters in the late texts. And Egyptian scribes were themselves inconsistent in their spellings.

Transliteration.

Throughout this book the transliteration of the Egyptian word is placed first in the entry, according to the plan followed in my Vocabulary to the Theban Recension of the Book of the Dead. Then follows the Egyptian word in hieroglyphs, frequently with a reference to the text where it is found, and then the meaning. Now, the exact meaning of many words is unknown, and can only be guessed at by the context. In some cases the context makes the meaning of an unknown word comparatively certain, but in others, especially where no probable Coptic equivalent is forthcoming, it does not, and then any meaning suggested is little else than the result of guesswork. In many cases, then, the English words that are set down as translations of rare and difficult Egyptian words must only be regarded as suggestions as to the probable meanings.

The meanings of many words unknown.

This is especially the case with certain words in the Pyramid Texts. The meaning of some of them is tolerably clear from the determinatives, but there are a considerable number of words in these difficult documents for which no one has so far proposed meanings that may be considered correct. The spells and magical formulæ which abound in these Texts are not only difficult to translate because of the words of unknown meaning in them, but also because it is not always clear where one word ends and the next begins. Even Maspero found himself unable to translate whole sentences and passages in them, and as none of the translations of them promised by German scholars has yet appeared, it seems as though the difficulties which they belittled in describing Maspero's edition of the Pyramid Texts have vanquished them.

Order of the letters.

The order of the letters in Birch's "Dictionary of Hieroglyphics" is as follows:— 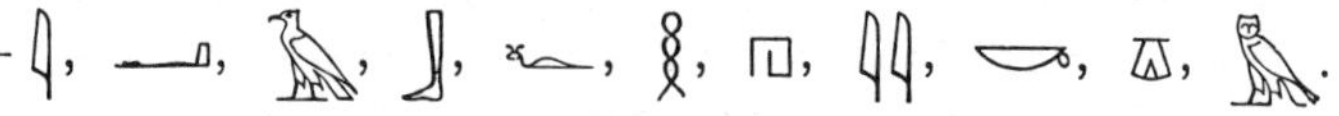
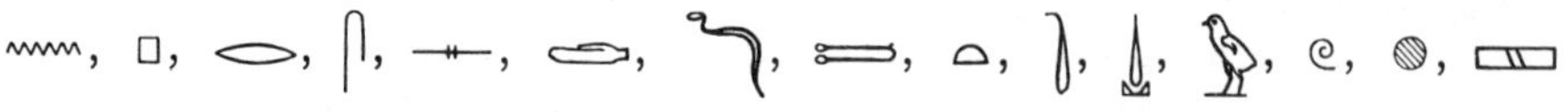

[1] *Catalogue of the Demotic Papyri in the John Rylands Library*, Vol. III. Manchester, 1909.

[2] *The Demotic Magical Papyrus of London and Leiden*, Vol. III. London, 1909.

[3] *Vocabulary to the Theban Recension of the Book of the Dead.* London, 1898.

In other words, he tried to make their order approximate to that of the letters of the English Alphabet. Birch.

In E. de Rougé's Egyptian Alphabet (*Chrestomathie Égyptienne*, Part I, Paris, 1867) the order of the letters is as follows :— E. de Rougé.

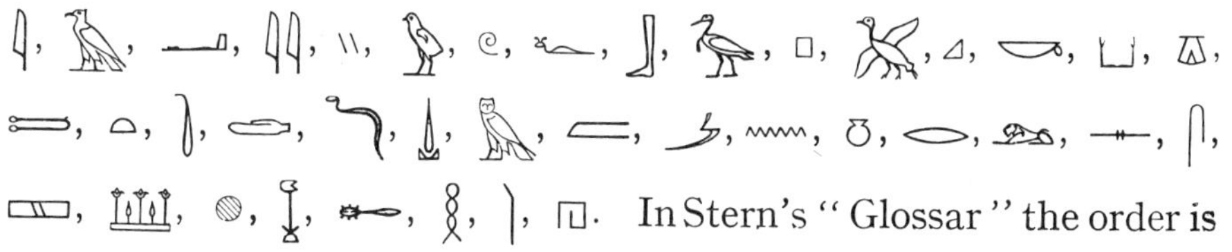

In Stern's "Glossar" the order is as follows :— Stern.

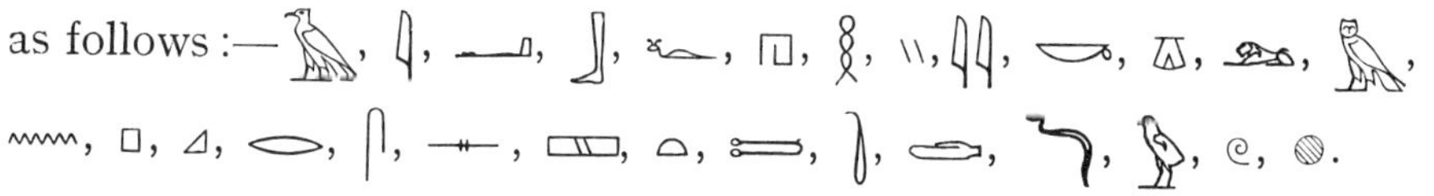

The order followed in this Dictionary is: Budge.

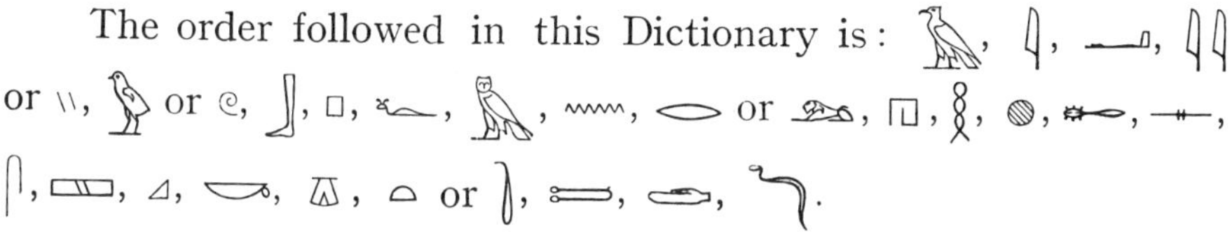

Among the words given in this Dictionary are many which are derived from demotic texts. As my knowledge of this branch of Egyptology is rudimentary I have relied for the correctness of their transcription into hieroglyphs chiefly upon the works of that erratic genius, E. Revillout, and Professor F. Ll. Griffith. These scholars have shown that Demotologists are able to transcribe demotic texts into hieroglyphs, and Birch's view that they were unable to do this is no longer tenable. About the correctness of the meanings of many demotic words given by them there can be no doubt, for the equivalents of a great number of them, and their counterparts in form, are to be found even in the existing Coptic "Scalae" and in the printed Coptic Vocabularies and Dictionaries of Peyron, Tattam and Parthey. Demotic words.

The references to original documents and to published editions of them in this Dictionary are, in respect of number, unsatisfactory. They represent a compromise, and will suffer the fate of all compromises, that is to say, they will satisfy nobody. In the great collection of slips which I made first of all there were to some words as many as sixty references, and the slips that contained only from six to twelve references were very few. To print all these was manifestly impossible, for the references would have occupied far more space than the Egyptian words and their meanings. It seemed at first that each word ought to be followed by a reference, but even so the References to publications.

references required as much space as the Egyptian words, and I decided that many references to the older printed literature must be cut out, and only a limited number to recent publications admitted. Further, it was clear that the names of authors and their papers printed in the *Recueil de Travaux*, the *Transactions* and *Proceedings* of the Society of Biblical Archæology, the *Archæologia* of the Society of Antiquaries of London, the *Aegyptische Zeitschrift*, and other scientific journals of the kind, would have to be omitted, and the name of the journal quoted in an abbreviated form. A list of the abbreviations of the titles of all books actually quoted will be found on pp. lxxv–lxxxvii. This is followed by a list of all the principal books that have been used or consulted in the writing of this Dictionary, so that the beginner may know to what books to turn in the prosecution of his studies.

Coptic forms of Egyptian words.

Following the meaning of the word and at the end of the entry is often given the equivalent of an Egyptian word in the latest stage of the language, *i.e.*, Coptic. In selecting these Coptic equivalents I have not copied them straight out of a Coptic Dictionary, but have satisfied myself that they bear the meaning which the Egyptian words have in passages in the Coptic versions of the Bible, and in Coptic patristic literature generally. Had the great *Corpus* of Coptic words upon which Mr. W. E. Crum has been at work for so many years been available[1] the number of Coptic equivalents quoted in this Dictionary would probably have been quadrupled. The Hebrew, Syriac, Arabic and other Semitic words quoted in the entries stand in a different relationship to the Egyptian, for they merely represent borrowings of words, usually by the Egyptians from the Semites, whilst the true Coptic words are native Egyptian. They seem to me to stand in quite a different category from the pronouns which were borrowed at a very early period by the Egyptians from the people whom, for want of a better name, we may call "Proto-Semites." And the greater number of them were certainly introduced into Egyptian texts after the Egyptians founded Colonies in Syria and Palestine by scribes who either knew no Egyptian words that were exactly suitable for their purpose, or who wished to ornament their compositions by the use of Semitic words or to show their erudition.

Mr. Crum's Coptic Dictionary.

Borrowed Semitic words.

[1] When the Great War broke out in 1914 Mr. Crum was in Vienna, and had his enormous mass of material with him. He succeeded in leaving the city, but his manuscripts remained there for a considerable time afterwards, and his work has been hampered in consequence, and the publication of his Coptic Dictionary delayed for five years.

In the transliterations of the Egyptian words in this Dictionary, I have followed the order of the letters of the Egyptian words, but I cannot think that these transliterations always represent the true pronunciation of the words. Thus in the word *ăăam* , a plant, it is impossible to think that the Egyptians took the trouble to pronounce two long vowels having exactly the same sound and to give  its value, always supposing it had a phonetic value in this word. The analogies in Coptic suggest that we should read the word simply ām, nevertheless the scribe wrote . Again in the word *Nenui*[*t*] or *Nui*[*t*] , the primeval watery mass, we have *n* + *en*  + *n* + *nu* , *i.e.*, four *n* sounds; that any Egyptian ever took the trouble to pronounce all of them in this word is inconceivable. It is possible that the scribe wished the reader to understand that one *n* had to be pronounced like the Spanish ñ or the Amharic ኘ, and wrote *n* four times to make certain that he did so. In many transliterations of Egyptian words I have added the letter *e*, not because I think it represents the vowel which the Egyptians used in these places, but merely to make the words pronounceable and therefore easy to remember. Thus the word , or , is transliterated *ḥes* by me, but the Coptic equivalent ϩⲱⲥ shows that the vowel sound between the two consonants was not an *e*, but something like an ŏ. On the other hand in 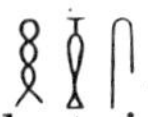, "to submerge," the Coptic equivalent ϩⲁⲥⲓⲉ suggests that in this word at least the vowel sound was that of some kind of *a*. And in *netchem* , or , "sweet," "pleasant," the Coptic equivalent ⲛⲟⲩⲧⲙ̅ suggests the first vowel sound in the word was *u* or *o* and the second that of some kind of *e* or *a*. Without vowels of some kind how can the name of the god , or , or , be pronounced? In transliterating I have written *en* or *ne*, and there is good authority for doing so, namely the most ancient Coptic papyrus Codex of the Book of Deuteronomy and the Acts of the Apostles.[1] Thus in ϩⲛ̅ ⲡⲏⲉⲓ ⲛ̅ⲧⲉⲕⲙ̅ⲛ̅ⲧϩⲙ̅ϩⲁⲗ (Deut. 13, 10) the line over the ⲛ̅s and the ⲙ̅ proves that the reader had to

Difficulties of transliteration.

Addition of the letter *e*.

Evidence of Coptic texts.

[1] Brit. Mus. MS. Oriental No. 7594. It was written not later than the middle of the fourth century of our Era. See my *Coptic Biblical Texts in the Dialect of Upper Egypt*. London, 1912. 8vo.

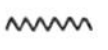

supply some vowel when pronouncing these letters, either an *a* or an *e*, probably the latter. And this was the case with several other letters besides ⲛ and ⲙ, for we have ⲁⲧⲉⲧⲛ̄ⲟⲩⲱϣⲃ̄ (Deut. 1, 41), ⲙ̄ⲡⲣ̄ (*ibid.* 42), ⲧⲉⲧⲛ̄ⲟⲩⲱϣϥ̄ (*ibid.*), ⲁⲩⲱ ⲛ̄ⲅ̄ ⲧⲃ̄ⲃⲟϥ (*ibid.* 4, 15), ⲛ̄ⲛⲉⲕⲣ̄ⲙ̄ⲛ̄ⲧ̄ⲣⲉ (*ibid.* 20), ⲙ̄ⲛ̄ ⲡⲉⲧⲛ̄ ϩⲗ̄ⲗⲟ (*ibid.* 23), ⲡⲛⲟⲩⲧⲉ ⲉⲧ ⲟⲛ̄ϩ (*ibid.* 26), ⲕⲁⲧⲁ ⲧⲉϩⲓⲏ ⲧⲏⲣⲥ̄ (*ibid.* 5, 33), ⲉ ⲧⲟⲟⲧⲕ̄ (*ibid.*), ϣⲁⲛⲧϥ̄ϥⲟⲧⲟⲩ ⲉ ⲃⲟⲗ ⲁⲩⲱ ⲛⲉⲩⲣ̄ⲣⲱⲟⲩ (*ibid.* 8, 24), ⲛ̄ⲅ̄ ⲧⲙ̄ ⲣ̄ ⲡⲱⲃϣ̄ (*ibid.* 25, 19), ϩⲛ̄ ⲟⲩⲱⲣϫ̄ (Acts 5, 23), ⲡⲛⲁⲩ ⲛ̄ ϫⲡ̄ⲥⲓⲧⲉ (Acts 10, 3), etc. From these examples we see that lines were-written over the letters ⲃ, ⲗ, ⲙ, ⲛ, ⲡ, ⲣ, ⲥ, ⲧ, ⲕ, ⲅ, ϥ, ϣ, ϩ and ϫ, and that in certain positions in words a helping vowel was necessary for their pronunciation.

Separate vowels in words.

The whole question of the use of the separate vowels which we find in Egyptian words is one of considerable difficulty, and it seems to me quite clear from the statements that are made on the subject by Egyptologists that no one has yet succeeded in solving the problem. It is quite obvious that the scribes systematically wrote certain words without vowels and expected the reader to supply them, *e.g.*, the name of the god 𓊪𓏏𓎛𓀭 PTḤ. Now, it is impossible to pronounce this name without adding one vowel at least, but there is nothing in Egyptian to show what that vowel must be or where it is to be placed. In the case of Ptḥ, the Greeks, who spelt the name Φθά, or Φθᾶ, supply the vowel, and suggest that the Egyptians pronounced it something like "Ptaḥ." Or, take the name of the god Horus, which the Egyptians wrote ḤER 𓎛𓁷𓂋𓅃, 𓅃𓊹, 𓅃𓀭, 𓁷𓂋𓀭 and 𓉺𓀭, without adding any vowel. The transcriptions of the name in Hebrew (הור), Coptic (ϩⲱⲣ) and Greek (Ὧρος) prove that the missing vowel is ō, but the Egyptian forms of the name give no indication of this fact. In the Pyramid Texts we find the form 𓎛𓁷𓂋𓅱𓅃 (M. 454) which was held by one Egyptologist to prove that the god's name terminated in *u*; but, according to M. Naville's view, which is probably correct, the 𓅱 is really the vowel that is wanting in the name, which we ought to read "Ḥur," or "Hor," as in Hebrew, Coptic and Greek. This same scholar thinks that another example of the use of the 𓅱 in this way is found in 𓊵𓏏𓊪𓅱𓏛, or 𓊵𓏏𓊪𓍢𓏛, variants of 𓊵, 𓊵𓊪, 𓊵𓏏𓊪, 𓎛𓊵𓏏𓊪, and 𓊵𓏏𓊪𓏛. As the Coptic form of the word is ϩⲱⲧⲡ̄, the ancient Egyptian form of the word clearly included

Egyptian abbreviations of words and names.

Vowels placed at the ends of words.

the vowel ō, and this is proved by the  or  in the first two forms of 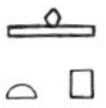 quoted above. It has seemed to me for several years past that the vowel signs which we find in many Egyptian words were intended not to be read necessarily as parts of the words, but only to indicate or limit their signification. But the subject is too large to discuss in an Introduction to a Dictionary, and demands a book to itself. Meanwhile, I understand that M. Naville is preparing a volume on the whole question, and as there is every reason to believe that he will present in a new light many important facts bearing upon Egyptian phonetics, its appearance is eagerly awaited.

Vowels as indications of the meanings of words or verbal forms.

The system of transliteration which I have used in this Dictionary is a modification of that which was employed by Birch and some of the older Egyptologists, and by Brugsch until the last years of his life. The following is the transliteration of the letters of the Egyptian Alphabet which Brugsch printed in the first volume of his *Wörterbuch* (1867):—

The Egyptian Alphabet in 1867.

	a		b		h		k
	à		p		ḥ		ḳ
	ā		f		χ		t
	i		m	 and	s	 or 	t
	ī		n		š		ṭ
	u		r		š		t́
	ū, ua (w)		l		k		t́

In 1880, the following modification of this Alphabet appeared in the fifth volume of his *Wörterbuch* (Folge und Umschreibung der alphabetischen Zeichen):—

The Egyptian Alphabet in 1880.

a. Vowels and half-vowels:—

 a.  à (א).  ā (ע).  i.  ī, y (י).  u, ō.

 u, w (ו).

c.[1] Consonants :—

𓃀	b, v (ב)	𓋴, 𓊃	s
𓃀𓅡, 𓃀𓅫	b (בּ)	𓈙	š, χ (sχ)
𓊪	p	𓆷	š (שׁ)
𓆑	f	𓈎	k, q (ק)
𓅓	m	𓎼	k, g (ג and غ)
𓈖	n	𓎡	k (כּ)
𓂋	r	𓏏	t (ט)
𓃭	l	𓍿, 𓍘	θ (ת, ס)
𓉔	h	𓂧	ṭ (ⲧ, ϯ)
𓎛	ḥ (ح)	𓆓	t′ (ז, צ)
𓐍	χ (ח, خ)	𓌉	t′(a) (צ)

The Egyptian Alphabet in 1891.

In 1891 (*Die Aegyptologie,* p. 94) he published a further modification of the Egyptian Alphabet which reads as follows :–

1.	𓇋	’ (ȧ)	9.	𓆑	f	17.	𓊃, 𓋴	s
2.	𓄿	ȝ (a)	10.	𓅓	m	18.	𓆷	š
3.	𓇌	” (ī)	11.	𓈖	n	19.	𓎼	g
4.	𓏭	″ (i)	12.	𓂋	r, l (r)	20.	𓎡	k
5.	𓂝	‘ (ā)	13.	[𓃭	rw] (l)	21.	𓈎	ḳ (q)
6.	𓅱	w (u)	14.	𓉔	h	22.	𓏏	t
7.	𓃀	b	15.	𓎛	ḥ	23.	𓍿, 𓍘	t (θ)
8.	𓊪	p	16.	𓐍	ḫ (χ)	24.	𓂧	d (ṭ)
						25.	𓆓	d (t′)

[1] **b** contains a list of double vowels and half-vowels.

In 1894 Dr. Erman proposed some modifications of this system of transliterating the Egyptian Alphabet, and printed the following (*Egyptian Grammar*, London, 1894, p. 6):—

The Egyptian Alphabet in 1894.

𓄿	ꜣ	𓆑	f	𓐍, 𓄡	} ḫ	𓎼	g
𓇋	ỉ	𓅓	m	𓊃, 𓋴	} s	𓏏	t
𓂝	ʿ	𓈖	n	𓈙	š	𓍿	ṯ
𓅱	w	𓂋	r	𓈎	ḳ	𓂧	d
𓃀	b	𓉔	h	𓎡	k	𓆓	ḏ
𓊪	p	𓎛	ḥ			𓇌	y 𓏭 ï

In 1911 he made the following changes and addition (*Aegyptische Grammatik*, Berlin, 1911, p. 20):—

The Egyptian Alphabet in 1911.

𓇋 ỉ or y. 𓂝 ʿ = ע. 𓂋 r = ר and ל. 𓉔 h = ה. 𓎛 ḥ = ח

𓐍 ḫ = ח̇. 𓄡 ẖ, 𓊃 = s. 𓋴 = ś. 𓈙 š = שׁ. 𓈎 ḳ = ק.

𓎡 k = כ. 𓏏 t = ת. 𓍿 = ṯ. 𓂧 d = ט. 𓆓 = ḏ. 𓇌 = y.

𓏭 = y (little yodh).

From these we see that Dr. Erman introduces the sign 𓄡 as a letter of the Egyptian Alphabet, and distinguishes between the two sibilants 𓊃 and 𓋴; that he gives *y* as an alternative value to 𓇋, and regards 𓏭 as a "little yodh," and that he retains ꜣ, ỉ and ʿ as the transliterations of 𓄿, 𓇋 and 𓂝 respectively. It is also to be noted that his system includes the letters ḫ, ẖ, ś, ṯ, and ḏ, making with ꜣ and ỉ seven new characters which must be specially cut for the compositor's use. There are many objections that might be urged against this system of transliteration, but the innovations in it are not worth discussion. It is sufficient to say that when the actual mistakes in the older system that was used by Birch, Lepsius, Brugsch and others are eliminated it remains, in my opinion, the best that has yet been proposed. The modifications which I have made in it for the purposes of this book are not in any way intended to be improvements or even corrections; they were made solely with the view of simplifying the transliteration for the use of the beginner, and of reducing the labour of the compositor. I have tried to get rid of as many letters with diacritical marks as possible, because they often

The simplified transliteration used in this book.

break off in the process of printing; but I have retained ȧ for 𓇋, ā for 𓂝, ḥ for 𓎛 and ṭ for 𓍿; three of these, ā, ḥ and ṭ, are familiar to every student of Oriental languages. I have rejected ꜣ and ỉ and ʿ; and letters with lines or a semi-circle under them, *i.e.*, ḫ, ẖ, ṯ, ḏ, and s with an accent (ś), I have eschewed entirely for the reasons given in the following paragraphs.

Maspero on Egyptian phonetics.

Maspero with infinite pains collected in his *Introduction à l'Étude de la Phonétique Égyptienne,* Paris, 1917, a number of examples illustrating the various vowel sounds which the Egyptians themselves gave to the signs 𓄿, 𓇋 and 𓂝. And from his conclusions it is clear that even though we transliterate 𓄿 by A, the A will not represent all the various modified sounds which the human mouth can give to that letter;[1] and this is also the case with 𓇋 and 𓂝. According to him the primitive phonetic value of the sign 𓇋 in Pyramid times was "un A moyen" like the French A in *patte, cage,* that is to say, an Ă, or an open Á which borders on É as in the popular pronunciation *Montp*É*nasse* for *Montp*Á*rnasse*; 𓄿 A is À *grave* bordering on Ô, as in the popular Parisian pronunciations gÒ*r* for *g*A*re,* or in the English A*ll,* *w*Os for *w*A*s*; 𓂝 is À guttural which recalls the sound of ע = ع, but does not correspond to it exactly and turns sometimes to the Á *aigu,* and sometimes to the À *grave.* In fact, we see that in archaic Egyptian "les phonèmes variés de la langue postérieure ne s'étaient pas produits encore, et qu'il n'y avait sous chacun d'eux, ainsi que sous chacun des signes reconnus pour consonnes par tous les savants 𓃀, 𓊪, 𓆑, 𓍿, 𓉔, etc., qu'un phonème unique, ou, si l'on veut, les groupes de nuances vocaliques que nous avons l'habitude de désigner par un signe unique." Accepting these conclusions heartily it has seemed to me quite unnecessary to use any other signs to represent 𓄿, 𓇋 and 𓂝 than a, ȧ and ā respectively.

𓄿, 𓇋 and 𓂝

[1] "Si donc nous disons que le signe A anglais figure une voyelle, il n'y a pas de raison pour que les signes 𓇋, 𓄿, 𓂝 ne figurent pas des voyelles. Bien entendu, je n'ai pas la prétention d'affirmer que, si 𓄿 par exemple sonnait A, il n'y avait sous ce signe qu'un seul des A possibles. Comme chaque modification de forme dans la bouche humaine produit une voyelle ou une nuance de voyelle différente, le nombre des voyelles et de leurs nuances est très considérable; aussi les signes que nous appelons *signes-voyelles* communément A, E, I, etc., représentent en réalité des groupes de nuances vocaliques différant très légèrement l'une de l'autre et l'on considérera les signes qui représentent chacun d'eux, 𓇋, 𓄿, 𓂝, en Égyptien comme couvrant chacun de ces groupes" (p. 119).

The sign 𓅱 is transliterated *u* throughout; it is no doubt equivalent both to ו and וּ, and I think it is a mistake to transliterate it always by *w*. The correct transliteration of 𓅓𓂝, or 𓂝𓅓, or 𓅓𓂝, or 𓅓𓂝 is a matter of difficulty. That 𓅓𓂝 was sounded in some way different from 𓅓 is clear, otherwise it would appear in words more frequently. It seems possible that the sign 𓂝 or 𓂝 added to the 𓅓 was intended to show that the 𓅓 was to be pronounced in one of the many ways in which *m* is sounded in African languages, but what that way was is not evident. When 𓅓𓂝 occurs at the end of an Egyptian transcription of the name of a locality in Palestine or Syria it may represent *mā*. In this book I have often transcribed 𓅓𓂝 by *m'*. And as regards 𓈖, when the Egyptian wrote 𓈖𓂋𓍿 the *n* was probably pronounced like the Spanish *ñ* or the Amharic ኝ *gn*.

The sign 𓅱.

The sign 𓅓𓂝.

𓈖 and 𓈖𓂋𓍿.

The signs 𓐍 and 𓄡 are transcribed throughout by *kh* and *kha* respectively. According to some authorities 𓐍 is represented in Coptic by ϩ and 𓄡 by ϧ, but the Copts did not observe this distinction carefully, for we find in Coptic texts ϩⲏⲓⲃⲓ and ϧⲏⲓⲃⲓ, ϩⲉⲙⲥ̄ and ϧⲉⲙⲥ̄, ϩⲣⲉ and ϧⲣⲉ, ϩⲱⲧⲃ̄ and ϧⲱⲧⲃ̄, etc. The absoluteness of the statement that 𓄡 can become in Coptic ϩ and ϧ but never ϣ, but that 𓐍 can become ϩ or ϣ, or ϧ or ϣ, has been disproved by Maspero,[1] and nothing more need be said about it here. In this Dictionary the words beginning with 𓐍 and those beginning with 𓄡 are separated into two distinct groups for the convenience of the beginner, but it has been thought unnecessary to use any specially distinctive signs for 𓐍 and 𓄡. As he will always have the Egyptian text before him, he can make no mistake. The χ is, of course, dropped.

𓐍 and ϩ.

𓄡 and ϧ.

In 1892, Professor Hommel pointed out in the *Zeitschrift für Aegyptische Sprache* (Bd. 30, s. 9 ff) that the Egyptians used two sibilants which were represented by the signs 𓊃 and 𓋴, and the fact is beyond dispute, as all will admit. But the texts prove conclusively that they ceased to distinguish between them in writing, except in the case of a few words at an early period, and that they used 𓊃 and 𓋴 indiscriminately when they wished to express the letter s. There is no doubt that 𓊃 must sometimes have had a somewhat different sound from 𓋴 for we find the

The sibilants 𓊃 and 𓋴.

[1] *Introduction à l'Étude de la Phonétique Égyptienne*, p. 46 ff.

word for "jackal" written 𓊃𓅜𓃀𓃢 or 𓊃𓃀𓃢 *sab* or *sb*, and the Hebrew word for the animal is *zĕēbh* זְאֵב. But we also find a form beginning with the 𓋴, thus 𓋴𓄿𓃀𓃢, and, as several variants of this form begin also with 𓋴, the form that begins with 𓊃 is not a very sure ground for the statement that 𓊃 = ז. The *z* sound must have been very rare in Egypt, for most of the words under ⲍ in the Coptic Dictionaries are of Greek origin; ⲍⲱⲛⲧ for ⲥⲱⲛⲧ (*see* Parthey's *Vocabularium*) seems to have been the result of careless pronunciation. When the Egyptians merged the sound of 𓊃 in that of 𓋴 is not known, but the merging must have happened long before the Christian Era began, for the Copts represent both signs by ⲥ. And the Egyptian transcriptions of Canaanite geographical names prove that both 𓊃 and 𓋴 represent ס and שׁ. In their transliterations of the signs 𓊃 and 𓋴 the German Egyptologists distinguish 𓊃 by *s* and 𓋴 by *ś*, but in this Dictionary I have followed the example of Birch and Brugsch and Maspero, and regarded them as having practically one and the same sound. Nevertheless, remembering the large number of words that begin with the signs 𓊃 and 𓋴, and with the view of simplifying the task of the searcher who may use this Dictionary, I have printed all the words beginning with 𓊃 in one section, and all those beginning with 𓋴 in the section following.

𓊃 rarely = ז.

𓊃 and 𓋴 = ס and שׁ.

By transliterating 𓈎 by *q*, a letter with a diacritical point (ḳ) has been got rid of and, though the transliterating of 𓎼 by g does not seem quite satisfactory, I have followed the example of the older Egyptologists in this particular.[1] The signs 𓏏 and 𓍘 are both transliterated by *t*, and by using *th* for 𓍿 the Greek θ and a letter with a line under it (*t̲*) are eliminated. In the case of 𓆓 I have retained the transliteration *ṭ* and have not adopted *d* by which it is now sometimes transliterated. Maspero has shown that in Semitic geographical names in the XVIIIth dynasty 𓆓 often represents the Hebrew ד, *e.g.*, in 𓈎𓆓𓏌𓊃𓅱, Heb. קָדֵשׁ, and 𓇋𓇋𓂋𓆓𓈖𓄿𓈙, יַרְדֵּן, but other names show that ד is represented in Egyptian by 𓍘, *t*, *e.g.*, 𓍘𓇋𓅓𓊃𓈎𓅱, Heb. דַּמֶּשֶׂק. At a later period 𓆓 is transliterated by ט, *e.g.*,

𓈎 = q.

𓎼 = g.

𓏏 and 𓍘 = t.

𓍿 = th.

[1] In one Coptic word, ⲕⲁϣ, "reed," the ⲕ represents 𓎼, for the hieroglyphic form is 𓎼𓄿𓈙𓇋𓇋𓆰; see Erman, *Aegyptisches Glossar*, p. 139, and Maspero, *Introduction*, p. 39.

in the name , the Aramean transcription of which is פטיסירי, and in the name , Abydos, the Aramean transcription of which is אבוט. In the Greek period  represents the Greek T, as in Κλεοπάτρα , and Δ, as in Δίος . In the Coptic period, when the hieroglyphs were no longer in use, the scribes wrote all the names which in the old language had a  or a  with θ. Finally, as Maspero admits[1] that the sound of  was not exactly that of the Greek Δ or the Arabic ذ, I have thought it best to retain *ṭ* as the transliteration of . It is possible that the sound of the Greek Δ did exist at one time in Egyptian, but when the Copts formulated their alphabet it had disappeared from the mouths of ordinary folk.

 = d (ד) or ṭ (ט).

There remains to mention now only the transliteration of  which in some recent works appears as *t'* or d with a line under it, *ḏ*. In the transcription of Semitic geographical names  represents both צ and ז, *e.g.*, , צִידוֹן and , גֶּזֶר. But there is abundant proof that it may be correctly transliterated by both *ts* and *tch*, and I have adopted the latter, which is pronounced like the *ch* in "child," or the *c* in "cicerone."

 = ts and tch.

Egyptian an African Language Fundamentally.

The alleged relationship of Egyptian to the Semitic languages.

During the years which I spent in collecting the materials for this Dictionary I looked eagerly in the texts for any evidence that would throw light on the relationship of the ancient Egyptian language to the Semitic languages and to the languages of North Eastern Africa. Though the subject is one of considerable importance philologically, it has never been, in my opinion, properly discussed, because the Semitic scholars who have written about it have lacked the Egyptological knowledge necessary for arriving at a decision, and the Egyptologists, with the exception of the lamented Burchardt, have had no adequate knowledge of Semitic languages and literature. Benfey came to the conclusion that the ancient Egyptian language had close affinity with the Semitic family of languages, but then he also said that the Semites belonged to a great group of peoples which not only included the

Benfey's opinion.

[1] *Introduction*, p. 30, Notre 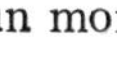 est donc, je pense, l'intradentale faible Δ, et il est à ce qui a été un moment à .

Egyptians, but all the peoples of Africa,[1] which is obviously absurd. Although his excursions into Coptic had disastrous results so far as his reputation was concerned, his view that there was a close affinity between the Egyptian and Semitic languages found acceptance with many scholars, among them being E. de Rougé, Ebers and Brugsch, all of whom were Egyptologists. Birch's view was that the "greater portion of the words [in the ancient Egyptian language] are an old form of the Coptic ; others, no longer found in that tongue, appear (to be) of Semitic origin, and have been gradually introduced into the language from the Aramaïc and other sources. A few words are Indo-Germanic."[2] Brugsch stated categorically that the oldest form of the ancient Egyptian language is rooted in Semitic, and he prophesied that one day philological science would be astonished at the closeness of the relationship which existed between Egyptian and the Semitic languages. He was convinced that they had a mother in common, and that their original home was to be sought for on the banks of the Tigris and Euphrates.[3] Brugsch held these views practically to the end of his life, for in his *Die Aegyptologie*, Leipzig, 1891, p. 91, he quotes from his *Wörterbuch* the words which he wrote in the preface in 1867. Stern, the eminent Coptic scholar, also declared that the Egyptian had an affinity with the Semitic languages, which shows itself in the pronominal formations and in the roots which are common to all, but thought that it separated itself from its Asiatic sisters at a very early period and developed along lines of its own.[4]

Brugsch on the Semitic origin of the Egyptian language.

Stern's opinion.

These views, which the older Egyptologists expressed in general terms, were crystallized by Erman in a paper which he contributed to the *Zeitschrift der Deutschen Morgenländischen*

[1] Benfey, *Über das Verhältniss der Aegyptischen Sprache zum Semitischen Sprachstamme.* Leipzig, 1844.

[2] Bunsen, *Egypt's Place*, Vol. V, p. 618.

[3] Es steht mir nämlich fest, dass die altägyptische Sprache, d. h. die älteste Gestaltung derselben, im Semitischen wurzelt. . . . Im voraus kann ich es weissagen, dass die Sprachforschung eines Tages erstaunt sein wird über das enge Band der Verwandtschaft, welches die ägyptische Sprache mit ihren semitischen Schwestern zusammenknüpft, und über die mir jetzt schon feststehende Thatsache, dass alle eine gemeinsame Mutter haben, deren Ursitze an den Ufern des Euphrat und Tigris zu suchen ist." *Wörterbuch*, Bd. I, p. ix.

[4] Es besteht eine alte verwandtschaft zwischen der ägyptischen, welche dem hamitischen stamme angehört, und den semitischen sprachen, wie sich unverkennbar noch in der pronominalbildung und in manchen gemeinsamen wurzeln zeigt ; doch scheint sich das ägyptische von den asiatischen schwestern früh getrennt zu haben und seinen eigenen weg gegangen zu sein. *Koptische Grammatik*, p. 4.

Gesellschaft in 1892.[1] In this he pointed out in a systematic manner the details of Egyptian Grammar that have their counterparts in the Semitic languages, and printed a List of the words that were common to the Egyptian and Semitic languages. Most of these words had been remarked upon by Brugsch in his *Wörterbuch*, but Erman's List heightens their cumulative effect, and at the first sight of it many investigators would be inclined to say without any hesitation, "Egyptian is a Semitic language." A very able comparative philologist of the Semitic Languages, Carl Brockelmann, impressed by the remarks of Brugsch quoted above and by this List, says that Egyptian must certainly be included among the Semitic Languages, and that the more the oldest form of it, such as that made known by the Pyramid Texts, is investigated, the more convincingly apparent becomes its similarity to the Semitic Languages. Like Brugsch, he thinks that it separated itself from its sister tongues thousands of years ago, and went its own way. According to him the Egyptian language developed more quickly than the languages of the other Semites, which was due partly to the mixing of the people caused by the invasion of the Nile Valley by Semites, and the rapidity with which the Egyptian civilization reached its zenith, much in the same way as English has gone far away from the other Germanic languages.[2] Wright thought that the connection between the Semitic and the Egyptian languages was closer than that which can be said to exist between the Semitic and the Indo-European. But he called attention to the fact that the majority of Egyptian roots are monosyllabic in form, and that they do not exhibit Semitic triliterality. He was prepared to admit that the "not a few structural affinities" might perhaps be thought sufficient to justify those linguists who hold that Egyptian is a relic of the earliest age of Semitism, *i.e.*, of Semitic

Recent views based on Brugsch's opinion.

Monosyllabic character of Egyptian roots.

[1] *Das Verhältniss des Aegyptischen zu den semitischen Sprachen* (Bd. XLVI), p. 93 ff.

[2] Es scheint sehr vieles dafür zu sprechen, dass die Aegypter eigentlich in diesen Kreis hineinzubeziehen sind. Je mehr die Forschung den ältesten Formenbau des Aegyptischen, wie er in den Pyramidentexten vorliegt, erschliesst, desto überraschender tritt Aehnlichkeit mit dem Semitischen zu Tage. . . . Durch die Vermischung der einwandernden Semiten mit den älteren, anderssprachigen Bewohnern des Niltals und durch die frühe Blüte ihrer Kultur sei das Aegyptische viel schneller und durchgreifender fortentwickelt, als die Sprachen der anderen Semiten, ähnlich wie das Englische sich unter denselben Umständen so weit von den anderen germanischen Sprachen entfernt hat. *Grundriss der vergleichenden Grammatik der semitischen Sprachen.* Berlin, 1908, p. 3.

speech as it was before it passed into the peculiar form in which we may be said to know it historically.[1]

Now no one who has worked at Egyptian can possibly doubt that there are many Semitic words in the language, or that many of the pronouns, some of the numbers, and some of its grammatical forms resemble those found in the Semitic languages. But even admitting all the similarities that Erman has claimed, it is still impossible to me to believe that Egyptian is a Semitic language fundamentally. There is, it is true, much in the Pyramid Texts that recalls points and details of Semitic Grammar, but after deducting all the triliteral roots, there still remains a very large number of words that are not Semitic, and were never invented by a Semitic people.

Egyptian fundamentally an African language.

These words are monosyllabic, and were invented by one of the oldest African (or Hamitic, if that word be preferred) peoples in the Valley of the Nile of whose written language we have any remains. These are words used to express fundamental relationships and feelings, and beliefs which are peculiarly African and are foreign in every particular to Semitic peoples. The primitive home of the people who invented these words lay far to the south of Egypt, and all that we know of the Predynastic Egyptians suggests that it was in the neighbourhood of the Great Lakes, probably to the east of them. The whole length of the Valley of the Nile lay then, as now, open to peoples who dwelt to the west and east of it, and there must always have been a mingling of immigrants with its aboriginal inhabitants.

Perpetual immigration into the Nile Valley.

These last borrowed many words from the newcomers, especially from the "proto-Semitic" peoples from the country now called Arabia, and from the dwellers in the lands between the Nile and the Red Sea and Indian Ocean, but they continued to use their native words to express their own primitive ideas, especially in respect of religious beliefs and ceremonies.

Borrowings from proto-Semitic.

Words like *tef* "father," *sa* "son," *sen* "brother," *ȧf* "flesh," *qes* "bone," *tep* "head," *ȧb* "heart," *ā* "hand," *tches* "self," *ka* "double," *ba* "soul," *ȧakh* "spirit," and scores of others that are used from the earliest to the latest times, are African and have nothing to do with the Semitic languages. When they had invented or borrowed the art of writing, they were quick to perceive the advantage of adding to their pictures signs that would help the eye of the

Addition of conventional signs.

[1] *Lectures on the Comparative Grammar of the Semitic Languages.* Cambridge, 1890, pp. 33–34.

reader, and convey to his mind an exact conception of what the writer intended to express. The names of the cardinal numbers show that the people who invented the words quoted above counted by fives, for they have words for "one" , "two" , "three" , "four" , and "five" , and their next number is "ten" . When they came in contact with the Semites they borrowed from them the numbers "six" , Heb. שֵׁשׁ, "seven" , Heb. שֶׁבַע, "eight" , Heb. שְׁמֹנָה, and "nine" Heb. תֵּשַׁע. In a similar manner they borrowed *t* as a sign of the feminine, and several of the pronouns, and at a much later period many of the Semitic words that were current at the time in Syria and Palestine. And it has always seemed to me that some of the aboriginal words of the primitive Egyptians found their way into neighbouring countries, where they still live. Thus the common Egyptian word *khefti* , "enemy," which has its equivalent in the Coptic *shaft* ϣⲁϥⲧ, is also found in Amharic under the form *shaftâ* ሽፍታ፡. The Egyptian word *ṭeng* , "pygmy," seems to be preserved in the Amharic *denk* ድንክ፡ The Egyptian word *ṭuat* , "morning," seems to survive in the Amharic *ṭuwat* ጧት፡; and with the Egyptian *Sa* (?) or "man," "person," may be compared the Amharic *saw* ሰው፡ "man or woman," "person."

Borrowing numbers.

Borrowing of the pronouns and the sign of the feminine.

Survivals in Amharic.

As none of the literature of the peoples who lived on each side of the Valley of the Nile has been preserved, we have no means of finding out how much they borrowed linguistically from the Egyptians or the Egyptians from them, but I believe the Egyptians were as much indebted to them as to the Semites. I do not for one moment suggest that such literature as the modern inhabitants of the Valley of the Nile and the neighbouring countries possess, whether it be those on the east or those on the west of the Nile, can be utilized for explaining ancient Egyptian texts, but the comparatively small amount of attention which I have been able to devote to the grammars and vocabularies of some of the languages now spoken in the Eastern Sûdân has convinced me that they contain much that is useful for the study of the language of the hieroglyphs. The ancient Egyptians were Africans, and they spoke an African language, and the modern peoples of the Eastern Sûdân are Africans, and they speak African languages, and there is in consequence much in modern native

Value of modern Sûdânî dialects for comparative purposes.

Sûdânî literature which will help the student of ancient Egyptian in his work. From the books of Tutschek,[1] Krapf,[2] Mitterutzner,[3] and from the recently published works of Captain Owen[4] and Westermann,[5] a student with the necessary leisure can collect a large number of facts of importance for the comparative study of Nilotic languages both ancient and modern.

The Introduction, Indexes, Semitic Alphabets, etc.

The Introduction.

In the introductory section of this book I have given a list of the commonest Egyptian signs, with their values as phonetics and determinatives, arranged practically according to the Lists of Egyptian Hieroglyphic Signs published by the eminent printing firms of Theinhardt in Berlin,[6] Holzhausen in Vienna,[7] and Harrison & Sons in London.[8] Certainly none of these lists is absolutely correct since the classification of several of the signs is the result of guesswork, for the simple reason that Egyptologists do not know what objects certain signs are intended to represent. The only native Egyptian List of Hieroglyphs known was published by Griffith, *Two Hieroglyphic Papyri from Tanis*, London, 1889, 4to, but this does not help us much in the identification of the hieroglyphs. The first printed List of Hieroglyphs was published by Champollion in his *Grammaire Égyptienne*, Paris, 1836, and contains 260 hieroglyphs. In 1848 Birch published a fuller List with detailed descriptions (see above p. xxxiii) in the first volume of the German and English editions of Bunsen's "Aegyptens Stelle." This he revised and enlarged, and republished in 1867, in the second edition of the first volume of the English edition, pp. 505–559. It contained 890 hieroglyphs and 201 determinatives were grouped separately. In 1851 E. de Rougé issued a List of hieroglyphs in his *Catalogue des signes hiéroglyphiques de l'Imprimerie Nationale*, Paris, 1851, and he reprinted it with explanations and descriptions in the first part

Lists of Hieroglyphic signs by Champollion, Birch, E. de Rougé and Brugsch.

[1] *Grammar of the Galla-Language*. Munich, 1845; and his *Lexicon*. Munich, 1841.

[2] *Vocabulary of the Galla-Language*. London, 1842.

[3] *Die Dinka-Sprache in Central Afrika* (with *Wörterbuch*). Brixen, 1866.

[4] *Bari Grammar and Vocabulary*. London, 1908.

[5] *The Shilluk People: their Language and Folklore*. Berlin, 1912; *Die Sudansprachen*. Hamburg, 1911; *The Nuer Language*. Berlin, 1912.

[6] *Liste der Hieroglyphischen Typen aus der Schriftgiesserei*. Berlin, 1875. This list was arranged by Lepsius.

[7] *Hieroglyphen*. Vienna (no date). This List contains all the unusual types which were specially cut to print Maspero's edition of the Pyramid Texts.

[8] *List of Egyptian Hieroglyphics*. London, 1892.

of his *Chrestomathie Égyptienne,* Paris, 1867. This contained about 340 hieroglyphs. A much fuller and more accurate List was published by Brugsch, *Index des Hiéroglyphes Phonétiques y compris des valeurs de l'Écriture Secrète,* Leipzig, 1872, and it contained 600 signs and their phonetic values, accompanied by references to pages of his *Wörterbuch,* and 147 determinatives. After the Lists given by Rossi in his Coptic Hieroglyphic Grammar[1] and by von Lemm[2] in his Egyptian Reading Book, no further attempt was made to discuss hieroglyphs generally until Griffith described 104 Egyptian characters in *Beni Hasan III,* London, 1896. Two years later he published *A Collection of Hieroglyphs,* London, 1898, which contained descriptions and identifications of 192 hieroglyphs illustrated by really good coloured pictures of the objects which they represented, copied chiefly from coffins and tombs of the XIIth dynasty. The most recently published List of Hieroglyphs is that given by Erman in the third edition of his *Aegyptische Grammatik,* Berlin, 1911. It contains about 660 hieroglyphs, not reckoning variants, selected from Theinhardt's List. In the List of Hieroglyphs given in the present work I have followed their order in the List of Messrs. Harrison & Sons, but have been obliged to alter the numbers of the characters. I have given all the ordinary phonetic values which the signs have when forming parts of words generally, but have made no attempt to give the word-values when they are used as ideographs. The values which many of the signs had when used in the so-called "enigmatic writing," and in the inscriptions of the Ptolemaïc Period are not given. Want of space made it impossible to include in this Introduction a list of the hieratic forms of hieroglyphs; for these the beginner is referred to Pleyte's *Catalogue Raisonné de Types Égyptiens Hiératiques de la Fonderie de N. Tetterode,* Leyden, 1865 (which contains 388 signs), and the works of Simeone Levi[3] and G. Möller.[4]

The selected Lists of Rossi, von Lemm, Griffith and Erman.

Lists of hieratic signs.

I have also given in the Introduction reproductions by photography of the Egyptian Alphabet as formulated by Young,

[1] *Grammatica Copto-Geroglifica con un' appendice dei principali segni sillabici e del loro significato.* Rome-Turin-Florence, 1877. It contains 386 phonetic signs and 124 determinatives.

[2] *Aegyptische Lesestücke.*

[3] *Raccolta dei Segni Ieratici Egizi nelle diverse epoche con i corrispondenti Geroglifici ed i loro differenti valori fonetici,* Turin, 1880 (contains 675 signs).

[4] *Hieratische Paläographie. Die Aegyptische Buchschrift in ihrer Entwickelung von der Fünften Dynastie bis zur Römischen Kaiserzeit.* Part I, Leipzig, 1909 (contains 719 signs); Part II, Leipzig, 1909 (contains 713 signs); Part III, Leipzig, 1912 (contains 713 signs).

Champollion, Lepsius, and Tattam, and reproductions of pages of Birch's *Sketch of a Hieroglyphical Dictionary*, Young's *Rudiments of an Egyptian Dictionary in the ancient Enchorial Character*, Champollion's *Dictionnaire Égyptien*, and Birch's *Dictionary of Hieroglyphics*. These works are not to be found in every public, still less private, library, and I believe that many a reader will examine and study them, if only from the point of view of the bibliographer.

Reproductions of pages of some early Egyptological works.

The indexes to the Coptic and to the non-Egyptian words and geographical names which are at the end of the book will show that a considerable number of Coptic, Hebrew, Syriac, Arabic, Ethiopic, Amharic, Assyrian and Persian words and names are quoted in this Dictionary. The beginner who wishes to examine these words will need to learn the alphabets of the principal Semitic languages, and as I know of no Egyptological work in which they are to be found, I have included them in this Introduction, and they follow the List of Egyptian Hieroglyphs.

Semitic alphabets.

Apologia and Thanks.

In the preparation of the manuscript of this Dictionary for the printer I have not spared labour, or trouble, or time or attention, and I have made every effort during the proof reading to reduce misprints to a minimum. I have copied too many texts in the course of my life not to know how easy it is for the attention to be distracted, and the eye to be deceived, and the hand to write something which it ought not to write when doing work of this kind. The professional copyists of the Book of the Dead, and the monastic scribes who laboriously transcribed Coptic, Syriac, Arabic and Ethiopic texts in Egypt, Ethiopia and Syria, made many mistakes, mis-spelt the words of the archetypes in their copies, omitted whole lines, and made nonsense of many passages by omitting parts of words and mixing together the remaining parts. It seems to me obvious from these facts that every one who undertakes a long and very tedious work like the making of an Egyptian Dictionary, must be guilty of the perpetration of mistakes, blunders, and errors in his copying, however careful he may be. In my work there will be found inconsistencies, misunderstandings, and misprints, and probably downright misstatements, and as Maspero said in his edition of the Pyramid Texts, "je le regrette sans m'en étonner. . . . C'est une infirmité de la nature humaine dont on finit par prendre son parti, comme de bien d'autres." Notwithstanding such defects I hope and believe that this Dictionary will be useful to the

The mistakes of scribes and transcribers, their errors and omissions.

beginner, and will save him time and trouble and give him help, and if my hope and belief be realized, the purpose of my friend who made the printing of the book possible will be effected, and my own time and labour will not have been wasted. Many, many years must pass before the perfect Egyptian Hieroglyphic Dictionary can, or will, be written, and meanwhile the present work may serve as a stop-gap.

It is now my pleasant duty to put on record my thanks and gratitude to those who have enabled me to produce this book. First and foremost they are due to the gentleman, who having discussed with me my plan for the proposed Dictionary and suggested certain modifications of it and additions to it, decided to defray the entire cost of its production. In spite of my entreaties he persists in remaining anonymous, and wishes to be known only as an English gentleman who is interested in everything that concerns the history, religion, language and literature of ancient Egypt, and in the language and literature of the Copts, that is to say, of the Egyptians who embraced Christianity. He is also deeply interested in the exploration of Western Asia, and has liberally supported all the endeavours made by the English to excavate the sites of the ancient cities mentioned in the Bible. Owing to the great advance in the price of materials, and the various rises in wages in the printing trades that have taken place during the War, twice or thrice I was on the verge of being obliged to stop the printing of this book, but my friend decided that the work should go on, and that the original plan as approved by him should be neither altered nor curtailed, and he furnished the means for continuing the work. What this means will be evident from the fact that since we began to print in July, 1916, the cost per sheet has increased by not less than 125 per cent.! In addition to this generous act I am indebted to my anonymous friend for ready help and sympathy during the last forty years.

Thanks to those who have made the publication of this Dictionary possible.

Great rise in wages and cost of production of this Dictionary.

I owe my wife many thanks for constant help in the sorting and incorporation of slips, and for assistance in the reading of proofs. She has also read for and with me the proofs and revises of every sheet of the book, and its completion is due largely to her help and encouragement.

To Mr. Edgar Harrison, partner in the firm of Harrison & Sons, I am indebted in another way. From start to finish he has taken the deepest interest in the printing of the Dictionary, and has done everything he could, both officially

Mr. Edgar Harrison.

and privately, to forward my work. During the War, when the resources of the Firm were strained to their utmost to carry out the urgent work which was thrust upon them by the Government, and when every available hand was pressed into this service, he somehow managed to keep going the composition of this book, and found means of machining each sheet when ready for press. Besides this, he had many hundreds of new characters cut, and spared no trouble in reproducing my manuscript, and whenever necessary he cast great quantities of new type to enable the composing to continue, and so avoided delay during the distribution of the type of worked-off sheets. At the present time his fount of Egyptian type is the largest and most comprehensive and complete in the world. At my request he has prepared a list of his Egyptian Hieroglyphic types which will be found at the end of the volume.* On the Continent great printing firms like Harrison & Sons, who enlarge and complete their founts of Oriental types, receive subsidies from Governments, or from Academies, but in England no subsidies or contributions are given to printers, and the satisfaction which they feel when they have done a public-spirited act of this kind is their sole reward. That Messrs. Longman cast at their own expense the fount of solid Egyptian type that was used for printing Birch's "List of Hieroglyphics," and his "Dictionary of Hieroglyphics," and that Messrs. Harrisons have cut, at their own expense, the very extensive and complete fount of linear hieroglyphic types used in the printing of the present work, will ever redound to the credit of the great company of English publishers and master-printers. Dedication: the coloured border was drawn by Mr. Alfred Caton.**

Messrs. Harrisons' fount of Egyptian type.

Finally, I mention with gratitude the help which I have received from Mr. A. E. Fish, the able compositor in the employ of Messrs. Harrisons who set the type of this Dictionary. He has shown great zeal and interest in the work, and his skill and great experience have triumphed over many difficulties, and made the proof reading easier. He is a worthy successor of Mr. Mabey, Messrs. Harrisons' great Oriental Compositor, who set the type for George Smith's monumental work *The History of Assurbanipal*, London, 1871, and of Mr. Fisher who set the type for my text volume of the *Book of the Dead*, London, 1894, published by the Trustees of the British Museum.

Messrs. Harrisons' Oriental compositor.

ERNEST WALLIS BUDGE.

British Museum,
February 25th, 1920.

* Omitted in this (1978) edition. ** In black and white in this (1978) edition.

A LIST

OF THE PRINCIPAL WORKS USED IN THE PREPARATION OF THIS DICTIONARY, AND OF THE ABBREVIATIONS OF THEIR TITLES BY WHICH THEY ARE INDICATED.

A LIST

Of the principal works used in the preparation of this Dictionary, and of the abbreviations of their titles by which they are indicated:—

I .. .. .. *Urkunden des Alten Reichs bearbeitet von K. Sethe.* Leipzig, 1903. Large 8vo.

II .. .. .. *Hieroglyphische Urkunden der Griechisch-Römischen Zeit bearbeitet von K. Sethe.* Leipzig, 1904. Large 8vo.

III .. .. .. *Urkunden der älteren Aethiopenkönige bearbeitet von K. Sethe.* Leipzig, 1908. Large 8vo.

IV .. .. .. *Urkunden der 18 Dynastie, Bände III und IV bearbeitet von K. Sethe.* Leipzig, 1906–09. Large 8vo. (In the Series *Urkunden des Aegyptischen Altertums.* Edited by G. Steindorff.)

Abbott Pap. .. .. Brit. Mus. Pap. No. 10183. The hieratic text was published by Birch in *Select Papyri.* London, 1860. Vol. ii, pls. 9–19.

A. E. .. .. .. Wilkinson, J. G., *The Manners and Customs of the Ancient Egyptians.* Ed. Birch. 3 vols. 1878. 8vo.

Alex. Stele .. .. Mariette, A., *Monuments Divers*, pl. 14.

Alt-K. .. .. .. Burchardt, M., *Die Altkanaanäischen Fremdworte und Eigennamen im Aegyptischen.* Leipzig, 1909–10. 4to.

Amamu .. .. Birch, S., *Egyptian Texts of the earliest period from the Coffin of Amamu in the British Museum.* London, 1886. Folio.

Ȧmen. .. .. .. The Book of Precepts of Ȧmen-em-ȧpt, the son of Ka-nekht, according to the Papyrus in the British Museum (No. 10474).

Amherst Pap. .. Newberry, P. E., *The Amherst Papyri.* London, 1899. 4to.

Anastasi I–IX. .. The Anastasi Papyri in the British Museum. Published by S. Birch. *Select Papyri in the Hieratic Character from the Collections of the British Museum.* London, MDCCCXLIII. Folio. Pl. 35 ff.

Annales .. .. *Annales du Service des Antiquités de l'Égypte.* Cairo, Vol. i. 1900. 4to. In progress.

Aram. Pap. .. .. Ungnad, A., *Aramäische Papyrus aus Elephantine.* Leipzig, 1911. 8vo. (No. 4 of *Hilfsbücher zur Kunde des alten Orients.*)

Asien .. .. .. Müller, W. Max, *Asien und Europa nach altägyptischen Denkmälen.* Leipzig, 1893. 8vo.

Ä. Z. .. .. .. *Zeitschrift für Ägyptische Sprache und Alterthumskunde.* Leipzig. 4to. Vol. i, 1863. In progress.

Banishment Stele .. The text is found in Brugsch, *Reise*, pl. 22.

Barshah. .. .. Newberry, P., *El-Bersheh.* Part i by Newberry and Fraser: Part ii by Newberry, Griffith and Fraser. London (undated). 4to.

B. D. .. .. .. The hieroglyphic text of the Theban Recension of the Book of the Dead. See E. A. Wallis Budge, *The Chapters of Coming Forth by Day.* Edited with a translation, vocabulary, etc. London, 1898. 3 vols. 8vo.

B. D. (Ani) .. .. THE BOOK OF THE DEAD: *Papyrus of Ani,* edited by E. A. Wallis Budge. London, 1890. Folio.

B. D. (Nebseni) .. Birch, S., *Photographs of the Papyrus of Nebseni in the British Museum.* London, 1876. Folio.

B. D. (Nu) .. .. THE BOOK OF THE DEAD: *Facsimiles of the Papyri of Hunefer, Anhai, Kerasher, and Netchemet, with supplementary text from the Papyrus of Nu.* London, 1899. Folio.

B. D. (Saïte). .. .. The hieroglyphic text of the Book of the Dead according to the Papyrus of Ȧuf-ānkh . It was published by R. Lepsius, *Das Todtenbuch der Aegypter nach dem hieroglyphischen Papyrus in Turin.* Leipzig, 1842.

B. D. G. .. .. Brugsch, H., *Dictionnaire Géographique de l'ancienne Égypte.* 2 vols. Leipzig, 1877–1880. Folio.

Beh. .. .. .. Rawlinson, H. C., The Persian Cuneiform Inscription at Behistun decyphered and translated. London, 1846. 8vo. (Forming vol. x. of the *Journal of the Royal Asiatic Society.*) See also *The Sculptures and Inscriptions of Darius the Great on the Rock of Behistûn* in Persia. Edited and translated by the late Prof. L. W. King, assisted by Mr. R. C. Thompson. London, 1907. 4to.

Beni Hasan .. .. Newberry, P. E., and G. W. Fraser, *Beni Hasan.* 2 vols. London, 1893. 4to.

Berg. I, Berg. II. .. von Bergmann, Ernst Ritter, *Der Sarcophag des Panchemisis* in the *Jahrbuch der Kunsthistorischen-Sammlungen des allerhöchsten Kaiserhauses.* 2 vols. Vienna, 1883–4. 4to.

Bibl. Egypt. .. .. *Bibliothèque Égyptologique publiée sous la Direction de G. Maspero.* Paris, 1893 (vol. i). 8vo. [At least forty volumes have appeared.]

Book of Breathings .. Brit. Mus. Pap. No. 9995, Budge, E. A. W., BOOK OF THE DEAD: *Facsimiles of the Papyri of Hunefer, etc.* London, 1899. Folio.

Book of Gates.. .. Bonomi, J., and Sharpe, S., *The Alabaster Sarcophagus of Oimenepthah I, now in Sir J. Soane's Museum.* London, 1864. 4to; Budge, E. A. W., *The Egyptian Heaven and Hell.* London, 1906, vol. ii.

Brugsch, Rec... .. Brugsch, H., *Recueil de Monuments Égyptiens.* Leipzig. Parts i and ii. 1862–3. 4to.

Brünnow .. .. Brünnow, R. E., *A Classified List of all simple and Compound Cuneiform ideographs,* etc. Parts i–iii. Leyden. 1887–89. 4to. The INDICES were published in 1897.

Bubastis	Naville, E., *Bubastis* (1887–1889), being the Eighth Memoir of the Egypt Exploration Fund. London, 1891. 4to.
Buch.	Bergmann, E. Ritter von, *Das Buch vom Durchwandeln der Ewigkeit* (in *Sitzungsberichte der Philosophisch-historischen Classe.* Bd. lxxxvi). Vienna, 1877, p. 369 ff.
Cairo Pap.	Photographs of Egyptian Papyri in the Egyptian Museum, Cairo.
Canopus Stele ..	See Lepsius, *Das bilingue Dekret von Kanopus,* Berlin, 1866, folio; and the facsimiles of the Hieroglyphic, Greek and Demotic texts published by Budge, E. A. W., *The Decree of Canopus.* London, 1904. 8vo, pp. 35–114.
Chabas Mél.	Chabas, F., *Mélanges Égyptologiques ;* 1er Série, Paris, 1862, 8vo; 2me Série, Chalon, 1864, 8vo; 3me Série, Paris and Chalon, vol. i, 1870, vol. ii, 1873.
Champ. Mon.	Champollion, J. F., *Monuments de l'Égypte et de la Nubie,* vols. i–iv. Paris, 1822. Folio.
Coptos	Petrie, W. M. F., *Koptos.* London, 1896. 4to.
Coronation Stele ..	The text of this stele was published by Mariette, *Monuments Divers,* pl. 9; Schaefer, *Urkunden III,* p. 81; and Budge, E. A. Wallis, *Annals of Nubian Kings,* p. 89 ff.
Culte Divin	Moret, A., *Rituel du Culte Divin.* Paris, 1902. 8vo.
Décrets..	Weill, R., *Les Décrets Royaux de l'ancien Empire Égyptien.* Paris, 1912. 4to.
De Hymnis	Breasted, J. H., *De Hymnis in Solem Sub Rege Amenophide IV conceptis* (lithographed).
Demot. Cat.	Griffith, F. Ll., *Catalogue of the Demotic Papyri in the John Rylands Library.* Manchester, 1909. Folio.
Denderah	Mariette, A., *Description Générale du Grand Temple.* Texte, Paris, 1880. 4to. Pl. Vols. i–iv and a supplementary volume. Paris, 1870–74. Folio.
Dêr al-B.	Mariette, A., *Deir el Bahari : documents topographiques, historiques et ethnographiques recueillis dans ce temple.* Leipzig, 1877. Folio.
Dêr al-Gabrâwî ..	Davies, N. de G., *The Rock Tombs of Deir el Gebrâwi.* Vols. i–iii. London, 1902. 4to.
Dream Stele	Text originally published by Mariette, *Monuments Divers,* pll. 7, 8; see also Sethe, *Urkunden* III, p. 57, ff; and Budge, E. A. Wallis, *Annals of Nubian Kings.* London, 1911, p. 71 ff.
Dublin Pap. 4. ..	Naville, E., *Das Aegyptische Todtenbuch* (Einleitung), Berlin, 1886. 4to, p. 80.
Düm. H. I.	Dümichen, J., *Historische Inschriften altägyptischer Denkmäler.* Leipzig, 1867 4to, and 1869 Folio.
Düm. Temp. Ins. ..	Dümichen, J., *Altägyptische Tempel-Inschriften in den Jahren* 1863–1865 *an Ort und Stelle gesammelt.* Leipzig. 1867. Folio.

Ebers Pap .. .. Ebers, G., *Papyros Ebers: das hermetische Buch über die Arzeneimittel der alten Aegypter in hieratischer Schrift.* Mit hieroglyphisch-lateinischem Glossar von L. Stern. 2 vols. Leipzig, 1875. Folio.

Ebers Pap. Voc. .. Stern, L., *Glossarium Hieroglyphicum quo papyri Medicinalis hieratici Lipsiae asservati et a clarissimo Ebers editi.* (Printed in the second volume of the preceding work.)

Edfu .. .. .. Dümichen, J., *Altägyptische Tempel-Inschriften,* vol. I. Leipzig, 1867. Folio.

Edict. .. .. .. Petrie, W. M. F., *Koptos.* London, 1896. 4to, pl. 8.

El Amarna .. .. Davis, N. de G., *The Rock Tombs of El Amarna.* 5 vols. (vol. i, 1903). London. 4to.

Eg. Res. .. .. Müller, W. M., *Egyptological Researches, Results of a journey in* 1904. Washington. Publication of the Carnegie Institution. No. 53. 1902. 4to.

E. T. .. .. .. *Hieroglyphic Texts from Egyptian Stelae,* etc., *in the British Museum.* Pts. i–v. London, 1911 (pt. i). Folio.

Excom. Stele .. .. Stele of the Excommunication now in the Egyptian Museum, Cairo. Published by Mariette, *Monuments Divers,* Paris, 1872–89, folio, pl. 10; Schäfer, *Klio,* Bd. vi, p. 287 ff.; and in *Urkunden der älteren Aethiopenkönige.* Leipzig, 1908. Large 8vo.

Famine Stele .. .. Brugsch, H., *Die biblischen sieben Jahre der Hungersnoth.* Leipzig, 1891. 8vo.

Festschrift. .. .. AEGYPTIACA. *Festschrift für Georg Ebers zum* 1 *März,* 1897. Leipzig, 1897. 8vo.

Festschrift, Leemans. Pleyte, W. (and others), *Études Archéologiques dediées à C. Leemans.* Leyden, 1885. 4to.

Gen. Epist. .. .. Maspero, G., *Du Genre épistolaire chez les Égyptiens de l'époque pharaonique.* Paris, 1872. 8vo.

G. I. .. .. .. Brugsch, H., *Geographische Inschriften: Die Geographie des Alten Aegyptens.* Leipzig, 1857. 4to.

Gnostic .. .. Griffith, F. Ll., and Thompson, H. F. H., *The Demotic Magical Papyrus of London and Leiden.* London, 1904–09. 8vo and folio.

Gol. .. .. .. Golénischeff, W., *Epigraphical Results of an excursion to Wâdî Hammâmât.* St. Petersburg, 1887, pp. 65–79, plates 1–18.

Gol. Pap. .. .. Golénischeff, W., *Les Papyrus hiératiques* 1115, 1116A *et* 1116B *de l'Ermitage Impérial à St. Pétersbourg.* St. Pétersbourg, 1913. Folio.

Goshen. .. .. Naville, E., *The Shrine of Saft el-Henneh and the Land of Goshen.* London, 1887. 4to.

Greene .. .. Greene, J. B., *Fouilles exécutées à Thèbes dans l'année* 1855. Paris, 1855. Folio.

Harris I. .. .. Brit. Mus. Papyrus No. 9900. For the facsimile see Birch, S., *Facsimile of an Egyptian Hieratic Papyrus of Rameses III in the British Museum* (Great Harris Papyrus). London, 1876. Long folio.

Harris 500 .. .. Brit. Mus. Pap. No. 10060. Facsimiles of several pages of this papyrus have been published by Maspero, *Romans et Poésies du Papyrus Harris No.* 500, Paris, 1879, and *Chants d'Amour*, etc., Paris, 1883.

Harris 501 .. .. Brit. Mus. Pap. No. 10042. See Chabas, F., *Le Papyrus Magique Harris*, Chalon-sur-Saône, 1860. 4to ; Budge, E. A. Wallis, *Facsimiles of Egyptian Hieratic Papyri in the British Museum.* London, 1910. Folio, pp. 34–40.

Hearst Pap. .. .. Wreszinski, W., *Der Londoner Medizinische Papyrus und der Papyrus Hearst.* Leipzig, 1912. 4to.

Hh. .. .. .. Text of Ḥer-ḥetep. A transcript of this text is given by Maspero, *Trois Années de Fouilles*, in *Mémoires de la Mission Archéologique Française au Caire*, 1881–84. Paris, 1884. Folio, p. 137 ff.

Horapollo .. .. Leemans, C., *Horapollinis Niloi Hieroglyphica edidit, ... item hieroglyphicorum imagines et indices adjecit.* Amsterdam, 1835. 8vo.

Hymn Nile .. .. Maspero, G., *Hymne au Nil publié et traduit après les deux textes du Musée Britannique.* Paris, 1868. 4to (lithographed) ; and *Hymne au Nil.* Cairo, 1912.

Hymn of Darius .. The text was published by Brugsch, *Reise nach der grossen Oase Khargah.* Leipzig, 1878, pl. 25–27.

Hymn to Uraei .. Erman, A., *Hymnen an das Diadem der Pharaonen* (in *Abh. K. P. Akad. der Wissenschaften.* Berlin, 1911. 4to).

I. H. .. .. .. Birch, S., *Inscriptions in the Hieratic and Demotic Character from the Collections in the British Museum.* London, 1868. Folio.

Ikhernefert .. .. Schäfer, H., *Die Mysterien des Osiris in Abydos unter König Sesostris III.* Leipzig, 1904. 4to. [In vol. iv of Sethe's *Untersuchungen zur Geschichte und Altertumskunde Aegyptens.*]

Inscription of Darius.. See under Hymn of Darius.

Inscrip. of Ḥenu .. Lepsius, C. R., *Denkmäler*, Abth. ii, Bl. 150*a* ; and Golénischeff, *Hammâmât*, pl. 15–17.

Israel Stele .. .. The inscription of Mer-en-Ptaḥ, which is found on the back of a stele of Ȧmen-ḥetep III (now in Cairo) ; published by Spiegelberg, *Aeg. Zeit.*, Bd. xxxiv, p. 1 ff.

Itinerary .. .. Parthey and Pindar, *Itinerarium Antonini et Hierosolymitanum.* Berlin, 1848. 8vo.

Jour. As. .. .. *Journal Asiatique.* Paris. In progress.

Jnl. E. A. .. .. *The Journal of Egyptian Archaeology*, vols. i–iv. London, 1914 f. 4to. In progress.

Kahun .. .. .. Griffith, F. Ll., *Hieratic Papyri from Kahun and Gurob.* 2 vols. London, 1898. 4to.

Ḳubbân Stele .. .. Prisse d'Avennes, *Monuments Égyptiens.* Paris, 1847. Folio, pl. 21.

Lacau .. .. .. Lacau, *Sarcophages antérieures au Nouvel Empire.* Cairo, 1903–4. (A volume of the great Cairo Museum Catalogue edited by Maspero.)

Lagus Stele .. .. Mariette, A., *Monuments Divers*, pl. 14.

Lanzone .. .. Lanzone, R. V., *Dizionario di Mitologia Egizia*, pts. i–v. Turin, 1881 f. 8vo.

Lanzone Domicilio .. Lanzone, R. V., *Le Domicile des Esprits ; Papyrus du Musée de Turin.* Paris, 1879. Folio.

Leemans Pap. Ég. .. Leemans, C., and Pleyte, W., *Papyrus Égyptien.* Leyden, 1839–1905.

Lib. Fun. .. .. Schiaparelli, E., *Il Libro dei Funerali ricavato da Monumenti inediti e pubblicato.* Tavole. Turin-Rome-Florence, 1881, folio ; Schiaparelli, E., *Il Libro dei Funerali degli antichi Egiziani tradotto e commentato*, vol. i, Rome-Turin-Florence, 1882, folio. See also *Atti della R. Accademia dei Lincei*, anno CCLXXXVII. 1890. Serie Quarta. Classe di Scienze morale, storiche e filologiche, vol. vii. Rome, 1890.

L. D. .. .. .. Lepsius, C., *Denkmäler aus Aegypten und Aethiopien.* Berlin, 1849. 4to, and twelve volumes of plates, large folio.

Leyden Pap. .. .. Gardiner, A. H., *The Admonitions of an Egyptian Sage from a papyrus in Leiden* (Pap. Leiden 344, recto). Leipzig, 1909. 4to.

Lieblein, Dict. .. Lieblein, *Dictionnaire de noms hiéroglyphiques*, vols. i and ii, Christiania, 1871, 8vo ; vols. iii and iv, Leipzig, 1892, 8vo.

Litanie .. .. *La Litanie du Soleil ; inscriptions recueillies dans les tombeaux des rois à Thèbes.* Leipzig, 1875. 4to.

Louvre C.14 .. .. This stele was published by Lepsius, *Auswahl der wichtigsten Urkunden des ägyptischen Alterthums*, Berlin, 1842, pl. 9 ; Prisse d'Avennes, *Monuments Égyptiens.* Paris, 1847, pl. 7 ; and see Maspero, *Trans. Soc. Bibl. Arch.*, vol. v, p. 555 ff.

Love Songs .. .. Müller, W. Max, *Die Liebespoesie der alten Aegypter.* Leipzig, 1899. 4to.

M. .. .. .. The funerary texts of King Meri-Rā , *i.e.*, Pepi I, and of King Mer-en-Rā I , published by Maspero, *Les Inscriptions des Pyramides de Saqqarah*, Paris, 1894, 4to ; and by K. Sethe, *Die Altägyptischen Pyramidentexte nach den Papierabdrücken und Photographien des Berliner Museums.* 2 vols, 1908–1910, Leipzig. 4to.

Mar. Aby. .. .. Mariette, A., *Abydos : description des fouilles.* Vol. i, Paris, 1869. Vol. ii, Paris, 1880. Folio.

Mar. Cat.	Mariette, A., *Catalogue général des Monuments d'Abydos découverts pendant les fouilles de cette ville.* Paris, 1880. Folio.
Mar. Kar.	Mariette, A., *Karnak : étude topographique et archéologique.* Leipzig, 1875. Text 4to. With a volume of plates, folio.
Mar. M.D.	Mariette, A., *Monuments divers recueillis en Égypte et en Nubie.* Paris, 1872–89. Folio. [With text by Maspero.]
Mar. Pap.	Mariette, A., *Les Papyrus Égyptiens du Musée de Boulaq,* 3 vols., Paris, 1871–6. Folio.
Mastabah	Mariette, A., *Les Mastabas de l'Ancien Empire.* Paris, 1882–85. Folio. [The work was edited by Maspero.]
Meir	Blackman, A. M., *The Rock Tombs of Meir.* London, 1914. 4to.
Mendes Stele	Naville, E., *The Store-city of Pithom and the Route of the Exodus.* London, 1885. 4to. Another transcript of the text will be found in *Aeg. Zeitschrift,* Bd. xxxii, 1894, p. 74 ff.
Merenptaḥ I	Dümichen, J., *Historische Inschriften,* Bd. I, Bl. 2 ff; Mariette, A., *Karnak,* pll. 52–55 ; and de Rougé, *Inscriptions Hiéroglyphiques,* p. 179 ff.
Methen..	Lepsius, *Denkmäler,* Abth. II, Bll. 3–7 ; Schäfer, *Aegypt. Inschriften aus den Königl. Museen zu Berlin,* Bd. I, Bll. 68, 73–87 ; Sethe, *Urkunden,* i, p. 1 ff.
Metternich Stele ..	Golénischeff, W., *Die Metternichstele in der Originalgrösse zum ersten Mal herausgegeben.* Leipzig, 1877. 4to.
Mission I, etc. ..	Maspero, *Mémoires de la Mission Archéologique Française au Caire.* Paris. Folio. Vol. i was published in 1884.
Moeller G.	*Die Beiden Totenpapyrus Rhind des Museums zu Edinburgh.* Leipzig, 1913. 4to.
Moeris	Lanzone, R. V., *Les Papyrus du Lac Moeris.* Turin, 1896. Folio.
Mythe	Naville, E., *Textes relatifs au Mythe d'Horus recueillis dans le temple d'Edfou.* Geneva and Basle, 1870. Folio.
N.	The funerary texts of King Nefer-ka-Rā Pepi II  published by Maspero, *Les Inscriptions des Pyramides de Saqqarah,* Paris, 1894, 4to, and by K. Sethe, *Die altägyptischen Pyramidentexte nach den Papierabdrücken und Photographien des Berliner Museums.* 2 vols. 1908–1910. Leipzig. 4to.
Nȧstasen	Lepsius, *Denkmäler,* Abth. V, pl. 16 ; Schäfer, *Die äthiopische Königsinschrift des Berliner Museums ; Regierungsbericht des Königs Nastesen des Gegners des Kambyses,* Leipzig, 1901, 4to ; and Budge, E. A. Wallis, *Annals of Nubian Kings,* London, 1911, p. 140.

Nesi Ȧmsu .. .. Budge, E. A. Wallis, *On the Hieratic Papyrus of Nesi-Ȧmsu, a scribe in the Temple of Ȧmen-Rā at Thebes, about* 305 B.C. London, 1891, 4to. (From THE ARCHÆOLOGIA, vol. lii); and Budge, E. A. Wallis, *Facsimiles of Egyptian Hieratic Papyri in the British Museum.* London, 1910. Folio.

Northampton Report Compton, W. G. S. S. (Marquis of Northampton), and Newberry, P. E., *Report on Excavations made at Thebes.* London, 1908. 4to.

Obel. Hatshep. .. Lepsius, C., *Denkmäler,* Abth. III, Bll. 22–24.

Ombos .. .. Morgan, J. de, *Catalogue des Monuments et inscriptions de l'Égypte antique,* vols. ii and iii. Vienna, 1894–99. 4to.

P. .. .. .. The funerary texts of King Pepi I  published by Maspero, *Les Inscriptions des Pyramides de Saqqarah,* Paris, 1894, 4to, and by K. Sethe, *Die altägyptischen Pyramidentexte nach den Papierabdrücken und Photographien des Berliner Museums.* 2 vols. 1908–1910. Leipzig. 4to.

Paheri .. .. .. Tylor and Griffith, *Ahnas el Medineh . . . . The Tomb of Paheri at El Kab.* London, 1894. 4to.

Palermo Stele .. .. Schäfer, H., *Ein Bruchstück altägyptischer Annalen* (Aus dem Anhang zu den Abhandlungen der Königl. Preuss. Akademie der Wissenschaften zu Berlin vom Jahre 1902). Berlin, 1902. 4to.

Pap. Ȧnhai .. .. Budge, E. A. Wallis, THE BOOK OF THE DEAD: *Facsimiles of the Papyri of Hunefer, Ȧnhai, Kerāsher and Netchemet,* etc. London, 1899. Folio.

Pap. Ani .. .. *Facsimile of the Papyrus of Ani in the British Museum* (ed., E. A. Wallis Budge), 2nd edition. London, 1890. Folio.

Pap. Hunefer .. .. Budge, E. A. Wallis, THE BOOK OF THE DEAD: *Facsimiles of the Papyri of Hunefer, Ȧnhai,* etc. London, 1899. Folio.

Pap. Koller .. .. Gardiner, A. H., *The Papyrus of Anastasi I and the Papyrus of Koller.* Leipzig, 1911. 4to.

Pap. Mag. .. .. Chabas, F., *Le Papyrus Magique Harris.* Chalon-sur-Saône, 1860. 4to.

Pap. Mut-ḥetep .. Brit. Mus. Pap. No. 10010. See Budge, E. A. Wallis, BOOK OF THE DEAD; *Chapters of Coming Forth by Day,* vol. i, p. xv. ff.

Pap. Nekht .. .. The Papyrus of Nekht in the British Museum (No. 10471); unpublished.

Pap. 3024 .. .. Lepsius, C., *Denkmäler,* Abth. vi, Bll. 111–112, and see Erman, A., *Gespräch eines Lebensmüden mit seiner Seele.* Berlin, 1896. [From the *Abhandlungen* of the *Königl. Preuss. Akad. der Wissenschaften zu Berlin* for 1896.]

Peasant	*Die Klagen des Bauern*, by F. Vogelsang and A. H. Gardiner. Leipzig, 1908. 4to (Berlin Museum; Hieratische Papyrus, 4, 5; Litterarische Texte des Mittleren Reiches).
Piānkhi Stele	For the text see Mariette, A., *Monuments Divers recueillis en Égypte et en Nubie*, Paris, 1872–89, folio, pll. 1–6; and Schäfer, *Urkunden*, iii. Leipzig, 1905. 4to, p. 1 ff.
Piehl	Piehl, E., *Inscriptions hiéroglyphiques recueillies en Europe et en Égypte*, Leipzig and Stockholm, pts. i and ii, 1886; 2nd Series, 1890–92; 3rd Series, 1895–1903. 4to.
Pierret Inscrip. ..	Pierret, P., *Recueil d'inscriptions inédites du Musée Égyptien du Louvre* (in *Études Égyptologiques*. Paris, 1873–78. 4to).
Precepts of Àmenemḥat	The text will be found in Sallier Pap. No. II, pp. 1–3, Sallier Pap. No. I, p. 8, etc.; see the article on the Millingen Papyrus by Griffith, F. Ll., in *Ae. Z.*, Bd. 34 (1896), p. 35 ff; Maspero, *Les Enseignements d'Amenemhaît 1er à son fils Sanouasrît 1er*, Cairo, 1904.
Prisse Mon.	Prisse d'Avennes, *Histoire de l'Art Égyptien d'après les Monuments depuis les temps les plus reculés jusqu'à la domination Romaine; Texte par P. Marchandon de la Faye.* Text (large 4to) and plates (folio). Paris, 1879.
Prisse Pap.	For the hieratic text see Prisse d'Avennes, *Fac-simile d'un Papyrus Égyptien en caractères hiératiques.* Paris, 1847. Folio.
P.S.B.A.	*Proceedings of the Society of Biblical Archaeology*, vols. i--xl. 1879–1918. Large 8vo.
Ptol.	Müller, C., *Claudii Ptolemaei Geographia*, 2 vols. Paris, 1883. The *Tabulae* to the above were published at Paris in 1901.
Qenna Pap.	Facsimile of the Papyrus of the merchant Qenna, , published by Leemans, C., *Papyrus Égyptien Funéraire Hiéroglyphique* (T. 2) *du Musée d'Antiquités des Pays Bas à Leide.* Leyden, 1882. Folio.
Quelques Pap... ..	Maspero, G., *Mémoire sur quelques Papyrus du Louvre.* Paris, 1875. 4to.
Rawl.	Rawlinson, Sir H. C., *Cuneiform Inscriptions of Western Asia*, vol. i, 1861; vol. ii, 1866; vol. iii, 1870; vol. iv, 1874; vol. v, 1880–84. London. Folio.
R. E.	*Revue Égyptologique*, ed. Revillout; see under Rev.
Rec.	Maspero, *Recueil de Travaux relatifs à la Philologie et l'Archéologie Égyptiennes et Assyriennes*, vol. i. Paris, 1880. In progress.

Rechnungen .. .. Spiegelberg, W., *Rechnungen aus der Zeit Seti I*, 2 vols. Strassburg, 1896.

Reise .. .. .. Brugsch, *Reise nach der grossen Oase Khargah in der Libyschen Wüste.* Leipzig, 1878. 4to.

Respirazione .. .. Pellegrini, *Il Libro della Respirazione.* Rome, 1904.

Rev. .. .. .. *Revue Égyptologique publiée sous la direction de MM. Brugsch, F. Chabas, and Eug. Revillout.* Première Année. Paris, 1880. The last volume (vol. xiv) appeared in 1912.

Rhind Math. Pap. .. Brit. Mus. Pap. No. 10057. Budge, E. A. Wallis, *Facsimile of the Rhind Mathematical Papyrus in the British Museum.* London, 1898. Folio.

Rhind Pap. .. .. Birch, S., *Facsimiles of two papyri found in a tomb at Thebes . . . . and an account of their discovery, by A. H. R.* London, 1863, long folio; Brugsch, *Rhind's zwei Bilingue Papyri hieratisch und demotisch.* Leipzig, 1865. 4to.

Rosetta .. .. Lithograph copy of the Rosetta Stone published by the Society of Antiquaries. London, 1803. Large folio. See also the photographic facsimile in Budge, *The Rosetta Stone*, vol. i. London, 1904.

Ros. Mon. .. .. Rosellini, I., *I Monumenti dell' Egitto e della Nubia*, vols. i–ix (text), Pisa, 1832–44, 8vo, and vols. i–iii, pll., large folio. [The original prospectus of this work was published in French and Italian in 1831, and was signed by Champollion le Jeune and Rosellini.]

Rougé, Chrest. .. Rougé, E. de, *Chrestomathie Égyptienne;* Première partie (lithographed), Paris, 1867, 4to; Deuxième Fascicule, Paris, 1868, large 8vo; Troisième Fascicule, Paris, 1875, large 8vo.

Rougé, E. de .. .. *Inscriptions et Notices recueillies à Edfou*, vols. i and ii. Paris, 1880. 4to.

Rougé, I. H. .. .. Rougé, E. de, *Inscriptions Hiéroglyphiques copiées en Égypte.* Paris, 1877–79. 4to.

Royal Tombs .. .. Petrie, W. M. F., *The Royal Tombs of the First Dynasty*, 3 vols. London, 1900–1. 4to.

Sallier I .. .. Brit. Mus. Pap. No. 10185. Facsimiles of the hieratic texts published by Birch, *Select Papyri.* London, 1843.

Sallier II .. .. Brit. Mus. Pap. No. 10182. Facsimiles of the hieratic texts published by Birch, *Select Papyri.* London, 1843.

Sallier III .. .. Brit. Mus. Pap. No. 10183. Facsimiles of the hieratic texts published by Birch, *Select Papyri.* London, 1843.

Sallier IV	Brit. Mus. Papyrus No. 10184. A facsimile of the hieratic texts was published by Birch, *Select Papyri in the hieratic character from the Collections in the British Museum.* London, 1843, pl. 144 ff. See also Chabas, *Le Calendrier de Jours Fastes et Néfastes de l'Année Égyptienne.* Paris and Chalon, 1863. 8vo.
Ṣȧn Stele	Lepsius, C., *Das Bilingue Dekret von Kanopus,* pt. i. Berlin, 1866. 4to.
Sarc. Seti I	Budge, E. A. Wallis, *The Egyptian Heaven and Hell,* vol. ii. London, 1906.
Scarabs of Ȧmenḥetep III	1. Marriage with Tī (Budge, E. A. Wallis, *Mummy,* p. 242). 2. Wild Cattle Hunt (Fraser, G. W., *P.S.B.A.*, vol. xxi, p. 156). 3. Lion Hunt (Pierret, *Recueil,* vol. i, p. 88). 4. Marriage with Gilukhipa (Brugsch, *Thesaurus,* p. 1413). 5. Making of an Ornamental Lake (Birch, *Catalogue of the Alnwick Collection,* p. 137).
Shipwreck	Golénischeff, W., *Le Papyrus No.* 1115 *de L'Ermitage Impérial* in the *Recueil de Travaux,* vol. xxviii, p. 73 ff; *Le Conte du Naufragé,* Cairo, 1912; and Erman, *Die Geschichte des Schiffbrüchigen* in *Aeg. Zeitschrift,* Bd. 43 (1906). 1 ff.
Sinsin I	Pellegrini, *Il Libro della Respirazione.* Rome, 1904.
Sinsin II	Pellegrini, *Ta Ša-t en Sen-i-sen-i meḥ sen,* ossia *Il Libro Secondo della Respirazione.* Rome, 1904.
Siut	Griffith, F. Ll., *The Inscriptions of Siut and Der Rifeh.* London, 1889. 8vo.
Sphinx	Piehl, K. (and others), *Sphinx, Revue Critique embrassant le Domaine entier de l'Égyptologie.* Upsala and Leipzig. 8vo. Vol. i, 1897.
Sphinx Stele	Lepsius, C. R., *Denkmäler,* Abth. iii, Bl. 68; and see Erman's summary of the readings of all the copies in vol. vi of the *Sitzungsberichte* of the Prussian Academy, p. 428 ff.
Statistical Tab. ..	Birch, S., *Observations on the newly discovered fragments of the statistical tablet of Karnak* (Jnl. Soc. Lit., vol. vii).
Stat. Taf.	Bissing, F. W. von, *Die Statistische Tafel von Karnak.* Leipzig, 1897. 4to.
Stele of Ḥerusȧtef ..	Text originally published by Mariette, *Monuments Divers,* pll. 11–13; see also Sethe, *Urkunden,* vol. iii, p. 113 ff; and Budge, E. A. Wallis, *Annals of Nubian Kings.* London, 1911, p. 117.
Stele of Nekht Menu..	For the texts see Prisse, *Monuments Égyptiens,* pl. 17, and Lepsius, C. R., *Denkmäler,* Abth. iii, pl. 114 i. For a transcript of the texts with English translations see Budge, E. A. Wallis, in *T.S.B.A.*, vol. xiii, p. 299 ff.

Stele of Ptol. I ..	For the text see Mariette, *Monuments Divers*, pl. 14, and *A.Z.*, 1871, p. 1 ff.
Stele of Usertsen III ..	Berlin, No. 14753. Lepsius, *Denkmäler*, Abth. ii, Bl. 136 (*i*).
Stunden	Junker, H., *Die Stundenwachen in den Osirismysterien.* Vienna, 1910. 4to. (*Denkschriften der Kaiserl. Akademie der Wissenschaften in Wien, Phil-Hist. Klasse*, Band liv.)
Suppl.	Brugsch, H., *Hieroglyphisch-Demotisches Wörterbuch* vols. v–vii. Leipzig, 1880–82. 4to.
T.	The funerary texts of King Tetȧ 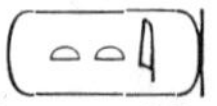 published by Maspero, *Les Inscriptions des Pyramides de Saqqarah*, Paris, 1894, 4to; and by K. Sethe, *Die Altägyptischen Pyramidentexte nach den Papierabdrücken und Photographien des Berliner Museums*, 2 vols. 1908–1910. Leipzig, 4to.
Tall al-'Amârnah ..	For the British Museum Collection of the Tall al-Amârnah Tablets see Bezold and Budge, *The Tell el-Amarna Tablets in the British Museum.* London, 1892. 8vo. For the texts of all the tablets in Berlin, Cairo and London see Winckler, H., *Der Thontafelfund von El Amarna.* Berlin, 1895. Folio. For translations see Winckler, H., *The Tell-El-Amarna Letters*, Berlin, 1896; and Knudtzon, J. A., *Die El-Amarna Tafeln*, Leipzig, 1907.
Tanis Pap.	Griffith, F. Ll., *Two Hieroglyphic Papyri from Tanis.* London, 1889. 4to.
Tell el-Amarna Tablets	Bezold, C., and Budge, E. A. Wallis, *The Tell el-Amarna Tablets in the British Museum, with autotype facsimiles.* London, 1892.
Theban Ost.	Gardiner, A. H., *Theban Ostraka*, pt. i, Hieratic Texts. London, 1913. 4to.
Thes.	Brugsch, H., *Thesaurus Inscriptionum Aegyptiacarum*, Abth. i–vi in 1 vol. Leipzig, 1883–91.
Thothmes III	Birch, S., *On a Historical Tablet of the Reign of Thothmes III recently discovered at Thebes.* London, 1861. 4to (*Archaeologia*, vol. xxxviii).
Todt. (Lepsius) ..	Lepsius, C. R., *Das Todtenbuch der Aegypter nach dem Hieroglyphischen Papyrus in Turin . . . . zum ersten Mal herausgegeben.* Leipzig, 1842. 4to.
Todt. (Naville) ..	Naville, E. *Das Aegyptische Todtenbuch der 18ten bis 20ten Dynastie.* Berlin, 1886. Large 8vo. In three vols. Vol. i, Text; vol. ii, Variant Readings; vol. iii, *Einleitung.*
Tomb of Ȧmenemḥat	Gardner, A. H., *The Tomb of Amenemḥet* (No. 82); illustrated by N. de G. Davies. London, 1915. 4to.

Tomb of Rameses IV, etc.	Lefébure, E., *Les Hypogées Royaux de Thèbes ;* Seconde Division. Publiées avec la collaboration de MM. Ed. Naville et Ern. Schiaparelli. [In *Mémoires de la Mission Archéologique Française,* vol. iii. Paris, 1890. Folio.]
Tomb of Seti I ..	Bouriant, U., Loret, V., Lefébure, E., and Naville, E., *Le Tombeau de Séti I.* [In *Mémoires de la Mission Archéologique Française,* vol. ii, *Les Hypogées Royaux de Thèbes.* Paris, 1886. Folio.]
Tombos Stele. ..	Lepsius, C. R., *Denkmäler,* Abth. iii, Bl. 5.
Treaty	Müller, W. Max, *Der Bündnissvertrag Ramses' II und des Chetiterkönigs.* Berlin, 1902. 8vo. (In *Mitteilungen der Vorderasiatischen-Gesellschaft.* 1902–5, 7 Jahrgang.)
T.S.B.A.	*Transactions of the Society of Biblical Archaeology,* vols. i–ix. 1872–1893. Large 8vo.
Ṭuat I, II, III, etc. ..	The various sections of the Book Åm-Ṭuat edited and translated by Budge, E. A. Wallis. *The Egyptian Heaven and Hell,* vol. i, London, 1906.
Turin Pap.	Rossi, F., *Papyrus de Turin,* Leyden, 1869–76. 4to.
Tutankhamen.. ..	Maspero, G., *King Harmhabi and Toutânkhamanou.* Cairo, 1912. Folio.
U.	The funerary texts of King Unȧs  published by Maspero, *Les Inscriptions des Pyramides de Saqqarah,* Paris, 1894, 4to, and by K. Sethe, *Die Altägyptischen Pyramidentexte nach den Papierabdrücken und Photographien des Berliner Museums.* 2 vols, 1908–1910. Leipzig, 4to.
Verbum Voc.	Sethe, K., *Das Aegyptische Verbum in Altägyptischen, Neuägyptischen und Koptischen,* vol. i, Lautlehre ; vol. ii, Formenlehre ; vol. iii, Indices (Vocabulary). Leipzig, 1899–1902.
Wazîr	Newberry, P. E., *The Life of Rekhmara, vezîr of Upper Egypt under Thothmes III and Åmenḥetep II* (circa 1471–1448 B.C.). London, 1900. 4to.
Westcar	*Die Märchen des Papyrus Westcar,* 2 vols. Berlin, 1890. Folio. (Berlin Museum : Mitt. aus den orientalischen Sammlung, Hefte 5 and 6.)
Wild Cattle Scarab ..	Fraser, G. W., *Notes on Scarabs, P.S.B.A.,* vol. xxi, p. 148 ff.
Wört.	Brugsch, H., *Hieroglyphisch-Demotisches Wörterbuch,* vols. i–iv. Leipzig, 1867–68. 4to.
Zodiac Dend.	DESCRIPTION DE L'ÉGYPTE. Antiquités, vol. iv. Paris, 1822. Folio. Pll. 19 and 20.

The following works, though not specially indicated, have also been used in the preparation of this Dictionary :—

Amélineau, E. .. *Essai sur l'évolution historique et philosophique des idées morales dans l'Égypte ancienne.* Paris, 1895. 8vo.

Amélineau, E. .. *Géographie de l'Égypte à l'époque Copte.* Paris, 1903. 8vo.

Amélineau, E. .. *Les nouvelles fouilles d'Abydos.* Paris, 1902. 4to.

Amélineau, E. .. *Morale Égyptienne quinze siècles avant notre ère : étude sur le Papyrus de Boulaq No.* 4. Paris, 1898. 8vo.

Amélineau, E. .. *Tombeau d'Osiris.* Paris, 1899. 8vo.

Arneth, J. .. .. *Aegyptische Sarcophages.* Göttingen, 1853. 8vo.

Arundale, F., and Bonomi, J. *Egyptian Antiquities in the British Museum.* London (no date). 4to.

Ball, J. .. .. *Kharga Oasis.* Cairo, 1900. 8vo.

Belmore, Earl of .. *Collection of Egyptian Antiquities*, 2 vols. London, 1843. Long folio.

Belmore, Earl of .. *Papyrus taken from a mummy at Thebes in* 1819.

Bergmann, E. Ritter von *Hieratische und hieratisch-demotische Texte.* Vienna, 1886. 4to.

Bergmann, E. Ritter von *Hieroglyphische Inschriften gesammelt. . . . in Aegypten.* Vienna, 1879. 4to.

Berlin Museum .. HIERATISCHE PAPYRUS : (1) *Rituale für den Kultus des Amon*, Leipzig, 1901, folio ; (2) *Hymnen an verschiedene Götter*, Leipzig, 1905, folio ; (3) *Schriftstücke der VI Dynastie aus Elephantine.* Leipzig, 1911. Folio.

Bezold, C. .. .. *Oriental Diplomacy.* London, 1893. 8vo.

Birch, S. .. .. *A Complete List of Hieroglyphic Signs according to their Classes.* [Being Appendix II of C. J. Bunsen's *Egypt's Place in Universal History*, vol. i. London, 1867. 8vo. pp. 601–620.]

Birch, S. .. .. *The Funeral Ritual or Book of the Dead.* [In Bunsen, *Egypt's Place*, etc., vol. v. London, 1867, pp. 123–333.]

Birch, S. .. .. *Dictionary of Hieroglyphics, ibid.*, pp. 335–586.

Birch, S. .. .. *Hieroglyphic Grammar, ibid.*, pp. 582–741.

Birch, S. .. .. *Catalogue of the Collection of Egyptian Antiquities at Alnwick Castle.* London, 1880. 4to.

Birch, S. .. .. *Historical Tablet of Rameses II, relating to the Gold Mines of Ethiopia.* London, 1852. 4to.

Birch, S. .. .. *The Papyrus of Nas-Khem.* London, 1863. 8vo.

Birch, S. .. .. *Two Egyptian Tablets of the Ptolemaic Period.* London, 1864. 4to.

Bissing, F. W. von. .. *Geschichte Aegyptens im Umriss.* Berlin, 1904. 8vo.

Boehl, F. M. T. .. *Die Sprache der Amarnabriefe.* Leipzig, 1909. 8vo.

Boinet, A. .. .. *Dictionnaire Géographique de l'Égypte.* Le Caire, 1899. 8vo.

Borchardt, L... .. *Das Grabdenkmal des Königs Ne-user-Rā.* Leipzig, 1907. 4to.

Borchardt, L... .. *Das Grabdenkmal des Königs Sa-hu-re.* Leipzig, 1910-13. 4to.

Bouriant, U. .. .. *Monuments pour servir à l'étude du Culte d'Atomou en Égypte* (*Mémoires* Inst. Franç. d'Arch. Orient. du Caire, tome viii).

Bouriant, U. .. .. Descriptions of Theban tombs in *Mémoires* of the Miss. Arch. Franç. au Caire, tomes vii, xviii, etc.

Brocklehurst Papyrus Photograph of, in 10 sheets. London, 1883. 4to.

Brugsch, E., and Bouriant, U. *Le Livre des Rois.* Cairo, 1887. 8vo.

Brugsch, H. .. .. AEGYPTOLOGIE: *Abriss der Entzifferungen und Forschungen auf dem Gebiete der Aegyptischen Schrift, Sprache und Altertumskunde.* Leipzig, 1891. 8vo.

Brugsch, H. .. .. *Drei Fest-Kalender des Tempels von Apollinopolis Magna in Ober-Aegypten.* Leipzig, 1877. 4to.

Brugsch, H. .. .. *Geographische Inschriften.* Leipzig, vols. i–iii. 1857–60. 4to.

Brugsch, H. .. .. *Hieroglyphische Inschrift von Philae.* Berlin, 1849. 8vo.

Brugsch, H. .. .. *Inscriptio Rosettana Hieroglyphica.* Berlin, 1851. 4to.

Brugsch, H. .. .. *Neue Weltordnung nach Vernichtung des sündigen Menschengeschlechtes, nach einer altägyptischen Ueberlieferung.* Berlin, 1881. 8vo.

Brugsch, H. .. .. *Shai an Sinsin.* Berlin, 1851. 4to.

Budge, E. A. Wallis .. *The Book of the Kings of Egypt,* 2 vols. London, 1908. 8vo.

Budge, E. A. Wallis .. *The Book of the Opening of the Mouth,* 2 vols. London, 1909. 8vo.

Budge, E. A. Wallis .. *The Liturgy of Funerary Offerings.* London, 1909. 8vo.

Budge, E. A. Wallis .. *The Greenfield Papyrus.* London, 1912. 4to.

Budge, E. A. Wallis .. *The Meux Collection of Egyptian Antiquities.* London, 1893. 4to.

Budge, E. A. Wallis .. *The Sarcophagus of Ānkhnesrāneferȧb.* London, 1885. 4to.

Bunsen, C. J. .. .. *Egypt's Place in Universal History.* Translation by Cottrell, vols. i–v. London, 1860–7. 8vo.

Burchardt, M., and Pieper, M. *Handbuch der Aegyptischen Königsnamen.* Leipzig, 1912 (pt. i). 8vo.

Burton, J. .. .. *Excerpta Hieroglyphica,* No. 1, Qahirah (Cairo), 1825-28. Long 4to.

Cailliaud, F. .. .. *Voyage à Méroë au fleuve blanc . . . . fait dans les années* 1819–22, vols. i–iv text 8vo., and a volume of plates, folio.

Cairo Cat. .. .. *Catalogue général des Antiquités Égyptiennes du Musée du Caire.* The volumes chiefly consulted were :—

Borchardt, L., *Statuen und Statuetten von Königen,* etc. Cairo, 1911.

Carter, H., and Newberry, P., *Tomb of Thothmes IV.* Cairo, 1904.

Chassenat, E., *2me Trouvaille de Deir-el-Bahari.* Cairo, 1907.

Quibell, J. E., *Archaic Objects.* Cairo, 1905.

Reisner, G. H., *Amulets.* Cairo, 1907.

Daressy, G., *Ostraca.* Cairo, 1901.

Daressy, G., *Fouilles.* Cairo, 1902.

Daressy, G., *Cercueils.* Cairo, 1909.

Lacau, P., *Sarcophages,* 2 vols. Cairo, 1903–08.

Lacau, P., *Stèles.* Cairo, 1909.

Lange, H. O., and Schäfer, H., *Grab- und Denksteine.* Cairo, 1903–08.

Maspero, G., *Sarcophages.* Cairo, 1908.

Chabas, F. .. .. *L'Égyptologie,* Série I. Années 1–4.

Chabas, F. .. .. *Une Inscription Historique du règne de Seti I.* 1856. 4to.

Chabas, F. .. .. *Les Maximes du Scribe Ani,* vols. i and ii.

Chabas, F. .. .. *Voyage d'un Égyptien en Syrie.* Paris, 1866. 4to.

Champollion, J. F. .. *Dictionnaire Égyptien.* Paris, 1841. Folio.

Champollion, J. F. .. *Grammaire Égyptienne.* Paris, 1836. Folio.

Champollion, J. F. .. *Monuments de l'Égypte et de la Nubie.* Paris, 1847–73 ; text, 2 vols., small folio, plates, four vols. in large folio.

Davies, N. de G. .. *The Mastaba of Ptah Hetep,* 2 pts. London. 1900–01. 4to.

Davies, N. de G. .. *The Rock Tombs of El Amarna,* 6 vols. London, 1903–08. 4to.

Delitzsch, F. .. .. *Wo lag das Paradies?* Leipzig, 1881. 8vo.

Description de l'Égypte Text, vols. i–xxiv. Paris, 1821–9. 8vo. Plates 11 vols. Folio.

Devéria, T. .. .. *Le Papyrus de Neb-qued.* Paris, 1872. Long folio.

Dümichen, J. .. .. *Baugeschichte des Denderatempels.* Strassburg, 1877. 4to.

Dümichen, J. .. .. *Geographie des alten Aegyptens.* 1877. 8vo.

Dümichen, J. .. .. *Zur Geographie des alten Aegyptens.* Leipzig, 1894. 4to.

Dümichen, J. .. .. *Der Grabpalast des Patuamenap,* 3 parts. Leipzig, 1884–94. 4to.

Ebers, G. .. .. AEGYPTIACA : *Festschrift für G. Ebers zum* 1 *März,* 1897. Leipzig, 1897. 8vo.

Eg. Exp. Fund .. *Atlas of Ancient Egypt.* London, 1894.

Erman, A. .. .. *Aegypten und Aegyptisches Leben im Alterthum.* Tübingen, 1884–7. 8vo.

Gardner, A. H. .. *Die Erzählung des Sinuhe und die Hirtengeschichte.* Leipzig, 1909. 4to.

Gardiner, A. H. .. *The Inscription of Mes.* Leipzig, 1905. 4to.

Gardiner, A. H. .. *Inscriptions of Sinai.* London, 1917. Folio.

Garstang, J. .. .. *Mahasna and Bet Khallaf.* London, 1902. 4to.

Garstang, J. .. .. *Meroë.* Oxford, 1911. 4to.

Garstang, J. .. .. *Tombs of the Third Egyptian Dynasty.* London, 1904. 4to.

Gauthier, H. .. .. *Le Livre des Rois d'Égypte,* 3 parts. [*Mémoires* of the *Inst. Franç. d'Arch. Orient.* Cairo. Vol. xvii.]

Gayet, E. .. .. *Stèles de la XIIme dynastie.* Paris, 1886. 4to.

Gensler, F. W. C. .. *Die Thebanischen Tafeln Stündlicher Sternaufgänge.* Leipzig, 1872. 4to.

Grébaut, E. .. .. *Hymne à Ammon-Ra.* Paris, 1874. 8vo.

Griffith, F. Ll. .. *A Collection of Hieroglyphs.* London, 1898. 4to.

Griffith, F. Ll. .. *Stories of the High Priests of Memphis.* Oxford, 1900. 8vo.

Groff, W. N. .. .. *Étude sur le Papyrus d'Orbiney.* Paris, 1888. 4to.

Guieysse, P., and Lefébure, E. *Le Papyrus funéraire de Soutimes.* Paris, 1877. Folio.

Hall, H. R. .. .. *Catalogue of Egyptian Scarabs,* vol. i. London, 1913. 4to.

Hall, H. R. .. .. *Coptic and Greek Texts of the Christian Period.* London, 1905. Folio.

Hammer, de .. .. *Copie figurée d'un rouleau de papyrus.* Vienna, 1822. Long 4to.

Hess, J. J. .. .. *Der Demotische Roman von Stne Ha-m-us.* Leipzig, 1888. 8vo.

Hess, J. J. .. .. *Der Demotische Teil der dreisprachigen Inschrift von Rosette.* Freiburg, 1902. 4to.

Hess, J. J. .. .. *Der Gnostische Papyrus von London.* Freiburg, 1902. 4to.

Hoelscher, U. .. .. *Das Grabdenkmal des Königs Chephren.* Leipzig, 1912. 4to.

Horrack, J. de .. *Les Lamentations d'Isis et de Nephthys.* Paris, 1866. 4to.

Ideler, J. L. .. .. *Hermapion sive rudimenta hieroglyphicae veterum aegyptiorum literàturae.* Leipzig, 1841. 4to.

Jéquier, G .. .. *Le Livre de ce qu'il y a dans l'Hades.* Paris, 1894. 8vo.

Jéquier, G. .. .. *Le Papyrus Prisse.* Paris, 1911. Oblong folio.

King, C. W. .. .. *The Gnostics and their remains.* London, 1864. 8vo.

Lacau, P. .. .. *Sarcophages antérieures au Nouvel Empire*, Fasc. 1 and 2. Cairo, 1903–4. 4to.

Lacau, P. .. .. *Stèles du Nouvel Empire.* Cairo, 1909. 4to.

Lanzone, R. V. .. *Les Papyrus du lac Moeris.* Turin, 1896. Folio.

Ledrain, E. .. .. *Les Monuments Égyptiens de la Bibliothèque Nationale*, vols. i–iii. Paris, 1879–81. 4to.

Lefébure, E. .. .. *Le Mythe Osirien*, pts. i and ii. Paris, 1874. 8vo.

Lefébure, E. .. .. *Traduction comparée des hymnes au soleil composant le XV chapitre du Rituel Funéraire Égyptien.* Paris, 1868. 4to.

Lefébure, E. .. .. *Les Yeux d'Horus : Osiris.* Paris, 1875. 8vo.

Legrain, G. .. .. *Le Livre des Transformations.* Paris, 1890. 4to.

Lemm, O. von. .. *Das Ritualbuch des Ammondienstes.* Leipzig, 1882. 8vo.

Lepsius, C. R. .. *Aelteste Texte des Todtenbuchs.* Berlin, 1867. 4to.

Lepsius, C. R... .. *Auswahl der wichtigsten Urkunden des Aegyptischen Alterthums.* Berlin, 1842. Folio.

Lieblein, J. .. .. *Index alphabétique de tous les mots contenus dans le Livre des Morts* publié par R. Lepsius, *d'après le Papyrus de Turin.* Paris, 1875. 8vo.

Lieblein, J. .. .. *Le Livre Égyptien*  *Que mon nom fleurisse.* Leipzig, 1895. 8vo.

Mallet, D. .. .. *Le Culte de Neit à Saïs.* Paris, 1888. 8vo.

Mariette, A. .. .. *Les Listes Géographiques des pylônes de Karnak.* Text and plates. Leipzig, 1875. 4to.

Marucchi, O. .. .. *Il grande Papiro Egizio della Biblioteca Vaticano.* Rome, 1888. 4to.

Marucchi, O. .. .. *Obelischi Egiziani di Roma.* Rome, 1898. 8vo.

Maspero, G. .. .. *Une Enquête Judiciaire à Thèbes.* Paris, 1872. 8vo.

Maspero, G. .. .. *Les Momies Royales de Deir el Bahari.* [In *Mémoires* of the French Archaeological Mission in Cairo, vol. i.]

Maspero, G. .. .. *Sarcophages des Époques Persanes et Ptolémaiques.* [See CAIRO CATALOGUE.]

Massey, A. .. .. *Le Papyrus de Leyde I*, 347. Gand, 1885. 4to.

Matter, J. .. .. *Histoire Critique du Gnosticisme*, vols. i–iii (text and plates). Paris, 1828. 8vo.

Morgan, J. de .. .. *Fouilles à Dahchour.* Vienna, 1895, 1903. 4to.

Naville, E. .. .. *The Cemeteries of Abydos.* London, 1914. 4to.

Naville, E. .. .. *Deir el-Bahari*, pts. i–vi. London, 1893–1907. Folio.

Naville, E. .. .. *The Eleventh Dynasty Temple at Deir el-Bahari.* London, 1907–14. 4to.

Naville, E. .. .. *Festival Hall of Osorkon II.* London, 1892. 4to.

Naville, E. .. .. *Inscription Historique de Pinodjem III.* Paris, 1863. 4to.

Naville, E. .. .. *Le Papyrus hiérogyphique de Kamara et le Papyrus hiératique de Nesikhonsou au Musée du Caire.* Paris, 1914. 4to.

Naville, E. .. .. *Le Papyrus hiératique de Katseshni au Musée du Caire.* Paris, 1914. 4to.

Pellegrini, A. .. .. *Nota sopra un' inscrizione Egizia del Museo di Palermo.* [In *Atti e Memorie della Società Siciliana per la Storia Patria.* Palermo, 1896. Large 8vo.]

Petrie, W. M. F. .. Works published by the Egypt Exploration Fund, the Egyptian Research Account, etc.

Piehl, K. .. .. *Dictionnaire du Papyrus Harris,* No. I. Vienna, 1882. 8vo.

Pieper, M. .. .. *Handbuch der Aegyptischen Königsnamen.* Leipzig, 1912. 8vo.

Pieper, M. .. .. *Die Könige Aegyptens zwischen dem mittleren und neuen Reiche.* Berlin, 1904. 4to.

Pierret, P. .. .. *Le Décret Trilingue de Canope.* Paris, 1881. 4to.

Pierret, P. .. .. *Études Égyptologiques.* Paris, 1874, 1878. 4to.

Pierret, P. .. .. *Vocabulaire Hiéroglyphique.* Paris, 1875. 8vo.

Pleyte, W. .. .. *Chapitres Supplémentaires du Livre des Morts,* vols. i-iii. Leyden, 1881. 4to.

Pleyte, W. .. .. *L'Épistolographie Égyptienne.* Leyden, 1869. 4to.

Pleyte, W. .. .. *Étude sur un rouleau magique (Pap. 348 Revers) du Musée de Leide.* Leyden, 1869–70. 4to.

Pleyte, W. .. .. *Études Archéologiques, linguistiques et historiques dédiées à C. Leemans.* Leyden, 1885. 4to.

Pleyte, W. .. .. *Les Papyrus Rollin.* Leyden, 1868. 4to.

Pleyte, W. .. .. *Papyrus de Turin.* Leyden, 1869–76. 4to.

Quibell, J. E. .. .. *Naqada and Ballas.* London, 1896. 4to.

Riel, C... .. .. *Der Thierkreis und das Feste-Jahr von Dendera.* Leipzig, 1878. 4to.

Rougé, E. de .. .. *Étude sur une Stèle Égyptienne.* Paris, 1858. 8vo.

Rougé, E. de .. .. *Recherches sur les Monuments qu'on peut attribuer aux six premières dynasties de Manéthon.* Paris, 1866. 4to.

Rougé, E. de .. .. *Rituel Funéraire.* Paris, 1861–76. Folio.

Rougé, J. de .. .. *Géographie Ancienne de la Basse-Égypte.* Paris, 1891. 8vo.

Sachau, E. .. .. *Drei Aramäische Papyrusurkunden aus Elephantine.* Berlin, 1908. 4to.

Schack, H., Graf von Schackenburg *Die Unterweisung des Königs Ȧmenemḥat I.* Paris, 1883. 4to.

Schack, H., Graf von Schackenburg *Aegyptologische Studien,* vols. i and ii. Leipzig, 1902. 4to.

Schack, H., Graf von Schackenburg *Das Buch von den Zwei Wegen der Seligen Toten,* pt. i. Leipzig. 1903. 4to.

Sharpe, S. .. .. *Egyptian Inscriptions from the British Museum and other sources.* London, pt. i, 1837 ; pt. ii, 1841 (First Series) ; Second Series, 1855. Folio.

Spiegelberg, W. .. *Aegyptologische Randglossen zum Alten Testament.* Strassburg, 1904. 8vo.

Spiegelberg, W. .. *Correspondances du temps des Rois-Prêtres.* Paris, 1895. 4to.

Spiegelberg, W. .. *Demotische Studien.* Leipzig, 1901–10. 4to.

Steindorff, G. .. .. *Das Grab des Ti.* Leipzig, 1913. 4to.

Steindorff, G. .. .. *Der Sarg des Sebk-o.* Berlin, 1896. 4to.

Stern, L. .. .. *The Hieroglyphic-Latin Vocabulary* in vol. ii of the *Papyros Ebers.* Leipzig, 1875. Folio.

Tylor, J. J. .. .. *Wall-Drawings and Monuments of El-Kab,* 2 vols. London, 1896–98. Folio.

Weigall, A. E. P. .. *A Report on the Antiquities of Lower Nubia.* Oxford, 1907. 4to.

Weill, R. .. .. *Recueil des Inscriptions Égyptiennes du Sinai.* Paris, 1904. 4to.

Wiedemann, A. .. *Sammlung Altägyptischer Wörter welche von Klassischen Autoren umschrieben oder übersetzt worden sind.* Leipzig, 1883. 8vo.

Wilkinson, J. G. .. *Facsimile of an inscription on a sarcophagus or mummy case.* [Brit. Mus. No. 10,553.] Published by Budge, E. A. Wallis, *Facsimiles of Egyptian Hieratic Papyri.* London, 1910. Folio.

Wilkinson, J. G. .. *Materia Hieroglyphica.* Malta, 1828. 4to.

A LIST

Of the most frequently used Hieroglyphic Characters with their Phonetic Values, together with their Significations when employed as Determinatives and Ideographs.

I.

MEN (**Standing, Sitting, Kneeling, Bowing, Lying Down**).

Number.	Hieroglyph.	Phonetic Value.	Signification as Determinative or Ideograph.
1		——	inactivity, inertness, inanition, exhaustion.
2		à	address, cry out, invoke. As an interjection, *hai*, *hi*.
3, 4		——	deprecate, propitiate.
5, 6		ṭua, àau	pray, worship, adore, entreat, praise.
7		hen	praise, exult, chant.
8		qa, ḥāā	high, lofty ; exult, make merry.
9		ān	go back, turn back, turn round.
10, 11		——	call, beckon.
12		——	see No. 7.
13		——	. . . .
14		àn	run.
15, 16, 17, 18		àb	dance, perform gymnastics.

Number.	Hieroglyph.	Phonetic Value.	Signification as Determinative or Ideograph.
19, 20		kes	bow, pay homage.
21		——	run away or run after something.
22, 23		——	pour out, micturate, *penq* .
24		——	make friends, be in league with someone, *ḥeter* ; be on brotherly terms with, *sensen* .
25		——	hide, to conceal, *ȧmen* .
26		——	dwarf, pygmy, *ṭeng* .
27, 28		——	image, figure, statue, *tut* , mummy, transformed dead body, *sāḥu* ; to stablish a custom.
29		——	eternity.
30		ur , ser	great, great one, a chief official, prince.
31		——	old, aged, *ȧau* , senior *semsu* .
32		——	strong, strength, *nekht* .
33		——	beat (?) strike (?)
34		——	shepherd (?) hunter (?)
35		——	to repulse, to drive away, *seḥer* .
36		——	to perform a ceremony (?)
37		——	shepherd.
38		——	the *ȧḥi*-priest .
39, 40		——	. . . .
41		——	strong, strength.
42		——	harper, play a musical instrument.

Number.	Hieroglyph.	Phonetic Value.	Signification as Determinative or Ideograph.
43		—	break up ground, plough.
44, 45		—	present, make an offering.
46		nini	pour out water.
47		—	purificatory priest.
48		—	sow grain; to use a throw-net in hunting.
49		—	skipping.
50		khus	build.
51		—	work a boring tool (?), drill.
52		qeṭ	build.
53		—	suspend, stretch out the sky, *ākh* .
54, 55		fa	carry, bear on shoulders.
56		—	= *kheṣteb* , lapis lazuli.
57, 58		qes	restrain, bind.
59		—	= *ḥeq* , governor.
60, 61		—	statue of king.
62, 63		—	king of Upper Egypt.
64, 65		—	king of Lower Egypt.
66, 67, 68		—	king of Upper and Lower Egypt.
69, 70		—	foreign potentate.
71		—	= *āti* king, prince.
72		—	child, infancy.
73, 74		—	sit.

Number.	Hieroglyph.	Phonetic Value.	Signification as Determinative or Ideograph.
75, 76		——	royal child.
77		——	. . . .
78, 79, 80		——	enemy, death, the dead, slaughter, = *khefti*  "enemy."
81		ḥāā 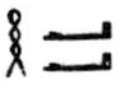	. . . .
82		m'shā 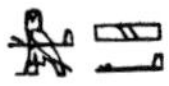	soldier of every kind.
83		——	soldier of every kind = *menfit* .
84, 85, 86		——	prisoner, captive, foreigner.
87		——	criminal.
88		——	execution, death.
89		——	man, *sa* , 1st person sing.
90		——	invoke, address, cry out to, interjection O or Oh! Hail! etc.
91,92,93		——	eat, drink, speak, and of everything which is done with the mouth.
94		——	inactivity, inertness, rest.
95		——	praise, *hen* .
96		——	pray, worship, adore, entreat; praise.
97, 98, 99		——	hide, *ȧmen* , conceal, protect (?)
100		——	play an instrument of music, harper.
101		——	drinking, offering (?)
102		——	offering.

Number.	Hieroglyph.	Phonetic Value.	Signification as Determinative or Ideograph.
103		——	hide, conceal, *ȧmen*.
104		uāb	priest.
105, 106, 107		——	pour out water, make a libation.
108		——	carry a load, *atep*, bear, support, *fa*.
109		——	var. of (?)
110, 111		ḥeḥ	great but indefinite number.
112		——	write.
113		——	. . . .
114, 115, 116		——	the blessed or holy dead.
117, 118		ȧ	a god or divine person.
119		——	the king holding the sceptre
120		——	the king holding the sceptre.
121		——	the king holding the whip.
122		——	the king holding the whip and sceptre.
123		——	the king wearing the White Crown and holding the whip and the sceptre.
124		——	the king wearing the Red Crown and holding the whip and the sceptre.
125		——	the king wearing the Red Crown and holding the whip and the *ānkh* "life."
126		——	the king wearing the White and Red Crowns and holding the sceptre.

Number.	Hieroglyph.	Phonetic Value.	Signification as Determinative or Ideograph.
127		—	the king wearing the Red Crown and holding the object .
128		—	the king wearing the White and Red Crowns and holding the sceptre .
129		—	shepherd, nomad, sentry, guard.
130, 131		—	. . . .
132, 133		—	sit as a king or noble, seat oneself.
134, 135		sheps 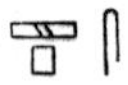	noble, honourable, revered, the sainted dead.
136, 137, 138, 139	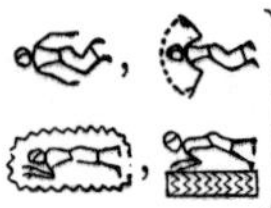	—	swim.
140		—	lie, recline.
141		kher 	fall, defeat, slaughter.
142		—	sickness, vomit.
143		—	reap.

II.

WOMEN.

Number.	Hieroglyph.	Phonetic Value.	Signification as Determinative or Ideograph.
1		—	woman, *sa-t*, 1st and 2nd pers. sing.
2, 3, 4, 5, 6, 7, 8		—	queen, lady of high rank, venerable woman.
9, 10, 11		—	woman beating a tambourine and playing a harp.
12		àri 	present at, in charge of, belonging to.

Number.	Hieroglyph.	Phonetic Value.	Signification as Determinative or Ideograph.
13, 14, 15	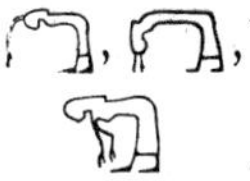	——	bend, bow, *geb*.
16		——	pregnant woman, *beq*.
17		——	parturient woman, give birth to, *mes*, *pāpā*.
18, 19		——	nurse, *menā*, dandle, rear a child, *renn*.

III.

GODS AND GODDESSES.

Number.	Hieroglyph.	Phonetic Value.	Signification as Determinative or Ideograph.
1		——	Àsàr (Osiris); usually written or.
2, 3		——	Ptḥ (Ptaḥ).
4, 5		——	Ptaḥ-Tanen.
6		——	Ptaḥ-Seker-Àsàr.
7		——	Menu (Min, Khem Àmsu).
8		——	Àmen (Ammon).
9		——	Àmen holding the sceptre.
10		——	Àmen holding Maāt.
11		——	Àmen holding the scimitar *khepesh*.
12		——	Àmen holding the sceptre.
13, 14, 15, 16, 17, 18, 19	   	——	Horus the Elder, Horus-Rā, Rā, the Sun-god.

Number.	Hieroglyph.	Phonetic Value.	Signification as Determinative or Ideograph.
20		—	Åmen-Rā, or Rā-Åmen.
21		—	Ḥeru-åakhuti (Harmakhis), or Horus of the Two Horizons.
22, 23, 24		—	Åāḥ , or Khensu , the Moon-god.
25, 26		—	Tcheḥuti (Thoth).
27		—	Set  (var. 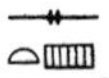), or Setesh 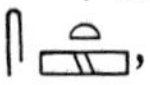, or Sutekh .
28		—	Ånpu (Anubis).
29, 30, 31		—	Khnemu (Khnoubis), Khnoumis, Khnum, Khneph, etc.
32		—	Ḥep, or Ḥāpi, the Nile-god.
33, 34		—	Shu, god of light and dryness.
35		—	Bes, a Sûdânî god.
36, 37, 38		—	Set as a warrior-god.
39, 40		—	the Bennu bird (phoenix).
41		—	Mestå, son of Horus.
42		—	Ḥāpi, son of Horus.
43		—	Qebḥsenuf, son of Horus.
44		—	Ṭuamutef, son of Horus.
45, 46		—	the Hare-god.
47, 48, 49, 50, 51, 52	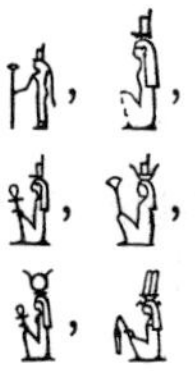	—	Åst or Set (Isis).
53, 54		—	Neb-t ḥe-t (Nephthys).

Number.	Hieroglyph.	Phonetic Value.	Signification as Determinative or Ideograph.
55		——	the sunrise.
56		——	Isis, Hathor or any cow-goddess.
57, 58		——	Net (Neith).
59, 60, 61, 62		——	the goddess Maāt.
63		——	the goddess Nut.
64		——	the goddess Serqet.
65, 66		——	the goddess Sekhmet.
67		——	the goddess Ānqet.
68		——	the goddess Sesheta.
69, 70, 71		——	of many goddesses.
72, 73		——	a guardian of one of the Seven Pylons.
74		——	goddess of Upper Egypt.
75		——	goddess of Lower Egypt.

IV.

MEMBERS OF THE BODY.

1		tep, tchatcha	first, foremost, top of anything, nod.
2		ḥer 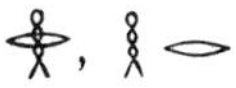	. . . .
3, 4, 5,	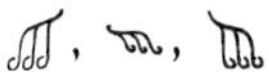	——	hair of men and animals, bald, lack, want, lacuna in manuscripts, colour, complexion.
6		——	lock of hair, side tress.
7		——	beard, *khabes* .
8		ȧr 	right eye, see, *ān* .

Number.	Hieroglyph.	Phonetic Value.	Signification as Determinative or Ideograph.
9		——	see, *ān*.
10		——	eye-paint (*koḥl*).
11		——	grief, tear, weep, *rem*.
12		——	left eye, see.
13		——	beautiful, *ān*.
14		——	see, behold, *peter*.
15		——	divine eye, right eye of Rā, *utchat*.
16		——	divine eye, left eye of Rā.
17		——	the two divine eyes, *utchatti*, , the eyes of Rā, *i.e.*, the Sun and Moon.
18, 19		——	need, what is required, *ṭebḥ*.
20		——	tear-drop of divine eye.
21		ȧr	pupil of the eye, death, destruction.
22		——	see, *maa*.
23, 24	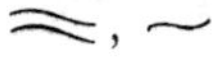	——	eyebrow.
25		——	ear, *mestcher*.
26		——	breathe, nose, nostril; the front of anything.
27		r, ra	mouth.
28		——	lip.
29		——	the two lips.
30, 32 32		——	eject spittle, vomit, efflux, exudation, moisture.
33		——	jaw-bone.
34		——	the two jaws.
35, 36	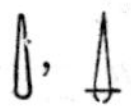	——	staff, to speak.

Number.	Hieroglyph.	Phonetic Value.	Signification as Determinative or Ideograph.
37, 38, 39		——	backbone, hew in pieces, dismember.
40		——	chine, sacrum, hew in pieces, dismember.
41		——	breast, nurse.
42, 43, 44		——	embrace, surround, happening, event.
45		ka	the double, person (?); strength of the *ka*, beauty of the *ka*.
46		——	ka-priest, *ḥem*, *ka*.
47, 48, 49, 50		n	lack, want, need, nothing, no, not.
51, 52		——	magnificent, splendid, *tcheser*.
53		khan	paddle, row a boat.
54		āḥa	fight, wage war, contend against.
55, 56		——	present an offering.
57		——	write.
58		khu	rule, direct, govern.
59, 60, 61		——	splendour, strength (?)
62		māk (?)	. . . .
63		ā, ṭet	give, *erṭa* or or.
64, 65		——	arm (*remen*), bear, carry, set in position, anything done with the arm.
66		——	give, *erṭa*.
67, 68		m, m'.	give.
69		āāi	wash, cleanse.
70, 71		——	strong, strength, *nekht*.

Number.	Hieroglyph.	Phonetic Value.	Signification as Determinative or Ideograph.
72		——	strength, rule, direct.
73		khu	rule, direct, govern.
74		shep	hand, take, receive.
75, 76		kep	press down (?).
77, 78		ṭ	hand, palm of the hand, *tcha-t*
79, 80		shep (?)	take in the hand, receive.
81		——	dew, *àaṭa*.
82, 83		——	grasp, lay hold on, *amm*.
84		——	finger, *tchebā*.
85		——	ten thousand, *tchebā*.
86		——	right, true mean, middle, *āqa*, witness, testimony, *meter*.
87, 88, 89, 90		——	take, take away.
91		——	nails, claws, talons.
92		men	present, offer.
93		met	phallus, front, male, masculine, procreate.
94		——	procreate.
95		ḥen	procreate.
96, 97		——	lead, guide, *seshem*.
98		——	testicles.
99		ḥem	female pudenda, female, woman.
100		——	go, walk, enter.
101		——	run, walk quickly.

Number.	Hieroglyph.	Phonetic Value.	Signification as Determinative or Ideograph.
102		——	come out, go out, go back, return.
103		geḥes, uār	run, flee, foot.
104		——	transgress, invade, attack.
105		——	stablish, falsehood, *gerg*.
106		q	. . . .
107		unem	eat, devour.
108, 109	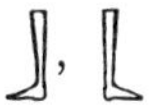	b	. . . . Compounds are *tcheb*, *āb*, , *ṭeb*, *khab*.
110, 111, 112	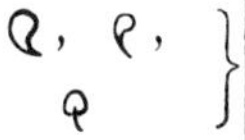	f	limb, flesh.

V.

ANIMALS.

1, 2		——	horse.
3, 4		——	bull, *ka*, ox, *àḥ*.
5		——	Apis Bull, sacred bull.
6		——	cow.
7		——	cow charging.
8		——	cow lying down or bound for sacrifice.
9		——	cow calving.
10		——	cow suckling her calf.
11		——	calf.
12		——	young ram, thirst.
13		àu	. . . .
14		ba	kudu, ram, soul, the god Khnum.

Number.	Hieroglyph.	Phonetic Value.	Signification as Determinative or Ideograph.
15		——	sacred ram of Åmen.
16		——	goat.
17		——	nobleman, elder ; var.  (?)
18		khan 	interior, skin, hide.
19, 20, 21		——	ape, monkey.
22		——	rage, fury.
23		——	dancing, merriment.
24, 25, 26		——	sacred ape, praise.
27		——	fight, quarrel.
28		——	ape bearing solar face.
29		——	ape wearing Red Crown.
30		——	ape of Thoth bearing the solar Eye (*utchat*).
31		——	hippopotamus-goddess (Ta-urt, Thoueris).
32		——	hippopotamus.
33		——	lion.
34		re, ru	. . . .
35, 36, 37		——	. . . .
38		neb 	image, sphinx.
39		——	sphinx (?)
40		——	bolt of a door.
41		——	the lion-gods of last evening and this morning.

Number.	Hieroglyph.	Phonetic Value.	Signification as Determinative or Ideograph.
42		—	leopard, cheeta.
43, 44, 45, 46		—	cat, give, gift.
47		—	dog.
48		—	wolf, wolf-god (?) Up-uat.
49, 50, 51, 52		—	jackal-god, Ånpu, judge.
53, 54		set	underworld.
55		—	fabulous animal, *khekh* .
56		un	hare.
57		—	wild animal.
58, 59		—	elephant.
60		—	bear.
61		—	rhinoceros.
62		—	giraffe.
63, 64, 65	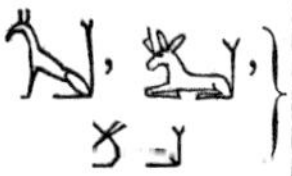	—	Set, or Setesh, or Sutekh, evil personified.
66		—	pig.
67		—	mouse, rat.
68		—	Āmem-mit, a composite monster, one-third hippopotamus, one-third crocodile, and one-third horse, which devoured the hearts of the wicked.

VI.

PARTS OF ANIMALS.

Number.	Hieroglyph.	Phonetic Value.	Signification as Determinative or Ideograph.
1		——	ass's head.
2		——	fore part of bull.
3		——	bull.
4		——	nose, breath, the front of anything.
5		——	the nose, breath, front.
6		——	throat and neck, head and windpipe, swallow.
7		——	cow-goddess.
8		——	respect, reverence, ***shefit*** 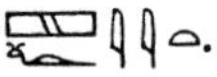.
9		——	. . . .
10		——	the Eight Gods (*Khemenu* ) of Hermopolis Magna.
11, 12		——	wisdom, knowledge, ***shesa*** 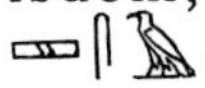.
13		——	strength, power.
14, 15, 16		——	fore part, front.
17		——	the lion-gods of yesterday evening and this morning.
18, 19, 20	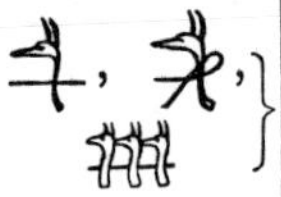	set	underworld.
21, 22		——	company, group.
23, 24, 25, 26	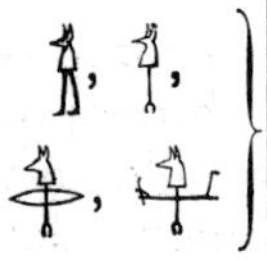	usr	strength.
27		——	moment, minute.
28, 29	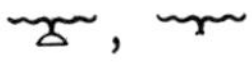	——	horns of kudu.

Number.	Hieroglyph.	Phonetic Value.	Signification as Determinative or Ideograph.
30, 31, 32	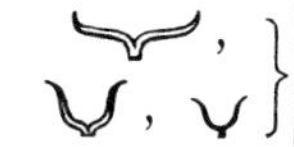	up	crown of the head, apex.
33, 34, 35		——	New Year's Day, *up renpit.*
36		——	the god Khnum.
37, 38, 39		——	rank, dignity, high position.
40		āb 	horn.
41, 42		beḥ , ḥu 	tusk, tooth.
43		——	hear, ear.
44		peḥ 	end, hinder part, attain, reach.
45		——	incantation, enchantment, *ḥeka* .
46		——	thigh, shoulder (?) strength.
47		——	pudenda of a cow, female.
48		——	constellation Meskhet (Great Bear).
49, 50		——	repeat, bone.
51, 52, 53, 54	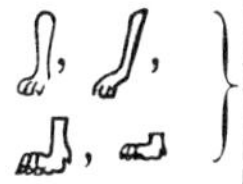	kap 	. . . .
55, 56, 57		——	skin, hide.
58, 59		——	striped or variegated hide.
60		——	shoot, aim at, target.
61		——	tail, rump, thorn, prickle, goad.
62		——	bone and flesh, flesh, joint, heir, posterity.
63		nes 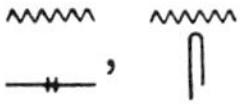	tongue, leader.
64		sma 	the lung or lungs, unite, join together.
65		——	the bull's skin in which the deceased was placed, *mesqat* .

VII.

BIRDS.

Number.	Hieroglyph.	Phonetic Value.	Signification as Determinative or Ideograph.
1		a	kite (?)
2, 3		ma	. . . .
4, 5, 6		ti 	eagle.
7, 8		neḥ 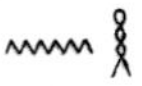	. . . .
9		——	Ḥeru, Horus; hawk, *bȧk* 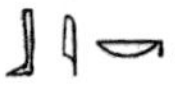.
10		——	Horus with whip.
11		——	Horus-Rā.
12, 13		——	Hawk of gold, a royal title.
14		——	king of the South and North.
15		——	king-god.
16		——	Rā-Harmakhis.
17	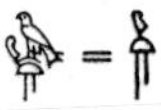	——	right, right-hand side, the West, *Ament.*
18	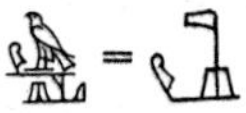	——	Under World, *Kher-neter.*
19		——	Horus, uniter of the Two Lands, a royal title.
20, 21		——	the god Sep.
22, 23, 24	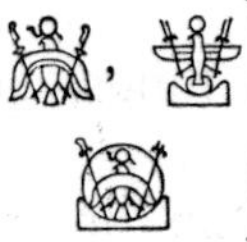	——	forms of Horus-Rā.
25		——	Horus or Rā in his disk.

Number.	Hieroglyph.	Phonetic Value.	Signification as Determinative or Ideograph.
26, 27		——	the goddess Hathor.
28		khu 	. . . .
29		——	sacred bird and image of a god.
30		——	Horus-Sepṭ.
31		ner , m[u]t	vulture, the goddess Mut, mother, year.
32		——	goddess Mut.
33		——	the goddess Nekhebit.
34		——	the goddesses Nekhebit and Uatchit, the tutelary goddesses of Upper and Lower Egypt respectively, *neb-ti* .
35		māk 	. . . .
36, 37		m	. . . .
38		mm	. . . .
39, 40, 41, 42, 43		ma, mā (?) m', mi (?)	. . . .
44		mer	. . . .
45		——	before, *em baḥ*.
46		mer , met 	. . . .
47		tekh 	. . . .
48		ȧakh 	light, radiance, brilliance, shine.
49		gem 	find, discover.
50		——	catch fish.

Number.	Hieroglyph.	Phonetic Value.	Signification as Determinative or Ideograph.
51, 52, 53, 54		——	ibis, the god Thoth, *tcheḥuti* 
55		ba , bak 	soul, dig.
56		——	souls, divine souls.
57, 58		——	nest.
59		——	lake with wild fowl, nest.
60		ba (?)	. . . .
61		——	. . . .
62		——	phoenix, *benu* 
63		——	. . . .
64		——	flood, inundate.
65, 66, 67		——	food, fatten.
68		——	red.
69, 70, 71		sa 	goose and duck, birds in general, insects, son, the Earth-god Geb.
72, 73	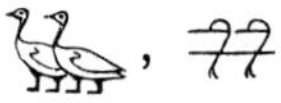	——	washermen.
74		——	shake, tremble.
75, 76	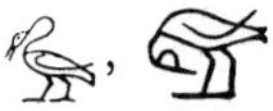	——	destroy.
77		——	enter.
78, 79		pa 	duck, waterfowl, flying.
80, 81		——	flying, flutter, hover, alight.

Number.	Hieroglyph.	Phonetic Value.	Signification as Determinative or Ideograph.
82		qema, then	flutter, hover, alight.
83		tcheb 	brick, seal.
84		ur	swallow, great.
85		——	small, little.
86		menkh 	. . . .
87, 88		——	people, mankind.
89		u	chicken, quail (?)
90		āu	. . . .
91		mau	. . . .
92		ṭu	. . . .
93		tha	. . . .
94		——	fear, terror.
95, 96		ba	the beatified soul.

VIII.

PARTS OF BIRDS.

1		——	goose, duck.
2		——	bird of prey, masculine.
3, 4, 5		peq 	. . . .
6		ȧakh 	bright, shining, etc., like .
7		——	. . . .
8		ȧmakh 	Eye of Horus.
9, 10	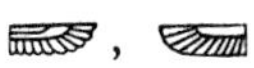	——	flying, wings.

Number.	Hieroglyph.	Phonetic Value.	Signification as Determinative or Ideograph.
11, 12	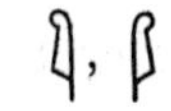	shu 	feather, truth, uprightness, integrity, *maāt* 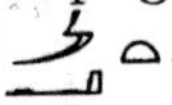.
13		——	Maāti, the two goddesses of Truth.
14		——	arm, cubit, carry.
15, 16		sha (?) 	claw of bird, talon.
17		——	cutting tool, nail, claw (?)
18		——	women, goddesses, cities; son = .

IX.

AMPHIBIA (REPTILES).

Number.	Hieroglyph.	Phonetic Value.	Signification as Determinative or Ideograph.
1, 2	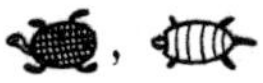	——	river turtle.
3		——	multitude.
4		——	. . . .
5, 6	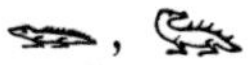	——	crocodile, wrath, rage.
7		——	sacred crocodile, the Sun-god (?)
8		——	Sebek , a Crocodile-god.
9		——	king, *Ati* 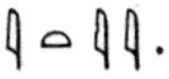.
10		k[a]m 	. . . .
11		——	frog, the Frog-goddess, *Ḥeqit* 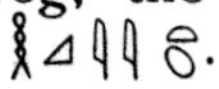.
12		——	tadpole, the number 100,000, *ḥefen* 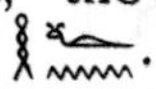.
13, 14, 15		——	serpent, goddess, priestess.
16		——	fire-spitting serpent or goddess.
17, 18		——	the goddess Meḥnit.
19		——	goddess.

Number.	Hieroglyph.	Phonetic Value.	Signification as Determinative or Ideograph.
20		——	goddess, Isis.
21		——	shrine of goddess, *àter* .
22, 23	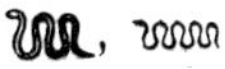	——	worm.
24		——	the loathly Worm *Āapep* .
25		tch	serpent.
26		——	. . . .
27		——	compound of ∩ = *metch* "ten," and  *tch*.
28		——	eternity, *tchet*.
29		——	compound of  *tch* and  *ḥ*.
30		f	snail (?), slug (?)
31		——	a sign formed by adding to on a sarcophagus in the British Museum (No. 32).
32		——	=  + or *s* + *f*.
33		——	to come out, *per* = .
34		——	go in, *āq* = 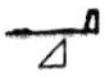 or .
35		——	serpent.
36, 37		——	spitting serpent.
38		——	serpent's head.
39		——	goddess.
40		——	collect, gather together, *saq* .

X.

FISH.

Number.	Hieroglyph.	Phonetic Value.	Signification as Determinative or Ideograph.
1, 2	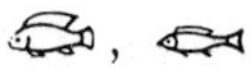	ȧn 	fish.
3, 4		—	fish, rise, mount up, foul, filthy.
5		—	fighting fish.
6, 7	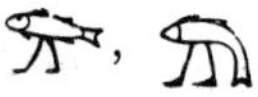	—	rise, mount up.
8, 9	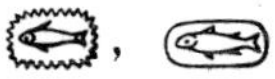	—	swim, shining, *ān* 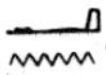.
10		—	. . . .
11, 12, 13	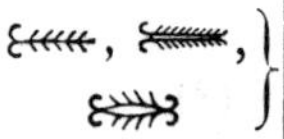	—	a deadly fish (?)
14		kha 	dead body.
15		—	cuttle fish (?) *nār* .
16		—	a fish.
17		—	*latus* fish (?)
18		—	*āntch mer*, an old title of the governor of a district.

XI.

INSECTS.

Number.	Hieroglyph.	Phonetic Value.	Signification as Determinative or Ideograph.
1, 2		—	bee, honey; hornet (?); king of the North.
3		—	king of the South and North, *Nesu Bȧt.*
4		—	the flying beetle *khepрer* , *scarabaeus sacer*; become, *kheper* .

Number.	Hieroglyph.	Phonetic Value.	Signification as Determinative or Ideograph.
5		——	flying, the winged solar disk of Ḥer-Beḥuṭet.
6, 7		——	alighting.
8		——	insect found in mummies.
9		——	fly, *āff* 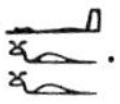.
10		——	grasshopper.
11, 12		——	scorpion, breathe; the goddess Serqit .
13		——	scorpion with the sign for eternity, *shen* .
14		——	. . . .

XII.

TREES, PLANTS, FLOWERS, ETC.

Number.	Hieroglyph.	Phonetic Value.	Signification as Determinative or Ideograph.
1, 2, 3		——	tree, sweet, pleasant.
4, 5, 6		——	tree.
7		——	palm tree.
8		——	plot of ground with a palm and an acacia tree.
9		khet 	tree, wood.
10, 11	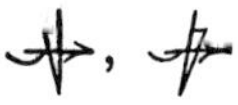	——	cutting wood.
12		——	growing grain plant.
13, 14	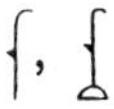	——	flourish, blooming, year, time in general, last year of a king's reign.
15, 16	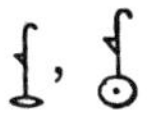	——	time.
17		——	flourish, *renp* .
18		——	long time.

Number.	Hieroglyph.	Phonetic Value.	Signification as Determinative or Ideograph.
19, 20	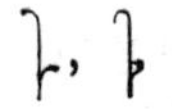	—	spring plant.
21, 22		—	thorn, goad.
23		—	the goddess Nekhebit and her town Nekheb (Gr. Eileithyiaspolis, Arab. Al-Ḳâb).
24		nen	written wrongly in later times .
25		su	plant of the South, king of the South.
26, 27, 28		res	the South.
29, 30, 31	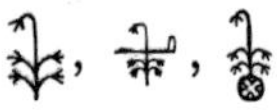	shemā	the South.
32		qemā	play music, musician.
33		—	see .
34		ȧ (ă, ĕ, ĭ)	. . . .
35		i	. . . .
36		ȧi	go, advance.
37		sekh-t	field, garden.
38		—	offering, oblation.
39, 40, 41	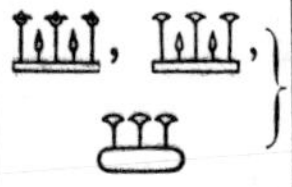	sha	field, garden, flood, inundation, = field in the South; = field in the North.
42, 43	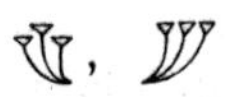	ḥen	plant, vegetable, herb, dried up.
44		ḥa	cluster of papyrus plants.
45, 46		—	papyrus swamp, the swamps in the Delta, the North.
47, 48		—	the South, Upper Egypt.
49, 50		uatch , utch	papyrus stalk.
51, 52		—	a plant of the South.

Number.	Hieroglyph.	Phonetic Value.	Signification as Determinative or Ideograph.
53		——	Upper and Lower Egypt, the Two Lands, *Taui*.
54		——	lotus in bloom.
55, 56, 57, 58, 59, 60	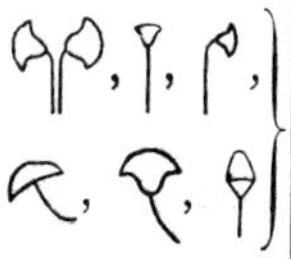	——	plants.
61		——	bud of a flower, *neḥem*.
62, 63	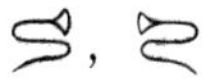	——	variants of *uṭen*, sacrifice, offering.
64, 65, 66, 67, 68	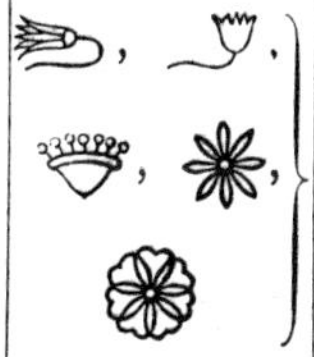	——	flower.
69		un	. . . .
70, 71	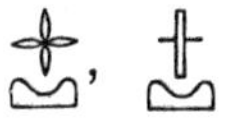	unṭu	. . . .
72		kha	part of a papyrus plant, leaf (?), the number one thousand.
73, 74	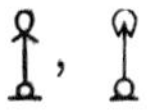	shen	. . . .
75		r =	. . . .
76, 77, 78		ḥetch	mace, club; white, shining.
79, 80	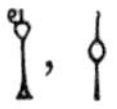	utch	knot-grass.
81, 82, 83	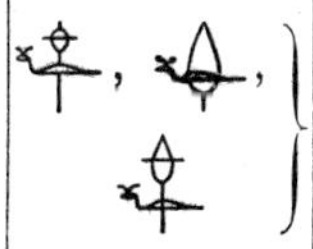	khesef	spindle; repulse.
84		mes	fly-flapper made of the tails of foxes.
85, 86		——	spelt, dhurra (?)
87		——	ear of corn.
88		——	growing grain.
89, 90	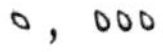	——	grain, corn.

Number.	Hieroglyph.	Phonetic Value.	Signification as Determinative or Ideograph.
91, 92	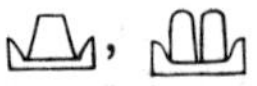	——	granary.
93, 94, 95, 96, 97	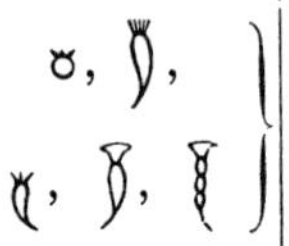	——	date, sweetness, pleasure, grow.
98, 99	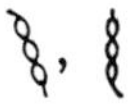	——	sweet, pleasant.
100, 101	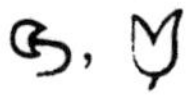	——	flower.
102		——	fig.
103, 104	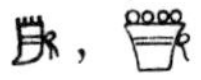	tcher 	bundle of plants or vegetables; boundary.
105, 106, 107, 108, 109,	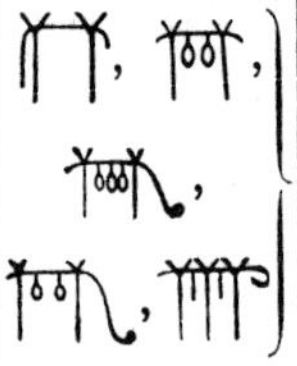	——	vineyard, pergola.
110		——	union of Upper and Lower Egypt.

XIII.

HEAVEN, EARTH, WATER.

1		——	heaven, sky, ceiling, what is above.
2, 3,	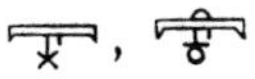	——	the night sky with a star hanging like a lamp from it, darkness, night.
4		——	rain or dew falling from the sky.
5		——	the sky slipping down over its four supports, storm, hurricane.
6		——	sparkle, shine, coruscate, lightning, blue-glazed faïence.
7		——	one half of the sky.
8, 9		——	sun, the Sun-god Rā , day, period, time in general.
10, 11, 12		——	the Sun-god Rā.

Number.	Hieroglyph.	Phonetic Value.	Signification as Determinative or Ideograph.
13		——	circle.
14		——	shine, rise (of a luminary), beings of light.
15		——	shine, lighten.
16		——	prepared, ready; the Dog-star Sepṭit.
17, 18, 19, 20, 21, 22	, , , , ,	——	winged solar disk.
23		——	walking disk.
24, 25	,	khā	rise (of the sun), coronation of a king.
26		——	nearly full moon.
27		——	crescent moon.
28		——	span, *shesp* .
29, 30	,	——	moon, month.
31		——	month.
32, 33 34	, ,	——	the half-month.
35		sba , ṭua	star, morning star, hour, time for prayer, pray.
36		——	the Under World, Ṭuat .
37, 38	,	ta	land.
39		——	the Two Lands, *Taui*, i.e., Upper and Lower Egypt.
40		——	"lands," *Taiu*, the world.
41		——	foreign country, the desert.
42		——	foreign land = + .
43		——	East.
44		——	West.
45		tchu , ṭu	mountain.

Number.	Hieroglyph.	Phonetic Value.	Signification as Determinative or Ideograph.
46		——	horizon.
47, 48	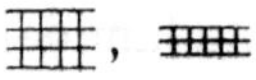	——	nome, district.
49		——	land.
50		——	river bank.
51		——	the eastern and western banks of the Nile, *i.e.*, Egypt.
52		——	boundary, limit.
53		ua , ḥer 	way, road, remote.
54		——	travel, traveller, journey afar.
55, 56, 57		m , ȧm 	side.
58, 59	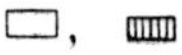	——	stone.
60, 61	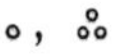	——	grain, powder.
62		n	. . . .
63		mu 	water, watery mass of the sky.
64, 65	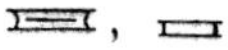	m	canal, any collection of water; written wrongly sometimes for *ȧu*  "island"; love, loving.
66, 67, 68, 69	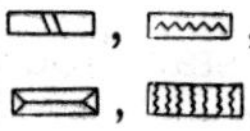	sh	lake, sea, ornamental water, *khent* .
70, 71, 72		——	horizon.
73		——	horizon.
74		——	the two horizons of the East and West.
75		ȧu 	island, *ȧu* .
76		——	bread, sacrificial cake.
77, 78, 79		sen 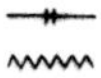	go, pass, like, similar.
80, 81, 82, 83, 84		——	pool, lake, sheet of water.
85, 86	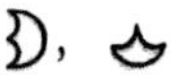	kha 	shellfish, cockle.

XIV.

BUILDINGS AND PARTS OF BUILDINGS.

Number.	Hieroglyph.	Phonetic Value.	Signification as Determinative or Ideograph.
1, 2	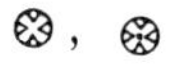	——	city, town.
3, 4, 5	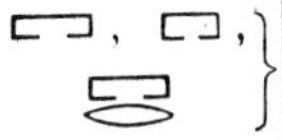	, late p or pa	house, any building, to come forth.
6		——	offerings to the dead, *i.e.*, offerings which appear at the command of the dead person, *per kheru* (*pert er kheru*),
7		——	treasure-house *per ḥetch*.
8		h	. . . .
9		mer , nem 	Mer, a name of Egypt.
10, 11, 12, 13	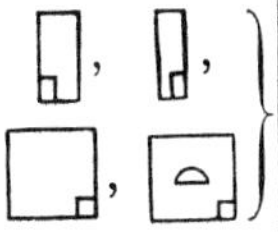	——	mansion.
14	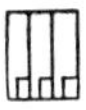	——	mansion with many rooms.
15	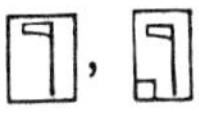	——	house of the god, temple.
16		——	"Great House," castle.
17		——	"Lady of the house," *i.e.*, the goddess Nephthys.
18		——	shrine, tomb.
19		——	"House of Horus," *i.e.*, the goddess Hathor.
20		——	"House of Nut," *i.e.*, the sky, heaven.
21		——	house of the king.
22		——	libation chamber.

Number.	Hieroglyph.	Phonetic Value.	Signification as Determinative or Ideograph.
23		—	palace.
24		—	palace of the god.
25		—	door, gateway protected by uraei.
26		—	title of a legal official.
27, 28, 29, 30	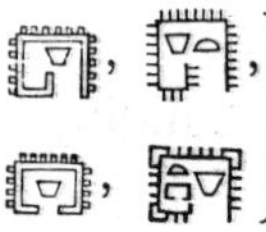	—	court, *usekht*, of palace or mansion.
31		—	wall.
32, 33	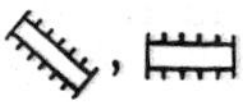	—	overthrow, throw down.
34		—	"White Wall," Åneb-ḥetch, *i.e.*, Memphis.
35, 36, 37		—	fortress.
38		—	shrine of a god with the two doors open.
39, 40, 41	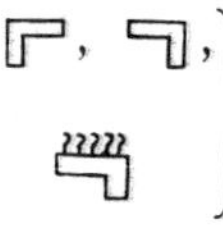	—	angle, corner, title of an official, *qenbt*.
42		ḥap 	hide, conceal; var. .
43, 44	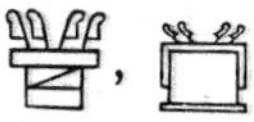	—	funerary coffer.
45, 46		—	pyramid.
47		—	obelisk.
48		—	memorial slab, boundary stone, landmark.
49		—	pillar.
50, 51, 52, 53, 54	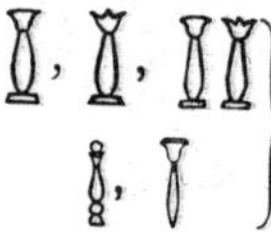	—	pillars with lotus and papyrus-shaped capitals.
55		—	capital of pillar.

Number.	Hieroglyph.	Phonetic Value.	Signification as Determinative or Ideograph.
56		——	decorate, adorn.
57		——	object (flint ?) used in birth ceremonies.
58		——	hall, council chamber.
59		——	bend, twist.
60, 61	,	——	festival of renewing the king's life, *ḥeb seṭ*, "festival of the tail" (?)
62		——	festival.
63, 64	,	——	stairway, stepped throne, ascend.
65		āa	open, door.
66		s	door-bolt.
67		——	travel, go, bring, carry.
68, 69	,	tches , thes	knot together.
70, 71	,	——	the god Menu.
72, 73	,	qeṭ	. . . .
74, 75, 76	, ,	——	funerary coffers.
77		——	shrine of Ptaḥ.
78, 79	,	——	door, gateway.
80		——	. . . .
81		——	chapel of the Ka.
82, 83	,	p	door (?)
84, 85, 86	, ,	——	great house, castle.
87		——	angle block (?)

Number.	Hieroglyph.	Phonetic Value.	Signification as Determinative or Ideograph.
88		——	funerary offerings of bread and beer.
89, 90, 91, 92, 93, 94, 95, 96, 97	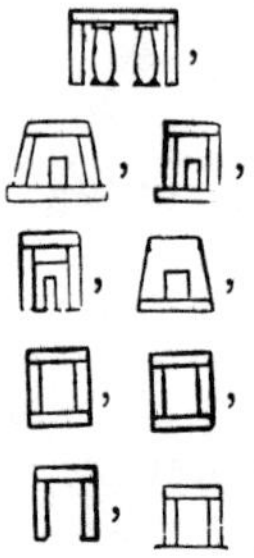	——	door, gateway.
98		——	a Sûdânî ḳubbah.

XV.

SHIPS, BOATS, SACRED BOATS, ETC.

Number.	Hieroglyph.	Phonetic Value.	Signification as Determinative or Ideograph.
1, 2, 3, 4, 5	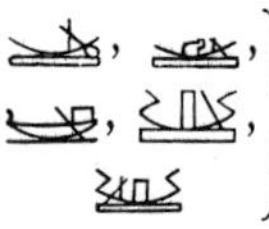	——	boat, ship, to sail, travel.
6		——	capsize, overturn.
7, 8	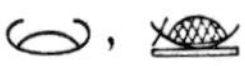	uḥā 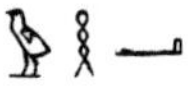	a loaded boat.
9		——	boat of Rā.
10		——	boat of the goddess Maāt.
11, 12	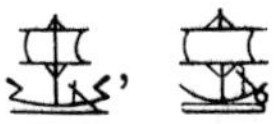	——	sailing, to sail upstream.
13, 14	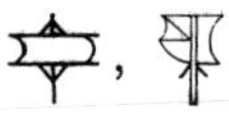	——	wind, air, breeze, breath.
15, 16		āḥā 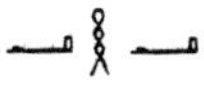	stand up.
17		——	steering pole or oar, helm.
18		——	rudder, voice, speech.
19		shesp 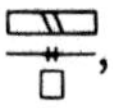, seshp 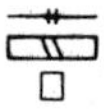, shep 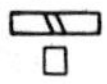	receive, take.
20, 21, 22	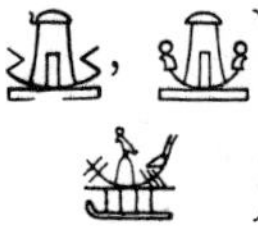	——	sacred boats for use in shrines and in religious processions.

XVI.

FURNITURE (SEATS, TABLES, CHESTS, STANDS).

Number.	Hieroglyph.	Phonetic Value.	Signification as Determinative or Ideograph.
1		s, ḥetem	seat, throne; the goddess Isis, *Ast* .
2	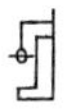	——	instrument for measuring.
3		——	chair, stool.
4, 5, 6, 7	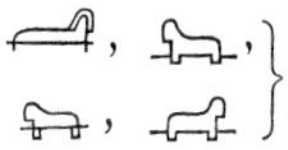	us	litter.
8		——	lie down, recline, sleep.
9		——	dead body, bier.
10		——	couch of Horus or Osiris.
11, 12	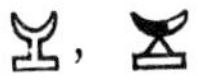	——	pillow, head rest, raise up.
13		s	. . . .
14	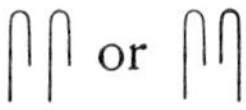	——	eight.
15		——	weaving tool or instrument.
16		ser	. . . .
17, 18		——	fractional number ($\frac{2}{3}$).
19		——	= *s-pekhar* .
20		sef	. . . .
21		= seshem	. . . .
22		——	offering, oblation, sacrifice; rest, set (of the sun).
23, 24, 25		——	stand for a vessel, down, under.
26		——	daily.

Number.	Hieroglyph.	Phonetic Value.	Signification as Determinative or Ideograph.
27, 28, 29, 30, 31	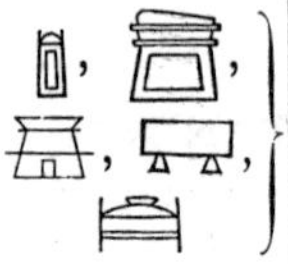	——	sarcophagus, funerary chest or coffer.
32		——	region, place.
33		tcheba, ṭeba	substitute, substitution, supply.
34		ȧn, ȧun	pillar, light-tower.
35		——	var. of preceding (?)
36, 37		hen	. . . .
38, 39	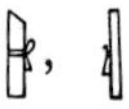	ȧs	. . . .
40		——	= = "book," or "offering."
41		——	Shesmu, the headsman of Osiris.
42		——	oil press, wine press.
43, 44, 45	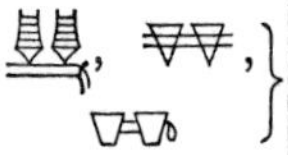	metcher, m'tcheṭ.	squeeze, press.
46		——	clothing, apparel.
47		——	lamp-stand.
48		——	ceremonial umbrella.
49		——	shade, shadow of the living or dead.
50		——	scales, balance, weigh.
51	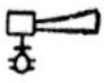	——	measurer of the hour, *unnu*.
52, 53	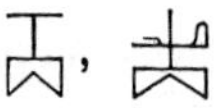	utchā or	right, correct, just, equable.
54, 55, 56, 57, 58	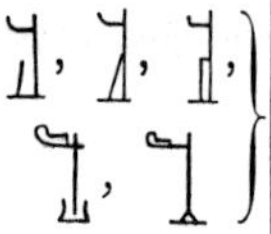	——	raise up, exalt.

Number.	Hieroglyph.	Phonetic Value.	Signification as Determinative or Ideograph.
59		maā	true, right, truth, integrity.
60		——	stand for sacred images, etc.
61		——	mirror.
62		——	weigh, balance.

XVII.

SACRED VESSELS AND FURNITURE.

Number.	Hieroglyph.	Phonetic Value.	Signification as Determinative or Ideograph.
1		——	altar with bread and beer on it.
2		——	stand with libation jars upon it.
3		——	altar.
4		——	altar.
5, 6	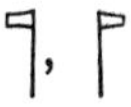	——	god, God.
7		——	divine mother.
8		——	Soter, Saviour-god.
9		——	Under World.
10		——	mistake for .
11		tchet , ṭeṭ	sacred object worshipped in the Delta, confounded with the *sacrum* of Osiris.
12		sma	unite, join.
13, 14, 15, 16	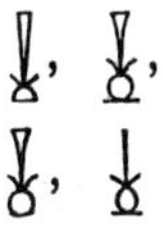	sen	two, friend, brother, associate.
17, 18		——	left *åab* , left side, ,
19		åm	what is in, who is in.

Number.	Hieroglyph.	Phonetic Value.	Signification as Determinative or Ideograph.
20		——	var. of *un-ṭu.*
21, 22		——	the goddess of Wisdom, Seshat.
23, 24, 25, 26, 27, 28, 29, 30		——	censer stands.
31		——	Khnemu.

XVIII.

CLOTHING, CROWNS, ORNAMENTS, ETC.

Number.	Hieroglyph.	Phonetic Value.	Signification as Determinative or Ideograph.
1		——	crown.
2		——	crown.
3		k (late)	covering for head and neck.
4, 5		——	the same with uraeus, symbol of royalty.
6		——	royal war helmet, *khepersh*.
7		——	crown of the South or Upper Egypt.
8		——	= + Upper Egypt.
9		net (late)	crown of the North or Lower Egypt.
10		——	= + Lower Egypt.
11		——	crowns of the South and North united, *sekhemti*.
12		——	cord.
13		u	cord measure, the number one hundred.
14		——	pair of plumes, *shuti*.
15		——	helmet with plumes.

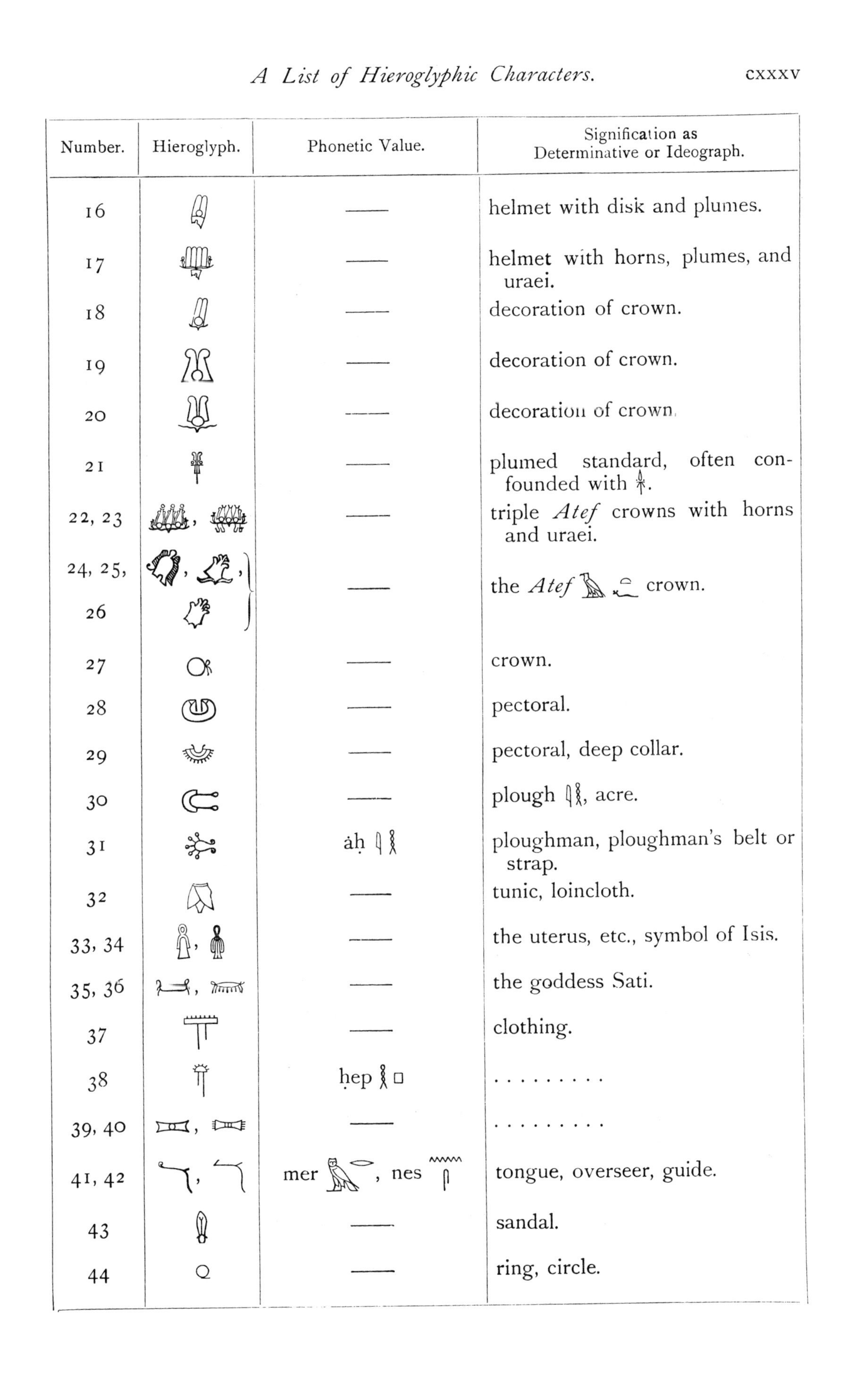

Number.	Hieroglyph.	Phonetic Value.	Signification as Determinative or Ideograph.
16		——	helmet with disk and plumes.
17		——	helmet with horns, plumes, and uraei.
18		——	decoration of crown.
19		——	decoration of crown.
20		——	decoration of crown.
21		——	plumed standard, often confounded with .
22, 23	,	——	triple *Atef* crowns with horns and uraei.
24, 25, 26	, ,	——	the *Atef* crown.
27		——	crown.
28		——	pectoral.
29		——	pectoral, deep collar.
30		——	plough, acre.
31		ȧḥ	ploughman, ploughman's belt or strap.
32		——	tunic, loincloth.
33, 34	,	——	the uterus, etc., symbol of Isis.
35, 36	,	——	the goddess Sati.
37		——	clothing.
38		ḥep	. . . .
39, 40	,	——	. . . .
41, 42	,	mer , nes	tongue, overseer, guide.
43		——	sandal.
44		——	ring, circle.

Number.	Hieroglyph.	Phonetic Value.	Signification as Determinative or Ideograph.
45		kheb	. . . .
46		——	unite, sum up, a total.
47		——	live, life.
48		——	seal-cylinder, seal, valuables.
49		——	seal-cylinder with cord, seal, what is put under seal.
50		——	"counterpoise" of collar, the *menȧt*, symbol of pleasure and gladness.
51		kap	incense, cense.
52, 53		——	provide, supply.
54		——	sistrum.
55, 56, 57, 58, 59, 60		——	mighty, powerful, direct, rule, emblem of authority, sceptre.
61, 62		——	present, offer.
63, 64, 65		——	right side, the West.
66, 67		——	fan, fly-flapper, air.
68		——	box that held the head of Osiris.
69, 70		——	district of the head box of Osiris, Abydos.
71		——	rule, reign, govern.
72		——	sheep and goats.
73		uas, tchām	sceptre, fine gold, serenity.
74		——	Thebes, *Uast*.
75		——	strength, strong.
76, 77, 78		——	term of Horus.

Number.	Hieroglyph.	Phonetic Value.	Signification as Determinative or Ideograph.
79, 80		——	symbol of Upper Egypt.
81, 82		——	symbol of Lower Egypt.
83, 84		——	whip.
85		——	. . . .
86		——	. . . .
87		——	the firstborn son of Osiris, Baba 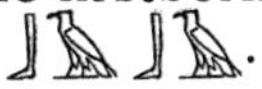.
88		——	White Crown with cord.
89		——	pectoral (?)
90	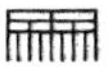	——	fringe of the "banner" of the Horus-names of kings, as in 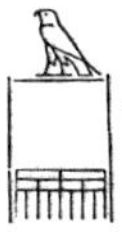.
91	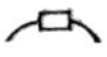	ā (?)	ass's load in a caravan.

XIX.

WEAPONS AND ARMS.

1, 2		——	boomerang, throw, foreign nations.
3, 4	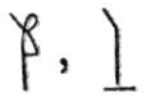	——	keep watch, be awake.
5		——	pillar support;  the four pillars of heaven.
6		——	calamity, disaster.
7, 8		——	carpenter's axe, work in wood.
9		——	battle-axe.
10		tep 	first, foremost, at the head.
11		——	scimitar, short, curved sword.
12, 13	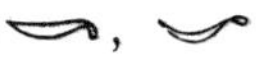	——	. . . .

Number.	Hieroglyph.	Phonetic Value.	Signification as Determinative or Ideograph.
14		——	mooring post, arrive in port, to land, die, end a journey.
15, 16		——	cut, inscribe a name, designate.
17		——	knife and block, slaughter.
18		——	a gory knife, slaughter.
19, 20	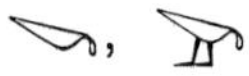	——	hone (?), slaughter, massacre.
21		——	razor (?), shave.
22, 23, 24	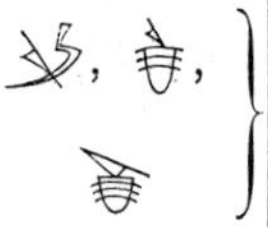	——	slaughter.
25		——	bow.
26, 27, 28, 29	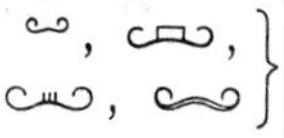	——	Nubian bow, symbol of Nubia and the Egyptian Sûdân.
30		——	extend, spread out, stretch out.
31, 32		——	arrow, shoot.
33		——	symbol of the goddess Neith as huntress.
34	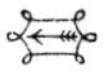	——	arrow in hide of a beast, hunt.
35		——	arrows and target.
36, 37, 38	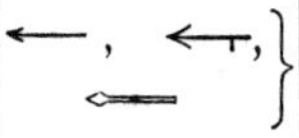	——	spear, pike, stab, transfix.
39, 40, 41	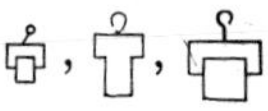	sa 	back, at the back of, hinder part.
42	 or 	āa 	great.
43		kha	. . . .
44		ṭebḥ 	a collection of weapons.
45, 46		——	chariot.
47		——	target (?) memorial stele.

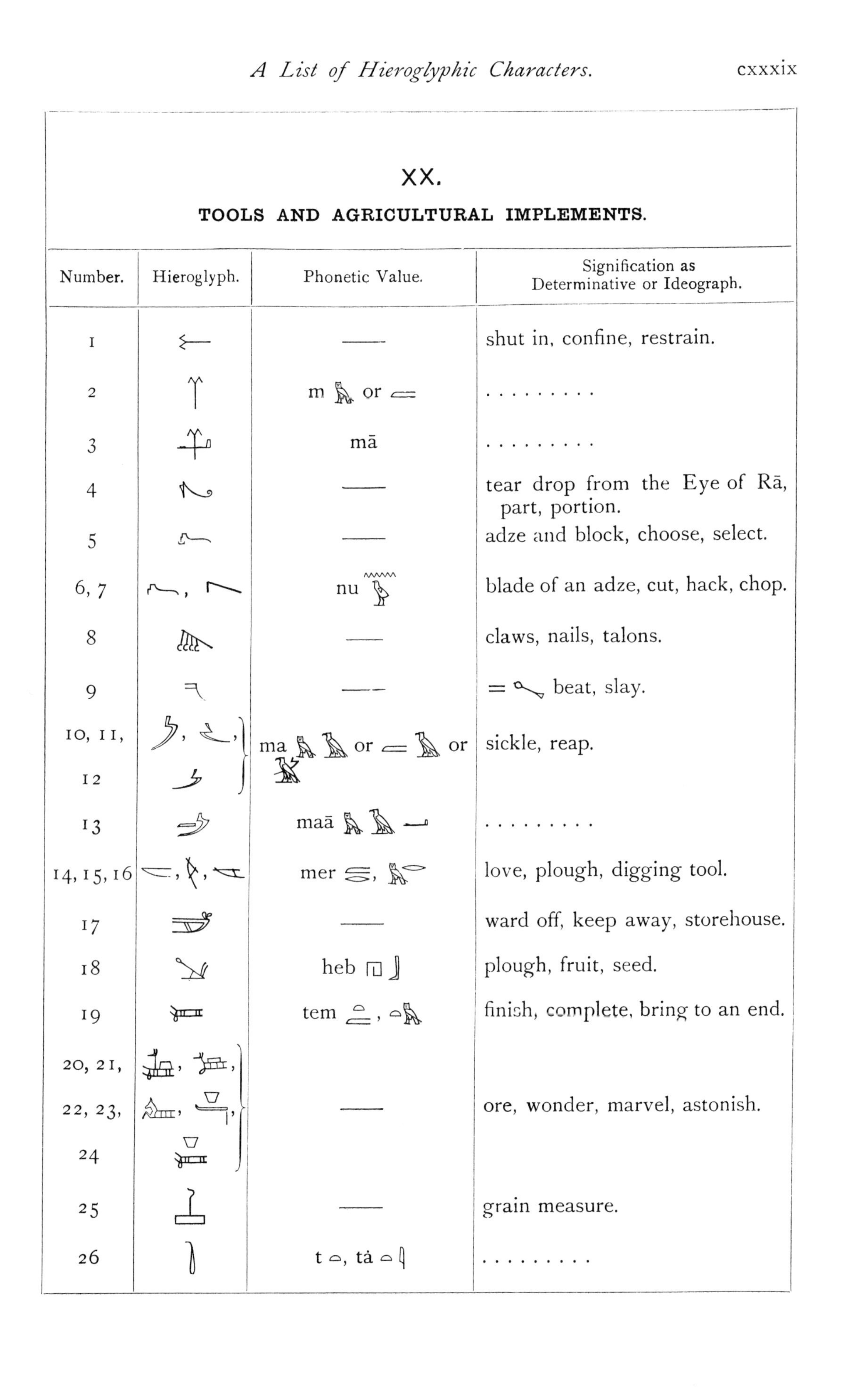

XX.

TOOLS AND AGRICULTURAL IMPLEMENTS.

Number.	Hieroglyph.	Phonetic Value.	Signification as Determinative or Ideograph.
1		——	shut in, confine, restrain.
2		m or	. . . .
3		mā	. . . .
4		——	tear drop from the Eye of Rā, part, portion.
5		——	adze and block, choose, select.
6, 7	,	nu	blade of an adze, cut, hack, chop.
8		——	claws, nails, talons.
9		——	= beat, slay.
10, 11, 12	, ,	ma or or	sickle, reap.
13		maā	. . . .
14, 15, 16	, ,	mer ,	love, plough, digging tool.
17		——	ward off, keep away, storehouse.
18		heb	plough, fruit, seed.
19		tem ,	finish, complete, bring to an end.
20, 21, 22, 23, 24	, , , ,	——	ore, wonder, marvel, astonish.
25		——	grain measure.
26		t , tà	. . . .

Number.	Hieroglyph.	Phonetic Value.	Signification as Determinative or Ideograph.
27		——	metal, mineral, heavy substance, weighty, salt, soda.
28, 29		tcha	fire stick or driil.
30		utcha	. . . .
31, 32, 33	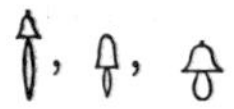	——	work in wood, excellent, fine, splendid.
34		mer	sick, diseased, pyramid.
35		——	handicraft, workmanship.
36		ab	. . . .
37		uba	open, make a way or passage.
38, 39		——	= ward off, keep away.
40, 41, 42		——	rub down to a powder, grind.
43, 44, 45	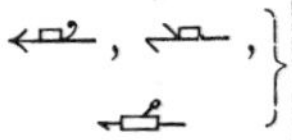	uā	pike, harpoon, the number one.
46, 47	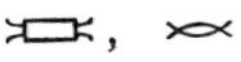	——	the goddess Neith.
48		——	razor, shave.
49, 50		——	follow as a friend or servant.
51		qes, qers	hollow reed, bone, to bury.
52		——	worker in stone or metal, metal founder, sculptor, artisan of Horus.
53, 54	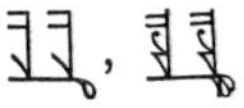	——	claw, talon.
55		ḥap, ḥep	= .
56, 57	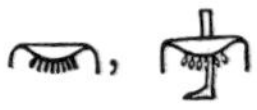	——	gold of every degree of purity (*nub*).
58		——	silver.
59		——	gold, *tchām* .

Number.	Hieroglyph.	Phonetic Value.	Signification as Determinative or Ideograph.
60		maā	truth, right.
61, 62		——	weave, net (snare).
63		ḥem	= .

XXI.

WOVENWORK, PLAITED ARTICLES.

Number.	Hieroglyph.	Phonetic Value.	Signification as Determinative or Ideograph.
1		——	cord.
2		u	measuring cord; the number one hundred.
3		set	. . . .
4		——	claw, talon.
5		au	wide, broad, spacious.
6		——	dignity, high rank, worth.
7		shes , qes	tie, bind, cordage.
8		——	constrained, suffering.
9		shen	. . . .
10		geb	packet, small bundle, sachet.
11		——	germinate, grow.
12, 13, 14, 15		——	roll of papyrus, tie up, bind together, come to an end.
16, 17, 18		——	fill, complete.
19		sheṭ	take, accept, receive.
20, 21,		——	= , the goddess Neith.
22, 23		āntch	sound, healthy.
24		——	the god Åtem .

Number.	Hieroglyph.	Phonetic Value.	Signification as Determinative or Ideograph.
25		—	foundation.
26		ua	. . . .
27		—	magical protection, amulet (*sa*).
28		shent	. . . .
29		—	knotted cord, magical knot (*sa*).
30		ḥ	. . . .
31		ḥer	. . . .
32		ḥā	. . . .
33, 34, 35		sek	. . . .
36		—	set, place, put, stablish.
37		—	is often written for or .
38, 39, 40		—	offering, oblation, sacrifice.
41		—	a sign composed of and . It occurs on sarcophagus No. 32 in the British Museum, and was cut on it when the sarcophagus of Queen Ānkhnesneferȧbrā was usurped by a man.
42		—	revolve, circle round, return, the bowels, the weight *ṭeben* .
43		th	. . . .
44		—	seize, grasp, capture, conquer.
45		—	swathe a mummy, embalm a body with unguents, spices, etc., the dead, to count up, reckon.
46		—	incense.
47		—	skin of an animal (?)

XXII.

VASES AND VESSELS, BASKETS, MEASURES, ETC.

Number.	Hieroglyph.	Phonetic Value.	Signification as Determinative or Ideograph.
1, 2		——	vases for unguents.
3		——	unguent, ointment, bitumen, naphtha; the goddess Bastt , and her city Bubastis.
4		——	libation jar, praise, commend.
5		——	coolness, refreshing.
6		——	the king's majesty, servant, kind of priest.
7		——	servant of the god, *ḥem neter*.
8, 9, 10	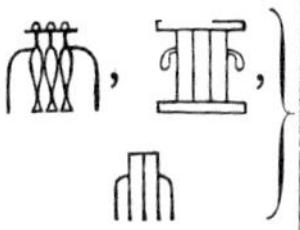	——	jar stand; be in front.
11		——	consort with, be joined to, unite; the god Khnemu .
12, 13, 14, 15	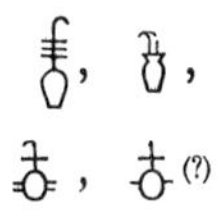	——	milk.
16 17, 18 19, 20	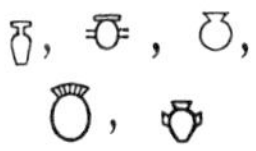	——	vase, vessel, pot, what is fluid, viscous, etc.; waiter, attendant, beer.
21		——	milk pot (?)
22		——	wine skin, wine.
23		nu	vase, vessel, pot, what is fluid or viscous, internal organ.
24		ȧn 	bring, bear, import.
25		——	heart.

Number.	Hieroglyph.	Phonetic Value.	Signification as Determinative or Ideograph.
26, 27, 28	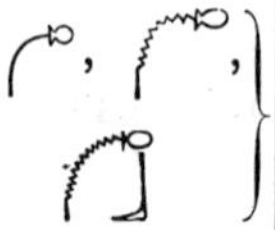	——	libation priest, clean, pure, holy.
29		——	clean, ceremonially pure, holy.
30, 31		mȧ , mer 	as, like, similar.
32, 33	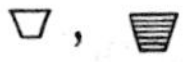	āb 	vase, vessel, pot, goddess, queen, mistress; broad, spacious, wide.
34, 35, 36	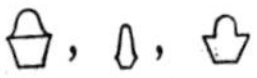	——	bread, cake, loaf, bread-offering.
37		——	pottery lamp (?)
38, 39		——	flame, fire, heat.
40		ba, b (in late times)	vase of burning incense (?)
41, 42		tcher 	limit, boundary.
43		g	. . . .
44		neb 	basket, receptacle for offerings.
45		k	. . . .
46		variant of	. . . .
47		——	vulva of cow.
48		——	pour out (?)
49		——	. . . .
50		——	festival.
51		——	. . . .
52	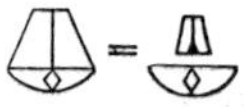	——	title of a priest *kheri ḥeb*, "he who hath charge of the festival."
53, 54	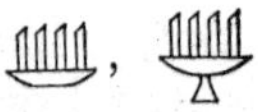	——	an offering.
55, 56, 57, 58, 59	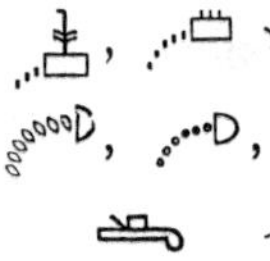	——	grain of all kinds.

Number.	Hieroglyph.	Phonetic Value.	Signification as Determinative or Ideograph.
60		——	cattle.
61, 62, 63		——	vessels in stone, the city of Abu or Elephantine.
64, 65, 66	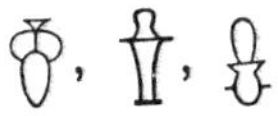	——	pottery jars, stone jars with covers, etc.
67		——	a kind of priest.
68, 69		ta 	heat, fire, furnace.
70		——	metal, especially copper or bronze.
71		——	the goddess Neḥeb-ka.

XXIII.

OFFERINGS, CAKES, ETC.

Number.	Hieroglyph.	Phonetic Value.	Signification as Determinative or Ideograph.
1, 2, 3	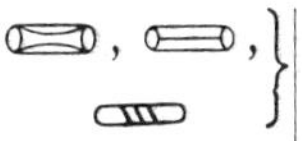	——	bread, cake.
4		——	the town Nekhen (Eileithyiaspolis).
5, 6	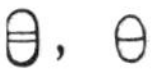	——	bread, cake ; father.
7, 8		——	bread, cake, shewbread ; primeval time.
9, 10		——	ennead.
11		——	circle, disk.
12, 13	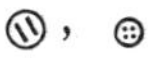	——	time.
14		kh	sieve.
15		——	river bank, land.
16		——	give, present.

XXIV.

WRITING AND MUSICAL INSTRUMENTS, GAMES.

Number.	Hieroglyph.	Phonetic Value.	Signification as Determinative or Ideograph.
1	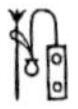	—	scribe's writing outfit, write, writing; rub down to powder, polish; variegated, stupid.
2		—	roll of papyrus tied round the middle, book, deed, document, register; of the abstract; group together.
3, 4	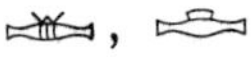	—	bag, sack.
5		—	harp, zither.
6, 7, 8		—	sistrum, castanets.
9		—	goodness, happiness.
10		—	the god Nefer-Tem .
11		sȧa 	recognize, know, understand.
12		men 	draughtboard.
13		—	draughtsman.

XXV.

STROKES AND DOUBTFUL OBJECTS.

1		—	a sign added for purposes of symmetry, *e.g.*, 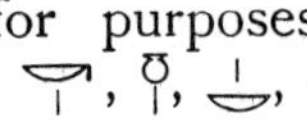, etc.
2, 3, 4		—	sign of the plural.
5, 6		i 	sign of the dual.
7, 8	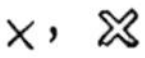	—	a pair of tallies = , count, tally, reckon, pass by, depart, etc.
9		—	the number ten.

Number.	Hieroglyph.	Phonetic Value.	Signification as Determinative or Ideograph.
10, 11, 12		——	objects of wood or wickerwork; terrify, terrible.
13		——	divide, cut.
14		t	. . . .
15		——	territory, estate; to complete; head, chief.
16		——	the oval round a royal name, *cartouche.*
17		——	beat, kill.
18		——	women's apartments.
19, 20		nem 	step, walk.

THE COPTIC ALPHABET.

COPTIC LETTERS.	COPTIC NAMES OF THE SAME.		PHONETIC VALUE.	NUMERICAL VALUE.	
Ⲁ	Alpha	Ⲁⲗⲫⲁ	a	ⲁ̅	1
Ⲃ	Bida	Ⲃⲓⲇⲁ	b	ⲃ̅	2
Ⲅ	Gamma	Ⲅⲁⲙⲙⲁ	g	ⲅ̅	3
Ⲇ	Dalda	Ⲇⲁⲗⲇⲁ	d	ⲇ̅	4
Ⲉ	Ei	Ⲉⲓ	e	ⲉ̅	5
				ⲋ̅*	6
Ⲍ	Zita	Ⲍⲓⲧⲁ	z	ⲍ̅	7
Ⲏ	Êta	Ⲏⲧⲁ	ê	ⲏ̅	8
Ⲑ	Thita	Ⲑⲓⲧⲁ	th	ⲑ̅	9
Ⲓ	Iauta	Ⲓⲁⲩⲧⲁ	i	ⲓ̅	10
Ⲕ	Kappa	Ⲕⲁⲡⲡⲁ	k	ⲕ̅	20
Ⲗ	Laula	Ⲗⲁⲩⲗⲁ	l	ⲗ̅	30
Ⲙ	Mi	Ⲙⲓ	m	ⲙ̅	40
Ⲛ	Ni	Ⲛⲓ	n	ⲛ̅	50
Ⲝ	Xi	Ⲝⲓ	x (ks)	ⲝ̅	60
Ⲟ	O	Ⲟ	o	ⲟ̅	70
Ⲡ	Pi	Ⲡⲓ	p	ⲡ̅	80
Ⲣ	Ro	Ⲣⲟ	r	ⲣ̅	100
Ⲥ	Sima	Ⲥⲓⲙⲁ	s	ⲥ̅	200
Ⲧ	Tau	Ⲧⲁⲩ	t	ⲧ̅	300
Ⲩ	Ue	Ⲩⲉ	u, y	ⲩ̅	400
Ⲫ	Phi	Ⲫⲓ	ph	ⲫ̅	500
Ⲭ	Chi	Ⲭⲓ	kh	ⲭ̅	600
Ⲯ	Psi	Ⲯⲓ	ps	ⲯ̅	700
Ⲱ	Au (Ô)	Ⲁⲩ	ô	ⲱ̅	800
Ϣ	Shei	ϣⲉⲓ	sh	—	
Ϥ	Fei	Ϥⲉⲓ	f	ϥ̅†	90
Ϧ	Chei (Xei)	Ϧⲉⲓ	ch	—	
Ϩ	Ḥori	Ϩⲟⲣⲓ	ḥ	—	
Ϫ	Djandjia	Ϫⲁⲛϫⲓⲁ	dj	—	
Ϭ	Tchima	Ϭⲓⲙⲁ	tch	—	
Ϯ	Ti	Ϯ	ti (di)	—	

The last seven letters are derived from Egyptian hieroglyphs (through Demotic); thus: ϣ from , ϥ from , ϧ from , ϩ from , ϫ from , ϭ from , ϯ from 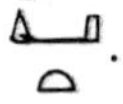.

* This sign represents the Greek sign ϝ Βαῦ, and has the value ⲥⲟⲟⲩ, *i.e.*, "six"; it is only used as a numeral.

† When a letter has a **double** line **over** it, its numerical value is increased a thousandfold, *e.g.*, ⲁ̿ = 1000, ⲃ̿ = 2000, etc.

THE HEBREW ALPHABET.

HEBREW LETTERS.	HEBREW NAMES OF THE SAME.		PHONETIC VALUE.	NUMERICAL VALUE.
א	Alĕph	אָלֶף	’	1
ב	Bêth	בֵּית	B, BH	2
ג	Gîmĕl	גִּימֶל	G, GH	3
ד	Dâlĕth	דָּלֶת	D, DH	4
ה	Hê	הֵא	H	5
ו	Wâw	וָו	W, U	6
ז	Zayin	זַיִן	Z	7
ח	Khêth	חֵית	KH (CH)	8
ט	Ṭêth	טֵית	Ṭ	9
י	Iôdh	יוֹד	Y	10
כ, ך*	Kâph	כַּף	K, KH	20
ל	Lâmĕdh	לָמֶד	L	30
מ, ם*	Mêm	מֵם	M	40
נ, ן*	Nûn	נוּן	N	50
ס	Sâmĕkh	סָמֶךְ	S	60
ע	‘Ayin	עַיִן	‘	70
פ, ף*	Pê	פֵּא	P, PH	80
צ, ץ*	Ṣâdhê	צָדֵי	Ṣ	90
ק	Ḳôph	קוֹף	Q	100
ר	Rêsh	רֵישׁ	R	200
שׂ	Sîn	שִׂין	S	300
שׁ	Shîn	שִׁין	SH	
ת	Tâw	תָּו	T, TH	400

* Form at the end of a word.

THE SYRIAC ALPHABET.

SYRIAC LETTERS.	SYRIAC NAMES OF THE SAME.		PHONETIC VALUE.	NUMERICAL VALUE.
ܐ	Âlaf	ܐܠܦ	’	1
ܒ	Bêth	ܒܝܬ	b, v (β)	2
ܓ	Gâmal	ܓܡܠ	g, gh	3
ܕ	Dâlath, Dâladh	ܕܠܬ, ܕܠܕ	d, dh	4
ܗ	Hê	ܗܐ	h	5
ܘ	Wâw	ܘܐܘ	w, u	6
ܙ	Zai, Zen, or Zayn	ܙܐܝ, ܙܝܢ	z	7
ܚ	Khêth	ܚܝܬ	kh (or) ḥ	8
ܛ	Ṭêth	ܛܝܬ	ṭ	9
ܝ	Yôdh	ܝܘܕ	y	10
ܟ ܟ	Kâf	ܟܦ	k, kh	20
ܠ	Lâmadh	ܠܡܕ	l	30
ܡ	Mîm	ܡܝܡ	m	40
ܢ ܢ	Nûn	ܢܘܢ	n	50
ܣ	Semkath	ܣܡܟܬ	s	60
ܥ	‘Ê	ܥܐ	‘ (guttural)	70
ܦ	Pê	ܦܐ	p, for ph	80
ܨ	Ṣâdhê	ܨܕܐ	ṣ	90
ܩ	Ḳôf	ܩܘܦ	q	100
ܪ	Rêsh (Rîsh)	ܪܝܫ, ܪܫ	r	200
ܫ	Shîn	ܫܝܢ	sh	300
ܬ	Tâw	ܬܐܘ	ṭ, th	400

THE ARABIC ALPHABET.

ARABIC NAMES OF THE LETTERS.		PHONETIC VALUE.	UNCONNECTED.	CONNECTED WITH PRECEDING LETTER.	CONNECTED WITH FOLLOWING LETTER.	CONNECTED WITH PRECEDING AND FOLLOWING LETTER.	NUMERICAL VALUE.
أَلِفْ	Alif	’	ا	ـا	—	—	1
بَآءْ	Bâ	b	ب	ـب	بـ	ـبـ	2
تَآءْ	Tâ	t	ت	ـت	تـ	ـتـ	400
ثَآءْ	Thâ	th	ث	ـث	ثـ	ـثـ	500
جِيمْ	Jîm	g, j	ج	ـج	جـ	ـجـ	3
حَآءْ	Ḥâ	ḥ	ح	ـح	حـ	ـحـ	8
خَآءْ	Khâ	kh	خ	ـخ	خـ	ـخـ	600
دَالْ	Dâl	d	د	ـد	—	—	4
ذَالْ	Dhâl	dh	ذ	ـذ	—	—	700
رَآءْ	Râ	r	ر	ـر	—	—	200
زَايْ	Zây	z	ز	ـز	—	—	7
سِينْ	Sîn	s	س	ـس	سـ	ـسـ	60
شِينْ	Shîn	sh	ش	ـش	شـ	ـشـ	300
صَادْ	Sâd	ṣ	ص	ـص	صـ	ـصـ	90
ضَادْ	Ḍâd	ḍ	ض	ـض	ضـ	ـضـ	800
طَآءْ	Ṭâ	ṭ	ط	ـط	طـ	ـطـ	9
ظَآءْ	Ẓâ	ẓ	ظ	ـظ	ظـ	ـظـ	900
عَيْنْ	‘Ain	‘	ع	ـع	عـ	ـعـ	70
غَيْنْ	Ghain	gh	غ	ـغ	غـ	ـغـ	1,000
فَآءْ	Fâ	f	ف	ـف	فـ	ـفـ	80
قَافْ	Ḳâf	k	ق	ـق	قـ	ـقـ	100
كَافْ	Kâf	q	ك, ك	ـك, ـك	كـ, كـ	ـكـ, ـكـ	20
لَامْ	Lâm	l	ل	ـل	لـ	ـلـ	30
مِيمْ	Mîm	m	م	ـم	مـ	ـمـ, ـمـ	40
نُونْ	Nûn	n	ن	ـن	نـ	ـنـ	50
هَآءْ	Hâ	h	ه	ـه	هـ	ـهـ	5
وَاوْ	Wâw	w	و	ـو	—	—	6
يَآءْ	Yâ	y	ي	ـي	يـ	ـيـ	10

THE ETHIOPIC SYLLABARY.

ETHIOPIC NAME OF THE LETTER.		PHONETIC VALUE.														
ሀይ፡	Hôy	H	ሀ	hă	ሁ	hû	ሂ	hî	ሃ	hâ	ሄ	hê	ህ	hĕ	ሆ	hô
ላዊ፡	Lâwî	L	ለ	lă	ሉ	lû	ሊ	lî	ላ	lâ	ሌ	lê	ል	lĕ	ሎ	lô
ሐውት፡	Ḥâwĕt	Ḥ	ሐ	ḥă	ሑ	ḥû	ሒ	ḥî	ሓ	ḥâ	ሔ	ḥê	ሕ	ḥĕ	ሖ	ḥô
ማይ፡	Mây	M	መ	mă	ሙ	mû	ሚ	mî	ማ	mâ	ሜ	mê	ም	mĕ	ሞ	mô
ሠውት፡	Sâwĕt	S (SH)	ሠ	să	ሡ	sû	ሢ	sî	ሣ	sâ	ሤ	sê	ሥ	sĕ	ሦ	sô
ርእስ፡	Rĕ's	R	ረ	ră	ሩ	rû	ሪ	rî	ራ	râ	ሬ	rê	ር	rĕ	ሮ	rô
ሳት፡	Sât	S (שׂ)	ሰ	să	ሱ	sû	ሲ	sî	ሳ	sâ	ሴ	sê	ስ	sĕ	ሶ	sô
ቃፍ፡	Ḳâf	Q	ቀ	qă	ቁ	qû	ቂ	qî	ቃ	qâ	ቄ	qê	ቅ	qĕ	ቆ	qô
ቤት፡	Bêt	B	በ	bă	ቡ	bû	ቢ	bî	ባ	bâ	ቤ	bê	ብ	bĕ	ቦ	bô
ታዊ፡	Tâwî	T	ተ	tă	ቱ	tû	ቲ	tî	ታ	tâ	ቴ	tê	ት	tĕ	ቶ	tô
ኀርም፡	Kharĕm	KH	ኀ	khă	ኁ	khû	ኂ	khî	ኃ	khâ	ኄ	khê	ኅ	khĕ	ኆ	khô
ነሃስ፡	Nahâs	N	ነ	nă	ኑ	nû	ኒ	nî	ና	nâ	ኔ	nê	ን	nĕ	ኖ	nô
አልፍ፡	'Alĕf	' (א)	አ	'ă	ኡ	'û	ኢ	'î	ኣ	'â	ኤ	'ê	እ	'ĕ	ኦ	'ô
ካፍ፡	Kâf	K	ከ	kă	ኩ	kû	ኪ	kî	ካ	kâ	ኬ	kê	ክ	kĕ	ኮ	kô
ዋዊ፡	Wâwî	W	ወ	wă	ዉ	wû	ዊ	wî	ዋ	wâ	ዌ	wê	ው	wĕ	ዎ	wô
ዓይን፡	'Ayĕn	' (ע)	ዐ	'ă	ዑ	'û	ዒ	'î	ዓ	'â	ዔ	'ê	ዕ	'ĕ	ዖ	'ô
ዛይ፡	Zay	Z	ዘ	ză	ዙ	zû	ዚ	zî	ዛ	zâ	ዜ	zê	ዝ	zĕ	ዞ	zô
የመን፡	Yaman	Y	የ	yă	ዩ	yû	ዪ	yî	ያ	yâ	ዬ	yê	ይ	yĕ	ዮ	yô
ደንት፡	Dant	D	ደ	dă	ዱ	dû	ዲ	dî	ዳ	dâ	ዴ	dê	ድ	dĕ	ዶ	dô
ገምል፡	Gamĕl	G	ገ	gă	ጉ	gû	ጊ	gî	ጋ	gâ	ጌ	gê	ግ	gĕ	ጎ	gô
ጠይት፡	Ṭayt	Ṭ	ጠ	ṭă	ጡ	ṭû	ጢ	ṭî	ጣ	ṭâ	ጤ	ṭê	ጥ	ṭĕ	ጦ	ṭô
ጰይት፡	Payt	P	ጰ	pă	ጱ	pû	ጲ	pî	ጳ	pâ	ጴ	pê	ጵ	pĕ	ጶ	pô
ጸደይ፡	Ṣadây	Ṣ	ጸ	ṣă	ጹ	ṣû	ጺ	ṣî	ጻ	ṣâ	ጼ	ṣê	ጽ	ṣĕ	ጾ	ṣô
ፀፃ፡	Dapâ	Ḍ (ض)	ፀ	ḍă	ፁ	ḍû	ፂ	ḍî	ፃ	ḍâ	ፄ	ḍê	ፅ	ḍĕ	ፆ	ḍô
አፍ፡	Af	F	ፈ	fă	ፉ	fû	ፊ	fî	ፋ	fâ	ፌ	fê	ፍ	fĕ	ፎ	fô
ፐ፡	Pâ	P	ፐ	pă	ፑ	pû	ፒ	pî	ፓ	pâ	ፔ	pê	ፕ	pĕ	ፖ	pô

Ethiopic Diphthongs.

ኰ	kuă	ኲ	kuî	ኵ	kuĕ	ኳ	kuâ	ኴ	kuê
ጐ	guă	ጒ	guî	ጕ	guĕ	ጓ	guâ	ጔ	guê
ቈ	quă	ቊ	quî	ቍ	quĕ	ቋ	quâ	ቌ	quê
ኈ	khuă	ኊ	khuî	ኍ	khuĕ	ኋ	khuâ	ኌ	khuê

Numerals.

፩	1	፬	4	፯	7	፲	10	፵	40	፸	70	፻	100
፪	2	፭	5	፰	8	፳	20	፶	50	፹	80	፲፻	1,000
፫	3	፮	6	፱	9	፴	30	፷	60	፺	90	፻-፻	10,000

THE AMHARIC SYLLABARY.

1 Gĭ‘z	2 Kâ‘ĭb	3 Sâlĭs	4 Râbĭ‘	5 Hâmĭs	6 Sâdis	7 Sâbĭ‘
ሀ ha	ሁ hu	ሂ hi	ሃ hâ	ሄ hê	ህ h, hĭ, hĕ	ሆ ho
ለ la	ሉ lu	ሊ li	ላ lâ	ሌ lî	ል l, lĭ, lĕ	ሎ lo
ሐ ḥa	ሑ ḥu	ሒ ḥi	ሓ ḥâ	ሔ ḥê	ሕ ḥ, ḥĭ, ḥĕ	ሖ ḥo
መ ma	ሙ mu	ሚ mi	ማ mâ	ሜ mê	ም m, mĭ, mĕ	ሞ mo
ሠ sa	ሡ su	ሢ si	ሣ sâ	ሤ sê	ሥ s, sĭ, sĕ	ሦ so
ረ ra	ሩ ru	ሪ ri	ራ râ	ሬ rê	ር r, rĭ, rĕ	ሮ ro
ሰ sa	ሱ su	ሲ si	ሳ sâ	ሴ sê	ስ s, sĭ, sĕ	ሶ so
ሸ sha	ሹ shu	ሺ shi	ሻ shâ	ሼ shê	ሽ sh, shĭ, shĕ	ሾ sho
ቀ qa	ቁ qu	ቂ qi	ቃ qâ	ቄ qê	ቅ q, qĭ, qĕ	ቆ qo
በ ba	ቡ bu	ቢ bi	ባ bâ	ቤ bê	ብ b, bĭ. bĕ	ቦ bo
ተ ta	ቱ tu	ቲ ti	ታ tâ	ቴ tê	ት t, tĭ, tĕ	ቶ to
ቸ tcha	ቹ tchu	ቺ tchi	ቻ tchâ	ቼ tchê	ች tch, tchĭ, tchĕ	ቾ tcho
ኀ kha	ኁ khu	ኂ khi	ኃ khâ	ኄ khê	ኅ kh, khĭ, khĕ	ኆ kho
ነ na	ኑ nu	ኒ ni	ና nâ	ኔ nê	ን n, nĭ, nĕ	ኖ no
ኘ ña (gna)	ኙ ñu	ኚ ñi	ኛ ñâ	ኜ ñê	ኝ ñ, ñĭ, ñĕ	ኞ ño
አ ’a	ኡ ’au	ኢ ’ai	ኣ ’â	ኤ ’ê	እ ’, ’ĭ, ’ĕ	ኦ ’o
ከ ka	ኩ ku	ኪ ki	ካ kâ	ኬ kê	ክ k, kĭ, kĕ	ኮ ko
ኸ k^{h}a	ኹ k^{h}u	ኺ k^{h}i	ኻ k^{h}â	ኼ k^{h}ê	ኽ k^h, k^{h}ĭ, k^{h}ĕ	ኾ k^{h}o
ወ wa	ዉ wu	ዊ wi	ዋ wâ	ዌ wê	ው w, wĭ, wĕ	ዎ wo
ዐ ‘a	ዑ ‘u	ዒ ‘i	ዓ ‘â	ዔ ‘ê	ዕ ‘, ‘ĭ, ‘ĕ	ዖ ‘o
ዘ za	ዙ zu	ዚ zi	ዛ zâ	ዜ zê	ዝ z, zĭ, zĕ	ዞ zô
ዠ dza	ዡ dzu	ዢ dzi	ዣ dzâ	ዤ djê	ዥ dz, dzĭ, dzĕ	ዦ dzo
የ ya	ዩ yu	ዪ yi	ያ yâ	ዬ yê	ይ y, yĭ, yĕ	ዮ yo
ደ da	ዱ du	ዲ di	ዳ dâ	ዴ dê	ድ d, dĭ, dĕ	ዶ do
ጀ dga	ጁ dgu	ጂ dgi	ጃ dgâ	ጄ dgê	ጅ dg, dgĭ, dgĕ	ጆ dgo
ገ ga	ጉ gu	ጊ gi	ጋ gâ	ጌ gê	ግ g, gĭ, gĕ	ጎ go
ጠ ṭa	ጡ ṭu	ጢ ṭi	ጣ ṭâ	ጤ ṭê	ጥ ṭ, ṭĭ, ṭĕ	ጦ ṭo
ጨ ṭcha	ጩ ṭchu	ጪ ṭchi	ጫ tchâ	ጬ tchê	ጭ tch, tchĭ, tchĕ	ጮ tcho
ጰ pa	ጱ pu	ጲ pi	ጳ pâ	ጴ pê	ጵ p, pĭ, pĕ	ጶ po
ጸ ፀ ṣa	ጹ ፁ ṣu	ጺ ፂ ṣi	ጻ ፃ ṣâ	ጼ ፄ ṣê	ጽ ፅ ṣ, sĭ, sĕ	—
ፈ fa	ፉ fu	ፊ fi	ፋ fâ	ፌ fê	ፍ f, fĭ, fĕ	ፎ fo
ፐ pa	ፑ pu	ፒ pi	ፓ pâ	ፔ pê	ፕ p pĭ, pĕ	ፖ po

Amharic Diphthongs.

ቈ qua	—	ቊ qui	ቋ quâ	ቌ quê	ቍ quĭ, quĕ	—
ኈ khua	—	ኊ khui	ኋ khuâ	ኌ khuê	ኍ khuĭ, khuĕ	—
ኰ k^{h}ua	—	ኲ kui	ኳ kuâ	ኴ kuê	ኵ kuĭ, kuĕ	—
ጐ gua	—	ጒ gui	ጓ guâ	ጔ guâ	ጕ guĭ, guĕ	—

THE PERSIAN CUNEIFORM ALPHABET.

A	𐎠	TH	𐎰	RA	𐎼
I	𐎡	DA	𐎭	RU	𐎽
U	𐎢	DI	𐎮	V	𐎺
ʿKA	𐎣	DU	𐎯	VI	𐎻
KU (QU)	𐎤	NA (I)	𐎴	S	𐎿
KH	𐎧	NU	𐎵	SH	𐏁
GA (GI)	𐎥	P	𐎱	Z	𐏀
GU	𐎦	B	𐎲	H	𐏃
C (TCH)	𐎨	M	𐎶	F	𐎳
J	𐎩	MI	𐎷	T	𐎬
DJ	𐎪	MU	𐎸	TR	𐏂
T	𐎫	Y	𐎹	𐏐 sign for division between words.	

 A — A 

a , in some respects = Heb. א.

a , an emphatic particle; 
, Peasant 181; ,
Peasant 180; Peasant B.I. 125; 
, Peasant 224. It seems to be used sometimes to mark a quotation like ሰ in Ethiopic (እፈቅደሰ: Brit. Mus. Orient. No. 678, Fol. III*a*, 1).

a , Rev. 12, 17, = , to come.

a , Berlin 2296, estate, farm.

a-t 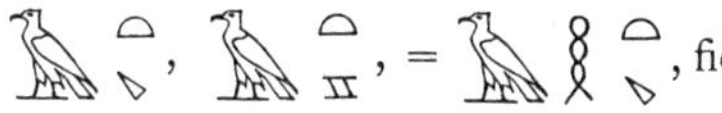, field.

a , Westcar 9, 16; 12, 25 . . . .

at , Litanie, p. 85, to bring forth.

aa = a-t 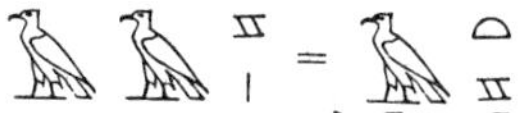, field, ground, territory, region; var. .

at, aat , staff, stick, stave.

aat , back.

aaa , U. 321, 535, T. 294 . . . .

aaā , to sleep, slumber; var. .

aaḥ-t , field; Copt. ⲓⲁϩ, ⲓⲟϩⲉ, ⲓⲱϩⲉ, ⲉⲓⲱϩⲉ.

aash , B.D. (Saïte) 115, 2, a god of slaughter; var. .

aati , be strong, hostile.

aati , enemy.

a-[t] , N. 920, the uraeus of Horus.

aȧu , to come.

aȧu , stick, staff, pole.

aȧ , see .

aȧr ,
, to tie, to bind, to restrain, to keep in restraint, to oppress.

aȧs , bile, gall; var. .

aȧsb , seat, throne, something fixed; compare יָשַׁב.

aā , to beget.

aāā 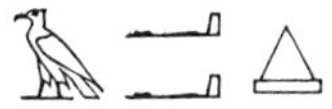, grave, tomb; varr. 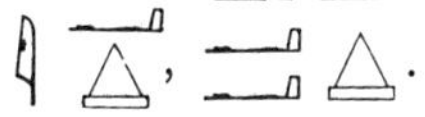.

aāu [illegible], U. 564, the hands; see [illegible].

aāā [illegible], Rev. 11, 131, to come.

aāāu [illegible], Lit. 17, journeyings, those who travel.

aāā [illegible], to sleep, slumber.

aāā [illegible],
[illegible], to punish, to do harm to some-one.

aāā [illegible],
[illegible], to plaster, to build, to bespatter, to make a charge against.

aāāu [illegible]
[illegible], Anastasi I, 28, 6 . . . .

aāā-t [illegible], Israel Stele 22.

aāā-t [illegible], vase, vessel, measure; plur. [illegible],
[illegible].

aāā , , , , , Rec. 14, 41, foreigner, interpreter (?).

aāā-tȧ , A.Z. 46, 143; , Rec. 14, 42, foreigner, barbarian.

aāiā , Thes. 1203, to extinguish, to put out a fire.

aāu , , case for a book; , tool-case; , case for arms (Lacau).

aāb-t , , , Rev. 16, 109, , , IV, 510; Excom. Stele 8; A.Z. 1908, 70; opposition, resistance, vexations, entreaty, calamity, ruin.

aāābu , , , , cup, bowl, vase, pail, measure.

aāābu , the little vase for incense which is attached to the handle of the censer.

aāfi , Ȧmen. 6, 15, 15, 9, a repulsive man.

aāān , , , , ape; plur. ; Copt. ⲉⲛ.

Aāni , B.D. (Saïte), 5, 5, the Ape-god.

Aāānu , the Ape-god Thoth.

aān (?) for , interpreter, foreigner.

aās , a weapon.

Ai , Ṭuat X, an ass-headed god; see .

ai , stalled ox.

air , , , stag; Heb. אַיָּל, Copt. ⲉⲓⲉⲟⲩⲗ, Arab. إيال, Assyr. *ailu*.

aish , Rev. 12, 44, truce; Copt. ⲉⲓϣⲉ.

aiq , Rev. 12, 45, reed, bulrush; var. .

ai-[t] , Rec. 36, 203, , Jour. As. 1908, 310, (?) , calamity, trouble, prejudice = .

ait , a kind of bread, or cake.

au , U. 390, , P. 336, , , , , to be long, to be large, to be wide, to be spacious; Copt. ⲱⲟⲩ. = the height of a spirit, B.D. 109, 8.

au, aui , , , , length, totality, all, throughout.

au-t , , length, largeness; , length of the earth; , , length of eternity; , , advanced in years; , advanced in iniquity.

au :— , T. 339, , N. 626, full of days; , Rec. 27, 219, long of stride; , P. 187, M. 349, N. 902, long of foot; , P. 215, abundant in offerings; , P. 602, wide of tail (a name of Isis); N. 802, 1155, long-haired.

au-t ȧb , dilatation of heart, swelling of heart, pleasure, joy, gladness; , A.Z. 1906, 127;  , "his heart was glad to do," Stele of the Dream, 18; , a god.

au-t ȧb , medicine for the heart (?).

au , to make an offering.

au-ā, au-t-ā 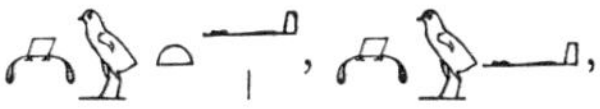 , gift, present, offering, alms, oblation, *i.e.*, "that of the open hand"; plur. 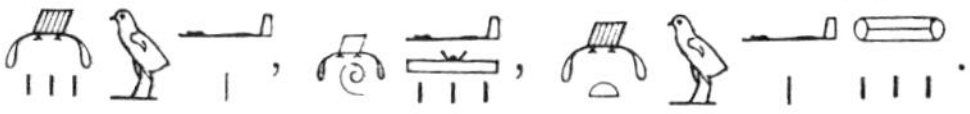.

Au-ā , the god of gifts, B.D. 99, 29; 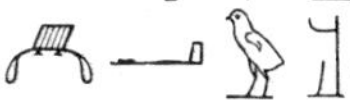, Ṭuat IV, a title of Horus and Thoth.

Au-t-ā , the name of a serpent on the royal crown.

Au-āu-Uthes (?) 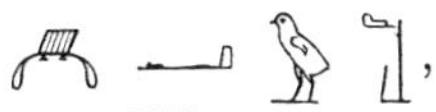, Ṭuat IV, a name of Thoth; see **Uthesu.**

au-ḥer , Peasant 271, a man of broad face (*i.e.*, sight).

Au-t-maātiu-kheru-maāt  , Ṭuat VI, a group of gods who gave alms when on earth.

Au-matu (?) , Ṭuat III, a god in the Herer Boat.

aui  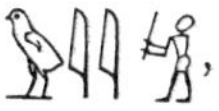, to stretch out, extend, IV, 498, 612.

au , Rec. 30, 187, , Rec. 26, 65, , to be strong, violent.

auit 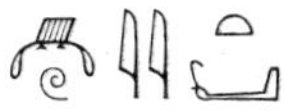, Rougé I.H., pl. 256, something promulgated, a decree.

aut , a kind of ochre.

au-t, Rec. 4, 121, bread, unguent.

au-t, U. 508, , , IV, 173, food, offering, sepulchral meals, supplies of all kinds.

au , Rec. 20, 42, splendour.

aui, Rev. 11, 166;  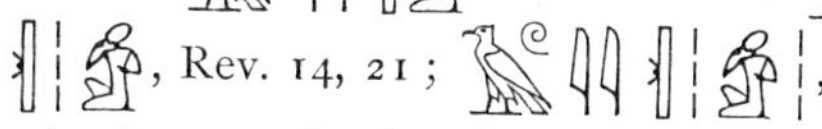, Rev. 14, 21; , glory, splendour, words of praise; Copt. ⲉⲟⲟⲩ.

auau , U. 539, T. 296, to rejoice.

au-t, rays of light, something bright.

au 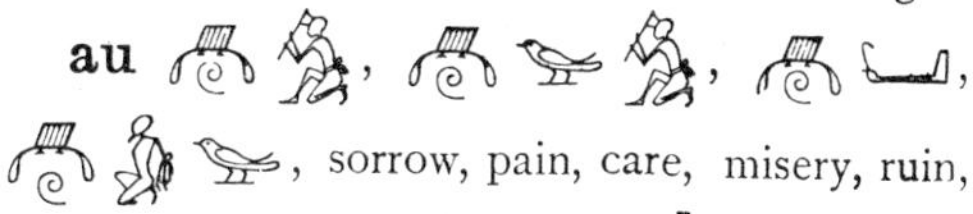, sorrow, pain, care, misery, ruin, sadness, the opposite of 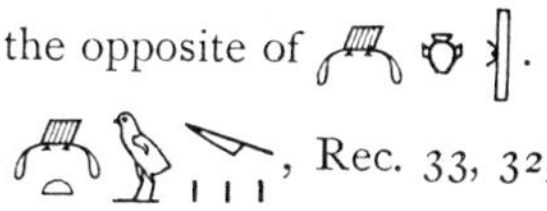.

au-t, Rec. 33, 32, slaughters, animals slaughtered for food.

au 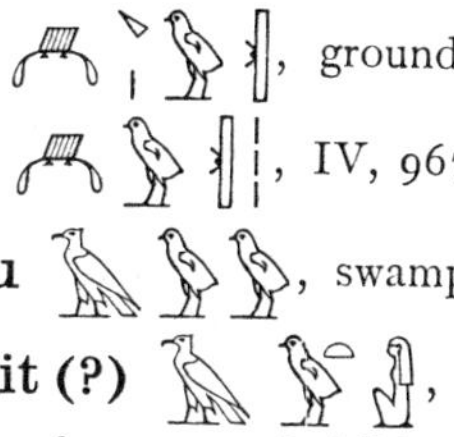, ground, region.

au, IV, 967, administration.

auu, swamp, marsh.

Auit (?), Wört. 32, 478, a goddess of nurses and children.

au , B.D. 130, 13, = , children.

au 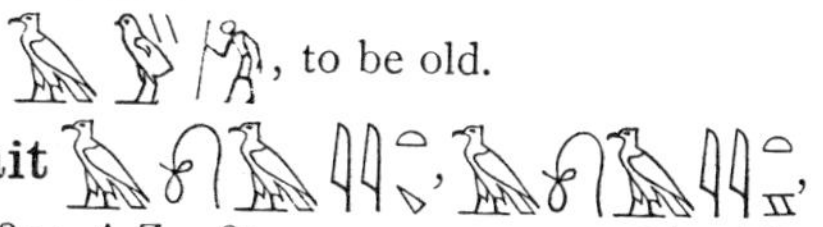, to be old.

auait, Supp. 383; A.Z. 1874, 90, a measure of land (?)

auas , to haul, to drag with a rope.

aui, to rebel, be violent, wicked.

auȧ 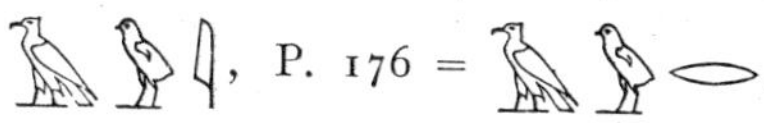, P. 176 = , N. 916.

auȧu , dog, jackal; compare ابن آوى.

aur , terror(?), restraint, violence.

aurf (?) , net; Copt. ⲁⲗⲟⲟⲩⲉ.

ausu , scales, balance.

ausek (ask) 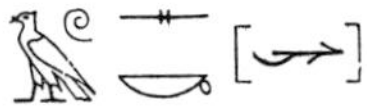, sceptre, stick, staff, rod.

ausha 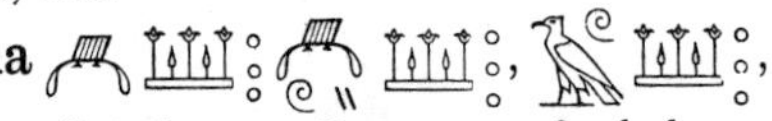, Wört. 144; Suppl. 514; Rev. 11, 138; balsam, incense, unguent of a light yellow colour.

ab-t , Rec. 34, 177, , gift, offering, sacrifice.

abu , elephant; plur. ; Copt. ⲉⲃ (in ⲉⲃⲣⲟⲥ).

abu , Suppl. 514;  (or ), elephant grass, or balsam.

ab, abu 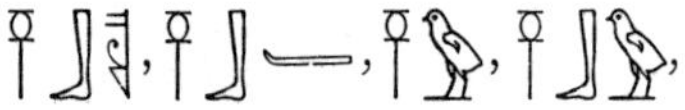, 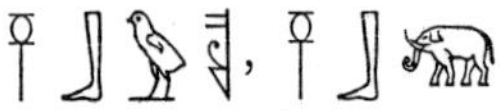, tusk of ivory; plur. 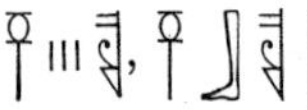, Pap. Koller 38; , ; var. , IV, 1149; 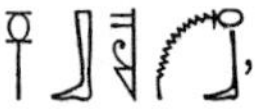, pure, *i.e.*, not rotten, ivory, IV, 329; ivory tusks and tooth,  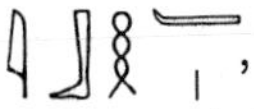, IV, 373.

Abt , the town of Abydos personified as a goddess.

ab , variegated, marked with different colours, streaked, striped; 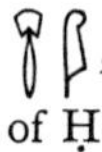, having feathers of different colours, a title of Ḥeru-Beḥuṭet.

abu , Rec. 30, 188, leopard.

ab, abi, abit , , Pap. Koller 4, 2, , leopard; leopard of the South, 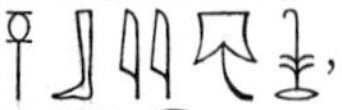, leopard of the North, 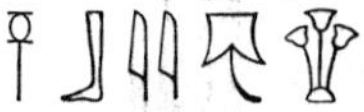; a leopard six cubits long, and four cubits in girth,  .

Abit 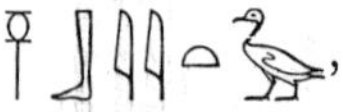, B.D. 76, 2; 104, 4, the mantis which guided the deceased into the Hall of Osiris; see  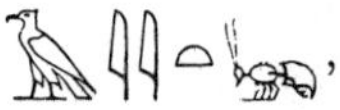, and .

ab , be thirsty; see [illegible].

ab [illegible], [illegible], Dream Stele 4; B.D. 19, 15; [illegible], Dream Stele 14, the left side; see [illegible].

ab [illegible], Hymn of Darius 17, the left eye of Rā.

ab [illegible], to wish for, to desire, to long for; see [illegible], [illegible], [illegible], Pap. Koller 3, 2, in order to, wishing to; compare אבה.

abeb, abebu [illegible], [illegible], [illegible] [illegible], to love, to wish for, to desire, to long for.

abeb-t [illegible], [illegible], IV, 975, 1092, wish, desire.

abu-t [illegible], kindly disposition.

abut [illegible], [illegible], [illegible], [illegible], Rec. 31, 26, [illegible], [illegible], forefathers, grandparents, ancestors, kinsfolk; [illegible], Hymn of Darius 19; compare אֲבוֹת.

ab [illegible], [illegible], to stop, to cease.

abu [illegible], [illegible], cessation; [illegible] [illegible], ceaselessly.

ab, abu [illegible], Edict 26, [illegible], [illegible], to brand; see [illegible], L.D. III, 184, 36.

ab , Rev. 11, 180, father; Heb. אָב.

aba-t , Rev. 14, 20, light; compare .

aban , Rev. 12, 69, alum; Copt. ⲱⲃⲉⲛ.

ab-lān-āthān-ālbā 
, Rev. 11, 180, a god. Gnostic ΑΒΛΑΘΑΝΑΛΒΑ.

abaḥi 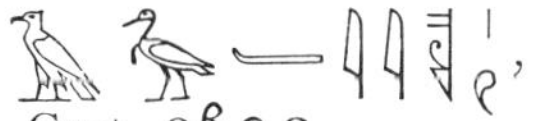, Rev. 13, 21, tooth; Copt. ⲟⲃϩⲉ.

abakh , to forget; Copt. ⲱⲃϣ.

abash , Jour. As. 1908, 267, , to forget; Copt. ⲱⲃϣ.

Abaqer , Mar. M.D. 49, Rec. 36, 86, Sphinx 1, 89; Alt. K. 3, name of a Libyan dog of Ȧntef-āa, the Slughi, كَلْب سلوقِيّ.

abatu , Rev. service, √עבד.

abit , Mar. Karn. 53, 35. . . . . . .

abmer , , pyramid tomb.

Abenti , Ṭuat I, a serpent-guide of the Boat of Ȧf.

abekh , , IV, 365, to mix with, to unite with, to penetrate, to enter in among, enter battle; see .

abkhekh , T. 385, M. 402, to clap the hands.

abs , Annales 9, 156, a kind of plant.

abka , see .

abt 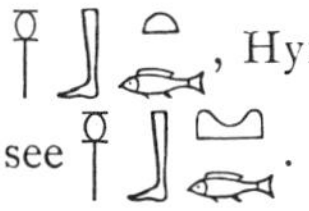, Hymn of Darius 11, a kind of fish; see .

abṭ , to shut, to bolt in.

abṭu , Pap. Ani, 1, 15, a mythological fish.

Aparius  = 'Απελλαῖος, a Macedonian name of a month, the Roman December.

Apuranițes 
 = 'Απολλωνίεης.

apḥ , Leyden Pap. 8, 13. . . . . .

apsu , birds.

apṭ , L.D. III, 65*a*, Rec. 4, 35, to flutter, to alight as a bird.

apṭ , goose, duck; plur. 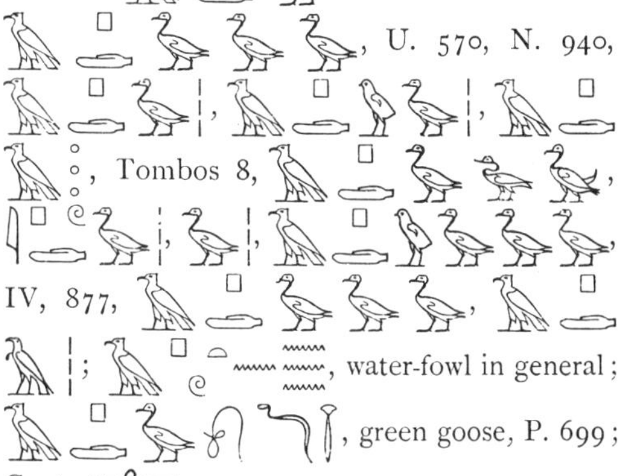, U. 570, N. 940, Tombos 8, IV, 877, water-fowl in general; green goose, P. 699; Copt. ⲱⲃⲧ.

apṭ , IV, 1047, staff (?).

af 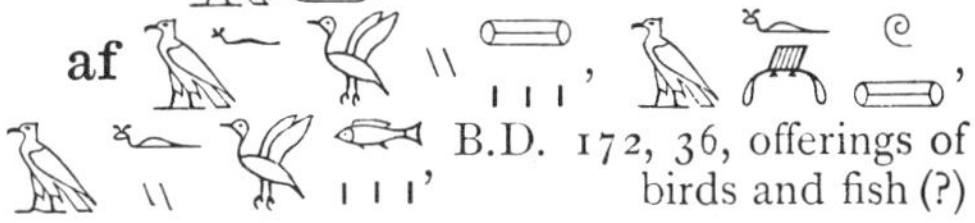, B.D. 172, 36, offerings of birds and fish (?)

af-t , P.S.B. 14, 232, gift, offering, present.

af , Hymn of Darius 38, might, strength (?)

afa , glutton, greedy man.

afa-[t] , greed, gluttony.

afau (?) , a kind of balsam, or medicine.

af, afau (?) 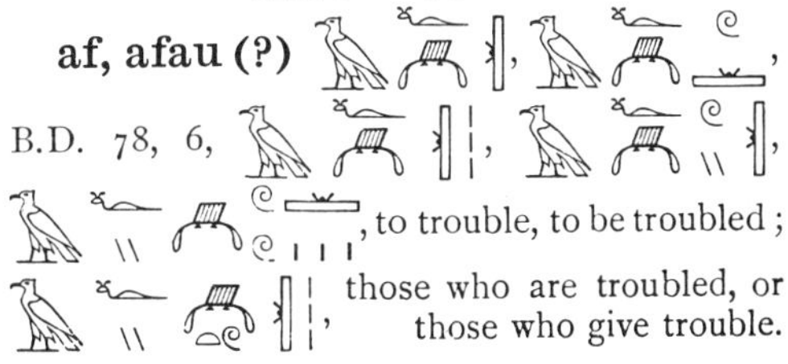, B.D. 78, 6, to trouble, to be troubled; those who are troubled, or those who give trouble.

afaf, to praise, to rejoice, to exult.

afit, flame, fire.

afu, to injure, to inflict an injury.

Afu, Ṭuat VII, the "Worm" Kheti.

afer, to burn, to be hot.

afri Verbum Voc., smoke, hot vapour.

aft, Rev. 13, 38, foot soldier (?)

afṭ, to bend the leg, to march, part of the leg.

am =, not.

am, amu, U. 177, , Rec. 3, 46, , , , , , ; to seize, to grasp.

amm, M. 742, , Rec. 31, 17, , , A.Z. 1905, 36, , to seize, to grasp.

amm-t, grasp, fist.

am, IV, 158, to understand, to know.

amam, Merenptaḥ 2, to know, to understand.

am, Ȧmen. 9, 19, to swallow.

am (read ḥem ?), Jour. As. 1908, 305, artisan.

am, to grieve, lament, to mourn.

amiu, mourners.

am, , to burn, to consume.

amm, , Rec. 16, 109, to burn, to consume.

am, amut, flame, fire; plur. , .

amait, island (?), land.

ama = , to see.

amȧ, ami, , , , , , , , , to mix together, to compound a medicine, to rub down drugs.

amȧ-t, something rubbed down, or crushed.

Amȧ, Tomb of Seti I, one of the 75 forms of Rā.

Amȧ-ȧmi-ta, Tomb of Seti I, one of the 75 forms of Rā (No. 63).

amȧu, Rec. 11, 153 . . . . .

amā-t (am-t), , , meal, pottage.

ami-t, Rev., the interior, nature; , a good disposition.

Amu, Ṭuat 11, a dawn-god.

ames, amsu, N. 803, , P. 169, , P. 614, M. 781, N. 1138, , , , , , , , , , , , , , , , rod of authority, sceptre, staff; , T. 14, two sceptres; plur. .

ames, , , A.Z. 1908, 17, the amulet of the sceptre.

ames-ȧb; Wört. 14.

ams-t = , liver.

Amtit, foreign tribes and peoples.

ani, Rev. 12, 19 = , to remove, to put aside.

an-t, Rev., removal.

anpa, Rev. 13, 14, an interrogative particle = .

ar, , be captured, be put in restraint, to strangle, to shut up, be netted.

arut, Rec. 31, 11.

ar, disgrace.

ar-t, hair, tress, lock of hair.

ar, , Rev. 13, 41, schoenus; var. .

ara, Rev. 11, 157, 12, 41, , Rev. 11, 161, , Rev. 12, 27, , Rev. 12, 32, , Rev. 12, 40, to go up, to embark in a boat, to bring, to be high; Copt. ⲱⲗ.

arar, , , Rev. 12, 23, 41, high, exalted; Copt. ⲱⲗ.

arri, Rev. 12, 113, vine; plur. , ; Copt. ⲉⲗⲟⲟⲗⲉ.

arb, Rev. 13, 63, to besiege; Copt. ⲱⲣⲃ̄.

arpsa-t, a kind of cake.

arf, Rev., rest, repose, death; Copt. ⲱⲣϥ̄.

Arsaṭnikus, , Rec. 33, 6, Aristonikos.

Arsinfau, II, 57, Arsinoë.

Arq-ḥeḥ, Rev. 11, 179 = Αλχαι.

ark-t, Rev. 5, 94, froth, foam, aphronitrum; Copt. ⲁⲗⲓϫⲓ.

arg, Rev. 11, 169, a member of the body; Copt. ⲁⲗⲁϫ.

Artakhshassha, , , A.Z. 49, 80, Artaxerxes.

Artakhshshs, Artaxerxes; varr. , , Pers. , Babyl. .

Artikastika, , B.D. (Saïte) 165, 3, a form of Åmen.

arṭȧ, Rev., to be safe, sure, security; Copt. ⲱⲣϫ.

artcha, Rev. 11, 157; Copt. ⲱⲣϫ.

ah, , , , , , , Rev. 13, 29, , , , Rev. 11, 123, pain, grief, trouble, loss, sorrow, poverty, misery, debility, destitution, sadness, ruin, woe; Copt. ⲁϩⲉ.

ahi, Rev., trouble, misery.

ahu, Peasant 249, a disturber, one who causes trouble.

ah, aha, Hymn of Darius 23, , cow, any cow-goddess.

Ahait, , , , L.D. 4, 82B, B.D. 162–4, (1) a form of Hathor; (2) wife of Osiris the Bull-god; and (3) mother of a Horus.

ahai, ahi, , , interjection O!

ahai, , Mar. Karn. 55, 62, camp; Heb. אֹהֶל (?)

ahi , to go (?), to march (?)

Ahit , B.D. (Saïte) 142, 5, 22, a goddess.

ahem , Rec. 16, 109, to advance.

ahem-t  , incense, unguent.

aheṭ , Rec. 16, 108, to groan, to grieve.

ahṭu, Rec. 32, 216, weak, powerless, grief.

aḥ-t , field, land, acre, ploughed or cultivated land; plur. 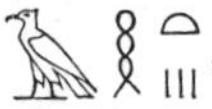, 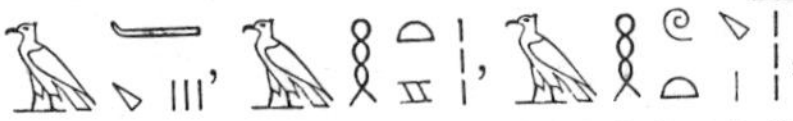, Åmen. 7, 14; Copt. ⲉⲓⲱϩⲉ, ⲉⲓⲟⲟϩⲉ, ⲓⲁϩ, ⲓⲟϩⲓ, ⲓⲱϩⲉ.

aḥ-t stat 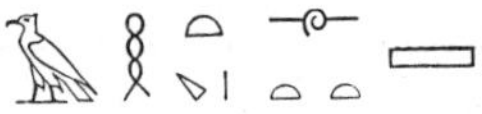, Thes. 1288, arura.

Aḥut-en-Åmentit , Ṭuat V, the estates of the blessed in Åment.

aḥ-t 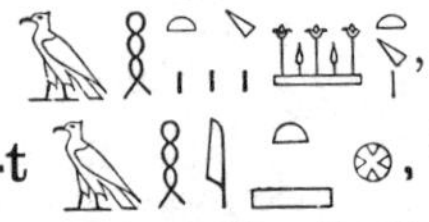, L.D. III, 229C, flax fields.

aḥȧ-t, the offering of a field.

aḥ-t-nu-ȧrr  Rec. 6, 7, vineyard; Copt. ⲓⲁϩⲁⲗⲟⲗⲓ.

aḥ-ḥet 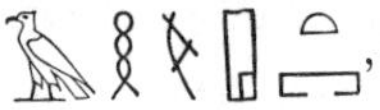, Akten. p. 340, the pit, or shaft, of a tomb.

aḥ 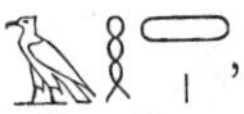, N. 281; , N. 281, 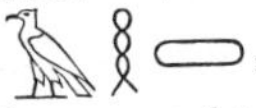, IV, 171, 754, a herb (?), a plant (?), a vegetable (?), pot-herb (?), a kind of bread, or cake.

aḥ, aḥu , meal, pottage; 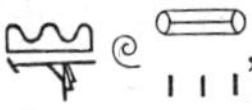, food.

aḥ-t , a kind of medicine.

aḥ , Rev. 11, 139, 12, 33, 50, evil, grief, disaster, prejudice; var. .

aḥ-t , entreaty, petition, prayer.

aḥ-ti 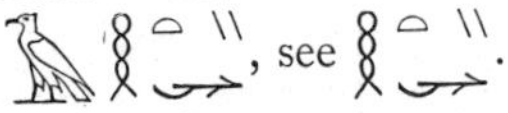, see.

aḥ-ti 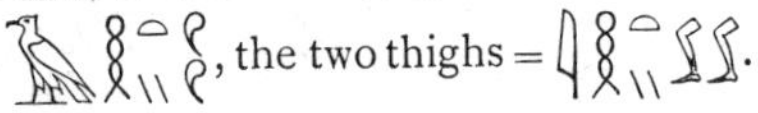, the two thighs =.

aḥaḥ , U. 50, to lighten (?)

Aḥa, Aḥu , P. 204, M. 331, , N. 850, Hh. 566, 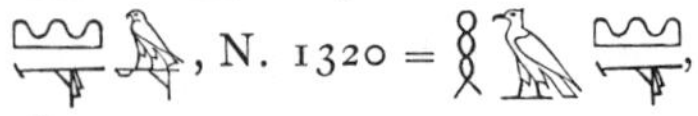, N. 1320 =, M. 699, , IV, 263, B.D. 40, 6, Rec. 29, 157, a form of Menu.

aḥā 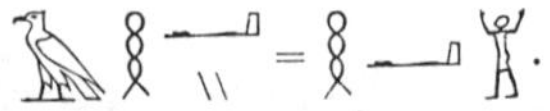.

aḥnu 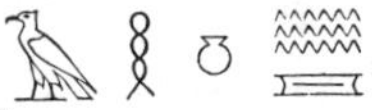, Rec. 12, 93 = , canal.

aḥs 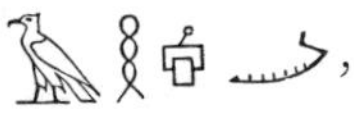, Rec. 13, 42, to harvest, to reap.

Aḥs 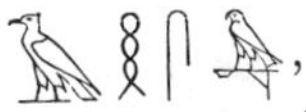, P. 668, the name of a Sûdânî god; varr. , M. 779, 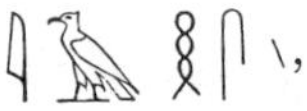, P. 200.

Akh-t , the first season of the year; see **Aakh-t**.

akh, M. 683, Rec. 26, 74, to bloom, to blossom, become green, green.

akhi [illegible], reed, water-plant; Heb. אָחוּ, Gen. xli, 2.

akh-t [illegible], N. 996, watered, or irrigated, land.

akhakh [illegible], to become green, to put forth shoots, to blossom.

akhakhu [illegible], Rec. 31, 28, [illegible], Åmen. 6, 9, [illegible], Rec. 15, 161, blossoms, flowers.

akhakh [illegible], P. 340, M. 641; [illegible], flowers (of heaven), *i.e.*, stars.

akhakh [illegible], night, darkness.

akh-t [illegible], thing, affair, business, matter of the day; plur. [illegible], Rec. 1, 48, Åmen. 8, 7, [illegible].

akhakh , bone; plur.  [illegible].

akh , Peasant 97; A.Z. 1866, 100, to withdraw an arrow from a quiver.

akhakh , Hh. 483, the tackle of a boat; var. akhut , Hh. 481.

akhā , to enter, to go.

akhā , , to carve, to engrave, to scrape, to shave off.

akhā-t 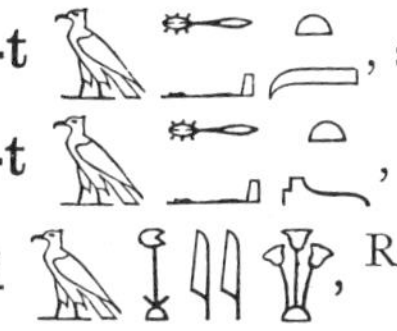, scar.

akhā-t, a disease of the womb.

akhai, Rev. 12, 46, to give quarter.

Akhabi 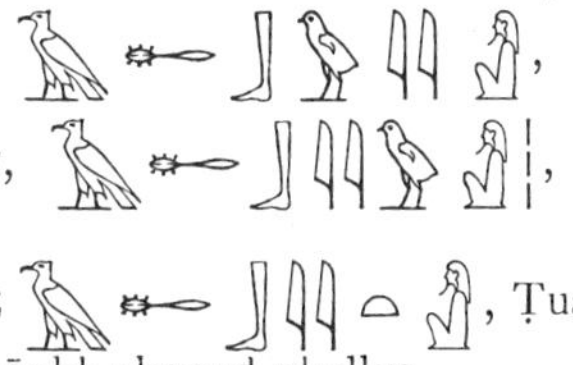, B.D. (Saïte) 153, 5, B.D. 153A, 11.

Akhabit, Ṭuat II, a god with an ānkh-shaped phallus.

Akhabit-ānkh-em-ṭesheri  , Denderah 1, 30, Ombos II, 2, p. 134, a goddess of the dead.

akhaḥ-t 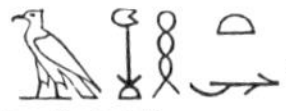, Rec. 13, 124, reed, papyrus; Copt. ⲁϫⲓ.

akhu , splendour, light, brightness; see.

akhu , U. 570, M. 823, light, beings of light; see [illegible].

akhu , U. 590, divine spirits; see **ȧakhu.**

Akhkhu , B.D. 153, 8 (Saïte), a god of vegetation.

akhef ..........

As-t, Rec. 30, 193, ll. 3, 4, A.Z. Bd. 46, 108, Isis; see **Ȧst** [illegible].

as , Rev. 12, 48,  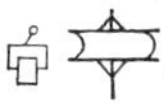, to be light, speedy. Coptic ⲁⲥⲓⲁⲓ (?)

as, asu , Peasant 277, , Rec. 12, 48, , Rec. 8, 135, , R.E. 6, 28, 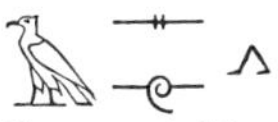, to make haste, to hurry to, to flow quickly, to run, to attack; Copt. ⲓⲱⲥ; 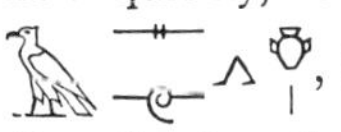, Rec. 13, 21, to judge hurriedly; , hasting with swift feet.

as-t , , Jour. As. 1908, 268, haste, hurry.

ast , hasters away, fugitives; running water.

asu, birds.

as , N. 296, 300, an offering.

as, Mar. Karn. 53, 35......

as, Hearst Papyrus, VIII, 14, Rec. 30, 183, , Tombos Stele 8, gall, gall-duct or gall-bladder (?), filth.

as , old (?); Copt. ⲁⲥ (?)

as-ti , testicles.

asi, Rec. 14, 69, payment, punishment; Copt. ⲟⲥⲉ.

asaka (ask) , Jour. As. 1908, 302, to delay; Copt. ⲱⲥⲕ.

asu , Hh. 230.......

asb , to burn, to consume by fire.

asbi[t] , flame, fire; plur. [illegible].

asbu , to reduce to powder, to crush.

Asbit , M. 237, N. 615, Denderah IV, 81, a fire-goddess.

Asbit 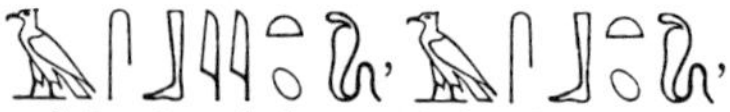, the goddess of the fourth hour of the day.

Asb , B.D. 69, 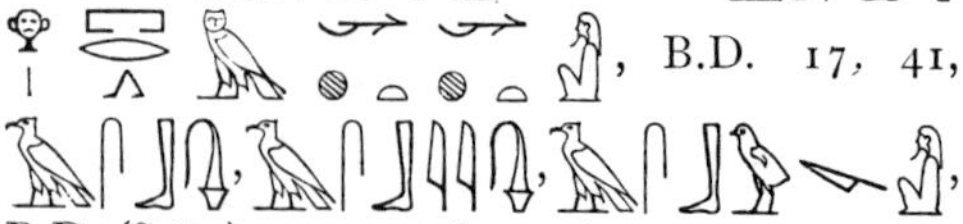, B.D. 17, 41, B.D. (Saïte) 147, 7, a fire-god.

asem , P. 375 = , a sceptre.

asen , Rev. 13, 111, to breathe easily or freely.

aseh , drum.

asekh 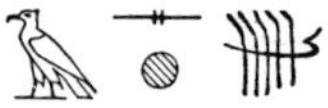, M. 224, N. 129, , to reap, sickle; Copt. ⲱϩⲥ ⲱⲥϭ.

asekh , Décrets 34, slaughter chamber (?)

asq 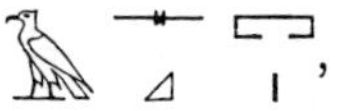, Rev. 14, 19, delay; Copt. ⲱⲥⲕ.

ast , clay, earth, chalk (?); , potter's clay.

ast , Jour. As. 1908, 300, ground, earth; Copt. ⲥⲏⲧ.

Asther 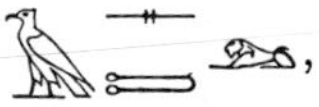, Annales III, 178, star; Gr. Ἀστήρ.

asṭa  (?), to tremble; see .

asṭeb 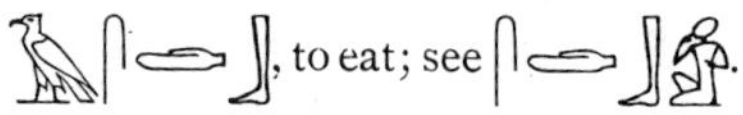, to eat; see .

ash 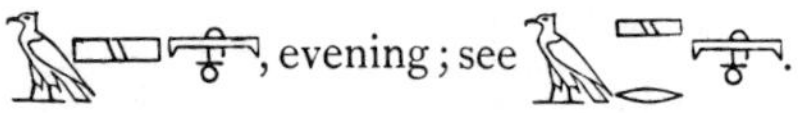, evening; see .

ash, ash-t , dog, jackal; var. .

ash , an offering made by fire.

ashash-t , IV, 482, = , flower.

asha , to scatter [sand 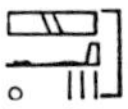].

ashȧḥu 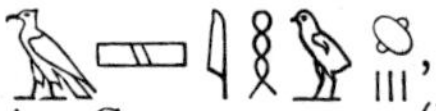, B.D. (Saïte) 42, 21, paralytic; Copt. ϣⲟⲩϩⲉ (?)

Ashu , B.D. 95, 2, a water-god.

ashu 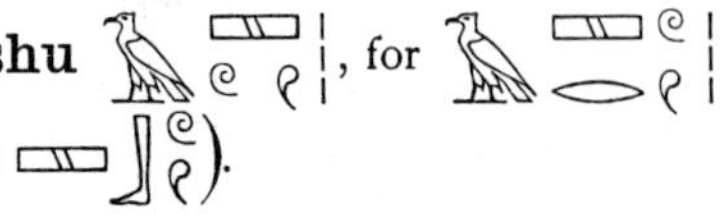, for , roast (meat).

Ashbu , B.D. 144, a fire-god in the 5th Ārit.

ashep 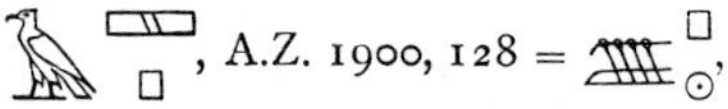, A.Z. 1900, 128 = , day, light.

asher , to burn, to melt, to roast, to try by fire.

asher-t 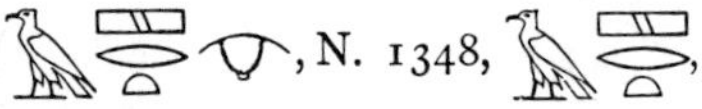, N. 1348, , U. 124, 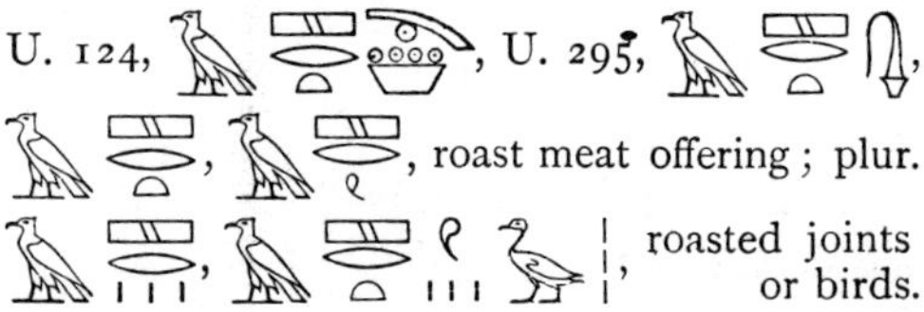, U. 295, , roast meat offering; plur. , roasted joints or birds.

asher , , evening; see .

ashṭu , plots of ground, estates.

aq, aqa , Peasant 259, 295, , to fail, to be weak, to be weary, to be tired, diminish, come to an end, be exhausted, perish, die; , to run aground; 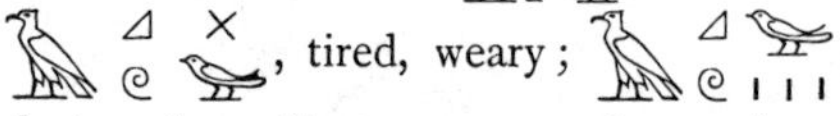, tired, weary; , ruin, destruction; Copt. ⲁⲕⲱ, and ⲁⲕⲟ in ⲧⲁⲕⲟ.

aqu , Peasant 1116B, 46, 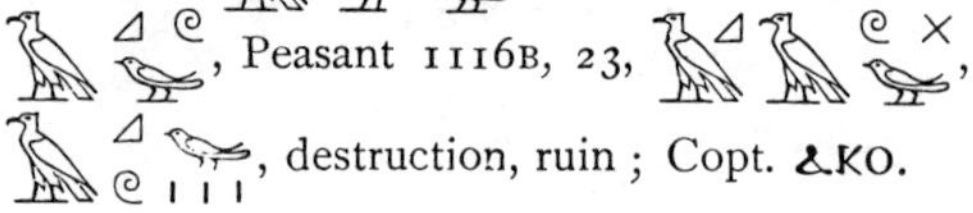, Peasant 1116B, 23, , , destruction, ruin; Copt. ⲁⲕⲟ.

Aq-t-er-pet , P. 645, name of the Celestial Ladder.

aqa , steps, height, a high place ; see .

aqa , filth, vomit =  .

aqau , a house-boat ; Arab. ذهبية.

Aqan , B.D. 99, Int. 4, the name of a god.

aqu (?) , Hh. 482, part of a boat.

aqb-t , arm, shoulder ; see .

Aqbut , Tombos Stele 4, a foreign people.

Aqbi , Book of Gates III, a serpent-god.

aqem , A.Z. 1898, 49, , Rev. 14, 10, to be sad ; Copt. ⲟⲕⲉⲙ.

aqen  ; see 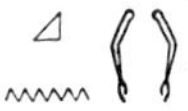.

aqers-t , tomb ; see .

aqretchna , IV, 669, a weapon, axe ; Heb. גרזן (?)

aqḥu , Rechnungen 70, , Rec. 29, 165, , Mar. Karn. 42, 22, , to work in wood, to be a carpenter, to hollow out a boat ; 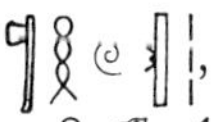, Rec. 21, 91, dressed timber ; caus.  .

aqḥu 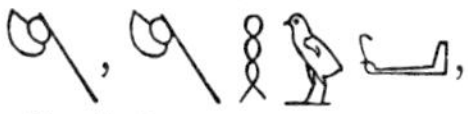, carpenter.

aqḥu 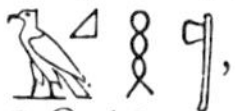, A.Z. 1905, 142,  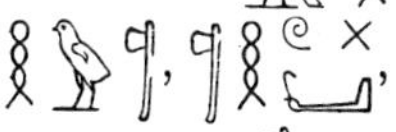, carpenter's adze, axe, battle-axe.

aqḥȧu , axe-men, soldiers.

aqḥ , clay, earth.

aqs , to move, to walk, to go.

aqs, aqs , to tie, to bind ; **aqsu** , bonds, fetters.

Aqeṭqeṭ ,  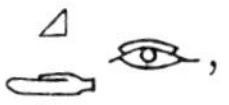, Hh. 101, [illegible], one of seven spirits who guarded Osiris.

ak [illegible], [illegible], to become weak, to feel pain or sorrow, destruction ; Copt. ⲁⲕⲱ.

aku-t [illegible], boils, blains, sores, pustules, any inflamed swelling.

aki-t [illegible], chamber, abode.

akuiu [illegible], Rec. 33, 7, [illegible], L.D. III, 194, 33, [illegible], aliens, foreigners, enemies.

Aker [illegible], U. 498, [illegible], T. 309, [illegible], T. 291, [illegible], U. 461, N. 850, [illegible], [illegible], Rec. 26, 65, [illegible], Rec. 31, 29, an Earth-god, who had a lion's body with a head at each end of it ; Copt. ⲁⲕⲱⲣⲓ.

Akeru [illegible], T. 319, [illegible], Rec. 30, 196, 31, 17, [illegible], N. 1386, [illegible] [illegible], a group of Earth-gods who are said to be the ancestors of Rā and of the Akhabiu-gods, B.D. 153A, 11, 23.

Akriu [illegible], B.D. 108, 13, a group of Earth-goddesses (?)

Akeru-tepu-ā-Akhabiu [illegible] [illegible], B.D. 153A, 11, the ancestor-gods who worked the net for catching souls.

Akeru-tepu-ā-Rā, B.D. 153A, 23, the ancestor-gods of Rā.

akrȧut, wagons; compare עֲגָלוֹת.

Akerta, U. 614, the name of a god.

ag, to lack, to want.

ag, U. 639, plant, shrub; see ; Copt. ⲁⲕⲉ, ⲟⲉⲓⲕ.

agg-t, a plant, a shrub.

agab, the Nile, water-flood, deluge; see .

agap, to destroy, to flood.

agb, U. 193, T. 73, N. 587, 605, , M. 227, , Rec. 26, 77, , the celestial waters, flood, stream, any large mass of water; , T. 56, M. 216; Copt. ⲱϭⲃ.

Agb, N. 706, , B.D. 189, 11, the primeval Water-god.

Agb-ur, P. I. 806, , U. 608, , T. I. 86, , N. 617, , the Great Agb.

agbȧ, U. 395, P. 384; see .

agb, an astronomical term.

ageb, knee; see .

ageb, Metternich Stele 179, to weep, to cry out; caus. .

agebgeb, P. 289, to shiver, to quake.

Agebsen (?), Ṭuat III, a goose-headed god.

at, atu, aṭ, a small portion of time, moment, minute, hour, the time of culmination of some act or emotion; , at this moment; , from hour to hour; , a happy time with the women.

at, B.D. 177, 7 = , not.

atu, , B.D. 154, 18, injury, harm.

at-t, loss, diminution.

at, loss, prejudice.

at, rebel, prisoner.

at, U. 456, P. 182, M. 285, , T. 249, , U. 370, N. 894, violence, wrath.

at, crocodile (?)

at, , evil-doer, enemy; plur. , enemies, fiends.

ati, , , , to be angry, to behave in a beastly manner.

att = , , destitute, poor, possessing nothing; Copt. ⲁⲧ.

ati, , , , Rev. 14, 15, he who is without, who has not, injury; , without failure, infallible.

at-t, a milch cow, cow suckling a calf.

at, Rec. 12, 10, vulva, uterus; Copt. ⲟⲧⲓ.

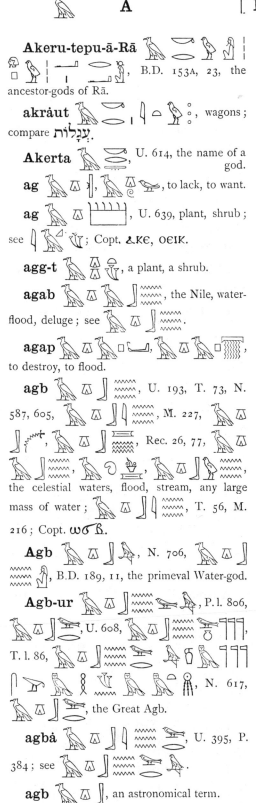

ati-t 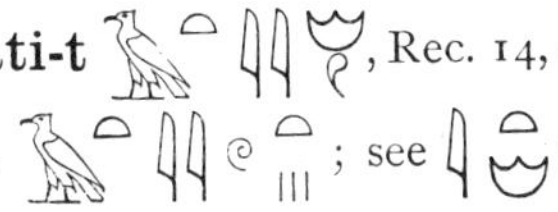, Rec. 14, 2, vulva, uterus ; plur. ; see ; Copt. ΟΤΙ.

at-t , bed, diwân, couch, bier ; var.

atit, atȧut , bed, couch, cushion ; plur.

atit , to nurse, nurse ; see

at-t 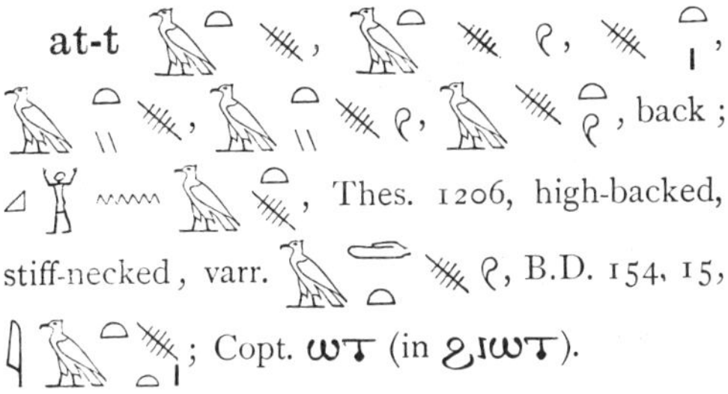, back ; Thes. 1206, high-backed, stiff-necked , varr. B.D. 154, 15, ; Copt. ωτ (in ϩιωτ).

at , standard, perch, resting place of a god or divine statue.

Ata-ra , Cairo Pap. 23, 4, a god in the form of a mummy.

atȧ , T. 200, P. 679, boat.

atȧ 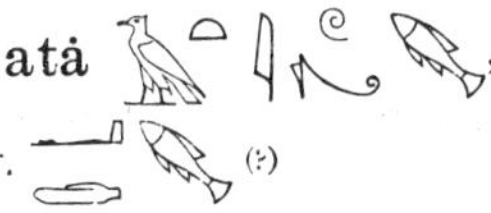, Rev., a kind of fish ; var.

Ati , Tomb Rameses IV, 28, a god.

atita , ministrant (?)

atu , Shipwreck 112, to trouble oneself.

atutu , B.D. 145, 4, 16, a kind of wood.

ateb , land, region.

ateb , sceptre (?)

atep , to load, to be laden ; master of a load, IV, 1076 ; Copt. ωτπ.

atep-t , A.Z. 49, 32, Jour. As. 1908, 282, load, burden ; Peasant 259 ; Copt. ετπω.

atepu , bearers of loads.

atep , chest for clothes.

atef , Rec. 27, 222, 31, 170, a crown of Osiris.

atf  incense, spices, sweet unguents.

atf , a tree.

atf , a cutting tool or instrument.

a-ten , A.Z. 1889, 71.

aten , Rev. 12, 10, ground, earth ; Copt ειτπ.

atr , river plants, papyrus.

atḥ , Rev. 14, 17, to draw a bow =

ath , U. 480, Rec. 26, 233, to nurse, to nourish.

ath-t , bed, couch, stool, chair, canopy.

athu  chair-bearer.

athu , Rec. 27, 85, air, wind.

athp , to load, be laden ; see ; Copt. ωτπ.

athput 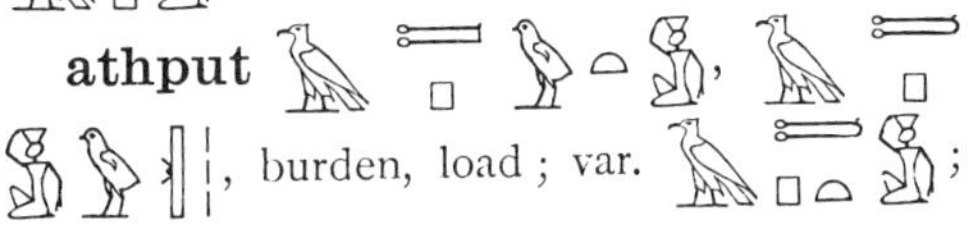, burden, load ; var. ; Copt. ετπω.

Athpi 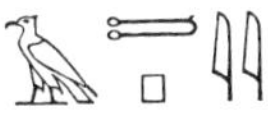, Ṭuat XI, a dawn-god.

aṭ, a small portion of time, moment.

aṭ-t, , back, rump.

aṭ, heart disease (?)

aṭi, , to be wounded, be afflicted.

aṭ-t, , inflammation of the eyes.

aṭ, , , , calamity.

aṭa, Rec. 10, 136, to suffer injury or loss.

aṭ, Rec. 26, 12, 27, 10, 31, 14, , , Rec. 27, 61, , , to be angry, to rage at.

aṭ-t, , Rec. 29, 157, wrath.

aṭu, a man of wrath.

aṭ-ḥa-t (?), a man of wrathful nature.

aṭu, Peasant 181, crocodile.

aṭ-t, to make ready a bed, to prepare (?), Leyden Pap. 9, 1, 14, 2.

aṭ, to burn; , fire, flames.

aṭȧu, B.D. 169, 12, garment, apparel.

Aṭau, Rec. 27, 60, a god.

aṭȧḥ; see .

aṭit, disease of the eyes.

Aṭu, Rec. 27, 220, a class of divine beings.

aṭu, to run, to flee, to make one's escape.

aṭep, , , Ȧmen. 12, 8, to load, be loaded; see .

aṭepu = , geese.

aṭf, a kind of balsam tree.

aṭf, incense.

aṭm, N. 982 . . . .

aṭḥ, , , papyrus swamp; see .

aṭsu, a kind of plant.

Aṭes-ḥeri-she, the herald of the 6th Ārit.

atch, calamity.

atcha, a bad act, wickedness, guile, fraud; Copt. ⲟϫⲓ.

atcha, chip of wood, splinter.

atchait, R.E. 4, 76, fraud, injustice, wickedness; Copt. ⲟϫⲓ.

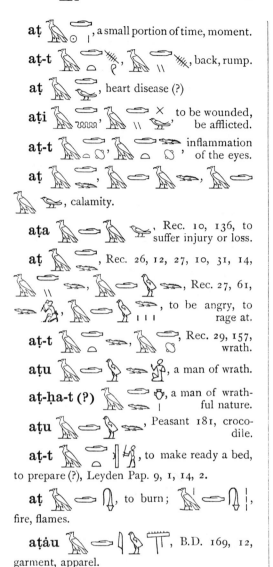

 Ȧ — Ȧ 

ȧ , represents a short sound of **a, e** and **i** in English.

ȧ , Rec. 31, 16, 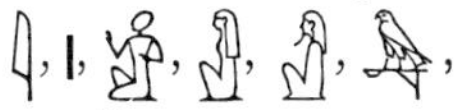, pronominal suffix, 1st person, I, me, my, etc.

ȧ 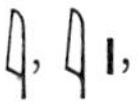, U. 173, T. 333, , P. 825, O, hail! , O my heart!

ȧ , he who, that which.

ȧ .

ȧ , old man.

ȧ  = **ȧu** , to come.

ȧ , P. 643, M. 680, N. 1242, to wash.

ȧ (?) , A.Z. 1908, 16, an amulet.

ȧ , a kind of plant.

Ȧ 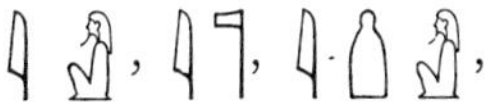, Rec. 30, 71 =  or , Thoth.

ȧa  = יָה in the name 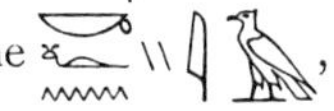, Asien u. E. p. 313, Lieblein Dict. No. 553.

ȧa 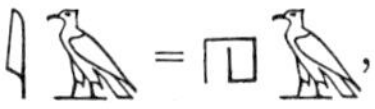, Rec. 32, 84, 34, 182.

ȧa , U. 442, P. 687, 703, N. 669, Rec. 31, 171, glory! praise.

ȧȧȧa , U. 609, acclamation; , Ȧmen. 14, 14, flattery.

ȧȧȧau , cries of joy.

ȧa , to cry out (?)

ȧa-t , moment; see .

ȧa-t , old woman; see .

ȧa-t , rank, dignity; see .

ȧa-t , cattle; see .

ȧa-t , backbone.

ȧa-t  (?) bounds (?), limits (?)

ȧa-t 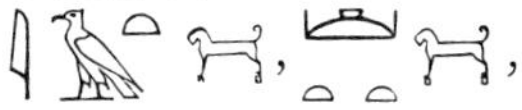, bier, grave; see **ȧa-t**.

ȧa-t , she who embraces, nurse.

ȧa-t , girdle (?)

ȧa-t [illegible], pain of body or mind.

ȧa-t [illegible], tomb, grave, sepulchre, dust heap; plur. [illegible], [illegible], U. 208, [illegible], P. 174, [illegible], A.Z. 1883, 65, [illegible], U. 587, [illegible]; gods of the tombs, [illegible], the tombs of Horus and Set; [illegible], [illegible], P. 668, M. 778, [illegible], P. 668, M. 778, [illegible], the two tombs of Osiris; [illegible], the 14 Ȧats, B.D. 149 and 150, [illegible], Book of Gates, 66; [illegible], B.D. 85, 17, the Western Ȧat; [illegible], IV, 882; [illegible], a sacred grove in Busiris; [illegible]; [illegible], the tomb of Osiris in Busiris; [illegible], "Ȧat of Life," the necropolis of the 8th Nome of Lower Egypt; [illegible], the tomb of Osiris in Mendes; [illegible], the Holy Ȧat, a locality in the nome of Gynaecopolites; [illegible], Metternich Stele 97.

Ȧa-t [illegible], the name given to the sections of the Kingdom of Osiris as described in B.D. 149.

Ȧat Ȧakhu, B.D. 149, the 3rd and 5th sections of Sekhet-Ȧaru.

ȧa-t, M. 689, the four Ȧats of Horus.

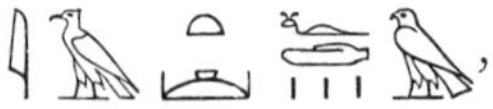

Ȧa-t-en-uābu, Rec. 31, 35, a mythological town.

Ȧa-t-ent-mu, B.D. 149, 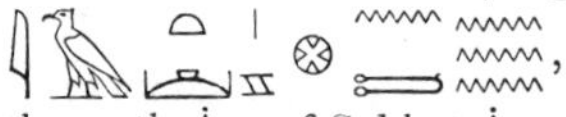 , B.D. (Nebseni) 17, the 13th Ȧat of Sekhet-Ȧaru.

Ȧa-t-en-setch-t, B.D. (Nebseni) 17, 43, a district of fire in the Ṭuat.

Ȧa-t-Ḥeru, , U. 208, P. 187, M. 351, N. 903, the divisions of the Kingdom of Horus in heaven.

Ȧa-t-Ḥeru-meḥti, P. 555, the domain of Horus of the North; 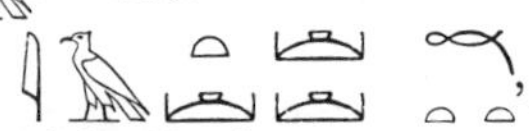 , P. 610, the domains of the North.

Ȧa-t-Ḥeru-resu, P. 555, the domain of Horus of the South; 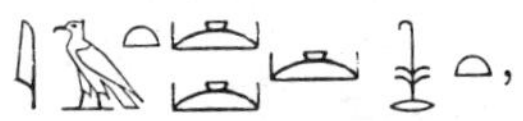 , P. 610, the domains of the South.

Ȧa-t Kher-āḥa, B.D. 149, the 14th section of Sekhet-Ȧaru.

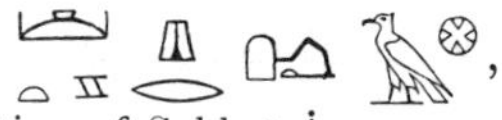

Ȧa-t Setesh-t, U. 208, , , P. 188, M. 351, N. 903, the divisions of the kingdom of Set, or Setesh, in heaven.

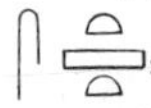

Ȧa-t-sharȧ, Rec. 31, 35, a mythological locality.

ȧa = , boat.

Aat, , , , the great canal of Heliopolis.

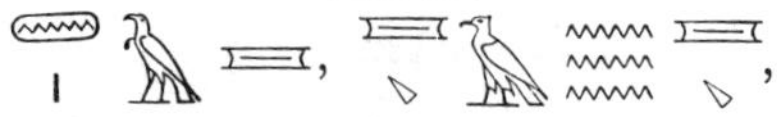

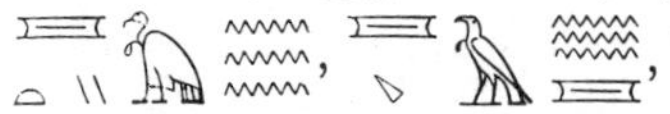

ȧa, , , , Rec. 13, 22, island; plur. , , , , Heb. אִי; , , , IV, 1098, islands of the Mediterranean; 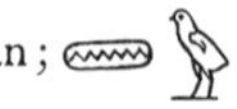 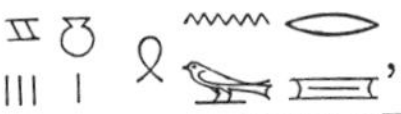 , islands of the Eastern Mediterranean; 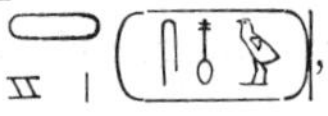 , island of Senefru; 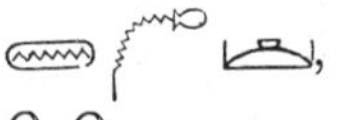 , the necropolis of Philae;  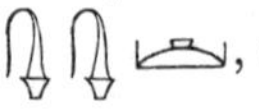 , the necropolis of Hermopolis.

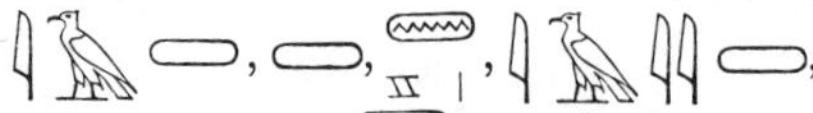

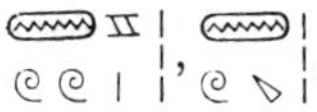

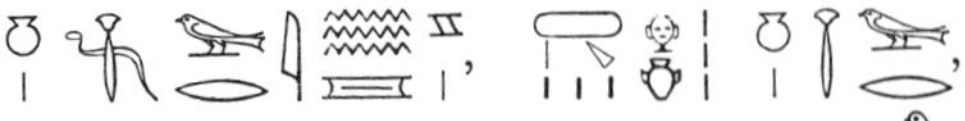

Ȧa-nsȧsȧ, N. 393, see Ȧa-nesrnesr-t.

Ȧa-nsernser-t, Rec. 27, 218; varr.  , Rec. 27, 217,  , Rec. 31, 17,  , Rec. 31, 173,   , Rec. 30, 71, , Rec. 31, 173, the "Island of Flame," a region in the Kingdom of Osiris.

ȧaa, ground, earth, rubbish-heap; plur. , Tutānkhȧmen 7.

ȧa-t, region, ground; , Mar. Karn. 52, 4, rubbish-heap.

ȧaut, waste lands, islands (?)

ȧa, Stele of Ḥerusȧtef 99, ox; plur. , cattle.

ȧa-t, De Hymnis 36, , an animal.

ȧa-t, P. 583, , , , , , stand for figures of gods and sacred animals, stand, perch; plur. , supports; , P. 411, M. 593, N. 1198.

ȧa-ti, columns; , two supports, U. 426, , T. 244.

Ȧa-t ent Up-uatu, B.D. 99, 16A, part of the magical boat.

ȧaa-t, P. 146, 364, 415, M. 185, 895, N. 1077, 1200, Rec. 31, 165, club, cudgel, mace, rod, sceptre, stick.

ȧa, pole, staff, stick.

ȧaa-t, Rec. 30, 191, plants, herbs, flax (?)

ȧaai-t, twig, branch, stick.

ȧaa-t, things with a strong smell.

ȧau, Hh. 550, things with a strong smell.

ȧaa, a kind of stone.

ȧaȧ, to glorify, to praise.

ȧaȧ-t, praise.

Ȧaȧit, B.D. (Saïte) 145, R. a goddess in the 17th Pylon.

ȧaȧā, to wash.

ȧaȧu, P. 437, 440, M. 651, 655, flourishers of sticks.

ȧaȧr = .

ȧaā, to bind an animal for sacrifice.

ȧaā, to burn, flame, fire.

ȧaāsh, to call, to cry out; Copt. ⲱϣ.

ȧaātchṭȧu, young man, youth.

ȧaātchṭȧ-t, maiden, virgin.

Ȧai, Ṭuat IX, an ass-headed god, the opponent of Āapep and Sessi; , the allies of the same.

Ȧaiu, Ṭuat IX, a group of gods who bewitched Āapep.

ȧait, old age.

Ȧait, B.D. 63A, 3, the "old gods," gods of olden time.

ȧaiu, second (?), moment (?), = (?).

ȧail, Rec. 21, 96, a horned animal; Assyr. 𒀀𒀀𒆍, W.A.I. II, 6, Col. 4, 11; Heb. אַיָּל.

Ȧau, Ṭuat I, a singing-god.

ȧau, praise, acclamation, adoration; Copt. ⲉⲟⲟⲩ.

ȧau, to be old, old.

ȧau-t, old age.

ȧau, A.Z. 1910, 117, old man, old god, veteran, aged folk; plur. , U. 513, , T. 325,

, , , , , .

ȧaut , , old woman; , Hh. 312, two goddesses.

Ȧau Nu, , B.D. 57, the primitive Sky-god.

ȧau-t , , , , , , official position, rank, dignity, position, professional occupation; plur. , , , ; , high offices; , T. 336, P. 811, M. 253, N. 639.

ȧauit , rank, dignity.

ȧauu , Rev. 11, 131, dignitaries.

ȧaui , to have power or rank.

ȧau-t , Israel Stele 24, , , , , , , , flocks, herds, cattle, sheep and goats; , Rec. 29, 148.

ȧaau , U. 392, strife (?) opposition (?)

ȧau-t , the sticker, the stabber.

ȧaau , B.D. 174, 10, double-plumed.

Ȧaau , Rec. 27, 60, a god.

ȧau , , , Ȧmen. 4, 6, to turn aside, to deflect from a course or purpose.

ȧaua , to bear, to carry.

ȧaua , , portable shrine or chapel.

ȧaui (?) , Rec. 21, 99, 100, P.S.B. 12, 123, 13, 574, a particle.

ȧauiti (?) , Mar. Karn. 54, 45, companies of troops.

Ȧaurmerrā , Jour. As. 1908, 312, a proper name (?)

ȧauhȧ , , Rec. 30, 72 . . . . .

ȧauḥu-t , , steering-pole, rudder; see **merḥu-t.**

ȧabi , , , , , , , left, the left side; , left foot; , , , the left eye of heaven, the moon.

ȧab-rek , P.S.B. 20, 203, [get] away to the left! Compare אַבְרֵךְ.

ȧabi-t , , , , the left eye of Rā, *i.e.*, the moon.

ȧab-t , U. 537, , T. 188, 295, , , P. 203, , , , , the east,

ȧabti , , N. 927, , U. 561, , , , , , , , , , left, eastern; plur. , P. 834, , N. 190, , Rec. 31, 169, , , , Rec. 35, 125, , , , , , , .

ȧab-t , T. 80, , M. 234, , N. 612, , , , , , the east wind.

Ȧab[it] , Ṭuat I, a singing-goddess.

ȧabtt , U. 298 = [illegible], T. 146, , , the east; Copt. ⲉⲓⲉⲃⲧ.

Ȧabtit , goddess of the East.

Ȧabtt , the name of a serpent of the royal crown.

Ȧabtt-ḥenā-ka-f 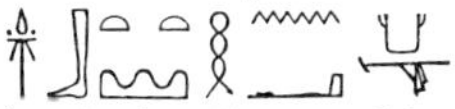 [illegible], B.D. 141 (Saïte), 18, the East and its double.

ȧab , N. 944, sceptre, ceremonial mace (?)

ȧabt , the head-box of Osiris at Abydos.

ȧabi , 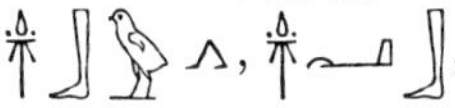, to lack, to want, to come to an end, to cease, to finish; [illegible], U. 285; [illegible], N. 719 + 11, ceaselessly; [illegible], ceaselessly day and night.

ȧab 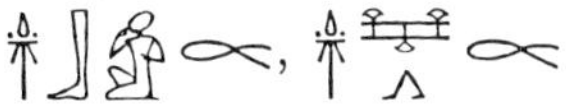, Rev. 11, 129, 136, decree, message.

ȧab , [illegible], Ȧmen. 17, 1, [illegible], to wish for, to desire, to love; [illegible], Ȧmen. 8, 13 . . . . . .

ȧabb , Rec. 32, 181, to love, to wish, to desire.

ȧab  [illegible], Rec. 19, 19, pleasure, desire.

ȧab-nut-f , "beloved of his city," a title of Ȧmen-Rā.

ȧab 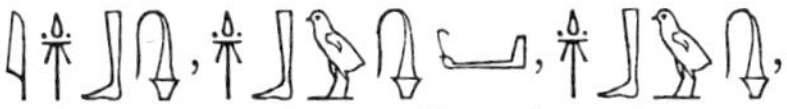, to burn, to flare up, to burn off, to brand.

ȧab  [illegible], L.D. III, 194, form, figure, similitude, statue, effigy, mark, sign.

ȧab , an animal marked for sacrifice.

ȧab 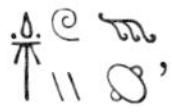, Sphinx III, 143, a mark on animals sacred to Set.

ȧab 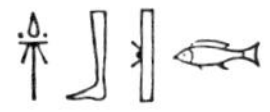, a mythological fish; Copt. ϯⲉⲫⲱⲧ (?)

ȧabi , [illegible], leopard, panther; plur. [illegible]; see [illegible].

ȧab 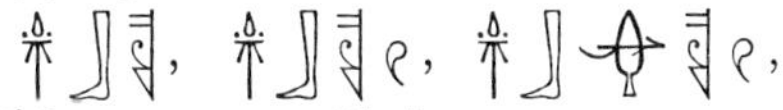, [illegible], ivory; see [illegible].

ȧab-t , enclosure, garden.

ȧab , a kind of cloth.

Ȧab[ut] , see [illegible], fathers, ancestors.

ȧab , [illegible], to cut, to slay, to smite, carved work.

ȧabtiu , fighters.

ȧabut , slaughters.

ȧabau ḥeru , Rec. 31, 171, "fighting faces" (?), the name of a company of gods.

ȧabi-t , the mantis.

ȧabis-t (?) , Nȧstasen Stele 61, eye-paint (?).

ȧabu , an official, butler (?); see [illegible].

Ȧabui , Rameses IV, 28, a singing-god.

ȧabnn , a kind of bird.

ȧabrek , Wört. 42, a vessel or instrument.

ȧabekh , L.D. III, 194, 9, [illegible], , [illegible], to pierce, to penetrate, to force a way among or into, to be permeated with; , mingled.

åabbkh , shrine, sanctuary.

åatbekhāb (?) 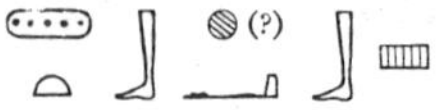, a kind of stone.

åabs , eye-paint.

åabet  = , the east, left side.

åabeṭ , a part of a crown mentioned with .

Åabṭu , Rec. 35, 56,  , B.D. 3, 1, 44, 11, 211, 3, B.M. No. 32, l. 123, 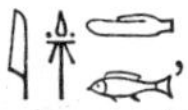, a fish that acted as pilot to Rā; var. ; Copt. ϯⲉϥⲱⲧ (?); , the holy åabṭ fish.

åapa , a baked cake; compare Heb. אפה.

åapatå , a baked cake.

åafut , N. 165, talons, claws.

åam , to tie, to bind.

åami 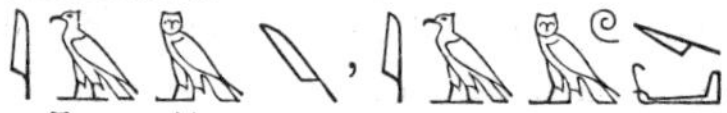, , to grasp, to seize.

åamåam , Thes. 1207, to be strong, effective.

åam , T. 85, M. 239, N. 616, to set fire to, to kindle.

åam , T. 334, , P. 826, palm tree; var. 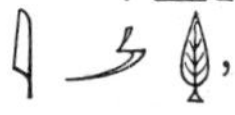, M. 249, , N. 704.

åam, åama , M. 249,  , N. 704, 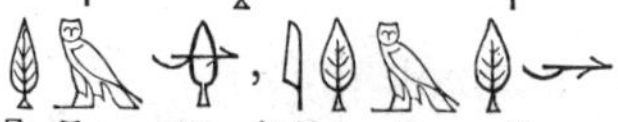, , , a kind of tree, date palm (?); plur. , , M. 720; , , Rec. 29, 152, , tree of life.

åam-t , T. 90, palm tree; var. [illegible], N. 620.

åama (?) [illegible], a wine, palm wine (?)

Åamtiu [illegible], the people of the Oasis of Jupiter Ammon.

åam [illegible], to arrive happily.

åam [illegible], [illegible], to deal kindly with, to be gracious to.

åama [illegible], [illegible], [illegible], [illegible], to be pleasant, to be benevolent, to be gracious.

åamåam [illegible], to treat very kindly; [illegible], [illegible], [illegible], good-hearted; [illegible] [illegible], "shadow, pleasant to thine eyes"; [illegible], kind of hand, benevolent.

åam-t [illegible], graciousness, grace.

åam [illegible], [illegible], Thes. 1205, graciousness.

åamit [illegible], [illegible], [illegible], [illegible], [illegible], [illegible], amiability, graciousness, pleasure, things which please.

Åammi [illegible], [illegible] [illegible], [illegible], gracious [god], a title of Rā; plur. [illegible], gracious gods.

Åamit [illegible], [illegible], the "gracious" goddess Hathor; [illegible] [illegible], name of the crown of Upper Egypt.

Åamu-t [illegible], U. 197, M. 229, N. 608, P. 230, T. 76, the name of a divine nurse.

Ȧamuti , Mission I, 596, Rec. 32, 177, kindly one, gracious god.

ȧam-t , house, tent, camp, station; plur. .

ȧamu , waggon load of some material.

ȧamu , IV, 657, weapons.

ȧam-t , a part of the body, intestines.

ȧam 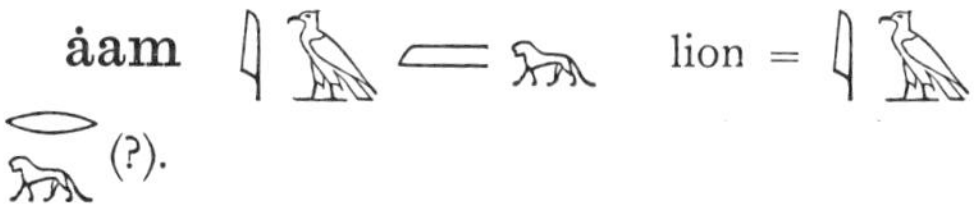 lion = (?).

Ȧamit , Asien u. E., p. 316, a god (?).

Ȧamit , a goddess.

Ȧanait , Rec. 2, 31, a goddess.

ȧaneb , L.D. III, 65A, 15; , A. Z. 17, 57, 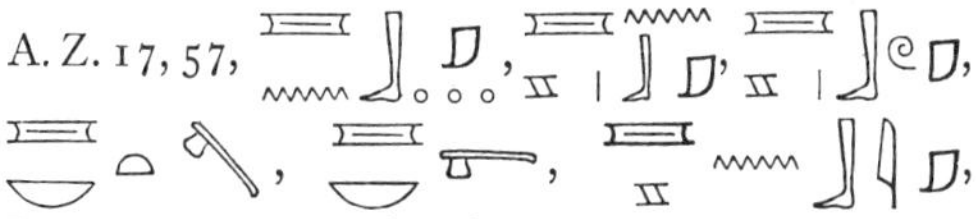, Rec. 36, 199, axe, battle-axe.

ȧaru , forms, transformations.

ȧarr-t, ȧarrut , vine; Copt. ⲉⲗⲟⲟⲗⲉ; plur. 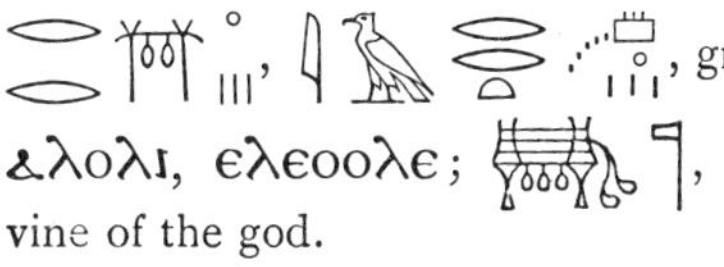, grapes; Copt. ⲁⲗⲟⲗⲓ, ⲉⲗⲉⲟⲟⲗⲉ; , P. 292, the vine of the god.

ȧar-t , , beans, berries (?).

ȧar-t , milk; Copt. ⲉⲣⲱⲧⲓ, ⲉⲣⲱⲧⲉ, ⲉⲣⲱϯ.

ȧar[r]t 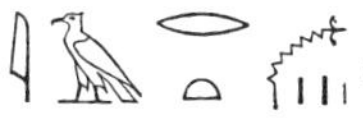, fish-spawn (?).

ȧaru , T. 395, U. 193, P. 234, M. 515, , Rec. 31, 26, reeds.

Ȧaru , the name of a celestial city.

ȧaaru , reeds.

Ȧaru, Ȧarr 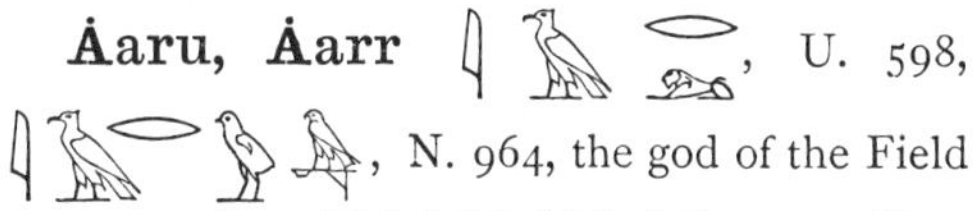, U. 598, N. 964, the god of the Field of Reeds, .

ȧar , Anastasi I, 23, 5, lion; Heb. אֲרִי.

ȧarȧar , Anastasi I, 23, 9, hero; compare Heb. אֲרִיאֵל.

ȧar , a kind of bird.

ȧar-t 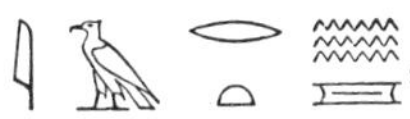, ditch; Copt. ⲉⲧⲟⲟⲣ.

ȧar , tress, lock of hair.

ȧar , sin, misery.

ȧarriu , B.D. (Saïte), 125, 43. . . .

ȧarȧṭ , to plant; see .

Ȧarāit , Uraeus-goddess.

ȧartiar , a kind of bird.

àah , unguent.

àahai , Rec. 34, 48, mourning, a cry of grief.

àahau , feeble, weak.

àahar , hut, tent; , tents made of camels' hair; Heb. אֹהֶל.

àahem , an ingredient in incense.

Àaheṭ 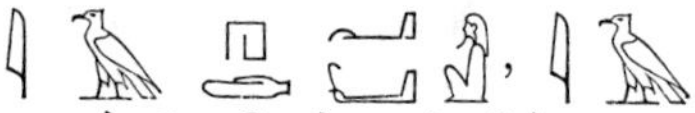 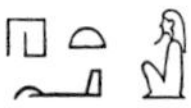 (varr. 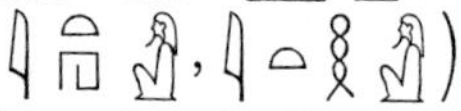), B.D. 78, 25, 26, a fighting god in the Ṭuat.

àaḥ 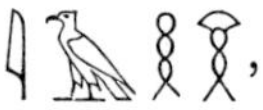, to set, to place.

àaḥ 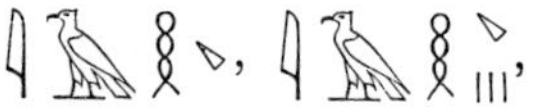, field, acre, estate.

Àaḥi ; see [illegible].

Àaḥui ; see [illegible].

Àaḥes 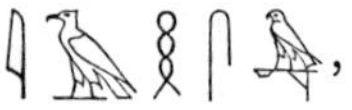, N. 936, [illegible] [illegible], P. 200, N. 936, an ancient Sûdânî god, "Head of the Land of the Bow,"  [illegible] (Nubia); varr. , P. 668, [illegible], M. 779.

àakhi 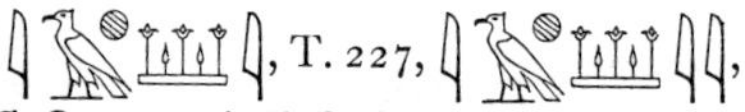, T. 227, P. 140, , U. 419, P. 247, 485, 617, M. 694, N. 1297, to flourish, to burst into flower, to bloom.

àakhi , to flood, to irrigate, to inundate.

àakh-t , 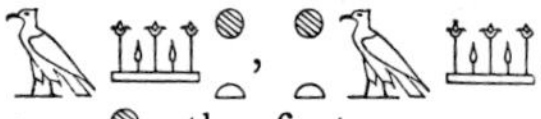, A.Z. 1904, 89, 147, [illegible], the first season of the Egyptian year (July 20–Nov. 15).

Àakhit (?) 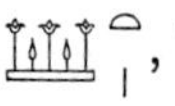, Ombos I, 90, goddess of the first season.

àakh 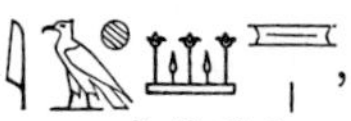, M. 684, pond, lake, large canal; plur. 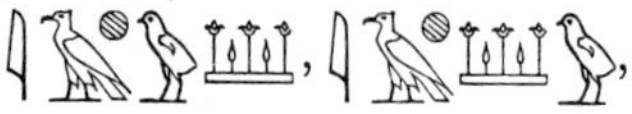, P. 123, N. 1040.

àakh-t , Àmen. 6, 2, 8, water plants; Heb. אחו, Gr. ἄχει, Copt. ⲁϧⲓ, ⲁϩⲉ.

àakhkh , neck, sinews (?)

àakhkh , night; var. [illegible].

Àakhabit , B.D. 145, (Saïte) 14, 52, a goddess of the 14th Pylon.

àakhu-t , L.D. III, 140c, fire.

àakhu[it] , night, evening; Copt. ⲉⲩϣⲏ.

Àakhuait , [illegible] [illegible], Ṭuat I, one of the twelve goddess-guides of Àf.

àakhu , N. 112, 124, [illegible], T. 292, , T. 399, Rec. 31, 17, [illegible], P. 2, 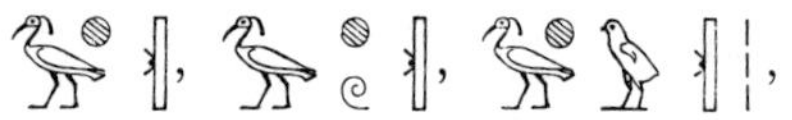, to shine, to be bright, fine, splendid, glorious, excellent, good, to be useful, to recite formulae.

àakhu-t , A.Z. 1904, 143, Metternich Stele 107, [illegible], Dream Stele 7, 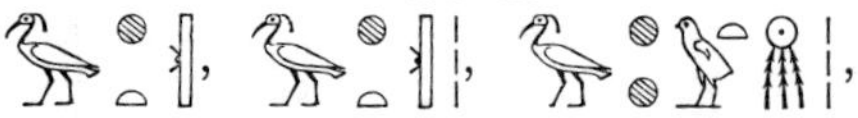, anything which is beneficial, good, splendid, benefit, strength, protection, advantage, credit, renown; 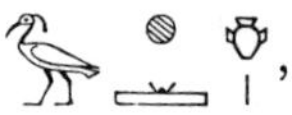, IV, 890; [illegible], excellent hearted.

Àakhu-menu 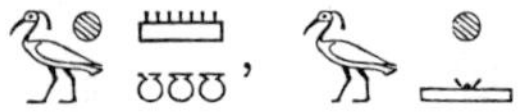, [illegible], a building of Thothmes III.

àakhu , , words of power, protective formulae, spells; [illegible] [illegible], Thes. 1295, the magical formulae of Thoth; [illegible], magical words.

ȧakhu, U. 622, P. 237, —, IV, 918, —, A.Z. 1900, 129, light, splendour, radiance, brilliance, glorious deeds, splendid acts, virtues, excellences, blessings, benefits; —, U. 636, —, the two gods Epiphanes.

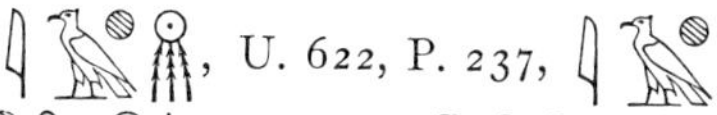

ȧakhu-t, the title of the priestess of the Nome Prosopites.

ȧakhut, Rec. 27, 219, beings of light, *i.e.*, wise, instructed folk.

Ȧakhu, Rec. 27, 59, —, P. 447, N. 656, 662, —, Rec. 30, 190, —, N. 1121, —, Pap. 3024, 65, —, Hh. 561, the Light-god; —, Rec. 31, 13, the Great Light, *i.e.*, the sun.

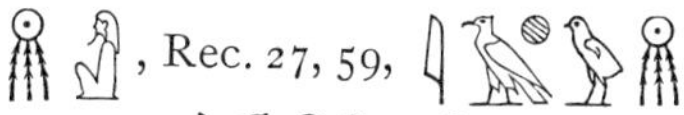

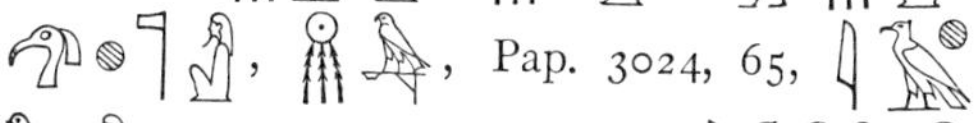

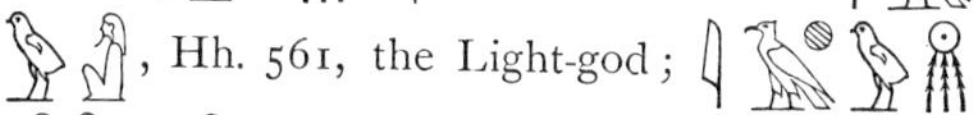

ȧakhu-t, T. 251, 321, —, U. 440, —, the Eye of Rā or Horus, the fiery light of the sun, a flame-goddess, the fiery uraeus on Pharaoh's crown, the name of a crown; —, the uraei on the royal crown.

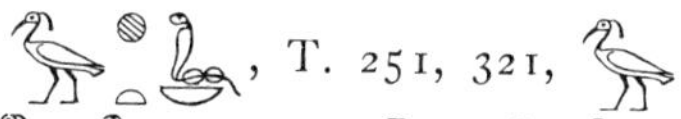

ȧakhu-ti, —, the two eyes of Horus or Rā, *i.e.*, the sun and the moon.

Ȧakhu-t, a name of Isis-Sothis.

Ȧakhuit, Ṭuat I, the fiery uraei-goddesses who light the way of Rā.

Ȧakhu, —, Denderah II, 10, one of the 36 Dekans; Gr. χυ.

Ȧakhu-nekhekh, Denderah II, 10, one of the 36 Dekans.

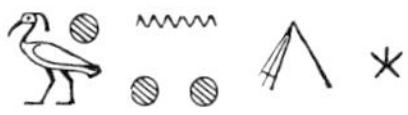

Ȧakhu-ra, Ṭuat XII, a singing dawn-god.

Ȧakhu-ḥeri-ȧb-Ḥe-t-āshemu, B.D. 141 and 148, the rudder of the eastern heaven.

Ȧakhu-ḥeri-ȧb, etc., B.D. 141 and 142, l. 26, the Light-god in the temple of the gods.

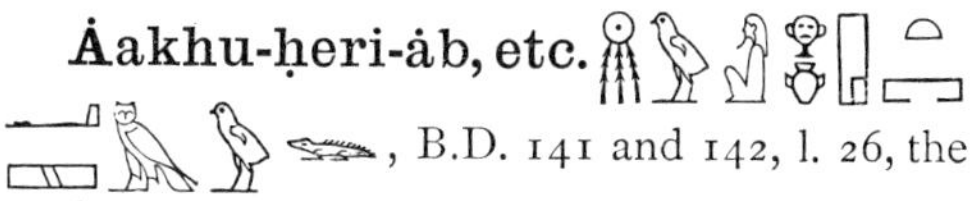

Ȧakhu-ḥetch-t, Cairo Pap. IV, 2, a god of the dead.

Ȧakhu-kheper-ur (?), B.D. 162, 7, the body of Rā in Ȧn.

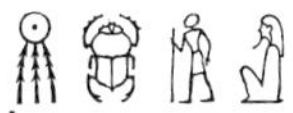

Ȧakhu-sa-ta-f, Denderah IV, 60, a warrior-god.

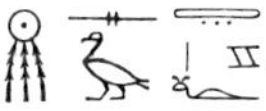

ȧakhu, to be or become a spirit; — B.D. 9, 6, "I am a spirit"; —, endowed with spirit, having become a spirit; see —, Rec. 33, 30.

ȧakhu, —, the spirit-soul of a god or man; —, Rec. 32, 182; —, a damned soul, Pap. 3024, 4; plur. —, P. 712, N. 1367, —, M. 268, 270, —, N. 888, —, N. 70, —, N. 888, —,

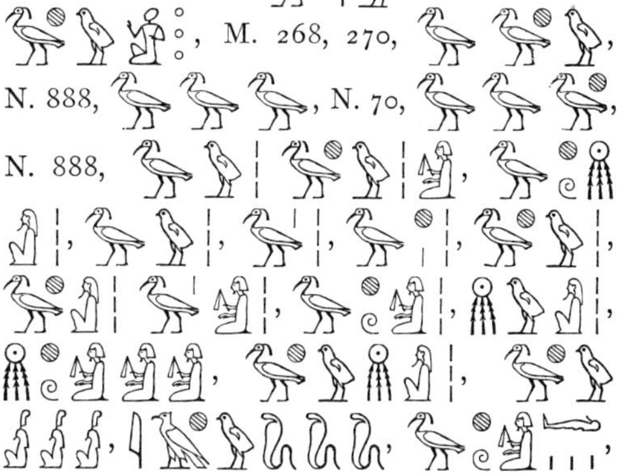

, A.Z. 1908, 115, , , spirits, the glorified spirits of the dead, the dead, the sainted dead; Copt. .

åakhu-t , , , a female spirit.

åakhu åqer , B.D. 91, 4, , a spirit whose mouth is able to recite spells with skill and knowledge; , B.D. 169, 15.

åakhu āper , B.D. 91, Rubric, a spirit equipped with amulets and spells.

åakhu ānkh , B.D. 65, 8, a living soul.

Åakhu , B.D. 64, 21, the spirit-souls of the dead who numbered , 4, 601, 200.

Åakhu , Berg. I, 13, a ram-headed god.

Åakhu , Denderah IV, 80; B.D. 149, the god of the 5th Åat.

Åakhu , B.D. 145A, the doorkeeper of the 17th Pylon.

Åakhui , Ṭuat II, a god with two lotus sceptres.

åakhuti , N. 760, , Lit. 90, the two spirits, *i.e.*, Isis and Nephthys.

Åakhuti , P. 642, , M. 677, , N. 1239, a pair of divine spirits.

Åakhu , Ṭuat VI, the spirit-souls of the gods of the Ṭuat.

Åakhu , U. 70, 275, 527, T. 174, 289, 330, P. 120, M. 155, N. 109, 331, 719, the spirit-souls of the gods.

Åakhu IV , B.D. 96–97, 3, the four spirits who follow the Lord of Things; , B.D. 17, 87, the seven spirits of Sepa; , B D. 149, II, spirits nine cubits high; , the ancestral spirits; (*sic*), the primeval spirits.

Åakhu VII , B.D. 17, 87, 100–106, the seven guardian spirits of the body of Osiris.

Åakhu VIII , Berg. I, 7, the four sons and the four grandsons of Horus.

Åakhu-åmi-Netå , P. 7, M. 10, , N. 114, the spirit-soul of Netå, *i.e.*, Osiris.

Åakhu-åkhmiu-seku , T. 289, N. 128, , M. 66, the spirit-souls of the imperishable stars.

åakhu , "Spirit-soul, Lord of Spirit-souls," a title of Osiris.

Åakhut-nebåt , Nesi-Amsu 27, 17, "Flaming Eye," *i.e.*, the goddess Sekhmit.

[Åakhu]-neb-s , Denderah IV, 84, the name of the 10th Pylon.

Åakh-su-āsh-mer-t-Uast , Rec. 17, 98, a Theban god (?)

Åakhu-Set-ḥeru-kheru , N. 952, the spirits of Set, celestial and terrestrial.

åakhu-t , T. 320, , U. 501, , , Rec. 31, 161, , the abode of the Light-god or Sun-god, the horizon; , the horizon of the sky; , the horizon of Manu, *i.e.*, the West.

Ȧakhut-en-ȧten, Berg. II, 13, a title of Nut.

ȧakhu-t ḥeḥ, , , eternal horizon, *i.e.*, the tomb.

Ȧakhuti, P. 642, , N. 1239, , , , , , , , , the god who dwelleth in the horizon.

ȧakhutiu, P. 357, , N. 1071, , Rec. 31, 171, , , , , , , , , the gods and beings of the kingdom of the Light-god.

Ȧakhu-t Khufu, the name of the pyramid of Khufu.

ȧakhu-t sheta-t, , the secret horizon, the name of a part of a temple.

ȧakhu, Rec. 27, 86, a kind of fish.

ȧakhuit (?), , , , , herb, reed, plant, grass, vegetation.

ȧakhu-t, , Rec. 27, 86, , , , soil, ground, land, earth.

ȧakhu meḥ, Suppl. 131, the name of a cubit.

ȧakhu-t, A.Z. 1906, 114, sacred cow.

Ȧakhmȧnsh, Achaemenes; Pers. , Beh. 1, 6; Gr. Ἀχαιμένης.

ȧas, to hasten; Copt. ιнc, ιωc.

Ȧas, , B.D. 102, 1, a god.

Ȧas-t (Ȧst), the goddess Isis = .

Ȧasabatiu, Harris Pap. I, 77, 3, name of a tribe or nation.

Ȧasakhr, name of a Hittite goddess.

Ȧasu, , T. 340, N. 628, a region in the heaven of Rā.

ȧasb, the name of a game.

ȧasb, throne, seat; compare Heb. יָשַׁב.

ȧasr, tamarisk tree; see .

Ȧasṭen, Berg. 1, 34, , B.D. 18, G. 1, Nesi-Ȧmsu 16, 6, , one of the eight ape-gods of the company of Thoth. He presided over the seven , Edfû 1, 25.

Ȧasṭes; see .

ȧash, to cry out, call, invite, ask for; Copt. ωϣ.

ȧash-t, cry.

Ȧasha, , , "the crier," *i.e.*, "roarer," a name of Set, or Typhon, jackal.

Ȧasha, a kind of dog or jackal.

ȧashaf, to burn.

ȧashatȧ, a kind of plant.

ȧashatȧ penu, a plant, rat's bane (?)

ȧaq, , U. 211, 562, P. 182, M. 256, , N. 894, to enter; see .

ȧaq, U. 283, N. 719 + 10, to rule, to govern.

ȧaqu, loss, want.

ȧaq-t, leek, onion; Copt. ⲏϫⲓ, ⲏϭⲉ; plur.  ,  ,  , Rec. 16, 2,   , Anastasi IV, 14, 12;  , Rec. 19, 92, seed of the same.

ȧaqu , , A.Z. 1874, 62, to bastinade.

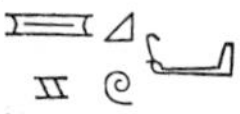

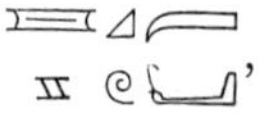

Ȧaqeṭqeṭ , B.D. 17, 102, one of the seven spirits who guarded the body of Osiris.

Ȧak , A.Z. 1906, 122, old man, senior; plur.  , B.D. 118, 2.

Ȧaku , B.D. (Saïte) 28, 1, a group of warrior-gods in the Ṭuat.

Ȧaka , , mason, stonecutter; plur. .

ȧakb , P. 106, N. 869,  , N. 761, 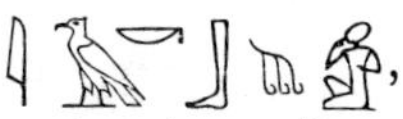 ,  , to weep, to grieve; Copt. ⲱⲕⲉⲉ.

ȧakbiu , , wailings, mourning, mourners.

ȧakbit , , a weeping, mourning.

ȧakbit , wailing woman; plur. , ,

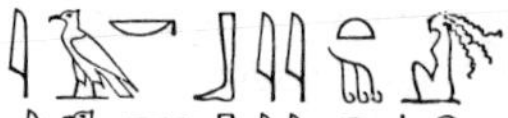

Ȧakebi , , , one of the 75 forms of Rā (No. 29).

Ȧakebi[t]  , Ṭuat VIII, the name of a Circle, .

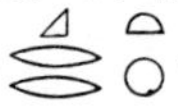

Ȧaker , Berg. I, 18, a protector of the dead.

Ȧaker , see .

Ȧag-t , a town in the Ṭuat.

Ȧagu-t , seed of a plant.

ȧat , to fail, be weak.

ȧat-t , weaknesses, defects; var. , Jour. As. 1908, 302.

ȧat , , , , , wound, injury, breach, stab.

ȧatiu , , slaughter houses.

ȧat-tiu , , Peasant 177, resister.

ȧat (?) , L.D. III, 140B, deadly country.

Ȧat , Mar. Aby. 1, 44, the god of the block of the goddess Sekhemit.

Ȧat-urt , , T. 98, P. 813, M. 243, a sky-god.

ȧat , speech (?)

ȧatatȧ , Koller Pap. 3, 1, , Anastasi IV, 2, 12, a kind of strong-smelling plant.

ȧatem , Prisse Pap. 11, 13 . . . . . .

ȧaten , disk of the sun; see .

ȧatru , stud bulls.

ȧath , Hh. 481, to lack.

ȧathu , Hh. 555, places of slaughter.

ȧatha , , Anastasi I, 11, 2, 21, 5, , what is this? compare Heb. אֵיזֶה.

ȧatha , Ȧmen. 15, 2, 18, 2, to seize.

ȧathamai, Anastasi I, 26, 8, part of a whip.

ȧatharȧa-t, Anastasi I, 18, 8, neighbourhood.

ȧathen, disk of the sun.

ȧaṭ, T. 399, M. 409, to descend.

ȧaṭ, Rec. 11, 71, mace (?)

ȧaṭ-t, …, …, moment, hour.

ȧaṭ-t, Rec. 33, 6, …, Rec. 21, 15, …, ground, place, region, field, meadow; plur. ….

ȧaṭ-t, …, marshy land, luxuriant meadow.

ȧaṭut, L.D. III, 140B, Rec. 14, 97, pastures, cattle-runs.

ȧaṭt-t, a stud cow; see ….

ȧaṭ-t, vine-land, vineyard.

ȧaṭ, …, …, …, …, …, dew, mist, vapour, rain-storm, moisture, exudation; Copt. ⲉⲓⲱⲧⲉ.

ȧaṭ, to hear (?)

ȧaṭ, ȧaṭ-t, …, …, child, youth, young man.

ȧaṭ-t, …, …, …, …, net, cord of a seal, a ceremonial bandlet; plur. ….

Ȧaṭ-t, B.D. 153A, the net of the Akeru gods for snaring the souls of the dead in the Ṭuat.

ȧaṭ-t, plague, disease, epidemic.

ȧaṭ-t, some strong-smelling substance.

ȧaṭ-t, ȧaṭi, …, …, …, …, Thes. 1199, …, Mar. Karn. 53, 39; Åmen. 4, 4, 21, 8, to vex, to injure, hurt, oppress, be hostile to, to be oppressed, desolate.

ȧaṭu, Rec. 10, 61, A.Z. 1905, 16, foes, enemies.

ȧaṭua, Israel Stele 17, to suffer, to be oppressed.

Ȧaṭ, T. 239, …, U. 419, the name of a sky-god.

Ȧaṭ, B.D.G. 78, a mythological locality.

Ȧaṭȧ, N. 908, …, P. 189, M. 357, a lake in the Ṭuat in which the righteous bathed.

Ȧaṭit, Love Songs 2, 8, a goddess, a friend of Osiris.

ȧaṭb, flood.

Ȧaṭen, the disk of the sun; see ….

ȧaṭn, some strong-smelling substance, dung(?); Copt. ⲉⲓⲧⲉⲛ.

ȧaṭr, …, stud cattle, a yoke of beasts; Copt. ϩⲁⲧⲣⲉ, ⲁⲟⲡⲉⲩ.

ȧaṭḥ, swampy land, marsh, papyrus swamp.

ȧatchn, disk = ….

ȧȧmiu, kinsfolk.

ȧā, ȧāi, U. 95, N. 373, …, Hh. 381, …, …, …, …, …, …, to wash, to bathe, to dip in water; …, Rec. 36, 162, indissoluble.

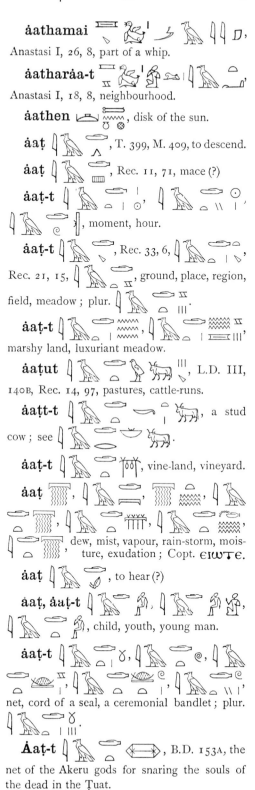

ȧāi-t, Rec. 30, 218, something washed; , Rec. 36, 162, things washed away.

ȧāi-ḥa-t (or ȧāi-ȧb), Israel Stele 3, , Peasant 206, to wash the heart, *i.e.*, to cool, to gratify the mind, to be appeased; , = ϵιω ϩητ.

ȧāi-ȧb en ȧten, Rec. 15, 46, joy of Åten.

ȧāiu-nub, gold-washer; plur. , L.D. III, 140c.

ȧāi, to remove, transport.

ȧā, Amherst Pap. 30, bowl, pot, vessel; plur. , .

ȧāi, Rec. 14, 122, to sport with, to hold or treat lightly.

ȧā = .

ȧā-t, U. 462, path, road, direction.

ȧāi, U. 562, P. 764, M. 765, , P. 658, to approach, go up to, to ascend, to rise, to reach up, to exalt; Copt. ⲁⲗⲉ.

ȧā, T. 268, M. 427, grave, tomb, sepulchre, monument.

ȧā = , .

ȧā, P. 65, 655, U. 120, , M. 760, , , , flesh and bone.

ȧāu, , T. 343, , P. 222, , Berlin 2296, food, offerings, morning meal.

Ȧāāu B.D. 5, 2, the ape-gods who praised Rā.

ȧā-tȧ, ... , Hh. 207.

Ȧā-t-nt-khert, B.D. 99, a part of the magical boat.

ȧāa-t, T. 15 . . . .

ȧāamesk, Hh. 204, ...

Ȧāi, Tomb of Seti I, one of the 75 forms of Rā (No. 55).

ȧāb, U. 507, , T. 321, , , U. 87, P. 364, , T. 366, to approach, to come towards, to meet.

ȧāb, , , , M. 127, to present a gift, to make an offering, an offering; , libation; varr. , , , , U. 223.

ȧāb-t, offering; plur. .

ȧābi, Hh. 195, to make libations.

ȧāb, to comb.

ȧāb, Rev. 13, 73, a measure = Gr. ἀρτάβης.

ȧāb, , , vase, bowl, vessel, pot.

ȧāb, table of offerings.

ȧābb, , Rhind Pap. 32, scarab, beetle.

ȧāper, Hh. 462, , to equip, be equipped.

ȧāf, , , to squeeze, press out oil or wine, to wring; var. .

ȧām, U. 512, 633, T. 324, to swallow, to eat; see , etc.

ȧān, to go back, return = , Rec. 30, 187.

ȧān, U. 527, , , , ape; plur. , P. 661, , P. 776, M. 772, , Rec. 31, 19; Copt. ⲉⲛ.

ȧāān , Rec. 30, 195, ape.

ȧāāni , Ȧmen. 17, 9, 22, ape.

ȧān 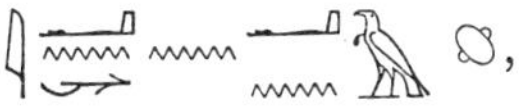, a box of ānti (myrrh).

ȧān , Peasant R. 186,  , to utter cries of joy or sorrow; var. ; , L.D. III, 140, cries, outcries.

ȧānu , U. 647 = 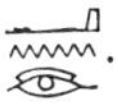.

ȧānȧ , ape; see 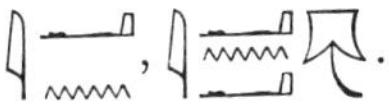.

Ȧānā 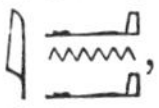, Ṭuat II, the Ape-god; plur. , "They praised Rā daily at dawn, and acted as his guides, and supported the Great Hand" (Ṭuat XI).

Ȧānāit 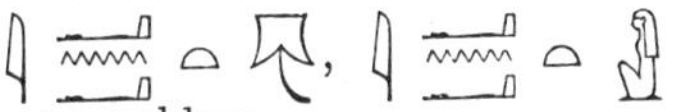, Rec. 30, 195, ape-goddess.

Ȧānā Ṭuati , one of the 75 forms of Rā (No. 69).

ȧānkh ; see .

ȧānkhu , N. 551, the living.

ȧār 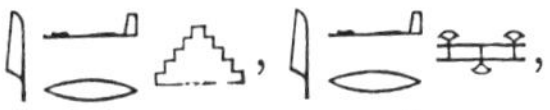, Hh. 395, to approach, to ascend; see ; Copt. ⲁⲗⲉ.

ȧār-t , U. 470, 630, P. 195, 660, 773, M. 369, 770, , P. 260, , 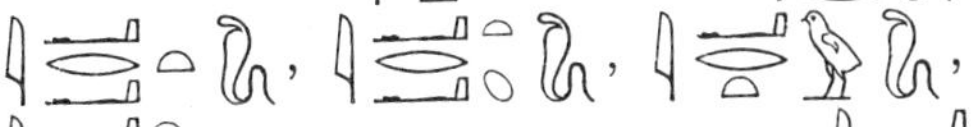, , snake, snake-goddess; plur.  , U. 394, , T. 305, 320, 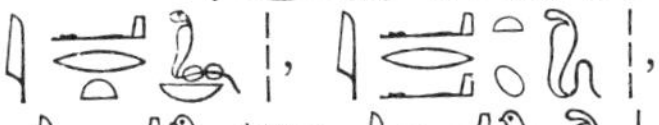, , .

Ȧār-ti , P. 542, , the two Uraei-goddesses, Isis and Nephthys (?)

ȧārārut  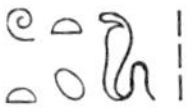, uraei, serpents.

ȧārut VII , the seven great Uraei.

Ȧārut , Hh. 376, the Uraeus-god.

ȧār-t [illegible], [illegible], the serpent amulet, [illegible], A.Z. 1908, 16.

Ȧār-t ānkh-t [illegible], Ṭuat VIII, the living Serpent-god.

Ȧārut ānkhut [illegible], Ṭuat IV, the uraei who burnt up the souls and shadows of the dead.

Ȧār-t per-t em Setesh [illegible] [illegible], N. 955, a serpent-goddess.

Ȧārā-t ḥeri ȧb ḥe-t neter [illegible] [illegible], B.D. 136, a uraeus-goddess.

ȧār [illegible], Hh. 472, [illegible], spiked reeds; Copt. ⲁⲣⲟ, ⲁⲣⲟⲟⲩⲉ.

ȧār [illegible], cypress trees; Copt. ⲁⲣⲟ.

ȧāḥ [illegible], P. 279, [illegible], T. 365, [illegible], N. 1103, [illegible], N. 944, [illegible], P. 203, [illegible], N. 1104, [illegible], [illegible], [illegible] [illegible], [illegible], [illegible], [illegible], [illegible], [illegible], [illegible], [illegible], [illegible], [illegible], [illegible], [illegible], the moon, Moon-god; Copt. ⲓⲟϩ, ⲓⲟⲟϩ, ⲓⲟⲓϩ; Heb. יָרֵחַ.

Ȧāḥ meḥ Utchat [illegible] [illegible], Quelques Pap. 41, the full moon.

Ȧāḥ ḥer res-t [illegible], Quelques Pap. 47, the moon at noon.

Ȧāḥ Ṭeḥuti (Tcheḥuti) [illegible] [illegible], Thoth the Moon-god.

ȧāḥ [illegible], U. 214, to break ground, to plough, to dig up earth.

ȧāḥu , field labourer, peasant.

ȧāḥ-t 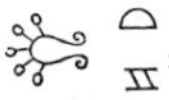, field.

Ȧāḥ-ur 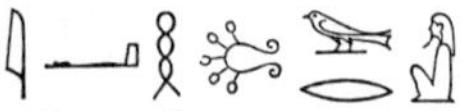, Rec. 26, 225, the name of a god.

ȧāḥ , to hold back (?), to restrain (?); , N. 764, restrain thy tears.

Ȧāḥ-rem-t , Rec. 37, 63, the "Drier of tears," title of a god.

ȧāḥ 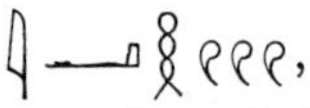, limbs, members, flesh,

Ȧākhbu , Ṭuat XII, a singing god.

ȧāsh 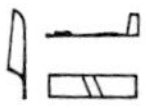, Rec. 4, 135, 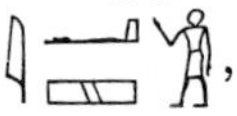, Berlin 6910, to cry out; see ; Copt. ⲱϣ.

ȧāsh en ḥa-t , pilot.

ȧāq , M. 728, T. 259, to enter; see āq .

ȧi 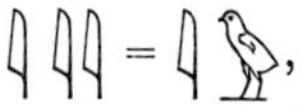, to be.

ȧiu (?) , Berg. II, 409, change, transformation.

ȧi 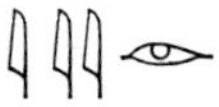, Rec. 3, 204, the evil eye (?).

ȧi , P. 184, M. 293, N. 897, , 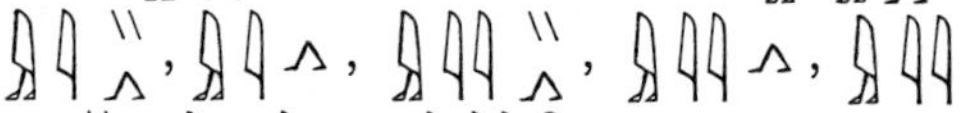, 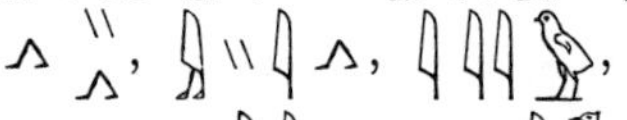, to go, to come; Copt. ⲉⲓ; , P. 137, , , to go, to come; , a coming; , come, come! , Rec. 30, 187, comers, comings, , P. 104, M. 71, N. 73.

ȧiu , those who shall come, *i.e.*, posterity.

ȧi ḥa 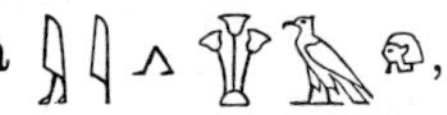, to get round, to circumvent.

ȧiu-ḥer-sa , Thes. 1297, , those who come after, posterity.

ȧi-t 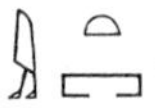, house, palace.

Ȧit 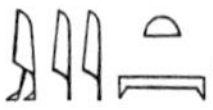, Berg. II, 13, a name of Nut.

Ȧi-em-ḥetep , a physician of Memphis who was deified and became the god of medicine and surgery and the art of embalming; he is called the son of Ptaḥ and was the third member of the triad of Memphis; Gr. 'Ιμοῦθης; 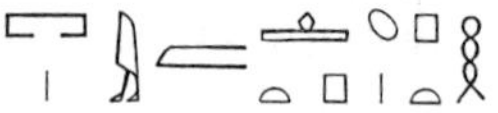 = τὸ 'Ασκληπιεῖον.

ȧi-t , evil hap, ill luck, unlucky event, wrong, injustice.

ȧi , Peasant 228, a kind of fish.

ȧia 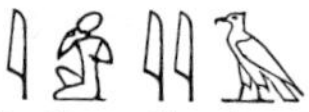, Rougé I.H. pl. 159, 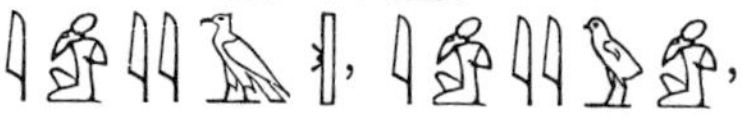, alas! O! hail!

ȧui (?) [illegible], certainly (?)

ȧiḥ [illegible], IV, 772, a plant.

ȧikha [illegible], Rev. demon, spirit; Copt. ⲓⲁ.

ȧitenn [illegible], ground, earth, mud, dung; Copt. ⲉⲓⲧⲉⲛ.

ȧu [illegible], pers. pron. 1st sing.

ȧu [illegible], to be; the Pyramid Text variant is [illegible], P. 164 = N. 859, and see U. 215, P. 652, 653, 654, M. 438, 560, 755, 756, 758, 759, N. 941, 1048, 1167, 1376.

ȧu-t [illegible], P. 693 (*bis*), act of being.

ȧu [illegible] = **er** [illegible]; [illegible], all; [illegible], above; [illegible], up to, until; [illegible], backwards, behind; Copt. ⲉⲡⲁϩⲟⲩ; [illegible], for the sake of; Copt. ⲉ ⲧⲃⲉ; [illegible], Rev., aussi bien qu'à.

Ȧu [illegible], Ṭuat XII, one of the 12 gods who towed the Boat of Rā through the serpent Ānkh-neteru, and who were re-born daily.

Áu-ānkhiu-f, Ṭuat XII, one of the 12 gods who towed the Boat of Rā through the serpent Ānkh-neteru, and who were re-born daily.

Áu, Mar. Aby. I, 44, a god.

Áu, Berg. I, 11, a god with two serpents.

áu, praise.

áu, limbs, members, flesh.

áu, Rev., bread, cake.

áu, U. 220, P. 212, 619, N. 759, 1303, T. 189, P. 676 = N. 1286, Stele of Ḥerusȧtef, 73, 100, 106, Rev. 12, 25, Rev. 12, 17, Rev. 14, 21, to come, to go; Copt. ϵι; T. 233; it hath gone out in peace; *explicit liber*.

áui, Rec. 32, 177, comer, leader.

áuiu, U. 506, Rec. 35, 138, passengers, passers, comers, goers.

áu-t, a going, a coming, errand, embassy.

áu-t en áthen, the course of the solar disk.

áu-t, goose pens, aviaries.

áuu (for **áur**?), light, brilliance, radiance; compare Heb. אור.

áu, Rec. 32, 78, Rev. 14, 19, child, heir.

áu-t, Rev. 11, 60, posterity.

áu-tu, Rev. 13, 14, growth.

áu, N. 760, to cry out, cry, outcry, wail.

áuáu, cry, outcry, wail.

Áu (?), T. 311, a group (?) of divine beings.

Áu-qau (?), M. 374, the name of a god.

áuáu, Mar. Karn. 53, 23, P.S.B. 13, 411, dog, jackal; plur.

áu-t . . . . , U. 605 . . . . . .

áu, to cut, to cut off; sticker; those who cut; var. (?)

áu = , river, stream.

áui = , to flood, to wet.

áu-t, offal, filth, = ; Jour. As. 1908, 261, foul or stinking water; filthy one.

áu, áu-t, sin, wrong, calamity, crime, disaster, deceit, evil, disgrace, offence, ill-luck, harm, injury, wickedness.

áui-t, Peasant 264, sin, sinful ones.

áutiu, Rev. 6, 156, foul ones, a group of gods in the Ṭuat.

ȧu 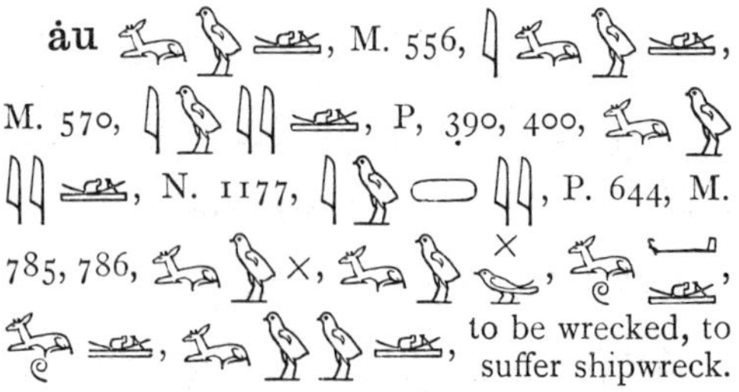, M. 556, M. 570, P, 390, 400, N. 1177, P. 644, M. 785, 786, to be wrecked, to suffer shipwreck.

ȧui , shipwrecked sailor.

ȧu , M. 201, , N. 679, nest, home.

ȧui (ȧi) 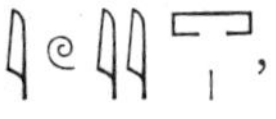, Rev. 12, 87, house; Copt. ⲏⲓ.

ȧuit , abode, house, court, temple, shrine, quarter of a town, camp, cattle-pen; plur. 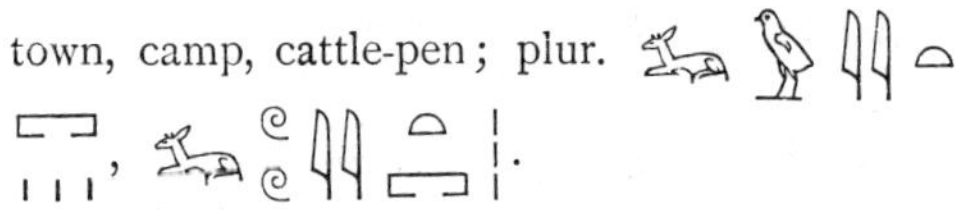.

ȧu ȧrpi 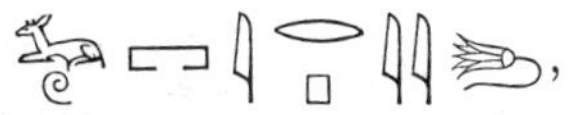, Rev. 14, 67, wine shop, tavern.

ȧuu-t , rank, dignity.

ȧu, ȧu-t 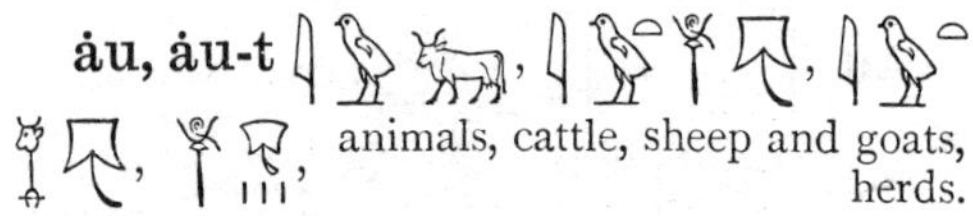, animals, cattle, sheep and goats, herds.

ȧua , ox; plur. 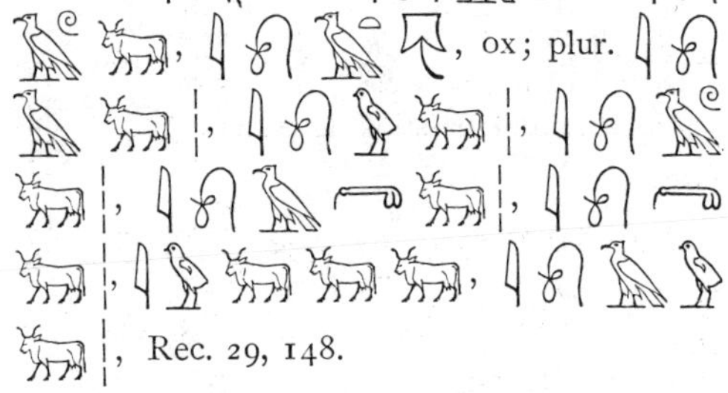, Rec. 29, 148.

Ȧua-en-Geb , B.D. 125, III, 30, name of the threshold of the Hall of Maāti.

ȧua , to travel, to go on a journey.

ȧua 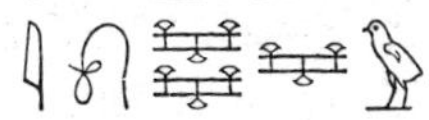, P. 381, ways, roads.

ȧua-t , a kind of fish.

ȧuaut , Hh. 330, old men, ancestors.

ȧua[ȧa]-t , girl, maiden.

ȧuaȧ , R.E. 3, 39, farmers, husbandmen; Copt. ⲟⲩⲟⲉⲓ.

ȧuaȧ , Jour. As. 1908, 285, Rev. 14, 52, pledge, guarantee.

ȧuai , Lit. 163 ....

ȧuai , roof (?)

ȧuai 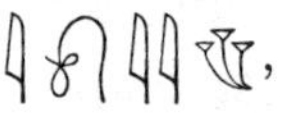, Mission 13, 127, plant, kind of tree, sycamore(?)

Ȧuai , Tomb of Seti I, one of the 75 forms of Rā (No. 60).

ȧuai-t , glue, flour (?)

ȧuamu , a kind of plant.

ȧuaḥ , Rec. 28, 205, and; Copt. ⲁⲩⲱ.

ȧuag , N. 997, to flow (?)

ȧuatȧ, ȧuaṭ 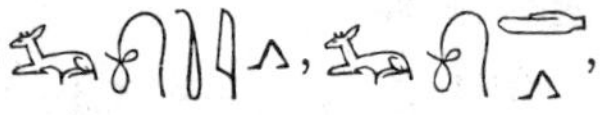, between; Copt. ⲟⲩⲧⲉ.

ȧuȧ , to be conceived = , **ȧur.**

ȧuȧ-t , A.Z. 1909, 127, old age.

ȧuȧ 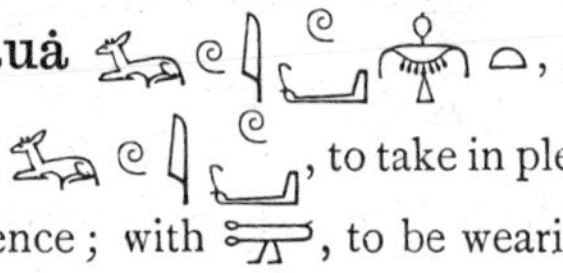, Jour. As. 1908, 285, to take in pledge, to commit violence; with 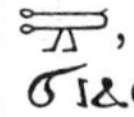, to be wearied or annoyed; Copt. ⲁⲟⲩⲱ, ϭⲓⲁⲟⲩⲱ.

ȧuȧu-t , chamber, abode (?)

ȧu-Ȧn (?) , N. 298A, club, mace.

ȧuā 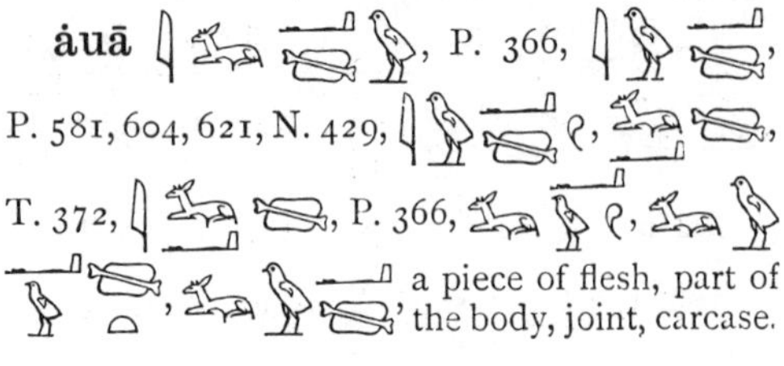, P. 366, P. 581, 604, 621, N. 429, T. 372, P. 366, a piece of flesh, part of the body, joint, carcase.

ȧuāā , , , , , , , , , flesh and bone, joint.

ȧuāu , N. 429, 1079, divine flesh, the god's body.

ȧuā , , , , , , , , , , , , heir, inheritor; plur , , heirs, progeny, posterity; , male heir.

ȧuāāu , Rec. 27, 85, offspring (of animals).

ȧuāāu , Rec. 21, 15, heirs.

ȧuā-t , Rec. 30, 196, , , , , , , , , , , heritage, inheritance.

Ȧuā-uā , Rec. 31, 24, the "One Heir," the name of a god (?)

ȧuāi-t , Stat. Taf. 10, , Rec. 13, 161, , , , , , Rec. 27, 204, , , , , a company of serfs or slaves, a body of soldiers, any group of men, civil or military, bodyguard, troop.

ȧuā , , to reward, to recompense.

ȧuā-t , IV, 1003, chamber, abode, house.

ȧuāā , gazelle, a horned animal.

ȧuāu , ring, bracelet (?)

ȧuāuit , Rec. 2, 111, dogs, jackals (?)

ȧuāft (?) , L.D. III, 229C, Suppl. 514 . . . . . .

ȧuār-t , joint, haunch.

ȧui , Rev. 11, 140, or; Copt. ЄΙЄ.

ȧui , P. 400 = , M. 570, , N. 1177, sailor.

ȧuiu , Israel Stele 10, old men.

ȧui , P. 644, to repulse (?)

ȧui-ḥa-t , Rev. 13, 7, , Rev. 13, 2, to be patient, long-suffering; Copt. ωοΥ Ν ϩΗΤ.

ȧui , Miss. 13, 127, a plant (?)

ȧui-t , grain measure.

Ȧuirna-t , Rec. 6, 6, the name Irene.

ȧuisu , pouch; Copt. ⲁⲥⲓⲟⲩⲓ.

ȧub-t , cake, bread.

Ȧuuba , B.D. 168, a god who bestowed peace on the dead.

ȧub-t (*sic*), net.

ȧubku , to weep; see .

ȧup , to open; see **up** .

Ȧup-ur , a god.

ȧuputi , , , , , , envoy, messenger; plur. , , , .

Ȧupasut 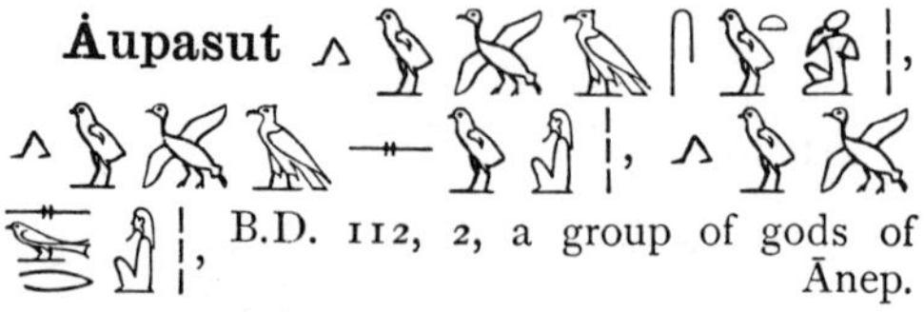, B.D. 112, 2, a group of gods of Ānep.

ȧupen 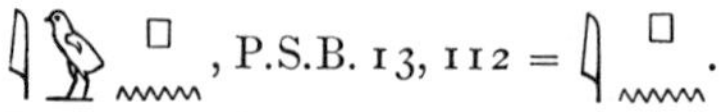, P.S.B. 13, 112 =.

ȧuf 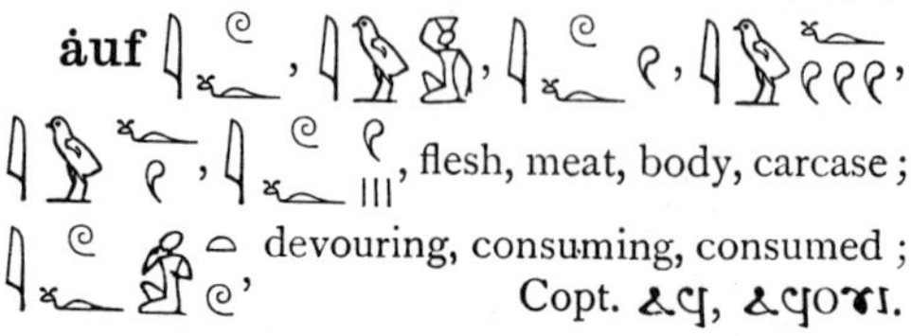, flesh, meat, body, carcase; devouring, consuming, consumed; Copt. ⲁϥ, ⲁϥⲟⲩⲓ.

Ȧuf , Berg. 1, 34, a dog-headed ape-god.

Ȧuf , Denderah 2, 49, a frog-faced ape-god.

Ȧufȧ , U. 533, the name of a serpent-god.

ȧuftȧ-t 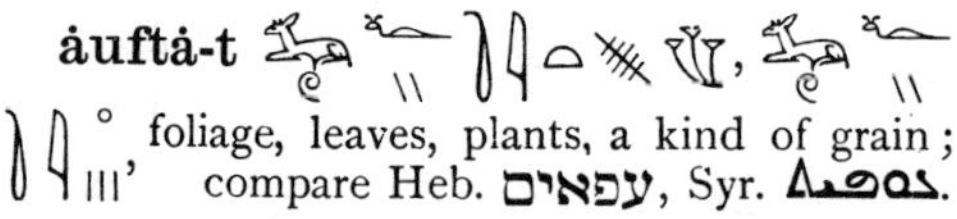, foliage, leaves, plants, a kind of grain; compare Heb. עפאים, Syr. ܐܒܐ.

ȧumā, ȧumāt , part of a waggon.

ȧumān (ȧmn) 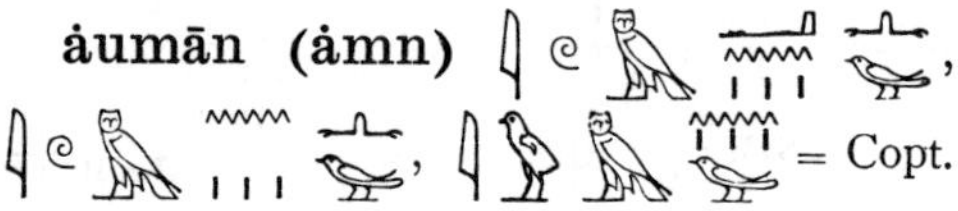 = Copt. ⲙⲙⲟⲛ.

ȧumi , fear, awe, reverence.

ȧumer (?) 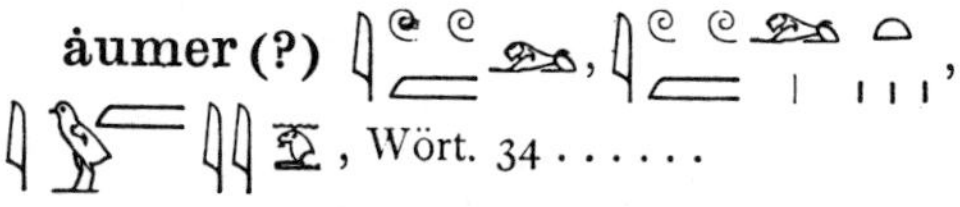, Wört. 34 ......

ȧums 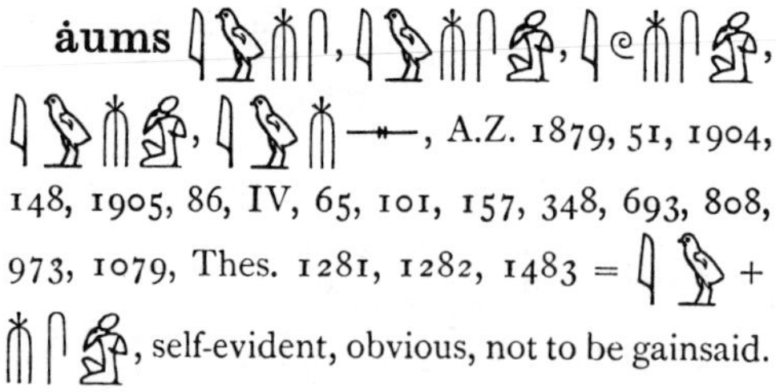, A.Z. 1879, 51, 1904, 148, 1905, 86, IV, 65, 101, 157, 348, 693, 808, 973, 1079, Thes. 1281, 1282, 1483 = +, self-evident, obvious, not to be gainsaid.

ȧunn (ȧnn) 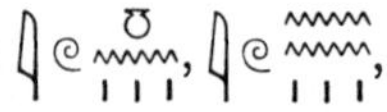, we; Copt. ⲁⲛⲟⲛ.

ȧun 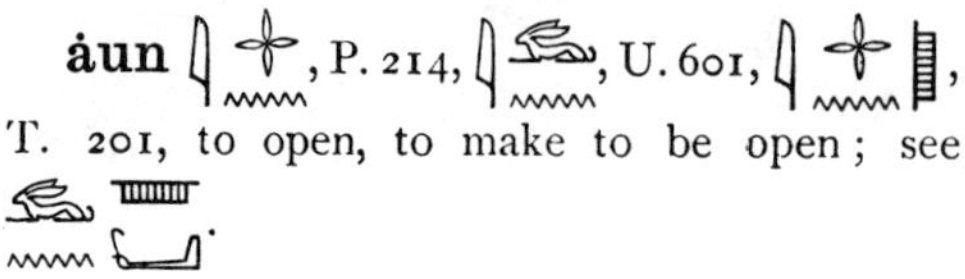, P. 214, U. 601, T. 201, to open, to make to be open; see.

ȧun-ra 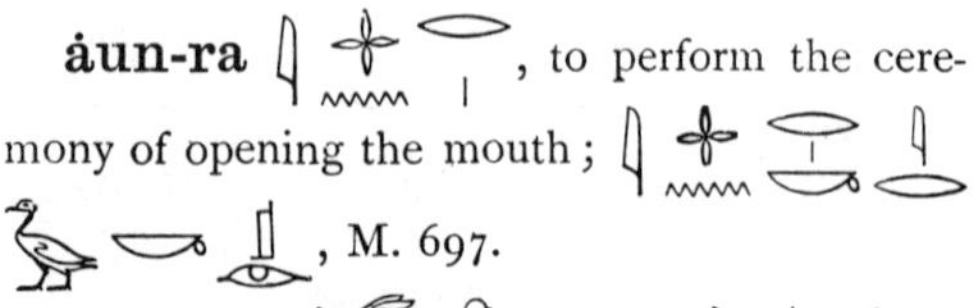, to perform the ceremony of opening the mouth; M. 697.

ȧun ḥer 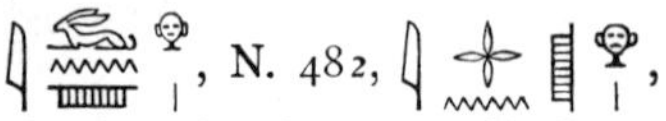, N. 482, N. 145, to open the face, *i.e.*, show oneself; Copt. ⲟⲩⲱⲛϩ.

ȧun 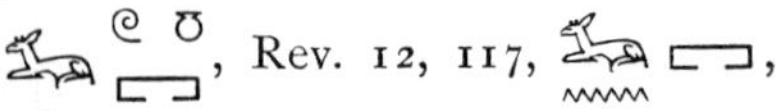, Rev. 12, 117, inner chamber.

ȧunn-t , A.Z. 1872, 37, Rec. 35, 125, shrine, sanctuary, part of a temple; plur., halls, courts.

ȧun 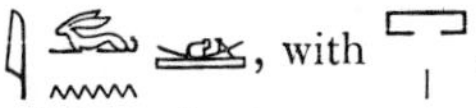, with, A.Z. 51, 72, cabin of a ship or boat.

ȧun 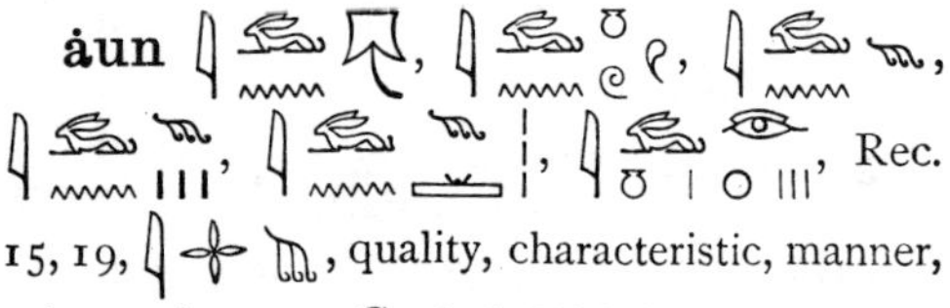, Rec. 15, 19, quality, characteristic, manner, colour, pigment; Copt. ⲁⲟⲩⲁⲛ.

ȧun , disposition, nature; good or kindly disposition.

ȧun , Rev. 12, 8, to load a ship; Copt. ⲁⲟⲩⲉⲓⲛ, ⲁⲩⲉⲓⲛ.

ȧun-t , garment, apparel, dress.

ȧunnu , P. 118, T. 171, M. 151, N. 106, abode, nest, home; T. 376.

ȧuna 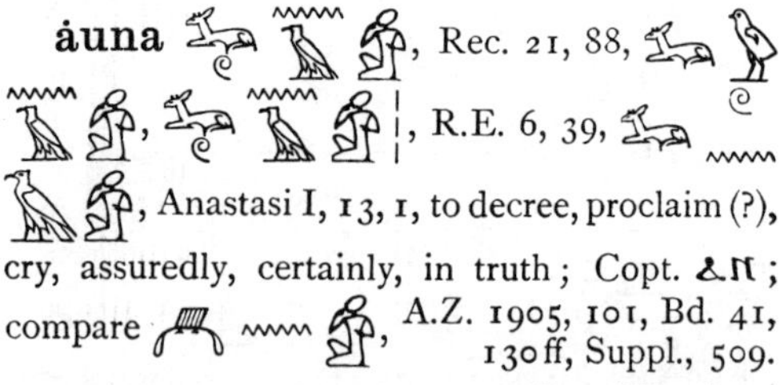, Rec. 21, 88, R.E. 6, 39, Anastasi I, 13, 1, to decree, proclaim (?), cry, assuredly, certainly, in truth; Copt. ⲁⲛ; compare, A.Z. 1905, 101, Bd. 41, 130ff, Suppl., 509.

Ȧun-āā-f 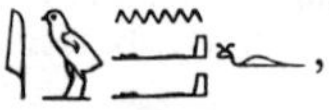, Ṭuat XI, a form of the god **Ȧf**.

ȧunit , L.D. III, 65A, 14, Rec. 27, 225, inner chamber, sanctuary.

Ȧunith 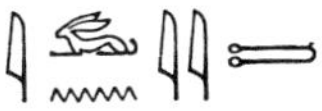, Ṭuat VII, a star-goddess.

Ȧunut , Rec. 31, 173, a group of divine beings (?)

ȧunf (?) , Rec. 31, 173 . . . . .

ȧunk ; var. , a medicinal plant.

ȧur , U. 198, , P. 575, 691, , N. 700, , M. 68, N. 49, , P. 98, , N. 750, to conceive, be pregnant, , T. 342, P. 221; compare Heb. הָרָה. Later forms are the following:—

ȧur   , Rec. 27, 57,  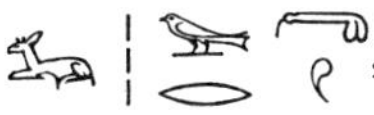, to conceive, be pregnant; , conceptions (?) Copt. ⲱⲱ.

ȧur-t   , T. 333, N. 703, the child conceived, pregnant goddess or woman.

ȧuru , human beings.

ȧurit , Rec. 30, 217,  , beans, Syrian beans; Copt. ⲁⲣⲱ.

ȧur , to separate (?)

ȧur 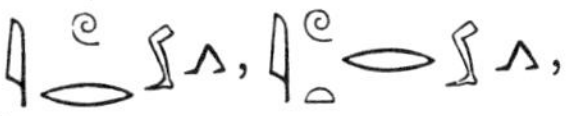, schoenus; see .

ȧur-t (ȧter-t?) , tomb, place of rest.

ȧur , stream, canal, river, arm of the Nile; see ; Copt. ⲉⲓⲉⲣⲟ, ⲉⲓⲟⲟⲣ, Heb. יְאֹר.

ȧur-āa , "great river"; var. , the Canopic arm of the Nile.

ȧur-t 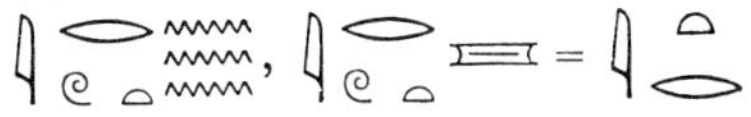 .

Ȧurȧuȧaqrsȧnq Rabati  , B.P. 162, a name of Par, a form of Rā.

ȧureḥ 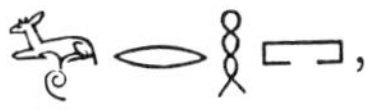, open space, area; see [illegible]; Copt. ⲟⲩⲣⲉϩ.

ȧurekhu [illegible], IV, 481, men who know, the learned; [illegible].

ȧurtchaȧȧu [illegible] [illegible], Koller Pap. 4, 4, staves.

ȧuh [illegible] [illegible] [illegible], to load, be loaded, bear, carry.

ȧuh-t [illegible], speech (?)

ȧuhamu [illegible], Theban Ost. No. 6 . . . .

ȧuhṭ-t [illegible], a medicinal wood or bark.

Ȧuheṭ [illegible], a god of the Ṭuat.

ȧuḥ  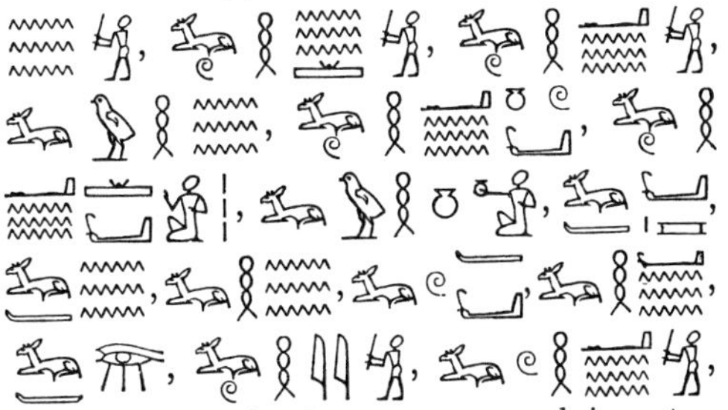, to inundate, to flood, to steep or soak in water, to moisten, to sprinkle, to shower, to pour out a libation.

åuḥ-t , lotion, liquid, flood.

åuḥu, to lament.

åuḥ , to cut away, to set free.

Åuḥu, a divine name of magical power.

Åuḥu-t (Åuḥit) , B.D. G. 292, a goddess of Philae; , Metternich Stele 189, the female counterpart of Un-Nefer and mother of Horus.

åuḥu 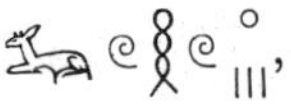, a kind of grain or seed.

åuḥa , Suppl. 513. ......

åuḥnu (?) 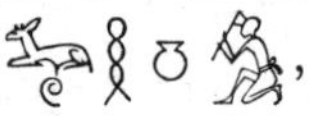, P. 1116, B. 20 ....

Åu-ḥer-åptes 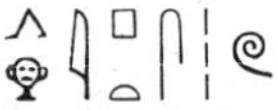, Ṭuat V, a god with a lasso who destroyed the dead.

åukhekh , 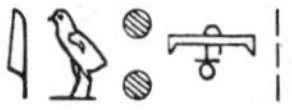, night, darkness.

åukhemu , IV, 480; see **khemu**.

Åukhemu urṭu 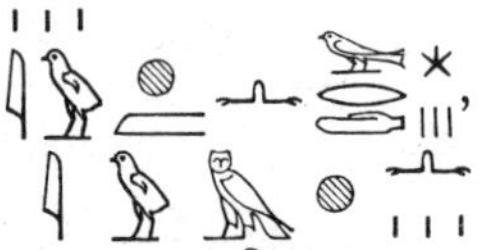, Mar. Aby. I, 8, 90, , the stars that do not rest.

Åukhemu-seku  , Mar. Aby. I, 8, 90, the stars that never perish.

Åukhemu-pen-ḥesb (?)  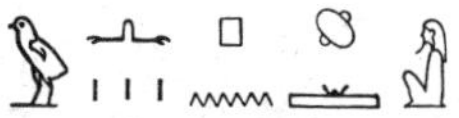, B.D. 189, 15, etc., a group of divine beings.

åukherru (?) . ....

åus , P.S.B. 14, 237, 3rd pers. sing. fem.; Copt. εc.

Åus-t, Mar. Aby. II, 16, Isis = 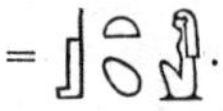.

åus(ås) , Rev. 14, 18, a perfume.

Åusårs (Åsåres) , Nesi-Amsu 28, 21, Osiris; see , Åsår.

Åusāsit , 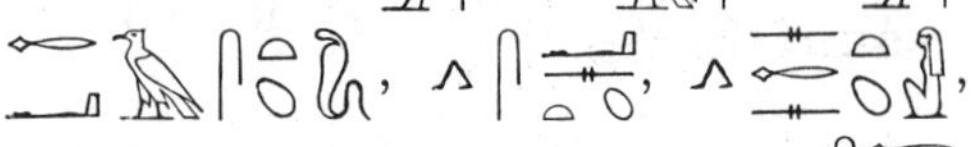, Nesi-Amsu 25, 22, Hymn of Darius, 31, 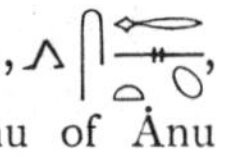, Harris I, pl. 1, a consort of Temu of Ånu ().

åusu , N. 659, what (?)

åusu, Peasant 148, , Åmen. 17, 18, , a small pair of scales held in the hand.

åusem , Rev., to prevent, to obstruct.

åusekh 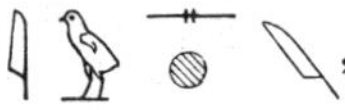, to reap; see 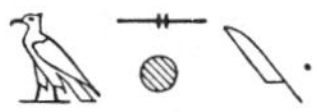.

åushesh , pottage, plaster, cake; Copt. ooγω.

åuqet , reeds used in a laboratory.

Åuqau, M. 374, N. 943, a name of the divine ferryman.

åukiu 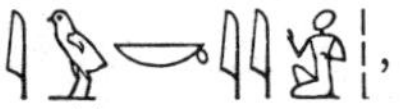, L.D. III, 219E, 17, quarrymen (?)

Åuker , Tomb of Rameses IV, 30, the god who bears on his back the solar disk, which is held in position by ropes in the hands of Nāri, Khessi, Åṭṭi and Rekhsi.

Åuger-t Åugertt , , a name of the Other World.

Åugeru , the gods of Åugert.

Åugerit, B.D. 64, 11, goddess of the Ṭuat of Ånu.

Åugerit-khenti-åsts 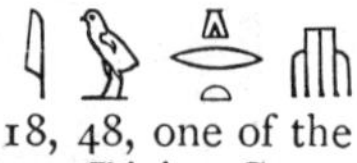 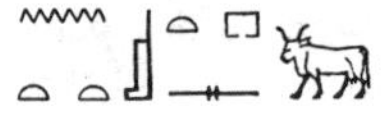, B.D. 141, 18, 48, one of the seven Divine Cows.

ȧut , Rev. 11, 143, who, which; Copt. ⲉⲧ.

ȧut ḥer , Rev. 11, 154; Copt. ⲉⲧ ϩⲏ.

ȧuti , , , , , = , who, or what, is not, without, lacking; Copt. ⲁⲧ.

ȧut , Rev. 11, 186, , Rev. 12, 29, , Rev. 14, 16, , Rev. 4, 74, between; Copt. ⲟⲩⲧⲥ.

ȧu-ti , Rec. 29, 157, 158, swathing, bandage; plur. .

Ȧuti , Tomb of Seti I, one of the 75 forms of Rā.

ȧuten-t , , Mar. Aby. I, 6, 31, Anastasi Pap. 1, 26, 1, , Rec. 21, 15, ground, dust, earth, dung; Copt. ⲉⲓⲧⲛ̄.

ȧuthth , Rev. 13, 3, between; Copt. ⲟⲩⲧⲉ.

ȧuṭ , Rec. 21, 98, between; Copt. ⲟⲩⲧⲉ; , Koller Pap. 1, 3, with, in charge of.

ȧuṭ , , Thes. 1296, , , , , to separate, to remove, to divide, to travel through; , to lead astray.

ȧuṭen-t , , , , dust, ground, earth; , Ȧmen. 9, 20, dung.

ȧuṭenb , incense (?)

ȧutchamāna (?) , Alt. K. 206 . . . .

ȧutchu , P. 146, 672, M. 661, N. 1276, , P. 672, to make an order or decree, to give a command.

ȧutcheb , river banks; see utcheb, .

ȧb , M. 407 = , T. 394, , , U. 16, 451, P. 110, 369, 653, 654, 833, M. 172, 754, 757, 759, N. 690, 1145; plur. , T. 181, P. 204, , Rec. 31, 28; , heart of the soul, Rec. 32, 79; , N. 27, the dictates of the heart; , heart's desire, U. 629. Later forms are:

ȧb , , , , , , , , heart, middle, interior, sense, wisdom, understanding, intelligence, attention, intention, disposition, manner, will, wish, desire, mind, courage, lust, self; plur. , , , , , , , Stunden 109; Heb. לֵב; , joy, gladness; , to eat the heart, *i.e.*, be sorry; , dense of heart; , , everybody, Rec. 33, 7; , thoughts, intentions; , heart of my heart, N. 350.

ȧb en Rā , "heart of Rā," a name of Thoth, , Rec. 26, 77.

Ȧb , Ȧmen. 14, 18, a god.

ȧb , the amulet of the heart; plur. , , heart of carnelian.

ȧb-ȧb , Rec. 27, 182, image, statue (?)

ȧb-t , , Thes. 1296, , middle room of a house, cabinet.

ȧb-t , bread, cake; plur. (?)

ȧb , , , , IV, 1131, calf.

ȧb, Anastasi I, 24, 8, Peasant B. 2, 117, to think, to suppose, to imagine, to let the fancy run free.

ȧb, U. 172, , to be thirsty; Copt. ειβε; , Rec. 26, 78, ; Arab. لاب.

ȧb-t, U. 196, , thirst.

ȧbb, T. 332, , N. 622, , to be thirsty.

ȧbi, Peasant B. 2, 118, thirsty man.

ȧb, U. 539, T. 296, vases.

ȧb, to mix.

ȧb-t, Peasant 130, 179, Rec. 32, 84, , Rec. 26, 8, , a walled enclosure, place of protection or of restraint, cave, abode, strong building, asylum, rest-house.

ȧb, pegs or stakes of a net or snare; var.

ȧbb, Rec. 30, 68, ropes of the magical boat.

ȧb, draughtsman.

ȧb, ȧbu, N. 737, ; var. **ȧab**, , to dance.

ȧbau, ȧba, M. 573, , P. 401, , N. 1180, dance [of the god].

ȧbau, dancer, dancing man; var. ; plur.

Ȧbti, Ṭuat I, a "dancer"-god who sang before Rā.

ȧb-t, (?) sistrum (?)

ȧb-t, sceptre; var.

ȧb, a spice offering (?)

ȧb, a kind of seed, or plant, used in medicine, lettuce; Copt. ιωβ (?); , *abu* of the South and North.

ȧbu (?), U. 326, excretions, saliva (?)

ȧb-t, something pure or holy; see .

ȧb, to cease, to stop, cessation; var.

ȧb-t, P. 579, path, road (?)

ȧb-t

Ȧb-ti, a goddess.

ȧba, U. 120, N. 429, a joint of meat.

ȧba, T. 350, P. 74, 109, N. 109, 973, to endow with soul, to make strong or courageous, to be filled with soul or strength.

ȧba, P. 165, M. 317, N. 821, to open.

ȧba, ȧbȧa, T. 182, N. 653, M. 164 = , P. 527, to marvel.

Ȧbait [ ], B.D. 76, 2, 140 (Saïte), the Mantis that guided the deceased.

ȧbait, Hh. 744, P.S.B. 14, 400, part of a rudder.

ȧbain, Rev. 13, 8, wretched man, poor; Copt. ⲉⲃⲓⲏⲛ.

ȧbau, Rec. 29, 148, small animals, sheep, goats.

ȧbar, P.S.B. 11, 266, with , in company with.

ȧbar, horse, stallion, horses, bulls; compare Heb. אָבִיר and אַבִּיר.

ȧbash-t, Anastasi Pap. IV, 14, 1, (*sic*), Gol. 6, 11, , Kahun 40, 23, a kind of cake or bread.

ȧbagi, N. 984, weak (?), helpless (?); see .

ȧbat-ta, Anastasi I, 23, 5, "thou hast destroyed"; √אבד.

ȧbata, servant, slave; Heb. עֶבֶד.

ȧbȧ-t, Rev. honey; Copt. ⲉⲃⲓⲱ.

ȧbȧ, Rec. 34, 121, a kind of unguent = , .

ȧbȧai, P. 588 . . . .

ȧbu, a tree sacred to Horus.

Ȧbuit, Denderah 4, 44, a "weeping"-goddess.

Ȧbu-ur, B.D. 42, 3, a god or goddess of the Block in the Ṭuat.

ȧbusuna (?), a sickness or disease.

ȧbem, Rec. 15, 5 . . . .

ȧbm[er]-t, grave, tomb.

ȧbn, Harris I, 63c, 15, Rec. 15, 199, , alum; Copt. ⲱⲃⲉⲛ.

ȧbns, calamint (?); Copt. ⲁⲃⲥⲱⲛ.

ȧbr, salve, unguent, ointment.

ȧbrȧu maā, genuine ȧbr.

ȧbheti, stone of Ȧbhet in Nubia, a precious stone, emerald (?)

ȧbeḥ, tooth; plur. , U. 41, 68, , N. 660, ; Copt. ⲟⲃϩⲉ.

ȧbḥ-t, tooth (?); , Hymn Nile 24, teeth, "biters."

ȧbḥ, Ebers Pap. 100, 9, 13, moist, wet.

ȧbeḥ, A.Z. 1899, 89, Rec. 23, 102, title of a priest.

ȧbḥu ⟨hieroglyphs⟩, IV, 386, to sprinkle, to moisten.

ȧbḥ-t ⟨hieroglyphs⟩, N. 524, a wooden object, goad (?)

ȧbḥn ⟨hieroglyphs⟩, T. 282, N. 132, to drive away.

ȧbekh ⟨hieroglyphs⟩, to proclaim.

ȧbkhȧ ⟨hieroglyphs⟩; var. **ȧabkh-t,** ⟨hieroglyphs⟩, ointment containing many ingredients.

ȧbekh (?) ⟨hieroglyphs⟩, U. 538, T. 295, P. 229 . . . .

ȧbes ⟨hieroglyphs⟩, U. 405, ⟨hieroglyphs⟩, P. 215, Rec. 31, 162, ⟨hieroglyphs⟩ = ⟨hieroglyphs⟩, to make to rise, to make to advance.

ȧbes ⟨hieroglyphs⟩, a kind of cap, headdress; var. ⟨hieroglyphs⟩, Rec. 5, 92.

Ȧbes ⟨hieroglyphs⟩, a god.

ȧbsa (?) ⟨hieroglyphs⟩, Peasant 25, medicinal plants, or seeds; ⟨hieroglyphs⟩, a kind of medicated oil.

ȧbsit ⟨hieroglyphs⟩, part of a boat; plur. ⟨hieroglyphs⟩, Rec. 30, 67.

ȧbsi ⟨hieroglyphs⟩, wolf, or jackal.

ȧbsha ⟨hieroglyphs⟩, gazelle.

ȧbk ⟨hieroglyphs⟩, ⟨hieroglyphs⟩, grief, wailing, weeping; see ⟨hieroglyphs⟩.

ȧbt ⟨hieroglyphs⟩, ⟨hieroglyphs⟩, ⟨hieroglyphs⟩, net, snare, trap; Copt. ⲁⲃⲱ.

Ȧbtka ⟨hieroglyphs⟩, B.D. 65, 8, a god who fettered Āapep.

Ȧbta ⟨hieroglyphs⟩, ⟨hieroglyphs⟩, Ṭuat I, one of the nine ape-porters.

ȧbeth ⟨hieroglyphs⟩, P. 616, M. 784, ⟨hieroglyphs⟩, N. 1144, to snare, to hunt with nets.

Ȧbeth ⟨hieroglyphs⟩, Ṭuat IX, god of the serpent Ṭepi.

ȧbthersu ⟨hieroglyphs⟩, an animal.

ȧbṭ ⟨hieroglyphs⟩, month; Copt. ⲉⲃⲟⲧ; plur. ⟨hieroglyphs⟩, T. 12, P. 657, 761, M. 764, ⟨hieroglyphs⟩, III, 140 = Pashons; ⟨hieroglyphs⟩, monthly festival; ⟨hieroglyphs⟩, the 12 monthly festivals; ⟨hieroglyphs⟩, the 2nd day of the month; ⟨hieroglyphs⟩, month by month.

Ȧbṭ ⟨hieroglyphs⟩. The gods of the 12 months, each containing 30 days, were:

Season	Month		God	
Season I.—ĀAKHET.	I	⟨hieroglyphs⟩	TEKHI	⟨hieroglyphs⟩
	II	⟨hieroglyphs⟩	PTAḤ ⟨hieroglyphs⟩, or MENKHET ⟨hieroglyphs⟩, or ȦPT ⟨hieroglyphs⟩	
	III	⟨hieroglyphs⟩	HET-ḤER ⟨hieroglyphs⟩	
	IIII	⟨hieroglyphs⟩	SEKHMET ⟨hieroglyphs⟩, or KAḤERKA ⟨hieroglyphs⟩	
Season II.—PERT.	I	⟨hieroglyphs⟩	MENU ⟨hieroglyphs⟩, or SHEFBETI ⟨hieroglyphs⟩	
	II	⟨hieroglyphs⟩	REKH-UR ⟨hieroglyphs⟩, or ⟨hieroglyphs⟩	
	III	⟨hieroglyphs⟩	REKḤ NETCHES ⟨hieroglyphs⟩	
	IIII	⟨hieroglyphs⟩	RENNUTET ⟨hieroglyphs⟩	
Season III.—SHEMU.	I	⟨hieroglyphs⟩	KHENSU ⟨hieroglyphs⟩	
	II	⟨hieroglyphs⟩	HERU-KHENTI-KHAṬIT ⟨hieroglyphs⟩	
	III	⟨hieroglyphs⟩	ȦPT ⟨hieroglyphs⟩	
	IIII	⟨hieroglyphs⟩	HERU-ĀAKHUTI ⟨hieroglyphs⟩	

àbṭ 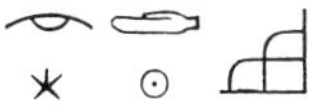, net = .

àbṭu , a temple of Shu.

àp , U. 216, P. 335, 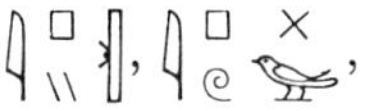, , to count, to reckon up, to number, to enumerate, to assess, to adjudge the value of, to appreciate, to measure; Copt. ωπ ; , the great counting, *i.e.*, last judgment; 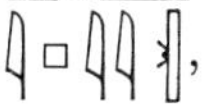, Rec. 26, 231.

àp-t , numbering, census, number, measure; Copt. ΗΠΕ ; 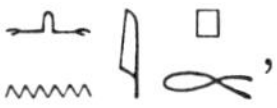, countless; , taxes.

àpp-t , reckoning, account.

àpp 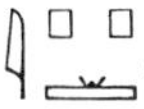, to count, etc. = 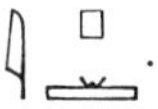.

àp-t 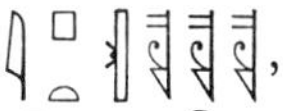, P. 557, a counting of bones; , counting up the members of the body to see that none is wanting.

Ápi-ábu 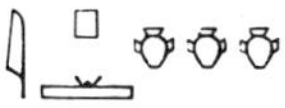, P. 541, 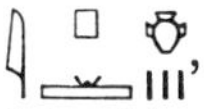, P. 697, "counter of hearts," a name of Anubis.

Ápi-áb-neter 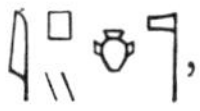, "reckoner of the heart of the god," a name of Thoth, .

Ápi-khenti-seḥ-neter , Rec. 20, 79, the god who makes a man to live 110 years.

Ápi-tchet-f , "counter of his body," a title of Osiris.

àp-t 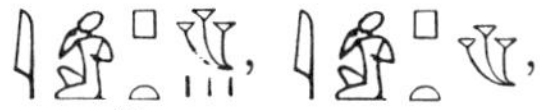, a kind of plant, papyrus (?)

àpu , papyrus (?), list, register of lands, rolls; 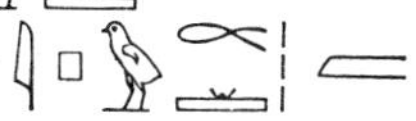 , estate rolls.

àp-t , Ámen. 8, 19, 18, 21, stick, sceptre, measuring rod, corn measure.

àp-t , Rec. 14, 56, a measure of corn = 40 , P.S.B. 14, 432, A.Z. 1904, 143; Heb. אֵיפָה, Copt. οιπε, Gr. (LXX) *οιφε*, *οιφει*.

àp-t 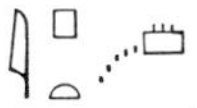 = the quadruple ḥeqet, and was the measure of a ration for beasts, R.E. 6, 26, Rec. 17, 159.

àp-t 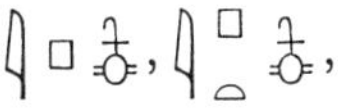, a vase or vessel.

àp-t , Rev. 11, 169, metal pot; plur. .

àp-t , Koller Pap. 38, refined (of gold).

àp-t 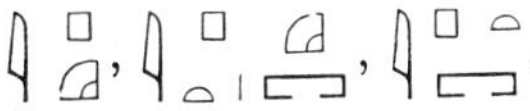, A.Z. 1912, 55, house, dwelling, palace.

àp-t nesu 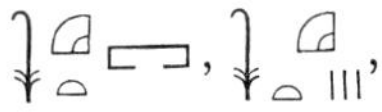, royal harîm.

àp-t ur-t , the great temple of Karnak; among its gates were: 1. 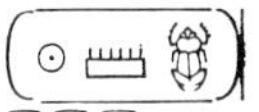 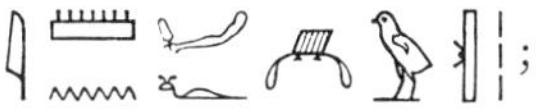; 2. ; 3. [illegible]; 4. [illegible]; 6. [illegible].

Ápàp [illegible], the month of επιφι.

àp (ḥeb-en-àp) [illegible], a festival in the month of παωπε.

Ápit [illegible], Wilkinson 3, 213, the tutelary goddess of **Ta-àpt,** [illegible], Thebes.

Ápàpit [illegible], Rev. 12, 1, a form of Hathor.

Ápit [illegible], L.D. 4, 30, Prisse, Mon. 36, Champollion, Mon. 1, 27, No. 4, one of the mother-gods of Egypt, nursing mother of Thebes, who appears in the forms of a woman and a woman-headed hippopotamus; her chief titles are: [illegible].

Ȧpit, the goddess of the 11th month of the year; Copt. єπнπ; varr.

Ȧpit-ḥemt-s, Rec. 34, 192, one of the 12 Thoueris goddesses.

Ȧpit-ȧakhut-theḥen, Ombos 1, 45, a hippopotamus-goddess.

Ȧpit-ur-t-em-khat-Nut, Rec. 34, 190, 192, one of the 12 Thoueris goddesses.

ȧp, stairs, staircase, steps.

ȧpȧp (pȧpȧ ?), tablet, plaque, tile, brick; compare Copt. ϕⲁϕє.

ȧpp, to journey, to traverse.

ȧpp-t, pill, pellet, round cake; pills, pastilles.

ȧp; see **up.**

Ȧp-t, Ȧpu-t, T. 312, N. 946, P. 650, 726, M. 751, the Messenger-god.

ȧp-ti (ȧupti), Rec. 21, 81, messenger, envoy.

ȧpa, P. 673, U. 604, M. 664, U. 476, N. 738, 1280, U. 477, N. 759, to make to fly, to fly.

ȧpapa, to fly.

ȧpa, A.Z. 1908, 27, house, dwelling, *harîm*; Copt. нπι.

Ȧpaȧ-f, P. 645, a proper name (?)

ȧpath, ȧpathȧ, M. 374, N. 934 . . . .

ȧpȧ, Rev., to think, to consider; Copt. ωπ.

Ȧpȧ, a goddess.

Ȧpi[t], U. 487, P. 640, M. 672, a god in the Ṭuat.

ȧpi-t, a measure for corn; Copt. οιπє.

ȧpi, Rev., judgment.

ȧpu, what is assessed, tax, tribute.

ȧpu, U. 190, dem. pron. plur. masc. these; fem.

ȧpui, these two (masc.).

ȧpf, U. 487, T. 203, P. 96, 310, N. 792, dem. pron. masc. this.

ȧpen, ȧpenu, these, these two (masc).

ȧpen, to play the tambourine.

ȧpeḥ, P. 163, to make arrive.

ȧpeḥ, pig.

ȧps, part of a boat, ribs (?)

Ȧpsit, Denderah 210, one of the 36 Dekans; Gr. ⲁϕοcο.

Ȧpsetch-t, Thes. 113, one of the seven stars of Orion; its god was Horus.

ȧpshen, a medicinal seed.

ȧpt, goose; plur. Rec. 18, 182; Copt. ωϐⲧ.

ȧpt, part of a ship.

ȧptu, Westcar 7, 1, Rec. 34, 118, A.Z. 1898, 147, cases for amulets; var.

åptui, T. 206, P. 40, 301, M. 610, 636, Hh. 312, these two (fem.).

åptf, Hh. 433, dem. pron. plur. of .

apten, åptenti, these two (fem.).

åpṭu, IV, 1149, Rec. 34, 118, furniture, beds, boxes.

åpṭ, goose; plur., Rec. 13, 2.

åpṭ, cup, pot; Copt. ⲁⲡⲟⲧ.

åpṭ, a measure.

Åptches, Annales I, 84 = .

Åf, god of the 6th day of the month.

åf, U. 268, 519, U. 535, flesh, meat, joint, member; plur., P. 89, IV, 1194; hidden body; bread, cake, food.

Åf, Åfu, the carcase of the Sun-god of night, or the dead body of Rā; he has the form of a ram-headed god, and his shrine is encircled by the serpent Meḥen.

Åf, Ṭuat V, a name of two man-headed sphinxes.

Åfi Åsår, Ṭuat VII, the flesh, *i.e.*, dead body, of Osiris.

Åfu fṭu, Thes. 122, the four gods who fought Set.

Åf-ermen-åri-f, an ape-headed associate of Thoth.

Åfu-ḥeri-khenṭ-f, Ṭuat II, an ape-headed god with a knife-shaped phallus.

Åfu Tem, Ṭuat VII, the "flesh of Tem," a god who devoured the enemies of Osiris.

åf, to turn, to twist, to revolve.

åf, serpent, viper; Heb. אֶפְעֶה, Arab. أَفْعَى, Eth. አፍዖት :

Åf, Ṭuat III, a serpent hostile to Rā.

åf, åf-t, a bed.

Åfå, Ṭuat I, an ape-god gatekeeper.

åffi, Ṭuat VIII, P.S.B. 7, 194, shrew-mouse, shrew-mouse god; Copt. ϩⲁⲃⲗⲉⲗⲉ.

åfen, U. 545, T. 300, 310, P. 232, to flee, to get back.

åfekh, U. 209, T. 310, to unloose, to untie, to unroll, to unpick, to disentangle.

åft, medicine for the eyes.

åfṭ, to rest, to repose, to sit.

åfṭ, bier; bed with fine linen bedclothes (Love Songs, 1, 4).

åfṭ, couch with cushions, bedstead like the Sûdânî عنقريب.

åfṭ, Peasant 48, Amherst Pap. 1, linen garment, piece of stuff, linen cloth, rectangular sheet or coverlet of a bed, square shawl or head-cloth, bed, bed-clothes.

åfṭ, a rectangular box or chest, a rectangular stone, a rectangular socket, a rectangle, Düm. T.I. I, 101, 4.

åfṭ, sarcophagus.

åfṭ, a rectangular plot of ground.

ȧfṭ, to flee, leap away, to jump up from the ground; IV, 697; Copt. ϥⲟⲩ.

ȧfṭ-t, sweat of the god; Copt. ϥⲱⲧⲉ, ϥⲟϯ, ϥⲱϯ.

ȧfṭ, four; four spirits, M. 405; Copt. ⲁϥⲧⲉ, ϥⲧⲟⲩ, ϥⲧⲱⲟⲩ, ϥⲧⲟⲟⲩ.

ȧfṭu, a fourfold garment.

ȧm, adverb; Copt. ⲙⲙⲁⲩ.

ȧm, U. 541, Rec. 27, 57, not, do not.

ȧm, within; see

ȧmi-t, U. 23, U. 387, M. 350, P. 187, between, among (?)

ȧmi-ut, Rec. 20, 42, between; between two, IV, 362; between the two legs, B.D. 174, 7; Unȧs is between them; between.

ȧmi-utȧ, P. 311, P. 185, between, among (?)

ȧmi-tȧ, P. 167, between; Rec. 30, 194, between the thighs of Isis.

ȧmi, some person or something which is in; plur. those who are in the waters.

ȧmi-t, she who is in, it which is in; plur. **ȧmiut**.

ȧmi-at, someone at the supreme moment of some emotion.

ȧmi-ȧb, one who is in the heart, darling, trusted one; fem. thy darling sister.

ȧmi-ȧb ā, IV, 1001, chief confidential friend.

ȧmi-ȧbṭ, he who served by the month, a priest.

Ȧmiu ȧmau, N. 1327, a group of gods (?)

ȧmi-ȧriti, pilot.

ȧmi-ȧs, he who is in the tomb, the name of a priest of the tomb.

ȧmi-ȧst-ā, the title of a priest; plur. M. 239, T. 322.

ȧmi-ȧst-ā em Ḥerset, an amulet (Lacau).

ȧmi-ā 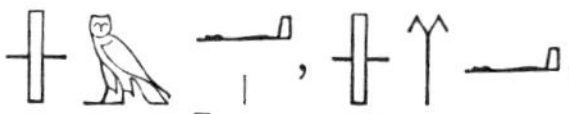, title of a priest of Ḥeru-ur; 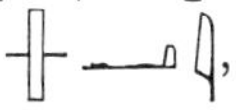, P. 674, M. 666; plur. , N. 1282.

ȧmi-āḥā 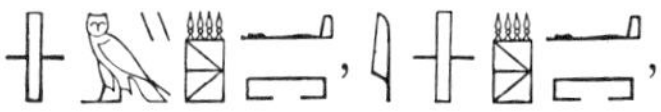, 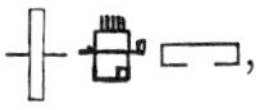, he who is in the palace, *i.e.*, the king.

ȧmi-uāb 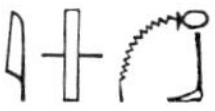, "dweller in the pure place," a title of a priest.

ȧmi-unnut , horoscope.

ȧmi-unnut , A.Z. 1899, 11, horoscopist.

ȧmi-unnut , guard; Copt. ⲉⲙⲛⲟⲩⲧ.

ȧmi-unnuit , Rec. 14, 13, a priest who served by the hour.

ȧmi-urt  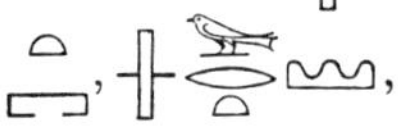, the port side of a boat when sailing northwards, the west.

ȧmi-urt-sa , a title of the king.

ȧmi-baḥ 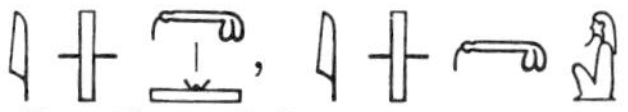, , he who is in front of or before; plur. , Rec. 36, 217, , , , Tombos 12.

ȧmi-per 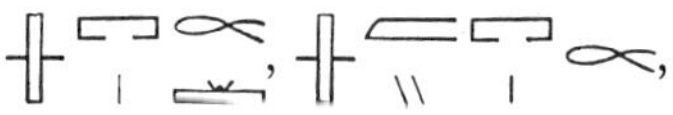, Rec. 19, 16, 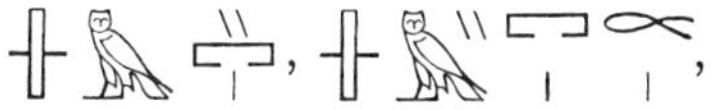, 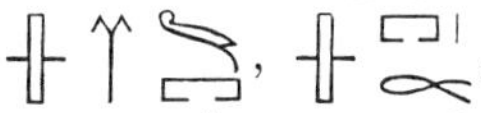, a will, conveyance of property, inventory of goods for testamentary purposes, title-deeds.

ȧmit-per , Methen 15, 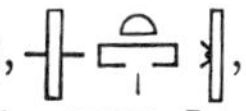, 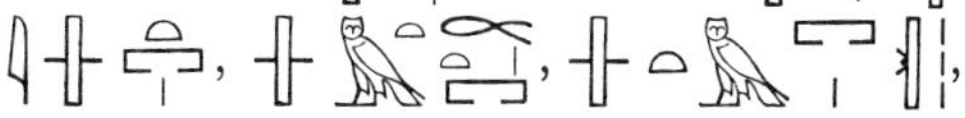, , will, testament, schedule of household goods.

ȧmiu-mitu , a name of the dead.

ȧmi-ren-f 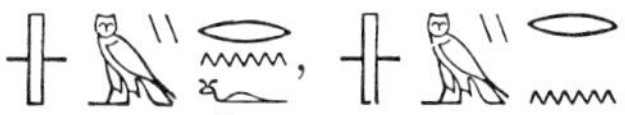, , a list of names, catalogue, register; plur.  , Rec. 21, 15, , registers, deeds.

ȧmi-hru 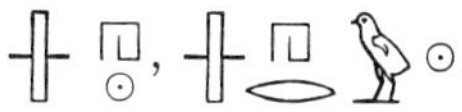, Rec. 15, 150, contemporary.

ȧmi-ḥa-t , Peasant 193, , he who is in front, leader.

ȧmit-ḥa-t , what is at the breast, in front.

ȧmiu-ḥat 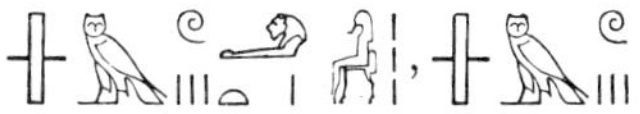 , ancestors, predecessors, beings of a former time.

ȧmiu-khat 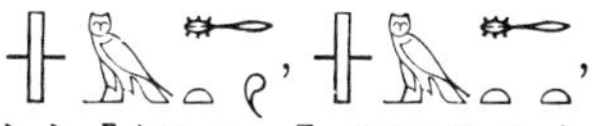, 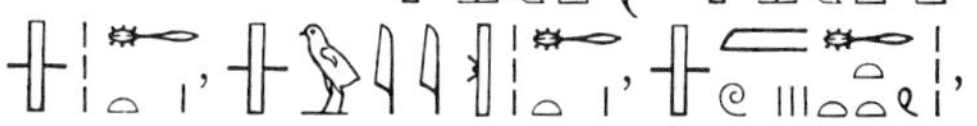, [illegible], viscera, intestines; [illegible], U. 511, [illegible], Rec. 31, 18, [illegible], Rec. 31, 29, [illegible], Thes. 1481, thoughts.

ȧmi-khent [illegible], he who is in front, leader.

ȧmi-khent [illegible], T. 29, [illegible], title of a priest; plur. [illegible].

ȧmiu-khen [illegible], palace officials.

ȧmi-khet [illegible], follower, companion, member of a body-guard; plur. [illegible], [illegible], [illegible].

ȧmiu-khet [illegible], N. 652, [illegible], those who come after, posterity; varr. , T. 180, M. 162, , P. 525.

åmi-sa , a title of a priest.

åmi-sa , he who is behind.

åmi-shepa (?) , U. 171 .....

Åmi-qerq-t , U. 530......

åmi-ta  , title of the chief priest of Letopolis.

åmiut-ta , herbs of the field.

Åmi-Ta-mer (?) 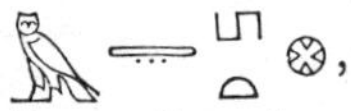, Rec. 33, 3, dweller in Ta-mer, *i.e.*, an Egyptian.

Åmi-taḥenb-t (?) , N. 1360 ....

åmi-tep , Rec. 30, 68, a rope of a boat.

åmiu-tcher , P. 161........

Åm-t (Åmit?) , the name of a serpent on the royal crown.

Åmi-Ånu , U. 254,  , N. 716, a title of Rā or Osiris.

Åmiu-åsu , M. 174, a group of gods whose abodes were hidden.

Åmi-Āntch-t 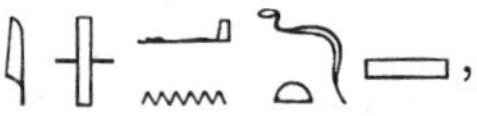, U. 256, 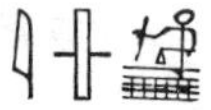, N. 717, a title of Osiris.

Åmi uåa-f , Ṭuat XI, one of the divine crew of the Boat of Rā.

Åmu-upt , T. 31, , N. 202, a form of the Sky-goddess Nut.

Åmi-Unu-meḥt , U. 265, "dweller in Hermopolis of the North," a divine title.

Åmi-Unu-resu , U. 264, "dweller in Hermopolis of the South," a divine title.

Åmi-urt , B.D. 145, 7, a cow-goddess.

åmi-ut 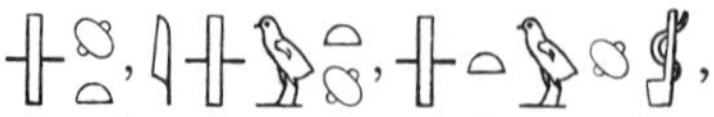, "dweller in the chamber of embalmment," a title of Anubis.

Åmi-ut , Rec. 36, 215, , the god of the 9th day of the month.

Åmi-utchat-såakhu-Åtemt 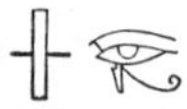 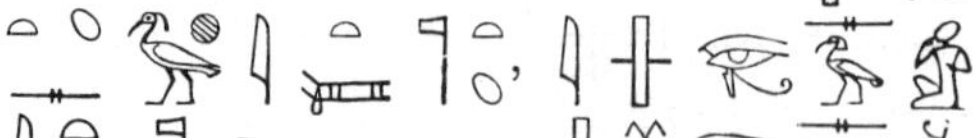 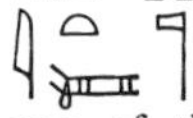, Rec. 34, 190, 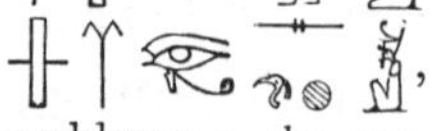, one of the 12 Thoueris goddesses; she presided over the month, 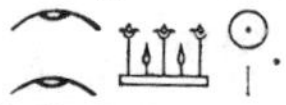.

Åmiu-baḥiu , B.D. 17, 59, the gods in the presence [of Osiris].

Åmiu-bagiu , Ṭuat VII, the "helpless" gods who lie on the back of the serpent Nehep.

Åmi-båk 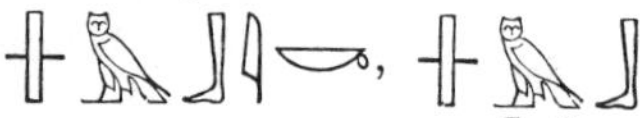 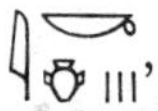, B.D. (Saïte) 125; see Åmi-besek [illegible] [illegible].

Åmi-beq [illegible], Cairo Pap. 23, 3, a god of the dead.

Åmi-Pe [illegible], Berg. 1, 11, a lion-god, a protector of the dead.

Åmi-pet-seshem-neterit [illegible] [illegible], [illegible], Ombos I, 48, Rec. 34, 180, one of the 12 Thoueris goddesses.

Åmi-pui [illegible], B.D. 25, 3; fem. [illegible].

åmi-mu [illegible], a title of Sebek.

Åmiu-Meḥnit [illegible], B.D. 168, the gods who are with Åfu-Rā.

Åmi-meḥen-f [illegible] [illegible], B.D. 64, 18, a title of Åfu, the dead Sun-god.

Åmi-naut-f [illegible], U. 331, [illegible], T. 300, a serpent-god of the "bush."

Ȧmi-Nu, Ṭuat VIII, the aged primeval Sky-god.

Ȧmi-nu-t-she (?), U. 266, the name of a god.

Ȧmi Nebȧui, Ṭuat II, the warder of Urnes in the Ṭuat.

Ȧm[it]-neb-s-Usert, B.D. 145, 146, name of the 9th Pylon.

Ȧmi-Nenu, N. 166, a name of the Sky-god.

Ȧmi-neḥṭ-f, N. 153, Rec. 30, 187, the name of a god.

Ȧmm-t Nekhen, the name of a serpent of the royal crown.

Ȧmi-Net, B.D. 146, the doorkeeper of the 7th Pylon.

Ȧmi-net-f, Ṭuat XI, the serpent guardian of the 10th Gate.

Ȧmi-neter, Ṭuat XII, a singing-god.

Ȧmi-Neṭȧt, U. 387, T. 346, P. 689, N. 114, a title of Osiris.

Ȧmi-Rerek (?), Quelques Pap. 79, title of a god (?)

Ȧmi-reṭ, U. 530, P. 674, M. 665, N. 1281, the name of a god (?)

ȧmiut-haiu, contemporaries.

Ȧmi-haf, B.D. 115, 6, a god who received a harpoon (māb,) from Rā, which was kept in Mābit, .

Ȧmi-hepnen, T. 308, the name of a god (?)

Ȧmi-hem-f, B.D. 108, 4, 5; see **Ȧmi-heh-f**.

Ȧmi-heh-f, B.D. 108, 4, 5, the serpent of the Mount of Sunrise who was covered with flints and metal; he was 30, or 50, or 70 cubits long, 3 cubits in girth, and his head was 3 cubits long.

ȧmiu-hetut, B.D. 100, 5, the apes that sing to the rising sun.

Ȧmi-Ḥe-t-ur-ka, U. 263, a title of Osiris and of Rā.

Ȧmi-Ḥe-t-Serqet-Ka-ḥetep-t, U. 257, a god.

ȧmi-ḥat, Tombos 6, the royal uraeus on the king's head.

Ȧmi-ḥent-f, M. 762, P. 665, a title of Osiris and of Rā.

Ȧmi-ḥer, Berg. I, 18, a protector of the dead.

Ȧmi-Ḥetep, Cairo Pap. 23, 3, a protector of the dead.

Ȧmi-Ḥetchpār, U. 259, N. 719, a title of Osiris and of Rā.

Ȧmiu khat Ȧsȧr, Ṭuat VII, the 12 gods who sleep on the serpent Nehep.

Ȧmi-khent-āat, Edfû I, 12, 15, a goddess of Edfû.

Ȧmiu-khet-Rā, Ṭuat IX, four gods who towed Ḥeru-ṭuati in his boat Khepri.

Ȧmiu-khet Ḥe-t-Ȧnes, B.D. (Saïte), 17, 40, a group of gods.

Ȧmiu-khet-Ḥeru, Ṭuat IX, four gods who towed Ḥeru-ṭuati in his boat.

Ȧmiu-khet-Teḥuti , Ṭuat IX, four gods who towed Ḥeru-ṭuati in his boat.

Ȧmi-suḥt-f , B.D. 17, 22 (Nebseni), a title of Rā; , , Denderah 4, 83, Todt. Lepsius 4, 83, B.D. 149, the god of the 9th Ȧat.

Ȧmi-sepa-f , P. 759, , P. 1656, , M. 962, the name of a god.

Ȧmi-Sepṭ-t , "a dweller in Sothis," a title of Horus.

Ȧmi-Seḥ , U. 260, a title of Osiris the god of Orion.

Ȧmi seḥseḥ 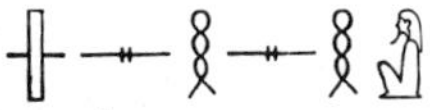, Rec. 31, 27, the name of a god.

Ȧmi-seḥ-neter , U. 258, a title of Anubis.

Ȧmi-seḥti 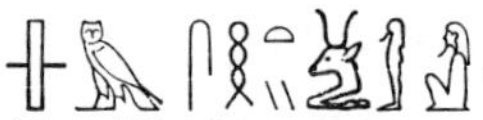, Nesi-Amsu, 10, 17, a title of Rā.

Ȧmi-sekhet-f 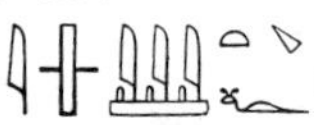, Ṭuat IX, a god of his domain.

Ȧmit-she-t-urt 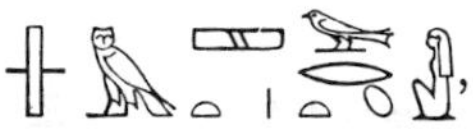, Ombos II, 130, a goddess.

ȧmiu-shemsu , those who are in the following of, the body-guard of a god.

Ȧmi-Sheṭ-t , N. 1360, title of Anubis.

Ȧmit-Qeṭem 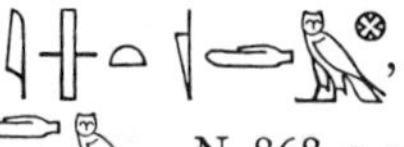, P. 204, M. 342, 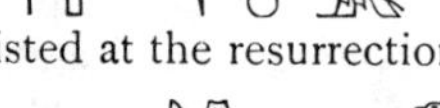, N. 868, a goddess who assisted at the resurrection of Osiris.

Ȧmi-kap 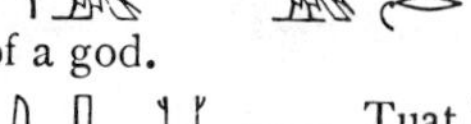, U. 258, N. 718, a title of a god.

Ȧmi-kar , Ṭuat I, a singing ape-god.

Ȧmi-keḥau , , T. 323, a god.

Ȧmi-ta 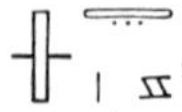, Rameses IX, 10, a serpent-god and associate of Tematheth.

Ȧmi-ta 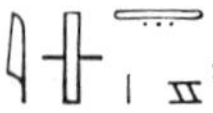, Ṭuat III, a god of the boat Pakht.

Ȧmi-ta , Berg. 1, 25, a lion-god.

ȧmi-ta-f 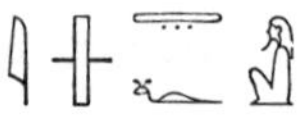, Rec. 6, 152, a title of Osiris.

Ȧmiu-ta (?) , B.D. 168, a group of gods who fed the dead.

Ȧmi-teḥenu , a title of Set.

Ȧmi-thepḥet-f 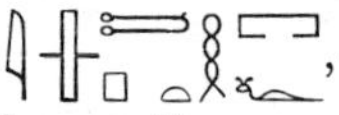,  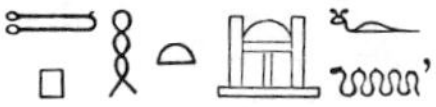, U. 332, T. 300, a title of several gods.

Ȧmi-Ṭuat , U. 466, a title of Horus.

Ȧmi-Ṭep , U. 261, a title of Horus of Buto.

Ȧmiu-ṭeser-t-tep  , B.D. 168, a group of benevolent goddesses.

Ȧmi-Ṭeṭ 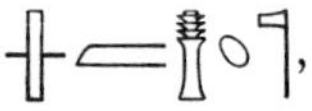, Rec. 4, 28, a title of Osiris (?)

Ȧmi-tchāāmu , T. 305, a title of a serpent.

Ȧmi-Tchebā kher-ut (?)  [illegible], T. 369, a title of Osiris.

ȧm [illegible], Rec. 11, 179, [illegible], [illegible], [illegible], [illegible], come! var. [illegible]; Copt. ⲁⲙⲟⲩ.

ȧm [illegible], U. 293, [illegible], N. 719 + 14, to be attacked.

ȧm, ȧmi [illegible], [illegible], [illegible], [illegible], Rec. 13, 20, [illegible], [illegible], Ȧmen. 12, 11, [illegible], Rev. 11, 138, [illegible], Rec. 14, 15, to eat; see [illegible], Rec. 29, 144; Copt. ⲟⲩⲱⲙ.

åm-ur, Rev., to overeat; Copt. ⲟⲩⲱⲙⲟⲩⲏⲣ.

åm-t, Israel Stele 7, , Rec. 17, 146, , P.E. 6, 22, food, fodder for horses and cattle, provender.

åm-t, T. 120, , U. 149, name of a wine.

åm, åm-t, , child, pupil.

Åm, B.D. G. 569, a form of Horus suckled by Renent, .

Åmit, Ombos II, 2, 195, a goddess of .

Åm[it], Ṭuat VIII, goddess of the circle Ḥetepet-neb-per-s.

Åm, Berg. 1, 34, a lion-god.

Åm, Berg. 1, 11, a jackal-headed god.

åm, Rec. 35, 56, , , Rec. 36, 213, to cry, to wail, to weep.

åmm, , , , , , , , to cry, cry out, to exclaim, to groan.

åm, A.Z. 1905, 107, woe!

åm, åm-t, , , , , (Lacau), staff, stick, standard.

åm, åmit, U. 458, , , , , to burn, to flame, to blaze, fire, flame; plur. , flames, fire-gods.

åmu (åmmu), , , , , , , , **(åam-t)** , , light, rays, beams.

åmemu, Todt. (Lepsius), 6, 43; see **Ḥenmemet.**

åmu, B.D. 148 (Rubric), colour, paint; see **åam.**

åmm, to make firm, to strengthen.

åmåm-t, strength.

åm, stuff, cloth, garment.

åm, , , Rec. 188, 13, 30, 72, stream, flood, deluge.

åm (åmm), , , , Hymn Nile 26, , , , Åmen. 20, 5, boat, ship.

åm (åmm), , , eyebrows.

åm (åmm), skin (?), cat.

åm (åmm), Rec. 31, 147, to be hard of hearing.

åm (åmm), Åmen. 12, 14, , patient, submissive.

åm (åmm), , , N. 170, 960, to putrefy, to rot, to ferment.

åm, filth.

åm (åmm), åmmit, , , , clay, like clay; Copt. ⲟⲙⲉ, ⲟⲙⲓ.

åm (åmm), raisins (?), fruit of a tree, dates (?)

åm (åmmu), P.S.B. 13, 411, fruit trees, palms.

åm (åmm), gracefulness of form, graciousness.

åm-ti, grace, graciousness.

Åma, Ṭuat XI, a dawn-god.

åma, to eat; Copt. ⲟⲩⲱⲙ.

åma, a staff.

ȧmau, borders, boundaries.

ȧmaā, M. 750, to make to travel.

ȧmam, house, tent.

ȧmam, date palm (?); plur.

ȧmam, kind, gracious, agreeable; , darling.

ȧmakh, Jour. As. 1908, 313, to honour, to worship, to be worthy of honour or worship; Copt. ⲙⲡϣⲁ; Rec. 23, 204.

ȧmakhu, Rec. 36, 78, U. 616, one who is bound to honour a master, or worship a god, vassal, one who is worthy to be honoured, revered, or worshipped; plur., P. 403, M. 576, paternal serfs, IV, 1054; , aged serfs, IV, 1045; , vassals of Osiris; fem.

ȧmakhi, Rec. 27, 53, serf, vassal of a god, person of honour.

ȧmakhit, female vassal (?), vassalage, fealty.

ȧmakhkh, Ȧmen. 11, 4, the venerable dead.

Ȧmakhu, P. 404, M. 576, N. 1183, the divine serfs in the Ṭuat.

Ȧmakhu nu Ȧsȧr, B.D. 141, the serfs of Osiris.

Ȧmakhu, N. 1200, the name of a god.

Ȧmakhui (?), Ṭuat XII, a god who towed Ȧf through the serpent Ānkh-neteru, and was reborn daily.

Ȧmakhit-f, Mar. Aby. 1, 45 . . . .

ȧmȧ, P. 258, T. 69, M. 224 = M. 492, like.

ȧmȧ, ȧmȧit, Rev. 11, 178, Rev. 13, 3, cat; Copt. ⲉⲙⲟⲩ.

ȧmȧ (?)-t, Rec. 31, 27 . . . .

ȧmȧr, U. 190, N. 601 = , T. 69, M. 224, like.

ȧmȧkheri, a kind of balsam tree, white manna tree.

ȧmma (read ȧmi ?), give, let, grant, I pray, make, cause; Copt. ⲙⲏⲓ, ⲙⲟⲓ.

ȧm (ȧmm), grain, wheat or barley.

ȧmȧa, Alt. K. 45, proper name (?); compare Heb. אֵם.

ȧmi, would that!

ȧmi-t, Rev., nature, disposition.

Ȧmi, Nesi-Amsu 30, 21, a name of the Eye of Horus.

Ȧmi, B.D. (Saïte) 110, 9, ibid. 153, 5, fire-god.

Ȧmit , , B.D. 164, 4, a name of Sekhmit-Bast-Rā.

ȧmitiu , dead person; plur. 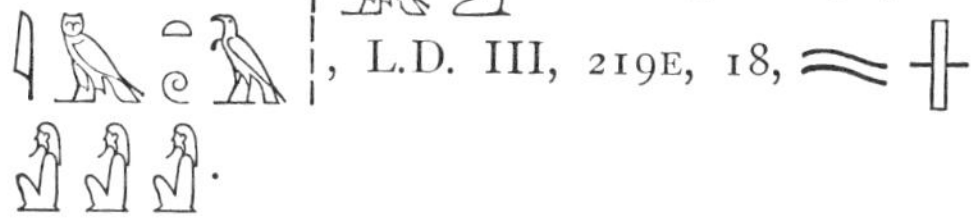, L.D. III, 219E, 18.

Ȧmutnen (?) , T. 49, 51, P. 160, a goddess of milch cows,  , and cows that give suck, .

ȧmn , R. 11, 140 = ⲁⲙⲙⲟⲛ.

ȧmen 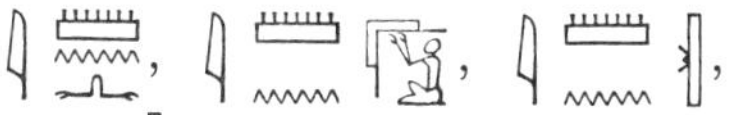, , Peasant 182, to hide, to conceal, to be hidden, secret, mysterious.

ȧmen , U. 508, hidden person or thing, concealed, secret, mysterious; plur.

Ȧmen 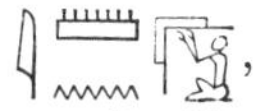, title of the high priest of the Gynaecopolite Nome.

Ȧmen , "hidden one," a name of the Devil.

ȧmen-t 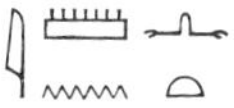, something hidden.

ȧmen-t 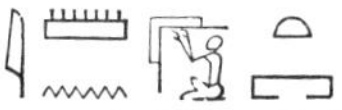, a hidden place, a sanctuary; plur. .

ȧmen ȧmen , U. 524, , T. 330, doubly hidden (?)

ȧmen-ȧb , to hide the heart, to dissemble.

ȧmen-ā 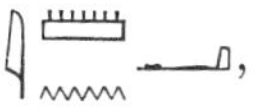, to conceal the hand.

Ȧmennu-āu , Ṭuat VII, 12 gods whose arms were hidden, and who lived with the body of Rā in Ḥet-Benben.

Ȧmen-ȧakhu , Ṭuat X, a destroyer of the dead.

Ȧmen-ren-f 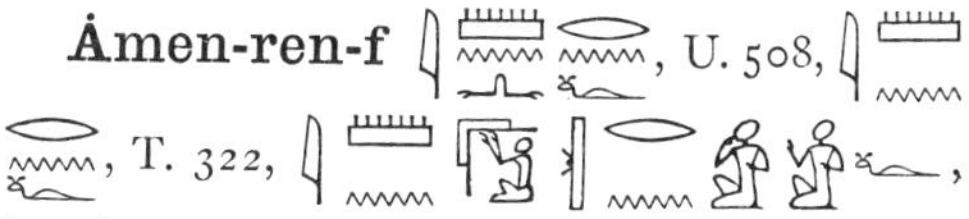, U. 508, T. 322, he whose name is hidden, a title of several gods, the great judge of the Ṭuat.

Ȧmen-ren-ḥer , Rec. 27, 55, the name of a god.

Ȧmen-ḥāu 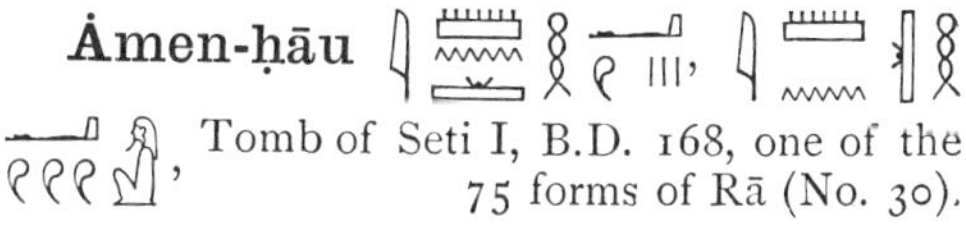, Tomb of Seti I, B.D. 168, one of the 75 forms of Rā (No. 30).

Ȧmen-Ḥeru , Ṭuat X, a destroyer of the bodies of the dead.

Ȧmen-khat , one of the 75 forms of Rā (No. 39).

Ȧmen-khat , Ṭuat X, the name of the Hand that holds Āapep by a chain.

Ȧment-seshemu-set 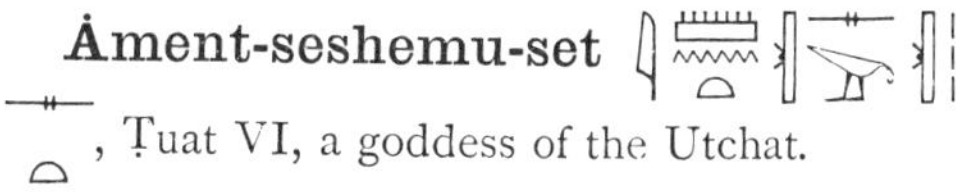, Ṭuat VI, a goddess of the Utchat.

Ȧmen , U. 558, P. 703, M. 478, Hh. 385, the god Ȧmen, "the hidden god" who is in heaven; Assyr., Heb. אָמוֹן, Nahum 3, 8, Copt. ⲁⲙⲟⲩⲛ, Gr. Ἄμμων.

Ȧmen-t (Ȧmenit) 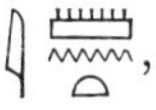, U. 558, , Hymn of Darius 23, fem. of preceding.

Ȧmeni , Rec. 3, 116, 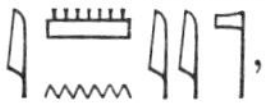, Edfû I, 9D, a form of Ȧmen and Rā.

Ȧmeni 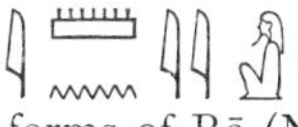, Tomb of Seti I, one of the 75 forms of Rā (No. 52).

Ȧmennu 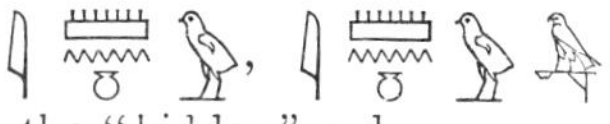, P. 266, N. 1246, the "hidden" god.

Ȧmenui , the dual Ȧmen.

Åmen-åab-t, Rec. 17, 119, Åmen as god of the East.

Åmen-åabṭi, Ḥerusåtef Stele 154, a form of Åmen worshipped in the Sûdân.

Åmen-åpt, Åmen of Karnak; compare Tell al-'Amarna.

Åmen-em-åpt, Åmen of Karnak; var. ; Gr. Ἀμενωφις.

Åmen-Menu, IV, 1031, Åmen + Menu.

Åmen-meruti, Åmen the beloved, or loving, god (?)

Åmen-naånka (?), B.D. 165, 4, a form of Åmen worshipped in Nubia.

Åmen net Nut (?), Ḥerusåtef Stele 34, Åmen of Thebes.

Åmen-neb-khart, Åmen as lord of the Nome of Heroonpolites.

Åmen-neb-nest-taui "Åmen, lord of the throne of the Two Lands," *i.e.*, Åmen of Karnak.

Åmen Nept, Dream Stele 8, Åmen of Napata (Gebel Barkal).

Åmen-Rā, Åmen + Rā.

Åmenit Rā, L.D. 4, 2, the female counterpart of Åmen-Rā.

Åmen-Rā-Ptaḥ, the triad Åmen + Rā + Ptaḥ.

Åmen-Rā-menmen-mut-f, Culte Divin, p. 124, Åmen-Rā as his mother's husband.

Åmen-Rā-neb-nest-Taui, Åmen-Rā, lord of the throne of the Two Lands, *i.e.*, Egypt, prince of Karnak, Nesi-Amsu 22, 1.

Åmen-Heb, Rec. 28, 182 = Ἀμενῆβις, Åmen of Heb, the capital of the Oasis of Khârgah.

Åmen-Rā nesu-neteru; Gr. Ἀμονρασωνθήρ, *i.e.*, Åmen-Rā, king of the gods; also

Åmen-Rā Ḥeru-åakhuti, the triad Åmen + Rā + Ḥeru-åakhuti.

Åmen-Rā Ḥeru-åakhuti Tem Kheperå Ḥeru, the double triad of Åmen + Rā + Ḥeru-åakhuti + Tem + Kheperå + Ḥeru.

Åmen-Rā setem (?) ua, Rec. 26, 57 . . . .

Åmen-Rā Ka-mut-f, Åmen-Rā as his mother's husband.

Åmen Ruruti, B.D. 165, 4, the triad Åmen + Shu + Tefnut.

Åmen-ḥap, an ithyphallic man-headed hawk-god, a form of Åmen-Rā.

Åment-ḥerit-åb-åpt, Champollion, Mon. IV, 332, 3, consort of Åmen as god of the Åpt.

Åmen-khnem-ḥeḥ, Åmen as god of eternity.

Åmen-sepṭ-ḥennuti (?), Nesi-Åmsu 17, 14, Åmen with the ready horns; Sepṭ-ḥennuti is probably the original of a title of Alexander the Great, Dhu 'l-Ḳarnên.

Åmen-qa-åst , Åmen of the exalted throne.

Åmen-kau 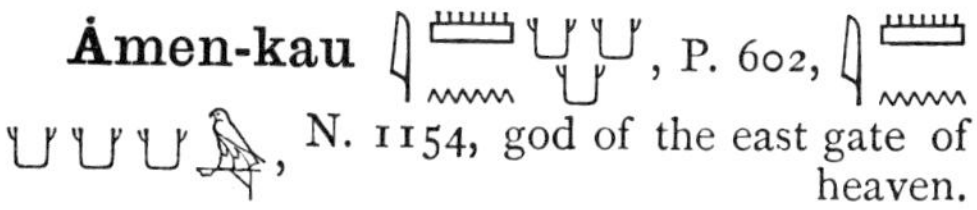, P. 602, N. 1154, god of the east gate of heaven.

Åmen-ta-Måt 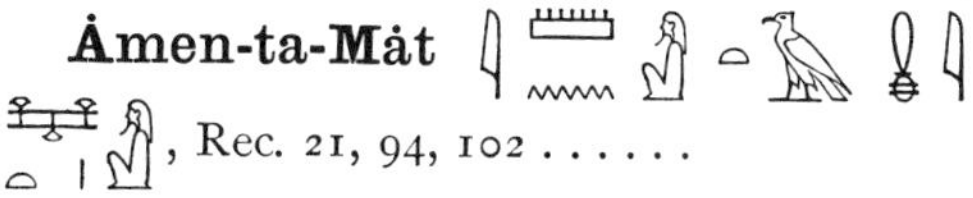, Rec. 21, 94, 102 . . . . . .

Åmen-Temu-em-Uas 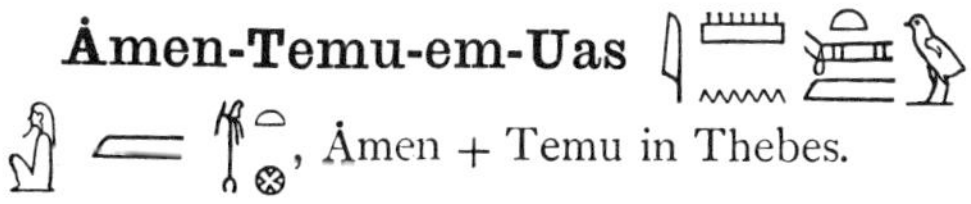, Åmen + Temu in Thebes.

Åmen Tehnit 
Rec. 14, 74, Åmen of Tehnit.

Åmen 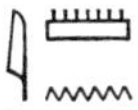, 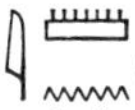, Lanzone, pl. 17, a frog-headed god, one of the eight elemental gods and goddesses, and grandfather of the Eight Gods; see **Khemenu.**

Åmen 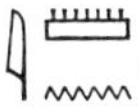, Pierret, Ét. 1, a lion-god.

Åmen 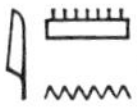, 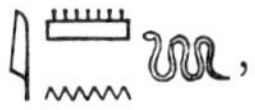, U. 543, T. 299, Ṭuat IV, a serpent-god.

Åmen-t 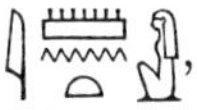, 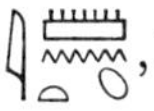, Lanzone, pl. 17, a serpent-headed goddess, counterpart of the preceding.

Åmen 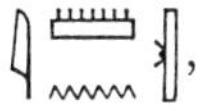, B.D. 168, a bull-god.

Åmen 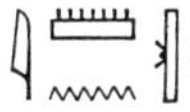 (?) Ṭuat VIII, one of the nine **Shemsu-Rā.**

Åmen-usr-ḥa-t 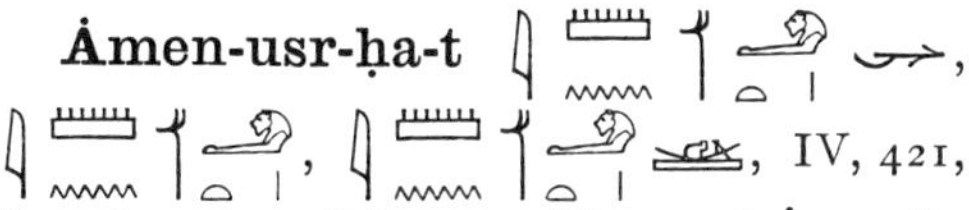, IV, 421, 895, the name of the sacred barge of Åmen-Rā at Thebes.

Åmen-Rā , an official; compare Am-mu-ni-ra , Tell al-'Amarna.

Åmen-Rā-em-usr-ḥa-t 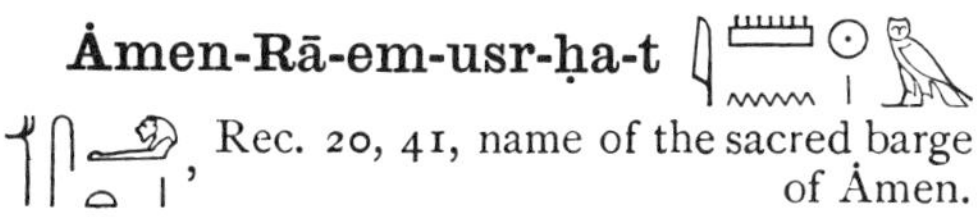, Rec. 20, 41, name of the sacred barge of Åmen.

Åmen-ṭa-f-pa-khepesh 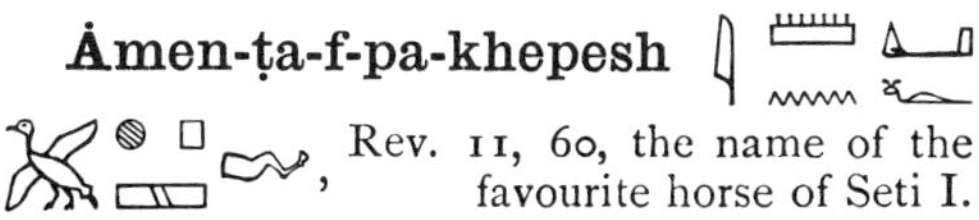, Rev. 11, 60, the name of the favourite horse of Seti I.

åmen 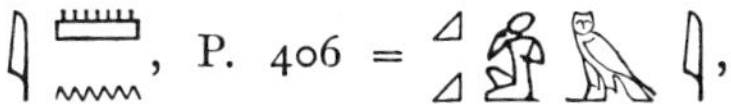, P. 406 =, M. 580, the right hand, right side; compare Heb. יָמִי.

åmen 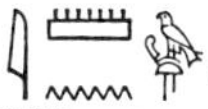, T. 360, P. 359, ,
N. 1073, 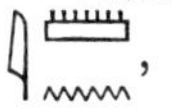, P. 406, right side, western; Heb. יָמִין.

åmen-t , P. 610, 
the West, the right side.

åmen-t , the right eye.

åmen-t , , T. 81, M. 234, N. 612, the west wind.

Åmen-t ,
Inscrip. of Darius 9, the west bank of the Nile and the land westwards.

åmenti , western; west wind.

Åmenti , Ṭuat III, the god of Åmenti or the West.

åmenti , 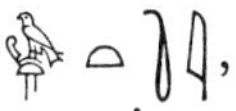, a denizen of Åmen-t, one belonging to Åmen-t, U. 578, N. 966.

åmentiu 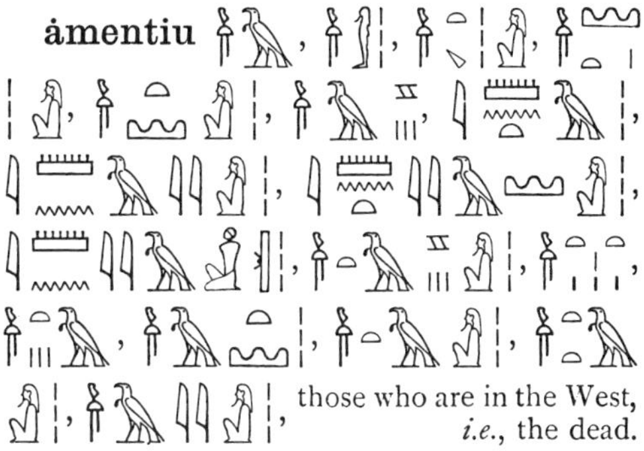, those who are in the West, *i.e.*, the dead.

Åmen-t 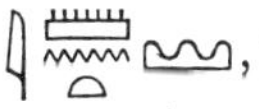, Tomb of Seti I, one of the 75 forms of Rā (No. 27).

Åmentt , the west, the abode of the dead, Dead-land; Copt. ⲉⲙⲛ̄ⲧ̄.

Åmentit 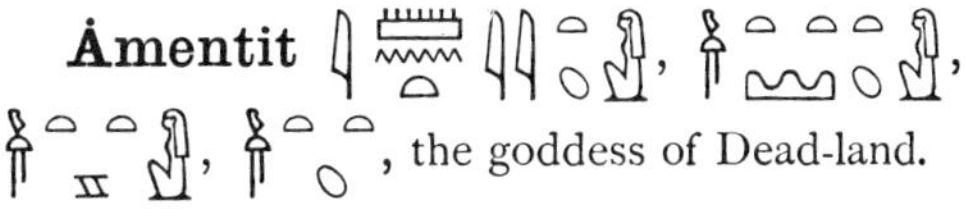, the goddess of Dead-land.

Åmen-t 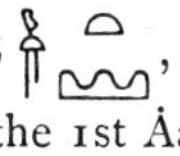, Ṭuat I, a singing-goddess; the name of the 1st Åat (B.D. 149).

Åmen-t-urt, Ṭuat I, a gate-goddess.

Åmen-t-Nefer-t, Ṭuat II, Berg. II, 3; (1) a goddess, the personification of the 1st division of the Ṭuat; (2) the name of the 15th Åat (B.D. 149); (3) a goddess who hid the deceased (Berg. II, 11).

Åmentt ermen, Ṭuat VII, a star-goddess.

Åmen-t-ḥep-neb-s, B.D. G. 494, goddess of the necropolis of Memphis and Abydos.

Åmen-t se[m]-t, the antechamber of the Ṭuat.

åmen-t, A.Z. 1908, 16, name of a vulture amulet.

åmen-t, name of a sceptre amulet (Lacau).

åmen, U. 335, T. 396, N. 1149, to make to arrive, or reach = .

åmenmen, to set in motion; see .

åmen, T. 340, N. 1352, to make firm, to stablish, to fortify; see .

åmenmen, Rec. 4, 121, Hymn of Darius 4, to stablish; see .

åmenu, made firm, established.

Åmenu - kherp (Kherp - Ḥe - t - Åmenu), a name of the pyramid of Åmenemḥat II.

Åmen-sekhem-f-au, name of a gate at Thebes.

åmeni-t, the regular daily sacrifice or offering; , IV, 1142, , Thes. 1253.

åmen, U. 589, M. 823, , N. 1338, , P. 669, N. 895, , M. 779, , P. 183, the daily sacrifice of a bull; plur. , U. 590.

åmenu, pasture; Copt. ⲁⲙⲟⲛⲓ.

åmenu, Rec. 36, 81, flower, plant.

åmenu, dove.

åmenḥu, , , sacrificial priest, butcher.

Åmenḥiu, B.D. 17 (Nebseni), 31, , a group of slaughtering gods.

åmer, , T. 264, P. 320, M. 129; see , to love.

åmer, , to be deaf.

åmer, an animal for sacrifice.

åmer-t, a staff, sceptre (?)

åmeh, Rec. 32, 67, a kind of incense, perfume.

åmeḥ, Åmen. 27, 13, , , P.S.B. 20, 195, , to absorb, to fill oneself full.

åmeḥ, T. 363, , N. 179, , Rev. 12, 59, to seize, to have power over; Copt. ⲁⲙⲁϩⲧⲉ.

Åmḥ-t, Åmmḥ-t, , , B.D. 72, 1, 149, the name of the 6th Åat.

åmḥ-t, , , , Rec. 4, 29, , , , , , , ,

, the Kingdom of Seker, the god of Death, at Ṣaḳḳârah. There was an ȧmḥ-t at Thebes also.

Ȧmḥit , the goddess of these kingdoms.

ȧmkhen , , T. 190, P. 676, to make a voyage, to travel through or about.

ȧmes , U. 296, N. 533, to conduct.

ȧmes , , crown, head-dress.

ȧms-t , , Ebers Pap. 47, 12, 81, 10, Rec. 7, 108, shrub, plant, flower; plur. , ; anethum, Gr. ἄνηθον, Copt. ⲁⲙⲙⲓⲥⲓ, ⲉⲙⲙⲓⲥⲓ.

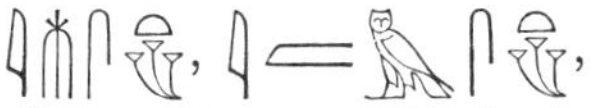

ȧms , , , Aelt. Tex. 38, , , staff of office, sceptre.

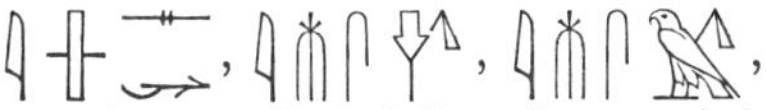

Ȧmsi , , , B.D. 17, 34, Todt. (Naville) II, 41, a title of Menu as the bearer of the sceptre **ȧmes**, .

ȧmes , to give birth to; see **mes**  ;  , born (plur.), N. 1229.

ȧmes , A.Z. 35, 16, , , , lie, untruth; see **ȧumes**, .

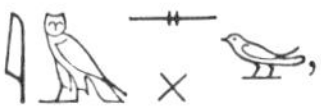

ȧms = , Rev. 14, 73, usury; Copt. ⲙⲙⲏⲥⲉ.

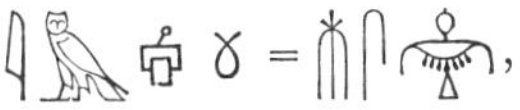

ȧmeska , , , skin, hide, leather.

ȧmset , Anastasi Pap. IV, 12, 3,  , the loins, reins, kidneys; Copt. ⲙⲉⲥⲧ ϩⲏⲧ.

ȧmset , , the great intestine.

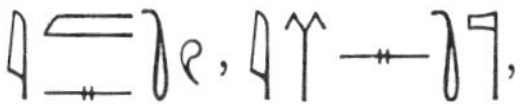

Ȧmset , P. 262, , N. 592, T. 60, P. 462, , M. 551, N. 1250, , N. 764, , P. 445, , Hh. 443, , , , , ; the following forms occur which suggest the reading **Ȧmges**: , P. 445, 706, M. 218, , P. 673, , N. 1279; Ȧmset was one of the four sons of Horus and assisted in embalming Osiris.

Ȧmset , , god of the 10th hour of the night.

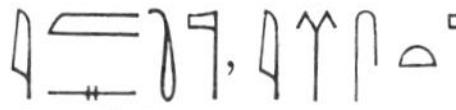

Ȧmset , , the god of the 4th day of the month.

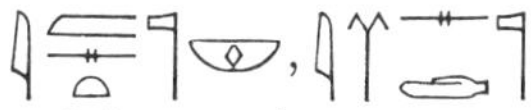

Ȧmestȧ-em-ȧbu , Denderah II, 10, one of the 36 Dekans.

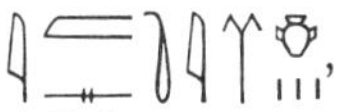

ȧmk , , T. 347, P. 535, 689, 690, N. 172, , to perish, to decay, to become corrupt.

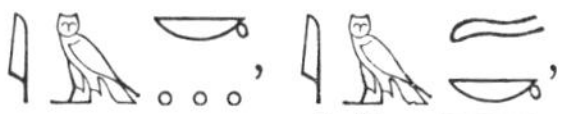

ȧmgaḥ , , , to be weak, to be sad; Copt. ⲙⲕⲁϩ (?)

Ȧmtt , Rec. 32, 80, a region.

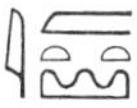

ȧm-ta  , U. 111, , a cake offering.

Ȧmtenni , Hh. 488, a magical name.

ȧmṭuit , , Rec. 31, 165, kinsfolk; see **unṭuit.**

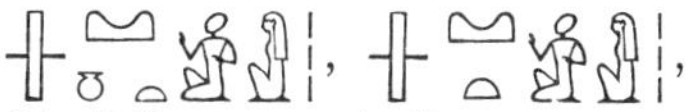

ȧmtchart , salve, unguent, ointment, , U. 297.

ȧmtcher , stronghold, garrison.

ȧn = Copt. ⲛ̄ⲧⲟ.

ån 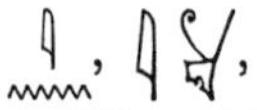, a mark of emphasis, an indication of the subject of a sentence.

ån , M. 624, 625, a particle = , P. 316, 317.

ån , interrogative particle; 
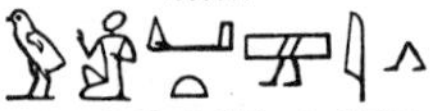, shall I send? 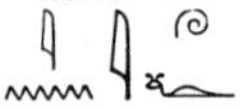
, where is he to-day? 
, do ye know? 
, shall then? , is it that not?
, who? , 
.

ån , a conditional particle, ; Copt. ⲉⲛⲉ (late form, 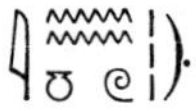).

ån , a post negative particle.

ån 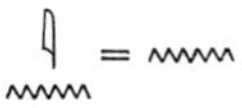, of, IV, 3, 140.

ån 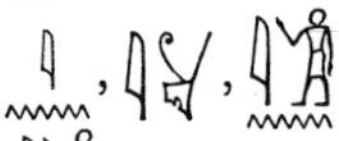, in, to, for, because, by.

ån 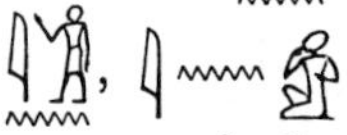, said by = , IV, 4, 220, 1141; var. , we say.

ån meru 
, so that.

ånn , pers. pron. 1st pers. com. we; Copt. ⲁⲛⲟⲛ.

ånn , an interjection.

ånn 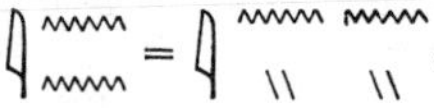.

ånn 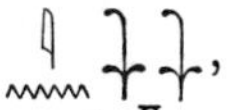, P. 318 = 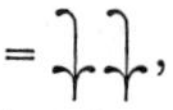, M. 626.

åni (?) , U. 2, ,
,
, to bring, to convey, to produce; , N. 1118, bringing; Copt. ⲉⲓⲛⲉ.

ånu , porter, carrier, bringer; plur. .

ån āu [illegible], to shut doors.

ån-uauai [illegible], bringer of reports, *i.e.*, herald.

ån utchat [illegible], to restore the light to the Eye of Rā.

ån em skhai [illegible], to put into writing.

ån-t reṭ [illegible], Tomb Åmenemḥat, p. 93, the name of a ceremony.

ån-shet [illegible], "fire bringer," *i.e.*, the fire stick.

ån-t, ånut [illegible], [illegible], something brought, conduct, lead; [illegible], offerings.

ån [illegible], U. 556, [illegible], M. 544, [illegible], T. 26, P. 440, gift, offering; plur. [illegible], T. 28, [illegible], M. 251, [illegible], P. 82, N. 788, [illegible], U. 212, 509, P. 688, [illegible], T. 323, [illegible], Rec. 32, 82, [illegible], T. 292. Later forms are the following:

ånu [illegible],
[illegible],
[illegible],
[illegible], gift, tribute, offerings, products, revenues, income, increase, wages, something brought in; Copt. ⲉⲓⲛⲉ; [illegible], Peasant 120, owner of merchandise.

ånit [illegible], things brought, offerings, etc.

ånit [illegible],
[illegible], date flour, offerings of flour.

ånu [illegible], IV, 1152, tools used in brickmaking.

ån-t [illegible], P. 172, [illegible], N. 939, watercourse, channel, valley.

Ån-t , Rec. 32, 82, the name of a serpent deity.

Ån , U. 272, 275, the name of a goddess.

Ån-t , Ṭuat III, the "bringer" of the Eye of Horus.

Åntit , Ṭuat III, a goddess who "brought" the pupils of the Eyes of Horus.

Ånniu , B.D. 89, 1, a god of offerings.

Ånith , Ṭuat VII, a star-goddess.

Ån-åri-t-Rā , Ṭuat III, a god of the Utchat, .

Ån-åtf-f , B.D. 92, 5, a form of Horus.

Ån-ā-f , Denderah III, 69, , B.D. 125, II, , a serpent-god, one of the 42 Assessors of Osiris.

Ån-ā-f , B.D. 17 (Nebseni), 26 ff., the executioner of Osiris.

Ån-urt-emkhet-uas B.D. 99, 15, name of the mast in the Magical Boat.

Ån-maāt , Ṭuat V, one of eight gods who burned the dead.

Ån-nef-em-hu , Berg. 1, 3, , Rec. 4, 28, one of the eight sharp-eyed custodians of the body of Osiris.

Ån-re-f B.D. 125, II; see **Maa-åntu-f.**

ån ḥa-ti , , to sacrifice a heart.

Ån-ḥer-t , , , , , Dêr al-Gab. 1, 18, , P.S.B. 7, 175, , Cairo Cat. 71, , , the god Onouris, the centre of whose cult was Abydos (This); Copt. ⲁⲛϩⲟⲩⲣⲉ, Gr. Ὀνοῦρις.

Ånḥer neb-māb , Ånher, lord of the harpoon.

Ån-ḥer Bast-utet-tha , Thes. I, 23, one of the 36 Dekans.

Ån-ḥer-Shu , , Lanzone, pl. 34, , Mission 13, 126, Ån-ḥer + Shu.

Ån-ḥer , B.D. 144, the Watcher of the 6th Ārit.

Ån-ḥetep , Ṭuat IV, a god in the Ṭuat of Seker.

Ån-ḥetep-f , , B.D. 125, II, one of the 42 Assessors of Osiris.

Ånṭaf , , U. 548, T. 303, a serpent fiend.

ån , , , , Rec. 32, 181, to turn back, to drive away, to repel.

ånån , T. 311, to turn back.

ånn , U. 297, T. 311, , T. 338, , T. 141, M. 198, , N. 537, to repel, to drive back.

ånni , T. 34, , N. 132, , M. 115, repeller.

ånti , , repeller.

ån-t , , a repelling, something returned.

ånn-t , a turning back.

ånn-t , P. 685, , N. 961, something repelled.

ånetnet , , , delay, withdrawal.

Ånen-reṭui , Ṭuat VI, ...

ån , , Rec. 6, 7, , Rec. 11, 143, , , IV, 546, to cut, to destroy, to reduce, to suppress, to obliterate a name.

ånån , knife, sword, to destroy.

ȧn, to fetter, to tie up, to bind, to wrap round, to rope up.

ȧn, cord, rope; plur. , Hh. 482.

ȧnȧu (?), , fetters, bindings.

ȧn, anew.

ȧn-t, , , , valley, *khor*, ravine; plur. , Hh. 229, , IV, 1026, , Rec. 29, 147, , upper valleys or ravines, valleys of the tombs.

ȧn-tt, , a region of valleys.

ȧn-t āa-t, M. 188, N. 694, the "Great Valley."

ȧn-t ānti, the valley of myrrh.

ȧn-t pa-āsh, valley of the cedar.

ȧn-t ḥeb, a funerary festival.

Ȧn-t-sekhṭu, Ṭuat XI, the pit of fire containing the damned standing on their heads.

Ȧn-tt Kek, B.D. G. 43, the "Valley of the Shadow," or "Dark Valley" through which souls entered the Kingdom of Osiris.

ȧn-t, one third of a second, the "twinkling of an eye."

ȧn, Rev. 11, 167, , , , = , stone; Copt. ⲱⲛⲉ, ⲱⲛⲓ; plur. .

ȧn, , = or , eyebrows.

ȧn, , , , , , , Ȧmen. 13, 1, Anastasi Pap. I, 25, 4, hair of any kind, covering, colour of hair, colour of face, complexion.

ȧnȧu, skin coverings.

ȧnuit, hair.

ȧn, the scale or rust of a metal.

ȧn, purple linen (?)

ȧn, Koller Pap. 3, 8, red cloth.

ȧn, , a kind of spotted fish, tilapia nilotica (?); plur. .

Ȧn-t, B.D. 15, 43, , a mythological fish, one of the two fish pilots of Rā.

Ȧn-t, Qenna Pap. 2, 8, a mythological boat of the Sun-god.

ȧn-t, sickness.

ȧn-t, the pallor of fever; Copt. ⲁⲟⲩⲁⲛ (?)

ȧn, some strong-smelling substance.

ȧn, juice, sap, drink of some kind (?)

ȧn, N. 535, 538 = , T. 294, 295 = , P. 229, pillar, column; plur. , P. 340, M. 642, , IV, 819, .

ȧn, Anastasi Pap. I, 15, 3, the shaft of an obelisk.

ȧn, Rec. 27, 87, mast for a sail (?)

ȧn, battering ram.

ȧn, a building (with pillars?) , M. 824, , .

ȧn-t, Rec. 10, 136, building, abode; , Rec. 30, 66.

ȧn, hall of a tomb; plur. , , graves, cemetery; , Rec. 8, 136, the slain.

ȧn-ti, T. 18, the two pillars of a palace, portico (?)

ȧn-t, , , Rec. 4, 121, , , a hall of columns, colonnade.

Ȧn, Ȧni, B.D. 15, 89, 1, a form of Osiris, the Moon-god; , Litanie 53, , Ȧn of the stars.

Ȧn-ȧ, P. 690, the divine father of Pepi I.

Ȧnit, B.D. G. 348, , Rec. 15, 162, the consort of Sȧaba, and mother of one of the seven forms of Harpokrates.

Ȧnit, Wilkinson A.E. III, 232, a form of Hathor and a goddess of childbirth.

Ȧnit, Rameses IX, pl. 10, directress of the serpent Neḥa-ḥer, .

Ȧnit, B.D. 169, 20, the habitation of the men-gods, Horus and Set.

Ȧn-mut-f, P. 828, N. 772, 781, , B.D. 18, I, , Denderah III, 35, , *ibid.* IV, 84, , , , , IV, 157, Beni Hasan III, 27, a god, whose exact functions are unknown. The original form of the name was, perhaps, ; see , P. 661, , P. 776, , M. 772.

Ȧn-mut-f, , (1) title of the priest at Denderah who personified the god of this name, (2) a bull-god, who presided over the 19th day of the month; (3) the god of the 9th hour of the night, , B.D. 111

Ȧnmut-f ābesh, Ombos I, 1, 252, a star-god.

Ȧn-mut-k, Mar. Mast. 1; var. = **Ȧn-kenmut**, .

Ȧnran (?), L.D. 3, 80, a form of Hathor.

Ȧn-ḥāā, , , a form of the Moon-god.

Ȧn-sebu, T. 289, , U. 419, the name of a god.

Ȧn-smeṭ, U. 421, , T. 241, a pillar of Osiris with the eyes smeared with stibium, a title of the Bull of Heaven.

Ȧn-k (?), P. 691, a title of Pepi I.

Ȧn-ken-mut, , , , , T.S.B.A. VII, 366, Mar. Aby. II, 23, 16, a god (?); see **Ȧnmutf.**

Ȧn-Kenset, U. 419, T. 239, title of a god (?)

Ȧn-tek (?), P. 690, the divine mother of Pepi I.

Ȧn-tt, the desert between the Nile and Red Sea.

Ȧn-tiu, , , , , , , , , , , the hill-men of the Eastern Desert, the Troglodytes, Eastern Desert tribes in general, their chief god was **Menu**; , , women of the Eastern Desert.

Ȧn-ti Set, a man of the Nubian Desert; plur. , , , , , Rec. 20, 43.

Ȧn-tiu Sett, the dwellers in the Eastern Desert as far north as Palestine.

ȧn-ti, P.S.B. 18, 37, , a Nubian bow.

ȧn-na, Rev. = , as an interrogative.

Ȧnana, Sphinx I, 258, the name of the original owner of the D'Orbiney Papyrus.

ȧnauasu , Methen 4, a title, or name of an office.

ȧnȧ , a kind of plant, twig, branch; plur. .

ȧnȧ 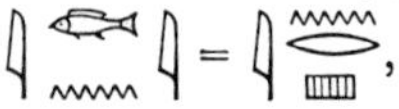, stone.

ȧnȧu, ȧnu 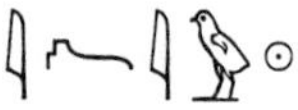, Rev. 11, 137, 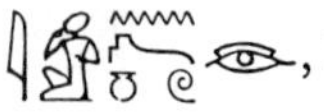, Rev. 11, 131, see! Copt. ⲁⲛⲁⲩ.

ȧnȧuȧu 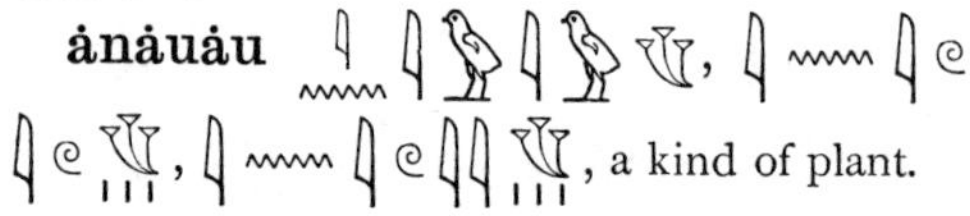, a kind of plant.

ȧnȧuba , Rec. 29, 165, [illegible], a bearing pole.

Ȧnȧushana , Anastasi Pap. IV, 1, 13, 1, Rec. 15, 110, a kind of plant.

Ȧnȧukar , , A.Z. Bd. 43, 97, the disease-fiend Ningal, [illegible].

ȧnȧr-t 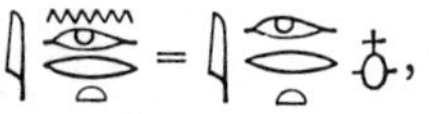, milk.

ȧnȧs , P. 618 = , N. 1299, to call.

ȧnā = [illegible], IV, 1161, with.

ȧnā , P. 567, chin.

ȧnāu , B.D. Nav. 15, 48, to blaspheme; var. [illegible].

ȧni [illegible], a man of On (Heliopolis), or singing-man of Denderah.

ȧni-tit , dancing-woman of Denderah.

ȧni 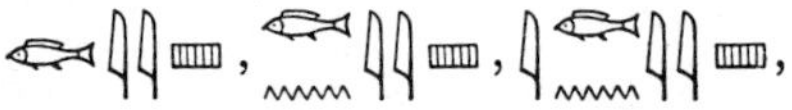, Jour. As. 1908, 292, stone; Copt. ⲱⲛⲉ.

ȧnit 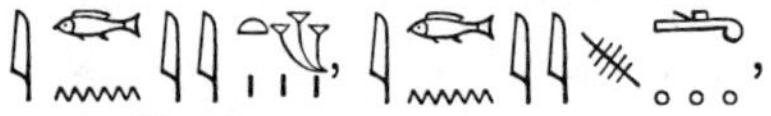, Rec. 5, 89, 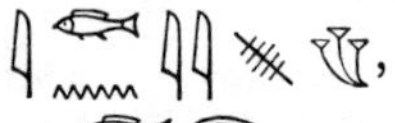, Rec. 16, 110, , twigs, palm-leaves, a kind of fruit; , Rec. 5, 93.

ȧnu , U. 392; see [illegible].

ȧnu , sandals.

ȧnu-t , P. 437, M. 651, boat (?)

ȧnun , herbs, plants.

ȧnuk , I; Copt. ⲁⲛⲟⲕ, Heb. אָנֹכִי.

ȧnuki [illegible], Rev. 11, 157, I; Heb. אָנוֹכִי.

ȧnuk-ḥu [illegible], Rev. 12, 87, I myself; Copt. ⲁⲛⲟⲕ ϩⲱ.

ȧneb 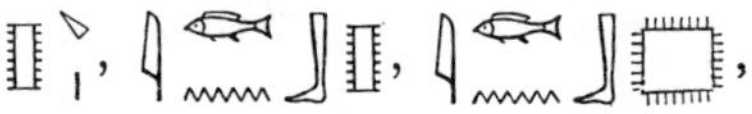, 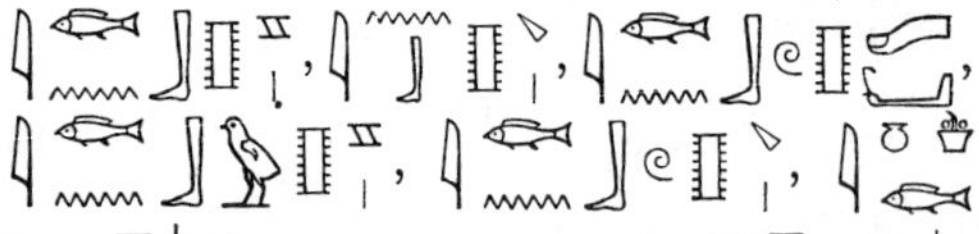, [illegible], Rec. 6, 9, wall; plur. [illegible], , Gol. 12, 100, [illegible], 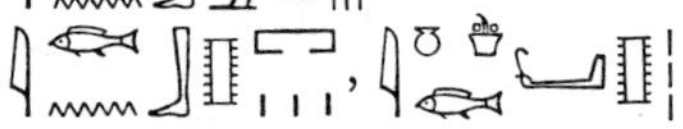, fortifications.

ȧneb-t 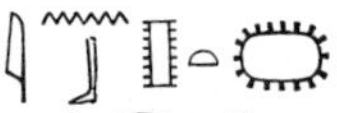, N. 955, [illegible], , [illegible], Anastasi Pap. V, 20, 2, a walled enclosure, a walled town, a palace, a fortress; plur. 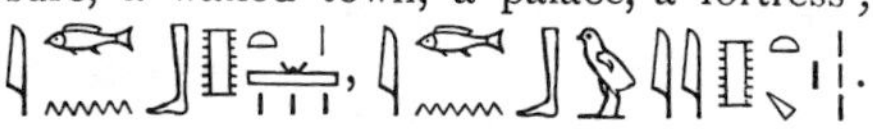.

Ȧneb [illegible], Israel Stele 3, a walled city.

ȧnbi [illegible], a walled district.

ȧnbit 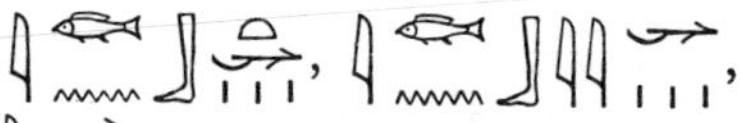, 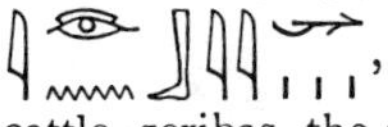, fenced enclosures, pounds for cattle, zeribas, the sides of a ship.

ȧnb 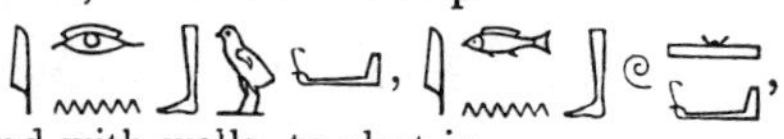, to surround with walls, to shut in.

ȧnbu 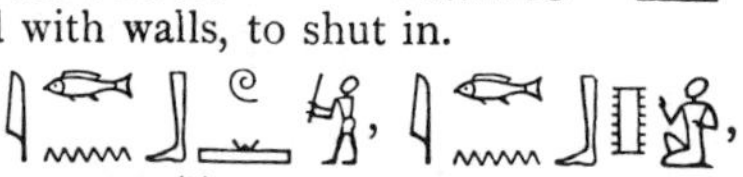, wall-builder, mason (?)

ȧneb-ḥetchtiu [illegible], inhabitants of Memphis.

ȧneb , de Rougé, Edfû 106, 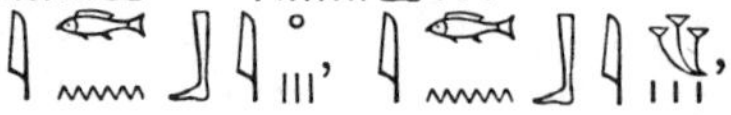,

Peasant 26, , Rec. 31, 26, a kind of medicinal plant, herb, or fruit.

ȧnb 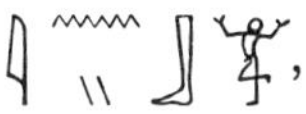, to dance, to perform acrobatic feats.

ȧnba , Ebers 100, 15 . . . .

ȧnbs (?) 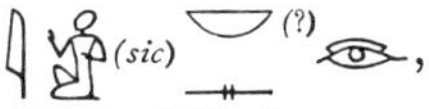 (sic) (?), A.Z. 1907, 46, title of an official of Thebes.

ȧneb-t (?), ȧneb-tȧ , P. 79, 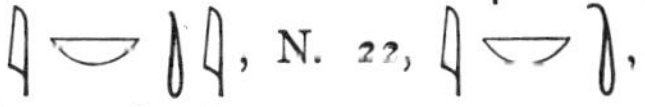 N. 22, M. 109, dual of , lord.

ȧnp , B.D. 188, 2 . . . .

ȧnp 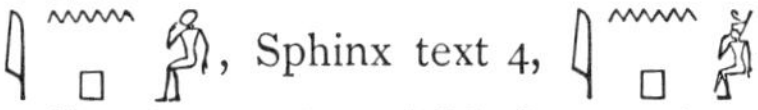 Sphinx text 4,  Thes. 1281, child, boy, prince, IV, 157, 898, 994.

ȧnp 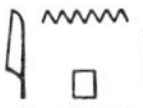, to swathe, to wrap round.

ȧnep , Rec. 29, 157, to decay, to stink.

Ȧnp, Ȧnpu , Peasant B 2, 115, 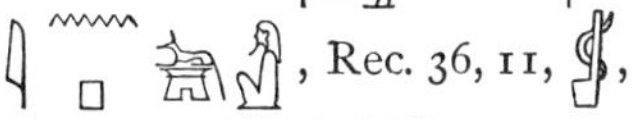 Rec. 36, 11, Rec. 2, 27, , the god Anubis, the judge of hearts (U. 220); Copt. ⲁⲛⲟⲩⲡ.

Ȧnpu , Edfû I, 14, the four forms of Anubis: (1) 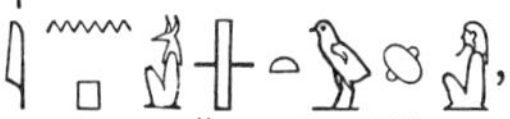, (2) (3) (4) .

Ȧnpit , Lanzone, pl. 31, consort of Ȧnpu.

Ȧnp-ȧmi-ut , B.D. 151, 156, , Anubis in the embalming chamber.

Ȧnp neb-Ta-tchesertt  , Anubis, lord of the cemetery.

Ȧnp heni , Ṭuat V, a jackal-headed god who guarded the river of fire, a form of Anubis.

Ȧnp-ḥeri-em-pet-ta-ṭuat  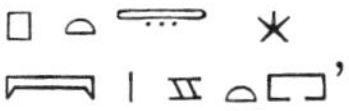, Cairo Pap. III, 5, Anubis, governor of heaven, earth and underworld.

Ȧnp khenti Ȧment , T. 387, U. 71, N. 331, , M. 403, Anubis, lord of Ȧment, the predecessor of Osiris.

Ȧnp khenti-seḥ-neter  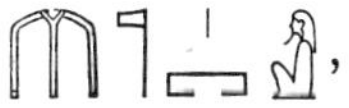, B.D. 117, Anubis, chief of the hall of the god.

Ȧnp khentȧ-ta-uāb  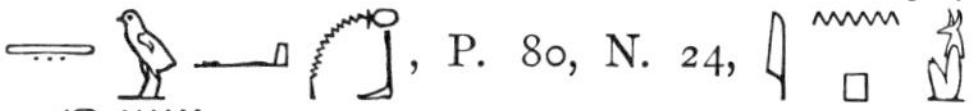 P. 80, N. 24, , Anubis, chief of the holy place.

Ȧnp Khenti Ta-tchesertt  , P. 707, Anubis, prince of the cemetery.

Ȧnp sa-Ȧsȧr , Anubis, son of Osiris.

Ȧnp , Anubis of various cities:  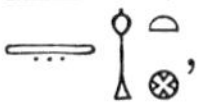, etc., Mar. Aby. I, 45, Nesi-Ȧmsu 25, 24.

Ȧnpu Uast  (?), Ṭuat III, Anubis of Thebes.

Ȧnp [illegible], Denderah IV, 83, god of the 14th Ȧat.

Ȧnp [illegible], Ombos I, 62, a hunting-god worshipped in the South.

ȧnp [illegible], a name of the 21st day of the month.

ȧnef [illegible] = [illegible].

ȧnf [illegible], [illegible], [illegible] [illegible] droppings from the eye, diarrhoea, any kind of bodily exudation.

ȧnem [illegible], [illegible], [illegible] [illegible], L.D. III, 140B = [illegible], who? Copt. ⲛⲓⲙ.

ȧnem [illegible], U. 543, [illegible], T. 298, [illegible], [illegible], [illegible], Rec. 30, 67, 191, 31, 162,

, Rec. 5, 90, skin of human beings, or animals, hide, pelt; Copt. ⲁⲛⲟⲙ; Rec. 30, 67.

ȧnemu, "skins," *i.e.*, human beings.

ȧnem-t, Rec. 14, 195, skin bottles, vessels of drink; plur., Rec. 16, 57.

ȧn-m'k-t, Greene II, 17, home, abode, dwelling.

ȧnmer, Rec. 33, 35 =, to love.

ȧnmesit, cloth, garment, apparel.

ȧnen; see **ȧn.**

Ȧnenit, B.D. 168, goddesses who bestowed virility.

ȧner, De Hymnis 44, shell of an egg.

ȧner, gravel, stone; Copt. ⲱⲛⲉ.

ȧnrit, stone, pebble, worked stone; plur.

Ȧner-ti, IV, 894, the two rocks near Al-Kâb;, B.D. 134, 6.

ȧner uā, IV, 932, monolith.

ȧner-en-bȧa, basalt.

ȧner-en-benu varr.), yellow sandstone.

ȧner-en-bekhenu, porphyry.

ȧner-en-ma, Rec. 3, 48, granite.

Ȧner-en-Maāt, Sinsin I, "stone of truth," a title of Osiris.

ȧner-en-ruṭ, sandstone.

ȧner-en-ruṭ-ent-ṭu-Ṭesher, Thes. 1286, red sandstone.

ȧner-en-sen-t, IV, 1174, a kind of stone.

ȧner ḥetch, white calcareous stone, limestone.

ȧner ḥetch-nefer-en-ruṭ-t, Thes. 1285, fine white sandstone.

ȧner sepṭ, prepared stone (?)

ȧner kam, black granite.

ȧnr, a vase (?)

ȧnr, skin head covering.

ȧnr, Anastasi Pap. IV, 9, a reptile (?), worm (?)

ȧnr ...., Birch I.H. 15, a kind of cake or bread.

Ȧn-ruṭ-f, "the place where nothing grows," a mythological locality at **Ḥensu**; var.

ȧnrana (alana), oak trees; Heb. אַלּוֹן or אֹרֶן.

ȧnrahama (ȧrhama), Anastasi IV, 14, 5, Harris I, 16A, 10, pomegranate; Heb. רִמּוֹן, Syr. ܪܘܡܢܐ, Arab. رُمَّان, Eth. ሮማን:, Copt. ϩⲉⲣⲙⲁⲛ.

Ȧnratȧt, the river Orontes.

ȧnhama, Harris I, 56A, 5, pomegranate; see ; var. .

ȧnhemen, IV, 73, Rec. 2, 107, , a fruit-bearing tree and the fruit thereof, pomegranate; see , etc.

Ȧnhetut, Qenna 4, 5, the singing ape-gods.

ȧnḥ, eyebrows; Demotic form, ; Copt. ⲉⲛϩ, ⲛ̄ϩ.

ȧnḥ, Rec. 8, 134, , to surround, to enclose, to embrace, to wrap round; , rimmed, or banded, with gold.

ȧnḥu, those who surround or encircle.

ȧnḥ, an enclosed place of protection, courtyard.

ȧnḥ, a word with a hidden meaning, a secret, a riddle.

ȧnḥ-t, vase, vessel.

ȧnḥasāp (?), a kind of unguent or salve.

Ȧn-ḥefta, Ṭuat IX, a guardian of the 8th Gate.

ȧnḥem, skin, colour, covering; mistake for .

ȧnḥem (?) U. 182, to carry off.

ȧnḥerḥer, to rejoice; see **nḥerḥer.**

ȧn-khu, Turin Pap. 67, 11, a kind of stone.

ȧnkhurȧsmara, Alt. K. No. 81, a precious stone.

ȧns-t, a title of the priestess of Bubastis.

ȧnes, P. 662, , M. 774, U. 398, T. 242, , a red bandlet, cloth, apparel; plur. , U. 423, .

Ȧnes-Rā, B.D. (Saïte) 42, 2, a god.

ȧns-t, the sole of the foot; plur. .

ȧns-t, the hoof of an animal.

ȧns-t, a kind of plant; Gr. ἀνίσον (?)

ȧns-t, Peasant 34, the seed of the same.

ȧnsu, Thes. 921, 941, king; see **nesu.**

ȧnsuti, Rec. 4, 25, , a reed case, box (?)

ȧnseb-t, U. 160, N. 511, to flame (?)

ȧnq, Rec. 17, 50, , to withdraw, to return (?)

ȧnq, U. 236, , P. 667, M. 777, , P. 601, , M. 447, ,

, , , , , Thes. 1296, , , , , Åmen. 13, 3, to embrace, to gather together, gird round.

Ȧnq-t , B.D. 153B, 3, the net used by the Akeru gods in snaring souls.

ȧnqȧ , Rec. 30, 67, cordage, tackle of a boat.

ȧnqefqef-t , Anastasi Pap. I, 24, 7, a part of a chariot, or harness.

ȧnk, ȧnnk , , , , , a kind of plant.

ȧnk , to tie, to fetter, to restrain.

ȧnk , fiend; plur. .

Ȧnku , Ṭuat VII, "the netter," a god who fettered the foes of Osiris.

ȧnt , to bind up or cripple [the toes].

ȧnt-t , , cord, rope, chain; pl. **ȧnt-ut**, , , , Rec. 31, 17.

Ȧnt-t , Ṭuat X, the chain by which Āapep is fettered to the earth.

Ȧntiu , Ṭuat X, a group of four gods who slew Āapep.

ȧnt , Hymn of Darius 13, to stifle, to choke, to close up.

ȧnti-tu , hindrance, obstruction.

ȧnt-t , N. 682. . . . .

Ȧnt-ti , , Nav. Lit. 64, a god.

ȧntu , L.D. III, 140B = ,

Ȧntriush , Darius; see ; Pers. , Babyl. .

Ȧntesh , Metternich Stele 73, a mythological animal.

ȧnth-t , fetter, cord, cordage, rope, tackle; plur. , U. 422, , T. 242, , , Rec. 30, 67, 187.

Ȧntheti , Tomb Seti I, one of the 75 forms of Rā (No. 64).

Ȧntheth , Ṭuat VI, a goddess, functions unknown.

ȧnthenem , I, 137. . . . . . .

ȧnṭ , , to be in need of, want, misery, sadness, disgust, trouble.

Ȧnṭebu , B.D. 99, 7, , a god.

ȧnetch , protector, defender, advocate, avenger; see , , T. 186, , , P. 366, 658, 764.

ȧnetch , to strike, P. 204.

ȧnetch ḥer , N. 709, , M. 242, , , , , salutation to thee! the opening words of many hymns; see .

ȧntch , , to suffer grief or pain, oppressed, depressed.

ȧntch-t , grief, sorrow, pain.

ȧntcher , , T. 386, M. 394, to grasp, to seize.

ȧr , a conditional particle, when, if.

ȧr , an emphatic particle; also used with other particles, *e.g.*, , , , , , , Rev. 6, 12.

ȧr = , more than; , , P. 92 = , N. 699.

ȧr , an old form of the preposition [illegible], at, by, to, towards, as far as, against, until.

ȧr  = preposition [illegible] to, towards, etc.

ȧr , Nȧstasen Stele 11, 22, 25, 26, 32 = preposition [illegible].

ȧr  = preposition [illegible] to, towards, from, etc.

ȧr-ḥer , , into the presence of someone; Copt. ⲉϩⲣⲉⲛ.

ȧr, ȧri , U. 586, P. 16, 96, [illegible], [illegible], [illegible], [illegible], P. 190, M. 392, [illegible], [illegible], [illegible], [illegible], M. 114, [illegible], [illegible], Rec. 21, 76, [illegible], [illegible], [illegible], [illegible], [illegible], [illegible], to make, to do, to create, to form, to fashion, to beget, to produce, to pass the time, to be made, done, created, etc., and used as an auxiliary; Copt. ⲉⲓⲣⲉ; , do not; Copt. ⲙ̅ⲙ̅ⲡ̅ⲣ, ⲙ̅ⲙ̅ⲡⲉⲣ;  Nȧstasen Stele 66 = ϣⲁⲛⲧⲉϥⲉⲓⲣⲉ.

ȧri [illegible], to visit,  [illegible], "any other man who visited Ȧmam"; [illegible] 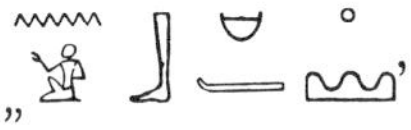, "I visited the mine region."

ȧri [illegible], to serve in the army, , "a second time I served."

ȧri [illegible], to amount to, 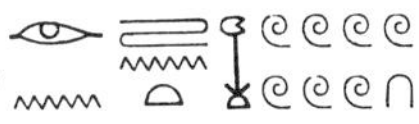 [illegible], IV, 666, "amounting to 1784 *teben*."

ȧri [illegible], to pass the time, [illegible] 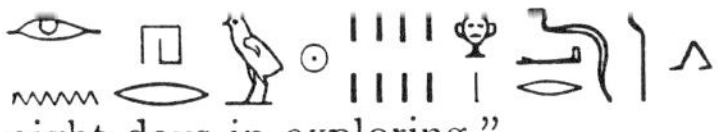, "I passed eight days in exploring."

ȧri abu 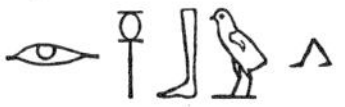, to make a stoppage, *i.e.*, to cease.

ȧri ȧau-t , to occupy an office, to enjoy a dignity, to exercise the functions of a certain office.

ȧri ȧakh , to benefit someone, to do good to.

ȧri ȧui 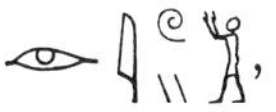, to praise, to perform a service of praise.

ȧri ȧb (?) 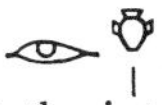, to do the will of someone, to carry out the intent of someone.

ȧri ȧr-t , to milk an animal.

ȧri ȧterti , to go through Upper and Lower Egypt.

ȧri ā (?) , to work the irrigation of a district.

ȧri ānkh , P.S.B. 10, 47, to take an oath, to perform what one has sworn to do.

ȧri ānt , worker on the nails, manicurist.

ȧri āntch , to heal, to make to recover, to restore to soundness.

ȧri ua-t (?) , to travel, to journey.

ȧri uat-shu 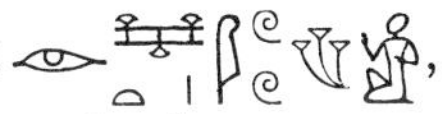, Rec. 19, 92, to work at the trade of a . . . . . .

ȧri utcha , to heal.

ȧri baka-t , to conceive, to become pregnant; Copt. ⲉⲣⲃⲟⲕⲓ.

ȧri-t pequ  to prepare food.

ȧri em ḥetep , to work contentedly.

ȧri ḥetep , to do what ought to be done.

ȧri em qaȧ , to make oneself like someone, to feign to be someone else, to disguise oneself, to pretend.

ȧri em ṭenȧ-t , to register oneself, to enrol one's name.

ȧri-t maāt , to practise right, to lead a life of integrity.

ȧri m'k-t , to protect, to spread the wings over young.

ȧri-t menkh-t , to do the very best work.

ȧri metcha 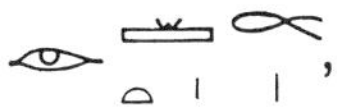, [illegible], to write a book.

ȧri en , made by, produced by,  "produced by the lady of the house," "born of the lady of the house."

åri ennu 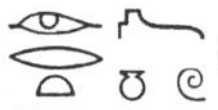, Rec. 21, 80, to do a thing continually.

åri nefer 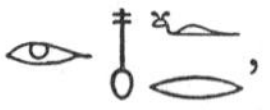, to perform a task well.

åri nefer-t 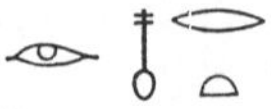, to have intercourse with a virgin.

åri neh 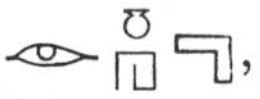, to protect.

åri nekhi , to protect.

åri nekhen 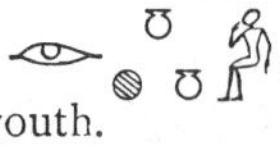, to renew one's youth, to act as a youth.

åri neter 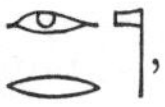, to deify.

åri netch , to shew pity, to protect.

åri-netchemm-t-åm-ḥenen  , P. 466, M. 529, N. 1108, to masturbate.

åri rethu åqeru 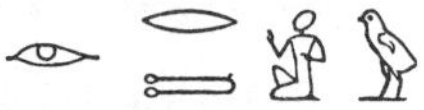 , to appoint "trustworthy people."

åri Haker , to celebrate the Haker festival.

åri hep er 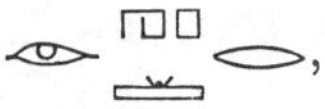, to set the law in motion against someone.

åri hru , to pass the day.

åri hru nefer 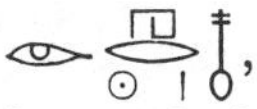, to make a day of rejoicing, to celebrate a festival.

åri hett 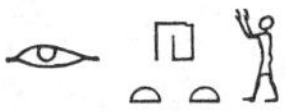, to praise.

åri ḥa 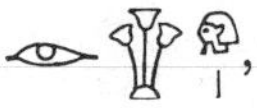, to make magical passes over the dead; , to make magical passes over the eyes.

åri-t ḥeb 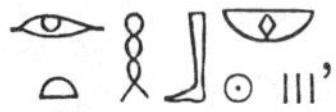, to celebrate a festival.

åri ḥebsu , to make cloth, *i.e.*, to weave.

åri ḥep-t 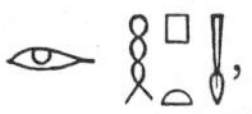, to work the paddle, *i.e.*, to row a boat.

åri ḥemu , to work the steering oar or rudder, to steer.

åri ḥem 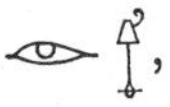, to work at a trade or handicraft.

åri ḥem-t , , to live with a wife; , to pass time in philandering.

åri ḥer , to terrify.

åri ḥes-t 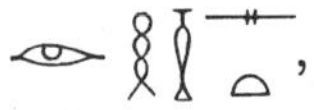, to do the pleasure of someone, to make someone pleased.

åri khet 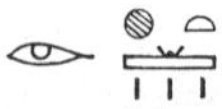, to do things, to be active, to acquire wealth, to sacrifice.

åri kheperu 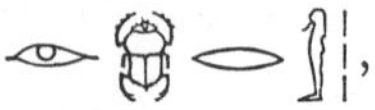, to effect transformations, to take different forms; 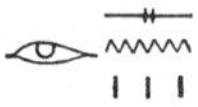 , they changed their forms.

åri kheru , Rec. 21, 87, to thunder.

åri kher-f 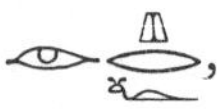, to perform his daily task.

åri sa , to make magical passes over someone.

åri sep sen 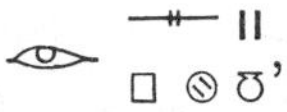, to repeat.

åri sem , to greet with good words; Copt. ⲣ̄ⲥⲙⲟⲩ (?)

åri senther [illegible], [illegible], to make an offering of incense, to cense.

åri sekhem [illegible], to play the sistrum.

åri sekheru [illegible], to devise plans, to arrange men's destinies, a title of one of the Khensu gods at Thebes.

åri sesh [illegible], to act as a scribe, to copy a document or book; [illegible], to act as a scribe, to copy; [illegible], [illegible], [illegible], to do into writing; [illegible] [illegible], IV, 1004.

åri seshsh [illegible], [illegible], to play, or rattle, the sistrum.

åri seshem kh[n]s [illegible], to praise.

åri seka [illegible], to plough.

ȧri-t setep sa (?) 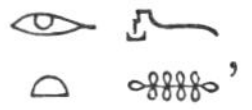, to make magical passes, to perform magical ceremonies with a view of securing protection from evil, to visit the Court.

ȧri shen , hairdresser; 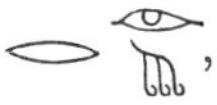, chief hairdresser at Court.

ȧri kat , "doer of the Splendid Works of the Lord of the Two Lands," *i.e.*, the royal Clerk of the Works.

ȧri gestep , to protect.

ȧri ṭa-t tep-f  , he who has laid his head upon the earth, *i.e.*, the dead man.

ȧri tcheṭ 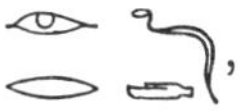, to make a speech, to say.

ȧriu , working men, slaves, servants.

ȧrit , working women.

ȧru, ȧriu 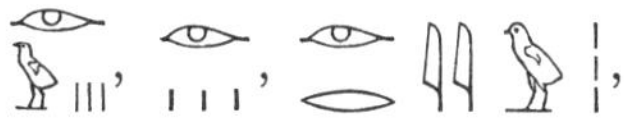, , , workers, doers, those who make, etc.

ȧri-t , IV, 901, made, artificial (of , lapis-lazuli).

ȧri-t 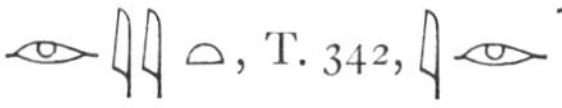, T. 342, P. 191, 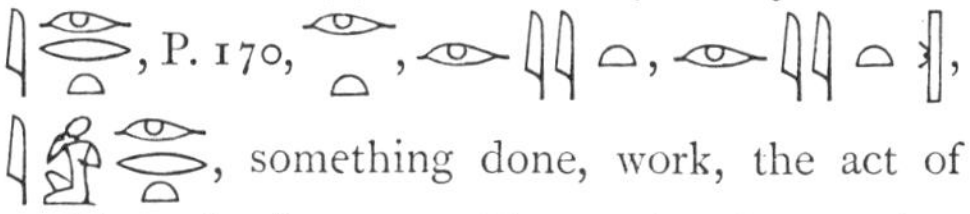, P. 170, something done, work, the act of working, deed, act, a thing to be done; plur. 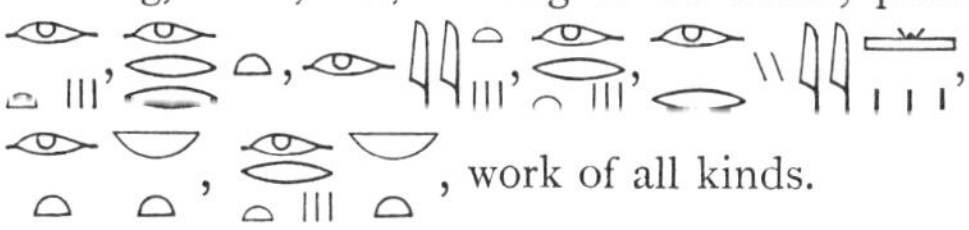, work of all kinds.

ȧri-t , creature; plur. creatures, human beings, mankind.

Ȧri , Rec. 32, 176, "worker," *i.e.*, the creative god, as opposed to the god whose heart is still, *i.e.*, , Osiris.

Ȧri 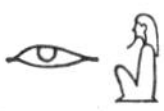, Ombos I, 1, 186–188, one of the 14 Kau of Rā.

Ȧriti , Rec. 15, 178, a goddess.

Ȧrit-ȧakhu , Ṭuat VII, a star-goddess.

Ȧri-Ȧmen 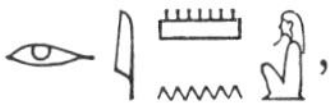, a god.

Ȧrit-ȧru (?) , Ṭuat VII, a star-goddess.

Ȧri-maāt 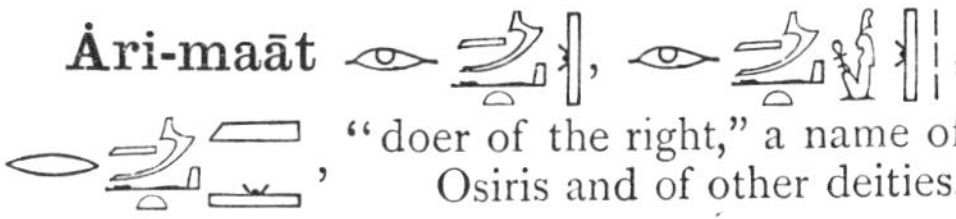, "doer of the right," a name of Osiris and of other deities.

Ȧri-em-ȧb-f , B.D. 125, II, one of the 42 Assessors of Osiris.

Ȧri-em-āua 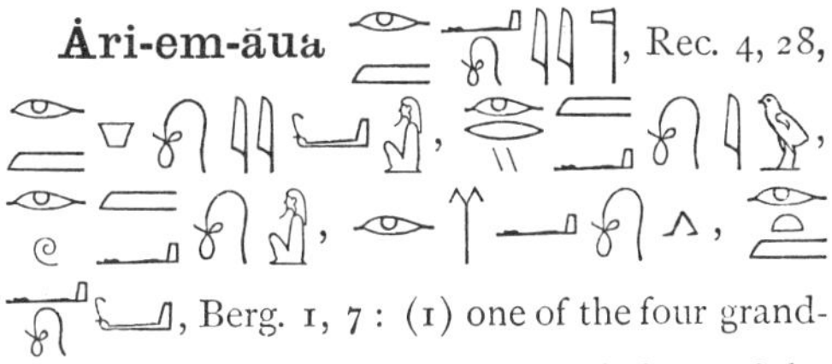, Rec. 4, 28, Berg. 1, 7: (1) one of the four grandsons of Horus; (2) god of the 6th hour of the night; (3) god of the 15th day of the month.

Ȧri-en-ȧb-f , B.D. 110, 42, a blue-eyed god in Sekhet-Ȧaru.

Ȧri-entuten-em-meska-en Nem-ur , B.D. 99, 19, the leathers of the magical boat.

Ȧri-ren-f-tchesef 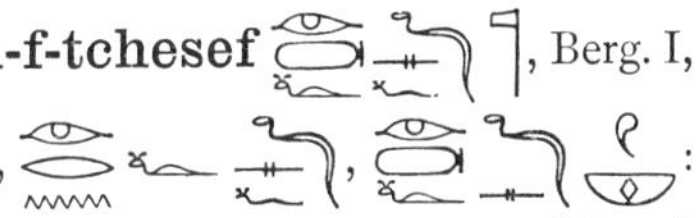, Berg. I, 7, Rec. 4, 28: (1) one of the four grandsons of Horus; (2) god of the 10th day of the month; (3) a part of the magical boat; (4) god of the 8th hour of the day.

Ȧri-ḥetch-f 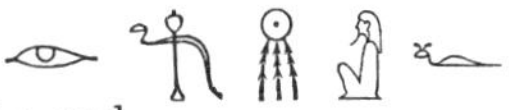, "creator of his light," a god.

ȧri-khet 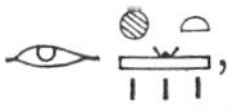, "maker of things," a title of several gods and kings.

Ȧriu-kamt 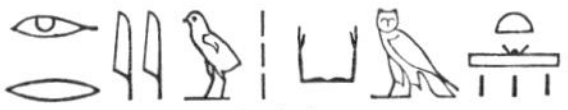, Ṭuat VI, the 12 gardeners of Osiris.

Ȧri-ta , Rec. 27, 189, a title of Ptaḥ.

Ȧrit-ta-theth (?) , Ṭuat X, a lioness-goddess.

Ȧri-tchet-f , the god and festival of the 9th day of the month.

ȧr , to see; compare Heb. רָאָה and Copt. ⲉⲓⲱⲣϩ (?)

ȧr , the pupil of the eye; Copt. ⲓⲟⲣϩ.

ȧr-ui , the two eyes. This reading is very doubtful; the correct reading is, perhaps, something like the Coptic ⲃⲁⲗ.

ȧr-t , , the eye; compare Copt. ⲉⲓⲁⲧ, a seeing, a looking, look, glance, the faculty or act of seeing, sight, vision; and ⲉⲓ in ⲉⲓⲉⲣⲃⲟⲟⲛⲉ, evil eye.

ȧr-t em ȧr-t , eye to eye.

ȧr-ti , U. 63, , U. 551, , , the two eyes; , eyes.

ȧr-ti en nesu , a title of an official.

ȧr-t nebt 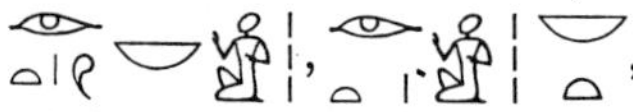, , "every eye," *i.e.*, all persons, everybody.

Ȧr-t (?) , B.D. 101, 4, the Eye of seven cubits with a pupil of three cubits.

Ȧr-t-ȧabt , Thes. 104, the left eye of Horus or Rā, *i.e.*, the moon.

Ȧr-t-uā 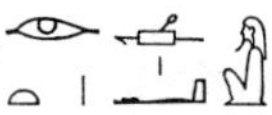, B.D. (Saïte) 115, 1, "one eye," a title of the Sun-god.

Ȧr-t-unem-t , B.D. 17, 71, the right eye of Rā, *i.e.*, the sun.

Ȧr-t-unemi , Thes. 104, a name of Sirius and Rā.

Ȧr-t-utt (?) , Rec. 30, 188, a goddess.

Ȧr-ti-f-em-khet 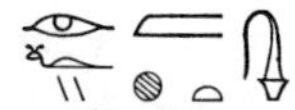, one of the 42 Judges in the Hall of Osiris.

Ȧr-ti-f-em-ṭes , B.D. 125, II, "Flint-eyes," or "Fiery-eyes," a god of Sekhem, one of the 42 Assessors; varr. 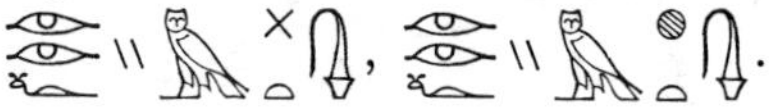.

Ȧr-ti-m-tches , Rec. 15, 17, one of the 42 Assessors of Osiris.

Ȧr-t Rā , , eye of Rā, the mid-day sun.

Ȧr-t-Rā-neb-taui 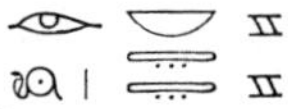, Ombos I, 1, 47, a serpent-goddess.

Ȧr-t-Ḥeru , N. 421, , 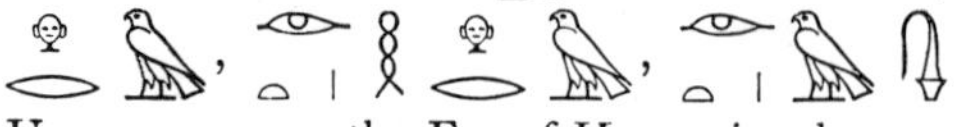, U. 91, 112, 117, the Eye of Horus, *i.e.*, the sun; fem. , Denderah IV, 81; , U. 37, the two eyes of Horus, one black, one white; , T. 196, P. 678, N. 1292, the southern Eye of Horus; , U. 37, the two Eyes of Horus =  and , P. 264, 265; 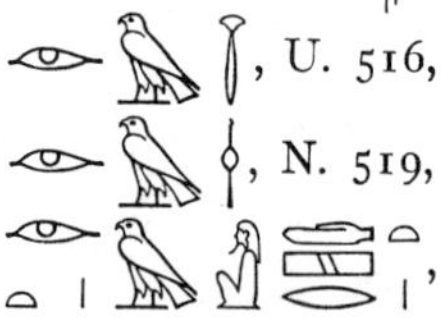, U. 516, the green Eye of Horus; N. 519, the white Eye of Horus; the red Eye of Horus.

Ȧr-t Ḥeru , U. 83, [illegible], [illegible], the Eye of Horus, a name given to offerings.

Ȧr-t Ḥeru ḥetch-t [illegible], a ceremonial garment.

Ȧr-t Khnemu [illegible], the Eye of Khnemu.

Ȧr-t Khnemu [illegible], P. 444, [illegible], M. 550, [illegible], N. 1130, "Eye of Khnem," the name of the boat of **Ḥer-f-ḥa-f.**

Ȧr-t Shu [illegible], Eye of Shu, *i.e.*, the day-sun.

Ȧr-t (?) Teb [illegible], T. 245, [illegible], 428, a god.

Ȧr-t (?) Tem [illegible], Pap. Mut-ḥetep 5, Eye of Tem, the setting sun; fem. [illegible], Denderah IV, 81.

Ȧr-ti-tchet-f (?) , the god of the 9th day of the month.

ȧr, ȧru , N. 119, 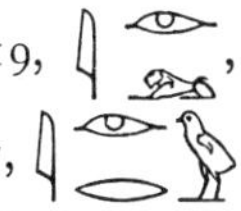, U. 421, , Rec. 27, 217, 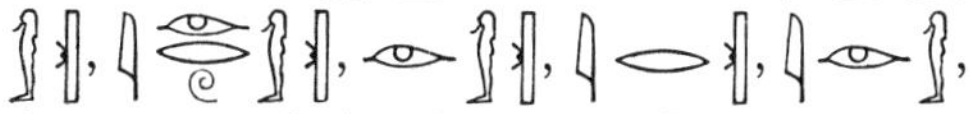 , form, figure, image, ceremony, rite; plur. , N. 213, , T. 241, P. 216, , T. 245, 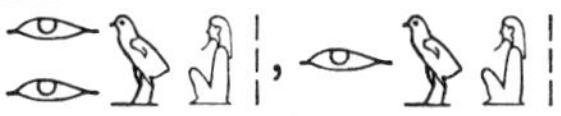, Rec. 33, 32, .

Ȧru , T. 245, 330, the divine forms in the Ṭuat.

ȧr 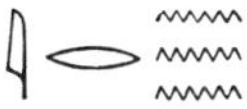, river; Copt. ⲉⲓⲟⲟⲣ.

ȧr-t , moisture, flow of water.

ȧr-āa , Ḥerusȧtef Stele 17, the Nile; Copt. ⲉⲓⲉⲣⲟ.

ȧrt-t 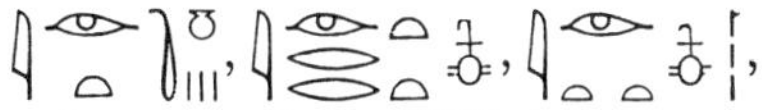, Rec. 27, 225, , 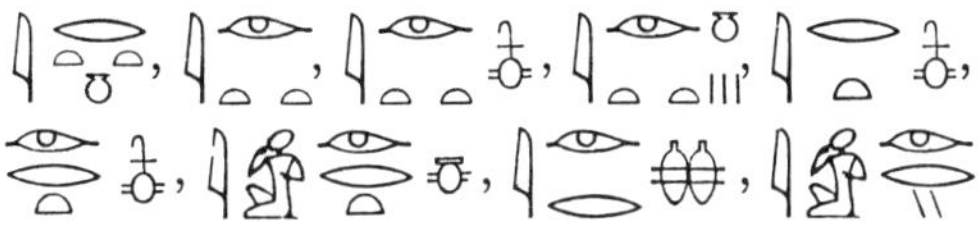, [illegible], Rec. 32, 183, , Rec. 13, 4, 21, milk; Copt. ⲉⲣⲱⲧⲉ; see [illegible].

ȧrtu (ȧrut) 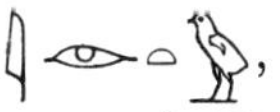, U. 68, [illegible], N. 327, [illegible], women who give suck, nurses (?)

ȧru , stalled ox; plur. , cattle for sacrifice.

ȧrit 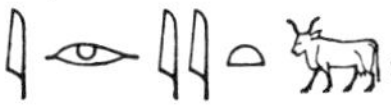, milch cow.

ȧr-t , beans; Copt. ⲁⲣⲱ, Arab. فول.

ȧr-ti 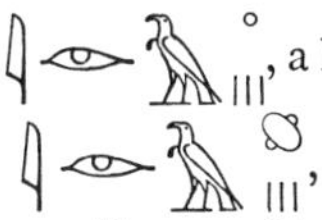, a kind of seed or grain (?)

ȧr-ti, some strong-smelling substance, or disagreeable sensation.

ȧr , to be oppressed; , Rec. 2, 109, greatly oppressed.

ȧr-ti 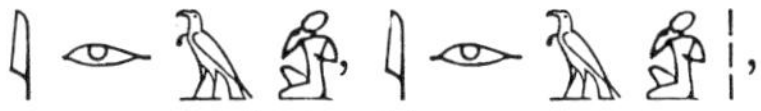, oppressed one, a man in trouble.

Ȧri-t , Ṭuat V, the gate of the 5th division of the Ṭuat.

ȧr-ut , part of the magical boat.

ȧr-tit, blue garment.

ȧr-ti, coloured cloth of which flags are made.

Ȧrti (?) , Ṭuat IX, a god who swathed Osiris.

ȧri 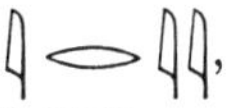, N. 391, [illegible], N. 1164, [illegible], P. 663, [illegible], P. 204, 961, , [illegible], he who belongs to something, or someone, one who is in charge, keeper; dual, , P. 391, M. 557, N. 1164; plur. , , P. 433, [illegible], M. 619, [illegible], N. 1224; Copt. ⲉⲣⲏⲩ.

ȧri , the man whose duty it was to attend to something; fem. [illegible].

ȧri , Rev. 11, 139, 12, 25, [illegible], friend, associate, companion.

ȧr-t 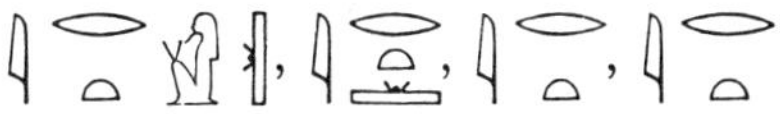, , [illegible], that which appertains to someone or something, the duty of someone, office, appointment.

ȧri ȧui [illegible], title of a priest of Upper Egypt.

åriu åakhut, dwellers in the horizon.

åri åru, title of the high priest of the 10th Nome of Upper Egypt.

Åri-år-t-tchesef, Rec. 4, 28, a god.

åri ås-t, throne attendant.

Åri-ås-t-neter, Ṭuat II, guardian of the divine throne.

åri āui, belonging to the arms, *i.e.*, bracelets, armlets.

åri ā-t, steward, housekeeper.

åri āa, N. 1074, P. 651, M. 752, porter, doorkeeper; plur.

Åri āui, B.D. G. 608, keeper of the Two Gates (Egypt); a title of Horus.

Åri-āa-em-ås-t-maāt, Cairo Pap. VII, 4, a lioness-goddess, keeper of the throne in the Hall of Judgment.

Åri-āa-en-Åsår, N. 1074, the doorkeeper of Osiris.

Årt-āa-nt-pet, P. 651, M. 752, the doorkeeper of heaven.

åri āau, ass-herd.

Åri-ānb-f, Ṭuat VIII, a dog-god in the Circle Åakebi.

åri ānti, Quelques Pap. 67, title of an official of the "House of Life,".

åri ārit, pylon-keeper; plur.

Åri-user-t, Thes. 100, the goddess Meḥennit.

åri pet, P. 299, belonging to the heavens, *i.e.*, divine being, or bird; plur., U. 430, T. 246, P. 391, M. 557, N. 1164, creatures of earth, T. 246.

Åri-peḥti, Denderah IV, 79, a bull-god.

åri-t peḥui, fil de perles (Lacau).

åri petch-t, bow-master, bow-bearer.

åri m'kha-t, master of the scales, a title of Anubis.

åri menkh-t, keeper of the wardrobe.

Åri meḥiu, Ṭuat V, the keeper of the drowned in the Ṭuat.

åri nit (?), steersman.

åri Nekhen, a title of high rank or learning; see **Nekhen**.

Åri-nebåui, Ṭuat I, keeper of the fire, stoker, a fire-god.

Åri-nefert, Ṭuat IV, keeper of the boat's tackle, a sailor of Åf's boat.

Åri-ti-nefert, keeper of the virgins.

åri neter, belonging to the god, sacred property.

Åri-t-neter-s, Ṭuat I, attendant on her god, a singing-goddess.

ȧri reṭui [hieroglyphs], belonging to the feet, *i.e.*, anklets.

Ȧri-reṭ-ur [hieroglyphs], P. 672, [hieroglyphs], M. 661, [hieroglyphs], N. 1276, "keeper of the Great Leg," a god.

ȧri reṭui [hieroglyphs], Rec. 33, 6, associate, companion.

Ȧriu-hut [hieroglyphs], B.D. 168, gods who directed the food supply.

ȧri ḥa-t [hieroglyphs], [hieroglyphs], [hieroglyphs], captain, title of a priest.

ȧri ḥeb [hieroglyphs], director of the festival.

ȧri ḥemu [hieroglyphs], steersman.

Ȧri-ḥems-nefer [hieroglyphs], [hieroglyphs], [hieroglyphs], [hieroglyphs], [hieroglyphs], [hieroglyphs], a Sûdânî god, whose wife was Tefnut; [hieroglyphs] [hieroglyphs] = Arensnuphis.

ȧri ḥenbiu [hieroglyphs], overseer of the cultivators.

ȧri kh-t [hieroglyphs], [hieroglyphs], storekeeper, revenue officer (?)

Ȧri-khabu [hieroglyphs], Ṭuat VI, master of the scythes, *i.e.*, of the Seven Reapers of Osiris.

ȧri khekh [hieroglyphs], [hieroglyphs], [hieroglyphs], belonging to the neck, *i.e.*, collar, necklet; [hieroglyphs]

ȧri sȧpu [hieroglyphs], B.D. 17, 123, keeper of the divine register of sins; plur. [hieroglyphs].

ȧriu surȧ [hieroglyphs], butlers, men in charge of drinks.

ȧri sba [hieroglyphs], door-keeper.

ȧri sebkh-t [hieroglyphs], gatekeeper.

Ȧriu sem-t (?) [hieroglyphs], B.D. 141, 61, the divine keepers of cemeteries.

ȧri seshem [hieroglyphs], Rec. 26, 7, keeper of the slaughter-house (?)

Ȧr-stau [hieroglyphs], a portion of the kingdom of Seker the Death-god.

Ȧriu-stau-ȧmenḥiu [hieroglyphs] [hieroglyphs], B.D. 17, 31 (Nebseni), the overseers of the slaughtering gods.

ȧri qeb-en-she-en-shet [hieroglyphs] [hieroglyphs], keeper of the bend in the Lake of Fire.

Ȧri kenem [hieroglyphs], Ombos I, 1, 252, the keeper of the Dekans.

ȧri-t ta [hieroglyphs], belonging to earth, *i.e.*, a man, or animal.

Ȧriu-ta [hieroglyphs], [hieroglyphs], U. 431, T. 246, the denizens of earth.

Ȧriu-ta (?) [hieroglyphs], B.D. 168, the four water-gods in the Ṭuat.

ȧri thetthet [hieroglyphs], Ȧmen. 22, 20 . . . .

ȧriu tha-t [hieroglyphs], Amherst Pap. 28, companions in theft, fellow robbers.

Ȧri-ṭes [hieroglyphs], Berg. I, 34, [hieroglyphs], Edfû I, 13D, keeper of the slaughtering knife.

ȧru [hieroglyphs], bandages, mummy swathings.

ȧr [hieroglyphs], to remove, to transport.

ȧr [hieroglyphs], [hieroglyphs], a measure of land.

ȧr-t [hieroglyphs], [hieroglyphs], a skin roll, a book; see [hieroglyphs].

ȧr-ti [hieroglyphs], the two jawbones, see [hieroglyphs].

ȧrr , Wört. 102, deaf (?)

ȧrr , grapes, grape seeds; Copt. ελοολε.

ȧrr 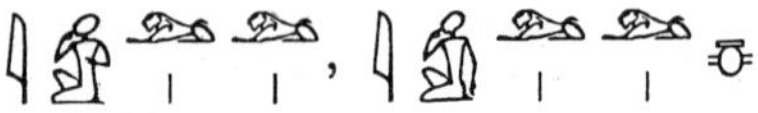, 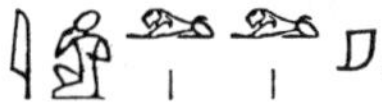, Alt. K. 106, a wine jar.

ȧrr-na 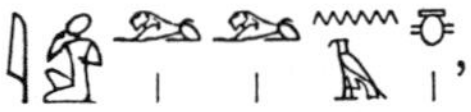 B.M. 5633, a pot (?)

Ȧrȧ , Ṭuat I, a singing-god.

Ȧrār-ti , two uraei-goddesses, Isis and Nephthys (?)

ȧri , knife, weapon.

Ȧri , A.Z. Bd. 38, 17, a proper name = אלי.

ȧri , Rec. 35, 57, name of a fiend, hostile being.

ȧri-t 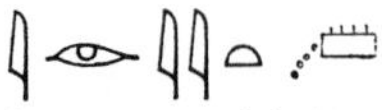, fruit, produce.

ȧri-t 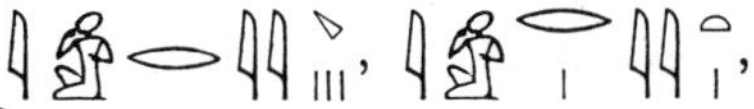, , land, estate.

ȧrutana 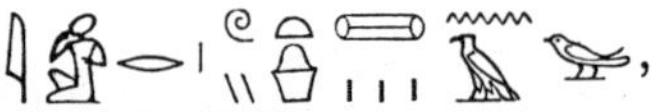, , Hearst Pap. Voc. the name of a disease.

ȧruṭ (?) 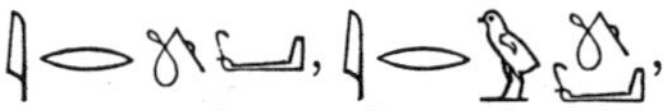, to tie, to fetter, to rob;  , poor man, one robbed of his goods.

ȧrb , to be shut in, driven in; Copt. ωρϐ.

ȧrabtu . . . . . , Annales 4, 129 . . . .

ȧrp , P. 724, 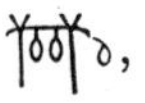, U. 43A, 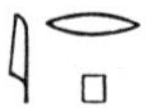 , P. 243, , P. 707, 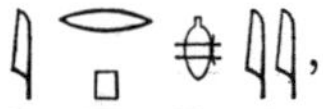, P. 98, , , 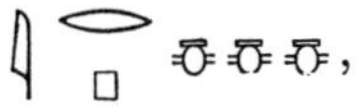, U. 194, , M. 719, N. 1327, wine; Copt. ηρπ;  , IV, 670, honey wine; 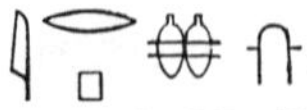, Rec. 13, 73, wine by measure; , wine shop; , wine cellar; , wine of the north; 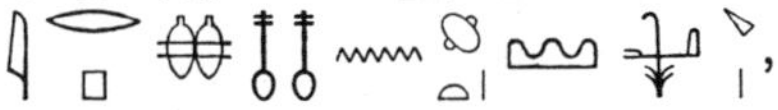, very fine wine of the Southern Oasis.

ȧrp 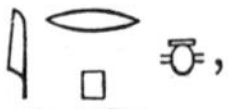, wine of various kinds and districts; [illegible], T. 120, wine of Pelusium; [illegible], T. 119; [illegible], U. 148, cedar wine; [illegible], T. 121, *ḥa* wine; [illegible], T. 122, wine of Syene.

ȧrp [illegible], wine plant, vine.

ȧrpi[t] [illegible], product, food.

ȧrp [illegible], Rec. 29, 158, to rot, to decay, to ferment.

ȧrpai [illegible], Rev. 12, 16 = [illegible].

ȧrpi [illegible], Jour. As. 1908, 300, temple = [illegible]; Copt. ρπε.

ȧrpi-t [illegible], wine cup (?) vase.

ȧref [illegible], B.D. 52, 3, an emphatic particle, [illegible].

ȧrm [illegible], L.D. ii, 49B, a word used in connection with a blowpipe.

ȧrm [illegible], a man of Aram (Syrian, Mesopotamian).

Ȧrmu (?) [illegible], Koller Pap. 4, 3, a tribe in the Sûdân.

Ȧrmau [illegible], Thes. 926, a god.

ȧrm' [illegible], [illegible]

, Treaty 10, with, along with; see ; Copt. ⲛⲉⲙ.

årmen , see **remen.**

Åranth 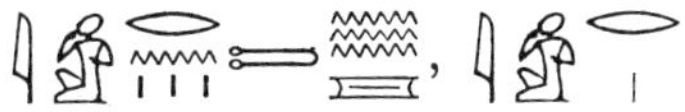 , the River Orontes.

År-ḥes 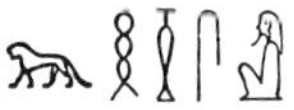, a lion-god.

årekh , U. 214, , Rec. 27, 57, to know, make to know; see 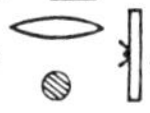.

årkhekh (?) , Theban Ost. No. 4, a mineral.

Årkhåm Khertt-neter 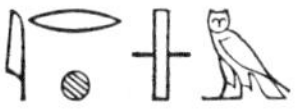 , B.D. (Saïte), pl. 72; Denderah 4, 83, a lioness-headed goddess in Åat XI.

åres , T. 286, 370, P. 69, 670, M. 174, N. 687, 760, 1272, to wake up.

Årsi 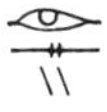, Gol. 10, 42, B.D. 181, 14, a god.

årr-sa 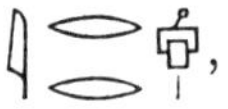, after.

Årsu , Obel. Ḥatshepset, Ḳubbân Stele 4, "his maker," the king's god (?)

Årsu , a Syrian general who ruled Egypt at the end of the XIXth dynasty.

Årsna-t  , Rev. 6, 6, 33, 3, Arsinoë.

årq , to roll up.

årq , A.Z. 1908, 16, name of a serpent amulet.

årqabas , Koller Pap. 4, 3, a kind of stone; compare Heb. אֶל־גָּבִישׁ, Arab. الجبس, crystal (?)

Årk , P. 266, N. 1244, a god.

Årkanåtchpan  , A.Z. 31, 101, Alt. K. 116, a god whose functions are unknown.

årk-tå , Rechnungen 59, a kind of wood.

Årt , Rec. 14, 11, , Mett. Stele, p. 19, note 15, a serpent-fiend in the Ṭuat.

Årtå , U. 534, T. 298, P. 231, a fiend in the Ṭuat.

årtåtchar , a kind of bird.

årth-t 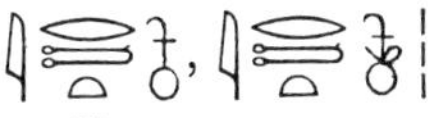, U. 20, T. 338, 368, P. 247, milk.

Årtheth-āa-sti (?) 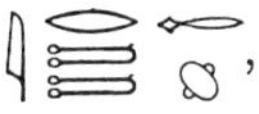, Tomb of Rameses IX, pl. 10, god of the serpent 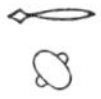.

årṭ , moisture, liquid.

årṭb [?] a measure; Copt. ⲉⲣⲧⲟⲃ, Gr. ἀρτάβη, Arab. ardeb.

åh , to utter cries of joy.

åhu , cries of joy.

åha , P. 42, M. 62, N. 29, O!

åhaa , IV, 895, shouts of joy.

åhai  , O! hail! hurrah! cries of acclamation.

åhahai [illegible] [illegible], joy.

åhå(hi ?) [illegible], T. 185, 287, P. 371, M. 820, N. 42, O! moan, cry, hail!

åhåh [illegible], U. 295, a shout of joy.

åhi [illegible] [illegible], a cry of joy, O! hail! hurrah!

åhit [illegible], a cry of joy.

ȧhh, ȧhhȧ, ȧhi 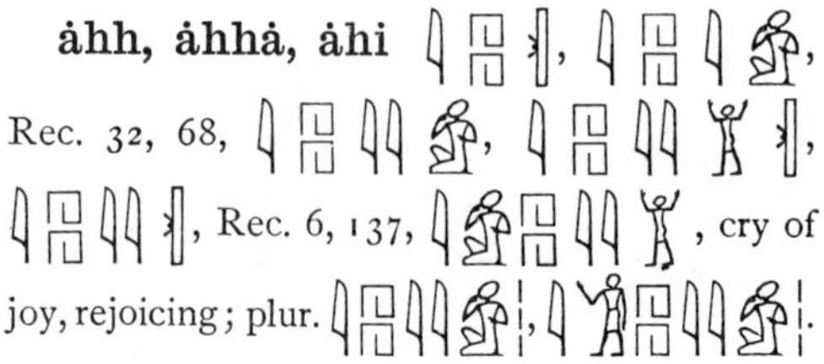, Rec. 32, 68, , Rec. 6, 137, , cry of joy, rejoicing; plur. .

ȧhhi , a festival.

ȧh 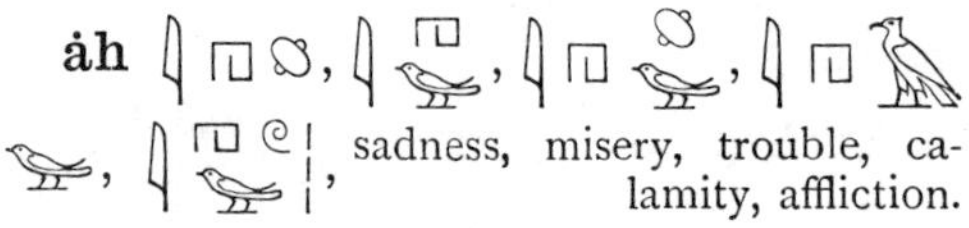, sadness, misery, trouble, calamity, affliction.

ȧhai , death cry, death sentence.

ȧhi , a cry of woe, death wail.

ȧhi 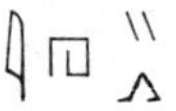, to make to go.

ȧha 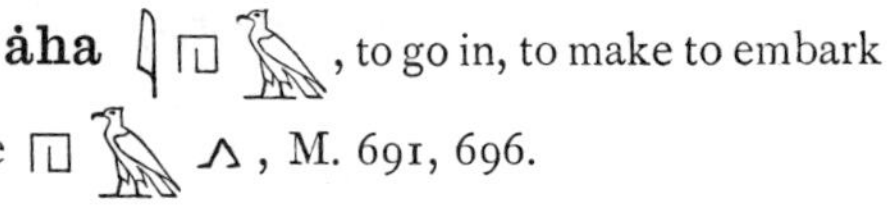, to go in, to make to embark; see , M. 691, 696.

ȧhai-t , , Mar. Karn. 52, 15, , A.Z. 83, 65, , cow-byre, stable, any outhouse on a farm, chambers, dock.

ȧhab 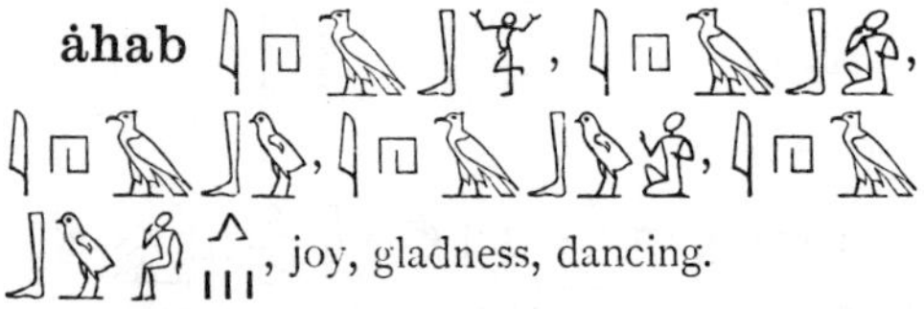, joy, gladness, dancing.

ȧhabu , P. 164, N. 861, dancer.

ȧhab 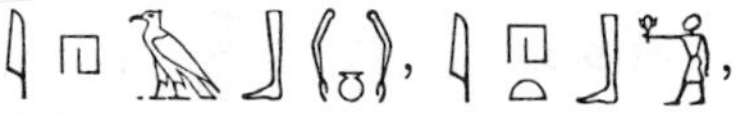, sistrum player.

ȧhab 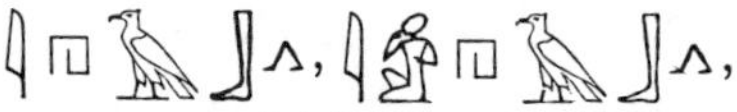, to send a messenger, to let fly (an arrow).

ȧham , Ȧhem, 10, 7, , Israel Stele 25, mourning, lament; Copt. ⲁϩⲟⲙ.

ȧham , to run aground (of a boat), to drive ashore (of a ship).

ȧhȧ 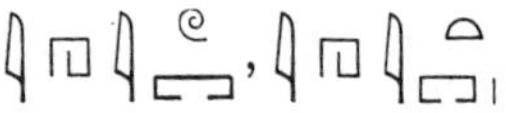 farm, homestead.

ȧhi , camp, courtyard; plur. , Israel Stele 7.

ȧhi n ȧua , house for cattle, cattle-shed.

ȧhi 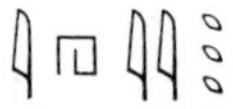, grain.

ȧhb 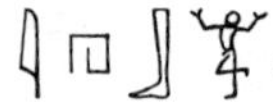, to rejoice, be glad.

ȧhbut , Rec. 10, 150, dancing-women, love-women, concubines; compare √אהב.

ȧhbu , IV, 504, a class of officials or workmen.

ȧhm 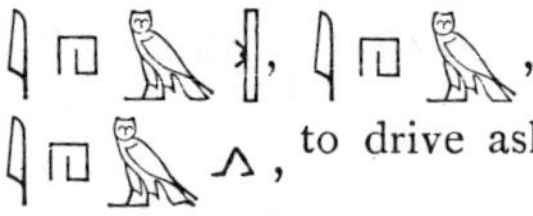, Rec. 30, 72, 33, 81, , to drive ashore (of a boat).

ȧhm , Rec. 30, 217, , Thes. 1199, , Thes. 1206, groaning, grief; Copt. ⲁϩⲟⲙ.

ȧhm-t 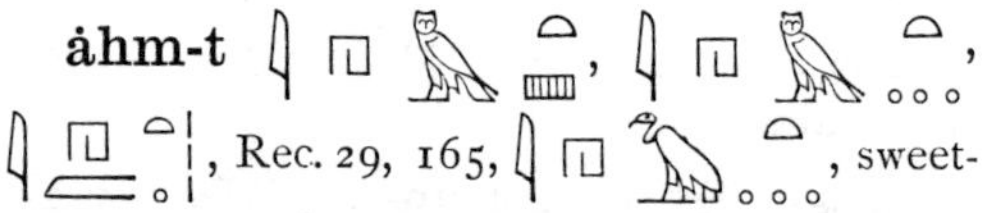, Rec. 29, 165, , sweet-smelling gum, incense, unguent.

Ȧhmesu , Rec. 30, 72, a god (?)

ȧhn 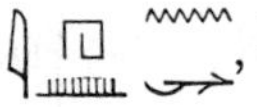, B.D. 145, 3, 12, a wooden instrument.

ȧhir (?) , Mar. Karn. 52, 7, camels'-hair tents; Heb. אֹהֶל.

ȧḥ 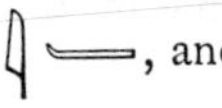, and; Copt. ⲟⲩⲟϩ.

ȧḥ 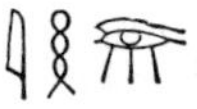, Mett. Stele 39, to cry.

ȧḥ, ȧḥi (?) 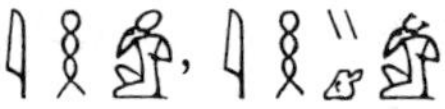, Israel Stele 22, cry of grief, Oh!

ȧḥ 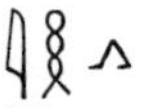, P.S.B. 24, 46, interjection, O!

ȧḥ , to go.

ȧḥ 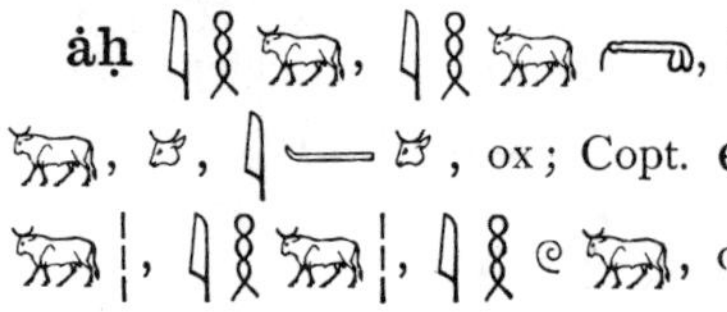, Rec. 21, 92, , ox; Copt. ⲉϩⲉ; plur. , oxen, cattle;

of the , foreign cattle; , , cattle of certain weight.

ȧḥ-t 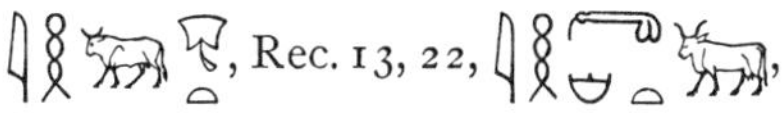 , Rec. 13, 22, , Bubastis A. 34, cow.

Ȧḥ-pet  , M. 704, "ox of heaven," the name of a star.

ȧḥ-ṭesher 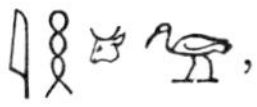 , P. 706, "red bull."

ȧḥ , pasture (?)

ȧḥ , , , , stall, stable, workshop; , stable of horses; , royal stable.

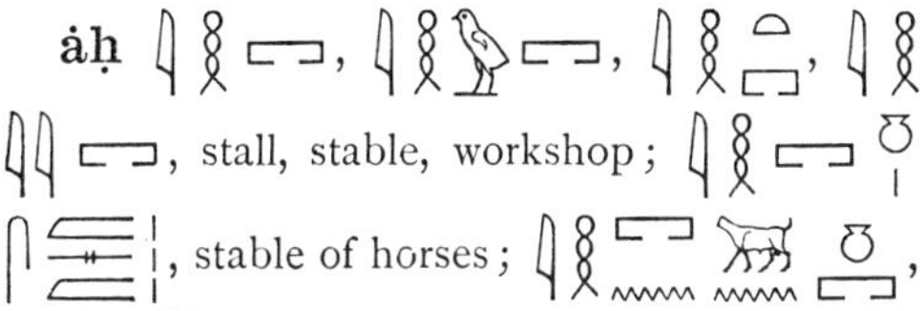

ȧḥ-t 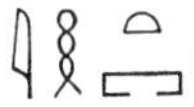 , a chamber in the Ṭuat.

ȧḥut , Rec. 2, 116, prisons.

ȧḥ , to be green (of land); see **āāḥ**.

ȧḥ-t , , , , , , acre, field, tillage, pasture, parcel of land; Copt. ⲉⲓⲱϩⲉ; plur. , , , , ; see **āāḥ**.

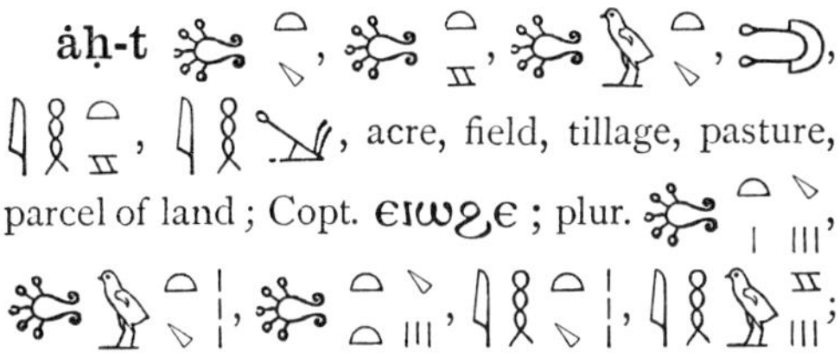

ȧḥuti , , , , , , , , , ploughman, field labourer, *fellâḥ*; plur. , , ; see **āāḥ**.

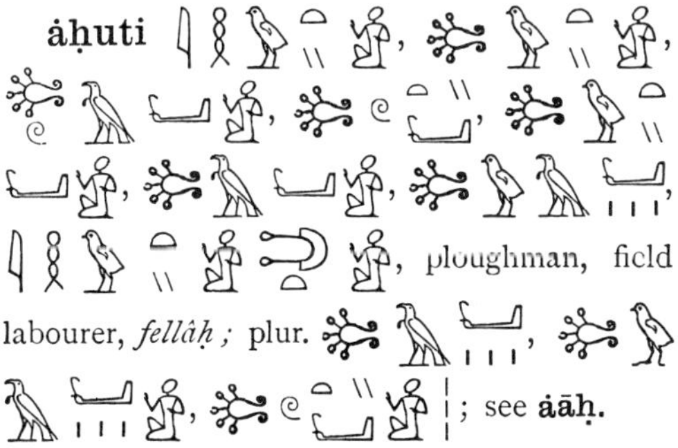

ȧḥ , , , , , U. 150, N. 458 = , T. 121, IV, 60, 767, 1078, Annales III, 109, to spread out a net, to lay a snare, to catch animals or birds, to surround with a wall, to enclose.

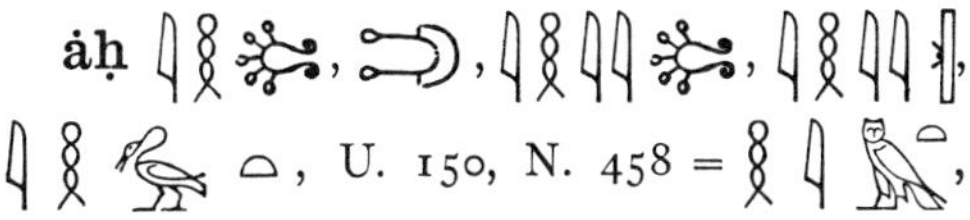

ȧḥ , , fishing net.

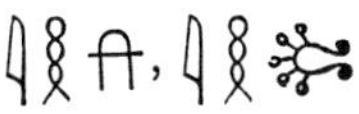

ȧḥ , a girdle, a collar, necklet, something worn round the neck or body.

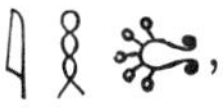

ȧḥ , rope, cord; plur. .

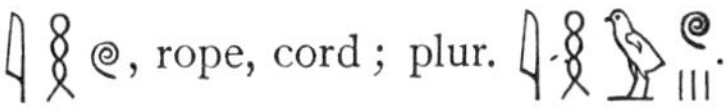

ȧḥ , papyrus, marsh flower; plur. , , ; Heb. אָחוּ.

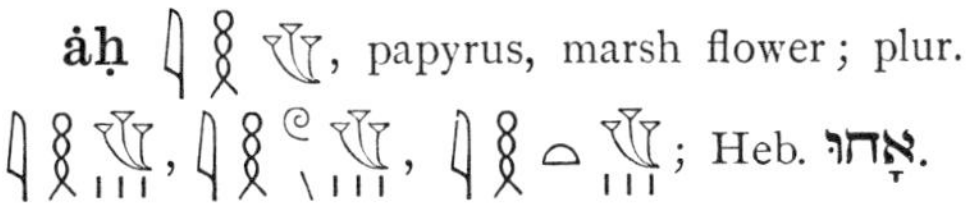

ȧḥ , , , , a kind of plant and its seed; , white ȧḥ.

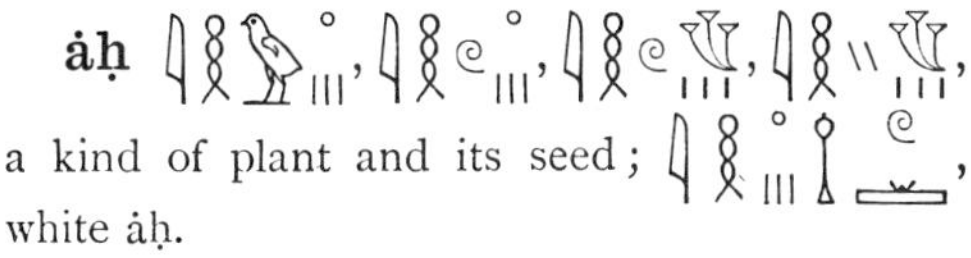

ȧḥ , , a kind of tree; plur. (?)

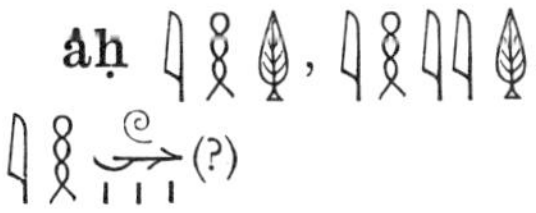

ȧḥ , Rec. 24, 161, the moon; see **āāḥ**; Copt. ⲓⲟϩ, Heb. יָרֵחַ.

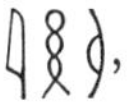

Ȧḥ , the Moon-god.

ȧḥ , lunar festival on the 18th day of the month.

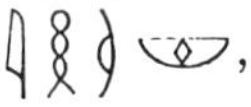

ȧḥ , white metal, silver (?)

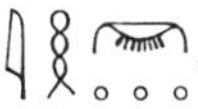

ȧḥu , limbs, members, flesh, body.

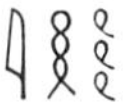

ȧḥ-ti , , soles of the feet (?)

ȧḥ , Wört. 107 . . . .

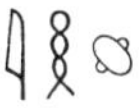

ȧḥ-t , , , steering pole, rudder, paddle; plur. , .

ȧḥȧḥ , , to work a paddle; , the sound of paddling.

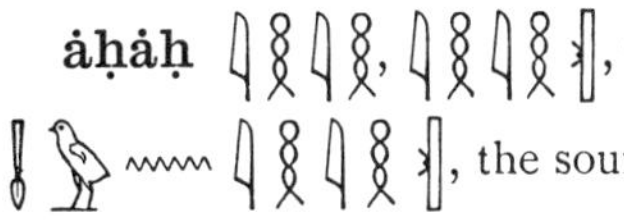

ȧḥ , U. 376, , , , to smite, to fight.

ȧḥ in , packets of arrows (Lacau).

ȧḥ , spears, arrows.

ȧḥa , to fight; see .

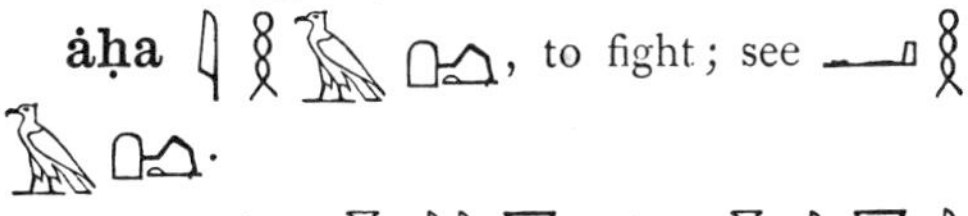

ȧḥai , = , some filthy animal.

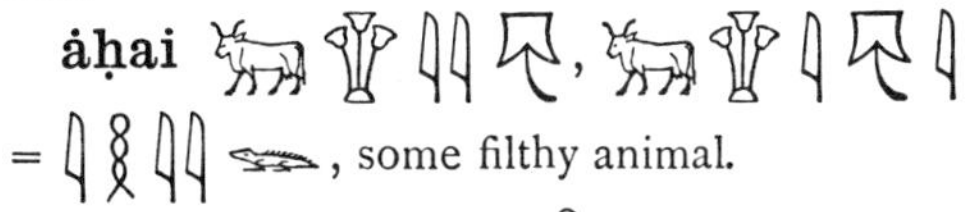

ȧḥai-t  , sistrum bearer.

åḥā =

åḥā-t , , , flesh, limbs.

åḥā , P. 175, to rejoice, , U. 166, , P. 194.

åḥā , , P. 450, 642, M. 461, 678, N. 1239, to rejoice, to acclaim, , N. 69, 649.

Åḥāp , the Nile-god.

åḥi , P. 364 = , N 1077, to smite, to strike.

åḥi , , U. 496, T. 319, to become dark.

Åḥi , Ṭuat VI, an attendant on the dead.

åḥi , "child," the name of the sun on New Year's Day.

åḥi, åḥit , , Rec. 30, 193, 31, 170, 171, , , , a priest or priestess who personified the god Åḥi.

Åḥi , , , B.D. 125, II, one of the 42 Assessors of Osiris.

Åḥi, Åḥui, Åḥai , , B.D. 102, 2, 149: (1) a form of Harpokrates; (2) the god of the 1st Åat; (3) the god of the 18th day of the month.

Åḥi-sa-Ḥe-t-ḥer , B.D. G. 348, a form of Harpokrates.

åḥu , a pair of clappers or castanets.

Åḥui , B.D. 124, 15 = (?), *i.e.*, Horus and Set.

åḥi , hair.

Åḥi , Edfû 1, 29, 7, a crocodile-fiend.

åḥi-t , fish-pond.

åḥiut (?) , a class of human beings, peasants (?); , a class of divine beings.

Åḥibit , B.D. 146, a goddess of the 17th Pylon.

åḥu (?) , , weakness, helplessness (?)

Åḥu (?) , B.D. 124, 8, a form of .

Åḥu , Rec. 30, 198 = , a form of Thoth; , Rec. 26, 211, ; var. of , Rec. 26, 228.

åḥun , , youth, stripling; plur. , , , divine child; , , Rec. 32, 176, young god.

åḥbenut (?) , ring, circle.

åḥem , P. 492, 493, 494, , N. 1101, to decree (?); , P. 276, M. 520, , N. 1101.

åḥemu , B.D. (Nebseni) 92, 13 . . . .

åḥems , M. 677, , N. 1240, to sit, to seat oneself.

åḥems , P.S.B. 14, 207, a child who was allowed to enter the royal nursery.

Åḥemt , N. 872, a warrior-god in the Ṭuat.

åḥenn , Mar. Karn. 54, 42 = (?)

åḥennu , U. 167, workmen, field-labourers; see .

åḥes , Wört. 550, to strike (?)

Åḥes , M. 779, a Sûdânî god; var. , P. 668.

åḥesmen , P. 292, packets of natron.

Ȧḥkai, Hh. 431, the god who composed magical spells for the gods.

ȧḥt-t, rent of a field or estate.

ȧḥt, liquor.

ȧḥt, the lung, or lungs.

ȧḥtit, neck, throat, windpipe, lung.

Ȧḥti, a name of Osiris as the throat and lungs of the dead.

Ȧḥti, L.D. 4, 82B, consort of Rerit (?)

ȧḥeth, U. 539, T. 296 . . . .

ȧḥṭ, chamber, stall, stable; see .

ȧḥṭi; see .

ȧḥetch ta, P. 432, M. 618, N. 1222, to dawn.

ȧkh, ȧkhi (?), , an interjection.

ȧkh = Copt. ⲁϧⲟ, why? what? where?

ȧkh, U. 424, , , , , , an interrogative particle: Why? what? in what manner? wherefore? how? Copt. ⲁϣ; , like what? , IV, 649; , for why?

ȧkh-rek, Rev. 30, 99, what is the matter with thee? Copt. ⲁϩⲣⲟⲕ.

ȧkh-t, , , , things, property, goods, possessions; see .

ȧkhit, product, revenue, food.

ȧkh, Rec. 30, 189, fertile land, grassland.

ȧkhkhut, plants and herbs, vegetables, verdure.

ȧkhȧkh, flowers of the sky, *i.e.*, the stars.

ȧkhȧkh, darkness, night.

ȧkhekh, , , , , , , , , , darkness, night.

Ȧkhkhi: (1) a doorkeeper in the Ṭuat; (2) the night personified.

Ȧkhekh, B.D. (Saïte) 98, 3, an associate of Shu.

ȧkhaȧr, Rec. 33, 120, street, quarter of a town.

ȧkhab, ȧkhb-t, , , pure water.

ȧkhabu, grain.

ȧkhȧ, , to flourish, to prosper.

ȧkhkhȧ, to be green, to flourish.

ȧkhāi, P. 614, , M. 780, N. 1137, to make to rise on a throne, to crown a man king.

ȧkhi, gladness, joy.

ȧkhi, upper region, sky.

ȧkhiu, spirits; Copt. ⲓϧ.

Ȧkhkhu, M. 409, , T. 399, , B.D. (Saïte) 98, 3, the Light-god; var. .

ȧkhu, beings of light, spirits; Copt. ⲓϧ.

Ȧkhuti, the two snake-goddesses, Isis and Nephthys (?)

ȧkhb, to feed (?)

Ȧkhpȧ = , Tomb of Seti I, one of the 75 forms of Rā.

åkhem, to be ignorant, to do nothing, to have nothing; see ; , IV, 201, inert, weak, feeble.

åkhem, åkhem-t , , without, lacking.

åkhm-t āua , P. 142, without sourness (of wine); var. , N. 885.

åkhm-t āma , N. 127, , T. 288, M. 65, , N. 885, without mouldiness, or staleness (of bread).

åkhem khestch , N. 885, , T. 288, M. 65, , N. 126, without going mouldy (of bread).

Åkhemit , U. 645, a goddess, consort of .

Åkhem åut , U. 477, , N. 747. . . . . .

Åkhem-upt-åmkhạu , U. 509, , T. 323, a hunting-god who bound the gods for slaughter.

Åkhmiu urṭu , , Hymn of Darius 14, B.D. (Saïte) 15, 2, 32, 2, 78, 28, 98, 3, 102, 2, the stars that never set (?)

Åkhem-urṭ-f , Ṭuat IX, a god who supplied souls in the Ṭuat with water.

åkhmiu urtchu , P. 382, N. 1157, , Rec. 26, 234, the never-resting stars.

Åkhemu-beṭesh[iu] , P. 241, a group of gods in the Ṭuat.

Åkhmui-remthu , U. 236, , N. 710, the two gods (Horus and Set) who weep not.

Åkhem-ḥep-f , Ṭuat IX, a god who supplied souls in the Ṭuat with water.

Åkhem-khems-f , Ṭuat IX, a god who supplied souls in the Ṭuat with water.

Åkhemu-seshåu , P. 241, a group of gods in the Ṭuat.

Åkhem-sek , an everlasting god who, under the forms of other gods, protected the members of the deceased. Each of the Cardinal Points possessed an Åkhem-sek.

Åkhem-sek , U. 218, 219, , P. 658, 763, a star near the pole, *i.e.*, a star that does not disappear till dawn; a never-failing, or imperishable, star; , a title of Rā, the "never-failing."

Åkhmiu-seku , , , , , U. 211, 214, 482, T. 289, 353, 366, 397, P. 158, 159, 181, 203, 308, 381, 412, 544, 701, M. 186, 285, 715, 749, N. 118, 839, 893, 944, 957, 990, 1196, 1219, 1329, 1342, Rec. 26, 234, 31, 21: (1) the "imperishable" stars, *i.e.*, the stars which never set below the horizon; (2) a group of 12 gods with paddles (Ṭuat X) who were reborn daily.

Åkhem-sek-f , Ṭuat IX, a god who supplied souls in the Ṭuat with water.

åkhkhm-t , U. 141, , T. 112, N. 449, fire.

åkhem-t , , bank of a stream, dam; see .

åkhm-t , A.Z. 1910, 125, pool, tank.

åkhemti , T. 238,  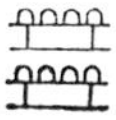, U. 418, the two regions (?)

Åkhmu-t , P. 319, , M. 626, a district (?)

åkhem , U. 509, , T. 267, 323, , N. 39, to seize, to smite, to grasp violently.

åkhkhm-t , U. 91,  , P. 624, M. 607, N. 1212, a smiting (?)

åkhen , 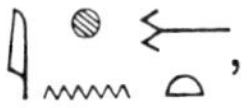, women's apartments; Gr. γυναικεῖον, seraglio, harîm.

åkhen , P. 603, to work a boat.

åkher , T. 246, 311, 346, 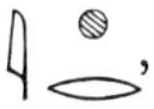, U. 430, Peasant 150, a conjunction, but, because, then; var. .

åkher , but, because, then.

åkher 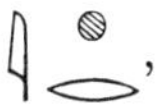, possession, property.

åkher , P. 228, , P. 701, M. 69, , Hh. 426, , to make to fall, to cast down, to bow oneself to the ground.

åkheriu , sacrifices.

åkheriu , the fallen in death, enemies, fiends.

Åkhsesf , 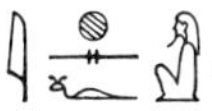, B.D. 75, 4, a god.

åkhet , U. 163, T. 134, N. 471, plant, wood, tree; Copt. ϣⲉ.

ås , T. 271, M. 33, an enclitic conjunction, often used as a mark of emphasis, or to draw special attention to the phrase to which it is attached; it also serves to mark an explanation, and may be translated "namely," "to wit," "that is," "behold" (Copt. ⲉⲓⲥ), etc.; 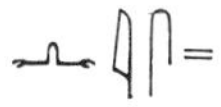 = but not; **åsk** , and **åst** , or **åsth** 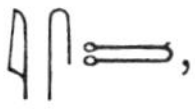, have a somewhat similar meaning.

ås , to call to, to hail; see **nås** .

ås , Rec. 28, 176, , to reckon a price, accountant.

ås-t 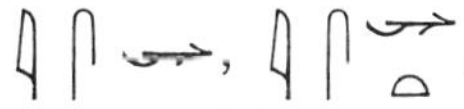, plank, beam, timber; Copt. ⲥⲟⲓ (?)

ås-t (or **st**) 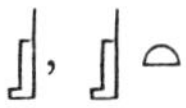, U. 222, 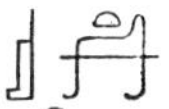, U. 391, [illegible], [illegible], Hymn of Darius 8, seat, throne, place, abode, tomb, room, chamber; plur. [illegible], U. 400, P. 608, M. 174, [illegible], N. 687, [illegible], [illegible], a piece of furniture; [illegible], U. 222.

ås-t åb [illegible], the dearest wish of the heart, heart's desire.

ås-t åmakh [illegible], a place where honour is paid to one.

ås-t ā [illegible], U. 507, [illegible]; plur. [illegible], T. 322 = [illegible], an assistant priest; plur. [illegible].

ås-t ā [illegible], an office, chancery.

ås-t āui [illegible], the place of the hands, *i.e.*, a possession.

ås-t āḥā en neb [illegible], L.D. III, 65A, 15, the place in the temple set apart for the king's use.

ås-t uāb-t [illegible], place of purity, bath (?), sanctuary.

ås-t ur-t [illegible], [illegible], Rec. 14, 17, great place, *i.e.*, heaven.

ȧs-t utcha-t 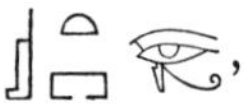, the position of the Eye of Rā in heaven.

ȧs-t maa , scene, spectacle.

ȧs-t maāt , 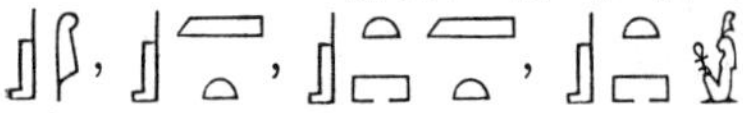, place of law, *i.e.*, the Kingdom of Osiris.

ȧs-t menȧ 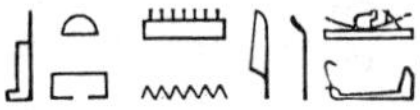, place of landing, landing stage, quay.

ȧs-t na shāu 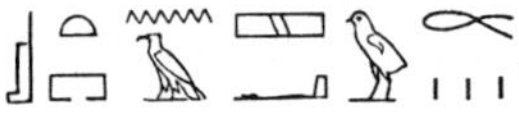, library, record-office.

ȧs-t neferu  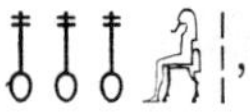, the seat of the happy, *i.e.*, heaven.

ȧs-t nefer-t 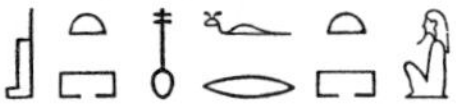, the cemetery.

ȧs-t nemm-t , place for walking, path, promenade.

Ȧs-t en-Net , a temple of Neith in the Gynaecopolite Nome.

ȧs-t ent senetchem  , resting place.

ȧs-t ḥeḥ (neḥeḥ) 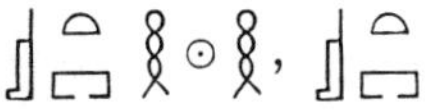 , "eternal home," *i.e.*, the tomb.

ȧsut neteru (Ḥe-t-ȧsut-neteru) 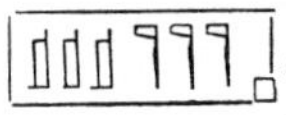, Palermo Stele, a sacred building.

ȧs-t ra 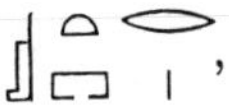, occasion for speech.

ȧs-t reṭui , place of the feet, one's accustomed place.

ȧs-t ḥer , in the phrase, , "under his supervision"; 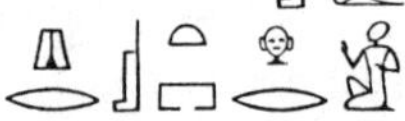, under my authority.

ȧs-t ḥert , the high place, *i.e.*, heaven.

ȧs-t . . . . .  (?) , place of sacrifice.

ȧs-t Ḥeru , seat of Horus, *i.e*, the royal throne.

Ȧs-t Ḥeqit , the temple of the Frog-goddess.

ȧs-t ḥetep 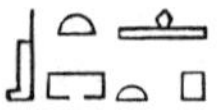, abode of peace, the tomb; plur. , place of the heart's rest.

ȧs-t khet 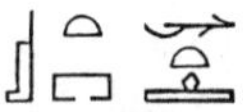, place of duty (?)

ȧsut sutsut , Anastasi I, 21, 8, 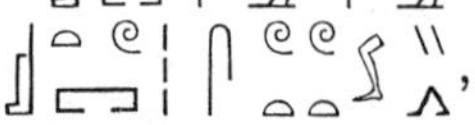, places for promenade.

Ȧs-t sutenit , a temple of Rā in Gynaecopolis.

ȧs-t smeter 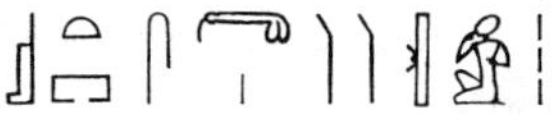, tribunal, judgment seat.

Ȧs-t-sen-ȧri-tcher 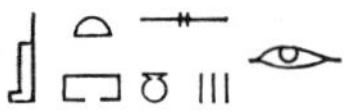 , Rec. 4, 28, a god (?)

ȧs-t sesh 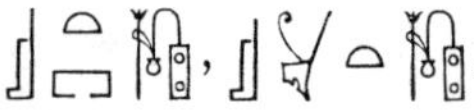, bureau, office, clerk's room.

ȧs-t segerȧ , Thes. 1480, place of silence, council hall.

ȧs-t qebḥ , place of refreshing, the bath (?)

ȧs-t qen-t 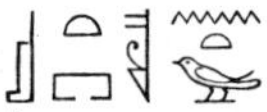, "bad place," *i.e.*, evil plight, critical state.

Ȧs-t-qerḥ-t 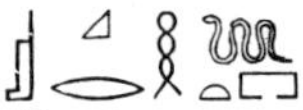, a sanctuary in the Heroopolite Nome.

ȧs-t taa [illegible], the place of fire in the Other World.

ȧs-t tcheb-t [illegible], Rev., place of retribution, hall of punishment.

ȧs-t tchef-t [illegible], store house, house for provisions.

ȧs-t tchesert [illegible], "holy place," sanctuary.

Ȧsut tcheseru [illegible], name of a building.

ȧs-ti [illegible], one in the place of another, deputy; [illegible], successor.

ȧst-ā , 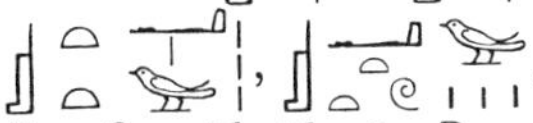, disease, fever;  , disease caused by a goddess.

Ȧst , N. 625, 903, 1139, , U. 181, 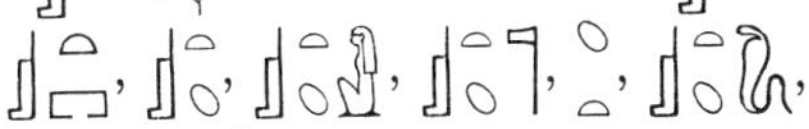, , Rec. 26, 235, the wife of Osiris and mother of Horus.

Ȧst Ȧment-t , Ṭuat V, Isis in the kingdom of Seker.

Ȧst Ȧnpu , Mar. Aby. I, 45, Isis-Anubis in Tept.

Ȧst urt em Ȧa-t-shā  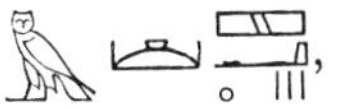, Mar. Aby. I, 44.

Ȧst ur-t-mut-neter 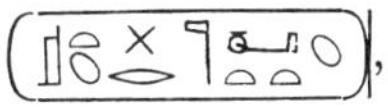, Mar. M.D. I, 33, Isis the Great, mother of the god [Horus].

Ȧst em Ȧst-āa-t , Mar. Aby. I, 45.

Ȧst em Per-mȧu  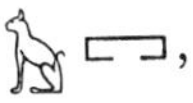, Mar. Aby. I, 45.

Ȧst em nebt ānkh , the goddess of the ninth hour of the day.

Ȧst em Semṭ-t (?) , Mar. Aby. I, 44, a form of Isis.

Ȧst em Shenȧs-t (?)  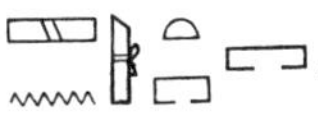, Mar. Aby. I, 44.

Ȧst em Ta-tcheser , Mar. Aby. I, 45, Isis in the Holy Land.

Ȧst-Meḥit 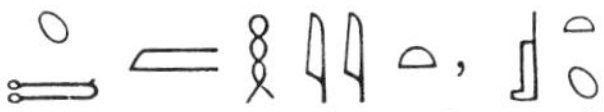 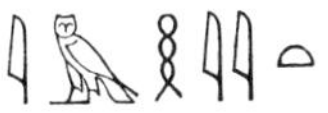, Ṭuat VI, a northern form of Isis.

Ȧs-t nekheb , Rec. 28, 182 = Ἐσεγχῆβις.

Ȧst-netrit-em-renus-nebu  , B.D. 119, Isis in all names.

Ȧst-netchit 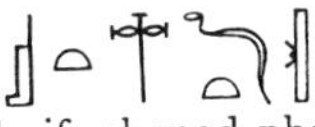, Ṭuat II, Isis the Avenger, with knife-shaped phallus.

Ȧst-Rāit-set (?) 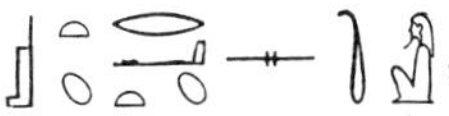, Ombos I, 1, 163, a lioness-headed form of Isis.

Ȧst-Sepṭit , Isis + Sothis.

Ȧst ta-uḥ , Rec. 24, 160, Isis, the Scorpion-goddess.

Ȧst , Ṭuat II, a uraeus in the Boat of Ȧf.

Ȧst 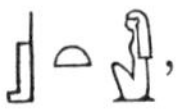, Tomb of Seti I, one of the 75 forms of Rā (No. 17).

Ȧsti , IV, 1085, wife of Thoth (?)

Ȧsti-pesṭ-t 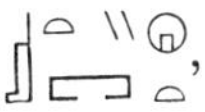, Ṭuat IX, a minister of Osiris.

ȧs-t 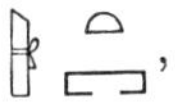, palace, any large building.

ȧs, ȧst 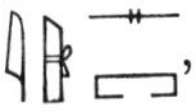, U. 296, , N. 534, 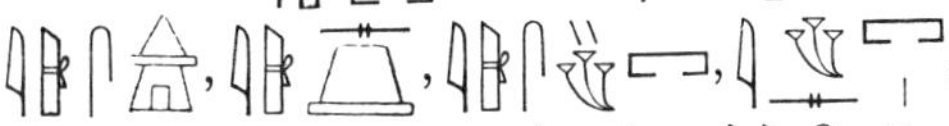, tomb, chapel of a tomb; [illegible], tomb; plur. [illegible], N. 707, [illegible], M. 174, [illegible], N. 637, [illegible], Rec. 31, 17, [illegible].

ȧs-t tchet 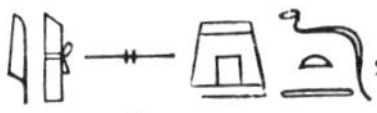, Rec. 29, 78, a tomb held in perpetuity.

ȧs-t 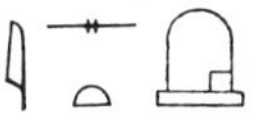, granary, silo.

ȧs-t [illegible], P. 338, 453, stelae, frontier stones, memorial tablets.

ȧs-t, ȧsit [illegible], workshop, factory; plur. [illegible].

ȧsui (?) [illegible], Rec. 28, 25, [illegible], Thes. 1290, [illegible], IV, 175, 1058, laboratory.

ȧs-en-sesh [illegible], copyists' room, chancery.

ȧs neteru, Ṭuat VIII, the workshop of the gods, a circle in the Ṭuat.

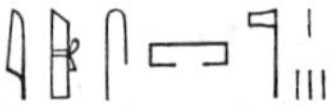

ȧs-t, workmen, gang of labourers;  , male and female servants.

ȧs, Rec. 15, 141,  , 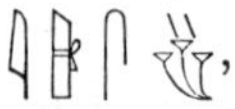 , reed, papyrus, herb, shrub, myrtle plant; plur. , , , Rec. 17, 146, , , , , .

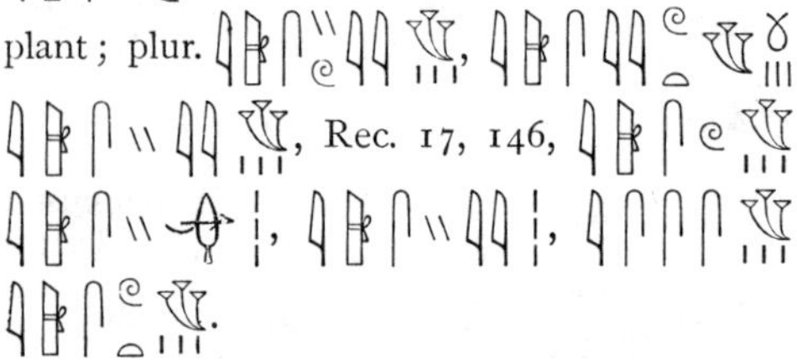

ȧsut, , , , , , old writings (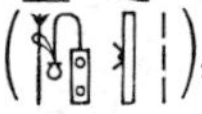), old registers or written regulations, old orders or rules; plur.  ; 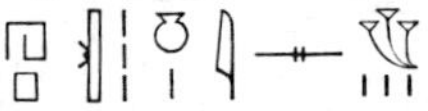 , old laws.

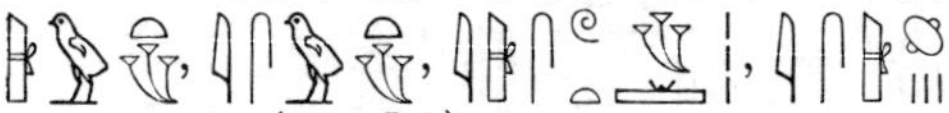

ȧsu, , , , old, ancient; , , , old, ruined; 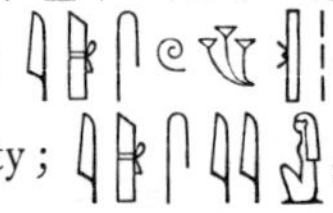 , Rec. 31, 146, old age, infirmity; , old woman.

ȧsiut, , , , rags, old pieces of cloth;   , old rags used for lamp wicks.

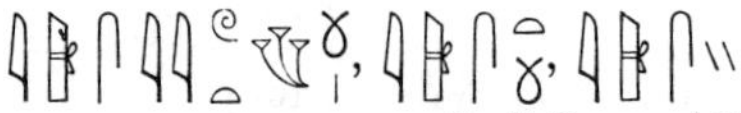

ȧsut, braid, cords, rope.

ȧs, Peasant B. 2, 103, 159, light in weight.

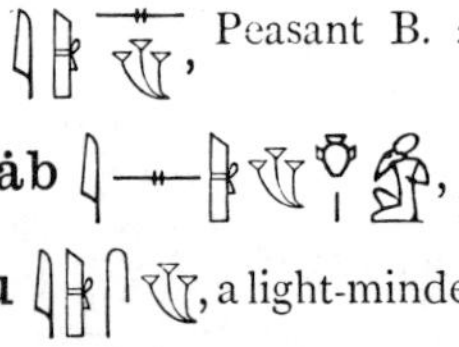

ȧs-ȧb, Peasant 209, light-minded, unstable.

ȧsu, a light-minded man, unreliable.

ȧs, , , , lie, sin, deceit.

ȧs, a disease of the belly.

ȧs, , , , , air, wind, breath; , , , , , , , , , wind, air, breeze, puff of wind.

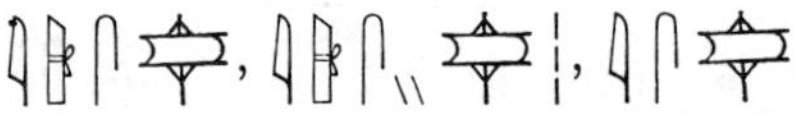

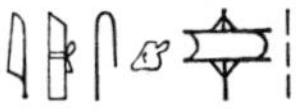

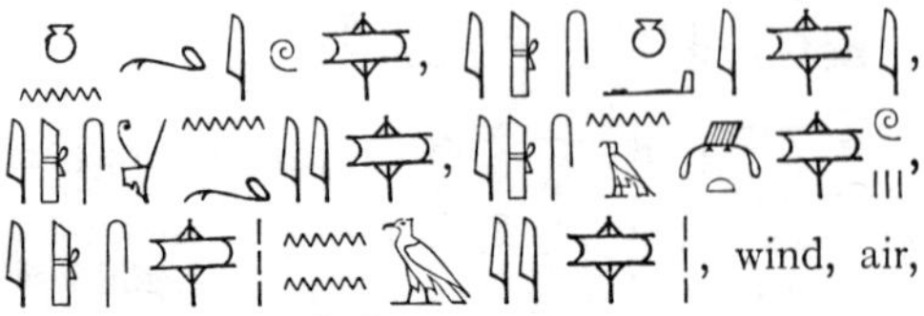

ȧs (?) ground, place.

ȧs, ȧsi, , , , who?

ȧs, ȧsi, U. 2, , U. 208, 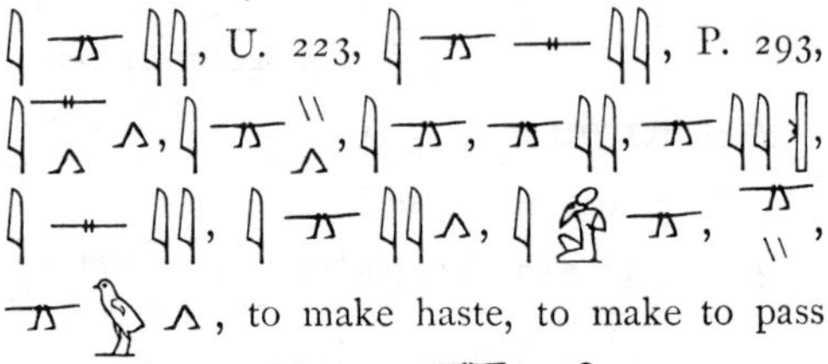 , U. 223, , P. 293, , , , , , , , , , to make haste, to make to pass quickly; Copt. ιωс; , IV, 809,  , U. 7.

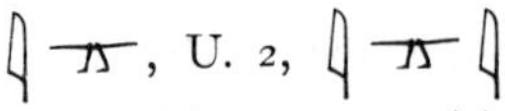

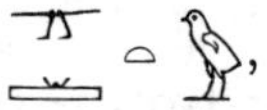

ȧs ḥaḳ, , , , IV, 659, 691, , Thes. 1297, quick spoil, spoil easily taken.

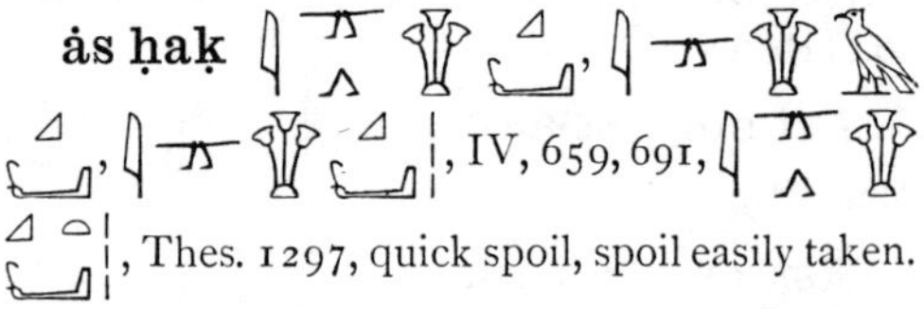

ȧsiȧsi (?) = (?) to stop, to hinder, to oppose.

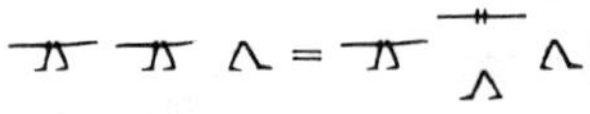

ȧsi, to pass away in decay; , incorruptible.

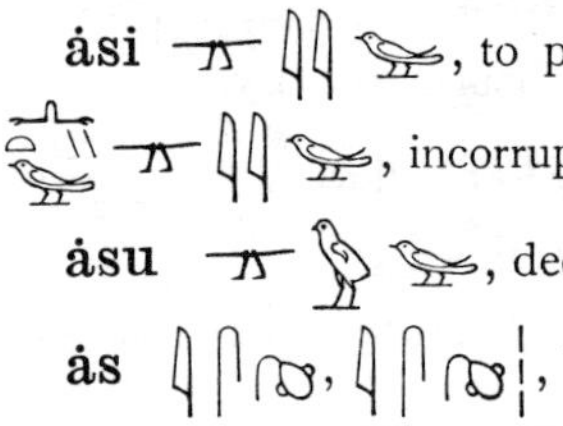

ȧsu, decay, destruction.

ȧs, , bile, gall.

ȧss, U. 534, T. 293, P. 539, to run, to move.

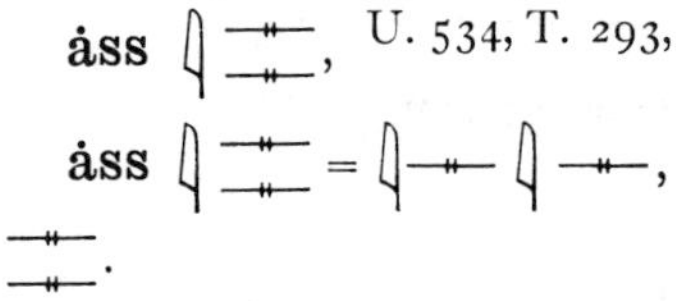

ȧss = , to punish; see .

ȧss, to fetter, to tie; , those whose heads are tied up.

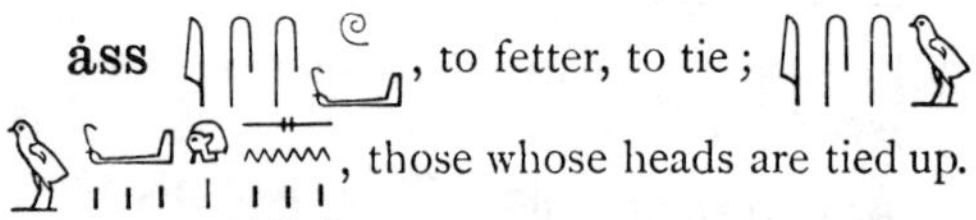

ȧss-t, rope, cord.

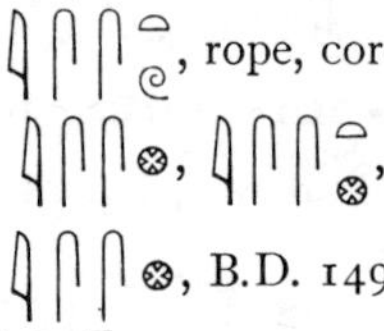

Ȧss-t, , Ṭuat VII, a town in the Ṭuat.

Ȧses, B.D. 149, the 7th Ȧat; var. (Saïte) .

åsa , T. 88, N. 618 ....

åsa , P. 12, [illegible], M. 14 = , N. 116, to watch, to guard, to pasture flocks.

åsa , P. 73, N. 15, [illegible], U. 125, [illegible], M. 701, P. 60, N. 1322, [illegible], T. 279, to come (?) to travel (?)

åsa-t 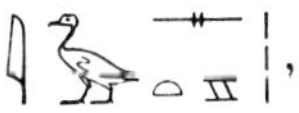, floor, ground, earth; Copt. ⲤⲎϮ.

åsa , T. 58, M. 217, N. 589, to fill full, to satisfy.

åsa .... , place of custody or restraint.

åsa (?) , Ȧmen. 22, 10 ....

åså 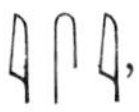, Rec. 34, 121 = [illegible], baton, club, mace.

åsaā , T. 268, to introduce; , M. 427.

åsȧu , M. 62, to lead.

Ȧsȧr , U. 2, , , 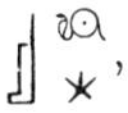, Rec. 30, 11, [illegible], Rec. 33, 30, 36, 209, , Berg. II, 11, , Buch. 51, [illegible], R.E. 1, 141, [illegible], Rec. 26, 224, 27, 56, 33, 28, A.Z. Bd. 46, 92 ff., [illegible] = Πολυόφθαλμος, the great Ancestor-god of the dynastic Egyptians. The origin of the god and the exact pronunciation of his name are not known. He was said to be the son of Shu and Tefnut and the grandson of Geb and Nut. He and his wife Isis and his brother and sister Set and Nephthys, and his son Horus, were brought forth by Nut at the same time. He was drowned in the Nile by Set and suffered mutilation, but he rose from the dead, and having been declared by the gods innocent of the charges brought against him by Set, became King of the Dead and giver of immortality to all who believed in him.

Ȧsȧrtiu , B.D. 89, 3, beings like unto Osiris.

Ȧsȧr-Ȧau-ȧmi-Ȧnu  , B.D. 142, 85, Osiris, the Aged One in Ȧn (Heliopolis).

Ȧsȧr-Ȧāḥ , Lanzone 42, , Osiris the Moon.

Ȧsȧr-ȧmi-ȧb-neteru 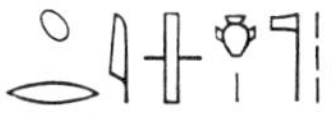, Ṭuat VI, Osiris, Darling of the Gods.

Ȧsȧr-Ȧn 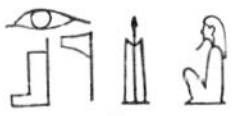, Denderah III, 35, Osiris, the solar god Ȧn.

Ȧsȧr-Ȧnpu 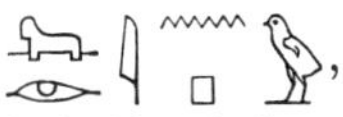, B.D. 168, Osiris + Anubis, a jackal-headed god.

Ȧsȧr Ȧḥti 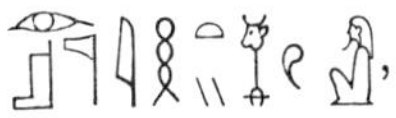, B.D. 142, 98, Osiris, the Lung-god and giver of breath to the dead.

Ȧsȧr-ȧs-ti , Ṭuat III, a form of Osiris, functions unknown.

Ȧsȧr-Ȧti , B.D. 142, 106, Osiris, the King.

Ȧsȧr-Ȧti 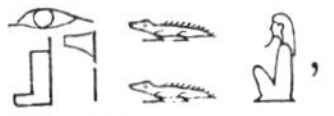, B.D. 142, 43, variant of preceding (?)

Ȧsȧr-Ȧti-ḥeri-ȧb-Abṭu  , B.D. 142, 93, Osiris of Abydos.

Ȧsȧr-Ȧti-ḥeri-ȧb-Shetat  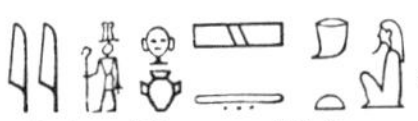, B.D. 142, 94, Osiris, king of the Ṭuat of Memphis and Heliopolis.

Ȧsȧr-ȧthi-ḥeḥ , Ṭuat III, Osiris, conqueror of eternity.

Ȧsȧr-ānkhti  , B.D. 142, 2, Osiris, the Living One.

Ȧsȧr-Ānti , Osiris, the Myrrh-god (?)

Ȧsȧr-Uu , B.D. G. 1064, a form of Osiris worshipped in Lower Egypt.

Ȧsȧr-up-taui 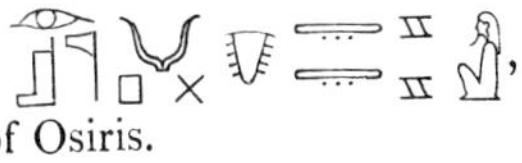, B.D. 142, 5, a form of Osiris.

Ȧsår-Un-nefer 
, B.D. 142, 1, , Mar. M.D. 1, 6, Osiris, the Good Being, true of word.

Ȧsår ur-pa-ȧsht 
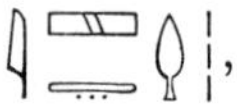, Nesi-Amsu 17, 15, Osiris, chief of the acacias.

Ȧsår-Utti , B.D. 142, 53, Osiris, the begetter.

Ȧsår-Bati-erpit 
, B.D. 142, 76, Osiris, the dual soul in Erpit.

Ȧsår-Ba-sheps-em-Ṭeṭ 
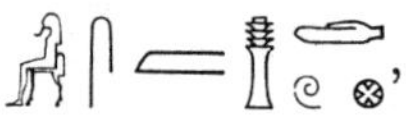 B.D. 142, 19, Osiris, the holy soul in Busiris.

Ȧsår-baiu-tef-f , B.D. 142, 72, Osiris, the souls of his fathers.

Ȧsår-Båti (?) , Ṭuat III, a form of Osiris.

Ȧsår-pa-meres , Annales VI, 131, a form of Osiris.

Ȧsår-p-ākhem , Denderah III, 10, Osiris, the divine Ākhem.

Ȧsår-Ptaḥ-neb-ānkh 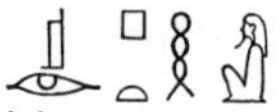
, B.D. 142, 15, Osiris-Ptaḥ, lord of life.

Ȧsår-Fa-Ḥeru , B.D. 142, 68, Osiris, carrier of Horus.

Ȧsår-em-Asher 
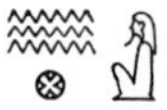, B.D. 142, 80, Osiris in Asher (part of Thebes).

Ȧsår-em-Ȧat-ur-t 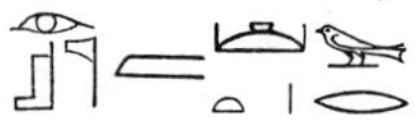
, B.D. 142, 62, Osiris in the Great Ȧat.

Ȧsår-em-Ȧnu 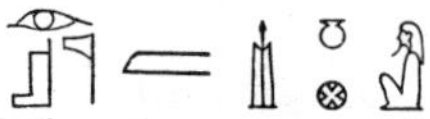, B.D. 142, 84, Osiris in Heliopolis.

Ȧsår-em-ȧsut-f-ȧmu-Re-stau 
, B.D. 142, 97, Osiris in all his shrines in Ṣaḳḳârah.

Ȧsår-em-ȧsut-f-ȧm-Ta-meḥ 
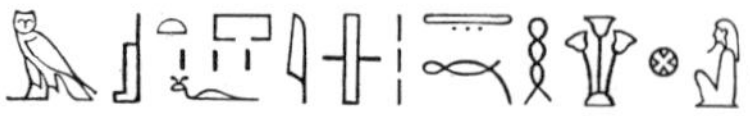, B.D. 142, 95, Osiris in all his shrines in the North.

Ȧsår-em-ȧst-f-em-Ta-shemā 
, B.D. 142, 144, Osiris in every shrine of his in the South.

Ȧsår-em-ȧst-neb-meri-Ka-f-ȧm
, B.D. 142, 146, Osiris in every shrine his Ka loves.

Ȧsår-em-Ȧtef-ur 
, B.D. 142, 50, Osiris in Ȧtef-ur.

Ȧsår-em-ȧter , B.D. 142, 104, Osiris in the river (?)

Ȧsår-em-Āper 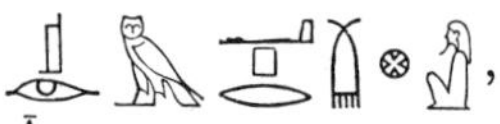, B.D. 142, 35, Osiris in Āper.

Ȧsår-em-ānkh-em-Ḥet-ka-Ptaḥ
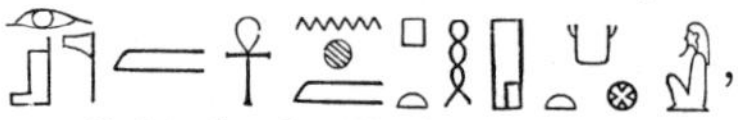, B.D. 142, 95, Osiris in the Ka-house of Ptaḥ (Memphis).

Ȧsår-em-Āntch , B.D. 142, 20, Osiris in Āntch.

Ȧsår-em-āḥā-t-f-em Ta-meḥt 
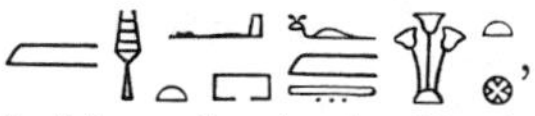, B.D. 142, 145, Osiris in his station in the North.

Ȧsår-em-Ākesh(?) , B.D. 142, 87, Osiris in Ākesh.

Ȧsår-em-Uu-Peg [illegible]
[illegible], B.D. 142, 69, Osiris in the great sanctuary of Abydos.

Ȧsår-em-Uḥet (?)-meḥt [illegible]
[illegible], B.D. 142, 61, Osiris in the Northern Oasis (Baḥrîyah).

Ȧsår-em-Uḥet (?)-rest [illegible]
[illegible], B.D. 142, 60, Osiris in the Southern Oasis (Khârgah).

Ȧsår-em-Båk [illegible]
[illegible], B.D. 142, 32, Osiris in the Hawk-city.

Ȧsȧr-em-Benben-t, B.D. 142, 83, Osiris in the sanctuary of the stone (obelisk) of the Sun-god.

Ȧsȧr-em-Bener, B.D. 142, 74, Osiris in Benr.

Ȧsȧr-em-Beṭshu, B.D. 142, 115, Osiris in Beṭsh.

Ȧsȧr-em-Pe, B.D. 142, 26, Osiris in Buto.

Ȧsȧr-em-Pe-Nu, B.D. 142, 88, Osiris in Buto of Nu.

Ȧsȧr-em-Per-ent-meḥ, B.D. 142, 12, Osiris in the sanctuary of the North.

Ȧsȧr-em-pet, B.D. 142, 47, Osiris in heaven.

Ȧsȧr-em-Per-ent-res, B.D. 142, 11, Osiris in the sanctuary of the South.

Ȧsȧr-em-Pesg-ra, B.D. 142, 44; var. , Osiris in Pesg-ra (?)

Ȧsȧr-em-Peṭet, Osiris in Peṭ.

Ȧsȧr-em-Maāti, B.D. 142, 70, Osiris in the city of Truth.

Ȧsȧr-em-Menȧ, B.D. 142, 71, Osiris in Menȧ

Ȧsȧr-em-Nefur (Tau-ur ?), B.D. 142, 40, Osiris in Nefur (?)

Ȧsȧr-em-Neruṭf, B.D. 142, 31, Osiris in the necropolis of Ḥensu (Herakleopolis).

Ȧsȧr-em-Netru, B.D. 142, 28, Osiris in Netr.

Ȧsȧr-em-Neṭit, B.D. 142, 41, Osiris in Neṭit, a place near Abydos where Osiris was slain by Set.

Ȧsȧr-em-Neṭbit, B.D. 142, 113, Osiris in Neṭbit.

Ȧsȧr-em-Netch-t; var. , B.D. 142, 24, Osiris in Netch.

Ȧsȧr-em-renuf-nebu, B.D. 142, 149, Osiris in his every name.

Ȧsȧr-em-Rert-nefu (?), B.D. 142, 55, Osiris in Rer (?)

Ȧsȧr-em-Reḥnen (var.), B.D. 142, 34, Osiris in Reḥnen.

Ȧsȧr em resu (?), B.D. 142, 25, Osiris in the South Land.

Ȧsȧr-em-Rastau, B.D. 142, 39, Osiris in the kingdom of Seker the Death-god.

Ȧsȧr-em-Henȧ, B.D. 142, 124, Osiris in Henȧ.

Ȧsȧr-em-Ḥetāa, B.D. 142, 89, Osiris in the Great House.

Ȧsȧr-em-ḥet-f-ȧmi-Ta-meḥ, B.D. 142, 46, Osiris in his temple in the North Land.

Ȧsȧr-em-ḥet-f-ȧmi-Ta-shemā, B.D. 142, 45, Osiris in his temple in the South Land.

Ȧsȧr-em-Ḥemag, B.D. 142, 86, Osiris in the Laboratory City.

Ȧsȧr-em-Ḥeser, B.D. 142, 21; varr. , Osiris in the City sacred to Thoth.

Ȧsȧr-em-Ḥeken, B.D. 142, 65, Osiris in Ḥeken.

Ȧsȧr-em-khakeru-f-nebu, B.D. 142, 152, Osiris in all his ornaments.

Åsår-em-khāuf-nebu, B.D. 142, 151, Osiris in all his manifestations.

Åsår-em-Sau, B.D. 142, 23, Osiris in Så.

Åsår-em-Sau-ḥeri, B.D. 142, 29, Osiris in Upper Sa.

Åsår-em-Sau-kheri, B.D. 142, 30, Osiris in Lower Sa.

Åsår-em-Så, B.D. 142, 78, Osiris in Så.

Åsår-em-Såti, B.D. 142, 79, Osiris in Såti.

Åsår-em-Sunnu, B.D. 142, 33, Osiris in Sunu (Syene).

Åsår-em-seḥ-f-nebu, B.D. 142, 147, Osiris in all his council chambers.

Åsår-em-Sesh, B.D. 142, 59, Osiris in the Nest-city, *i.e.*, his birthplace.

Åsår-em-sek-f, B.D. 142, 54, Osiris in his feathered headdress.

Åsår-em-Seker, B.D. 142, 66, Osiris in Seker (Death-god).

Åsår-em-Sekri, B.D. 142, 37, Osiris in the city of Seker.

Åsår-em-Sekti, B.D. 142, 54, Osiris in the Sekti Boat.

Åsår-em-Shau, B.D. 142, 67, Osiris in Sha.

Åsår-em-Shenu, B.D. 142, 64, Osiris in Shenu.

Åsår-em-Qefṭenu, B.D. 142, 36, Osiris in Qefṭenu.

Åsår-em-qemauf-nebu, B.D. 142, 148, Osiris in all his creative works.

Åsår-em-gerg-f-neb, B.D. 142, 150, Osiris in his every settlement.

Åsår-em-ta B.D. 142, 48, Osiris in the Earth.

Åsår-em-taiu-nebu, B.D. 142, 81, Osiris in all lands.

Åsår-em-Ṭep, B.D. 142, 27, Osiris in Buto.

Åsår-em-Ṭesher, B.D. 142, 58, Osiris in the Red City.

Åsår-em-Tchatchau, B.D. 142, 25, Osiris in the Chiefs.

Åsår-nub-ḥeḥ, B.D. 142, 75, Osiris, gold of millions of years.

Åsår-Neb-Åment, Ṭuat III, Osiris, Lord of Åment.

Åsår-Neb-ānkh, B.D. 142, 3, Osiris, Lord of Life.

Åsår-Neb-ānkh-em-Abṭu B.D. 142, 90, Osiris, Lord of Life in Abydos.

Åsår-Neb-peḥti-petpet-Sebåu, B.D. 142, 96, Osiris, Lord of Might, crusher of the rebels.

Åsår-Neb-er-tcher, B.D. 141, 4, Osiris, Lord to limit of the Earth, *i.e.*, Osiris Almighty.

Åsår-Neb-ḥeḥ, B.D. 142, 57, Osiris, Lord of Eternity.

Åsår-Neb-ta-Ānkh B.D. 142, 22, Osiris, Lord of the Land of Life.

Åsår-Neb-taiu-Nesu-neteru, B.D. 142, 73, Osiris, Lord of Lands, King of the gods.

Åsår-Neb-Ṭeṭ, B.D. 142, 91, Osiris, Lord of Busiris.

Åsår-Neb-tchet , B.D. 142, 56, Osiris, Lord of Eternity.

Åsår-Nemur , Metternich Stele 87, 88, Osiris + Mnevis; , the tomb of Osiris Mnevis.

Åsår Nesu-båt  Ani Pap. 19, Lit. 9;  B.M. No. 236, Osiris, king of the South and North.

Åsår-nesti 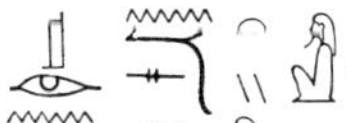, B.D. 142, 49; var. 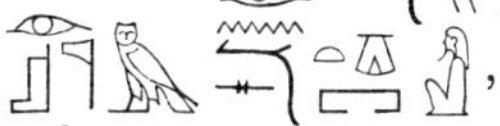, Osiris, belonging to the throne.

Åsår-ḥeri-åb Åsher  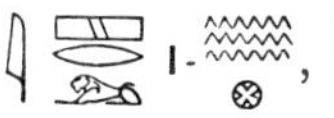, Nesi-Åmsu 17, 16, Osiris in Åsher (part of Thebes).

Åsår-ḥeri-åb-se[m]-t , B.D. 143, 18, Osiris in the desert (*i.e.*, Necropolis).

Åsår-Ḥeri-shā-f  , B.D. 142, 76, Osiris on his sand.

Åsår-Ḥeru , Osiris + Horus.

Åsår-Ḥeru-åakhuti , B.D. 142, 100, Osiris + Harmakhis.

Åsår-Ḥeru-åakhuti-Tem  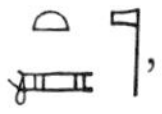, Osiris + Harmakhis + Temu.

Åsår-ḥeq-taiu 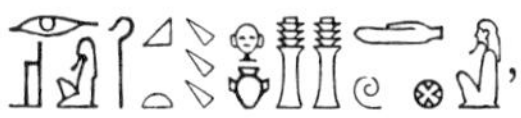, B.D. 142, 18, Osiris, Governor in Busiris.

Åsår-Ḥeq-tchet-em-Ånu  , B.D. 142, 52, Osiris, Governor of Eternity in Ån (Heliopolis).

Åsår-Khas 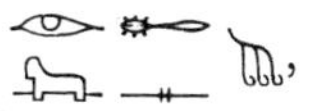, Annales XIII, 277, a form of Osiris.

Åsår-Khenti Åmentt   , Osiris, Chief of Åmentt, Osiris, Chief of those who are in Åmentt.

Åsår-Khenti-Un , B.D. 142, 6, Osiris, Chief of Un.

Åsår-Khenti-peru (?) 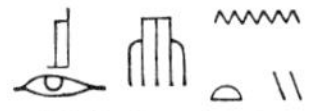 , B.D. 142, 72, Osiris, Chief of the temples.

Åsår-Khenti-men-t-f 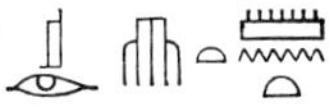 , P. 706, Osiris, Chief of his . . . . .

Åsår-Khenti-nut-f 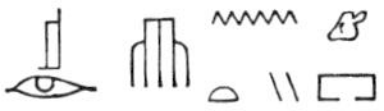 , B.D. 142, 42, Osiris, Chief of his town.

Åsår-khenti-nep[r]  , B.D. 142, 7, Osiris, Chief of corn (all kinds of grain).

Åsår-Khenti-Nefer  , B.D. 142, 69, Osiris, Chief of Nefer.

Åsår-Khenti-Rastau  , B.D. 142, 16, Osiris, Chief of Rastau of Seker (Death-god).

Åsår-Khenti-seḥ-kaut-f  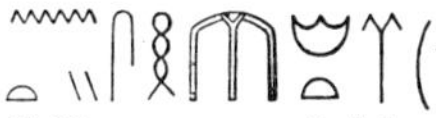 (var. [illegible]), B.D. 142, 77, Osiris, Chief of the house of his Cows.

Åsår-Khenti-shet-āa [illegible] [illegible], B.D. 142, 82, Osiris, Chief of the Lake (?), Pharaoh.

Åsår-Khenti-geti-åst (?) [illegible] [illegible], B.D. 142, 92, Osiris, Chief of . . . . . .

Åsår-Khenti-Tenn-t [illegible] [illegible] (var. [illegible]), B.D. 142, 10, Osiris, Chief of Tenen.

Åsår-Kherp-neteru [illegible], Ṭuat III, Osiris, Director of the gods.

Åsår-Sa [illegible] [illegible], B.D. 142, 71, Osiris the Shepherd.

Åsår-sa-erpit [illegible]; varr. [illegible], [illegible] [illegible], B.D. 142, 14, Osiris, son of the two Erpti.

Ȧsȧr-Saḥ , 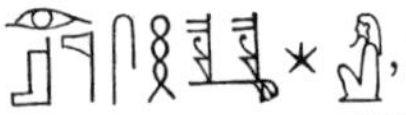, B.D. 142, 8, Osiris + Orion.

Ȧsȧr-Sep 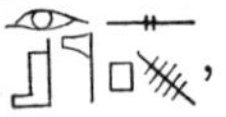, Rec. 3, 46,  , Rec. 14, 13, Osiris + Sep.

Ȧsȧr-Sepa , , B.D. 142, 9, Osiris Sepa, Osiris, the holy worm (?) of the Souls of Ȧn.

Ȧsȧr-seḥ , B.D. 142, 99, Osiris of the Council Hall.

Ȧsȧr-Sekri 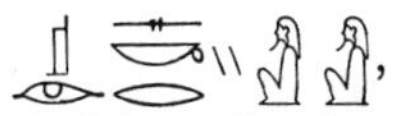, B.D. 142, 51, Osiris + the god of the coffin, *i.e.*, Seker.

Ȧsȧr-Sekri-em-Sheta-t  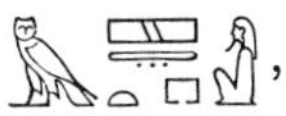, B.D. 142, 51, Osiris + Seker in Sheta, the modern Ṣaḳḳârah.

Ȧsȧr-Ka-Ȧment , Ṭuat III, Osiris, Bull of Ȧment.

Ȧsȧr-Ka-ḥeri-ȧb-Kam  [illegible], B.D. 142, 97, Osiris, Bull in Egypt.

Ȧsȧr-Taiti , B.D. 142, 75, Osiris, the swathed one.

Ȧsȧr Ṭu-Ȧmentt 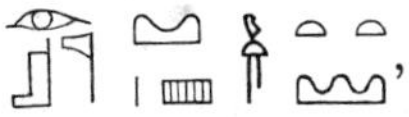, Osiris of the Mountain of Ȧmentt.

Ȧsȧr-Ṭem-ur , [illegible], B.D. 142, 50, Osiris, the great Executioner (?)

Ȧsȧr-Ṭet-Sheps 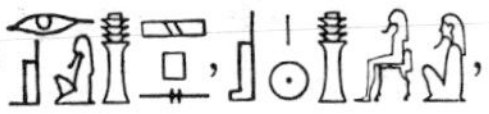, Osiris, the holy Ṭet.

Ȧsȧr , Ṭuat II, the name of a term.

Ȧsȧr , Ṭuat VI, one of the nine spirits who destroy the wicked, soul and body.

Ȧsȧr-merit , a place in the Athribite Nome.

ȧsā , U. 296 = [illegible], N. 533, to introduce, to make approach.

ȧsi.... , Rec. 31, 12.......

ȧsu 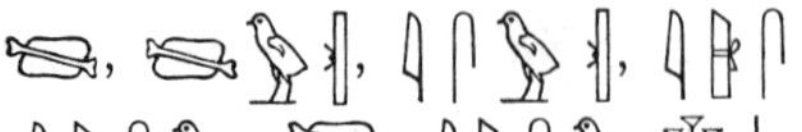  , reward, recompense, return, substitution, price, payment, remuneration, retribution, equivalent; Copt. ⲁⲥⲟⲩ; , those who are rewarded; [illegible] [illegible], in return for; [illegible], as a reward; , Rec. 20, 40, to endow.

ȧs-ui (?) 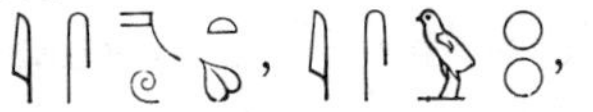, the testicles.

ȧsu-t (?) 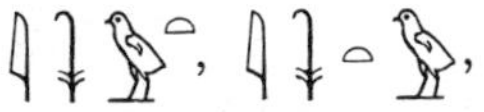, P. 260, M. 494, an explanatory particle.

ȧsua-t 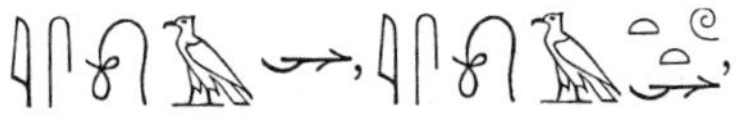 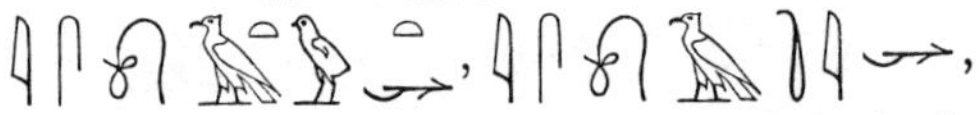, P.S.B. 19, 261, Rechnungen 59, board, plank, beam, seat, throne; plur. ; Heb. אֲשִׁיָּה, Arab. آسية, Syr. ܐܣܝܬܐ.

ȧsb-t  , P.S.B. 24, 47, L.D. III, 194, 47, seat, throne; compare Heb. √ יָשַׁב.

ȧsbu , Rec. 6, 9, rebels, evil men.

Ȧseb 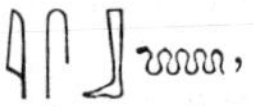, Berg. I, 34, [illegible], Rec. 4, 28, a benevolent serpent-god.

Ȧsbit , a goddess.

Ȧsbu-peri-em-khetkhet  [illegible], Edfû I, 10G, one of the eight sharp-eyed servants of Osiris.

Ȧseb , Hh. 328; see [illegible].

ȧsbar, ȧsbur  [illegible] [illegible], Anastasi I, 24, 2, [illegible]

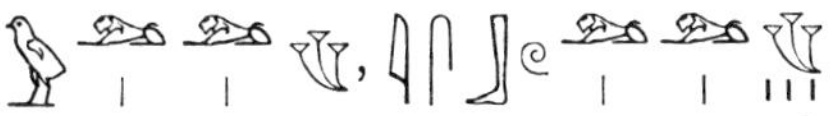, bush, thicket, undergrowth, scrub, thorn growth; compare Heb. שִׁבֹּלֶת.

àsbur 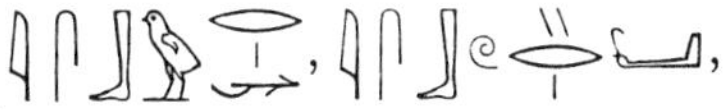, 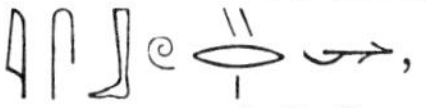, Anastasi I, 26, 8, Koller Pap. 1, 5, 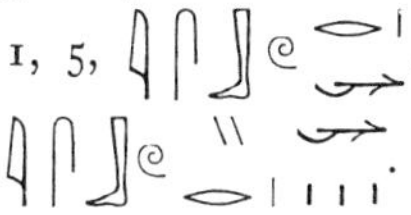, whip, beating stick; plur.

àsp , U. 137, T. 108, N. 445, to be offered; see 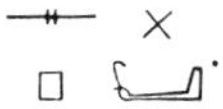.

àsp 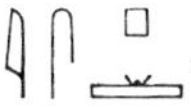, to keep count of something, to reckon up.

àsp , pain, grief;  his belly is in pain.

àspu 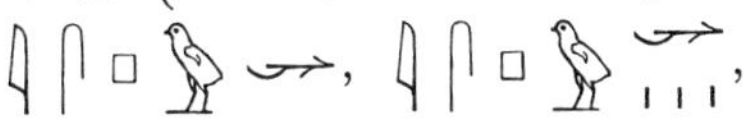, sledge, bearing pole, wood packing, timbers.

àsp-t 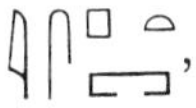, Israel Stele 12, throne; see .

àsp-t , P.S.B. 13, 424, Ḥeruemḥeb (Masp.) 18, seat of royalty, palanquin.

àspat , Koller Pap. 1, 4, quiver; plur. , Mar. Karn. 53, 35; A.Z. 17, 57, quiver filled with arrows; Heb. אַשְׁפָּה; Assyr. ishpatu, plur. , Sennach. VI, 56.

àsepsep (?) 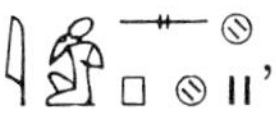, Anastasi I, 14, 3, 15, 4, slope of side of an inclined plane (?)

àspr 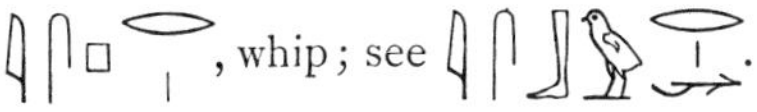, whip; see.

àspṭ , Rec. 8, 171, sledge.

àsf , U. 120, to cut off; var. 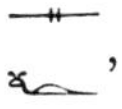, N. 429.

àsf-t 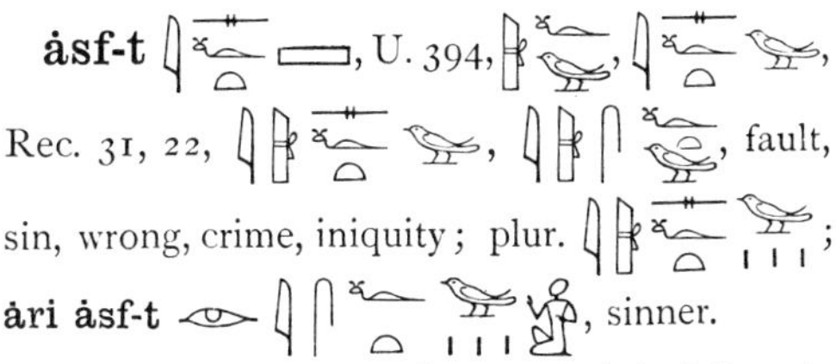, U. 394, Rec. 31, 22, fault, sin, wrong, crime, iniquity; plur.; **àri àsf-t**, sinner.

àsfetiu , evil men, criminals, fiends, sinners; var.

àsfa , Rec. 31, 11, a group of gods (?)

àsfekh , P. 643, M. 679, N. 1241, to do away, to cast aside.

àsfekk 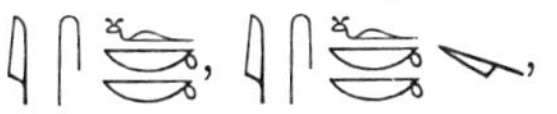, U. 58, N. 310, to split, to sacrifice (?)

àsfekk-t 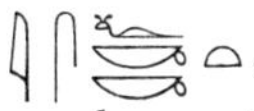, slaughter (?)

àsmar 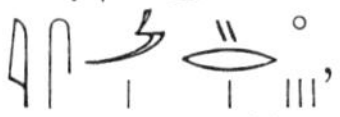, Turin Pap. 67, 11, a kind of stone, emerald (?)

àsmen 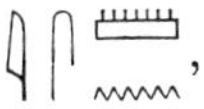, U. 26, P. 409, M. 586, N. 1191, , Rec. 11, 90, to stablish, make firm.

àsmer 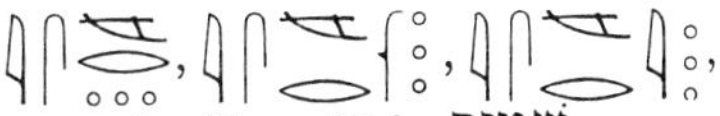, σμύρις, emery powder (?), or Heb. שָׁמִיר.

àsmes 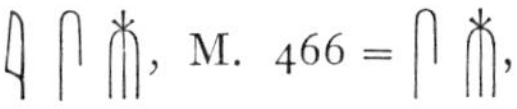, M. 466 = , P. 243, , Rec. 11, 90, to give birth to.

Àsmet , M. 663, one of the four sons of Horus; see **Mestà**.

àsen, àsenn 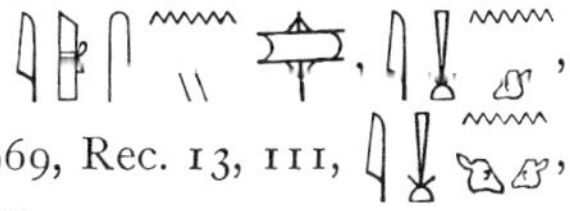, T. 289, M. 66, N. 969, Rec. 13, 111, N. 128, 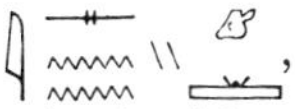, to sniff, to smell, to kiss, to make friends with, to fraternize.

àsenn, àsensen , 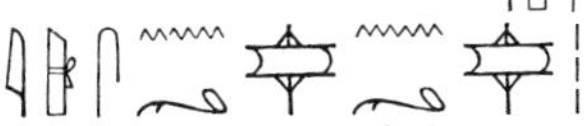, air, wind, breeze.

àsen-ta , to smell or kiss the earth in homage; 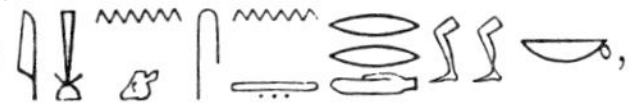, N. 114.

ȧsni, P. 608, , P. 631, , M. 498, , N. 1080, to make to open.

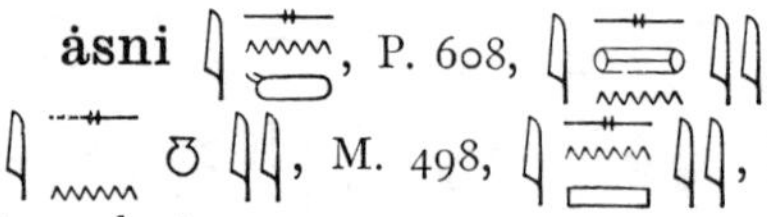

ȧsenut, P. 360, N. 1074, hire, fee, boat-fare.

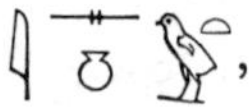

ȧsensh (?), U. 375, T. 19, , T. 356, P. 322, 668, , P. 196, M. 628, N. 928, 1080, to push back doors, to open.

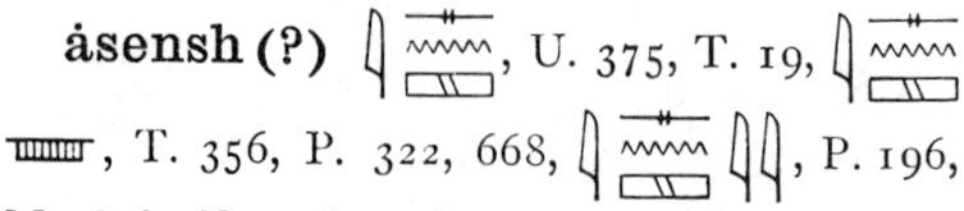

ȧsnet, a ceremonial bandlet; plur.

ȧser, N. 294, staff, mace.

ȧser, N. 755, , U. 188, T. 66, M. 221, N. 598, , , , P.S.B. 8, 158, , , tamarisk tree; plur. , , foliage, branches, etc.; Heb. אֵשֶׁל, Copt. ⲟⲥⲓ, ⲟⲥⲉ.

Ȧser-t, , U. 188, T. 66, M. 221, N. 598, a sacred tree whence came Up-uatu, , B.D. 42, 4.

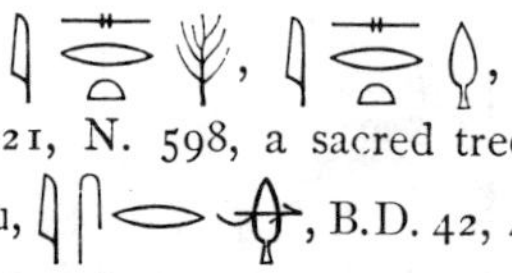

Ȧser, B.D. 178, 14, a town in the Other World (?)

ȧsr, Rec. 17, 155, a foreigner (?) prisoner (אסיר) (?)

ȧsru (?), Rec. 8, 171, article of furniture.

ȧsruṭ, N. 738, to make to grow; see .

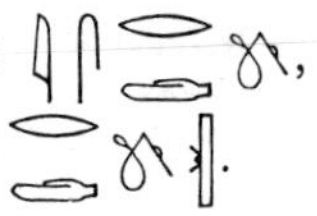

ȧseh, B.D. (Saïte) 110 . . . .

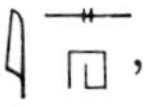

ȧsha, linen bandlet (?)

ȧsha (?), Décrets 28, 29 . . . .

ȧshabu, a kind of animal.

ȧshabu, P.S.B. 13, 412, whips made from the skin of the same.

ȧsḥ, U. 388, to make to travel.

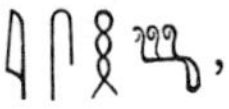

ȧsḥetch, T. 281, N. 130, to shine; see **ḥetch.**

ȧskh, , , , , to reap; Copt. ⲱⲥϩ; see .

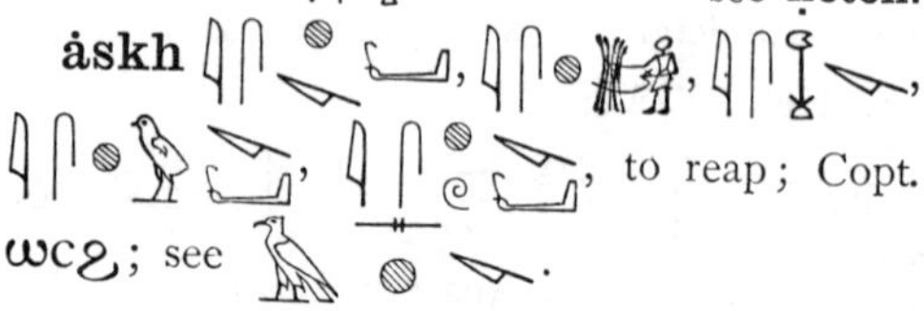

ȧskha, T. 199, N. 1295, to call to mind, to remember.

Ȧskhit (?), Berg. 1, 23, a wind-goddess.

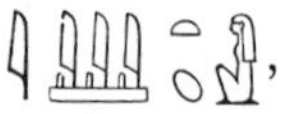

ȧsshau, U. 124, N. 433 . . . . . .

ȧsesh, U. 140, T. 111, N. 448 . . . . . .

ȧsshem, N. 762; see **seshem.**

ȧsq, , , to cut, hack in pieces, to decapitate.

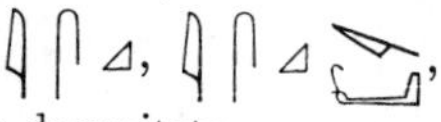

ȧsq, , , , , , to linger, hesitate, delay; Copt. ⲱⲥⲕ̄.

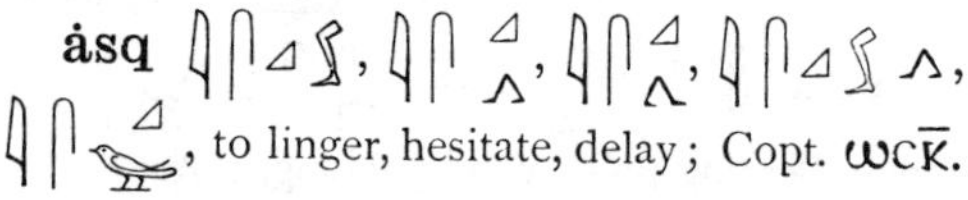

ȧsqer (?), P.S.B. 12, 250, to beat, to fight.

ȧsk, , , an explanatory particle.

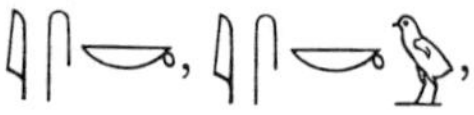

ȧsk, U. 481, P. 188, M. 354, N. 144, 906, to draw, to strengthen.

ȧska (?), Décrets, Vocab. to plough.

Ȧsken, P. 79, M. 109, N. 23, , M. 708, , P. 379, , N. 1324, M. 333 . . . .

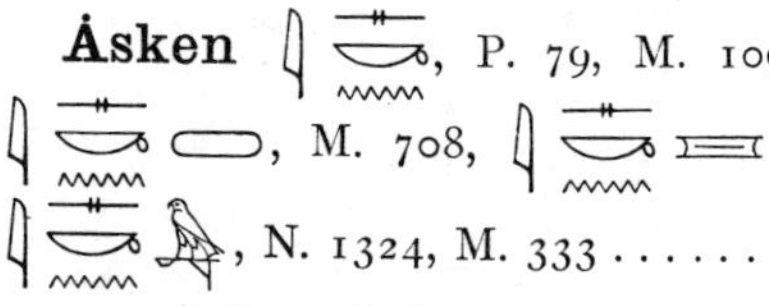

ȧst, , , Rec. 19, 187 ff. (many examples given), an explanatory particle; var. .

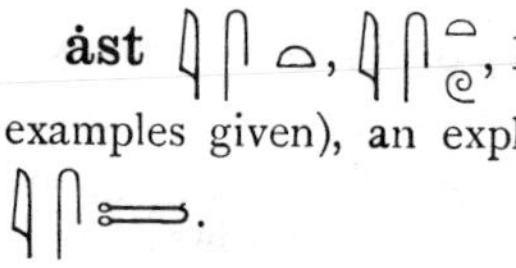

ȧsti, Mar. Karn. 54, 1, report, document.

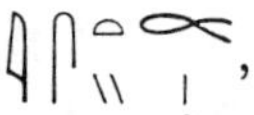

ȧst, , , to tremble, shake (of the limbs).

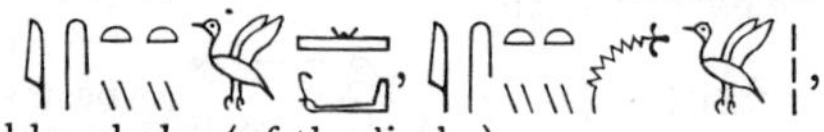

ȧsta = , to hasten.

ȧstit, unguent, incense (?)

ȧsti, a deceitful man, liar (?)

ȧstb = , seat, throne (?)

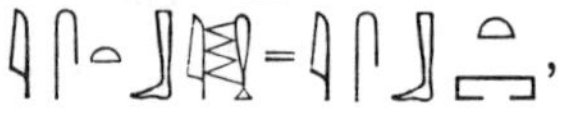

Ȧsten 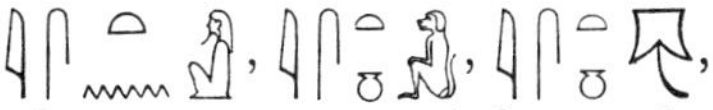, , P.S.B. 20, 142, , , a sacred ape, an incarnation of Thoth; the 'Οστάνης of Democritus of Abdera.

ȧsten , to tie up, to lace up, to tie round, to envelop, to fetter.

ȧsteḥ , to beat down.

ȧsth 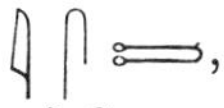, U. 224, P. 102, M. 89, N. 96; see , an explanatory particle.

Ȧsth Thaȧth , Ṭuat VI, Isis, the clother [of Osiris].

Ȧsthen 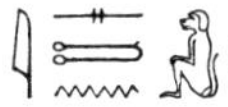; see .

ȧsṭ , P. 125, M. 136, N. 647, spittle, saliva.

Ȧsṭ 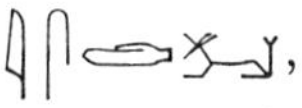, U. 388, a name of Set (?)

ȧsṭṭ 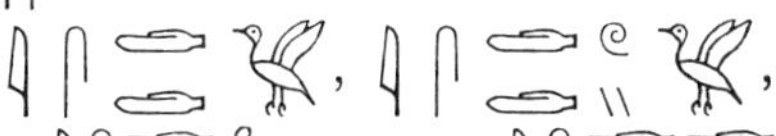, Thes. 1202, 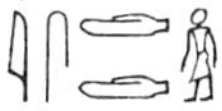, Rec. 9, 61, 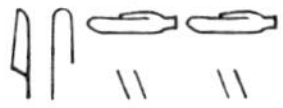 , , L.D. III, 194, 21, , to make to tremble; Copt. ⲥⲧⲱⲧ.

ȧsṭu , N. 944, chest (?), coffer (?)

Ȧsṭen  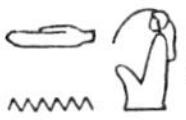, P.S.B. 20, 140; see .

ȧsṭes , U. 401, knife, dagger (?)

Ȧsṭes 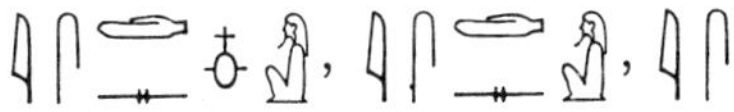 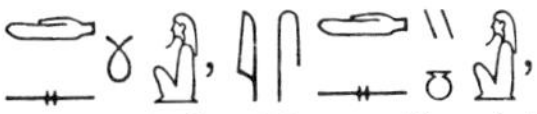, B.D. 17, 89, B.M. 32, l. 245, 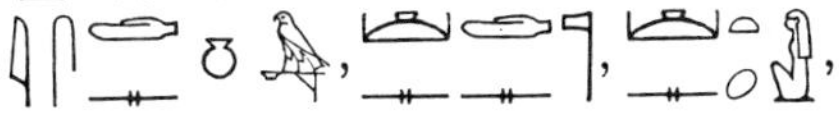, one of the Company of Thoth.

ȧstch , U. 455, 601, 609, to cast out, to shoot, to hurl, to break.

Ȧstcheṭ , B.D. 149, a fiery region in the 12th Ȧat.

ȧsh-t 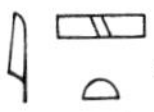, U. 512, P. 693, 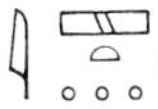, N. 708, , thing, possession; 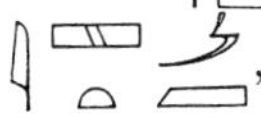, legal possession.

ȧsh-t 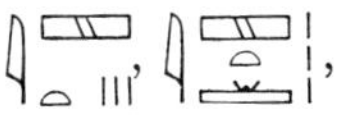, Rec. 31, 165, wealth, goods = , U. 185, T. 324, and .

ȧsh-tt , T. 344, meat and drink offering (the five offerings).

ȧsh-tȧ 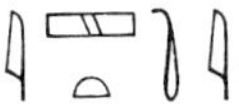, N. 972, to make a possession of.

ȧsh-t 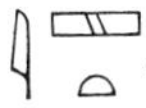, food, meal, ration.

ȧsh-t-f khu 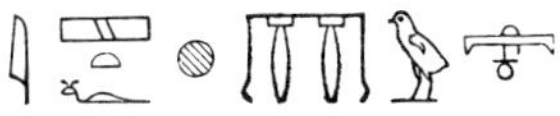, evening meal.

ȧsh-t-f ṭuat [illegible], morning meal.

ȧsh [illegible], an offering.

ȧshsh [illegible], P. 125, [illegible], N. 663, 695, [illegible], M. 93, [illegible], to spit out, to evacuate, to pour out.

ȧshu [illegible], U. 333, outpourings, emissions, sweatings.

ȧshshu [illegible], [illegible], U. 15, emission, saliva, efflux.

ȧshsh [illegible], [illegible], to bear, to carry.

ȧshsh [illegible], Rec. 32, 67, perfumes, unguent (?)

ȧshaf [illegible], [illegible] [illegible], to break, contrition; Copt. ⲟⲩⲱϣϥ.

ȧshakhar [illegible] [illegible], Alt. K. 152, a disease.

ȧshā [illegible], U. 552, [illegible], P. 425, M. 608, to cut.

ȧshā-t [illegible], piece, something cut off.

ȧshu [illegible], to dry up; see **Shu** [illegible].

ȧshui 〔hieroglyphs〕, P. 447, 〔hieroglyphs〕, M. 541, 〔hieroglyphs〕, N. 1122, to raise up, to elevate.

ȧshep 〔hieroglyphs〕, cucumber; Copt. ⲉϣⲟⲟⲛ.

ȧshf 〔hieroglyphs〕, a liquid, unguent (?)

ȧshem 〔hieroglyphs〕, M. 114, 〔hieroglyphs〕, M. 201, 559, N. 1160, 1166, 〔hieroglyphs〕, U. 488, T. 193, to make to go.

ȧshem-t 〔hieroglyphs〕, P. 96, 〔hieroglyphs〕, M. 114, 〔hieroglyphs〕, N. 41, a going; 〔hieroglyphs〕, Anastasi I, 24, 4, journey, travel.

ȧshem sek 〔hieroglyphs〕, the imperishable stars; var. 〔hieroglyphs〕.

Ȧshemiu seku 〔hieroglyphs〕, Thes. 59 = 〔hieroglyphs〕, a group of four jackal-gods who towed the Boat of Rā.

ȧshems 〔hieroglyphs〕, to make to follow.

ȧshen 〔hieroglyphs〕, U. 267, to furnish, to ornament, to encompass with.

ȧsher 〔hieroglyphs〕, fire, flame.

ȧsher 〔hieroglyphs〕, roast meat.

ȧsherȧu 〔hieroglyphs〕, daily burnt-offering.

ȧshes-t 〔hieroglyphs〕, M. 271, 〔hieroglyphs〕, N. 756, 〔hieroglyphs〕, N. 888, Hh. 429, 〔hieroglyphs〕, 〔hieroglyphs〕, Rec. 26, 225, 29, 151, 31, 90, 〔hieroglyphs〕, 〔hieroglyphs〕, 〔hieroglyphs〕, interrogative particle, who? what? where? why? wherefore? 〔hieroglyphs〕, Peasant 129.

ȧshesep 〔hieroglyphs〕, to make to shine.

Ȧshesp 〔hieroglyphs〕, light-god.

Ȧshespi-khā 〔hieroglyphs〕, Thes. 31, the goddess of the 4th hour of the day.

ȧshesep 〔hieroglyphs〕, bandage, garment.

ȧshespit 〔hieroglyphs〕, 〔hieroglyphs〕, 〔hieroglyphs〕, a booth in a garden, a summer house, a niche in a temple, a chapel, hall.

ȧshesn 〔hieroglyphs〕, to utter a cry of joy.

ȧsht 〔hieroglyphs〕, to compel; see 〔hieroglyphs〕.

Ȧshtit 〔hieroglyphs〕, Berg. 1, 14, a light-goddess.

ȧsht, ȧshṭ 〔hieroglyphs〕, 〔hieroglyphs〕, 〔hieroglyphs〕, 〔hieroglyphs〕, a kind of tree, persea (?) sycamore fig; plur. 〔hieroglyphs〕, 〔hieroglyphs〕, 〔hieroglyphs〕, 〔hieroglyphs〕, 〔hieroglyphs〕, the holy ȧsht tree in Heliopolis; 〔hieroglyphs〕, a title of Rā.

Ȧshteth 〔hieroglyphs〕, U. 360, a city in Sekhet-Ȧaru; var. 〔hieroglyphs〕, N. 1074.

ȧshṭ 〔hieroglyphs〕, U. 154, 〔hieroglyphs〕, 〔hieroglyphs〕, 〔hieroglyphs〕, 〔hieroglyphs〕, 〔hieroglyphs〕, Rec. 15, 107, P.S.B. 13, 499, sycamore figs; 〔hieroglyphs〕, 〔hieroglyphs〕, fruit of the sycamore.

Ȧshṭ 〔hieroglyphs〕, B.D. 17, 21, a mythological tree in Ȧnu by which sat the Great Cat (Rā).

Ȧshṭṭ 〔hieroglyphs〕, Hh. 438, a god.

ȧq 〔hieroglyphs〕 = 〔hieroglyphs〕; 〔hieroglyphs〕, 〔hieroglyphs〕 = 〔hieroglyphs〕.

ȧq 〔hieroglyphs〕, 〔hieroglyphs〕, to lose, to be injured; Copt. ⲁⲕⲟ, ⲁⲕⲱ.

ȧqa-t 〔hieroglyphs〕, 〔hieroglyphs〕, 〔hieroglyphs〕, loss, injury, ruin, destruction.

ȧq-t 〔hieroglyphs〕, a kind of drink.

ȧq-t 〔hieroglyphs〕, A.Z. 35, 17, 〔hieroglyphs〕, Rev. 12, 48, reed; Copt. ⲁⲕⲉ.

ȧqi 〔hieroglyphs〕, reed; Copt. ⲁⲕⲉ.

ȧqi-t 〔hieroglyphs〕, Nȧstasen Stele 48, some kind of gold ornaments or figures; var. 〔hieroglyphs〕 (l. 50).

åq 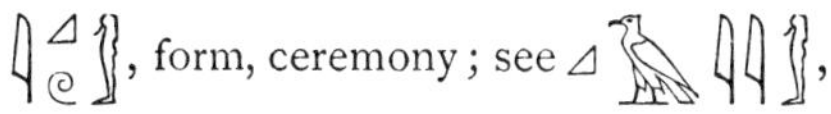, form, ceremony; see,

åqa , Åmen. 26, 16, to come.

åqa , to dance (?); perhaps =, to be high;, U. 186, T. 65, M. 220, N. 597, 847.

åqai 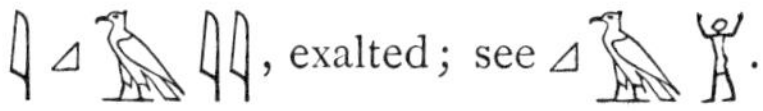, exalted; see.

åqau , Rec. 27, 218,, P. 199,, N. 935, exalted (?)

Åqauasha , Mar. Karn. 52, 1, a Mediterranean people.

åqar , fishing tackle.

åqeb , to double.

åqep 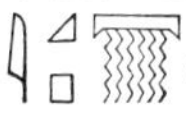, Hymn of Darius 12, storm.

åqem 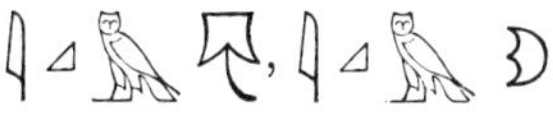, shield, buckler.

åqmu , N. 766 . . . .

Åqen , B.D. 168, a protector of the dead.

åqer 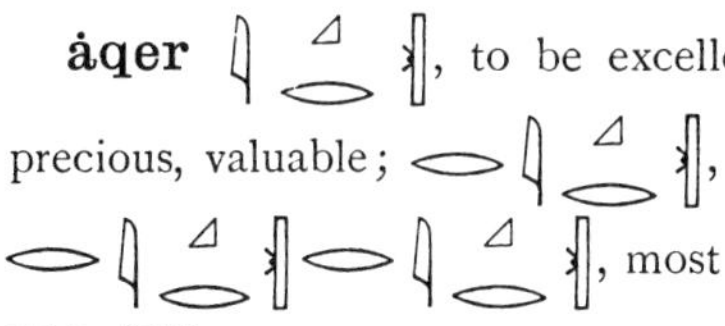, to be excellent, perfect, precious, valuable;, excellently;, most excellently; Heb. יָקָר.

åqer-t , something excellent or precious.

åqeru ; fem., the perfect ones, a title of the beatified.

Åqeru , P. 92, M. 121,, N. 699, the "perfect" gods.

Åqru , T. 305, a mythological serpent.

Åqrit 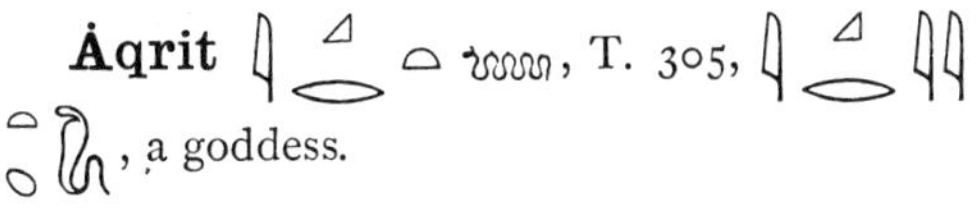, T. 305,, a goddess.

Åqrit Khenti-ḥe-t-set 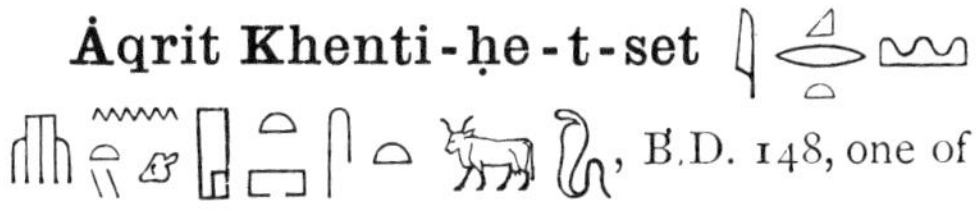, B.D. 148, one of the seven divine cows.

Åqertt , Berg. II, 12, the "perfect land," the Other World.

åqer , a plant.

åqer , a kind of wood.

åqrå (qeri?) , bolt.

Åqeh , B.D. 168, a protector of the dead.

Åqhit 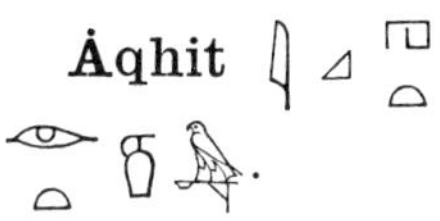, U. 556, a goddess, the.

åqḥ 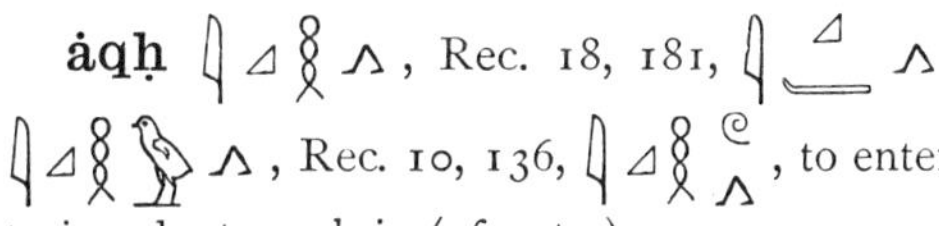, Rec. 18, 181,,, Rec. 10, 136,, to enter, to invade, to rush in (of water).

åqḥ , light (?)

åqḥu 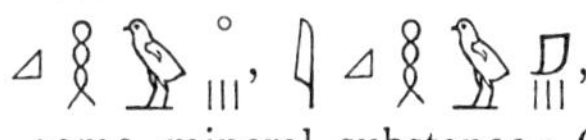, IV, 726, a metal, some mineral substance; Copt. ⲕⲉϩⲕⲉ (?).

åqes , to cut.

Åqes 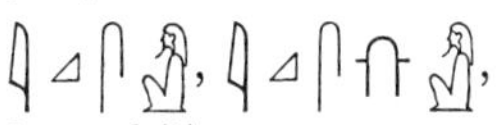, Rec. 32, 81, the name of a god (?)

åqes , to be vile.

åqes-t , vile, wretched, a vile thing.

åqeṭ 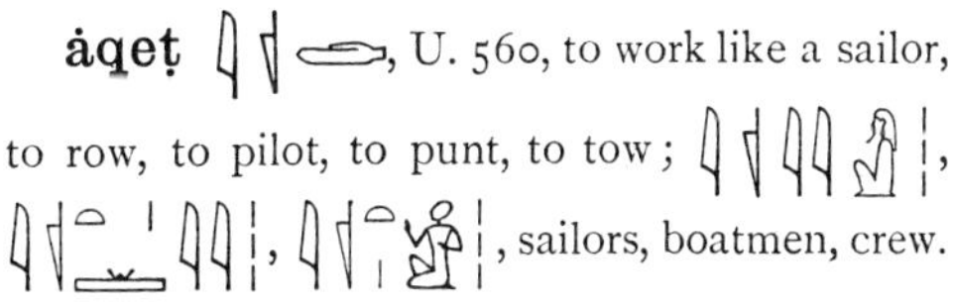, U. 560, to work like a sailor, to row, to pilot, to punt, to tow;,,, sailors, boatmen, crew.

åqeṭṭiu ,,, sailors, servants;,,, divine sailors in the Boat of Rā.

åqeṭṭiu qerås , Rec. 36, 78, funerary bearers.

àqeṭ 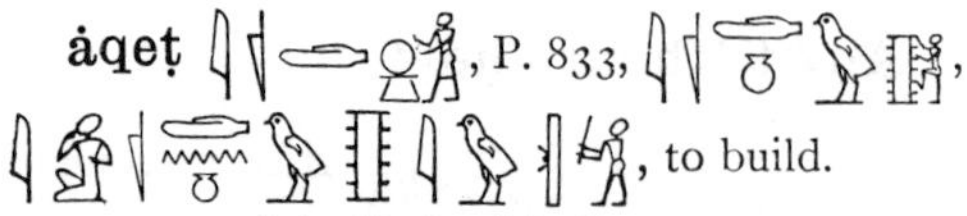, P. 833, , to build.

àqeṭu 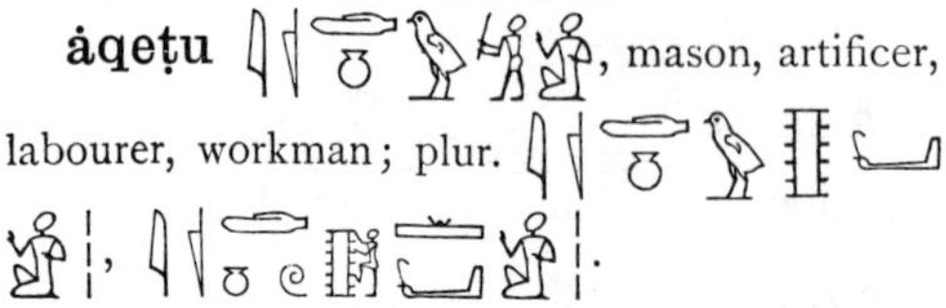, mason, artificer, labourer, workman; plur. , .

àqeṭ-t 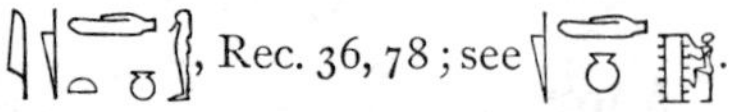, Rec. 36, 78; see .

àqeṭ 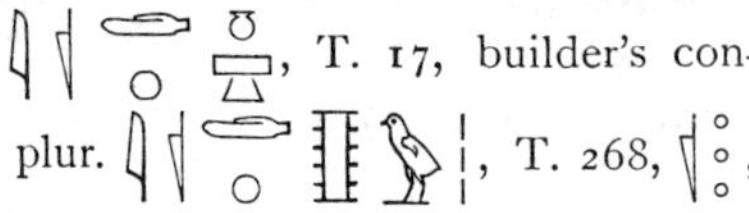, T. 17, builder's construction; plur. , T. 268, , M. 426.

àqeṭ , , builder's plan, design, draft.

àk 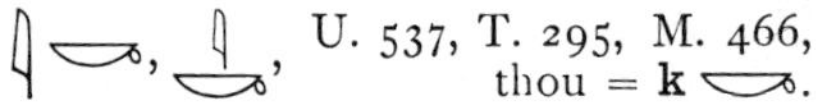, , U. 537, T. 295, M. 466, thou = **k** .

àk , to suffer injury, be lost or destroyed.

àkiu , lost ones, things destroyed; , the damned.

àk-t , pain, injury, something lost.

àkk 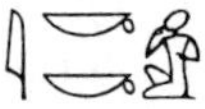, cry, song.

àk, àku 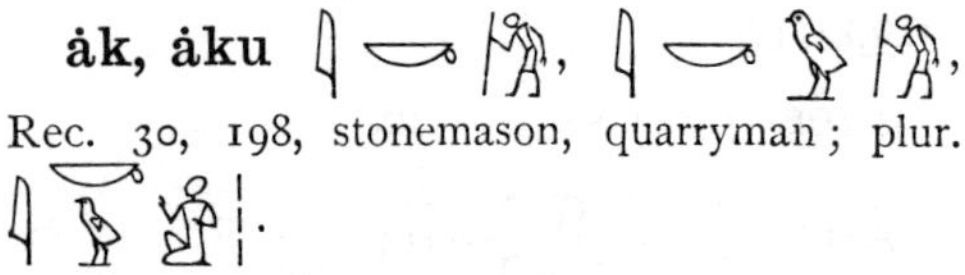, , Rec. 30, 198, stonemason, quarryman; plur. .

àk-t (?) , Hh. 451 ....

àku , stone quarry.

àk-t 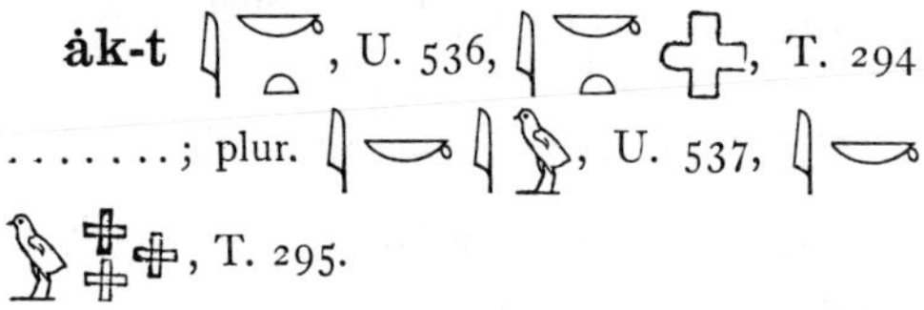, U. 536, , T. 294 ....; plur. , U. 537, , T. 295.

àka-t , estates, lands.

àka , A.Z. 1874, 64, sesame seed (?); Copt. OKE.

àkam 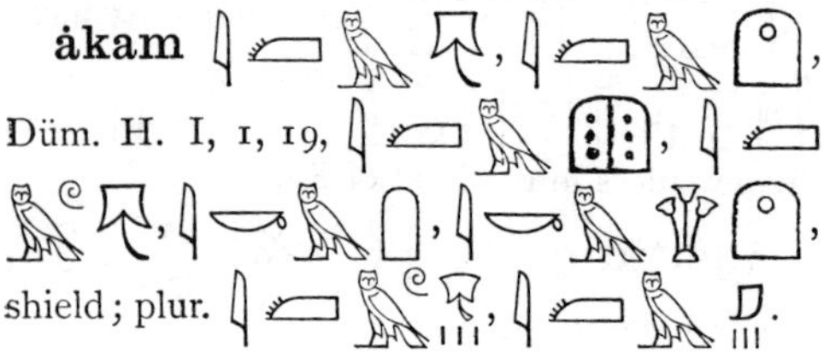, , Düm. H. I, 1, 19, , , , , shield; plur. , .

àkamu , wretched, miserable, patient; Copt. ωκεμ.

àkana 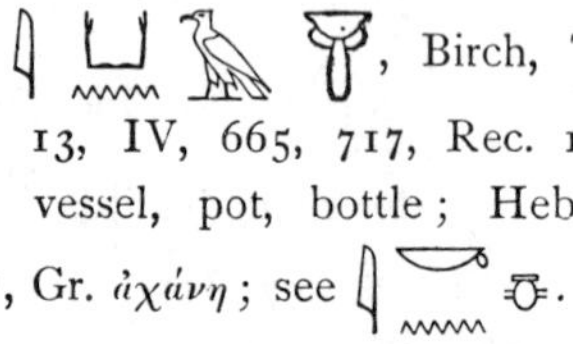, Birch, Thothmes III, p. 13, IV, 665, 717, Rec. 17, 76, basin, bowl, vessel, pot, bottle; Heb. אַגָּן, Syr. ܐܓܢܐ, Gr. ἀχάνη; see .

àkà 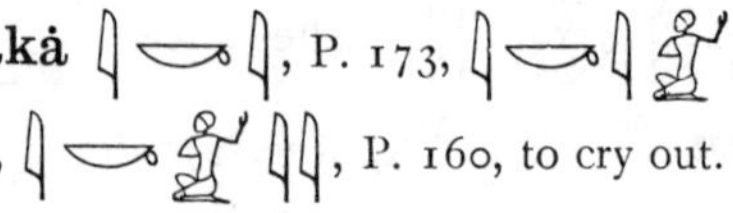, P. 173, , T. 51 + 1, , P. 160, to cry out.

àkkà 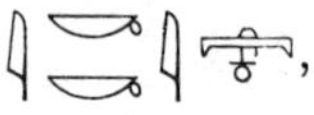, night, darkness.

àkàu .... , P. 223 ......

Àkànhi , U. 327, the name of a serpent-god or fiend.

àki 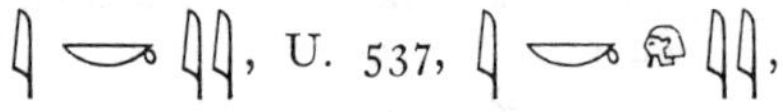, U. 537, , T. 295 ....

Àku , Ṭuat III, a god or animal in the Ṭuat.

àku-ta 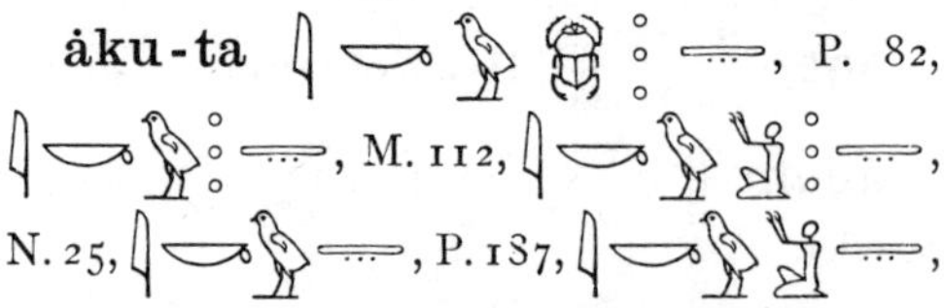, P. 82, , M. 112, , N. 25, , P. 187, , M. 348, N. 901, bowings to the earth (?)

àkeb 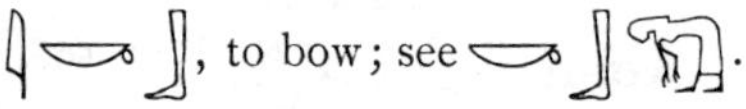, to bow; see .

àkeb 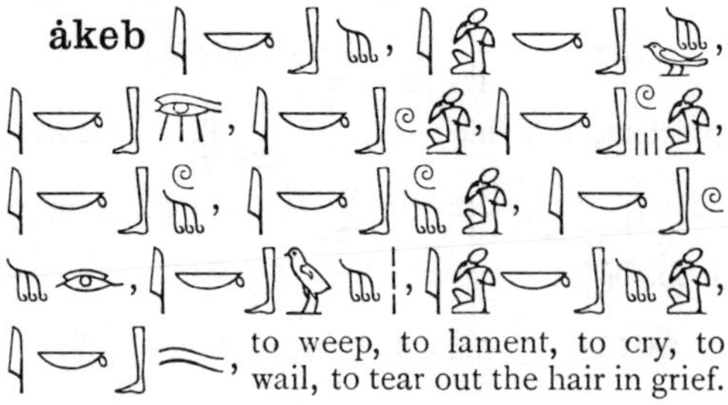, , , , , , , , , , to weep, to lament, to cry, to wail, to tear out the hair in grief.

àkebu , Àmen. 18, 5, weepers, mourners.

àkbit 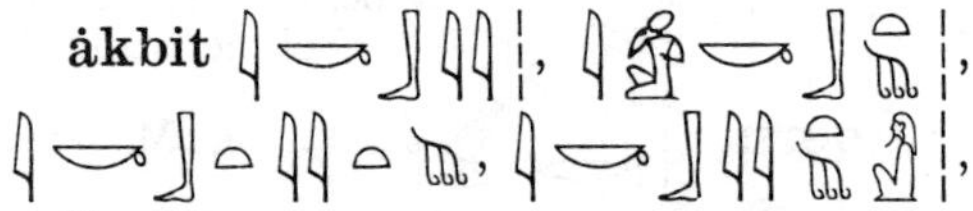, , , , wailing women.

Àkbiu 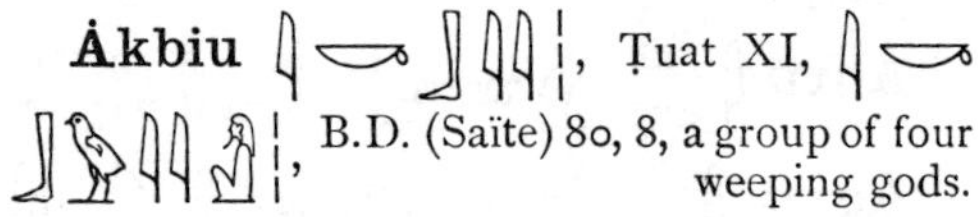, Ṭuat XI, , B.D. (Saïte) 80, 8, a group of four weeping gods.

Àkbit 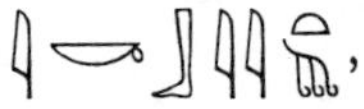, Ṭuat III, a weeping goddess.

Åkeb, Edfû I, 80, , the Nile and its flood.

åkbu, Rec. 22, 103, resin for fumigating purposes.

åkep, rain-flood, storm, torrent.

åkem, buckler; plur. (Lacau).

åken, bowl, basin; Heb. אַגָּן; see ; compare Assyr. "bowls," Rawlinson, C.I.W.A. I, 23, 122.

åken, a kind of stone (?)

åken-t, U. 611, resting place (?)

åken-t, domain, estate, abode (?)

åken, to make, to fashion.

åken, to salute, to address.

åken, Rec. 1, 48, , a digging tool, hoe, plough, pick; plur.

Åkniu, B.D. 127B, 14, a class of gods like Osiris.

åkenu, Åmen. 13, 6, 24, 3, some evil quality, lying (?)

Åken-åb, Ṭuat I, a doorkeeper god.

Åkenh, U. 544, the name of a serpent.

Åkenhå, T. 299, the name of a monster serpent; var. U. 327.

Åken-tau-keha-kheru, B.D. 144, the doorkeeper of the 6th Ārit.

Åkenti, B.D. 146, the door-keeper of the 7th Pylon; varr.

Åker, an Earth-god; see

Åkeru, Hh. 213, the gods who guarded the great tunnel through the earth.

Åkes, B.D. 149, the 9th Āat; var. (Saïte)

åkeshti, Rev. 13, 3, Cushite, Nubian (adjective).

Åkesh, Rev. 14, 13, a Nubian; plur. , Rev. 13, 3, , Rev. 12, 52; Copt. ⲉϭⲱϣ.

Åkshit, B.D. G. 134, a cow-goddess of Oxyrhynchus, mother of Apis.

åg, stream, flood.

ågu, a plant or herb; var.

åga . . ., P. 564 . . . . . .

åga, A.Z. 1869, 86, a kind of wood.

åga, to quiet, to subdue.

Åga, B.D. 78, 35 (Saïte), a god.

Ågaå, T. 293, Rec. 29, 157, 159, a god, a form of Anubis (?)

Ågau, B.D. 64, 19, a title of Anubis (?)

ågap, flood, rainstorm.

Ågiu, Ṭuat VIII and X, the souls of the drowned in the Ṭuat.

ågit, åggit, a kind of garment (?)

Ȧggit-ḥebsiṭ-bag, etc. 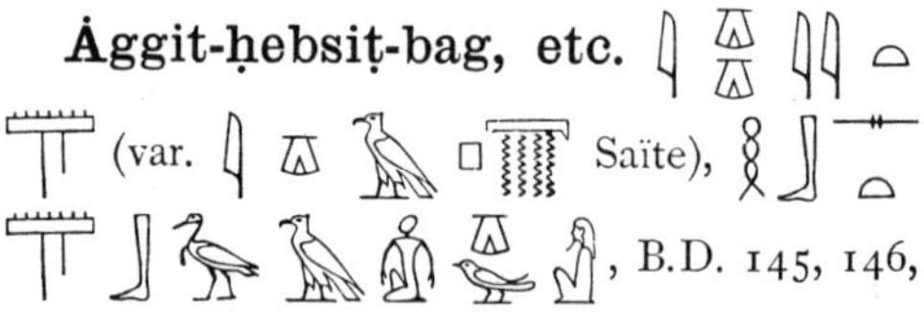 (var. Saïte), B.D. 145, 146, the name of the 7th Pylon.

ȧgb , to bow, to do homage, to be subdued.

ȧgb , flood; Copt. ⲱϭⲃ̄.

ȧgbu 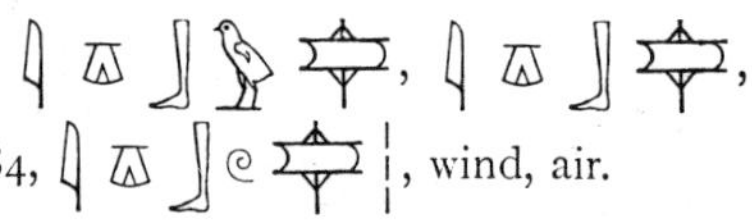, Rec. 27, 84, wind, air.

ȧgep 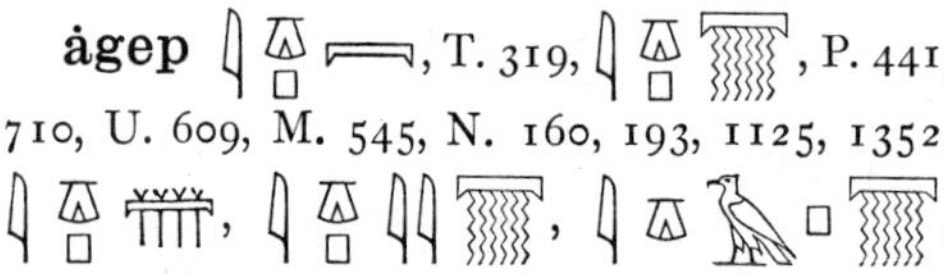, T. 319, P. 441, 710, U. 609, M. 545, N. 160, 193, 1125, 1352, rain storm, tempest, flood; Copt. ϭⲏⲡⲓ.

ȧgep 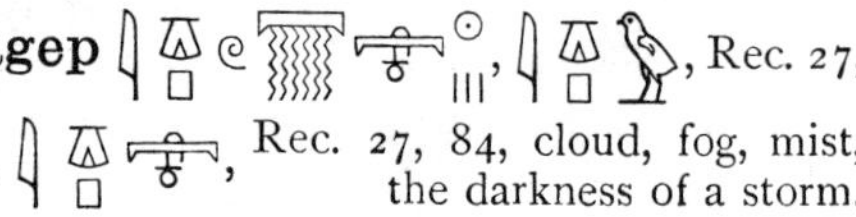, Rec. 27, 219, Rec. 27, 84, cloud, fog, mist, the darkness of a storm.

ȧgem , to discover.

ȧger 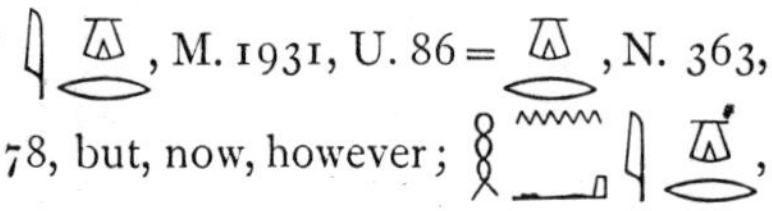, M. 1931, U. 86 = , N. 363, Rec. 29, 78, but, now, however; I, 36, yea, even.

ȧger 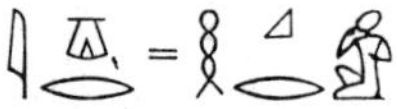, IV, 236, hunger.

ȧger 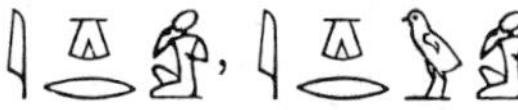, Rec. 31, 20, to make silent, to quiet.

Ȧgeriu 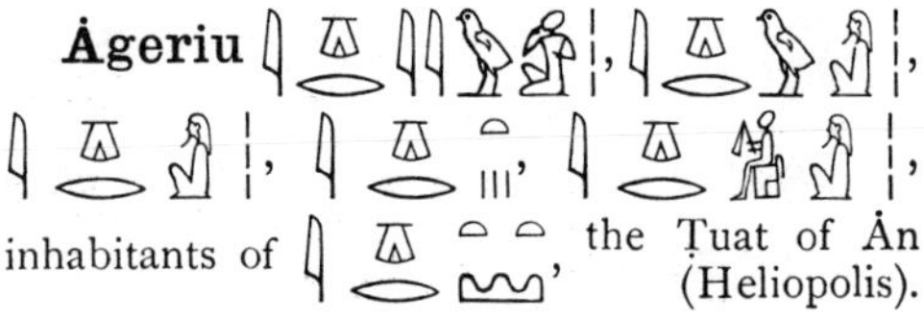, inhabitants of the Ṭuat of Ȧn (Heliopolis).

Ȧger , B.D. (Saïte) 64, 19, Rec. 30, 192, 31, 20, a god.

Ȧgrit , B.D. (Saïte) 64, 19, a goddess.

Ȧgrit , the goddess of the 5th hour of the day.

Ȧgeru , B.D. 110, 5, a group of gods in Sekhet-Aaru.

Ȧgertt , B.D. 137, B. 13, 17, the abode in the Ṭuat of the souls from An.

ȧges , P. 438, M. 653, side, half.

Ȧgest 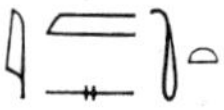; see **Ȧmset.**

ȧt 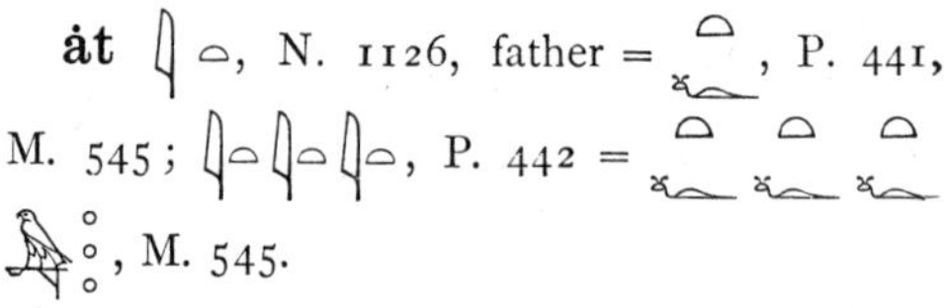, N. 1126, father = , P. 441, M. 545; , P. 442 = , M. 545.

ȧt 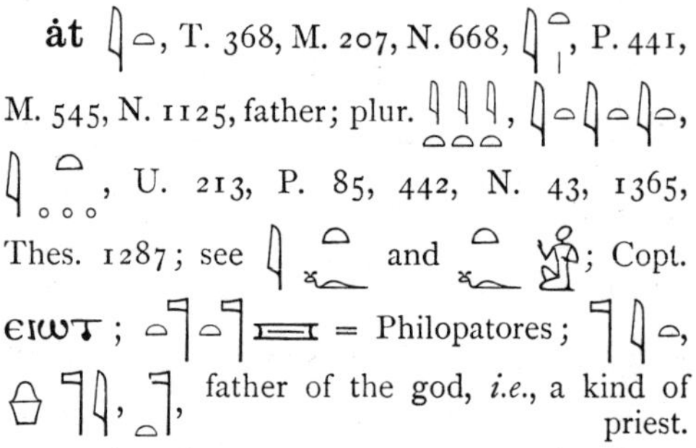, T. 368, M. 207, N. 668, P. 441, M. 545, N. 1125, father; plur. , U. 213, P. 85, 442, N. 43, 1365, Thes. 1287; see and ; Copt. ⲉⲓⲱⲧ; = Philopatores; father of the god, *i.e.*, a kind of priest.

ȧt 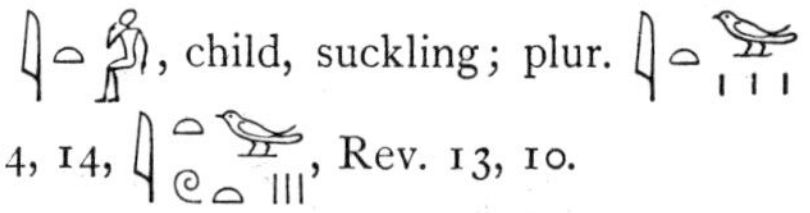, child, suckling; plur. , Rev. 14, 14, Rev. 13, 10.

ȧt-t , nurse.

ȧt, ȧtȧ 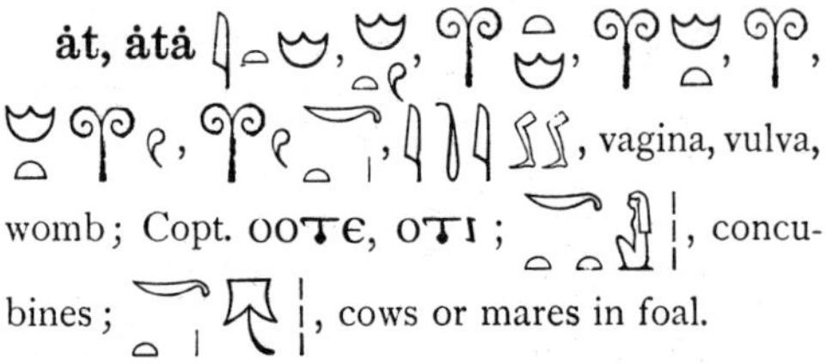, vagina, vulva, womb; Copt. ⲟⲟⲧⲉ, ⲟⲧⲓ; , concubines; , cows or mares in foal.

ȧt , P. 287 ......

ȧt 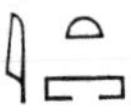, house.

ȧt 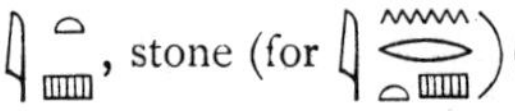, stone (for)(?)

ȧt 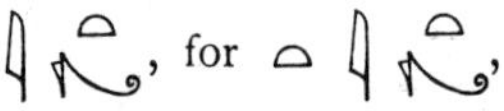, for , part, portion; Copt. ⲧⲟⲓ.

ȧt , Rec. 20, 91, fluid, liquid.

ȧt , to smite, to pierce, to beat, to constrain.

ȧti , beater, scourger.

ȧt , N. 747 ......

ȧt , T. 182, P. 529, M. 165, N. 653, twig, branch (of a palm).

åt-t , a cord net; plur. [illegible], cords.

åt, åta , P. 94, M. 118, N. 57, a kind of red cloth.

Åt , Rec. 29, 149, a god.

åt , king, prince; see [illegible].

åt 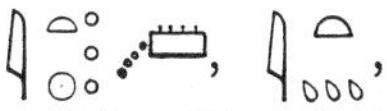, T. 289, P. 621, N. 824, , corn, grist; Copt. ϵιωⲧ.

åti 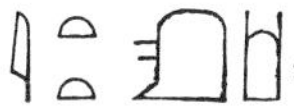, P. 703 = [illegible].

Åti-t-khau 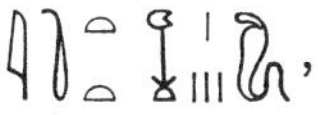, a title of the crown of Upper Egypt.

åta , boomerang.

Åtar , the name of a fiend.

Åtar , B.D. 164, 9, a Nubian (?) dwarf-god, son of Rā.

åtå , dew, moisture; Copt. ϵιωⲧϵ.

Åtå , N. 766, an associate of Shu.

åti 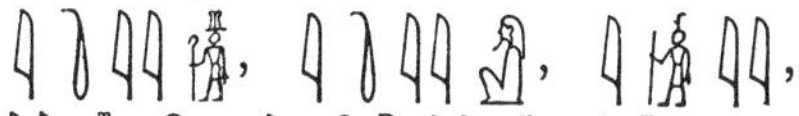, , , Rec. 16, 68, , king, prince, chief, sovereign, suzerain.

åti , Rec. 3, 116, [illegible], [illegible], king.

Åti , Ṭuat VI, a crocodile-god.

Åtiu , the bandaged gods, *i.e.*, the divine mummies.

Åttiu , fiends, the damned.

Åti-baiu , I, 148, the name of a pyramid.

Åtu , U. 632, [illegible], T. 306, an associate of the Serpent-god .

åtu , P. 505, 507 (with [illegible]) . . . .

Åtum 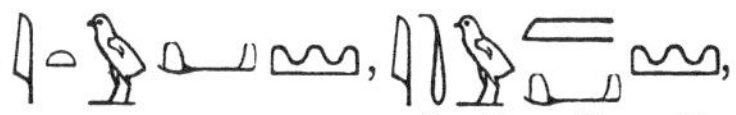, Asien, p. 316, a Syrian god; fem. [illegible], wife of Reshpu; compare Heb. אֲדוֹם.

åtur , to come out, to flow, to march.

åtur , [illegible], [illegible], river, flood, arm of the river, lake, basin; see **åter, åtru.**

Åtur āa 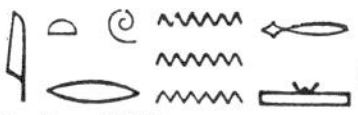, a name of the Canopic arm of the Nile.

åtur 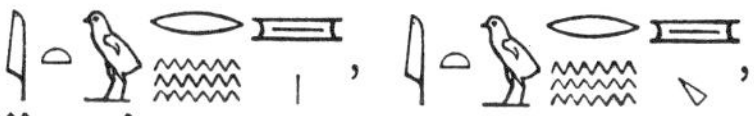, [illegible], a measure of land, stade, league.

Åtur-meḥ , Thes. 1251, Lower Egypt.

Åtur-res , Thes. 1251, Upper Egypt.

Åtur-ti 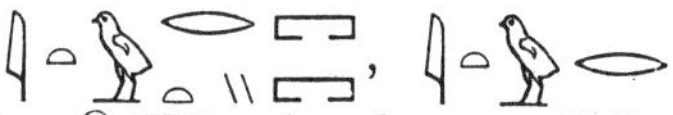, [illegible], the two chief temples of Upper and Lower Egypt, the two halves of Egypt, the northern and southern halves of the Egyptian sky; [illegible], U. 418, P. 453.

Åtur-ti 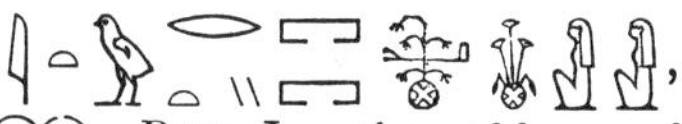, [illegible], Berg. I, 9, the goddesses of the same.

åtuḥi 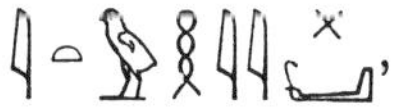, see [illegible].

åteb , territory, estate, land; see **åṭeb.**

åteb 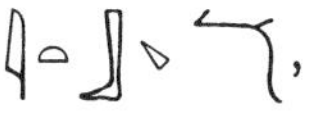, tongue.

åteb , Rev. 13, 62, to be removed; Copt. ⲟⲩⲱⲧⲉⲃ.

åtep , to load, to be laden; Copt. ⲱⲧⲡ.

åtpå , bark, boat.

àtf 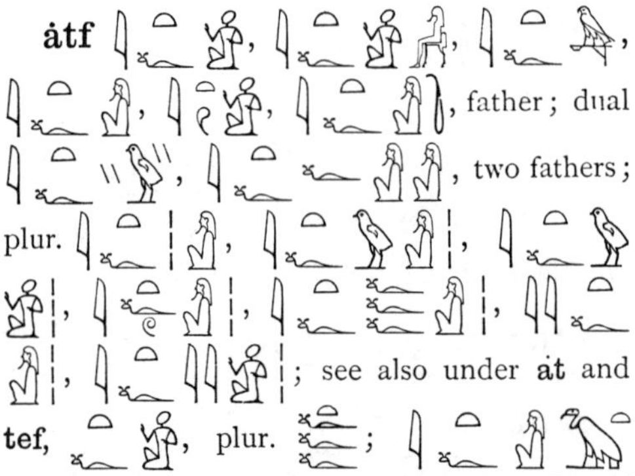, father; dual, two fathers; plur.; see also under **àt** and **tef**, plur.; , L.D. III, 140D., father and mother of all mankind; Copt. ЄΙⲰⲦ.

Àtf-meri 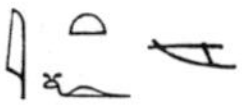, = Philopator.

Àtf neter , "father of the god," title of a priest, or father-in-law of the king; plur. 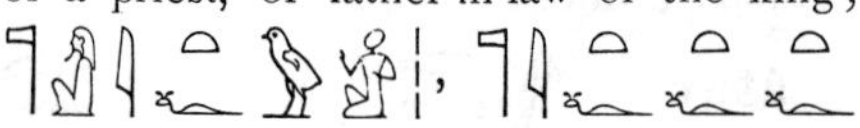 , IV, 349.

Àtf, Àtfa-t , Rev. 13, 121, , the serpent on the royal crown.

Àtfa-ur , T. 274, , P. 26, M. 37, N. 67, a god.

àtem 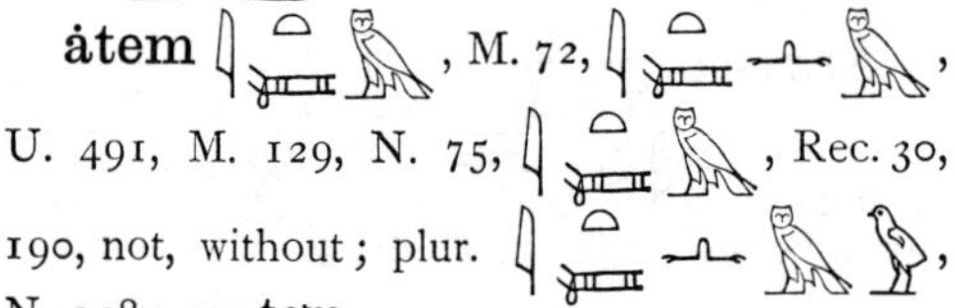, M. 72, U. 491, M. 129, N. 75, Rec. 30, 190, not, without; plur. N. 938; see **tem**.

àtmu , U. 602, N. 749, P. 204, N. 1231, those who are not.

Àtmu , the damned; see .

àtem , to shut, to close, to make an end of.

Àtem 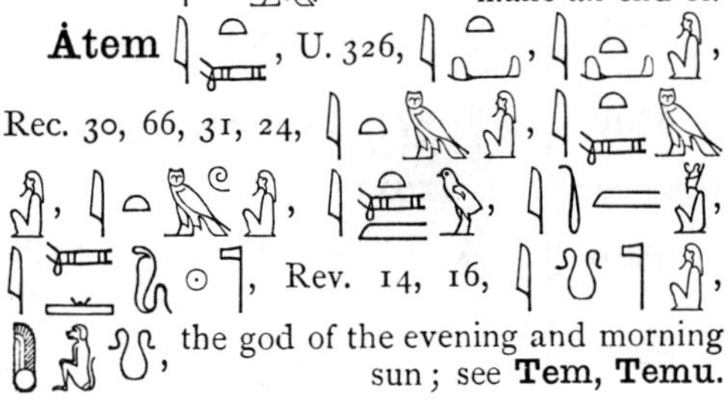, U. 326, Rec. 30, 66, 31, 24, Rev. 14, 16, the god of the evening and morning sun; see **Tem, Temu**.

Àtemit 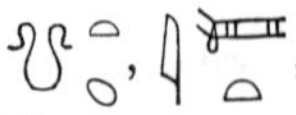, U. 218, the female counterpart of Tem.

Àtem 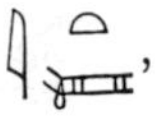, Goshen, Pl. 2, a dog-headed bow-god.

Àtem Kheprà , Àtem + Kheperà, the union of the evening and morning Sun-gods.

àtemu-t 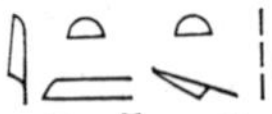, knives.

àtemti , one who destroys.

Àtemti, Ṭuat III, a goose-headed god.

àtem 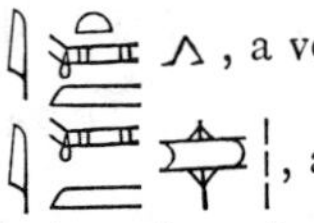, a verb of motion.

àtem, air, wind.

àtmà-t 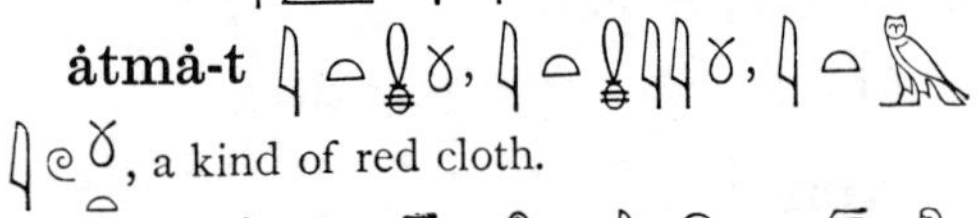, a kind of red cloth.

Àten , Rec. 27, 55, 31, 174, , Rec. 4, 128, 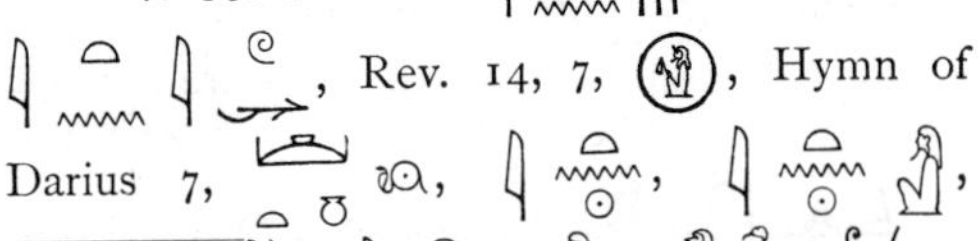, Rev. 14, 7, Hymn of Darius 7, , the disk of the sun, the disk stands still, Metternich Stele, 207; , disk with two horns; , A.Z. 1901, 63, the name of the barge of Àmenḥetep III.

Àten VII 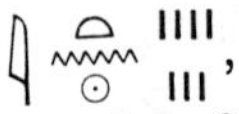, B.M. No. 32, l. 253, the seven disks of the Sun-god.

Àten-ur-nub , a serpent-headed supporter of the throne of Rā.

àten , mirror.

àten , to act as a deputy; see.

àtenu 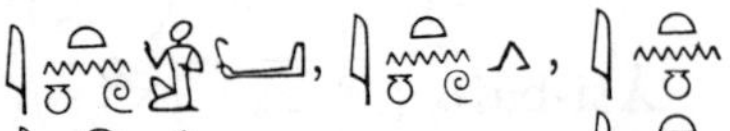, 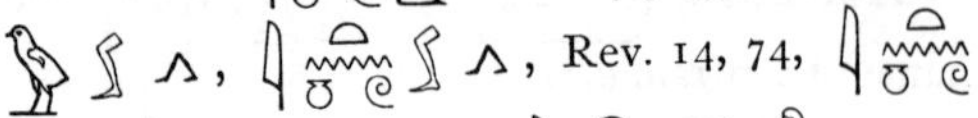, Rev. 14, 74, 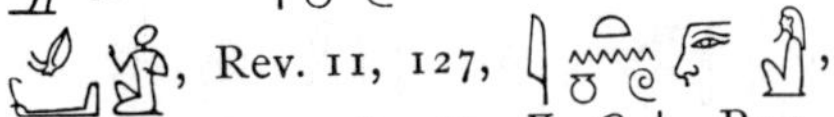, Rev. 11, 127, vicar, deputy, *wakîl*; 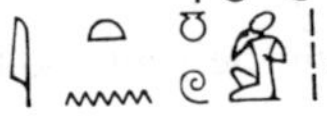, Rev. 12, 18, directors (?)

åten-t, staff of office, mace.

åten, to push aside, to repulse; var., to resist authority, to revolt.

åtenu, Mar. Aby. II, 30, 37, revolt.

åtenu, rebels, fiends.

åten, Thes. 1295, Anastasi I, 5, Hymn of Darius, 12, Rev. 12, 10, Rev. 14, 11, an opening, air hole (?), place of restraint (?) prison (?); ....

åtenut, circle, horizon.

åten, Rec. 15, 43, Rev. 13, 67, ground, dust, earth, land, estate, farm; Copt. ⲉⲓⲧⲛ̄.

åten, to bind, to tie.

åten-petch-t, L.D. III, 55B; IV, 194, stringer of bows, bow-bearer.

åtennu, knots, difficult points in a book or argument; untier of knots, *i.e.*, solver of difficulties.

åtennu, part of a book, or of its binding.

åten, a kind of plant.

åter-t, Rec. 31, 162, a hall, a large or small building, a cell or shrine of a god, *e.g.*, of Åmen at Elephantine.

återti, N. 719, P. 218, N. 831, Rec. 26, 234, 27, 218, 219; see **åturti**.

Återti, Denderah IV, 67, the name of a funerary coffer; Rec. 5, 92, the shrine of Osiris.

Åter-t meḥ-t, P. 612, Lower Egypt; the goddess of Lower Egypt.

Åter-t shemā-t (?), P. 612, Upper Egypt; the goddess of Upper Egypt; the two sides of the southern heaven.

åter (?) ....., the belt of Orion (?)

åtru, to pour out.

åtr, åtru, Rec. 31, 168, plur. L.D. III, 140B, Treaty 30, Hh. 269, P. 425, M. 92, 607, Rec. 26, 65, 80, 29, 146, river, stream, canal, Nile; Copt. ⲉⲓⲟⲟⲣ, Heb. יְאֹר.

åtru, Nile festivals.

åtru, Hh. 373, watered land, a watering place; Rec. 20, 41.

Åtru-neser-em-khet, B.D. 149, the 13th Åat.

ȧter, ȧtru , , , , , , , , , a distance of between 1,500 and 1,600 metres, or 3,000 cubits, the schoenus of 30, 32, 40 or 60 stadia, Rec. 15, 164 ff. The square  , = 18,200 aruras = 182,000,000 square cubits. The ȧter of Edfû = 14,000 cubits = 4·2 miles = 40 stadia, P.S.B. 14, 409.

ȧter , Jour. As. 1908, 302 =  , limit; Copt. ⲁⲣⲏϫ.

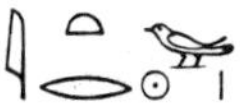

ȧtru , , time, season, year; plur. 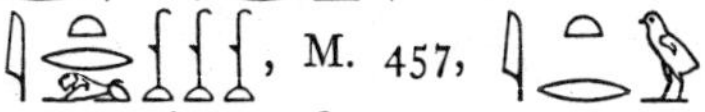 , M. 457, 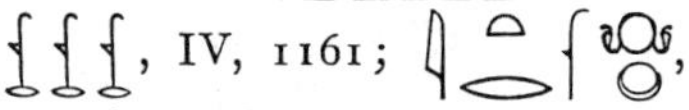 , IV, 1161; , Rec. 3, 49, morning and evening.

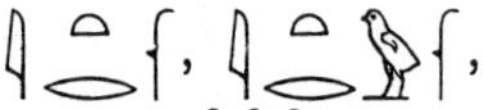

ȧter , Rec. 4, 28, , Rec. 3, 49, papyrus, the cord of a papyrus roll.

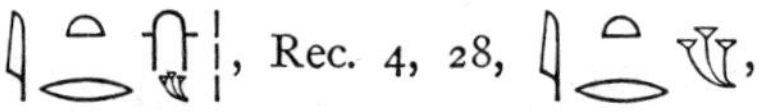

ȧter , yoke of animals; , , stud cattle; Copt. ϩⲁⲧⲣⲉ.

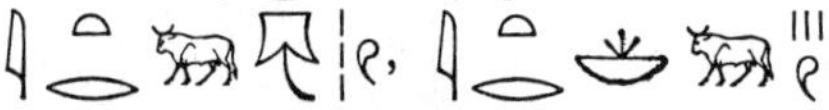

Ȧthabu , B.D. 163, 1, a town in Egypt or the Ṭuat.

ȧtḥ , U. 89, , P. 366, , , Rec. 27, 230, 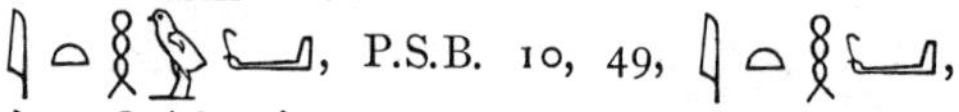 , P.S.B. 10, 49, , , , , , U. 442, to drag, to haul, to draw, to harness, to yoke, to pull, to tow a boat, to constrain, to restrain;  , to string a bow; 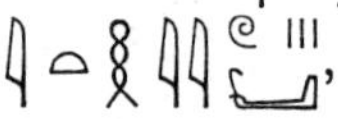 , "pull ye!" Copt. ⲱⲧϩ.

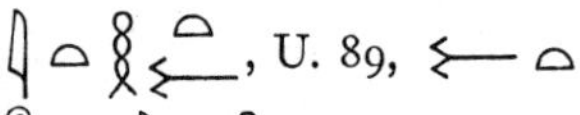

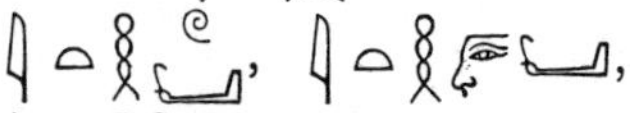

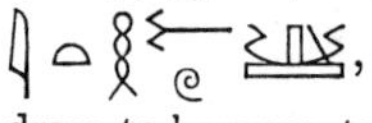

ȧtḥ , , place of restraint, prison, fort.

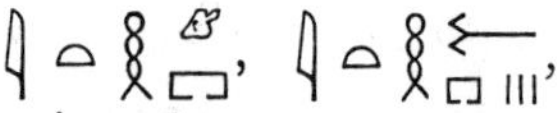

ȧtḥu , prisoners.

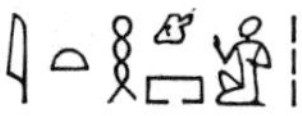

ȧtḥ , fields.

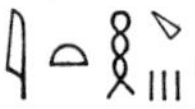

ȧtḥ , , , , , papyrus swamp, marshy land.

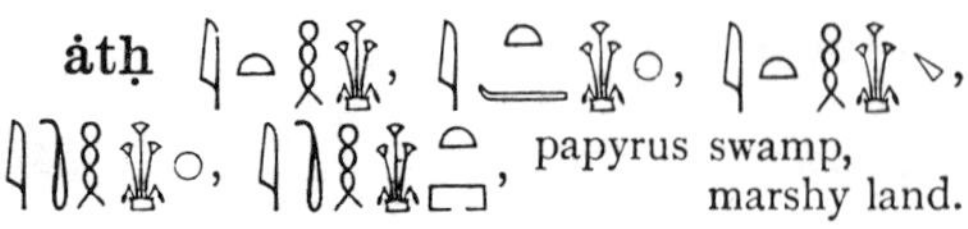

ȧtḥu , swamp plants, marsh vegetation.

ȧtḥ , U. 89, N. 366, a cake-offering.

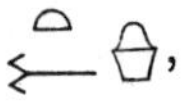

ȧtḥ-t 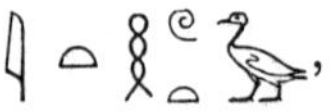 , a kind of bird, crane (?)

ȧtḥāa , N. 1126, crane.

ȧtkh , to brew beer; , brewer (?); see .

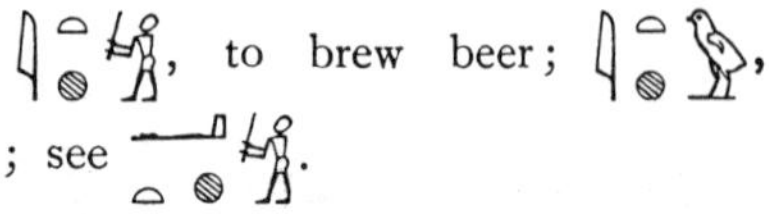

ȧtsef , cake; var. , .

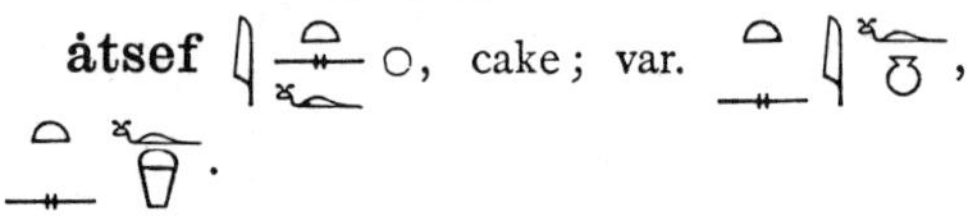

ȧth , Thes. 926 . . . . . .

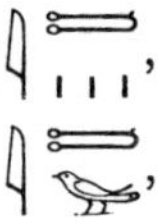

ȧth , Mett. Stele, 120, to hurt (?), hurtful (?)

ȧthth-t 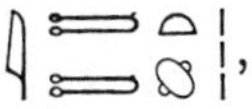 , bloody pus.

ȧthth , N. 953, , , to twitter, to pipe like a bird, to quack like a duck.

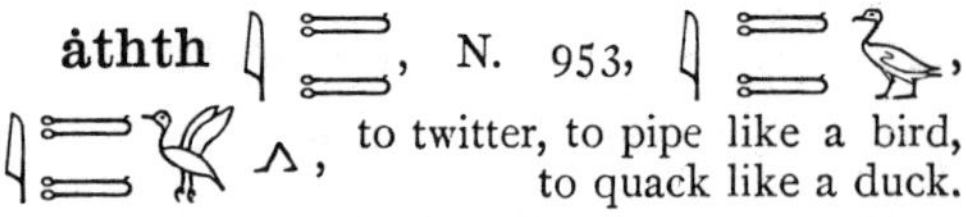

ȧthi en 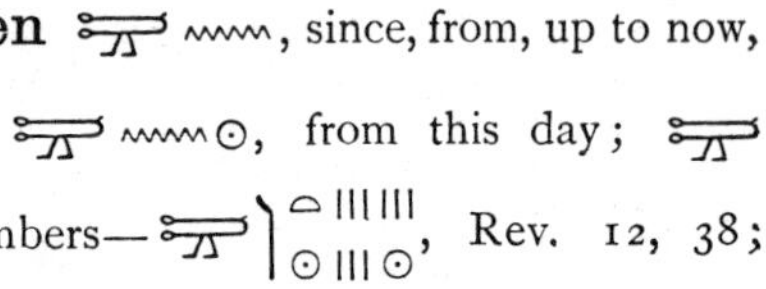 , since, from, up to now, hitherto; , from this day; with numbers— , Rev. 12, 38; Copt. ϫⲓⲛ.

ȧth , U. 537, , T. 26, N. 209, , U. 1, 564, P. 340, N. 1221, 1231, 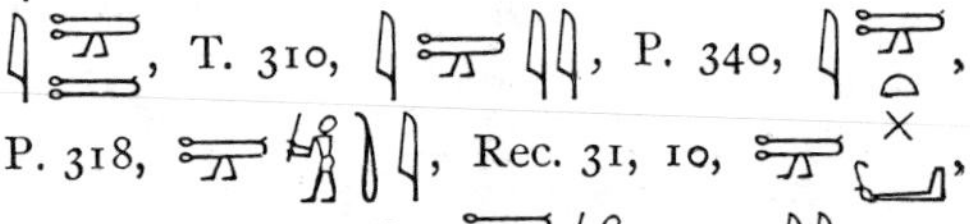 , T. 310, , P. 340, , P. 318, , Rec. 31, 10, , , , , , , , , to seize, to steal, to snatch away, to conquer, to capture, to plunder, to carry off, to transfer, to remove; Copt. ϫⲓ.

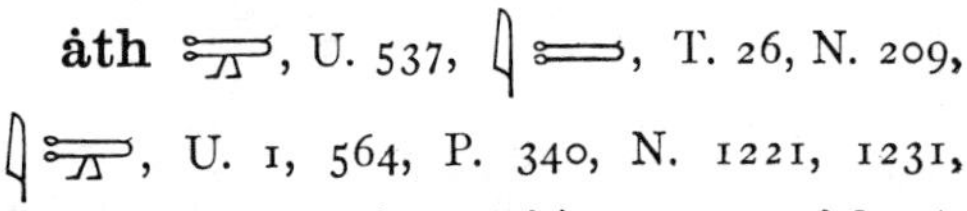

ȧthu , Amen. 19, 1, , robber, seizer, conqueror; plur. 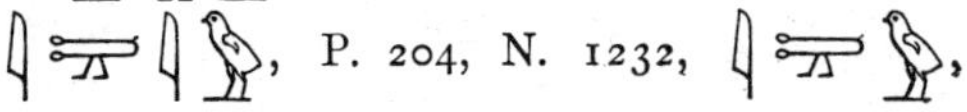 , P. 204, N. 1232, ,

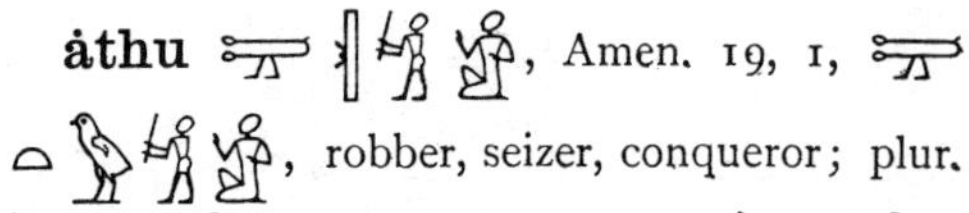

N. 1231, , , IV, 667, foragers; , conqueror of Egypt; , ravisher of women; , stealer of hearts.

Ȧthtiu-ȧbu , B.D. 27, 1, the robbers of hearts.

ȧthit , what is seized, forage, plunder.

ȧthi ȧu-t 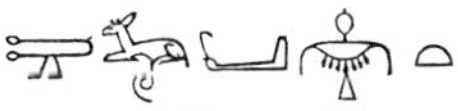, Jour. As. 1908, 294, to torment; Copt. ϭⲓ ⲁⲟⲩⲱ.

ȧthi mit , Jour. As., 1908, 293, to set out; Copt. ϫⲓ ⲙⲟⲉⲓⲧ.

ȧthi en qes 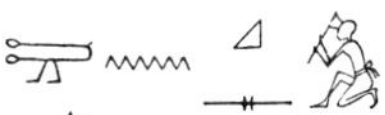, Rev. 14, 67, , Rev. 13, 30, [illegible] 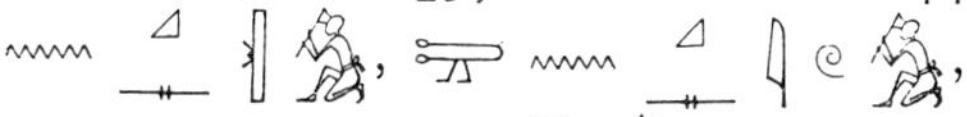, Rev. 11, 146, 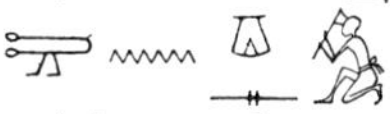, Rev. 14, 67, to wrong, to do violence; Copt. ϫⲓ ⲛ̅ϭⲟⲛⲥ̅.

ȧthi ḥer , B.D. G. 281, [illegible] , Rev. 11, 138, to shew favour, to accept the person of someone; Copt. ϭⲓ ϩⲟ.

ȧthi ḥetr 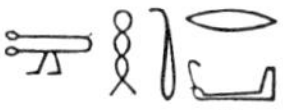, Jour. As. 1908, 252, to have power over; Copt. ϫⲓ ϩⲧⲟⲣ.

Ȧthit-em-āua  , B.D. 99, 23, a bolt peg in the magical boat.

Ȧthi-hru-em-gerḥ 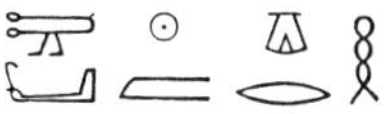 [illegible], Ṭuat III, a god.

Ȧthi-ḥeḥ , Ṭuat III, a title of Osiris.

ȧtha, ȧthai , Israel Stele, 53, 24, , ibid. 6, 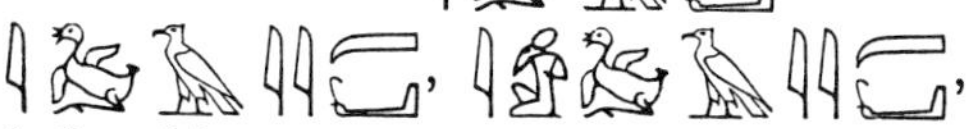, [illegible], to seize, to snatch away, to carry off, to lay violent hands on, to steal.

ȧthau , Peasant, 192, , Rec. 21, 79, thief, robber; plur.  .

ȧthap , T. 23, ...

ȧthar , Alt. K. 193, prisoner; Heb. אָסִיר (?).

Ȧthep 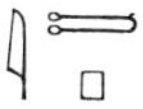, Ṭuat I, a singing-god.

Ȧthemti 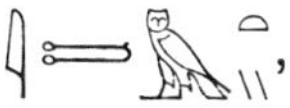, Ṭuat III, a goose-god in the Ṭuat.

ȧthen , 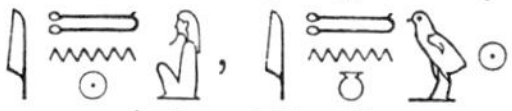, the disk of the sun; plur. [illegible].

Ȧthen . . . . .  [illegible], Rec. 27, 55, 29, 152, the name of a god.

ȧthen [illegible], to push aside, to repel.

ȧthnu [illegible], deputy, chief.

ȧthnu [illegible], foes, enemies, rebels.

ȧther , time, season; varr. [illegible].

ȧthes [illegible], to beget, to raise up children.

ȧthtcha [illegible], Rev. 12, 11, restraint, prison; Copt. ⲧⲁⲧϩⲟ.

ȧṭ, ȧṭi , U. 416, [illegible], to cense, to pour out a libation.

ȧṭ-t [illegible], incense.

ȧṭ-t [illegible], an incense offering.

ȧṭ [illegible], M. 693, [illegible], P. 416, M. 596, N. 1201, [illegible], Rec. 31, 169, , IV, 222, 615; dew; plur. 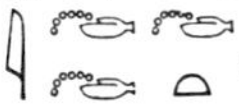, U. 565; see [illegible]; Copt. ⲉⲓⲱⲧⲉ.

ȧṭ 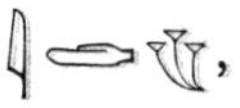, Mett. Stele, 53, swampy land.

ȧṭ-t , U. 115, N. 424, a cake-offering.

ȧṭ , rich, abundant, multitudinous.

ȧṭ-ui(?) 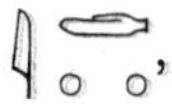, the pupils of the eyes.

ȧṭ , child; plur. [illegible].

ȧṭi-t , girl, maiden.

ȧṭ 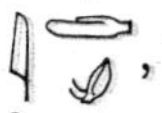, U. 608, Rec. 26, 67, [illegible], to be deaf, deafness.

ȧṭṭ-ti (?) 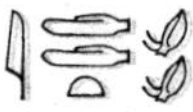, Ebers Papyrus, 99, 14, 15, deaf ears (?).

ȧṭ (?) , part of a plant, *e.g.*, **ȧṭ-en-ȧam** [illegible]; **ȧṭ-en-ȧḥ** [illegible]; **ȧṭ-en-āru** [illegible]; **ȧṭ-en-rega** [illegible], Rec. 15, 119, 120.

ȧṭ , a kind of bird.

ȧṭ 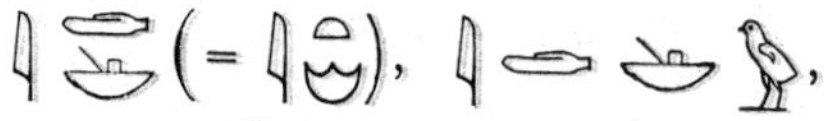, IV, 159, uterus; Copt. ⲟⲟⲧⲉ, ⲟⲧⲓ, ⲟⲧⲧⲉ.

ȧṭ , Rec. 26, 235, to seize, to grasp, to smite.

ȧṭiu, ȧṭṭiu , smiters, slaughterers.

ȧṭ-t 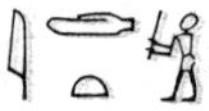, slaughter, a smiting.

ȧṭ 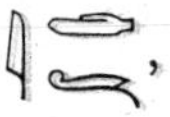, Wört. Supp. 170, the cord of a papyrus roll.

ȧṭ-t , net, cordage, bag.

ȧṭ , P. 705, to be fat, strong.

ȧṭ , to be oppressed, afflicted.

ȧṭ , perdition, destruction, death.

ȧṭu , IV, 480 . . . .

ȧṭa-t , oppression, misery, miserable state.

Ȧṭa-t , M. 703, a mythological locality.

Ȧṭau(?) , Rec. 31, 19, the name of a god.

ȧṭa , U. 332, 479, T. 300, P. 655, M. 366, 759, N. 141, [illegible], Anas. I, 26, 2, to make, to cause, to grant, to give.

Ȧṭṭi , Tomb Rameses IV, 29, 30, Rec. 6, 152, a supporter of the Disk.

Ȧṭu , B.D. 149, the 11th Ȧat.

ȧṭua 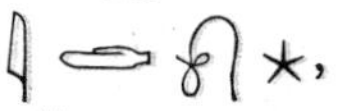, T. 289, M. 66, [illegible], Rec. 30, 185, to praise.

ȧṭeb 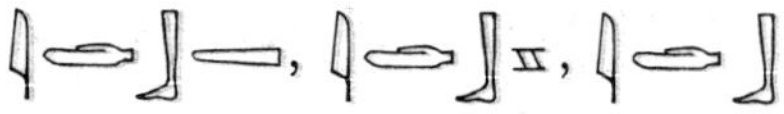, Rec. 25, 191, land which the waters of the Nile can reach; plur. [illegible], T. 334, P. 376, N. 1157, [illegible], Rec. 31, 174, flooded Nile banks.

ȧṭebui 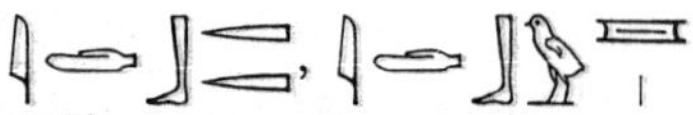, P. 90, 603, 718, N. 698, [illegible], the two banks of the Nile, *i.e.*, all Egypt.

ȧṭeb , A.Z. 1879, 54, plum tree (?)

ȧṭb , Ḥerusȧtef Stele, 93, Nȧstasen Stele, 61, to reward, to punish.

ȧṭbana , Harris Pap. 501 . . . .

ȧṭep 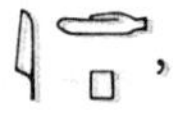, U. 15, to taste.

ȧṭep 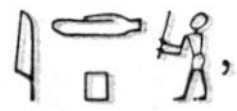, load; Copt. ⲱⲧⲡ.

ȧṭep-t , place for loading up, station, khân.

ȧṭep 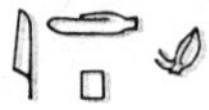; see **ṭep** .

Ȧṭem' , Alt. K. 106, Edomite.

Áṭem, god of the setting sun; see .

áṭmá, N. 972, to make like.

áṭmáit, P. 692, , M. 592, N. 1197, , , , , , , , the name of a garment or article of apparel made of dark red cloth.

áṭen; see **áṭ** and **át.**

áṭen, Ámen. 10, 12, , Ámen. 25, 19, god of the solar disk.

áṭen, ear; Heb. אֹזֶן.

áṭen, , , , , , , to act as deputy, to rule for someone else, to serve as wakîl.

áṭen, , to enter as deputy on some service.

áṭenu, Edict 16, , , , , , , , deputy, agent, vicar, wakîl; var. .

áṭnu tent - ḥetru, Rec. 17, 145, deputy-master of the horse.

áṭnu pa-menfit, deputy-general of the army.

áṭnu . . . . per-uatch-ur, deputy-sealer of the maritime department.

áṭnu bánti, deputy-confectioner.

áṭenut, Ḥerusátef Stele 91 . . . . . .

áṭenu (?) . . . .

áṭen-t, part, division.

áṭer, P. 186, 344, 609, M. 301, N. 899; , , to destroy, to do away, to remove, to chastise.

áṭeriu, A.Z. 1869, 134, destroyers (?)

áṭerit, B.D. 125, III, 16, calamities, destruction.

Áṭerásfet, N. 980, "Destroyer of sin," the name of a god.

áṭer, , stud cow or bull; plur. , Coptos, Pl. 18, .

áṭeru, IV, 745, geese kept for breeding purposes.

áṭer, , an internal organ of the body.

áṭrut, P. 661, , P. 778, M. 772, garments, bandages, swathings, bandlets.

áṭeru, Ebers Pap. 109, 9 . . . .

áṭre, Harris Pap. 501 . . . .

áṭre - gaha, Harris Pap. 501 . . . . .

áṭḥ, áṭḥu, , , , , , swamp, marsh, fen-district, a common name for land in the Delta; plur. , .

áṭḥi[t], marsh plants, reeds, etc.

áṭḥi, , the swamp-dweller, fen man, Delta man.

áṭheḥ(?) (?), to block up, to obstruct.

àṭḥ , 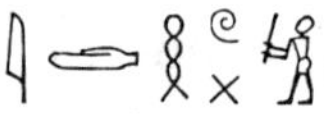, Amen. 23, 20, to pull, to draw, to haul, etc.; see àṭḥ 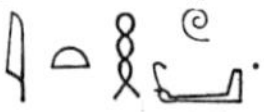.

Àṭḥu , Rec. 31, 171, the name of a god.

àṭekh 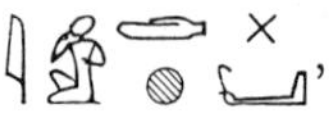, to make to fall, to make tremble.

àṭsh 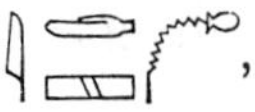, Hymn of Darius 25, to spit (?)

àṭga , , head-cloth, garment.

àtch ḥer , U. 357, P. 204 = .

àtchanr , Birch, In. Hier. Ch. 29, 3, to rejoice; compare Heb. אצל (Alt. K. 209).

Àtchai , B.D. G. 769, Osiris in the Fayyûm.

àtchartà , Alt. K. 210, a pot, vessel.

àtchbu , ground, land; see .

àtchbā , fingers, U. 552; Heb. אֶצְבָּעוֹת.

àtcher , , limit, boundary; Copt. ⲁⲣⲏϫ.

àtcherà 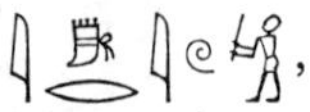, Rhind Pap. 34, as long as.

àtcher 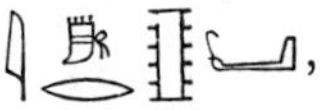, to make strong, to fortify (?)

àtcher-t 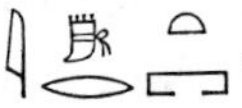, IV, 1175, fortress.

àtchḥu , wet lands, marshes, swamps.

àtcheṭ , , , U. 270, P. 652, 655, M. 76, 193, 754, to make a reply, to speak.

àtcheṭut , , words, utterances, speech, divine talk.

Ā

ā = Heb. ע.

ā , piece, one, a, an, pair; see the following eleven examples:—

ā ār-t , a uraeus amulet.

ā , a plant or flower; , an unbu plant.

ā menḥ-t , an amulet.

ā en-meri-t , Rec. 21, 21, a port, harbour; Copt. ⲁⲛⲉⲙⲣⲱ.

ā em-khet-em-āsh , a censer.

ā en-ḥetrȧu , a body of cavalry.

ā en-saga , Anastasi I, 25, 6, a piece of sackcloth.

ā en-thebut , a pair of sandals, white , or black .

ā en-senther , a censer.

ā shem-reth , an amulet.

ā tchet , an amulet.

ā , in compound prepositions, etc.:— , Rec. 21, 21, truly; Copt. ⲛⲁⲙⲉ; , before; , a second time; , , at once, immediately; ; before, in the presence of; , at once.

ā , hand, authority; , under the authority of.

ā , , , the forearm, the hand, the prominent part of a thing; , tip of the nose; , , Rec. 21, 21, hill top; Copt. ⲁⲛⲧⲱⲟⲩ; , handle of a quiver.

ā , used with verbs of motion (Copt. ϭⲓⲛ, ϫⲓⲛ):— , a fighting; , a flight; , a journeying, or , , a going, a passage; , a journeying; , a mighty battle; , an eating.

āui , P. 643, 666, , P. 256, , , , , , , , , , , , the two forearms, the two hands; , IV, 161, by my two hands actually.

āut , family.

āiu , "hands," *i.e.*, workmen, labourers.

ā-n-Ḥeru , "arm of Horus," *i.e.*, censer.

Ā-saḥ , "arm of Orion," the name of a Dekan.

Āui-f-em-kha-nef , Ṭuat XI, a double serpent-headed god.

Āui-en-neter-āa , etc., B.D. 153A, 12, the "hands" of the net for snaring souls.

āui , , armlets, bangles, bracelets; var. (?)

āuāu , arm ring, bangle, bracelet.

ā , Anastasi I, 26, 6, pole of a chariot.

ā , Anastasi I, 20, 6 . . . .

ā 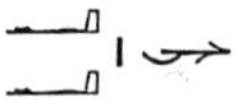, Gol. 12, 104, handle (?)

ā , Sphinx II, 174, Décrets, 100, caravan (?), or some article used in carrying goods in the desert on asses or camels (?) ;  , a caravan of Metcha. Some think that , dragoman, interpreter, P.S.B.A. 37, 117–125, 224.

ā , Mar. Karn. 54, 42, state, condition, means; , L.D. III, 140B, means of keeping alive; 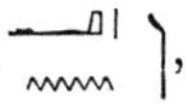, Rec. 21, 21 ; Copt. ⲁⲛϭⲃⲁ.

ā , region, place, *e.g.*, , the region of the Shasu; , the southern region; 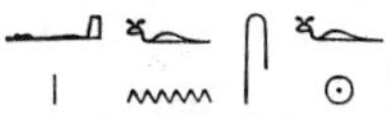, his place of yesterday; 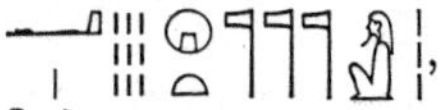, estate of the gods;  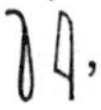, east side, etc.

āui-sem-t 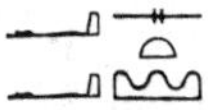, IV, 574, hilly country.

āui-ṭu , IV, 388, hilly country.

ā 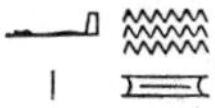, Rec. 18, 181, 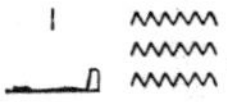, Rec. 10, 136, 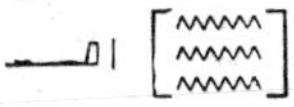, Kahun Pap. 100, dam, dyke.

ā-t 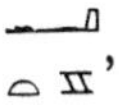, domain, estate, plot of ground; 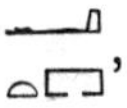, Rec. 11, 174, bank of river.

ā-t 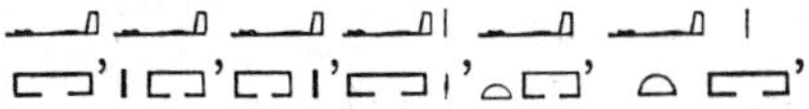, R.E. 11, 125, chamber, house, palace, temple; Copt. ⲏⲓ.

ā-t ȧrp , wine-shop, wine-cellar.

ā-t bener-t 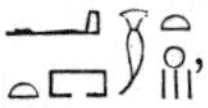, IV, 1141, date shop or store.

ā-t nem , Rec. 12, 32, sleeping room (?)

ā-t nemm-t , chamber in which men and bodies were dismembered or dissected.

ā-t nett , cistern.

ā-t en reṭui 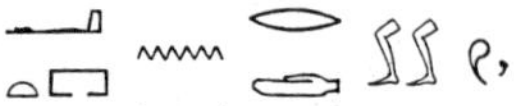, Rev. 11, 169, foot-cases, sandals (?)

ā-t ent-khet , Thes. 1254, summer-house.

ā-t ḥeq-t 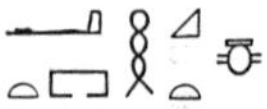, beer shop.

ā-t seba  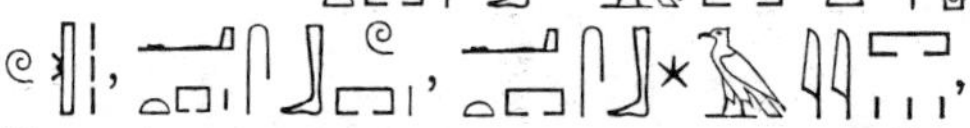, Rec. 18, 63, school, college; Copt. ⲁⲛⲍⲏⲃⲉ.

ā-t tau 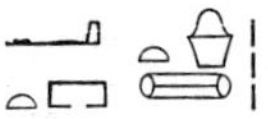, baker's shop.

ā-t , limb, member, piece; plur. , U. 219, [illegible] [illegible].

ā-ti [illegible], Hh. 433, [illegible], the two members.

ā-t neter [illegible], the god's body.

ā-t uā-t em ȧner [illegible], a single piece of stone, monolith; [illegible], Mar. Karn. 42, 16.

ā, āi [illegible], [illegible], to cry out, to speak loud, to recite; see [illegible].

ā [illegible], Oh! Alas!

ā [illegible], U. 575, [illegible], P 695, Methen 8, charter, writing. register, list, document, will, original document, roll, deed, order, edict; plur. [illegible].

ā-ti [illegible], Rec. 21, 14, [illegible], L.D. III, 229C, list, register, catalogue; plur. [illegible], Amherst Pap. 29; [illegible], P.S.B. 19, 261.

ā, to grow (of the moon).

ā, darkness, night.

ā-t, goat.

ā, , , , , , Amherst Pap. 30, a vessel, a pot, a measure, pot of incense.

ā, a measure; , a half measure.

ā-t, , Rev. 14, 9, mistress, great lady, queen; = , P.S.B. 20, 191.

ā, , great one, chief.

ā ā, god twice great (Thoth).

ā mes, first born, eldest born.

ā, āa, , , , , B.D. 125, III, 14, IV, 650, Wazîr 10, Pap. 3024, 151, here, hereabouts.

āa, āai, , , to journey, to travel (?)

āa = .

āa-t, , , house, abode, estate, domain.

āa-t-shetat, "hidden chamber," *i.e.*, the sanctuary of a temple.

Āa, Āai, , B.D. 125; see **Āati**.

āa, U. 324, , , , , , , leaf of a door, door, cover of a sarcophagus. Dual: **āaui**, U. 269, , M. 778, , N. 1101, , P. 276, , , Rec. 29, 153, , , , , , , , , , , the two leaves of a door, door; **āau, āaiu**, T. 288, 391, , , , , , Rec. 27, 231, 30, 67, , , , , , , , , , doors.

āau, , doorkeeper, πασπτοφόρος.

āa ur, "great door," title of a high official.

Āaiu-en-sbaiu-Ṭuatiu, , B.D. 141, 58, the doorkeepers of the doors of the Ṭuat.

Āaiu-shetaiu, B.D. 141, 56, the gods of the secret doors.

āa, āai, , , , , , , , , , , to be great, to be large, to be mighty, to be spacious or abundant, to be powerful; , great; Copt. ⲁⲓⲁⲓ. The ordinary use of **āa** is illustrated by the following:—

āa ȧb, , N. 651, B.M. 138, great of heart, *i.e.*, proud, arrogant.

āa ȧru, great of forms, *i.e.*, of very many forms.

āa baiu, great of souls, *i.e.*, of mighty will.

āa peḥti, , great of valour, most brave.

āa maā-kheru, great of truth-speaking, most truthful.

āa-mu, great of water, the **Āamu.**

āa mertu, greatly beloved.

āa nerut 
[illegible], great of terror, most terrible, most victorious.

āa nekhtut , most strong.

āa ra 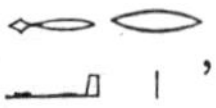, great of mouth, *i.e.*, boastful, insolent.

āa rennu , great of names, a title of Thoth.

āa ḥerit , great of terror, most terrifying

āa khāu , great one of risings, a title of Rā.

āa kheperu , great of transformations, *i.e.*, of many changes.

āa khenu 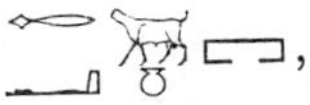, of large interior (of a barge).

āa senṭ 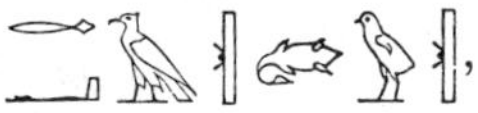, most fearful.

āa sheps , most holy, most august.

āa en shefit 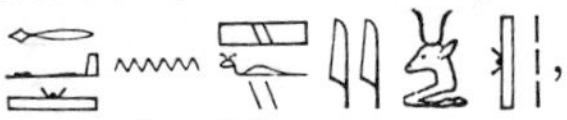, most terrible, or most awe-inspiring.

āa-āa , to be doubly great.

āa-āaȧu , very great men.

āau , very, exceedingly.

āa  or [illegible],
[illegible], great, grand, mighty, important, noble, lofty, weighty, chief; fem. [illegible],
[illegible]; dual, masc. [illegible],
fem. [illegible], N. 1385, [illegible]; [illegible],
Thoth, the twice great; plur. [illegible],
.

āḳ 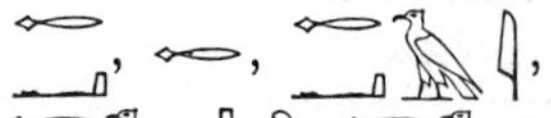, P. 696, [illegible]
, Rec. 31, 29, a great person, chief, officer, governor, noble, a great god as opposed to a little god ;
plur. , T. 325, [illegible],
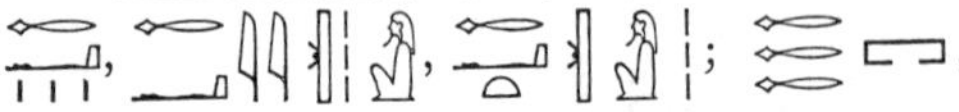,
nobles of the palace; , very, very great gods.

āa-t 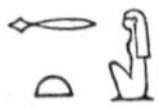, a great goddess; [illegible], two great goddesses.

āa ȧḥenut-ḥen-f 
[illegible], director of the royal corvée.

āa ā-t 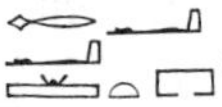, marshal of the court.

Āa-t-em-Ȧneb-ḥetch 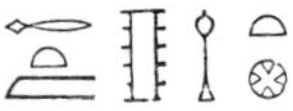, B.D.G. 57, a gate at Philae.

āa em āḥā 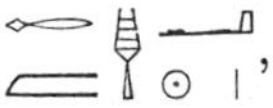, a man advanced in age.

āa en uāb , chief libationer.

āa en utcha , director of storehouse (Bêt al-Mâl).

āa en per 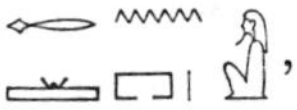, steward, major-domo.

Āa-m'k ,
[illegible], name of the sacred boat of Edfû.

āa en mu , head of the stream.

āa en mer 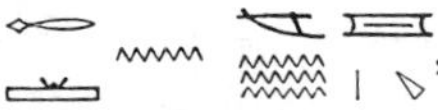, chief of the port, harbour master.

āa en sa , phylarch.

āa en qeṭut , director of marines.

āa kha 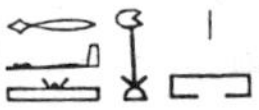, chief of the diwân.

Āa , U. 513, [illegible]
[illegible], T. 325, a fire-god.

Āai , Rec. 6, 137, a god of the dead.

Āait 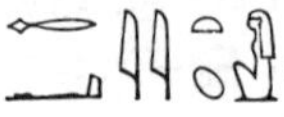, Ombos II, 132.

Āa-t-ȧakhu , Ṭuat IX, a singing-goddess.

Āa-t-Āaṭ-t  , Ṭuat IX, a singing-goddess.

Āa-āmi-khekh 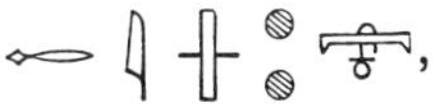, Thes. 31, the god of the 12th hour of the day.

Āa-āru , B.D.G. 104, Osiris of Athribis.

Āa-t-āru , Ṭuat IX, a fiery, blood-drinking serpent.

Āa-āter , Ṭuat I, a singing-god.

Āa-perti 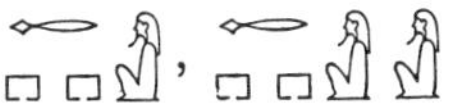, Rec. 21, 14, Pharaoh; see **Per-āa.**

Āa-peḥti 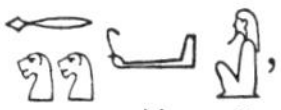, Denderah IV, 63, a bull-god; , Rec. 21, 14, a title.

Āa-peḥti-petpet-khaskhet  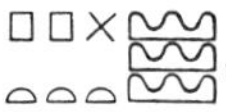, Lanzone 106, a composite hawk-crocodile-cat-bull-lion-goose-ape-ram-god.

Āa-peḥti-reh 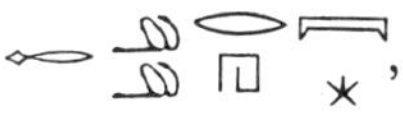, a god of a Dekan.

Āa-peḥti-rehen-pet-ta , Denderah II, 10, one of the 36 Dekans.

Āa-nest , Ṭuat VI, a god (?)

āa-hemhem  (Demotic form), "Great of roarings," a name of Āmen.

Āa-ḥerit , Ṭuat VI, a god of terror.

Āa-kheru 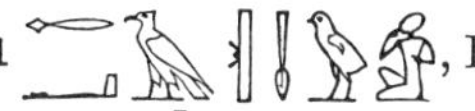, B.D. 144, the Watcher of the 7th Ārit.

Āa-kherpu-mes-āru 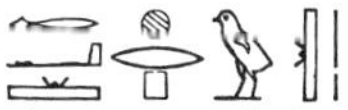 , Ṭuat X, the name of the door of Ṭuat X.

Āa-saaḥ 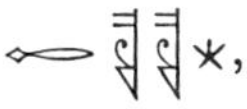, Tomb of Seti I, one of the 36 Dekans.

Āa-t sāpu , P.S.B. 25, 218, a title of Sekhmit.

Āa-sekhemu , B.D. 149, the god of the 11th Āat.

Āa-sti , Tomb Rameses IX, pl. 10, a serpent-god.

Āa-t-Setkau , Ṭuat VIII, the name of a Circle.

Āa-shefit 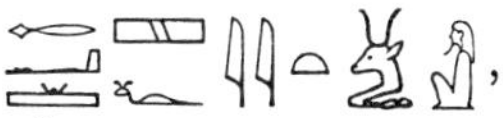, a title of several solar gods.

Āa-t-shefit , Thes. 28, , Denderah III, 241, , Berg. II, 8, the goddess of the 4th hour of the night.

Āa-shefit , Denderah IV, 84, the name of the 4th Pylon.

Āat-Shefshefit , Ṭuat VIII, the gate of the 9th division of the Ṭuat.

Āa-t-qar-uaba  , Nesi-Āmsu 32, 49, a serpent-fiend.

āa , to beget, to generate.

Āa-pesṭ-rehen-pet , Denderah II, 10, one of the 36 Dekans.

āa , a disease of the genital organs.

āa , Ebers Pap. 99, 12, hair of the pubes.

āa, āa-t  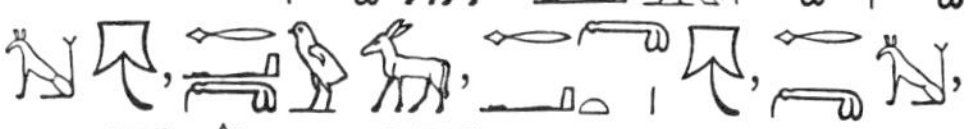, [illegible], [illegible], Rec. 25, 192, [illegible], Koller Pap. 1, 3, [illegible], Bubastis 34A, [illegible], ass, she-ass; plur. [illegible], [illegible], [illegible], [illegible], [illegible], [illegible], Rec. 25, 195, [illegible], Rev. 13, 35.

Āau , [illegible], B.D. 125, III, 12, the Ass-god, a form of Rā.

āaut [illegible], [illegible], Rec. 30, 67, [illegible], [illegible], pillars, colonnade.

Āaut-ent-Khert-neter 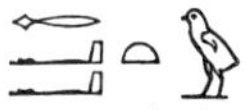 [illegible], B.D. 99, 13, oar-rests of the magical boat.

āa-t, Rev. 12, 63, 70, a bandlet, a garment, woven work; plur. ; Copt. ЄΙⲀⲀⲨ (?)

āa-t, Rec. 20, 40, , stone of great price or value, gem, amulet, tumour; plur. , , rare stones; , N. 743, pots of precious stones.

āaut, āut, , glands of the throat and neck.

āa to beat (?)

āaā , M. 136, , N. 185, 647, well, fountain; plur. , P. 411, M. 588, , N. 1194, , Rec. 26, 224.

āaāui, U. 576, N. 965, the two sides of the ladder.

Āai, the Phallus-god.

Āai, Tomb of Seti I, one of the 75 forms of Rā (No. 34).

āai-t , , house, abode, chamber.

āai-t, roof (?) ceiling (?)

Āait-ȧr-t, B.D.G. 147, the place of sunset.

āai, flame, fire, heat.

āaiāai, to rejoice, to exult.

āau , , , Rec. 18, 183, to speak with violence, to curse, to abuse, to blaspheme; Copt. ⲞⲨⲀ.

Āau, Ṭuat IV, a jackal-headed porter.

āau, to flourish.

āau, flax, linen; Copt. ΙⲀⲨ, ЄΙⲀⲀⲨ.

āaua , , to steal, to rob, to plunder.

āauait, B.M. 657, a reaping.

āauȧu, boy, girl, maiden.

āab, to be acceptable to anyone, to please; , Peasant 42, , Amherst Pap. I, things or feelings which produce pleasure.

āab-t, U. 579, , T. 383, , U. 193, , T. 73, , P. 161, , P. 372, , N. 1148, , P. 610, , M. 203, N. 685, , N. 703, , , Rec. 26, 235, 31, 164, offering, sacrifice, sepulchral meals. Later forms are:— , , , , , , , , , , , , , .

āab-t, vessel for ceremonial purification.

āabb, ābb , , spear, harpoon.

Āabi, B.D. (Saïte) 78, 38 a god.

āabu, a kind of herb?

āaber-t, balsam, unguent.

āabes, fire, flame.

āabag , [illegible], Rec. 32, 86, to be weak, or helpless.

āabṭ , slave, worker; Heb. אֶבֶד, or עוֹבֵד.

āap 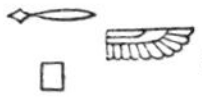, to fly; Heb. עוּף.

Āapep 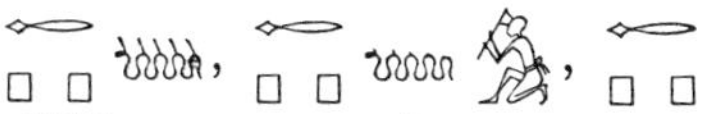 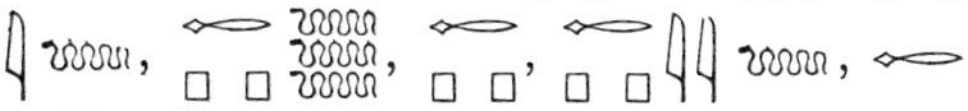, [illegible], Rec. 6, 158, a monster mythological serpent which produced thunder, lightning, storm, hurricanes, mist, cloud, fog, and darkness, and was the personification of evil. He was called by 77 "accursed names"; Copt. ⲁⲫⲟⲫⲓ, ⲁⲫⲱⲫⲓ.

āapi 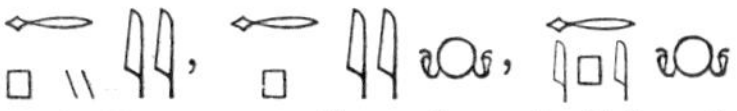, [illegible], the winged disk, the summer solstice.

Āapit , a goddess.

āapinṭ , unguent, incense (?)

Āapef , [illegible], B.D. 39, 2, a serpent-fiend.

āafa , to be greedy, glutton.

āam , to clasp, to grasp, to seize.

āam , , an Asiatic, a nomad of the Eastern Desert; plur. [illegible], 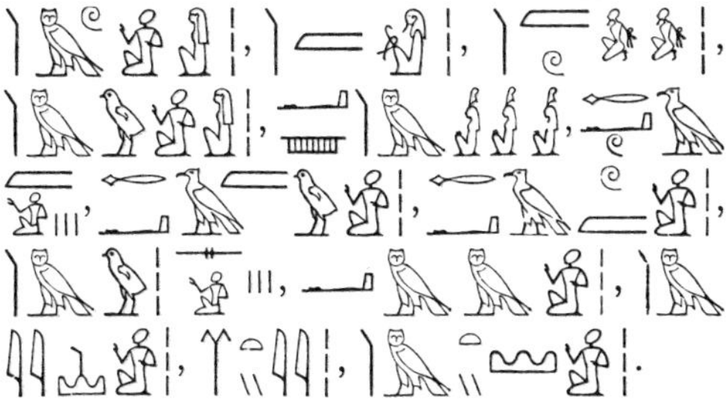.

āamu , [illegible], Rec. 33, 118, [illegible], shepherd, nomad, herdsman, farmer; plur. [illegible] [illegible], fellaḥîn.

āamit , IV, 743, , an Asiatic woman; plur. [illegible], Rec. 10, 150.

Āamu , Ṭuat V, the souls of the Āamu in the Ṭuat.

āam 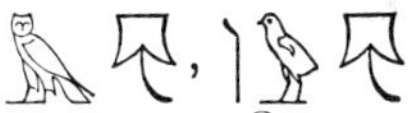, animal, beast; 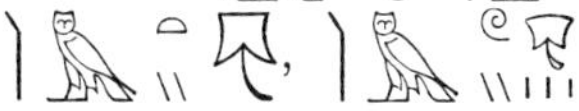, cattle, the sacred animals of Egypt, *e.g.*, Apis, Mnevis, the ram of Mendes, etc.

āam , to bring down birds and animals with a boomerang.

āamu , IV, 335, throw-stick, boomerang; plur. [illegible], boomerangs (?) nets (?)

āam , crystal, some kind of sparkling stone.

Āam , B.D. (Saïte), 62, 2, a god.

āam' , to eat, to understand, to perceive.

āamut  , Hymn to Uraei 25, a kind of plant.

āamm ḥa-t , R.E. 4, 75, sweet, pleasant.

āamāa , part of a bed.

āamāq 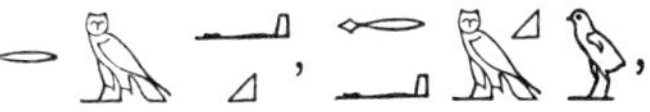, , valley; Heb. עֵמֶק.

āamāṭi 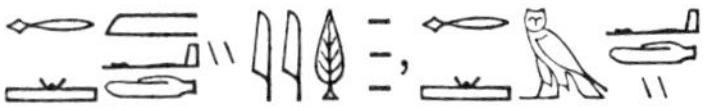 , part of waggon.

āameḥ 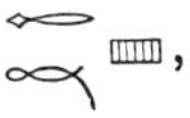, B.D. (Saïte) 30, 4, a kind of stone.

āanniu 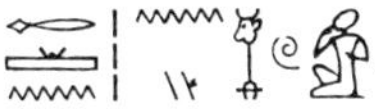, ape; Copt. ⲉⲛ.

āann , to sing; Heb. עָנָה, Arab. غَنَّى.

āanatả , singing-woman (?)

āanb-t , axe, hatchet; plur.  .

āanra, pebbles, round stones.

āanratȧt, Gol. 5, 14, 15 = , or , upper chamber, balcony; Heb. עֲלִיָּה.

āanḥ, a winding serpent.

āankh (Demotic form), to live, life; Copt. ⲱⲛϩ, ⲱⲛϧ.

āankh, Rec. 33, 137, to swear an oath; Copt. ⲁⲛⲁϣ.

āant, spice, perfume = .

āar (āal), to ascend; Copt. ⲁⲗⲉ.

āar-t, a kind of stone, a natural block of stone (?)

āarara, Anastasi I, 23, 3, pebbles; Copt. ⲁⲗ.

āarā, a part of a building; , Rec. 3, 55, tenons of a coffin.

āaref, Rev. 11, 184 = ; Copt. ⲱⲣϥ, ⲱⲣⲉⲃ.

Āar-n-āaref, Rev. 11, 184, Horus of bandages; Copt. ⲟⲣⲡⲟⲩⲱⲣϥ.

āarsh, cult, service.

āarshan, Rec. 21, 91, lentils, beans; Copt. ⲁⲣϣⲁⲛ, ⲁⲣϣⲓⲛ.

āaratȧ, Rec. 21, 82, an upper chamber; Heb. עֲלִיָּה.

Āartȧbuhait, Harris 501, B. 9, a female demon.

Āaḥ, the Moon-god = .

Āaḥpi, Annales III, 179, a god.

Āasit, L.D. 3, 138, Lanzone 140, Rec. 13, 78, a goddess of war and of the chase.

Āasiti-Khar, Rec. 7, 196, the name of a goddess of Syria.

Āaserttu; see .

Āasek, M. 143, N. 648, a god.

āashasha-t, throat, gullet.

āasharana, a kind of seed or fruit.

āashaq, to oppress, oppression, to usurp, violence; Heb. עָשַׁק.

āaqer, 2, 68, 8 . . . .

āag, Peasant 185, , to beat, to bastinado.

āag-t, nail, claw, toenail, hoof; plur. , P. 310, , Rec. 30, 72.

āag-t, the oil made from the āgit plant, .

āagit, an offering of some kind.

āag = .

āagartȧ, , L.D. III, 219E, 19, , chariot; Copt. ⲁϭⲟⲗⲧⲉ, Heb. עֲגָלָה.

āagasu 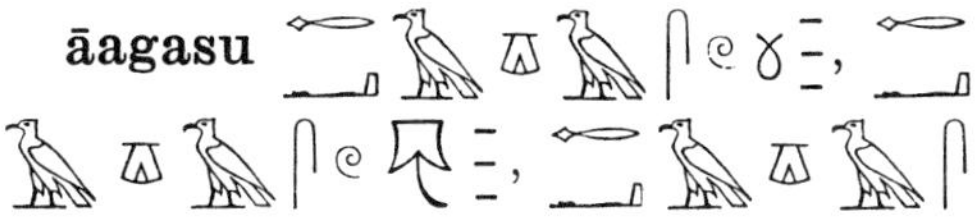 , Gol. 13, 107, [illegible], Sallier Pap. II, 4, 2, 5, 8, cord, belt [illegible]rdle (?); Heb. עֶכֶם (?)

Āagm' , the name of a fiend.

āatkh , a woven stuff.

āaṭ , a piece of fertile ground.

Āaṭ-en-sekhet 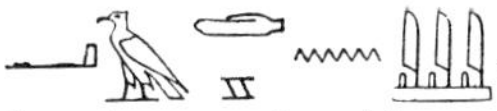, B.D.G. 136, the second station on the old caravan road between the Nile and the Red Sea.

āaṭ-t , a kind of bread-cake.

āaṭ-t , Sall. II, 3, 1, 2, Rec. 35, 161, gate sockets (?) slabs of stone.

Āaṭi , [illegible], B.D. 125, one of the 42 assessors of Osiris.

Āaṭiu  [illegible], Tomb Seti I, one of the 75 forms of Rā (No. 23).

āaṭ , of a livid colour, pale (of the face), yellow; Copt. ⲟⲩⲟⲧⲟⲩⲉⲧ.

āaṭna 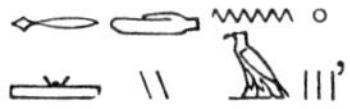, lentils; Heb. עֲדָשׁ.

āaṭṭȧu , men who conspire.

āatch , pallor, paleness (of the face); Copt. ⲟⲩⲟⲧⲟⲩⲉⲧ.

āatch-t , fat, grease.

āatchamm , a kind of oil.

āatchar , to help, to assist; var. [illegible].

āatchr-t , a kind of balsam tree.

āȧu, āȧuā , Rec. 30, 196, heir.

Āȧu-taui , B.D. 125, III, 38, a title of Thoth.

Āȧbṭ , the name of a mythological fish.

āā , to bring, to carry.

āā 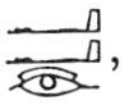, Rec. 10, 61, 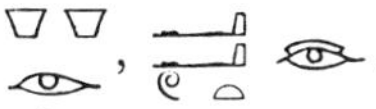, , A.Z. 1877, 61, to doze, to be drowsy, to sleep.

āā , tomb, pyramid.

Āātt , the pyramid region, the necropolis, the Other World.

Āātt , Berg. II, 11, a goddess, the personification of the pyramid district.

āā, āāi , [illegible], to cry out, to shout, to speak loudly.

āā 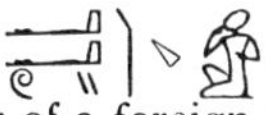, Rec. 14, 42, foreigner (?) speaker of a foreign tongue (?)

āā , joy.

Āā , Denderah IV, 79, an ape-god who slew Āapep.

āā 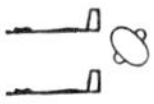, filth (?)

āā , flesh and bone, heir, inheritance, posterity; an accursed heir [illegible].

āāu , seed.

āā , to tie, to bind, to compress = [illegible] (?) = Copt. ⲱϥⲉ.

āāa , Aelt. Tex. 28, a kind of tunic.

āāa , Nav. Lit. 26 . . . .

āāam , [illegible], a kind of plant.

āāam , the seed of the same.

āāb, Annales III, 110, a vessel, a bowl, a copper vessel, spoon.

āāb, to card wool, to comb; , L.D. III, 65A, 15 . . . .

āābṭ, incense vase.

āāf, to squeeze out, to wring out, to press out oil, to strain; Copt. ωϥε.

āām, canal.

Āām, Edfû I, 81, a name of the Nile.

āām, an earthenware vessel (?)

āān, ape; plur. ; Copt. εn.

āānā, ape; plur. , Koller Pap. 4, 3.

Āān, Berg. I, 19, a minister of the dead.

Āānu, Jour. As. 1908, 313, the ape-god; Copt. εn.

Āānāu, B.D. 126, 2, the four ape-gods who judged the dead.

āān, Jour. E.A. III, 105 . . . .

āān, camp, place, tent, station.

āāḥ, to rejoice.

āāḥ, Rev. 11, 151, cattle; Copt. εϩε.

Āāḥ-ti, a pair of goddesses.

āina, a kind of stone.

āut, sheep and goats, animals, flocks; , animal kept in a shrine; , sacred animal.

āu-t, desert game.

āu-t-neb- etc. , all kinds of four-footed beasts.

āu, wretched, miserable.

āu-t, a beast of a man; plur. .

āu, sins, evil deeds (?)

āu-t, stick with a curved end (Lacau).

āu-t, U. 283, , M. 766, , P. 659, , staff, crook, sceptre (?)

āu, M. 253, to travel.

āu-t (?), a call house (?)

āu, a kind of wood.

āuāu, Thes. 1203, Rec. 8, 136, to smash, to crush.

āua, āuai, Peasant 292, , Thes. 1252, , R.E. 6, 26, , to steal, to rob, to injure, to do violence, to break, to plunder, to waste, to reap grain.

āuaṇ 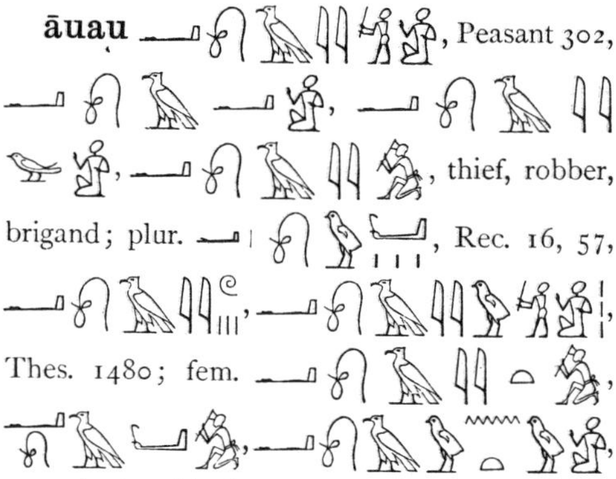, Peasant 302, thief, robber, brigand; plur. Rec. 16, 57, Thes. 1480; fem. one who is robbed.

āua-t 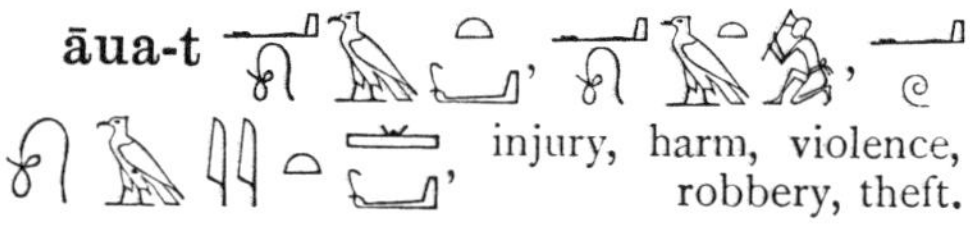, injury, harm, violence, robbery, theft.

Āuai 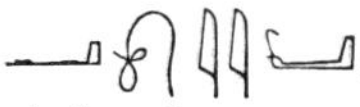, Ṭuat III, a winged serpent-headed god.

Āuait , B.D. 17, 26, a goddess who kept the register of the punishments inflicted on the foes of Osiris.

āua , P. 442, N. 1127, P. 142, Rec. 30, 191, to ferment, to become sour.

āuait , some kind of fermented drink.

āuab , courtyard; see **uba**.

āuā , to give a gift, to present.

Āuāḥa (Āḥa) , Mission 13, 126, a goddess.

āubbu 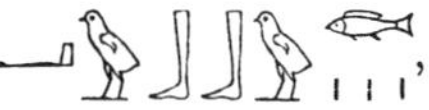, Peasant 229, a kind of fish.

āun 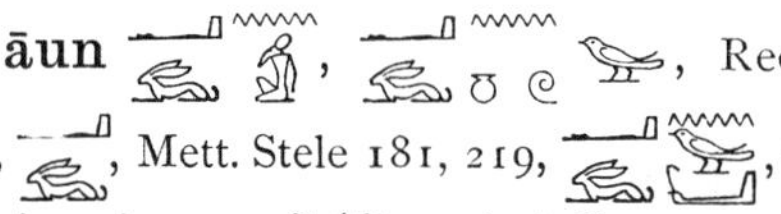, Rec. 36, 78, Mett. Stele 181, 219, to cry out in pain, to wail (like a jackal).

āun , to rob, to steal, to plunder, to commit deeds of violence.

āun-t , robbery, violence.

āunu 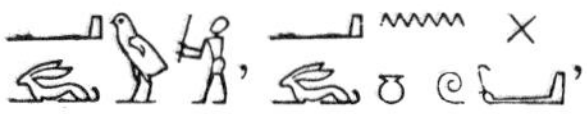, robber, ravager, oppressor.

āun-ȧb 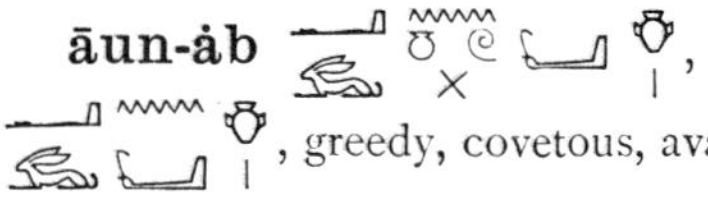, Thes. 1207, greedy, covetous, avaricious.

āunuti , Ȧmen. 10, 10, robber.

Āun , a god.

Āun-ȧb , Mett. Stele 189, the scorpion that stung Horus and killed him.

āun-t 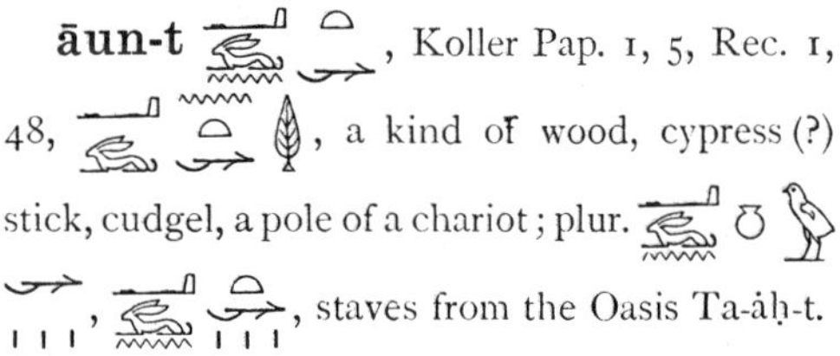, Koller Pap. 1, 5, Rec. 1, 48, a kind of wood, cypress (?) stick, cudgel, a pole of a chariot; plur. staves from the Oasis Ta-āḥ-t.

āun , to sleep, to slumber.

āunra , pebble, stone; plur.

āuratchaut (ārtchatu) , charioteers (?)

āuq , stream, canal.

āug , to heat, to cook (?)

āutcharu , auxiliaries, a class of soldiers.

āutcharu (ātcharu) 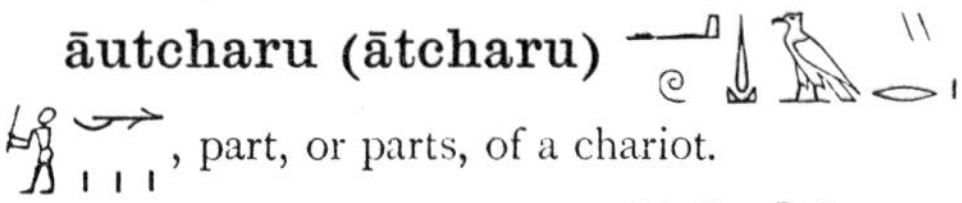, part, or parts, of a chariot.

āutchatȧ (ātchatȧ) , Alt. K. 306 . . . .

āb , to be renowned, famous, strength (?)

āb 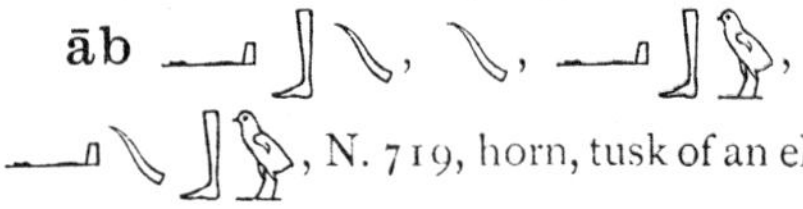, U. 270, N. 719, horn, tusk of an elephant;

plur. , U. 270, , N. 719; dual, , , Rougé, I.H. II, 114; = Dhu'l Ḳarnên; , he with horns ready to gore; , U. 577, the four horns of the bull of Rā, the four horns of the world.

ābāti (?) , Thes. 1198, the gorer.

āb , tusk of ivory; see **ab** , .

Ābui , Ṭuat V, , B.D. (Saïte) 64, 14, a god who burnt the dead.

Ābu-tt , the name of a serpent on the royal crown.

āb , B.D. (Saïte) 134, 4, a star.

Āb-peq (?) , Tuat IV, an ally of Neḥeb-kau.

Ābet-neteru-s , Ṭuat X, a lioness-goddess.

āb seshu , , , title of Thoth and of a kind of priest.

Āb-shā , , Ṭuat VII, a crocodile-god which guarded the "symbols."

Āb-ta , Ṭuat IX, a serpent-gatekeeper.

āb , a kind of incense.

āb, ābā , , to resist, to revolt against, to oppose by force.

ābb , to fight, to hurl a spear or any weapon.

ābut , opposition, resistance.

āb , , , resistance, opposition, what is opposed to existing things.

āb , , , enemy, rebel, fiend.

āb , to sink, to drop back, to diminish (of the Nile).

āb , , Rougé, I.H. II, 125, to sink into [the ground] through fear (of the feet).

ābāb , , to push a way into, to open up.

āb, ābā , , , Thes. 1483, , , , , A.Z. 79, 51, IV, 101, 368, 751, to contradict, to gainsay, to oppose in speech; , Rec. 10, 61, to contradict his statement; , Mar. Karn. 44, 35, contradiction.

ābāb , Rec. 8, 124, , Rec. 23, 203, , to contradict, to gainsay.

ābāb-t , , R.E. 7, 24, contradiction.

āb , , , to face someone or something, to meet, to join, to unite with; **em āb** , , U. 16, 568, T. 372, N. 751, , , , , , , , , , , , , together with, face to face with, opposite; **er āb** , P. 815.

ābu , Rec. 3, 116, cattle for sacrifice.

āb , , a bird with a loud harsh voice.

āb , to weave.

ābāb , to weave.

Ābuti , the two weavers, Isis and Nephthys.

āb, to purify, to make clean.

ābu, P. 449, N. 912, , , , purifications, cleansings, libations, washings with water.

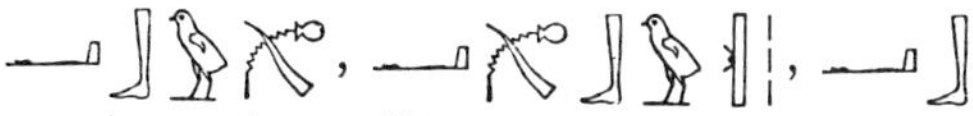

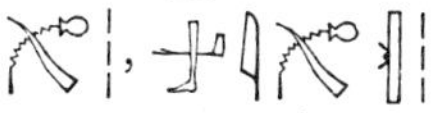

ābit, offering.

āb, āb-t, , , , a vessel, vase of purification.

āb, to embalm.

āba, P. 175, , , , to make an offering, to present a propitiatory gift.

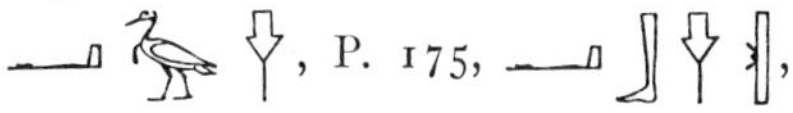

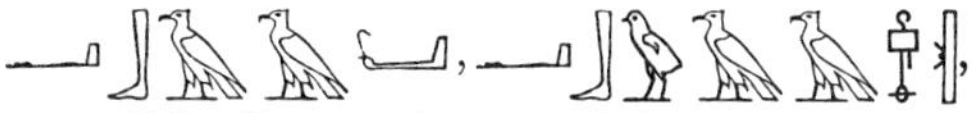

ābu, ābut, , , , , , , a gift, an offering; plur. , P. 552, , T. 258, , Rec. 33, 5, , ibid. 29, 156, , , , , .

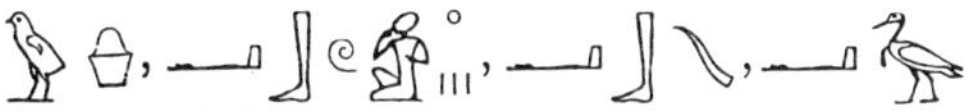

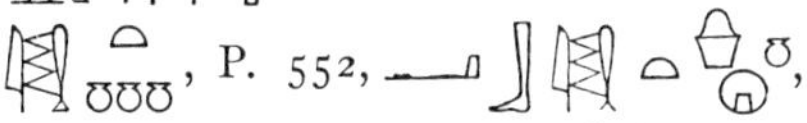

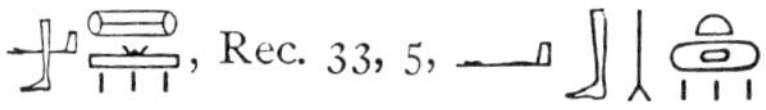

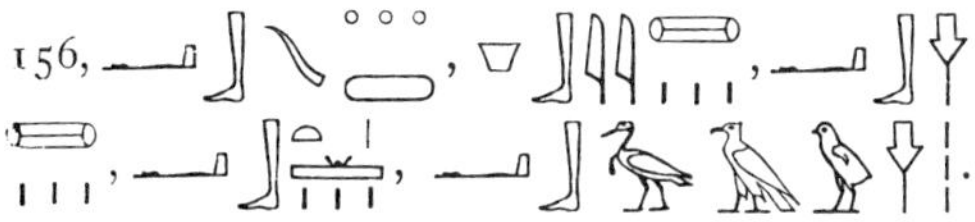

Āb, Ṭuat II, a grain-god.

Āba-taui, Hh. 456 . . . . . .

āba, , , , , , N. 1072, altar, a table for offerings.

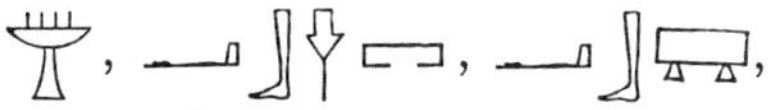

āba, , , , , , a slab of stone on which offerings were placed.

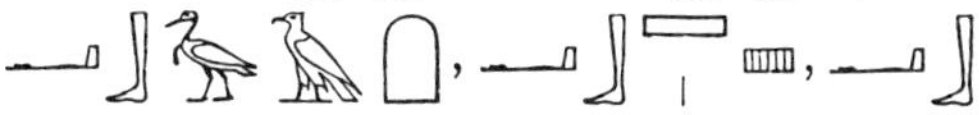

āb, a kind of stone; plur. .

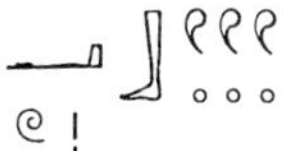

āb-t, N. 503, a kind of grain.

āb[a]u, Peasant 24, a kind of stone.

ābiu, , , the gods who slay.

āb-t, Palermo Stele, , sanctuary, shrine, any holy place; = Ισειον.

ābu, a festival at which the making of offerings was obligatory; plur. , , , L.D. III, 194, 35.

āba, , , T. 227, P. 708, Rec. 31, 166, to penetrate, force a way into.

āba, P. 339, , M. 641,  , Rec. 27, 231, to act as captain, to direct.

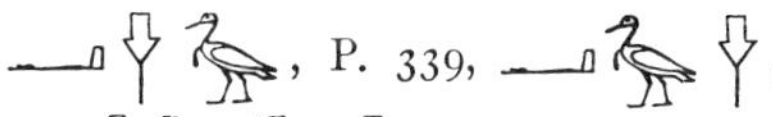

āb, āba, U. 274, N. 798,  , U. 473, P. 311, 613, , N. 673, , U. 206, sceptre, staff, stick.

ābit, , , , , staff, stick.

ābut, P. 186, , M. 301, P. 666, staff.

ābb-t, staff, sceptre, stick.

āb-t, kidney, testicle.

ābu, A.Z. 49, 59 . . . . . .

āb, Rec. 11, 92, , , , , , to shine, to show different colours, "shot" as in "shot" silk.

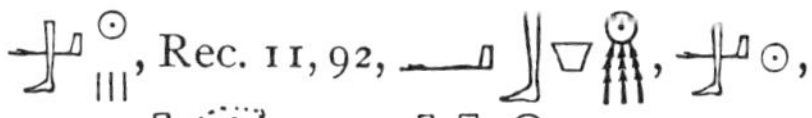

āb, , , , variegated, spotted; , spotted or speckled or striped plumage.

āb shuti, Thes. 414, he of the variegated wings, a title of Horus of Edfû.

ābu, people, men and women.

ābi, animal, reptile, or insect (?)

ābāb, Rec. 20, 41 . . . .

ābābu, Rec. 15, 178, to rejoice, to dance.

ābb, to see.

ābb, , to desire, to love, to be desired.

ābb, to fly, the flying scarab; var., the flier.

ābb, , , beetle, scarab.

Ābb, B.D.G. 1394, a form of Osiris.

āba, , , , to see.

ābā āui, to open the hands in greeting.

ābut, , ropes, bonds, fetters.

Ābbut, Ṭuat IX, the nets (?) used in snaring Āapep.

Ābbuitiu, Ṭuat IX, three gods who fettered .

ābu, , , Rec. 16, 3, , a mass of plants or flowers, bouquet.

ābnekh, , , frog (?) toad (?)

Ābrāskktiāks = 'Αβρασαξ, Leemans, Papyrus III, 210–213.

ābeḥ-t, P. 334, , M. 637, , P. 552, , Hh. 227, 247, to pour out water or seed, to create, to make, to fashion.

ābesh, vase, pot, vessel.

ābesh, U. 622, , U. 539, T. 296, P. 230 . . . . .

Ābesh, Ṭuat X, a form of Ptaḥ.

Ābesh, Thes. 112, one of the seven stars of Orion.

Ābesh, a benevolent serpent-god.

ābesh, T. 119, 318, N. 1344, a kind of wine.

āp, R.E. 3, 111, a pyramid tomb, Apis tomb; , Apis tomb of Memphis (?)

āp, P. 703, , , , , , a verb of motion, to travel, to go, to go in, to go out, to escape, to walk, to march, to journey, , tramplings under foot.

āp, , , , , , to fly, the winged disk, the summer solstice.

Āpi, , Rec. 35, 56, , , , Rec. 14, 7, the "flier," a name of the Sun-god; , the rising sun.

āpu, Hymn of Darius 37, scarab, beetle.

Āp-ur, B.D.G. 798, Osiris in the form of a beetle.

Āpep; see .

Apāp, B.M. No. 383; see and ,

āpāp, ground, earth, estate.

āpāp, brick or tile kiln.

āpi, Rev. 12, 91, account = .

āpenn-t, , serpent, worm.

āper, P. 663, 783, M. 775, , , P. 178, T. 321, U. 507, , M. 268, , N. 888, , , , , , , to be equipped, to be provided with, furnished (of a house); , Hymn of Darius 38.

āper , 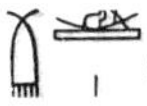, a boat equipped with everything necessary and a crew; , Thes. 1296.

āperu 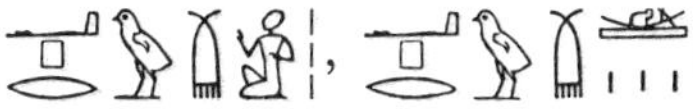, , crew of a boat or ship; , P. 396, M. 564, N. 1171.

āperu 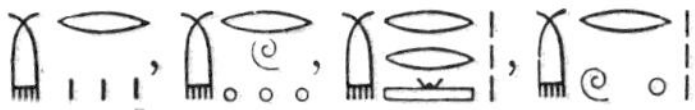, 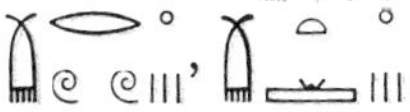, ornaments, fittings, chains attached to jewellery, accoutrements, furnishings; , the equipment of the royal barge; Mar. Karn. 53, 36, a woman's outfit.

āper , mantle, garment.

Āperit , a name of the Eye of Horus.

āper , the name of the 21st day of the month.

Āper , the god of the town of Āper.

Āper-peḥ , Berg. 1, 18, a protector of the dead.

Āper-peḥui , Thes. 818, Düm. Temp. Insch. 25, Rec. 16, 106: (1) a hawk-god, patron of learning and letters, who was one of the seven sons of Meḥurit; (2) a watcher of Osiris.

Āper-t-ra , Ṭuat I, a singing-goddess.

Āper-ḥer Nebtchet , Ṭuat XI, a form of the rising Sun.

Āper-ta , Tomb of Seti I, one of the 75 forms of Rā (No. 45).

āper , a kind of goose; the egg of the āper goose.

Āpriu 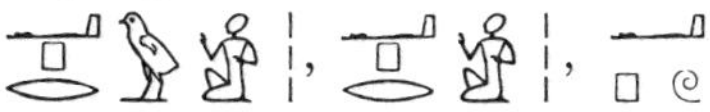 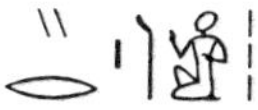, Harris I, 31, 8, a class of foreign stonemasons; var.  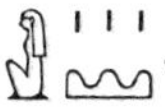, L.D. III, 219E, 17. They were once identified with the Hebrews.

āpesȧustāas , Rev. 11, 185 = ἀψευστως, unfeigned.

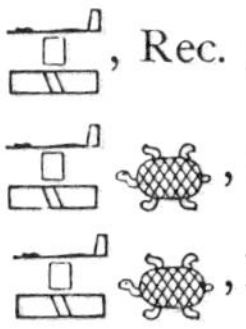

āpesh, Rec. 5, 97 . . . .

āpesh, tortoise, or turtle.

Āpesh, B.D. 161, the Turtle-god.

Āpshait , B.D. 36, 1, an insect which devoured the dead.

āpshut 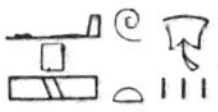, a kind of beetle; plur. of  (?)

āf, āff , Rec. 30, 201, 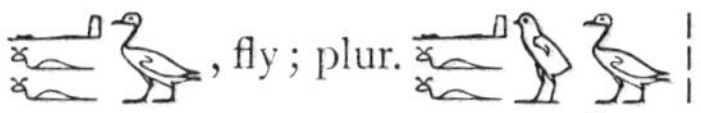, fly; plur. Rec. 31, 15; Copt. ⲁϥ.

āf ȧbȧ-t , Rev. 13, 20, honey fly, *i.e.*, bee.

āf 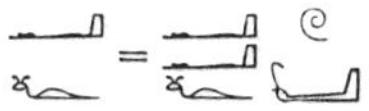; Copt. ⲱϥⲉ.

āff , crown, helmet, hat, diadem, cap.

āfāf , crocodile.

āf-t , Rev., gluttony.

āfa , plants, vegetables.

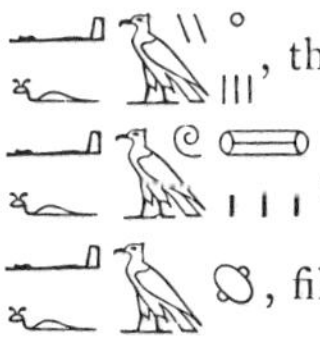

āfa, the seed of the same.

āfa, food, bread.

āfa, filth, dirt.

Āfat , Ṭuat VI, a god in mummy form.

Āfau , Ṭuat II, a god of one of the seasons of the year.

Āfa , T. 339, N. 951, N. 626, a class of divine beings in the Other World.

āfait 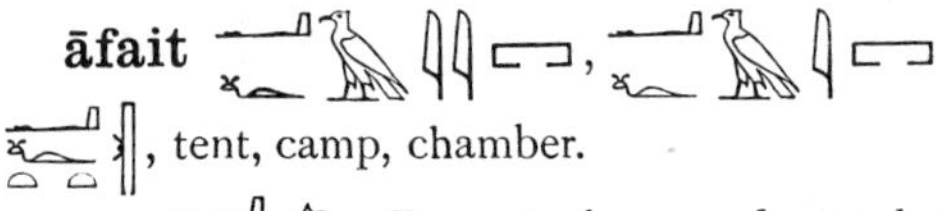, tent, camp, chamber.

āfā , Rev., to be greedy, a gluttonous man.

āfā 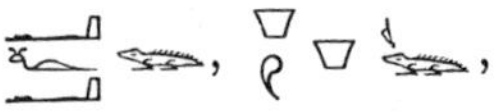, evil, calamity, crocodile.

āfen 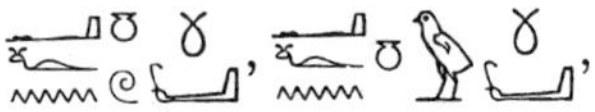, to bind, to tie, to tie something on.

āfen-t 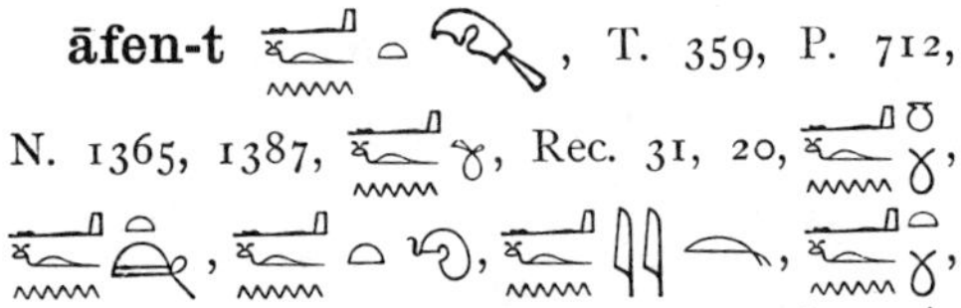, T. 359, P. 712, N. 1365, 1387, Rec. 31, 20, head-cloth, headdress, wig; plur. .

āfnut 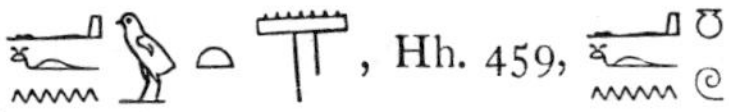, Hh. 459, 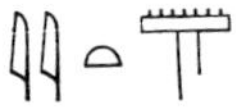, bandlet.

āfen-t 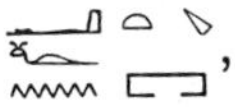, haunt, retreat, hiding place.

Āfnuit 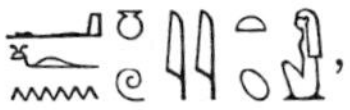, Ombos 2, 133, a goddess.

āfs 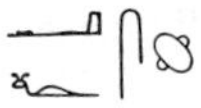, a disease of the eye.

Āfkiu , a group of gods.

āfṭit 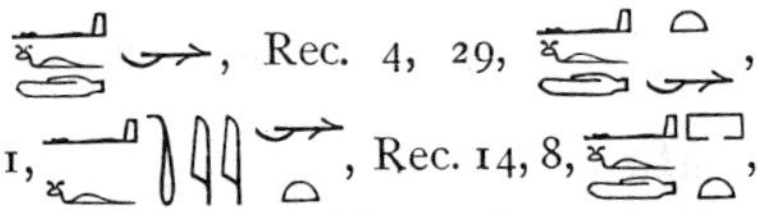, Rec. 4, 29, Rec. 8, 171, Rec. 14, 8, , Rec. 3, 56, , Rec. 30, 198, box, coffer, chest, coffin, sarcophagus; , Rec. 30, 187, 195, 31, 163, 32, 79.

āftch-t 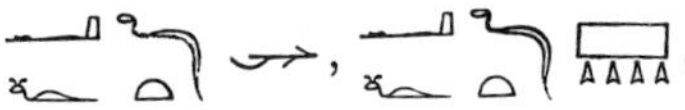, box, chest, sarcophagus.

ām 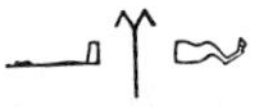, fore-arm, thigh (?)

ām , to grasp, fist.

ām 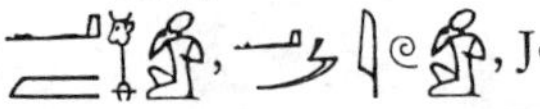, Jour. As. 1908, 290, to know, to understand; 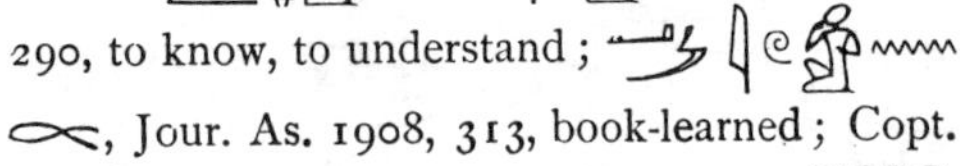, Jour. As. 1908, 313, book-learned; Copt. ⲉⲓⲙⲉ.

ām 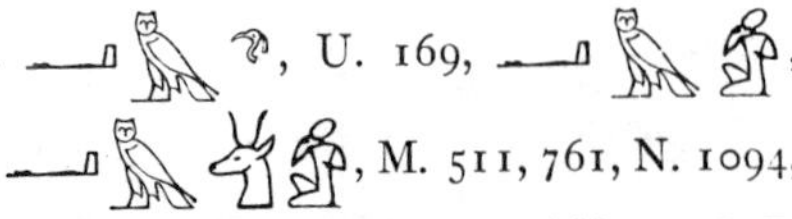, U. 169, P. 655, M. 511, 761, N. 1094, , to eat, to swallow, to devour.

ām-ḥa-t , to eat the heart, to feel remorse, to repent.

āmaāma-t , to devour.

ām-t , something that is eaten, food; Rec. 30, 195, flesh for eating.

ām , food.

āmām , food.

ām'it 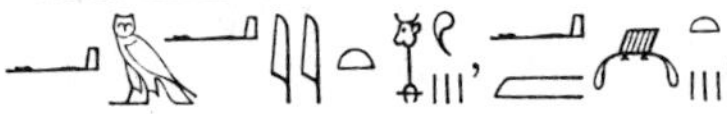, flesh-food.

Ām , Nesi-Àmsu 32, 36, devourer, a title of Āapep.

Ām , P. 445, M. 552, N. 1132, a god who fed on the hearts of the dead.

Āmām 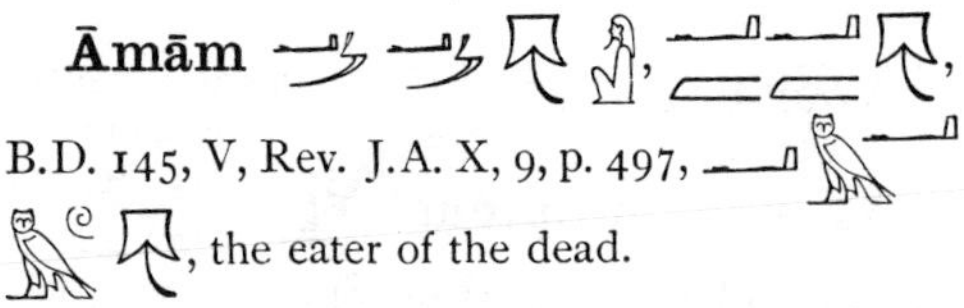, B.D. 145, V, Rev. J.A. X, 9, p. 497, the eater of the dead.

Āmiu , eaters (of the dead), a class of fiends.

Ām-àutiu (?) , Ṭuat III, a keeper of the Third Gate.

Ām-àsfetiu 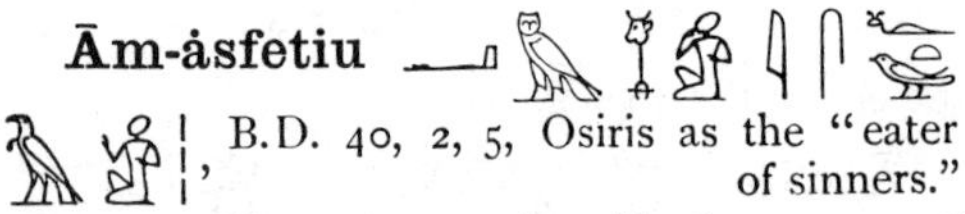, B.D. 40, 2, 5, Osiris as the "eater of sinners."

ām-ā , Rec. 31, 10, "eater of the arm," a mythological pig associated with Osiris.

Ām-ā, Ṭuat VI, the name of the pig in the boat.

Ām-ā-f, , B.D. 11, 2, a god.

Ām-āa, , , , , "eater of the ass," the name of a serpent which attacked the Sun-god.

Ām-āau, , B.D. 40, 1, a name of Āapep.

Āmu-āau, Ṭuat II, an ass-headed god with a knife-shaped phallus.

Āma-āsht, Rec. 13, 31, "eater of many, the name of a fiend.

Ām-baiu, "eater of souls," the name of a fiend.

Ām-mit, Ṭuat II, , , Papyrus of Ani, Pl. 3, a monster, part crocodile, part lion, and part hippopotamus, , which devoured the dead.

Ām-emit, B.D. 168, a goddess who strengthened the dead.

Ām-ḥeḥ, B.D. 17, 43, an invisible dog-faced god, who devoured human hearts in the River of Fire, and voided filth.

Āma-kha-t, Rec. 15, 17, one of the 42 assessors of Osiris.

Ām-khaibitu, Āmam-khaibitu, , , B.D. 125, II, one of the 42 assessors of Osiris; var.

Ām-khu, Ṭuat VI, a serpent-god who devoured the shadows and spirit-souls of the foes of Rā.

Āmāmti kheftiu, Ṭuat II, "eater of foes," an avenging goddess in the Ṭuat.

Ām-t-tcheru, , Ṭuat II, a goddess.

āmu, seed of a certain herb or plant.

āmām, a kind of plant or herb.

āmm, the roe of a fish, eggs, intestines.

āmu, āmāui (?), , pillars.

ām, weaving instrument or machine, shuttle of a loom (?)

āmām (āmm), to throw the boomerang, to catch in a net?

āmām, a garment, ornament.

āmām-t, , estate, parcel of land.

āmām (ām), places with water in them, wells, pools.

āma, N. 885, , T. 288, M. 65, , N. 126, to go sour (of wine).

āma-t, Rec. 29, 148, staff.

āma, a kind of stone.

āma, to winnow grain.

āmam, , , Rec. 21, 79, , , to perceive, to understand, to comprehend, to see, to know; , to show, to instruct; Copt. ⲉⲓⲙⲉ.

āmam, Āmen. 10, 1, , Āmen. 14, 17, ,

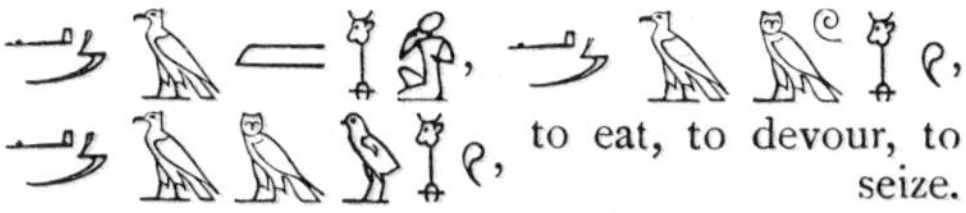 to eat, to devour, to seize.

Āmam  Nesi-Åmsu 32, 21, Rec. 14, 12, a name of Āapep.

Āmam-år-t (?) 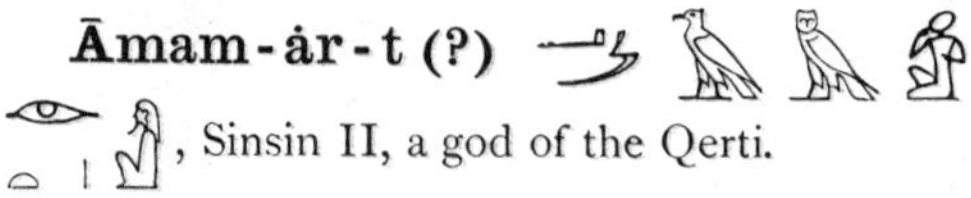 Sinsin II, a god of the Qerti.

āmam  a herb; the seed of the same.

Āmamu , an Asiatic people.

āman 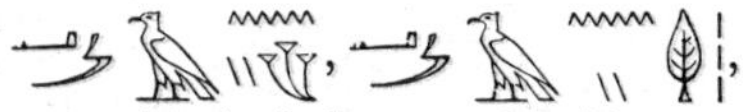, Rhind Pap. 32, a kind of plant, garden (?)

Āmanḥ 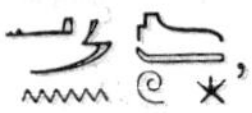, the god of the 11th hour of the day.

āmar , travellers (?)

āmå, āmā , R.E. 11, 122, clay; Copt. ⲟⲙⲙⲉ, ⲟⲙⲙⲓ.

āmā , Rec. 30, 196, to nurse.

āmā , T. 17, a plant (?)

āmā, āmām 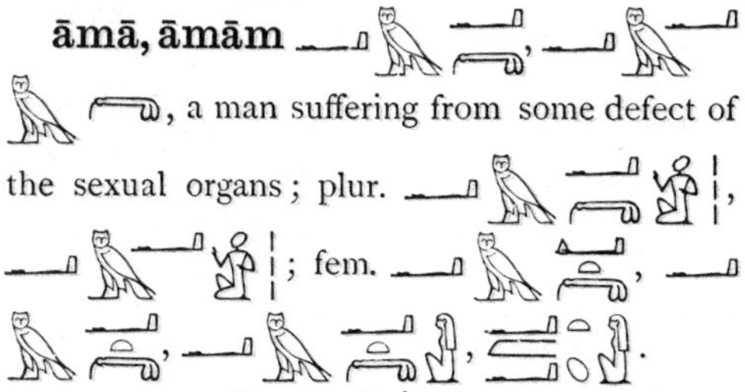 a man suffering from some defect of the sexual organs; plur.; fem.

āmā  Åmen. 24, 13, a disease of the sexual organs.

āmā-t , a liquid.

āmā 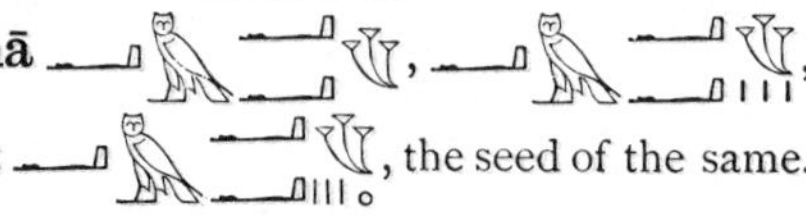 a herb; the seed of the same.

āmāa-t  Rec. 29, 148, boomerang, net (?); var.

āmāṭi-t , a kind of land.

āmu  Hh. 221, to be sour (of beer and wine).

Āmu , Ṭuat V, a fire-god.

āmth 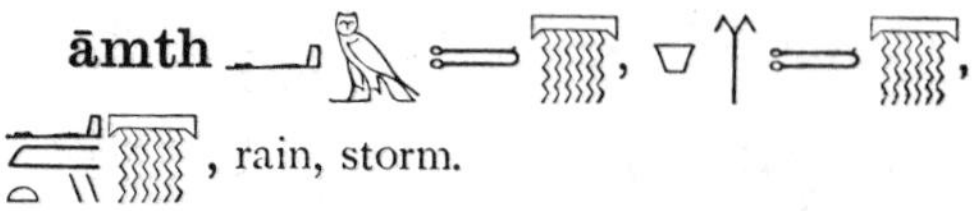 rain, storm.

āmṭ , to be languid, to collapse.

ān 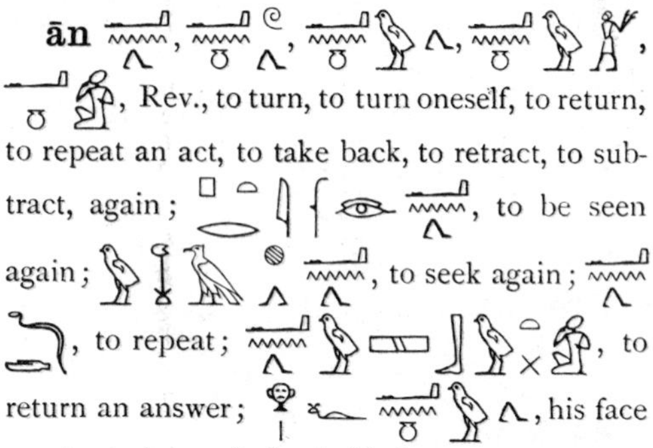 Rev., to turn, to turn oneself, to return, to repeat an act, to take back, to retract, to subtract, again; to be seen again; to seek again; to repeat; to return an answer; his face was turned round, *i.e.*, behind.

ānn , Peasant 299, L.D. III, 140B, to return, to turn back.

ānnu  one who returns from he grave; those who return.

āni , "the turner back," a title of Horus.

ānān 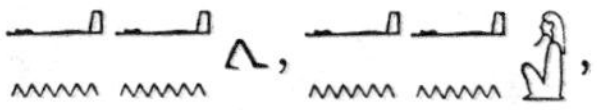, to turn back.

ānān  to gainsay, to contradict, rejoinder.

ān 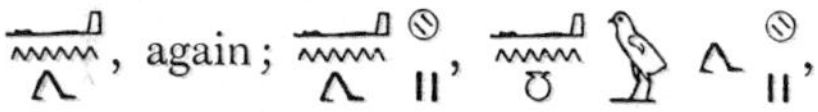 again; again again, on the contrary; Copt. ⲟⲛ.

ānn 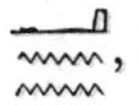, P. 509 . . . .

Ānn ābui (?) , the god of the 24th day of the month; he is gazelle-headed.

ān 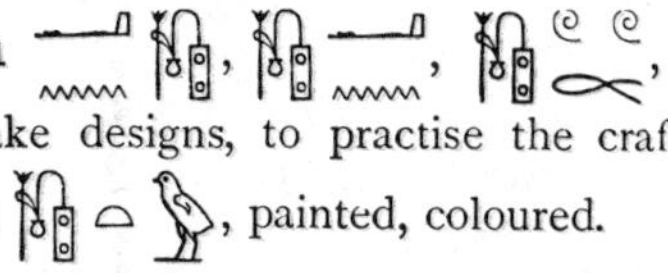 to paint, to make designs, to practise the craft of the artist; painted, coloured.

ān 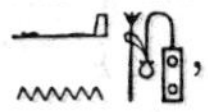, a letter of invitation from a woman.

ān mess , Rec. 1, 48, a kind of painted cloth.

ān ruṭ 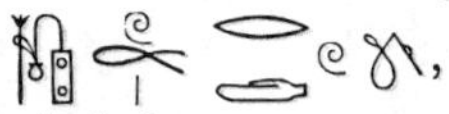, Rec. 1, 48, a kind of painted cloth.

ān nesu 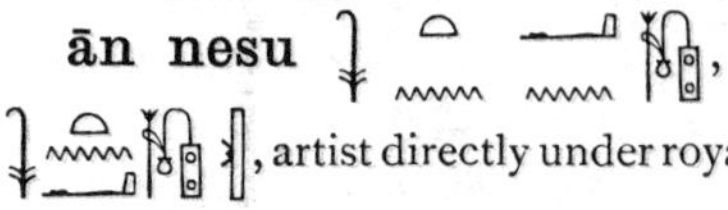 B.M. 145, artist directly under royal patronage.

ān, Rec. 6, 127, Treaty 4, a writing tablet, a flat thin writing board, plaque; plur.

ān en ān, the tablet of the artist's palette.

āniu (?), plaques, wooden tablets.

ānu, fine limestone from Ṭûrah.

ānu, Peasant 17, blocks of limestone.

ān, Thes. 1198, to turn a glance towards something.

ān, to be pretty or beautiful, beauty, beautiful, pleasant, delightful, gracious; splendid.

ān, Thes. 1481, Thes. 1482, a man of noble qualities, a cultured man, a good man; plur.

ānu, a beautiful object; dual; plur.

ānu-na, Mar. Aby. I, 9, 10, what is pleasing.

ān-t, a beautiful goddess, or woman.

ān-ḥa-t, Anastasi I, 23, 8, a fine or beautiful disposition, a noble heart.

ānu nekhti, B.D.G. 1116, the beauties of the warrior.

Ān, Berg. I, 16, an antelope-headed god who beautified the faces of the dead, and removed blemishes from the skin.

Ān-t-mer-mut-s, T.S.B.A. 3, 424, a goddess.

Ān-em-ḥer, T.S.B.A. 3, 424, a god.

ān, Rec. 3, 49, 5, 88, a kind of dry incense.

ān, well, fountain; var.; Heb. עַיִן.

ān, ānti, mud (Lacau).

ān, ape; Copt. ⲉⲛ.

Ān, Ṭuat XII, a mythological serpent.

Ānit, Denderah III, 12, a female counterpart of Osiris.

ān-t, a sharp-edged or pointed tool, adze, axe, auger, bradawl.

ān-t, a knife.

ān-t, U. 537, T. 295, claw of a bird or animal, talon, nail of the hand or foot; plur., P. 425, M. 737, N. 1233, 1213, P. 608, N. 798, P. 612, Rec. 31, 171, to cut the nails; to rub down the nails.

Ān-t-ent-Ptaḥ, B.D. 153B, 6, "Ptaḥ's claw," a part of the magical net.

Ān-t-tep-t-ānt-Ḥet-Ḥeru B.D. 153A, 19, a part of the magical net.

ān . . ., a kind of cattle.

ānān, the nape of the neck.

ānān, ānān-th, wigs, headdresses.

ān-t, ring, seal, signet.

ān-t [ ], a vase, vessel.

ānnu, Rec. 31, 18, cords, ropes.

ān, , Rec. 8, 138, to cry out, to entreat, to beseech as a captive.

ānāni, cry, appeal.

ān, a mythological fish; see **ānṭ**.

āni, U. 633, nape of the neck (?)

ānu, ānnu, , Rec. 13, 15, a kind of tree.

ānu-t, ray of light, beam; Copt. ⲟⲩⲉⲓⲛ.

ānut, ulcers, boils, sores.

ānutiu (?), Rec. 14, 42, , L.D. III, 219E, 17, , a class of foreign workmen (?)

Ānā, Ṭuat IX, a god, son of Ḥeru-àmi-uàa, a hawk-headed lion.

ānārt, a kind of worm.

Ānutàt; see .

ānb, , , to surround, to bind, to tie, to grip, to clutch, to seize prey.

ānb, a bundle.

ānb thema-t, IV, 1124, ; IV, 1131 . . . .

ānb, , grape, vine; Heb. עֵנָב.

ānberu, Peasant 115, basket, crate.

ānep, Mar. Aby. I, 6, 47 . . . .

ānep, , the festival of the 20th day of the month.

ānep, the third quarter of the moon; one of the seven stars of Orion (Thes. 112).

ānem, a kind of precious stone.

ānem-t, falsehood, lies, no, not so (?)

ānḥeb-t, a kind of bird.

ānkh, U. 191, T. 71, M. 225, N. 603, , , , , , to live, to live upon something, life; Copt. ⲱⲛϩ.

ānkh —, "life, stability, prosperity (or, content)"; , "life, all prosperity, all stability, all health, [and] joy of heart," a formula of good wishes which follows each mention of the king's name in official documents. See the following examples.

ānkh —, P. 652, life and content for ever! , P. 18, M. 20, N. 119, all life and content for ever!

ānkh —, T. 338, N. 626, life, strength, health!

ānkh —, , , the name of a college of priests.

ānkh —, "repeating life," a formula used sometimes in the place of maā-kheru.

ānkh —, Rec. 29, 184, "to whom life is given."

ānkh —, , "ever-living," a title of gods and kings.

ānkhu, Edict 17, man, citizen.

ānkhu nu nut, , Rec. 16, 70, citizen; fem. , Rechnungen 71; plur. .

ānkh-t, , , U. 192, T. 71, M. 225, N. 603, Rec. 31, 32, , , a living person (fem.) or thing; , "living fire."

ānkhi, ānkhu, , , , a living being, a living thing; plur. , , , , , , , ,

, , , , , , , , , , living beings, men and women.

ānkhu , M. 723, , N. 57, , P. 17, , N. 986, , P. 94, M. 118, , N. 1327, , Rec. 26, 236, "the living," *i.e.*, the beatified in heaven.

ānkh , house, living place.

ānkhu nu menfit , military folk.

ānkh – , living persons.

ānkh , an amulet.

ānkh , , M. 145, N. 649, "living," the name of a beetle.

ānkh , Berl. 2312, a name of the tomb.

Ānkh-t , the "land of life," *i.e.*, the Other World.

Ānkh Uas-t , Rec. 19, 89, "life of Thebes," a palace of Rameses II.

ānkh merr , an amulet.

ānkh neter , A.Z. 1908, 16, "god's life," name of a serpent amulet.

ānkh neter , Rec. 12, 79, a parcel of sacred ground.

Ānkh , life personified, the name of a god.

ānkh , star; plur. , , , stars, planets (?)

Ānkhiu , , Thes. 133, "living ones," *i.e.*, the 36 Dekans.

Ānkh , P. 174, , P. 672, , M. 661, N. 1276, the son of Sothis, or .

ānkh-t , , , "living one," a name of the Eye of Horus and of Tefnut.

ānkh-ti , , the two Eyes of Horus or Rā, *i.e.*, Sun and Moon.

Ānkhi , Ṭuat X, the god of time and of the life of Rā.

Ānkhit , Ṭuat IV, the name of a monstrous scorpion

Ānkhit (?) , Ṭuat IX, a fiery, blood-drinking serpent-god.

Ānkhit , , , , "living one," the name of a goddess.

Ānkhit , Rec. 11, 178, a uraeus-goddess.

Ānkhit , Ombos I, 1, 46, a hippopotamus-goddess.

Ānkhit , Ṭuat VII, a woman-headed-serpent.

Ānkh-ȧb , Ṭuat V, a guardian of the river of fire of Seker.

Ānkh-ȧru-tchefa , , Ṭuat VII, a serpent-guardian of Ȧfu-Ȧsȧr.

Ānkhit-unem-unt , , , Rec. 34, 190, one of the 12 Thoueris goddesses; she presided over the month .

Ānkh-f-em-fentu , B.D. 144, the doorkeeper of the 5th Ārit.

Ānkh-f-em-khaibitu , Ṭuat XI, a serpent-god with a pair of wings and two pairs of human legs and feet; from his body sprang Tem, the man-god.

Ānkh-em-fenth , Berg. I, 15, a form of Bes.

Ānkh-em-maāt , Berg. I, 12, a god of Truth.

Ānkh-em-neser-t , Berg. II, 9, the goddess of the 8th hour of the night.

Ānkhit ent Sebek, B.D. 125, III, 30, the name of the socket of a bolt in the Hall of Maāti.

Ānkh-neteru, Ṭuat XII, the monster serpent through the body of which the Boat of Åf was drawn by 12 gods daily at dawn.

Ānkhit-ermen (?), Ṭuat XII, a wind-goddess of dawn.

Ānkh-ḥer, Ṭuat VI, a guide and protector of souls and spirits.

Ānkh-ḥetch, Ṭuat X, a goddess who touches her lips with the tip of her fore-finger.

Ānkh-Sepṭit, Ṭuat VIII, a serpent-god in the Circle Āa-t-setekau.

Ānkh-s-meri, Denderah II, 11, one of the 36 Dekans.

Ānkh-ta, Ṭuat X, a serpent-god of the dawn.

Ānkhti, "the living one," a title of Osiris.

ānkh, , , , , to swear an oath; , to take an oath; , to swear a tenfold oath; , to swear by the life of the god; , he swore by the life of Pharaoh; Copt. ⲁⲛⲁϣ.

ānkh, , , , oath; , king's oath.

ānkhu, , goat, any small domestic animal; plur. , Mar. Karn. 54, 60, , , E.T. 1, 53, .

ānkh, , , grain, corn, wheat.

ānkh-t, victuals, food, vivers.

ānkhit, goose-food.

ānkh, , , , , flower, flowers.

ānkh – , , , plant or wood of life, *i.e.*, corn, grain, food.

ānkh-t, , , , P. 93, M. 117, Rec. 31, 113, 161, staff, stick, stalk.

ānkh, ear; dual , , , , , Åmen. 3, 9, , , , , the two ears; ; the ears of a god; , a god's title.

ānkh-ti, the two ears, *i.e.*, leaves of a door.

ānkh-ti, Rec. 11, 178, , , the two eyes.

ānkh, a kind of metal.

ānkh, , , , , a mirror; , mirror in its case; , A.Z. 1908, 20, the mirror amulet; , mirror for daily use; of various metals, *e.g.*, , , .

ānkh shau, a seal (Lacau).

ānkh-t, , a vase, vessel; plur. , .

ānkh, unguent.

Ānkh-taui, "life of the Two Lands," or "Memphis plant."

ānkhȧm, , , a flower used in funeral

wreaths; plur. 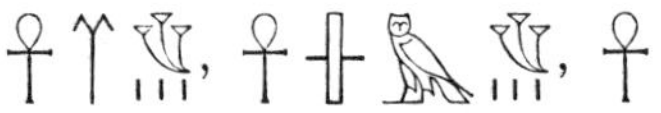
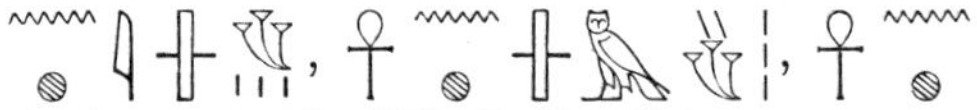
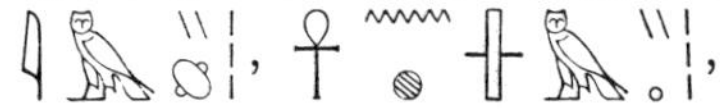 the seed of the same.

ānkhus 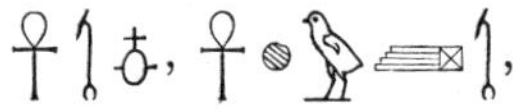, milk.

ānsh , Rec. 3, 152, to live, life; see [illegible].

Ānsh-senetchemnetchem 
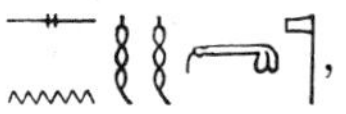, Denderah IV, 59, a bull-god, guardian of a coffer.

ānq [illegible], Rec. 12, 30, beam of a plough.

Ānq [illegible], a god in the Ṭuat; see [illegible] or [illegible].

Ānqit [illegible], a Nubian water-goddess, of Sûdânî origin, who with Khnemu and Sati formed the great triad of Elephantine and Philae. Champollion (Panthéon, p. 20) compared her with 'Εστια.

Ānqnāamu , Alt. K. 273 = Heb. יָקְנְעָם, ען קנעם.

ānt, āntiu 

, myrrh.

āntiu – āntiu uatchiu 
, fresh myrrh.

āntiu – āntiu en ḥemut 
[illegible], women's myrrh.

āntiu – āntiu nu tekhu 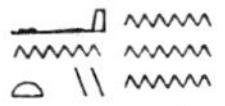
[illegible], moist myrrh as opposed to dry myrrh.

āntiu – per āntiu , myrrh store.

āntiu – perit-en-āntiu 
, seed of the myrrh shrub.

āntiu – khet-en-āntiu 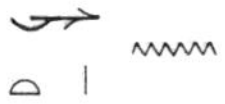
, wood of the myrrh shrub.

Ānti [illegible], the Myrrh-god.

ānti , an image made of myrrh, used in funerary ceremonies.

Āntȧt , B.M. No. 646;
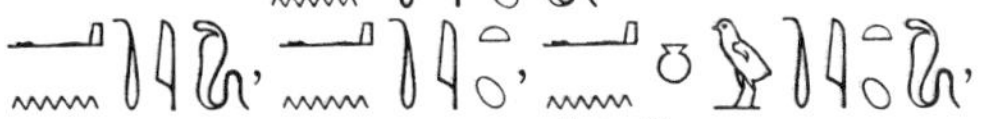
Chabas, Pap. Mag. 207, 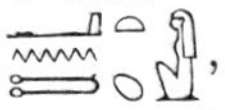, a war-goddess of Asiatic origin, who was adopted by the Egyptians, and stated by them to be the daughter of Set; Heb. ענת.

Āntit [illegible]; see [illegible].

Āntu, Ānth 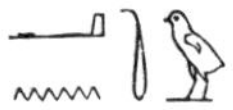, [illegible]; see [illegible]
.

Ānthet , Düm. H.I. I, 19; see
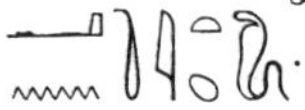.

Ānthrtȧ , Treaty, 28, a Hittite goddess.

ānṭ 
, to have or possess nothing, to lack, to want, to be destitute, destitution, to diminish.

ānṭ , the destitute man; plur.
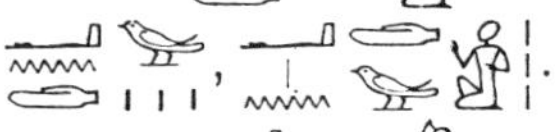.

ānṭ , calamity, trouble.

ānṭ-t [illegible], the minority, as opposed to [illegible], the majority.

ānṭ [illegible], deeds of violence.

ānṭ 
, to cut, to slay; see **āṭ** ,
.

ānṭ [illegible], part of a fowling net.

ānṭ, to know, to perceive.

ānṭ, , , to be sound, in good condition, to be well, to get better; , IV, 1024, healthy; varr. , .

ānṭi, , , he who is well, sound, firm, healthy, prosperous.

ānṭ-t, A.Z. 1908, 16, name of an amulet.

ānṭ, bank, side.

ānṭ, , ground, field, soil, cultivated lands; plur. , .

Ānṭit, , , , , Rec. 14, 165, the Boat in which Rā sailed from dawn to midday.

ānṭ, , , , , , , , light.

ānṭ, , , , , , fat, grease, manure; , unguent; , fresh grease; Copt. ωτ.

ānṭȧ = , myrrh.

ānṭ, a kind of fish.

Ānṭ-mer pet a title of the Nile-god.

Ānṭi, B.D. 125, II, one of the 42 assessors of Osiris; see **Āaṭi.**

ānṭu Hearst Pap. 11, 6, Leyden Pap. 4, 11, vase, vessel.

ānṭit, vase, vessel, pot.

ānṭu, B.D. 130, 30, darkness.

Ānṭu, a locality in the Ṭuat.

āntch, destitute; see **ānṭ**.

āntchut , the poor, the destitute.

āntch, a vessel.

āntch, P. 615, M. 783, N. 1143, the tip of a wing.

āntch, P. 643, claw, talon, nail.

āntch-t, Rec. 5, 90, a drug from which a tincture was prepared.

āntch, Rec. 27, 60, , light, radiance, splendour.

Āntch, M. 253, a name of the sun when in the sky.

āntch, , king.

āntch, to know.

āntch, P. 186, N. 900, to be strong, sound, healthy.

āntch, , , sound, firm, strong; , strong men; see **ānṭ.**

āntch-ur, , B.D. 41, 5, a guide of the dead.

āntch, M. 696, a kind of cloth (?)

āntch, fat, grease.

Āntcheṭ, , , the Boat in which Rā sailed from sunrise until noon; see **Māntchet, Māṭet,** etc.

āntch-t, P. 406, M. 580, N. 1185, , U. 298, , M. 709, , , field, pasture, lake, pool.

Āntch-mer, B.D.G. 130, a form of Osiris worshipped at Ḥebit.

āntch-mer, , P. 80, M. 110, N. 23, , , Royal Tombs, I, 43, , , a very ancient title meaning chief, governor, etc.; , N. 851, the chief of the gods; , IV, 952, the chief of the nomes.

Āntch-mer 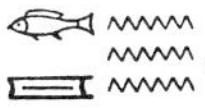, B.D. 17 (Nebseni), a lake in Sekhet Åaru.

Āntch-mer-uatch-ur , B.D. (Saïte), 110, a lake in Sekhet Åaru.

ār 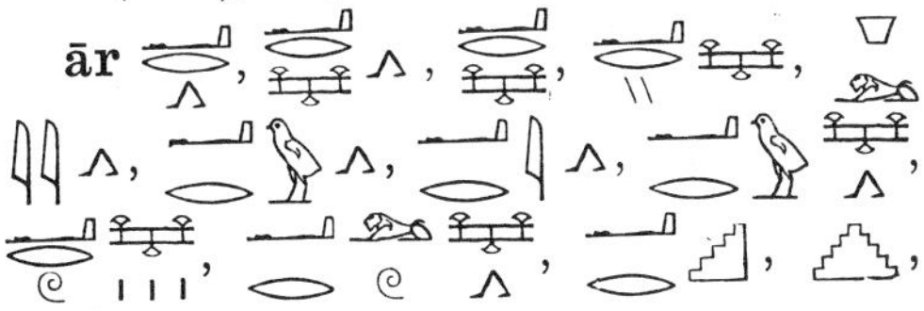
, to come or go up to some one or something, to ascend; Copt. ⲁⲗⲉ, ⲱⲗ, Heb. עָלָה.

āri , he who goes up; plur. .

ārār , to go up, to rise up, to ascend.

ār , steps, stairs, staircase.

Ār-neb-s , Denderah IV, 84, the name of the 2nd Pylon.

ār-t , Peasant I, 305, Rec. 26, 225, , Thes. 1296, rush, reed, stalk of a plant, reed for writing; plur. [illegible].

ār-t 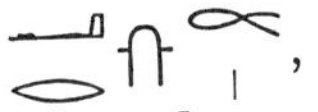, Amen. 15, 20, 19, 5, 21, 13, , a book, a roll, register, document, a writing, a leather scroll or roll, parchment, deed; plur. 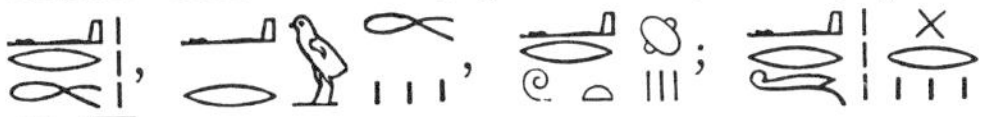
[illegible], great rolls of skin.

āru hau , Rec. 21, 85, day books, daily account books.

ār-t 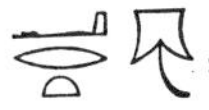, skin, skin-roll; compare Heb. עוֹר.

ār-t 
[illegible], goat, gazelle, ibex, ram, any horned animal; Copt. ⲉⲟⲩⲗ, Heb. אַיִל, Eth. ሀየል፡, Arab. اِيَّل, Syr. ܐܝܠܐ.

ār , lion; Heb. אֲרִי.

ār 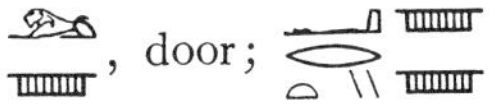, the two leaves of a door.

ār 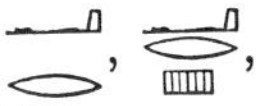, Rec. 5, 93, a writing tablet; , P. 186, M. 300, 899, a writing tablet with two leaves, or two tally sticks made of palm wood.

ār 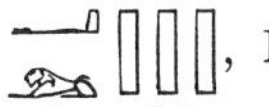, M. 207, , N. 669, wooden objects, poles (?).

ār 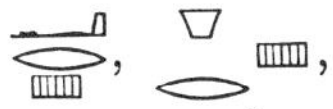, a kind of Nubian stone, pebble; plur. 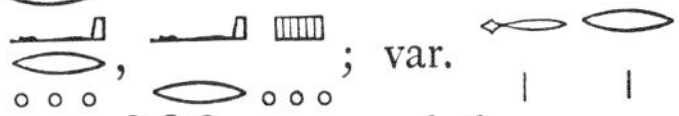
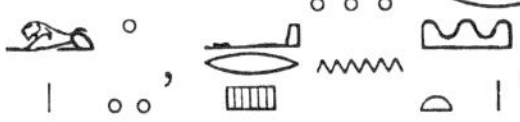 stone of the mountain, rock.

ār , pill, grain, pellet.

Ār 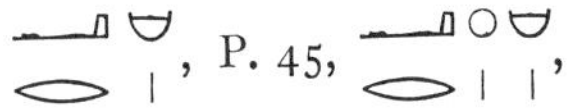, N. 31 . . . .

ār , Ḥenu 4, to complete, to finish.

ārr , Thes. 1205, to be efficient, capable.

ārār , Thes. 1319, [illegible]
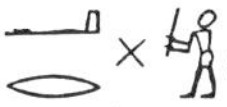, Anastasi I, 267, [illegible], to bring to an end, to finish, to repair, to make good, to complete; Copt. ⲗⲟⲟⲗⲉ, ⲗⲁⲗⲱ.

ārār , Rec. 21, 90, 92, to fulfil, to agree to a proposition, to fall in with.

ār 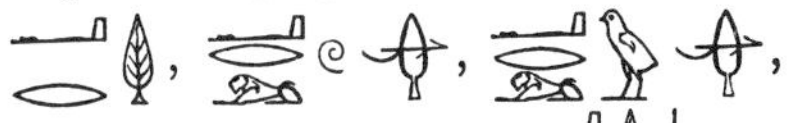, a kind of tree, terebinth; plur. [illegible], Heb. אֵלָה.

ār , a kind of shrub.

ārār 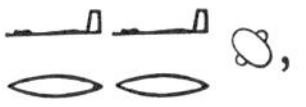, Anastasi V, 13, 4 . . . .

ār-t , jaw-bone, the lower jaw; dual. [illegible], U. 26, Rec. 5, 91, 30, 68, [illegible]; plur. [illegible]. The early Egyptians thought that the lower jaw was formed of two parts.

ār-t , [illegible], P. 604; Rec. 29, 156, 30, 67, 31, 18, haunch, tail.

ārār 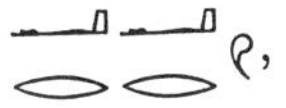, rump (?) tail (?).

ār-t , a kind of bird.

ār-t 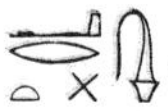, fire, flame.

ār-t 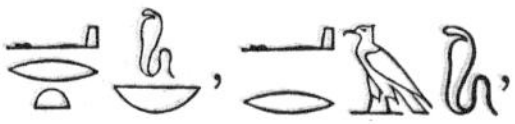, Rec. 11, 178, uraeus.

ārti , the two uraei-goddesses Isis and Nephthys; , two great uraei-goddesses.

ārut ānkhut 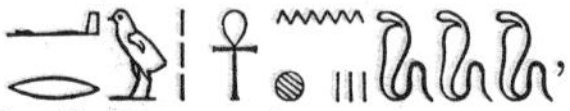, B.D. 125, III, 44, the living uraei.

ārār-t 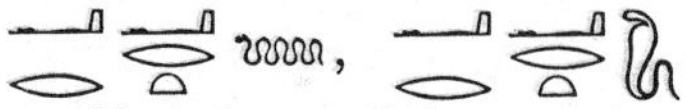, uraeus, uraeus-goddess, uraeus-diadem.

ārār-ti 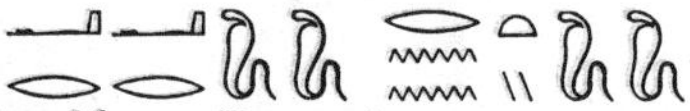. the two uraei-goddesses Renenti.

Ārt 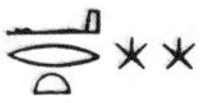, Tomb of Seti I, 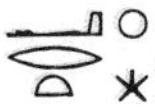, Tomb of Rameses IV, , Annales I, 87, one of the 36 Dekans; Gr. 'Ερῶ.

Ārit 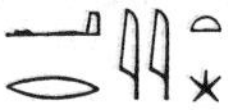, Denderah II, 10, one of the 36 Dekans; varr. 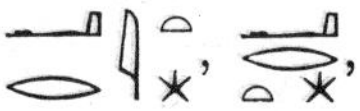, 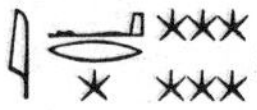; Gr. Αρου.

ār 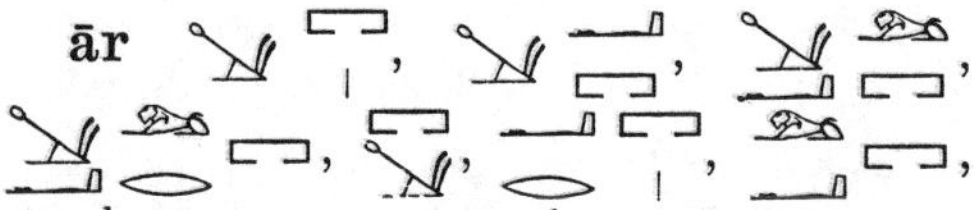, storehouse, treasury, magazine.

ār-t , shrine, chamber.

ārȧu , Rev., outcries of pleasure or pain.

Ārȧtsia 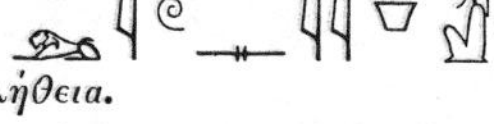, Rev. 11, 185 = Gr. 'Αλήθεια.

ārȧṭ 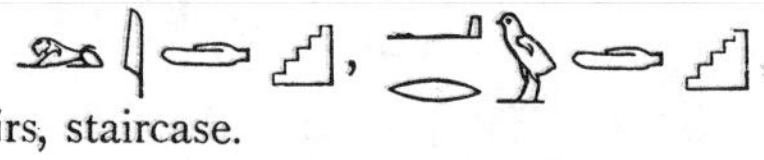, steps, stairs, staircase.

ārā-t 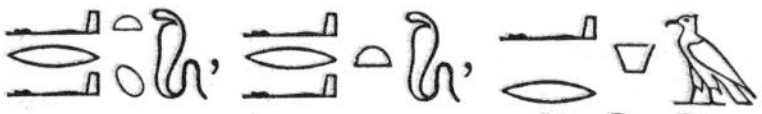 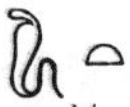, Rec. 13, 24, uraeus; 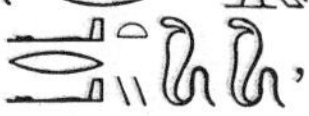, 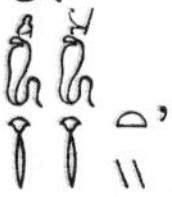, two uraei; compare Copt. ⲟⲩⲣⲁⲥ (?).

ārrā-t 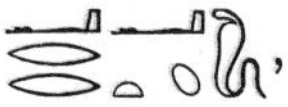, uraeus-goddess.

ārāit 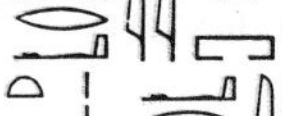, a hall, chamber; plur. 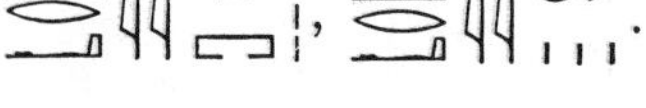.

ārit, ārrit 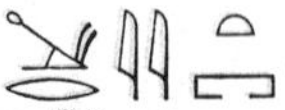, Thes. 1480; , 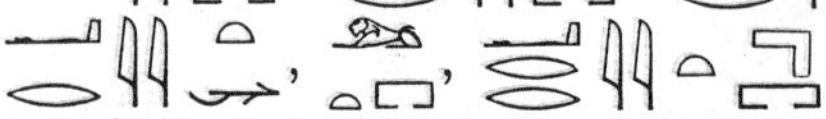, door, gate, hall of a palace, judgment hall, cabin of a boat; plur. 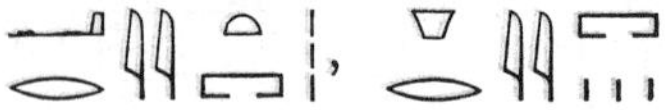, Rec. 11, 173.

Ārit , a division of the Ṭuat. The Ārits were seven in number 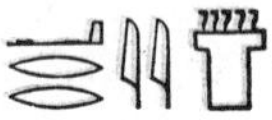 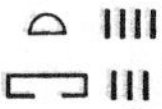, and each was in charge of a doorkeeper, a watcher, and a herald; see B.D. 144.

āri , light, fiery one.

Āri, Ārit 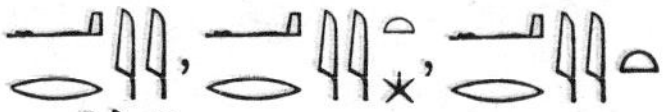 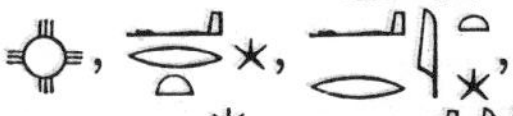, the name of a Dekan; Gr. Αρου; , the star of Āri; Copt. ⲁⲣⲟⲩ, ⲉⲣⲟⲩ.

ārit 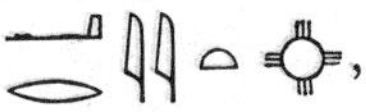, an internal organ of the body (?)

āri 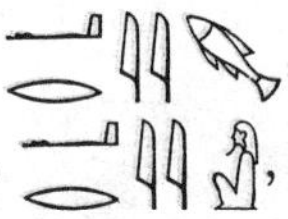, a kind of fish.

Āri, B.D. 125; see **Ȧaṭi**.

āri (ārri) , breeze, wind.

Āriti [illegible], [illegible], [illegible], [illegible], Edfû I, 79, a name of the Nile-god and of his Flood.

ārut, ārrut , M. 743, [illegible], N. 898, [illegible], P. 185, [illegible], door, gate, gateway, hall; plur. [illegible], [illegible], T. 247, [illegible], [illegible].

āru [illegible], Rev. 11, 179, 184, child; Copt. ⲁⲗⲟⲩ.

āru [illegible], Rev. 13, 15, perhaps; Copt. ⲁⲣⲏⲩ.

ārb, fume, flame, a burning; Copt. ⲉⲗϩⲟⲃ, ⲉⲗϩⲱⲃ.

ārp-t, Rec. 31, 23 = .

ārp-t, vase, pot, vessel.

ārf, , , , , , to grasp, to enclose, to collect, to twine, to weave; Copt. ⲱⲣϥ; , holder of [many] dignities; a pluralist.

ārf, , , purse, bag, bundle, packet; plur. ; , two packets, one of sulphate of copper, one of stibium.

Ārf, B.D.G. 653, a serpent water-god.

ārn-t (?), a beer-pot.

ārsh, to suffer pain, to be in restraint.

ārsh, Rev. 12, 86 = ; Copt. ⲣⲟⲟⲩϣ.

ārsh, Jour. As., 1908, 305, to be amazed or stupefied; Copt. ⲱⲛϣ.

ārq, , P. 422, 612, M. 603, N. 813, 1208, , , , , , , , , , , L.D. III, 194, , Anastasi IV, 12, 1, , , , , (1) to complete, to conclude, to finish, to make an end of, to abstain; (2) to swear an oath, to take an affidavit; Copt. ⲱⲣⲕ.

ārq en neter, to swear by God.

ārqu, , , an educated man, a wise man, counsellor, an expert, an adept.

ārq, , the end of anything, the last.

ārq ta, end of the earth.

ārqit, decree, decision, the conclusion of a matter.

ārqi, , , , , , Rec. 3, 50, , Rec. 2, 111, the end of a period, the last day of the month; var. (Nāstasen Stele); Copt. ⲁⲗⲕⲉ.

ārq renpet, the festival of the last day of the year.

ārq ȧb, Thes. 1481, , finished in heart.

ārq, a book, roll, writing.

ārq, Rec. 3, 49, , , to tie up, to wrap up, to cover over, to put on a garment, to bind round, to wriggle (of a serpent).

ārq, , , girdle, tie, bandlet.

ārq ḥeḥ, Thes. 1253, , , Rec. 15, 173, necropolis.

Ārq-ḥeḥtt, the Other World.

ārq, A.Z. 1874, 64, vase (?) a measure.

ārq, part of a chariot.

ārq ur, , Sphinx, 2, 8; , , , , silver; Gr. ἄργυρος.

ārtch, Jour. As. 1908, 276, Rev. 14, 43, pledge, money deposit, money.

āḥ, U. 162, T. 133, = , carobs.

āḥ , , moon; see .

āḥ , , to till the ground, to dry tears .

āḥ-t , N. 512, P. 592, net (?)

āḥu , , P. 615, M. 782, 785, N. 1141, cordage, tackle, ropework.

āḥ-t , U. 214, Thes. 1253, , , a large house or building, palace, chapel.

āḥ-ā , title of the high priest of the Nome Prosopites.

āḥa , Rev., oxen; , Rev. 13, 73, sacred oxen; Copt. ⲉϩⲉ.

āḥa , U. 538, , , , , , P. 229, , Lagus Stele, , , , to fight, to do battle, to wage war; , Amherst Pap. 26.

āḥa-ā , U. 560, , T. 170, , M. 179, , N. 689, , , , , , , , to fight, to do battle, to wage war.

āḥati, āḥauti, , Rougé I.H. II, 114, , , , , , , , warlike man, warrior, soldier, fighter, a fighting bull; Copt. ϩⲟⲟⲩⲧ; plur. , , , , , .

āḥati , , "slayer," the title of a priest of Ȧnḥer in Sebennytus; var. .

āḥa , a fighting animal, the Set animal (?)

āḥa , , the "fighting" fish, latus Niloticus (?)

āḥa-t, , a fighting ship, ship of war; , a name of the sacred boat of Sebennytus.

āḥa , Koller Pap. I, 4, , arrow, spear, weapon of war; plur. , Mar. Karn. 53, 36, , , packets of arrows; , weapons of bronze.

āḥa-t taui , Rec. 22, 107, day of the fight between the South and the North.

Āḥaui , N. 755, , , , , , Pellegrini II, 31, B.D. 75, 5, the two Warriors, *i.e.*, Horus and Set.

Āḥatiu , , B.D. 28, 3, the "Fighters," a group of gods in animal form.

Āḥa-āui , B.D. 64, 48, a warrior-god.

Āḥa-nebt-benu , Denderah IV, 63, a warrior-god of Denderah.

Āḥau-ḥeru , U. 400, , B.D. 168, the "fighting faces" in the Ṭuat.

Āḥa-Ḥeru , Denderah III, 36, a god of Denderah.

Āḥa-sati-neterui , Denderah III, 36, a god of Denderah.

āḥa , unlucky, unfavourable, bad, as opposed to , good. Used in calendars.

āḥa , Peasant 278, , Peasant 258, , IV, 1077, to make water, to empty oneself.

āḥā , U. 277, N. 719, [illegible]
, [illegible], [illegible], [illegible], [illegible], Mar. Karn. 52, [illegible], Rec. 13, 30, [illegible], Rec. 6, 8, to stand, to stand still, to halt; Copt. ⲱϩⲉ.

āḥā with **n** , [illegible], [illegible], [illegible], used as an auxiliary verb, *e.g.*, [illegible]
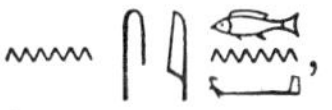, [illegible] [illegible], [illegible]
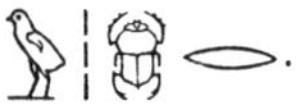.

āḥāiu , [illegible], P. 408, M. 584, N. 1189, , N. 1189, , Rec. 17, 147, those who stand in their appointed places.

āḥāu neb , Thes. 1282, the royal stand in a temple.

āḥāit , [illegible], [illegible]
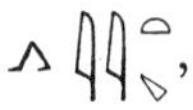, support, prop of the sky, pillar.

āḥā , Rec. 1, 48, wooden staff, prop, stick.

āḥāu , [illegible], [illegible], supports, things that make stable.

āḥā ȧri 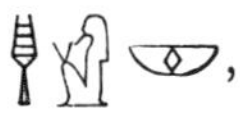, the name of the festival of the 29th day of the month.

Āḥā , [illegible], [illegible],
, B.D. 168, [illegible], Denderah III, 14, [illegible], Berg. I, 6, a serpent-god, an ally of Set.

Āḥā-āḥā 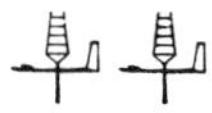, Rev. 6, 116, a god.

Āḥāit 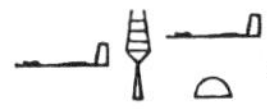, Ṭuat X, 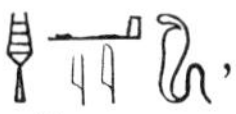,
[illegible], [illegible], Rec. 6, 116, [illegible], Rec. 27, 189, a lioness-goddess.

Āḥāu , Ṭuat III, a goddess.

Āḥā-ȧb , Ṭuat XII, a supporter of the disk.

Āḥā-nurṭ-nef , Ṭuat VIII, a gate in the Ṭuat.

Āḥā-notoru , the door of the 5th hour of the night.

Āḥā-rer 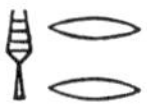, Ṭuat XII, one of 12 gods who towed the boat of Åf through Ānkh-neteru; as a dawn-god who was reborn daily.

Āḥā-sekhet , Ṭuat IX, a god—functions unknown.

āḥā, āḥāit (?) , Anastasi I, 243, , [illegible], [illegible], Rec. 13, 127, [illegible], [illegible], stele, tablet, hill.

āḥāu ; Rec. 20, 40, station, stele (?) tablet (?)

āḥāu , P. 651, M. 728, , N. 752, boundaries, landmarks, delimitation posts.

āḥāu , [illegible], [illegible],
, place, post, station, position, condition, state.

āḥāu , T. 329, [illegible], U. 520, [illegible], [illegible], [illegible], [illegible], [illegible],
[illegible], [illegible], [illegible], [illegible], Rec. 12, 118, time, period of time, lifetime, a man's age; , lifetime upon lifetime; Copt. ⲁϩⲉ.

āḥāu — , the gods who measure the lives of men in Åment.

āḥā, advanced in life, aged, very old (of a man).

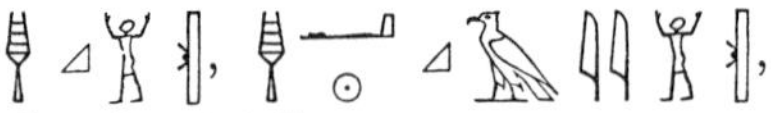

āḥā-t, lifetime, period of time; plur., ages; a period of ten days.

āḥā en ḥeḥ, a life of millions of years.

āḥāi, a standing still, pause, interval.

āḥāit, noon, a name of the goddess of the 5th hour of the day.

Āḥāit, Thes. 31, the goddess of the 6th hour of the day.

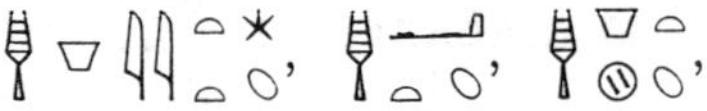

Āḥāit, Denderah II, 55, III, 24, a disk goddess and one of the seven goddesses who supported the sky.

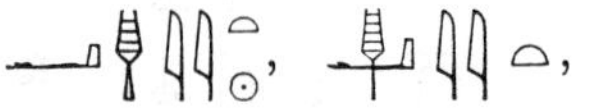

āḥā, colonnade (?) a high building.

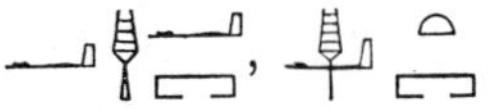

āḥā-t, tomb, grave; see **māḥā-t**; plur.

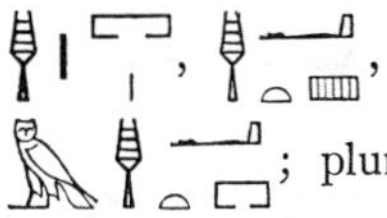

āḥāit, grave, tomb.

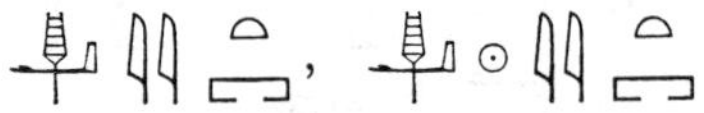

āḥāu, tomb, sepulchral stele, memorial slab.

āḥā, Rechnungen 48, 58, amount, value (?)

āḥā, a method of reckoning.

āḥā, circumference, circuit, extent, range, compass.

āḥā, a number, a quantity, sum total.

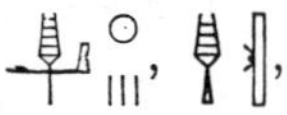

āḥā, E.T. 1, 53, food, provisions, stores, heaps of grain, wealth, riches, abundance; Annales III, 110, a heap offering containing provisions of all kinds.

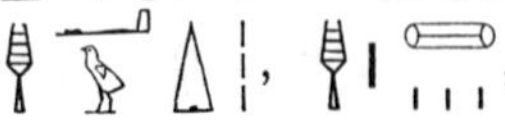

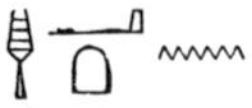

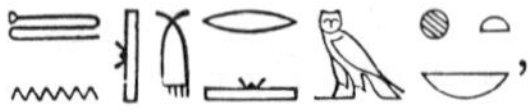

āḥāiu, men provided with stores, well-to-do folk.

āḥā, IV, 755, jar, vase.

āḥā-t, stiff, hard, the nape of the neck.

āḥā, limbs, members; see **ḥā**.

āḥā, ship; plur., Rec. 33, 67, battle ships.

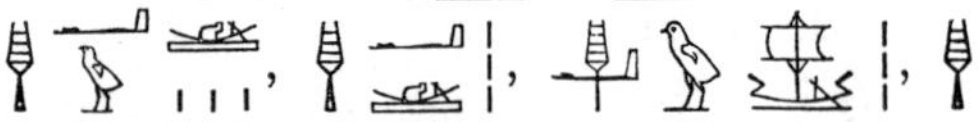

āḥāit, boat; plur.

āḥā-apṭu (?), Rechnungen 35, boat for the transport of birds.

āḥāu, P. 441, M. 545, P. 164, M. 328, N. 859, N. 953, 1125, a kind of bird, crane.

āḥb-t, M. 637; see P. 334.

Āḥeth, Ṭuat IV, a region in the Ṭuat of Seker.

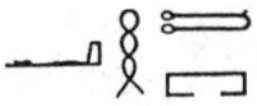

ākh, to boil, to cook.

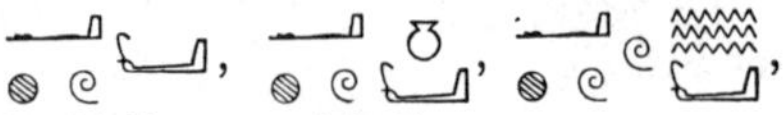

ākh, T. 85, N. 616, M. 239, N. 254, fire-altar, brazier, offering by fire; plur., L.D. III, 65A, 15.

ākhȧ, furnace; fireplace; Copt. ⲁϣ.

ākh-t, P. 652, brazier, fireplace; plur., N. 754.

ākh, De Hymnis, 47, L.D. III, 65A, 18, L.D. III, 65, 18, to raise up on high, to hang out in the height, to soar, to be poised in the air, to hang a man; suspended; = Copt. ⲉϣⲧ.

Ākhi-ā-n-Beḥuṭ, Denderah III, 68, a solar god.

ākhekh, night, darkness, night personified.

Ākhekhtiu, B.D. 145 V (Saïte), a group of serpent-fiends.

ākh, Rec. 27, 86, to soar in the air, to mount up, to fly.

Ākhekh, Thes. 1199, 1203, R.E. 6, 41, gryphon, the "flying" animal.

ākhai, Hh. 540, a kind of bird (?) to fly (?)

ākhi, a kind of bird; plur., Koller Pap. 2, 3, Anastasi IV, 2, 5.

ākh-t, Rec. 30, 71.

ākhkh, to advance, to attack.

ākh, reeds, grass, sedge.

ākhabṭȧt (?), T. 309, ...

ākhamu, ornamental models (?)

ākham, the image or symbol of a god; plur., L.D. III, 65A, 9, N. 152.

ākhami, figure of a sacred animal.

ākhamit, Rev. 14, 7, eagle; Copt. ⲁϧⲱⲙ.

ākham, to destroy, to beat to death.

ākhan, to sleep, to close the eyes.

Ākhan-ȧri-t, Ṭuat VII, a serpent doorkeeper of the 6th Gate; var.

Ākha-ḥer, a serpent-god.

ākhm, to put an end to, to destroy; var.

ākhm, U. 334, Rec. 31, 31, Rec. 31, 168, to extinguish a fire or flame, to quench thirst; varr., Copt. ⲱϣⲙ.

ākhmiu , those who extinguish.

ākhmut , A.Z. 84, 88, those who wash clothes, laundrymen;  [illegible], Annales IX, 156.

ākhm , to fly (?) to glide about (?)

ākhm , Hymn of Darius, 31, , image or symbol of a god; plur. 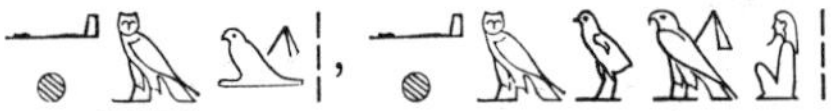, 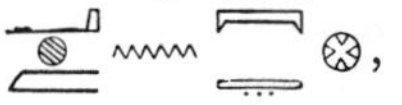, images of heaven, the earth, and the Ṭuat;  [illegible], images of sacred animals.

Ākhmu , see 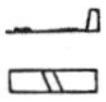 [illegible].

ākhm , ; plur. , Rec. 3, 53, 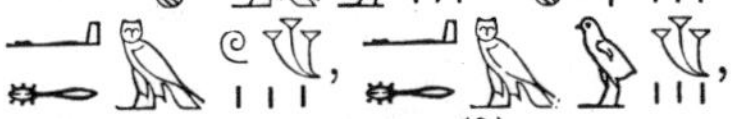, plant, shrub, flax; Copt. ⲁϣⲙⲓ (?)

ākhm , a parcel of land, river bank; plur. [illegible], Rec. 2, 129, , [illegible], B.D. 99.

ākhn 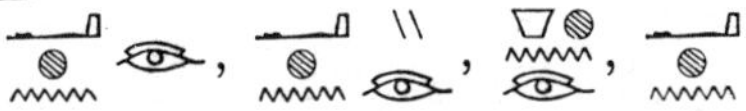, [illegible], to shut the eyes, to sleep.

Ākhn-ȧrti-f , B.D. 64, 13, a god.

ākhn 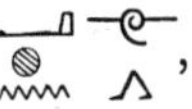, IV, 639, sledge, a piece of furniture.

ākhnuti   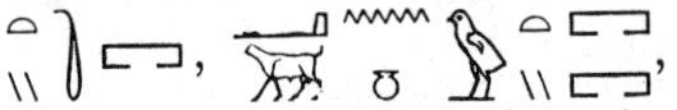, Pharaoh's private apartments in the palace, the royal quarters, the Cabinet, the Court, the Administration.

āsa 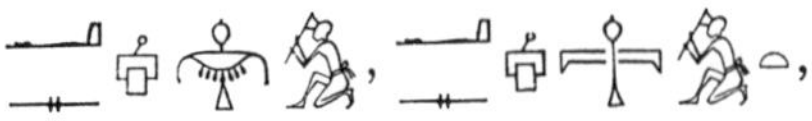, Rev., wrong, retribution.

Āstȧrtȧt  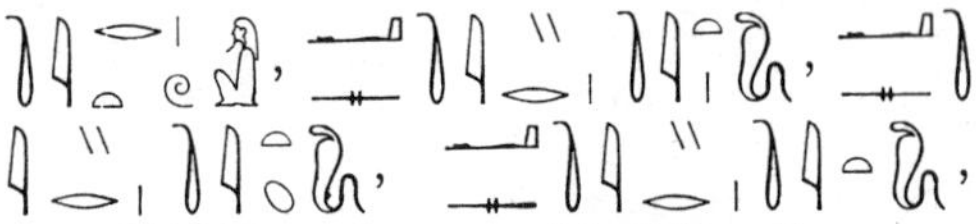 , Ashtoreth, Ashtoroth; Heb. עַשְׁתֹּרֶת, עַשְׁתָּרוֹת, Assyr. [illegible]

Āsthȧreth 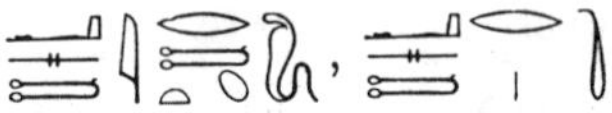 [illegible], Naville, Mythe, pl. 4, Ishtar, Astarte, Ashtoreth, an Asiatic goddess of war and the chase, whom the Egyptians identified with Isis and Hathor; see Tell el-Amarna Tablets (B.M.), p. xlii; 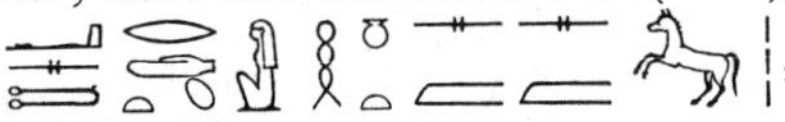, Ashtoreth, lady of horses.

Āsthert 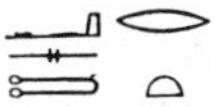, Rev. 12, 1, Ishtar; see [illegible].

āsh , , Rev. 11, 136, [illegible] , Rec. 3, 152, [illegible], N. 842, [illegible], to cry out, to call, to call out, to summon, to invoke, a call, a cry for help, to lament, to groan; Copt. ⲱϣ.

āsh en-utchu-t , Rev. 13, 75, [illegible], Rev. 14, 36, order, command, invocation.

āsh-seḥni 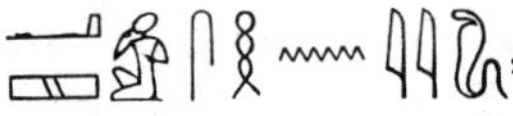, Rev. 12, 42, to command; Copt. ⲟⲩⲉϩⲥⲁϩⲛⲉ.

āsh , P. 168, M. 323, [illegible], Ȧmen. 27, 11, 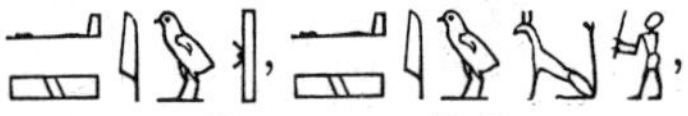, to call, to cry out; 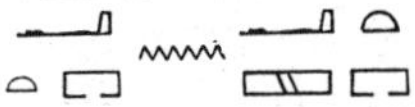, house of appeal.

āshaut , screams, cries of pain, those who cry or lament.

āsh , wicked word, curse.

Āsh-kheru, Berg. I, 18, a ram-headed god.

āsh, Rec. 29, 146, ..., cedar wood, cedar tree; plur. ..., Thes. 1287, new cedar; ..., Thes. 1323, cedar treated in a particular way; Assyr. ushu, Rost, Tig. Pil. III.

āsh, U. 61, Thes. 1286, ..., P. 526, N. 843, 993, ..., T. 278, a salve or ointment made from cedar oil.

āsh, U. 148A, a kind of wine = ..., T. 118, 119, N. 456A.

āsh, ..., Åmen. 9, 2, a kind of Sûdânî beer.

āsh, vase, vessel, pot.

āshi, cauldron.

āsh, a bronze fire-stand.

āsh, corruption.

āsh, to come = ... (?)

āsh, Anastasi I, 17, 2, meals, food.

āshāsh-t, ..., Åmen. 14, 8, throat, gullet.

Āsha, P. 345, ..., Åmen. 19, 2, to be much or many, to be abundant, to happen often or frequently; Copt. ⲁϣⲁⲓ.

āsh, ..., N. 981, ..., much, many, numerous, overmuch; ..., however many there may be; ..., very many.

āsha-t, P. 167, ..., M. 322, ..., Rec. 26, 230, ..., a large company, crowd, multitude, mob, any large assembly of people, the majority; Copt. ⲟϣ, ⲱϣ, ϣⲱ; **āsht-urt**, ..., a vast multitude; **āsht-nepit** ..., producing great quantities of grain; **āsht-ra** ..., to babble, to talk overmuch; **āsht-renu** ..., many-named; **āsht-ḥebu** ..., [god of] multitudinous festivals; **āsht-ḥefnu** ..., myriads of hundreds of thousands; **āsht-ḥeru** ..., many-faced; **āsht-kheperu** ..., of multitudinous forms; **āsht-kheru ḥer meṭ-t** ..., speaking very loudly and very often.

Āshit-åbu, Ombos III, 2, 132, a goddess.

Āsh-ḥeru, Ṭuat VI, a five-headed serpent which enclosed the body of Åf.

Āsh-t kheru ḥer meṭ-t ..., the name of one of the 42 judges in the Hall of Osiris.

āsha-t ... = ..., or ..., village, town.

āshait, ..., quay, haven, port, landing-place on a river bank.

āsh åt (?), bird kept for breeding purposes.

āsha, Rev., a rich man, man of easy circumstances.

āshā, food.

āshā-t, knife, weapon.

Āsheb, Denderah IV, 61, an ape-headed warrior-goddess.

āshem, U. 515, T. 327, M. 485, , figure or symbol of a god or sacred animal; plur. , Rec. 27, 53, 58; , U. 575.

āshem, plant, shrub, branch; plur. , branches.

āshem, a form of evil.

āshem, to destroy, to bring to an end, to diminish; var. , undiminished.

Āshemeth, Ṭuat XI, a hawk-headed servant of Rā.

āshgaȧ, Ȧmen. 6, 14, 7, 17, , 18, 12 . . . . .

āshgāgā, Rev. 12, 39, to cry out; Copt. ⲁϣⲕⲁⲕ.

āshṭ, a fat bird (?)

āq, a sign of addition.

āq, Rev. 11, 131, , to go in, to enter; , those who go in; , going in and out, entrance and exit; , sunrise or sunset.

āqāq, Mar. Karn. 52, 19, , to go in, to enter, to invade a country frequently, to raid a country.

āq, a priest who goes in to read the service.

āq ȧb, a right-hearted man.

āqiu, those who enter, ingoers, people who are in the habit of frequenting a place.

āqt, things that enter, entrances.

āqu, income, revenue.

āq-em-seḥ, to praise.

Āq-ḥer-ȧmi-unnut-f, B.D. 17, 104, Rec. 4, 28, , Edfû I, 10E, one of the eight watchers of Osiris.

āq, flux, menses.

āq-t, exit.

āq, bread, bread-cake; plur. , bread baked by fire, toast (?); Copt. ⲟⲉⲓⲕ.

āqu ȧmenit, the daily offering of cakes and bread.

āqā, Rechnungen 41, , "great bread," a kind of confectionery.

āq m'ti, cake with some kind of sweet stuff in it.

āq sher, Rechnungen 41, "little bread," short-bread (?)

āq, bread made of fine flour.

āq-ui (?) (*sic*), jaw-bones or cheek-bones.

āq, , P. 642, N. 1240, a garment (?)

āq, Rev. 11, 170, to destroy, be destroyed; Copt. ⲁⲕⲱ.

āq, , , , Åmen. 9, 20, , , , , , to keep the true mean, to be right, to behave rightly, exact, correct, right, proper; = .

āq maāt, strict justice.

āq ḥati, Israel Stele, 15, upright, to come to a right determination.

āq ṭ, even-handed justice.

āq—em āq, , opposite, exactly facing.

er āq, opposite, exactly facing.

āq, righteousness and justice personified.

āq åb, , , , Thes. 1251, 1481, , true, true-hearted, of right mind.

āqa, Rec. 3, 115, a trustworthy servant (?)

āq, , , , , the exact middle, the culminating point of a star or heavenly body.

āqait, Peasant 158, equilibrium.

āqa, a right lead, true guidance.

āq, āqau, , , U. 508, T. 322, Rec. 26, 64, , , , , cord, rope, tow-rope; plur. , U. 639, , , Rec. 31, 27, .

Āqa-uben, etc., B.D. 99, 25, name of the steering pole of the magical boat.

āq, Rec. 1, 48, , reed, a kind of wood.

āqa, B.D. 99, 3, to feed, to give (?)

Āqa, Sarc. Seti I, a form of Geb, god of food.

āqai (?), boat (?)

āqem, Rev. 11, 129, sad, wretched; Copt. ⲱⲕⲙ.

Āqen, Ṭuat VII, Hh. 426, a god in the Ṭuat; varr. , .

Āqennu-ḥeru, Rec. 36, 215, a group of gods.

āqr, a measure.

ākk-t, Rechnungen 41, , , , P.S.B. 19, 261, , Rec. 23, 203, a bread cake baked in the ashes; Copt. ϭⲁⲁϭⲉ, Gr. κακεῖς (Strabo, 824), Chald. כַּעֲכָא, Arab. كَعْك, Pers. كَاك, Syr. ܟܥܟܐ = ܟܥܟܐ.

āka, a drowning man.

ākai, a plant, shrub.

ākriu, Rec. 13, 12 = .

ākr, Rev. 12, 25, casque; Copt. ⲁⲕⲗⲏ.

āg, whip, flail.

āg-t, U. 157, , , , , food, a kind of grain.

āgut, , a plant, mint, peppermint (?)

āg-t, , , an offering of some kind, bolts, nails, metal pegs.

āga-t, Rec. 15, 142, nail, claw, hoof; dual, hoofs; plur. Kubbân Stele, 5.

āgau bolts, pegs, nails (?)

āga to nail, to drive pegs into something, to beat, to hammer.

āga to be hot, to burn, to be burned.

āga a kind of drink, a medicine.

āga a kind of unguent, ox-fat (?)

āgait a plant, a shrub; the seed of the same.

āgait a substance used in making a sacrifice.

āgai Åmen. 25, 15, to drown.

āgaina a kind of plant or herb.

āgana rod, staff, part of a staff.

āgariu Rec. 4, 29, ball (?)

āgas food (?)

āgit a herb, plant, shrub.

āgn support of a vessel, stand.

āgsu IV, 1120, goat-hide.

āt, ātu staff, stick, cudgel.

ātāt Rev. 12, 16, Jour. As. 1908, 258, to strike, to beat, to inflict pain; suffered, endured.

ātāt Rev., sin, folly.

āt to turn away from, to hate.

āt fat; Copt. ⲱⲧ, ⲱⲑ.

āt-t pool, lake (?)

āti Rec. 16, 70, confectioner, pastry-cook.

āteb Rec. 16, 110, tomb.

āteput seed of some kind.

āteru B.D. 169, 4 . . . . .

ātekh to crush, to bruise, to pound, to strain through a rag, to boil, to cook food, to make up a prescription.

ātekh to knead dough, to rub down.

ātekh Amherst Pap. 34, to crush grain for beer; brewers.

ātshai Rev., useless, incapable; Copt. ⲁⲧϣⲁⲩ.

āthen Rec. 15, 187 . . . . . .

āṭ Rougé I.H. II, 114, to suppress, to subdue.

āṭ Rec. 6, 7, defeat, depression, suppression.

āṭāṭ Rev., loss, damage, injury.

āṭ slaughter.

āṭu nub gold-beaters.

āṭ sound, strong; see .

āṭ Nåstasen Stele, 17, Rec. 14, 12, the two banks of the Nile.

āṭ fat, oil; Copt. ⲱⲧ.

Āṭu a mythological fish; see **ānṭ**.

āṭ-t the boat of the morning sun; see **āntch-t**.

āṭ house, abode.

āṭ ḥeq-t Åmen. 24, 22, beer-house.

āṭ , Åmen. 16, 4, 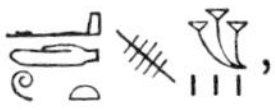, Åmen. 17, 6, , 18, 20, a plant.

āṭa , clothing, cloaks.

āṭi 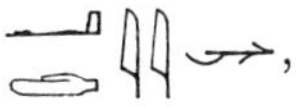, B.D. (Saïte), 125, 55, a post (?)

āṭi , Rec. 13, 27, member (?)

āṭma , Rec. 14, 178, an offering.

āṭen 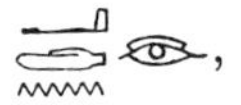, Rec. 25, 126; beauty.

āṭch , boy; see .

ātch , name of a staff or club.

ātch-t , Rec. 27, 218, daggers (?)

ātchātch 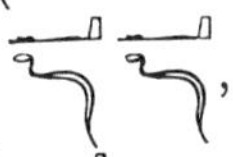, B.D.G. 1063,   (*sic*), Hymn Darius 16, , to hail, to greet, to praise, to rejoice, to shout for joy, to dance.

Ātch-t år-ti  , Rec. 30, 201, the name of a god or goddess.

ātcha , , , to commit a crime, to do evil, to oppress, to rob, to act unjustly, wicked, evil, deceit, falsehood.

ātcha , , robber; , man of guilt; plur.  .

ātcha , Anastasi I, 26, 2, , Israel Stele, 15,  , Rec. 19, 91, , P.S.B. 10, 44, to tell lies, to deceive, to give false evidence; Copt. ⲟϫⲓ.

ātchaå 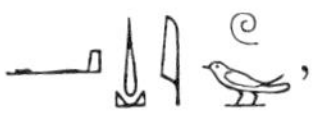, Rec. 21, 88, injustice, falsehood; Copt. ⲟϫⲓ.

ātchå , Rev. 12, 69, a lying spirit.

ātchaut , wrong, injury, injustice, extortion, oppression.

ātchau (?) , errors, mistakes.

ātcha , wind, breeze.

Ātcha , P. 497, a mythological city.

ātchan , Rev. 14, 9, to be defective, to fail, to cease; Copt. ⲱϫⲡ.

ātchar [illegible], help, assistance; compare Heb. אֵזֶר.

ātcharan [illegible], Ebers Pap. 63, 9, saffron as used in medicine; compare Arab. زعفران (?)

ātchā [illegible], to joke, to jest.

Ātchen [illegible], the name of a demon.

Ātchnit [illegible], the female counterpart of the same.

ātchn-t [illegible], [illegible], arm ornament (Lacau).

ātchṭ [illegible], [illegible], Rec. 21, 81, P.S.B. 31, 13, [illegible], [illegible], [illegible], child, boy, girl, young man, young woman; plur. [illegible], [illegible], [illegible], [illegible].

i  or \\, sometimes the equivalent of the Heb. י.

i 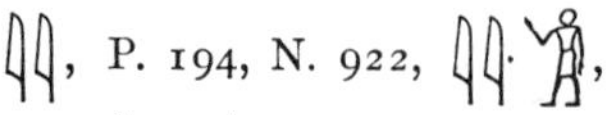, P. 194, N. 922, , P. 183, N. 662, an exclamation.

i , U. 494, 539, T. 295, P. 229, N. 946 . . . .

i-t 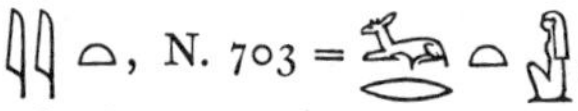, N. 703 = , P. 824, a woman who has conceived.

i-t , Rec. 31, 174, grain, food.

ia , P.S.B. 31, 11, Rec. 21, 5, 79, , Rec. 21, 78, 88, a particle of exclamation.

iu, iu-t , a particle of exclamation.

iau , P.S.B. 13, 425, goats.

iaur-t , river, stream, ditch (?); Heb. יְאֹר, Copt. ειερο, ειοορ.

iati (?) , calamity, misfortune.

iat-t , Rev. 14, 12, dew; Copt. ειωτε.

iaṭ-t 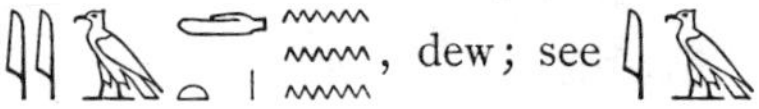, dew; see 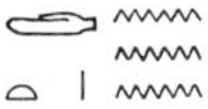.

iā (ȧȧā ?) , 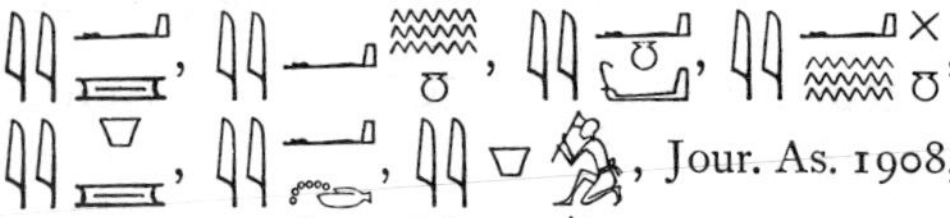, Jour. As. 1908, 254, to wash; 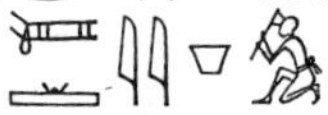, unwashed, impure; Copt. ειωι.

iā ḥa-t (?) 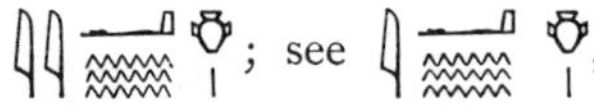; see , .

Iāa (?) , Rev. 11, 184; Heb. יָהּ, Gnostic ιω.

iāab , weariness, fatigue; Copt. ειααβε.

iāb , Rev. 12, 114, to conquer.

iām , Rev. 12, 68, sea; Heb. יָם.

iār 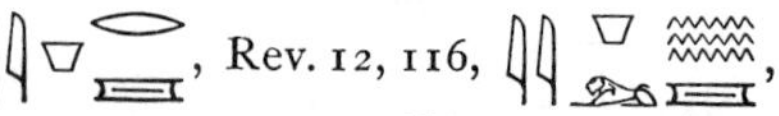, Rev. 12, 116, , Rev. 11, 174, , Rev. 13, 65, river; Heb. יְאֹר.

iār , Rec. 13, 25, brilliance, splendour; Copt. ιαλ, ιελελ.

Iāh-ā 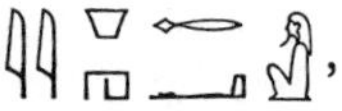, Rev. 11, 180, 182, Jâh the Great; Gnostic ιαυω.

Iāqebher 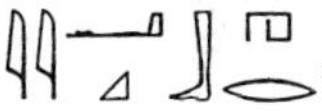, Alt. K. II, 86, Verbum Vocab. These words do not mean "Jacob God," but "Jacob hath . . . . . .,"  being a verb.

iuā (?) , Peasant 28, a fisherman of some kind.

Iba , Nesi-Ȧmsu 32, 38, a title of Āapep.

Iban , Nesi-Ȧmsu, 32, 20, a title of Āapep.

ium (ȧȧum ?) 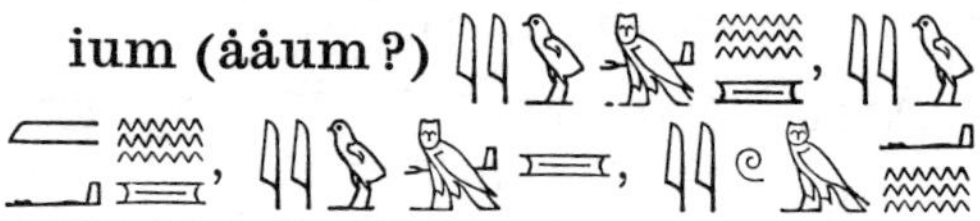, , , sea, river; Heb. יָם, Copt. ειομ, ιαμ, ιομ;  , the great sea of Qeṭ-t, or Asia Minor.

iur (?) 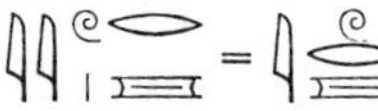; Heb. יְאֹר.

iba 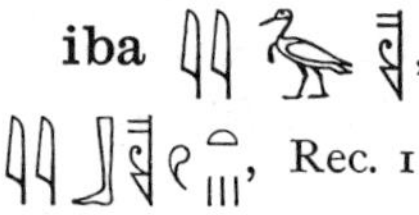, Rev. 14, 2, claw; plur. , Rec. 14, 10; Copt. ειβ.

iba , Jour. As. 1908, 262, weakness; Copt. ιαβι.

iban  Rec. 13, 41, ebony; Heb. in plur. הָבְנִים, Ezek. 27, 15.

ibr [illegible], [illegible], flood or rush of water in a river; Heb. יָבָל.

ibsha-t 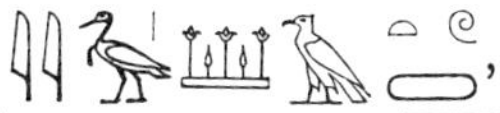, a kind of cake or bread; compare Heb. √יבש.

im , Mar. Karn. 54, 52, , [illegible], Rev. 13, 61; plur. [illegible], Rev. 13, 40, sea, river; Heb. יָם, Copt. ⲉⲓⲟⲙ, ⲓⲟⲙ.

Im'r , Alt. K. 217, a proper name.

inu 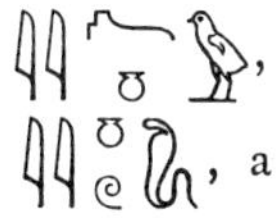, water.

Inu, a goddess.

inbu , Anastasi IV, 15, 3, a kind of wine; compare [illegible] and [illegible].

inm'  [illegible], Treaty 30, sea; Heb. יָם.

inra 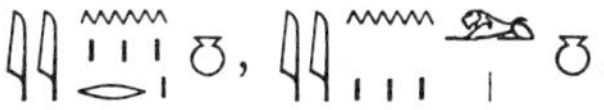, Paheri 7, pot, vessel, wine jar.

Inḥem  [illegible], A.Z. 38, 17, the official Yankha-mu; Tell el-Amarna [illegible]; Heb. ינחם.

Inḥerpes 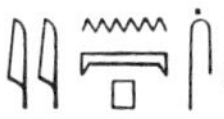, a proper name.

inkuun  [illegible], Ebers Pap. 98, 20, grass or seed.

intch-ḥer , Rec. 13, 2; see [illegible].

ir (il) , mirror; Copt. ⲉⲓⲁⲗ.

ir , something foul or unpleasant.

ir , P. 243 = [illegible], M. 446, [illegible], P. 815, to conceive.

ir , Rev., river.

irsh (?) , Rev. 12, 67, a kind of stone.

Irqai , B.D. 165, 8, a name of Åmen.

Ihit , Mission XIII, 149, a cow-goddess.

ihȧ 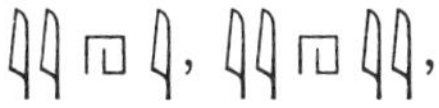, P. 84, T. 318, O!

iḥ 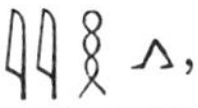, IV, 305, to toil at the oars.

iḥi 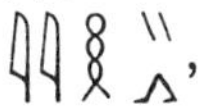, P.S.B. 24, 46, a particle of exclamation.

iḥa , T. 304, alas!

ikh , to hang out, to suspend in the air.

is 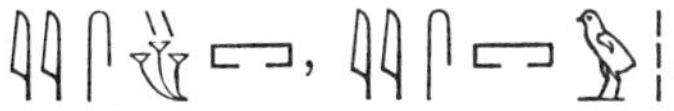, tomb; see [illegible].

is , Rev., to make haste; Copt. ⲓⲏⲥ.

isaṭṭ 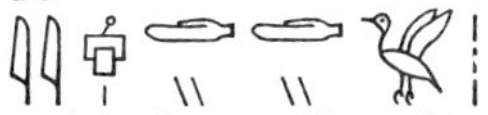, Anastasi I, 24, 8, to tremble, hover (like a bird).

isf-t , sins, faults, transgressions; see [illegible].

isr , stalks of papyrus, [illegible] [illegible].

Isrȧar , Israel Stele, 27, Israelites; from Heb. יִשְׂרָאֵל.

it , P. 371, father; plur. [illegible].

it , Rev. 11, 163, , dew; see [illegible]; Copt. ⲉⲓⲱⲧⲉ.

iti , grain.

ititi , to sound a trumpet.

Ituā Bār , Asien 98, Alt. K. 241, a proper name; Heb. ירעבעל(?)

ithit-t 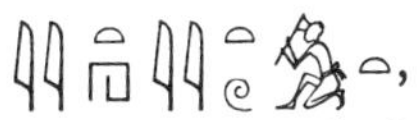, Rev., importunity.

iṭ 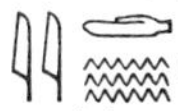, dew; see [illegible].

iṭāa 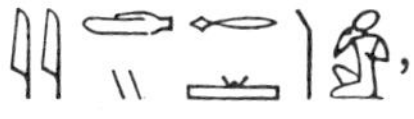, one who knows; Heb. יוֹדֵעַ.

itchar , potter (?); Heb. יוֹצֵר.

U

u ; Heb. ו.

u , they, them, their.

u , Rec. 3, 221, serpent or serpent-god.

u (?), uu (?) , district, estate, domain.

u (?) , Anastasi I, 12, 3, Brit. Mus. 321, officer (= ?).

u (?) , to build.

u (?) , Rec. 21, 14, a kind of well or spring in the Great Oasis.

u (?) , Rev. 13, 113, roll, documents.

U , Rec. 30, 191, a mythological city.

U , B.D.G. 1110, a god of Denderah.

u (?) , Jour. As. 1908, 261, remote, afar; Copt. ОΥЄІ.

uai , N. 708, , Àmen. 18, 7, , to be away from a person or place, to go away, be remote, afar off, absent; Copt. ОΥЄ; , being afar off.

ua , to remit a tax, to abolish an impost.

uaiu , travellers, remote (of countries).

ua , something which happened a long time ago.

uai-t , a distant thing.

uaua (?) the name of the moon on her 12th day.

ua-t , U. 70, , U. 399, , P. 330, , way, road, path, journey; dual, ; plur. , various ways; **ua-t neter** , the road followed by the procession in which the figure of a god was carried; , traveller, he who is on the road.

uau , L.D. III, 140B, a flat field.

ua-t , a garden walk.

ua-t ent reth , "road of all men," *i.e.*, a common highway.

ua-t mitu , the roads of the damned.

uatu neferut , good roads, roads easy to travel.

Uatiu , road-gods.

Uat-Ḥeru , P. 160, the path of Horus, *i.e.*, heaven.

ua-t mu (?) , a watercourse, water channel.

ua-t ḥit , rain channel.

uau 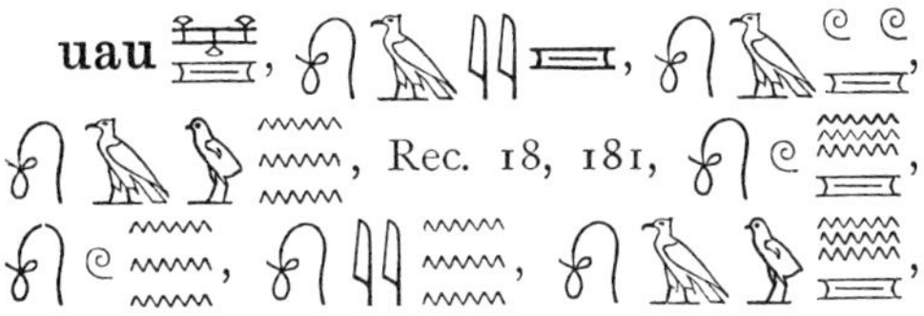 Rec. 18, 181, stream, watercourse.

uau en uatch ur 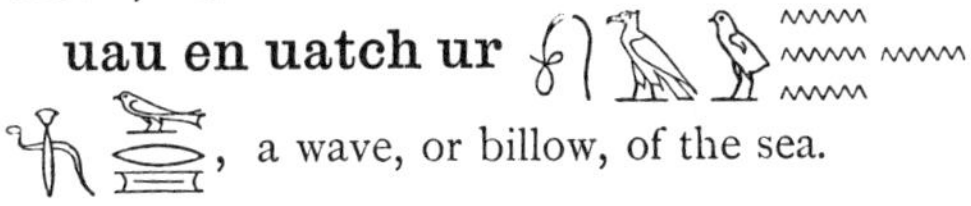 a wave, or billow, of the sea.

uau en åter  Mar. Karn. 42, 22, river flood.

ua  to be about to do something; going to ruin; with, about to burst into flame.

ua 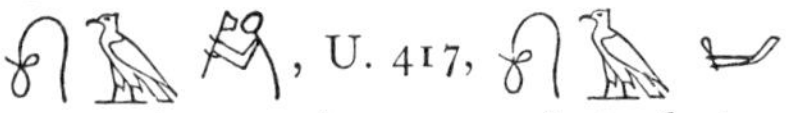 U. 417, T. 237, to attack, to smite, to smash, to destroy, to vanquish.

ua 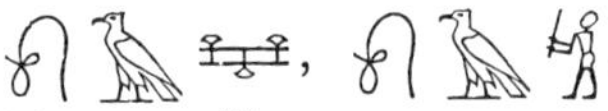 Peasant 291, to drive away (?)

uaua 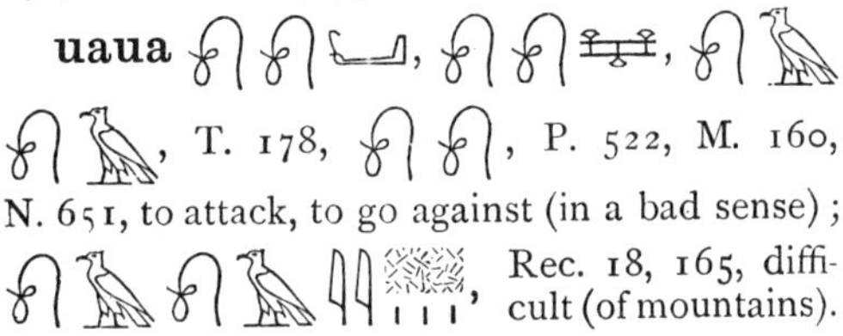 T. 178, P. 522, M. 160, N. 651, to attack, to go against (in a bad sense); Rec. 18, 165, difficult (of mountains).

ua 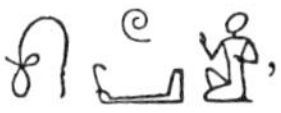, warden, governor.

uai 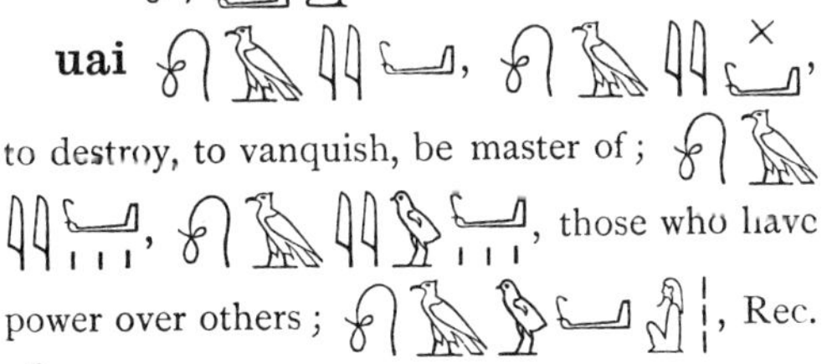 to destroy, to vanquish, be master of; those who have power over others; Rec. 26, 230.

ua  to bear, to carry away, to grasp.

ua ḥa-t , uplifted in heart, glad.

Ua , B.D. 170, 2, a birth goddess (?)

Ua-ḥa-t , Ṭuat XII, a dawn-god.

uaa  to think, to meditate, to take counsel; the king communed with his heart.

uaua-t , Wört. 326, Wört. Supp. 383 . . . .

uaua 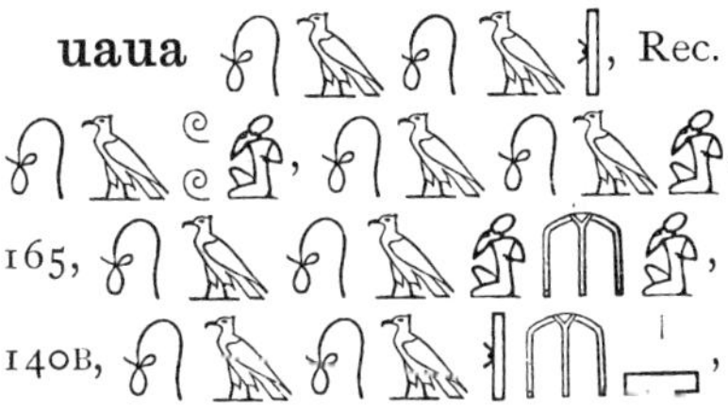 Rec. 29, 164, Rec. 18, 165, L.D. III, 140B, Tutānkhåmen 12, to take counsel, to discuss, to deliberate, to talk things over.

uaua sekheru , Kubbân Stele 8, to devise plans.

uaua 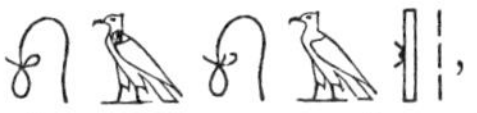, Demot. Cat. XIII, a word used in connection with money.

ua , Jour. As. 1908, 267, to blaspheme, to speak evil of some one, to plot rebellion; Copt. ⲟⲩⲁ.

uaiu , blasphemers.

uau-t  blasphemy; plur.

uati  rebel; plur.

uaua , to plot rebellion, to curse the king, to blaspheme.

uauai , to answer (?) Copt. ⲟⲩⲱ.

uai  Rev., death, destruction, the end; Copt. ⲟⲩⲱ.

Uai , "Rebel," "Blasphemer," a title of Āapep.

Uaiu , the associates of Āapep.

uai , Rec. 29, 157, to stink, foul, bad, stinking.

ua 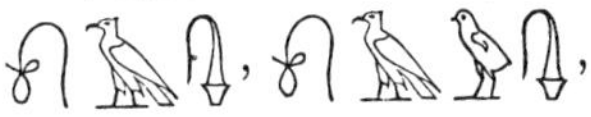, to burn, to be hot.

uaa-t , flame, fire.

uaua-t , Rec. 14, 176,  , fire, flame; plur. , 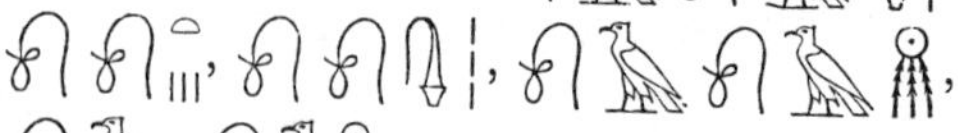, .

uauau , radiance, light, fiery splendour.

ua , Rec. 31, 31, a rope, a fetter, a bond; plur. 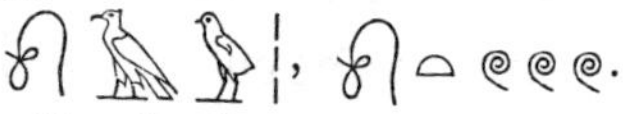.

uaua-t 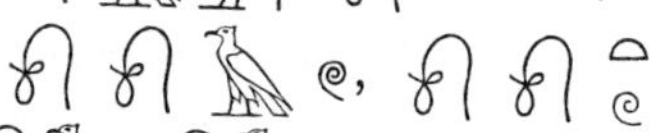, Thes. 1285, 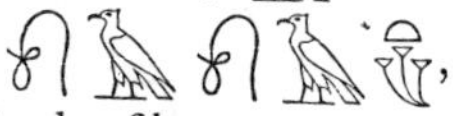, a measuring line, cord of palm fibre.

uaua-t, uauait 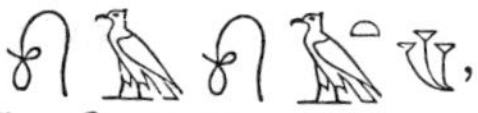, foliage, hair; plur. .

Uauaiu , Rec. 14, 106, a tribe or people.

ua[ua] , the seed of a plant.

uaua-t , a part of the head.

uaårekh 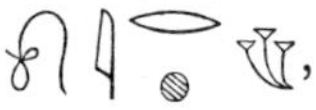, to blossom.

uaā 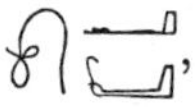, to carry off.

Uaiput , B.D. 177, 7, a group of four cow-goddesses.

Uauamti ; see , B.D. 125, II.

uab  = Copt. ⲟⲩⲃⲉ.

uab  , a plant, flower, blossom; plur. , Hymn Darius 24.

uabu , garden (?) cultivated land of some sort.

uab-t , the sides of a crown.

uabs (?) , green plants.

uapt 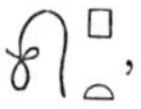, U. 369 . . . . . .

uapi (upi?) , a judgment, a judicial decision.

uam 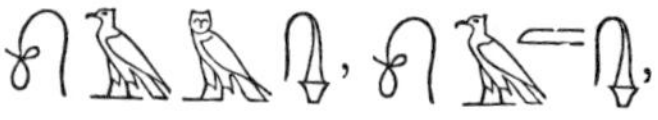, to be hot, to burn.

uam , a plant;  , the seeds of the same (used in medicine).

uami , Rec. 30, 66, a part of a ship (?)

Uamemti , B.D. 125, II, one of the 42 assessors of Osiris.

Uamemti   , Ṭuat IX, X, a monster mythological serpent, a form of Āepep.

Uamemtiu [illegible], Ṭuat X, a group of five serpents who are fettered by Geb.

uanu (?) [illegible], Rec. 4, 21, a grain-bearing plant.

uani [illegible], Rev. 14, 21, garland, crown = [illegible].

uanen [illegible], that which is.

uaneb [illegible], herbs, plants.

uanr [illegible], mat.

uar [illegible], to conceive = [illegible].

uar [illegible], to tie up, to lace up.

uar [illegible], a measuring cord or rope, cord of a net; plur. [illegible].

Uar-t-neter Semsu [illegible], B.D. 153A, 21, the name of a rope of the magical net.

uara 
, reed, a reed flute or pipe.

uar-t , a bird with a shrill note.

uarr 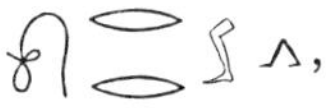, title of an official, governor (?)

uaruti , Mission V, 521, the two thighs.

uarp , to send; Copt. ⲟⲩⲱⲣⲡ.

uarh 
, to rejoice, to dance, to leap with joy; var.
.

uarḥ , Rec. 3, 35, 
, a space suitable for building; var.
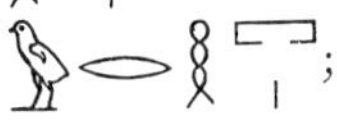; Copt. ⲟⲩⲣⲉϩ.

uarḥ-ntu , Rec. 16, 57 . . . .

uarkh ,
, to be green, to become green, to flourish.

uarkh-t 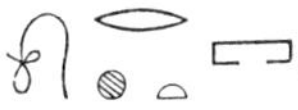, Rec. 10, 136,
, space, area, hall, court of a temple; Copt. ⲟⲩⲣⲉϩ.

uarkhut (?) 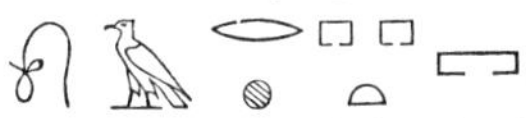, the chambers in which Hathor assisted the dead.

uars-t 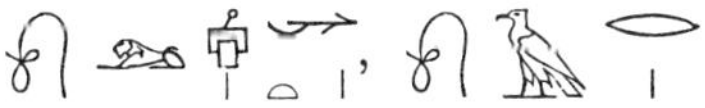
, head-rest; Copt. ⲟⲩⲣⲁⲥ.

uarsh , to enjoy.

Uarkatȧr , Rec. 21, 81, a Syrian shipmaster.

uartȧ , rose; Copt. ⲟⲩⲉⲣⲧ, Arab. وَرْد.

Uartȧ , Rec. 21, 78, a Syrian shipmaster.

uarṭ , part of the ornamentation of a crown.

uahr 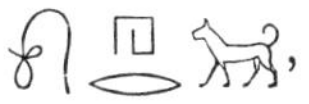, dog; Copt. ⲟⲩϩⲟⲣ.

uaḥ , T. 224, , U. 528, P. 91,
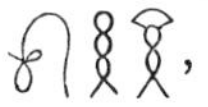, M. 120, T. 332, , N. 961,
, Rec. 27, 224, 29, 148, ,
,
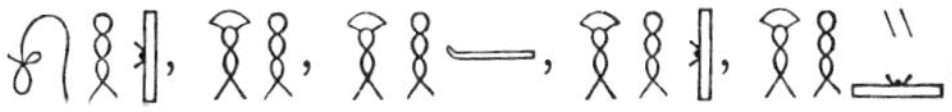,
, Ȧmen. 2, 3, 10, 9, , Ȧmen. 23, 14, 26, 10, to set, to plant, to place in position, to leave behind, to fasten, to set before, *i.e.*, to offer, the acquittal of a court, to pitch a camp.

uaḥ ȧb , Rec. 16, 56, , Peasant 219, to set the heart or mind to do something or on something, to set in the heart, to pay heed; 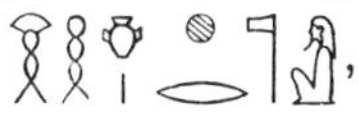, devoted before the god.

uaḥ ȧhi [illegible]. Rec. 8, 133, to pitch a camp.

uaḥ ākh [illegible], Rec. 6, 10, to offer up a burnt offering.

uaḥ ākh [illegible], a fire-altar, fire-place.

uaḥ ākh [illegible], N. 999, the name of a fire festival.

uaḥ neḥb-t [illegible], to lay a stone.

uaḥ er ta [illegible], to lay down (arms).

uaḥ tchatcha (?) [illegible], U. 283,
[illegible], N. 26, [illegible], N. 1214,
[illegible], Thes. 1285,
[illegible], to bow the head frequently, to do honour, multiplication (of figures); [illegible]
[illegible] = 1185 × $\frac{1}{20}$.

uaḥ-t [illegible], Anastasi IV, 2, 11, Koller Pap. 2, 9, an instrument used in carrying loads.

uaḥit 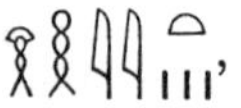, Annales III, 109, places for alighting; see .

uaḥ , to offer libations, water carrier (?)

uaḥ , Rev. 12, 135, libation priest; Gr. χοαχυτης.

uaḥit 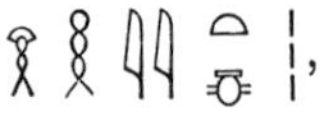, libations, libation vessels (?)

uaḥ-t , Annales III, 110, offerings.

uaḥȧ , Rev. 6, 7, gifts, benefactions.

uaḥit , N. 1226, [illegible], M. 622, [illegible], P. 435, [illegible] [illegible], T. 267, [illegible], M. 424, [illegible], a divine offering.

uaḥ 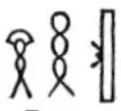, Mar. Karn. 53, 25, in swearing:—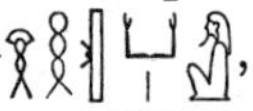, "I swear by my Ka"; [illegible] , "I swear by the Ka of Ptaḥ."

uaḥ 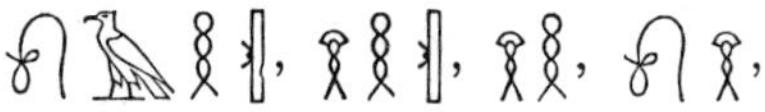, 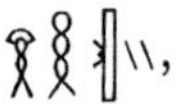, to add to, to increase, to grow, to become many or much; , frequent journeyings; , in addition to; , besides; Copt. ⲟⲩⲱϩ.

uaḥi[t] , increment, growth, increase, plentiful, abundant.

Uaḥit 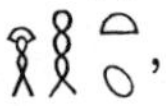, Berg. I, 14, a lioness-headed goddess.

Uaḥ-qaȧ-f , Rhind Pap. 26, , "he who increases his form," a title of the Moon-god.

uaḥit 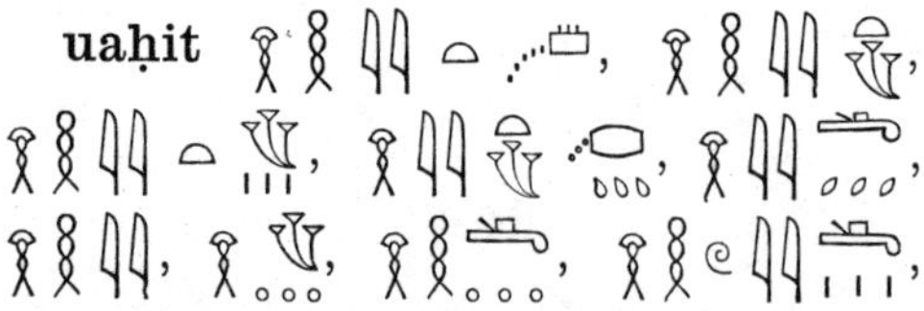, 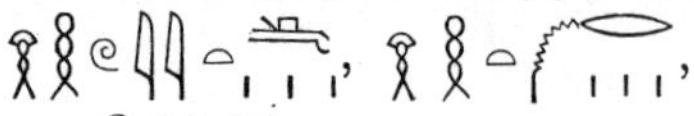, spelt, grain; var. .

uaḥ-t 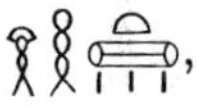, food.

uaḥ , wreath, crown, necklace (?)

uaḥ 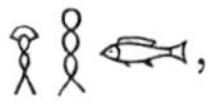, a kind of fish.

uaḥ , Rec. 14, 67, [illegible], Rec. 16, 70, fishermen; Copt. ⲟⲩⲟϩⲓ.

uaḥȧ (?) , Rev. 12, 62, 66 = Copt. ⲟⲩⲟϩ.

Uaḥtiu , the dwellers in the Oasis country; , Rec. 10, 150, Oasis women.

uakh , U. 519, P. 277, 697, Rec. 31, 28, [illegible], P. 361, N. 1075, [illegible], to be green, to flourish; [illegible], T. 336, P. 816, N. 644, full of blossom, blooming, flourishing.

Uakh-t , a green or fertile region, a name of the Great Oasis.

uakhkh-t , P. 399, M. 570, N. 1176, garden, pool with plants growing in it.

Uakh , B.D. 110, a lake full of green plants in Sekhet-Åaru.

uakh 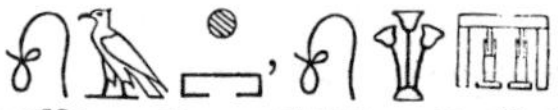, Rec. 26, 2, [illegible], [illegible], [illegible], [illegible], [illegible], a large chamber, hall of a palace, hall of columns, colonnade, a country house.

uakh , to seek after; Copt. ⲟⲩⲱϣ.

uakhr , a hall or chamber with plants in it.

uas 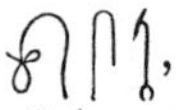, P. 359, N. 762, 910, 1073, [illegible], [illegible], [illegible], [illegible], [illegible], a sceptre; [illegible], P. 659, M. 767, the **uas** and the **tchām** sceptres.

uas , physical and mental well-being, content, serenity; , "life, stability, content"; [illegible], P. 18, [illegible], P. 624, sound, well, content.

uas-t (?) 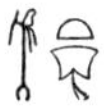, a kind of animal, dog (?)

Uas , Mar. Karn. 42, 16, Thebes personified.

Uasit , consort of Uas.

Uasit 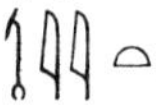, Ṭuat X, a lioness-goddess of the Eye of Horus.

uas 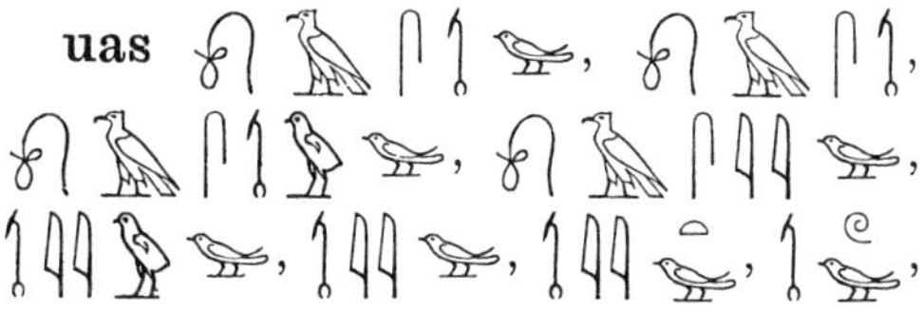, to be in a ruined state, crumbling to ruin, ruined, decayed, weak, feeble; , in a most ruined state.

uas , to work in wood, to saw.

uasuas , to cut, to stab, to saw; see .

uasam , to be in a ruined state; var.

uasakh 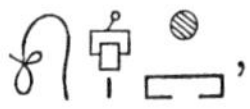, chamber, large room, hall; see **usekh-t**.

Uasȧr (Uasri) , 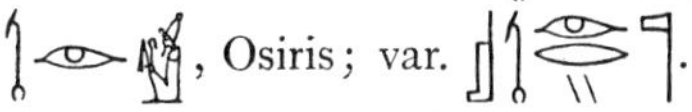, Osiris; var.

uasm (?) , to be ruined, destroyed.

uasmut (?) , ruin.

Uasri , a title of Osiris.

uasg , a large wide board (?)

uasṭen 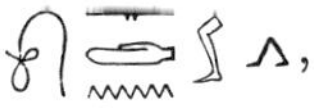, to move with long strides; see **usten** ; Copt. ⲟⲩⲟⲥⲑⲉⲛ.

uash 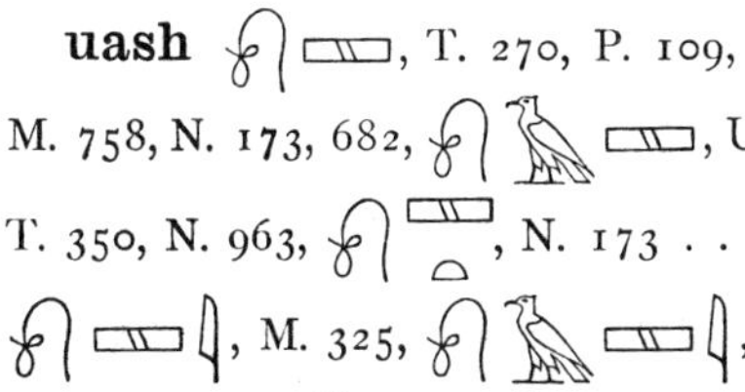, T. 270, P. 109, 372, 654, M. 758, N. 173, 682, U. 94, 536, T. 350, N. 963, N. 173 . . . . , M. 325, P. 163.

uash , Hh. 211 . . . . .

uash-t 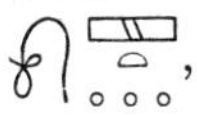, P. 555 . . . . .

uash , to greet, to adore, to worship, to praise, to magnify, to wish; Copt. ⲟⲩⲱϣ.

uashu , praises, cries of joy.

uashiu , those who sing praises.

uash-t , praise, adoration.

uashesh , a skin disease.

Uasheshu 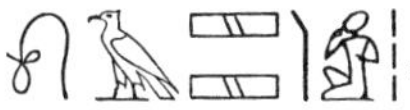, a foreign people or nation.

uasha 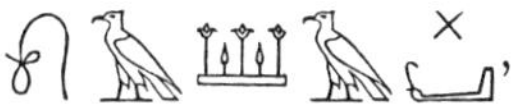, Rec. 21, 98, to carry (?) to be carried (?)

uashat-t , a disease of the eye.

uashatȧ-ti , P.S.B. 13, 412, a chronic sufferer from eye disease (?)

uashb-t , a kind of medicine (?) medicaments.

Uashba 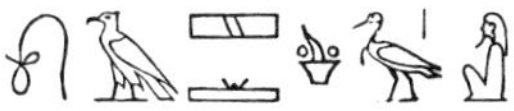, Tomb of Seti I, one of the 75 forms of Rā (No. 46).

uashk , Hh. 363 . . . .

uag 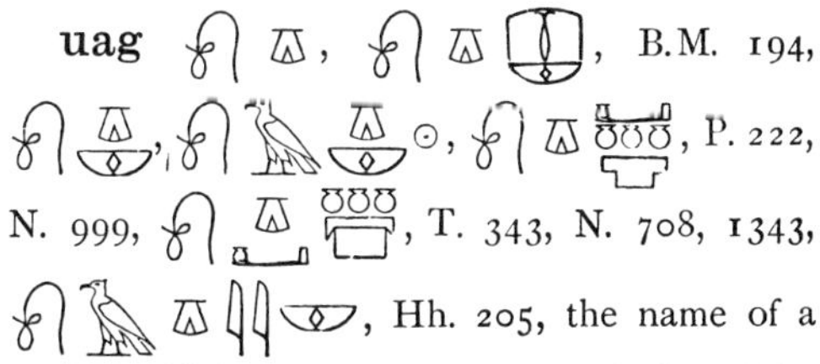, B.M. 194, P. 222, N. 999, T. 343, N. 708, 1343, Hh. 205, the name of a festival which took place on the 18th day of the month Thoth.

uag , to cry out, to shout.

uat , Jour. As. 1908, 295, to depart; Copt. ⲟⲩⲱϯ.

uati 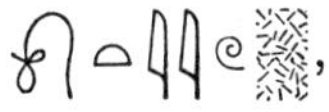, creation, production.

uatemtȧ, Anastasi I, 7, 3.......

uaths-t, what is held up, above, heaven, sky.

Uathesit, Berg. II, 13, "Raiser," a title of Mut.

uaṭ, way, road = .

uaṭu, a kind of plant used in medicine.

uatch, U. 185, , to be green, to be young and new, to thrive, to prosper, to flourish, be fertile; Copt. ⲟⲩⲱⲧ; , U. 566.

uatch-t, P. 413, M. 591, N. 1197, , green, fresh, youthful, something green.

uatchuatch, P. 419, M. 600, N. 1205, yellowish-green, or green; Copt. ⲟⲩⲉⲧⲟⲩⲟⲧ.

uatchuatch, yellowish-green coloured light.

uatchuaṭch-t, Rec. 27, 218, something yellowish-green in colour.

uatchut, , green things, growing crops, plants, herbs, vegetables; , young trees.

uatchuatch, , herbs, vegetables; Copt. ⲟⲩⲟⲧ-ⲟⲩⲉⲧ.

Uatchit, , the Green Land, a name of the Delta.

uatch-t, a part of the body, eye (?)

uatch-t, Berl. 7272, "fresh meat," *i.e.*, uncooked meat.

uatch-t, uatchit, B.M. 448, , a ceremonial bandlet made of green cloth or linen.

uatch-t, P. 614, M. 781, N. 1138, , the Green Crown.

uatch, U. 566, , green feldspar, sulphate of copper, root of emerald, turquoise; , green stone of Bakhet, *i.e.*, Sinai (?); , green stone of the South, perhaps the emeralds of Gebel Zâbarah; , green stone of the North.

uatch-t, , an amulet made of "root of emerald" stone, either in the round , or sculptured in relief on a plaque, ; green stone in general.

Uatch, 1. the sceptre of feldspar with which Horus fought against the foes of Osiris: it proceeded from Uatchit, , N. 705; 2. , the sceptre of Isis, B.D. 105, 4.

Uatch-en-theḥen-t, B.D. 125, III, 24, the crystal sceptre which the Fenkhu gave to the deceased.

uatch, U. 65, , T. 334, , N. 411, , N. 708, , eye-paint containing sulphate of copper.

uatch, ointment containing sulphate of copper.

Uatch-ȧr-ti (?), B.D. 32, 8, green of eyes, or strong sighted (?)

Uatch-ān, T. 145, M. 198, N. 540, the name of a sacred boat.

Uatch-ur , T. 275, P. 690, N. 67, 

, "the Great Green water," *i.e.*, the sea, the ocean; , the islands of the Mediterranean.

Uatch-ur , Ombos I, 1, 83: (1) the god of the Mediterranean Sea, , T. 338, P. 28, M. 610; (2) a name of the great celestial sea, , B.D. 17, 45.

uatch ra , a goose with a green beak.

uatch ḥa-t, Rec. 29, 148, a bird with a green breast; plur. .

uatch , a stick, withy, twig, pillar, support, column; Copt. ⲟⲩⲉⲓⲧ; , T. 198, P. 678, two pillars connected with .

uatchit 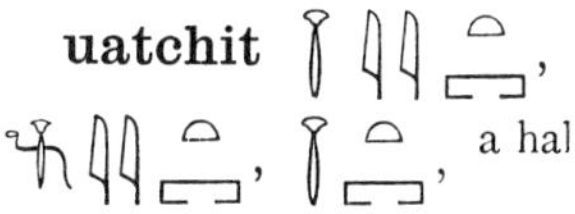, Hymn Darius 35, a hall with pillars in it, colonnade.

uatchi[t] 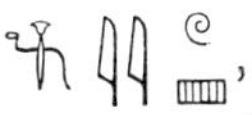, stele, memorial tablet; Copt. ⲟⲩⲟⲉⲓⲧ; var. 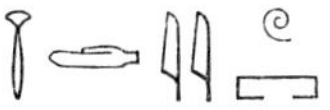.

uatch , altar, tablet for offerings.

uatch , IV, 1157, a kind of loaf or cake.

uatch 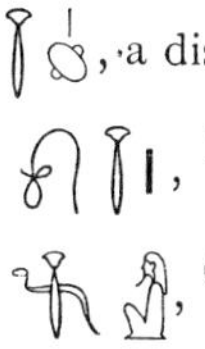, a disease of the belly.

Uatch, N. 705, "green one," a divine proper name.

Uatch, Ombos I, 1, 186–188, one of the 14 Kau of Rā.

Uatchit 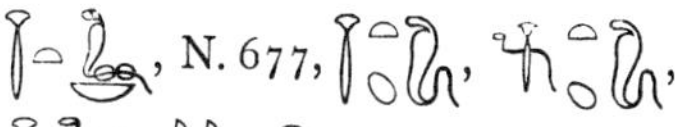, N. 677, , Rec. 30, 186, , an ancient serpent-goddess. The centre of her cult was Per-Uatchit (Buto), in the Delta. She was the chief goddess of the North. 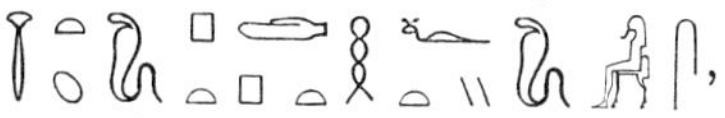, Berg. I, 8, Uatchit, the holy double goddess of Pe-Ṭep; 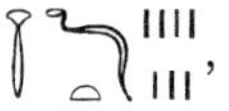, Rec. 30, 186, the seven companions of Uatchit.

Uatch-tî 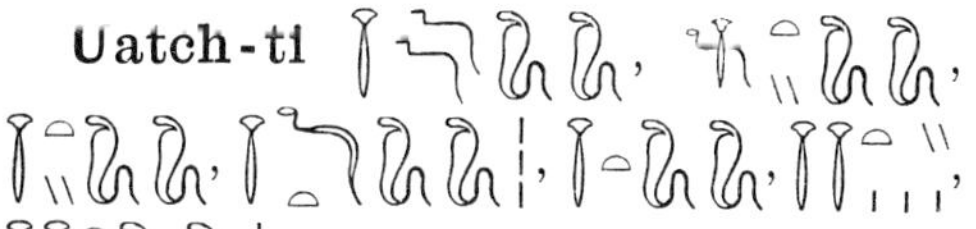, , the two goddesses Uatchit and Nekhebit, the two uraei on the brow of Rā.

Uatchit , a foreign land (?)

Uatch-àu-mut-f , Berg. II, 9, an ape-headed keeper of the 9th hour of the night.

Uatch-āab-f-tep-sekhet-f  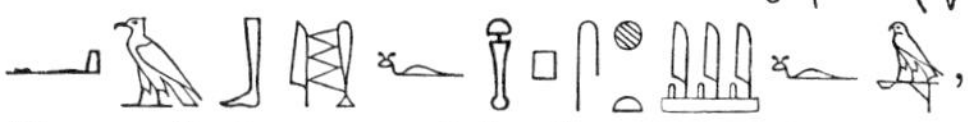, T. 333, P. 825, one of the four bulls of Tem.

Uatchit neb-[t]-kek , Ombos I, 111, a hawk-headed serpent-goddess.

Uatch-Neser-t 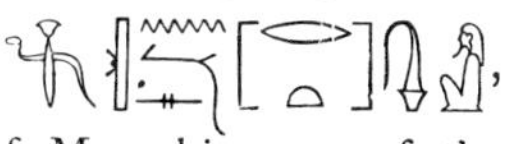, B.D. 125, II, a god of Memphis, one of the 42 assessors of Osiris.

Uatch-neterit , Ombos 2, 132.

uatch-t rār (?) , Rev. 14, 18 . . . .

Uatch-reṭ 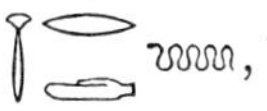, Denderah IV, 65, a serpent associate of Horus.

Uatch-ḥer , Ṭuat IV, "Green-face," a god.

Uatchit-tcheserit , a goddess (?)

uatch , to violate.

uatchāi , a kind of flower.

uatcheb [hieroglyphs], Mar. Karn. 54, 42, to present, to bring forward, to recoil (?)

uatchnȧ [hieroglyphs], a flute, reed pipe.

uatchḥ [hieroglyphs], IV, 587, child.

uatchḥ [hieroglyphs], Bubastis 51, altar, altar pitcher.

uȧ [hieroglyphs], pronoun, 1st pers. sing.

uȧ [hieroglyphs] = mark of dual masc. = later [hieroglyphs].

uȧ-t [hieroglyphs], P. 308, a cake, a loaf (?)

uȧ [hieroglyphs], mummy case.

uȧ [hieroglyphs], the latus fish.

uȧ [hieroglyphs], A.Z. 49, 134–136, Mar. Karn. 55, 61, [hieroglyphs], Ebers Pap. 109, 8, [hieroglyphs], R.E. 6, 26, to remove, to set aside, to withdraw (from the sum); [hieroglyphs] A.Z. 47, 134–136, setting aside, not counting.

uȧa [hieroglyphs], ship, boat; [hieroglyphs].

uȧa nesu [hieroglyphs], the boat of the king, *i.e.*, the royal barge.

uȧa en tcha [hieroglyphs], Nȧstasen Stele 39, a kind of boat used in the Ṣûdân.

uȧa-ui [hieroglyphs], the two great boats [of the Sun-god], *i.e.*, the Sekti boat and the Āntchti boat.

Uȧa penāt [hieroglyphs], Ṭuat III, a mythological boat.

Uȧa em Meḥṭit [hieroglyphs], Mar. Aby. I, 45, the sacred boat of Meḥṭit.

uȧa en maāti [hieroglyphs], boat of Truth, a mythological boat.

Uȧa en Neh-t [hieroglyphs], A.Z. 35, 19, a boat in [hieroglyphs].

uȧa en Rā [hieroglyphs], B.D. 141, 5, the boat of Rā.

uȧa en Kheperȧ [hieroglyphs], the boat of Kheperȧ.

uȧa en Tef [hieroglyphs], B.D. 164, 3, the boat of the Father.

uȧa en Tem [hieroglyphs], the boat of Tem.

Uȧa herr [hieroglyphs], Ṭuat III, a mythological boat.

uȧa ḥeḥ [hieroglyphs], the "boat of Millions of Years," a name of the boat of Rā.

Uȧa-ta [hieroglyphs], Ṭuat III, the boat of the earth; [hieroglyphs], Ṭuat II, the four boats of the earth.

Uȧa Tesṭes [hieroglyphs], Ṭuat VII, a star-goddess.

uȧa [hieroglyphs], Ȧmen. 24, 19, to praise.

uȧa-t [hieroglyphs], a kind of bird.

uȧa-t [hieroglyphs], nausea, vomiting.

uȧauȧa [hieroglyphs], Anastasi I, 28, 3, to be weak, loose, flabby.

uȧauit [hieroglyphs], the weakness of old age, tottering, feeble.

uȧu [hieroglyphs], Rec. 32, 15 . . . . . .

uȧn , [illegible], [illegible]
[illegible], [illegible], [illegible],
[illegible], to put aside, to shift, to depart from, to transgress.

uȧnf (?) 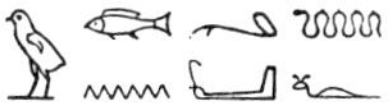, to turn into worms, become maggoty.

Uȧnṭit , a goddess, Ombos 2, 133.

uȧḥ ; see [illegible], carob fruit.

uȧth-ȧb (?) , U. 460, son of [illegible].

Uȧṭȧṭ 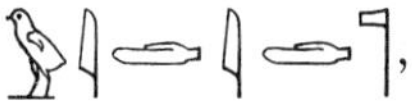, Aelt. Texte 3, 35, a god (?)

uā , an interjection.

uā , curse.

uā 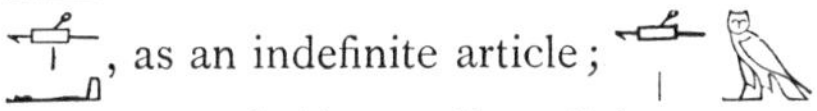, as an indefinite article; [illegible]
, a festival; [illegible], a door;
, a servant of thine.

uāu 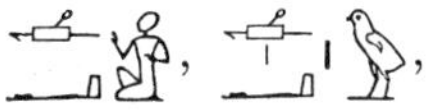, [illegible], a man, a person, anyone.

uā , U. 316, N. 1238, [illegible], P. 641,
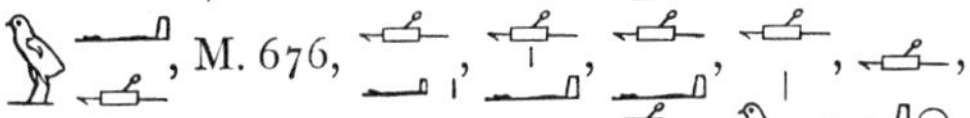, M. 676, [illegible], [illegible], [illegible], [illegible], [illegible],
one, single, only one; fem. , [illegible],
P. 617, 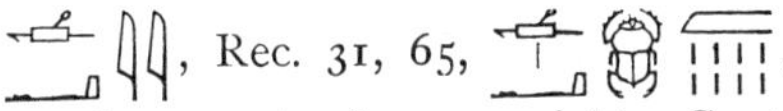, Rec. 31, 65, [illegible], Rec. 23, 196, one who became eight; Copt. ⲟⲩⲁ, ⲟⲩⲁⲓ.

uā-t 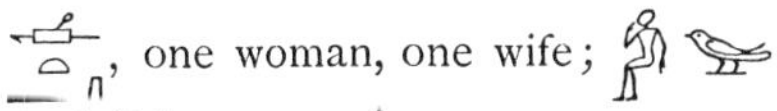, one woman, one wife; [illegible]
, 70 children, the children of one wife.

Uā 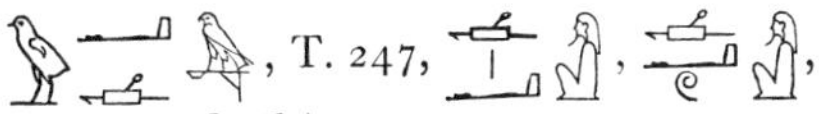, T. 247, [illegible], [illegible],
One, *i.e.*, God; 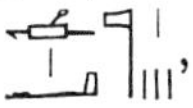, number one of the gods.

uā 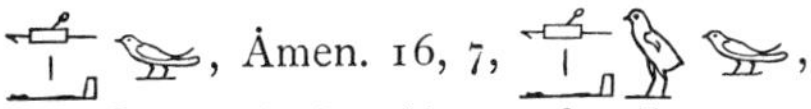, Ȧmen. 16, 7, [illegible],
, [illegible], [illegible], [illegible],
only one, sole, solitary, alone.

uāāu 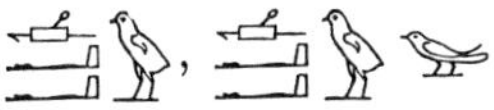, [illegible], one, only one, alone, favourite.

uāā-t 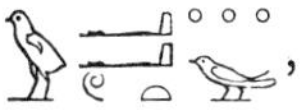, loneliness.

uāiu 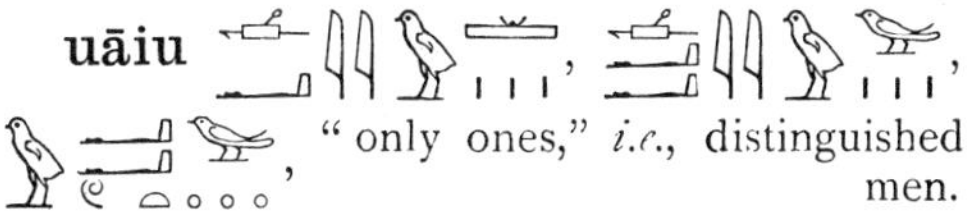, [illegible],
[illegible], "only ones," *i.e.*, distinguished men.

uāti 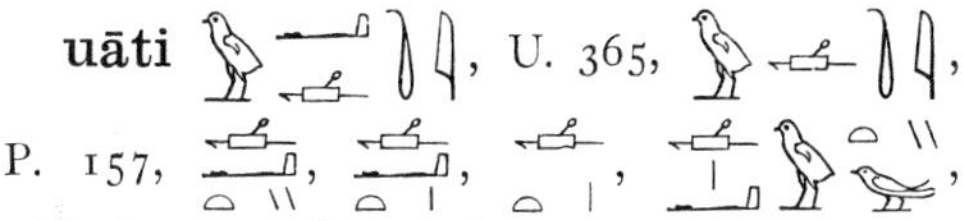, U. 365, [illegible],
P. 157, [illegible], [illegible], [illegible], [illegible],
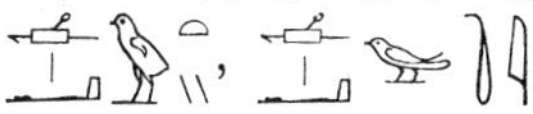, [illegible], only one, sole; fem.
, [illegible], Israel Stele 12; [illegible], the only God; 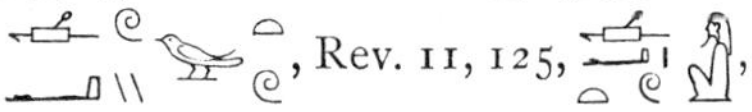, Rev. 11, 125, [illegible],
Mar. Karn. 53, 28, royal statue; Copt. ⲟⲩⲁⲁⲧ.

uā uā , N. 784, [illegible],
Rec. 30, 187, , [illegible],
[illegible], [illegible], [illegible], one only, one alone; 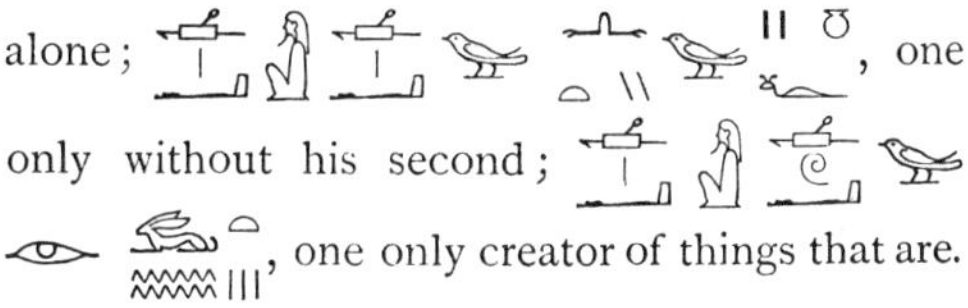, one only without his second; [illegible]
[illegible], one only creator of things that are.

uā 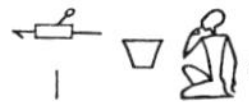, Jour. As. 1908, 285, to set apart something for a purpose.

uā 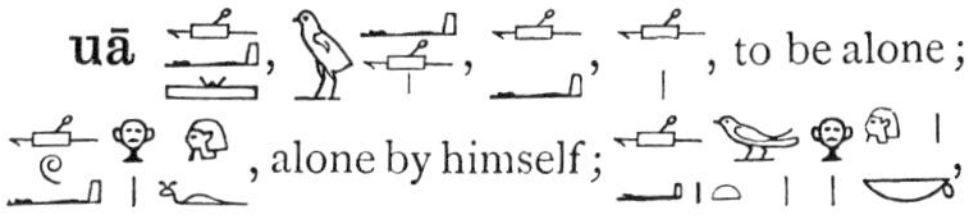, [illegible], [illegible], [illegible], to be alone;
[illegible], alone by himself; [illegible],
alone by thyself.

uā ȧb 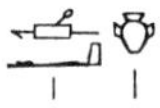, "one heart," a title (?)

uā — 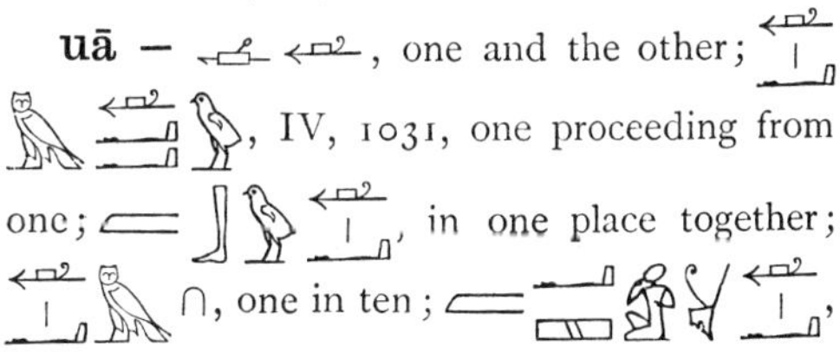, one and the other; [illegible]
[illegible], IV, 1031, one proceeding from one; [illegible], in one place together; [illegible], one in ten; [illegible], with a common cry; 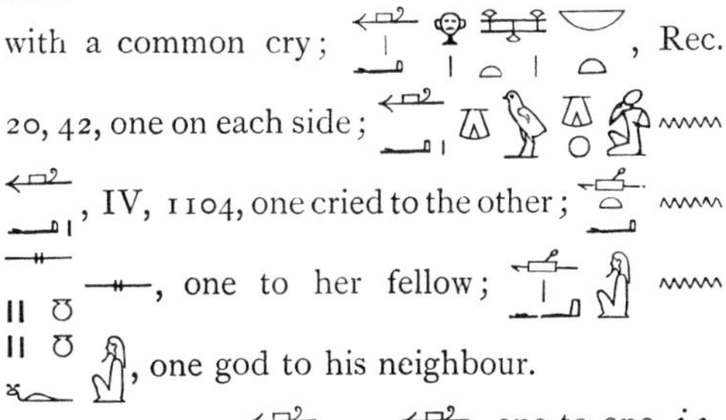, Rec. 20, 42, one on each side; [illegible]
[illegible], IV, 1104, one cried to the other; [illegible]
[illegible], one to her fellow; [illegible]
[illegible], one god to his neighbour.

uā en uā 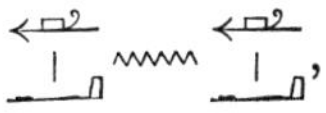, one to one, *i.e.*, one to another.

uā neb, every one, everybody; , Rec. 20, 41, everybody is like his neighbour.

uā ḥer uā, one on the top of the other.

uā ḥer khu, B.M. 196, one by reason of his abilities or qualities; , IV, 1026, he was unrivalled.

uā-ḥer-...., an object—use unknown (Lacau).

uā .... ki ....., the one .... the other; fem. ...., B.D. 161 (Rubric 2).

Uā, U. 432, , T. 247, the ONE, later , , , a title of Rā, Osiris, Åmen and other gods, and of the deceased as a divine being: thus Pepi II is , N. 952.

uā-t, the name of one of the eyes of Rā.

uā-t, , the name of a crown, or diadem.

Uāuti, B.D.G. 659, , , a name of Hathor.

Uāuti, B.D. 164, 1, Moret, Culte, 140, *i.e.*, ONE, a title of Neith and of Sekhmit-Bast-Rā.

Uā-uben-em-Åāḥ, B.D. 2, 1, a title of Osiris.

Uā-pesṭ-em-Åāḥ, B.D. 2, 2, a title of Osiris.

Uā em Uā, B.D. 42, 17, "One [proceeding] from One," a title of Osiris.

Uā-menḥ, B.D. 7, 1, "One of wax," *i.e.*, the wax figure of Āapep which was burnt ceremonially.

Uā seqeb, B.D. 105, a god.

uā-t, a piece; , a piece of åsha cloth.

uāāu, private chamber, or apartments.

uā, Düm. H.I. I, 26, 27, , spear, lance.

uā-ti, a staff with a jackal's head.

uā-ti, a hair tail, a tail.

uā-ti, , the Lion, a sign of the Zodiac.

uā-ti, , , a kind of goat.

uā, P. 98, M. 68 = , N. 48, flesh and bone, heir, heritage.

uā-t, P. 57, 122, N. 661, flesh, heir.

uā, P.S.B. 13, 303, , , , , , , , , an officer, master, lieutenant, an official of any kind; plur. .

uā en menshu, master of the boat, captain.

uā en khenu, master mariner.

uā, a kind of fish.

uā, , , to smite, to slay, to smash.

uāuā, , , to slay, fight, battle, slaughter; , Rec. 15, 171, eight leagues of slaughter.

uāa, Åmen. 11, 16, , , to cry out, to conjure, to blaspheme, to curse; demotic form, , Rev. 11, 164.

Uāau, , , B.D. 144, 147, the herald of the 3rd Ārit.

uāa , Rev. 12, 212, flax; Copt. ⲓⲁⲩ, ⲉⲓⲁⲁⲩ.

uāȧb 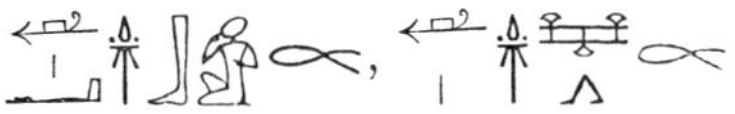, Rev. 11, 136, will, pleasure.

uāi, uāit 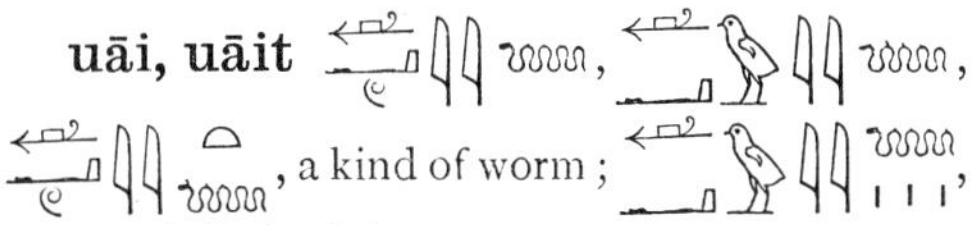, a kind of worm; worms, bait for fish.

uāu , box, casket.

uāuti , a kind of star, comet (?)

uāb , U. 573, P. 322, 607, M. 222, P. 191, N. 967, U. 188, P. 123, Rec. 31, 13, 31, 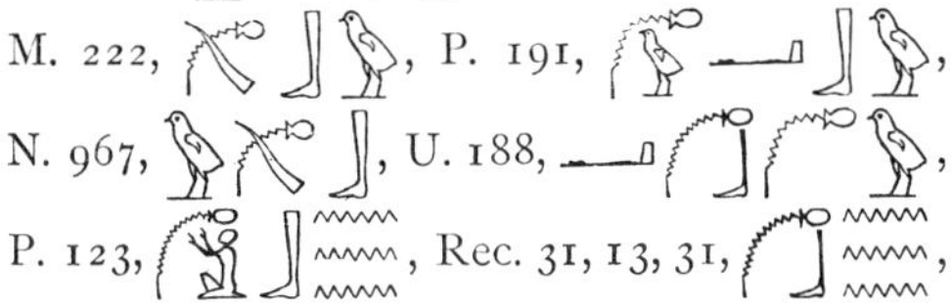 , to be innocent, guiltless, to be clean, to be purified, to be ceremonially pure or clean, to purify, to purify oneself, a cleansing, clean, to wash clean, pure, holy; Copt. ⲟⲩⲟⲡ.

uāb āui , clean-handed.

uāb ra , of pure mouth, clean speech.

uābu ḥeru , beings with clean or pure faces.

uāb , holy man, priest, libationer; Copt. ⲟⲩⲏⲏⲃ; plur.  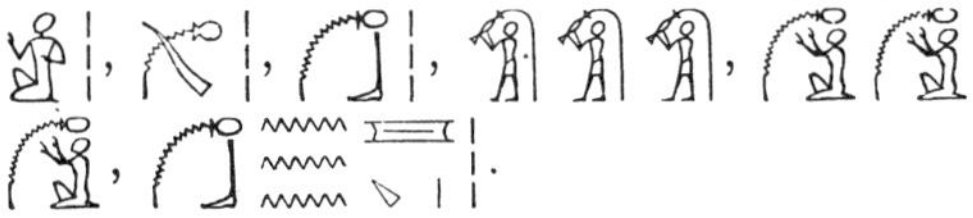.

uāb āa  , high priest, chief priest; plur.

uāb āa-ȧmi-hru-f  , the high priest of the day.

uāb Sekhmit , Ebers Pap. 99, 2, 3, exorcist.

uāb-t ȧbṭ , the month's duty of a priest.

uābu 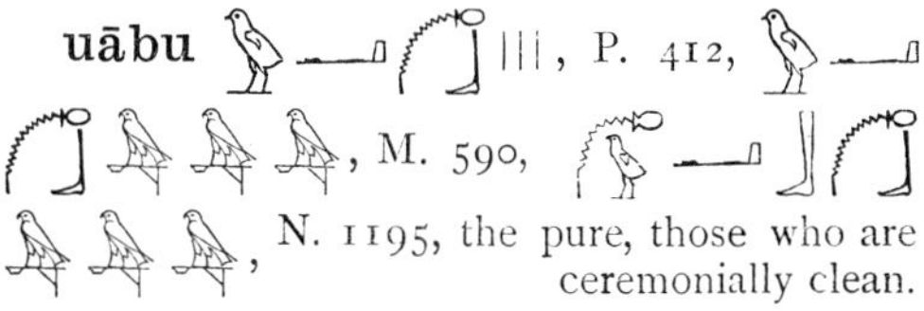, P. 412, M. 590, N. 1195, the pure, those who are ceremonially clean.

uābti , Rec. 36, 78, one morally pure.

uābtiu, uābut (?) 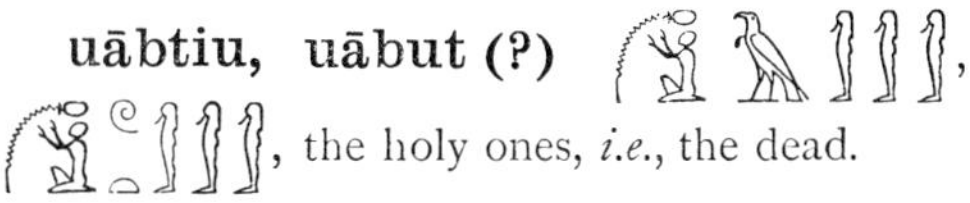, the holy ones, *i.e.*, the dead.

uāb , to pour out a cleansing liquid, to pour out libations.

uābu 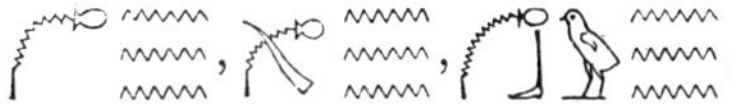, libation, a sprinkling with water in which incense has been dissolved; plur.  .

uāb-t , a pure meat offering; plur.  .

uābit 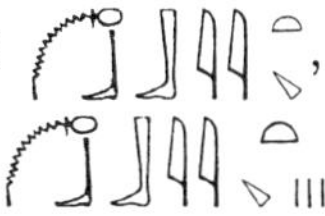, P.S.B. 16, 132, offering; plur.

uāb  , Rec. 27, 223, holy raiment or vestment, apparel which is ceremonially pure.

uāb-t  , U. 581, P. 608, N. 52, 962, Rec. 31, 163,  , a place ceremonially pure, a holy place, a sanctuary, a place where purification was effected, a wash-house, a bath; Copt. ⲟⲩⲁⲁⲃ; , doubly pure place, twice pure place.

uāb , a vessel of holy water (?)

uāb-t 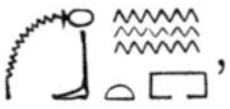, , the chamber in a temple in which the ceremonies symbolic of the mummification of Osiris were performed; it was commonly called 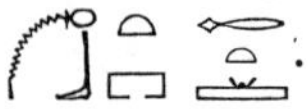.

uāb-t 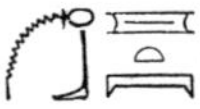, the holy place, a name of heaven.

Uābit , Berg. II, 14, a name of Nut.

Uāb-t 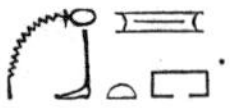. a sanctuary of Libya-Mareotis.

uāb 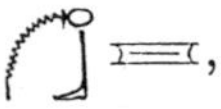, [illegible], [illegible], base, pedestal, socket.

uāb-t , Rec. 17, 4, tomb.

uābut (?) , Edict 15, breweries (?)

Uāb åsut 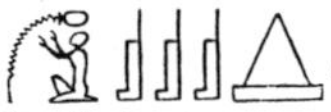, the name of the pyramid of Userkaf.

uāb ..... 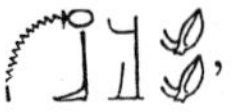, IV, 1031 ....

Uāb ur , "great sanctuary," a name of Osiris.

uābāb-t , U. 452, holy offerings.

uāf , [illegible], [illegible], [illegible], [illegible], [illegible], [illegible], [illegible], to tie, to bind, to wring, to twist, to fetter, fetter, tie, band; [illegible] [illegible], Rev. 13, 4, to oppress; [illegible] [illegible], Ḳubbân Stele 1; 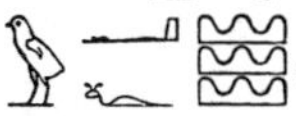, L.D. III, 55A; Copt. ⲱϥⲉ.

uām , to slay (?)

uān 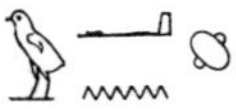, M. 826, [illegible], [illegible] [illegible], Rec. 13, 15, 15, 107, [illegible], [illegible], [illegible], [illegible], Rec. 13, 15, cedar; 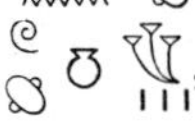, the fruit of the cedar.

uān , to kill, to slay.

uār , Rec. 22, 2, 31, 31, [illegible] , Mar. Karn. 53, 37, 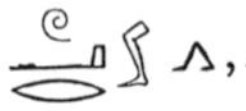, Åmen. 11, 7, [illegible], [illegible], [illegible], , Rec. 21, 77, to come forth (of a child from the womb), to take to flight, to escape, to depart, to melt away.

uāru , Peasant 208, fugitive (?) flight (?)

uār-t , N. 1196 [illegible], T. 399, P. 378, 412, M. 590, [illegible], [illegible] [illegible], [illegible], [illegible], [illegible], [illegible] [illegible], thigh, foot and leg; dual , [illegible], the two thighs; Copt. ⲟⲩⲉⲣⲏⲧⲉ.

Uār-t , [illegible], [illegible], one of the 36 Dekans; Greek *ουαρε*.

uār-t , [illegible], [illegible], [illegible], [illegible], [illegible], [illegible], [illegible], [illegible], Rec. 26, 229, a piece of ground, the quarter of a town, a place of bifurcation, bend; plur. , Rec. 33, 33, 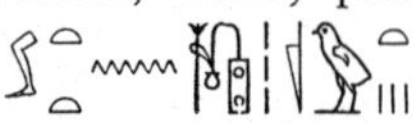, Rec. 11, 35, the artists' quarter.

uār-t , [illegible], Rec. 29, 146, [illegible], [illegible], [illegible], [illegible] [illegible], bend of a canal or lake.

uār-t , the necropolis at Abydos.

uār-t , [illegible], [illegible] [illegible], the name of a bend in a hill, or of a portion of the mountain at Abydos, which was sacred to Osiris; near it was a passage or corridor, with a canal in it or near it, by which offerings were supposed to be transported to the Other World.

uār-t āa-t , B.D. 86, 9, the name of a place where offerings were made at Abydos; , the great Uār-t.

Uār-t neb-t ḥeteput 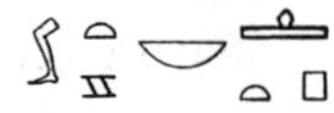 , the uār-t of offerings at Abydos.

uār-t, B.D. 150, 14, 5, a sacred place at.

uār-t, B.D. 153B, 10, the site of a moon-temple ( ).

Uār-t, , B.D. 98, 2, 86, 9: (1) a region in the Ṭuat; (2) the passage by which souls went to the Ṭuat.

Uār-t ent åkhemiu-seku, N. 1196, a mythological locality.

Uār-t ent Åst, etc., etc., B.D. 99, 25, 26, the keel (?) of the magical boat.

Uār-t ent båa, etc. etc., B.D. 153A, 13, the name of a part of the magical net.

Uār-t ent mu (?), B.D. 149, a place in the 13th Åat.

Uār-t ent she, B.D. 149, a place in the 11th Åat.

uāruti, Rechnungen 56, , , Rec. 9, 35, , inspector, overseer, ranger; , overseer of the governor's dining room.

uārit, , fem., mistress.

uār, juniper (?) (perhaps =); plur. .

uār-t, part of a ship, gangway plank (?)

uāri, Rev. 14, 17, to flow over or away; Copt. ⲟⲩⲱⲗⲉ.

uārirāu(?), Rev. 14, 12, singers, waiters; Copt. ⲟⲩⲉⲗⲟⲩⲉⲗⲉ.

uāḥ, , grain, an offering of grain.

uāḥ, a meat offering.

uāskhi (uskhi), Rev. 11, 168, something woven.

ui, mark of the dual masc., *e.g.*, , two great obelisks; , two great mighty gods; , doubly good is thy rising.

uiui (?), Anastasi I, 3, 7, light = (?)

ui, pers. pron. 1st sing.

ui, P. 163, N. 854, , Rec. 27, 56, , Rec. 30, 185, an interjection, an exclamation.

ui, Rev. to go away; Copt. ⲟⲩⲉⲓ.

ui, , , to reject, to cast aside, to throw away.

Ui-ermen (?), B.D. 99, 26, the worker of the sail in the magical boat.

ui-t, chamber, room.

uiā, , , , Rev. 14, 16, husbandry, agriculture; compare Copt. ⲟⲩⲟⲉⲓⲉ.

uip, Rev. 11, 184, judgment, decision.

uin, Rev. 11, 182, , Rev. 11, 178, , Jour. As. 1908, 289, light; Copt. ⲟⲩⲟⲉⲓⲛ.

uin, to open; see .

uin, , , window; Copt. ⲟⲩⲱⲓⲛⲓ in ⲙⲁⲡⲉⲣⲟⲩⲱⲓⲛⲓ.

Uinn, Rev. 13, 107, *i.e.*, , Greece, Greek; Heb. יָוָן.

uit , Rev. 13, 104, 15, 16, , stele; plur. , Rev. 13, 38, , Rev. 12, 59, a stone stele.

uiti 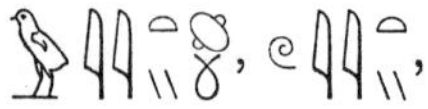, embalmed body.

uiti , a dresser of the dead, embalmer.

ub [illegible], heart; see **åb** [illegible].

ub 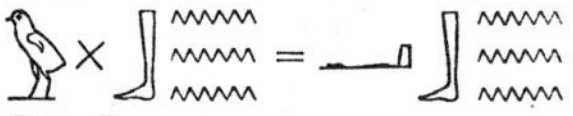.

ub [illegible], Rec. 12, 32, limit, frontier.

ub [illegible], Rev. 11, 124, , Rev. 13, 22, 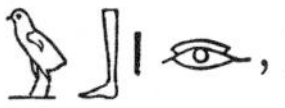, Jour. As. 1908, 291, , Rev. 13, 41, 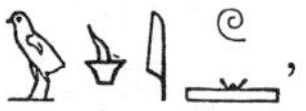, Rev. 13, 8; , Rev. 11, 146, 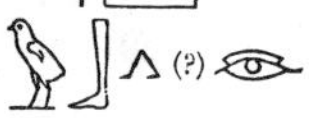, opposite, facing; Copt. ⲟⲩⲃⲉ.

ub (ubub?) [illegible], Wört. 248.

ubub [illegible], to break open.

uba 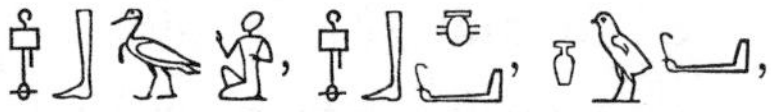, , Peasant 176, , servant, butler, workman, artisan; var.; plur. 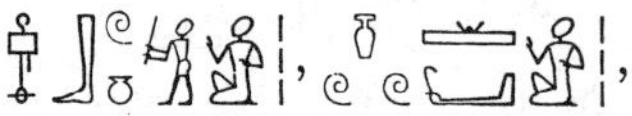, , a kind of priest (?)

ubait , , servant, handmaiden.

uba [illegible], work, toil.

uba rau 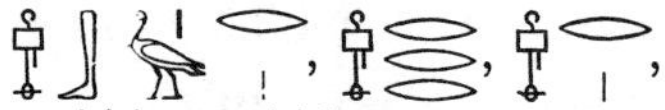, , Rec. 35, 56, , , A.Z. 1868, 89, 1874, 89, howsoever many there may be, whatsoever, et cetera; Copt. ⲟⲩⲏⲣ.

uba , to dig out ore, to hew stone in a quarry, to quarry stone.

ubait åner , stonebreaker, quarryman.

uba [illegible], P. 66, N. 685, [illegible], N. 703, P. 171, , P. 46, M. 597, N. 1202, 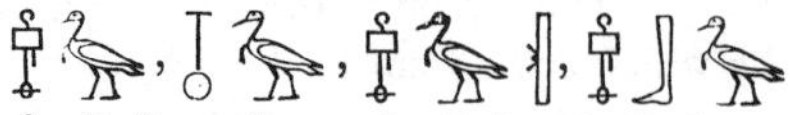, , , to open, to open up a country, to penetrate, to make a way into a foreign land, hence to raid, to invade, to enter.

uba åb , to open the heart, *i.e.*, to confide, to speak freely.

uba āui , to open the arms in greeting.

uba ra , to open the mouth.

uba khnem-t , to open a well.

uba-t , entrance.

uba (ta?) [illegible], A.Z. 1901, 63, a festival.

uba 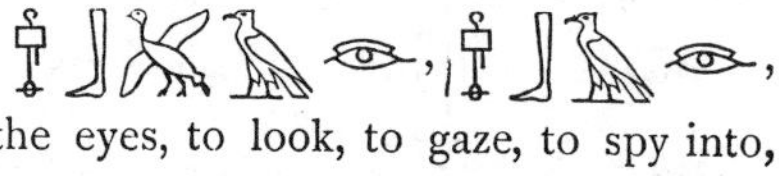, to open the eyes, to look, to gaze, to spy into, to examine; , open thou thine eyes.

uba-t , , [illegible], forecourt, courtyard; plur. [illegible], 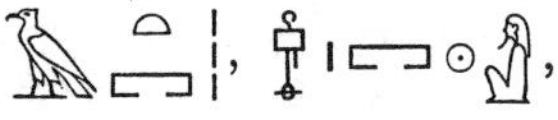, court of Rā (in a temple).

uba, part of a doorway, or of a door (?)

Uba . . ., Denderah IV, 84, a god of the 11th Pylon.

Uba-em-ṭu-f, the god of the 11th hour of the night.

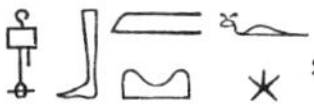

Ubaukhikh-tepi-nehet-f, T. 333, P. 826, M. 249, N. 203, one of the four Bull-gods of Tem.

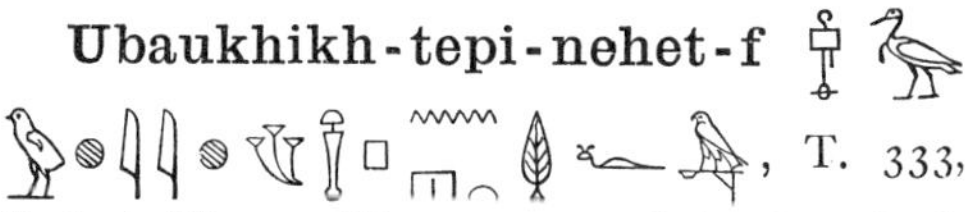

Uba-ta, B.D. 153A, 25, a god of the net of the Akeru gods.

Uba-taiu, Nesi-Åmsu 32, 22, a title of Āapep.

uba, to flame up, to become excited.

ubash, Rev. 11, 173, white; Copt. ⲟⲩⲃⲁϣ.

ubak, to shine, to be abundant.

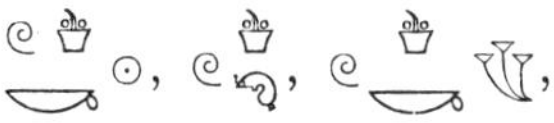

ubag; see

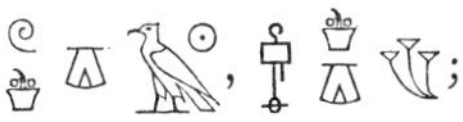

Ubå, Lanzone, Domicilio, Pl. 8, a god of the Ṭuat.

uben, to advance.

uben, U. 484, U. 223, U. 290, N. 719, T. 46, Rev. 13, 40, to rise, of a planet or any celestial body, to illumine, to shine; 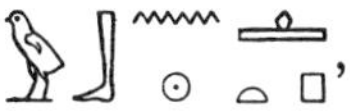 , rising and setting of the sun.

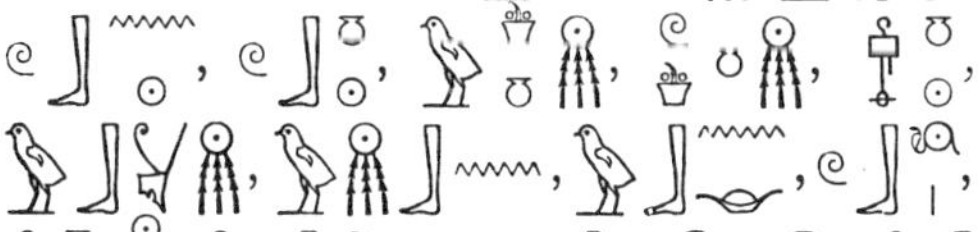

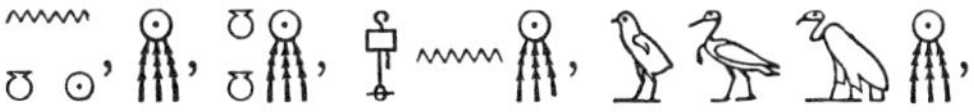

ubnit, Rev. 14, 12, light, splendour.

uben, B.M. 236, celestial bodies which give light, luminaries, rays of light.

uben, to dawn, the sunrise.

uben-t, the place where the sun rises.

uben, "he who thrusts himself up," a name of the Sun-god.

Uben-urr, M. 754, P. 744, a title of Rā.

ubenit, a name of the 1st hour of the day.

uben ḥeḥ, the festival of the 13th day of the month.

ubni, Rec. 18, 182, "the thruster up," a name of the solar disk.

Ubennå, N. 705, a form of the Sun-god.

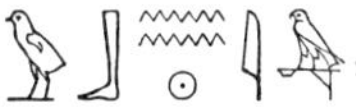

Uben-ån, Tomb of Seti I, one of the 75 forms of Rā (No. 53).

Uben-em-nubit, the name of a goddess (Hathor).

uben, Peasant 252, to overflow, to be abundant.

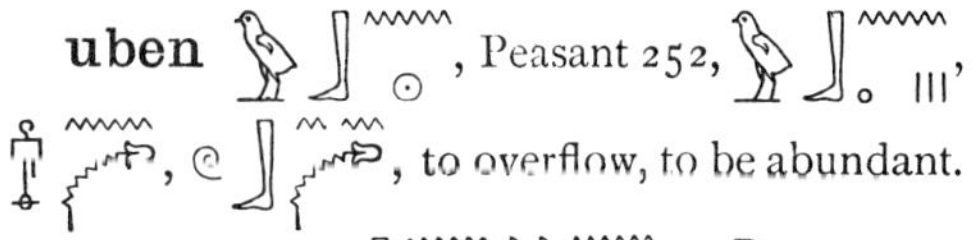

ubni[-t], Rec. 21, 14, well.

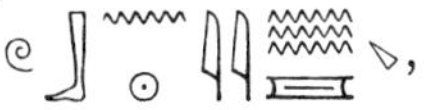

uben, Edict 28, to wound, to make blood flow.

uben, uben-t, wound, stripe, blow, sore.

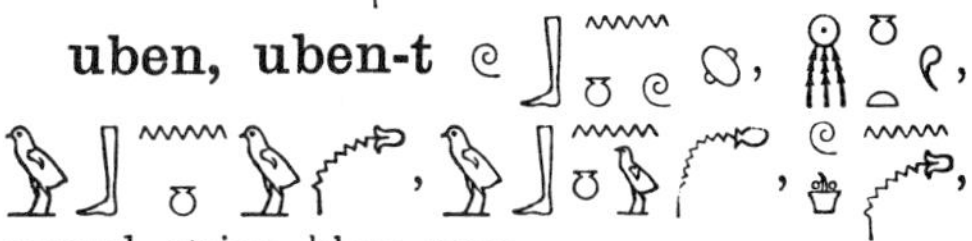

uben, Peasant 30, a kind of plant or seed.

Ubentui , P. 648, 
, P. 720, ,
M. 747, two sons of Rā (?)

ubr , a kind of disease (?)

ubekh 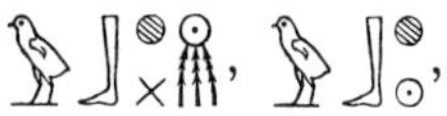, to shine, be bright.

ubekh-t 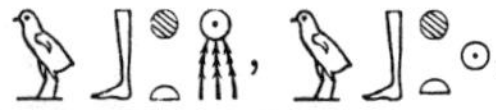, Hymn Darius 21, light, brilliance, blaze.

Ubekh-t , the name of a temple of Isis and Nephthys.

ubekh , white; Copt. ⲟⲩⲃⲁϣ.

ubekh-t , Åmen. 21, 1, , clothing, cloth, woven stuff, apparel; plur. 
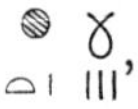, Koller Pap. 3, 1, Anastasi IV, 2, 12.

ubekh , a hide, a skin, skin dress.

ubes , Wört. 15, Suppl. 251, to lay up a store of corn (?)

ubes , an aromatic plant.

ubes 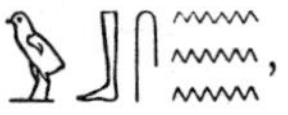, B.D. 130, 8, a water flood (?)

Ubesu , B.D. 130, 32, a group of fiery beings in the service of Shu.

Ubes-ḥer-per-em-khetkhet 
, B.D. 17, 105, one of the seven spirits who guarded the body of Osiris.

ubt , to burn.

ubti , burner, blazer, blazing.

ubṭ, ubṭṭ 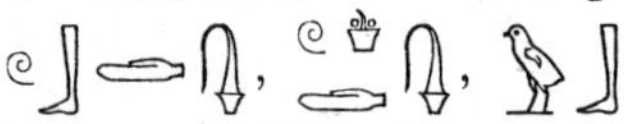
, to set fire to, to scald, to burn, to be burned, to sting (of an insect).

ubṭ 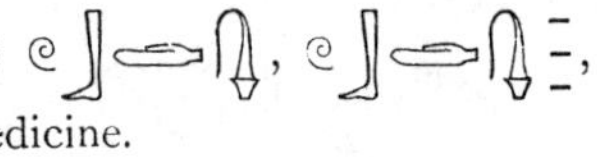, an astringent medicine.

ubṭ-t 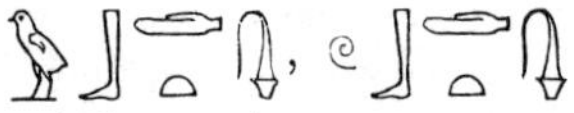, an inflamed sore, inflammation, cancer, gangrene, a burning.

up , Rec. 21, 14, , except, but.

up er , except, but, with the exception of.

up ḥer , L.D. III, 140c, , Israel Stele 5, ,
, except, but; 
, except thyself.

up , Rev., joy, gladness.

up, upp , M. 214, , U. 14,
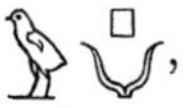, U. 27, , N. 64, T. 283, P. 50, 140,
204, M. 169, [illegible],
[illegible],
[illegible], Jour. As. 1908, 287, to open, to open up, *i.e.*, inquire into a matter, to try and decide a case in law, to decree, to judge, to pass judgment.

upi [illegible], Rec. 29, 145, opener; plur. [illegible], T. 357, P. 42, N. 29.

up-t ent ḥemut [illegible], A.Z. 35, 17, women who have borne children (?)

up en khat [illegible], opener of the womb, *i.e.*, firstborn, firstling.

up-t [illegible],
[illegible], Rec. 33, 137, judgment, sentence, doom, verdict.

up-t mitu [illegible], death sentence.

up-t Åmentiu [illegible], the judgment of those in Åmenti.

up-t meṭtut [illegible], the judgment of words and deeds.

upi [illegible], work, business affairs, worker.

up-t [illegible], work, business, daily duty;
[illegible], blacksmiths at [their] work.

up-t, income, revenue, daily supply; plur., U. 509.

uput, , , , , , lists of things, inventories, catalogues, accounts, registers, documents.

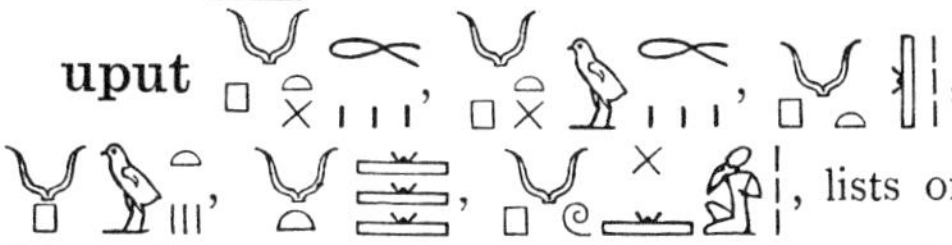

uput, lists of the people, *i.e.*, census.

upu-t, , , , , , , , , , , , T. 219, , , , , message, embassy, order, decree, errand, command, mission, duty, commission.

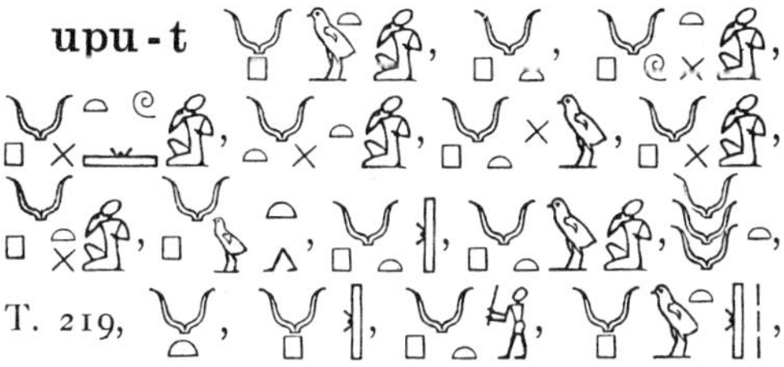

upu-t nesu, a royal commission.

uput renp-t, an annual mission.

up, leader, chief.

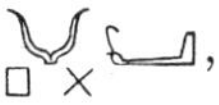

upp, , judge; plur.

upu, , , judges.

uputi, , , N. 597, 898, , , , U. 511, T. 323, M. 602, N. 1048, , M. 517, , N. 1098, divine messenger, envoy of the gods; plur., U. 186, , U. 208, , N. 749, , P. 454. Later forms are the following:—

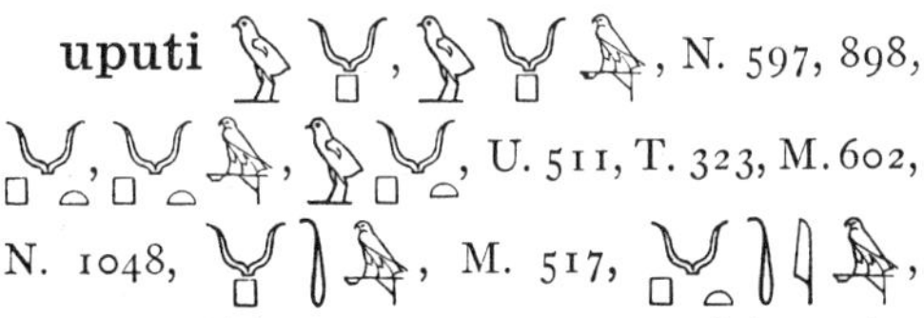

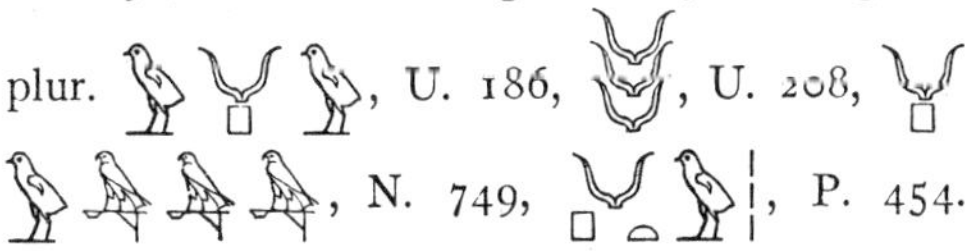

uputi, , , , , , , , , , , , , , envoy, messenger; plur., , , , , , , , , , , , , , , , , .

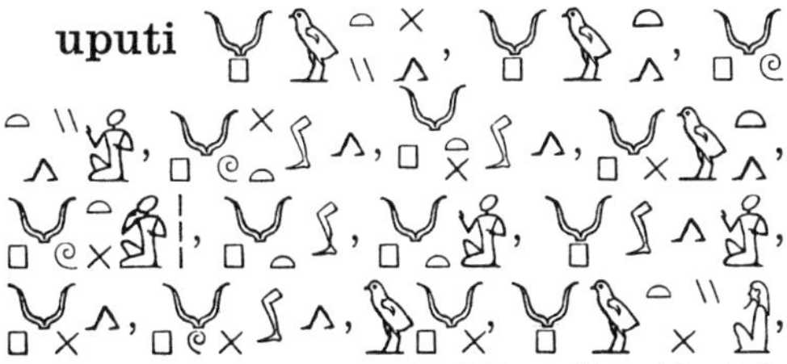

uputi nesu, , , king's messenger.

upit, the New Year festival; , A.Z. 1912, 55, festival, rejoicing.

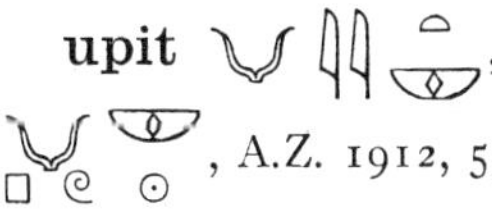

up-āaiu-ḥetut-Net, , the festival of the opening of the doors of the houses of Neith.

up uat, to open the way, *i.e.*, to act as a guide.

up m'tennu. to open the way, *i.e.*, to act as guide.

up re, U. 253, P. 214, , P. 589, 601, , , , , , , , the ceremony of "opening the mouth" of the deceased; 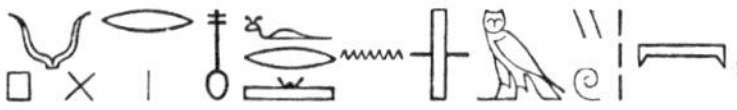 , the successful "opening the mouth" of those who are in heaven.

up re, the book or service of the "opening the mouth";  , Mar. Aby. II, 37, regulations.

up-t renp-t, , , , the opening of the year, *i.e.*, the New Year.

up-t renp-t, , , , , , , to keep the festival of the New Year, the New Year festival;   , the festival of the New Year of the ancestors.

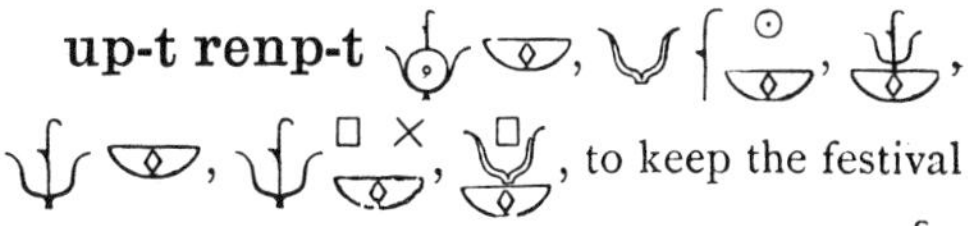

Up reḥui, , "judge of the two men" (Horus and Set), a title of the priest of Thoth of Hermopolis Parva.

up-t khenṭ , Hh. 447, the fork of the legs.

Up , , Denderah 4, 79, an ape-god of Edfû.

Up-t, Upti , U. 511, , T. 323, , Lanzone, 20, , Rec. 33, 32, , B.M. 32, 487, a title of several gods.

Upit , a serpent-goddess.

Upåu , T. 357,  , N. 176, a title of Ånpu.

Upåu , P. 42, M. 722,  , M. 62, , N. 29,  , N. 719, *i.e.*, Ånpu and Up-uatu.

Upåst , Ṭuat I, a light-god.

Upu , Ṭuat VI, one of the nine destroyers of souls.

Upu , Ṭuat IX, god of the serpent Shemti.

Upu Åqa , U. 186, , T. 65, M. 221, 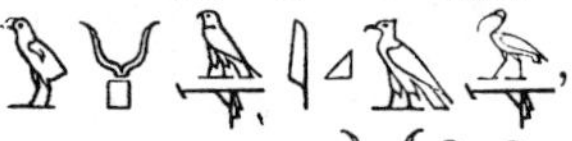, N. 597, a form of Thoth (?)

Up-uatu 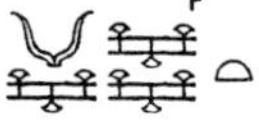, P. 542,  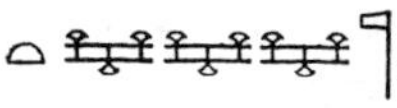, N. 490, 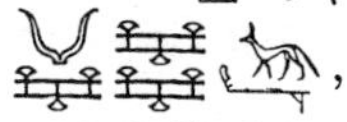, U. 187, T. 66, M. 221, N. 598, , Hh. 364, 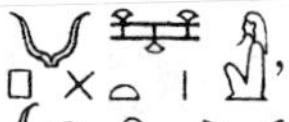, 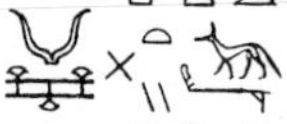,  , , , , , , the "opener (*i.e.*, guide) of the roads" for the dead on their way to the Kingdom of Osiris; see A.Z. 1904, 97 ff., Rec. 27, 249.

Up-uatu [illegible], [illegible], [illegible], Ṭuat I, Denderah 2, 10: (1) a singing-god; (2) one of the 36 Dekans.

Up-uatu meḥu [illegible], a title of Anubis.

Up-uatu meḥu kherp-pet [illegible] [illegible], B.D. 103, opener of the ways of the North, director of heaven, a title of Anubis.

Up-uatu shemā [illegible], [illegible] [illegible], the opener of the ways, *i.e.*, the guide to the South, a title of Up-uatu; he is also called [illegible], B.D. 102.

Up-f-senui [illegible], T. 341, [illegible], P. 140, [illegible] [illegible], N. 655, "he judgeth the two brothers," a title of Thoth.

Up-maāt [illegible], [illegible], Berl. 6910, a title of Thoth.

Up-meḥ [illegible], Ombos 1, 143, a god, Anubis (?)

Up-neterui [illegible], [illegible], [illegible], U. 408, "judge of the two gods" (Horus and Set), a title of Thoth and of a priest.

Up-hai [illegible], Rec. 6, 156, a god of the dead.

Upt (Uputi?) Ḥeru [illegible] [illegible], M. 449, N. 1259.

Upt (Uputi?)-ḥeḥ [illegible], B.D. 34, 2, a title of Rā.

Upt (Uputi?)-ḥeka [illegible], a god connected with enchantments.

upit-khaibiut [illegible], Rec. 31, 167, judge of shadows.

upi-khenu [illegible], U. 445, [illegible], T. 255, a title of the servants of Set.

Upi-sekhemti (?) [illegible], Ṭuat I, a jackal-headed singing-god.

Upi-shet [illegible], Ṭuat IX, a fiery, blood-drinking serpent.

Up-shāt-taui [illegible], Rec. 27, 56, a god.

Upi-shemā [illegible], Ombos 1, 143, "opener of the South," a title of Up-uatu.

Upi-......, "opener of time," *i.e.*, the god with whose existence time began.

Upi-taui, , , a title of Osiris and Rā.

Upt-taui, Ṭuat XI, a form of Åf, the dead Sun-god.

Upit-taui, , Ṭuat XI, a fire-goddess.

Upi-ṭuui, N. 969, a title of Rā.

Upi-Ṭuat, Ṭuat IV, Horus, guide of the Ṭuat.

up-t, U. 504, , T. 320, , T. 339, , M. 410, , N. 951, , , , the top of the head, the crown, the skull, a covering for the head; plur. , , U. 509, T. 323.

up-t Åmentt, , , the top part of Åmenti, the brow of Åmenti; , Rā in the zenith; , lord of the zenith.

up-t pet, the top of the head of the Sky-goddess, the crown of the sky.

Up-t-ent-mu, B.D. 149, a region in the 11th Åat.

Up-t-ent-khet, B.D. 149, the name of the 2nd Åat.

Up-t-ent-Geb, B.D. 12, 2, a name for the surface of the earth.

Up-t-ent-Qaḥu, B.D. 149, the name of the 8th Åat.

Up-t she, the crown of the lake.

Up-t ta, , , the crown of the earth.

Up-t Tenen-t, the name of a uraeus crown.

upt, geese, birds; see

up, destruction, to perish (?)

upu, a tool for opening or cutting through, a saw.

Upu, filth, a name of Set.

ups, Hymn Darius 11, to burn up, fire, heat.

ups, , Rhind Pap. 18.....

Upsit, , , , , , , , , , , , L.D. V, 17c, a fire-goddess of the First Cataract.

Ups-ur, , Nesi-Åmsu 25, 5, 9, the divine fire which consumed Āapep.

upsh, , Rec. 11, 153, , , , Rec. 27, 87, to give light, to illumine, to shine, to flood with light.

Upshit, Ṭuat I, a light-goddess.

upsh, N. 491, , P. 488, , P. 658, , P. 764, , M. 765, star, luminary.

upsh, Thes. 923, sleep, dream; Copt. ⲟⲃϣ.

uptiu, judges.

uf, ufā, , , , to have power, authority, to punish (?)

ufa, , , Peasant 108, event, happening.

ufa, , , , , lung; Copt. ⲟⲩⲱϥ.

Ufå, U. 533, a hostile serpent-fiend.

ufḥ, to burn, to blaze.

umm (?) Stat. Tab. 5, a kind of grain (?)

umu, U. 417, 515, greedily.

umt, Rec. 12, 109, to copulate.

umt-t, Rev. 8, 139, phallus.

umt, Thes. 1201, , chiefs, leaders, men; , Thes. 1206, a dense mass of people.

umt, , girdle, belt, band, bandlet, binding, name of a garment.

umt, , , , to be thick, thickness, thick, denseness, padded (of cloth), studded (of a door); Copt. ⲟⲩⲙⲙⲟⲧ.

umt ȧb, , thick or dense of heart, obstinate, firm (?)

umt, Thes. 1251, , , a room, a hall, a part of a large building.

umt, Thes. 1322, to build massive walls.

umt, , , , , Annales III, 109, , a thick wall, a bulwark, a tower, a citadel; plur. ; Copt. ⲟⲩⲟⲙⲙⲧⲉ.

umtut, beams of timber.

umt-t ta, B.D. 64, 7. . . . .

umtch-t, bulwark, wall, defence.

un, , ye, you, they, them, their.

un, we, us.

un, unn, as an auxiliary verb: , she said to him; , his elder brother became like a leopard; , the seven Hathors came; , if there be a petitioner.

un, unn, P. 235, , N. 669, , , , , , to be, to exist, to become; , B.D. 42, 19, , P. 16, M. 118, N. 118, being, existence; , N. 959, those who are; , P. 167, , M. 322, , Rec. 21, 41 = ⲟⲩⲛϯ; Copt. ⲟⲩⲛ, ⲟⲩⲟⲛ.

unun, , T. 170, M. 179, to be.

unun-t, something that is.

unun neb-t, all that is.

unn-t, , , , , , , Rec. 16, 60, things which are, things which exist, what is, goods, stuff, property; , he is non existent; , non-existent; , let it never be.

unnu, , Ȧmen. 17, 5, being, existence.

un maāt, , , very truth, the absolute truth; , indeed, most assuredly.

un ḥer mu, to be in the following of, loyal, to be of the same kidney.

unnu, a living man, a human being; plur. , , , , , ,

, , , , , men and women, human beings, people; , strong men.

unnu , a man of means, as opposed to .

unnit , , inhabitants.

unnu , child, infant.

unnu , cattle (?)

un-t , a part of the body.

Un , P. 175, , N. 947, the god of existence, the son of Ȧpt; , Rec. 36, 210.

Untȧ , T. 292, a light-god; see .

Unnti , , the name of a god, the god of existence.

un-t , Rev. 12, 68, hare.

Unnit , , , , , the name of a goddess.

Unnuit , Denderah IV, 81, , a hare-goddess, a watcher of the bier of Osiris.

Unu-t , , Rec. 34, 182, the name of a serpent tiara, or crown.

Unun-t , the name of a serpent on the royal crown; var. , IV, 286, 288.

Unt-ābui (?) , goddess of the 27th day of the month.

Un[t]-baiusit , Ombos 2, 131, a goddess.

Unn-em-ḥetep , B.D. 110, 28, the 1st division of Sekhet-Ȧaru.

Unn-Nefer , , , , , , , , , , , , , a title of Osiris; , Un-Nefer, the son of Nut; , Unn-Nefer, dweller in Abydos; Gr. Ὀννωφρις, Copt. ⲟⲩⲉⲛⲟϥⲣⲉ, ⲟⲩⲉⲛⲛⲁⲃⲣⲉ, ⲟⲩⲉⲛⲁⲃⲉⲣ.

Unn-nefer Ḥeru-ȧakhuti , B.D. 15, 1, Un-Nefer Harmakhis.

Un-nefer-Rā , Pap. Mut-ḥetep 5, 19, Un-nefer + Rā.

Unun[it]-ḥer-tchatcha-f (?) , Denderah I, 30, a lioness-headed goddess.

Uni-sheps , , , Rec. 13, 38, Berg. I, 9, a name of Osiris.

un , , , , , , Rec. 26, 10, , , , , , to do wrong, to commit a sin or a fault, defect, error, fault, mistake, offence, defective, light or worthless.

un , a sinful or erring man, a cheat.

un-ȧb , Berl. 7272, evil-hearted man.

unnui , evildoer.

Unnu , Mag. Pap., a serpent-fiend.

un-ti , , transgressor, offender.

Un-ti , , , Hymn Darius 11, Nesi-Ȧmsu 32, 29, 51, a duck-headed fiend, and a form of Āapep.

un, unn , T. 271, , Åmen. 26, 11, , Rev. 11, 70, 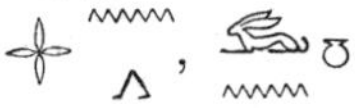 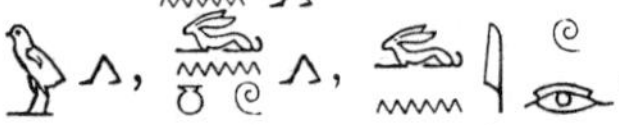, Rev. 13, 55, to leap up, to rise up, to run, to run away from, to move; , Rec. 27, 56, her heart leaped; Copt. ⲟⲩⲉⲓⲛⲉ.

unun 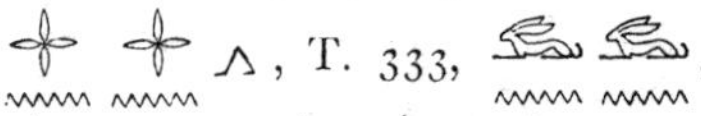, P. 42, 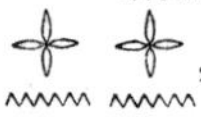, M. 63, 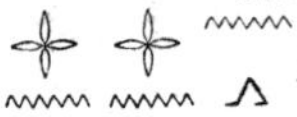, N. 30, 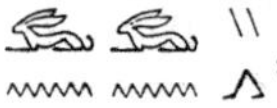 De Hymnis 36, to spring up, to leap.

unȧ-t 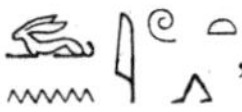, journey, course.

un ṭet  Rec. 15, 158, to lift the hand, *i.e.*, to help.

un , Rec. 2, 29, , 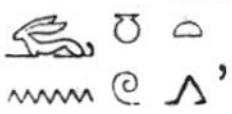, to reject, to turn back, to set aside.

Unt 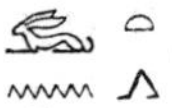, B.D. 149, the 12th Āat.

un-t 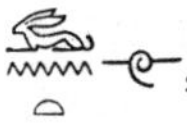, carpenter's drill-bow (Lacau).

un, unit 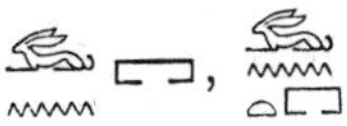, Rec. 34, 120, 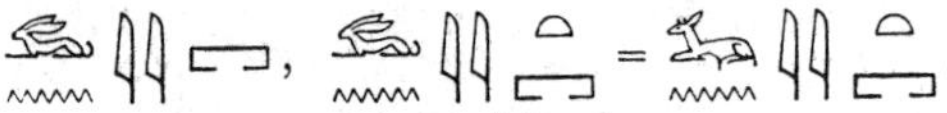, Rec. 27, 225, , Rec. 2, 111, , Rev. 13, 63, room, chamber, a square box; 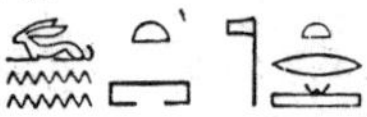, Thes. 1285, sanctuary.

ununȧ-t , U. 461,  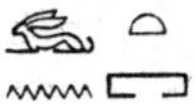, chamber, sanctuary.

un-t 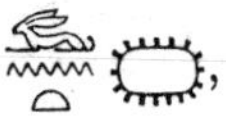, fortress; plur. 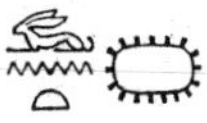 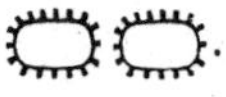.

un 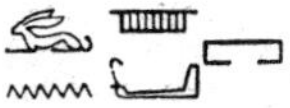, dovecot, aviary (?)

un, unn   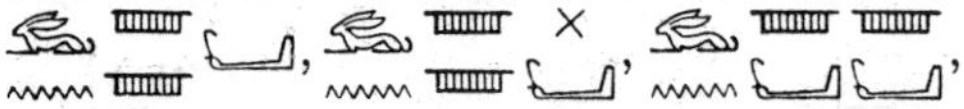 , to open, to open fetters (to unfetter), to open a mare (*i.e.*, to stab her), to be open; 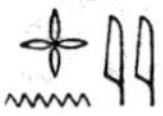, P. 196, N. 928; Copt. ⲟⲩⲱⲛ.

uniu 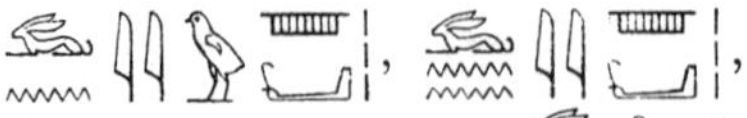 openers, scatterers, door openers; 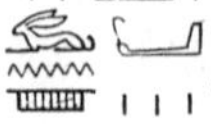, open (plur.).

Unn-uiti , Buch 63, a sacrificial priest.

Un-ti , opener, piercer, stabber, title of a priest as the slayer of the sacrificial beast.

un āui , to open the hands, *i.e.*, to praise.

un āaui nu pet 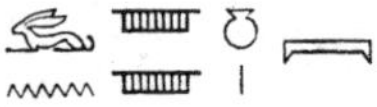, a title of a prophet of Thebes.

un per [illegible], [illegible], Rec. IV, 29, festal procession.

un ra [illegible], [illegible], [illegible], he who performs the ceremony of opening the mouth, a title of priests of various gods.

un ra en ȧmḥ-t [illegible] [illegible], a priestly title.

un ḥer [illegible], [illegible], [illegible], [illegible], to show oneself, to make oneself public, publicity, manifest, known to everyone; [illegible], Rec. 31, 25; Copt. ⲟⲩⲱⲛϩ.

un ḥer ḥebu [illegible], festivals during which the faces of the gods were uncovered.

un ḥer [illegible], [illegible], [illegible] [illegible], mirror.

un ṭet [illegible], open-handed.

Unniu-ākhmiu-setch-t [illegible] [illegible], B.D. 141, 64, a group of fire-gods.

Un-ḥat [illegible], the porter of the 2nd Ārit.

Un-ta [illegible], Ṭuat I, a doorkeeper-god.

un [illegible], N. 733, to eat, to feed upon.

un, to be shaved clean, to pluck out the hair.

unit, baldness.

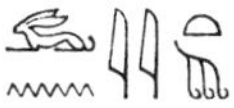

un, hair, or foliage, which has been cut off.

unun, Rec. 27, 219, Hh. 298, to tremble, to bristle (of the hair).

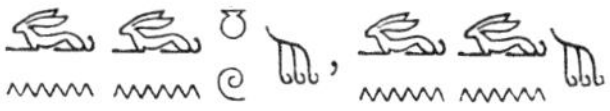

unun, to do work in the field, to sow seed (?)

un-t, cypress.

un, Rec. 31, 175 . . . .

un-t, T. 314, rope, cord.

unun, to argue, to dispute; see

unnȧ, N. 705 . . . .

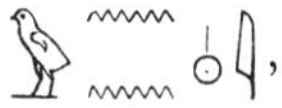

Unȧs Nefer ȧsut, the name of the pyramid of Unȧs.

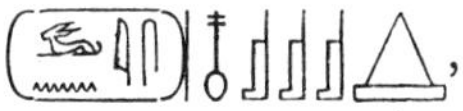

unām (?), B.D. 137A, 48, a reed (?) tube.

uni, unin, Rev. 11, 178, Rec. 27, 84, light; Copt. ⲟⲩⲟⲉⲓⲛ.

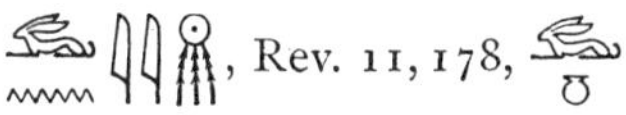

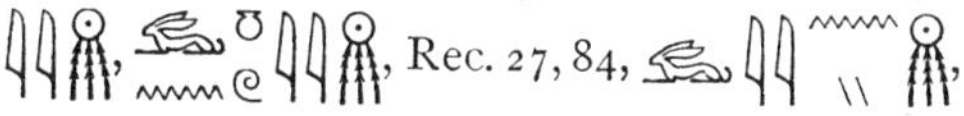

Unit, Tomb of Rameses VI, Pl. 50, a star-goddess.

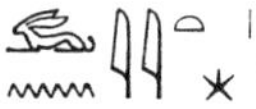

unin, to open, opening.

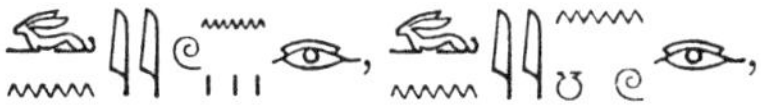

unu-t, Ȧmen. 5, 18, Rec. 3, 49, Rev. 13, 3, Rev. 11, 162, hour, time, regular duty, service; plur. U. 399; at once; Copt. ⲟⲩⲛⲟⲩ.

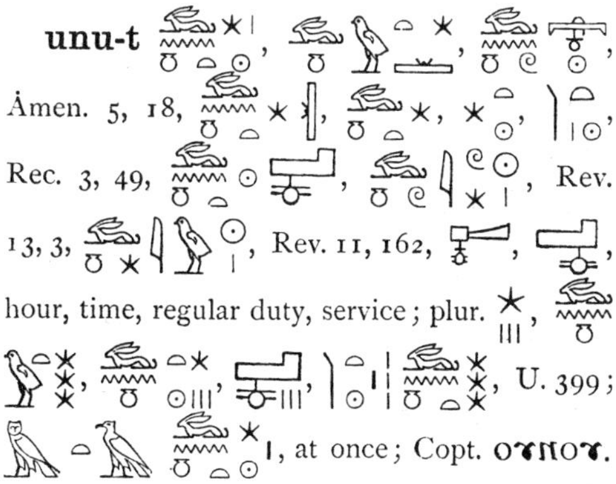

unu-t, Thes. 1483, hourly service, service reckoned by hours; a servant at Court.

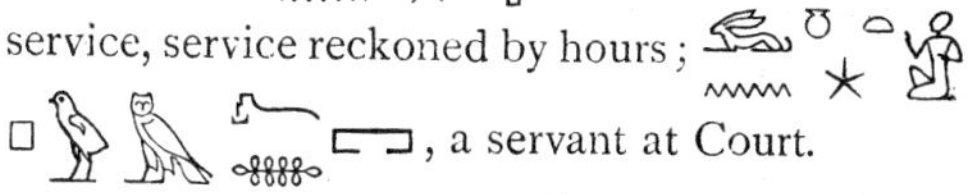

unu-t, priests who served in courses, priests of the hour, lay servants of a temple, priests in ordinary; horoscopists (?)

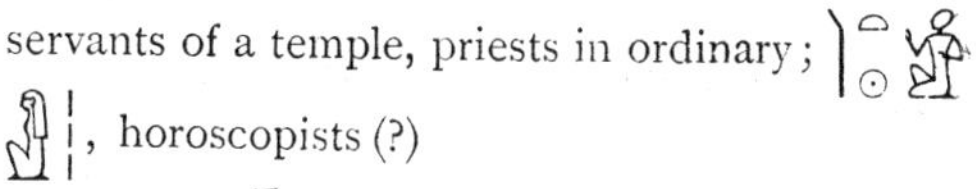

Unti, Ṭuat X, B.D. 15 (Litany), 136A, 7, a light-god, and the god of an hour.

Unu-t, Rec. 30, 186, hour-goddess; plur. hour-goddesses of the night.

Unut-ȧmiut-Ṭuat, Ṭuat IV, the 12 hour-goddesses who were divided into two groups by

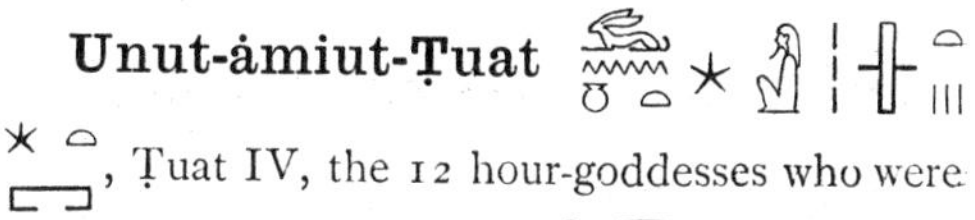

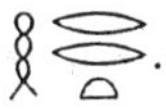

Unut-netchut, Ṭuat XI, a group of eight goddesses who smote the serpent, and sang hymns to the rising sun.

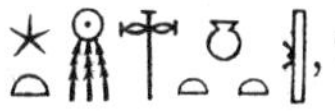

Unut-Sethait, Ṭuat X, a group of 12 goddesses who made the hours to advance.

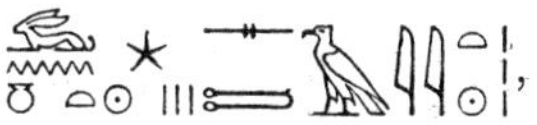

unb, B.D. 28, 1, plant, bush, shrub, undergrowth, flower; Rev. 13, 22.

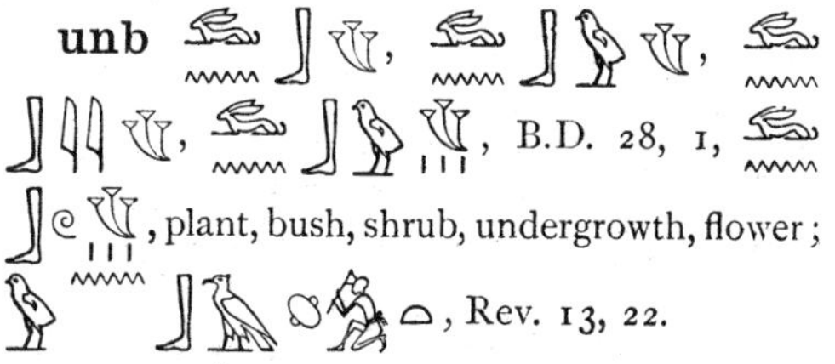

Unb, T. 39, the divine sprout, plant or shoot proceeding from 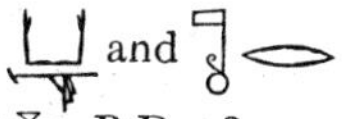 and ; B.D. 28, 1, a form of Rā.

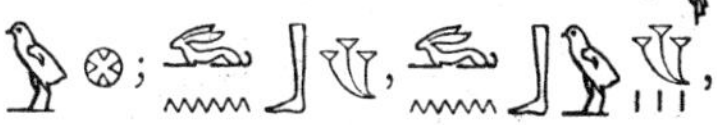

Unb-per-em-Nu  , B.D. 42, 24, a title of Rā and Osiris.

unp , , to cut, to stab, to slay.

unp-t , waste, ruin, destruction.

unpep-t 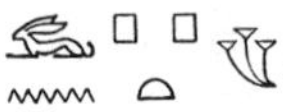, staff, stick.

unp-t , plants, shrubs.

Unpep-t-ent-Ḥe-t-Ḥer  , B.D. 125, III, 35, a mystical name of the left foot; varr. 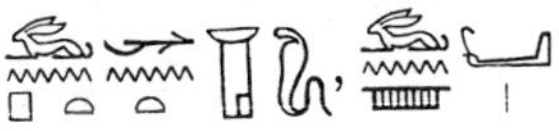 .

Unpi , a name of Horus.

unuf , Rev. 13, 7, joy, gladness.

unf , Rec. 2, 116, 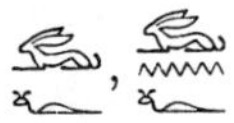  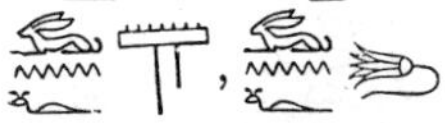, Rev. 16, 152, to rejoice, to be glad, gladness; Copt. ⲟⲩⲛⲟϥ.

unf ȧb 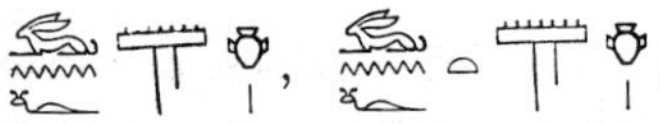 , to be glad, joy, gladness, a man of happy disposition.

unf , to undo, to unloose, to uncover.

unemi , M. 580, , N. 1186,  , right, right side, right hand; Copt. ⲟⲩⲛⲁⲙ.

unemtiu , those on the right side.

unemi  , Hymn Darius 17, the right eye of Rā, *i.e.*, the day, or Shu.

unemȧ , M. 337 =  **unemi**, N. 862; , T. 70, P. 67, 180, 411, 607 = , M. 280, 588, P. 273 =  , N. 892; 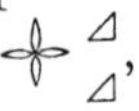, T. 70 = 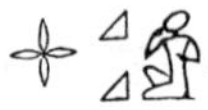, M. 224 = 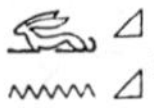, U. 191; , Rec. 27, 220, 225 = ; [illegible] = [illegible] [illegible], Rec, 29, 149, to eat; Copt. ⲟⲩⲱⲙ; [illegible], to eat, U. 90 = [illegible], P. 367 = [illegible], U. 42; [illegible], N. 1186, [illegible], M. 313 = [illegible], N. 847. Later forms are:—

unemi [illegible], [illegible], [illegible], [illegible], [illegible], to eat, to gnaw, to devour; Copt. ⲟⲩⲱⲙⲓ; [illegible], eaters; [illegible], dining room.

unemi [illegible], to drink; [illegible] [illegible], thou drinkest beer.

unem-t [illegible], U. 191, [illegible], T. 70, [illegible], M. 225, [illegible], food. Later forms are :—

unem-t [illegible], [illegible], [illegible], bread, cakes, food.

unemit [illegible], a consuming fire.

unem snef [illegible], a disease; Copt. ⲟⲩⲁⲙⲥⲛⲟϥ (?)

Unem-ȧb-nt-menḥu-ḥeq-uȧa [illegible], Denderah I, 30, a lioness-goddess.

Unem-utch-bāḥ-ȧb 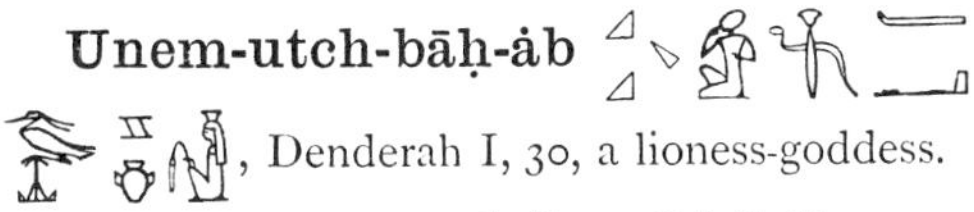, Denderah I, 30, a lioness-goddess.

Unemiu baiu , eaters of heart souls, a class of devils.

Unem-besku , B.D. 125, II, one of the 42 assessors of Osiris.

Unem-ḥuat , a turtle-headed god of the 3rd day of the month.

Unem-ḥuat-ent-peḥui-f 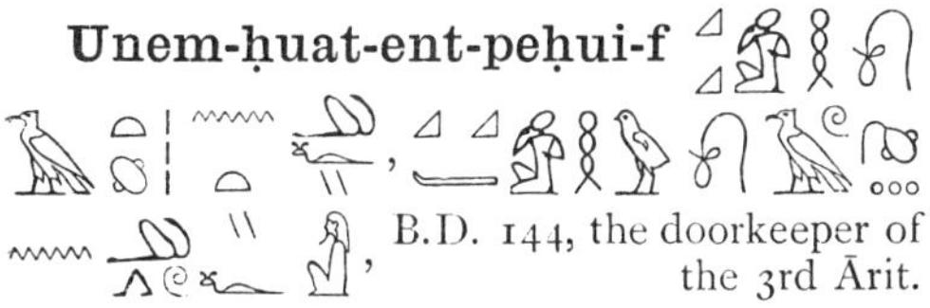, B.D. 144, the doorkeeper of the 3rd Ārit.

Unem-snef 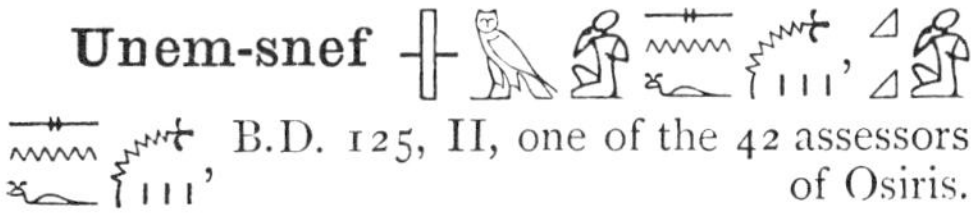, B.D. 125, II, one of the 42 assessors of Osiris.

unmes , IV, 988 . . . . .

Un-ermen-ṭu , Ombos I, 1, 252, a star-god.

unḥi 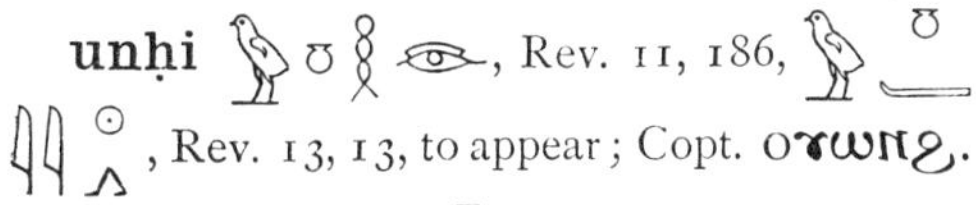, Rev. 11, 186, Rev. 13, 13, to appear; Copt. ⲟⲩⲱⲛϩ.

unḥ , garlands of flowers.

unkh 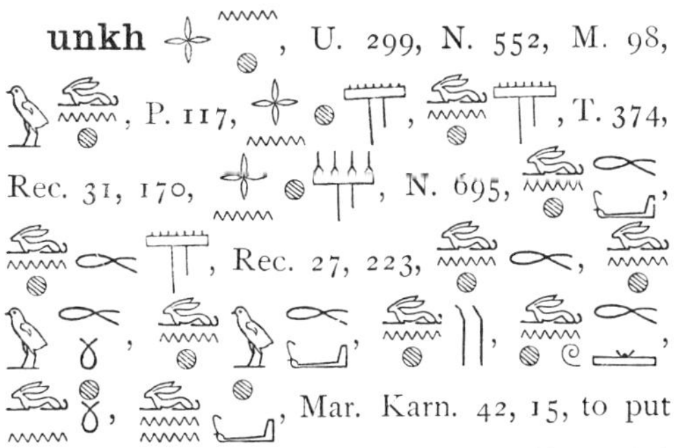, U. 299, N. 552, M. 98, P. 117, T. 374, Rec. 31, 170, N. 695, Rec. 27, 223, Mar. Karn. 42, 15, to put on garments, to dress, to array oneself, to gird oneself; 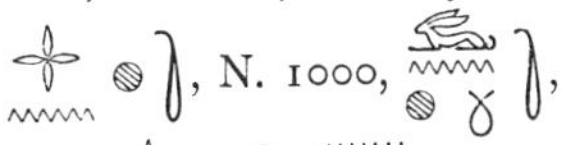, N. 1000, arrayed.

unkhu 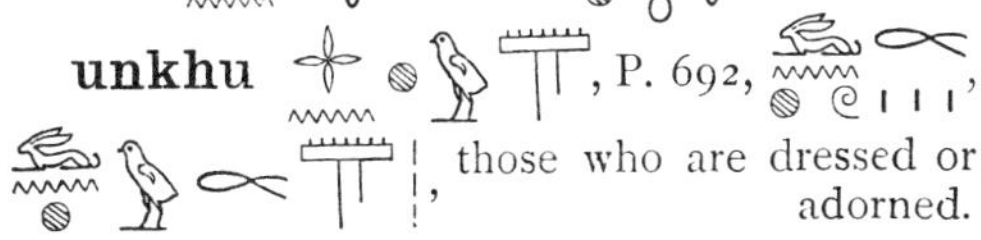, P. 692, those who are dressed or adorned.

unkh 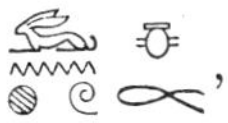, to oil and bind up the hair, to make the toilette.

unkh 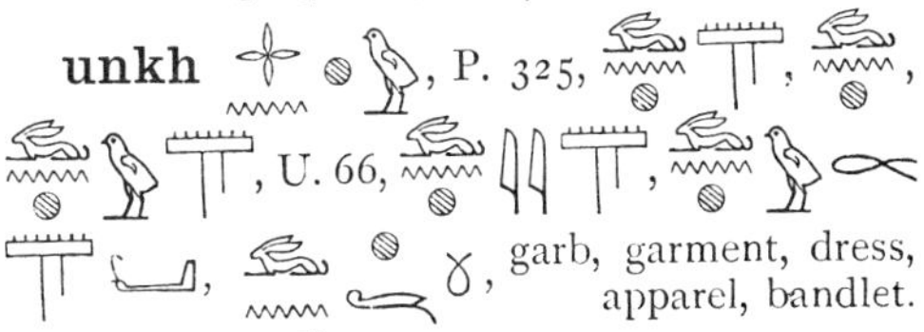, P. 325, U. 66, garb, garment, dress, apparel, bandlet.

unkhit , bandage, bandlet.

unkh , diarrhoea.

unkh , to bite, to gnaw.

unkh , to wound, to gore.

Uneshit 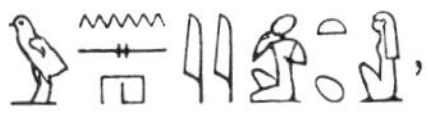, Ombos III, 2, 133, a goddess.

unsh 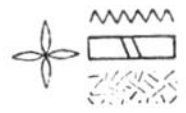, P. 605 . . . .

unsh 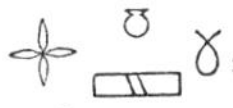, clothing.

unsh 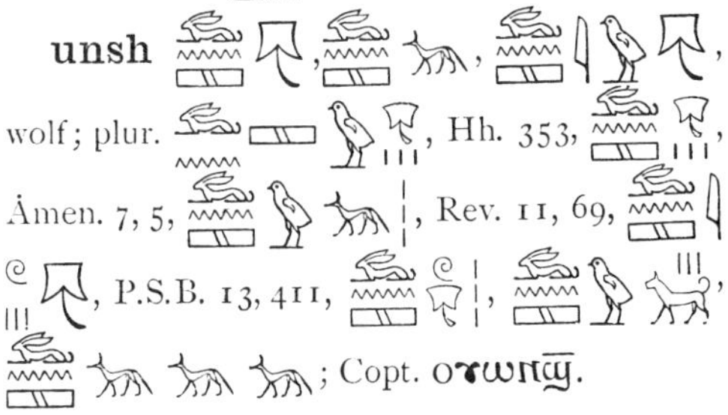, wolf; plur. Hh. 353, Ȧmen. 7, 5, Rev. 11, 69, P.S.B. 13, 411; Copt. ⲟⲩⲱⲛϣ.

unnshnesh 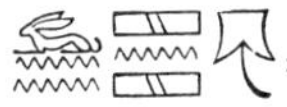, a kind of dog, or the skin of a dog.

unsh-t 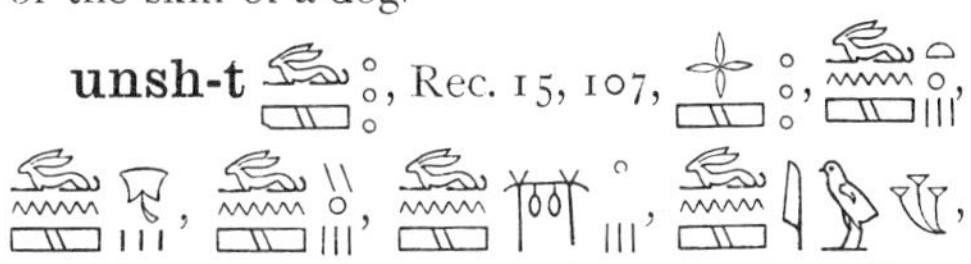, Rec. 15, 107, a kind of plant, wolf's-bane (?) coriander; Copt. ⲃⲉⲣϣⲛⲟⲩ, ⲃⲉⲣϣⲉⲩ.

unsh-t , a sledge for stone.

Unshet 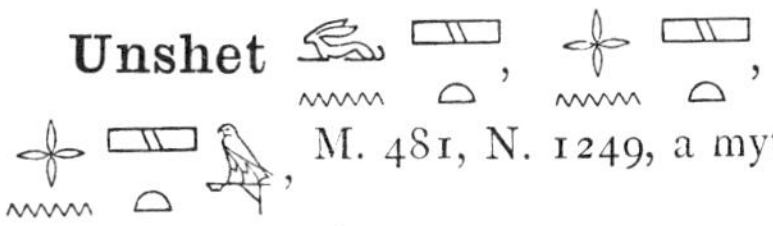, P. 268, M. 481, N. 1249, a mythological being.

Unshtȧ 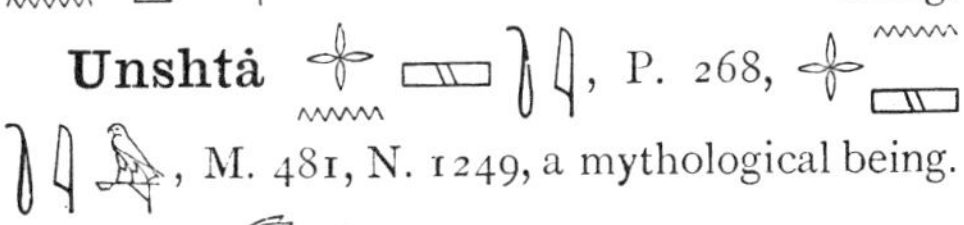, P. 268, M. 481, N. 1249, a mythological being.

unsh , to travel, to run.

unshnesh , to run, to run quickly.

Ung  , P. 160,  , M. 297,  , P. 160, N. 898,   , P. 185,  , Louvre C, 15, a son of Rā, who bore the heavens on his shoulders, 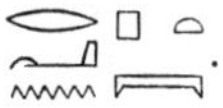 .

Ungit  , Rec. 3, 116, a goddess.

unges (?) , , messenger (?) envoy (?)

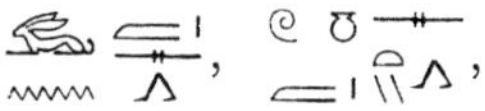

untiu   (?) = (?), laundrymen, washers.

Unth 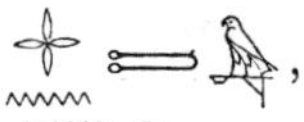 , M. 477, a god; var. 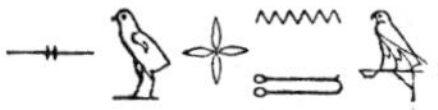 , N. 1245.

unṭu  , Sphinx XVI, 164 = cattle from which the horns have been sawn off.

unṭu (?)  , Rec. 29, 148, , , , ox, cow, calf, goat, etc.; plur. ; , calves,  , goats, 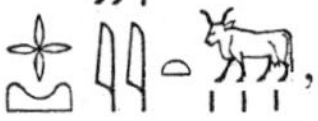 , cattle.

unṭu  , garment, loin cloth; plur. 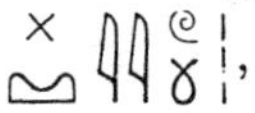 , Anastasi IV, 3, 1, Koller Pap. 3, 2, 4, 6.

Unṭu  , the name of a fiend.

unṭu  , evil hap, calamity.

unṭuit , , , men and women, people, society, folk; varr. , , , , .

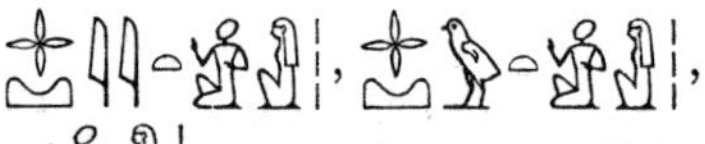

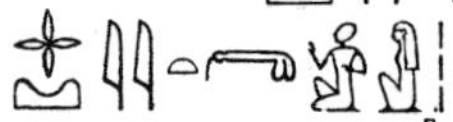

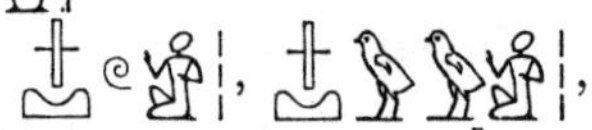

unṭu , , Rec. 20, 47, part of a ship, part of the barge of Åmen.

unṭu  , things.

Untchut (?)  , T. 200,  , P. 679, a divine pilot (?)

uńtchar , Gen. Epist. 103, a fish-pond.

untcher (?)  , P. 605 . . . . . .

ur , , , , , , great, much, superior, very, greatness, great size; dual , , , ; plur. , , ; , P. 808, great piece of flesh from the joint.

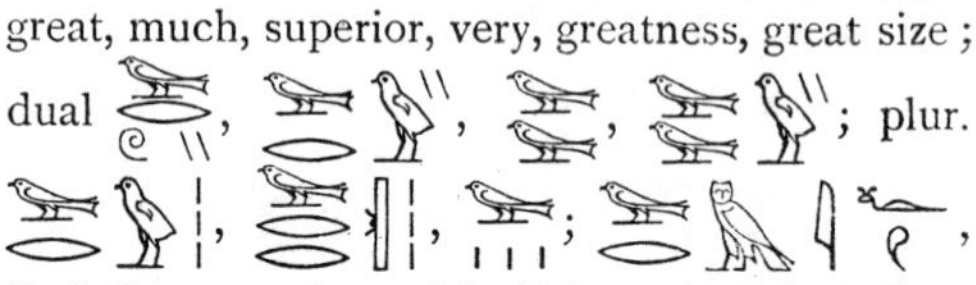

ur , U. 215, , , , , , , , , , , , , , , , , , , great man, great god, prince, chief, noble, eldest son, senior; plur. , , , , , , , , , , ; , a conquered chief;  , chief of chiefs; , noble men and women.

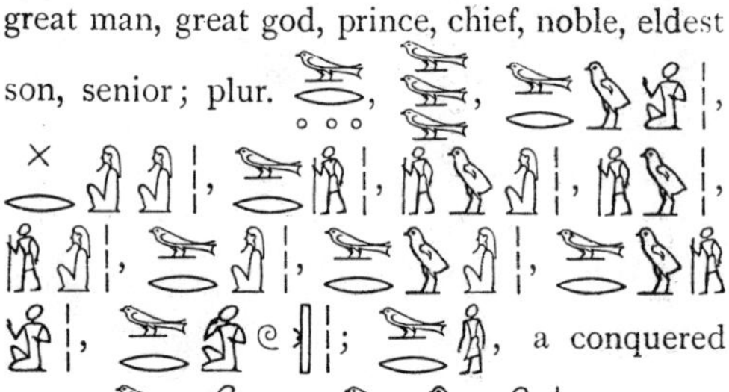

ur-t , , , , , , Rec. 5, 90, great woman, great thing, great, eldest; plur. , , .

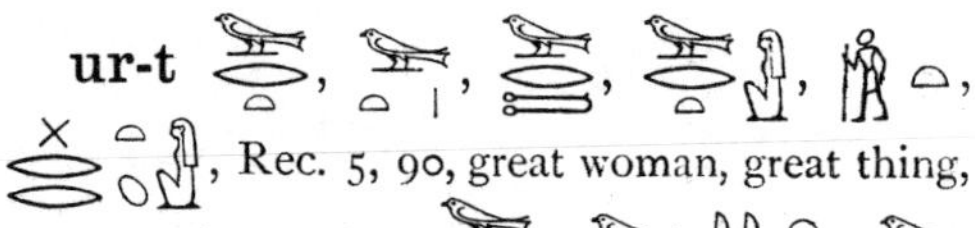

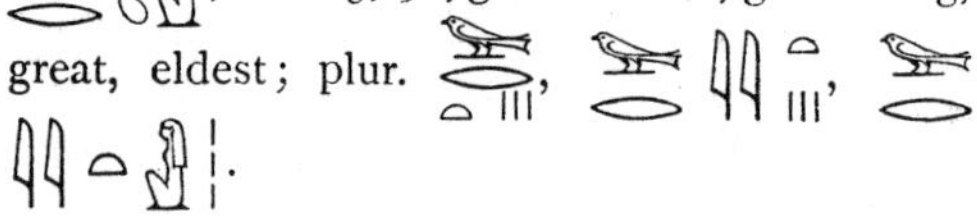

ur , Anastasi I, 27, 8, , very great, how very great; Copt. ⲟⲩⲏⲣ.

ur , great; , greater than; , , great two times, twice great; , very much, very many many times; , because of the greatness of.

ur āa, king; Copt. ογρo.

ur-t āa-t, queen.

ur khet (akh-t), great in possessions, rich.

ur khert, great in property, rich.

urr, U. 235, P. 659, 744, M. 754, to be great, to make great, to increase, to grow large; , P. 156, 646, , P. 716, N. 786, , great.

Ur-t, , , title of the high-priestess of Saïs.

Urti, the title of the two high-priestesses of the Heroopolite Nome; , N. 1385, two great goddesses.

ur-t, urr-t, U. 272, , N. 719, , , , , , , , a name of the crown of Upper and Lower Egypt.

Ur-tt, the name of a serpent on the royal crown.

Ur-ā, the title of a priest.

Urttbu, the name of a serpent on the royal crown.

Ur-ma, , , , , , T.S.B.A. 8, 326, , a title of the high-priest of Heliopolis; plur. .

ur-menfitu, chief of soldiers = Gr. στρατηγός.

Ur-neruti, great of victories, most victorious, a common title of kings.

Ur-nekhtut, the name of a chamber in the temple at Edfû.

Ur-en-senṭ, a title of gods and kings meaning he who is greatly feared.

Ur-Rā, the title of a priestess of the Busiris Nome.

Ur-res, great one of the South (?) great one of the Ten of the South (?) a title of a high official; plur. , IV, 1104.

Ur-res-meḥ, , , A.Z. 1907, 18, IV, 412, great one of the Ten of the South and of the Ten of the North.

Ur-ḥāu, a title of the chief priest of Saïs.

Ur-ḥeb, , , M. 213, N. 684, a proper name, or title.

Ur-ḥeba, a title of the chief priest of the Nome Prosopites.

ur-ḥemut, chief of the smelters.

ur-ḥeka, , , "great of words of power," a tool or instrument used in the performance of magical ceremonies.

Ur-ḥekau, Ṭuat III, the name of a sceptre, and of a staff used by magicians in working spells.

urit-ḥekau, P. 100, M. 88, N. 95, a sceptre of Horus and Set (?)

urit-ḥekau, a serpent-amulet, a vulture-amulet (Lacau).

Ur-ḥekau, a collar-amulet.

ur-ḥekau, , , , , he who is great in words of power, or enchantments, *i.e.*, a god or man who is a magician.

Ur-ḥekau, a title of Set.

Urit-ḥekau, U. 269, 271, , M. 129, , , a name of the crown of the North, or of its goddess.

Urit-ḥekau , M. 129, , Rec. 32, 80, a name of the crown of the South, or of its goddess.

Urti-ḥekau 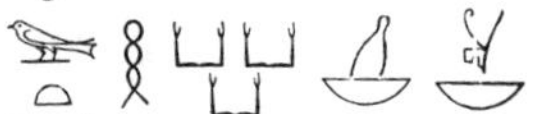, , the crowns of the South and North.

Urit-ḥekau , 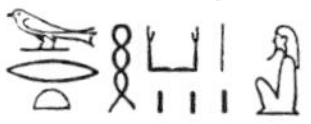, a royal crown.

Ur-Khāfrā , the name of the pyramid of King Khāfrā.

Ur-kherp-ḥemut , , the great director of the hammer, a title of the high-priest of Ptaḥ of Memphis; , two high-priests of Ptaḥ.

Ur-senu , "chief physician," a title of a priest of Saïs; 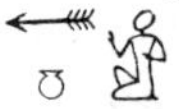 = Copt. ⲥⲁⲉⲓⲛ.

ur-sunt , paymaster.

ur-shāt , mighty one of slaughters, *i.e.*, great slaughterer.

ur-shefit , , mighty one of terror, *i.e.*, terror inspiring.

ur-qāḥu , B.D. 60, 3, chief of districts, title of an official.

Ur V , Mar. Aby. I, 44, chief of five gods, a title of Osiris and of the high priest of Thoth.

ur-ṭeb 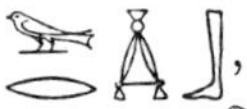, a priest's title.

Ur-t ṭekh[en]t 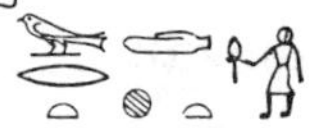, title of a priestess of Heliopolis.

Uru 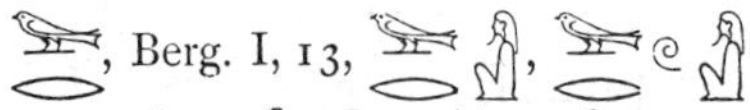, Berg. I, 13, B.D. 32, 1, 9, , great god, Great God.

Ur 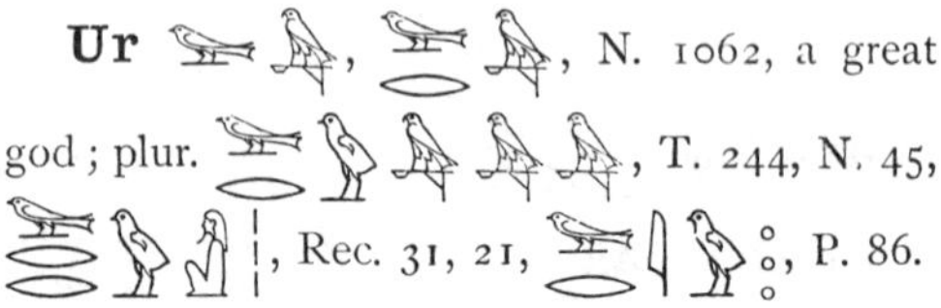, N. 1062, a great god; plur., T. 244, N. 45, Rec. 31, 21, P. 86.

Urȧ 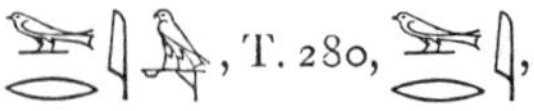, T. 280, P. 61, M. 29, great god.

Urur , twice great god.

Urrtȧ 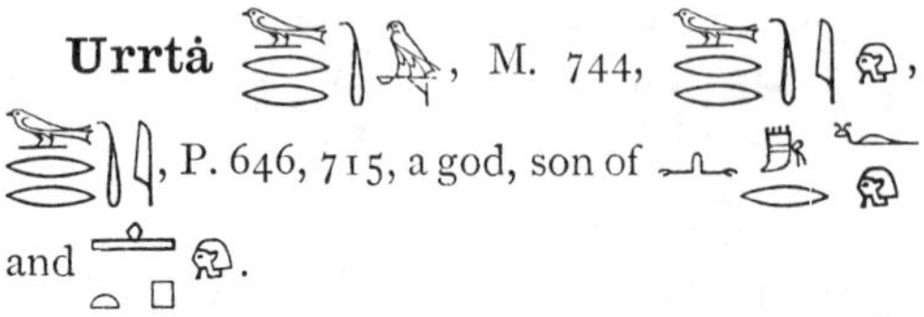, M. 744, P. 646, 715, a god, son of … and … .

Urui , the two great gods, *i.e.*, Horus and Set.

Uru 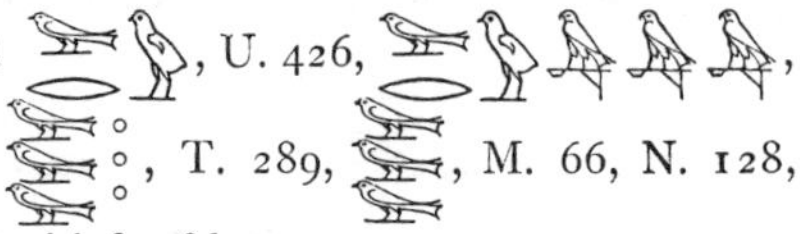, U. 426, T. 244, T. 289, M. 66, N. 128, the great chiefs of heaven.

Uru , Ṭuat II, a group of gods who lightened the darkness; compare Heb. אוֹרִים.

Urit 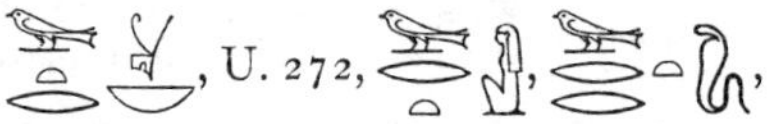, U. 272, B.D. 100, 4: (1) one of a group of four goddesses; (2) a protector of the dead.

Urit 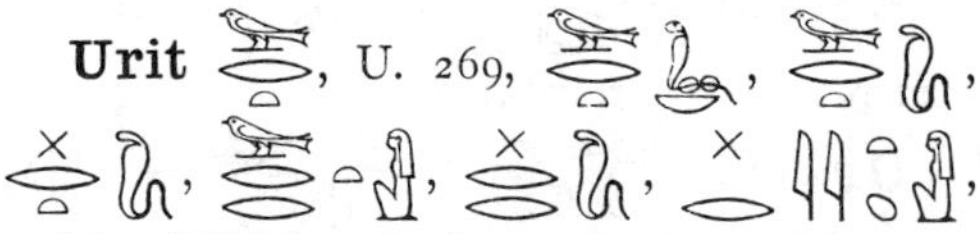, U. 269, a title of Neith and of several other goddesses.

Urti 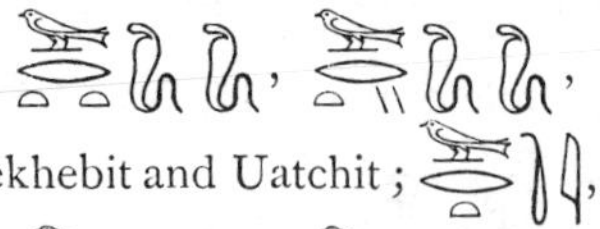, the goddesses Nekhebit and Uatchit; N. 1385.

Urit 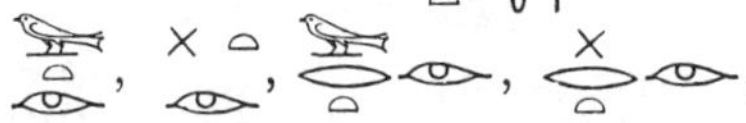, a name of an eye of Horus, the moon.

Ur-at , Sinsin II, a god of Kher-Āḥa.

Urit-ȧb-er-tef-s , Ombos III, 2, 130.

Ur-ȧmi-Sheṭ 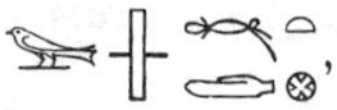, U. 529, a title of Horus.

Urit-ȧmi-t-Ṭuat 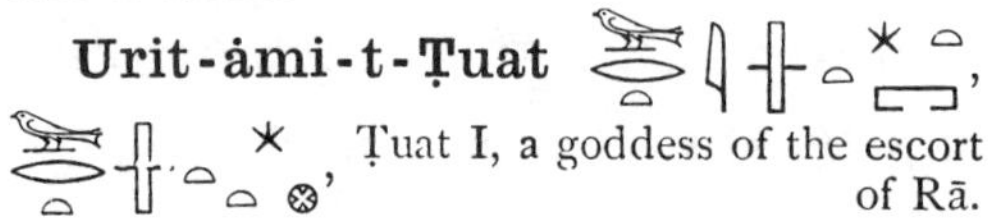, Ṭuat I, a goddess of the escort of Rā.

Ur-àres, Uràrset 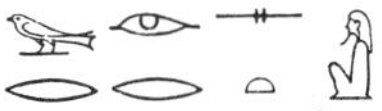, , B.D. 102, 6, 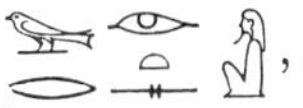, a god of a boat; Saïte var. [illegible].

Ur-ā , P. 164, 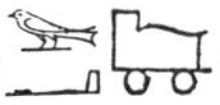, N. 861, [illegible], U. 68, P. 328, the name of a goddess.

Ur-urti 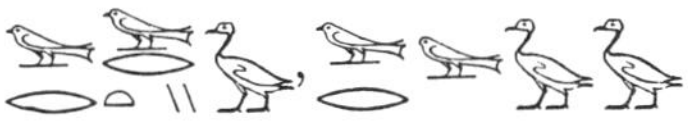 [illegible], B.D. 64, 16, a title of Isis and Nephthys.

ur-baiu , [illegible] great of souls, *i.e.*, strong-willed, a title of gods and kings.

Ur-peḥui-f , B.D. 144, 20, a god.

Ur-peḥti 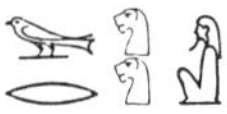, Mar. Aby. I, 44, , Denderah IV, 78, a doorkeeper-god.

Ur-maati-f , B.D. 115, 9, a god.

Urit-em-àb-Rāit , Ombos III, 2, 133, a form of Hathor.

Ur-em-Neṭàt , N. 1345, a title of Horus and Osiris.

Ur-mentch-f , N. 754, a title of Horus.

Ur-mert-s-ṭesher-sheniu  [illegible], B.D. 141, 20, 148, one of seven Cows.

Urit-em-sekhemu-s  , the goddess of the 4th hour of the day.

Ur-metuu-ḥer-àat-f  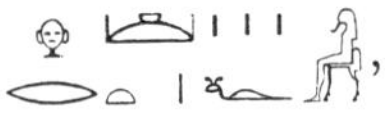, Rec. 26, 227, a god (Osiris?)

Uru-nef-ta-seṭau-nef-pet  , U. 215, a title of Horus.

Ur-nes  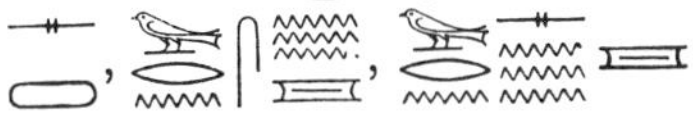, the name of a portion of the river in the Ṭuat.

Urit-en-kru (?) , Ombos I, 1, 47, a lioness-headed hippopotamus-goddess of Ombos.

Ur-henu 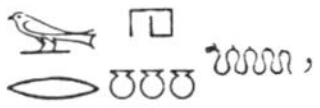, Mission 13, 225, a water-god.

Ur-henhenu [illegible], B.D. 3, 2, a water-god.

Ur-ḥeb , M. 213, [illegible] [illegible], N. 684, an associate of Ta, Geb, Àsàr and Ànpu.

Ur-ḥeka , Denderah III, 36, a god of Denderah.

Urit-ḥekait , Denderah IV, 78, a form of Hathor as a fighting-goddess.

Ur-ḥekau , a name of Set of Ombos, [illegible], U. 285.

Urit-ḥekau , U. 269, N. 719, [illegible], U. 271, [illegible] [illegible], a goddess of spells and enchantments, who was identified with Isis, Hathor, Bast, Sekhmit, etc.

Urti-ḥekau 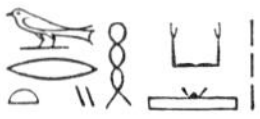, Rec. 32, 80, , [illegible], the two goddesses Nekhebit and Uatchit.

Urti-ḥethati , B.D. 189, 21, goddesses of Ànu.

Ur-khert , Denderah IV, 80, a jackal-god in the 2nd Àat.

Ur-khert 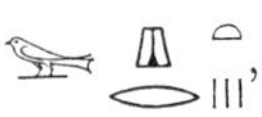, Ṭuat VII, a star-god.

Ur-sa-Ur , N. 656, a title of Osiris.

Ur-saḥ-f , Lanzone 176, a god, Rā or Osiris (?)

Ur-senu , B.D. 17, 32 (Nebseni), a chief of the torture chamber of Osiris.

Ur-senṭ, , Denderah IV, 78, Berg. 1, 35: (1) a double bull-god; (2) a jackal-god who befriended the dead; (3) a god of Edfû.

Ur-sekat, , U. 420, T. 240, a god of ploughing in the Ṭuat.

Ur-sheps-f, , P. 672, N. 1271, a son of Ptaḥ.

Urit-shefit, goddess of the 4th hour of the night.

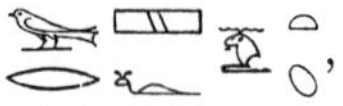

Ur-ka-f, T. 87, , M. 240, , N. 618, a form of Horus.

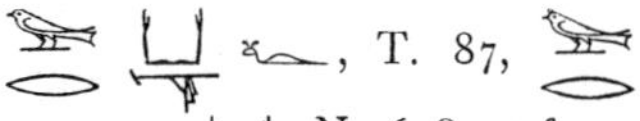

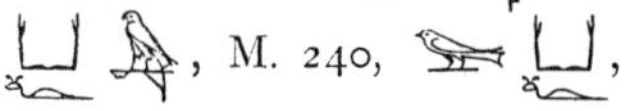

Ur-gerti, a star-god.

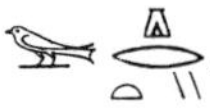

Urui-ṭenṭen, Naville, Mythe, a title of Horus of Edfû.

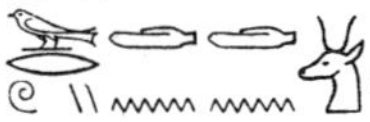

ur, large house, mansion, palace.

ur, , , a joint of meat, a meat ration; 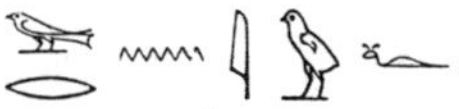 ,  , 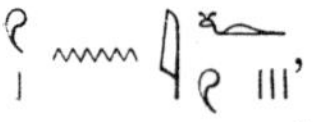 , a large piece or slice of flesh off a joint.

ur, a violent wind, gale, storm (?)

ur, N. 976, part of a ladder (?)

ur, , pig.

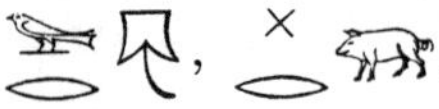

ur, flame, fire.

ur-t, a funeral chest.

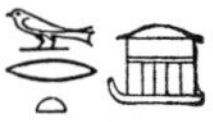

ur-t, N. 507, a large (?) cake.

ur-t, a large boat.

Ur-t, B.D. 110, a lake in Sekhet-Àaru.

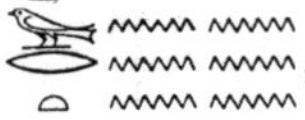

ur, U. 284, N. 719, lake; plur. , U. 291, , M. 729, , N. 1330.

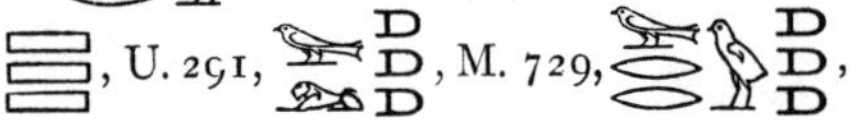

ur-t, the funeral mountain, the grave.

Urtt, a name of the Other World.

urr-t, a place (?)

ur, helpless, miserable.

urr, Ḥerusâtef Stele 101, to be abased, to be destitute.

urr-t, Rec. 3, 57, hairy head.

Urȧ[tenti] [ ], Rec. 20, 81, a good demon.

urāi (?), a garment, a bandlet.

urit, , , , a mass of water, flood, a name of the sky.

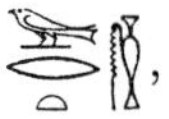

urit, , , pylon, a house, a large chamber, hall.

urri, Rev. 11, 136, 171, , Rev. 11, 173, 12, 15, , Jour. As. 1908, 208, to delay, 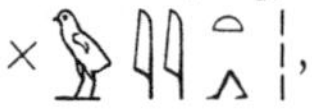 , Mar. Aby. I, 6, 42; Copt. ϩⲣⲟⲩⲣ.

urrat, Rev. 12, 47, delay.

Urit, B.D. 125, II, 23, a town in Egypt or in the Ṭuat.

urrit, , , , , , chariot; , , , , .

urit, a kind of garment.

uri, to be hairy; compare Copt. ⲟⲩⲗⲁⲓ (?)

urmu,  , title of priests of Rā and Mnevis.

urmu, , , Nile-flood.

Urm'r, Thes. 1203, a Libyan king.

urmit, a disease of the belly.

urmu, battlement, protective works.

urḥ, N. 307, P. 238, Rev. 5, 96, to rub with oil or salve, to anoint, to smear.

urḥu, P. 692, anointed ones.

urḥ-t, unguent.

urḥ, Rev. 14, 40, plot of ground, court; Copt. ⲟⲩⲣⲉϩ.

urkh, Rev. 11, 134, court; Copt. ⲟⲩⲣⲉϩ.

urkh, to become green, to flourish.

urkh, to guard, to protect.

urs, head rest, pillow; plur., cedar wood pillows; meru wood pillow; alabaster pillow; wooden pillow.

urs, to overturn; Copt. ⲟⲩⲱⲗⲥ̄.

urs, Rev. 13, 19; herb, Copt. ⲟⲩⲣⲓⲥ.

ursh, to become green, to flourish.

ursh, U. 451, P. 165, N. 799, Hh. 224, Rec. 31, 30, Rev. 13, 3, to pass the time, to keep a watch, to observe astronomically, watcher, observer, observatory; Copt. ⲟⲩⲣϣⲉ.

ursh-t, watch, vigil.

urshu, Rec. 21, 14, festivals kept in the Great Oasis.

ursh, watcher; plur., Rev. 14, 2.

Urshu, T. 387, M. 403, N. 719, N. 736, T. 289, N. 737, P. 204, N. 11, N. 849, the watchers, a class of divine beings.

Urshiu, Tomb of Seti I, three Hour-gods who make one of the 75 forms of Rā (No. 67).

Urshu Pu, P. 71, M. 102, N. 11, the tutelary gods of Pe (Buto).

Urshu Nekhen, P. 72, M. 102, the tutelary gods of Nekhen.

Urek = , an Earth-god.

Urti-ḥa-t, Thes. 83, "Still-heart," a title of Osiris.

urṭ, to rest, be motionless; Copt. ⲟⲩⲣⲟⲧ.

urṭ, the setting of a star.

urṭ-t, immobility, cessation.

urṭu, L.D. III, 140B, a fainting or exhausted man.

Urṭ, Ṭuat VI, a motionless god = **Urṭ-ȧb** (or **ḥa**).

urṭu, see **ȧkhmiu urṭu**.

Urṭ-ḥa-t, B.D. 1, 13,

64, 42, 145, I, 1, 182, 1, 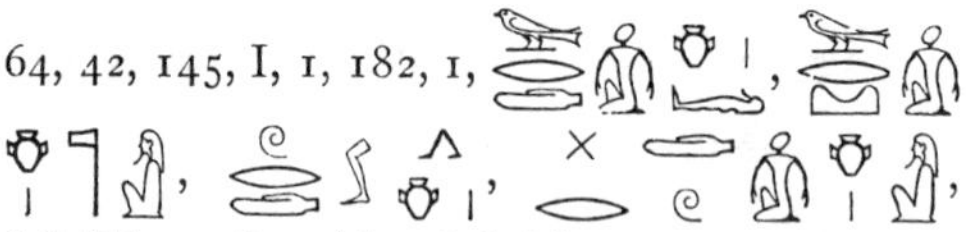, “Still-heart,” a title of Osiris, a name given to any mummy.

urṭ , a kind of bird.

urtch , U. 13, to stop, to cease.

uhi 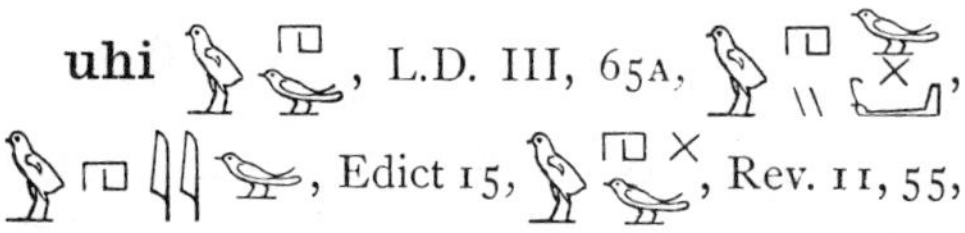, L.D. III, 65A, Edict 15, Rev. 11, 55, , Rev. 8, 134, to fail, to err, to miss the mark (of an arrow), to escape, to manage to avoid something, to be a defaulter; 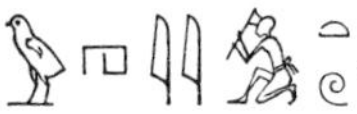, deprived.

uhi , one who is stripped or robbed, deprivation (?); , a fiend.

uh-t , Peasant 292, failure, ruin.

uhiu (?) , Rev. 13, 37, defaulters.

uhiu , Thes. 1322, things decayed or rotten.

uhi , Rev., scorpion; Copt. ⲟⲩⲟϩⲉ.

uha , Åmen. 14, 11, 12, 19, 2, , Mar. Karn. 54, 42, to fail, to miss the mark, etc. (as **uh** ); to fail.

uhaha , to fail.

uhamu , to repeat, to recite; Copt. ⲟⲩⲱϩⲙ̅.

uhan , to destroy, to overthrow.

uhan-t , ruin, ruins.

uhas , Anastasi I, 25, 7, to be exhausted, to be weary of, to be careless about.

uhȧ , a disease of the belly.

uhȧ , to decay, to become putrid, to rot.

uheb 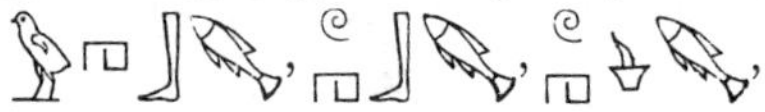, a kind of fish.

uhem , hoof, claw of a bird; , Rec. 23, 198, a horned animal.

uhem 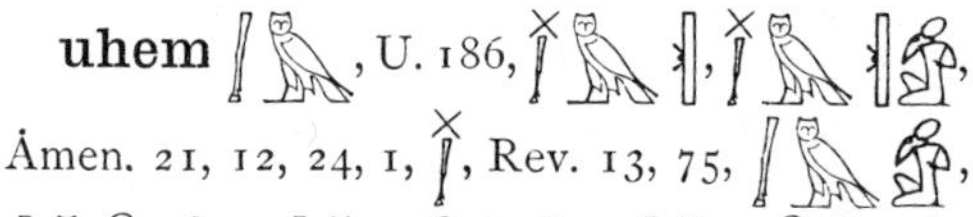, U. 186, Åmen. 21, 12, 24, 1, Rev. 13, 75, , to repeat, to narrate, to recount, to tell a story, to tell a dream; 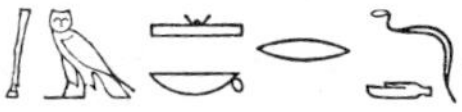, Speak again! Copt. ⲟⲩⲱϩⲙ̅.

uhem ānkh , renewing life, repeating living; , water which renews life.

uhemu , P.S.B. 10, 47, , , a “teller,” registrary, herald, lay priest, recorder, orator, proclaimer; plur. , Rec. 21, 92.

uhem-ti , narrator.

uhem āa , IV, 972, the great recorder; 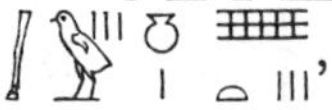 IV, 1120, recorders of the Nomes.

uhem en se[m]-t neb , "teller of every land," dragoman, Foreign Office messenger.

uhem nesu , the king's herald.

uhem nesu tep , king's herald-in-chief.

Uhemu 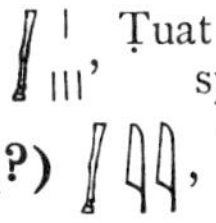, Ṭuat IX, the gods who recite spells to bewitch Āapep.

Uhemi (?) , Ṭuat X, a god of the 9th Gate.

Uhem-ḥer , B.D. 123, 3, a god.

Uhem-t-ṭesu, etc. 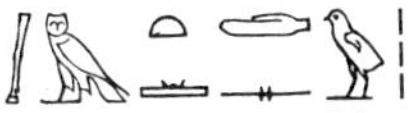, etc., B.D. 145, 146, the 11th Pylon of Sekhet-Ȧaru.

uhem , , Jour. As. 1908, 256, to renew, to repeat an act, to do something often; , Rec. 16, 57, renewing the race; Copt. ⲟⲩⲱϩⲙ̅.

uhemit, uhemmit , , repetition.

uhem-t , what is repeated, something that is renewed; , a revolution (of a star).

uhemuti , second, duplicate, like; , without his like, unequalled.

uhem–

em uhem , a second time, anew.

em uhem ā , a second time, anew.

mit em uhem , death a second time, the second death.

n mut-f em uhem  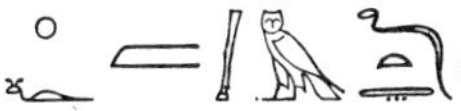, he shall never die a second time.

Uhem ānkh , Edfû 1, 80, 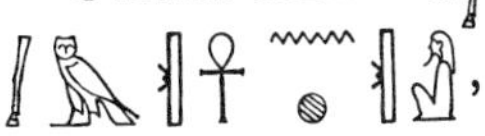, a title of the Nile-god.

uhemu āḥa , to renew a fight, repeat an attack.

uhem menu 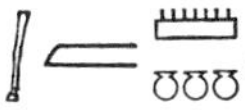, Rec. 20, 42, 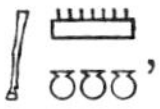, IV, 358, to repeat monuments, *i.e.*, to multiply buildings.

uhem meṭu , to repeat words.

uhem ra , IV, 414, multiplying speech (?)

uhem renp , renewing youth.

uhem ḥer , "he who renews [his] face," the name of a god.

uhem khā , repeater of risings, *i.e.*, Rā.

uhem sesheṭ , renewing the bandlet.

uhem qaȧs , to renew fetters, *i.e.*, to increase them.

uhem qai , renewer of form, *i.e.*, the moon.

uhem qeṭ-t , renewer of form, *i.e.*, the moon.

uhem 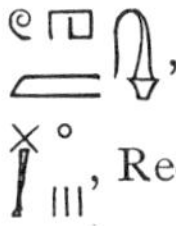, to burn up, to blaze.

uhem , Rec. 15, 127, grains of incense.

uhen 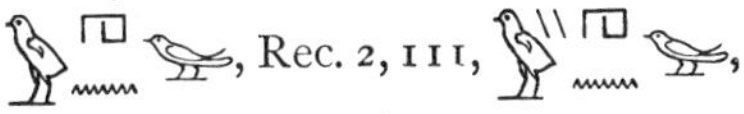, Rec. 2, 111, , Rec. 20, 43, failure, decay, ruin.

uhen , filth (?)

uhen , Ȧmen. 8, 3, 12, 3,  , to destroy, to overthrow, to drag down, to lay waste.

uhnen 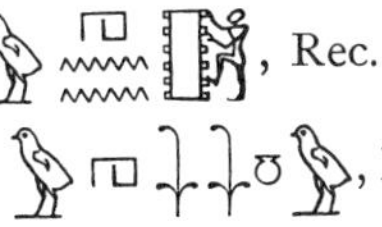, Rec. 31, 173.

uhennu , P. 471, M. 539, N. 1118, to remove.

uher , house dog; Copt. ⲟⲩϩⲁⲣ, ⲟⲩϩⲟⲣ.

uḥ [illegible], U. 297, T. 141 = [illegible], M. 198, N. 537, to be strong (?)

uḥuḥ , Rec. 15, 57 . . . . . .

uḥ , U. 295, N. 529, to cry out.

uḥuḥ 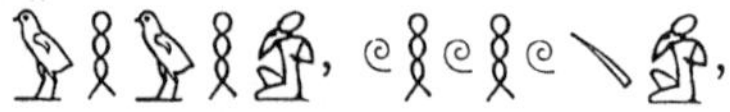, Åmen. 26, 7, to bay, to bark, to cry out.

uḥ 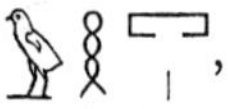, a place of abode, encampment, compound; Copt. ⲟϩⲉ.

uḥ, uḥa 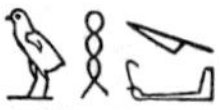, Rec. 16, 127, 

to hew or cut stone, to quarry stone, to break stone, to excavate; , to reap corn; , to prune vines, to harvest grapes.

uḥa 
, a disease, stone in the bladder.

uḥḥ , El-Amarna V, 33, abortus; Copt. ϩⲟⲩϩⲉ.

Uḥa , B.M. 32, 383, a fiend in the Ṭuat.

uḥa-t 
, pot, kettle, roasting dish, brazier, any kind of cooking pot; plur. 
, U. 513, T. 326.

uḥau , Annales III, 110, increment, addition.

uḥā 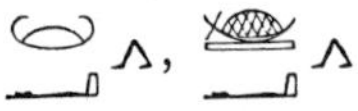, to inspect, to examine into.

uḥā 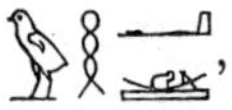, N. 1345, 1346, 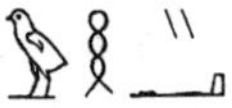
[illegible], N. 766, [illegible], T. 183, 233, [illegible],
[illegible], [illegible], Rec. 27, 55, 30, 198,
[illegible], IV, 162, [illegible], N. 806, [illegible],
[illegible], Anastasi I, 1, 7, [illegible], Israel Stele 16, [illegible], [illegible], [illegible], [illegible],

, Åmen. 27, 14, 15, to untie, to loosen, to set free, to release, to solve a riddle, to unravel a problem, to separate (heaven from earth, Thes. 1283), to return in the evening.

uḥā sennti 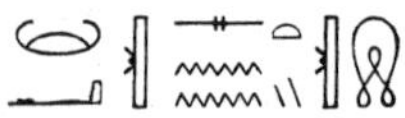, to open a way through the outer enclosure of a building.

uḥā thess-t 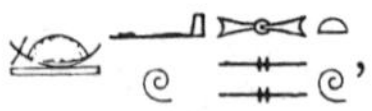, to unpick a knot, to disentangle a difficult matter, to explain riddles.

uḥā ṭerf 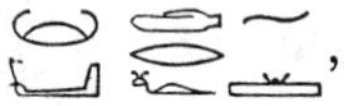, IV, 969, to decipher writing.

uḥā , Rec. 6, 11, , a matter which has to be explained, problem, riddle, parable; plur. , Åmen. 3, 10.

Uḥā-ḥa-t , a guide of Åf through the Gate of Saa-Set.

uḥā åb (or **ḥati**) , Mar. Karn. 36, 26, ,
, Rec. 24, 185, wise, understanding of heart, able, competent; , skilfully coloured.

uḥā-ṭet , a man with clever, skilful hands and fingers.

uḥā tchatcha , to revere, to bow down to.

uḥā 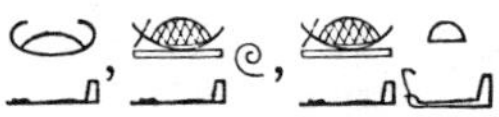, to cast a line, to stretch a cord, to use a rope; , Thes. 1285, to stretch out a builder's cord to show the size of the building.

uḥā ,
[illegible], to work a line or net in fishing and fowling.

uḥā [illegible], [illegible], [illegible],
[illegible], fisherman, fowler, hunter; plur.
[illegible], [illegible], [illegible]
[illegible]; Copt. ⲟⲩⲟϩⲓ.

uḥā (remu) , Peasant 230, fisherman; plur. , Rec. 13, 203, , fisherman to the Court.

uḥā , a kind of fish (synodontis shall); plur. , , Rec. 30, 217.

uḥā-t 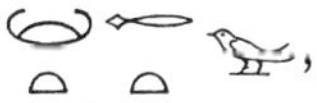, the [festivals of the] great and little fishing.

uḥā , to wound, to stab with a knife, to sting (of a scorpion).

uḥā-t , Metternich Stele 73, , Rec. 15, 145, Rev. 13, 41, scorpion; 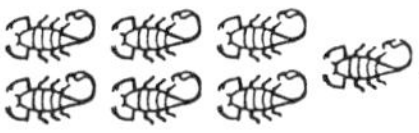, the seven scorpions of Isis; Copt. ⲟⲩⲟⲟϩⲉ, ⲟⲩⲟϩⲉ.

uḥā , to feed, food, provisions, superfluity.

uḥāi, a kind of grain or seed.

uḥā, plants, flowers (?)

uḥi, a stage of a journey, a halting-place.

uḥit 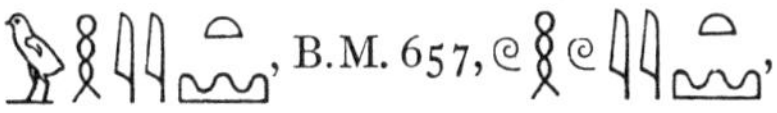, B.M. 657, encampment or village of nomads in the desert; plur. 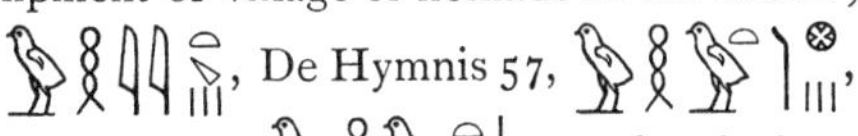, De Hymnis 57, Mar. Aby. I, 7, 68, , Tombos Stele 5, 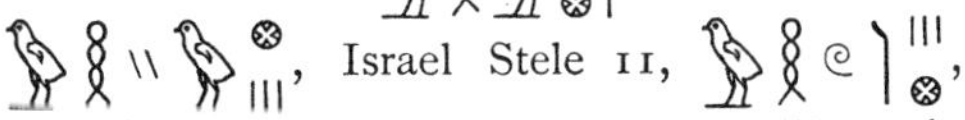, Israel Stele 11, Rougé I.H. Pl. 256, Rec. 31, 39, villages in East Africa, the Sûdân, the Eastern Desert, etc.

uḥut , foreign settlements.

Uḥuit   , the nomads of the Sûdân, East Africa, Syria, Palestine, Arabia, etc.

uḥi 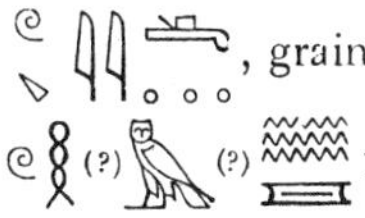, grain. Ȧmen. 23, 20 .....

uḥem, Rec. 3, 30, to repeat; Copt. ⲟⲩⲱϩⲙ̄.

uḥer 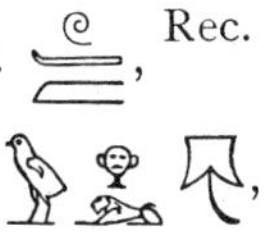, Rev. 12, 53, dog; Copt. ⲟⲩϩⲟⲣ.

uḥes , to beat down, to slay.

uḥsut , Hh. 354, filth, dust, dirt.

Ukh (?) 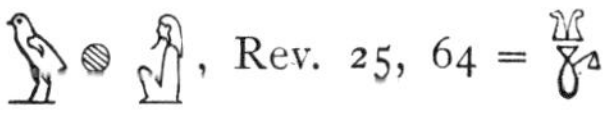, Rev. 25, 64 = or .

ukh-t 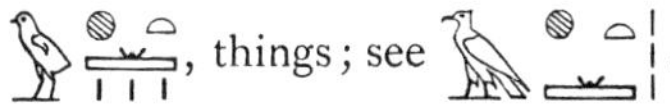, things; see.

ukha 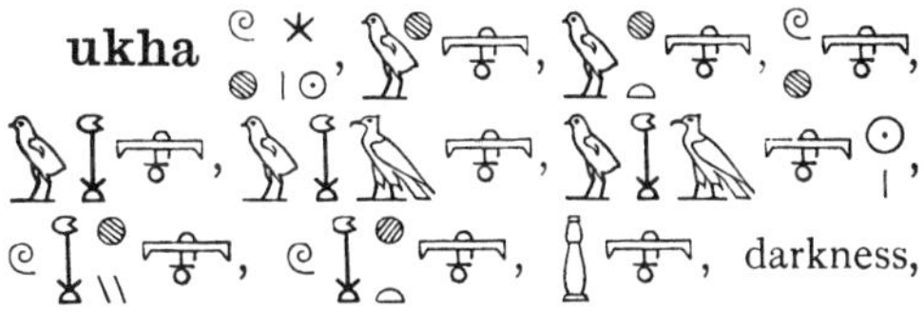, darkness, night; Copt. ⲉⲩϣⲏ.

ukha 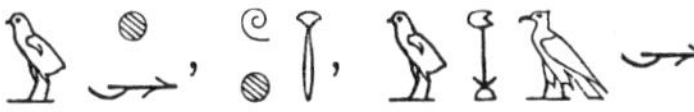, Mar. Aby. I, 6, 37, 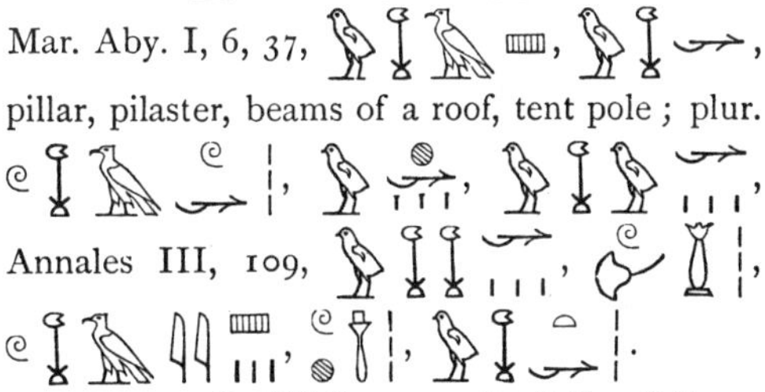, pillar, pilaster, beams of a roof, tent pole; plur., Annales III, 109.

ukha-t , portico, colonnade, pillar.

ukhatu-t , Ḥerusȧtef Stele 59, part of a building.

ukha 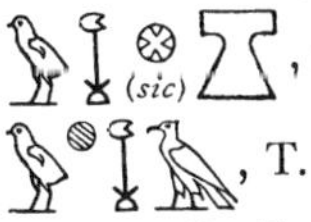, fire altar.

ukha, T. 288, P. 609, M. 406, 735, N. 806, 1332, , T. 371, N. 126, , T. 392, L.D. III, 140, 6, Rev. 14, 136, 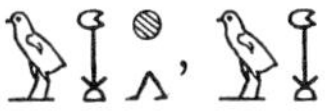 , to seek, to enquire for; Copt. ⲟⲩⲱϣⲉ.

ukhakh , Ȧmen. 9, 14, 19, 19.

ukha , , , to let fall, to have a miscarriage, to purge, to place, to set down something; , Rec. 30, 67.

ukha kha-t , to evacuate.

ukha theb-t , base of a pyramid.

ukha-tȧ , a pair of sandals or shoes (Lacau).

ukha , P. 671, M. 661, , N. 1275, , a cake offering.

ukha.... , an amulet (?)

ukha , , whirlwind, storm (?)

ukha , Peasant 287, , , to play the fool, to be foolish, simple, ignorant, neglectful, careless, stupid, slothful, etc.

ukha, ukhau , R.E. 8, 73, , Peasant 218, , , , , fool, ignoramus, simpleton, boor, the unlettered man, sluggard; plur. ; L.D. III, 16A, 8, , defects, crimes, acts of folly.

ukha , , , note, letter, despatch, roll, document; plur. , , Rec. 21, 83, , Rec. 21, 83.

ukha , N. 753, claws, nails, hooks.

ukham (?) , Theb. Ost. 15K = (?)

ukhikh (?) , T. 333, , M. 249, N. 703, , P. 826, a plant-god (?)

ukheb , to shine, to be bright.

ukher , , Rechnungen 63, granary, warehouse, wharf, dock, dockyard; plur. .

ukher-t , a wooden tool or instrument, appliance; plur. , Hh. 436, , , Rec. 31, 86.

ukhes (?) , P. 461, N. 1098 = , M. 517.

ukhes nemmȧt , B.D. 125, II; see .

ukhtu , port, harbour.

ukheṭ-t (?) , boat.

ukheṭ , IV, 1082, , , , to be in a state of collapse, to be in pain, to be painful, to be inflamed (of a sore, or of the heart), to feel hurt, , Rec. 31, 168.

ukhṭi , a man in a state of collapse.

ukheṭ-t , , , , , , , , pain, sickness, inflammation.

ukheṭ , to be treated with drugs, embalmed. Also used of words of the wise which are "preserved," or stored up.

ukhṭu , , Peasant 272, long-suffering.

ukheṭ ḥat , tolerant, forbearing; plur. .

us = , to be broad, wide.

use[kh]-t ā , long-armed, a far-reaching hand.

usi , , , much, exceedingly, quite, wholly.

us-t , , , , hall, a building of some kind; plur. , , Rec. 27, 222.

us , Famine Stele 31, , , , , , to be empty, to come to an end.

us-t , , , , , , decay, ruin, misery, the lack of something, emptiness.

us , to destroy, to do away something.

us , to saw; Copt. ⲟⲩⲉⲓⲥⲉ, ⲃⲓⲥⲉ.

us-t , , , , , something sawn off, sawdust, scrapings.

us-t , A.Z. 1908, 12, the amulet of the sceptre.

usaf (usf) , Rev. 12, 115, , Jour. As. 1908, 486, to lose, to lack; Copt. ⲟⲩⲱⲥϥ.

usam (usm) , Rev. 11, 134, 160, 172, crushed, broken.

usar , Rev. 13, 8, strong man; see .

Usar, User , , , , , , , , , , Pierret, Inscrip. II, 130, A.Z. 1879, 126, Berg. I, 6, late forms of the name of Osiris.

usaḥ , to advance.

usakh-t (uskh-t) , Rev. 13, 30, hall; plur. , Rev. 14, 13, asylums, refuges.

usash , Rev. 14, 22, hall; see .

usaten (usten) , Rev. 11, 178, , , to enlarge = ; Copt. ⲟⲩⲉⲥⲑⲱⲛ.

Usāau , B.D. 144c (Saïte), a goddess.

useb , to heap up.

usf , Peasant 257, B. 2, 107, , Edict 30, , IV, 353, , to be lazy, idle, slothful; Copt. ⲟⲩⲱⲥϥ.

usfa , , laziness, supineness, sloth, idleness, sluggishness, , Anastasi VII, 12, 1, Sallier II, 14, 9.

usfu , Peasant 284, B 2, 109, , lazy man.

usfa , a kind of marsh bird.

usfau , snarers of the same.

usem , bowels, intestines.

usen , to make water.

useni , a title of the Ram-god.

user , , , , T. 72, , U. 192, , Rec. 31, 165, , , , to be strong, to be mighty, to be rich; , rich in houses.

user , IV, 972, strong one, *i.e.*, oppressor.

userit  Rec. 5, 90, 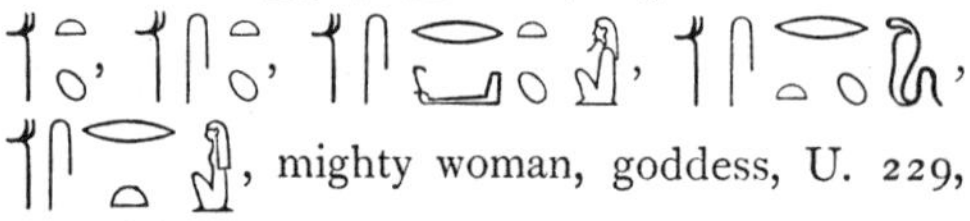 mighty woman, goddess, U. 229, a wealthy woman, Metternich Stele 55; plur. , T. 306.

user-t 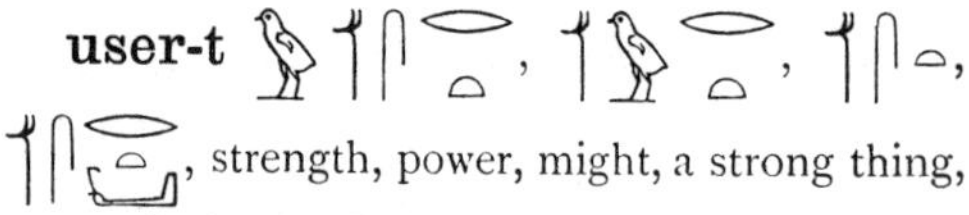 strength, power, might, a strong thing, riches (, Åmen. 9, 6).

useru 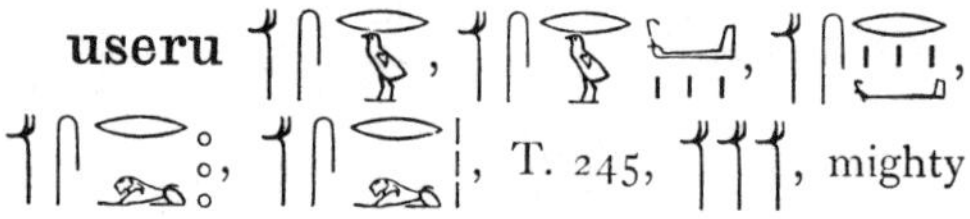 T. 245, mighty ones, powers, strong beings.

User , Rec. 30, 198, the god of strength.

User , Ombos I, 1, 186–188, one of the 14 kau of Rā.

User-ti , a god.

Userit  U. 229, a goddess of .

User-t , B.D. 41 (Saïte), a lake in Sekhet-Åaru.

Userit 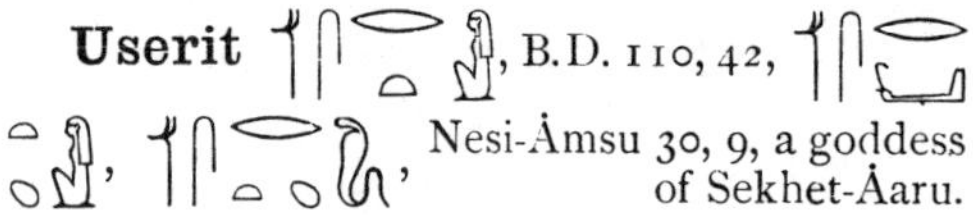 B.D. 110, 42, Nesi-Åmsu 30, 9, a goddess of Sekhet-Åaru.

User-Ba , B.D. 65, 4, a title of Rā and of Osiris.

User-baiu-f-em-Uatch-ur 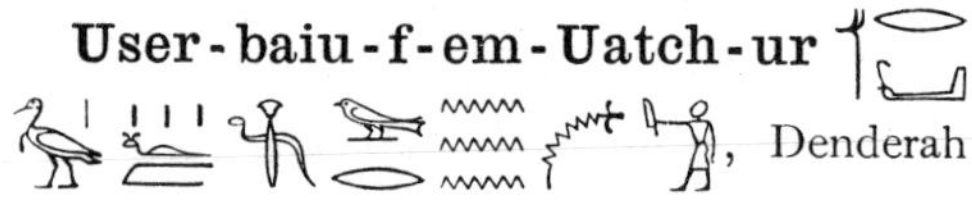, Denderah IV, 63, a warrior-god.

User-Rā , Ṭuat VI, a name of a standard in the Ṭuat.

User-ḥa-t , "strong heart," the name of a god.

User-ḥati 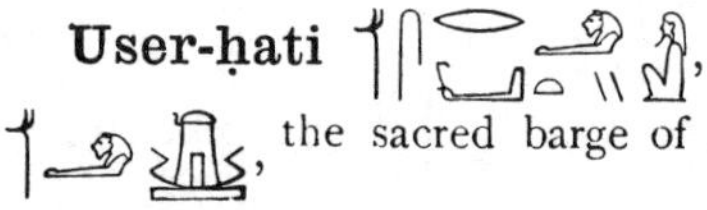 Rec. 21, 76, the sacred barge of Åmen-Rā at Thebes.

User-t (?) Geb , Ṭuat VI, the jackal-headed stakes to which the damned were tied in the Ṭuat.

user-t 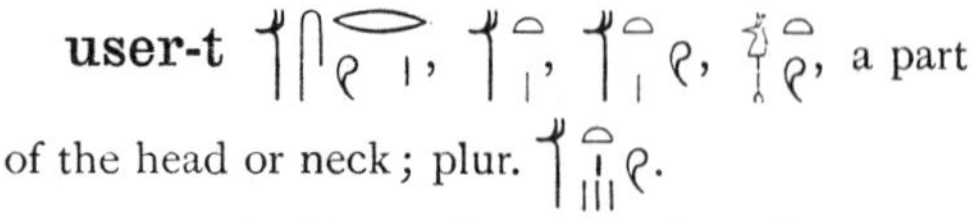 a part of the head or neck; plur. .

user , to steer, rudder, steering pole, oar, paddle; plur. 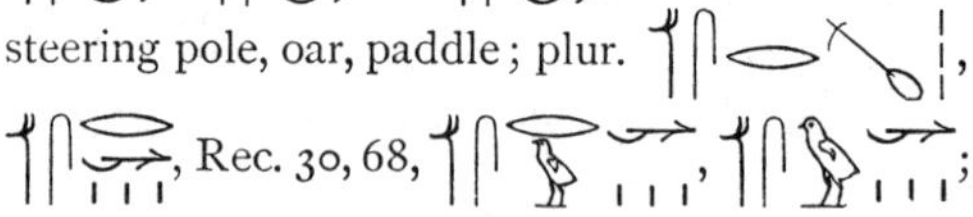 Rec. 30, 68, ; Copt. ⲟⲩⲟⲥⲣ̄, ϭⲟⲥⲉⲣ.

useru , rowers, IV, 305.

user-t 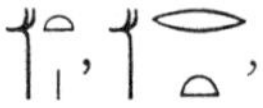, U. 423, T. 242, a kind of sceptre.

user-t , flame, fire.

userti , Tanis Pap. 18, two leathern objects.

useḥ 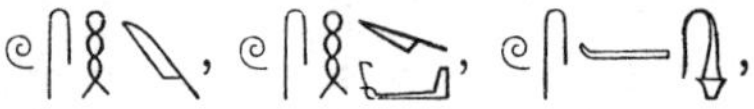, to cut in pieces, to cut through, to shave, to destroy.

useḥ 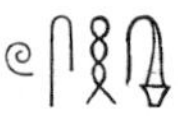, to destroy by fire.

usekh 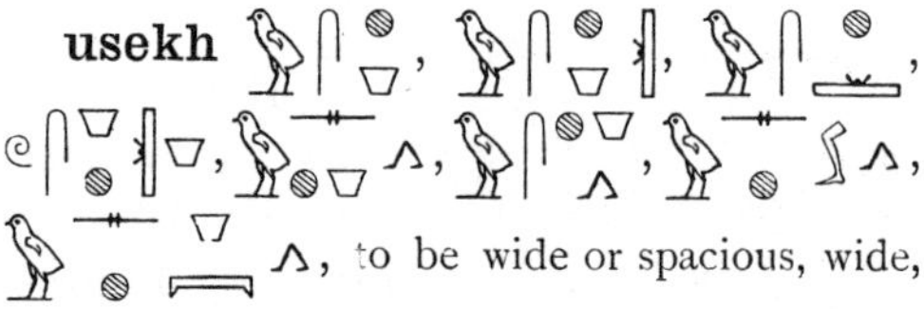, to be wide or spacious, wide, to be in a spacious place, to be spread out, to be empty, vacant; Copt. ⲟⲩⲱϣⲥ̄; 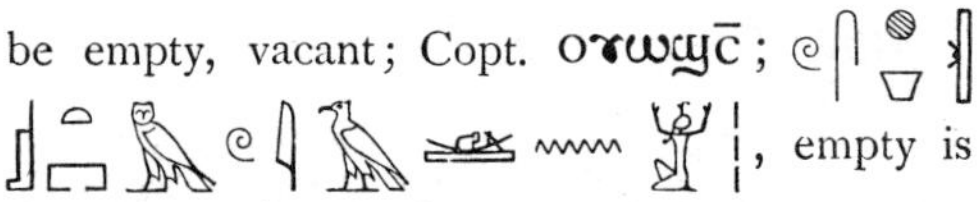, empty is the throne in the boat of millions of years; 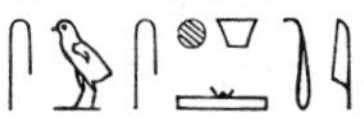, made spacious.

usekh-t , width, breadth; , the width of his two arms.

Usekh[-t]-åst-ānkh[-t]-em-snef , Denderah I, 30, Ombos II, 2, 134, a lion-god and lioness-goddess.

Usekh-nemmåt 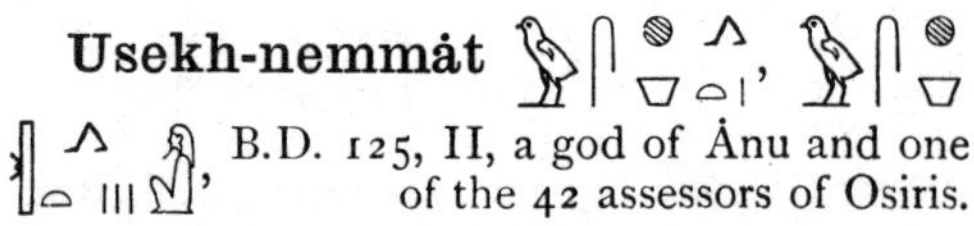 B.D. 125, II, a god of Ånu and one of the 42 assessors of Osiris.

Usekh-ḥer : B.D. 28, 5, a title of Rā.

Usekh-t ḥett , a uraeus-goddess.

usekh-t 
(*sic*) 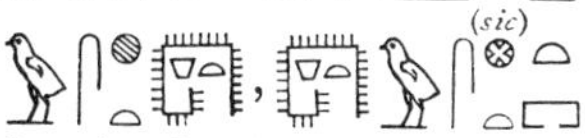 Ḥerusȧtef Stele 7,
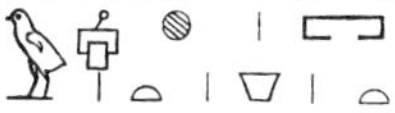, hall, any large chamber.

usekh-t ȧsq , waiting room.

usekh-t Ȧsȧr , a title of the tomb.

usekh-t en bunr 
, outside hall.

usekh-t ent Maāti 

, hall of the two gods of Truth, or the Judgment Hall of Osiris.

usekh-t . . . . . , the hall of the people in a temple, the outer court.

usekh-t ḥebit , IV, 344, festival hall.

usekh-t ḥetep 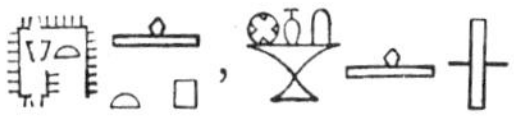
, the hall in the tomb in which the offerings were presented, and the offering itself.

Usekh-t Sekh-t Ȧanru 
, hall of the Fields of Reeds (the Elysian Fields).

Usekh-t Seṭ 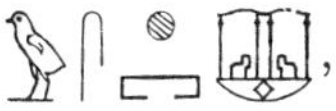, the hall of a temple in which the Seṭ Festival was celebrated.

Usekh-t Shu , "hall of Shu," a name of the sky, or of the space between the earth and the sky.

Usekh-t Geb , "hall of Geb," a name of the earth.

usekh , a wide-mouthed vessel.

usekh-t 
, a broad flat-bottomed boat; plur. , Koller Pap. 3, 6.

usekh 

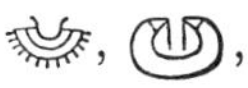, collar, pectoral, breast ornament; plur. 

usekh-ti , Rec. 4, 26.

usekh , A.Z. 1908, 15, the amulet of the collar or pectoral; , pectoral of mother of emerald; , of various kinds of stones; 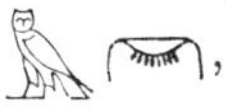, in gold; , in silver; , in lapis lazuli; 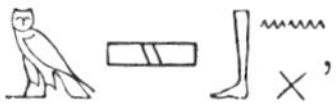, in wood; , in tchām metal.

usekh-en-bȧk , A.Z. 1908, 18, the "hawk-collar" amulet.

usekh-en-Mut 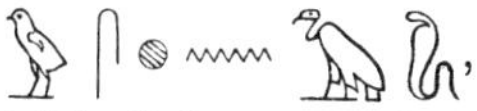, A.Z. 1908, 18, "collar of Mut," the name of an amulet.

usekh-en-Nebti , A.Z. 1908, 18, "collar of Uatchit and Nekhebit," the name of an amulet.

usekh-en-Khens [illegible], A.Z. 1908, 18, the collar of Khensu, an amulet.

usekh-en-tchet [illegible], A.Z. 1908, 18, "collar of eternity," the name of an amulet.

usekh [illegible], B.D. 172, 23, to plate with metal; [illegible], thy limbs are plated with gold.

usekh [illegible](?) Rec. 31, 170 . . . .

usesh [illegible], to be wide = [illegible].

usesh-t [illegible], hall = [illegible],

usesh, collar, necklace.

usesh , , to make water, to evacuate; later form, .

usesh-t , U. 159, T. 344, , Hh. 448, , , , Rec. 29, 150, , , , , , Hh. 372, urine, evacuation, excrement in general.

ussha, to cut off.

ust-t , , Ḳubbân Stele 31, roll, letter, document, despatch; plur. , Berl. 7272.

usta, to tow, to drag, to draw.

usten , Israel Stele 12, , , , Edict 23, , , , , , , to walk with long steps, to stride, to step out; Copt. ⲟⲩⲉⲥⲧⲱⲛ.

usten re, to open the mouth wide.

usten reṭ, to walk with long strides, *i.e.*, boldly.

ustenu, Rougé I.H. 256, a kind of officer.

usten, a spacious room.

Usten, a title of the Nile-god and of his flood.

Usten = , an ape-god.

usthen , , IV, 1075, 1189, to stride; Copt. ⲟⲩⲟⲥⲑⲉⲛ.

Usṭ, B.D. 148, the herald of the 2nd Ārit.

Usṭen, Åmen. 15, 10, 26, 5, 17, to walk with long strides, to stretch, to extend.

Usṭen, Ombos II, 2, 200, a lake-god, a title of the Nile-god.

ustchefa, Gen. Epist. 64, vainly (?)

ush , , , , , , , , Ḥeruemḥeb 23, Rev. 11, 150, to be empty, to be decayed or destroyed, or ruined, effaced (of an inscription), bald, hairless, to fall out (of the hair), to lack; , , deprived, robbed; Copt. ⲟⲩⲉϣ.

ushsh, to lack, to be deprived of.

ush, omission, space, interval, a sign used in papyri to mark a lacuna.

ush, nothing, emptiness.

ush åmi, Rev. 12, 21, one-armed, one-handed.

ush up-t, Rev. 13, 63, headless.

ush ḥat, Pap. 3023, 85, senseless, stupid (?)

ush-t, A.Z. 1900, 128, a hair ornament.

ush , , , , darkness, night; Copt. ⲟⲩϣⲏ.

ush , , pelican (?)

ush, Rec. 4, 121, to eat; var. .

ush, to make water.

ushsh , , to make water.

ush-t , , urine, evacuation.

ush, to play the harp.

ush , , Åmen. 26, 13, , , to cry out, to praise, to adore, Caus. .

ushush, to crush, to pound.

usha, to masticate, to chew.

usha, to fatten geese or cattle.

usha ȧḥu, R.E. 6, 26, herdsman, pasturer or fattener of cattle, or perhaps fattened cattle; compare.

ushau (?), fattened geese.

usha-t, a place where birds or animals were fattened.

usha, IV, 502, 1095, 1208, to babble, to revile, to abuse, to curse.

usha, revilings, cursings, words of ill omen.

usha, Hymn Darius 3, to pour out, to scatter, to spread, to rub into powder.

usha-usha, Anastasi I, 26, 1, to beat, to beat flat, to smash, to strike, to break into; Copt. оуєϣоуωϣ.

usha-t, darkness, night, sunset.

ushait, night.

Usha-t, Denderah II, 10, 11, one of the 36 Dekans; Gr. Ουεστε.

Ushat-bakat, Denderah II, 10, Annales I, 84, one of the 36 Dekans; Gr. Ουεστε-Βικωτι.

ushauti; see **Shabti.**

usham, a sacrificial bucket.

Ushatȧspi, Hystaspes; Pers., Beh. I, 4, Babyl., Gr. Ὑστάσπης.

Ushati, Tombs of Seti I, Rameses IV; see **Usha-t.**

ushā, to gnaw, to chew, to bite, to masticate, to eat, what is eaten, food; P.S.B. 13, 412, the gnawing of a worm at a tooth.

ushā, a disease of the mouth, itching of the mouth.

ushu, dry, arid, desert, parched.

Ushur-ḥa-t, Berg. I, 10, an ibis-god.

usheb, Rev. 14, 14, to answer, to make a defence; to make an answer or an excuse; to answer at the right time; Copt. оуωϣв.

usheb-t 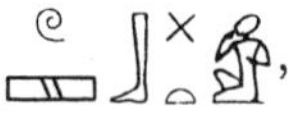, Israel Stele 15, 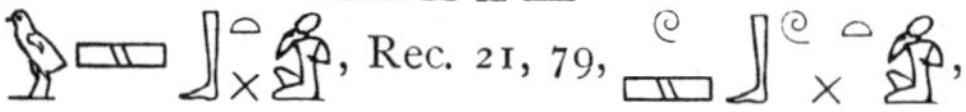 Rec. 21, 79, Åmen. 4, 11, 11, 18, , answer, deposition, statement, advocacy, speech in defence of something, the subject under discussion.

ushbit , Mar. Karn. 52, 17, answer, deposition.

ushebti ; see **Shabti.**

ushbit , a wailing woman; plur. .

usheb 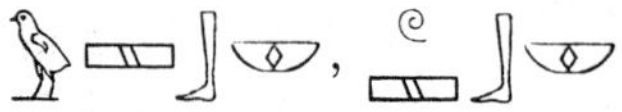, the name of the 27th day of the month.

usheb 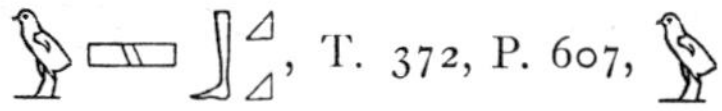 T. 372, P. 607,  U. 499, M. 717, , N. 709, to eat, to consume, to feed on, to swallow.

usheb-t 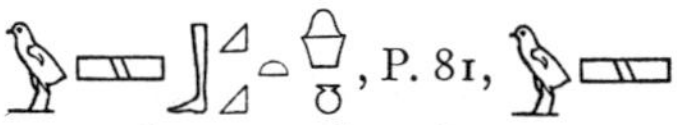 P. 81,  M. 111, N. 25, food, meals for the dead.

usheb 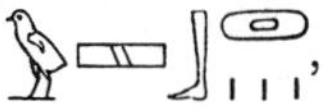 Rec. 26, 224, cakes, loaves of bread.

usheb-t , edible grain or seeds, medicaments, drugs.

ushbit 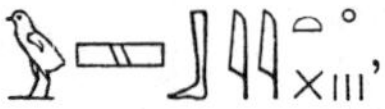, pearl beads.

Usheb , B.D. (Saïte) 144E, a fire-god.

usheb , Rec. 3, 49, vase, pot, vessel, cup.

usheb , to cut, to carve, to engrave.

usheb , B.D. 110, 16, to be begotten (?)

usheb-usheb , Hh. 424 . . . .

ushem 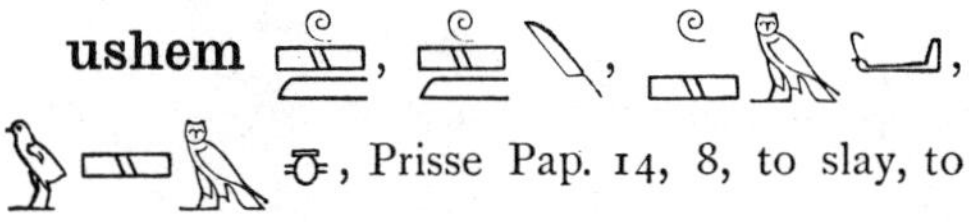, Prisse Pap. 14, 8, to slay, to crush, to chop up, to split, to pound together.

ushem-t , something crushed or split, powdered substance.

Ushem-ḥat-kheftiu-nu-Rā  , Ṭuat I, goddess of the 1st hour of the night.

Ushem-ḥat-kheftiu-s 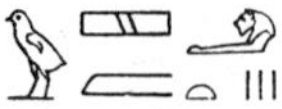 , Ṭuat I, one of the 12 guides of Åf.

ushem 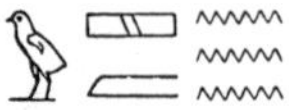, to mix together; Copt. ⲟⲩⲱϣⲙ.

ushem , a measure, libation bucket (?)

ushem , Rec. 28, 166, the hair of a grain plant, beard of grain.

ushen 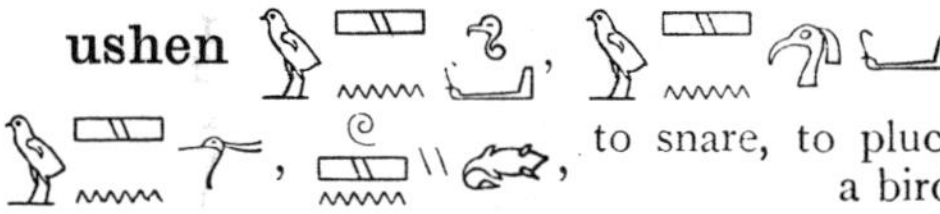, to snare, to pluck a bird.

ushnu , netted birds, feathered fowl.

usher , Hh. 308, Rec. 26, 80, to be parched, to be dried up (of pools of water), to be burnt up (of grass).

usher 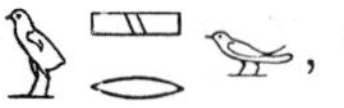, Tombos Stele 6, , to lack, to be empty, to be consumed, bare, bald, destitute, helpless.

usher 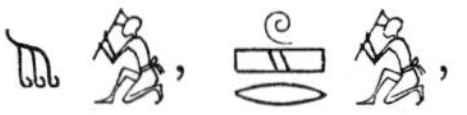, Metternich Stele 242, annihilation, emptiness, a term of abuse.

usht 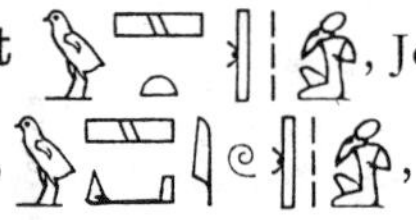, Jour. As. 1908, 268, to adore, Rev. 13, 39; Copt. ⲟⲩⲱϣⲧ.

usheṭ 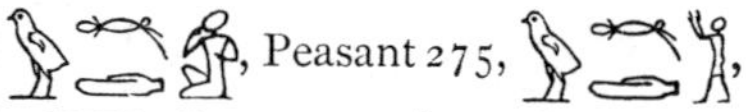 Peasant 275, , Åmen. 10, 8, , Rec. 26, 5, to beseech, to ask, to enquire after, to interrogate, to cross-examine, to greet, to salute, to cry out to, to pray to; Copt. ⲟⲩⲱϣⲧ.

usheṭ-ti, Rec. 21, 98, crier.

usheṭu, Peasant 216, a person addressed.

usheṭ, (late form), to pray to, to supplicate.

usheṭ-t, sickly appearance (?)

Uqeṭ-neferu, name of a palace of Nefer-ḥetep.

Ukesh-ti, Rec. 13, 26, Nubian (adjective); compare Copt. ⲉϭⲱϣ.

ug, to be burned, to burn.

Ug, Uga, Edfû I, 78, a title of the Nile-god.

uga-t, Rechnungen 58, Rev. 11, 174, Rec. 30, 67, part of a boat; plur. Nav. Mythe 7, Rec. 30, 67.

Ugaiu, B.D. 99, 22, 23, the eight pegs of the magical boat which represented the four sons and the four grandsons of Horus.

uga, B.M. 448, the name of a festival.

uga, Ȧmen. 23, 15, to eat, to chew and swallow.

ugȧ, ugȧu, P. 774, P. 775, P. 661, to eat, to chew and swallow; "he does not swallow [it], he spits [it] out."

ugit, Peasant 253, something eaten, what has been chewed.

ugait, jawbone; Copt. ⲟⲩⲟⲟϭⲉ, ⲟⲩⲟϭⲉ, ⲟⲩⲟϫⲓ.

uga, Ȧmen. 3, 12, to be weak, the helplessness of old age.

ugaȧ, pit, well, pool, stream.

ugap, Ȧmen. 8, 6, to overthrow, to sweep away; Copt. ⲟⲩⲱϫⲡ, ⲟⲩⲱϭⲡ.

ugam', Thes. 1206, a kind of myrrh.

ugas, Anastasi IV, 15, 7, P.S.B. 10, 469, to slit, to split open, to stab, to gut a fish.

ugep, to overthrow, to destroy; Copt. ⲟⲩⲱϭⲡ, ⲟⲩⲱϫⲡ.

ugem, IV, 687, a kind of grain (?)

uges, to cut open, to gut a fish or an animal.

ugsu, P. 1116B, 31, slit fish, or fish fillets (?)

uges, geese which have been drawn.

ut, Rev. 13, 37, other; Copt. ⲟⲩⲉⲧ.

ut, Rev. 12, 69, to go away; Copt. ⲟⲩⲱϯ.

ut, Rev. 5, 18, to order, to issue commands.

uti, to command.

ut, to be called, to name.

utu, an official (?) crier (?)

ut, Rec. 33, 33, to tie up, to swathe, to wind bandages round a dead body, to mummify, to embalm; Copt. ОΤ.

utaut, swathings, mummy bandages.

uti, an embalmed body; plur.

ut, utu, uti, embalmer; plur. Rec. 27, 230.

utiu IV, the four embalmers, *i.e.*, the four sons of Horus.

ut, utiu, coffin, mummy case, cartonnage case; plur.

uti, Rev. 12, 40, destruction.

Utt = the Evil One.

utu, Rev. 13, 22, sepulture, death.

Utu (?), B.D. 99, 30, a god who assisted in sailing the magical boat.

utaḥ, Gol. Pap. 9, 26; var. ibid. 23.

Utȧnu (?), the name of a god.

ut, tile, slab.

ut, bronze.

ut, Rev. 14, 49, plants, vegetables =

ut, Rev. 11, 167, "green," *i.e.*, new (of leather).

utut, Rev. 13, 15, 19, 14, 18, Rev. 15, 17, green things, vegetables, papyrus shoots; Copt. ΟΥΟΤΟΥЄΤ.

ut, T. 311, a kind of plant (?) in

utit, grain, seed.

utt, P. 172, U. 216, to beget, to produce; P. 698; see Rec. 29, 164, procreation.

utut, M. 464, to beget.

utu, Rev., males; Copt. ϨΟΟΥΤ.

Utt, B.D. 110, the god of generation in the Ṭuat.

Utt, "begetter," a title of several solar gods; he begot himself; he begot his own organs of generation, Culte Divin 122.

utti, "begetter," a name of Rā.

Utit, a title of Hathor.

Utet-f-em-utcha, a god of one of the Dekans.

Utet-f-em-pet , Denderah II, 10, a lion-headed god, one of the 36 Dekans.

Utet-f-em-ḥer 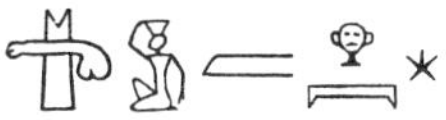, a star.

Utet-neferuset 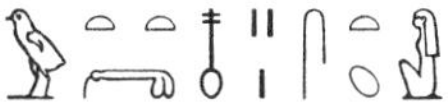, Ombos 2, 131, a goddess.

Utet-ḥeḥ , B.D. 17, 48, the everlasting god of generation, or begetter of eternity.

Utet-tef-f , the god of the 29th day of the month.

utt , P. 68, 167, 689, M. 196, 321, N. 35, 838, the uraeus of Nekhebit.

utti (?) , P. 167, N. 841, the two uraeus-goddesses (?)

Utu-Shu , T. 183, , N. 766, the two Nebti of Nenu, .

utt , to heat, to burn, to boil up, to cook.

Utau 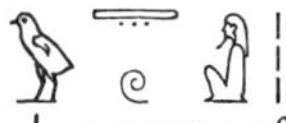, Ṭuat III, [illegible], [illegible], a group of four gods with hidden arms.

Utau Åsår , B.D. 168.

Utau-ta , a group of gods.

uteb , Jour. As. 1908, 275, excess; Copt. ⲟⲩⲱⲧⲃ.

uteb , Rhind Pap. 44, to survive (?)

uteb , bank of a river; see **utcheb.**

uten , to make an offering.

uten , offering; Copt. ⲟⲩⲱⲧⲉⲛ.

uten (?) , a kind of tree.

uten (?) , Ebers Pap. 60, 13, fat (?) grease (?)

uten , Anastasi I, 25, 3, to breach a wall, to bore through; , Rev. = Copt. ⲟⲩⲱⲧⲉⲛ.

uten , to be heavy, a weight.

utenu , Rec. 26, 65, a name of the crown of the North.

Utenu , N. 951, a group of beings mentioned with the [illegible] .

utens , Wört. 308, a stone.

uter , some moist substance, entrails (?)

utriu , ochre used in painting.

uteḥ , Rev. 11, 169, 12, 25, 85, founded, cast; Copt. ⲟⲩⲱⲧϩ.

utekh , Annales III, 109, 11, [illegible], Tombos Stele 9, IV, 84, 767, to move, to march.

utshi , a kind of stone.

uteth , P. 355, N. 1069, to seize.

Uteth , [illegible], T. 286, P. 37, 355, N. 1069, a god (?) a form of Thoth.

uteth 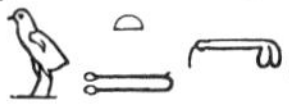, to beget; later form, [illegible].

uth , Rev. 13, 95 = [illegible], reed.

uthut , Tombos Stele 9, IV, 84, fertile, prolific.

uthes 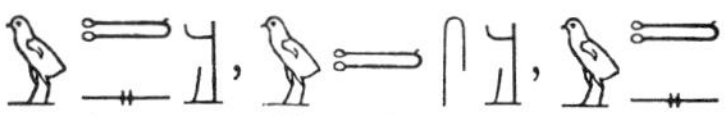, [illegible], [illegible], to lift up, to bear up, to support, to raise, to wear, to carry.

uthesu [illegible], those who lift up.

uthes , to be lifted up (in a bad sense), to be arrogant, proud, pride.

uthes ka [illegible], haughty, arrogant, conceit, pride.

uthes-t 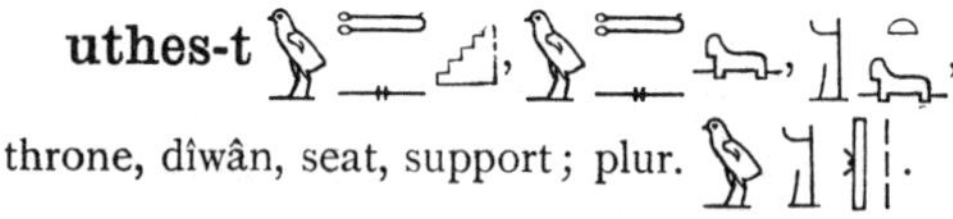, [illegible], [illegible], throne, dîwân, seat, support; plur. [illegible].

uthes-t 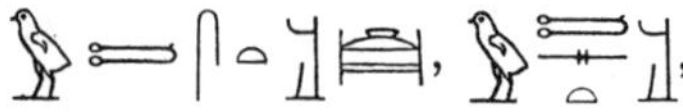, [illegible], support, prop, stay.

uthesit 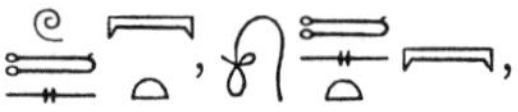, [illegible], heaven, height, a name of the sky and of the Sky-goddess.

Uthes , N. 976, a god, the son of [illegible].

Uthesit 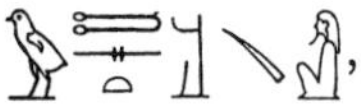, Hh. 361, a god, or goddess, heaven (?)

Uthesu 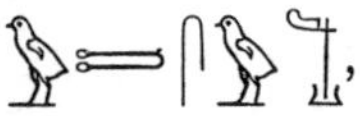, a title of Thoth.

Uthesu 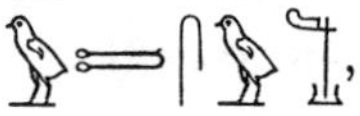, Ṭuat IV, Horus as a supporter of the Utchat.

Uthes-ur 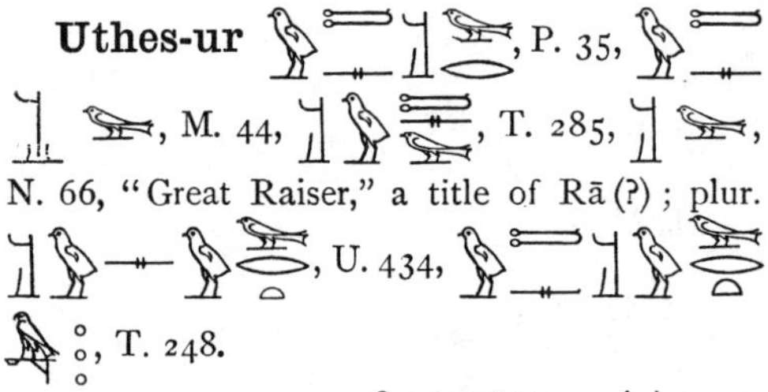, P. 35, [illegible], M. 44, [illegible], T. 285, [illegible], N. 66, "Great Raiser," a title of Rā (?) ; plur. [illegible], U. 434, [illegible], T. 248.

Uthes-neferu 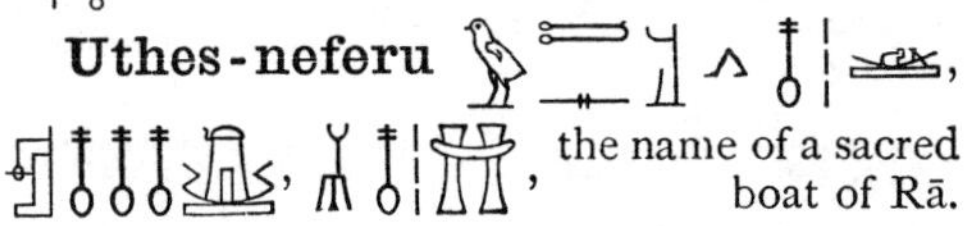, [illegible], [illegible], the name of a sacred boat of Rā.

Uthesi-ḥeḥtt , Buch. 45, the country of resurrection.

uṭ , to dismiss; Copt. ⲟⲩⲱⲧⲉ.

uṭi 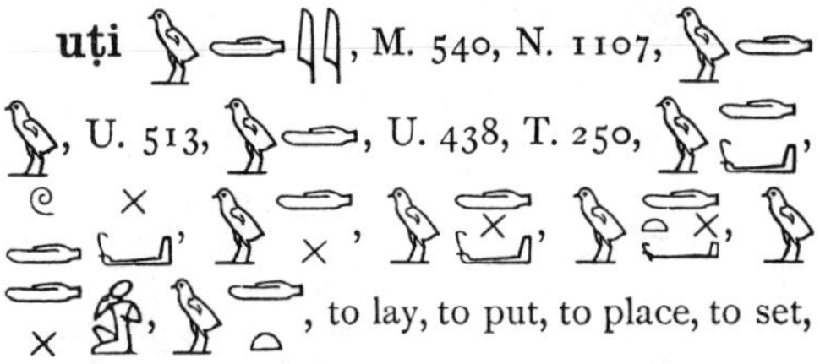, M. 540, N. 1107, [illegible], U. 513, [illegible], U. 438, T. 250, [illegible], [illegible], [illegible], [illegible], [illegible], [illegible], to lay, to put, to place, to set, to thrust, to thrust out, to push, to throw, to shoot out, to cast out, to emit a word or cry, to dart out, to void (dung); , IV, 968.

uṭ-ā 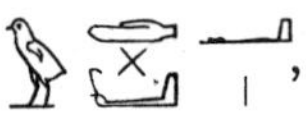, to thrust out the arm in hostility.

uṭ , B.D. 190, 6, shot with stars.

uṭ-t sau , the ejaculation of magical formulae or spells.

uṭ qen , Thes. 1480, violent man; plur. [illegible].

uṭṭ 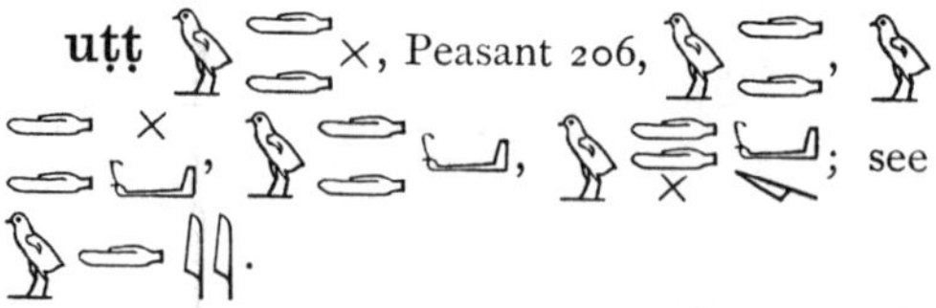, Peasant 206, [illegible], [illegible], [illegible], [illegible]; see [illegible].

uṭṭut enuiu 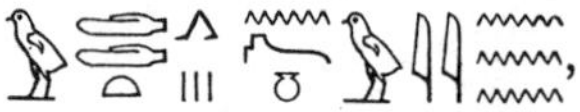, shooters forth of water.

uṭ , Rec. 36, 218, to shoot out fire.

uṭṭ 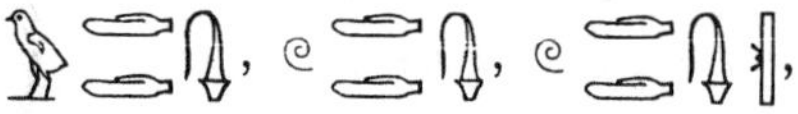, [illegible], [illegible], to burn.

Uṭ-āui 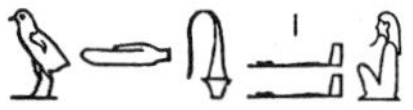, Rec. 31, 13, "fiery hands," the name of a god.

uṭ , [illegible], to write, to inscribe, to engrave, to draw up a list of "strong names."

uṭ 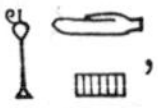, stele, tablet; see **utch.**

uṭiu , Rec. 36, 78, embalmers; see **utiu.**

uṭu, uṭ-t , [illegible], see **utchu,** [illegible].

uṭeṭ , [illegible], [illegible], [illegible], to decree, to order; see **utchu,** [illegible].

uṭu , commander, leader.

uṭṭ-t , [illegible], [illegible]. command, behest, decree, order.

uṭṭ , [illegible], [illegible], [illegible], cerebrum, brain (?)

uṭaiu , B.D. 92, 4, strong (?)

uṭit 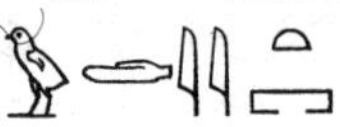, chamber.

Uṭu 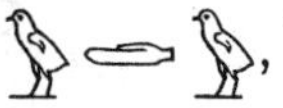, Ṭuat X, a solar-god or hour-god.

uṭeb 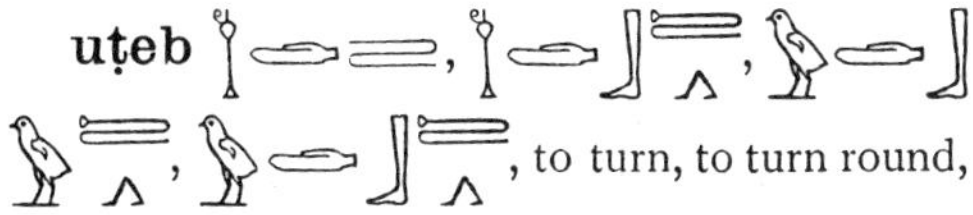, to turn, to turn round, to change; Copt. ⲟⲩⲱⲧⲃ̄.

uṭeb 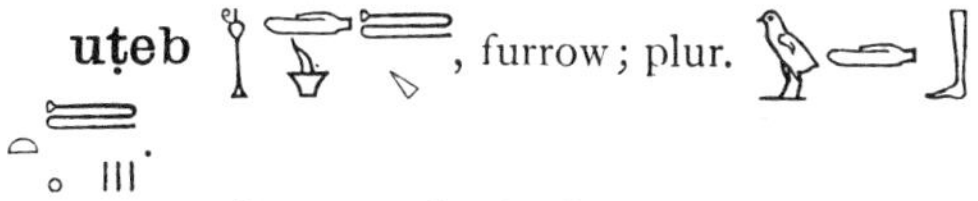, furrow; plur.

Uṭeb 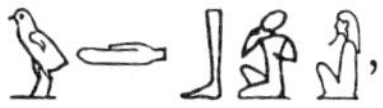, Rev., a god (?)

uṭpu , U. 175, 184, vase.

uṭfā  . . . .

uṭef 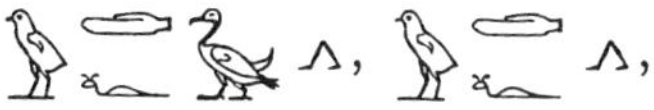, Shipwreck 70, Peasant B. 2, 122, to delay; var. .

uṭen 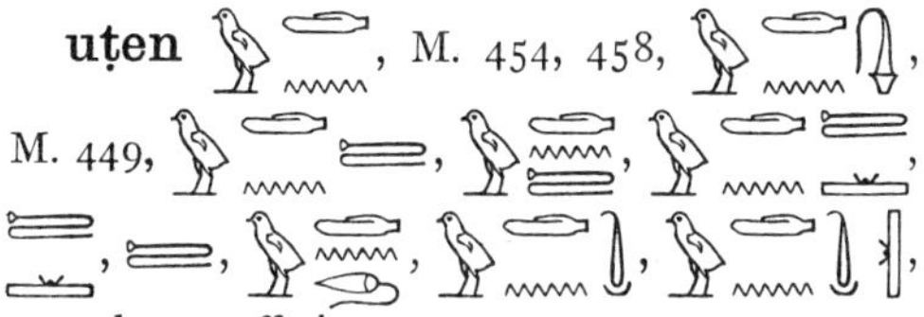, M. 454, 458, M. 449, to make an offering.

uṭen , offering, gift; plur., N. 791; IV, 748, the evening offering.

uṭen-t 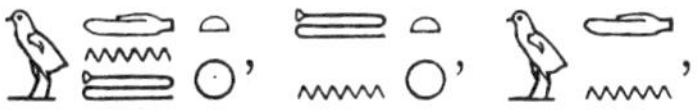, U. 42A, cake, cake offering.

uṭen-t , P. 95, 289, 625, M. 696, something offered, gift.

uṭen , altar.

uṭenit 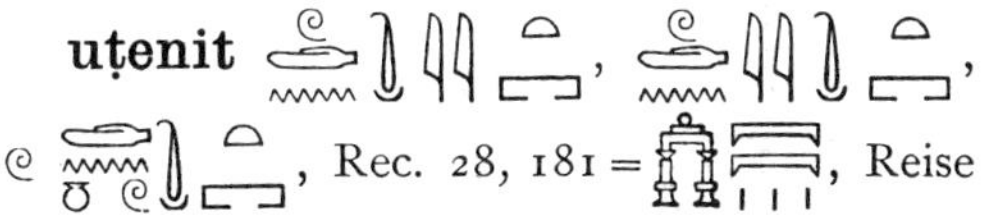, Rec. 28, 181 =, Reise 27, 35, a shrine at Memphis.

uṭen-t (read **ṭeben-t)** 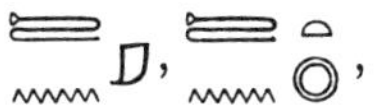, ring, the ring of a balance.

uṭen , to stretch out, to extend.

uṭen , to breach a wall, to bore, to penetrate.

uṭen 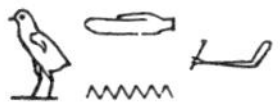, to copy, to write.

Uṭennu 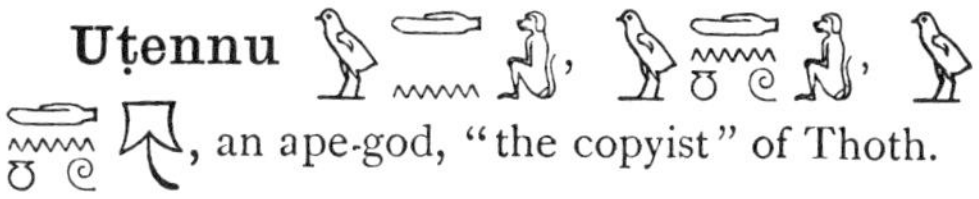, an ape-god, "the copyist" of Thoth.

Uṭen , Berg. I, 20, an ape-god, a friend of the dead.

uṭen , to be heavy.

uṭen 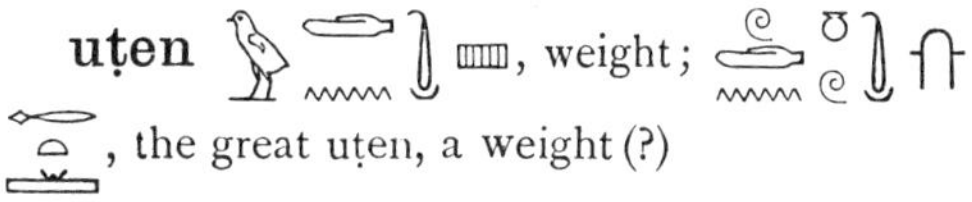, weight; , the great uṭen, a weight (?)

uṭen-ā 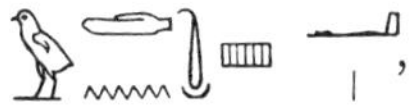 L.D. III, 65A, heavy-handed.

uṭensu , B.D. (Saïte) 153, 6, 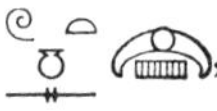, Düm. K.I. 70, a kind of stone.

uṭer , funerary vases.

uṭhu , U. 582, a table or altar for offerings; Copt. ⲟⲩⲱⲧϩ.

uṭhu 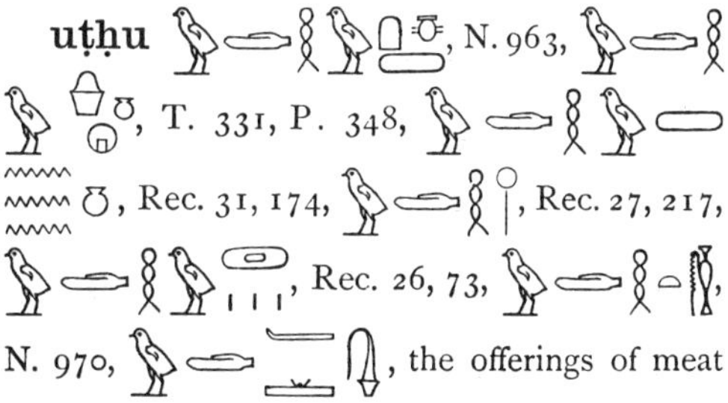, N. 963, T. 331, P. 348, Rec. 31, 174, Rec. 27, 217, Rec. 26, 73, N. 970, the offerings of meat and drink which were set on the altar.

Uṭekh , the god of embalming.

utch , to give an order, to command, to decree; compare Heb. צִוָּה.

utchtch 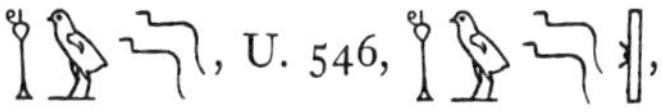, U. 546, Hh. 547, to command.

utch , U. 175, command, order, decree, record, will, testament; plur. 〔hieroglyphs〕,

〔hieroglyphs〕, 〔hieroglyphs〕, 〔hieroglyphs〕, to make decrees; 〔hieroglyphs〕, a decree in writing;

〔hieroglyphs〕, 〔hieroglyphs〕, royal decree or proclamation; 〔hieroglyphs〕, stablished by decree.

utch-t 〔hieroglyphs〕, 〔hieroglyphs〕, 〔hieroglyphs〕,

〔hieroglyphs〕, 〔hieroglyphs〕, 〔hieroglyphs〕, law, statutory decree, edict of a Council; plur. 〔hieroglyphs〕,

U. 601, Décrets 27, 〔hieroglyphs〕, 〔hieroglyphs〕;

var. 〔hieroglyphs〕.

utchtch-t 〔hieroglyphs〕, T. 290, decree, document.

utch tep 〔hieroglyphs〕, chief command.

utch meṭu 〔hieroglyphs〕, 〔hieroglyphs〕, 〔hieroglyphs〕,

〔hieroglyphs〕, to command, to give an order, to issue orders, to promulgate an edict.

Utch-meṭu 〔hieroglyphs〕, Ṭuat IV, V, the god of a persea tree in the Ṭuat of Seker.

Utch-meṭu-Åsår 〔hieroglyphs〕, Ṭuat I, a term which precedes the boat of Åf.

Utch-meṭu-Rā 〔hieroglyphs〕, Ṭuat I, a term which precedes the boat of Åf.

Utch-meṭu-kheperå 〔hieroglyphs〕, Ṭuat I, a term which precedes the boat of Åf.

Utch-meṭu-Tem 〔hieroglyphs〕, Ṭuat I, a term which precedes the boat of Åf.

Utchnef 〔hieroglyphs〕, N. 946, the name of a god.

Utch-nes[r] 〔hieroglyphs〕, 〔hieroglyphs〕, "fire-shooter," one of the 42 judges in the hall of Osiris.

Utch-rekhit 〔hieroglyphs〕, B.D. 125, II, one of the 42 assessors of Osiris.

Utch-ḥetep 〔hieroglyphs〕, N. 971

〔hieroglyphs〕, B.M. 32, 473, a god of offerings.

utch 〔hieroglyphs〕, 〔hieroglyphs〕, 〔hieroglyphs〕, 〔hieroglyphs〕, 〔hieroglyphs〕,

〔hieroglyphs〕, 〔hieroglyphs〕, 〔hieroglyphs〕, 〔hieroglyphs〕,

〔hieroglyphs〕, memorial tablet or stone, landmark, pillar, boundary stone, inscribed stele or tablet; plur. 〔hieroglyphs〕, 〔hieroglyphs〕.

utch en Åakhut-Åten 〔hieroglyphs〕,

〔hieroglyphs〕, a boundary stone of the capital of Åmenḥetep IV.

utchit 〔hieroglyphs〕, 〔hieroglyphs〕, a memorial stone, or tablet, or building; Copt. ⲟⲩⲟⲉⲓⲧ.

utchit 〔hieroglyphs〕, 〔hieroglyphs〕,

Rec. 21 94, 〔hieroglyphs〕, a tomb and its garden, a memorial building.

utch 〔hieroglyphs〕, 〔hieroglyphs〕, 〔hieroglyphs〕, 〔hieroglyphs〕,

garland, crown, flower; plur. 〔hieroglyphs〕, 〔hieroglyphs〕.

utch uauat 〔hieroglyphs〕, a plant.

utch fai 〔hieroglyphs〕, a plant.

utch nuḥ 〔hieroglyphs〕, a plant.

utch sirḥatå 〔hieroglyphs〕, a plant.

utchi-t 〔hieroglyphs〕, 〔hieroglyphs〕, part of a boat; plur. 〔hieroglyphs〕, Rec. 30, 66.

utch 〔hieroglyphs〕, 〔hieroglyphs〕, 〔hieroglyphs〕, a red fish; plur. 〔hieroglyphs〕, 〔hieroglyphs〕.

utch 〔hieroglyphs〕, unguent, eye-paint.

utch 〔hieroglyphs〕, 〔hieroglyphs〕, 〔hieroglyphs〕, 〔hieroglyphs〕,

〔hieroglyphs〕, 〔hieroglyphs〕, 〔hieroglyphs〕, to send out, to go on an expedition, to make a journey, to travel, to stray, to roam, to march.

utchi-t 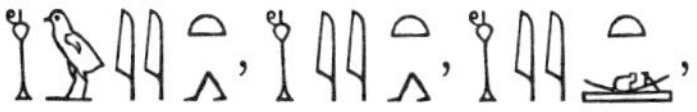
, Rec. 20, 42,
, Thes. 1218, expedition, campaign by land or water, voyage, escape.

utchi-t ent nekht 
[illegible], victorious campaign.

utchuiu , Israel Stele 24, cattle turned out to graze where they please.

utcha 

, to be healthy, to be sound, to be safe, to be strong, to set in a fitting order or condition, safe, sound, whole, intact, healthy, strong, flourishing; [illegible], life, strength, health! (added after the king's name); 
[illegible], Rec. 16, 56, salutations to you!; 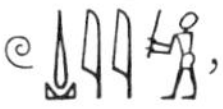, Rev. 12, 10, salutation, greeting; Copt. ⲞⲨϪⲀⲒ, ⲞⲨⲞϪ.

utcha , protective strength.

utcha , IV, 969, a safe man.

utcha-t 

, Rec. 24, 164, objects that bring strength and protection to those who wear them; , staff of protection.

utcha-t sa , amulets [giving] the fluid of life.

utcha 
, a breast ornament, pectoral, breast plate.

utcha-ba-f , a title of the high-priestess of Memphis.

utcha ra , to speak firmly.

utcha ḥa-t 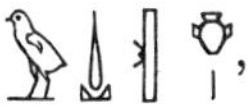, bold, fearless.

utcha sep , strength with good luck.

utcha ṭet 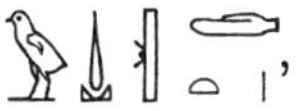, firm-handed, to act with decision.

Utcha , N. 956, 1182, the god of strength, son of Utcha and Utchat, .

Utchat , Berg. II, 14, a form of the Sky-goddess Nut.

Utcha-ḥa-t , B.D. 70, 1, a god.

utcha-t , Nåstasen Stele 64, temple, storehouse.

utcha Åmen. 9, 1, , storehouse, warehouse, stable (?) the bêt al-mâl of the Arabs; plur. [illegible], IV, 1144; 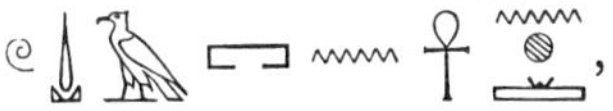, Åmen. 4, 1.

utcha-t , Rechnungen 41,
, what remains, the rest, arrears, remainder.

Utcha-t [illegible], one of the 36 Dekans.

utchait , Rec. 13, 25, 14, 2, a constellation.

utcha 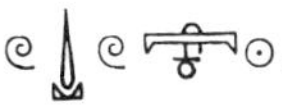, the early dawn (?)

utchai 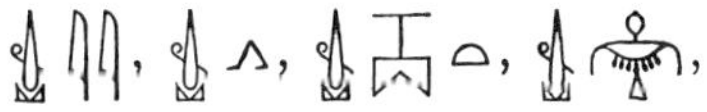, Rev., to pay, payment.

utcha 
, to go, to go forth, to come, to betake oneself to a place, to advance.

utchai , a going forth.

utcha-t , a journey.

utcha-t , 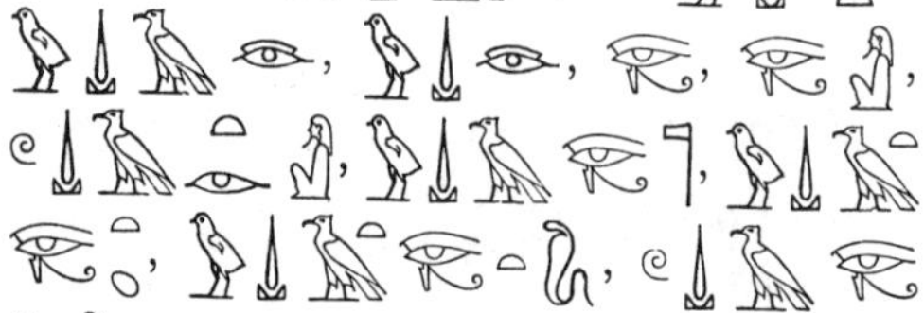 , the eye of Horus, the eye of Rā, the amulet of the solar eye, which gives the wearer strength; plur. , eyes.

Utcha-t , "Eye," a name of heaven, or the sky.

Utcha-t , the eye of Ḥeru-ur, and later of Horus and Rā.

Utcha-t , the right eye of the Sky-god, *i.e.*, the Sun.

Utcha-t , the left eye of the Sky-god, *i.e.*, the Moon.

utchati 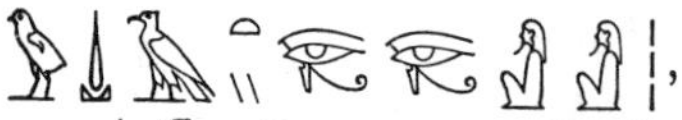, Rec. 32, 177, 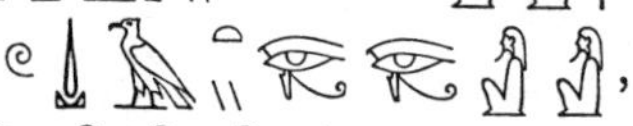, , , B.D. 163, 9, , , the two eyes of the Sky-god, *i.e.*, the Sun and Moon.

Utchait , B.D. 14, 6, the goddess of the eye of Horus.

Utchait  , the goddess of the moon.

Utchat . . . . . . , Ṭuat XII, one of 12 air-goddesses of the dawn who assisted in towing the boat of Åf.

utcha-t åakhut  , the eye of the Light-god.

utcha-t meḥ-t , the northern or right eye of Horus.

Utchat-Sekhmit 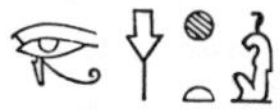, B.D. 164, 9, a form of Mut (?)

Utchat-Shu-em-pet-em-åri-t-set , Rec. 34, 190, one of the 12 Thoueris goddesses, she presided over the month 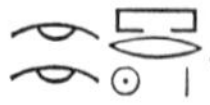.

utcha-t shemā , the southern or left eye of Horus.

utchā , U. 289, , T. 282, 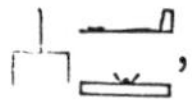, Rec. 31, 17, , Rec. 27, 219, 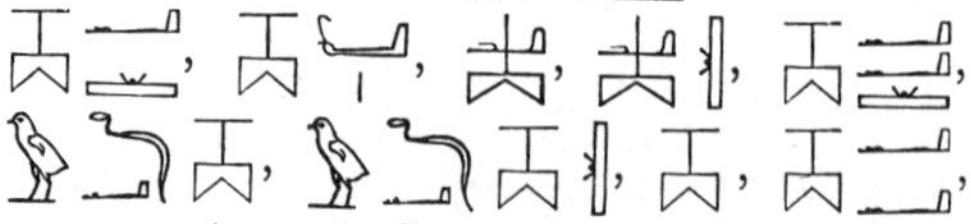, , U. 595, 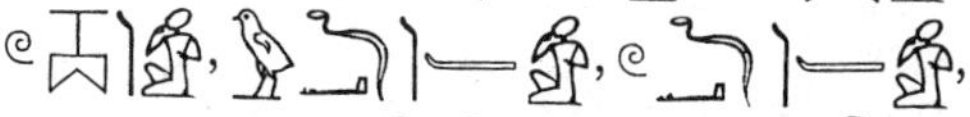, Anastasi I, 25, 5, 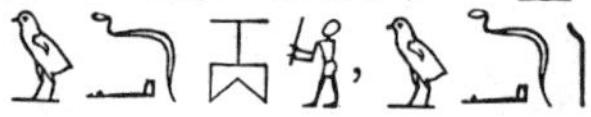 , Mar. Karn. 52, 5, to decide, to judge, to pass sentence, to rectify; Copt. ⲟⲩⲱⲱⲧⲉ.

utchāiu , judges, judged ones.

utchā 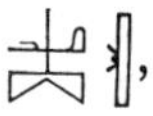, to balance;  , B.D. 117, 3.

utchā-t 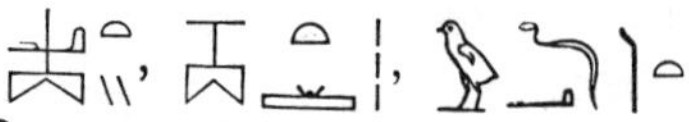 , decision, judgment.

utchā-t [illegible], a woman who has been put away or repudiated, outcast.

utchā aḥ-t [illegible], to define the bounds of estates and to settle their limits.

utchā meṭu [illegible], P. 630, [illegible], N. 1374, [illegible], P. 264, 313, [illegible], Rec. 31, 163, [illegible], IV, 1107, [illegible], to weigh words, to try cases, to judge; [illegible], in the place of judgment, *i.e.*, in court.

utchā-ra [illegible], Anastasi I, 24, 1, decision, judicial sentence.

utchā rut  (var. ), Peasant 216 . . . .

utchā ḥatu , to judge hearts or dispositions.

utchā senu sen  , Peasant 234, to judge between two rivals.

utchā senemm , B.D. 19, 10 (variant of ), to decide a case.

utchā 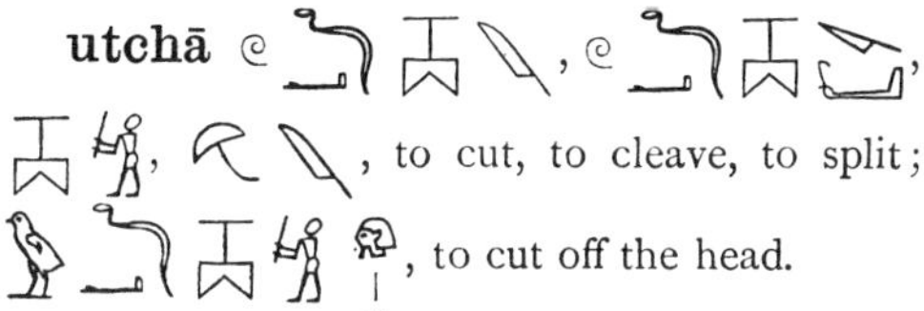, to cut, to cleave, to split; to cut off the head.

utchāiu , executioners.

utchā , tremblers (?)

utchā , a kind of sceptre (Lacau).

Utchā , Denderah IV, 61, a hawk-headed warrior-god.

Utchā , A.Z. 1910, 17, a god.

Utchā-aāb-t , B.D. 54, 3, 56, 3, the protector of the egg laid by .

Utchā-fenṭ (?) , Mar. Aby. I, 45, a god who dwelt in .

Utchā-mestcher (?) 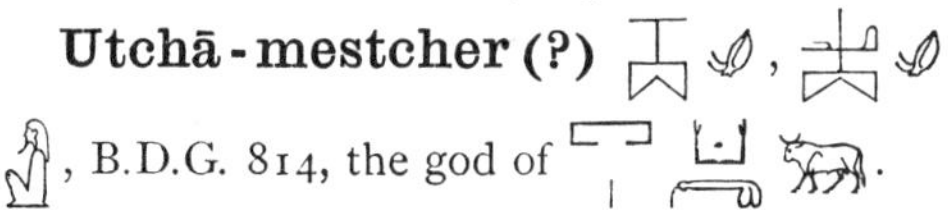, B.D.G. 814, the god of .

utchāi-t , a fruit.

utchā 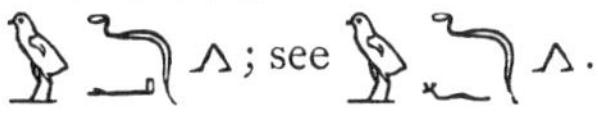; see .

utcheb 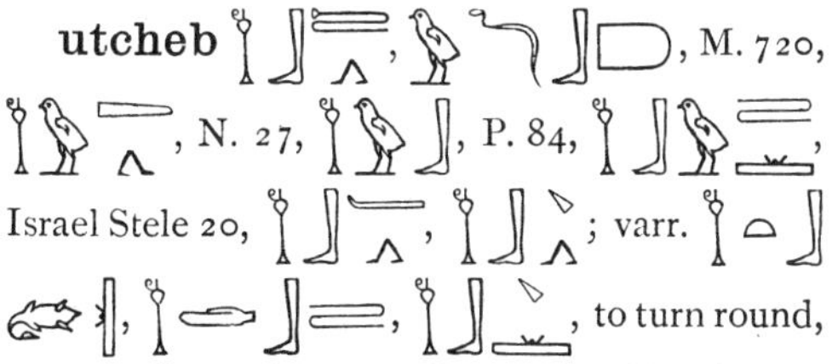, M. 720, N. 27, P. 84, Israel Stele 20; varr. , to turn round, to go back or about, to change the direction, to change, to bend down (of the top of a tree, N. 27); Copt. ⲟⲩⲱⲧⲃ̄.

utcheb 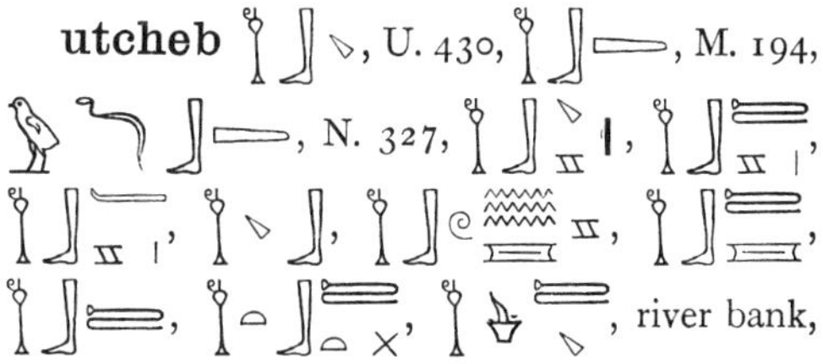, U. 430, M. 194, N. 327, river bank, any ground by the side of a canal or stream; plur. 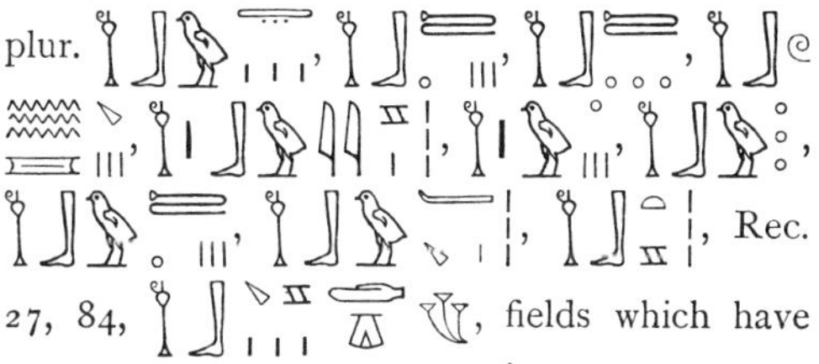, Rec. 27, 84, fields which have been planted; Copt. ⲟⲩⲱⲧⲃ̄.

utcheb-t , riparian cultivators.

utcheb , I, 26, 37, something paid in to a temple, , a heap of offerings.

utcheb 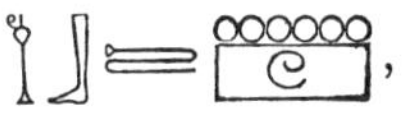, carpet, floor covering.

utcheb-ti , P.S.B.A. 1884, 187, Sphinx 16, 182, a wrong reading (?); see under sem.

utchbes , to be green.

utchef , to tarry, to delay.

utchef-t , a bird.

utchfa-t 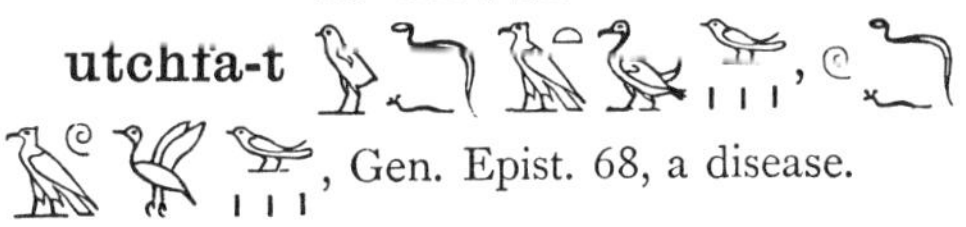, Gen. Epist. 68, a disease.

utchen , Peasant 145, flood, stream.

utcheḥ 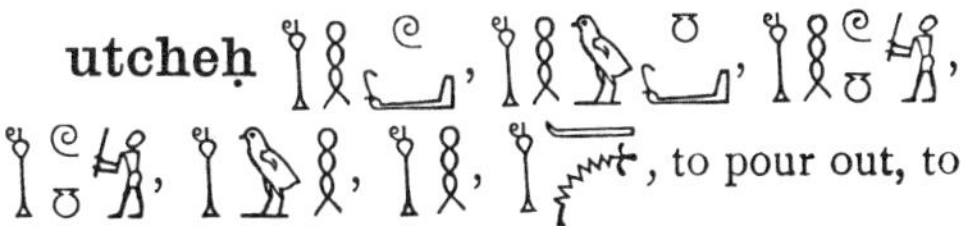, to pour out, to evacuate, to smelt; Copt. ⲟⲩⲱⲧϩ̄.

utcheḥ , 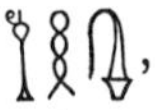, IV, 695, 731, an offering by fire, to apply fire to a metal, *i.e.*, to smelt, to sparkle (of precious stones).

utchḥu 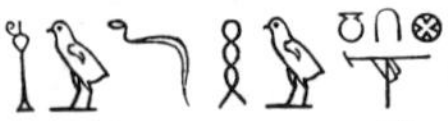, , , , , 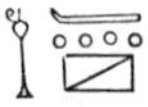, 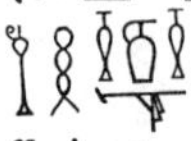, , , altar, table of offerings.

utcheḥ 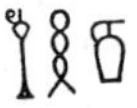, , altar vessel; plur. , Rec. 26, 73, , IV, 1150, 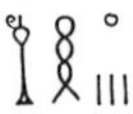, 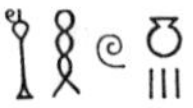, .

utcheḥ , 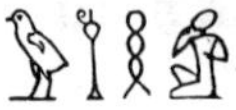, T. 360, P. 602, N. 803. . . . .

utcheḥ , , Thes. 1281, , IV, 157, 926, child, babe.

utchṭ , to walk, to go on.

 B

b  = Heb. ב.

b , abode, place; see .

b , Rev. 12, 113, plant, bush; see .

b (bu) , people; see  .

B (Bu?) , B.M. 32, 383, a fiend in the Ṭuat, demon, devil in general.

B 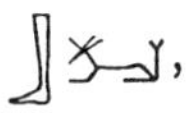, Nav. Mythe, , the name which Set assumed when he took the form of a hissing serpent, .

ba 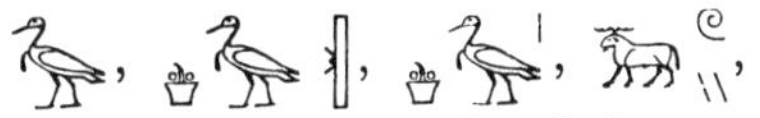, to have a soul; , N. 986, , N. 17 = , P. 75, T. 271, , U. 235, , Rec. 33, 30, endowed with soul.

ba , U. 159, , , T. 319, , T. 202, Rec. 27, 228, soul;  , Jour. As. 1908, 303, , the heart-soul, might, power, strength, courage; plur. , P. 655, , , , Rev. 11, 186, , the Baï of Horapollo; , a beatified soul; , Westcar 7, 25, a damned soul; , P. 163, , N. 854.

B 

ba , heart-soul; 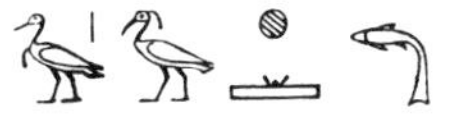 , B.D. 180, 10, soul, spirit, and body; , B.D. 91, 4, soul, spirit, and shadow; [illegible], B.D. 183, 35, body, double, and spirit; [illegible] [illegible], B.D. 169, 3, thy soul is in heaven, thy body is under ground.

ba āper [illegible], a soul equipped with amulets, spells, etc.

baiu mitu [illegible], dead, *i.e.*, damned, souls.

baiu menkhu [illegible], perfected souls, *i.e.*, the beatified.

ba en nub [illegible], B.D. 89, 12, "soul of gold," *i.e.*, an amulet.

Ba [illegible], [illegible], [illegible], [illegible], [illegible], B.D. (Saïte) 163, T. 349, M. 596, 722, N. 657, 719, 1202, 1328, the Soul-god; plur. [illegible], Rec. 30, 67, divine soul-gods; [illegible] [illegible], "I enter as Ba, I come out as Ru."

Bait [illegible], [illegible], Hh. 455, the Soul-goddess.

Baiti [illegible], the two divine souls, U. 159, T. 130, P. 648, 720, [illegible], M. 747, [illegible], U. 569, P. 572, [illegible], [illegible], [illegible]; [illegible], [illegible], the two souls in the two Thafui.

Baiti , Ṭuat I, the two Soul-goddesses.

Baiti ; see **Reḥti,** .

Ba-åab-t , P. 670, N. 1272, , the Soul-god of the East; plur.  .

Bait-åabt , the Soul-goddess of the East.

Baiu-åabtiu , B.D. 109: (1) the gods who sang at dawn and turned into apes when the sun had risen; (2) the three gods Ḥeru-åakhuti, the Calf of Kherå and the Morning Star.

Baiu-åmiu-neteru 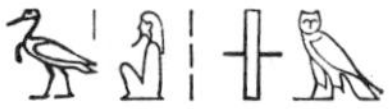 , the souls dwelling in the gods.

Baiu-åmiu-she-Neserser  , Ṭuat VIII, a group of nine gods.

Baiu-åmiu-Ṭuat , the souls dwelling in the Ṭuat.

Ba-åmi-ṭesher-f  , N. 657, the soul dwelling in his redness.

Ba-Åment , B.D. 168, the soul of Åment that fed the dead; plur. 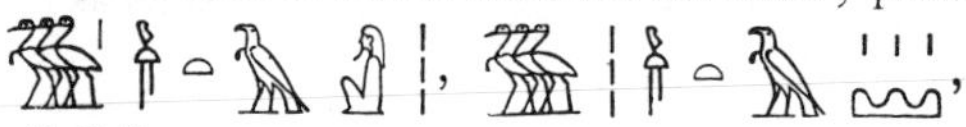, [illegible].

Baiu-Åmentiu , Thes. 59, B.D. 108, 15, 16, Tem, Sebek, and Hathor.

Baiu-Åment , Ṭuat IX, the gods who towed the serpent-boat Khepri.

Baiu-Ånu , B.D. 115, 10, Rā, Shu, and Tefnut.

Ba-āa , "great soul," *i.e.*, Åf, the night Sun-god.

Ba-ānkh , N. 1252, Nesi-Åmsu 25, 23, "living soul," a title of Osiris of Ṭeṭ.

Ba-ānkh , a soul that has renewed its existence in heaven; plur.  [illegible].

Ba-Āshem , M. 785, the soul of the divine image.

Ba-irqai , B.D. 165, 8 (Saïte), a title of Åmen.

Ba-utet-åru , Denderah IV, 79, a bull-god of generation.

Ba-Pu , a hawk-god.

Baiu-Pe (Pu) , U. 585, P. 471, B.D. 112, 13, Horus, Mestå, and Hāpi.

Baiu-periu , B.D. 168, the souls who open the mouths of the dead, *i.e.*, perform the ceremonies that effect their resurrection.

Bafermit (?) , Ṭuat V, one of the eight fire-gods who burn up the dead in the Ṭuat of Seker.

Ba-merti  = Παμύλης (?) Plutarch, De Iside, § 12.

Ba-en-Shu  [illegible], "soul of Shu," a name for the wind.

Ba-t nefer-t , A.Z. 1867, a title of Hathor.

Ba-Nekhen , the "soul of Nekhen," a jackal-god.

Baiu-Nekhen , P. 471, M. 537, 804, B.D. 113, 11, , the souls of Nekhen, *i.e.*, Horus, Ṭuamutef, and Qebḥsenuf, B.D. 113.

Ba-Rā 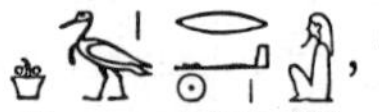, Tomb of Seti I, one of the 75 forms of Rā (No. 5).

Ba-ti-erpit 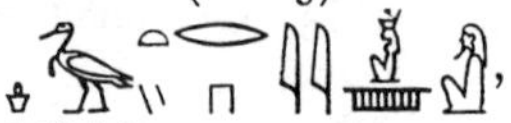, B.D. 142, 76, a name of Osiris.

Baȧt-erpit, T. 174, , M. 156, , N. 109, , B.D. 142, 14, Osiris as the soul of Isis and Nephthys.

Ba-ḥeri-ȧb-baui-f , "soul dwelling in his two souls," a title of Osiris.

Ba-khati , Ṭuat III, a goddess associated with Horus.

Ba-kha-t-Rā , B.D. 140, 6, 7, a form of Rā.

Baiu-Khemenu , B.D. 114, the souls of Hermopolis.

Baiu-khenu , Thes. 59, the gods of the 1st day of the month.

Baiut-s-ȧmiu-ḥeḥ , Ombos 2, 132, a goddess.

Ba-sheps , B.D. 142, 19, "holy soul," a title of Osiris.

Baiu-shetau , , Ṭuat III, the "secret, *i.e.*, invisible, souls," a class of beings in the Ṭuat.

Ba-ta , , Ṭuat I, an ape-god.

Baiu-ta , B.D. 168, Ṭuat VII, the souls of the earth.

Ba-tau , P.S.B. 27, 186, A.Z. 1907, 98, a very ancient god: in late times Cynopolis was a centre of his cult.

Ba-Tathenn , Ṭuat VII, soul of the Earth-god Tathenn.

Bau-tef-f , B.D. 142, 20, a title of Osiris.

Ba-tcheser , "holy soul," a form of Osiris.

Ba , Ṭuat III, the soul of the god Ȧf which was swallowed by the Earth-god.

Ba , the Ram-god, god of virility and generation. The worship of the Ram of Mendes was founded in that city in the IInd dynasty. The Ram-god, , in Ṭuat XI was a god of offerings.

Ba , , , the Ram-god of Ṭeṭ and Ḥensu.

Baiu , Berg. 66, the soul-gods of Ṭeṭ.

Ba-ȧakhu-ḥā-f , Rec. 8, 199, a ram-headed god.

Ba-ȧmi-Shu , B.D. 17, 17 (Nebseni), the soul dwelling in Shu.

Ba-ȧmi-Tefnut , B.D. 17, 18 (Nebseni), the soul dwelling in Tefnut.

Ba-ȧri , a ram-headed god.

Ba-utcha-ḥāu-f , a ram-headed god.

Ba-Baiu , Pap. Mut-ḥetep 5, 20, "soul of souls," a title of Osiris.

Ba-pefi , Denderah IV, 84, a ram-headed god of the 8th hour of the night.

Baui-f-ȧmui-Ṭeṭ , B.D. 17, 17, 18 (Nebseni), the souls of Rā and Osiris.

Ba-em-uār-ur (?) , Mar. Aby. I, 44, a god of Abydos, a form of Osiris.

Ba-en-Ȧsȧr . B.D. 17, 111, the soul of Osiris, one of the tetrad of divine souls that dwelt in Ṭeṭ.

Ba-en-Rā , B.D. 17, 17 (Nebseni), the soul of Rā, one of the tetrad of divine souls that dwelt in Ṭeṭ.

Ba-en-ḥeḥ , Pap. Ani 19, 3, "everlasting soul," a title of Osiris.

Ba-en-Shu, soul of Shu, one of the tetrad of divine souls that dwelt in Ṭeṭ.

Ba-en-Geb, soul of Geb, one of the tetrad of divine souls that dwelt in Ṭeṭ.

Ba-neb-Ṭeṭ-t, the ram of Mendes, a form of Osiris.

Ba-neb-Ṭeṭ-ānkh-en-Rā, Cairo Pap. III, 4, the soul of Osiris, the life of Rā.

Ba-neteru, a ram-god in the Ṭuat.

Ba-ḥeka, Rec. 8, 199, a ram-god.

Ba-sheft-ḥa-t, a god composed of four ram-gods, *i.e.*, the souls of Rā, Osiris, Shu, and Khnemu.

Ba-Ṭaṭa, Berg. II, 5 =, a form of Osiris.

ba, ram, sheep; Gr. βῆ, ovis longipes.

Ba-seḥ, I, 15, an estate of Methen.

Baiu, Zod. Denderah, one of the 36 Dekans.

Baiui (?), one of the 36 Dekans; Gr. BIOY.

Baiu-ānkhiu, Thes. 133, the 36 Dekans.

Ba-qeṭ-t, the 29th Dekan; Gr. BIKΩT.

ba-t, illumination, light, splendour.

ba with, N. 671, to pay homage (?)

ba (baba), to wonder, to admire; see.

ba-t, Rev. 13, 28, quality, characteristic.

ba, book, papyrus roll, service, liturgy, document; plur, Rec. 32, 178.

bai àb, Rev. 11, 129,, Rev. 11, 136, bearer of a message =.

baiu-rā, Rev. 2, 351, book; plur..

Ba, B.D. 163, 14, the Leopard-god.

ba, T. 144,, U. 472, P. 204, N. 548,, P. 169,, I, 127,, Rec. 30, 186,, Rec. 36, 215, leopard skin, a skin garment; plur., Rec. 36, 215.

ba meḥt, A.Z. 1902, 98, leopard of the North.

ba resu, A.Z. 1902, 98, leopard of the South.

Bai, Hh. 439, the Leopard-god.

Baba, B.D. 17, 44 (Nebseni),, Hh. 240,, first-born son of Osiris, who took the form of a typhonic animal; he presided over the phallus, and devoured the dead; Gr. Βέβων, Βεβῶνα (Plutarch, De Iside, § 62).

Babai, the eldest son of Osiris.

ba, to mock, to sneer, to scorn.

ba , N. 552, Rev. 11, 130, to plough, to dig, to hew stone, to break through, to force a way, to hack, to mince, to cut up.

ba bait , to dig out foundations for a house.

baba 

, to work a plough or some other digging tool, to wield a battleaxe in fight, to lay about one with weapons.

baba , to use force.

bait , Åmen. 10, 2, a cutting, hacking.

bau , in the phrase 

, B.D. 172, 36 . . . . .

bai  field labourer, ploughman.

babaiu , workmen, ploughmen, field labourers.

ba- . . . . 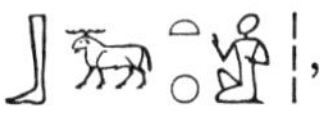, workers in mud, brickmakers (?)

ba (baba) 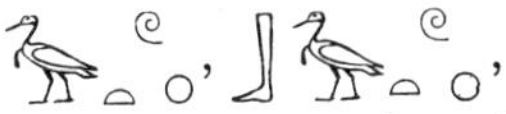, hole in the earth, den, cavern, cave; plur. , sepulchres, tombs.

ba-t , Rec. 27, 221, ground, earth, cavern (?)

baba 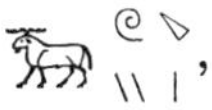, Thes. 1200, ,

, Israel Stele 57, meadow land.

ba-t , tomb; perhaps = בַּיִת, house.

baiu (?) , holes in the ground, caves.

baba , U. 312, 

, cave, cavern, den, lair of an animal, abode in the earth, hole in the ground; Copt. ⲂⲎⲂ; plur.

.

baut , Leyd. Pap. 13, 4, Rev., household servants, house-dwellers.

ba-t , Rec. 27, 86, honey (?)

ba , gland (?) matter (?)

baa , U. 543, 544, some substance (white ).

ba-t 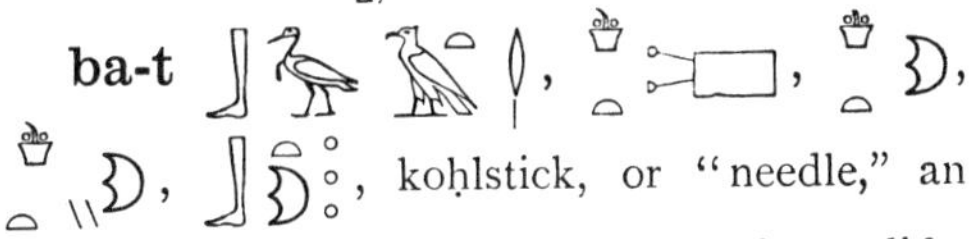, kohlstick, or "needle," an instrument for applying eye paint to the eyelids.

ba-t , U. 159, fruit of some kind; see .

baba-t , T. 130A, fruit of some kind.

bai , a kind of grain or seed.

baba-t , a kind of grain.

ba  a grain measure = $4\frac{1}{2}$ hen.

ba , a measure for liquids, contents half a hen.

ba-t 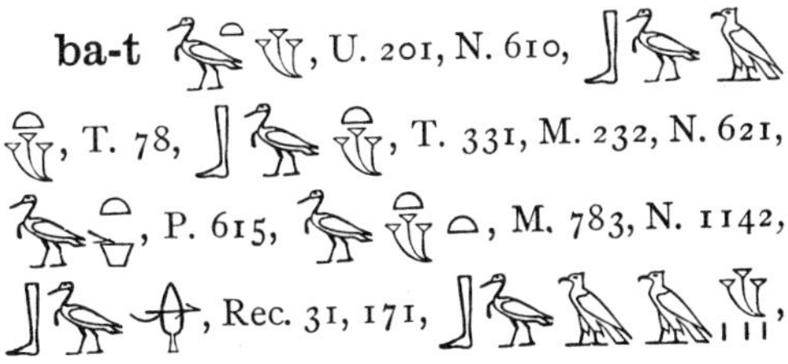, U. 201, N. 610, T. 78, T. 331, M. 232, N. 621, P. 615, M. 783, N. 1142, Rec. 31, 171,

Peasant 14,  bush, thicket, branch, undergrowth; Copt. ⲃⲱ.

baba 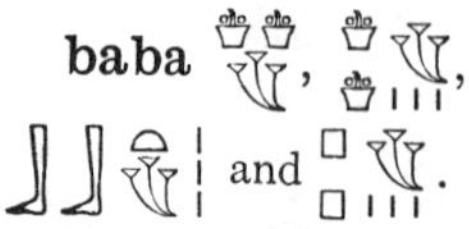 plant, plants, herbs; see and.

ba , staff, stick.

baa 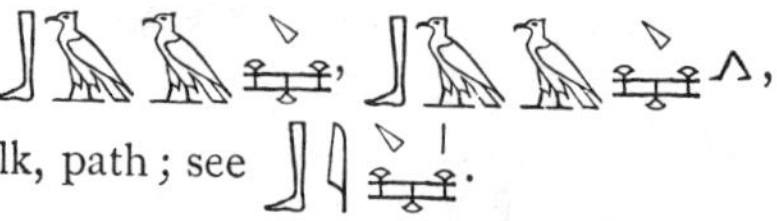 paved walk, path; see.

baba-t  Berl. 6910, stream, source of a river.

baba , drink, liquid; see **beb**.

baba-t 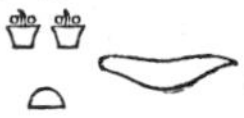, pectoral.

babȧa  necklace of beads, pectoral; see.

baȧa  canal, stream; Copt. ⲃⲟ.

baȧa , a moist substance of some kind, honey (?)

baȧa , bands, cords, palm-fibre, tendrils of a plant or tree (?)

baȧa-t  Rec. 18, 183, a cake, loaf, food =.

baȧu , evil word, curse.

Baȧur , Baal; Heb. בַּעַל.

Baȧbu , P. 568, god of the breast.

baȧrut  wells, pools; Heb. בְּאֵרוֹת.

baāit 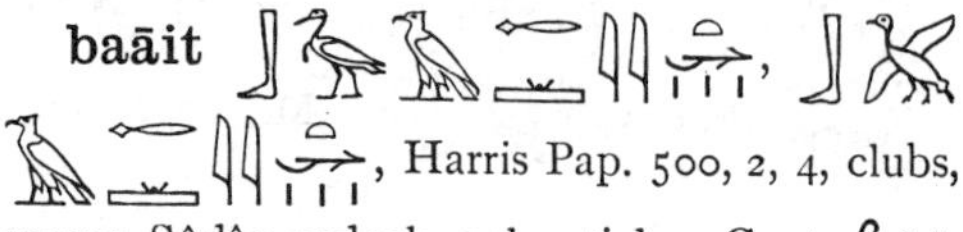 Harris Pap. 500, 2, 4, clubs, maces, Sûdân cudgels, palm sticks; Copt. ⲃⲁⲓ.

bai , a digging tool.

Bai  a form of Osiris and Rā.

bai , Rec. 23, 198, a priestly title.

baui , B.D.G. 214, the two nobles, *i.e.*, Horus and Uatchit of Pe-Tep (Buto).

bai , boat.

bai-t , mantis.

Bai-t , B.D. Nav. 76, 1.

Babait (?)  Hh. 468; var.

bai-ut , marvels, wonders.

bai-ārq 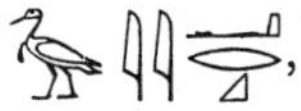, A.Z. 1877, 32, mat covering.

bain-t , Rev. 14, 11, harp; Copt. ⲃⲟⲓⲛⲓ.

bain , Jour. As. 1908, 287, wretched, miserable; Copt. ⲉⲃⲓⲏⲛ.

bairi 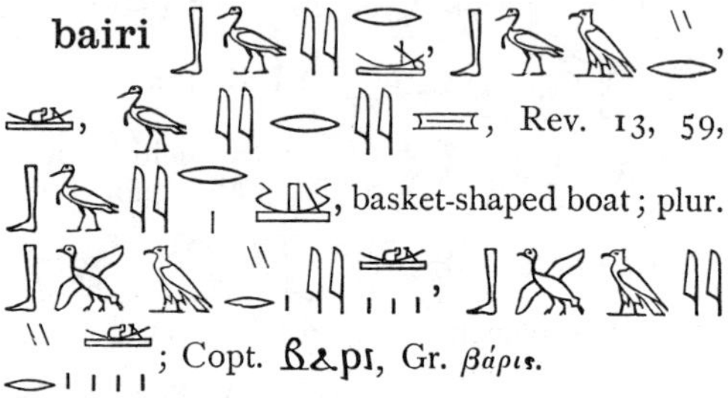 Rev. 13, 59, basket-shaped boat; plur.; Copt. ⲃⲁⲣⲓ, Gr. βάρις.

bairi 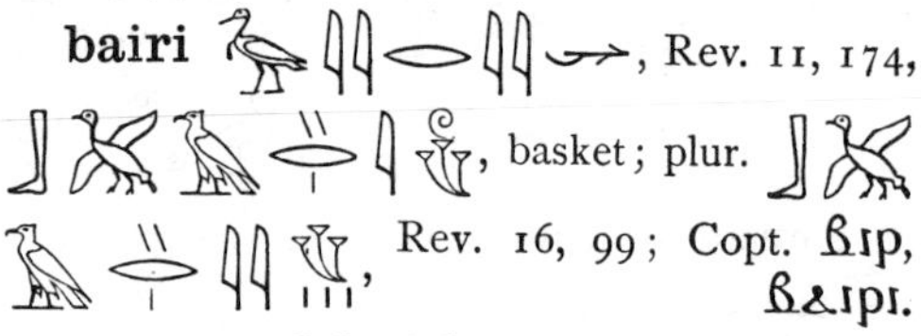 Rev. 11, 174, basket; plur. Rev. 16, 99; Copt. ⲃⲓⲣ, ⲃⲁⲓⲣⲓ.

bairriu , Koller Pap. I, 3, 4, a kind of wood used in making chariots.

bait  house; Heb. בַּיִת.

baiti , king of Lower Egypt; Gr. Βιτης (?)

bau , boat.

Bau , U. 565; see **Bakhau,** .

baun (?) , to bay (of a dog).

Bautcha , Denderah IV, 60, a warrior-god.

Babau (?) , Rec. 14, 175.

baba , to fly.

babaga , Mar. Aby. I, 8, 97, to scrutinize, to examine carefully.

Babȧ, Babi , U. 532, , U. 644; see **Baba.**

Baabi , the eldest son of Osiris.

Babi 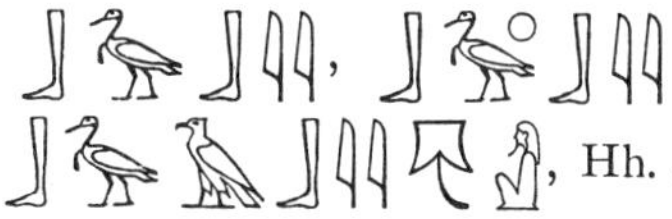, , U. 610, 644, , Hh. 446; see **Baba.**

Babuu , a fiend in the Ṭuat; see **Babuȧ.**

Babuȧ , P. 604, a god with a red ear and dappled haunches; , a name of Set (?)

ban , Rec. 14, 21, herd of cattle.

ban-t , , , breast, a pair of breasts.

banban 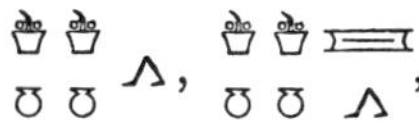, , to overflow, to flood.

ban , Rec. 11, 138, 12, 15, , Rev. 13, 26, bad, evil, enemy.

ban , , Rec. 5, 90, date palm; see **bnr**; Copt. ⲃⲛⲛⲉ.

ban 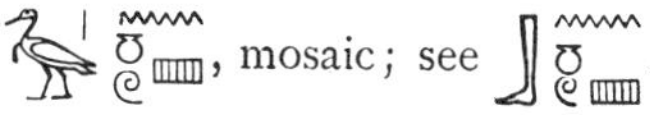, mosaic; see .

bann-t 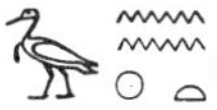, Rev. 14, 34, pill, bolus.

bann , box, chest, harp (?)

Banȧathana , Mar. Aby. II, 50, a Semitic proper name.

Ban-Āntȧ , Alt. K. 343, a Semitic name of a man.

banpi , Rev. 11, 141, 12, 18, iron; Copt. ⲃⲉⲛⲓⲡⲉ.

Bant-Ānt 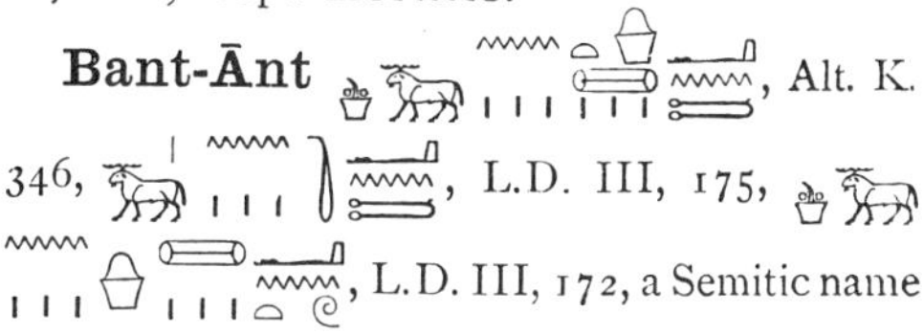, Alt. K. 346, , L.D. III, 175, , L.D. III, 172, a Semitic name of a woman; compare בנת־ענת.

banṭ 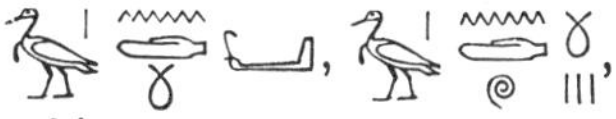, , to tie, to bind, swathings.

banṭi[t] , a vegetable garden.

bar (bal) , blind (?); Copt. ⲃⲉⲗⲗⲉ.

Bar , Rev. 12, 31, Baal; Heb. בַּעַל.

bar (bal) 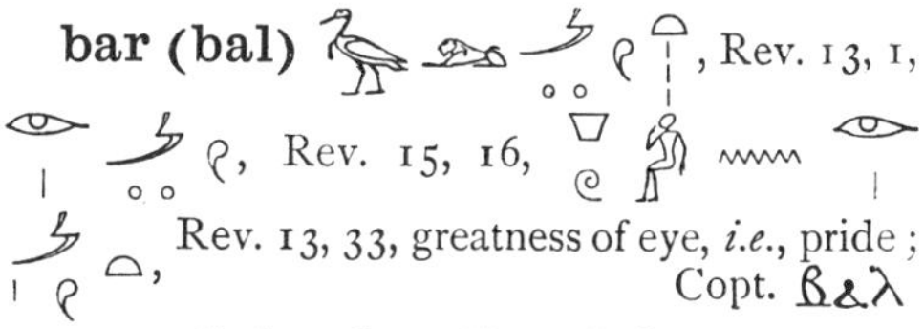, Rev. 13, 1, , Rev. 15, 16, , Rev. 13, 33, greatness of eye, *i.e.*, pride; Copt. ⲃⲁⲗ

bar , , IV, 783, well; Heb. בְּאֵר.

barrȧ , a kind of cake.

Barȧst , a name or title of Bast (?)

bari , Rev. 13, 4, to swallow; compare بلع.

bari 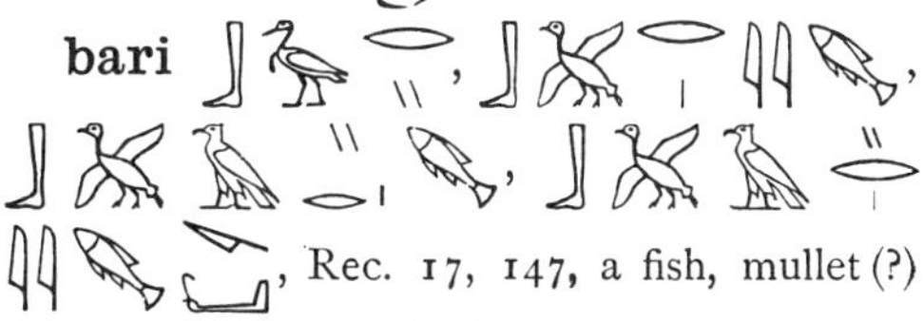, , , , Rec. 17, 147, a fish, mullet (?) plur. .

bari ȧn , spotted mullet (a Tanis fish).

bari  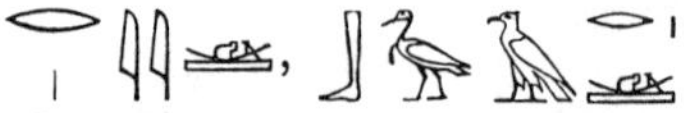, Rec. 21, 77, , , boat, ship; Copt. ⲃⲁⲣⲓ.

bari , Rev. 12, 17, Rev. 12, 30, chariot; Copt. ⲃⲉⲣⲉϩⲉ.

barit , Düm. H.I. I, 15, 30, cage of wickerwork.

bari 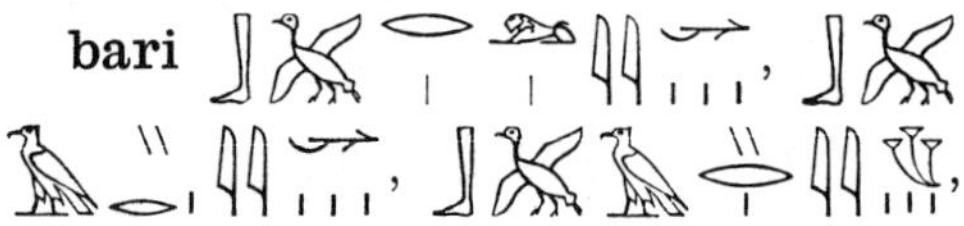, cypress wood (?)

barbar , Rev. 13, 20, grain; Copt. ⲃⲗ̄ⲃⲓⲗⲉ.

barbar-t , Rev. 5, 88, the knob of the crown of the South, grain, seed, berry, any rounded thing; compare Copt. ⲃⲗ̄ⲃⲓⲗⲉ.

barbar , Rec. 16, 139, to soak, to macerate, to boil; Copt. ⲃⲉⲣⲃⲉⲣ.

[ba]rbȧr  , Rev. 11, 180, to empty (?) lay waste; Copt. ⲃⲟⲗⲃⲗ̄.

barbas , a pot, vessel of some kind.

Barhm , a Nubian tribe which lived on the eastern and south-eastern borders of Egypt; Gr. Βλέμυες; see Strabo XVII, Pliny V, 8, Pomponius Mela I, 4, etc.

barek-t , Rev. 11, 146, pool; Heb. בְּרֵכָה.

bareka , to bless; compare Heb. √ברך in Piel.

baraka , Düm. H.I. I, 28, 29, 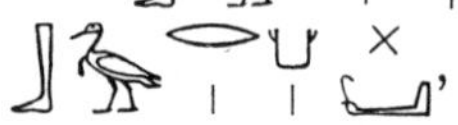, to bow the knee in homage; compare Heb. בָּרַךְ.

bareka 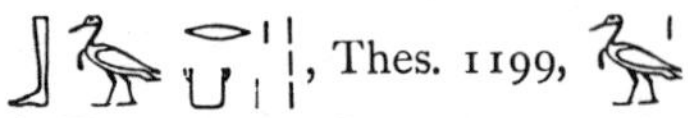, Thes. 1199, 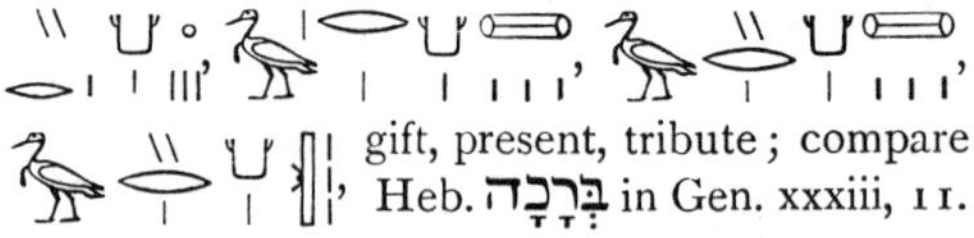, gift, present, tribute; compare Heb. בְּרָכָה in Gen. xxxiii, 11.

barekatȧ , pool, pond, lake; Heb. בְּרֵכָה.

Barkatȧthua  , B.D. 162, 7, a name of the body of Rā in Ȧnu.

barga , to be in want, empty, destitute.

barga , to illumine, to give light; compare Heb. בָּרַק, Arab. بَرَق.

bargtȧ  , Rev. 11, 156, 158, pool; Heb. בְּרֵכָה.

bartȧ, barth  , covenant, contract; Heb. בְּרִית.

bah , to snuff, to inhale.

bahaiu , fans.

baht (?) 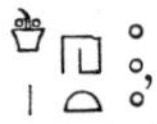, a kind of precious stone, emerald (?); compare בַּהַט, Esther i, 6.

baḥ   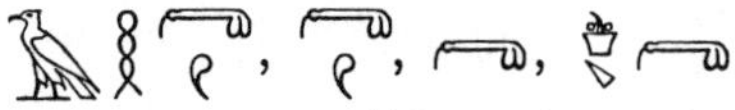, Jour. As. 1908, 311 (var. 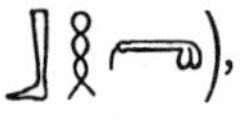), the phallus of man or animal, member; Copt. ϥⲁϩ.

baḥu (?) , Berg. 28, men, people.

baa[ḥ]ut , virility.

baḥ — m baḥ , , , , , , , Rev. 13, 31, before, in the presence of; plur. , ; Copt. ⲙ̀ⲡⲉⲙⲑⲟ; **m baḥ ā** , before, of old time; **m tcher baḥ** , U. 319, before; **tcher baḥ** . before.

baḥit , a garment (Lacau).

baḥen , to slay.

baḥen , knife.

baḥs , Rev. 14, 44, , Rec. 25, 14, calf; Copt. ⲃⲁϩⲥⲉ.

bakh , , to bear, to give birth to.

bakhbakh , A.Z. 1908, 117, to enjoy.

Bakhau , B.D. 108, 1–8, the Land of the Sunrise where Rā speared Set.

bakhannu , Rev. 11, 131, paraschistes.

bakhen , , pylon; see .

bas , , , the little waterpot on the scribe's palette; see **pes.**

basti , , salve, unguent.

Bastt , P. 290, , P. 569, , N. 861, , , Rec. 31, 31, , Rec. 27, 229, , , , , , , , an ancient cat-headed fire-goddess of the Eastern Delta. Her favourite cities were Bubastis in the Delta and Tar in Nubia.

Basti , , B.D. 125, II, one of the 42 assessors of Osiris.

Bast-sheshȧ-ȧrit (?) , a lioness-goddess, a form of Bastt.

Bastt Tar , Bast of Tar, an ancient town in the Sûdân.

basa , panther skin.

Basa , , the god Bes; Gr. βης.

basan-t , , Anastasi I, 27, 7, A.Z. 1911, 53, , , , chisel, graver.

basannt (?) , things worked with the chisel.

bash , Rev. 14, 1, , , Rev. 12, 14, to vomit.

basha , , , , , to slit, to cut, to split, a cutting tool.

bashȧ , Jour. As. 1908, 261, to desert; Copt. ⲃⲱϣ.

baq , to anoint, to rub with oil; , anointed.

baq , , , , , , IV, 1058, , Loret, Flo. Phar. 95, oil, unguent, salve, ointment; Copt. ⲫⲁⲕⲓ (?)

baq-t, U. 170, P. 652, M. 773,  (*sic*), oil tree, olive; plur. ; U. 170, the olive tree in On; P. 652, M. 773, the olive tree of heaven.

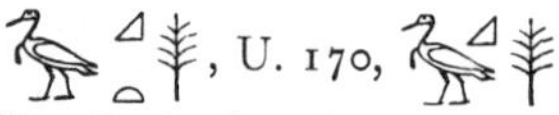

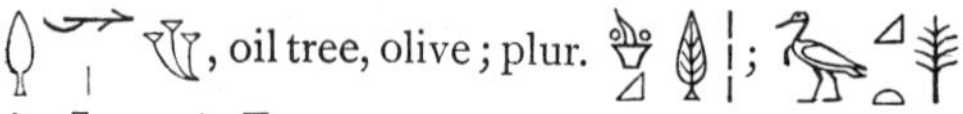

Baq-t, U. 170, M. 753, the mythological olive tree of Heliopolis.

baq, IV, 896, 925, to dazzle, to be bright, to be happy, Hymn to Uraei, 24.

baq, a prosperous man.

baq, clear, bright, shining.

baq, to be protected.

Baqbaq, Thes. 818, Rec. 16, 106, a hawk-god with a bull's head.

Baqbaq, Berg. I, 14, a protector of the dead.

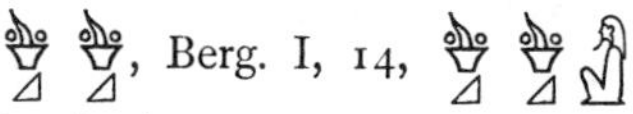

baq, to be with child, pregnant; Copt. ⲂⲞⲔⲒ.

baq, to beat (?) to slay (?)

baqr, stairs, steps.

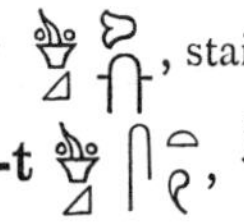

baqs-t, jawbone, cheek (?); Copt. (?)

bak = .

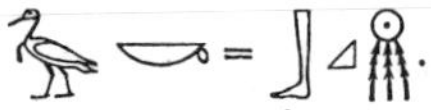

bak, Rev. 12, 65, hawk; see **bȧk**; "hawk of gold," an amulet; Copt.

bak, to work, to labour, to toil, to serve, to do service, to pay tribute; Rec. 20, 40, to be worked upon (of engraved objects)

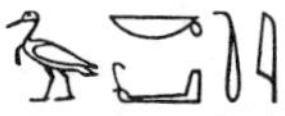

bak, work, labour in the field, service; plur. Rec. 20, 40, products; IV, 665, product of Syria; the best of the products.

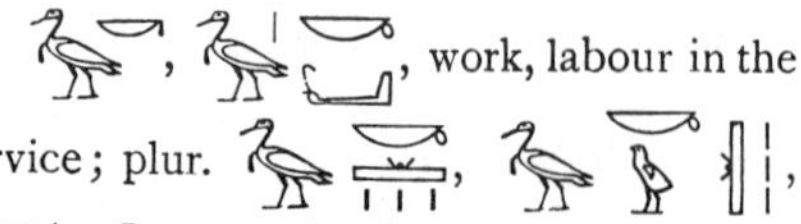

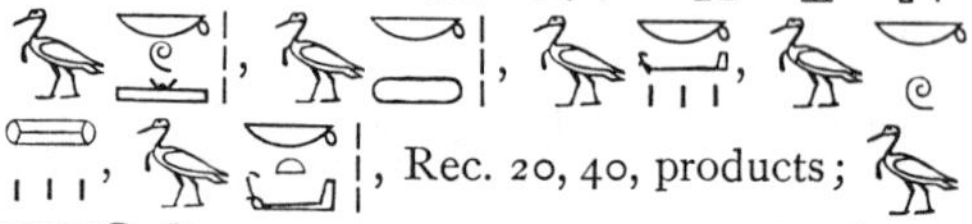

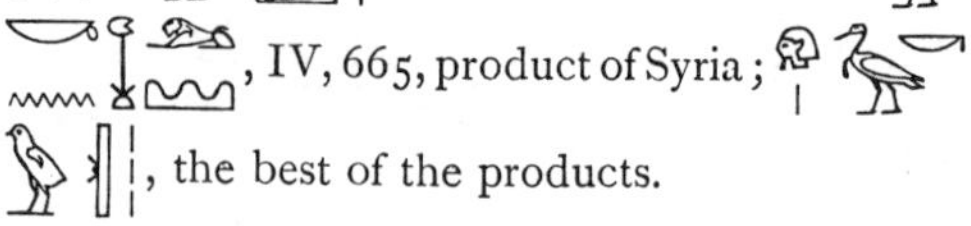

bak-t, gift, tax, tribute, burden, assessment, vassalage.

bak, Rec. 21, 86, Åmen. 6, 16, manservant, slave, workman, labourer, member of the corvée; fem. 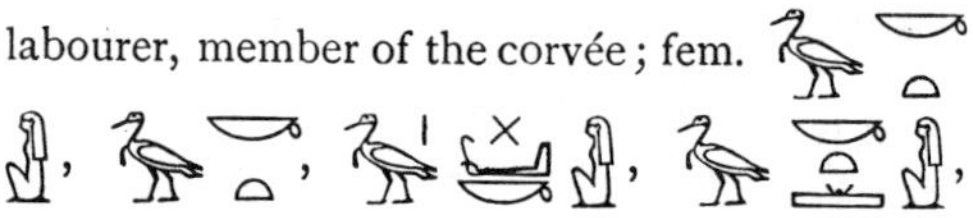 maidservant, slave woman; plur.

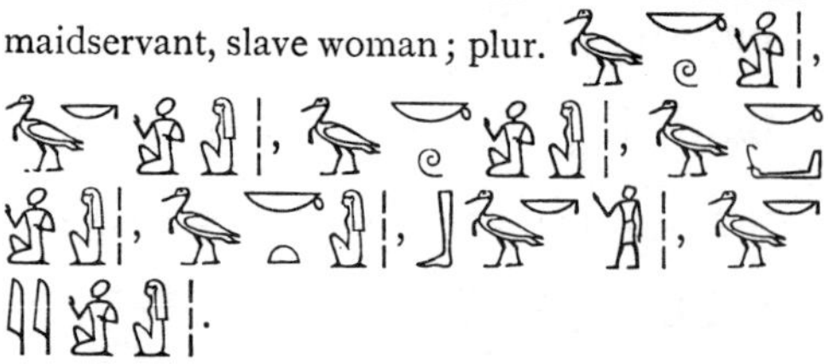

bak-keriu, Mar. Karn. 55, 65, tax-paying subjects.

bakȧu, servants, people attached to the service of the god.

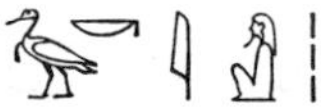

Bakȧ, "worker," a name of the Sun-god.

bak, Rev., reward, price, wages; Copt. ⲂⲈⲔⲈ.

Bak; var. Zod. Denderah, one of the 36 Dekans.

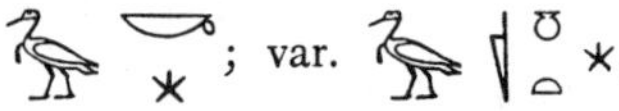

Baktiu (?), Thes. 133, a name of the Dekans.

bak, ladder = , frame, woodwork.

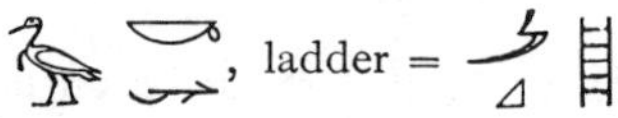

bak, city, town; Copt. ⲂⲀⲔⲒ.

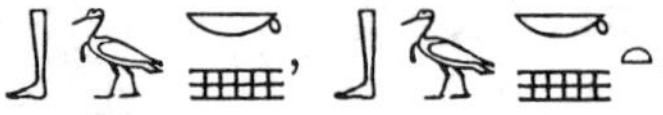

bak  , to bless; compare Heb. בָּרַךְ.

bak  , olive oil.

bakbak  , IV, 506, a mineral substance (?)

baka  , to be pregnant; Copt. ⲂⲞⲔⲒ.

bakaut  , pregnant women.

baka 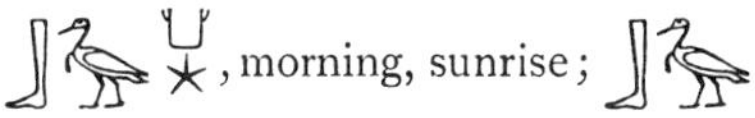 , morning, sunrise; 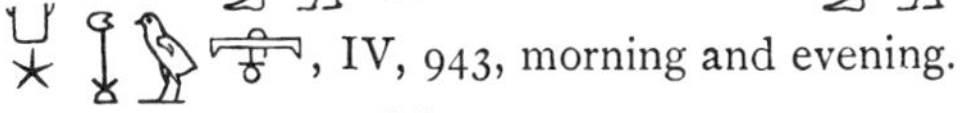 , IV, 943, morning and evening.

baka-t  , A.Z. 1905, 27, place, region, precinct; plur. 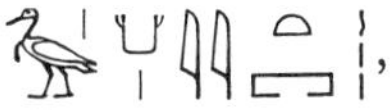 , Mar. Aby. I, 19, 3, Ḥeruemḥeb 24.

Baka, Bakait  , a common name for settlement, inhabited district, place, region; Copt. ⲂⲀⲔⲒ.

bakaa  , the sacred bark of Horus.

baka  , Anastasi I, 23, 7, cleft in a rock, gorge, a kind of tree; Heb. בָּכָא.

bakaȧ  , a kind of plant, or tree (olive?).

bakȧ  , platform, foundation, base.

baki  , Rev., shipwreck; Copt. ⲂⲒϪⲒ.

bakr  , stairs, steps; see .

bag  , hawk; see 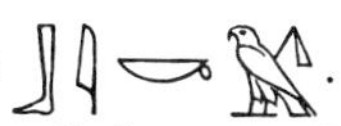 .

bag 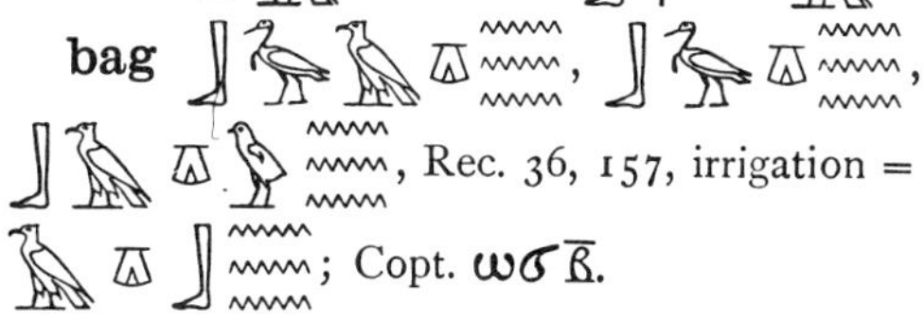 , Rec. 36, 157, irrigation = ; Copt. ⲰϬⲂ̄.

bag-t  , breast, the two breasts.

bag  , Rec. 36, 78, , to be weak, to be tired, to be feeble, helpless, inactive, wretched, needy, empty of strength.

bag  , Rec. 31, 30, laxity, slackness, exhaustion.

bagȧ  , T. 346, P. 689, inactive, immovable.

bagi  , helpless one, exhausted man, dead person; plur. 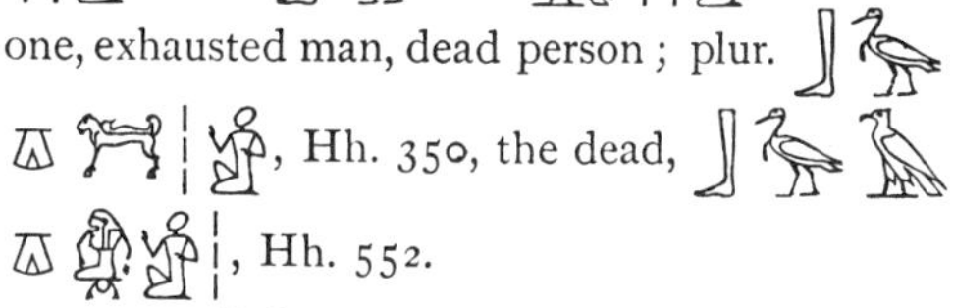 , Hh. 350, the dead, , Hh. 552.

bagi  , an inactive god; plur.  .

baga  , Rec. 17, 147, , a kind of fish.

bagȧsa  , Rec. 21, 14, revolt, rebellion, riot.

bagas  , the name of an animal.

bagrthȧ-t  , Israel Stele 11, Rec. 20, 31 . . . . .

bags-t 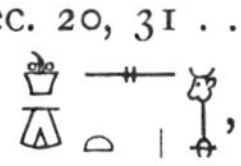 , collar, necklace.

Bags 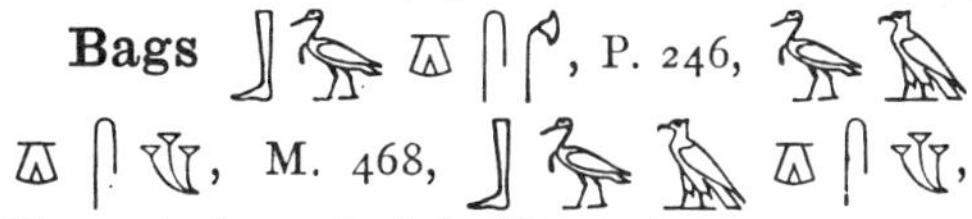 , P. 246, , M. 468, , N. 1058, the god of the lily, or lotus.

bagsu , , dagger; var. .

bat, bait , Rev. 11, 167,  , Rev. 12, 110, , Rev. 13, 28, , palm branch; Copt. ⲂⲎⲦ.

bat , cornstalk; dual .

bat 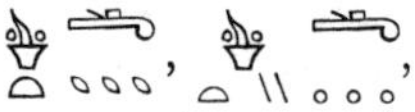, Rec. 3, 57, spelt; see **beṭ-t**; Copt. ⲂⲰⲦⲈ, ⲂⲰϮ.

bat 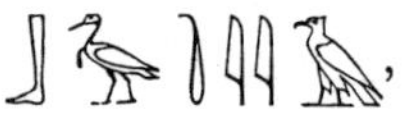, IV, 785, house; Heb. בַּיִת.

bat-ar , Bethel; Heb. בֵּית־אֵל.

bati , Rev. 13, 25, horror, abomination; Copt. ⲂⲰⲦⲈ.

batiu , A.Z. 1908, 121, B.D. 146, 38, fiends, red-haired devils, filthy and abominable creatures; Copt. ⲂⲞⲦⲈ, ⲂⲞϮ.

Bata , P. 267, , M. 480, , N. 1248, a bull-god with two faces,  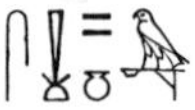; var. **Betch** , Rec. 26, 132, and see A.Z. 1906, 77.

Bata 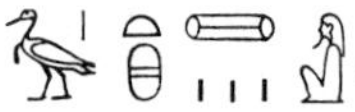, A.Z. 1880, 94, P.S.B. 27, 186, a god of war and the chase.

Bata-āntȧ-t 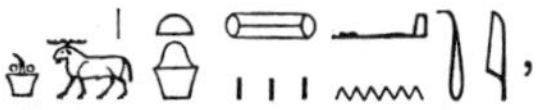, L.D. III, 172, 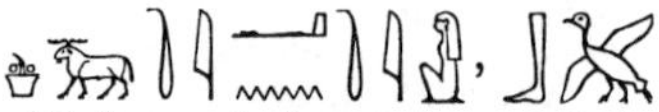, , IV, 786, a Semitic name of a woman; compare Heb. בת־ענת.

batauȧ 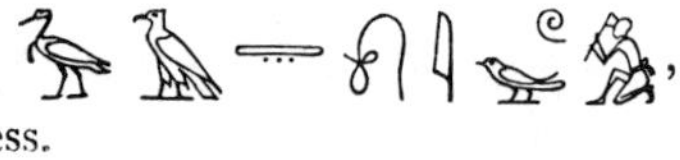, evil, wickedness.

batanȧ-t  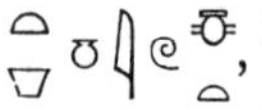, Rev. 12, 62, plate, dish, stew-pan; Gr. βατάνη.

batȧ-t , P.S.B. 27, 186, part of a waggon, chariot (?)

baten , Rev. 13, 112, 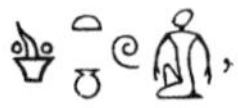, enemy, rebel.

Baten 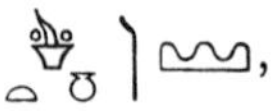, the country of the enemy.

batsh , weak, helpless.

batgeg , to be strong, to cut, violent.

Batgeg 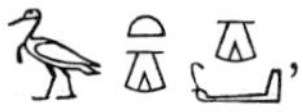, Denderah III, 8, a hawk-god.

batgā 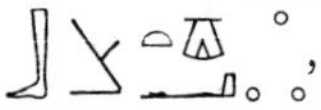, a kind of stone.

Bathit 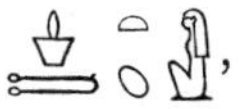, Rev. Arch. 1874, 287, a title of Isis-Hathor.

Bathaḥ 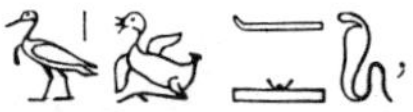, Alt. K. 393, a goddess.

Bathresth (?) , Ṭuat V, a crocodile-god by the River of Fire.

baṭ-t , spelt (?); Copt. ⲂⲰⲦⲈ.

baṭn [illegible], Anastasi I, 28, 3 = [illegible], to be wrapped up or involved in some matter.

Baṭr [illegible], Rec. 21, 77, king of Thakasa.

baṭḳek [illegible], to smite, to shatter.

batcha [illegible], a kind of pot, or vessel.

batchan [illegible] [illegible], Amherst Pap. 26, [illegible] [illegible], staff, stick, the bastinado-stick, stave, cudgel.

batchar [illegible], [illegible], stick, staff; plur. [illegible], [illegible].

bȧ , pavement; var. 
.

bȧ , flower, palm (?) garland, plant (?)

bȧa ,
, plants, thicket, bushes, a kind of herb.

bȧ, bȧa , Hearst Pap. 2, 9 . . . .

bȧ , grain.

bȧa-t ,
, cake, loaf, a tablet of incense; plur. 
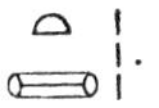.

bȧ , a cry.

bȧ-t , cry, speech (?)

bȧbȧ , a cry of joy (?) to mutter spells or incantations.

bȧ-t , sack, bag, chest, baggage.

bȧ-t 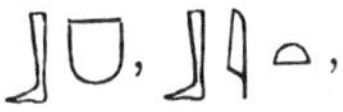, IV, 637, a drinking vessel.

Bȧ-t , B.D. 41, 4, a city in the Ṭuat.

bȧ-t , IV, 1140, , Rev. 11, 182, honey; Copt. ⲉⲃⲓⲱ; 
, like bees abounding in honey.

bȧa , to rebel, to revolt.

bȧa — em bȧa , with , a strong negative; 
, Ebers Pap. 97, 13 ff., A.Z. 1905, 104, 1907, 133.

bȧ-t , Berl. 2296, , Berl. 17021, , Rec. 16, 56,
, IV, 994, , IV, 903, , character, quality, disposition, characteristic, moral worth, reputation; plur. 
, Anastasi I, 1, 5, , Gol. 13, 129, , Thes. 1483, , IV, 505.

bȧa-t bȧn , evil-natured.

bȧa-t nefer-t , Gol. 14, 145, well-disposed.

bȧai [illegible], Rec. 20, 43, to wonder, to cause wonder, to do a wonderful thing, to be amazed, to be astonished, to consider marvellous or wonderful.

bȧa-t [illegible], [illegible],
[illegible], A.Z. 1905, 100, [illegible]
[illegible], [illegible], [illegible], [illegible],
[illegible], [illegible], IV, 1077, [illegible], wonder, wonderful, something to be amazed at, a marvellous act or deed, a surprise; Copt. ⲉⲃⲏ; plur. [illegible], P.S.B. 21, 3, [illegible],
[illegible], Hymn Darius 7, [illegible], [illegible]
[illegible], [illegible], [illegible],
[illegible], [illegible],
[illegible], [illegible], [illegible]
[illegible], Mar. Karn. 54, 47.

bȧa — em bȧa [illegible], extraordinary; [illegible], bon à merveille; [illegible], truly wonderful [ointment].

Bȧaiti [illegible], A.Z. 1905, 32, "wonderful one," a title of a god.

bȧa [illegible], to work a mine, to dig out ore.

bȧa [hieroglyphs], T. 253, 284, P. 214, M. 31, N. 64, [hieroglyphs], P. 310, [hieroglyphs], N. 983, [hieroglyphs], N. 18, 264, 957, [hieroglyphs], N. 796, [hieroglyphs], M. 765, [hieroglyphs], P. 52, [hieroglyphs], P. 76 = [hieroglyphs], M. 106 = [hieroglyphs], N. 18, metallic substance, copper; [hieroglyphs], N. 789, [hieroglyphs], metal of the North; var. [hieroglyphs]; [hieroglyphs], metal of the South; var. [hieroglyphs]. Later forms are:— [hieroglyphs], [hieroglyphs], [hieroglyphs], [hieroglyphs], [hieroglyphs], [hieroglyphs], [hieroglyphs], [hieroglyphs], IV, 1111, [hieroglyphs], [hieroglyphs], [hieroglyphs], [hieroglyphs], [hieroglyphs], [hieroglyphs], [hieroglyphs], [hieroglyphs], [hieroglyphs], [hieroglyphs], [hieroglyphs], [hieroglyphs], ingots of gold, [hieroglyphs], Rec. 20, 40.

Bȧa-em-seḥ-t-neter [hieroglyphs], the name of an instrument used in the ceremony of "opening the mouth."

bȧa en pet [hieroglyphs], L.D. III, 194, [hieroglyphs], [hieroglyphs], [hieroglyphs], Rec. 32, 129, iron of the sky; Copt. ⲂⲈⲚⲒⲠⲈ.

bȧa nu ta [hieroglyphs], earth-iron (?)

bȧa kam [hieroglyphs], black basalt.

bȧa [hieroglyphs], [hieroglyphs], [hieroglyphs], [hieroglyphs], [hieroglyphs], [hieroglyphs], [hieroglyphs]

[hieroglyphs], the sky, heaven, the material of which heaven was supposed to be made.

Bȧa [hieroglyphs], I, 55, [hieroglyphs], [hieroglyphs], [hieroglyphs], [hieroglyphs], Shipwreck, 23, [hieroglyphs], [hieroglyphs], [hieroglyphs], [hieroglyphs], [hieroglyphs], [hieroglyphs], [hieroglyphs], the mine-region in the Sûdân and Sinai; [hieroglyphs], P. 789; [hieroglyphs], mines.

b[ȧa]-t [hieroglyphs], mine (in Sinai).

Bȧau [hieroglyphs], Rec. 31, 169, [hieroglyphs], B.D. 80, 14 = [hieroglyphs], a sky-god.

bȧa [hieroglyphs], A.Z. 71, 141, capital of a pillar.

Bȧa-ḥeri-ȧb-pet [hieroglyphs], B.D. 153B, 7, the weight of the magical net.

Bȧa-ta [hieroglyphs], Ṭuat IX, a monster serpent with a head at each end of his body.

bȧa [hieroglyphs] = [hieroglyphs], tooth.

bȧak [hieroglyphs], [hieroglyphs], Hymn Darius 1, 6, hawk; see [hieroglyphs].

Bȧak-t [hieroglyphs], the hawk-god of iron (?)

bȧu [hieroglyphs], Peasant 223 = [hieroglyphs].

bȧuk [hieroglyphs], grains, seed, vegetables (?)

bȧuk [hieroglyphs], [hieroglyphs], [hieroglyphs], hawk, the hawk-god of heaven, a name of Ȧmen-Rā; plur. [hieroglyphs].

bȧbȧ [hieroglyphs], Rec. 29, 159, to kill, to slay.

Bȧbȧ [hieroglyphs], B.D. 93 (Saïte), 2, a title of Set; see **Baba.**

bȧbȧ [hieroglyphs], Hearst Pap. VI, 8 . . . .

bȧb-t , B.D. (Saïte), 133, 3 ....

bȧf , to see, to look; see [illegible].

bȧn , to be evil, to be wicked; Copt. ⲃⲱⲱⲛ.

bȧnȧ 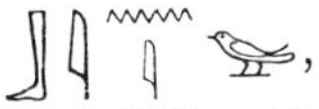, a bad man.

bȧn-t , evil, wrong, sin, misery, wretchedness; plur. , , , most wicked, or evil, wholly bad; Copt. ⲉⲃⲓⲏⲛ.

Bȧn , evil personified, the devil.

bȧn , sweet, pleasant = [illegible].

bȧn-t , harp; Copt. ⲃⲟⲓⲛⲏ, ⲟⲩⲱⲓⲛⲓ.

bȧn , to play a harp.

bȧn , javelin, spear.

bȧn-t , palm = [illegible].

bȧnr , [illegible], Ȧmen. 6, 11, 13, 6, to be sweet, gracious; see [illegible].

bȧnr-t 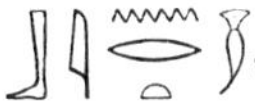, sweetness.

bȧnr , dates.

Bȧnr-ra-t , Ombos III, 2, 131, a goddess.

bȧḥ 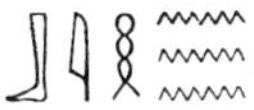, flood, inundation.

bȧḥ 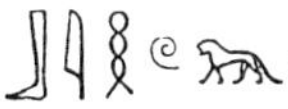, IV, 998, lion.

bȧḥes 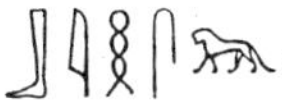, a young fierce lion (?)

bȧqer , excellent, good = [illegible].

bȧk , Rec. 27, 59, to twitter, to cry (?)

bȧk , M. 183,  , hawk; fem. ; plur.  [illegible], U. 525, P. 173, N. 684, [illegible] [illegible], Rec. 26, 79, [illegible], B.D. 42, 101, [illegible], U. 209; Copt. ⲃⲏϭ, Gr. Βαΐηθ, Horapollo, I, 7.

, living hawks.

Bȧkui (?)  [illegible], B.D. 64, 4, the double Hawk-god.

Bȧk , B.D. 110, 15: (1) a hawk-god, 1000 cubits long, in Sekhet-Ȧaru; (2) a god of letters, one of the Seven Wise gods, Düm. Temp. Inschr. 25; (3) a hawk-god in Ṭuat III.

Bȧk — , Rec. 11, 70, a divine hawk with parti-coloured plumage.

Bȧk-t , Ṭuat III, a hawk-goddess.

bȧk , L.D. III, 65A, 17, [illegible] [illegible], Rec. 16, 57, [illegible], [illegible], [illegible], IV, 897, the hawk-boat of Horus, barge, boat in general.

Bȧk-t , U. 578, N. 966, a town in the Ṭuat.

Bȧt, Bȧti , Rec. 27, 218, [illegible], N. 1346, [illegible], [illegible], , T. 352 = , king of the North (as opposed to , **nesu**, king of the South), king of Lower Egypt; Gr. Βιτης; plur. , P. 684, [illegible], M. 477, N. 1245, [illegible], P. 266, [illegible] [illegible], IV, 85, [illegible], IV, 169, [illegible] [illegible], Tombos Stele 14, [illegible], [illegible]

, Thes. 1287, kings of the South and North; , king of the kings of the North.

bȧti , a title of two priestesses.

bȧti – , IV, 1015, the "two ears of the king of the North," title of an official.

bȧti khā , the festival of the king of the North.

Bȧti , B.D. 41, 4, a dweller in Ȧmenti, king of the North (?)

Bȧti Bȧti 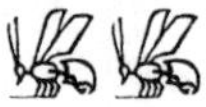, Ṭuat III, a form of Osiris.

Bȧtiu , N. 1245, , Ṭuat VI, the deified kings of the North.

Bȧtiu , Ṭuat VI, a group of four gods in the Ṭuat.

bȧt . . . . . , , the title of a very high official, meaning something like "bearer of the seal of the king of the North"; plur. .

Bȧtḥeḥ (?) , a god.

bȧth 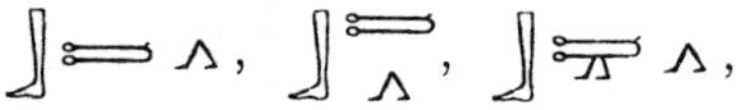, 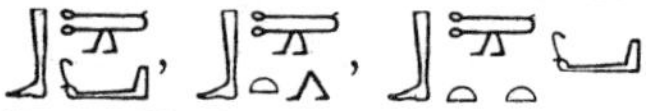, U. 212, 371, P. 41, N. 659, 1159, to walk, to run, to leap, to leap in, to leap out, to escape, to hasten, to depart.

bȧth 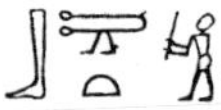, to carry off, to seize.

bȧth 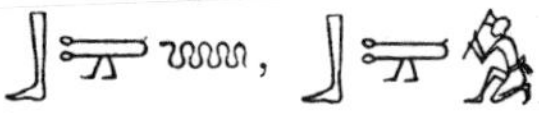, evil, destructive, the name of a devil.

Bȧth 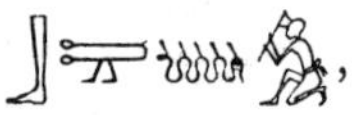, Nesi-Ȧmsu 32, 45, a form of Āapep.

bȧth , Berl. 3024, 113, a sick man, one vexed with the devil of a disease.

bȧthi 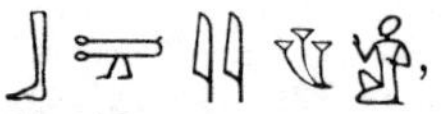, Northampton Rep. 11, profession.

bȧthiu 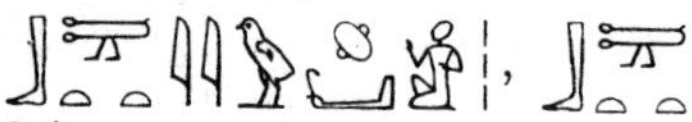 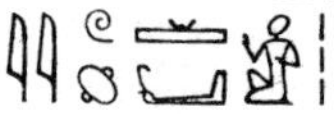, professional men (?)

bȧṭ , a disease of the eye.

bā , A.Z. 42, 107, Koller Pap. 4, 8.

bā 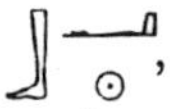, to shine, be bright.

bābā 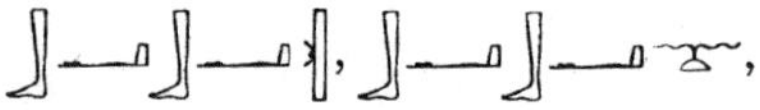, , Mission 13, 143, to shine, to give light, splendour; Copt. ⲃⲟⲩⲃⲟⲩ.

bā, bāāȧ 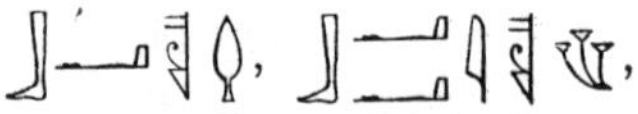, sticks of palmwood; plur.  , Rec. 16, 97; Copt. ⲃⲁⲓ.

Bā , Nav. Lit. 80, the name of a god.

bāā 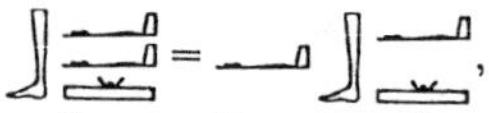, contradiction.

bābā 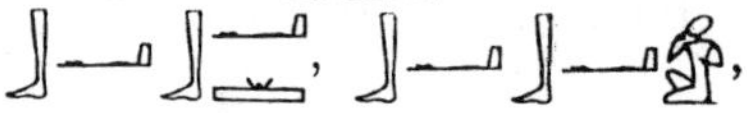, Rec. 4, 121, to converse, to speak in a contradictory manner.

bāā (?) 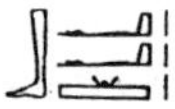, a kind of disease.

bāā , to sip, to lap, to moisten (the lips ?)

bābā  , to make wet, to moisten, to sip, to lap; Copt. ⲃⲉⲃⲉ.

bābā , P. 540, to smear oneself in blood.

bābā-t [illegible], stream, canal, river.

bābā [illegible] [illegible], Rec. 2, 15, smelter.

bāa [illegible], [illegible], Ȧmen. 16, 19, 21, 2, 27, 1, [illegible], Tomb Ram. III, 79, 10, to explain (?)

bāuḥu [illegible], flood; see **bāḥ**.

bān [illegible], P. 277, M. 521, N. 1102, stream (?) lake (?) pool.

bān-t [illegible], Rec. 30, 72, T. 26, P. 389, N. 165, 208, neck, throat, bosom.

bān [illegible], to mount an object in metal, to plate, to inlay.

bānȧ 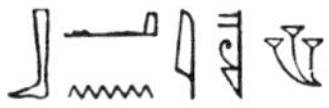, a kind of plant.

Bānti , Ṭuat X, a dog-headed ape-god.

bār 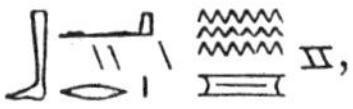, a mass of water; compare Heb. בְּאֵר.

Bār 

, Baal, a Syrian god of war and the chase, sometimes identified by the Egyptians with Set; Heb. בַּעַל.

Bār-m'hr , a judge in the Ḥarîm Conspiracy; compare בעל־מהר (Devéria).

Bārtȧ , Ba'alath בַּעֲלַת, Bêltis, the consort of בַּעַל צְפוֹן (Exod. xiv, 2, Numb. xxxiii, 7, Asien 315).

bāḥ, bāḥȧ , N. 996, [illegible], T. 368, P. 47, 548, , N. 33,
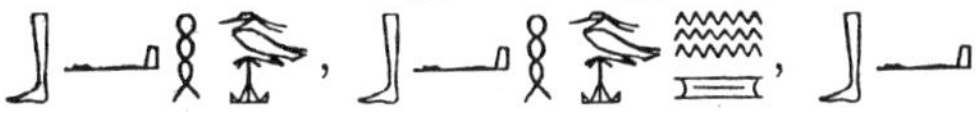

, to flood with water, to submerge, to be flooded; [illegible]
, M. 335, [illegible], M. 334, , P. 708; [illegible]
, Rec. 21, 14, irrigation officer.

bāḥ 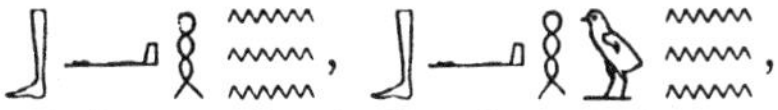, T. 243, P. 608, water-flood, abundance of water.

Bāḥ , "Waterer," a title of the Nile.

Bāḥ 
, B.D. 64, 20, 136B, 7, the god of the Nile-flood.

bāḥ 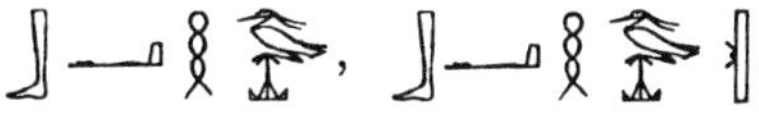,
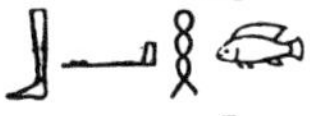, to be abundant.

bāḥ 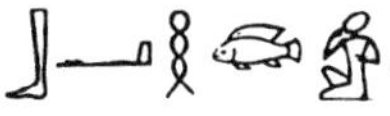, Pap. 3024, 87, a man overwhelmed with misfortunes.

bāḥ-t , T. 82, M. 236, N. 613, I, 34, an abundant food supply, bounty, abundance; [illegible], an abundant harvest.

bāḥ, bāḥȧ 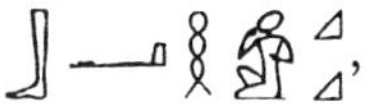, N. 1326, [illegible], P. 81, [illegible], M. 111, [illegible], N. 25, giving meat and drink in abundance, to feed full.

bātha , Nástasen Stele 39, vessel, pot.

bi 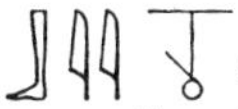, Lacau . . . .

bi , IV, 612, to make a wonder of.

bi-t , A.Z. 1905, 14, a wonder; plur. [illegible], [illegible], IV, 340, 347.

biu , B.D. 138, 7, "wonderful" (?)

Bi 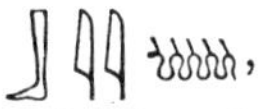, the name of a fiend.

Bit 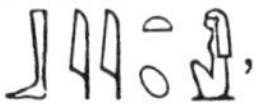, B.D. 145R, a form of Hathor.

bina , A.Z. 1908, 85, the phoenix bird; Gr. φοῖνιξ.

bu , Ȧmen. 9, 1, [illegible], a sign of negation, not; Copt. ⲙⲉ.

bu ȧr , do not = Copt. ⲙⲉⲣⲉ.

bu pu , Rec. 21, 79, [illegible], [illegible], [illegible], [illegible], P.S.B. 14, 330; fem. [illegible].

bu pu uā , no one.

bu pu-t 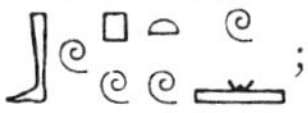; Copt. ⲙ̄ⲡⲁⲧⲉ.

bu pui-tu , A.Z. 1908, 73 ff., not; Copt. ⲙ̄ⲡⲉ.

bu ān , ungracious, unpleasant, malignant.

bu [illegible], [illegible], [illegible], [illegible], [illegible], [illegible], place, house, site ([illegible], B.D. 81B, 6); Copt. ⲙⲁ; [illegible], place of wine;

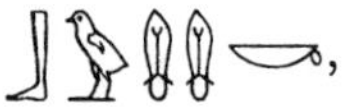, U. 12, 34, 80, 345, N. 262, 349, 560, place where thy feet are.

bu ȧakhu , Gol. 14, 144, the best, excellence.

bu ȧqer  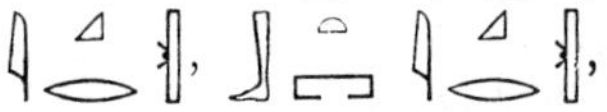, place of strength or perfection, *i.e.*, strength, wisdom, perfection.

bu uā , one place ; , in one or the same place, together.

bu uāb , place of purity, *i.e.*, cleanness, purity.

bu ur , place of greatness, *i.e.*, majesty, riches, prosperity.

bu bȧn 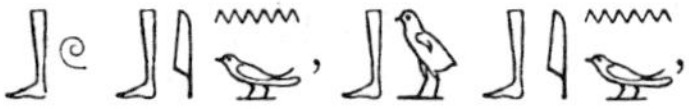, place of evil, *i.e.*, wickedness, evil, misery, wretchedness.

bu maā 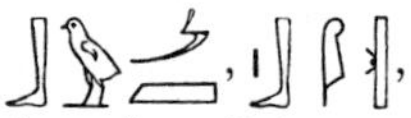, Rec. 35, 126, , I, 79, 14, 971, Rec. 35, 73, place of truth, *i.e.*, truth.

bu menkh 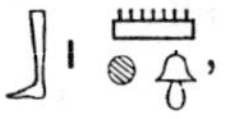, Rec. 16, 56, perfection.

bu neb 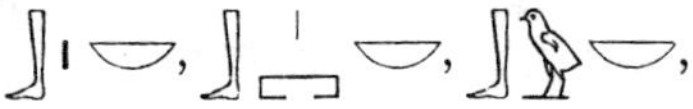, , every place, everywhere.

bu nebu, bu nebt ,  , Peasant 262, 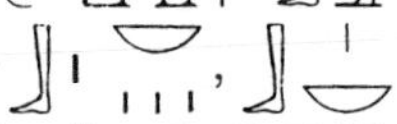, 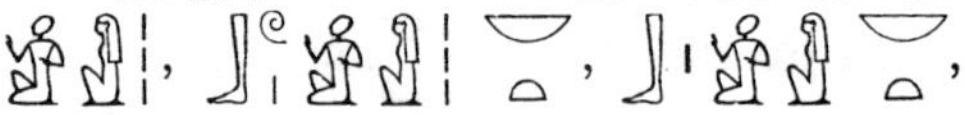, IV, 835, Berl. Pap. 3024, 108, all men, everybody, men in general, , B.D.G. 1064.

bu nefer 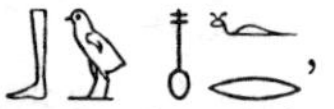, Peasant 197, , place of happiness, *i.e.*, happiness, felicity ;  , Peasant 288, happy folk ; 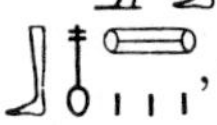, the happiness caused by plenty of food.

bu bu nefer , P. 174, N. 942.

bu n r 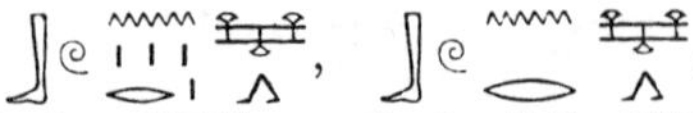,  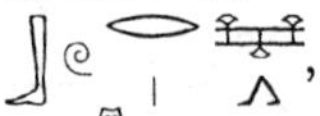, Ȧmen. 12, 12, 24, 1, with  and  outside ; Copt. ⲃⲟⲗ.

bu ḥuru , Peasant 167, 263, badness, wickedness, shameful.

bu ḥer sekheru , Gen. Epist. 68 . . . .

Bu ḥeḥ 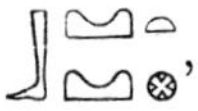, place of eternity, a name of the Other World.

bu khenti , disaster, misfortune.

bu kher , place below, *i.e.*, under.

bu sa , protection, the place where protective magic is worked.

bu sa 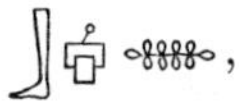, after (?) ; Copt. ⲙⲉⲛ-ⲉⲛⲥⲁ (?)

bu kiu 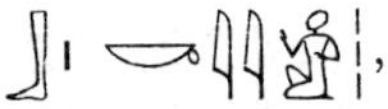, A.Z. 1906, 160, 1907, 99, foreigners, strangers, foreign (?)

bu ga , Anastasi I, 7, 2 ; var. [illegible] ; see **beg.**

bu tem [illegible], perfection, completeness, conclusion.

bu ṭu [illegible], [illegible], Peasant 214, calamity, evil, iniquity, misfortune.

bu tcheser [illegible], [illegible], Rec. 33, 3, sanctuary, holy place.

bu-t [illegible], a kind of fish.

bu [illegible], [illegible], U. 189, P. 687, M. 223, N. 977, [illegible] [illegible], to abominate, to hate, to hold to be hateful or accursed.

but 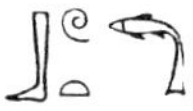, Ȧmen. 13, 17, , [illegible], [illegible], T. 344, abomination; , [illegible], Gol. 12, 97, loathsome thing; Israel Stele 9.

buiti , Tombos Stele 4, hateful persons, abominable beings or things.

but ka , a hateful person.

But-Menu 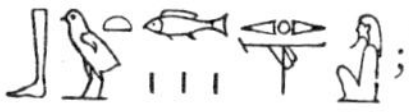; see **Besu-Menu.**

but (bes-ut?) , to come forth (?) place of issue (?)

but (?) , some kind of workman.

bu , beams, rafters.

bubu 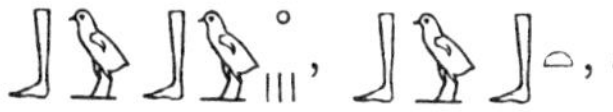, a seed or grain offering.

bubu , rings, annular ornaments.

bua , place; see .

bua-t, buai-t , Berl. 3024, 92, [illegible], [illegible], high ground, high place, hill, high rock.

bua 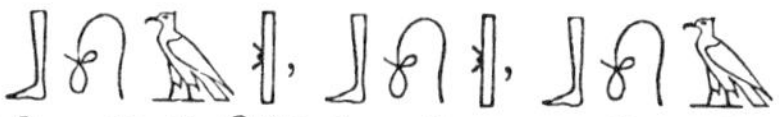, [illegible], [illegible], to be great, to be wonderful, or marvellous, to hold to be wonderful, to magnify;  [illegible], thou art more wonderful than those who are in thy train.

bua-t , Rec. 14, 97, [illegible], Ḳubbân Stele 31, marvels, wonders.

bua 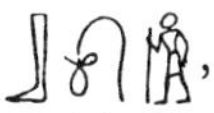, A.Z. 35, 17, [illegible], [illegible], Rhind Pap. 54, [illegible] , Ȧmen. 3, 5, 26, 14,  [illegible], chief, mighty one, magnate, lord, overlord, nobleman; plur. , [illegible], , Leyden Pap. 13, 14, [illegible] [illegible], Hymn to Nile 3, 14.

Bua-tep , Tomb of Seti I, one of the 75 forms of Rā (No. 42).

buȧait , wonders, marvels.

bun , 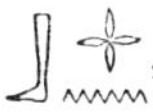, P. 425, M. 608, N. 1213, claw, nail, talon.

Bun (?) , B.D.G. 1194, a serpent-fiend and form of Set.

Bun-ā , Tuat XII, a singing dawn-god.

bunes 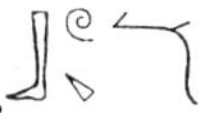, to eat, to devour; see [illegible].

burqa , Verbum 14, to shine, to lighten, to glimmer, to sparkle, bright, shining; Copt. ⲃⲣⲏϫ, ⲃⲣⲏϭⲉ, Heb. בָּרָק.

buha , fugitive, he who flies, coward.

buḥnra , , Love Songs 2, 11, to mock at, to laugh at; Heb. בָּהַל.

busu (?) 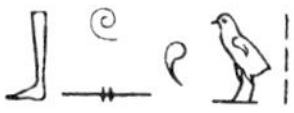, cheeks (?)

busa 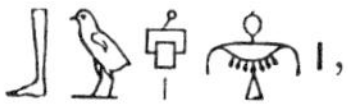, Demot. Cat., some silver object given in dowries.

bug-[t] , Rev. 14, 107, pregnant woman.

buṭ 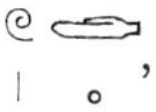, barley; Copt. ⲃⲱⲧⲉ, Gr. ὄλυρα.

buṭ , a kind of offering, incense (?)

butchiu , those who are burned or scalded.

beb , to be violent.

bebu, B.D. 161, 4, strong man.

beb, to go round, to revolve, to circulate.

beb, a metal pectoral or breast-plate, collar; , uraeus headdress (?)

beb, beb-t, , Rec. 27, 86, , cave, cavern, cavity, hole in the ground, hiding-place, den, lair; Copt. ⲃⲏⲃ.

beb-t, the deep part of a stream, source; , Berl. 19286, depth of the Nile; see ; , deep water, , IV, 464, B.M. 374.

Beb , , B.D. 17 (Nebseni), 125, II, 6, , Rec. 27, 84, the first-born son of Osiris who ate the livers of the dead; see **Baba, Babai, Babi**; Gr. Βέβων.

Bebi, the eldest son of Osiris; see .

Bebi, B.D. 18, I, 1, a dog-headed god of the dead.

Bebti (?), B.D. 17 (Nebseni), 44, the guardian of the Bend of Àmente.

Beb-ti, Mar. Aby. I, 45, the god of .

beb-t, , Rec. 31, 14, a kind of herb or flower.

bebait, , B.D. 104, 5; see

bebuit, IV, 1164, , , a kind of wig.

bebut (?), arrows.

bebnth (benbenth?), U. 539, , T. 295 . . . .

bepi, B.D. 168, Qerr-t X . . . . . .

bef, to see, to look at.

Befen, , Metternich Stele 51, one of the seven scorpions of Isis.

Befen-t, consort of Befen.

bmāi (bum'i), IV, 781 = = בָּמוֹת, high places.

ben, Àmen. 27, 1, not; Copt. ⲡ̄; = .

benȧ, not.

ben, N. 799 = **benr**, P. 152.

ben, , evil, wickedness, wretchedness; see ; Copt. ⲃⲱⲱⲛⲉ.

ben-t, Metternich Stele 35, evil.

benu, evil one, wicked man; , Rhind Pap. 18.

benȧ, Rev., , , , Rev. 13, 9, badness, evil, wickedness, sensual, bad; varr. , , Rev.; Copt. ⲃⲱⲱⲛⲉ.

ben ḥa-t, IV, 1075, evil-hearted, rebel.

Ben, , Rec. 26, 233, a god of evil.

ben-t, , , harp; Copt. ⲃⲟⲓⲛⲉ.

benben-t, , B.D. 145, 8, Rechnungen 58, 59, a kind of wood, palm-stick.

benr, to escape, to flee, to pass away, to be dissolved, to go on.

benȧ, Jour. As. 1908, 262, to go, to come.

benben , , , IV, 925, to hasten, to come.

ben , B.D. 39, 11, to copulate.

benu , male, man.

benben , Nesi-Åmsu 508, to copulate.

benn , IV, 943, B.D. 17, 135, , Rec. 32, 68, to copulate, to beget, to be begotten, virile, phallus.

Benen , a god of generation, a form of Menu.

Benni , Ṭuat IV, a phallic god.

ben-t , a portion of the body; plur. .

ben-ti , two egg-shaped organs of the body.

ben-ti , , the two breasts of a woman; see ,

ben-t, benut , , , , , boil, pustule, abscess, gangrene, pus.

benn-t , , some ball-shaped object, ball, eye-ball, apple of the eye; , the two eyeballs.

benn-t , Ebers Pap. 35, 9, eye-ball (?)

benn , amulet, the evil eye, witch-craft; Copt. ⲂⲰⲰⲚ.

benn , rings, bracelets.

ben-t , Rec. 15, 152, , cincture, belt, girdle, .

benn , B.D. 145, 36, a kind of wood.

Benn , Ṭuat VIII, a light-god of the 7th Pylon.

benben , , , , , , , , the stone symbolic of the Sun-god, obelisk, pyramid; see .

benben-t , Mission 13, 61, , Rec. 4, 30, the sanctuary of the benben or sun-stone.

benben-t , , , , IV, 590, , the pyramidion of an obelisk, the top of a pyramid.

benben-t , , , , a pyramid tomb, tomb in general; , B.D. 172, 30, bier.

benben , N. 971, a fire offering [in the house of Seker]; , N. 663.

Benben , Mar. Aby. I, 44, a solar-god (?)

Benben , N. 971, a light-god in the temple of Seker.

Benbeniti , , Ṭuat I, Tomb of Seti I, one of the 75 forms of Rā (No. 74).

benben ; see .

benau , L.D. III, 194, 12 . . . . . .

benȧ , IV, 1183, , Rev. 12, 62; see .

benȧ-t , sweetness; see .

benȧ ȧri , well-doing, gracious.

benȧ , young palms, palm shoots.

benȧ , , , date wine.

bnānā , B.D. 134, 7, to bathe (?)

bni , swallow; Copt. ⲂⲎⲚⲈ, ⲂⲎⲚⲒ.

benu-t, , , , IV, 831, a kind of stone, pebbles, flints; , , the ore of copper (?) a stone used in medicine.

benuit, corn-grinders, querns.

benu-t, , cakes, loaves.

benu, N. 757, claws, nails, talons; see **bun.**

benu, Nȧstasen Stele 38, bowl, vessel.

bennu, to set something in metal.

benu, , , Rec. 29, 146, , , , , , , Metternich Stele 92, the benu bird; , Rec. 30, 72.

Benu, B.D. 17, 25, a bird-god sacred to Rā and Osiris, and the incarnation of the soul of Rā and the heart of Osiris; Venus as a morning star was identified with him; Benu was self-produced, and the bird appeared each morning at dawn on the Persea Tree in Ȧnu; the Greeks connected it with the Phoenix; see Herod. ii, 73, Pliny N.H. x, 2, Pomponius Mela iii, 8, Tsetzer, Chil. v, 397.

Benuf, P. 662, , P. 782, an enemy of Osiris (?); var. , M. 774.

Beneb, Rec. 16, 150, a native of Beneb.

benpi = Copt. ⲁⲓⲡⲉ.

benpi, Rev. 12, 25, , Rev. 12, 26, , Rev. 13, 41, iron; Copt. ⲃⲉⲛⲓⲡⲉ.

benf, A.Z. 1892, 29, , Rec. 31, 31, exudation or emission from an animal or reptile.

Benf, Metternich Stele 58, one of the seven scorpions of Isis.

benr, , , , IV, 651, 661, , , with and , outside, exit; Copt. ⲃⲟⲗ; see **bu n r** .

Benr, B.D. 142, III, 25, a town of Osiris.

benr, "sweet water," a name of the Nile.

benrȧ, T. 345, , , , , , , , , , Rec. 29, 155, , , , , , dates; , fresh dates, IV, 171; Copt. ⲃⲛ̄ⲛⲉ, ⲃⲏⲛⲛⲉ.

benrȧ-t, , , , date palm; Copt. ⲃⲛ̄ⲛⲉ.

benrȧu, , , , , , Rec. 32, 178, date wine; , new date wine.

benrȧ-t, date wine.

benrȧti, Rec. 19, 92, , labourer in a palm grove.

benrȧ, , , , , to be sweet, sweet, to be grateful to the senses; , nice; , N. 799, , P. 152, sweet things.

benr-nes-t, sweet-tongued, speaker of fair things.

benr-re, sweet-mouthed.

benrȧ benrȧ, very sweet, very nice.

benrit, U. 163, T. 134, P. 640, T. 182, sweetness, a favour, anything sweet or pleasant or nice; plur. E.T. 1, 53, B.D. 179, 7.

benri, benriti, Leyden Pap., confectioner, sweetmeat-maker; plur.

bennḥu, to turn away, or aside; Copt. ⲫⲟⲛϩ (?)

benkh, Rec. 15, 127, to make an incision in bark; to cut.

bensh, bolt, part of a door; plur. B.D. 125, III, 27.

beng, a kind of bird.

beng . . . . . .

bent, benti, dog-headed ape; plur.

Benti, Ṭuat II, a singing ape-god; plur. Ṭuat I.

Benti-àri-àḥe-t-f, Ṭuat VI, an ape-god.

Benti, B.D. 17, 124, Isis and Nephthys in ape forms.

Bent (?), P. 161, T. 210, the son of Uat-Ḥeru.

Bentui, P. 648, P. 720, M. 747, two fiends in the Ṭuat.

benṭ-ti, the two breasts; varr. = ; Copt. ⲙⲛⲟⲧ.

benṭ, to copulate, phallus.

benṭ, Rec. 11, 62, to tie, to bind, to bind with spells.

benṭ, A.Z. 1905, 39, to groan, to moan.

benṭ, Thes. 1202, Israel Stele 10, an exclamation of grief, woe! alas!

bentch-t, Mission I, 159, Rec. 29, 157, vineyard, pergola.

bentch-ut (?), Mar. Mast. 181, 186, vineyard, estate.

ber, outside, exit, gateway; Copt. ⲃⲟⲗ (ⲉⲃⲟⲗ).

ber, Rev., eye; Copt. ⲃⲁⲗ; dual

brr (?), to become hard, to ossify.

berber, pyramid, stone with a pyramidal top; see

berber, a loaf of bread of a pyramidal shape.

berber, to cast out, to wreck, to overturn; Copt. ⲃⲉⲣⲃⲱⲣ.

brā, Rev. 2, 351, basket; Copt. ⲃⲓⲣ, ⲃⲁⲓⲣⲓ.

berkaru, Ḥerusàtef Stele 40, beads (?) some kind of metal ornaments.

Berqer, Rec. 35, 57, name of a fiend used in magic.

berg, to force open a door; Copt. ⲫⲱⲣϫ.

beh , IV, 711, Statistical Tab. 39, to flee, to run away.

behau 
, he who runs away, coward.

beh , earth, ground, place.

beh 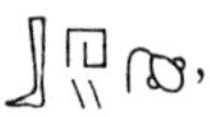, some odoriferous substance, incense (?)

beha-t , Koller Pap. 4, 6,
, Rec. 16, 69, Anastasi IV,
16, 5, ,
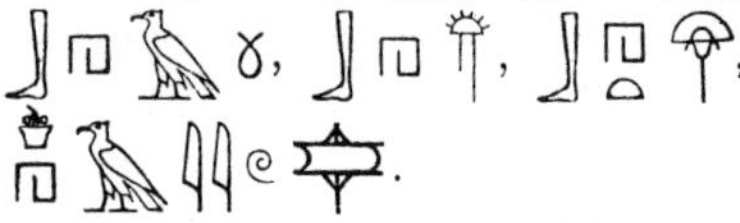, fan; plur. .

behen ,
, to cover over, cover, covering, coverlet, veil.

Behthu , Rec. 36, 169, a class of gods (?)

beḥ , IV, 1081, a part of the body.

beḥ , prepuce; Copt. ϥⲁϩ

beḥ , what is in front.

beḥ , , a measure.

beḥ , Rec. 4, 32, shrubs among which Osiris was buried.

beḥḥ , a kind of shrub.

beḥu 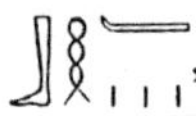, teeth, tusks = 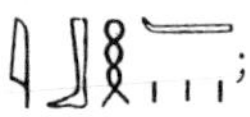;
Copt. ⲟⲃϩⲉ.

beḥ 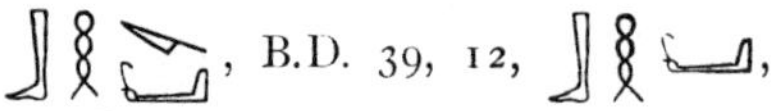, B.D. 39, 12,
, to cut, to kill, to hack, to carve, to hew stone.

beḥ-t 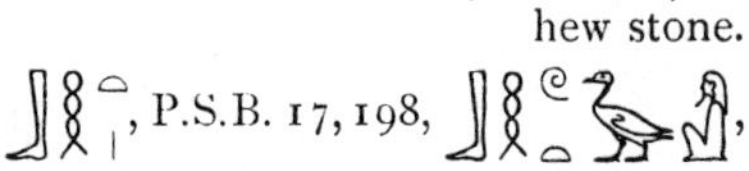, P.S.B. 17, 198,
P.S.B. 17, 197, , "the tearer," a kind of bird.

beḥu , P.S.B. 10, 48, a class of servants or workmen.

beḥḥu (?) , hyena.

beḥa , Rec. 1, 49, to break or tear in pieces.

beḥā , to set (offerings), a kind of fish.

beḥā ; see **bāḥ**.

Beḥus , B.D. 109, 9, the calf of Kherȧ (?) a soul of the East, the calf star, the morning star.

beḥus 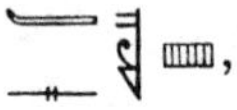, a kind of stone.

Beḥuka ,
, Mar. Aby. I, 49, Sphinx I, 88, Abbott Pap. 2, 10, 11, the name of a swift Libyan dog of Ȧntef-āa.

beḥukaȧ , Mar. Mon.
Div. 49, Rec. 36, 86 = 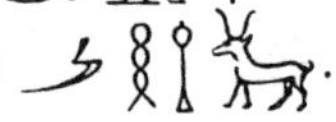.

Beḥutit 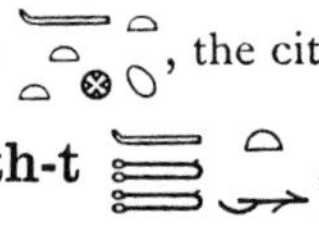, the city-goddess of Edfû.

beḥuthth-t , mast, pole, flagstaff.

beḥuṭ-t 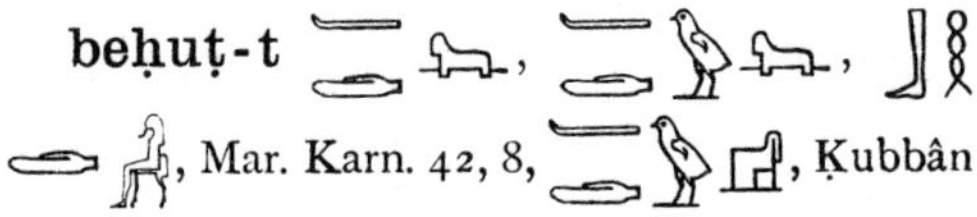, Mar. Karn. 42, 8, Ḳubbân
Stele 8, , seat, throne, throne on steps, stairs, seat of a god.

Beḥuṭ-t 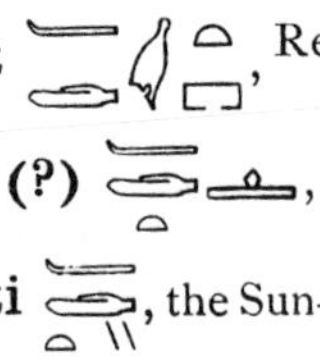, Rec. 29, 190, a shrine in Lower Egypt.

beḥuṭ-t (?) , tablet for offerings, altar.

Beḥuṭ-ti , the Sun-god of , whose form was that of a beetle.

beḥuṭṭ 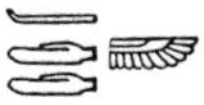, to spread out the wings.

beḥen 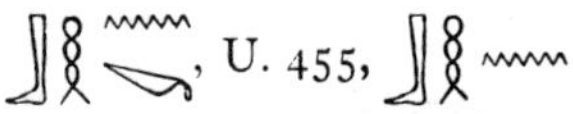, U. 455, T. 17,
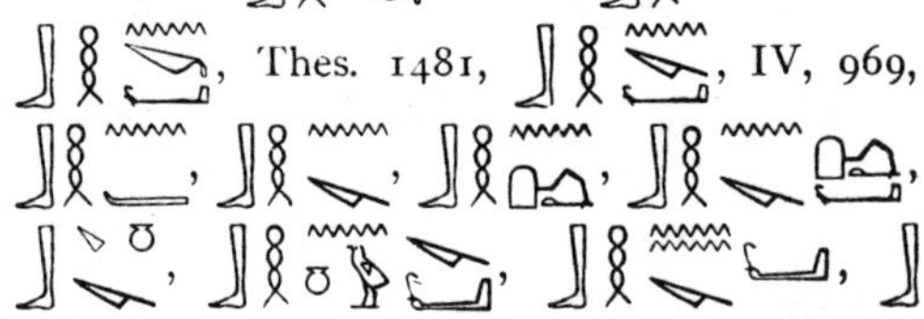, Thes. 1481, IV, 969,
, to slay, to cut in pieces, to stab, to pierce, to perforate a body.

behen , baleful, deadly.

Beḥen-t , Ṭuat I, a light-goddess.

beḥenu , Rec. 31, 31, deadly serpents in the Other World.

beḥen 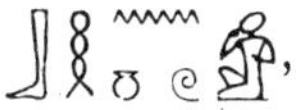, P.S.B. 13, 412, to bark.

beḥenu , B.D. 24, 2, fighting dogs.

beḥes 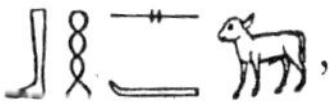, U. 20, [illegible], , [illegible], calf; plur. [illegible], P. 45, [illegible], M. 63, [illegible], N. 31, [illegible] [illegible], P. 604, [illegible], [illegible] [illegible], [illegible], Rec. 4, 30, [illegible] [illegible], a sucking calf.

beḥes 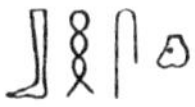, calf.

beḥes , IV, 893, [illegible], [illegible], [illegible], to hunt, to follow the chase.

beḥsȧu , hunter.

beḥes , a hunt, game.

beḥqa , P. 1116B, 57 . . . .

beḥt-ti 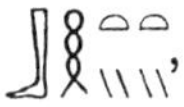, Rec. 12, 211, two thrones, or double throne; see .

beḥṭ , seat, throne.

bekh-t , quantity, amount.

bekhkh , U. 611, N. 643, Hh. 414, 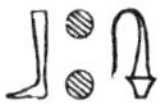, Rec. 31, 168, to be hot, to burn, flame, heat, fire, fiery; , T. 336.

Bekhkhi , Ṭuat VIII, the name of the 7th Gate.

Bekhkhit 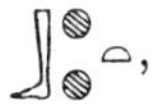, Ṭuat X, a light-goddess of dawn.

Bekhbekh , [illegible], B.D.G. 453; var. [illegible],

bekh 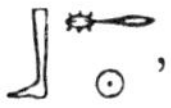, to give light, to light up, to illumine.

Bekh , B.D.G. 200, a black-haired bull-god of Hermonthis, the Living Soul of Rā, the Bull of the East, and the Lion of the West; Gr. Βακις, Macrobius, Sat. I, 26, Aelian, De Nat. An. XII, 11.

bekh , A.Z. 1910, 112, to give birth, to produce.

bekh-t 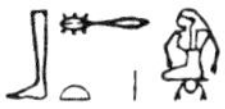, what is born, produced.

bekhb[ekh]? , a kind of tree

bekhen , to cut, to saw.

bekhen 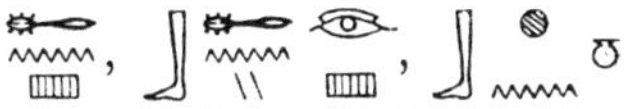 , , a kind of stone from Wâdî Ḥammâmât, basalt, diorite; plur. [illegible], Rec. 20, 41.

bekhen-t  , Thes. 1286, [illegible] [illegible], IV, 167, [illegible] [illegible], gate-house, pylon; plur. , Berl. 7262; [illegible], Rec. 8, 9, [illegible], Rec. 20, 40, [illegible], the two towers of a pylon; [illegible], IV, 365, two great towers.

bekhnu , Rec. 20, 85, a fortified town; plur. [illegible], Rec. 19, 16.

Bekhen , B.D. 165, 1, a proper name (?)

bekhes 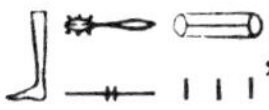, bread, cakes.

bes , A.Z. 1908, 17, an amulet.

bes , T. 321, P. 398, M. 568, N. 1175, to flame up, to be hot.

besit , flame, fire, blaze.

bes , flame, fire, blaze; plur. , L.D. III, 140c.

Besu-en-setch-t , B.D. 125, III, 23, the fire of the 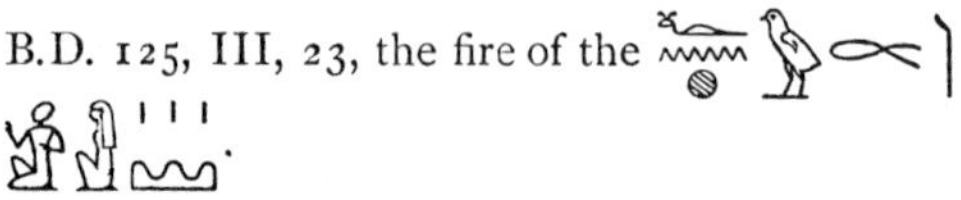.

Besi , Ṭuat X, god of the fire-stick and maker of fire.

Besi, Ṭuat I, a singing ape-god.

Besit 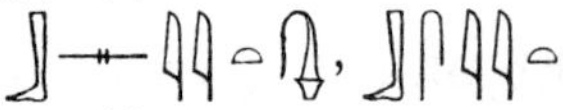, Ṭuat I, a serpent fire-goddess.

Besu-Menu , B.D. 125, III, 35; see **Besu-Aḥu.**

bes , instructor, teacher, schoolmaster; see .

besu 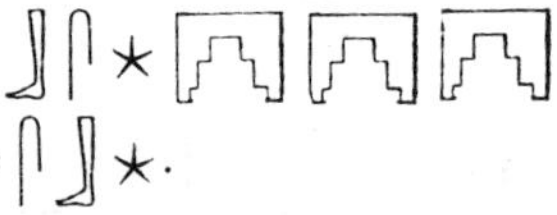, P. 797, doors; see.

bes, besi 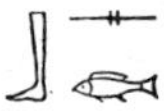, Rec. 31, 162, 171, 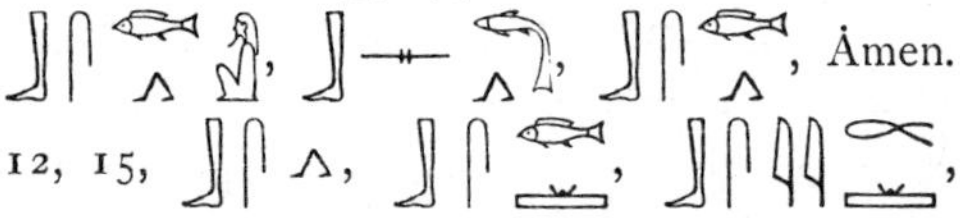, Ȧmen. 12, 15, 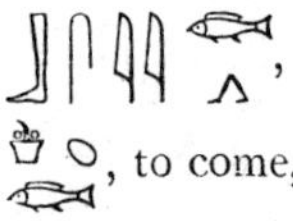, Anastasi I, 26, 4, 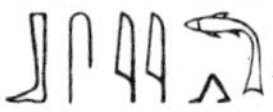, to come, to come on, to advance, to progress, to rise (of the Nile), to grow up, to swell, to lead a force against a town, to enter upon [the study of literature]; 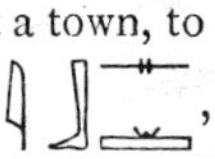, P. 215; Copt. ⲟⲩⲓⲥⲓ.

bess , Peasant 211, Rec. 18, 183, , IV, 505, Love Songs 7, 6, to advance, to rise, to pass on, to pass up.

bes 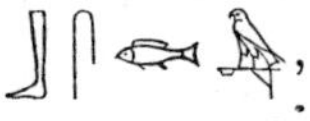, IV, 157, to induct a priest.

bes-t, bes-tu 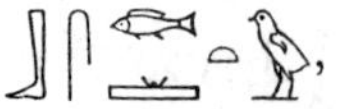, induction (of a king); , advanced (in years), swollen (of a river) passage.

bestuu (?) , N. 754 . . . . .

bes , IV, 159, Thes. 1282, 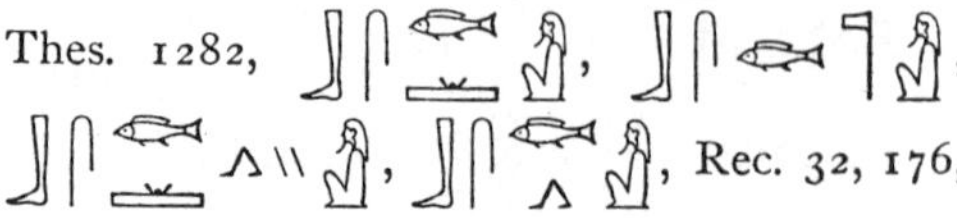, Rec. 32, 176, form, figure, body, statue, a visible image of a god, a re-incarnation (?); plur. .

Besi 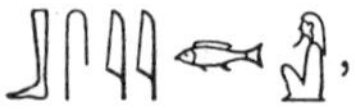, a hawk-god, one of the 75 forms of Rā (No. 68).

Besu-Aḥu (?) , B.D. 125, III, 35, a magical name of the right foot of the deceased.

Bes-ȧru , a title of Rā.

Bes-t-ȧru-ānkhit-kheperu , the name of the IXth division of the Ṭuat.

Besi-ā , Nav. Lit. 30, the name of a form of Rā.

Besi-em-ḥe-t-kauit 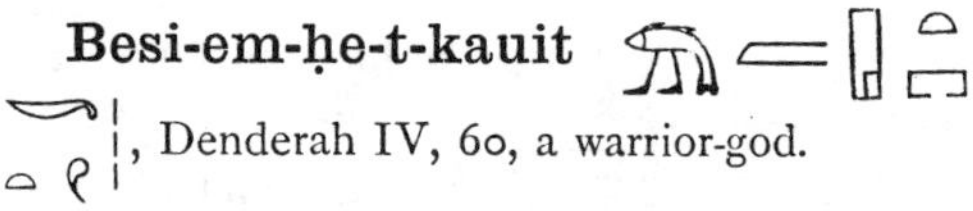, Denderah IV, 60, a warrior-god.

Besi-neḥeḥ , "advancer [through] eternity," a title of Rā and of other gods.

Besi-sāḥu 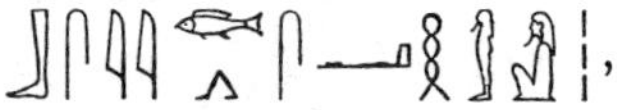, Nav. Lit. 68, a title of Rā.

besit 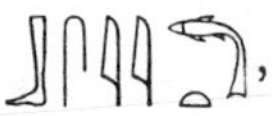, a swelling in the body, boil, pustule, abscess.

bes 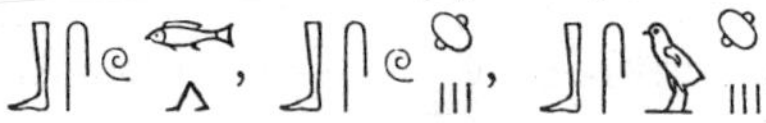, a disease of some kind which is accompanied by boils or sores, or swellings.

bess , foetid matter, pus, humours, excretions.

bes 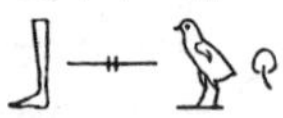, a part of the body, mucous membrane (?)

bes , Rec. 24, 163, unguent vase, oil bottle; , , the oil bottle used in the ceremony of "opening the mouth."

bes , pomegranates.

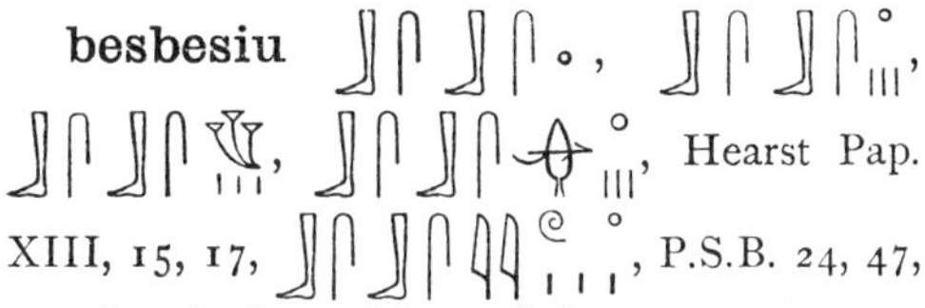

besbesiu , , , , Hearst Pap. XIII, 15, 17, , P.S.B. 24, 47, a seed or herb used in medicine.

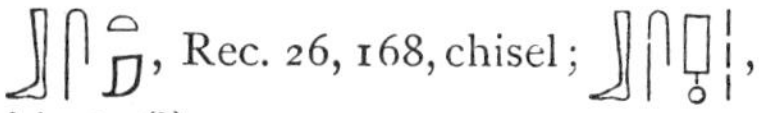

bes-t , Rec. 26, 168, chisel; , chiselled objects (?)

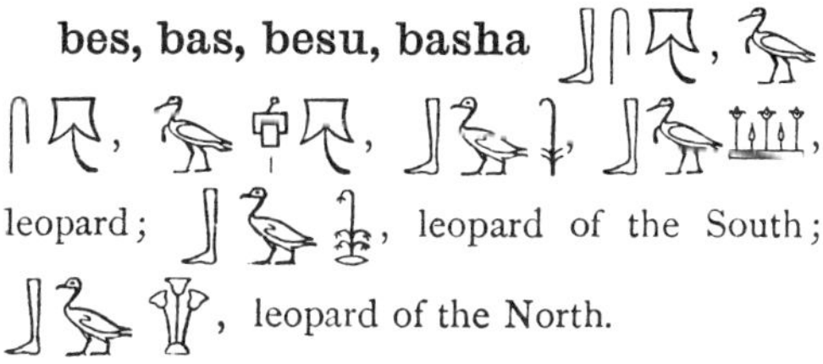

bes, bas, besu, basha , , , , , leopard; , leopard of the South; , leopard of the North.

bes-t , female leopard.

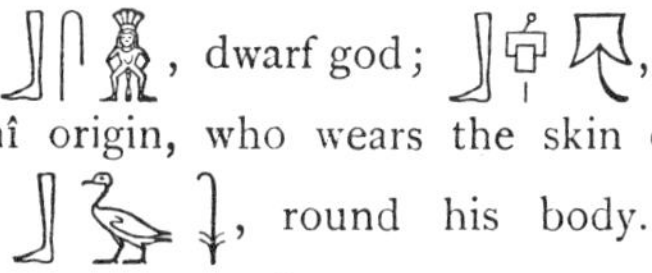

Bes , dwarf god; , a god of Sûdânî origin, who wears the skin of the leopard, , round his body. He was the god of:—(1) music, dancing, and pleasure; (2) war and slaughter; (3) childbirth and children. In late times he was symbolic of the destructive and regenerative powers of nature, and was the lord of all typhonic creatures; Copt. ⲂⲎⲤ.

besbes , a kind of goose.

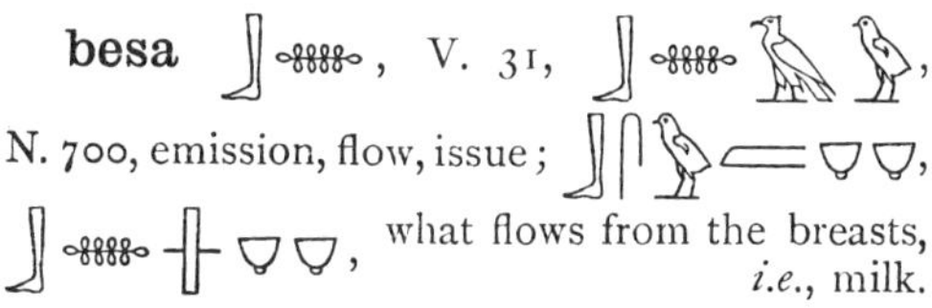

besa , V. 31, , N. 700, emission, flow, issue; , , what flows from the breasts, *i.e.*, milk.

besa , back, loins.

besa , , , a short tunic, waistcloth, loin band.

Besa , Ṭuat II, a corn-god.

besb[es] (?) , Rec. 30, 188 . . . .

besn 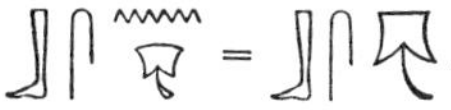.

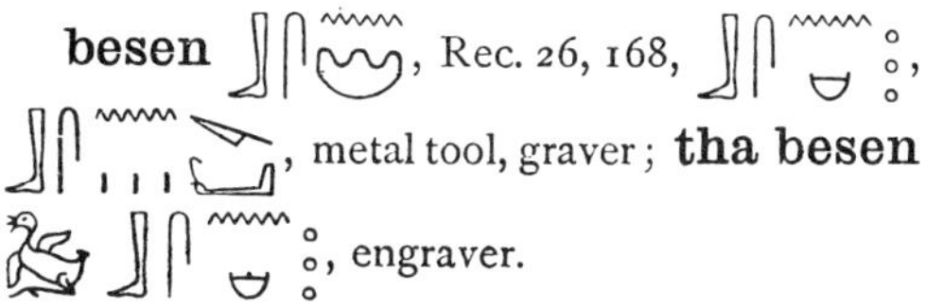

besen , Rec. 26, 168, , , metal tool, graver; **tha besen** , engraver.

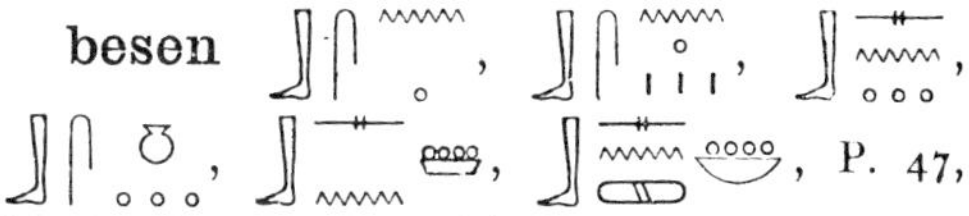

besen , , , , , , P. 47, M. 64, N. 33, 504, a kind of seed, some substance burnt at the inauguration of a temple.

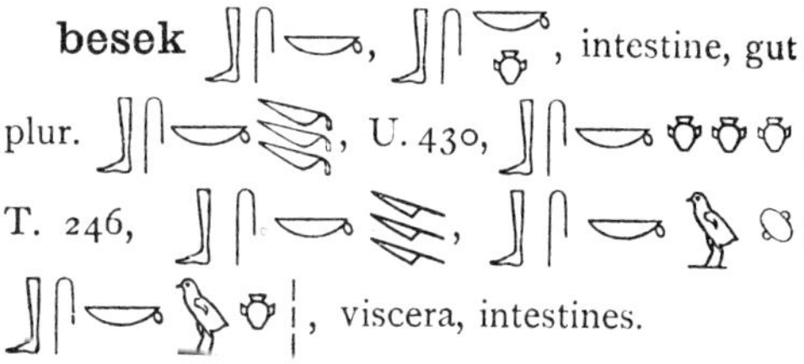

besek , , intestine, gut; plur. , U. 430, , T. 246, , ; , viscera, intestines.

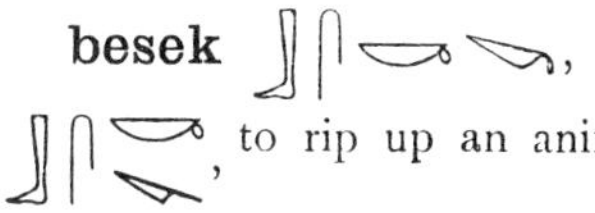

besek , P. 540, U. 527, , to rip up an animal, to cut out the intestines, to gut.

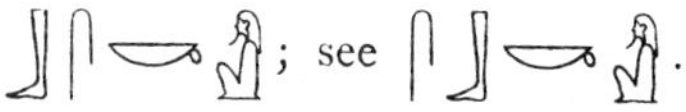

Besek ; see .

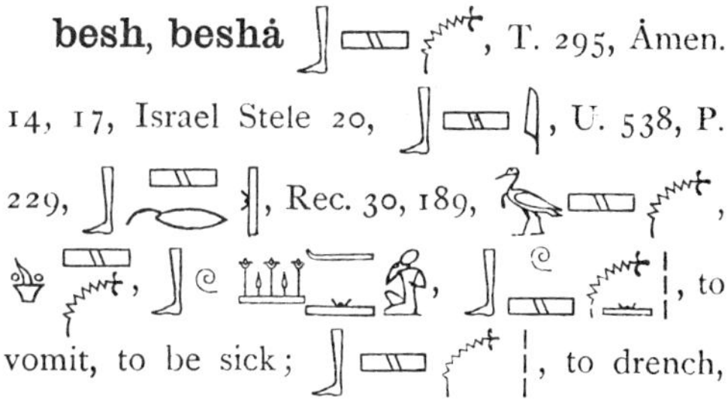

besh, beshȧ , T. 295, Ȧmen. 14, 17, Israel Stele 20, , U. 538, P. 229, , Rec. 30, 189, , , , , to vomit, to be sick; , to drench, to be drenched.

besh-t 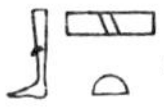, U. 148, T. 119, N. 456.

beshu , spittle, excessive saliva, vomit.

beshsh , P. 661, 775, .

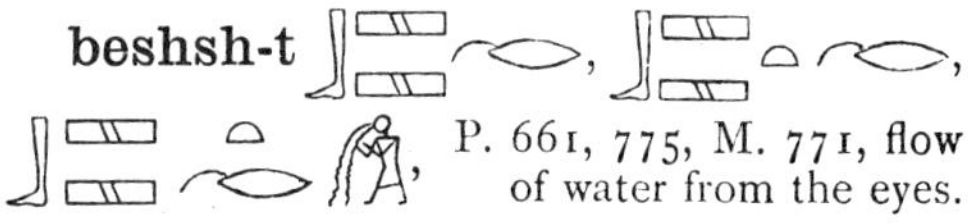

beshsh-t , , , P. 661, 775, M. 771, flow of water from the eyes.

besh , dust; Copt. ⲟⲉⲓϣ (?)

beshsh , , sticks of incense.

beshu (?) , B.D. 108, 5 metal scales or plates.

besh 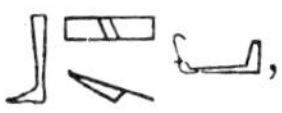, Annales V, 34, to slay, to kill.

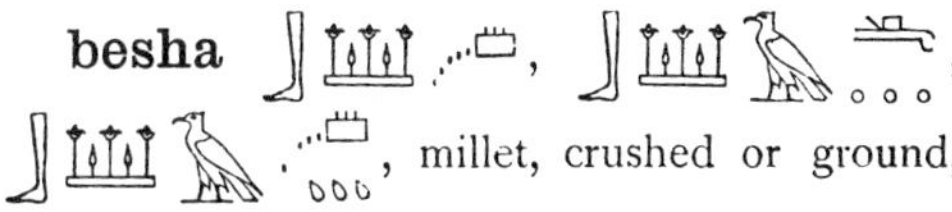

besha , , , millet, crushed or ground, millet flour, dhurra for making beer.

besht 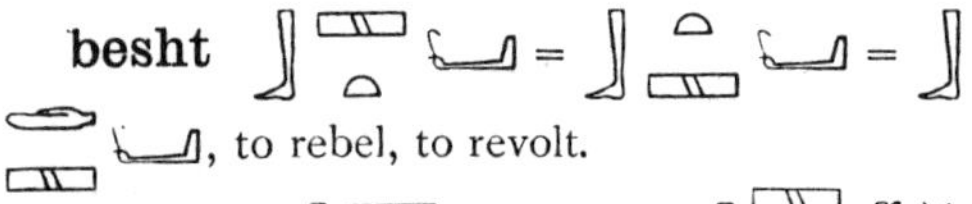, to rebel, to revolt.

besht-t 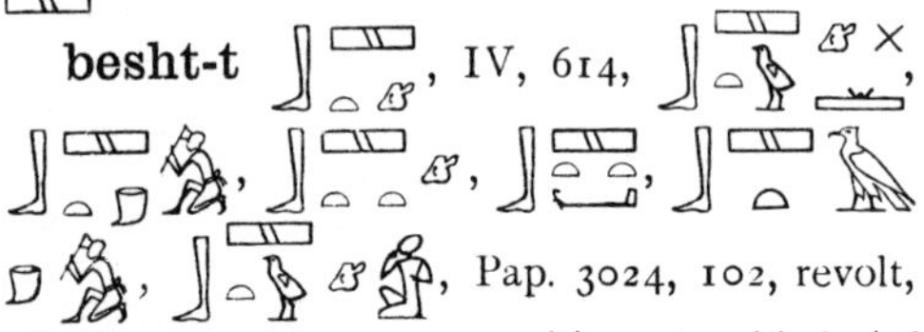, IV, 614, Pap. 3024, 102, revolt, rebellion, resistance, opposition, troubled (of water).

beshtiu 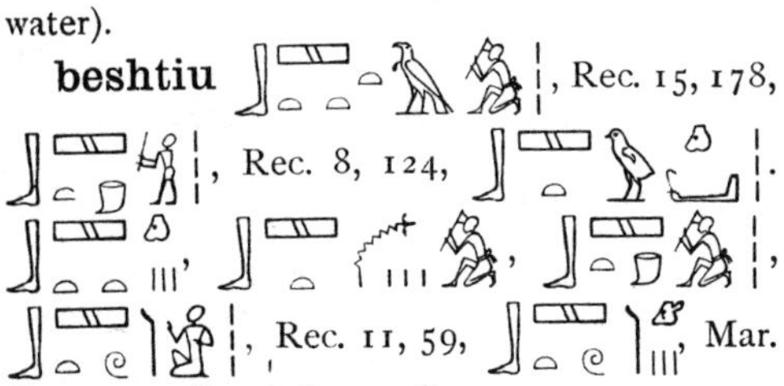, Rec. 15, 178, Rec. 8, 124, Rec. 11, 59, Mar. Karn. 52, 18, rebels, revolters.

beshth 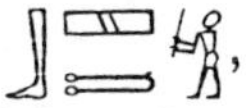, to revolt, to rebel.

besht̩ 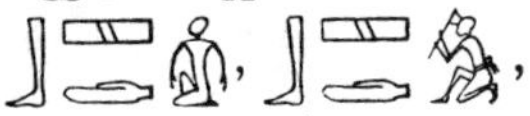, to revolt, to rebel.

besht̩u , rebels; see

beq 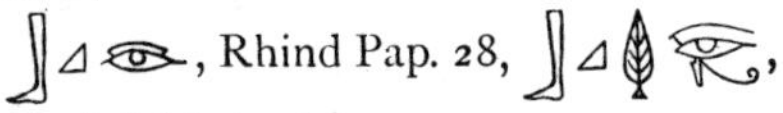, Rhind Pap. 28, to see, to be bright, to shine.

beq 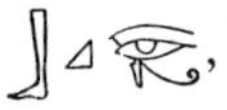, the shining, or bright, Eye of Horus.

beq-t , heaven, sky.

Beq , Ṭuat XII, a dawn-god, who towed Af through the serpent Ānkh-neteru, and was reborn daily.

Beq , B.D. 145, 10, 74, a god.

Beq , B.D. 146 (Saïte), the door-keeper of the 3rd Pylon.

beq-t , olive tree.

beq , IV, 688, olive oil, unguent compounded of olive oil.

beq-t , Ebers Pap. 90, 7.

beq uatch 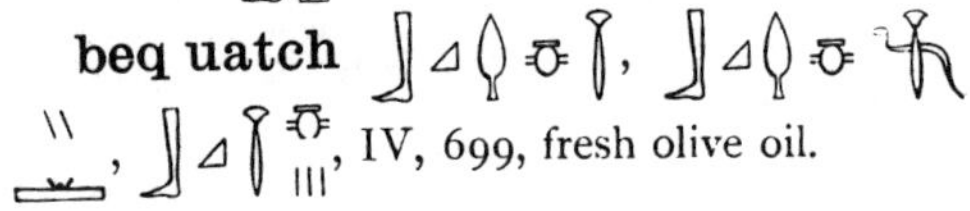, IV, 699, fresh olive oil.

beq netchem , IV, 699, sweet olive oil.

beq t̩esher , red olive oil, *i.e.*, old olive oil (?)

beq ḥa-t 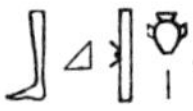, "oily-hearted," to be deceitful, to flatter, to be insincere.

beq 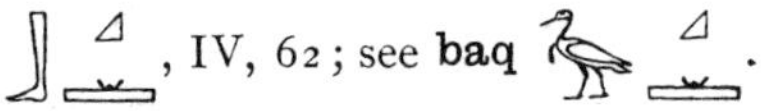, IV, 62; see **baq** .

beq , chief, overseer.

beq , Metternich Stele 7, to cry out.

beq 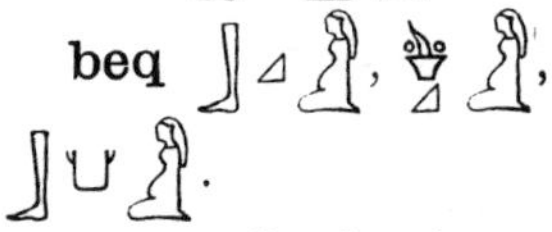, to be with child; see .

beqa , to shine, to be bright, to flourish.

beqa , light, sunrise, shimmer.

beqi , to flow, to descend.

beqbeq 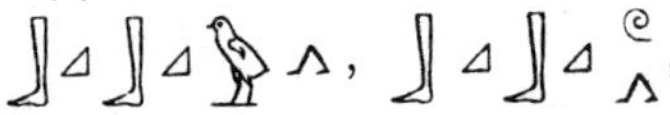, to pour out, to flow; compare Heb. √בקק.

beqen 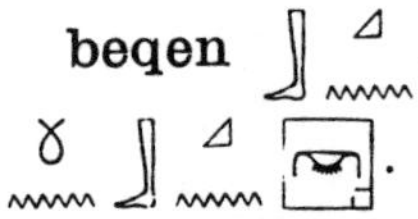, IV, 640, a kind of altar, .

beqenqen , an object carried in a procession.

beqen , a kind of plant.

beqenu , warrior, armed soldier.

beqer 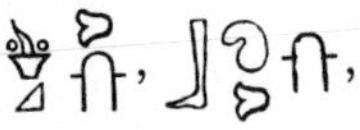, steps, stairs, stair-way.

beqes , a Nubian precious stone.

beqs-t 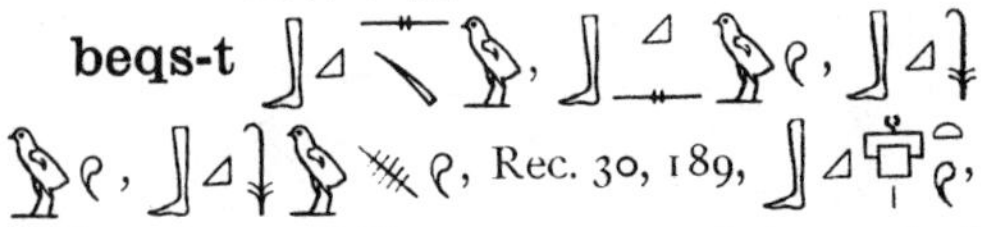, Rec. 30, 189, A.Z. 1900, 20, B.D. 31, 4, 133, 4, lower part of the body, tail, bowels, belly; plur. 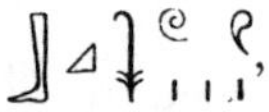, Ebers Pap. 65, 10, 16, , Rec. 26, 230; , "eye in his belly," a god; , Rec. 30, 68.

beqsu , U. 310, , U. 320, armlet (?); plur. , U. 517.

beqsu (?) N. 159, a part of a grasshopper, .

beqsu , B.D. 149, I, 5, scales, balance.

Beqtui (?) , the name of a god.

bek , , U. 362, hawk; see ; Copt. ⲂⲎϬ.

Beku , U. 570, N. 752, hawk-gods.

Bekut , U. 209, hawk-goddesses.

bek = , to work, to labour.

bek , Rec. 12, 36, ladder, steps, tribune = .

bek-t , the morning sky.

beka , , to shine, to illumine, to be bright; compare Heb. √בקר.

bekau , , light, radiance, splendour.

beka , , morning, to-morrow morning; compare Heb. בֹּקֶר; , P. 618, 619, N. 1303, T. 229, 230, yesterday.

beka-t , morning, morning light, light of dawn, as opposed to , darkness, night; compare Heb. בֹּקֶר.

bekau (?) , T. 230, , M. 690 . . . . . .

beka , Mar. Karn. 44, 42, Annales V, 95, , to bulge out, to swell (of the belly of a pregnant woman); Copt. ⲂⲞⲔⲒ.

beka-t , Rec. 27, 56, , , a pregnant woman; , a cow with young.

beka-ti , the breasts when swollen with milk.

Beka-t , , , , , , the name of one of the Dekans; Gr. ΒΙΚΩΤ.

beka , weak, feeble = , B.D. 32, 9.

beker , steps, stairs.

beg , , Rec. 30, 6, to see, to shine, to be splendid.

beg , , , , , , , to be exhausted, weak, feeble, destitute of strength, helpless, helpless one, tired, weary.

begg , to be helpless, do nothing, be inert.

beg-t , chamber of a sick person.

begi , IV, 1156, , Ȧmen. 4, 10, , , , , , the weak, the helpless, the inert.

begaȧu , place of helplessness, the grave.

beg , to cry out.

bega , , , moan, cry, weeping, lamentation, sighing, groaning.

begau , Peasant 138, shipwrecked man; Copt. ⲂⲒϪⲒ.

bega , a kind of fish; var. .

begarthȧt , Israel Stele 11, cave; compare Heb. מְעָרָה.

begas , feeble, weak, little, diminutive; plur. , B.D. 147, IV, 8.

begas-ḥa-t , Love Songs 4, 10, to be troubled in mind.

begasu , a wild animal.

begas , B.D. 38B, 4, part of a boat.

begen 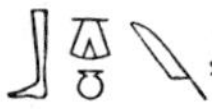, knife.

beges 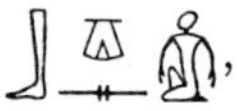, to be weak or miserable, to be in want, empty; var. .

begs-t , weakness, feebleness, helplessness; , IV, 470.

begsu , trouble, misery.

beges , neck (?) a part of the body.

begs-t 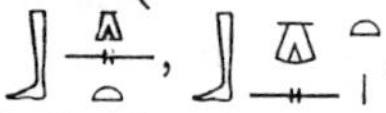, A.Z. 1908, 17, B.D. 136B, 8, necklace, collar, an amulet; var. 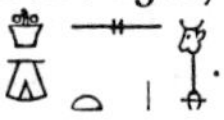.

beges , , dagger, poignard.

beges , a kind of shrub.

bet , to be an abomination, to be regarded as loathsome.

beta 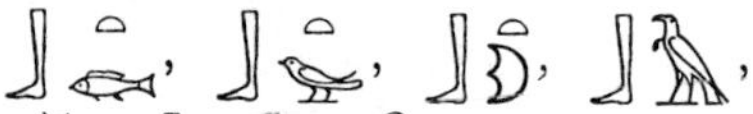, , Åmen. 4, 19, , Åmen. 11, 6, , , , evil, evil thing, iniquity, wickedness, bad, abomination, sin, fault, offence, crime; plur. , , , Israel Stele 15, , , , a great crime [worthy of] death; Copt. ⲃⲱⲧⲉ.

betau , an abominable man, a man ceremonially unclean.

betu-t tcheser-t , A.Z. 35, 16, a special abomination.

betu , a kind of fish.

bet , plant, flower.

bet , grains, seed.

bet 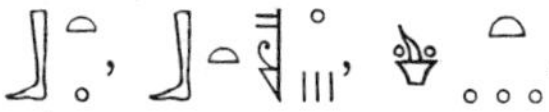, resin used in making incense.

bet (?) , house, place; Heb. בַּיִת; 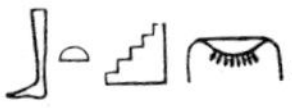, Nåstasen Stele 34, the throne of gold; , original place, the old home.

bet , shepherd, herdsman.

bet [illegible], to shine.

Bet-neters [illegible], Ṭuat XII, a dawn-goddess who towed Åf through the serpent Ānkh-neteru and was reborn daily.

betbet [illegible]; see [illegible].

betȧ [illegible] = [illegible], ore.

beti [illegible], Rec. 3, 48, a mould.

beti ḥa [illegible], Rec. 3, 52, the back of the mould.

beti ḥer [illegible], the front of the mould.

beti senu [illegible], Rec. 3, 50, the two halves of the mould.

betu [illegible], Rec. 12, 145, a sacred tablet (?)

betnu , , Rec. 1, 46, rebel, foe, fiend, enemy; plur. .

Betnu , foreign rebels.

beten ḥa-t , IV, 969, disaffected, discontented, hostile in intent, rebellious.

betnu , dog-headed apes.

betnu , swift, agile.

betḥ-t (?) 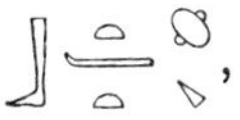, IV, 893, the tusk of an elephant.

betsh , to be faint, to be feeble, weak, or helpless; see 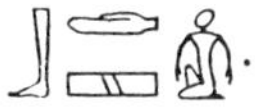.

betshu , helpless but evil-disposed beings, both men and spirits.

betek , to fall, to drop, to fail.

betektek , to fall.

betek , rebel, foe; plur. .

betek , filth, misery.

beth 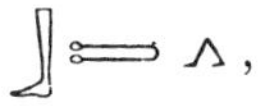, P. 41, M. 62, N. 29, to run quickly, to hasten.

bethau 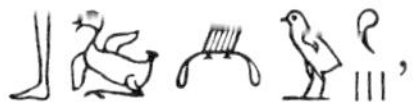, Rec. 31, 169 . . . .

bethenu , Thes. 1480, IV, 968, to be rebellious or hostile.

bethenu , foe, enemy.

bethen ḥa-t 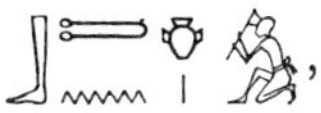, Rec. 17, 44, 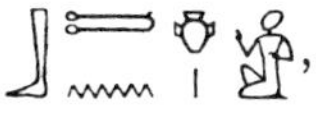, disaffected, disloyal, rebellious.

bethesh 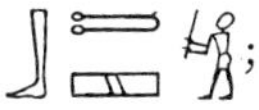; see 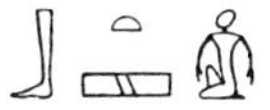 and .

beṭ-t 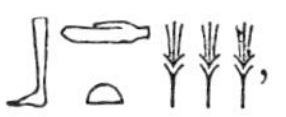, T. 289, 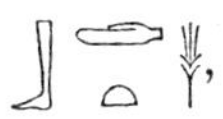, M. 66, 824, N. 119, 129, 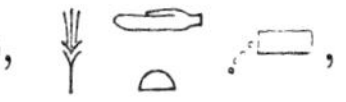, 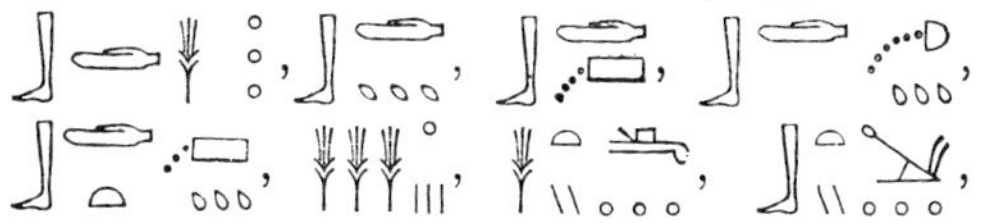, , spelt, millet, dhurra, barley; Copt. ⲃⲱⲧⲉ.

beṭ-t 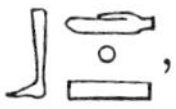, a heap of dhurra.

beṭ-t ḥetch-t , , Rec. 12, 85, white millet.

beṭ-ṭesher-t 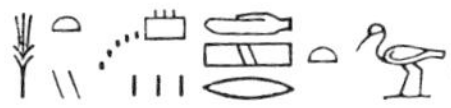, red millet.

beṭ , to burn, to burn incense; 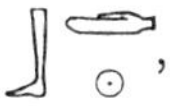, to illumine, to shine.

beṭṭ , U. 359, to smell of incense.

beṭ , U. 102, [illegible], P. 125, [illegible], [illegible], natron, saltpetre, incense; [illegible] [illegible], incense chamber.

beṭȧ [illegible], censing, one who censes.

Beṭu [illegible], P. 469, M. 533, N. 1112, beṭu incense deified.

beṭṭ-t [illegible], a kind of plant or herb used in medicine.

beṭṭka [illegible], water-melon; plur. [illegible], [illegible]; Heb. אֲבַטִּחִים, Copt. ⲃⲉⲧⲧⲕⲉ, Arab. بِطِّيخ.

Beṭ-ti [illegible], B.D. 31, 3, the opponent of the Crocodile-fiend Sui; var. (Saïte) [illegible].

Beṭbeṭ [illegible], B.D.G. 1064, a goddess.

beṭ 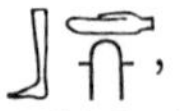, Rec. 43, 48, 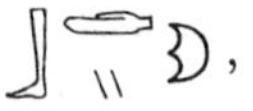, the mould in which the figure of Osiris was made at Denderah.

beṭ , Nȧstasen Stele 20, throne of gold ([illegible]) with steps.

beṭi , abominable person or thing; Copt. ⲂⲞⲦⲈ.

beṭen , B.D. (Saïte), 40, 3, , to compress, to bind.

beṭen , to tie, to bind, fillet, bandlet.

beṭen , foe, enemy, fiend, evil spirit.

beṭniu 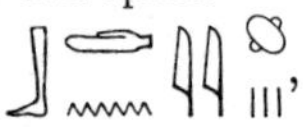, enemies, foes.

Beṭen 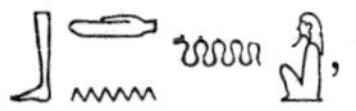, Annales, 3, 177, a star-god.

beṭesh , P. 241, to dissolve, to be dissolved, poured out like water.

Beṭshet , T. 85, , M. 239, N. 616, a god who presided over burnt offerings.

Beṭsh-āui , Rec. 30, 67, a god.

beṭsh , 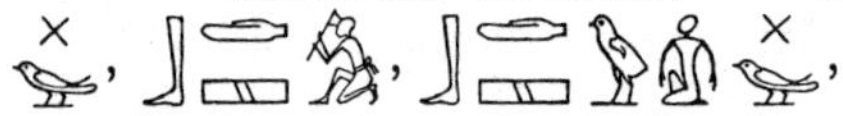, to be weak, helpless, exhausted, powerless, impotent.

beṭsh 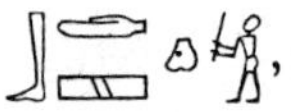, to be angry.

beṭshu, beṭshut 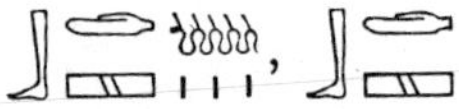, , impotent but ill-disposed beings, gods, men, fiends, etc.; , , , impotent rebels.

Beṭesh , the devil of revolt.

Beṭshu (?) , Nesi-Ȧmsu, 32, 42, a form of Āapep.

beṭek , [illegible], guide (?)

Betch , Rec. 12, 145,  , Rec. 31, 31, Annales 10, 192, A.Z. 1906, 79, , Rec. 36, 214, *i.e.*, , a bull-god.

betch , U. 418, , T. 239,  . . . .

betcha 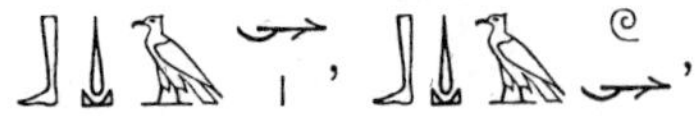, stick, staff, some wooden tool or instrument; , Rec. 30, 67, parts of a ship.

betcha , cooking pot, vessel; plur. 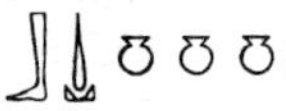; Copt. ⲂⲒⲜ.

betchen 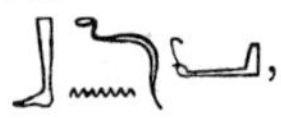, Rec. 29, 157; var. [illegible].

betchentchen , IV, 1076 . . . .

 P

p ; Heb. פ.

p, pi 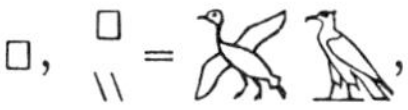, demonst. pron. masc. sing.; **p + n (pen)** 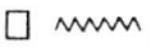, what belongs to; **p + å** , IV, 143, what is mine.

p, på 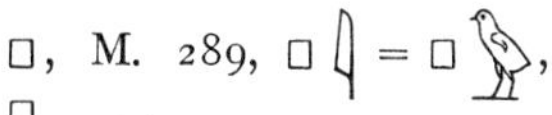, M. 289, P. 182, N. 895 = , this.

p , an article of furniture, base of a stand.

pe-t 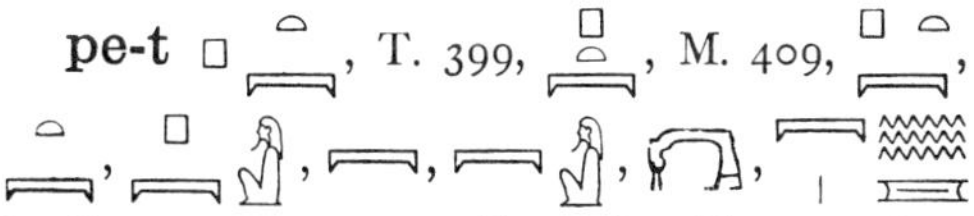, T. 399, M. 409, , the sky, heaven, Rev. 13, 2, Rev. 13, 40; plur. 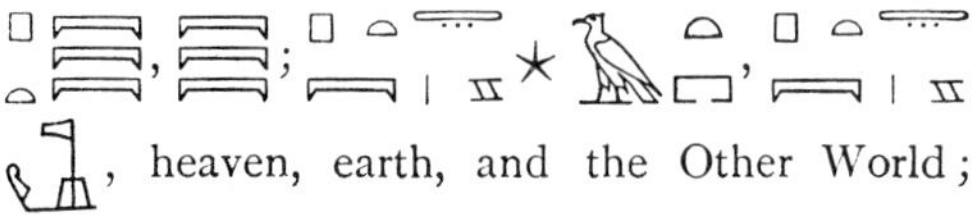, heaven, earth, and the Other World; , all heaven; Copt. ⲡⲉ.

pe-t pe-t 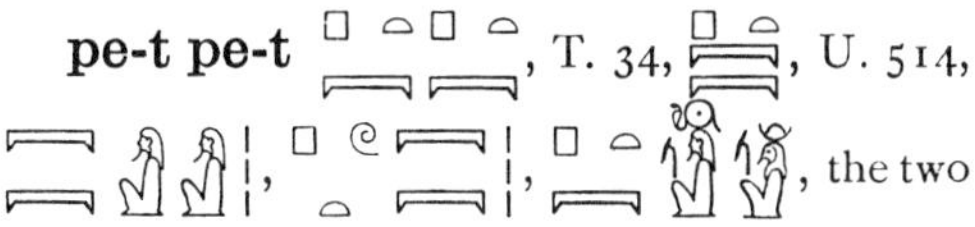, T. 34, U. 514, the two halves of heaven, the day and the night sky.

pet-ti temtå , U. 514, T. 326, the two heavens or skies.

pe-t , sky, the four quarters thereof: 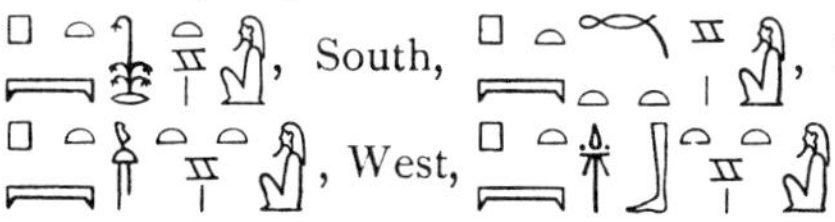, South, North, West, East.

petiu , heavenly beings.

pa , demonst. pron. sing. masc; Copt. ⲡⲁⲓ, ⲡⲏ.

pa-å , Nåstasen Stele 27, my.

P 

pai , demonst. pron. masc. sing.; Copt. ⲡⲁⲓ, ⲡⲏ. With suffixes:—

pai-å , my, mine (masc.),  (fem.); Copt. ⲡⲱⲓ.

pai-k , thy, thine (masc.); , Rev. 11, 124; Copt. ⲡⲱⲕ.

pai-t , thy, thine (fem.).

paituk , III, 143, thy.

pai-f , Åmen. 6, 3, his; Copt. ⲡⲱϥ.

pai-s 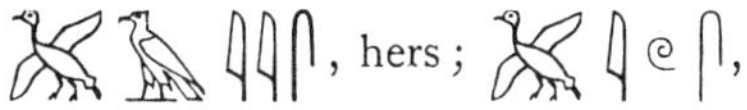, hers; Rev.; Copt. ⲡⲱⲥ.

pai-n , Rec. 26, 153, our; later Rev. 11, 141, 12, 46; Copt. ⲡⲱⲛ.

pai-ten , your; Copt. ⲡⲉⲧⲉⲛ.

pai-sen , their.

paiu 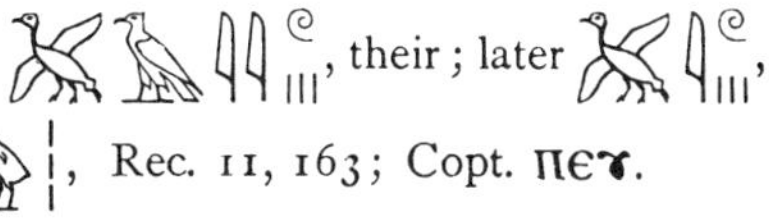, their; later Rec. 11, 163; Copt. ⲡⲉⲩ.

pau , those.

pa-un , a particle, = then, in that case.

Pa-åri-sekhi , a title of Khensu of Thebes.

Pa-åh-nersmen  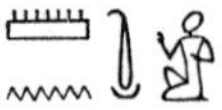, Rec. 31, 36, the owner of a town.

pa-āa-n-ursh , Rec. 21, 22, guardian; Copt. ⲡⲁⲛⲟⲩⲣϣⲉ.

Pa-ium'-t Åsår  , the port of the sacred boat of the Busirite Nome.

Pa-bār , *i.e.*, הַבַּעַל; see **Bār**.

Pa-Bekhennu , B.D. 165, 1, a title of Åmen.

Pabekht-ḥes-en-pa-ḥes  , Rec. 31, 35, a town in the Delta.

Pa-nemmå , B.D. 164, 9, a son of Rā.

pa Rā , the Sun; Copt. ⲫⲣⲏ.

pa ḥa-t , Ebers Pap. 14, 3, a kind of medicine.

pa , transcribed in the Tanis papyri by ; see **per**.

pa, pai , P. 164, M. 327, N. 858,  U. 568, N. 751,  to fly; later 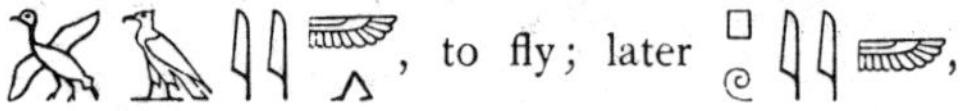, preserved in Copt. ⲡⲁⲡⲱⲓ.

pai , Rec. 12, 39 = Copt. ϭⲓⲫⲉⲓ.

pai , louse, lice; Copt. ⲡⲏⲓ.

pait , feathered fowl, birds; , Rec. 32, 67, water fowl.

pa-t , N. 952, a kind of garment, or apparel.

pa 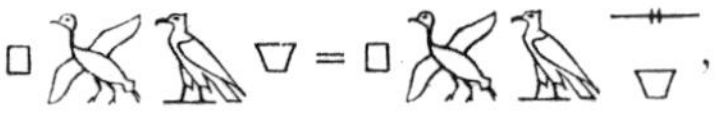, cup, pot.

pa-t , liquor, drink.

pa , to be, to exist.

paut , beings, men; women.

pau-t 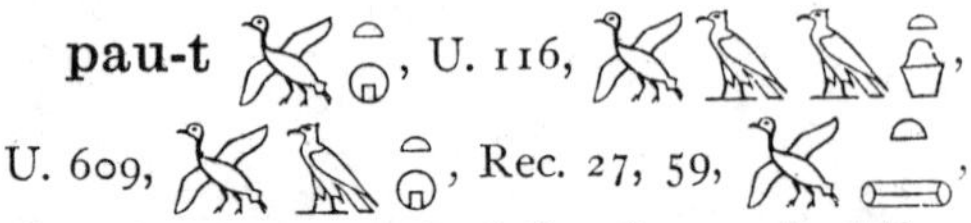 U. 116, U. 609, Rec. 27, 59, 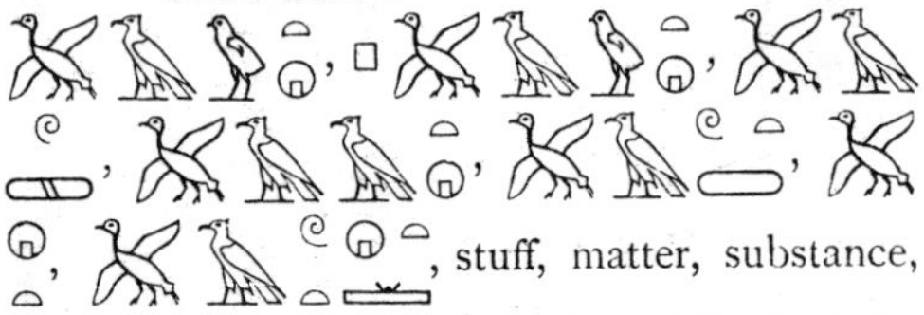, stuff, matter, substance, the matter or material of which anything is made, dough, cake, bread, offering, food, product; plur.  U. 559, Åmen. 9, 7.

pautiu , Rec. 3, 116, primeval beings (?)

pau 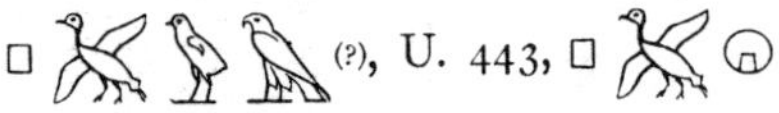 (?), U. 443,  (?), T. 253, primeval time (?)

pa-t , primeval time, remote ages; , not from the oldest time, *i.e.*, never before; , Thes. 1285, the first beginning.

paut ta , Rec. 27, 28, 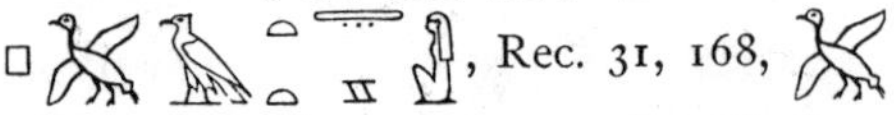 Rec. 31, 168, , primeval time, remote ages.

pauti taui (?) 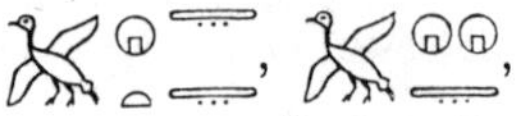, 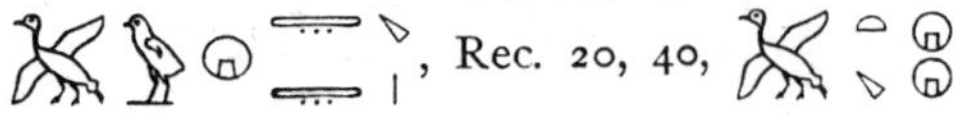 Rec. 20, 40,

, , , IV, 1168, the beginning of time, the creation, primeval time; , since the creation.

Pauti taui (?) , Rec. 32, 63, , A.Z. 1900, 31, a title of Àmen-Rā as the representative of the primeval god of Egypt.

Pau , Rec. 27, 224, the primeval god. This name perhaps means "he who is," "he who exists," "the self-existent."

Pauti , IV, 517, a title of the primeval god.

Pauti , U. 437, , T. 250, , , , B.D. 15, 10, , B.D. 79, 3, , N. 67, , P. 97, M. 67, , Berl. 2293, , , B.D. 15, 11, , B.D. 15, 7, , , Rec. 26, 77, , B.D. 85, 9, , B.D. 145, 84, , IV, 807, B.D. 39, 18, , , Rec. 27, 60, 220, 31, 167, , , , , , , , , , the primeval god, the god who created himself and all that is. The dual form of the name refers to his rule of Upper and Lower Egypt.

pa-t (paut) en neteru , N. 709, "company of the gods."

Pau-t-then-ta , Rec. 27, 221, a god.

Paā-t , P. 417, M. 597, N. 1202, a lake in the Ṭuat.

paāthaḥ (?) , a kind of cake.

paāsh , a kind of bird, pigeon (?)

paāt-t , various kinds of woods, or barks, used in medicine; see , Hearst Pap. IX, 13.

Pai , , , Ṭuat XII, Demot. Cat. 422, a god.

Pait , Metternich Stele 96, the consort of .

Pain , a lake in the Ṭuat.

pair , Nāstasen Stele 34, the river, the stream; Copt. ⲡⲓⲟⲟⲣ.

Pais , a Hittite proper name.

pait , B.D. 125, III, 30, a part of a boat.

pait = , house.

pait , , Hearst Pap. IX, 13, a kind of seed used in medicine.

paur , Rechnungen 17, 1, 12, Hearst Pap. XI, 6; , , , new wine.

pafi , , that; see .

pant , Jour. As. 1908, 265 = ⲡⲉⲛⲧ.

Panti-baf-em-khen-tchet-f 
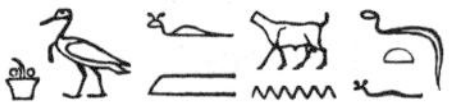, a beetle-headed throne-bearer of Harmakhis Temu.

Pannṭu (?) , Berg. II, 9, the ibis-headed guard of the 11th hour of the night.

parān , *i.e.*, , Nåstasen Stele 40, 44 = ϫⲓⲛ.

Paru , B.D. (Saïte) 162, 1, 165, 1, a Nubian god, a form of Rā.

Pariukas 
, B.D. 165, 1, a title of Åmen.

Parhaqa Kheperu 
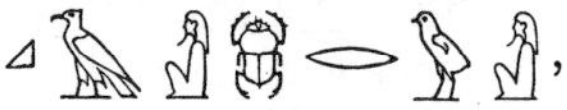, B.D. 164, 3, the consort of Sekhmit-Bast-Rā.

Parhu , IV, 324, a prince of Punt.

partha[l] , Anastasi I, 23, 4, Alt. K. 418 . . . .

parthal , iron, iron weapons; compare Heb. בַּרְזֶל.

pahu , to-day; Copt. ⲡⲟⲟⲩ.

paḫrer 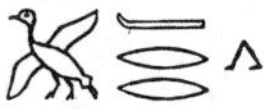, to run, to revolve, to circle; see [illegible].

pakh [illegible], U. 551, to attack.

pakh , a kind of herb.

Pakhit ,
[illegible], Rec. 26, 229, a cat-goddess, or a lion-goddess. The chief seat of her cult was at Beni Hasan in a sanctuary now called the Speos Artemidos.

pakhar 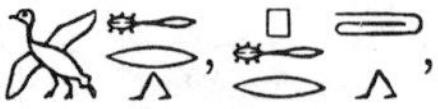, to go about, to run.

Pakhenmet 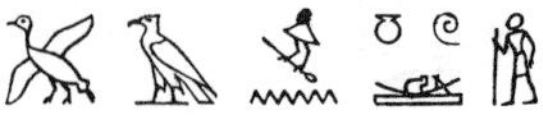
, A.Z. 1901, 129 . . . . .

pakhst-t 
, a kind of plant or vegetable.

Pakhet , Ṭuat III, a mythological boat with ends in the form of lions' heads.

pakheṭ 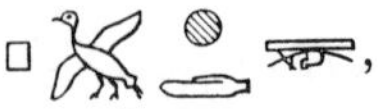, T. 314, to overturn, to capsize, to be upset or overturned.

pas , the name of the object [illegible].

pas 
, Rec. 26, 228, the little pot for water attached to a painter's palette.

pasa 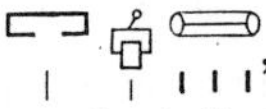, cakes, loaves.

pasasa , Edict 15,
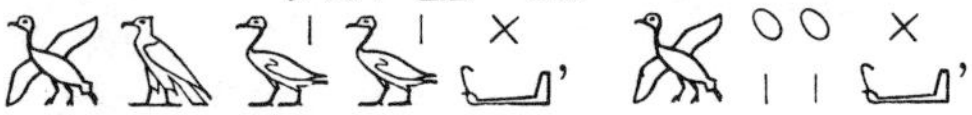, Rec. 1885, 43, 15, toil (?) labour (?)

pasef , U. 109, N. 418, to bake, to cook; see [illegible].

pasen 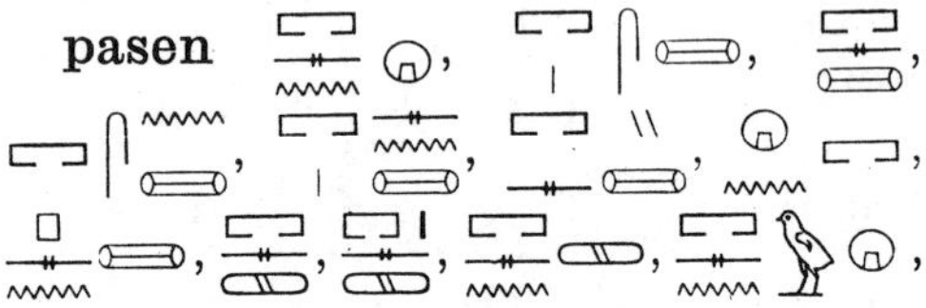
cake, loaf; plur. [illegible].

Paseru , B.D. (Saïte) 165, 1, a title of Rā or Åmen.

paskh , T. 311; 
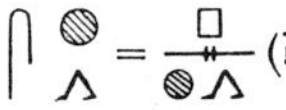 (?)

Pasetu , B.D. (Saïte) 112, 1, a god, a divine title.

Pashakasa , B.D. 164, 2, a god, son of Parhaqa-Kheperu and Sekhmit-Bast-Rā.

Pashemt-en-Ḥer 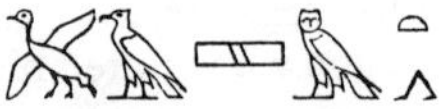
, A.Z. 1901, 129, "the passage of Horus," the name of a month.

paq, cake, loaf; plur. , P. 161, , Rec. 31, 172.

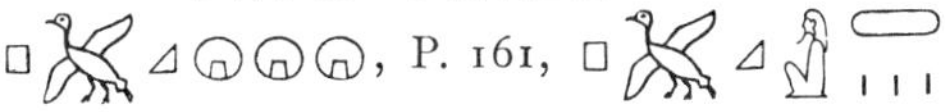

paq, Rec. 31, 162 . . . .

paq-t, N. 937, ladder.

paqit, shard, shell; 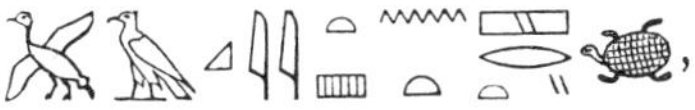 , tortoise-shell, turtle-shell.

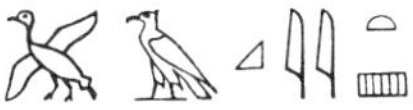

paqru, Peasant, 230, a kind of fish.

Paqrer, Dream Stele 36, "the Frog," a proper name = Copt. πεκροϒρ.

pakaka, Nȧstasen Stele, 48 = πεϮκωκ (?)

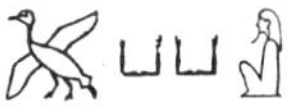

Patheth, U. 615. . . . .

Patheth, Ṭuat I, a singing ape-god.

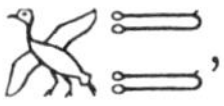

paṭ (paut), , Hh. 460, cake, loaf, bread; plur.  .

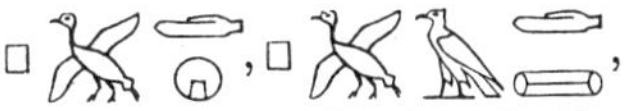

paṭ, salve, ointment.

paṭ, a kind of dove; Copt. ϵποϯ.

paṭ, foot; Copt. πατ, φατ; see  .

paṭ, , , fountain.

paṭenu, Ḥerusȧtef Stele 52, a metal vessel.

patch, U. 486, , P. 168, , , U. 450, , , , matter, substance, ball or tablet or cake of incense, cake of bread, a fruit (?); plur. , Rec. 31, 28; , Hh. 341.

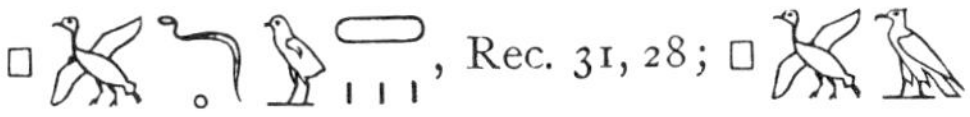

pȧ, U. 190, 195, P. 610, a demonstrative pron. = , ; , U. 190, 520 = , T. 70, 329.

pȧpȧ, Ȧmen. 12, 16, , Rec. 26, 47, to make bricks; Copt. παπϵ, φαφϵ.

pȧpȧ-t, part of a ship.

Pȧn, Ṭuat II, a god.

pȧs-t, cake, loaf.

pȧt, Rec. 30, 201, cake.

pȧt, , he who; Copt. πετ.

pȧtha (?), Ȧmen. 24, 9, moulder, smiter (?)

pā, ancestor.

pāit, a mortal man; plur. , ; , the face of a man, a human face.

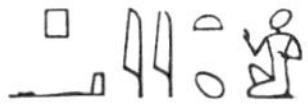

pā-t, U. 480, P. 216, T. 375, , P. 166, , N. 142, , Sphinx III, 129, IV, 1045, , , , , , , , , , men and women, mortals, mankind, people, a class of people or spirits.

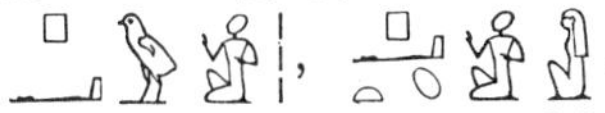

Pāt, Denderah III, 77, a group of beings in the Ṭuat.

pāpā, Rec. 36, 79, , , , , to bring forth, to bear, to give birth to; , born of.

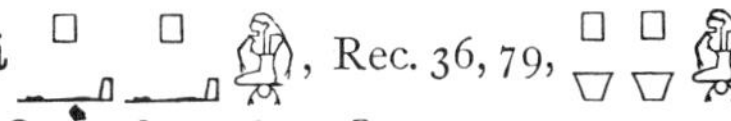

Pāpā[it] , Denderah, I, 6, a birth-goddess.

pā , flame, fire, spark; plur. [illegible].

pāpā , [illegible], [illegible]. to shine, to illumine.

pā-t , L.D. III, 229c, , Rec. 14, 166, a kind of farm land.

pā-t , Rec. 31, 169, a knife.

pā-t 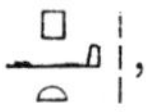, furniture, seats (?) chairs (?)

pāpāit 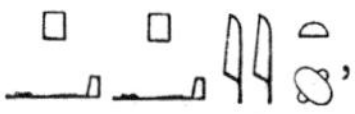, a kind of grain or seed with a pungent odour or taste.

pān , M. 127 . . . . (play on the name Rapān , the chief of the gods).

Pānȧri , Ṭuat IX, a god.

P-ānkhi , Ṭuat X, a form of Kheperȧ.

Pāhāaref 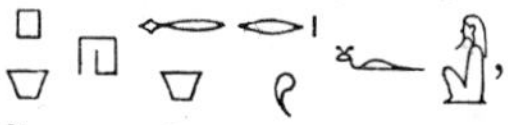, Rev. 11, 184, a god; Copt. ⲡⲁϩⲟ ⲣⲟϥ.

pāt 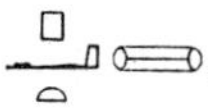, 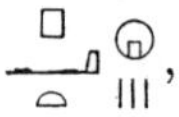, loaf, bread, food.

pāt , dove; Copt. ⲉⲡⲟϯ; var. [illegible].

pāṭ-t , dove; see [illegible], and [illegible].

pātch 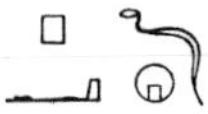, [illegible], a circular object, disk, cake, round tablet, loaf.

pi , Rec. 15, 175 = ⲡⲉ.

pi 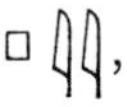, belonging to :—[illegible], Nás-tasen Stele 44, my; [illegible], his; [illegible], her; [illegible], thy.

pi, pi-t 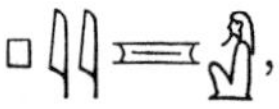, Rev. 11, 141, [illegible], Rev. 13, 31, heaven; see [illegible].

Pit 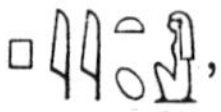, Lib. Fun. II, 87, goddess of the town of Pu, , Buto.

pi 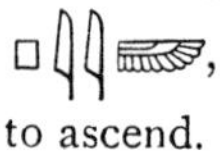, [illegible], [illegible], [illegible], to fly, to ascend.

piu (?) , Rec. 27, 86, birds.

pip 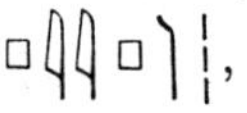, Rec. 10, 150, foreign dancing-women.

pi , flea; Copt. ⲡⲏⲓ, ⲫⲉⲓ; plur. [illegible].

pi-t 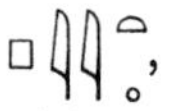, pill, globule.

pif , IV, 141, his.

pinaks , [illegible], Rev. 14, 36, tablet; Gr. πίναξ.

Pi-neter-ṭuau 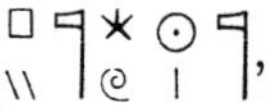, Lanzone, 20, the god of the planet Venus; he had a man's head and a hawk's head.

pir 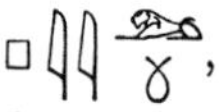, [illegible], Rec. 4, 22, 24, cloth of flax, a strip of linen, bandage, bandlet, linen cloth of all kinds; [illegible], threads of flax; see [illegible].

pis , her, hers.

pituk , Nástasen Stele 45, thy.

pu , [illegible], a demonstrative particle (masc.). = [illegible], a weakened form of [illegible], sing. fem. [illegible] and [illegible]; plur. [illegible], fem. [illegible]; dual [illegible], fem. [illegible], [illegible], [illegible].

pu 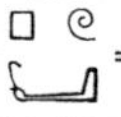 = [illegible], to make bricks; Copt. ⲡⲁⲡⲉ, ⲫⲁⲫⲉ.

pu-ti 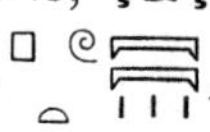, A.Z. 1900, 27, the heavens.

puȧa , cake, loaf; plur. [illegible], Rec. 32, 181, [illegible], Rec. 32, 183.

pui , [illegible], [illegible], [illegible], [illegible], [illegible], a demonstrative particle, a weakened form of

pui , to fly; see .

pui , Åmen. 10, 5, 13, 8, 22, 22, to fly.

pui , birds, feathered fowl.

puiu 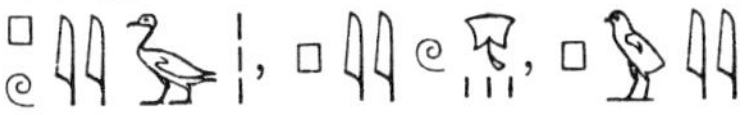
, fleas.

pup , Rec. 26, 47, , to mould, to make; 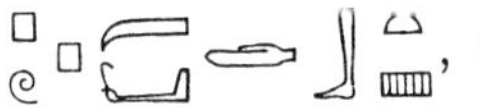, to make bricks; Copt. ⲡⲁⲡⲉ, ϕⲁϕⲉ.

punen , Rec. 8, 76 . . . .

pur, purå , beans, peas; Heb. פול, Arab. فول.

purš h 
, to separate, to divide, to split; compare Heb. √פרש, Copt. ⲡⲱⲣϣ.

pus , ink jar; see .

pusa 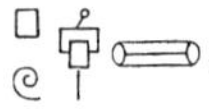, a cake, a kind of bread.

pusasa , Anastasi IV, 14, 10, to divide, to separate, to distribute, division.

puga , stick, staff, a piece of wood; plur. .

puga 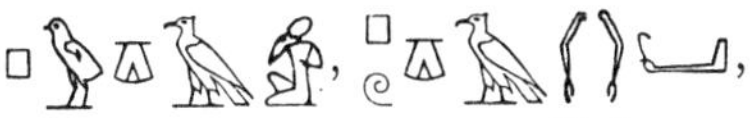, to divide, to open, to be opened; see .

puga , a measure for honey equal to one quarter of a hin.

puga , Love Songs 1, 8, camping ground, encampment, camp, compound.

puga 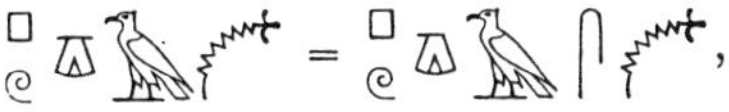, to spit.

pugas , Åmen. 10, 20, 23, 16, to spit; see 

put 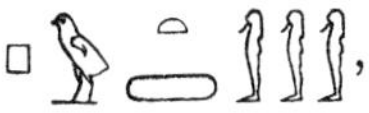, a name for the dead.

Putukhipa , Treaty 38, a princess of the Kheta.

putrå , Leyd. Pap. 3, 7, 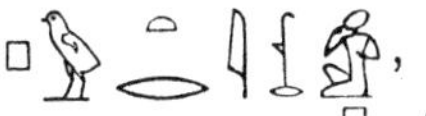, B.D. 17, what? The later form is **peti** . This word is connected with , to see, and means probably, "make to see," "demonstrate," as in , "explain now what this is (or, means)."

putchu , a chair of office or of state.

Pebaf , Ṭuat III, a god with horns on his head.

p-b-maāi (?) , Rhind Pap. 12 . . . .

pep 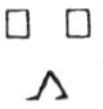, to go, to march.

pep 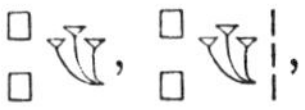, a plant or herb used in medicine, pepper (?)

pepå , boat.

pepi, pip , to make bricks; see **pup** [illegible].

P-pesṭit-neteru [illegible], a name of Hathor.

pef [illegible], a demonst. particle, that; fem. [illegible]; plur. [illegible]. In the Pyramid Texts it is sometimes placed before the substantive, *e.g.*, [illegible], P. 615, M. 783, N. 1143; and see P. 674, etc.

pfa [illegible]
[illegible], that.

pefi [illegible]
[illegible], that.

Pefi [illegible], that damned one, *i.e.*, Āapep.

pef-qa-ḥer [illegible], a title of honour.

pefes, Berl. 7272, to boil or roast, to cook; Copt. ⲡⲓⲥⲉ, ⲡⲉⲥ.

pefs genn, Amherst Pap. 34, oil-boiler.

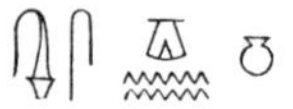

pefss, B.D. 172, 34, to roast, to cook; Copt. ⲡⲓⲥⲉ.

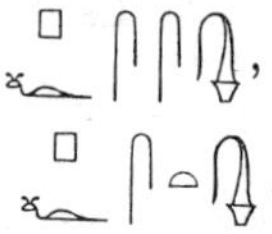

pefs-t, a roasting, cooked food.

pefsit, something roasted, cooked food.

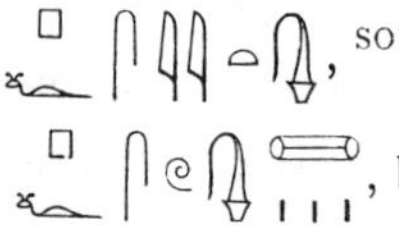

pefsu, baked cakes.

Pefset-ākhu-f, B.D. 145A (Nav. II, 156), a god.

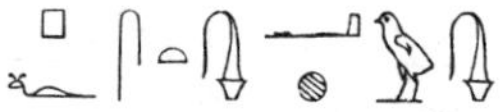

pen, a demonst. particle, this; fem. 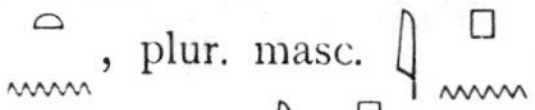 , plur. masc. , fem. , dual masc. , fem. 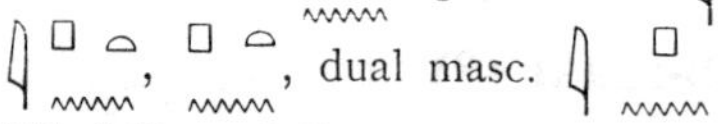 . **Pen** usually follows the substantive, but in the Pyramid Texts it is sometimes placed before it, *e.g.*,  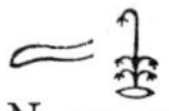 "on this south side," P. 615, M. 783, N. 1142; see also U. 580, etc.

pen, peni, this, as opposed to 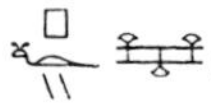 , that.

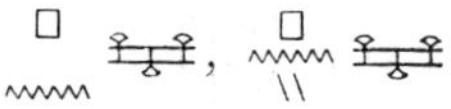

penn, U. 253, a demonst. particle, this; see

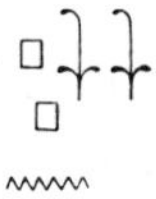

pen, penn, Ebers Pap. 60, 11, to overthrow, to thrust together; Copt. ⲡⲱⲱⲛⲉ.

Pen, B.D. 98, 6, a god; Saïte var. 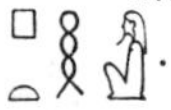 .

penpen, Chab. Mél. II, 262, a kind of stuff or garment.

peni, B.D. 149, III, 3 . . . .

penu, mouse; plur.  , Berl. 6910; Copt. ⲡⲓⲛ.

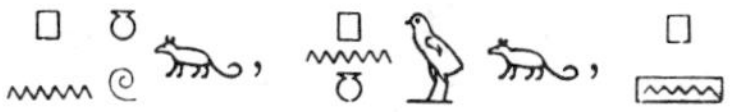

Penu, B.D. 33, 2, a mythological mouse or rat.

penu, ratsbane.

penu, Tombos Stele 5 . . . .

penpen, a kind of fish.

Penȧp-t, A.Z. 1901, 129, 1906, 137, the month Paopi; Copt. ⲡⲁⲁⲡⲉ, ⲡⲉⲟⲡⲓ.

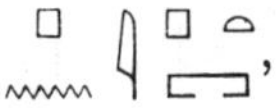

Pen-Ȧmen-ḥetep, A.Z. 1901, 129, 1906, 137, the original form of the name of the month Phamenoth; Copt. ⲡⲁⲣⲙϩⲁⲧ, ⲡⲁⲣⲉⲙϩⲁⲧⲡ, ⲫⲁⲙⲉⲛⲱⲑ.

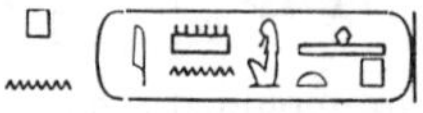

Pen-ȧnt, A.Z. 1906, 137, the original form of the name of the month Paoni; Copt. ⲡⲁⲱⲛⲓ.

penā, to overthrow, to overturn, to capsize, to reverse; Copt. ⲡⲱⲱⲛⲉ.

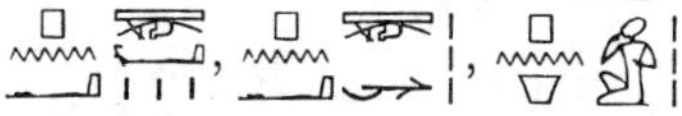

penā, Peasant 112, the going back of a crop of grapes; 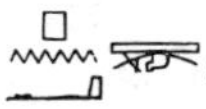 , Rec. 27, 85; to balance the tongue, 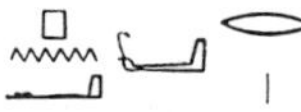 , P.S.B. 10, 49.

penā-t, Ȧmen. 3, 14,  , overthrow.

Penā-t, Ṭuat III, a mythological boat.

penāit, a portion of a river with rocks in it.

P-neb-taui, Morgan, Ombos 156, 181, a god, son of Ḥeru-ur and Tasent-nefer-t.

P-nefer-nehem, a form of Horus.

P-nefer-enti-nehem, a form of Horus.

Penramu, a group of gods.

Penrent , A.Z. 1906, 137, the original form of the name of the month Pharmuthi; Copt. ⲫⲁⲣⲙⲟⲩⲑⲓ, ⲫⲁⲣⲙⲟⲩⲧⲉ, ⲫⲁⲣⲙϩⲟⲧⲓ, ⲫⲁⲣⲙⲟⲑⲓ.

penreḥer (?) , a measure (?)

Penhuba  , Nav. Lit. 29, a name of Rā.

Pen-ḥesb (?) , B.D. 189, 15, 17, etc., a god of offerings.

Penn-Khenti-Ȧmenti  , Cairo Pap. III, 3, a serpent-headed god of the Mesqet.

pens 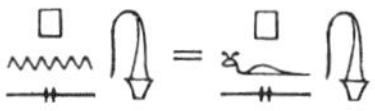 (?) to burn, to roast, to cook.

pensu , Rec. 9, 93, joint of meat.

pens-t, pensit 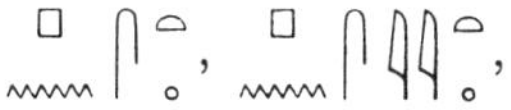, pill, globule, bolus.

pens , a kind of ground.

pens 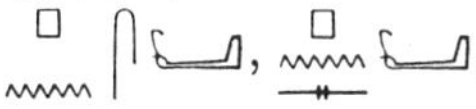, to eradicate.

Pensu-ta (?) , , B.D. 62, 4 . . . .

pensa 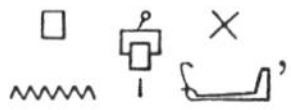, Anastasi IV, 2, 10, 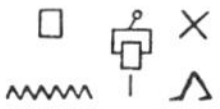, Koller Pap. 2, 8, to cut off.

pensa 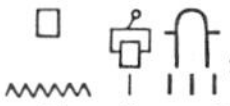, fans for the kitchen fire.

pensh 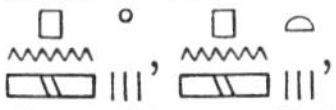, Ebers Pap. 65, 4, a kind of seed used in medicine, juniper berries? compare Heb. בְּרוֹשׁ.

ponq 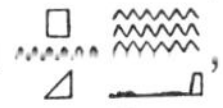, Peasant 278, , Peasant 220, 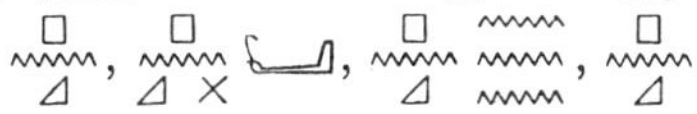 , IV, 839, B.D. 99, 21, 189, 13, to pour out, to empty a vessel, to make water; Copt. ⲡⲱⲛⲅ.

penq , U. 470, , T. 222, , P. 184, , M. 294, , N. 897, , Anastasi I, 13, 3, to bale water out of a boat; Copt. ⲡⲱⲛⲧ.

penga , , to split, to divide, to separate; compare Heb. √פלג; Copt. ⲡⲱⲗϭ.

penti , Rec. 15, 175, he who.

Pentauru , Rev. 6, 24, a famous scribe, or perhaps author.

Penti, Peti , , B.D. 50A, 5, 50B, 5, a god.

penṭ , worm, snake, serpent; Copt. ⲃⲛ̄ⲧ, ϥⲛ̄ⲧ.

Penṭ, Pentch , , the name of a god.

Penṭ-tȧ , T. 337, , P. 816, N. 644, a title of Rā.

Penṭen , U, 280, a bull-god (?)

Penṭer [illegible], Ṭuat XI, Hh. 154, a ram-god who prepared offerings for Rā.

Pentch [illegible], Hh. 327, a title of the Nile-god.

Pentchen [illegible], A.Z. 1910, 128, the name of a god.

per [illegible], [illegible], house, palace, seat of government; plur. [illegible], [illegible], U. 431, P. 401, N. 1180, [illegible], [illegible], IV, 1095, [illegible] [illegible], double house, B.D. 159, 2, [illegible], I, 81;

neb-t per [illegible], mistress of the house, *i.e.*, a legally married wife.

perit [illegible], house, the land about a house, corn-land (?); plur. [illegible], Metternich Stele 8, [illegible] [illegible], A.Z. 1900, 30, [illegible], B.D. 15, 34.

perit [illegible], Mar. Aby. I, 6, 47, women of the chamber.

peru (pestchu) [illegible], Rec. 5, 91, the group of gods of one shrine.

per aqur [illegible], Rev. 12, 107 . . . . . .

Per-àbu 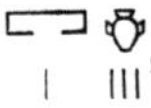, B.D. 26, 2, "house of hearts," the Judgment Hall of Osiris.

Per-. . . . -àmi-ā-āḥa 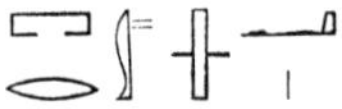 , Ṭuat X, the gazelle-headed fire-stick that supplied Rā with fire.

Per-Àmen 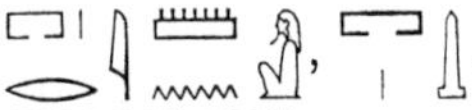, Rev. 11, 178, 14, 33 = ⲡⲉⲣⲉⲙⲟⲩⲛ.

Per-àrp 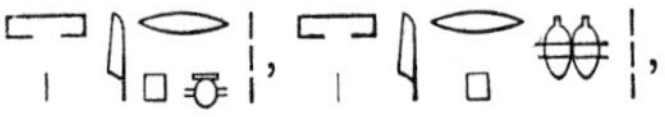, wine cellar.

Per-āa 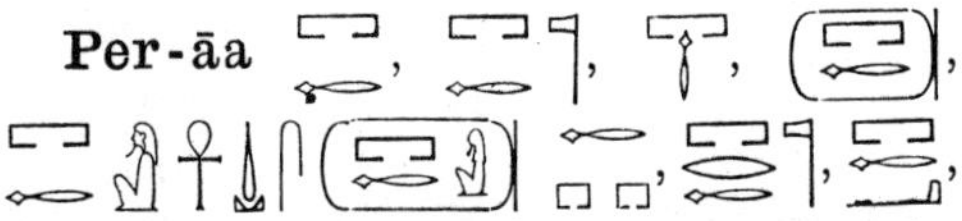, B.M. 241, "great house," *i.e.*, palace, Pharaoh; Copt. ⲡ̄ⲣⲟ, Heb. פַּרְעֹה. Later per-āa was a title assumed by mere officers, *e.g.*, , "the per-āa of the king." It is sometimes placed inside a cartouche with the royal name, *e.g.*, 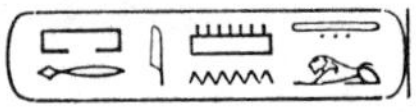.

per-āa , I, 149, Pharaoh's man.

Per-āa 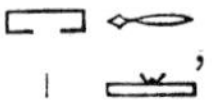, "great house," a name of the Necropolis.

per-ānkh 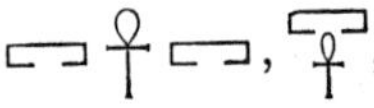, Thes. 1254, , "house of life," a name for the school or college of the temple.

per-ānkh 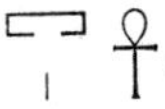, mirror case; see .

Per-ānkh-àru-t 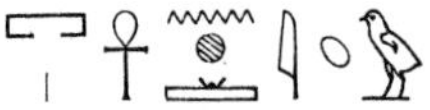 , a chamber wherein funerary ceremonies were performed.

per-ānti 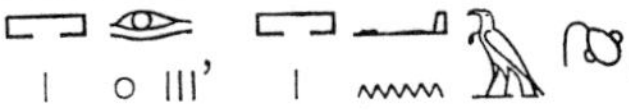, funerary coffer.

per-ār , store-city, magazine.

per-āḥa (?) 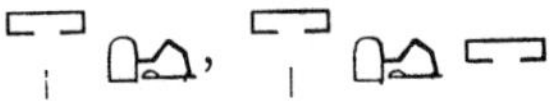, I, 138, armoury.

per-āq-t , bread store, pantry.

per-uāb , coffer.

per-ubekh-t , a chamber in a temple.

per-ur 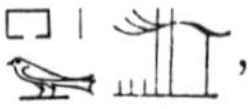, T. 284, P. 35, M. 43, N. 65, , IV, 1071,  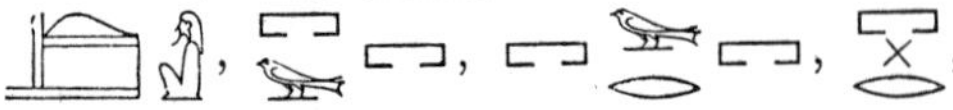, 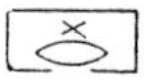, a holy place, sanctuary, the chamber of a sanctuary, a name of the sky or heaven.

per-ur-em-nub-t , , Berg. 37, a chamber in the tomb.

peru-uru VI 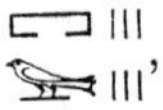, the six great courts of justice.

Per-ba-tet . Rev. 11, 128 = , Busiris.

per-Bàti , house of the king of the North.

Per-pestch-neteru , , house of the nine gods.

per-em-nub , gold house, *i.e.*, the sarcophagus chamber; var. 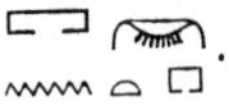.

perma (?) , summer-houses, booths.

peru-maāu (?) , Rec. 6, 12, , Rec. 6, 15, temples; the reading is probably **mau**.

peru-Manu [illegible], P. 506, temples in the Ṭuat (?)

Per-mit (?) [illegible], Rev. 16, 129 . . . .

per-menàu [illegible], B.D. 64, 5, the house of those who have arrived in port, *i.e.*, the tomb.

peru-mesu-nesu [illegible], the apartments of princes and princesses.

per-meṭu [illegible], house of speech, council chamber (?)

per-metcha [illegible], Mar. Aby. I, 6, 34, [illegible], [illegible], A.Z. 1906, 124, [illegible], L.D. III, 184, 27, library, registry, chancery.

Per-en-båkh-t , Rec. 31, 35 . . . .

per-en-per-ānkh 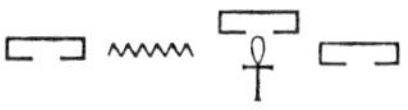, school, college.

per-neheh 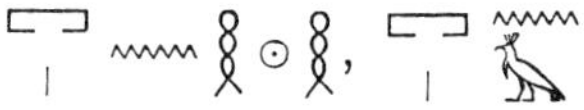, 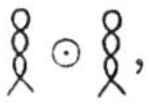, house of eternity, *i.e.*, the grave, the tomb.

peru-nu-seshu 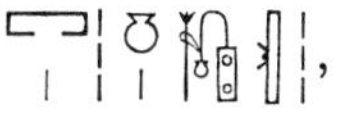, houses in which plans and designs were drafted and copied.

per-en-teka , A.Z. 1887, 115, furnace; Copt. ⲡⲓⲛⲧⲱⲕ.

peru-nub 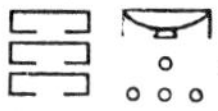, IV, 1072, places wherein gold was worked; [illegible], B.M. 174.

Per-nefer 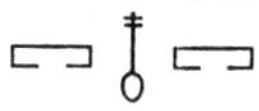, Rec. 33, 31, 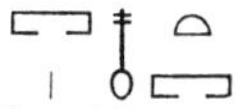, Rec. 5, 88, the chamber in a temple in which the ceremonies of the resurrection of Osiris were performed.

per-nem-t 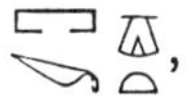, U. 295, the divine slaughter-house.

per-nesu , , king's house, palace, royal property.

Per-neser 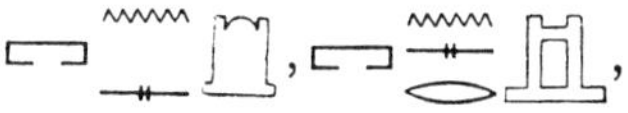, M. 380, N. 656, "house of flame," *i.e.*, sanctuary (?)

Per-neser, 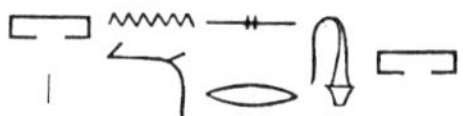, B.D. 25, 3, a fiery region in the Ṭuat.

per-neter 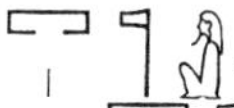, the god-house, shrine or sanctuary; , the house of the great god.

per-Ru (?) . . . . . . 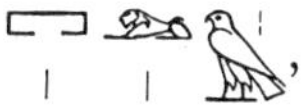, P. 294 . . . .

Per-ḥatu 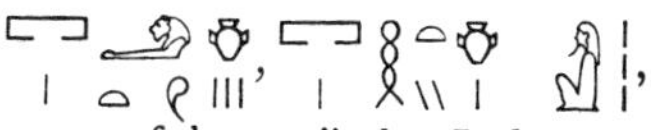, B.D. 26, 1, "house of hearts," the Judgment Hall of Osiris.

Per-ḥu , Rec. 30, 4, the temple of the Sphinx.

per-hemt , the house of women, *i.e.*, ḥarîm.

Per-Ḥenu 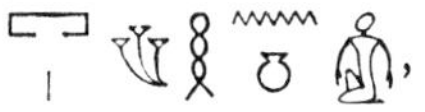, Ḥenu 9 . . . . .

peru-ḥeru , , Berl. 2296, "houses above," *i.e.*, celestial mansions.

per-ḥer-ḥetep 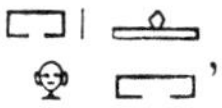, Décrets 19, offering chamber.

per-ḥeḥ 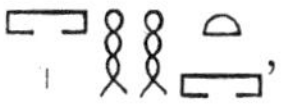, "house of eternity," *i.e.*, the tomb.

per-ḥesb , the office in which slaves and goods were taxed, *e.g.*:  , IV, 1051, stores office; IV, 1051, slave office; IV, 1052, agricultural office; IV, 1052, metals office.

per-ḥetch , 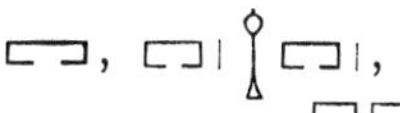, treasure-house, store-house, treasury; plur. 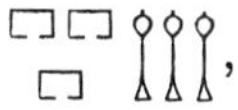, IV, 1143.

perui-ḥetchui , B.M. 174, 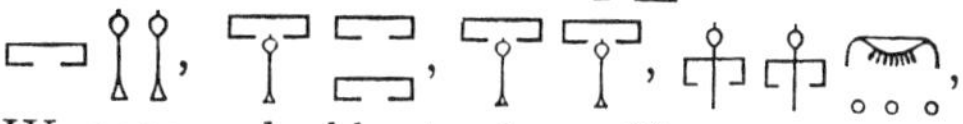, IV, 1030, a double storehouse (?)

peru-ḥetch 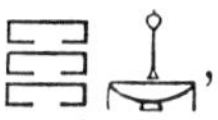, IV, 1072, houses in which silver was worked.

per-kha-renput , Ḥerusâtef Stele 57, house of a thousand years.

Per-khut 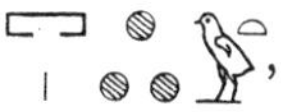, M. 728, N. 1329, ...

per-khen 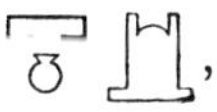, P. 648, 721, M. 748, [illegible], libation chamber.

per-khenr (?) 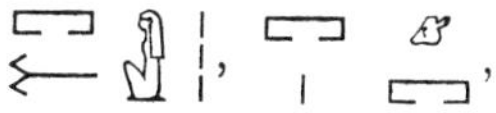, house wherein women were secluded, ḥarîm.

Per-Saḥ , Rec. 16, 129, house of Orion.

persen [illegible], cake; see **pasen**.

Per-seḥep 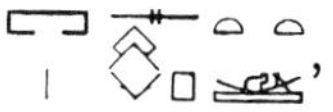, B.D. 104, 5, the place whither the mantis led the deceased.

Per-Seker-neb-Seḥetch, Piānkhi Stele 81, a temple of Seker near Kher-āḥa.

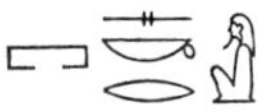

per-sha, III, 143, garden.

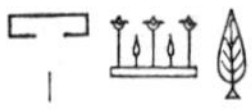

Per-sha-nub, Nȧstasen Stele 32, a temple on the Island of Meroë.

per-shesth-t, an estate of Methen in the Delta.

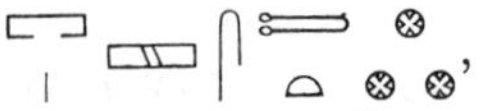

per-qebḥ, house of coolness, place of refreshment.

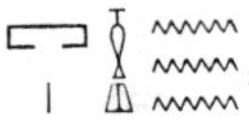

Per-Qebḥ, Pap. Ani, 2, 16, a region of refreshing in the Ṭuat.

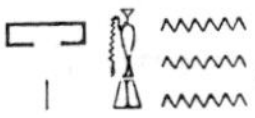

Per-Kemkem, B.D. 75, 4 . . . . . .

Per-Keku, B.D. 78, 4, , a region of darkness in the Ṭuat.

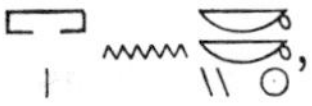

per-ṭuat, Rec. 36, 1 ff., : (1) "chamber of the Other World," *i.e.*, a chamber of a tomb wherein offerings were made, and wherein the liturgy of funerary offerings was recited; (2) a dressing room.

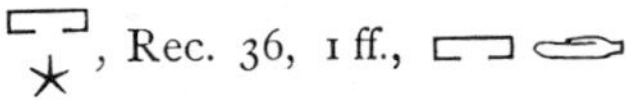

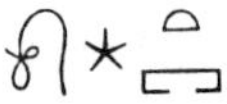

per-tcha-t, a part of the body (?)

per-tchet, house of eternity, the tomb.

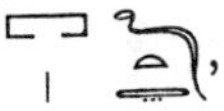

per =, a sign of subtraction.

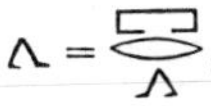

per, , , , , , , Rev., , Jour. As. 1908, 277, to go out, to go forth, to go away, to depart, to leave one's country, to withdraw from a place, to proceed from, to be born, to arise from, to flow out, to empty itself (of a river), to issue, to escape, to march to an attack, to come up or sprout (of plants), to manifest oneself, to appear, to run out, to expire, to perish, to be sacrificed, to pass a limit, to evade a calamity; Copt. ⲡⲉⲓⲣⲉ, ⲡⲓⲣⲉ (?); , , , coming out and going in.

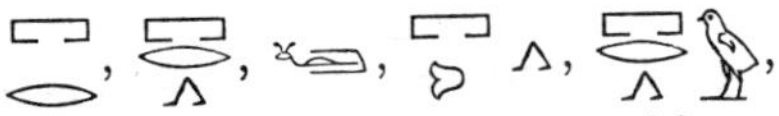

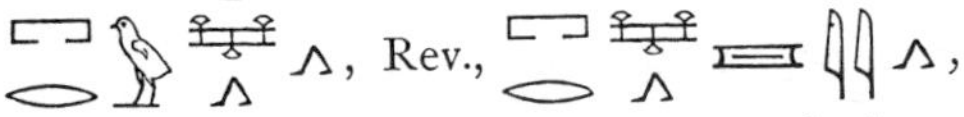

perr, , P. 633, M. 504, N. 1087, , Rec. 26, 229, , U. 343, ; see .

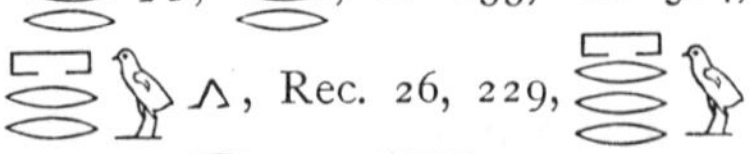

per, peru, , , (*sic*), what comes forth from the mouth, *i.e.*, word, speech.

perȧ, peri, U. 12, , , , he who comes forth, he who appears, he who attacks, he who is prominent; plur., T. 45, P. 87, M. 53, N. 69, , , , ; , Rec. 31, 171.

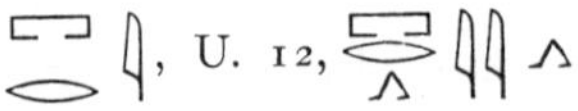

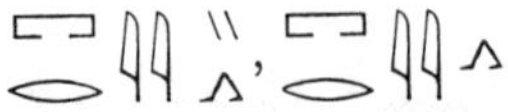

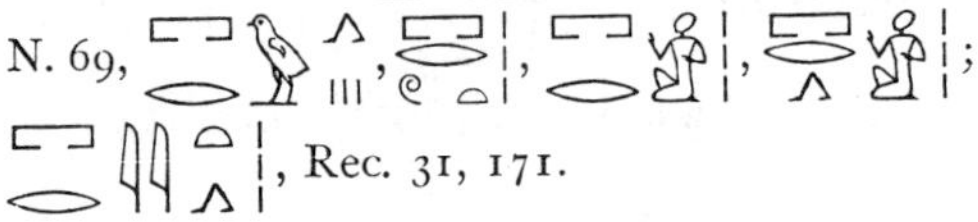

peri, fighting man, soldier (?) bold warrior (?) mighty man of war.

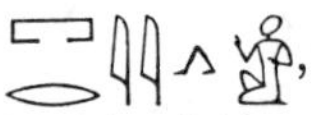

perru, , , Rec. 31, 162, those who come out or go out, attackers.

per-t, , , , , Metternich Stele 55, exit, issue, what comes forth, manifestation, outbreak of fire, offspring; plur. .

perr-t, T. 270, M. 437, ; see  .

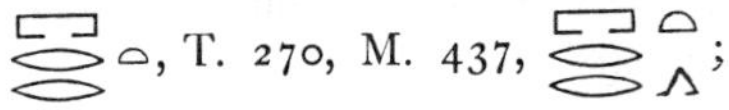

peru, A.Z. 1908, 70, expenses, outgoings; , Peasant 295, crops; , Peasant 325, a "righteous result," as opposed to 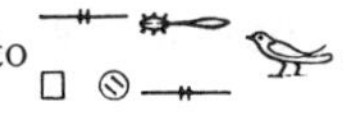 .

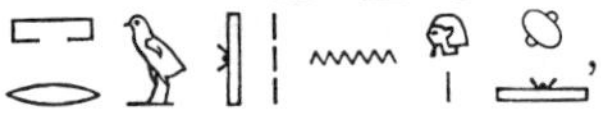

per-t, , , battlefield (?)

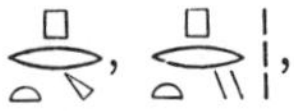

per-t, vigour, strength, attack.

perti, B.D. 134, 5, , , U. 13, , U. 36, , , mighty one, might, strength, a professional soldier.

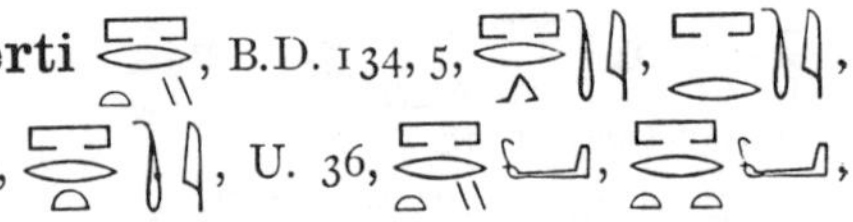

per-ā, Rec. 15, 150, , , , power, strength, violence, struggle, contest, activity, war, bravery.

per-ā, , , , hero, mighty man, warrior, fighter, soldier, a high-handed man; plur. , .

per-ā ḥa-t, hero, brave man; , words of boldness or courage.

per ḥa-t, Ȧmen. 22, 14, , a bold, brave man.

per-t en ḥa-t, bravery, pride.

peru ḥa-t, Rec. 16, 57, thoughts or emotions of the mind.

per em-baḥ, to appear in the presence of someone.

Per em hru, Pyr. § 2206, , , , , , , "Coming forth by day," or, "Coming forth into the day," or "Coming forth from the day." A general title of the series of Chapters which is commonly known as The Book of the Dead.

per-t, , a journey into the open country.

per ha, Leyd. Pap. 6, 12, to be crowded, thronged.

per ḥer ta, to appear on the earth, *i.e.*, to be born.

per kheru, Rec. 14, 46, produce (of the farm).

Per-kheru, a name of the Inundation.

Perit, Ṭuat IX, a singing, fighting-goddess.

Pertiu, Ṭuat III, , the fighting gods of heaven, divine warriors.

Periu, Ṭuat XI, a group of four gods who prepared the sky for Rā.

Perru, , , U. 418, T. 239, a group of gods.

Perimu (?), Ṭuat VIII, one of the nine bodyguards of Rā.

Perit-em-up-Rā, Ṭuat XII, a fire-goddess, a foe of Āapep.

Peri-em-ḥāt-f, "he who proceeds from his body," *i.e.*, the self-produced, a title of Rā.

peri-em-khetkhet, B.D. 125, II, 8, "coming forward and retreating," used of the Flame-god Nebȧ , who alternately grew and diminished.

Peri-m-khet-maa (?)-em-ḥer-f, Berg. I, 3, one of the eight watchers of Osiris.

Peri-em-qenb-t, Denderah IV, 62, a serpent-god.

Peri-em-tep-f, a god of the Arsinoïte Nome.

Peri-em-thet-f, Denderah IV, 62, an ape-headed warrior-god.

Perui neterui, the two Epiphanes gods.

per-t-er-kheru, , , , , , , , , , , , , , , , , , the offerings which appeared in the tomb when the deceased uttered their names with his voice; , Thes. 1252, to recite prayers for sepulchral offerings.

per-t-er-kheru nesu 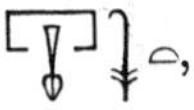, P. 363A, 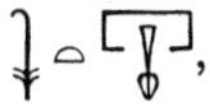, U. 86A, royal sepulchral offerings.

per , funerary offerings.

per 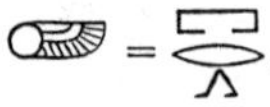, to rise (of the sun).

per 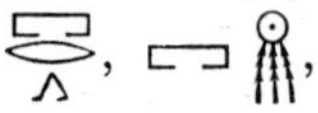, splendour, to shine; Copt. ⲡⲉⲓⲣⲉ ⲉⲃⲟⲗ.

per-t 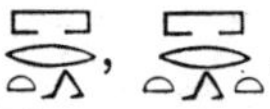, the appearance of a heavenly body, or of the figure of a god or goddess, which was usually celebrated by a festival.

per-t āa-t  [illegible], the "great appearance," or the great festival; a ceremony in the miracle play of Osiris; , the great day of grief, *i.e.*, the day of the death of Osiris.

per-t 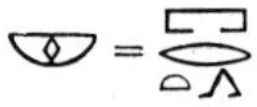, appearance, festival.

Per-t , a festival held on the 26th day of the month; , a festal procession.

Per-t Up-uatu 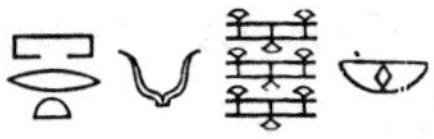, the appearance of the god Up-uatu, or his festival.

Per-t Bars-t , a festival.

Per-t Menu  , the festival of Menu on the 30th day of the month.

Per-t Nu , the festival of Nu, the Sky-god.

Per-t neterui 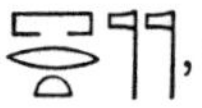, the festival of the appearance of the two gods; var. .

Per-t Sepṭ-t 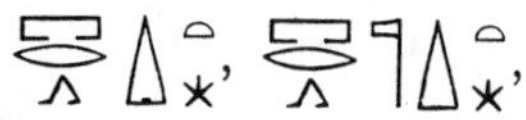 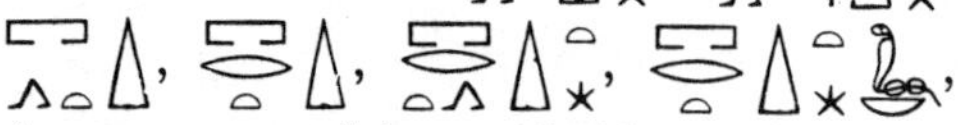, the appearance of the star Sothis.

Per-t Sem 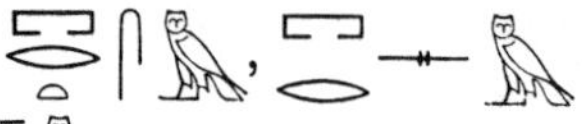 [illegible]; see .

Per-t Setem  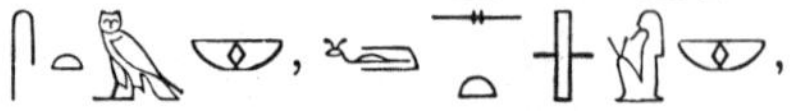, a moon-festival on the 4th day of the month.

Per Shu , a festival of Shu.

Per-t tep-t , the "chief festival."

per-t  [illegible], Jour. As. 1908, 290, the 2nd season of the Egyptian year which contained the four months ⲧⲱⲃⲓ, ⲙⲉⲭⲓⲣ, ⲫⲁⲙⲉⲛⲱⲑ and ⲫⲁⲣⲙⲟⲩⲧⲓ ; Copt. ⲡⲣⲱ.

Perit [illegible], Ombos I, 1, 90, goddess of the 2nd season of the Egyptian year.

per-t, perr-t 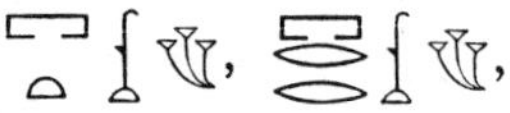, sprout, plant, vegetable.

per-t 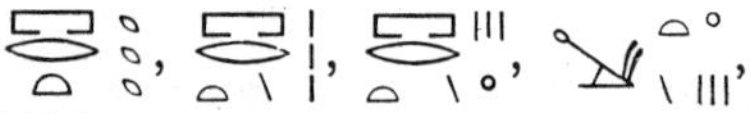 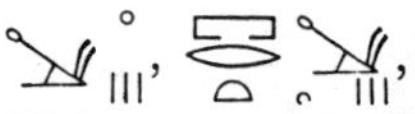, Thes. 1203,  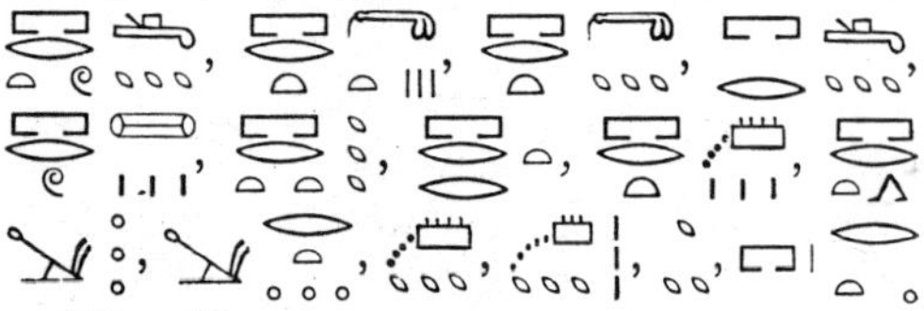 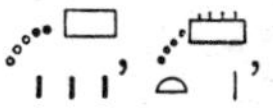, Peasant 294, grain, corn, wheat, field produce, fruit of any kind; Copt. ϥⲣⲉ, ⲃⲣⲏⲧⲉ, ⲉⲃⲣⲏⲧⲉ, Heb. פְּרִי.

per-t 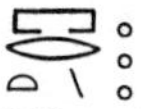, grains of any substance, *e.g.*, , grains of myrrh; [illegible] , grains of cassia.

per-t seshu 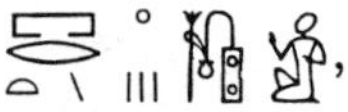, Precepts Åmenemḥat 1, 13, the produce of the scribe, *i.e.*, literary productions.

per-t shemā-t 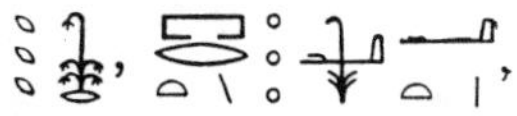, grain of the South, dhurra (?)

per-t shen  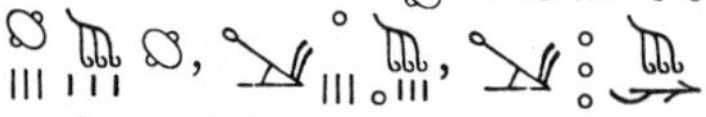, the aromatic seeds or fruit of a plant; Copt. ⲃⲉⲣϣⲛⲟⲩ, coriander seed (?)

per-t shesp, B.D. 189, 16, light-coloured grain from which beer was made.

per-t kam, B.D. 189, 16, black grain, dark-coloured grain from which cakes were made.

per-t ṭesher, B.D. 102, 5, red grain from which beer was made.

per-t, Rec. 29, 164, , Israel Stele 27, seed, progeny, posterity, descendants.

peru, Décrets 9, men attached to a royal granary.

per, , , , to see, sight, vision, aspect, appearance; see .

pera, to see.

Per-neferu-en-neb-set , , , Thes. 28, , , Berg. 11, 8, the goddess of the 12th hour of the night.

per-t, , crime, sin.

per, Excom. Stele 5 . . . . . .

perper, Metternich Stele 192, to run swiftly, to leap about, to be agitated; compare Heb. פַּרְפַּר, √פָּרַר.

perȧ, Thes. 1296, , IV, 890, 938, fighting, battle, field of battle.

perȧ, warrior, hero; plur. , L.D. III, 65A, heroes.

perā Israel Stele 23, unstopped (of wells).

perā = , a bird; Copt. ⲡⲉⲣⲁ (?)

peri, , bandlet, turban, strip of linen cloth.

perri, Rev., wild ass; compare Heb. פֶּרֶא, Isaiah xxxii, 14.

Perriṭes, Rec. 33, 3, Ros. Stone 4, transcription of the Greek name Pyrrhides.

perp, abominable (?) contemptible.

per-em-us, A.Z. 1874, 148, edge, ledge, slope of a pyramid = πυραμὶς (?)

perḥ, to march about; see .

perkh, Rec. 11, 167, , Rec. 5, 95, , Rec. 14, 136, to divide, to separate; Copt. ⲡⲱⲣϣ.

perkh-t, cloth, napkin; Copt. ⲫⲟⲣϣⲓ.

perkh, A.Z. 1905, 19, , flower, bloom; Heb. פֶּרַח.

persh, Rec. 7, 113, , Rec. 15, 107, , Hearst Pap. 8, 8, coriander seed; Copt. ⲃⲉⲣⲉϣⲉⲧ.

persh-t, destruction, ruin.

persh, to stretch out; Copt. ⲡⲱⲣϣ.

Perqsaṭus, Rec. 33, 3, transcription of the Greek name Pergasidos.

pertcha, to split, to divide, to separate; Copt. ⲡⲱⲣϫ.

pertchan (?), a kind of stone.

peh, to rend (?); , U. 534, T. 294.

pehsa, Rev., prey; Copt. ⲡⲁϩⲥ.

Pehtes, Sphinx 1, 89, Mar. Mon. D. 49, a dog of Ȧntef-āa; the word means "black," , Rec. 36, 86.

peḥ 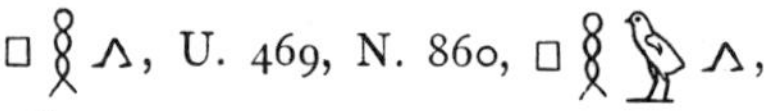, U. 469, N. 860, P. 379, 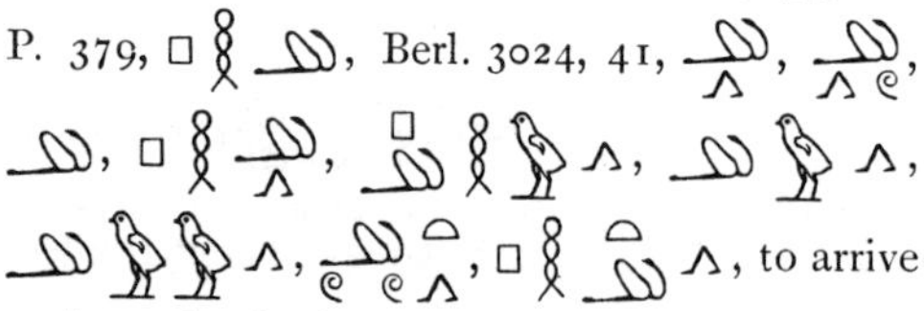, Berl. 3024, 41, to arrive at the end of a journey, to attain to a place or object, to reach; Copt. ⲡⲱϩ.

peḥ remu , Peasant 207, to catch fish; 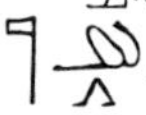, Chab. Pap. Mag. 170, to work magic.

peḥ ḥa-t , to attain the heart's desire.

peḥ, peḥ-t 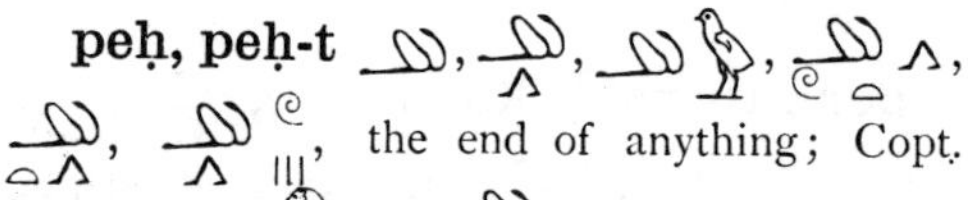, the end of anything; Copt. ⲡⲁϩⲟⲩ: , its beginning to its end (of a book), Berl. 3024, 155, 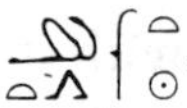, end of the year; , at the end of the night, or perhaps "in the deepest night";  = Copt. ⲉⲡⲁϩⲟⲩ.

peḥu , IV, 1129, beyond.

peḥui 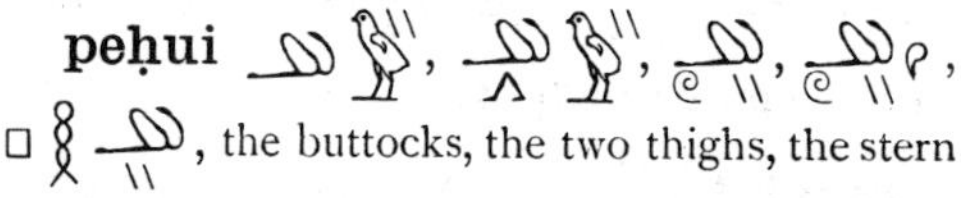, the buttocks, the two thighs, the stern of a boat, the base of an obelisk, the back generally; 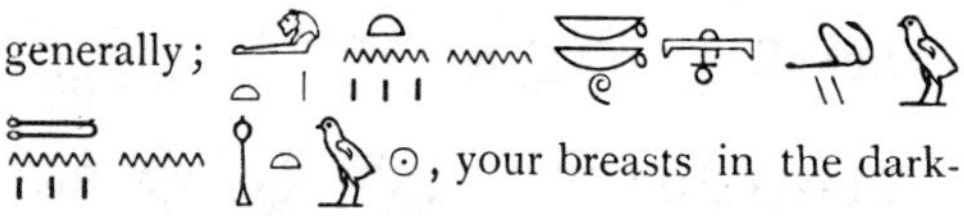, your breasts in the darkness, your backs in the light; Copt. ⲡⲁϩⲟⲩ.

peḥuiu , Thes. 1484, IV, 974, back (of a man), the end.

peḥuit 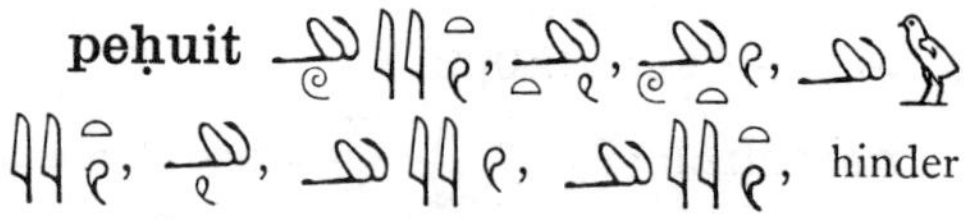, hinder parts of a man or animal, back of the neck, back, rump, fundament, anus.

peḥu , A.Z. 45, 133, rump-steak.

peḥuti , the last comer.

peḥuiu , IV, 650, the rear-guard of an army.

peḥ-āḥā-t , IV, 1116, "remnant of the navy."

peḥu , the ends of leaves, tops of plants.

peḥ ...... , bolts of a door.

peḥuit 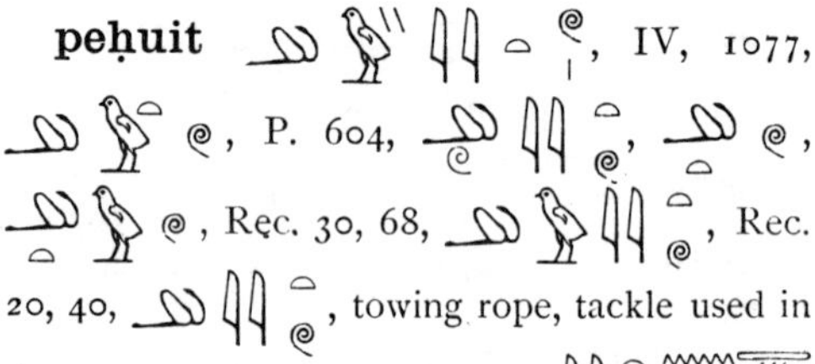, IV, 1077, P. 604, Rec. 30, 68, Rec. 20, 40, towing rope, tackle used in the stern of a boat or ship; 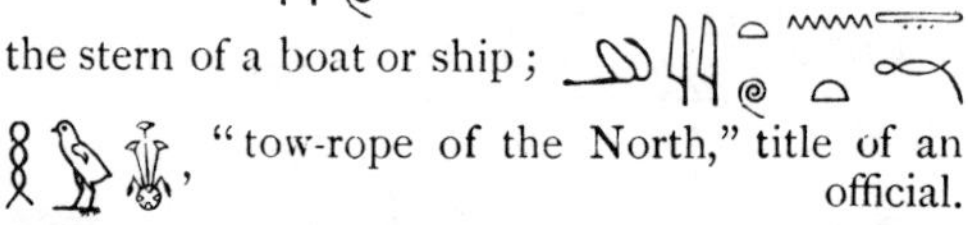, "tow-rope of the North," title of an official.

Peḥui-utchait 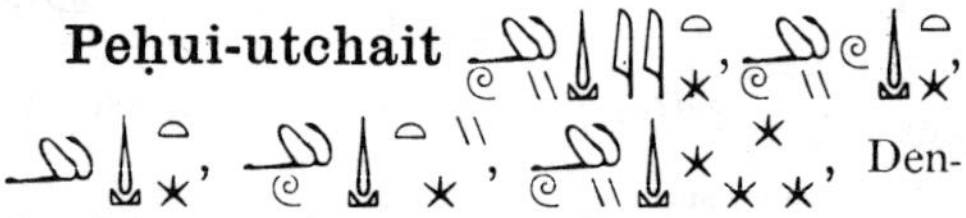, Denderah II, 10, Seti I, Rameses IV, one of the 36 Dekans; Gr. *φουτητ*.

Peḥui-ḥer 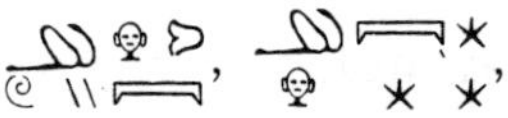, one of the 36 Dekans; Gr. *φουορ*.

Peḥ-khau (?) 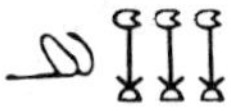 Annales I, 84, one of the 36 Dekans.

Peḥ-Sepṭ-t , the name of the 22nd day of the month.

peḥu , swamp, marsh, low-lying land; plur. 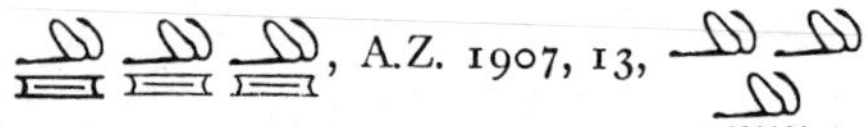, A.Z. 1907, 13, 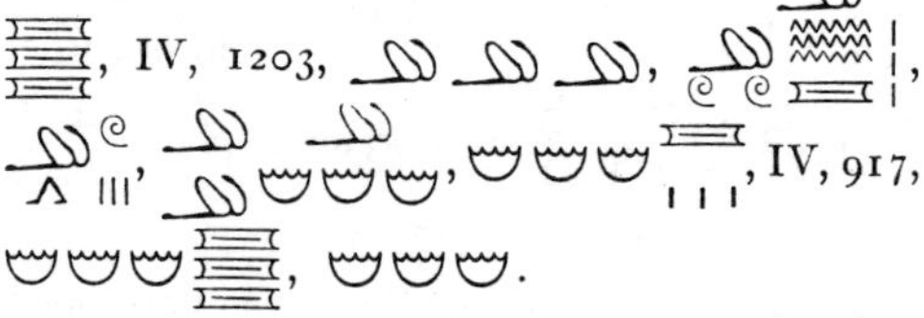, IV, 1203, IV, 917.

Peḥu pa ta en Uatch-t  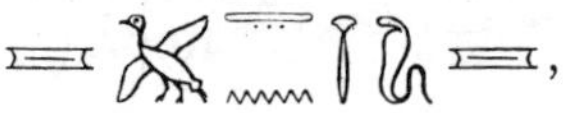, the swamp land of the town of Buto.

peḥu Sati 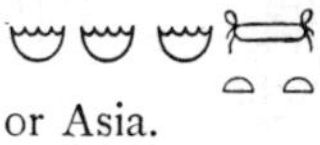, the swamps of Eastern Egypt or Asia.

peḥu ta , IV, 648, the swamps of the earth (Egypt?).

peḥu taui , IV, 617, the swamps of all lands.

Peḥ-åm (?) , Ombos I, 1, 236, a lake-god.

Peḥ-årti (?) , Ombos I, 1, 335, a lake-god.

Peḥ-ustt , Ombos I, 1, 334, a lake-god.

Peḥ-reṭui (?) , Ombos I, 1, 335, a lake-god.

Peḥ-Ḥerui , Ombos I, 1, 336, a lake-god.

Peḥ-kharui (?) , Ombos I, 1, 335, a lake-god.

Peḥ-sekhet 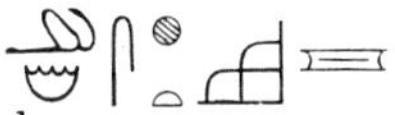, Ombos I, 1, 336, a lake-god.

peḥ-t , lion (?) strength (?)

peḥt 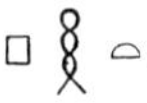, M. 144, A.Z. 1900, 128, , P. 525, , Jour. As. 1908, 277, strength, might, power, bravery, renown.

peḥti 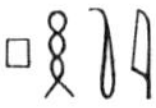, T. 271, P. 343, , N. 122, Rec. 27, 59, , Rec. 26, 66, 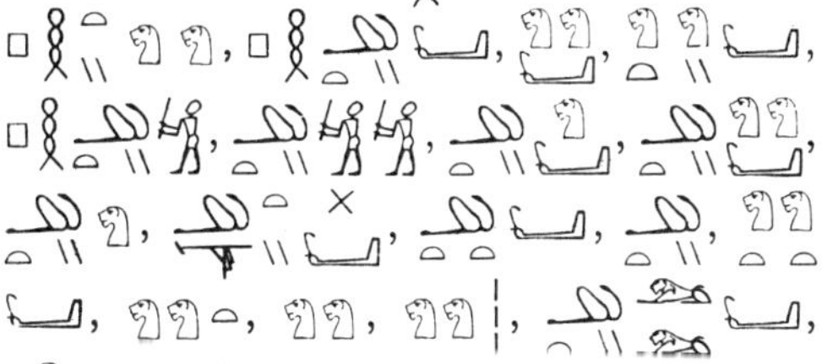 , IV, 657, , strength, might, glory, renown, fame; 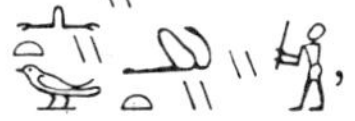, weak; Copt. ⲡⲁϩⲧⲉ in ⲁ-ⲡⲁϩⲧⲉ.

peḥti – , exceedingly mighty, or glorious; Copt. ⲁ-ⲡⲁϩⲧⲉ.

peḥti , to restrain, to turn back.

Peḥ-ka-åmi-Qebḥ 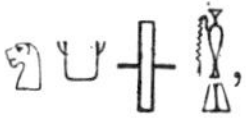, P. 169, , P. 789, a region in the sky.

peḥ , P. 706 . . . . . .

peḥn 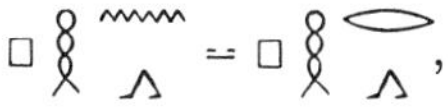, or 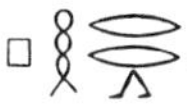.

peḥer , P. 164, 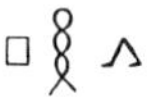, M. 328, N. 860, to run, to traverse; , N. 788.

peḥrer  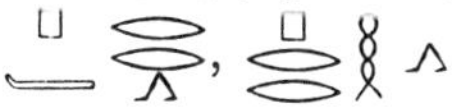, Rec. 35, 126, 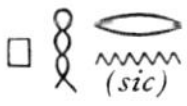 (sic) , to run, to traverse a district or country, to follow a course of action.

peḥreri 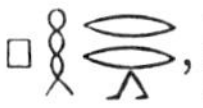, Mar. Karn. 82, 14, a kind of soldier, scout (?)

peḥreri , 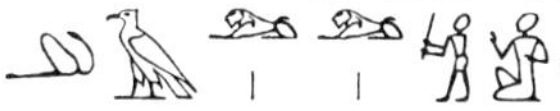, runner, messenger, envoy, courier; plur. .

Peḥreri , B.D. 89, 2, "Runner," a title of the Sun-god.

peḥrer-t , a journey; [illegible] [illegible], the circuiting of the Apis Bull (Palermo Stele), the ceremonial running of the bull before capture for sacrifice.

peḥṭ, peḥtch [illegible], [illegible], [illegible], to cut through, to split, to divide; Copt. ⲫⲱϫⲓ.

pekh [illegible], U. 144, T. 115, N. 452, a kind of grain.

pekhkh [illegible], Hearst Pap. 8, 13, a plant used in medicine.

pekh-t [illegible], [illegible], a kind of seed used in medicine.

pekh [illegible], [illegible], to split, to divide; Copt. ⲡⲁϩ, ⲡⲉϩ, ⲡⲱϩ, ⲫⲱϩ.

pekh [illegible], [illegible], [illegible], piece, bit, slice, morsel, portion, ration, bread-offerings.

pekh [illegible], [illegible], a part of a ship.

pekh-t [illegible], a death-trap, snare; Copt. ⲡⲁϣ.

pekh (?) , curse, spell, imprecation, incantation; plur. .

pekhpekh 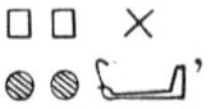, A.Z 1874, 65, to crouch.

pekhpekh 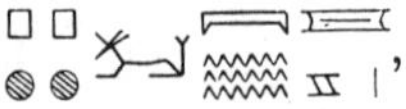, Åmen. 4, 15, hurricane, thunderstorm.

Pekhit , Nesi-Åmsu 30, 25, , a goddess of destruction who took the form of a cat or lion.

pekh , A.Z. 1906, 111, upright, sincere, prudent.

pekh ḥa-t , IV, 890, wise.

pekha 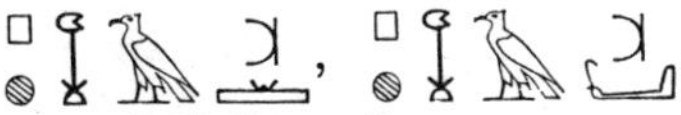, 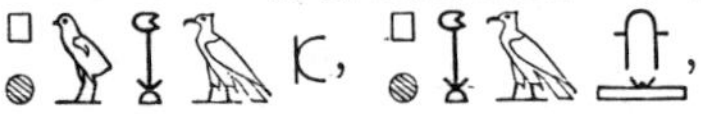, to split, to divide, to cut off, to separate, to purge; Copt. ⲡⲁϩ, ⲡⲉϩ, ⲡⲱϩ.

pekha meṭtut  , Anastasi I, 28, 3, the splitting of words.

pekha-t , Love Songs 1, 12, , ibid. 4, 6, : (1) splinter, shoot, bud; (2) trap, snare; (3) peg, clamp, bolt, floor of a chariot; plur.  , Åmen. 18, 2, , Rev. 11, 141, , IV, 1081.

Pekhat , B.D. 164 (Saïte), a vulture-goddess, a form of Mut.

Pekhat , a cat-goddess, or lioness-goddess.

pekhaåu , cleaver of the water (applied to the Abṭu fish).

pekhar , U. 437, 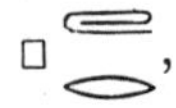, T. 249, M. 114, 621, , Rec. 27, 217, , , to revolve, to go round about, to encircle, to make a circuit, to traverse; varr. 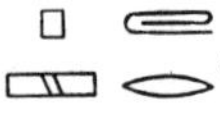, P. 96, N. 41, , N. 625, , Rec. 20, 40, 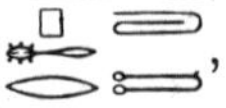, surrounded.

pekharr , T. 338, to go round, to circuit; var. 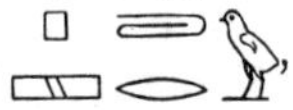, N. 625.

pekhar-pekhar , T. 316, P. 307, to revolve, to circuit.

pekhar-t , U. 400, , , IV, 1077, circuit, journey.

pekharut 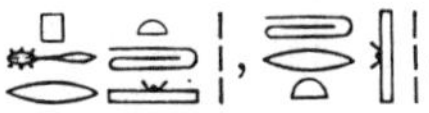, methods of procedure, changes, vicissitudes.

pekhar em-sa , to follow about; , P. 1116B, 55.

pekhar nes-t [illegible], successor to the throne; var. [illegible].

pekhar ḥa [illegible], to turn backwards; [illegible], making a circuit of the walls (a ceremony).

pekhar shut [illegible], IV, 655, at the turn of the day; [illegible] the turning of the shadow.

pekhar khet [illegible], to retreat, to withdraw.

pekhartiu [illegible], A.Z. 45, 138, [illegible], L.D. 3, 140B, "runners," lightly armed infantry who guarded the frontiers.

Pekhari [illegible] [illegible], Ṭuat XI, a serpent-warder of the 11th Gate.

Pekhariu-åmiu-pe-t [illegible] [illegible], T. 326, [illegible], U. 514, beings who assisted in the boiling of the gods.

Pekharit-ānkh [illegible], Ṭuat VIII, a serpent deity in the circle Āat-setekau.

Pekharer [illegible], B.D. 141, 148, the name of the rudder of the western heaven.

pekharit , , Rec. 33, 5, 33, 6, , , , revolution (of time), the course of time, circle, the rolling year; , Berl. 3024, 20, "a circle is life."

pekharu , P. 416, M. 596, N. 1201, course of time, revolution of the sun.

pekhar , general, universal (of a festival), common.

pekhar with **thes** , conversely.

pekhar , a place for walking about in in the court of a temple, cloisters.

pekhar-t , , peristyle of a court; plur. .

pekhar , , Gol. 10, 39, ground, territory, a kind of land; plur. (?) , IV, 902.

pekhar-pekhar (?) , vortex, eddy (?)

pekhar ur , IV, 613, 697, , Rec. 27, 190, , A.Z. 1905, 15, the "Great Bend," the bend of a river.

pekhar ur shen ur , Rec. 32, 68, Great Bend of the Great Circuit.

pekhar , , , Rev. 13, 40, , Rev. 12, 70, to bewitch, to work enchantments by means of drugs.

pekhar-t , , , , Love Songs 1, 7, drugs, medicines, remedy, antidote, healing pills; Copt. ⲡⲁϩⲣⲉ.

pekhat , Rev. 11, 179, , Rev. 11, 184, to incline, to cast down; Copt. ⲡⲁϩⲧ, ⲡⲉϩⲧ, ⲫⲁϧⲧ, ⲡⲱϩⲧ.

pekhes , to split; see .

pekht , P. 603, , Rec. 27, 228, , IV, 897, , , to reject, to repel, to thrust aside, to cast down; **pekhṭ,** ; Copt. ⲡⲱϩⲧ.

pekht , "tearer," a title of a bird.

pekht-t , Rec. 30, 192, a bird that tears its prey.

Pekht, Pekhth , , a lioness-goddess; the chief town of her cult was , near the modern village of Beni Hasan; see .

pekhṭ , , , , Leyd. Pap. 8, 13, to throw down, to overturn, to upset; Copt. ⲡⲁϩⲧ, ⲡⲉϩⲧ, ⲡⲱϩⲧ, ⲫⲁϧⲧ.

pes , B.D. 175, 8, , , water-pot of a palette.

pes , a kind of plant.

pesi, pess , , , , , , , Hearst Pap. 11, 6, to boil, to roast, to cook, to light a fire for cooking purposes; Copt. ⲡⲓⲥⲉ, ⲡⲟⲥⲉ.

pes-t, pess-t , , roasted or boiled meats.

pesit , cooked food.

pes , , cake, loaf of bread.

pessa , Rechnungen 78, cooked food.

pessa , baker, confectioner who made , , .

pessi ȧnsi , Rec. 19, 92, hot-presser of flax (?)

pessa 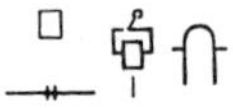, flower-basket, flower-stand, fan for the kitchen fire, sack; plur. 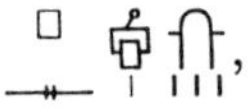, Koller Pap. 4, 3.

pesi 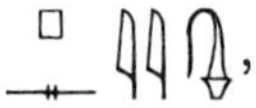, Rev. 14, 68, a tax (?)

Pesi[t] 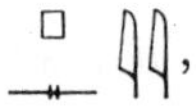, Ṭuat XI, a goddess of the desert [illegible].

Pesi[t] 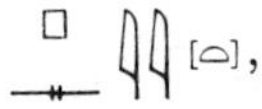, Ṭuat XI, a fire-goddess in the Ṭuat.

Pesiu 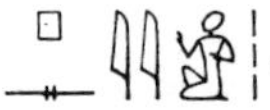, Excom. Stele 5 . . . . .

pesag , to spit.

pesag , spittle.

pessu 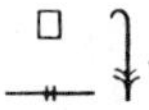, Rev. 14, 73, liability.

pesuṭ 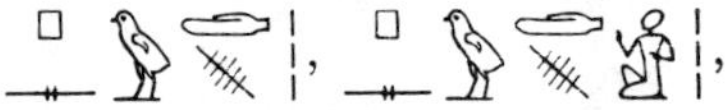, IV, 749, Anastasi I, 5, 7, , backs of men, helpers, assistants.

P-seb-uā 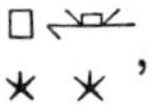, Zod. Denderah, the 19th Dekan.

pesef 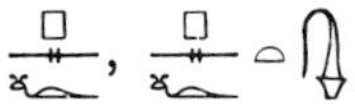, Peasant 246, to cook, to boil, to roast; see 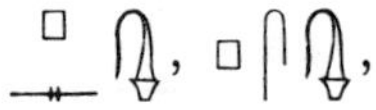, and .

pesefu , Rec. 15, 15, cook.

pesen 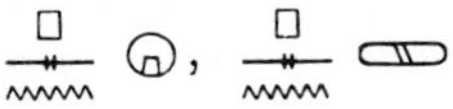, U. 109A, N. 418A, a cake of bread.

pesḥ 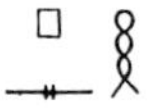, U. 314, 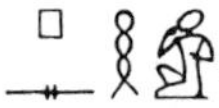, T. 335, M. 246, N. 637, 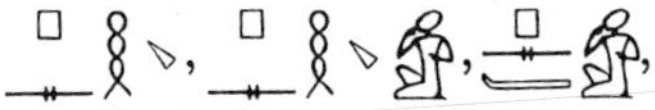, 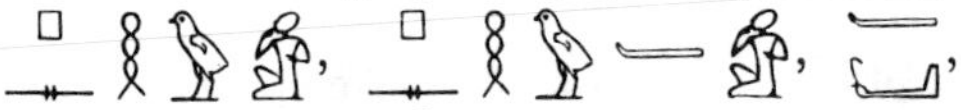, 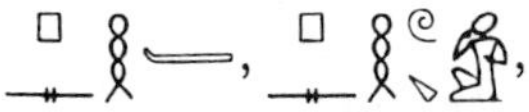, to bite (of an insect), to gnaw, to sting, to devour, to eat; , Nav. Bubas. 34A.

pesḥ-t 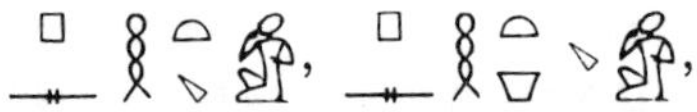, 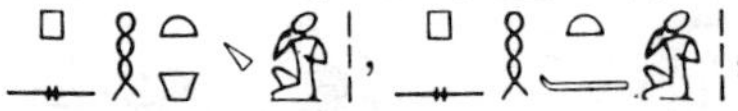, bite, sting of an insect or reptile.

peskh 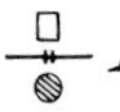, to split; see [illegible].

peskh 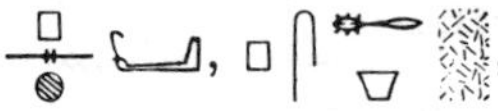, Rec. 27, 224 . . . . . .

Pesekhti 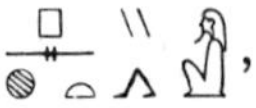, B.D. 64, 26, the name of a divine envoy.

pess-t 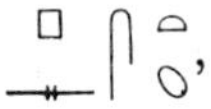, granule, pill.

pesesh , U. 26, , Rec. 31, 27, [illegible], Dream Stele 6, 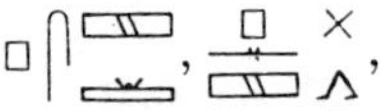, 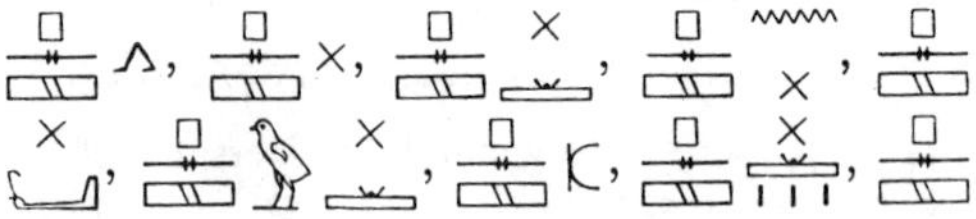 [illegible], to cleave, to split, to slit, to divide, to divide with, to share or participate with some one, to open the legs or arms, to distribute; Copt. ⲡⲱϣ.

pesshu , Peasant 248, one who divides, adjudicator.

pesshe-t 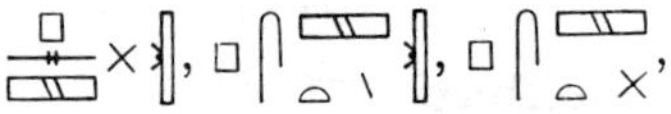, 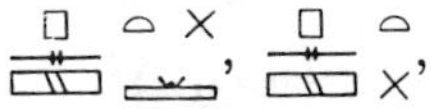, ration, allowance, share, division, allotment, lot, part, portion, division; [illegible], the half of anything; [illegible], [illegible], ĀZ. 35, 6, the two halves, the two portions; 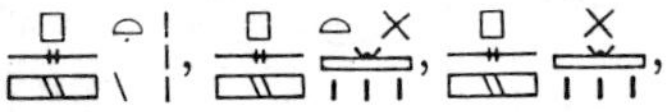, divisions, borders, boundaries; Copt. ⲡⲁϣⲉ.

pesesh-t en uat 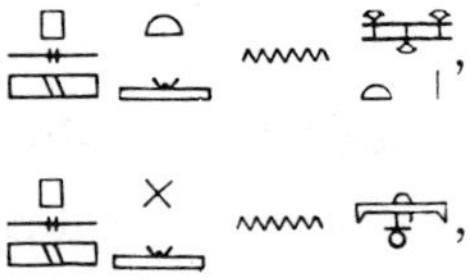, Rec. 14, 97, half-way.

pesesh en gerḥ, IV, 839, midnight.

pesesh-t 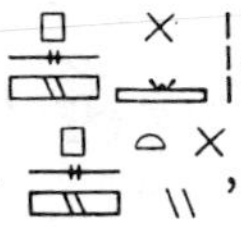, separation.

pesesh-ti, distributor.

Peseshti 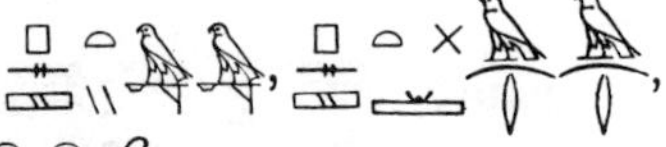, IV, 560, [illegible], the two divisions of Egypt, one belonging to Horus and the other to Set.

pesesh-t nu Ḥeru [illegible] (var. [illegible]) [illegible], the division or share of) Horus, *i.e.*, the South of Egypt.

pesesh-t nu Set [illegible], the division or share of Set, *i.e.*, the North of Egypt.

pesesh-t , , mat, carpet.

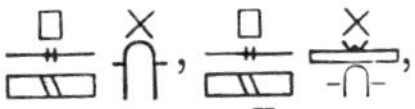

pesesh-t , , bandlet, bandage, strip of linen.

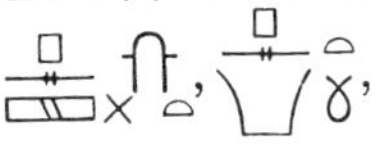

pesesh-kef , U. 26A, , , , the name of the principal instrument used in the ceremony of Opening the Mouth; see **peshen kef**  .

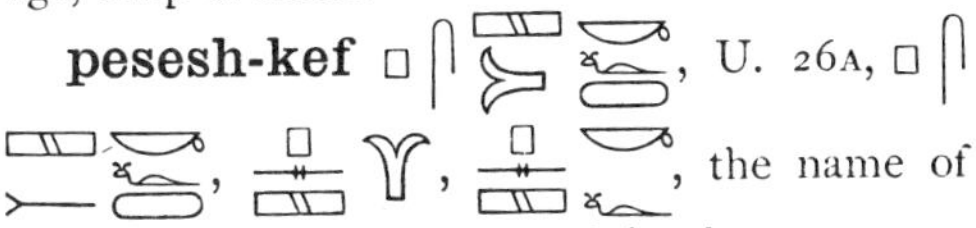

pesg , U. 214, , to spit with the intent to heal, or to curse, *e.g.*, when reciting incantations against Āapep; Copt. ⲡⲁϭⲥⲉ.

pesga , , spittle, saliva, rheum, any matter ejected from the body.

pesg , T. 11, N. 958, , , Rec. 30, 189, 31, 28, to anoint.

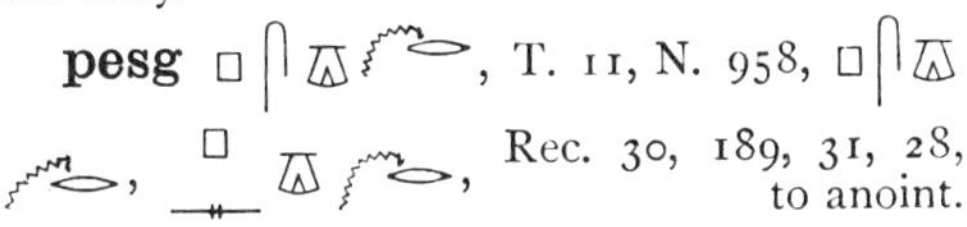

pesg  , to bite, to prick, to perforate.

pesg , , IV, 670, a log, a kind of timber.

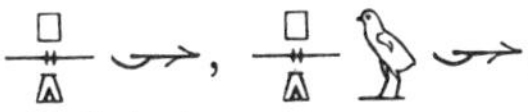

pest (pesṭ-t) , , back, backbone; see .

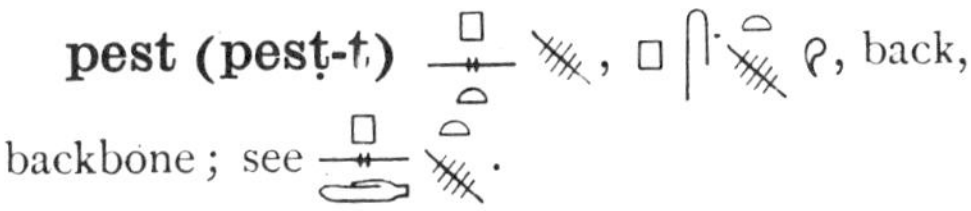

pest , ; to shine, to give light, to illumine; see .

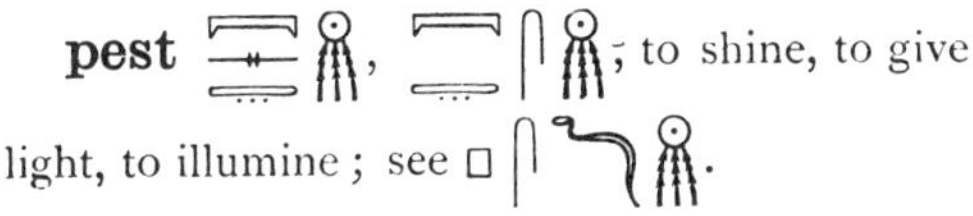

Pestit (Pesṭit) 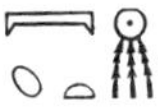 , the goddess of sunrise.

pest (pesṭ-t)  , gum or seed used in medicine.

Pest-taui (Pesṭit-taui) 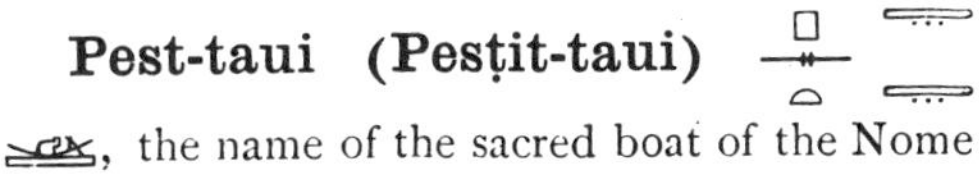 , the name of the sacred boat of the Nome Busirites.

pesṭ-t , , , , , IV, 1101, IV, 809, , back, backbone, vertebrae.

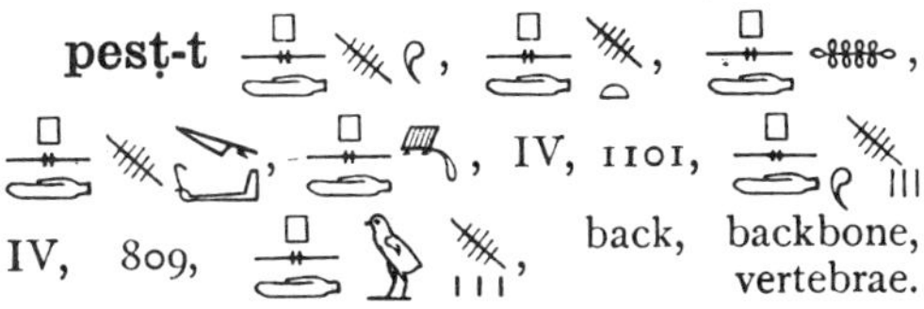

pesṭit , , "backs," men and women, people.

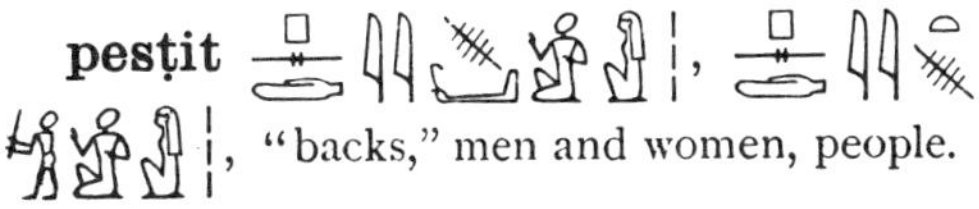

pesṭiu åmiu Ånu , B.D. 136A, 10, the sacred bones in Heliopolis.

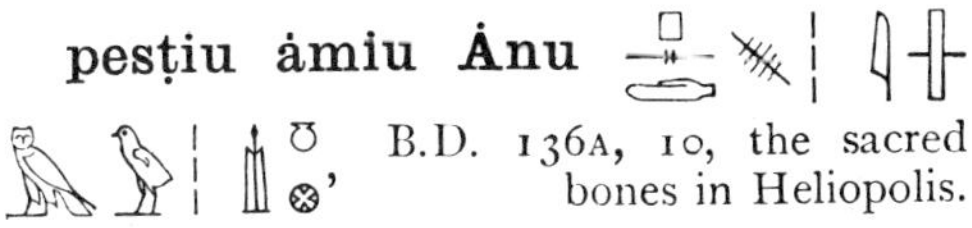

pesṭ-t (?)  , the backbone (of Osiris).

pesṭ , , , nine; see ; Copt. ⲯⲓⲧ.

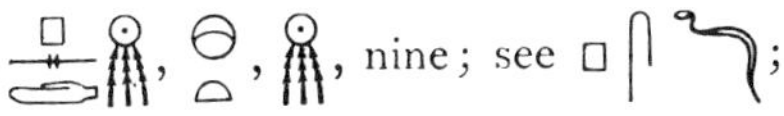

pesṭ , , , , , Rec. 27, 88, , , to shine, to illumine.

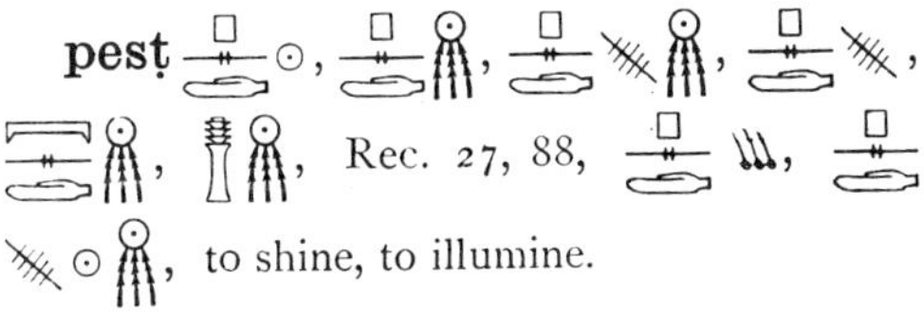

pesṭ , , to spread out like the light, or the sky.

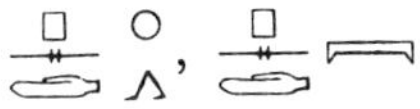

pesṭ tep  , B.D. 17, 133. . . . . .

pesṭ-t , ray of light; plur. .

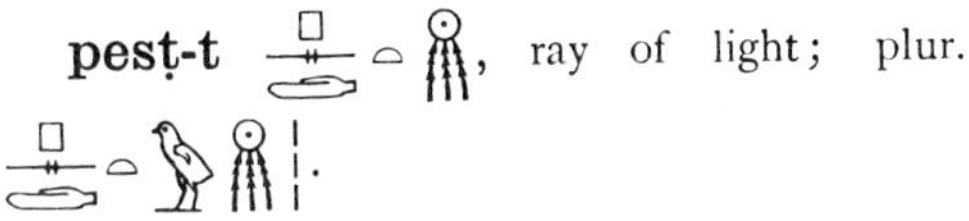

Pesṭit  , the 6th Gate of the Ṭuat.

Pesṭ-ti (?) , , Ṭuat XI, the light-disk that guided the boat of Åf into the dawn.

Pesṭu 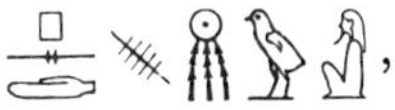 , B.D. 74, 2, a light-god.

Pesṭ-er ab  , a name of a god.

Pesṭ  , the festival of the 1st day of the month.

Pesṭit-khenti ḥert , , Rec. 34, 91, one of the 12 Thoueris goddesses; she presided over the month .

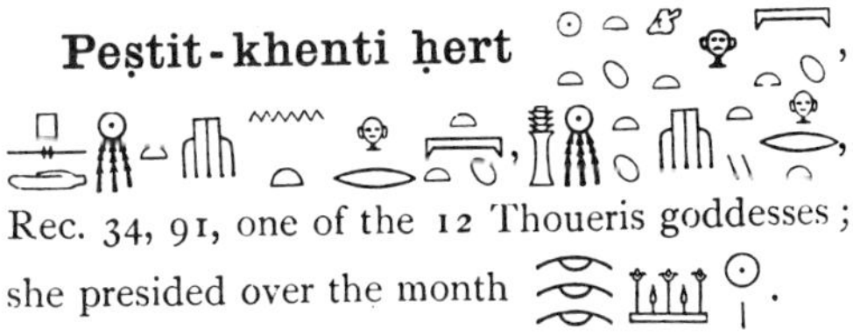

Pesṭ-taui 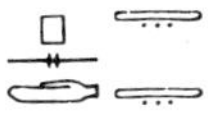 , the name of the sacred boat of the Nome Libya Mareotis.

pesṭ , , , Hearst Pap. 8, 18, , Rec. 27, 86, seed of some kind used in medicine.

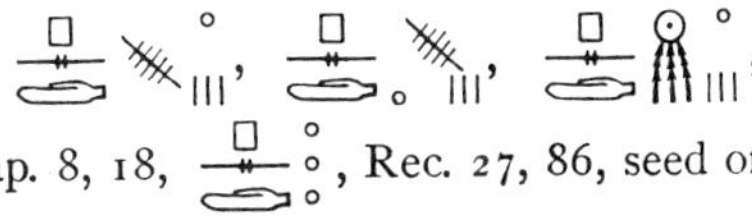

pesṭu 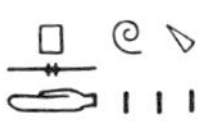 , Rec. 19, 19. . . . .

pestch , T. 174, P. 163, N. 856, 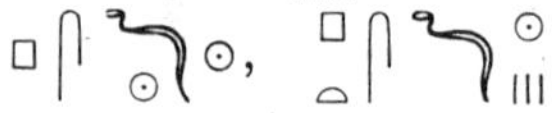 , to shine, to illumine.

pestch  , back, backbone, vertebrae; plur. 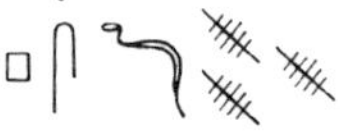

pestch 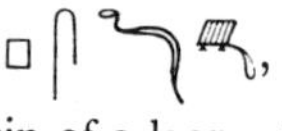, IV, 373, the back part of the skin of a leopard.

Pestchet , T. 238, 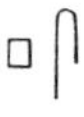 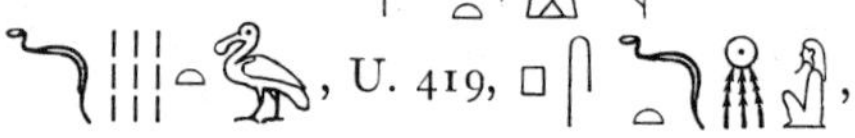, U. 419, Rec. 31, 170, a god.

pestch 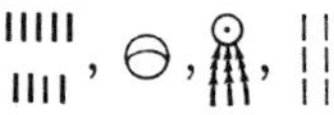, nine; fem. 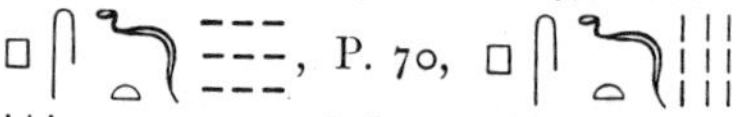, P. 70, M. 100, 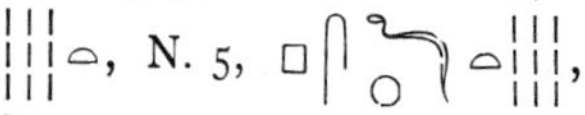, N. 5, T. 308, P. 456, ; Copt. ⲯⲓⲥ, ⲯⲓⲧ, etc.

pestch nut 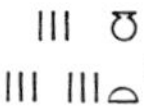, ninth.

[pestch . . . .] , ninety; Copt. ⲡⲥ̄ⲧⲁⲓⲟⲩ.

pestch — ḥeb enti pestch , , 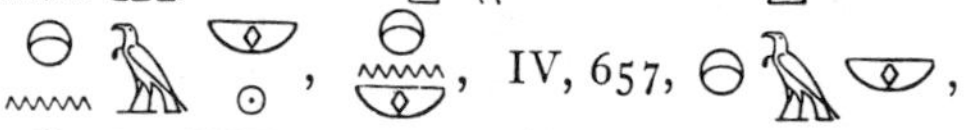, IV, 657, 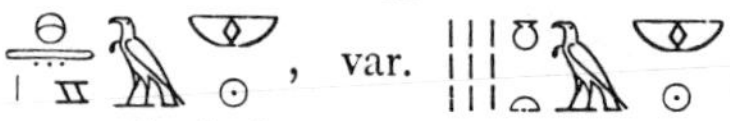, var., the new moon festival.

pestch (?) , nine-thread stuff.

pestch-t , It is probable that the true reading is Pauti, which is the name of a very ancient god; see 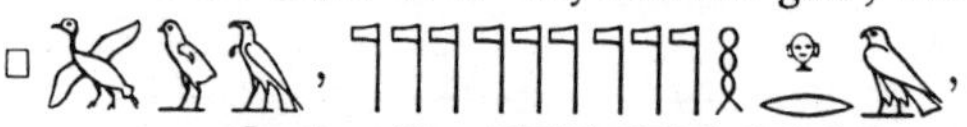, U. 443, 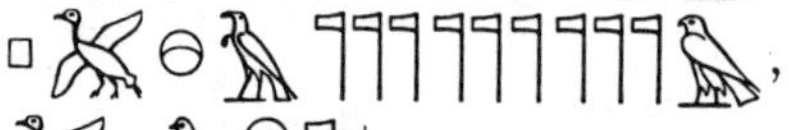, T. 253, , B.D. 125, I, 12. The reading pestch-t is due to the confusion of the signs 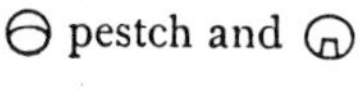 pestch and paut.

pestch - t (?) 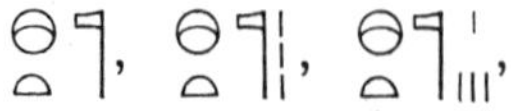, 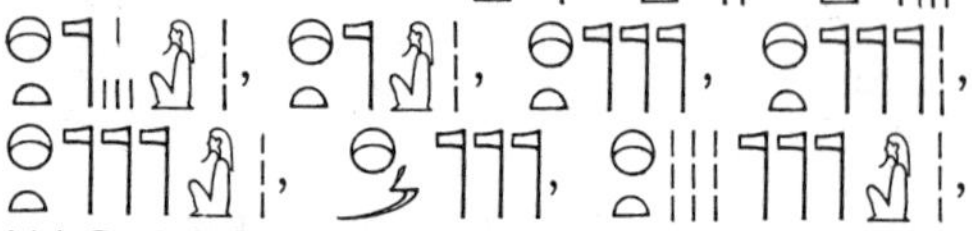, , Rec. 31, 163, the first and greatest nine gods. Late forms are 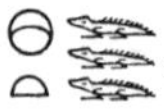, Sphinx 4, 123, and .

pestch-t āa-t , U. 251, P. 26, T. 273, M. 36, N. 67, 647, 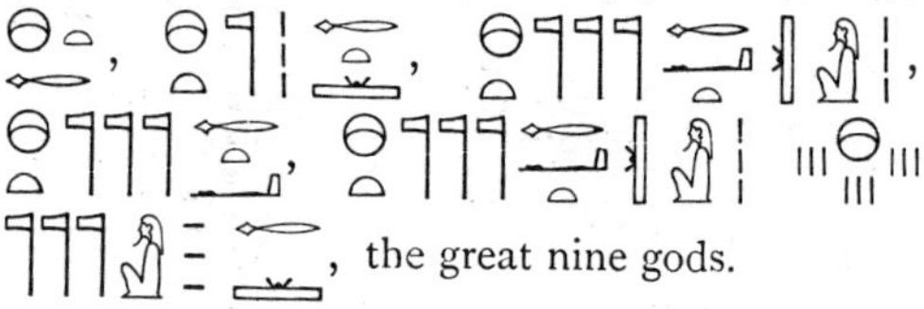, the great nine gods.

pestch-t netches-t , U. 251, the little nine gods.

Pestch - ti (Pauti)  , U. 188, T. 30, 67, 362, M. 67, 203, 222, 322, 461, 462, 463, 464, 465, 466, 582, N. 684, 751, 790, 1137, 1188, 1189, 1321, 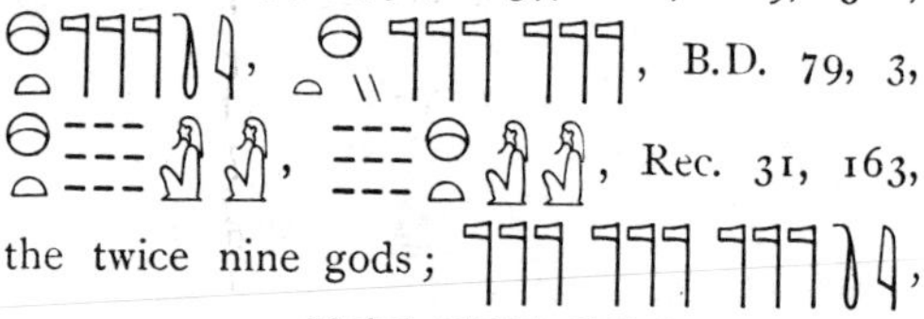, B.D. 79, 3, Rec. 31, 163, the twice nine gods; U. 179, 480, , P. 602, N. 47, 1267, M. 453, the very great twice nine gods.

pestchiu (?) 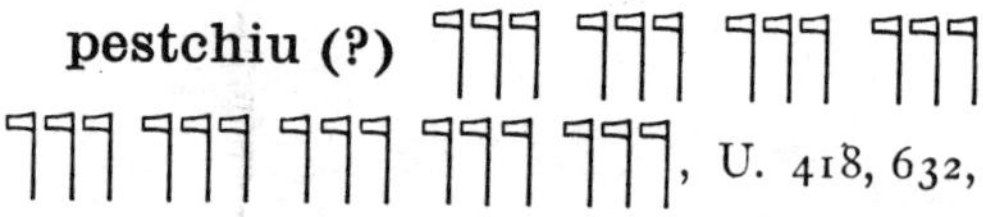, U. 418, 632, T. 238, 307, P. 218, the three companies of the gods, *i.e.*, the great gods of heaven, earth, and the Ṭuat = 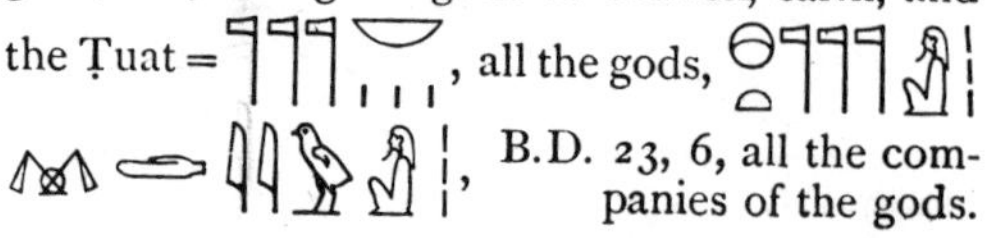, all the gods, B.D. 23, 6, all the companies of the gods.

pestch-t 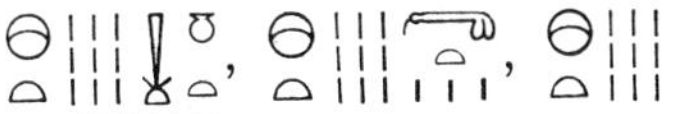 , etc., up to , the 9th nine gods.

Pestch-t Åakbit  , B.D. 168, the nine weeping goddesses.

Pestch-t åmiu-khet Åsår   B.D. 168, the gods in the train of Osiris.

Pestch-t åmiut Sar 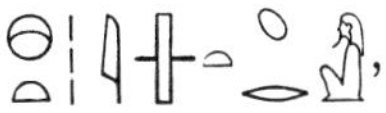, the nine gods of Osiris in the 6th Gate.

Pestch-t åmeniu Åsår  , B.D. 168, the nine gods who hid Osiris.

Pestch-t åmeniu āu 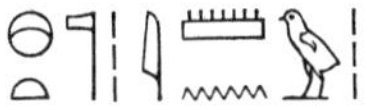  B.D. 168, the nine gods of the hidden arms.

Pestch-t årit pe-t  , P. 298–300, the nine gods of heaven.

Pestch-t årit ta  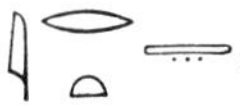, P. 298–300, the nine gods of earth.

Pestch-t nåk-t Āapep  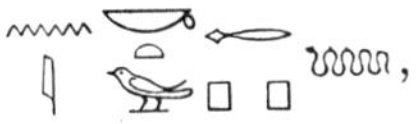, the nine gods who slew Āapep.

Pestch-t resit , B.D. 168, the nine watchers.

Pestch-t ḥeq Åment  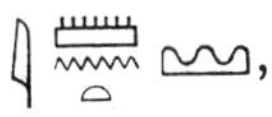, B.D. 168, the nine gods of the governor of Åment.

Pestch-t sau åmiu Ṭuat 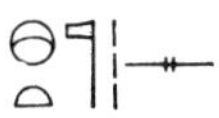 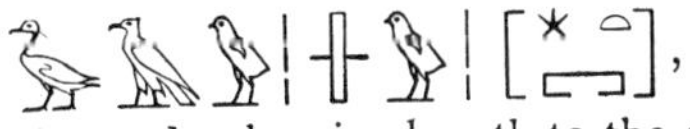, B.D. 168, the nine gods who give breath to the dead.

Pestch-t pestch , T. 308, the nine bowmen of Horus.

pesh  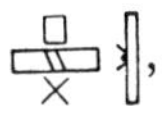, to divide, to split, to cut, to separate, to distribute, to share;  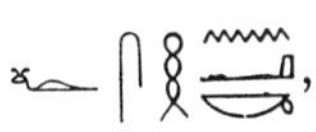, no other god shared her with thee; Copt. пωϣ.

pesh-t  Israel Stele 17, part, portion, share, division.

pesh-ti , the two halves of heaven, the South and the North.

peshå 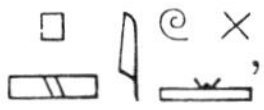, Rec. 21, 15, part, lot.

pesh 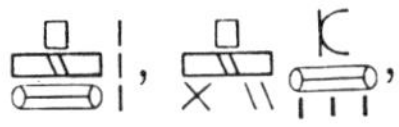, rations, offerings, products.

peshut (?) 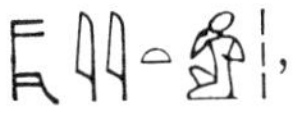, Israel Stele 25, , Kubbân Stele 5, , rebels (?)

pesh-en-kef 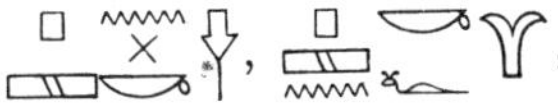, an instrument used in the ceremony of "Opening the mouth." Read **peshen-kef.**

Pesh-f-ḥeteput , Denderah IV, 84, 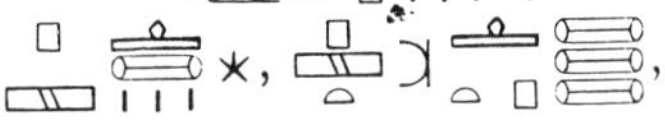, Berg. II, 8, a guardian of the 3rd Pylon.

peshsh 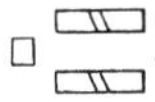, M. 69, 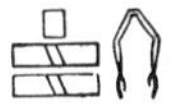, P. 103, [illegible], T. 279, P. 61, M. 156, N. 89, 989, to spread out the legs; [illegible], to spread out the arms, to divide.

pesh [illegible], to spread out the wings, to fly.

pesh-t [illegible], the bending or stringing of a bow.

peshen [illegible], U. 444, [illegible], T. 253, [illegible], N. 755, [illegible], [illegible], Åmen. 13, 18, to cleave, to divide, to split, to separate from.

peshen-t [illegible], divisions, shares in an inheritance.

Peshnå [illegible], T. 311, a town in the Ṭuat (?)

peshen-t [illegible], Ebers Pap. 84, 3, a seed used in medicine.

pesher [illegible], U. 260, M. 787, [illegible], P. 96, 713, [illegible], P. 96, [illegible], N. 41, [illegible], N. 661, [illegible], N. 625, to revolve, to make a circuit, to turn the face round; see [illegible].

pesher-t 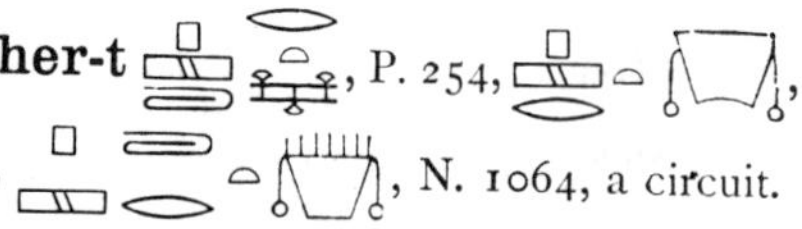, P. 254, M. 475, N. 1064, a circuit.

peshes 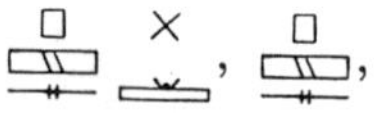, to divide, to cleave, to split.

peshes-t , division, share.

pesht 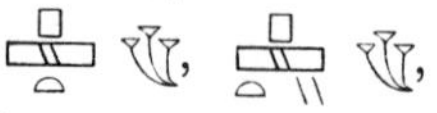, flax; Heb. פִּשְׁתָּה, פֵּשֶׁת.

peq 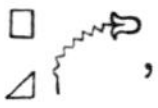, to pour out.

peq 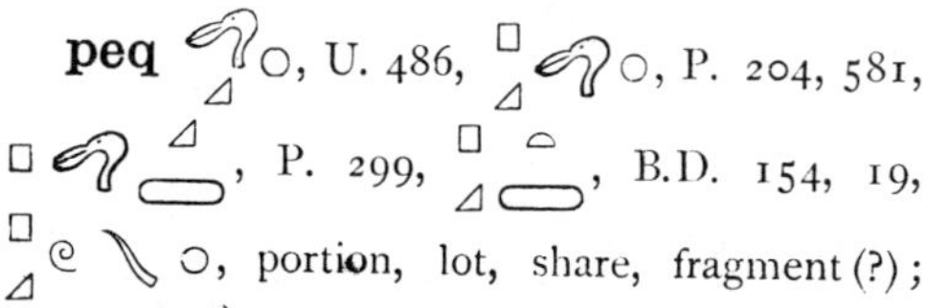, U. 486, P. 204, 581, P. 299, B.D. 154, 19, portion, lot, share, fragment (?); plur. 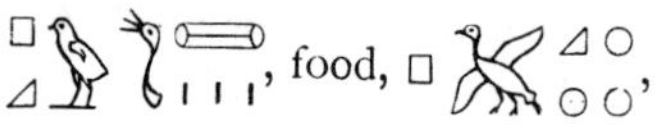, food, P. 161.

pequ , a seed or fruit.

peq-t 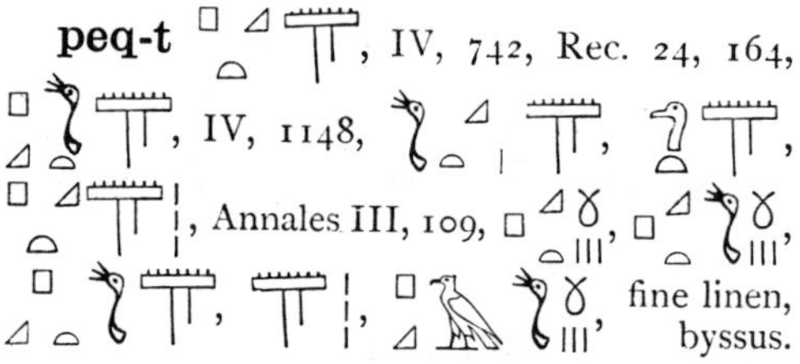, IV, 742, Rec. 24, 164, IV, 1148, Annales III, 109, fine linen, byssus.

peq - t 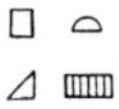, potsherd, earthenware, crockery.

peqit , shell of an animal or of a fish.

peqȧ 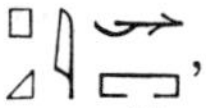, a holy temple (of Osiris ?) at Abydos; see , IV, 98, the festival of Peqȧ.

peqer , Rec. 11, 84, , an object made of peqer-wood in the tomb of Osiris.

Peqer-t 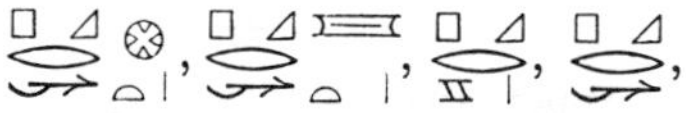, 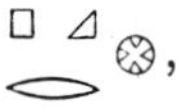, the name of the portion of the plain of Abydos that contained the tomb of the early king which was believed to be that of Osiris.

peqer , a tree, or group of trees, that grew at Abydos by the tomb of Osiris.

peqer 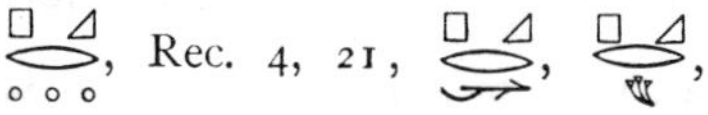, Rec. 4, 21, sesame seed, poppy seed; Copt. ⲫⲁⲕⲓ.

peqru , Hearst Pap. 15, 3, intestinal worms.

pek , Ȧmen. 23, 11, thy, thine; Copt. ⲡⲉⲕ.

pek , to spread out, to separate; Copt. ⲡⲱϭⲉ.

peki 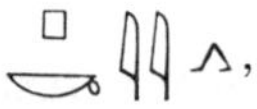, Rev. 11, 165, to be timid.

pekȧ en-ḥa-t , cowardice, Copt; ⲡⲁⲕⲉⲛϩⲏⲧ.

peki 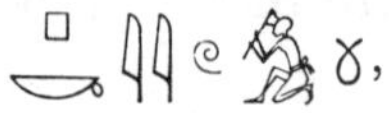, mourning apparel.

peksa , Rev. 14, 18, spittle; Copt. ⲡⲁϭⲥⲉ.

peg 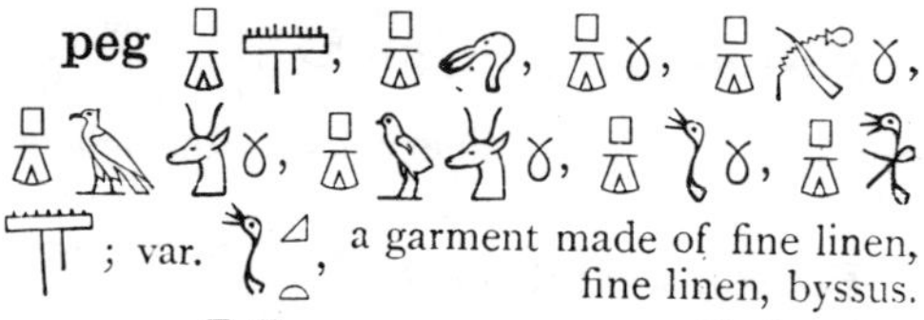; var. a garment made of fine linen, fine linen, byssus.

pega , Rec. 31, 22, ibid., IV, 1110, A.Z. 1910, 117, Thes. 1295, (?) Rhind Pap. 48, to divide, to cleave, to open, to spread out, to open the arms or legs, to embrace someone, to unroll papyri, to lay open, to spread out.

peg, pega-t 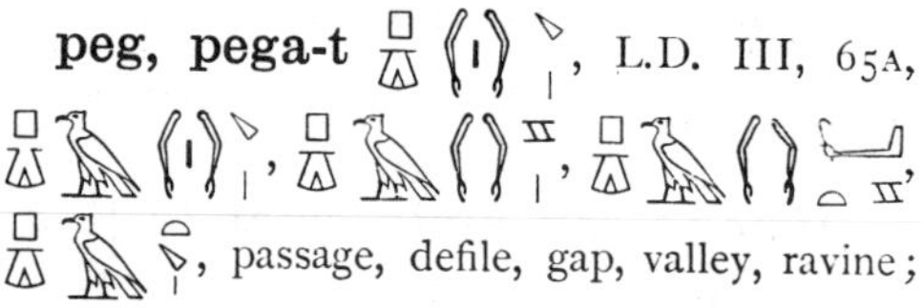, L.D. III, 65A, passage, defile, gap, valley, ravine; plur. 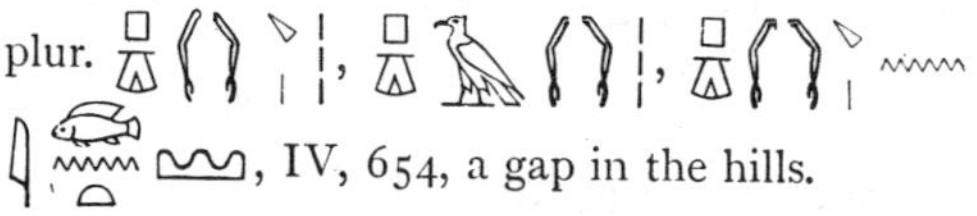, IV, 654, a gap in the hills.

Pega , N. 792, T. 202, a god.

peg , part, piece, portion.

peg , B.D. 145, 79, to unfold, to explain.

peg , to set at rest, to quiet.

peg, IV, 755, A.Z. 45, 133, a bowl, a vessel, a measure; plur.  , Hh. 455.

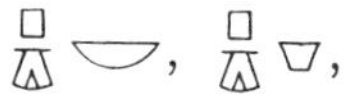

peg, Ḥerusàtef Stele 27, A.Z. 1890, 24 ff., a measure of weight = $\frac{1}{128}$ of the 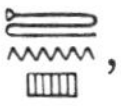 , or $\frac{1}{4}$ of the , or $\frac{5}{3}$, or 0,7106 grammes.

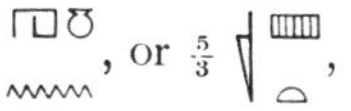

pegg-t, Hearst Pap. 13, 6, a kind of insect.

pega, a vessel of some kind.

pega, a metal object.

pega, Rec. 11, 69, dust, earth (?)

Pega, B.D. 169, 18, a town or city.

pega, a kind of cake or bread.

pegas, , , to spit, spittle, saliva; Copt. ⲡⲁϭⲥⲉ.

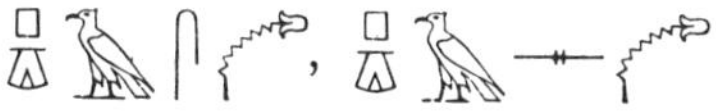

pegs, , to spit, spittle.

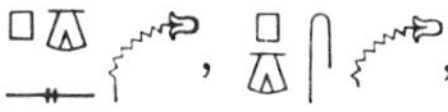

pegs, tied round with something, girt about with.

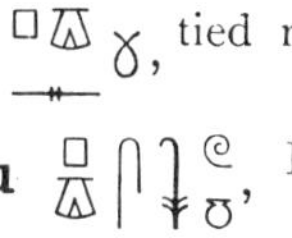

pegsu, Rechnungen 76, pot, vessel.

pet, cake, bread, food.

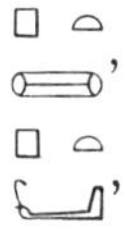

pet, to break open; varr. 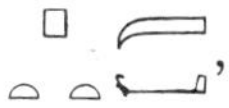 , 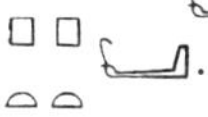 .

pett, to crush, to break; see  .

pet, Rev. 11, 125, to pursue; Copt. ⲡⲱⲧ.

petȧ, Rev. 13, 29, runner.

petpet, T. 35, N. 133, , M. 116, , , , to bruise, to beat down, to trample down, to smite, to crush in pieces; Copt. ⲡⲟⲧⲡⲧ.

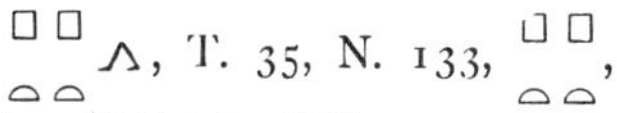

pet, footstool, footboard, socket, plinth, pedestal, stand.

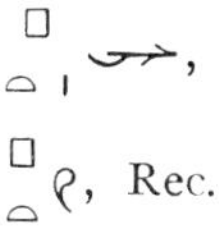

pet, Rec. 15, 17, sceptre, staff.

pet, U. 584 , M. 796; see **petr**  .

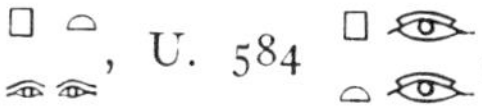

pet, , flood, inundation.

Petu, Edfû I, 81, a title of the Nile-god.

Pet, III, 141 = **Ptaḥ**  .

Petit, Metternich Stele 51, one of the seven scorpion-goddesses of Isis.

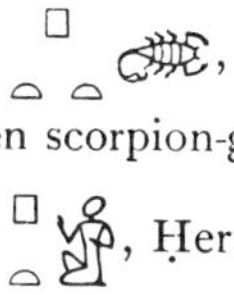

pet-ȧ, Ḥerusàtef Stele 5, what is to me, my; var.  .

petȧ, see **petrȧ**  .

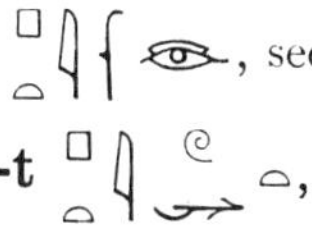

petȧ-t, Rev. 14, 5, bow; Copt. ⲡⲓⲧⲉ.

peti, , = , , what?

peti eref su, , , B.D. 17, "what is it?" literally, shew (or, explain) what it is (*i.e.*, means).

Peti, , , B.D. 50A, 5, a god.

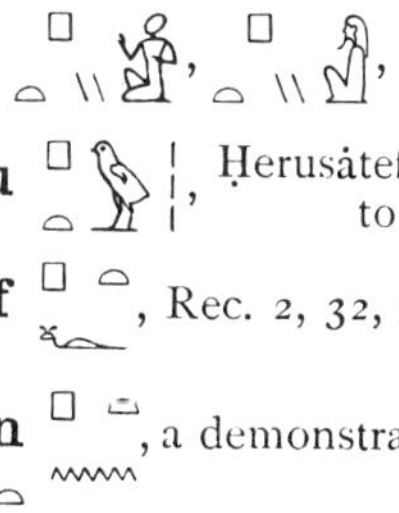

pet-u, Ḥerusàtef Stele 96, what is to them, them, their.

petef, Rec. 2, 32, this.

peten, a demonstrative pronoun, this; see  .

pet-nȧ, Ḥerusàtef Stele 110, what is to me, my, mine.

petr, , , an interrogative particle, what?;  , what is the matter?

petr, petrȧ, , , to explain, to say, to declare, to show, to reveal.

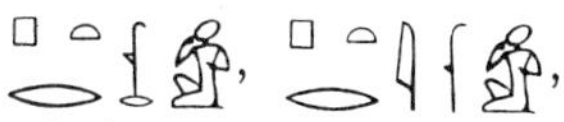

petr 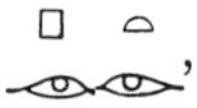, U. 385, , U. 576, 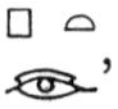, P. 181, M. 284, N. 893, , N. 965, 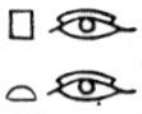, U. 584, M. 794, 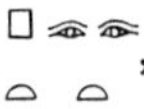, P. 667, M. 776, , U. 504, to see, to look.

petriu 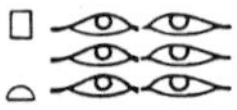, N. 656, 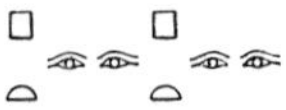 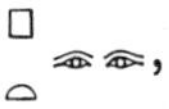, M. 381, those who have sight, those who see.

petr — Later forms are: 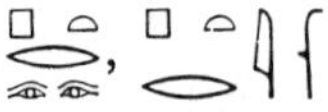 , Treaty 8, 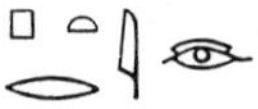  Ȧmen. 15, 7, 18, 6, 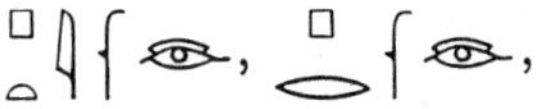 .

petrȧ 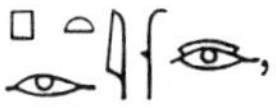, Leyd. Pap. 7, 10, glance, glimpse, a sight of anything; , things seen.

petrȧ-t , A.Z. 76, 100, a look-out place, watch tower.

Petr 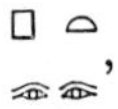, P. 414, M. 593, , N. 1198, , U. 576, , P. 236, 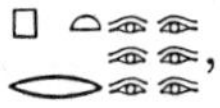, N. 965, a region of heaven.

Petrȧt , P. 332, 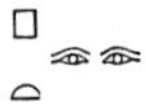 , M. 634, , a lake in the Ṭuat.

Petrȧ , N. 662, , , Rec. 31, 13, 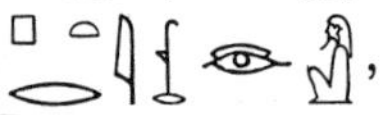, B.D. 68, 3, a sky-god.

Petrȧ 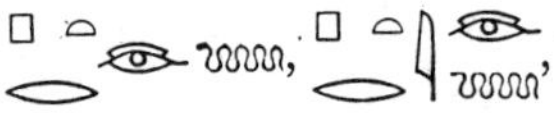, Ṭuat XI, the name of a fiend in the Ṭuat.

Petrȧ-ba  , Nav. Lit. 28, a name of Rā.

Petrȧ-neferu-nu-nebt-s  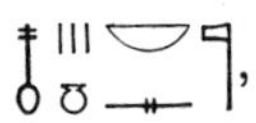, Denderah IV, 84,  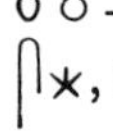, Denderah III, 24, 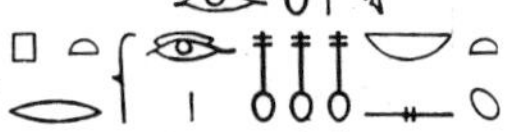 the goddess of the 12th hour of the night.

Petrȧ-sen [illegible], B.D. 99, 28, the stream on which the magical boat sailed.

petr [illegible], Rec. 5, 94, [illegible], Rec. 5, 95, [illegible], Anastasi IV, 3, 1, cord, thread, cord of a seal, wick of a lamp; plur. [illegible], Koller Pap. 3, 2; Heb. פְּתִיל.

pteḥ [illegible], Rev. 14, 13, to beg, to ask, to pray; Copt. ⲧⲟⲃϩ, ⲧⲱⲃϩ, ⲧⲱⲃⲁϩ, a prayer.

pteḥ [illegible], [illegible], to open, to make open-work, to engrave; var. [illegible].

Pteḥ [illegible], Rec. 31, 16, [illegible], [illegible], P. 672, 807, N. 618, 634, 1277, [illegible], [illegible], the architect of heaven and earth, the mastercraftsman in working metals, sculptor, designer, and the fashioner of the bodies of men; he was the blacksmith, sculptor, and mason of the gods. His chief forms are:

Pteḥ-āa-resu-ȧneb-f [illegible], Ptaḥ the Great, South one (?) of his wall.

Pteḥ-ur [illegible], Ptaḥ the Great, the heart and tongue of the gods, [illegible].

Pteḥ-Nu [illegible], [illegible], Ptaḥ, creator of the sky.

Pteḥ-neb-ānkh [illegible], Ptaḥ, lord of life.

Pteḥ-neb-qeṭ-t [illegible], Ptaḥ, lord of the artist's designing and painting room.

Pteḥ-nefer-ḥer [illegible], Ptaḥ of the beautiful face.

Pteḥ-re [illegible], B.D. (Saïte), 47, 15; see **Ḥept-shet.**

Pteḥ-res-àneb-f , Ptaḥ, south of his wall: one of the forms of Ptaḥ of Memphis.

Pteḥ-res-àneb-f 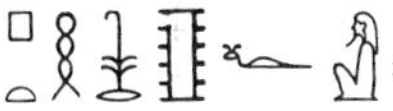, , the god of the month Paophi.

Pteḥ-Ḥāp , Ptaḥ united to the Nile-god.

Pteḥ-kheri-beq-f  , Rev. 2, 63, Ptaḥ beneath his olive tree.

Pteḥ-smen-Maāt 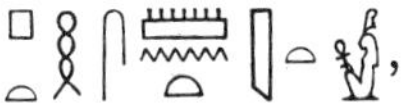, Ptaḥ stablisher of law.

Pteḥ-Seker (Sekri)  , Ptaḥ united to Seker, the old god of Death, lord of the necropolis of Memphis, *i.e.*, Ṣakkârah. He symbolized the dead Sun-god.

Pteḥ-Sekri-Àsàr , the triune god of the resurrection.

Pteḥ-Sekri-Tem 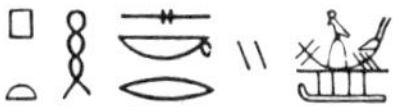 , B.D. 15, 2, a triad of Memphis.

Pteḥ-Tanen , the union of Ptaḥ with the primitive Earth-god Tanen, or Tenen, ; varr. , 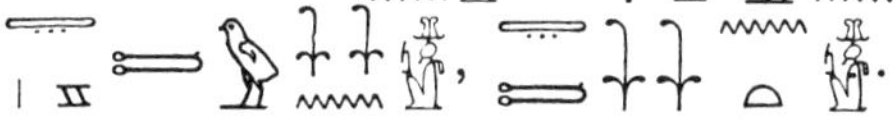.

Pteḥ-ṭeṭ , Ptaḥ and the god of the Ṭeṭ pillar.

Pteḥ-ṭeṭ-sheps-àst-Rā  , B.D. 142, IV, 26.

pteḥti 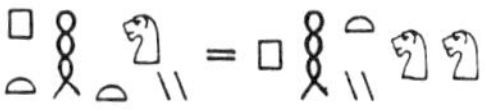.

petekh , P. 604, , N. 1155, , P. 1116B, 31, , to cast down, to fall.

petekh sa , Leyd. Pap. 8, 14. . . .

petsh 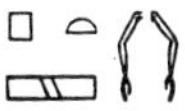, Rec. 27, 84, , to fall (?)

peth 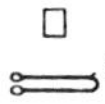, U. 534, T. 294, to tear, to rend.

petthai , Rechnungen 69; compare Syr. ܦܝܬܐ, Arab. فض. . . . . .

pethan (?) , ball, tablet (Lacau).

pethrà 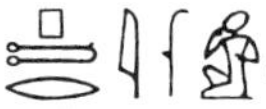, Metternich Stele 45; see **petrà** .

peṭ , foot, paw of an animal; plur. , Mar. Aby. I, 6, 34, knees; , two-legged; , four-legged; Copt. ⲡⲁⲧ.

peṭ , servant, footman; plur.  , IV, 501.

peṭu , Rev. 6, 9, foot-soldiers, infantry; [illegible], captain of footmen; [illegible], chief of the hill district.

Peṭti [illegible], a tribe or nation.

peṭu-t (petsu-t) [illegible], Anastasi I, 12, 2, 16, 3, chest, box, book-box.

peṭ [illegible], Israel Stele 5, to run away, to flee, to hasten; [illegible], Rev. 13, 35; Copt. ⲡⲱⲧ.

peṭpeṭ [illegible], Hh. 174, to take to flight.

peṭu [illegible], Rec. 11, 72, fugitives.

peṭ [illegible], Mar. Karn. 53, 33, [illegible], to open out, to spread out, to be wide, spacious, extended.

peṭ-ti [illegible], strider.

peṭ-àb(?) [illegible], N. 666; see [illegible].

peṭ āui [illegible], Metternich Stele 74, to open the arms, to embrace.

peṭ nemm-t [illegible], to walk with long strides.

peṭ setu 
[illegible], Mar. Aby. I, 7, extent of a coast or land.

Peṭ-she 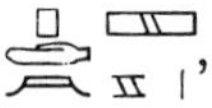, B.D. 141–142, 92, a sanctuary of Osiris.

Peṭu-she (?) , M. 699, , P. 442, a mythological town.

peṭ-sheser , Thes. 1285, [illegible], Annales 3, 109, [illegible], IV, 837, Palermo Stele, etc., to mark out the size and extent of a proposed building with the builder's cord.

peṭ-sheser , IV, 169, Thes. 1287, the festival of stretching the cord.

Peṭ[it] , Berg. II, 13, "spreader," a title of the Sky-goddess.

Peṭit ȧbut , P.S.B. 25, 18, a title of Sekhmit.

Peṭ-ā 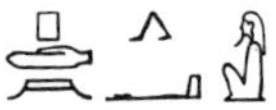, he of the extended arm, *i.e.*, Osiris.

Peṭ-āḥāt 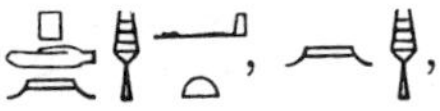, Ṭuat III, a god.

Peṭ, Peṭ-ra , B.D. (Saïte) 125, 40, 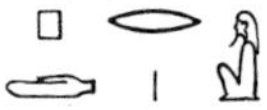; see **Ḥepṭ-ra.**

peṭ , IV, 977, A.Z. 1905, 27, to bend a bow.

peṭ-t, petch-t 
[illegible], bow; plur. [illegible]
[illegible]; see [illegible]; Copt. ⲡⲓⲧⲉ, ⲫⲓⲧ.

peṭ-ti , the double bow.

peṭ-t 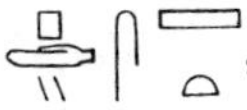, A.Z. 1908, 20, the bow and arrow amulet.

peṭ-t Khar , IV, 712, a Syrian bow.

peṭṭiu 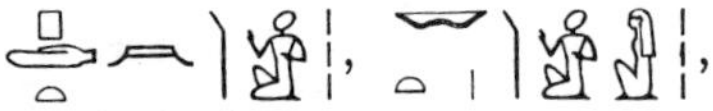, foreign bowmen, barbarians.

peṭ-t , a measure for cloth, [illegible], or incense, IV, 756.

peṭ 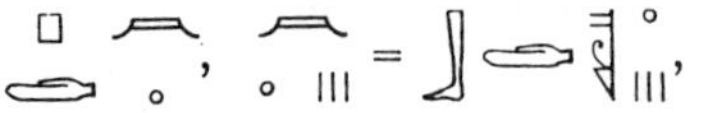, incense, unguent.

peṭ 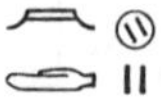; see [illegible], perfume.

peṭṭu , Ebers Pap. 93, 20; Hearst Pap. 11, 10, pustules (?)

peṭ , P. 307, goose, duck.

[Peṭaparā ], Potiphar; Heb. פּוֹטִיפֶרַע, Gr. Πετεφρῆ.

peṭer , a basket made of plaited reeds or cords, lamp wick; var. 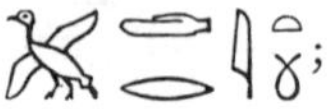; compare Heb. פְּתִיל.

peṭkh 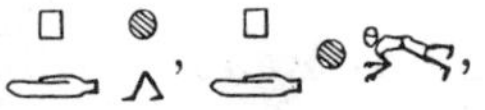, Thes. 1198, 1201, to throw down, to be brought low.

peṭkh-t 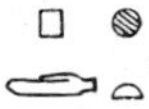, defeat, overthrow.

peṭes , a covering, wrap, bag (?); [illegible]
[illegible], IV, 630, wrap for clothes, holdall;
[illegible], IV, 31.

peṭes , Rec. 8, 171, box, chest.

peṭsut , Gol. 12, 82, tracts of land, marches of country.

peṭes ,
[illegible], to lay waste, to destroy, to attack (?)

peṭsu , opener, breaker, destroyer.

peṭs-t , ball, globule, bolus, pill; plur. [illegible], Rec. 19, 19.

Peṭsu , B.D. 62, 4, a magical name.

peṭesh 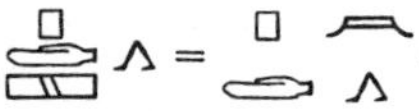 (?)

Peṭṭhi 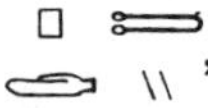, Ṭuat X, a bowman-god.

petch , to sharpen (?)

petch 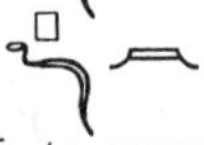, [illegible], P. 704, [illegible], M. 205, N. 666, to spread out, to stretch out, to bend a bow.

petch-t , something flexible.

petch-t ḥa-t , N. 408, expansion of heart, joyful; , M. 205, [illegible], N. 666.

petch nemtt ,  P. 187, M. 349, N. 902, he who walks with long strides.

petch-t , bow, bowman; plur. , T. 308, [illegible].

petchti , bowman, archer, foreign soldier; Copt. ⲣⲁⲙⲙⲛⲓⲧⲉ; plur. , U. 497, T. 308, P. 204, 683, N. 759,   , Tell el-Amarna, **pidati**, P.S.B. 1892, 347, Zeit. für Ass. 1892, 64, 65; 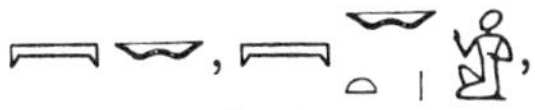, chief bowman; plur. .

Petchtiu 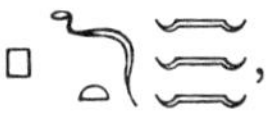, T. 308, 319, U. 497, the bowmen of Horus who were either nine 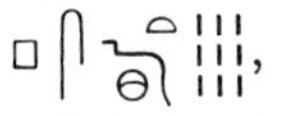, T. 308, or seven , T. 306, in number.

petchtiu pesetch (?) 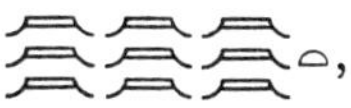, N. 665,   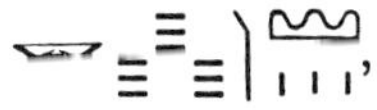, III, 138, the nine peoples in the Sûdân whose principal weapons were bows and arrows.

petchtiu pesetch (?) 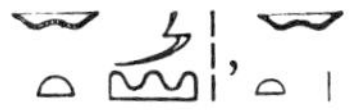, , Harris Pap. I, 4, 5, Metternich Stele 160, var. of preceding.

petchtiu menshu , naval archers.

petchtiu shu (?) , Mar. Karn. 53, 24, , Rec. 19, 18, bowmen, or hunters, of the desert.

Petch-āḥā , Lacau, a god.

Petch-taiu , Hh. 332, a title of the Nile.

petchu 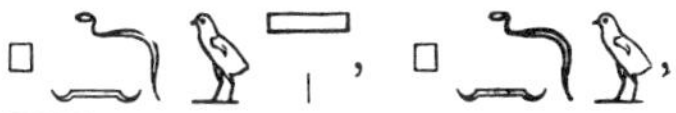, , P. 607, N. 757, 797, 849, 1126, canal, stream, lake; plur. , P. 76, [illegible], P. 73, [illegible], N. 13.

petchṭu  , P. 204, 442, canal (?)

Petchu 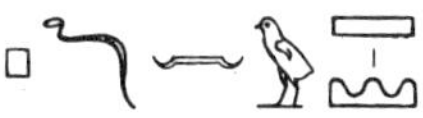, U. 557, a district in the Other World.

petch-t [illegible], P. 340, , T. 314, perfume (?)

petchpetch , Rec. 17, 18, , U. 25, perfume, incense.

petchpetch , U. 356, N. 70, 233 = .

petcha , Rev. 13, 28, to copulate; compare Arab. فَجَّا.

petchu , an offering.

[illegible] F — F [illegible]

f  = Heb. ב and ף.

f , P.S.B. 14, 141, he, his, its.

f , form of pron. 3rd pers. sing. when following a noun in the dual, *e.g.*, 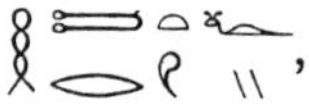,

.

fi aa-t (?) , Rev. 13, 15, = ϥⲓ ⲙⲟⲟⲩ or ϥⲁⲓ ⲙⲟⲟⲩ.

fi  with 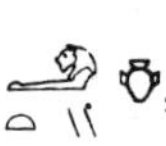, to feel disgust, nausea.

fu (fṭu) 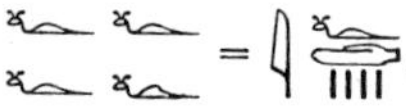, four.

fa-t , cordage, tackle; [illegible], U. 537 (?)

fa, fai , M. 359, , T. 8, N. 910, 1382, , P. 347, , M. 648, , , L.D. III, 229c, 14, to carry, to bear, to lift up, to get up from sleep, to start a journey; Copt. ϥⲉⲓ.

fai, faȧu , P. 347, , 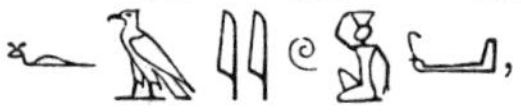, bearer, carrier, carrying.

fai , to lift up the feet in flight, *e.g.*,  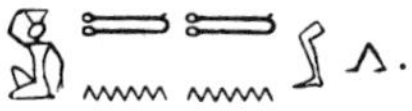.

fai , P. 311,  , bearer, carrier, support, supporter; plur. , Rec. 32, 98, , , Peasant, 324, weighers.

fait , support, supporter (fem.).

fait (?) , Rev., support.

faa , [illegible], Rec. 30, 189,  [illegible], something carried or borne or lifted up; , Rec. 36, 157, weighings.

fa-t [illegible], interest on money.

fa-t , Rec. 14, 166, a raised seat.

fai 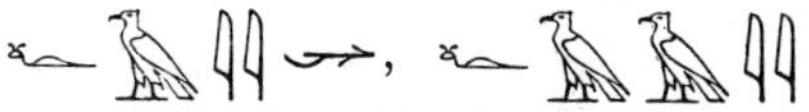, , a litter, a kind of sedan chair.

fai [illegible], the bearer-in-chief who carried the king's stool.

fau , P. 186, M. 346, N. 900, Décrets 27, , forced labour, corvée.

fa-ā 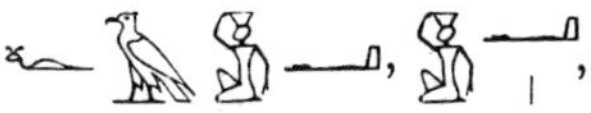, IV, 1031, to lift up the hand and arm.

fa-t-ā , Rec. 36, 160.

fa-ākhu, to kindle fire on the altars.

fai-m'rka [ ], Rec. 21, 86. . . . . . .

fa-t-m'her-t, IV, 1020, milk-carrier.

fa-nifu(tau), A.Z. 1907, 82, to hoist the sail, to set sail for a place.

fa-ḥer, to lift up the face, to be bold; , "those who lift up their faces."

fai-ḥeteput, Rec. 19, 92, bouquets-carrier.

fai-ḥetch, to present an offering of silver.

fa-khet, to make offerings.

fa-t kheft ḥer, N. 277, a presentation of an offering to the deceased.

fai-senter, to present an offering of incense.

fa-shep-en-qen, Rec. 33, 3, "carrier away of the prize of bravery"; Gr. ἀθλοφόρος.

fa-t-tep, the rearing of the head of a serpent before striking.

fa-ṭenȧ, , Rec. 33, 3, "bearer of the basket [of sacred offerings]"; Gr. κανηφόρος.

Fai, Ṭuat XI, a god who bore the serpent Meḥen to the East daily.

Fait, , , Rec. 27, 190, Denderah II, 55, a goddess who supported the western quarter of heaven.

Faiu, B.D. 168, the "bearer"-gods.

Faiu, Ṭuat III, eight gods who carried the boats and .

Fai-ȧr-tru, Ṭuat III, a god of the seasons, or year (?)

Fai-Ȧsȧr-mȧ-Ḥeru, Ombos I, 1, 64, a jackal-god.

Fai-ā, B.D. 165, , Hymn Darius 38, , , the god of the lifted arm, a title of Menu, Ȧmen, and other gods of generation.

Fai-ākh, B.D. 149, a god of the 2nd Ȧat.

Fai-pet, B.D. 149, a god of the 7th Ȧat.

Fai-m'kha-t, Ṭuat VI, B.D. 105, 6, a god whose body formed the pillar of the Great Scales.

Fai-Ḥeru, "carrier of Horus," a name of Osiris.

fa-t, cake, loaf.

fa-t, U. 417, , , U. 92, N. 369, an offering.

fai, loads of food, provender, etc.

fa (?) t, a kind of seed.

fai, , Harris Pap. I, 16B, 5, a kind of plant, a net made of palm fibre.

fai, a kind of precious stone.

Fai, Rec. 13, 27, a mythological serpent.

fau, worm = .

fau , riches, things that are broad or wide; , , "doors, great, high, broad."

fau , Rec. 32, 176, , Rec. 32, 179, gladness (?)

fanṭ 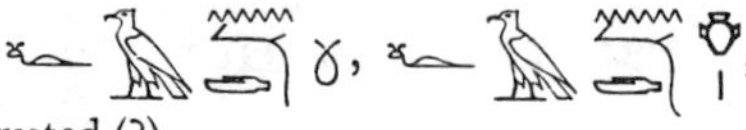, to be disgusted (?)

faka-t 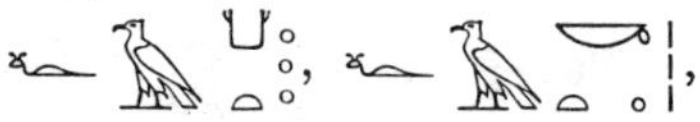, turquoise, malachite, mother of emerald; see 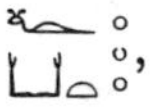, and .

Faku , Hh. 423, Rec. 31, 31; see 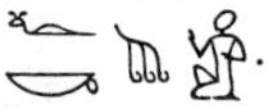.

fat , U. 417, , T. 237, things that cause disgust, abominations; see .

fȧ , hair; Copt. ϥⲱ, ϥⲱⲓ.

fȧth , Rougé I.H. II, 114, 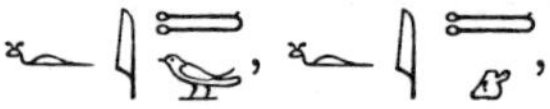, Thes. 1206, to be dirty, to be despised, contemned.

fāu , wicked, evil, wrong.

fāq 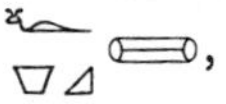, to bestow, to grant.

Fāgit 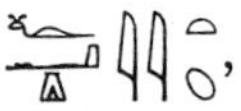, B.D.G. 243, a goddess of Nekhebet.

fi 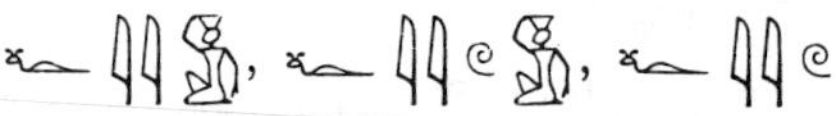 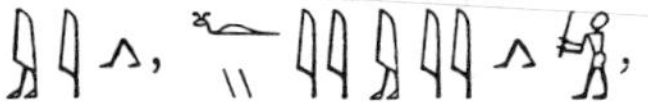, Rec. 11, 165, , to bear, to bring, to carry; , Rec. 13, 26 = ϥⲓ ⲛ ϩⲟ; Copt. ϥⲓ.

fiu , bearers, carriers, porters.

fi 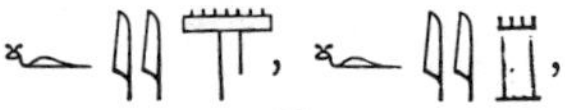, garment, covering.

fitr 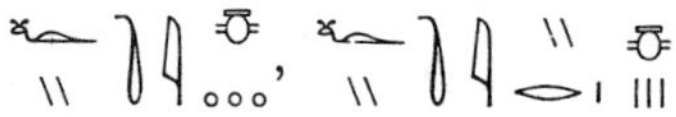, fat, grease; Heb. פֶּדֶר.

fua (?) , Rev., stone, mountain.

fefȧ 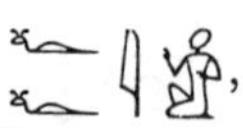, Amherst Pap. 1 . . . .

fen , Peasant 232, Rec. 29, 164, Tutānkh. 9, weak, helpless, weary of heart.

fennu , tired or feeble man.

fennu 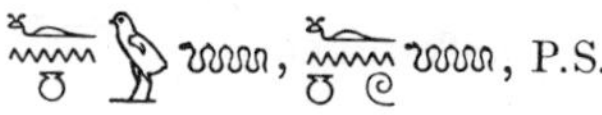, P.S.B. 13, 412, worm, serpent; see 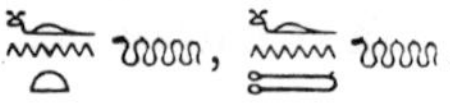.

fenui , T. 302 . . . . . .

fenuḥ (fenḥ) , to create, to propagate.

fenb , Wört. Supp. 497, bandy-legged.

fenkhu , E.T. 1, 53, , B.D. 125, I, 12, offerings [for the spirits].

Fenkhu 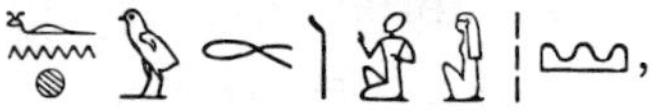, B.D. 125, III, 23, 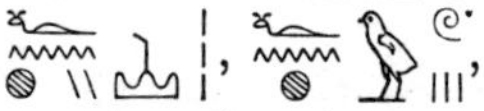, Rec. 31, 31, A.Z. 1908, 85, [illegible], [illegible], [illegible], L.D. III, 16A, [illegible], foreigners, [illegible], IV, 807, the lands of the Fenkhu; Gr. Φοίνικες.

feng [illegible] (?), [illegible], to evacuate, to make water; see [illegible].

fent [illegible], Annales 9, 156, some metal objects (?)

fenṭ [illegible], Anastasi I, 23, 8, [illegible], nose; see [illegible] and [illegible]; Copt. ϣⲁⲛⲧⲉ.

fent-neb [illegible], every nose, *i.e.*, everybody.

Fenti [illegible], [illegible], B.D. 125, II, "he of the nose," *i.e.*, one of the 42 judges in the Hall of Osiris, a name of Thoth.

Fenti-en-ānkh [illegible], "nose of life," a title of Osiris.

fent, worm, serpent; plur.; Copt. ϥⲛⲧ.

Fentu, B.D. 1B, 10, the "worms" of Ȧmente who devoured the dead.

fenth, T. 298, U. 543, worm, serpent; plur., Rec. 31, 15.

Fenth-f-ānkh, Denderah IV, 72, a title of Osiris.

fenṭ, Rec. 16, 59, to be disheartened.

fenṭ, Ȧmen. 24, 4, nose; plur., IV, 662, noses, nostrils.

Fenṭi, B.D. 125, II, a form of Thoth; one of the 42 Assessors of Osiris.

Fenṭ-t ānkh, A.Z. 1908, 120, "nose of life," *i.e.*, living nose, a name of Osiris.

Fenṭ-pet-per-em-Utu (?), B.D. 99, 30, a name of the ground over which sailed the magical boat.

fenṭ, worm, serpent; see.

fentch, U. 565, P. 216, Rec. 30, 200, nose; see; Copt. ϣⲁⲁⲛⲧ.

Fentchi, a name of Thoth; var.

Fentchti, Sphinx, II, 81.

F-ḥes-em-tep-ā (?), a crocodile-god, god of the 2nd day of the month.

fekh, U. 285, 362, P. 539, Rec. 11, 67, to unloose, to undress, to detach, to strip, to raid, to destroy, to ruin, to overthrow a wall, to relax the hold on, to leave someone or something.

fekhkh, U. 180, B.D. 178, 8, to break, to break through.

fekhfekh, N. 656, to break, to destroy, to ruin.

Fekhu = .

fekh-t, characteristics, distinguishing marks.

Fekh-ti (?) (?), Mar. Aby. I, 44, two sacred objects in .

fekhā, P. 1116B, 61, to seize, to grasp; see (U. 176).

fekhen, to refuse, to fail.

fekhen-t, Rec. 5, 95, twisted or plaited fibre-work.

fes, P. 682, to bake, to boil, to cook; see, Copt. ⲫⲁⲥ, ⲫⲥⲥ, ⲫⲓⲥⲓ, ⲫⲟⲥⲓ.

fess, U. 511, T. 324, to roast, to cook; see, and.

feqq, to eat, to feed.

feqa-t, to feed, food.

feqa, Hearst Pap. 1, 1, cake, loaf; plur.

feqau 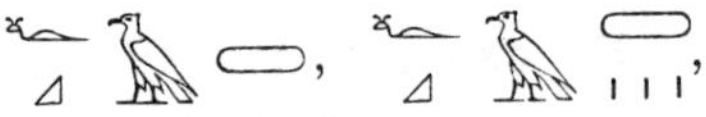 Peasant 301, manure for fields.

feqa , M. 695, , 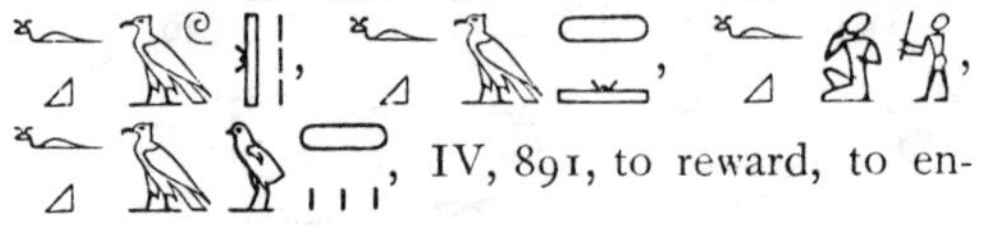 IV, 891, to reward, to endow, to subsidize, to bribe.

feqa 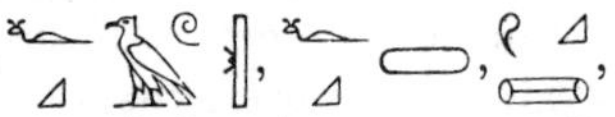, reward, gift; plur. 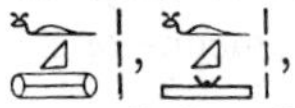, Thes. 1122, 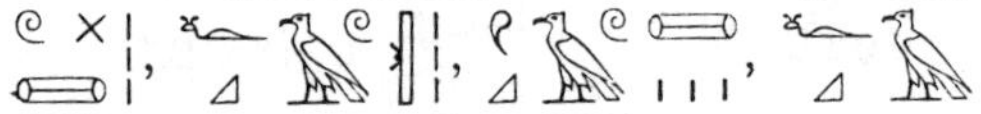 Åmen. 21, 3, 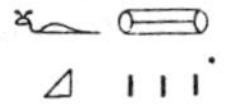.

feqa , Rec. 32, 183,  Anastasi IV, 2, 10, , Koller Pap. 2, 8, to pull off, to pluck, to cut; Copt. ϥⲱϭⲓ.

feqa , Hymn Darius 38 . . . .

feqn , IV, 1082, to be paid or rewarded.

fek , to destroy; Copt. ϥⲟϫ.

fek , a title of the high-priest of the Nome Hermopolites.

fekti 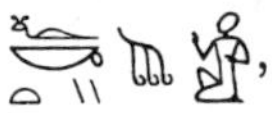, Rec. 5, 90, a priest of the resurrection of Osiris.

fekti åmi seḥti 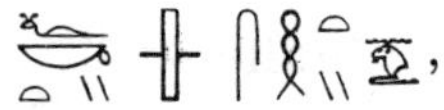, Rec. 15, 173, title of the high-priest of Tanites.

fekk , to drive away.

fekat , N. 891, turquoise, malachite, mother-of-emerald; see 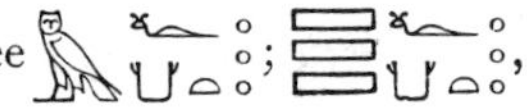, N. 170, lakes of turquoise.

fekat , N. 700, the stars.

feka 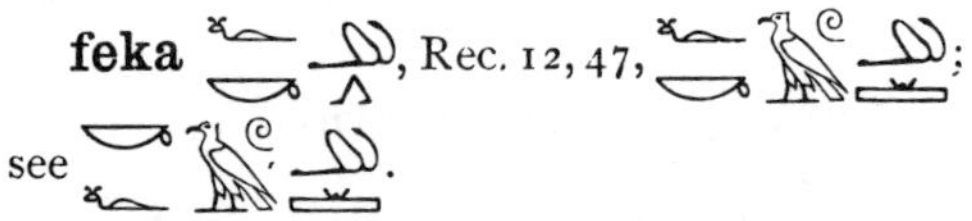, Rec. 12, 47; see.

fekth , a shaven man.

fekthu 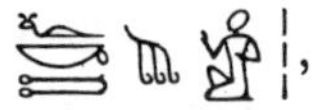, the high-priests of Abydos.

fega 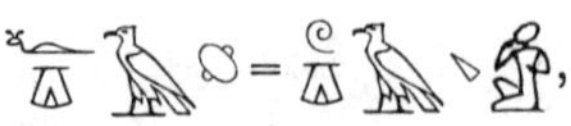, to chew (?)

fega , B.D. 153B, 19, to make water; see .

fegn , Rec. 29, 156, 31, 18, 174,  to make water, to evacuate, to empty the belly.

fet , to feel disgust, to be nauseated, to regard as profane or abominable, disgust, nausea, decay, failure of courage, discouragement; Copt. ϥⲱⲧⲉ, ϥⲱϯ.

fet-tå , Koller Pap. 1, 7 . . . . . .

fetfet 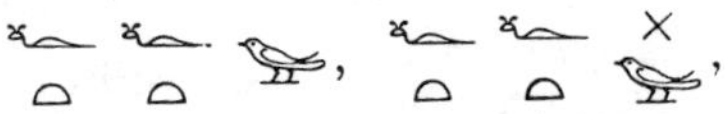, Hymn to Nile 4, 9, to be tired out (in body), wearied (in mind), to feel loathing or disgust.

fet , Anastasi I, 24, 8, loathing, disgust.

fetfet 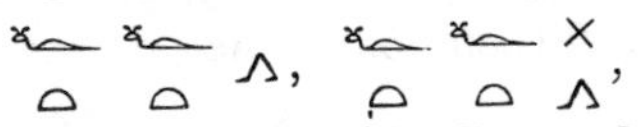, De Hymnis 39, A.Z. 1905, 15, Ebers Pap. 108, 14, to leap (of fish), to wriggle, to crawl (of insects, worms, etc.); see 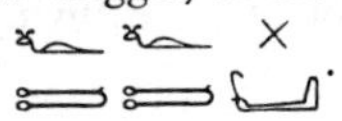.

fettu (fetfetu) , fish.

fetfet , worm.

fetu , worms.

fettit 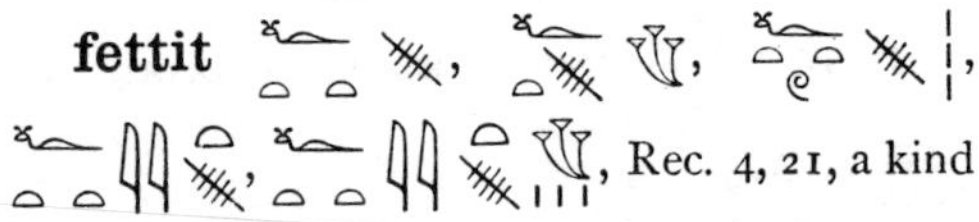, Rec. 4, 21, a kind of plant, stalks of plants or wheat, barley, etc.; see 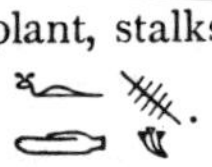.

fet, fetit [illegible], sweat; Copt. ϥⲱⲧⲉ.

fetf (?) [illegible], garment, apparel.

fetq [illegible], to hack in pieces.

fetk (?) [illegible], U. 175, bread, food.

fethfeth [illegible], to crawl, to wriggle.

fethth, Rec. 29, 157, to become worms, to decay.

feṭ, N. 761, , P. 439, M. 655, , , , , Rec. 27, 218, 31, 24, IV, 327, 352, 918, to cut, to pluck, to hack at, to tear out, to dig up by the roots; Copt. ϥⲱⲧⲉ.

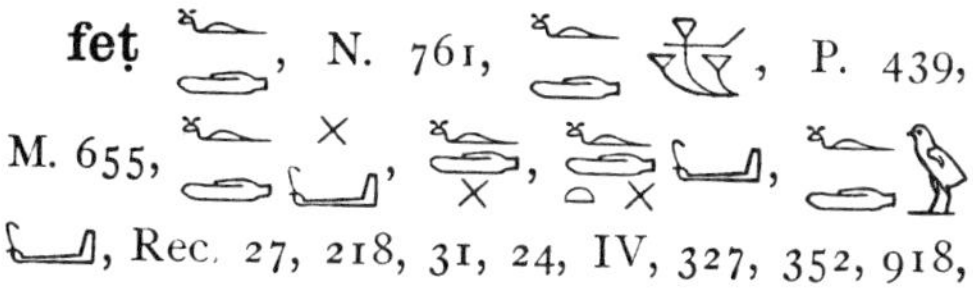

feṭ, , to feel disgust or nausea.

feṭ ḥa-t, despair, disheartened.

feṭit, Rev. 6, 22, loathing, disgust.

feṭ, to sweat.

feṭ-t, , , , , T. 362, P. 293, 535, N. 484, 697, sweat, secretions of the body, humours; Copt. ϥⲱⲧⲉ.

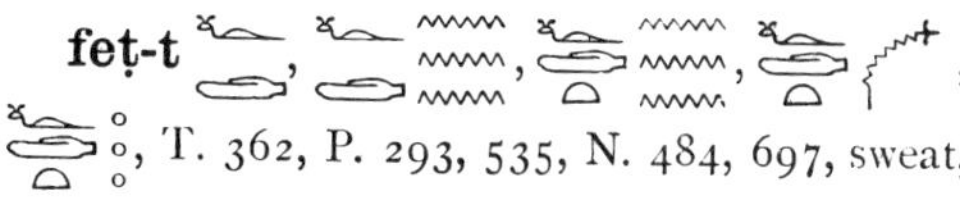

feṭ, sweat of Ḥep, *i.e.*, Nile-water.

feṭfeṭ, some sweet-smelling ointment.

feṭ, a kind of plant.

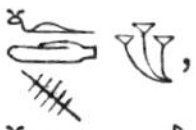

feṭ, box, coffer.

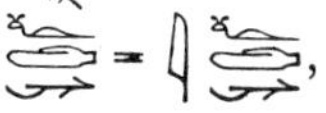

fṭu, , , U. 369, T. 91, , , P. 233, 537, N. 102, (?), , , , four; is often used as mark of the plural, *e.g.*, Rec. 27, 225; Copt. ϥⲧⲟⲟⲩ; , four; , , U. 577, N. 966, four horns; , N. 964, the four gods; 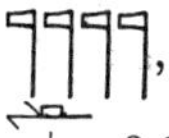   , a god with "four faces on one neck."

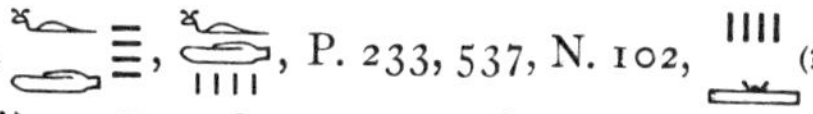

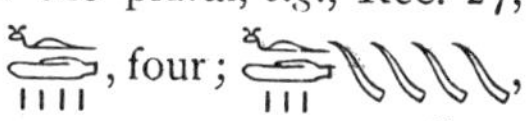

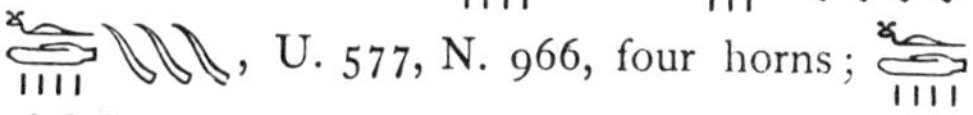

fṭu-nu, , , P. 659, 768, , N. 761, , U. 452, , , , Rec. 31, 24, fourth; fem.  .

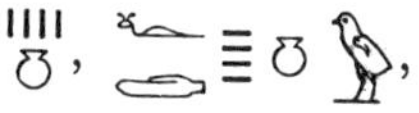

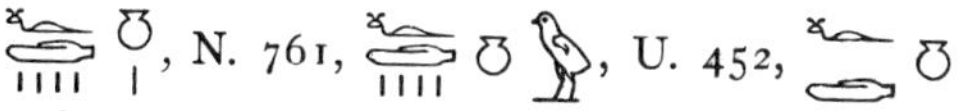

Fṭu àakhu, , , U. 473, 475, P. 115, M. 96, N. 102, the four spirits of Ånu.

Fṭu neteru mesu Geb, P. 691, four gods who ate figs, drank wine, and used perfume, etc.

Fṭu neteru khentiu ḥe-t āa-t, N. 964, the four divine chiefs of the palace.

Fṭu neteru tepiu Mer-Kenstà, P. 337, M. 639, the four gods of the lake of Nubia.

Fṭut netherit, T. 206, a group of four goddesses.

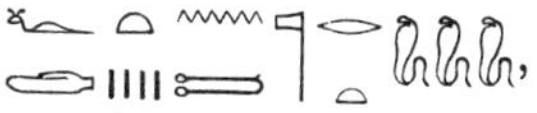

Fṭu rutchu, U. 553, four divine servants of the sandals of Osiris.

Fṭu ḥāau, , P. 281, , M. 525, a group of four singing-gods who sat under the fort of Qat,  .

Fṭu ḥeru, P. 419, N. 1206, M. 601, the god of four faces.

feṭr, to rub away; Copt. ϥⲱⲧⲉ (?)

feṭq, Peasant 129, 257, , Peasant 173, , Thes. 1199, , , , , , to cut, to cut off, to hack at, to destroy, to be destroyed, to rip up.

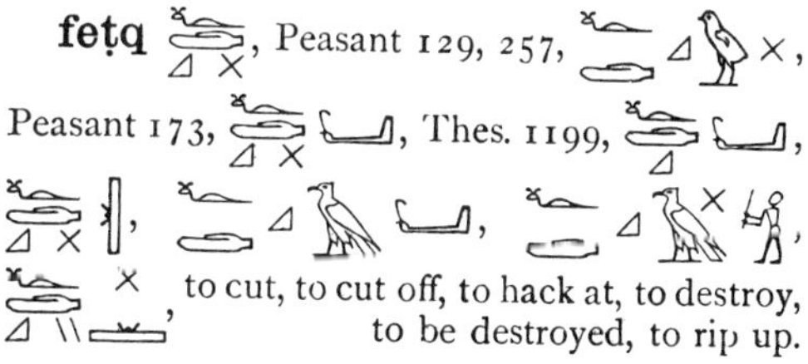

feṭq, Jour. E.A. 3, 98, slice, portion.

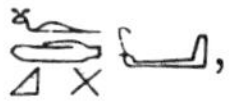

feṭqu, destruction, damage.

feṭk, , , to reap, to cut, P. 439, M. 655.

M

m  = Heb. מ, ם.

m'  , probably represents the peculiar sound which is often given to "**m**" by the natives in many parts of the Sûdân and East Africa; the sound of  must have been different from that of  , and the or in it represents some blurred vowel-sound.

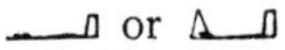

m , , , , , , a preposition: in, into, from, on, at, with, out from, among, of, upon, as, like, according to, in the manner of, in the condition or capacity of.

m au-t tchet 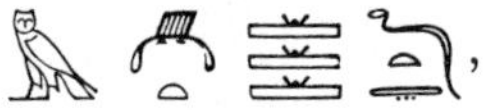 , Décrets 9, 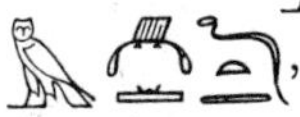 , everlastingly, eternally.

m åmenit , perpetually, daily.

m åsu , , in return for, as payment for, as a reward for.

m āb , U. 364, , , , together with, facing, opposite to.

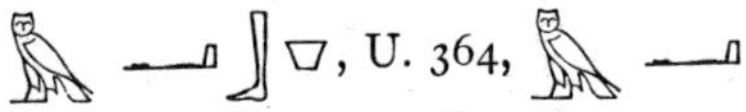

m āqu 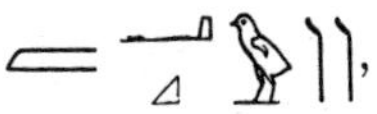 , B.M. 138, with, opposite.

m uaḥ , , besides, in addition to.

m uā  , alone.

m unu-t 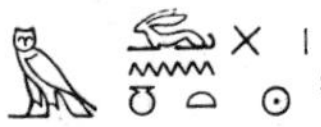 , at the moment, immediately.

m uhem , , , , repeating, a second time.

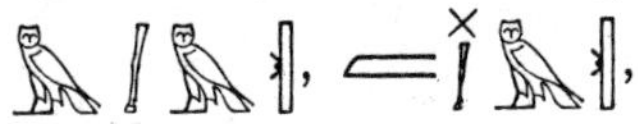

m uhem ā , , , a second time.

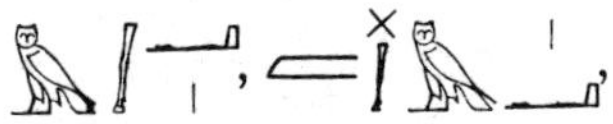

m baḥ , U. 7, 321, , U. 353, , , , , , , , , , Shipwreck 67, , Junker, Stunden 51, 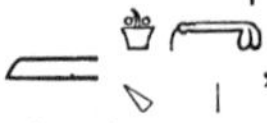 , literally "at the prepuce of," *i.e.*, in the presence of, before; Copt. ⲙ̀ⲙⲁϩ.

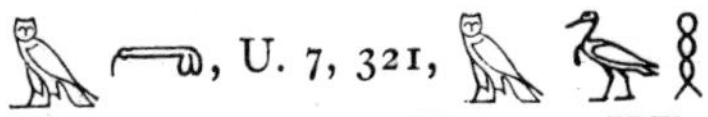

må baḥ , U. 322, , U. 321.

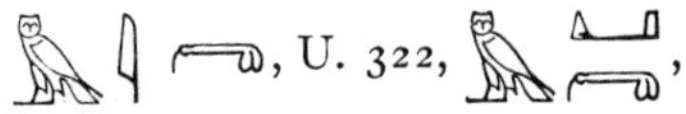

m baḥ ā , , of old time, before.

m paitu  , before, not yet; Copt. ⲙ̀ⲡⲁⲧⲉ (?)

m peḥui  , endwise, rearward.

m pekhar  , round about.

mm , U. 194, 571, T. 396, P. 308, Rec. 32, 85, IV, 157, , , , , , Treaty 31, , Treaty 32, among;  , Sanehat 23, 9, B.D. 83, 4.

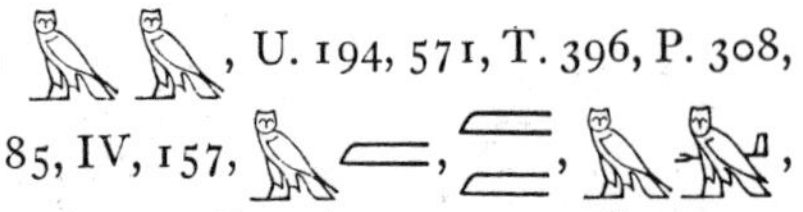

m mat  , anew, afresh.

m mått , , Rec. 3, 49, likewise, similarly.

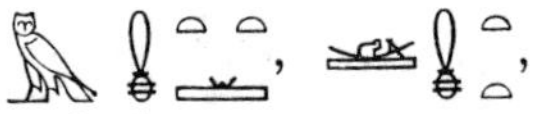

m må qeṭ , , Rec. 32, 180, conformably, in the likeness or manner of.

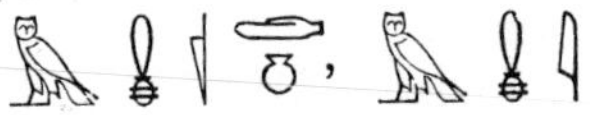

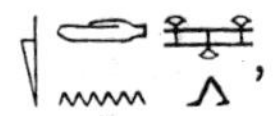

m m' m' 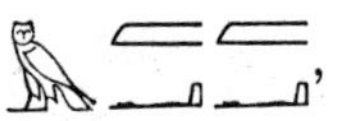 , IV, 1024, with, among.

m men-t  , daily.

m meni  , daily; Copt. ⲙ̄ⲙⲏⲛⲉ, ⲙ̄ⲙⲏⲛⲓ.

m mer 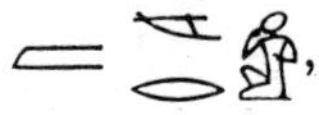 , therewith, in order that; varr. , .

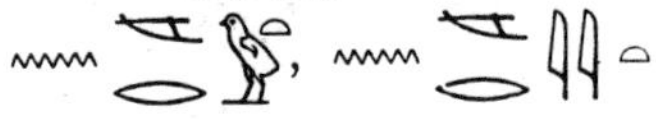

m meḥ, Rev. 11, 138, before; Copt. ⲙ̄ⲙⲁϩ.

m nen, Rev. 12, 85 = , like this, the same.

m nsa, Rev., after; Copt. ⲙ̄ⲛ̄ⲛ̄ⲥⲁ.

m rā, Rec. 21, 84, 85, surely, verily.

m re pu, or, on the contrary, alternatively.

m ruti, , , Åmen. 11, 9, outside.

m rekh, knowingly, wittingly.

m hau, , in the neighbourhood of.

m ḥa, , behind, near, close.

m ḥa-t, , at the front of, at the point of, in the bows of a boat.

m ḥa-t ā, B.D. 92, 5.

m ḥer, , , , Rec. 36, 78, opposite, in the face of someone or something, towards.

m ḥeri, , above.

m ḥer ȧb, within.

m ḥetep, successfully, satisfactorily.

m khem, , ignorantly, unwittingly, without, not possessing.

m khen, U. 384, , T. 250, M. 569, P. 411, , Rec. 31, 19, , , Rec. 33, 27, , , , , , , , in the inside; Copt. ϩⲛ̄.

m khen ā, , forthwith.

m khent, at the head of.

m kher, , , among.

m khet, U. 9, 75, 354, N. 336, , , , , , after, behind, in the following of, in accordance with, what follows, posterity, futurity; , IV, 350, declared to posterity; , he considers not futurity.

m khet, assistant of; , assistant artisan; , assistant ka-priests; , palace watcher.

m khetiu, divine followers, those who are in the train of the god.

m sa, , Rev. 11, 138, at the back of, after, behind; , singers to the harp; , in the train thereof; , Rec. 11, 147, after them; Copt. ⲛ̄ⲥⲱⲟⲩ.

m sa-t, after; Copt. ⲛ̄ⲥⲁ.

m sep, at once, forthwith.

m sep uā, at one time, at once, unanimously.

m sen-t, round about.

m seḥetch, evident, evidently, plainly.

m sekhan, suddenly; Copt. ⲥϣⲛⲉ.

m sesheta, secretly, in a hidden manner.

m seti (?) , in front of.

m setut 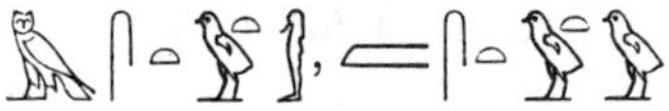
, Rec. 13, 116, in accordance with statute, conformably to the law, rightly.

m shes , exceedingly; Copt. ⲉⲙⲁϣⲱ (?)

m shes maā 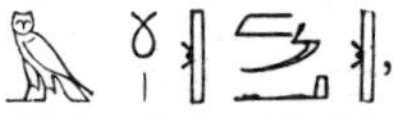, Mar. Aby. I, 9, 107, rightly (?) conformably (?)

m qab 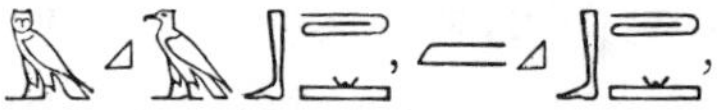, in the belly of, in the midst of.

m qeṭ , round about, in the circle of.

m tep , upon, on top of.

m thut 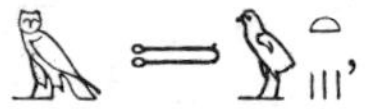, Rec. 36, 216 = , within.

m ṭet , since, when.

m tcheb (ṭebu) , in payment for, in return for.

m tcher 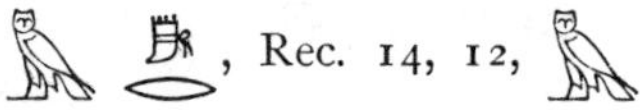 Rec. 14, 12,
, by the hand of.

M (Åmit)-ågeb , Ombos 2, 133, a goddess.

M (Åmit)-up-tef , Ombos 2, 130, a goddess.

M (Åmit) - Ḥāp 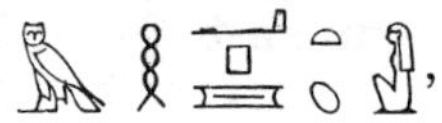, Ombos 2, 131, a goddess.

m 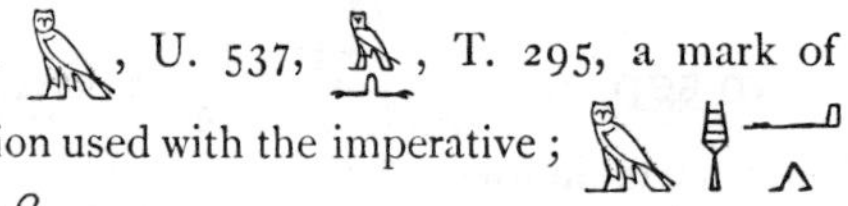 U. 537, T. 295, a mark of negation used with the imperative;
, B.D. 30B, 2, stand not up against me; 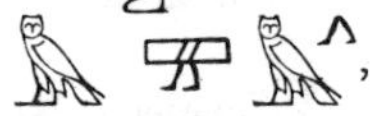, B.D. 33, 2, advance not; , B.D. 40, 2, eat me not; Copt. ⲙ̄.

m  P. 636 = M. 513 =
N. 1096 = 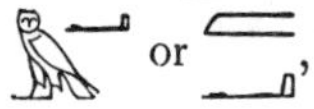 or, see, behold.

m, må, mi 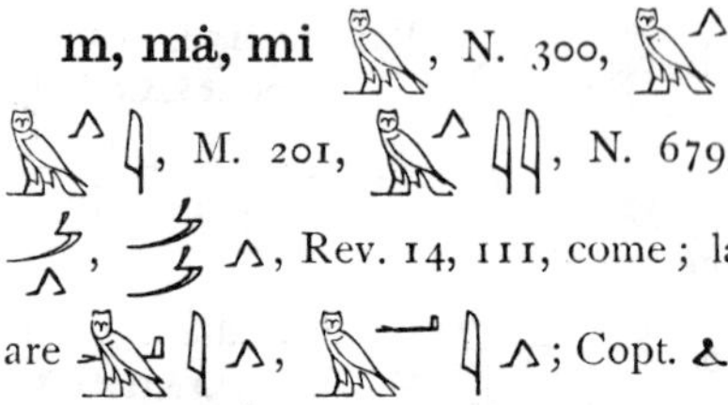 N. 300, T. 208, M. 201, N. 679, T. 342, Rev. 14, 111, come; later forms are; Copt. ⲁⲙⲟⲩ.

mm 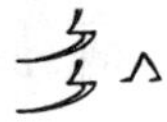, to come.

m , to grasp.

m , death; see **mut**.

maa 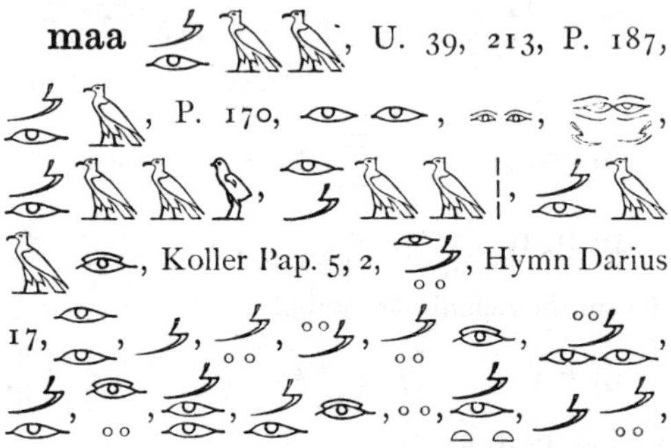 U. 39, 213, P. 187, P. 170, Koller Pap. 5, 2, Hymn Darius 17,
Rev. 11, 140, to see, to examine, to inspect, to perceive, to look at;  IV, 1006; seen, visible.

maa-t  sight, vision, something seen, tableau; things seen, visions.

maa-t , an inspection.

maaå , U. 180, seer.

maau  seer, watcher, he who keeps a look-out on a fort; plur. T. 42, P. 89, M. 51, N. 37, U. 584, M. 795, Rec. 30, 190.

Ma-ur , Palermo Stele, the title of the high-priest of Anu.

maa, a place for keeping watch.

mau-ḥer, thing by which one sees the face, *i.e.*, mirror.

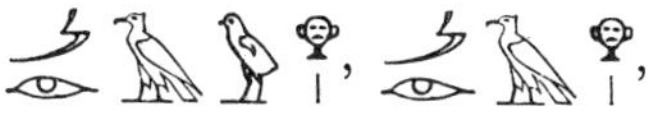

Maa, the "Seer," a divine title.

Maait (?), Ombos 2, 131, a goddess.

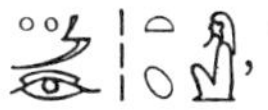

maau-ti, Rec. 14, 165, the two divine eyes.

Maa-åb(ḥa)-khenti-åḥ-t-f, Ṭuat VI, a god.

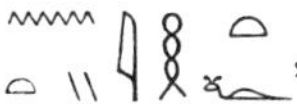

Maa-åntu-f, B.D. 125, II, one of the 42 assessors of Osiris; varr.

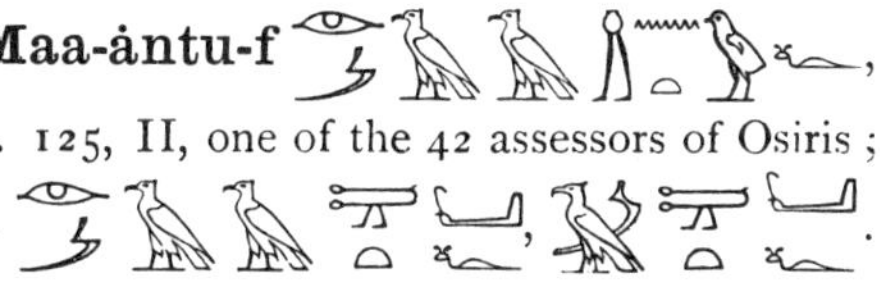

Maa-åntu-f, B.D. 99, 23, a bolt peg in the magical boat.

Maa-åri-f (?), a title of the Sun-god.

Maa-åtf-f-kheri-beq-f, B.D. 17, 60, one of the seven spirits who guarded the tomb of Osiris.

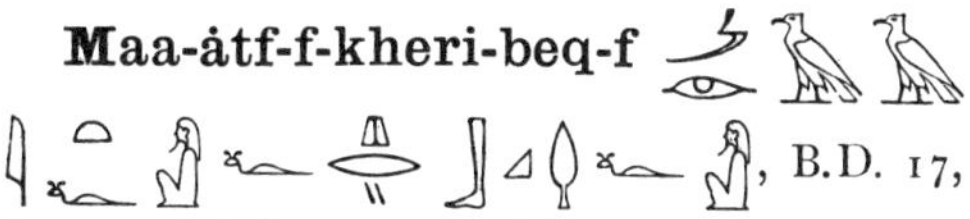

Maa-åtht-f, B.D. 149, a god of the 14th Åat.

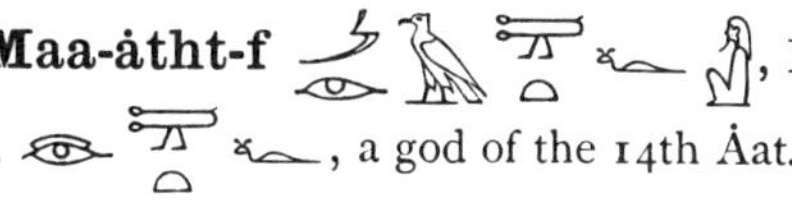

Maa-ā, Ṭuat I, a singing-god.

Maa-f-ur, Rec. 34, 67, a god.

Maa-mer-f, the god of the 26th day of the month.

Maa-mer-tef-f, the festival of the 26th day of the month.

Maau-m-ḥerui (?), U. 606, a god (?)

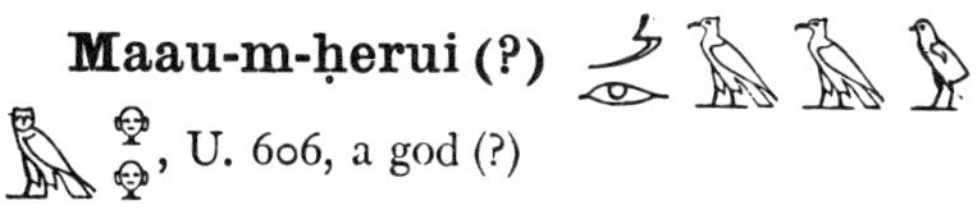

Maa-m-gerḥ, etc.,    Rec. 4, 28, B.D. 17, 105, Edfû 1, 10H, one of the seven guardian spirits of Osiris.

Maa-neb-Tem-Kheper, Ombos II, 1, 108, a lion-goddess, a form of Sekhmit.

Maait-neferu-neb-set, Ṭuat I, a goddess, one of the 12 who guided Rā.

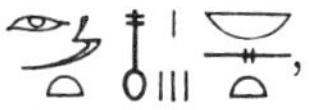

Maa-neferut-Rā, Ṭuat XII, goddess of the 12th hour of the night.

Maa-en-Rā, Ṭuat I, an ape-god door-keeper.

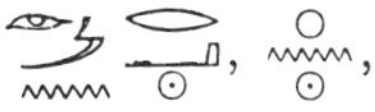

Maa-neter-s (År-t-neter-s ?), Ṭuat I, a singing-goddess.

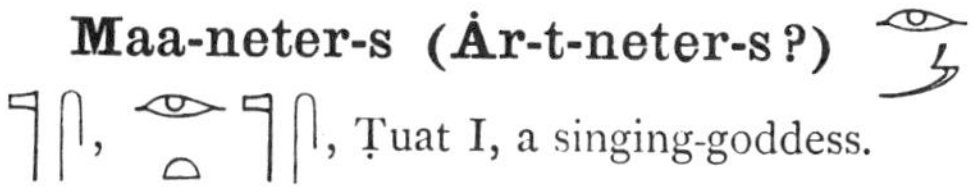

Maa-ḥa-f, U. 489, M. 362, a ferry-god.

Maa-ḥa-f, U. 489, T. 193, P. 676, 677, M. 549, N. 918, 1129, 1287, B.D. 153A, 2, the ferryman of Osiris.

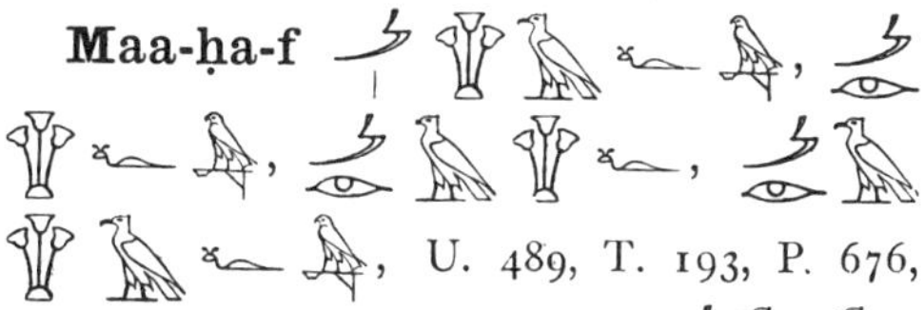

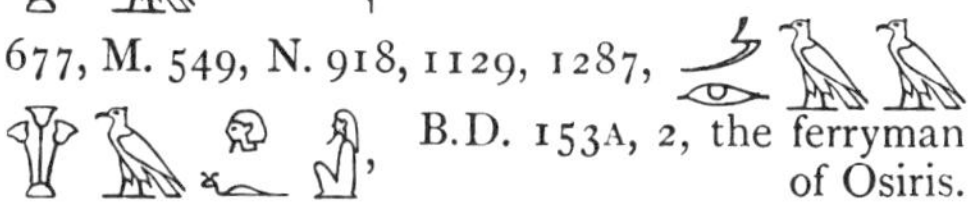

Maa-Ḥer, the fiery flash that "cometh forth from the eye of Horus,"

Maa-ḥeḥ-en-renput, B.D. 42, 13, a magical name.

Maa-sa-s (År-t-sa-s ?), B.D.G. 735, a form of Hathor of

maaiu su (?), B.D. 125, III, 12, beings in the Other World.

Maa-set 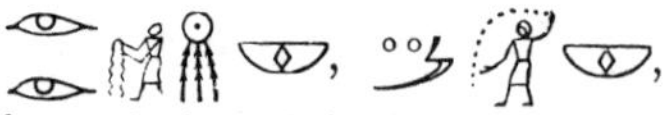, the festival of the 13th day of the month.

Maa-setem (?) , Nesi-Ȧmsu 9, 18, a god.

Maatet (Ȧr-ti) , Metternich Stele, 51, one of the seven scorpion-goddesses of Isis.

Maa-tuf-ḥer-ā , B.D. 17, 142, name of the storm-god .

Maa-tepu-neteru , Ṭuat XII, a singing dawn-god.

Maa-tef-f (Ȧr-ti-tef-f) 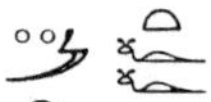 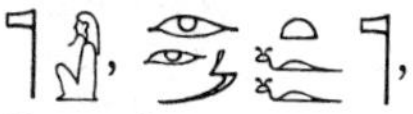, Rec. 4, 28, , Berg. I, 7, an ape-headed god, a grandson of Horus; he presided over the 7th hour of the day and the 8th day of the month.

Maa-tef-f , 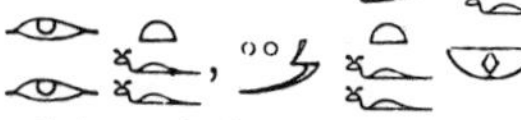, the god and festival of the 8th day of the month.

Maa-tcheru (Ȧrit-tcheru) [illegible] , Ṭuat III, a form of Osiris.

ma, maȧu , P. 82, , M. 112, , antelope, gazelle; plur. ; see .

maa [illegible], U. 289, , N. 541, , III, 140, [illegible], III, 143, , Rec. 11, 180, lion; plur. , Shipwreck 30, 96; Copt. ⲙⲟⲩⲓ.

mai , Metternich Stele 81, lion.

ma-t , Rec. 26, 229, [illegible] 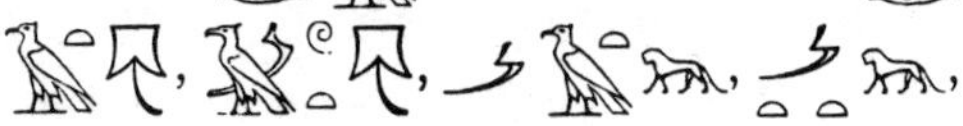, lioness; Copt. ⲙⲓⲉ, ⲙⲓⲏ.

ma-ḥes [illegible], T. 165, 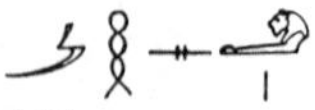, N. 688, , , lion with a fierce eye that fascinates; plur. , P. 310, N. 732.

Ma-ḥes , Dream Stele 2, [illegible], a lion-god.

ma [illegible], scabbard (Brugsch).

ma 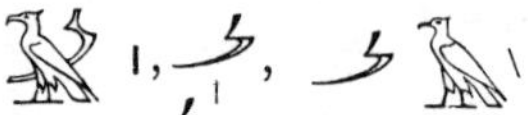, part of a ship or boat; , Rec. 30, 66, the fore **ma**; , Rec. 30, 66, the aft **ma**; , Rec. 30, 67, the double **ma**.

ma , Rec. 15, 18, to reap(?) to harvest.

ma, mau-t , 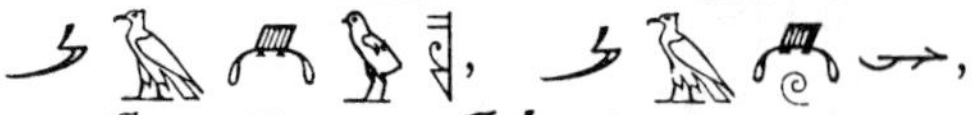, , Rec. 11, 123,  [illegible], IV, 666, spear handle, stalk of a plant, staff; plur. [illegible], IV, 732.

ma-t 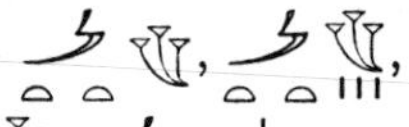, Rec. 16, 8 ff., 27, 219, [illegible], safflower(?); two other kinds are distinguished: one of the hills [illegible], and the other of the Delta [illegible] (or, [illegible]); Copt. ⲙⲉⲧⲁⲓⲟ.

ma-t, maut 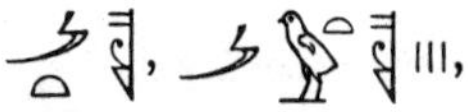, Rec. 31, 21, 170, [illegible], incense.

ma [illegible], to burn up.

ma, to slay; see .

ma, to make ready, to prepare.

ma, to wrap up in.

ma (?), Thes. 1296, , Rec. 16, 70, , Rev. 11, 146, 12, 23, a gathering of people, troop, recruits (?)

ma, maā, , temple, temple estates and landed property; plur. , , , , , , , , .

ma, , Rev. 11, 125, 142, 12, 42, 13, 32, , Rev. 12, 49, temple.

ma-t, Rec. 20, 149, , , , Rec. 25, 191, land close to a river or the sea, low-lying land, island; plur. , IV, 747, , , , , islands of the sea; Copt. ⲙⲟⲩⲓ.

ma, locality (?)

ma-ti, , , testicles.

maiu (?), De Hymnis 41, seed (?) offspring (?)

ma, mai, maui, T. 254, , Rev. 13, 76, , , , , , U. 445, , , , Ḥerusȧtef 61, , to be new, to make new, youth, freshness, young, fresh.

mai-t, U. 443, , T. 253, , something new, new, newly; , U. 720, , , , renewed.

mau-t, , , IV, 894, , something new, new.

ma = , like, as; , like, likeness, the like.

mama (mm), Décrets, 14, conformably to.

mama, to give light.

mama, to fan, to make air.

mama, , , Rec. 11, 142, the dûm palm (?) or its fruit; plur. , , , , , , .

mama en khann-t, a kind of fruit tree.

mamȧ, date-grove gardener (?); plur. , Rec. 15, 18.

maȧu, De Hymnis 28, , , , , lion, cat; plur. ; , the lion or cat of the god .

Maȧu, Nesi-Ȧmsu 32, 48, a lion-headed serpent, a form of Āapep.

Maȧu-ḥes, , ,

, IV, 617, , , Rec. 23, 71; 36, 176; , , Annales VI, 226, a lion-god, the Soul of Bast, Nesi-Âmsu 30, 24, , Rec. 2, 110; Greek Μίυσις.

maȧu-ḥetch , N. 26, , Koller Pap. 3, 6, , , , antelope, oryx, gazelle; see .

maȧ , , the name of a star.

maȧ , a metal object; see .

maȧui , , , Rev. 11, 133, 151, 154, , Rev. 13, 15, region, island; Copt. ⲙⲟⲩⲉ.

maȧr , , , , IV, 1139, Berl. Pap. 3024, 128, , , , , , to be miserable, misery, wretchedness, poverty, affliction.

maȧr , Peasant 204, , Peasant B. 2, 112, , , IV, 972, Berl. 3024, 22, a poor man, one of humble condition, or one in a miserable or oppressed state; plur. .

maȧs , , , , a part of a crown.

maȧs , to slay, to kill.

maā , , , , , , , , , , , , to give, to present, to offer, to make an obligatory or statutory offering, an offering, sacrifice in general; , to pay such an offering.

maāu , , , products of a country, gifts (?)

maāmaā , Décrets 19, order, will, wish, command.

maā , a legal rite or ceremony; plur. .

maā , , , , , , , , , , , , , , to be true, to be upright, true, truthful, veritable, real, actual; Copt. ⲙⲉ, ⲙⲏⲓ.

maā-t , P. 93, truth, integrity, uprightness, justice, the right, verity, genuineness, law; Copt. ⲙⲉ, ⲙⲏⲓ.

maā-t – un maā-t , very truth:— , a well-doing god indeed; , in very truth the heart of Osiris hath been weighed; , indeed I fought strenuously.

maā-t – shes maā-t , , , to do a thing "regularly and always," or a very large number of times.

maā-t ȧb (or **ḥa-t**), true or righteous of heart.

maāti, righteous; Copt. ⲙⲙⲏⲧ.

maāti, IV, 970, IV, 971, Thes. 1482, IV, 1080, a righteous, just and truth-speaking man; plur. the righteous dead.

maā-t thy genuine friend; U. 455, a real form; Just judge, a title of Thoth; a man of truth; doubly true; the king's truth; the scales balance exactly; beautiful truth; truly honest; to straighten the legs; real lapis-lazuli, real turquoise; a veritable royal scribe, as opposed to an honorary one; a real smer uāt; truth twofold, *i.e.*, really and truly; Berl. 6910; Rev. 12, 66 = Copt. ⲝⲓⲛⲙⲙⲉ.

maā-kheru, U. 453, P. 171, M. 266, P. 662, M. 773, P. 587, N. 982, Rec. 33, 34, P. 778, Rec. 31, 281, Rec. 33, 36 [to be declared to be] "true of voice, or word" in the Judgment, *i.e.*, to be innocent, to be justified like Osiris; Maā-kheru (fem. maāt-kheru) always follows the names of the dead, it being assumed that they have been declared innocent, as was Osiris; I am innocent before the Great God; innocent before the great company of gods; thou art innocent a million times over; innocent, or justified, in peace; with victory [and] in innocence.

maā-kheru B.D. 19, 1, a crown of innocence, a garland of triumph.

Maā, U. 220, P. 400, M. 571, N. 1178, Ṭuat XI, god of law, order, truth, integrity, etc.

Maā em Ȧmentt, Mar. Aby. I, 45, the Truth-goddess in Amentt.

Maā-t, N. 154, 1224, 1279, a goddess, the personification of law, order, rule, truth, right, righteousness, canon, justice, straightness, integrity, uprightness, and of the highest conception of physical and moral law known to the Egyptians.

Maāt, Berg. I, 16, a goddess who opened the mouth of the deceased.

Maāti 
[illegible], B.D. 125, I, [illegible]
[illegible]
[illegible], U.453, [illegible], IV, 1082,
[illegible], IV, 1220, the two goddesses of Truth, *i.e.*, Isis and Nephthys, who assisted at the Great Judgment.

Maātiu , Anastasi I, 3, 3, 
, gods of truth.

Maā-ȧb 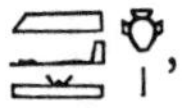, Ṭuat VI, a keeper of the 5th Gate.

Maā-ȧb-khenti-ȧḥ-t-f 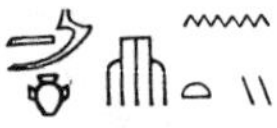
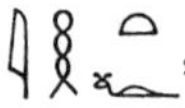, Ṭuat VI, a god.

Maātiu-ȧmiu-Ṭuat 
, the souls of the truthful in the Gate Saa-Set.

Maā-uatu 
, Tomb of Seti I, one of the 75 forms of Rā (No. 48).

Maā-ennuḥ 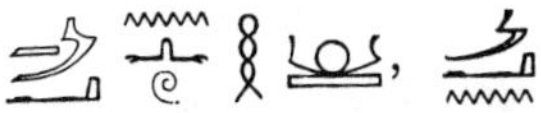
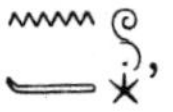, Thes. 31, the god of the 11th hour of the day.

Maā-ḥer-pesh-ḥeteput 
, Mythe 2, a defender of Osiris.

Maāti-khenti-ḥeḥ 
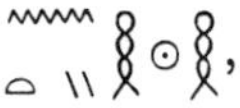, Cairo Pap. III, 3, a goddess of Mesqet.

Maātiu-kheriu-maāt 
, the gods who possess Truth.

Maāti , P. 567, [illegible]
[illegible], P. 573, [illegible]
[illegible], N. 171, the boat of Truth.

Maāti 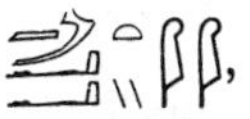, the name of the 1st field in the Ṭuat.

Maāti , the region where the Maāti-goddesses administered the affairs of heaven and judged the souls of men.

Maāti , B.D. 125, III; 24, the place where the deceased buried the flame of fire and the crystal sceptre, etc., varr. 
[illegible].

maāti 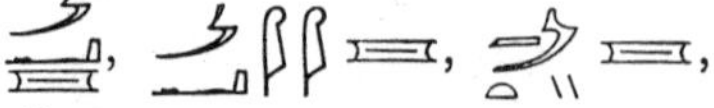
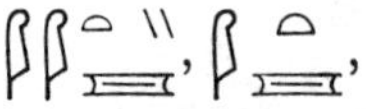, Nile swamp, marsh in general.

Maāti 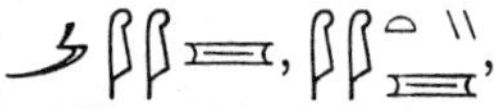, Edfû I, 80, a name of the Nile-god and his Flood.

maā 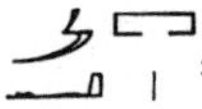, Nâstasen Stele 61, 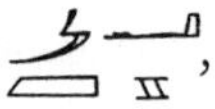, place, court of a house or temple.

maā 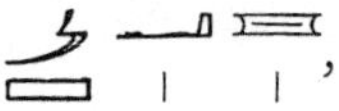, P. 247, 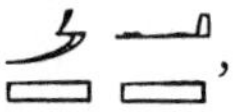,
[illegible], M. 469, N. 1058, [illegible]
[illegible], Thes. 1296, shore, bank of a river, flat near the mouth of a river;
, a promenade by the river (?);
, the river-gate of a building.

maā 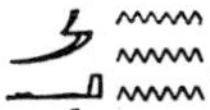, Thes. 1251, salt water.

maā 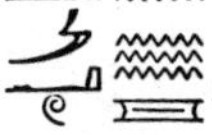, current of a stream.

maā , Rec. 16, 129, [illegible],
[illegible], Hymn Darius 8, [illegible],
[illegible], to go, to journey, to go straight to a place.

maāmaā , Rec. 35, 126, to go, to travel.

maāiu , IV, 655, advance guard, pioneers, soldiers.

Maā-ḥer , Berg. II, 8,
[illegible], the guardian of the 4th hour of the night.

Maā-ḥer-Khnemu , Denderah IV, 84, the guardian of the 4th hour of the night.

maā 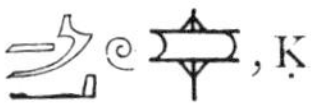, Ḳubbân Stele 31, 
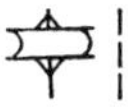, Åmen. 10, 11, 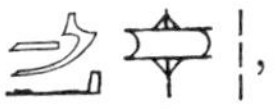, Hymn
Darius 6, 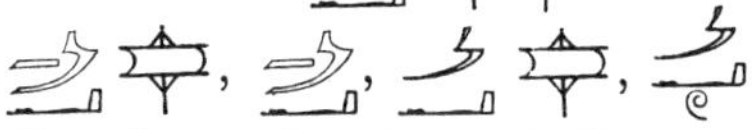
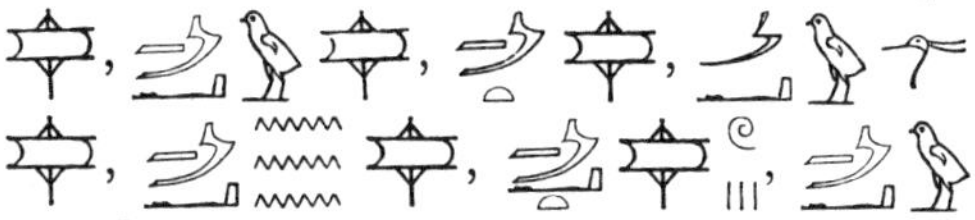
, to sail, wind, breeze; 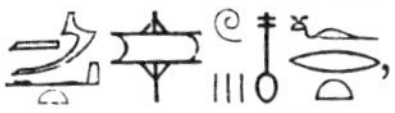,
a fair wind; ,
puffs of wind.

maā 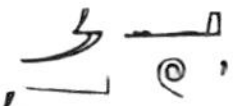, Rec. 31, 21, cordage of a
boat; , Rec. 31, 161, cordage of the
bow of a boat; , Rec. 30, 67,
, Leyd. Pap. 3, 11; ,
Rec. 30, 67.

maā 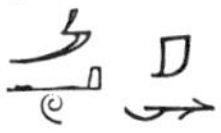, Rechnungen 77, hook, clasp.

maāiu 
, bronze fastenings, staples, ring-fastenings;
varr. 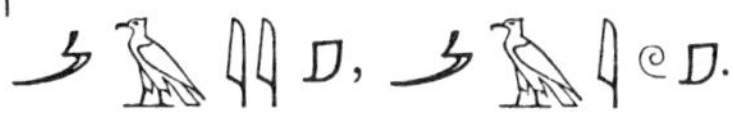.

maā 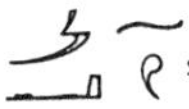, eyebrow.

maā-ti ,
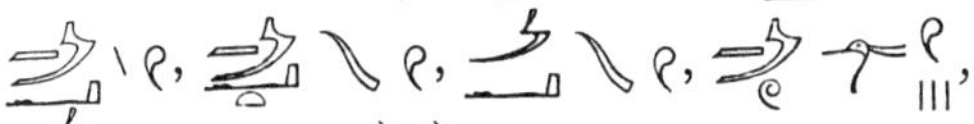,
, the temples of the head, forehead (?)

maā 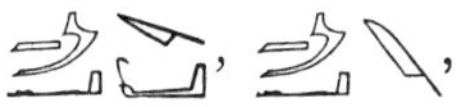, to kill, to slay.

maā , boat.

maān (?) , to fetter.

maār , to be
oppressed, bound, miserable; see 
.

maār , to see, to keep a look-out.

maār , watch-tower, look-out place.

maāḥetch , onyx stone.

maāsu-t 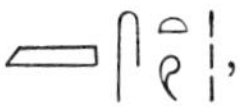, liver.

Maāstiu 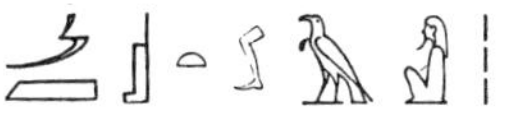, Rec. 33, 32, the gods of the northern constellations.

maāshqu , Annales IV, 130, 9, a piece of armour.

maāk ,
to protect, protector.

maātārtā , a kind
of fruit.

Maāāṭ , the boat of the
rising sun; see **Māntchit.**

mai , T. 254, new, once again.

mai [illegible], metal fastening; see
[illegible].

mai [illegible], Rec. 14, 66,
island; Copt. ⲙⲟⲩⲓ.

mai-t [illegible], abode, dwelling, workshop.

mait [illegible],
[illegible], reed, flute.

mau [illegible]; varr. [illegible]
[illegible], cat; Copt. ⲉⲙⲟⲩ.

Mau [illegible]
[illegible], a lion-god, or a cat-god; see **Māu** and **Māi.**

mauu [illegible], Tomb of Åmen-emḥat 56.......

mau [illegible], softness, gentleness.

maut (?) [illegible]
[illegible], Hymn to Nile 3, 8, dead fish.

mau-t [illegible]
[illegible]

, IV, 806, light, radiance, brilliance, splendour ; Copt. ⲙⲟⲩⲉ.

Mau  , the Light-god ; var. .

mau , Rev. 13, 8, to think, to ponder, to bear in mind, to remember, to fix the attention on something, mind, memory ; Copt. ⲙⲉⲩⲓ, ⲙⲉⲉⲩⲉ ;  , "one cannot call to mind the name of everything."

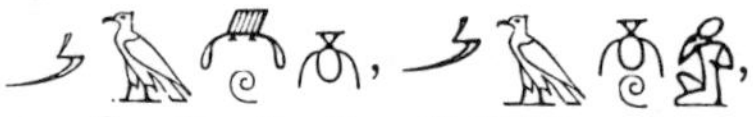

mau-t , the part of a story to be remembered, the sum, or total, or conclusion of a matter, the moral of a tale.

mau-t , P. 424, M. 607, N. 1212, club, staff.

mau-t , stave, staff, pillar of a balance ; plur. Stat. Tab. 35.

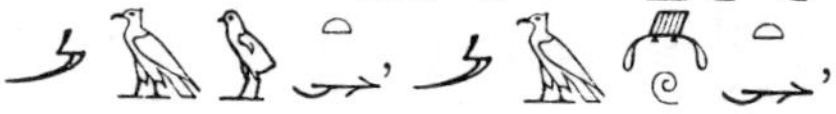

maui (?) 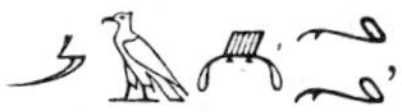 , the leg bones of a bird.

mau-t  , Theban Ost. C. 1, anus (?)

maur  , Åmen. 19, 5 . . . . . .

mauhi  , Rec. 14, 20 =  , crown.

maut 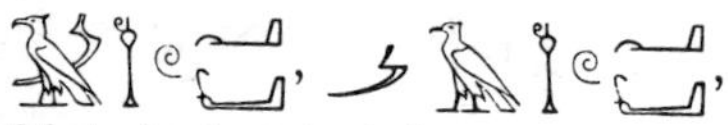 , P.S.B. 27, 186, to load, to be laden.

maut 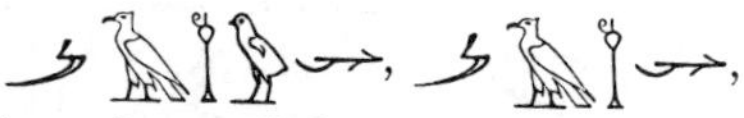 , bearing pole, yoke, staff for carrying objects ; compare Heb. מוֹט.

maf-t 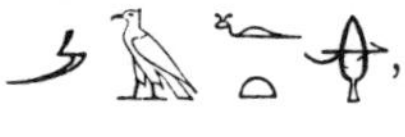 , a kind of tree.

maft , an animal of the lynx or leopard species with powerful claws ; see 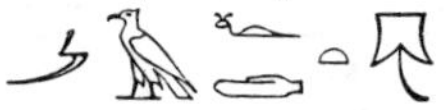 .

Maft , B.D. (Saïte) 34, 2, 39, 3, the Lynx-god (?)

mafṭ , to spring up, to jump, to leap.

mafṭ-t , U. 313, , U. 548, , T. 303, 310, , P. 425, , M. 608, , N. 1213, , Rec. 30, 67, an animal of the lynx or leopard species, with powerful claws ; the form on the Palermo Stele is 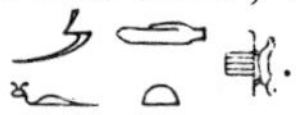 .

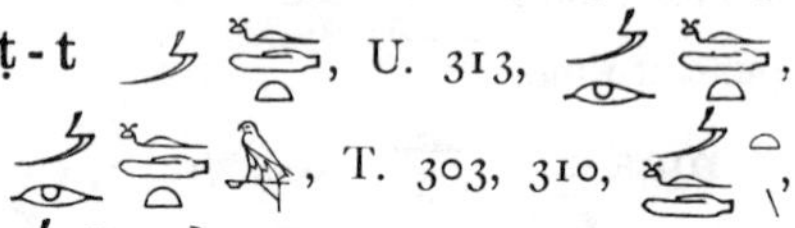

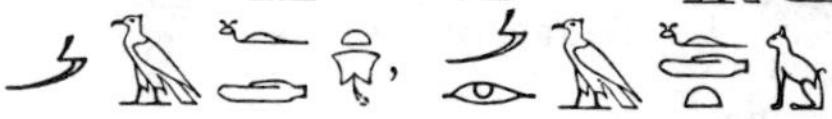

mamu , runners.

mamu  , Mar. Karn. 55, 65, to see, to know ;  , to inform.

mamu  , Rec. 15, 18, to cut, to kill, to reap.

mann 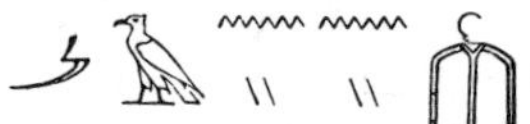 , Rec. 28, 163, to twist, to turn round, curved, bow-shaped.

manu 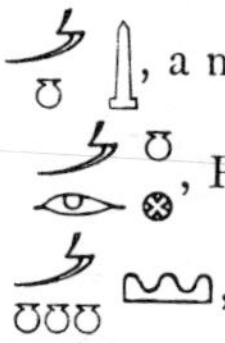 , a monument, pillar, stele.

Manu , P. 506, a town or city (?)

Manu , B.D. 15, 168, Circle XII, , the land of the setting sun, the West.

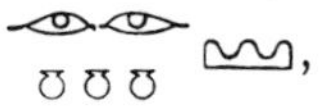

maanra-t , Leyd. Pap. 37, watch-tower, beacon-tower ; compare Heb. מְנוֹרָה.

mar , , see .

mar-ti , the two eyes.

mar-t , , Rec. 20, 41, , watch-tower, chamber for watching star risings.

Mar-t , Berg. II, 13, the region where certain stars rose, .

maråa , Anastasi I, 25, 9, to hasten, to flee.

mahet , , , , , , , doorway, gate chamber, door, gate tower, vestibule; see .

mahṭ-t , gate chamber; see .

maḥ , , , A.Z. 1880, 94, to beat the hands together, to clap.

maḥ-t , , plaudit, clapping of hands.

maḥi , Rev. 14, 19 = , wing; Copt. ⲙⲉϩⲉ.

maḥ , B.D. 51, 2, part of a boat; var. .

maḥ , , , flowers for garlands or wreaths; , , , , floral crowns, wreaths of flowers, garlands, chaplets; , chaplet of innocency.

maḥa , , , the back of the head and neck.

maḥn , Rec. 13, 12, lair, den, a filthy place.

maḥetch , white gazelle, antelope; plur. .

makh , Rec. 36, 162, , , IV, 614, to burn, to smelt; Copt. ⲙⲟⲩϩ.

Makhi , Ṭuat II, a god of one of the seasons of the year.

makhan , slime, mud (Lacau).

mas , T. 363, N. 179; see .

masu , N. 798, , P. 710, N. 1353, knives, daggers, weapons.

mas , to cut.

mas , , bull.

mas , to be shut in, to be kept in restraint.

mas-t , U. 486, M. 668, , Rec. 21, 77, , , thigh, a disease of the thigh; var. , U. 419, T. 239.

masti , , , , , , , , , pair of thighs, the two hip bones.

Mastiu , B.D. 130, 12, , , Rec. 33, 32, the gods of the Thigh (Great Bear).

Mast-f , B.D. 130, 19, a god of the Thigh.

mas-t 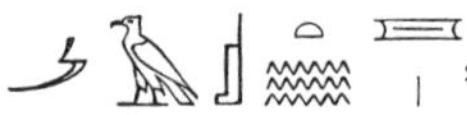, sandbank, shallow of a stream, shoal water.

mas-ti 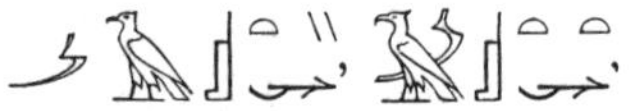, the supports of a seat, a part of a boat or ship.

Maskhemi[t] , Rec. 12, 40, a goddess.

masher , to roast.

maq-t , A.Z. 1907, 123, fire, flame, torch, brand.

maq-t , U. 493,  [illegible], U. 576, [illegible], P. 645, [illegible], P. 182, 471, 804, M. 537, 777, N. 975, 1115, [illegible], N. 965, [illegible], [illegible], Rec. 29, 148, [illegible], [illegible], ladder, mast; Copt. ⲙⲟⲩⲕⲓ.

Maqet , U. 493,  [illegible], N. 946, [illegible], P. 192, [illegible], N. 918, , B.D. 98, 4, the Ladder whereby Osiris ascended into heaven.

maqaqa-t , Anastasi IV, 2, 10, , Koller Pap. 2, 8, ploughed land; [illegible] , ploughed fields (?)

maqar  [illegible], Rec. 15, 16, stick, staff; Heb. מַקֵּל; Eth. በቀልት:

maki 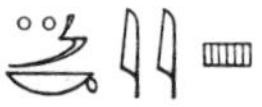, a mineral from the Sûdân, haematite (?)

mag , B.D. 140, 11, a kind of precious stone.

magsu 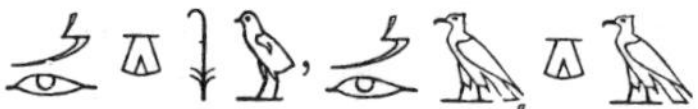 , , A.Z. 131, 171, dagger, poignard; see .

mat , Pap. 3024, 61, [illegible] [illegible], [illegible], [illegible], [illegible], [illegible], [illegible], [illegible], [illegible], the red granite of the First Cataract; see [illegible], [illegible], [illegible].

mat ruṭ-t , the living granite rock.

mat , B.D. 27, 5, [illegible], stupid, ignorant.

mat 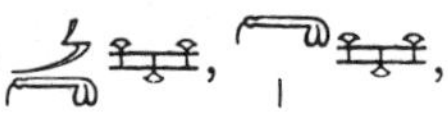, way, path; Copt. ⲙⲟⲉⲓⲧ.

Matȧit 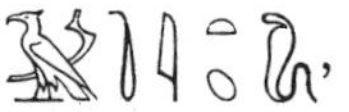, Rec. 17, 120, a goddess.

matȧuahar  , Dakhel Stele, 17, 18, a Libyan title.

Matit , Ṭuat III, [illegible] [illegible], B.D.G. 242, a form of Hathor.

math , granite; see 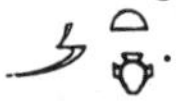.

math 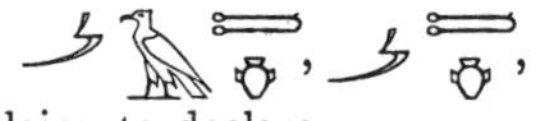, A.Z. 1901, 43, to proclaim, to declare.

Mathit , P. 727, [illegible], P. 650, , M. 751, a tree-goddess who assisted the deceased in climbing into heaven.

maṭ 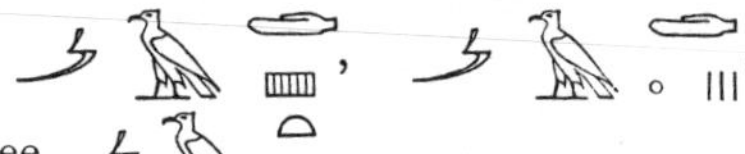, granite; see .

maṭṭ 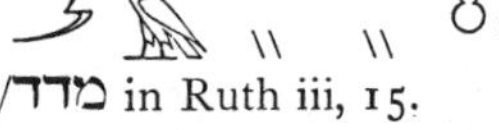, pot, vase; compare √מדד in Ruth iii, 15.

maṭiu , Mar. Aby. I, 8, 79, a class of priests

maṭ , a kind of bandlet.

maṭu 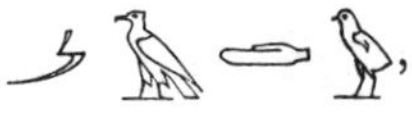, ignorance, stupidity.

maṭu , Prisse 13, 2, , Rec. 19, 93, staff, stick, cane.

maṭpen , A.Z. 1908, 17, a kind of amulet.

matchu , U. 557 . . . .

mȧ  — as well as, by the:  , gods like men, gods as well as men; , by the million; , by the ten thousand.

mȧ , P. 656, M. 761, , like, as, according to, inasmuch as, since, as well as, together with; early forms are:— [illegible], M. 626, [illegible], T. 365, [illegible], N. 856, [illegible], N. 71, [illegible], N. 956, Hh. 351; [illegible], A.Z. 1900, 128; [illegible], Ḥerusȧtef Stele 79, 86.

mȧ , like what? how?; , like what did they do? *i.e.*, how did they act?

mȧ  – **mȧ enn** , N. 1096, , [illegible], like this, in this wise; [illegible], P. 636, [illegible], M. 513.

mȧ nti , , Lit. 73, like him who, like that which, or the things which.

mȧ r , in proportion to; Gr. *κατὰ λόγον*.

mȧ qeṭ, mȧ qeṭ-t , Rec. 29, 153,  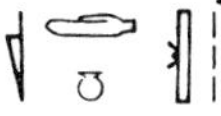, after the manner of, in the form of.

mȧ tcher baḥ , I, 139, from remote time.

mȧu , to be like.

mȧut , a man of the same kidney, like, equal, fellow, companion, associate, fellow-worker; plur. .

mȧtu 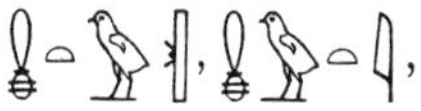, T. 270, [illegible], similar in form or nature, likeness; [illegible], similitudes.

mȧti , Thes. 1297, [illegible],  [illegible], similitude, likeness, copy, resemblance; [illegible], [illegible], likeness, I, 139; [illegible], statue, image, likeness; [illegible], divine type; [illegible], his divine companions.

mȧtt , , Rec. 3, 50, the like, likeness, copy, similitude; [illegible] with [illegible] likewise; [illegible], Rec. 6, 8, like them; [illegible], Rec. 35, 204, repetition of an act; [illegible], Rev. 13, 10, 14, 10.

mmȧu (mȧu) , to take a mould for making a copy or cast of something.

mȧ , metal rings.

mȧ , cat; fem. [illegible], .

mȧt, mȧit , , Jour. As. 1908, 265, way, path, road; [illegible] , path of the two hands, *i.e.*, rectitude; , course of action; Copt. ⲙⲟⲉⲓⲧ.

mȧām , Rev., misery.

màāḥā-t , , tomb, grave; see ; Copt. ⲙϩⲁⲁⲩ.

màāsh , , abundance, many; Copt. ⲙⲏⲏϣⲉ.

màì , part of a ship.

màì-t , Rev. 13, 27, 14, 8, , Rev. 13, 8, place; Copt. ⲙⲁ.

màì-t , Leyd. Pap. 13, 13, pots, vases.

màì, màì-t , Koller Pap. 4, 3, , , B.D. 33, 2, , cat (lion); , "little cat," a woman's name, "pussy"; Copt. ⲉⲙⲟⲩ.

Màì , B.D. 145A, the door-keeper of the 12th Pylon.

màu , T. 315 . . . . . .

màu , , lion; plur. , ; Copt. ⲙⲟⲟⲩⲓ.

màu , , cat; Copt. ⲉⲙⲟⲩ.

màu-t , she-cat.

màui , , he-cat.

Màu , the cat sacred to Bast of Bubastis. It is probable that the sacred cat possessed certain distinguishing marks, as did the Ram of Mendes and the Apis and Mnevis Bulls.

Màu , , B.D. 17, 20; 33; 145, 8, 32, a cat-god, a form of Rā who lived by the Persea tree in Ȧnu, and cut off the head of Āapep daily; for his converse with the Ass, see B.D. 125, III.

Màu-āa , Tomb of Seti I, one of the 75 forms of Rā (No. 56).

Màuti , , U. 558, T. 332, , Tomb of Seti I, one of the 75 forms of Rā (No. 33); see **Rurutà**.

Màti , , , , Lit. 33, a cat-god or lion-god.

Màti , Ṭuat XI, a cat-god who guarded his Circle.

màb , P. 427, M. 611, N. 1215, a plant.

màm (?) , T. 365, P. 85, 160, 163, 193, N. 921, as, like; see and , N. 856; = , N. 71.

màmr , a kind of seed, or herb.

màn , , , , to-day; , , daily; , , , daily; Copt. ⲙⲏⲛⲉ.

màn-t , , daily food or provisions.

màna , Rec. 29, 7, , A.Z. 1912, 103, daily intercourse, familiarity, daily work.

màn-t , Gol. 13, 125, , Rev. 6, 29, Rec. 29, 7, land which is worked by forced labour.

màn , a bandlet.

mànu , speckled, streaked, variegated, pied.

mànb , , , Rec. 33, 75, 199, (*sic*) , axe, weapon.

mànkh-t , tassel, part of a collar; see .

màr , U. 194, T. 74, P. 185, 319, 636, M. 298, N. 7, 899, , P. 162, 441, 602, M. 410, , M. 545, N. 856, , M. 511, N. 1093, as, like; see and .

mȧr ; see .

mȧra , Rev. 11, 187, abyss; Copt. ⲙⲏⲣⲉ.

mȧhȧaaȧ , to lament.

mȧḥ , rudder, paddle; plur. , ; see **māḥu**, .

mȧḥu , Rec. 30, 185, paddles, oars.

mȧḥ , cord, bandlet, tiara, garland (?)

mȧs-t , U. 419 = , T. 240, , , Rec. 26, 74, , , , , , , , liver.

mȧsu-t , P. 5, M. 6, , , , , , , N. 113, ornament attached to the Crown of the South that fell or rested on the shoulders.

Mȧs-t , the name of a serpent of the royal crown.

mȧs , Rev. 11, 184, child; Copt. ⲙⲉⲥ.

mȧs-ut , , Peasant 22, a kind of plant.

mȧsu , to work in metal or stone, to carve a statue.

Mȧskhen-t , , the name of a goddess; see **Meskhen-t.**

mȧk , A.Z. 1905, 108, thou; Copt. ⲙⲙⲟⲕ.

mȧka , some strong-smelling substance.

mȧka-t , Rec. 16, 93, a kind of grain, or seed, aniseed (Loret); Copt. ⲉⲙⲕⲏ.

mȧt , , a bandlet, a tiara or crown.

mȧṭa , P. 705, jawbones (?) of a bull.

mā , A.Z. 1884, 80, P.S.B. 13, 562; and see P.S B. 24, 349.

mā (ma (?) mi (?)) , who? what? Heb. מִי, מָה.

mā (ma (?) mi (?)) , , , , , who is it?; , what are they?; , why? wherefore? for what reason?; , like what?; , how many?; , , what then?

mā (mi ?) , , , , , see, behold; , see thou; varr. , , , .

mā , , a preposition:—by the hand, or arm, of, from, through, by means of, because; , together with; Copt. ⲛ̄ⲧⲉ.

mā-ti (mi-ti ?) , Rosetta Stone 9, inasmuch as.

mā (mi ?) , , a conjunction; also used as an imperative, grant, give; Copt. ⲙⲏⲓ.

mā (mi ?) , , , , , , , , , , prithee, let me, grant, permit, O let, would that, give; , grant us; , grant thou; , grant ye to me.

mā (mi ?) , , Rhind Pap. 38, , , , , , , , , , , , ,

, , , come; plur. , , .

mā , altar slab, table for offerings.

mā , , breath, wind, air.

mā (mi, mu) , , , , , , A.Z. 1905, 25, water, a collection of water, sea, lake; Heb. מַיִם.

māi (mi) , , , Rec. 27, 86, , , Rougé I.H. II, 17, Düm. H.I. I, 19, , , , , the seed of men, essence.

māi (mi-t) , , , , , , urine; , urine.

māi (mi) , divine seed, royal seed.

māmā (mimi) , fountain; Copt. ⲙⲟⲩⲙⲉ.

mā-t , right feeling, rectitude; see **maā-t.**

Mā-t (?) , B.D. (Saïte) 125, 61, a god.

māu (?) , , , ; see .

māā (?) , Rec. 35, 138, to sleep.

māā-t (mā-t) , , , , place, house.

m'āa-t , , , salt or soda water (?); var. .

m'āa , , , to strike, to beat the hands or feet with a stick, bastinado.

māui , U. 576, N. 965, the two sides of a ladder.

M'au-taui , B.D. 125, III, 34, the name of a god.

M'anaqraṭa , a proper name; Gr. Μενεκρατεια.

m'at , dead body, mummy.

māȧ , hair, lock, tress.

māȧ (mai) , , , ring, handle (?)

māȧtu (mȧaut) , some kind of wooden objects in the sanctuary of Horus.

māȧrȧu (mȧrȧu) , groom, syce.

m'inikhsa , Pap. Koller, 4, 1, a kind of wood.

māiḥa (miḥa) , Rev. 13, 26, hesitation.

māitut (mitut) , Rev. 14, 12, places.

m'iṭṭ , path, road; Copt. ⲙⲟⲉⲓⲧ.

m'u , stinking fish; var. .

m'uai-ā , fight, struggle.

M'uskian , a proper name, Moschion.

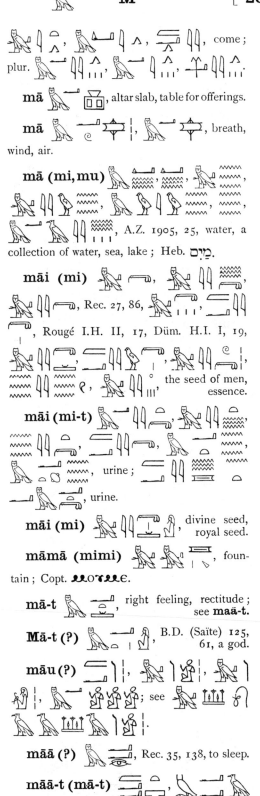

M'uit, a water-deity, a name of the heavens personified as a woman; see .

m'uf, helper, ally, servant.

māunfu (m'unfu), IV. 730, Anastasi I, 5, 5, "those who are with him," *i.e.*, allies, auxiliaries, guardians, protectors.

Māri (Mari?), Israel Stele, 18, a defeated Libyan king.

Māresar (Mursar?), Treaty, a Hittite king.

māuḥ, P. 163, N. 857, Hh. 311, oar, paddle.

Māuthenre (Muthenr), Treaty, a Hittite king.

māba, Rougé, Chrest. II, 110, thirty, Copt. ⲙⲁⲁⲃ.

mābiu (?), Thes. 1202, Rev. 2, 12, the 30 judges, human or divine; one of the 30 judges.

mābiu —, president of the Thirty; president of the Southern Thirty; president-in-chief of the Southern Thirty.

mābit, P.S.B. 8, 238, Hh. 718, Rec. 16, 129, the court in which the Thirty sat.

māba, P. 424, N. 1212, Rec. 22, 21, (*sic*), M. 607, A.Z. 1905, 23, pike, lance, spear, harpoon; plur. Nesi-Åmsu, 31, 17.

mābti, spear maker (?)

Mābiu, Berg. 72, the harpoon-gods (?)

Māpu (M'pu), a title of honour (?)

māfekh (m'fekh), place of unloading a boat, landing-place; see .

māfesh (m'fesh), A.Z. 1879, 20, to land, to unload a boat.

māfqṭȧ (m'fqṭȧ), vase, bottle, jar, vessel.

māfka-t (m'fka-t), Palermo Stele, turquoise; real turquoise, as opposed to the paste imitation.

mām, to destroy.

Mām, Ṭuat VII, a monster serpent-god, from whose body 12 human heads appeared; he was also called Kheti

m'maām , balsam, unguent.

māmā (mimi) , Shipwreck, 164, giraffe = , IV, 948.

mān (m'n) , , Rec. 21, 14, 82, 88, Åmen. 19, 18, 22; 26, 20, , A.Z. 1876, 121, without, there is not; Copt. ⲙ̀ⲙⲙⲟⲛ.

mānn (m'nen) , , , to fetter, to tie round, to wind round, to entwine.

mānnu (m'nen) , , cord, rope.

Mānn (M'nen) , Ṭuat VII, the rope used to tie up Qan.

M'neniu , , , Ṭuat X, two serpents in the Ṭuat.

māna (m'na) , Amherst Pap. 26, to fetter, to strike, to beat.

mānfi , , he who is with him, *i.e.*, helper, ally.

mānkh-t , , A.Z. 1908, 18, , , , pendant, a part of a collar, something worn on the neck, an amulet.

M-ānkhti , Ṭuat IV, a form of Osiris.

Māngabtȧ , Rec. 21, 77, a captain of Tanis.

māntȧu (m'ntȧu) , leather trappings or straps of a waggon or chariot.

m'ntȧtchu , leather straps of a chariot.

m'nthai , out of danger (?)

Mānṭit , U. 293, , , the boat of the rising sun. Later forms are: — , , , , , , , , , , ; see **Māntchit.**

Mānṭet ; see **Māntchit.**

m'ānṭṭ , to cut, to hew, to dig out.

m'nṭatȧ , Mar. Karn. 53, 36, equipment, furnishing, jewels, ornaments.

Māntchit , Palermo Stone, , U. 293, N. 719, P. 670, , T. 222, , T. 293, , M. 658, , M. 176, , , Rec. 32, 81, , Hh. 399, , the boat of the morning sun.

m'ntcheqtȧ , P.S.B. 13, 411, pot, flask; Heb. מוּצָקָה.

mār , , yonder; Copt. ⲙ̀ⲙⲏⲣ.

mār, mār-t , , , , , , , to dress, to clothe, dress, girdle, tie, band, bandlet, garment, apparel, fine raiment.

mār , Pap. 3024, 41, , , IV, 1080; var. , to be happy, to flourish, to prosper; , without thee the carrying out of a matter prospereth not; , a flourishing time.

mār-t, A.Z. 35, 16, favour.

mār , a shrub or tree.

mārr, a cake, loaf.

mārȧau (?), groom, syce, herd, servant; plur.

Mārȧiu (?), Thes. 1203, , Israel Stele 9, 14, , Mar. Karn. 52, 13, a Libyan king who attacked Rameses III.

māri (m'ri), metal fitting of a door.

māri-ghāri, Rev. 11, 181 = μαριχαρει, "May I rejoice!"

mārina, IV, 892, , lord, chief, officer; Syr. ܡܪܝܐ (?); plur. , Thes. 1208, , two lords.

m'ruatȧ, Demot. Cat. 354.

mārrȧa-t, cudgel, stick for beating animals with.

mārḥu, mārkh, Koller Pap. 1, 5, lance, spear; Heb. רמח.

m'rkh-t, ointment.

Mārsar, a king of the Kheta.

mārsh (?), Rec. 3, 46, red ochre, cakes (?) Copt. ⲙⲉⲣϣ, ⲙⲟⲣϣ.

mārqaḥt, booty (compare Heb. מַלְקוֹחַ), flight (compare Heb. √רחק)

Mārqatȧ (M'reqtȧ), Pap. Mag. 162, B.D. 165, 8, a name of Ȧmen.

m'rakau (?), Rec. 21, 86, gifts, tribute.

m'rkabtȧ-t, chariot; Copt. ϭⲉⲣⲉϭⲱⲱⲧ, Heb. מֶרְכָּבָה.

m'rkatȧ-t, a thin piece of wood.

m'rtȧ, kind, value.

m'rṭ, L.D. III, 194, 27, , success (?)

m'rṭ, food (?)

māh (m'hi), , Rec. 31, 147, , to forget, to neglect, to delay, to hesitate.

m'heh, to delay, to hesitate.

m'h-t, forgetfulness, neglect, delay.

m'hau-t , tribe, clan, family, kith and kin, tribesmen, relatives, mob, crowd of people, generations (?)

m'ha-t , pot, vase, vessel, milk-can; plur. 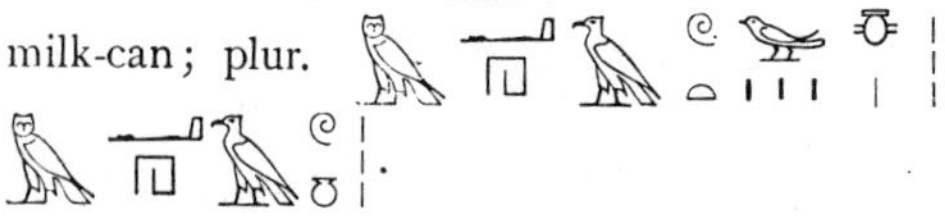.

m'hanu 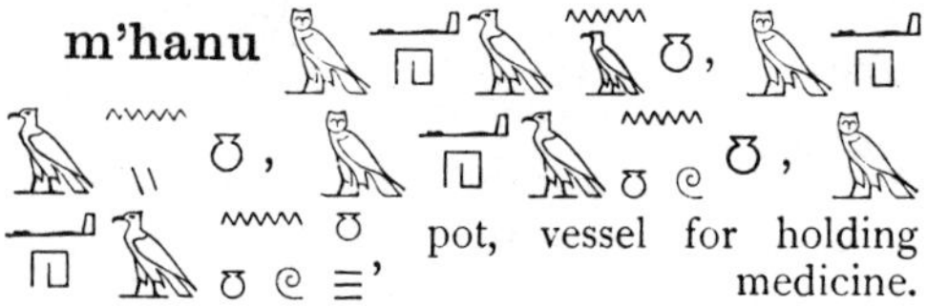 pot, vessel for holding medicine.

m'hani 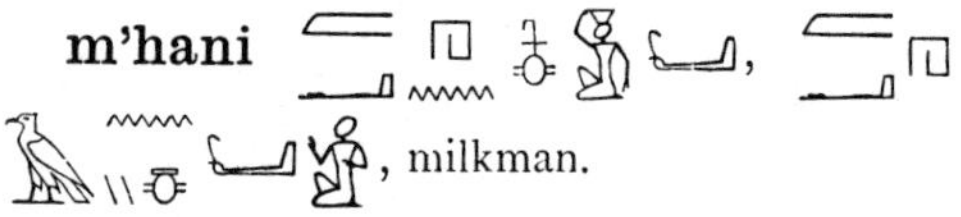, milkman.

m'hani , Rec. 19, 96. sarcophagus, coffin, part of a shrine.

m'hari 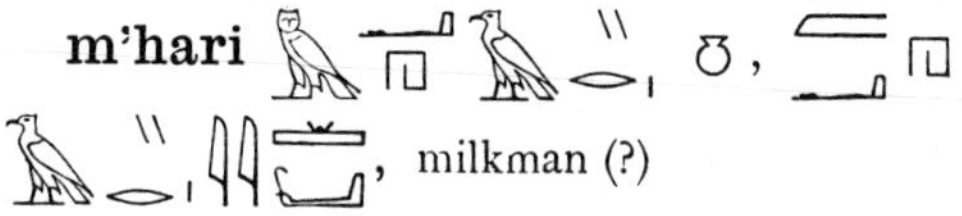, milkman (?)

m'har , the title of an officer, a skilled or clever man.

M'har-bār  = Mahar-Baal, מהר־בעל.

m'hasun (?) 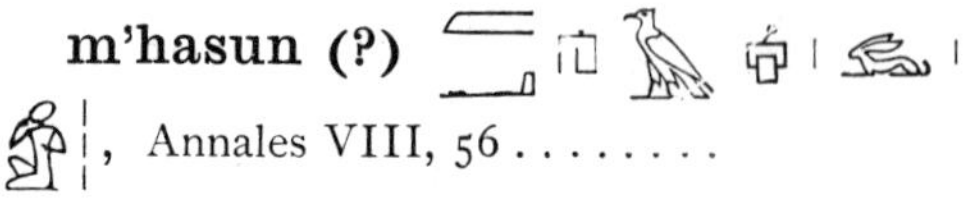, Annales VIII, 56 . . . .

m'haṭṭi , fire, flame, burner.

m'hȧ-t 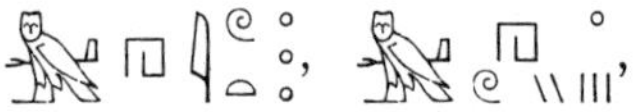, a seed or grain.

m'hui , vessel for holding milk, pot; plur. 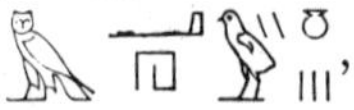, Hearst. Pap. 9, 2.

m'hua 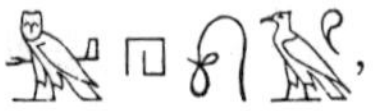, Rec. 33, 121, relation.

m'hen 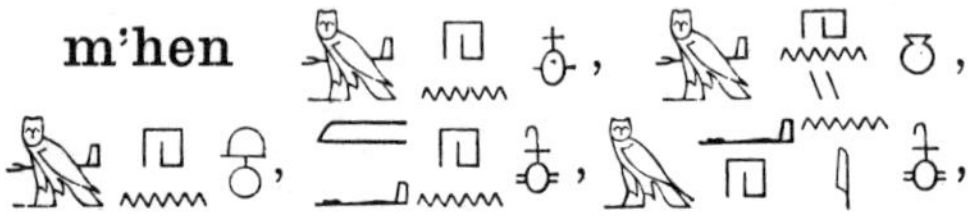, vessel for milk, milk-pot.

m'hen 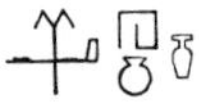, milk-vessel.

m'henu 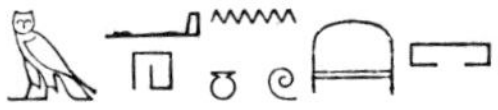, Åmen. 3, 13, treasure-house.

m'her , Wört. Suppl. 563, to be skilled, expert.

M'her , a title of Āapep.

m'her , vessel, pot; plur. 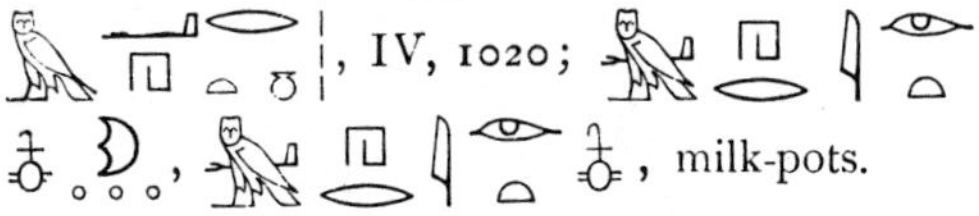, IV, 1020; milk-pots.

m'her 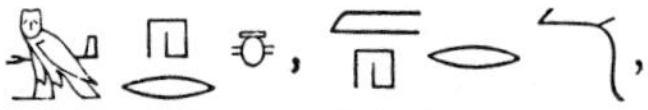, to suckle, to nourish, to be nourished.

m'herȧ , sucking-child, babe.

ṁ'heru 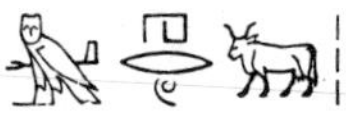, young cattle, milk-calves.

m'het 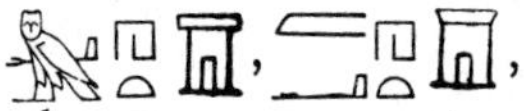, entrance, door; see 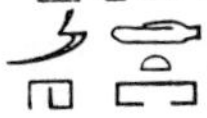 and .

māḥ (m'ḥi) 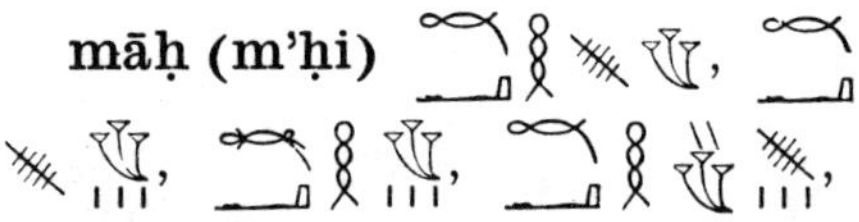, flax; Copt. ⲙⲁϩⲓ.

māḥ , P. 169, staff, cudgel (?)

māḥ 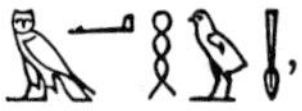, T. 199, P. 786, paddle, oar.

māḥa (?) , T. 170, , M. 179, , N. 689, ...

māḥā , standard.

māḥā-t , grave, tomb, sepulchre; plur. ; Copt. ⲙϩⲁⲁⲩ. Late form .

māḥi (m'ḥi) , to direct, to supervise.

m'ḥutchartȧ , , pool, lake.

m'ḥenk , Peasant 170, friend, client, benefactor, associate.

Mākh , Denderah IV, 68, a funerary coffer of Osiris.

m'kht . . . . , metal objects.

m'kh-t , Ebers Pap. 13, 14, a beating, a pounding.

m'khai , , , , , , , , to weigh, to measure, to ponder, to judge.

m'kha-t , , Peasant 312, , Åmen. 17, 22, , , , , , , , , , , a pair of large scales mounted on a pillar for weighing bulky or heavy objects; Copt. ⲙⲁϣⲓ; , salesman; , balance of the earth.

M'khaȧ-t , Pap. Ani, sheet 3, Ṭuat VI, the Great Scales of the Hall of Judgment wherein souls were weighed.

M'kha-t-ent-Rā , B.D. 12, 2, , the Scales of Rā.

m'kha , Rechnungen 63, scale-room (?)

m'khai , , , , Rev. 14, 136, , to strike, to fight, to contend; Copt. ⲙⲓϣⲉ.

m'khaiu , fight, fighters, foes.

m'kha , Thes. 1200, , Thes. 1210, , to burn up, fire, flame.

m'kha , , , , to tie, to bind, to despoil (?)

m'khau , trappings of a chariot, or part of the chariot itself.

M'khait , B.D. 1, 29, the sledge of the Ḥennu boat.

m'khāq-t , , , , , neck: Copt. ⲙⲁⲕϩ.

m'khau , IV, 671, a kind of animal.

m'kham'khaut 
, Love Songs 7, 3, purslane, a succulent herb ; Copt. ⲙⲉϩⲙⲟⲩϩⲉ.

M'khan 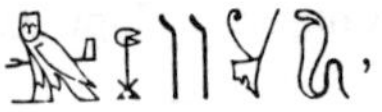, B.M. 32, 470, a goddess.

mākhat (m'kht) 

, intestines ; 
 to turn the stomach, to make one sick ; Copt. ⲙⲕⲁϩⲧ.

m'khaṭ-ti , strife, striver, fighter.

m'khṭȧ , Demot. Cat. 356, northwards = .

mākhiu 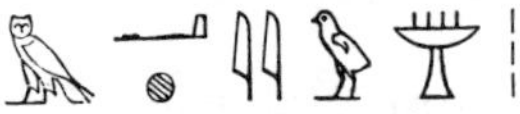, fire-altars, braziers on stands filled with fire.

Mākhiu , B.D. 141, 63, the gods of fire-altars.

M'khiȧr (?) , the word from which was derived the name of the month Mekhir.

M'khiȧru (?) , the god of the 6th month, whose name is preserved in the Copt. ⲙⲉⲭⲓⲣ.

M'khir , A.Z. 1901, 129, the month Mekhir ; Copt. ⲙϣⲓⲣ, ⲙⲉⲭⲓⲣ.

m'khitȧ (?) 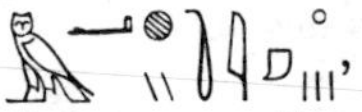, Mar. Aby. II, 6, 7, 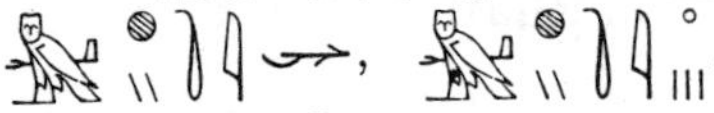,
, metal inlayings.

m'khen 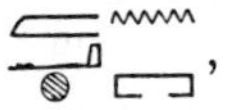, cabinet, closet, chamber.

m'khen-t , B.D. 24, 4,

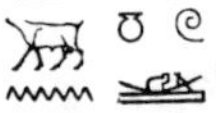, Ȧmen. 27, 2, ,
, ferry-boat.

m'khen-t 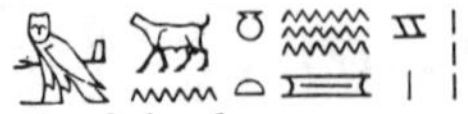, Love Songs, 2, 5, the craft of the ferryman.

m'khennuti ,
Ȧmen. 12, 9, 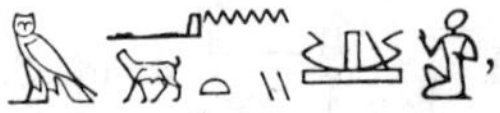, ferryman.

M'khenti 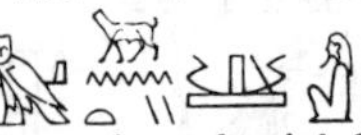, the god of the magical ferry-boat, the celestial ferryman.

m'kheru ,
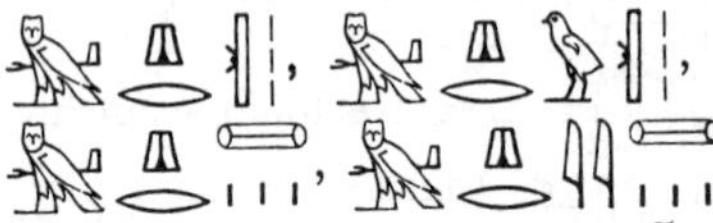, Thes. 1480, Leyd. Pap. 103, food, provisions ; IV, 968, , sustenance, means of subsistence, maintenance, articles of tribute, gifts, offerings.

m'kher , price, dowry, value, wages ; Heb. מְחִיר, Assyr. makhîru ; Rawlinson, C.I., V, 9, 49 ; Ass. Wört. 404, makhîru.

m'kher, m'kher-t ,
Ȧmen. 9, 1, 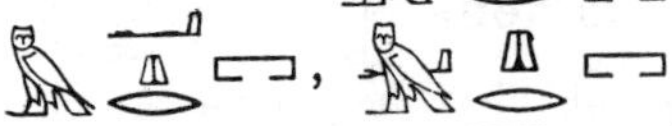,

, granary, barn, magazine, storehouse, warehouse ; , Westcar, 12, 24.

M'kheskhemuit (?) 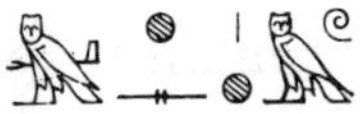
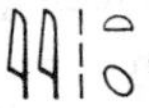, the goddess of the 11th hour of the night.

m'khtem-t [illegible], enclosure, fold, shelter.

mās (m's) [illegible], IV, 983, 1022,
Shipwreck 175, [illegible], IV, 659, 953, 1086, [illegible], IV, 899, [illegible]
[illegible], Rec. 21, 92,
[illegible], Rec. 18, 182, [illegible],
[illegible],
Rec. 27, 223, [illegible], to bring, to lead forward, to pass on or into, to come in with something.

m's-t, passage.

m'su, bearer; , IV, 1007, offerings-bearer.

m's, bouquet, bunches of flowers, garlands.

m's, hair (?)

m'sakh, pot of oil, unguent, to anoint (?); compare Heb. מַשְׁחִית, 2 Kings xxiii, 13.

m'sakh-t, Rec. 21, 77, 96, wine-jar, wine-skin.

m'saqa, Koller Pap. 1, 7, to work in bronze, wrought metal work, sculpture.

m'satȧḥ, Alt. K. 503 . . . . . .; compare Heb. מִשְׁתֶּה, feast, revel.

m'sua (?) I, 127, a product of the Sûdân.

m'seḥ, Nâstasen Stele 12, 52, to march, to go.

m'sha, Demot. Cat. 391, to go; Copt. ⲙⲁϣⲉ.

m'sha, evening; see .

m'shu, IV, 894, sword, dagger.

m'sha, to gut fish, to draw game, to split open.

m'shaȧb, place for drawing water; compare Heb. מַשְׁאָב, Judges v, 11.

m'shaiu, Anastasi I, 26, 6, Koller Pap. 2, 1, , traces of a chariot (?) bindings of a bow.

m'sha (m'shasha ?), Ȧmen. 27, 17 . . . . . .

M'shauasha, a Libyan tribe or people.

m'shap, Ȧmen. 16, 17, 19, 19, 20, 12, 27, 3 . . . .

m'sharar, Koller Pap. 2, 1, part of a waggon (?)

M'shashar, a Libyan name.

m'shaq, Ȧmen. 9, 14 . . . . . .

m'shakabiu, Rec. 15, 143, 17, 147, , great or mighty men, overseers, inspectors, tax-gatherers; compare √שׁגב.

M'shaken, Thes. 1203, a Libyan king.

m'shaṭi, joiner, table-maker, cabinet-maker.

m'shā, Thes. 1202, Israel Stele 6, , Rec. 8, 134, to march, to go, to travel; II, III, 141, to march at the double; Copt. ⲙⲟⲟϣⲉ.

m'shāi, traveller, envoy; plur. , Koller Pap. 5, 2.

m'shā-t , , journey.

m'shāu , soldier; plur. , , , , I, 101, army, host, troops; , cavalry soldiers.

m'shā , unguent, spice, incense.

m'shā re , a kind of unguent.

m'shāfiu , Ȧmen. 7, 4 . . . . . .

m'shepn-t , a kind of disease.

m'sheshm-t , a kind of disease.

m'sheru , , , Rec. 29, 155, 31, 15, , Berl. 3024, 81, , , , , , , , , , , evening, night; Copt. ⲉⲩϣⲏ.

M'sherr , the City of Night in the Ṭuat.

m'shtau , B.D. (Nav.) II, 108 = .

m'sheṭit , , , , A.Z. 17, 4, , Rec. 13, 21, ford; compare Copt. ⲙⲉϣⲱⲧ (?) , the ford of the Orontes.

m'shṭ , nest.

m'sheṭ , to travel, to go about, to inspect; Copt. ⲙⲟⲩϣⲧ.

māq (m'q) , , to slay, to hack in pieces, to chop up, knife.

m'q-t , ladder; , Rec. 36, 78; Copt. ⲙⲟⲩⲕⲓ.

m'qaār , , , , , a baker's fire shovel.

m'qar-t , a kind of onion (?) portulaca, purslane, sedum (?); , water onion.

m'qaḥa ; see **m'kḥa**, .

m'quráu , , , saddle-gear, loads for a beast, pack-saddles (?)

m'qnas , Rec. 11, 96 (in cartouche) = Lat. Magnus.

m'ki , , , , , , , , , , to protect; , Koller, Pap. 3, 4, protector of the people.

m'kiu , protectors.

m'kit , , , , , , , Rec. 27, 58, , , , protection, protectress.

m'kit , Rec. 5, 88, a covering.

m'kti , , protector.

m'kit 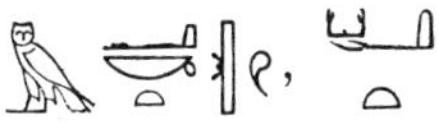, Ebers Pap. 101, 13, A.Z. 1908, 116, support of the heart.

m'ki[t] , protector of the house, housewife.

m'kit , storehouse, station, place; 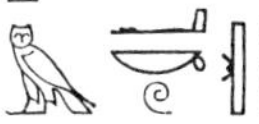, what is stored, provisions (?)

m'k-pa (?) , Rev. 12, 97, to reclaim a property.

M'ket-åri-s 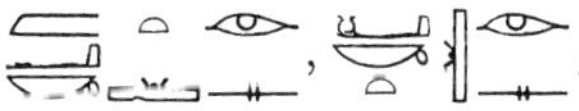 Ṭuat I, a goddess, guide of Rā.

M'k-neb-set , Thes. 31, , Denderah III, 24, , Berg. II, 9: (1) goddess of the 3rd hour of the day; (2) goddess of the 10th hour of the night.

māk (m'k) 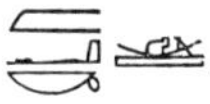, boat; plur.  [illegible], Mar. Karn. 53, 24

m'k-t 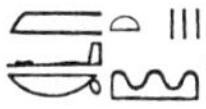, regions, districts.

m'k 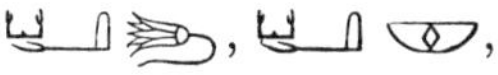, to rejoice.

māk (m'k) , , Åmen. 18, 10, , Rev. 3, 40, linen, bandlet, a kind of cloth.

Māk (M'k) , the name of a crocodile.

m'ka , see! behold!

m'ka-t  , base, place, seat, stand, bench, bed, bier, couch.

M'katu , a boundary god (?)

m'ka , Shipwreck, 29, 99, brave, bold.

M'kam'r , Rev. 21, 98, a Syrian.

m'karbutå  [illegible], chariot; see 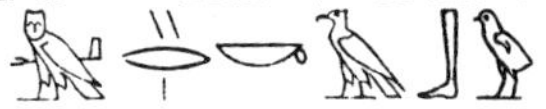 [illegible].

m'katåu , charms, amulets, protective talismans.

m'ki , Rec. 16, 93, dung, excrement (?)

m'kfitiu  [illegible], turquoise.

mākmārtå (m'km'rtå)  [illegible], Åmen. 7, 6, cloth, a garment.

m'kr , Tanis Pap. 15........

mākråiu (m'kriu) 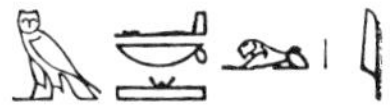 [illegible], merchants; Heb. מכר.

m'kḥa , Åmen. 24, 5, , Thes. 1482, [illegible], Mar. Aby. I, 9, [illegible], to turn the back on, to turn away from, to neglect, to put behind one, to set aside, to disregard, to be negligent or careless.

m'kes , a sacred stone object held by Osiris.

m'ktål   [illegible], tower; Heb. מִגְדֹּל, Copt. ⲙⲉϭⲧⲟⲗ, ⲙⲓϫⲧⲟⲗ.

Mäg, M'ga  [illegible], Pap. Mag. 388, Rec. 35, 57, a crocodile-god, son of Set.

m'ga , foe, enemy.

m'ga 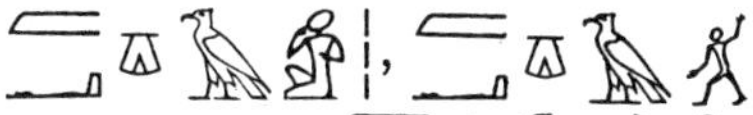 [illegible], Hymn to Nile 2, 13,  [illegible], to command, to issue orders, to instruct.

m'ga , commandant, the chief of the corvée, instructor.

m'gau , a corvée gang (?)

m'ga-t , Hymn to Nile 11, 9, arrow, weapon; a stick for beating the hands or feet; Copt. ⲙⲁⲕⲁⲧ.

m'ga , a kind of plant used in medicine.

m'ga , oven, fireplace, fire (?)

m'agaār , oven, fireplace, fire (?)

m'ga-t , sadness, grief, affliction.

m'gartȧ 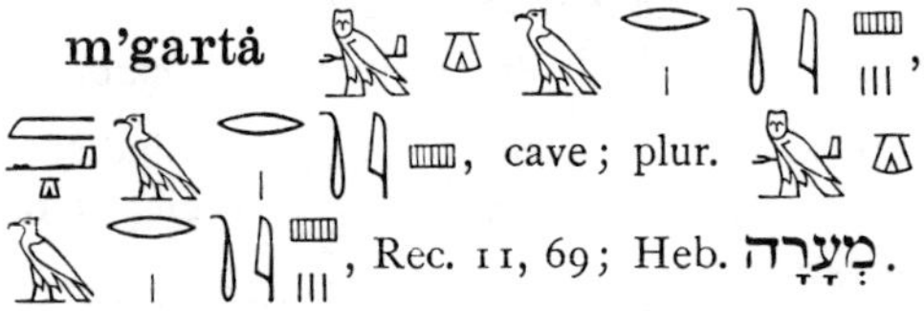, cave; plur. Rec. 11, 69; Heb. מְעָרָה.

m'gas , armlet.

m'gaṭir , tower, fortress; Heb. מִגְדָּל.

m'gȧ , B.M. 138, child (?)

m'gi , to be in despair.

māt 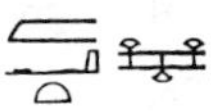, way, road, path; Copt. ⲙⲱⲓⲧ.

māt , a kind of cloth.

māt 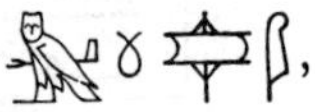, Rev. 13, 32 = Copt. ⲙⲁⲧⲉ, ⲉⲙⲁⲧⲉ.

māt , a river boat.

Mātt (Mutt) 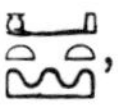, Berg. II, 11, a name of Ȧmentt.

Māāti (M'āti) 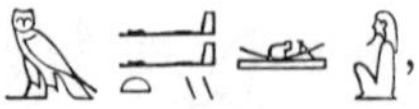, the boat of the morning sun; see **Māntch-t.**

māti (m'ti) , steersman, boatman.

m'ta , to fetter, to bind to stakes.

m'ta 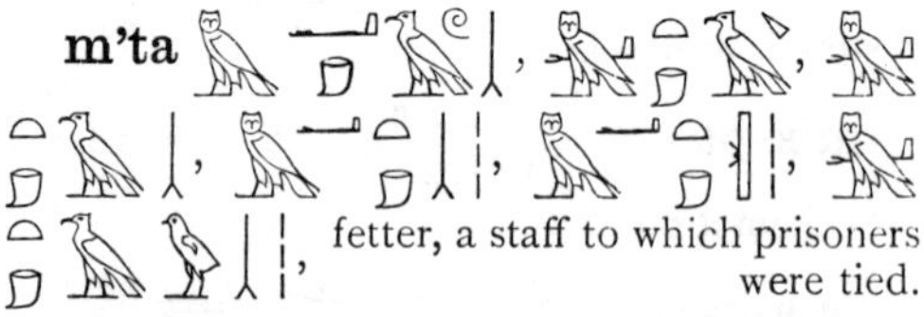, fetter, a staff to which prisoners were tied.

m'tait , chief of a tribe.

m'tȧtcha , Anastasi I, 26, 8, leather thongs.

m'ti , grief, bitterness.

m'ten 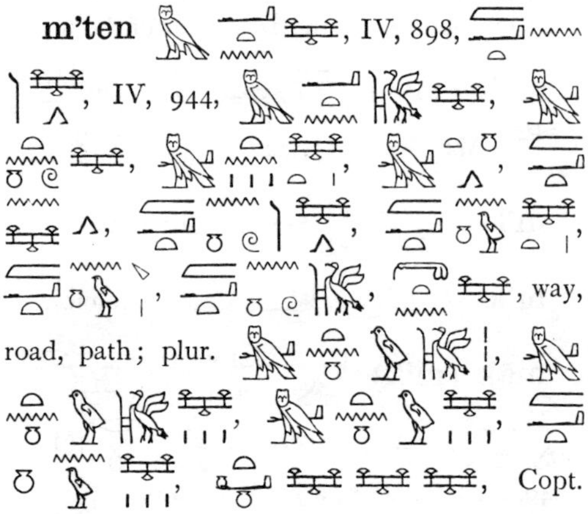, IV, 898, IV, 944, way, road, path; plur. Copt. ⲙⲟⲉⲓⲧ, ⲙⲱⲓⲧ.

m'tenu , leader, guide.

m'ten 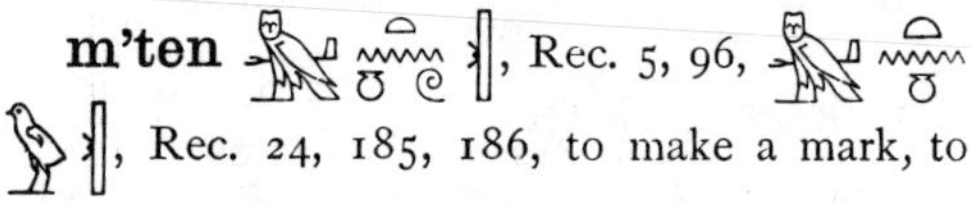, Rec. 5, 96, Rec. 24, 185, 186, to make a mark, to draw designs or pictures on stone, to mark a word; , L.D. III, 194, 14, things inscribed.

m'ten 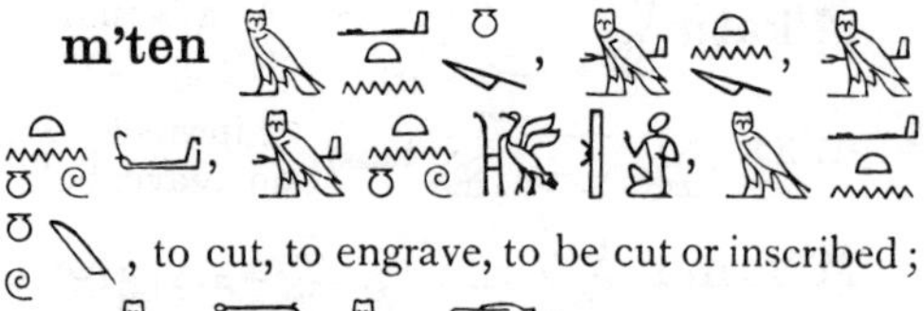, to cut, to engrave, to be cut or inscribed; varr. .

m'tenu , a written legend, story, inscription.

m'ten , an amulet.

m'tenu , cutter, engraver.

m'ten , P.S.B. 13, 413, to rest, to be quiet; Copt. ⲙⲟⲧⲉⲛ.

m'tenu . . . , dam (?) sluice (?)

māth (m'th) 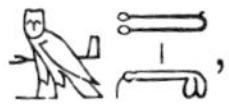, Hymn Darius 38, phallus; var. [illegible].

m'tha  [illegible], Rev. 13, 6, A.Z. 1900, 20, 1905, 36, phallus; , thy phallus and testicles.

M'tha au , "Long Phallus," a title of Osiris.

m'tha   [illegible], Hearst Pap. 10, 9: (1) to bind, to tie, to twist, to weave; (2) to anoint.

M'tharima(?) , L.D. III, 164, the name of a Hittite.

m'then , [illegible], way, road; plur. [illegible] 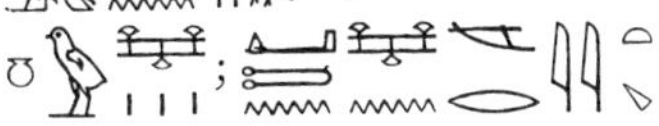, IV, 729, road along the sea coast.

m'then , road-man, guide, chief of a tribe, shêkh.

M'thenu 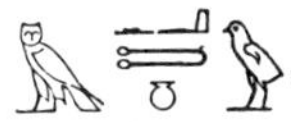, Ṭuat VIII, one of the bodyguards of Rā.

M'thra 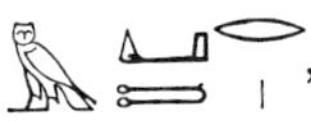, Mithras (in the name 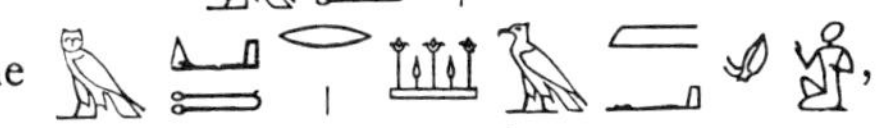, Mithrashamā, A.Z. 1913, 122).

M'āṭ-t , the boat of the morning sun; see **Māntchit.**

Māṭi (M'ṭi) , a title of Set.

m'ṭ [illegible], Mar. Aby. I, 6, 41, , Åmen. 3, 18 = [illegible].

m'ṭa , cloth.

m'ṭen-t  , way, road, path; plur.  [illegible].

m'ṭen 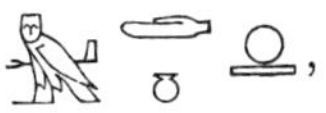, to equip (?) to bestow (?)

m'ṭen 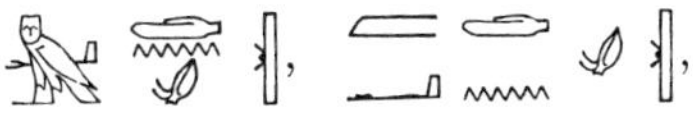, Rougé I.H. 158, to listen, to obey, to accept, to agree to, to be content; [illegible], Rev. 13, 15; compare Copt. ϫⲛⲁ.

m'ṭennu 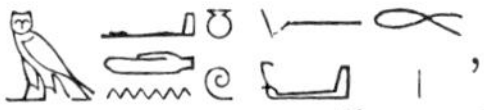, Åmen. 17, 14, inscribed, written; plur. [illegible] [illegible], Ameni Å. 2, 1.

m'ṭeḥ , IV, 778, to hew, to cut.

m'ṭes  , Anastasi I, 1, 8, to stab, to kill, to be sharp like a knife, to be keen, to be jealous; , Thes. 1481, IV, 969, "knife-hearted," *i.e.*, jealous (?)

M'ṭes 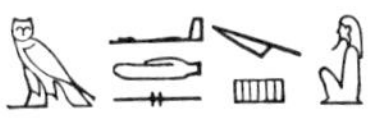, B.D. (Saïte) 17, 67, 39, 2, 146L, a warrior-god.

M'ṭes-åb , an ibis-headed god in the Ṭuat.

M'ṭes årui (?) 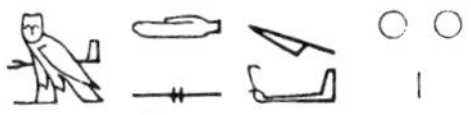 , Edfû I, 10, , Berg. I, 3, 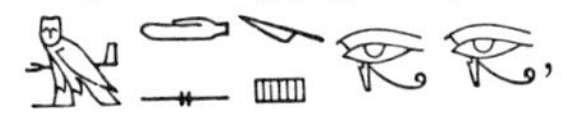, a group of "sharp-eyed" gods who watched over Osiris.

M'ṭes-sma-ta  , Ṭuat IV, the door of the 2nd section of Rastau

m'tcha , phallus, male.

m'tchaȧ , phallus.

m'tchaȧu , to hunt.

m'tchai 

[illegible], Koller Pap. 2, 4, Anastasi IV, 2, 6, , IV, 996, hunter of the Western Desert, soldier.

M'tchaiu 

, IV, 990, nomad hunters; at a later period, soldiers, town-guard, police; Copt. ⲙⲁⲧⲟⲉⲓ, ⲙⲁⲧⲟⲓ.

M'tchau , the Hunter-god.

m'tcha , Ȧmen. 15, 2, a kind of husbandman.

m'tchaȧ 
, grain, arable land.

m'tchait , Ȧmen. 15, 16, grain crops.

m'tchab 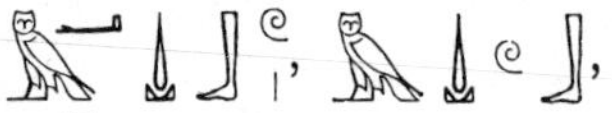, a fetter, chain, rope (?)

m'tchab-t 

, a tool or instrument, or part of a ship or boat; sometimes rendered pump.

m'tchar , to obey (?) to be content.

m'tcharȧ 
, a plaiter of crowns.

m'tchaqatȧ , Ȧmen. 26, 11, pot, vessel.

m'tcheqtȧ 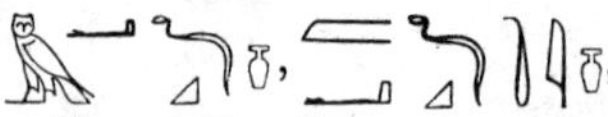
, a pot or bottle.

m'tcheṭ , Tombos Stele 15, , Peasant 212, 
, Thes. 1295, to squeeze, to press, to follow closely or strenuously, to tread, to force, to crush, to be urgent, insistent, the necessary result (Gol. 13, 123).

m'tcheṭ , the extract or juice of something, something squeezed or pressed out, decoction, solution.

m'tcheṭ 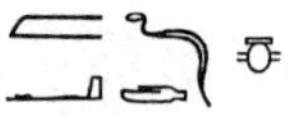, salve, ointment, unguent.

M'tcheṭ , B.D. 17, 34: (1) a bull-headed god; (2) a lion-headed god; (3) an invisible god in the House of Osiris who burned up the enemies of Osiris.

m'tcheṭfet , a tool or instrument.

mi , Rec. 11, 178; Copt. ⲙⲁⲣⲉ.

mi 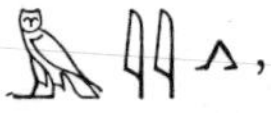, Rec. 27, 57, , T. 342, Come! Copt. ⲁⲙⲟⲩ.

mi , an optative particle, O that! Would that!

mir-ti , Rev. 11, 168, Copt. ⲙⲏⲣⲉ.

miha 
, Rev. 12, 112, 13, 32, wonder, admiration; Copt. ⲙⲟⲉⲓϩⲉ, ⲙⲟⲓϩⲉ.

mikh , Rev. 13, 1, fight; Copt. ⲙⲓϣⲉ.

Mi-sheps , , B.D. 172, 11 . . . . . .

mit , Jour. As. 1908, 264, way, path; Copt. ⲙⲱⲓⲧ.

mit , T. 290, , N. 167, , N. 129, , Hh. 344, to die.

mitiu , , , , L.D. III, 65A, 5, the dead, defeat, slaughter.

mui , to flow.

mui , water.

mui , , Peasant, 220, 279, essence, seed, urine.

mu , IV, 649, on the water of someone, *i.e.*, dependent upon someone; , Dream Stele 30, who was on his water, a dependant, a follower; , of one water, *i.e.*, of the same kidney; , "knowing my water," *i.e.*, knowing my position of vassal.

mu , Rec. 14, 97, , , , , , , Rec. 27, 83, 85, water, any large mass of water, water-supply, stream, canal, lake, liquid, essence, seed, sap; , De Hymnis 41; , the things that live in the water; , the brow of the water; , stars of the water; , flood of water.

mu-t , lake, pond; , Rec. 27, 84, river bank.

mui-t , , , seed, urine; var. ; Copt. ⲙⲟⲟⲩ.

Mu , Berg. 29, the divine essence of Osiris.

Mu , the Water-god, the personification of the celestial waters.

Mui-t , U. 181, , , , : (1) the goddess of the primeval waters; (2) the consort of Uatch-ur.

mu Ȧmentt , the water of Ȧmenti.

mu āa , great water, flood.

mu uru , high Nile-floods, full Inundations.

mu uḥā-t (?) , Rec. 21, 97, ...

mu bȧn , bad water, *i.e.*, water broken by rocks.

mu betesh-t , troubled waters.

mu em setch-t , water with fire [in it], *i.e.*, boiling water.

mu nu ȧr-t , , Peasant B 2, 119, waters of the eye, *i.e.*, tears.

mu nu āa , water from a vase.

mu nu ānkhȧmu , solution of ānkhȧm flowers.

mu nu ānti , myrrh water, liquid myrrh.

mu nu pet , , water of the sky, *i.e.*, rain.

mu nu mesten , a kind of solution used in embalming.

mu nu ennu , water of the Inundation.

mu nu Rā , water of Rā, celestial water, the water on which Rā sails.

mu nu Ḥāp , , water of Ḥāp, *i.e.*, Nile-water.

mu nu ḥesmen 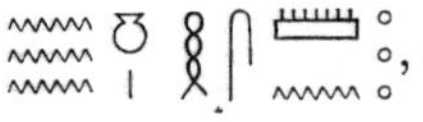, a solution of natron.

mu nu khnem-t , water from a well or cistern;
, water of the western well.

mu nu Khnemu , water of Khnemu.

mu nu qamȧi ; solution of incense.

mu nu tekhu , a solution of a herb used in embalming.

mu nefer 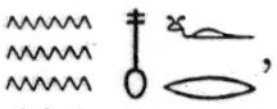, sweet water, *i.e.*, water neither brackish nor salt.

mu netem , Jour. As. 1908, 291, sweet water.

mu netri 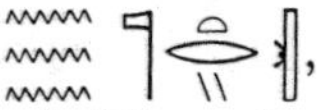, Thes. 1207, divine essence, seed of the god.

mu renp , T. 181,
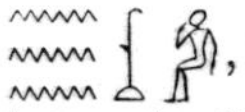, Edfû I, 77, M. 40, "Water of rejuvenation": (1) a title of Osiris; (2) a title of the Nile-god and his flood.

mu ḥai , Rec. 31, 30, rain water (?) Copt. ⲙⲟⲩⲛϩⲱⲟⲩ.

mu ḥit , Tombos Stele 8, a raging rain torrent.

mu ḥua , rain water;
, Ḥerusȧtef Stele 14, a beneficial rain; Copt. ⲙⲟⲩⲛϩⲱⲟⲩ.

mu Kher-āḥa 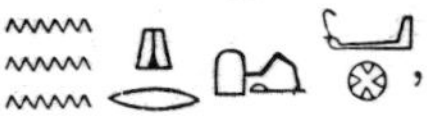, the canal of Kher-āḥa.

mu khet , the current of a stream.

mu setchit 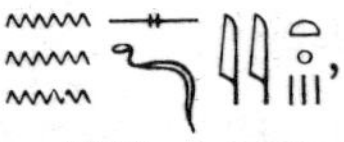, a medicinal solution.

mu qeṭ, etc. 
, Tombos Stele 13, water that turns round as one descends the river in going south.

mu ṭu , foul water, foetid liquid, pus.

mu (?) 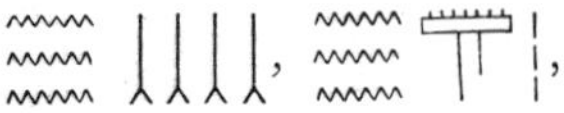, B.D. 110, 35, a kind of woven stuff.

mu , jester, buffoon.

muu , dwarfs.

mu — . . . . . 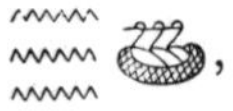, N. 769, 770, 778 . . . .

mu (?)-t , Anastasi I, 23, 3 . . . .

mumu (?) , U. 417, 554, T. 238, , T. 303 . . . .

mu-t 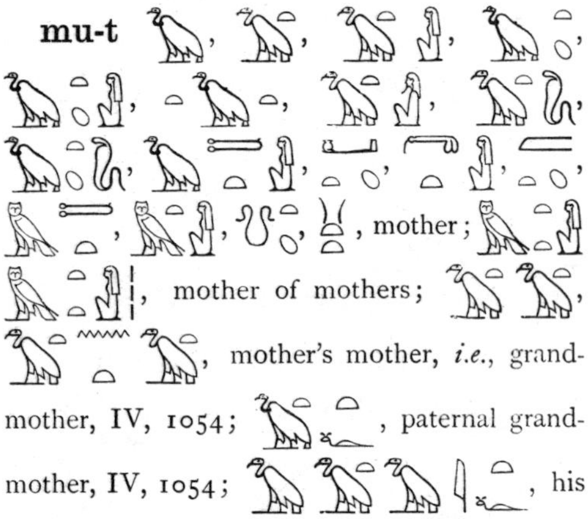
mother; mother of mothers; mother's mother, *i.e.*, grandmother, IV, 1054; paternal grandmother, IV, 1054; his father's great grandmother; Copt. ⲙⲁⲁⲩ.

mu-ti 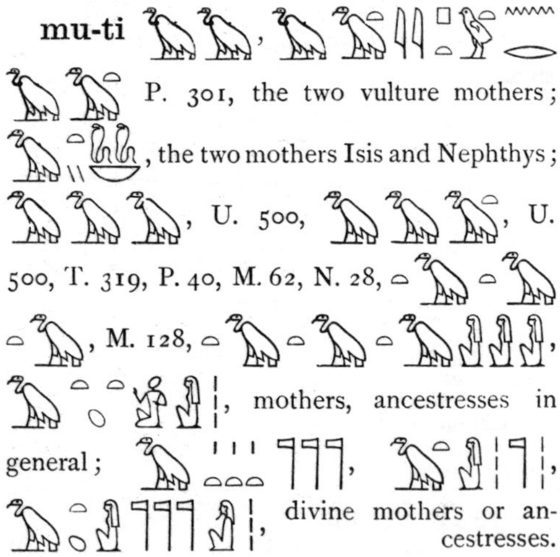
P. 301, the two vulture mothers; the two mothers Isis and Nephthys; U. 500, U. 500, T. 319, P. 40, M. 62, N. 28, M. 128, mothers, ancestresses in general; divine mothers or ancestresses.

mu-t ent ḥemt , mother of the wife.

mu-t, Dream Stele 24, , mother-cow, mother of a cow-goddess.

Mu-t, the "Mother"-goddess of all Egypt, who in late times was said to possess, like Neith, the power of parthenogenesis; , Mut in the horizon of heaven; Gr. Μουθ, Μουθις.

Mu-t, B.D. 164 (Rubric); Lanzone, 136–138, a goddess with three heads (one of a lioness, one of a woman, and one of a vulture) and a pair of wings and a phallus. Under this form she was called Sekhmit-Bast-Rā.

Mu-t . . . . neteru, Ombos I, 1, 46, a woman-headed hippopotamus-goddess.

Mu-t urit, a goddess of the Natron Valley.

mu-t meri = Philometor.

mu-t neter, (1) mother of the god, a title of Isis and other great goddesses; (2), title of the high-priestess of Letopolis.

Mu-t-hertȧu, Rev. 9, 28, the name of a horse of Rameses II.

mu-t, IV, 1125, , B.D. 125, I, 14, the weight used in a pair of scales.

mu-t, Rec. 5, 90, vase, pot, vessel.

muȧ, , Berg. 29 = **kuȧ**, .

muḥu, paddles, oars.

mukha, Jour. As. 1908, 272 = , , to burn, to blaze; , Rev. 14, 10, fiery-[eyed].

mukharer, Rev. 13, 13, scarab, beetle; Gr. κάνθαρος.

mukhen-t, ferry boat; **m'khen-t** .

Musta, Ṭuat IV, a goddess of food.

mushmush, to beat, to strike; Copt. ⲙⲉϣ, ⲙⲁϣ.

mukes, Rec. 15, 17, a kind of sceptre.

mut, , , , , to die; , he killed himself, he died by his own hand; , U. 206, , Rec. 31, 27, dead; , T. 235; Copt. ⲙⲟⲩⲧⲉ, ⲙⲟⲟⲩⲧ, Heb. מוּת.

mut, mit, , U. 224, 491, N. 914, , P. 85, , , Mar. Karn. 53, 21, , , , death; , Berl. 3024, 130, "death is in my face daily"; Copt. ⲙⲟⲩ, Heb. מָוֶת.

muti, miti (?), U. 96, , , dead, dead person or thing; plur. , P. 453, 650, , P. 374, M. 206, 361, N. 667, , , , , , , , the dead, the damned.

muti-t, miti-t (?), a dead woman.

mutmut, contagion, a deadly disease.

Muti-khenti-Ṭuat, Ṭuat IX, a hawk-god of offerings.

Muthenith, Ṭuat IV, a goddess.

mbenai, Rev. 11, 163, hither; Copt. ⲉⲙⲛⲁⲓ.

mbentiu (?), the apes in the 1st division of the Ṭuat.

mpaitu; Copt. ⲙ̄ⲡⲁⲧⲉ.

mput (?), disaster, trouble (?)

mefak, turquoises, emeralds.

mefakitiu (with), the gods of the turquoise land, *i.e.*, Sinai.

mefkh, to untie, to release, to loosen.

mefkh-t, Verbum II, 686, to pass corn through a sieve.

mefka-t, T. 99, P. 180, , Rec. 27, 224, , , IV, 888, turquoises, malachite, emeralds.

Mefkait, Rec. 31, 172, goddess of the turquoise land, *i.e.*, Sinai.

mefg, , turquoise, malachite; see .

mm, T. 268, M. 423, Thes. 1295, a preposition: with, among, etc.; var. , , .

mem (?) = .

mem, , , , , , , coriander seed, caraway seed, cummin.

mem, , Mar. Mast. 306, 474, IV, 948, hyena.

mem, a sanctuary of Sebek in the Prosopite Nome.

Mema-āiu, Ṭuat VII, a star in the Ṭuat.

memḥet, IV, 484, = , a chamber in the domain of Seker.

Memḥit (Meḥit), B.M. 32, 169, an associate of Ptaḥ and Neith.

memkh, Lateran Obel. = , unknown.

memsher = , evening, night.

men, , Rev. 11, 149, 12, 48, good! perfect!

Men, not to have, to be without.

men, , to suffer pain, to be sick or diseased, to be weak, to be in labour.

men-t, , , , , , Peasant 250, , , pain, sickness, sorrow, suffering, mourning, disasters, sore places, wounds, fatigue, calamity.

men, IV, 972, , a sick man.

men, , , A.Z. 1908, 17, an amulet, a kind of ornament.

men, , , , , , , Rev., to remain, to abide, to continue, to be permanent, to be stable, fixed, abiding, stablished; , , doubly firm; , , things that abide, hence possessions; , everlasting inscriptions; Copt. ⲙⲟⲩⲛ.

men — er men m 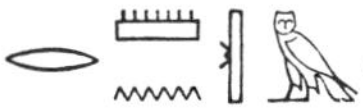, to remain by, a compound preposition: unto, until.

men-t 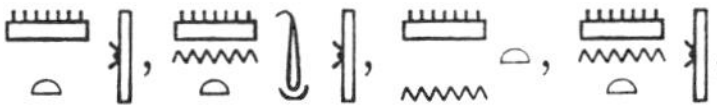, something which is firm, abiding, stand, position, habitation, stability, staying power.

menn-t 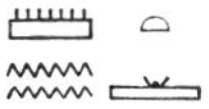, permanent one (fem.).

menmen 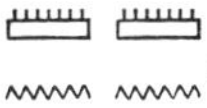, Ptol. I Stele 18, stable, permanent, abiding.

men-t, men-tȧ 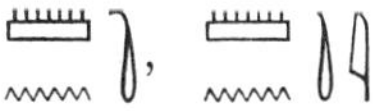, P. 183, N. 876, regularly, consecutively.

menu , firm, permanent, stable one.

men ȧb (or ḥa-t) 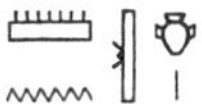, IV, 616, firm of heart, bold, brave, resolute.

men reṭui , firm of the two feet, determined, persistent.

men , that which endureth, a name of the sky.

Ment , P. 537, a goddess from whom proceeded 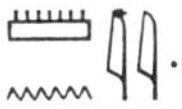.

Menu-ȧb , Ṭuat VIII, a member of the bodyguard of Rā.

Men-ā 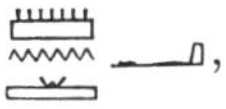, Ṭuat IX, a god who swathed Osiris.

Men-āḥ-ḥetch-tt , the name of a serpent on the royal crown.

Men-urit , Ombos 2, 131, a goddess.

men-t [illegible], Rec. 21, 80, , , daily; Copt. ⲙⲏⲛⲉ.

men-t ent rā neb 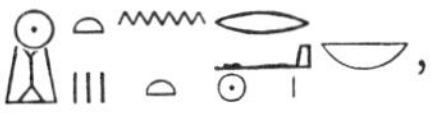, , IV, 490, 491, 754, 904, regularly, every day.

meni  with , Rev. 13, 2, daily; Copt. ⲙⲙⲏⲏⲛⲉ.

menu 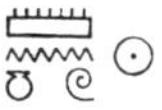, Ȧmen. 24, 15,  , Ḥerusȧtef Stele 67, daily.

men , daily gift or offering; plur. 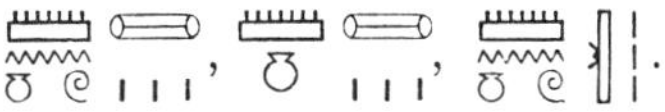.

menu , P. 373 = 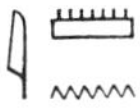, N. 1149, daily offerings or ceremonies.

menit 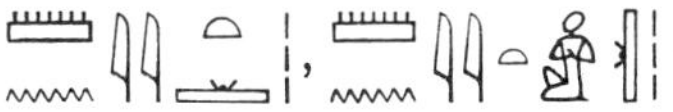 = 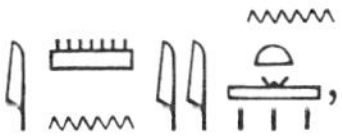, daily offerings.

men 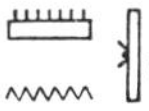, Rechnungen 45, calculation, statement.

men , Rec. 36, 90, "profondeur dans le sens horizontal."

men-t 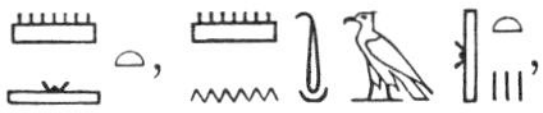, Rev. 13, 8, nature, kind, manner; Copt. ⲙⲓⲛⲉ.

men 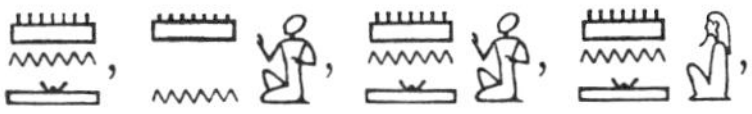, A.Z. 1908, 37, such and such a man, so-and-so; , Rec. 31, 11, I am so-and-so, the son of so-and-so; , Peasant 231, such as they.

men-t , such and such a woman.

men-t 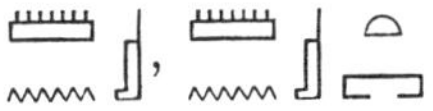, place, abode, habitation; plur. [illegible].

menu, mennu [illegible], Rec. 13, 11, [illegible], IV, 1113, [illegible], Tombos Stele 10, IV, 1120, [illegible], [illegible], Rec. 20, 40, [illegible], IV, 739, camp, fort, station, fortress, caravanserai, stronghold; plur. [illegible], Israel Stele 23, [illegible], IV, 1105, [illegible].

men en Abu [illegible], B.M. 169, fort of Elephantine.

menu [illegible], Tombos Stele 6, boundaries.

meni, to set up a memorial.

menu, U. 605, Rec. 34, 117, shrine, pavilion.

menu, Palermo Stele, , monument, monuments, temples, commemorative buildings of colossal scale, obelisks, palaces, walls, etc.; , monuments made of basalt (?); Copt. ⲙⲁⲉⲓⲛ, ⲙⲁⲉⲓⲛⲉ, ⲙⲁⲉⲓⲛⲓ.

men, a colossal statue of a god or king; plur. ; Copt. ⲙⲁⲉⲓⲛ.

meni, image, statue; plur.

men, a kind of stone, block of stone, slab; plur. , bases of statues, large pedestals.

men, meni, mountain, stone hill; dual, , Rec. 27, 84.

Menmentt, Rec. 36, 81, mountain, necropolis.

Ment, P. 665 = , the West.

men, to set down.

menmen, IV, 1105, Rec. 31, 15, to move, to move towards or away, to quake; Copt. ⲙⲟⲛⲙⲉⲛ.

menmen, A.Z. 1900, 30, 1905, 37, 1908, 6, to remove, to set aside, to carry off, to steal.

menmen ta, Rev. 11, 141, earthquake.

Menmenit, Ṭuat IV, a three-headed serpent-god bearing six stars and 14 human heads.

Menmen[it], B.D.G. 259, a form of Hathor adored in the Fayyûm.

Menmenu-ā, a title of Menu.

Men-mut-f, Pap. Mag. 54, a form of Åmen.

men, the pinion or leg of a bird (?).

men-ui (?), the two shoulders; , Ṭuat XI.

menu, a kind of priest, ministrant; plur.

Menui (?)-ḥer pet, Annales III, 177, a goddess.

men, seat, buttocks.

meni, Rev. 11, 167, leg, thigh.

men-t, thigh.

men-ti, U. 389, P. 253, P. 201, 611, N. 812, 937, 1063, Metternich Stele 156, , the two thighs, and the part of the body above them, the buttocks.

men-ti Nut, P. 401, M. 572, N. 1179, the two thighs of the goddess Nut.

menti, P. 79, N. 23, , M. 109, N. 760, thighs.

menmen, to meet together.

Men-t, a god.

Meni, Ṭuat VI, a god.

men-t, Thes. 1202, plant, shoot.

menit, roots, stalks, stems.

meni-t, a kind of wood; varr. , .

menu, , , , , , Åmen. 6, 11, , Rec. 15, 162, , IV, 687, 730, 1104, 1165, grove, avenue of trees in a garden, plantation, shrubbery.

men, , domestic animal; plur. **menut**, , Nåstasen Stele 40, , Rev., cattle, sheep and goats.

men-t, Rev. 12, 70, cow.

menmen, bull; , Menu-Åmen, the bull of his mother.

menmenu-t, , , , , flocks and herds, cattle in general.

Menu, Palermo Stele, , Décrets 9, , U. 377, 537, , M. 699, N. 719, 725, 899, 1280, , P. 185, , T. 295, A.Z. 1908, 38, , Rec. 31, 31, , , , Hh. 90, an ithyphallic god of generation, and the god of the 5th month; Gr. Μὶν; = , L.D. III, 283, Burton, Excerpta 4, A.Z. 1867, 33.

Menu-fai-ā, Hymn Darius 37, Menu of the lifted arm.

Menu-neb-semt, Gol. 11, Menu, lord of the deserts.

Menu ḥeri åb P-ḥapti, Berg. II, 410, Menu, dweller in P-Ḥapti.

Menu-åāḥ, Quelques Pap. 38, Menu as a moon-god.

Menu-Åmen, a dual god of generation.

Menu-Åmen-Rā-ka-mut-f, Denderah I, 23, Menu + Åmen-Rā + Kamephis.

Menu-nesu-Ḥeru, Denderah IV, 62, , B.D. 110, a warrior bull-god.

Menu-Ḥeru, Menu + Horus.

Menu-Ḥeru-fai-ā, Mar. Aby. I, 49c, Menu + Horus.

Menu-Ḥeru-netch-tef-f, B.D. 145, V, 75.

Menu-Ḥeru sa Åst, Menu as son of Isis, a god of Coptos.

Menu-Khenti-Ḥe-t-Seker, Edfû I, 12, 17, a form of Menu worshipped at Edfû.

Menu-qeṭ, Denderah IV, 80, B.D. 149, the god of the 1st Åat; var. .

men, dove, swallow; plur. , Peasant 27, .

mennu, Ḥerusåtef Stele 47, a vessel in the form of a dove or swallow.

men-t, , a kind of bird, swallow (?) dove (?) pigeon (?); Copt. ⲃⲏⲛⲉ.

Men-t , B.D. 86 and 147, the swallow, sacred to Serqit, the daughter of Rā, and an incarnation of Isis.

meni-t 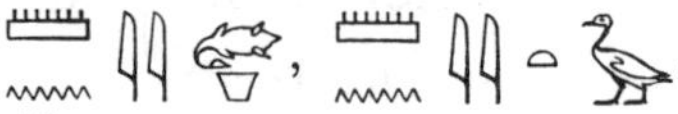, dove, swallow (?)

menu-t , U. 134A, N. 442A, the offering of a dove or swallow.

men 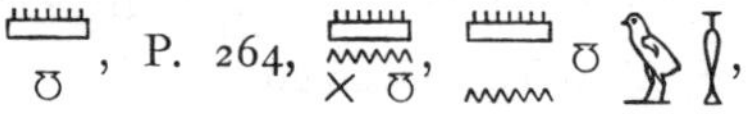, A.Z. 1900, 130, pot, vase; 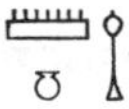, pot of white stone; 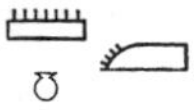, pot of black stone.

men-t 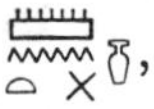, P.S.B. 13, 412, Rec. 17, 145, 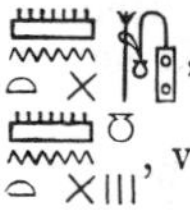, pot, vessel, a wine measure; plur., vessels to hold medicine.

men 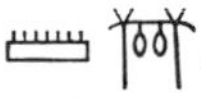, wine.

menu 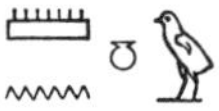, a tool (?)

menu , a club, a weapon (Lacau).

mennu 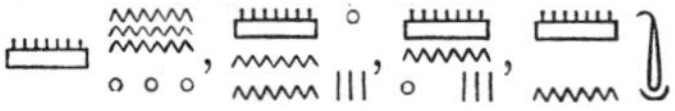 , gum, resin, manna.

menen (?) , an eastern drug from Phoenicia or Arabia, used in mummification.

men ḥetch-t 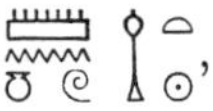 white manna, a kind of drug.

mennu en Tchah  , Annales IX, 155, manna from the country east or north-east of the Delta.

menen-t 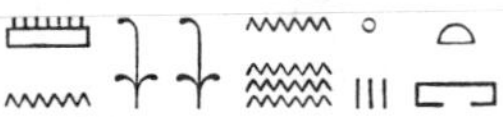, the mummification chamber.

men , a piece of cloth or stuff, sheet, garment; plur.  , T. 387, M. 403.

men kam 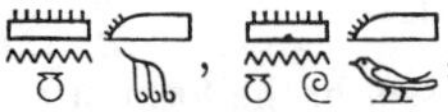 black cloth.

men 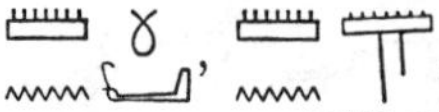, an offering of cloth, a bundle of linen; , linen for sacred purposes.

meni , linen cloth.

menui , linen cloth.

men , fire, flame, heat; var. 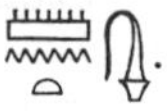.

men , venom, poison (?)

men-t, fire, flame.

men, men-t 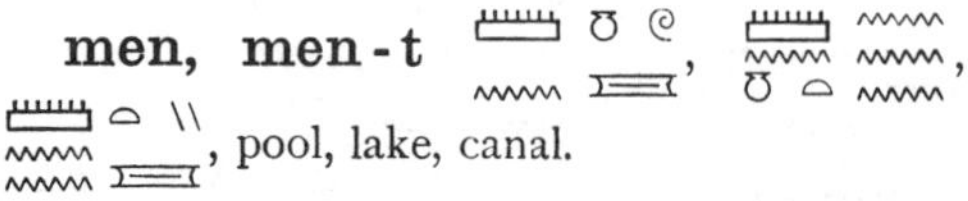, pool, lake, canal.

menȧ, meni 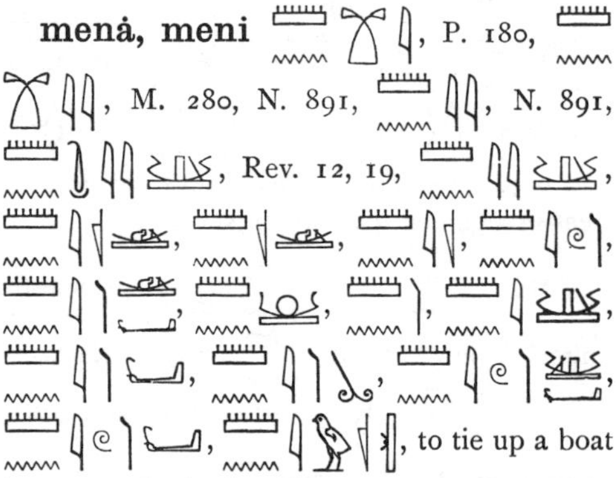, P. 180, M. 280, N. 891, N. 891, Rev. 12, 19, to tie up a boat in port, to lead a boat into port, to tether cattle, to gain access to a woman; , Rec. 21, 79, moored; Copt. ⲙⲟⲟⲛⲉ.

menȧ hepu , Ḥeruemḥeb 6, to administer laws, to enforce laws.

mennȧ 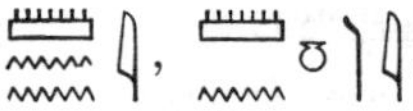, P. 617, to arrive in port.

menn-t , arrival in port.

men, arrival in port.

menu, Nȧstasen Stele 12, a quay, harbour.

menȧ, harbour, haven.

menȧu-t  , IV, 692, 732, harbour, haven; plur.; Copt. ⲙⲁⲛⲟⲩ, ⲙⲟⲟⲛⲉ.

menȧ-tu 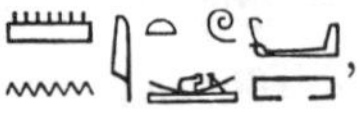, arrival in port.

menu-t , Nástasen Stele 10, a landing; Copt. ⲙⲟⲟⲛⲉ.

men-t 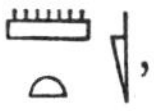, a post, boundary mark; plur. .

mená-t , , Rec. 30, 68, 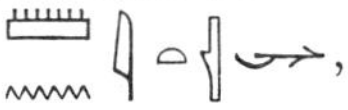, Shipwreck 4, mooring post; , two stakes for tying up a boat.

menáu , stakes to which prisoners to be executed were tied.

mená, meni , P. 180, 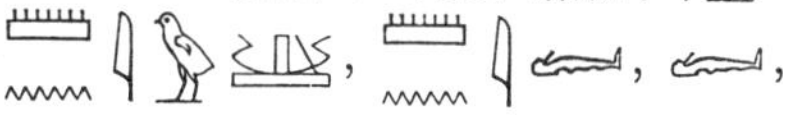, A.Z. 1908, 118, to arrive in port, to die; , a happy death.

mená-t 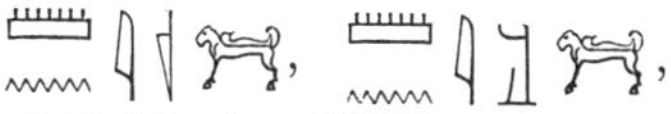, , Berl. 2296, death; 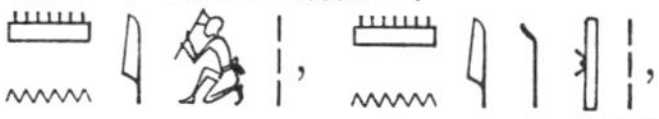, , dead things, the dead; 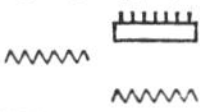 , deathless; , the death cry, the wailing of women for the dead.

men 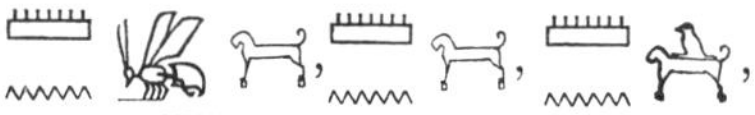, 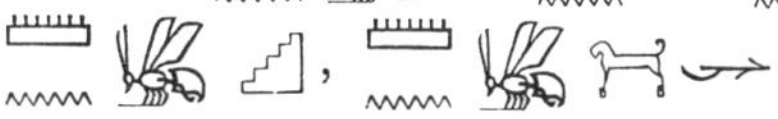, funeral couch, death bed, bier.

mená-t , U. 422, , , 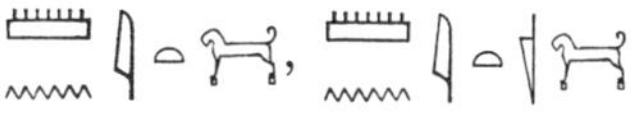, funeral, death bed, bier, funeral couch; plur. 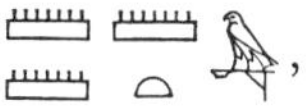, T. 241.

mená-t , M. 709, ligature, bandage, wrapping; , Rec. 30, 185, funerary swathings (?)

Menát 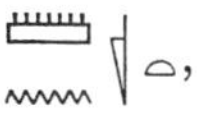, P. 155, , N. 785, a god (?)

Mená-t urit , N. 949, 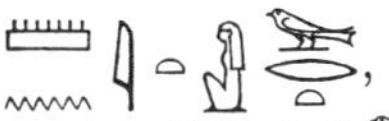, M. 396, , N. 811, , N. 7, a goddess (?)

Menánt-urit , P. 163, , M. 415, a goddess.

men 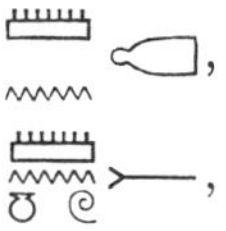, P. 684 (division of word doubtful).

men Tur. Pap. 19, to offer (?)

men 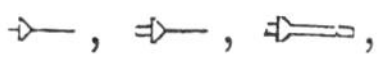, M. 124, N. 427, 646 = , in U. 118, to bring, to present, to offer.

mená, menáu apṭu , P. 604, , to herd cattle, shepherd, herdsman; [illegible], A.Z. 1905, 119, gooseherd.

mená-t, menit [illegible], IV, 917, 1059, [illegible], an amulet worn to give physical happiness, ornaments worn on ceremonial occasions; plur. [illegible], [illegible]; it was made of [illegible], [illegible], [illegible], [illegible], etc.

Menát [illegible], P.S.B. 13, 331, a name of Hathor.

mená-t [illegible], a kind of bird, swallow (?) dove (?)

mená-t [illegible], a kind of gum, resin.

mená [illegible], [illegible], a vase, a pot, a measure.

Menát [illegible], the name of a star (?) in the northern heaven.

Menátiu [illegible], Nav. Lit. 100, a group of warrior-gods.

menáná [illegible], [illegible] [illegible], [illegible], [illegible], to arrive in port, to die.

menáná (?) [illegible], A.Z. 1905, 103, mina, a weight; compare Heb. מָנֶה,

menā (?) , box, draught box, writing tablet.

Menā , , , T. 227, P. 181, N. 892, a lake or canal; , P. 171.

menā-t , P. 615, , M. 781, , N. 1139, , , , , , , , , , nurse; , T. 23, , P. 739, two sister-nurses; , nurses; Metternich Stele 246, 247; Copt. ⲙⲟⲟⲛⲉ.

Menāt , N. 1139; , Lanzone 112, the Nurse-goddess Isis.

Menā-t N. 759, a nursing-goddess.

Menā-t urit , , IV, 920, 921, great nurse, a title of several goddesses.

menāut , milch cows.

Men-ānkh Nefer-ka-Rā , the name of the pyramid of King Nefer-ka-Rā.

meni , P. 537, a proper name (?), .

Meni , Ṭuat III, a form of Osiris.

meni , soldier.

meni , to kill men in honour of a chief.

meni-t , foe, enemy.

meni , , Rec. 14, 51, , to plough, to till the earth, to cultivate, to break up.

meni , Anastasi I, 1, 8, ploughman, labourer, peasant; plur. ; varr. , .

Mennu , a dog belonging to Set.

Mennui , Ṭuat X, a pair of serpent-supporters of the solar disk; var.

Menu-ur , Ṭuat VI, a crocodile (?)-god.

menu-nār (?) , , acacia wood or gum (?)

menur , Stunden 44 . . . .

menur , to asperge, to pour out a libation (?)

menur (?) , , , a kind of incense, bitumen (?)

menuḥ , papyrus, water plants.

menuḥu-t (?) , U. 462, firmament.

menusa , Wört. 657 . . . . . .

menpeḥ-t , Rec. 24, 164, , Rec. 18, 177, , nipple of the breast; dual .

m nef , Nȧstasen Stele 8, III, 143, from it; Copt. ⲙⲙⲟϥ.

menf-t , , , bracelets, armlets, rings, jewellery, etc.

menfit (?) , rings, jewellery.

menfer-t , , ring, a kind of ornament (of the feet); plur. , , , rings for the arms and feet.

Men-nefer Meri-Rā 
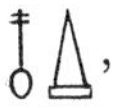, the name of the pyramid of Meri-Rā.

menfti , , a kind of soldier who was armed with a shield; plur. [illegible], IV, 660, [illegible], IV, 911, , Mendes Stele.

menfeṭ , soldier, plur. [illegible].

menfṭ-ti (?) 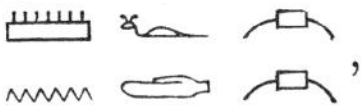, rings, bracelets, jewellery.

Menmu-t urit , T. 290 . . . .

menmens 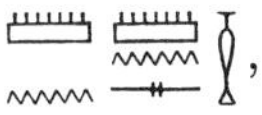, P. 606, vessel, vase (?)

Menrir (Menlil)   (*sic*), a Nubian god; see **Merur, Mandulas.**

menhiu 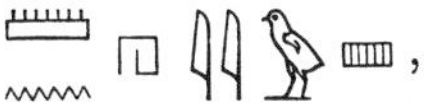, A.Z. 1899, 96, stone.

menhep 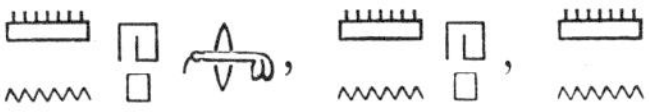 [illegible], to copulate. marriage, spouse.

menhes 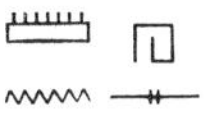; see [illegible].

Menhesȧu 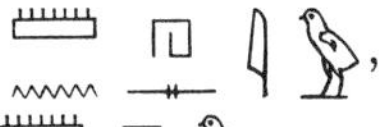, P. 673, M. 664, N. 1280, [illegible], P. 94, M. 118, N. 56, a group of gods who watched over the South, [illegible], Ta-shemā.

menheṭ 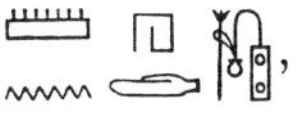, IV, 509, register, writing tablet.

menhetch 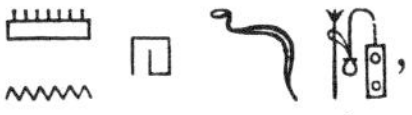, P. 185, M. 200, N. 899, A.Z. 1908, 47, register, writing tablet.

menḥ 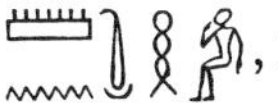, Rec. 13, 10, [illegible], [illegible], boy, youth, young man.

menḥ-t 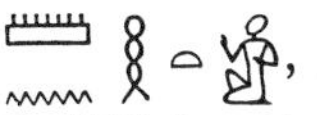, girl, maiden (?); , Rec. 15, 142, young sow.

menḥ-t 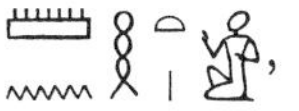, belonging to the corvée (?)

menḥ 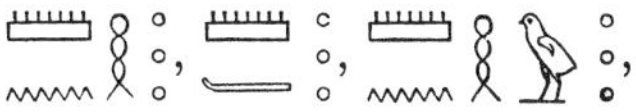, IV, 480, 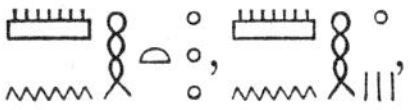, wax; Copt. ⲙⲟⲩⲗϩ.

menḥiu 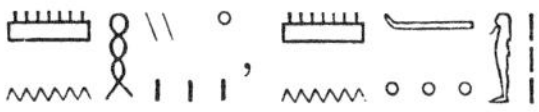, Rec. 16, 110, things made of wax, wax figures.

menḥ-t 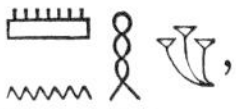, Rec. 29, 148, [illegible]  [illegible], water plant, papyrus; plur.  [illegible].

menḥ-t 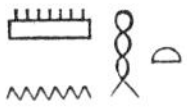, an amulet in the form of a serpent.

menḥut , common soldier.

menḥu , to sacrifice, to offer up an animal.

menḥu 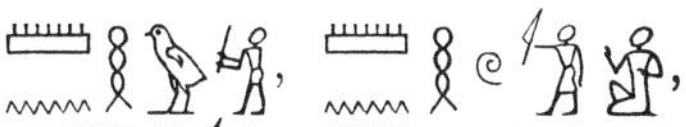, , sacrificial priest, slaughterer, butcher, slayer, executioner.

Menḥu , "slaughterer," a title of several gods.

Menḥu , Denderah IV, 62, [illegible], B.D. 17, 142, the butcher-god who slew sacrificial animals and the foes of the gods.

Menḥi 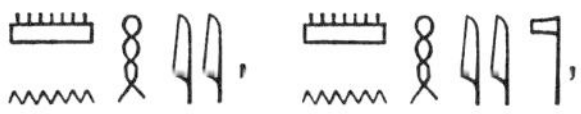, the Executioner-god, the Butcher-god.

Menḥi , Ṭuat VIII, a god of the Circle Seḥert-baiu-s.

Menḥi 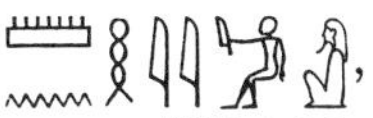, Nesi-Ȧmsu 33, 6, a slaughtering-god; [illegible], B.D. (Saïte) 17, 57, the companions of the same.

Menḥit , [illegible], Lanzone 287, Denderah IV, 78, a lioness-goddess, mother of Shu.

Menḥit 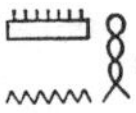, IV, 479, , 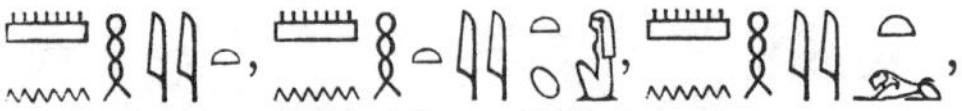, , a lioness-goddess, consort of Shu.

Menḥi-khenti-Seḥetch 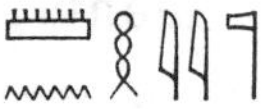 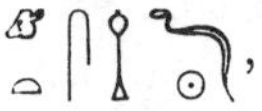, Piānkhi Stele 83, a god.

menḥȧ , P. 311, , P. 613, a kind of bird (?)

menḥitȧ , Rev. 6, 24, a king's gift; compare Heb. מִנְחָה.

menkh 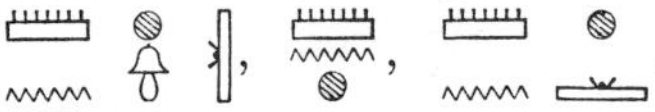, 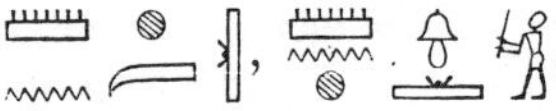, Ȧmen. 14, 11, to award, to reward, to recompense, to pay back, to confer a gift or an honour, to be good, gracious, perfect, well-doing, beneficent; 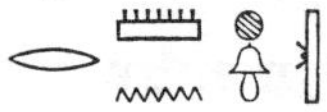, in a proper or becoming manner; 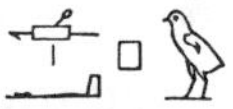 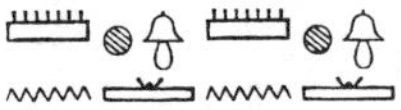, IV, 1071;  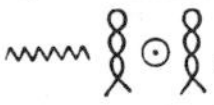, perfect for ever, good to last for all time; , the two beneficent gods (Euergetai).

menkh-t 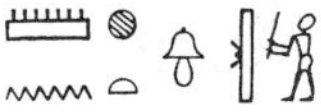, Ȧmen. 19, 14, 22, , Rec. 21, 79, 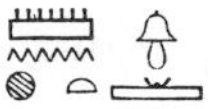, 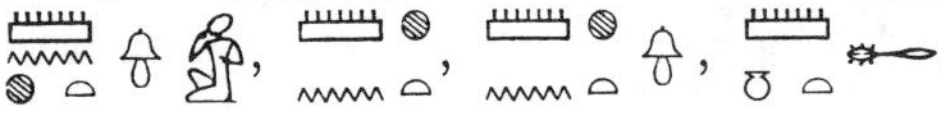, something that is correct, perfect, excellent, good, solid (of buildings), beneficent, excellence; , perfect in the knowledge of spells; 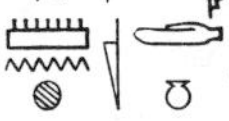, of gracious disposition.

menkhu 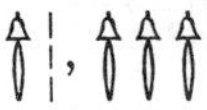, good deeds, benefits, benefactions, excellences, perfections.

menkhut , good counsels, counsels of excellence.

menkh 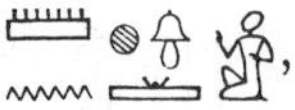, a well-conducted child.

menkhu , loyal and well-trained servants.

menkh ȧb (or ḥa-t) , IV, 1044, a man of right disposition.

menkh 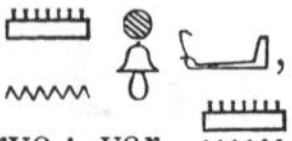, to work in wood, to cut, to carve; var. 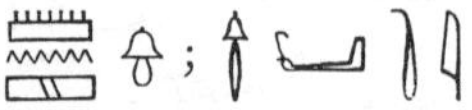, worked; Copt. ⲙⲟⲩⲛⲕ.

menkhu , carpenter.

menkh-t , work produced by the carpenter, inlaid work, fretwork.

menkh 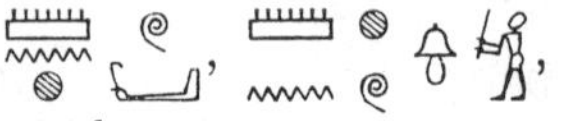, to be tied, to be fastened.

menkh 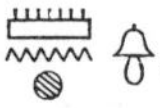, clapper, tongue of a bell.

menkh-t 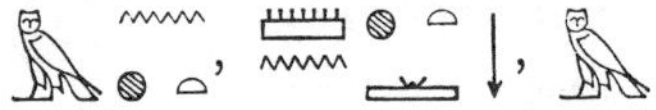 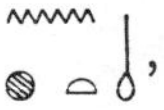, a tool or instrument, chisel, a forked staff.

menkh 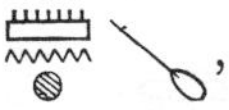, an offering.

menkh-t 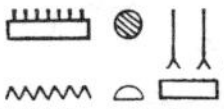, T. 389, P. 592, 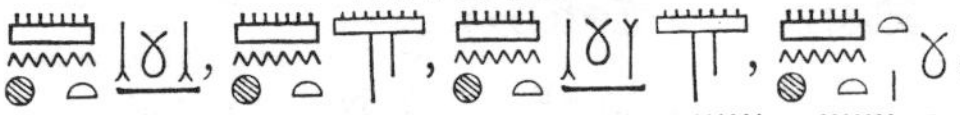, [illegible], Thes. 1207, [illegible], [illegible], a piece of cloth or stuff of any kind, bandlet, veil, a ceremonial girdle or fillet, a change of raiment; plur. [illegible], IV, 1147, 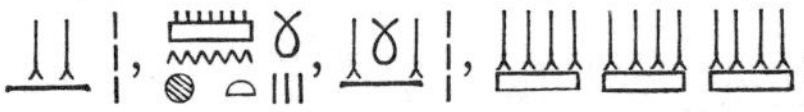, P. 408, M. 584, N. 1189. The following bandlets were used during the performance of the ceremony of Opening the Mouth :—

menkh-t ȧns [illegible], or [illegible], the red bandlet.

menkh-t ȧrun (?) [illegible], the blue bandlet.

menkh-t ȧṭmȧ [illegible], or [illegible], a bandlet made of ȧṭmȧ cloth (damûr?).

menkh-t āa-t [illegible], the great bandlet.

menkh-t uatch-t [illegible], or [illegible], the green bandlet.

menkh-t ḥetch-t [illegible], the white bandlet.

Menkh 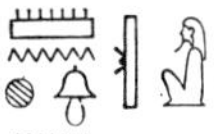, B.D. 96, 5, a god.

Menkh , a god who presided over the 2nd month; Copt. ⲠⲀⲞⲠⲒ.

Menkh 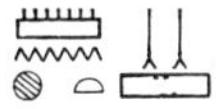, Ṭuat IX (1) a god who swathed Osiris; (2) an object worshipped in Per-Neteru (Mar. Aby. I, 44).

Menkh-qa-haḥetep 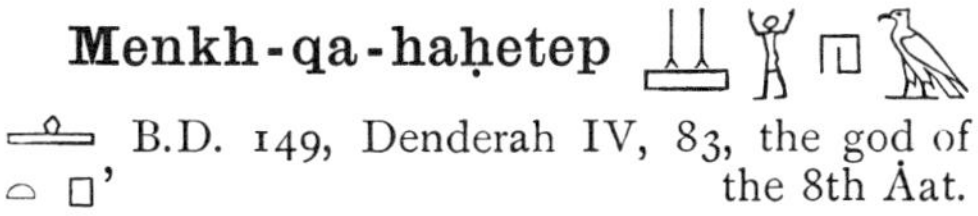 B.D. 149, Denderah IV, 83, the god of the 8th Åat.

mens-t ḥer-t 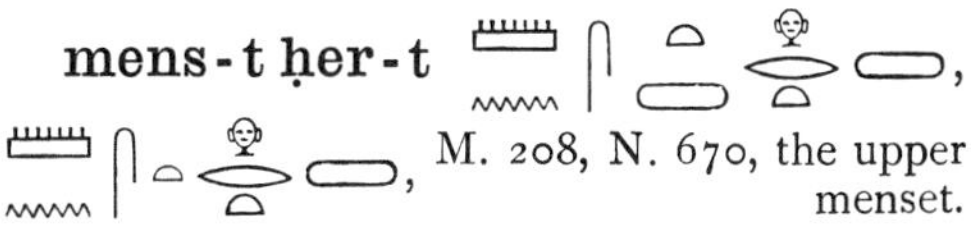, M. 208, N. 670, the upper menset.

mens-t kher-t 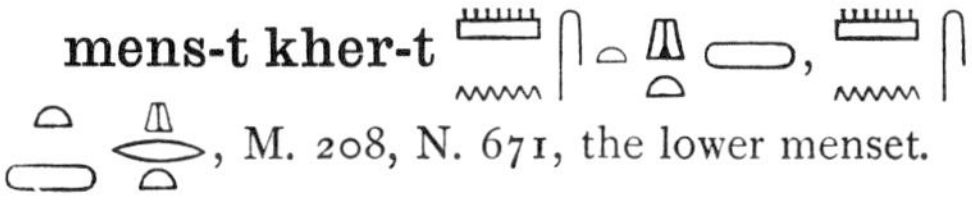, M. 208, N. 671, the lower menset.

mens-ti , legs, knees (?)

mensa , Rev., after, afterwards; Copt. ⲘⲚ̅ⲚⲤⲀ.

mensa (?) 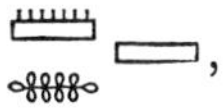, U. 31A, 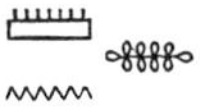, N. 259A, sour milk (?)

mensa , jar, vase, jug; , two jars or jugs.

mensas 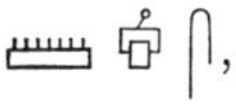, Rev. 13, 91, after, afterwards; Copt. ⲘⲚ̅ⲚⲤⲰⲤ.

mensub (?) 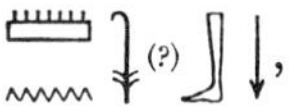, spear, javelin, weapon.

mensh 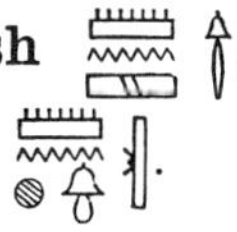, excellent, good, sound, solid; see.

menshu 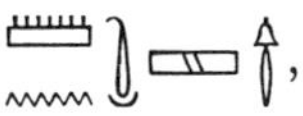, Rev. 13, 5, benefactor.

mensh-åb 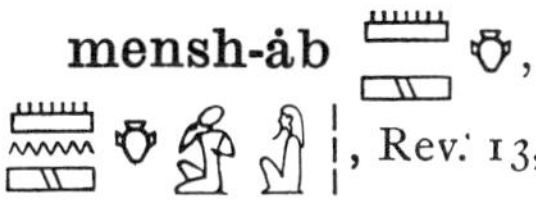, generous, beneficent; Rev. 13, 31, kindly deeds.

mensh 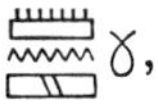, Rec. 4, 24, 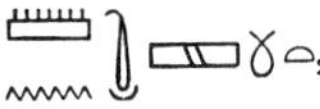, Rev. 13, 2, bandage, cord, tie, bond; see 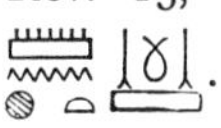.

mensh 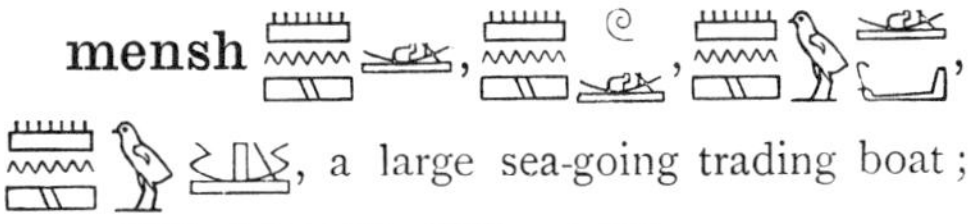, a large sea-going trading boat; plur. 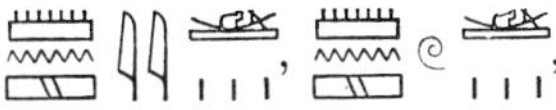, A.Z. 1905, 15.

mensh 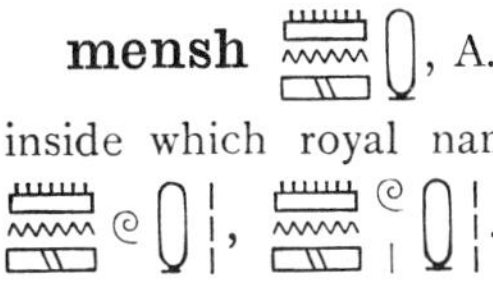, A.Z. 1906, 158, the oval inside which royal names are written; plur.

mensh-t 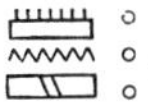, Thes. 1323, Rec. 3, 50, , Hearst Pap. 11, 9, minium, a substance used by painters.

menq 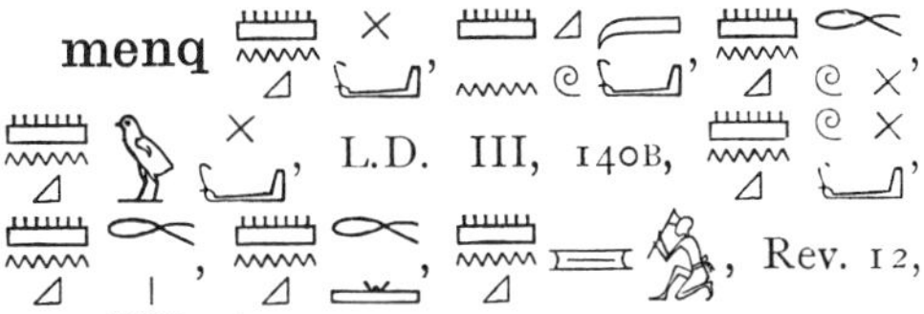, L.D. III, 140B, Rev. 12, 116, , Rev. 11, 160, 167, to bring to an end, to finish, to complete, to make an end of, to destroy; Copt. ⲘⲞⲨⲚⲔ, ⲘⲞⲨⲢⲔ.

mennq , Rev. 13, 37, to complete.

menq 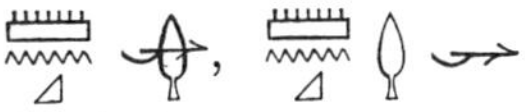, Hearst Pap. 5, 17, a kind of tree.

Menqit 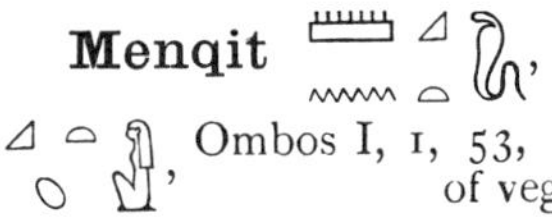, B.D. 101, 11, 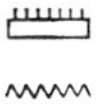, Ombos I, 1, 53, Berg. 71, a goddess of vegetation and gardens.

Menqit 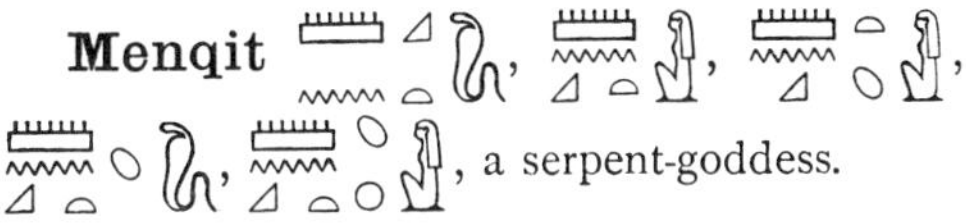, a serpent-goddess.

menqi[t] 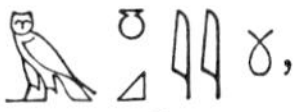, Rev. 11, 167, stuff, cloth.

menqeb , P. 352, 581, a cool shady seat, place where the jars of wine were stored.

menqeb(ḥ)-t 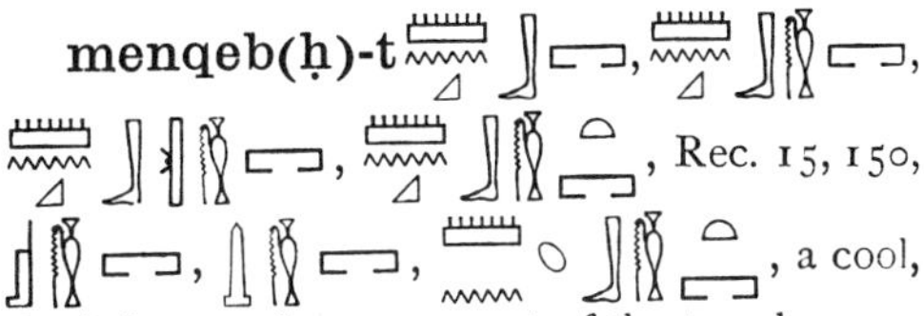, Rec. 15, 150, a cool, shaded room for rest, a part of the temple.

Menqeb , Thes. 818, , Rec. 16, 106, a man-headed hawk-god; var. (Saïte) **Menqebå** , B.D. 101, 8, a god.

menqebit, Rec. 34, 124, the amulet of the serpent's head.

menqebit, collar or pectoral to which the serpent amulet was attached.

menqerit, Rec. 34, 124; var. of .

menk, Jour. As. 1908, 313, end, finish; Copt. ⲙⲟⲩⲛⲕ, ⲙⲟⲩⲣⲕ.

menk-t, see .

menker-t, an animal's tail worn as an ornament by men.

Menkerit, Ṭuat X, a lioness-goddess.

Mengabu, B.D. (Saïte) 99, 4, a god.

ment, ment-ti, the two breasts of a woman; see and .

menti = , an amulet.

menti = (?), the two eyes.

ment (?), Excom. Stele 1 . . . .

Mentiu, IV, 200, L.D. III, 16A, L.D. III, 16A, 17, robbers of the desert, cattle men in the Sûdân.

Mentiu nu Satt, IV, 372, the thievish nomads of the Eastern Desert and Southern Syria.

Ment, the War-god of Thebes; Gr. Μωνθ.

Mentit, Edfû I, 20, 5, a goddess of Edfû.

Ment-safi (?), a proper name (Menthesuphis ?).

mentȧ, N. 850 = , P. 204 + 4 (Pyr. 1015).

mentȧi, Rev. = Copt. ⲙⲛⲧ + ⲉⲓ.

mentār, Rev., ascent; Copt. ⲙⲛⲧ + ⲱⲗ.

menti, Rev. 13, 19, 15, 16, compatriot (?)

menti, a Typhonic animal of the wolf species.

mentef, he, it; Copt. ⲛ̄ⲧⲟϥ.

mentnakh-t, Rev. 13, 13, 20, strength, power; Copt. ⲙⲛⲧ-ⲛⲁϣⲧⲉ.

mentek, thee, thou; , Gen. Epist. 67, 68, , Rec. 21, 78.

menth-ti, the two breasts; see and .

Menthu, IV, 808, nomad hunters and robbers of the Eastern Desert and Southern Syria. They were famous for their beards—, T. 353, N. 174, "like the beards on the Menthu."

Menthu, P. 241, M. 784, B.D. 140, 6, 171, an ancient war-god of Hermonthis near Thebes.

mentha, B.D. 114, 2, 5, a mythological town.

menṭ, an unknown object.

menṭ-t, , , Love Songs, I, 5, , , the breast, the bosom of a woman; , Nâstasen Stele 33, the left breast; dual , , , , , , , , , , Rec. 4, 122, ; Copt. ⲙⲉⲛⲟⲧ.

menṭiṭi, the two breasts.

menṭ-àb (?), Rec. 11, 65, of bold intent.

menṭ-ti, , the pupils of the eyes.

Menṭef-t, N. 1228, , P. 204, a god.

mentch, U. 30, , U. 31, P. 602, N. 487, A.Z. 1908, 38, Rec. 31, 21, , Rec. 27, 232, breast; , the left breast, P. 606; dual **mentch-ti**, T. 360, N. 700, 982; plur. , P. 302, , Rec. 30, 196; , teats of a cow, N. 802, 1387, , , T. 360, , , N. 1155, , P. 712, , , N. 1365.

mentch, a kind of seed or grain.

mentchi, safe, secure.

mentchu, N. 996, plaited beards.

mentchem, , , Peasant 133, , Rev. 8, 171, a kind of basket, wickerwork bed.

mentchem, A.Z. 68, 12, sweet scent.

mentcher, Sphinx II, 83, cerebellum; Copt. ⲁⲛⲧⲉⲗⲉⲙ (?)

mer, a particle of prohibition; Copt. ⲙⲡⲱⲣ (?) ⲙⲡⲣ (?)

mer = = , like, as.

mer-tt, Rec. 3, 50 = = , copy, likeness.

mer, a sea-going ship.

mer, P. 485, , P. 484, , , , , , , , , , Fest-schrift 117, , A.Z. 1905, 19, any collection of water, lake, pool, cistern, reservoir, basin, canal, inundation, flood, stream; plur. , M. 729, N. 1330, , P. 123, , U. 533, P. 427, M. 611, N. 1216, , P. 68, , P. 245, , P. 414, M. 593, N. 1198, , , , , ; Copt. ⲙⲏⲣⲉ.

mor, swampy land.

mer, , IV, 630, libation tank.

mer, Rec. 21, 78, , the basin of a harbour, port, quay, harbour.

merà, IV, 1077, flood, bodily excretion.

merit, celestial lake, heaven, sky.

Merit, Mareotis.

merit, A.Z. Bd. 35, 17, , Ȧmen. 4, 12, IV, 729, A.Z. 1874, 148, river bank, landing stage, sea coast, port, quay, dam; Copt. ⲉⲙⲣⲟ.

merit, lake, reservoir.

merit, merut, Rec. 33, 30, boats, shipping in port.

merit, Berl. 3024, 75, crocodiles which bask on the river bank.

merti, Love Songs 3, 7, , canal, quay.

mer-t, beyond, on the other side; Copt. ⲙⲏⲣ (?)

Mer, B.D.G. 617: (1) a sacred serpent kept at Edfû; (2) the protecting spirit of the Inundation.

Merit, a goddess of the Inundation.

Mer-ti, Rec. 20, 42, the two goddesses of the Inundation, Southern and Northern.

Merit meḥ, Pap. Anhai, the goddess of the Inundation in the North.

Merit shemā, Pap. Anhai, the goddess of the Inundation in the South; the two goddesses of the Inundation.

Mer-asbiu, B.D. 63, 2, the lake of Fire in the Ṭuat.

Mer-ȧāru, P. 234, , P. 464, N. 1381, , M. 526, , N. 1119, a lake in Sekhet-Ȧaru.

Mer (She ?)-ȧārut, Ṭuat IV, the lake of Uraei in the Ṭuat.

Mer-Maāti, B.D. 17, 52–55, the lake of Truth in Rastau.

Meru-em-M'fkat, B.D. 39, 18, the turquoise pools in the Ṭuat.

Mer-menā, P. 180, M. 282, N. 892, a lake in the Other World from which the blessed drank.

Mer-en-amu, B.D. 98, 7, a fiery lake in Sȧsȧ.

Mer-en-ȧakhuti, the lake of the gods of the Horizon.

Mer (She)-en-ānkh, Ṭuat IV, the bath of Rā which was kept by 12 jackal-gods.

Mer-en-maātiu, the lake of the gods of Truth.

Mer-en-Māa-t, B.D. 17, 46, a bath of the gods in the Ṭuat.

Mer-en-Ḥeru, B.D. 13, 1, the lake of Horus in the Ṭuat.

Mer-en-ḥesmen, B.D. 17, 46, the natron lake in the Ṭuat.

Mer-en-ḥetem, M. 552, N. 1132, the lake of destruction.

Mer-en-Kha,

, T. 37, P. 247, 332, M. 469, 635, N. 1058, a lake in the Ṭuat.

Mer-en-Sȧsȧ , U. 393, 506, T. 321, a lake, or island (ȧa ?), of fire in the Ṭuat.

Mer-en-serser , Ṭuat VIII, a lake of fire in the Ṭuat.

Mer-en-seḥetep , B.D. 96, 7, the lake of propitiation in the Ṭuat.

Mer-en-ṭesṭes , B.D. 15, 8, a lake in the Ṭuat.

Mer-en-ṭesṭes , a lake in the Great Oasis.

Mer-Nu , B.D. 39, 2, the lake in which the serpent-fiend Rerek was drowned.

Mer-neter , the lake of the god.

Mer-Ḥepu , U. 419, T. 239, a lake in the Ṭuat.

Mer-ḥeḥ , B.D. 131, 10, the lake of one hundred thousand years.

Mer-Ḥetep , B.D. 110, 6, a lake in Sekhet-Ȧaru.

Mer-Kharu , B.D. 109, 3, the lake of the herons in the Ṭuat.

Mer-khebu , Ṭuat III, the lake of boiling water with a foetid smell; to the righteous the water is cool and sweet.

Mer-Sab , U. 481, N. 144, jackal-lake in the Ṭuat; plur. , P. 245, N. 1057.

Meru-smen-ā , P. 699, lakes of the smen geese.

Mer-Seḥseḥ , P. 178, M. 269, N. 888, a lake in the Ṭuat.

Mer-sekhnit , Denderah I, 6, a goddess of .

Mer-shesh (?) , B.D. 98, 8, , a lake in the Ṭuat.

Mer-Kenstȧ , P. 337, , P. 336, 462, 638, M. 517, , N. 1099, the Nubian lake.

Mer-Ṭuattȧ , N. 144, , U. 481, , N. 1153, the lake of the Ṭuat; plur. , P. 245, N. 1057, , P. 353.

mer , T. 266, M. 421, , T. 283, , P. 50, , M. 31, , N. 64, , , , , , P. 64, , , , , U. 224, Rec. 27, 224, , , , to love, to desire, to wish for, to crave for, to will; Copt. ⲙⲉ.

mer——mer , Pap. 3024, 150, 151.

mer-mer , Israel Stele 22, lovely, amiable.

mer , , Rev. 11, 138, love, desire; , according to our wish.

mer-t , , U. 454, , , love, desire, wish, something loved, longed or wished for; , T. 26, N. 208.

mer-t ȧb , IV, 1023, willingly.

merr , , , , P. 216, , , to wish for, to desire, to love.

merriu 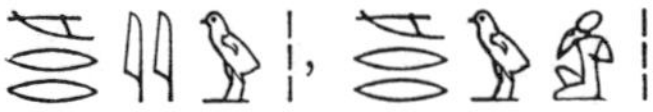, those who love, lovers, friends.

merr-t , P. 69, N. 36, IV, 1045, love, desire, wish, something longed or wished for; plur. [illegible].

merrut , love, desire, wish.

merut , , , love.

merut , beloved woman, sweetheart; [illegible], Metternich Stele 87, , L.D. III, 140B, , 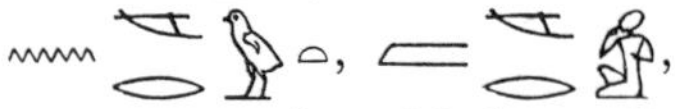, wishing that, so that; 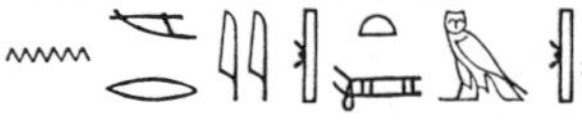, wishing that not.

meruti , [illegible], P.S.B. 25, 218, beloved; Copt. ⲙⲉⲣⲓⲧ.

merȧ , Hymn Darius 19, lover, friend.

meri  , [illegible], U. 532, lover, a loved one, something loved.

meriu , beloved one, darling.

meriti , U. 532, [illegible] [illegible], Rec. 4, 135, 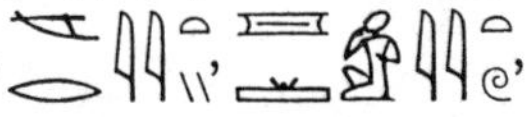, Jour. As. 1908, 278, beloved; Copt. ⲙⲉⲣⲓⲧ.

merit 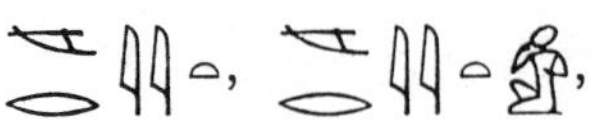, love, desire, wish; [illegible], Amherst Pap. I, love-spells or love-letters.

mer-ni , Pap. 3024, 104, lovable.

meri reth , benevolent, loving mankind; Gr. φιλάνθρωπος.

mer-t , title of a priestess in Hermopolis.

mer , Rec. 3, 47, a festival.

mer-t , Rec. 11, 142, gladness.

mer  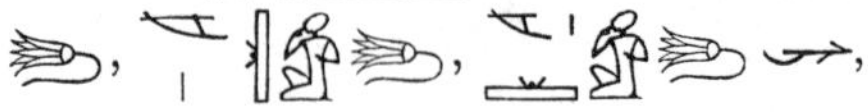, Rev. 11, 133, 12, 8, 56, pleasure boat; Copt. ⲙⲉⲗⲱⲧ (?)

Merr , "beloved one," a title of several gods.

meri 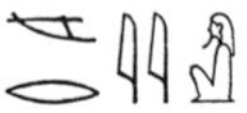, a title of several gods.

Meriti , [illegible], a Mareotic form of Osiris.

Meriti 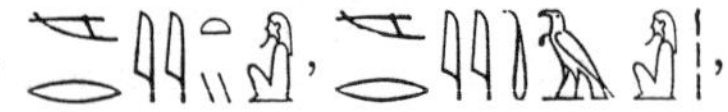, Berg. 50, a god.

Meriti, Meritti  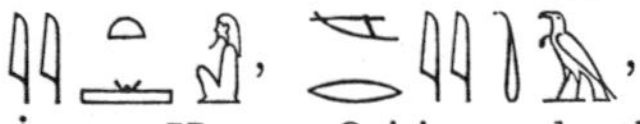, a title of Rā, Ȧmen, Horus, Osiris, and other gods; plur. , Hymn Darius 38, a pair of goddesses.

Merti , Hymn Darius 8, the primeval gods and goddesses.

Meru-ā , B.D. (Saïte) 68, 2, a god; fem. [illegible], B.D. (Saïte) 99, 20, 140, 7.

Meri-f-uā , a guardian of Osiris.

Meri-f-ṭa ..... , Denderah IV, 59, a guardian of Osiris.

Meri-maāt 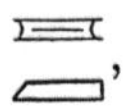, Berg. I, 12, a god in the Ṭuat.

Meri-mut-f  [illegible], Denderah III, 36, , B.M. 46, 681, [illegible], Rev. 37, 70, [illegible], Rec. 37, 14, [illegible], [illegible], Rec. 12, 1, a form of Khnemu, lord of Khāi, [illegible].

Mer-en-āui-f, Ṭuat XI, a form of Åf.

Mer-ent-neteru, Ṭuat XI, a goddess seated on two serpents, a wind-goddess of the dawn (?)

Merit-erpā-neteru (?), Ombos 2, 131, a goddess.

Mer-segrit, Lanzone 127, , Rec. 2, 32, "lover of silence," a serpent-headed goddess, whose cult was common in the hilly cemetery of Western Thebes.

Mer-setau, etc., etc., B.D. 145, 146, name of the 18th Pylon.

Meri-tef, B.M. 46631, , Ombos 2, 131, a goddess.

mer-t, , funerary chest or coffer.

mer, Rec. 16, 70, , Rec. 12, 12, servant, peasant, dependant.

merȧ, a female slave.

mer-t, Palermo Stele, Rec. 26, 236, Rec. 31, 26, , , , Décrets 9, , IV, 1147, , , , , Dream Stele 40, , serfs, servants, vassals, peasants, hereditary servants on an estate; , , IV, 1081, , Décrets 14, , IV, 972; , IV, 408, chief of the peasants.

mer, meru, , , IV, 656, Metternich Stele 117, desert, plain, mountain.

mer-tt, desert land, waste, wilderness.

mer, , , , , , , , Rev. 11, 124, 12, 29, overseer, chief officer, head, superintendent, director, foreman; plur. , , .

mer ȧau-t, IV, 1118, inspector of dignities of the highest kind.

meru ȧuāāut, heads of families, shêkhs of tribes.

mer ȧḥ-t, IV, 1110, , overseer of the estates, land superintendent.

mer ȧḥu, , inspector of cattle.

merā (?), A.Z. 1908, 45, chief of the caravan, , chief of caravans; see Sphinx XIV, 172, and *supra* p. 106A.

mer ā en set (?), N. 1002, chief of the mountain tract.

mer ābu (?), Anastasi IV, 3, 1, Koller Pap. 3, 1, inspector of horned cattle (?)

mer ābu . . . . . . shu, inspector of horn, hoof, and feather, *i.e.*, overseer of all the cattle and feathered fowl; , Rec. 17, 4, inspector of horn, hoof, feather, and metal.

mer ānṭ, overseer of the storehouse.

mer u (?), IV, 1115, , Peasant 193, district inspector.

mer uȧau, A.Z. 45, 124, overseer of the boats, captain of the fleet.

mer unut, Rec. 17, 149, a kind of priest (?)

mer per , IV, 1071, chief of the house, steward, major-domo ; plur. 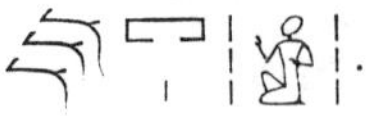.

mer per ur 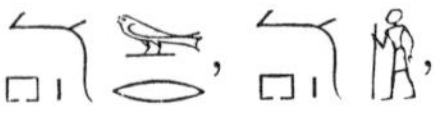, chief steward.

mer per nub 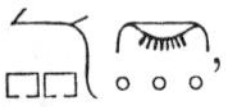, overseer of the gold foundry ; , IV, 421.

mer per ḥetch , overseer of the silver foundry.

mer per ḥetch , governor of the treasury ; , IV, 421 ; 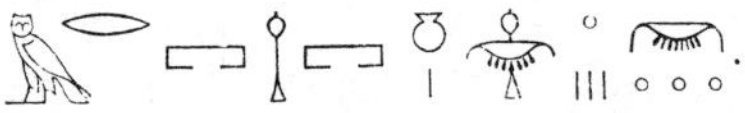.

meru mau (?) 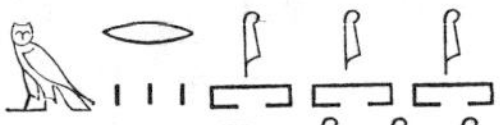, Rec. 6, 6, , Rec. 33, 3, overseers of sacred property.

mer mau , 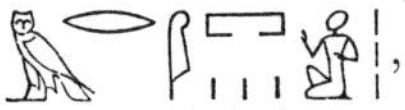, overseer of the servants on a temple estate or on private property.

mer m'khen 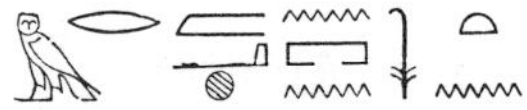 [illegible], chief of the royal cabinet.

mer menmen , Rev. 11, 180, overseer of cattle.

mer mer[it] , Rec. 21, 81, port-master, harbour-master.

mer mesentiu 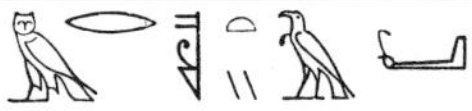 [illegible], overseer of the blacksmiths.

mer m'shāu 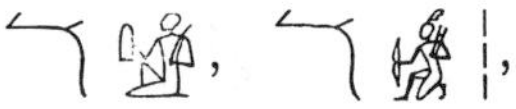, , P.S.B 21, 271, general, commander of an army ; Copt. ⲗⲉⲙⲙⲏⲏϣⲉ.

mer m'shāu , title of the high-priest of Mendes.

mer m'shāu ur , commander-in-chief.

mer met , a captain in charge of ten men.

mer metcha-t 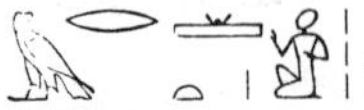, overseer of the keepers of the books.

mer nu-t 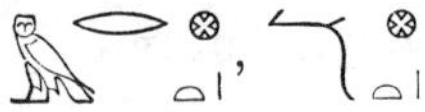, governor of the town, mayor.

mer resu , overseer of the South.

mer ḥe-t urt VI 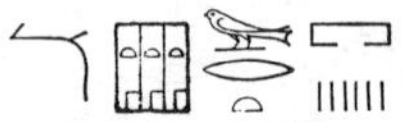, IV, 1118, overseer of the six courts of justice.

mer ḥe-t ka , keeper of the Ka-chapel.

mer Ḥanebu (?) 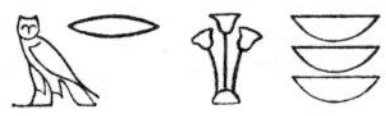, Rec. 28, 25, governor of the Greeks.

mer ḥem nesu , inspector of the royal slaves.

mer ḥem neter  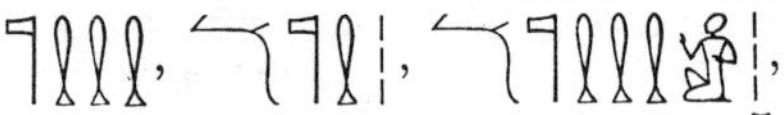, IV, 927, inspector of the servants of the god ; [illegible] , inspector of the priests of the South and North.

mer khent (?) IV 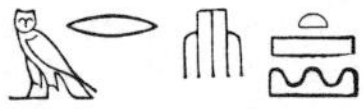 [illegible], I, 100, the four overseers of the pleasure gardens.

mer khert neter , overseer of the cemetery ; 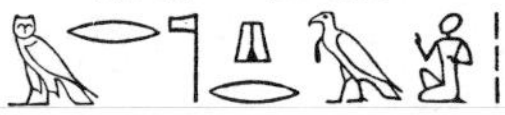, overseer of the cemetery workmen.

mer khetem-t  [illegible], IV, 1106, keeper of the seal.

mer khetemu , , overseer of the keepers of the seal ; , keeper of the seal of the palace.

mer sau resu , Décrets 18, chief of the classes of the South.

mer sunu 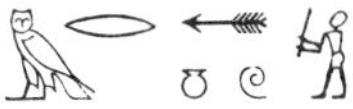, Amherst Pap. 42, archiatros.

mer seba , an officer on a boat.

mer semt åabtt 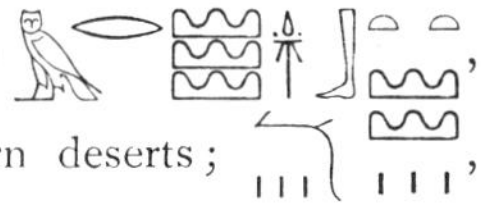, governor of the eastern deserts; , governors of deserts.

mer sekhtiu , chief of the peasant field-labourers.

mer sesem , chief officer of cavalry.

mer sesh(?)ā nesu  , keeper of the king's correspondence.

mer shen-t , chief of enquiry; Copt. λⲁϣⲁⲛⲉ (?); , Rec. 24, 189 = Gr. λεσῶνις.

mer shen-ti , chief of the double granary.

mer shenār  , chief of a temple storeroom.

mer shent 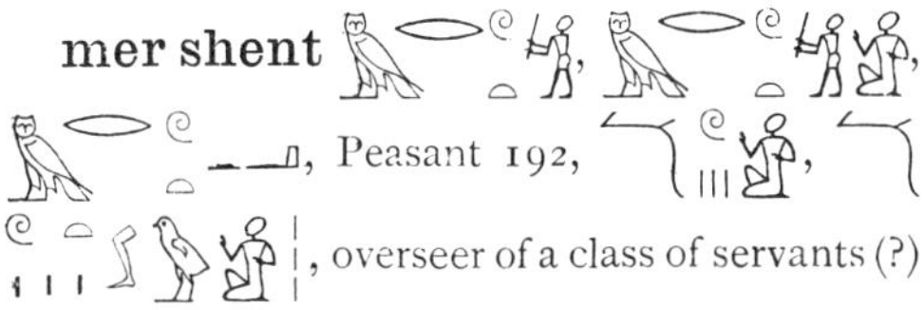, Peasant 192, , overseer of a class of servants (?)

mer kat , director of public works, clerk of the works.

mer thetḥu , inspector of the . . . .

mer tcheb 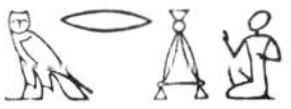, Décrets 18, chief of payments, chief accounting officer.

mer , to see, to look at.

mer-t 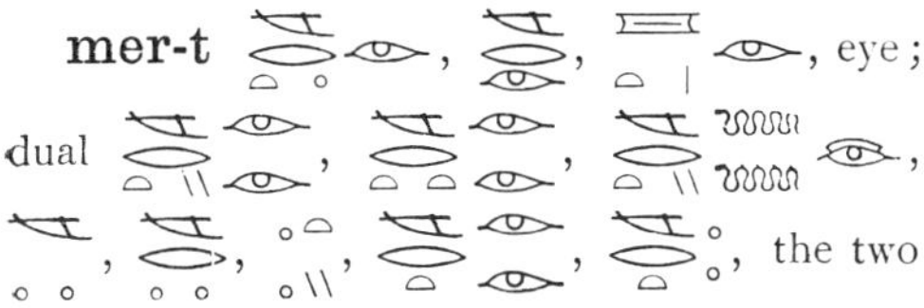, eye; dual , the two eyes; 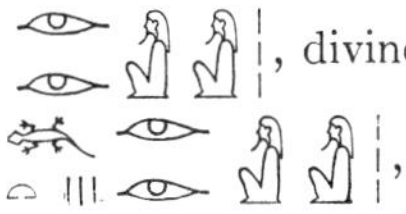, divine eyes, sun and moon, etc.; , many-eyed, "full of eyes"; , "all eyes," *i.e.*, everybody, people in general; Copt. ⲃⲁⲗ.

merit , eyes

Merit 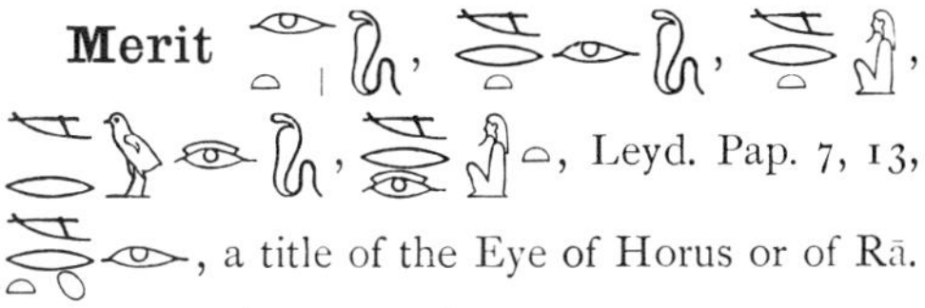, Leyd. Pap. 7, 13, , a title of the Eye of Horus or of Rā.

Merit , B.D. 99, 24, name of a part of the magical boat.

Merti 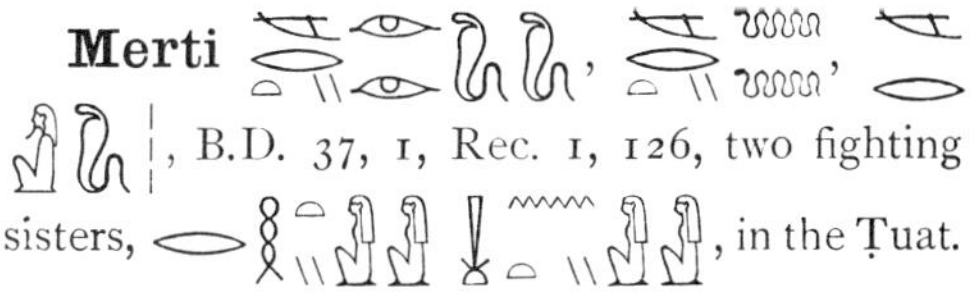, B.D. 37, 1, Rec. 1, 126, two fighting sisters, , in the Ṭuat.

Mer-åakhu, etc. , Thes. 18, one of the 36 Dekans (?)

Merti seti , the name of the 13th day of the moon.

mer 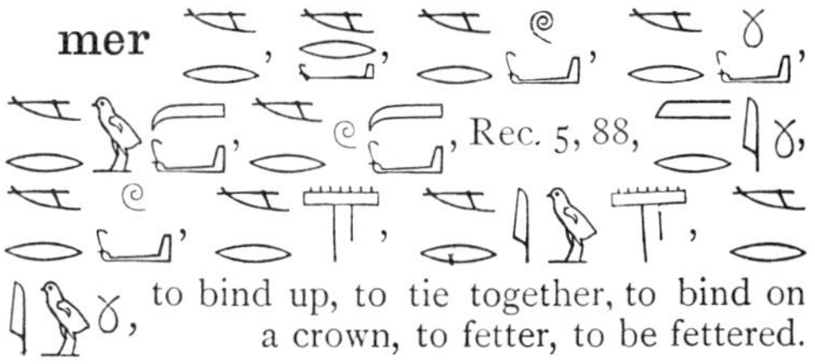, Rec. 5, 88, , to bind up, to tie together, to bind on a crown, to fetter, to be fettered.

mer-t , Rec. 31, 174, , Rec. 12, 25, , Love Songs 2, 6, band, bandage, girdle, fillet, tie; plur. 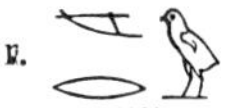 , bundles of clothes; Copt. ⲙⲟⲩⲣ.

mer-t , house, palace.

mer-t 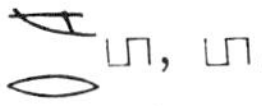, Metternich Stele 72, 119, 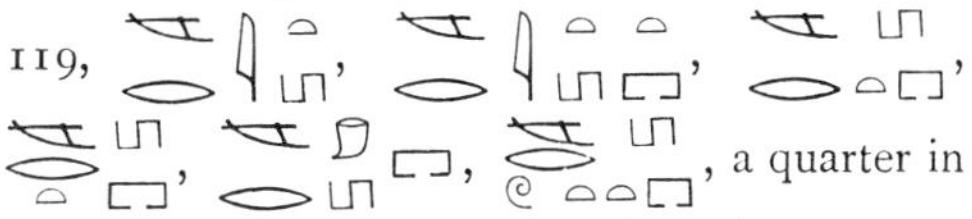, a quarter in a town or village, street or lane in a town, market-place; plur. 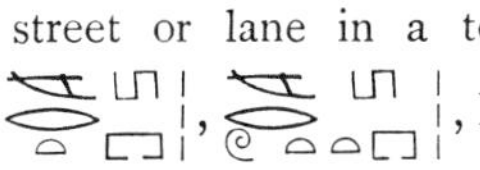, Rev. 11, 110; , house to house.

merr-t, Peasant 300, , a quarter of a town or village, street corner, market; plur. .

mer-ti, the two halves of heaven.

mer-t, cow (?)

Mer-ur, B.D. 99, 19, , Rev. 11, 130; see **Nemur.**

mer, merȧ, , , , Rec. 4, 30, to guide (?)

mer, Palermo Stele, , , , , IV, 1149, the morus tree.

merit (?), Rec. 3, 48, , U. 664, , , , Rec. 5, 88, , Love Songs 1, 12, , staff, plank, etc., of the wood of the morus tree; plur. , .

Merit, B.D. 169, 18, a mythological mulberry tree.

mer-t, a writing instrument.

mer, N. 258, milk pot.

merrit, Shipwreck 164, vessels or pots.

mer, hero, brave man; , Rev. 12, 45.

mer, U. 607, P. 286, , , Ȧmen. 25, 21, , , , to be sick, to suffer pain, to grieve, to be sad, to feel sympathy for someone.

meru, Pap. 3024, 131, a sick man.

mer ȧri, a sick man.

mer-t, , , P. 830, M. 448, N. 465, 773, , , , , , Rev. 14, 12, sickness, illness, pain, sorrow, cruelty, grief, fatal disease; , Rec. 31, 30, , Pap. 3024, , sickness.

mer (mut), Ȧmen. 21, 10, , , to die, dead, death.

merti (miti), , , the dead, the damned.

Mer, A.Z. 49, 55, the damned one, a name of Set.

Mer, B.D. 65, 9, a protector of the dead.

Mer[it], Denderah IV, 84, , ibid. III, 24, name of the goddess of the 8th Pylon.

Merit-neser-t, , Thes. 28, the goddess of the 8th hour of the night.

Merit nesru, Ṭuat I, a fire-goddess.

mer, M. 202, , N. 681, , N. 682, , , , Ȧmen. 2, 9, pyramid, tomb; plur. , , .

mera, , , Rev. 11, 151, 174, 12, 19, ships, fleet; , Rev. 12, 8, sailor (?)

mera-t, Rev. 14, 11, fullness; compare Heb. √מלא.

Merȧ  an ancient name of Egypt; **Pa-ta-Merȧ** 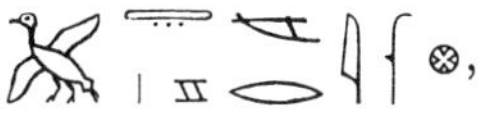, the land of Merȧ = Gr. Πτιμύρις.

meri , a kind of stone.

merina  , IV, 665, captive chiefs; compare Heb. מרין (?)

merua , Rec. 15, 158, weak, wretched.

Merur (Melul)  , a Nubian god worshipped at Talmis and Kalâbshah (Mandulas).

merurit , a kind of bird.

meruḥ 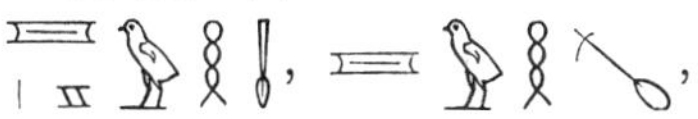, steering oar, paddle.

merukh-t , "measurer," a name of the left eye of Horus, *i.e.*, the moon; var. .

Merbȧa 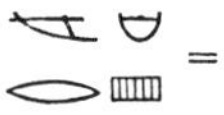 = Μιεβίς, a king of the Ist dynasty.

mermer  , title of an official.

Mermer , B.D. 75, 3, a god.

Merna, IV, 691 ....

merḥ, to anoint, to rub with oil or fat.

merḥ-t 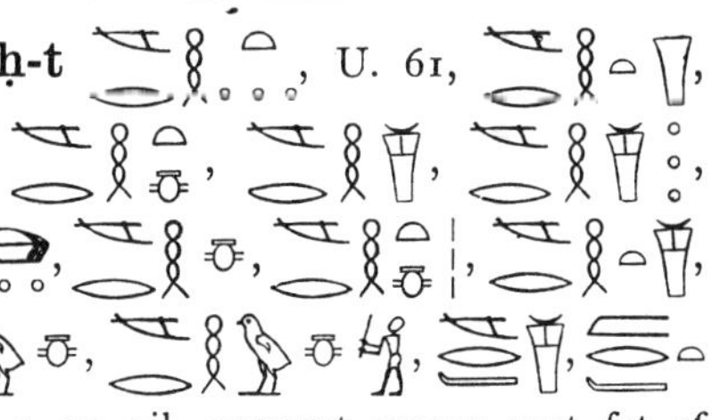, U. 61, N. 313, , Rec. 4, 30, oil, unguent, grease, suet, fat of any kind; Copt. ⲃⲣⲉϩⲓ, ⲙⲙⲣⲏϩⲉ.

merḥ-tȧ 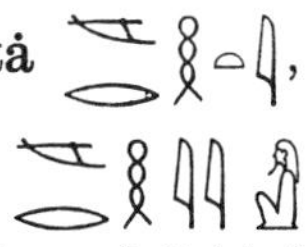, unguent or perfume maker.

Merḥi, Mar. Aby. I, 79, a bull-god, a form of Osiris (?)

Merḥu , the god of perfume (?)

Merḥuit, T.S.B.A. III, 424, a cow-goddess of.

merḥ 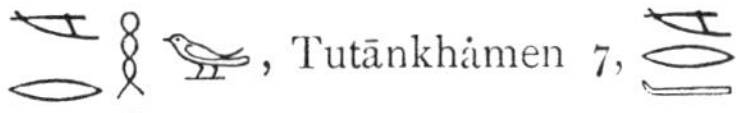, Tutānkhāmen 7, , Rec. 16, 57, , A.Z. 35, 19, to destroy, to wipe out, to delete or obliterate, to perish;  , A.Z. 35, 19, ineffaceable.

merkh , U. 420, T. 240, to measure (the day).

merkh-t 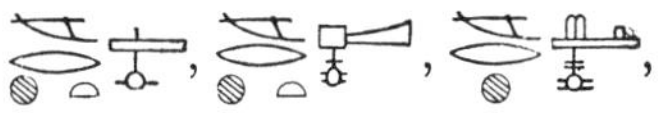, A.Z. 1870, 156, 1899, 13, , Rec. 15, 141, a measurer of time, water-clock (?); Gr. ὡρολόγιον.

merkh-t , Mythe 24, 107 .....

merkh, Rev. 11, 124, 138, 140, to fight, to wage war; Copt. ⲙⲗⲁϩ.

merkhȧ 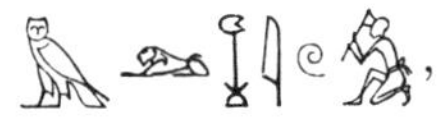, Rec. 13, 42, , war, strife, fight.

Meres 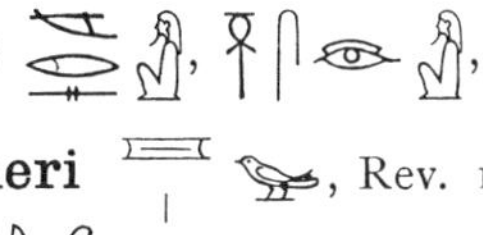, a god.

Mersheri, Rev. 12, 9, 29 = 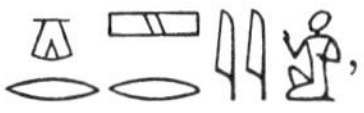, Calasirites.

mertit (merit) 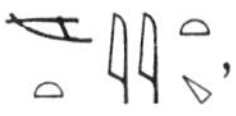, a piece of ground.

mhi , to forget, delay, hesitation; not forgetting my rule.

mhait , roof (?)

mhani (?), A.Z. 1900, 27, a limb or member of the body.

Mehȧt , T. 50, 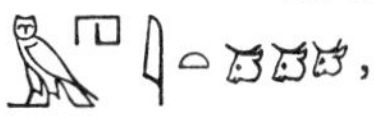, P. 160, a group of cow-goddesses.

mhu, Rev. 12, 8, , Rev. 12, 118, , Rev. 12, 108, , Rev. 11, 124, , IV, 648, tribe, clan, family; see

mhu-t , , coition, begetting, begetter.

meher , milk vessel; plur. , IV, 743, , Thes. 1288, IV, 172.

mehri , milkman.

Mhettut , Ṭuat I, the ape-gods who sang to Rā at dawn.

meḥ (mmeḥ) , Rev. 12, 31 = Copt. ⲙ̄ⲙⲁϩ, before.

meḥ , a sign placed before ordinal numbers: , first; , , second; Copt. ⲙⲉϩ.

meḥ , P. 421, , , , , , cubit, *i.e.*, seven handbreadths or 28 fingerbreadths or 0·525 metre, or about 20 inches; Copt. ⲙⲁϩⲉ; , 10 cubits multiplied by 10; , Ḥerusȧtef Stele 60, 132.

meḥ nesu , , the royal cubit. The 28 fingerbreadths of the royal cubit, , were under the protection of the following gods:—(1) Rā, (2) Shu, (3) Khent, (4) Geb, (5) Nut, (6) Osiris, (7) Isis, (8) Set, (9) Nephthys, (10) Horus, (11) Mestȧ, (12) Ḥāpi, (13) Ṭuamutf, (14) Qebḥsenuf, (15) Thoth, (16) Sep, (17) Ḥeq, (18) Ȧrimāua, (19) Maantef, (20) Ȧrireneftchesef, (21) Ḥeka, (22) Sepṭu, (23) Seb(?), (24) Ȧnḥer, (25) Ḥeruȧua, (26) Sheps, (27) Menu, (28) Uu.

meḥ netches , the little cubit containing six palmbreadths and 24 fingerbreadths.

meḥ , Palermo Stele, a ship 100 cubits long.

meḥ , P. 123, M. 215, N. 686, , P. 417, M. 412, 597, 1202, , , , , , , , , Rec. 33, 4, , , , to fill, to fill full, to be full, filled, to be occupied with; , T. 227, , , U. 174, ; Copt. ⲙⲟⲩϩ.

meḥ-t , M. 412, , N. 708, , N. 1191, , fullness;

meḥ-t ra , Ȧmen. 14, 17, 15, 10, mouthful of bread; , fulfilment of affairs, *i.e.*, the day's work.

meḥ ȧb , , , Anastasi I, 14, 5, to fill the heart, to satisfy, to be content, content; , a person who fills the heart, beloved one, darling.

meḥ ȧb menkh , IV, 1001, perfect filler of the heart, a title.

meḥ ānkhui Ḥeru , IV, 1040, filling the ears of Horus.

meḥ un , A.Z. 1912, 33, Rechnungen 34, poultry yard; Copt. ⲙⲁϩⲟⲩⲁⲗ.

meḥ utcha-t , the filling of the eye, *i.e.*, full moon on the last day of the 2nd month of Pert, the 6th month of the Egyptian year.

meḥ mestcher-t , Anastasi IV, 3, 1, to fill the ear, to listen attentively.

meḥ reṭui , to use the legs to good purpose.

meḥ seka , to occupy oneself with ploughing.

meḥ qenȧ , Shipwreck 133, to fill the bosom, *i.e.*, to embrace.

meḥ qeṭ-t , Rev. 13, 3, to act with great prudence; Copt. ⲙⲟⲩϩ ⲕⲁϯ.

meḥ , Rev. 14, 40, the perimeter of a town.

meḥ-t (?) , U. 261, abundance.

mḥa , addition, increment, increase.

Meḥiu (?) , B.D. 180, 18, a god (?)

Meḥi , B.D. 168, a serpent-deity.

Meḥit , , a goddess associated with the god Ȧn-ḥer.

Meḥit , B.D.G. 1268, , Denderah II, 66, , the goddess of the North.

Meḥit , Ṭuat IV, , Pap. Ani 20, 9: (1) a goddess, warder of the serpent Nehep; (2) a uraeus on the brow of Rā.

Meḥ-f-meṭ (?)-f , the god of the 16th day of the month.

Meḥ-maāt , Ṭuat III, a god.

Meḥit-Tefnut , Edfû I, 20, 6, a double-goddess of Edfû.

meḥ 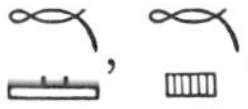, Rev. 5, 95, to be inlaid with something; , inlaid with precious stones; 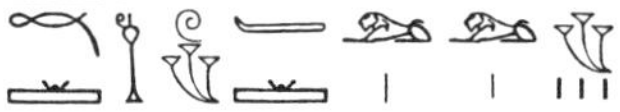 , covered with flowers of all kinds.

meḥ 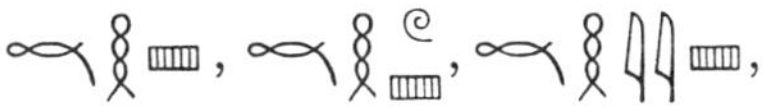, a kind of stone, agate (?)

meḥ , stones for inlaying.

meḥ-t , a plaque.

meḥ 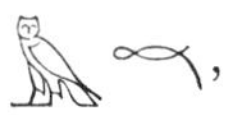, T. 267, , N. 39, 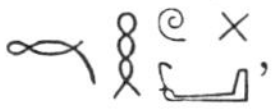, A.Z. 1872, 21, , Thes. 1205, IV, 600, 648, to seize, to have or hold as a possession; 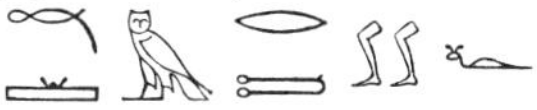, to lay hold of his feet.

meḥ 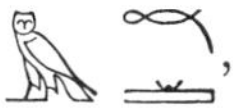, something captured, prisoner.

meḥt , Rev. 12, 37, , Rev. 14, 37, to have power over, to have possession of; Copt. ⲁⲙⲁϩⲧⲉ.

meḥi 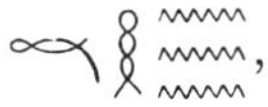, T. 268, 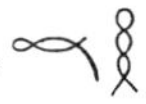, M. 425, , N. 945, , 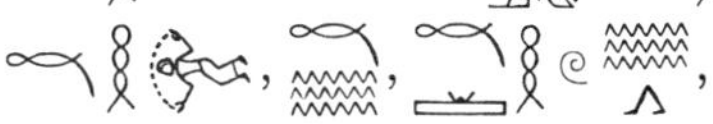, Ȧmen. 6, 5, 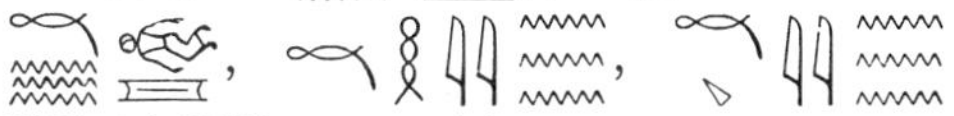, [illegible], [illegible], to be submerged, drowned.

meḥ-t nub [illegible], the washing out of gold from quartz or mud.

meḥu [illegible], a drowned man.

meḥiu [illegible], [illegible], [illegible], Ṭuat X, [illegible], [illegible], [illegible], the drowned.

meḥ [illegible], submerged land.

Meḥi [illegible], [illegible], the canal of the Nome Metelites.

meḥuiu [illegible], the flood that destroyed mankind.

meḥi [illegible], Rec. 10, 136, flood.

meḥit [illegible], [illegible], [illegible], [illegible], [illegible] [illegible], [illegible], Metternich Stele 202, Pap. 3024, water-flood, rainstorm, a mass of water, essence.

meḥit Agbȧ [illegible] [illegible], U. 620, the flood of Agbȧ, *i.e*, the mass of celestial water above the earth.

meḥai 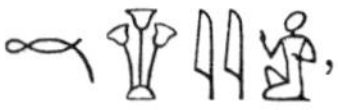, fuller, washerman.

meḥi 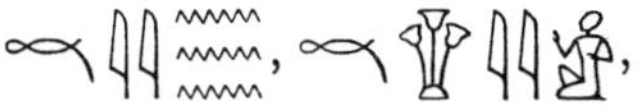, Rev. 6, 136, title of a priest.

meḥi sem (?) , Rev. 3, 45, title of a priest.

Meḥi 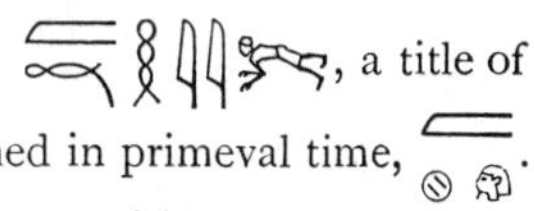, a title of Osiris who was drowned in primeval time.

Meḥi 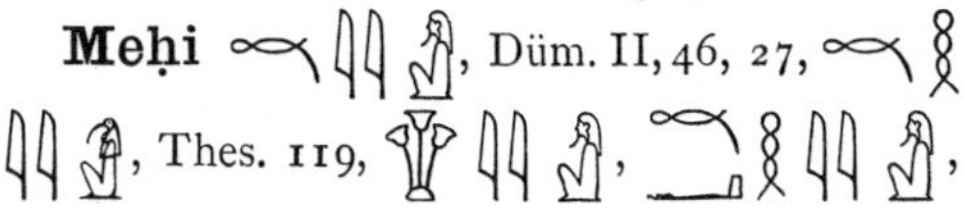, Düm. II, 46, 27, Thes. 119, B.D. (Saïte) 109, 7, a title of Thoth as god of the Inundation.

Meḥit 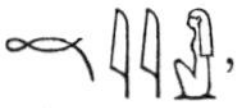, B.D.G. 292, a goddess of the Nile-flood.

Meḥt-urit 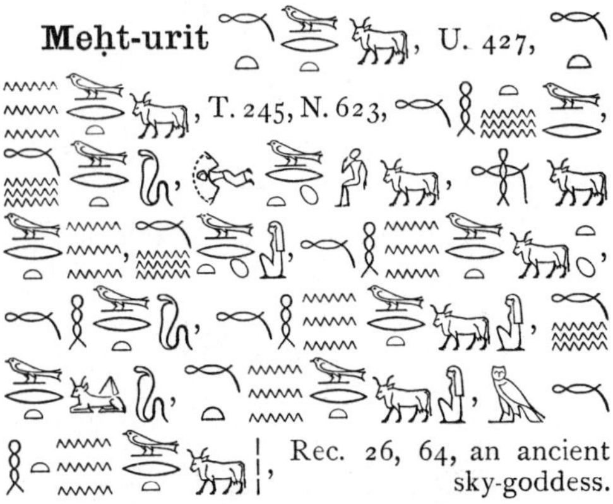, U. 427, T. 245, N. 623, Rec. 26, 64, an ancient sky-goddess.

meḥit 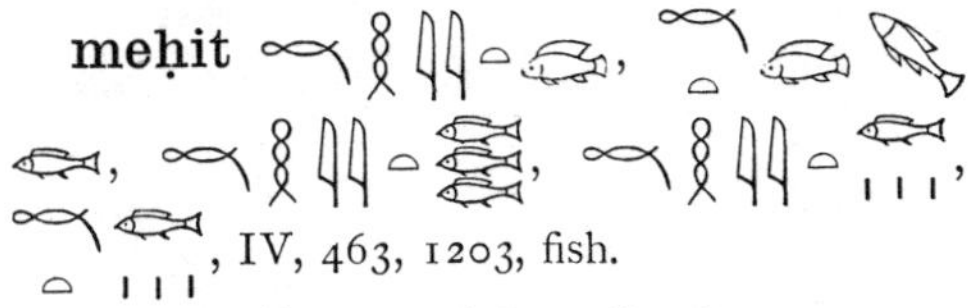, IV, 463, 1203, fish.

meḥu , fisherman.

Meḥ-t 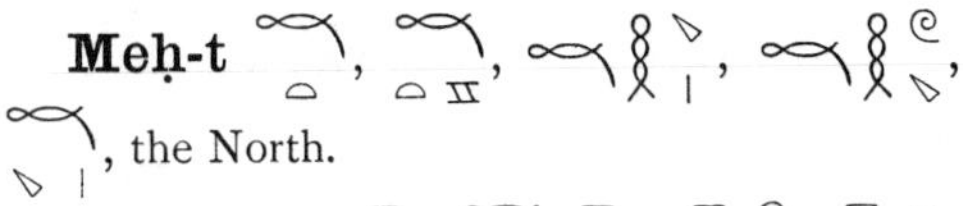, the North.

Meḥ-t , North-land, *i.e.*, the Delta.

Meḥit 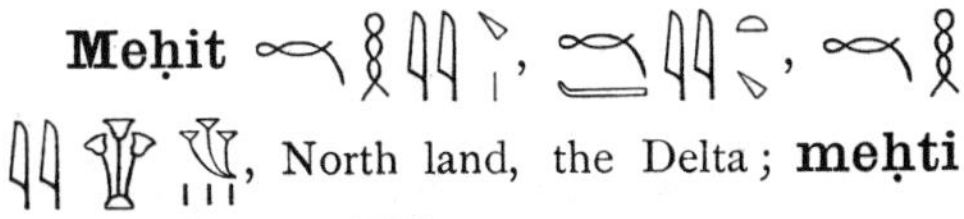, North land, the Delta; **meḥti**
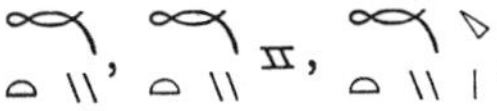, northern.

meḥti 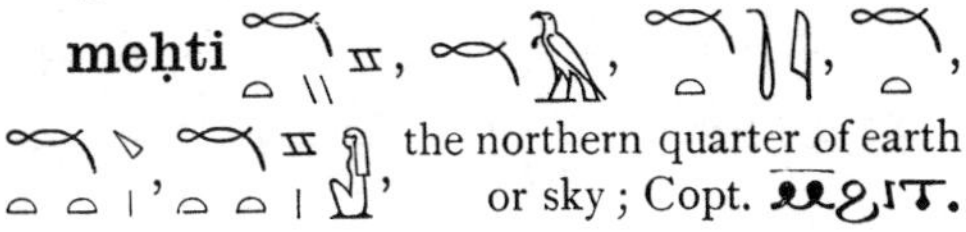, the northern quarter of earth or sky; Copt. ⲙⲉϩⲓⲧ.

Meḥtiu , those who live in the North.

Meḥtiu , P. 829, IV, 612, Dream Stele 41, northern tribes, gods of the North.

meḥti (?) , grain of the North.

meḥti — 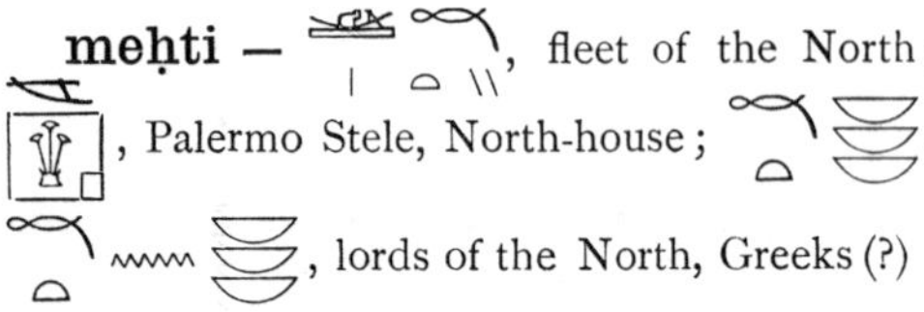, fleet of the North; Palermo Stele, North-house; lords of the North, Greeks (?)

meḥti-àmenti 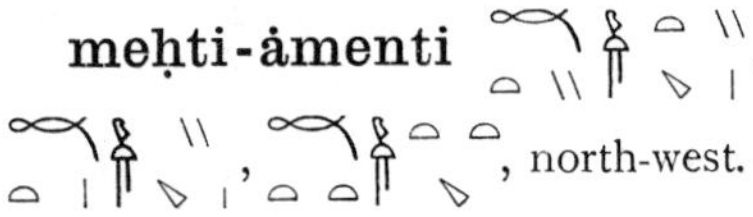, IV, 657, north-west.

meḥit 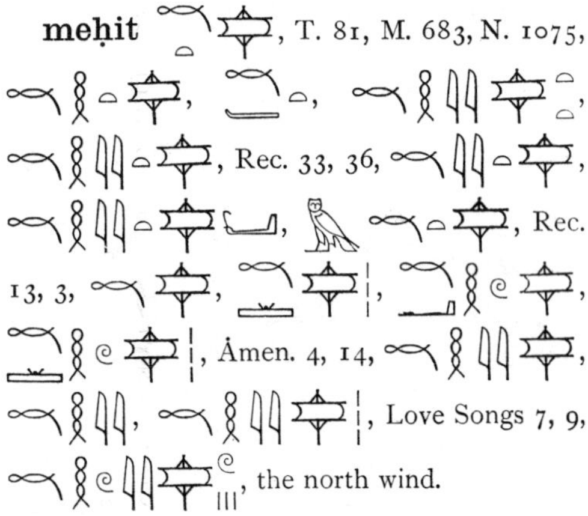, T. 81, M. 683, N. 1075, Rec. 33, 36, Rec. 13, 3, Åmen. 4, 14, Love Songs 7, 9, the north wind.

meḥut , P. 362, 707, A.Z. 1907, 3, Rec. 33, 36, the north wind.

Meḥit-per-t-em-Tem, etc. 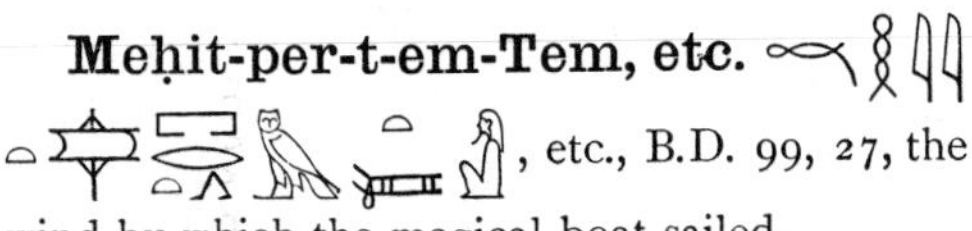, etc., B.D. 99, 27, the wind by which the magical boat sailed.

meḥ-t , fan, fly-flapper.

meḥ-t 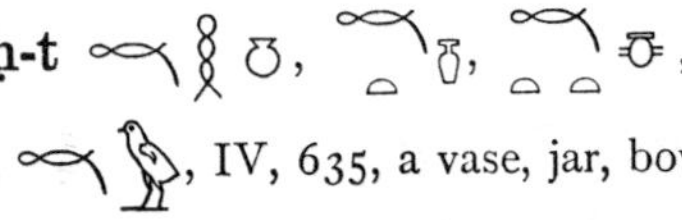, Rec. 17, 145, IV, 635, a vase, jar, bowl.

meḥut 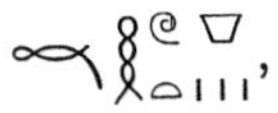, offerings.

meḥti , oil, unguent, salve.

meḥ-t, , , , Israel Stele 6, crown, plume, feather-crown; plur. , Koller Pap. 4, 1, 6.

meḥ, , to crown, to be crowned.

meḥ, , , , , , , , bandlet, fillet, garland, crown, girdle; plur. , , , , , P. 426, M. 610, N. 1215; Copt. ⲙⲁϩⲉ.

meḥ, , , linen thread.

meḥi (m'ḥi), Rec. 12, 211, , Rec. 4, 25, , , , , Leyd. Pap. 5, 5, flax, linen; Copt. ⲙⲁϩⲓ.

meḥ, I, 129, Pap. 3024, 68, , Metternich Stele 199, , to have a care for, to be anxious about, to be sorry, to brood over.

meḥi, , Hymn to Nile 3, 9, , , Pap. 3024, 30, , P. 1116B, 18, wretched man, miserable.

meḥ-t, , , care, grief, anxiety, thought.

meḥ sa, , , , , , , , = (?)

meḥ-t sa, care, anxiety.

meḥ, Rec. 15, 17, nest; , Rec. 13, 15.

meḥa-t, Leyd. Pap. 2, , P. 644, tomb, sepulchre.

Meḥānuti (Meḥnuti)-Rā, , B.D. 180, 31, a god (?)

meḥi, shining one.

meḥuar, pigeon tower; Copt. ⲙⲁϩⲃⲁⲗ (?)

Meḥun, , , a harvest-god.

meḥ-f (?), a kind of stone.

meḥn-t, , , , , , , Rec. 3, 50, house of the North.

meḥn-t (?), north winds.

meḥen, a covering.

Meḥen, , , , Ṭuat VII, , , , a serpent-god who protected Áfu-Rā in the Ṭuat.

Meḥnit, B.D. 131, 9, , B.D. 168, , , , , , , , Rec. 27, 88, , , , , Hymn Darius 29, a serpent-goddess, uraeus crown.

Meḥni, Ṭuat XI, one of 12 gods who carried Meḥen.

Meḥen-ȧpni (?), Ṭuat X, a serpent-god, each half of whom had three heads and three necks and rested on a bow.

Meḥen-ta, , Ṭuat VIII, a goddess in the Circle Ḥetepet-neb-per-s.

Meḥen-ti, Denderah IV, 60, a guardian of a coffer.

meḥenk, , , one to whom things are given or offered.

meḥra (meḥa), Rev. 12, 38, clan, tribe; (?) U. 296, N. 534, store chamber of tomb.

meḥs, blain, boil, sore.

meḥs (?), IV, 266, , the crown of the North.

meḥtep, needle; Copt. ϩⲁⲙⲛ̄ⲧⲱⲡ.

meḥṭ-t, B.D. 96, 97, 7, ...

mekha, to burn, to be hot or fervent.

mekha, N. 759, IV, 72, to turn to, to run towards.

mekha-t, Rec. 30, 67, intestines; Copt. ⲙⲁϩⲧ.

mekha-t, Rec. 32, 78, Rec. 30, 189, Rec. 13, 31, pillar-scales, balance; Copt. ⲙⲁϣⲉ.

mekhai, carpenter; Copt. ϩⲁⲙϣⲓ.

mekhaut, Barshah 1, 14, 11, shelters (?) on the river.

mekhar, Rev., war, fight; Copt. ⲙⲗⲁϩ.

mekhar-t, Rev. 13, 59, army.

mekharr, Rev. 12, 70, scarab.

mekhi, Verbum I, 396, Rev. 12, 34, to beat, to strike, to fight; Copt. ⲙⲓϣⲉ.

mekhen, N. 293A, club.

mekhnu, A Z. 1868, 38, saw.

mekhn-t, T. 220, P. 615, U. 468, M. 786, Rec. 26, 64, N. 913, 1172, 1287, A.Z. 1894, 119, ferry boat; plur. M. 782, 785; var. **meshen-t**, P. 400, 651, 676.

mekhent, mekhentȧ, P. 183, N. 896, 913, T. 190, P. 396, M. 290, 571, N. 565, Rec. 26, 64, Hh. 379, Hh. 425, U. 556, N. 1184, god of the divine ferry, ferryman; var. P. 405.

M-khenti-ȧr-ti, N. 660: (1) a form of Horus; (2) B.D. 168, a crocodile-headed god.

M-khenti-ur, Rec. 37, 59, a form of Ptaḥ.

M-khenti-Ṭefnut, Rec. 37, 61, a form of Ptaḥ.

M-khenti-Sekhem, U. 532, a title of

mekhsefu 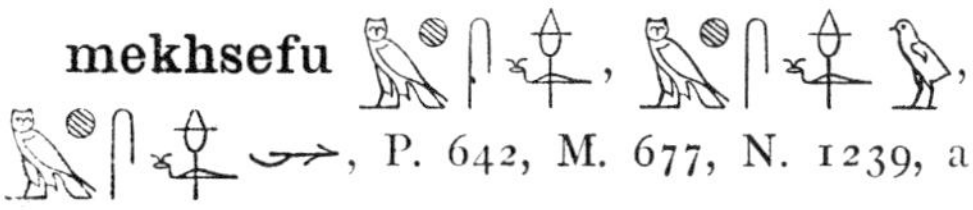, P. 642, M. 677, N. 1239, a kind of ceremonial staff or weapon.

mekht , Rec. 27, 77 = ȧmiu khet, subordinates.

mes 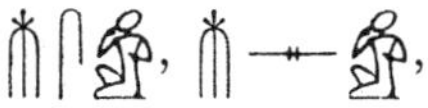, Pap. 3024, 142, a conjunctive particle: yet, moreover; 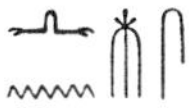 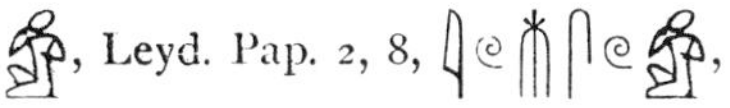, Leyd. Pap. 2, 8, Leyd. Pap. 3, 4.

mes , an amulet worn by women to obtain easy labour.

mesi , Rec. 27, 228, 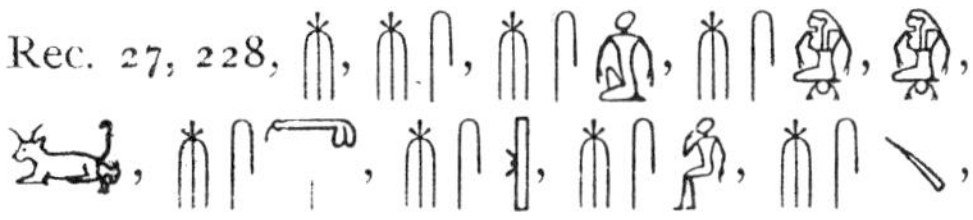, to bear, to give birth to, to produce, to fashion, to form, to make a likeness of; 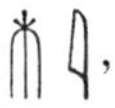, P. 613, T. 359; 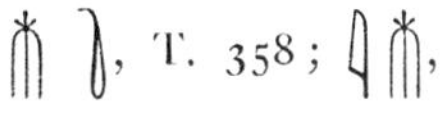, T. 358; to make to be born.

mes en , born of, brought forth by.

mess , U. 597, to bear, to produce.

messuth 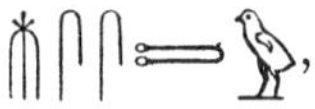, birth.

mesmes , to bear, to produce.

mesmes , Rev. 11, 110, to set in order (?)

mesmesiu , children.

mesi , bearer, producer; plur. P. 711, N. 1355.

mesi , midwife; Copt. ⲙⲉⲥⲓⲱ.

mes-t , U. 197, Mission 13, 51, genetrix; , bearer of a man child.

mess-t 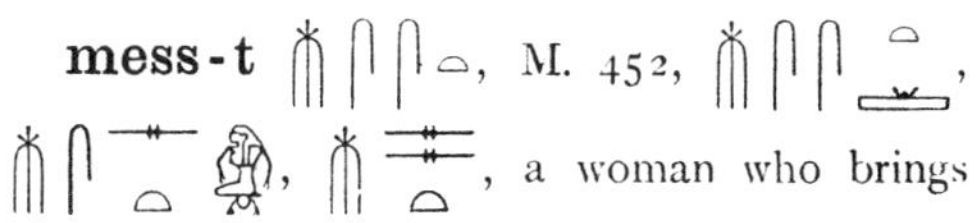, M. 452, a woman who brings forth, something which is born or produced, birth.

mesut , U. 43, M. 681,  birth.

mesti , Rev. 14, 19, childbirth.

mes-t 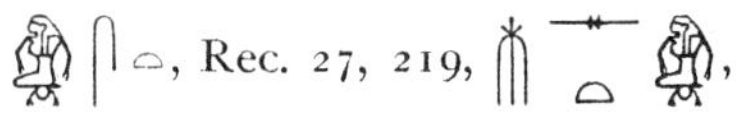, Rec. 27, 219, Rec. 27, 228,  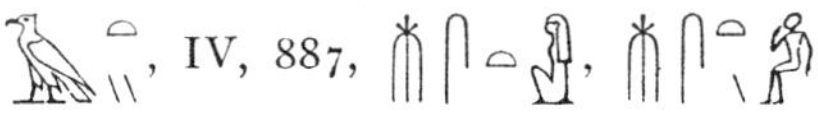, IV, 887, birth, something produced.

mes[ut] 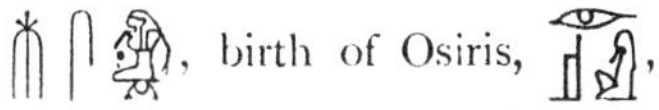, birth of Osiris, of Horus, , of Set, of Isis, of Nephthys, ; these births were observed on the five epagomenal days of the year.

Mesut Neprȧ , "birth of the Grain-god," the name of a festival.

Mesut-Rā , "birth of Rā," *i.e.*, the month Mesore (Demotic form).

mes — hru mesut  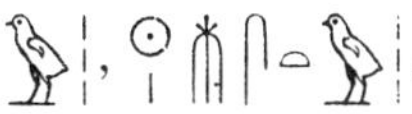, birthday.

mes-t 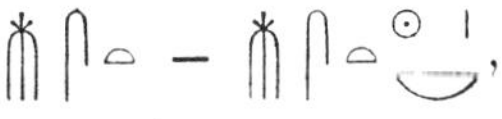, IV, 700, laying [eggs] every day.

mes  , Rec. 30, 190, , child, son; plur. 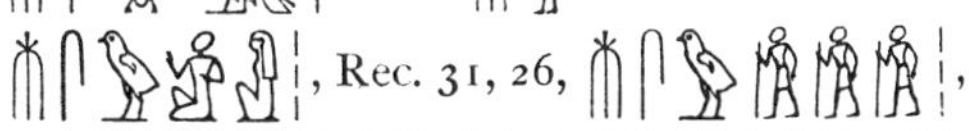, Rec. 31, 26, IV, 1102, 

, , , , , , , , Rec. 29, 28, , Rec. 29, 77, , , , Rec. 32, 82, , children.

messu , IV, 614, children.

messiu , P. 171, 177, , , those who are born, children.

mesit , T. 284 = , P. 53, , M. 32, , N. 65, , , children; , P. 593, race, family.

mes , a baby; , baby 15 months old; , a weaned child.

mes-t , Pap. 3024, 76, , , a female child.

mesu nebu , all who are born, *i.e.*, all mankind.

mesu nt mu (?) , offspring of the Water-god, *i.e.*, plants.

mesu ḥemt , female children.

Mesu Ḥeru , Quelques Pap. 43, a class of embalmers.

mesu ḥesiu , sons of quakings (?) terror-stricken beings.

Mesu-khenti-Āat , Quelques Pap. 43, a class of embalmers.

Mesu seru , children of noblemen.

Mesti , , A.Z. 1910, 117, IV, 84, "begetter," a name of Åmen, , Tombos Stele 10.

Mesti , the two divine parents of Rā ( ).

Mesut , children of Osiris, divine beings.

Mesu , the gods who begat their own fathers, divine beings.

Mesu beṭesh-t , , , , , , children of revolt, *i.e.*, the rebels who followed Set.

Mes-pet-åaṭ-t-em-ḥer-f , Denderah I, 30, Ombos II, 2, 134, a lion-goddess.

Mes-peḥ , B.D. 146, the doorkeeper of the 2nd Pylon; var. Mes-Ptaḥ, .

Mes-t pekh-t , B.M. 32, ll. 409, 495, a mythological bird of prey.

Mes-Pteḥ , the warder of the 2nd Ārit, B.D. 145.

Mesi mesu , Hymn Darius 2, producer of [his] children, a title of Rā.

Mesu Nut , , , N. 960, B.D. 175, 1, children of Nut, *i.e.*, Osiris, Isis, Set, Nephthys and Horus.

Mes-en-Ḥeru-neb-t-ḥefiu , Denderah IV, 63, a hawk-headed god.

Mesui neterui , the two divine children.

Mesu Ḥeru , P. 599, , P. 600, , T. 281, N. 131, , B.D. 137A, 17, , Mar.

Aby. I, 44, , the four sons of Horus, viz., Mestȧ, Ḥāpi, Ṭuamutef and Qebḥsenuf.

Mesu Ḥeru , Edfû I, 15A–H, the four sons and four grandsons (Ȧrimāuai, Maatefef, Ȧrireneftchesef, and Ḥeq) of Horus.

Mesu Ḥeru , Ṭuat XI, four chains that fetter Āapep.

Mes-sepkh 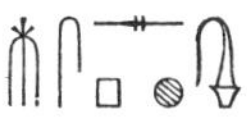, B.D. 145, a god.

Mesu-serȧt-beqt 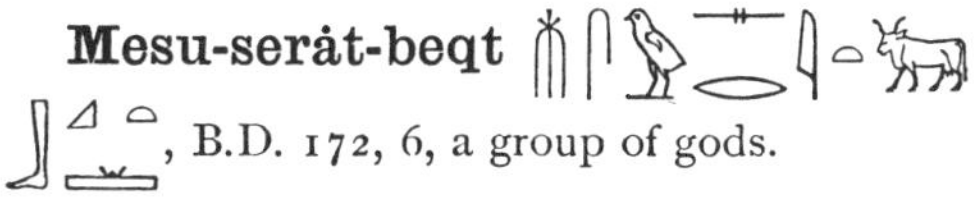, B.D. 172, 6, a group of gods.

Mesu Set 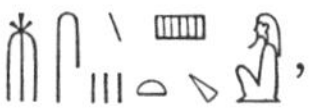, children of Set, *i.e.*, fiends.

Mesu-qas , Ṭuat X, a title of the four sons of Horus as fetterers of Āapep.

Mesu Temu , N. 960, *i.e.*, Shu, Tefnut, Geb, Nut, Osiris, Isis, Set, Nephthys.

Mesi temu em uhem 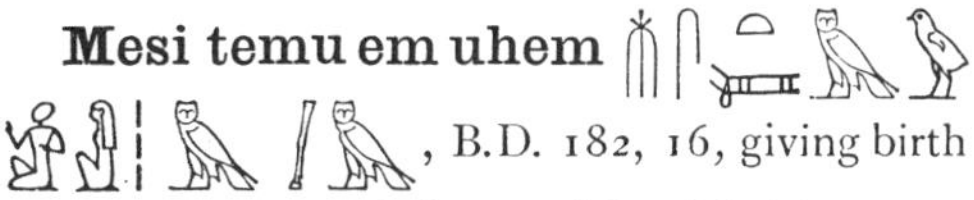, B.D. 182, 16, giving birth to mortals a second time, a title of Osiris.

Mesit-tches-s 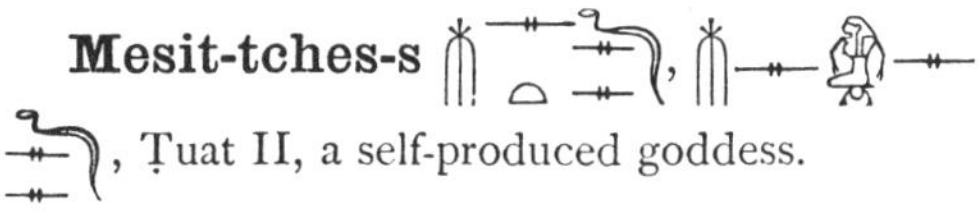, Ṭuat II, a self-produced goddess.

mes (?) , Rev. 12, 47, bull calf; plur. , heifers; Copt. ⲙⲁⲥⲉ.

mess , Stat. Tab. 52, bull-calf.

mesit , foals.

mesi , to cut, to carve, to sculpt, to fashion a figure or statue; 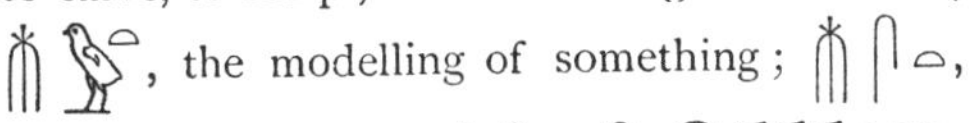, the modelling of something; plating (with metal); 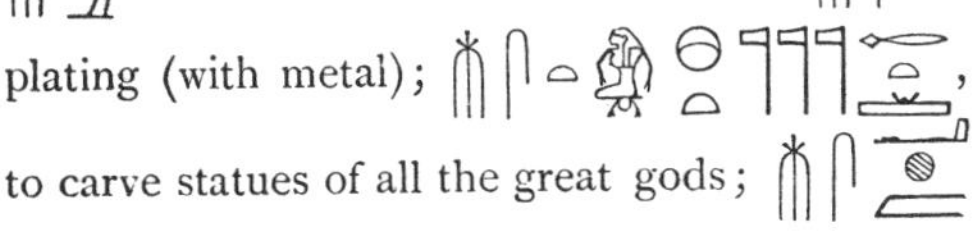, to carve statues of all the great gods; 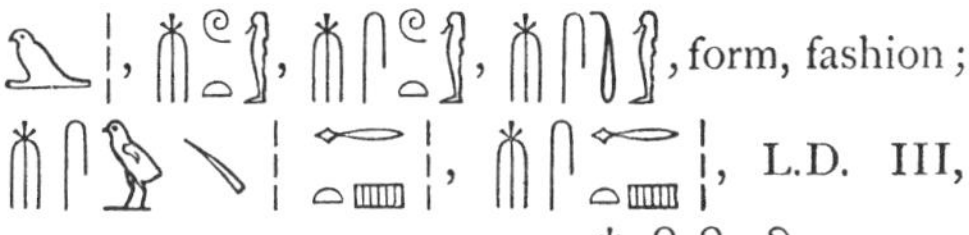, form, fashion; L.D. III, 219, 3, 18, stone carvers; 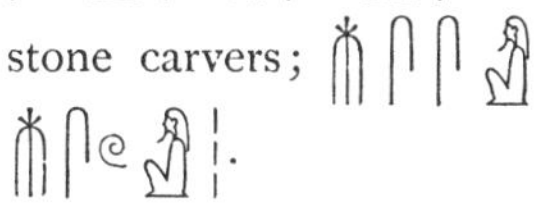, divine statue; plur.

mes , Rev. 11, 169, foundry.

Mes 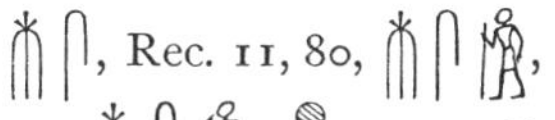, Rec. 11, 80, Rec. 21, 3, chief prince; , Rec. 17, 98, overseer of a cemetery.

mes , Metternich Stele 34, to weave, to spin.

mes-t 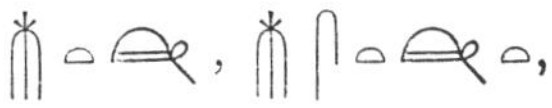, bandlet, tiara, turban.

mes , lock of hair, curl.

mes , to turn round from, to avoid.

mes 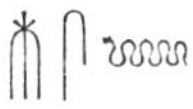, serpent, Horapollo Μεισί.

mesut 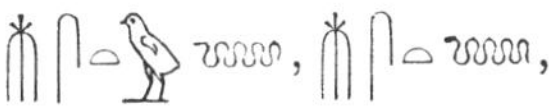, serpent.

mes-t 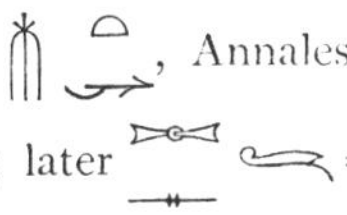, Annales I, 87, one of the 36 Dekans; later = Θοσολκ.

mesit 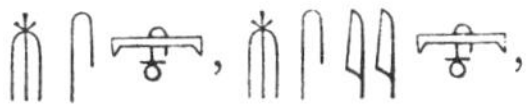, eventide, darkness; var. .

mesit 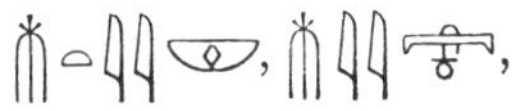, Thes. 478, a festival.

mes , supper, evening bread.

mesit 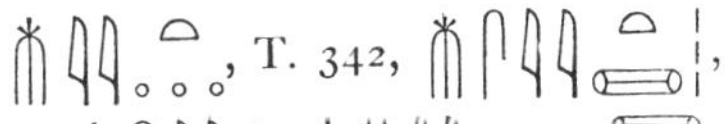, T. 342, Pap. 3024, 81, 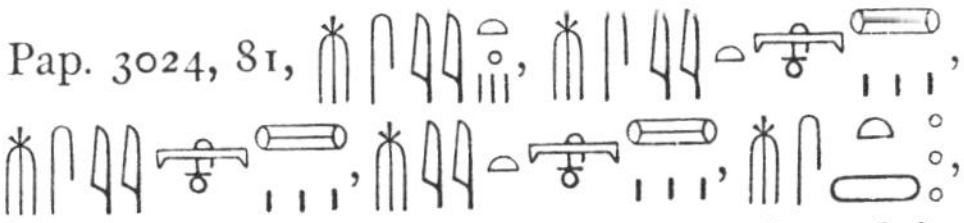, Rec. 4, 121, evening meal, supper, cakes of the evening.

mesut 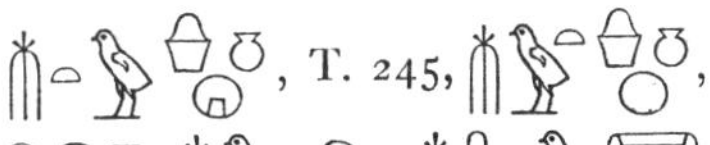, T. 245, T. 343, , , food, provisions for the night; IV, 108.

mes-t , grain (?), U. 138, a kind of loaf or cake; var. cakes.

mes 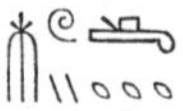, crop, grain.

mes , A.Z. 1900, 37, a kind of disease (?)

mes , L.D. III, 219, 19, to drag.

mes , to lead, to bring, to transfer.

mes-t 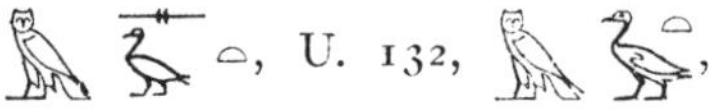, U. 132, N. 440, a bird (?)

mes , to walk.

mesmes , P. 254, M. 475, N. 1064, to journey, to travel.

mesmesu , steps (?) stridings (?)

mes-t 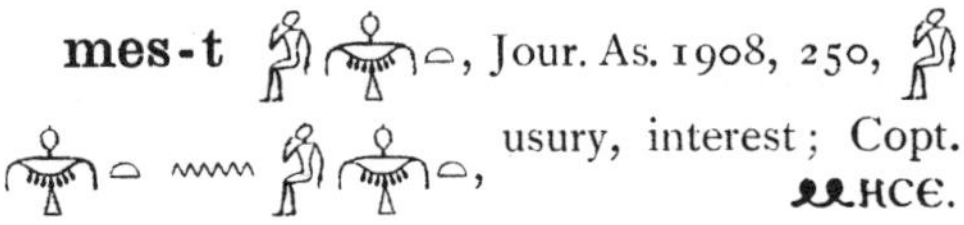, Jour. As. 1908, 250, usury, interest; Copt. ⲙⲏⲥⲉ.

mes (?) 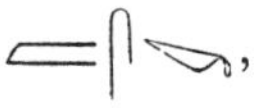, to slay.

mess 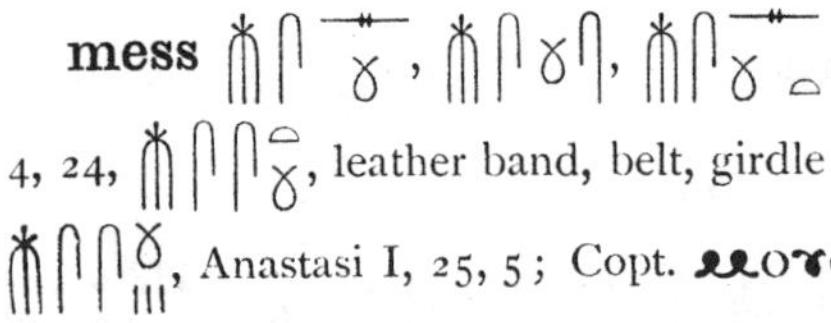, Rec. 4, 24, leather band, belt, girdle; plur. Anastasi I, 25, 5; Copt. ⲙⲟⲩⲥ.

mess 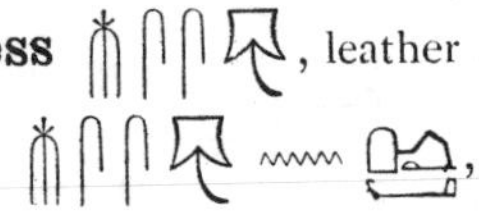, leather armour, buckler, shield; a fighting coat made of leather.

mesa-t, mesȧ-t , a kind of goose, or powerful waterfowl.

mesit 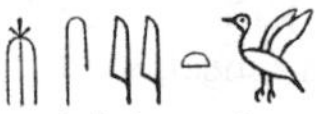, Pap. 3024, 93, birds, waterfowl (plur. of preceding ?).

msaḥ , Rev. 12, 67, Rev. 13, 14, crocodile; Copt. ⲙⲥⲁϩ.

mesȧntf (?) , a portion of the lower part of the body.

mesȧnṭ 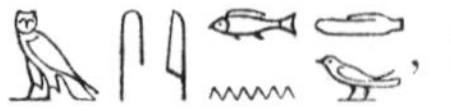, Pap. 3024, 58, to cause trouble.

Mesānuit (?) 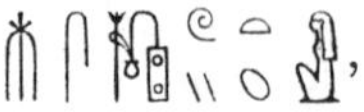, Ombos 2, 132, a goddess.

Mesit , B.D. (Saïte), 136, 1, a god.

Mesu , A.Z. 1905, 104, a man's name, Moses (?)

mesur , a drinking bowl.

mesut (?) , clothes, apparel.

mesbeb (?) 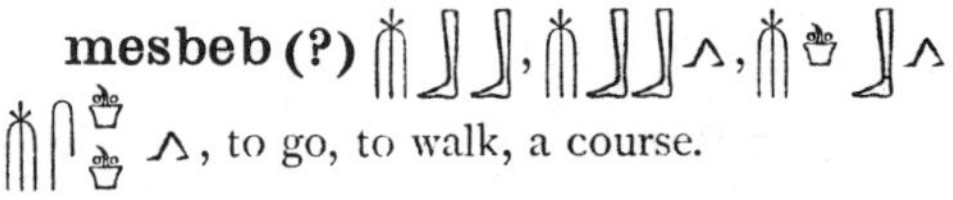, to go, to walk, a course.

mesbeb (?) , plated, banded with metal, framed.

mesbeb (?) 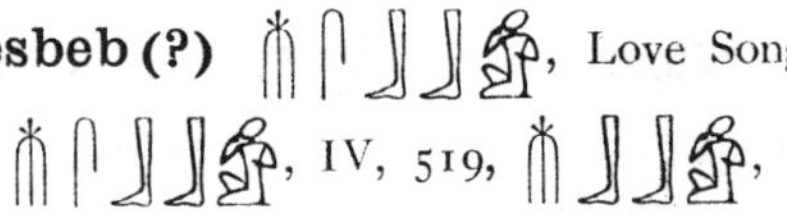, Love Songs 4, 10, IV, 519, to think (?)

mesper tep , the 1st mesper, *i.e.*, the 3rd day of the month, which was sacred to Osiris.

mesper sen-nu 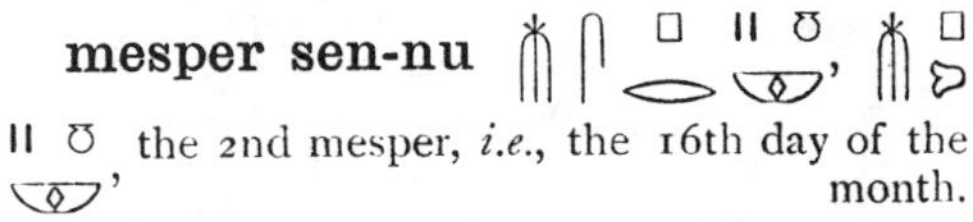, the 2nd mesper, *i.e.*, the 16th day of the month.

Mesperit , Ṭuat I, the goddess of the 6th hour of the night; varr.

mespertiu , coppersmiths.

msef , Rev. 2, 43 = Copt. ⲡⲥⲁϥ.

mesen (?) , U. 421, T. 241 ....

mesen , Ȧmen. 12, 19, to defend, to protect.

mesen , , to weave, to spin.

mesen-t 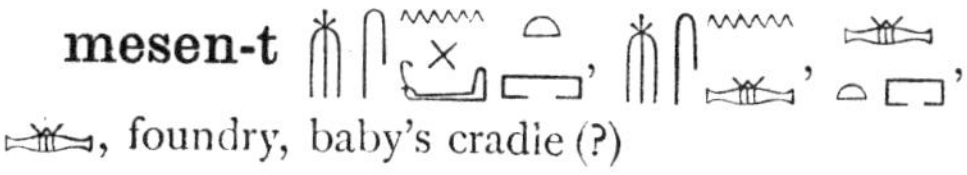, foundry, baby's cradle (?)

Mesen , Berg. I, 34, an ape-headed fire-god.

mesen , Rev. 14, 69, to form a property or estate.

mesen 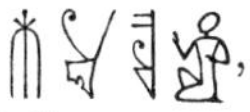, a metal worker; plur. 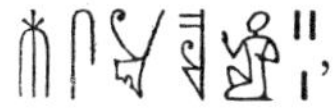, Rec. 16, 116.

mesen , Herusȧtef Stele 35, 36, 37, some kind of metal objects.

mesnu , spearmen.

Mesen 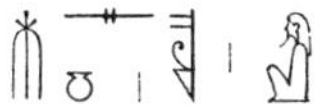, Rec. 27, 223, the Blacksmith-god; his associates were the  .

Mesniu, Mesentiu , 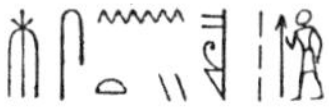, Nav. Mythe 7, the blacksmiths of Horus who made harpoons, spears, etc.

mesenti 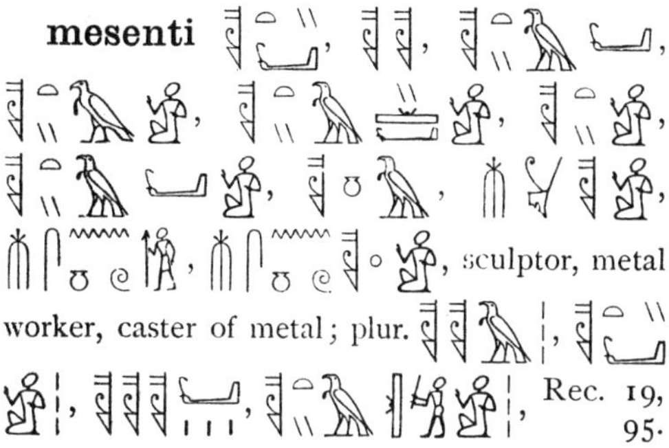, sculptor, metal worker, caster of metal; plur., Rec. 19, 95.

Mesenti , the title of the high-priest of Apollinopolis (Edfû).

mesentiu , sacrificial priests (?)

mesnȧ (?) , knife, dagger.

mesner-t , tunic.

mesneḥ , 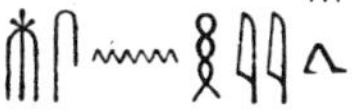, A.Z. 1905, 19, Leyd. Pap. 2, to turn about, to turn away, to turn back.

Mesnekhtit 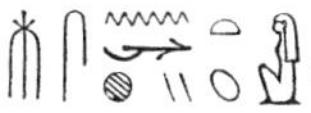, Berg. 67; see **Meskhenit.**

mesenti , foundation; see 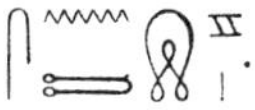.

mesr-t , Rec. 30, 67, parts of a ship, ribs (?)

meshai , Rec. 11, 66, to turn oneself round.

meseḥ 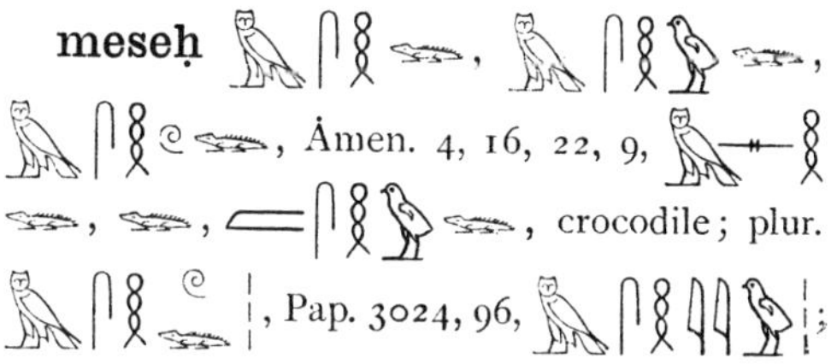, Ȧmen. 4, 16, 22, 9, crocodile; plur., Pap. 3024, 96; Copt. ⲙⲥⲁϩ, Ass. namsukha , (Talbot, Jour. R.A.S. 19, 133, Broken Obelisk I, 29), Gr. χάμψαι.

meseḥ-t , a female crocodile.

mesḥu , the four crocodiles of the Cardinal Points; see B.D. 32.

Mesḥu VIII , B.D. 32, the eight crocodiles of the Ṭuat. The Theban Recension mentions four only, .

meseḥ , Ebers Pap. Voc., a drug made of the member of the crocodile, an aphrodisiac (?)

mesḥu (?) 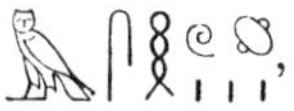, the dung of the crocodile.

meseḥ , Rev. 11, 92, Rev. 14, 14, to turn round, to turn away.

meseḥ , to slay, to cut, to divide.

mesḥep 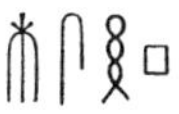, something hidden or concealed.

meskh-t , lake, pool (?); plur., Rec. 33, 5.

meskh-t , IV, 1060 . . . .

meskh-t, forearm, thigh (?); var. .

Meskh-ti, Meskh-t, U. 567, , N. 214, , Rec. 31, 170, , , Rec. 27, 226, , P. 671, M. 660, N. 1275, , , the constellation of the Great Bear.

Meskh-ti, Thes. 124 ff., the Great Bear, depicted as a bull-headed heart, or a bull-headed bull's haunch with seven stars. It was the abode of the soul of Set.

Meskh-ti, Ṭuat XI, a form of Åfu-Rā.

meskh-t, ribbons, veils.

meskha, Rec. 14, 119, , to rejoice, joy, gladness.

meskha-ti, a mistake for , the two nostrils.

Meskha-t kau, U. 220 . . . .

meskhā, diadem, crown.

meskhāu, P.S.B. 15, 32, 33, splendour (?)

meskhen-t, an instrument in the form of a thigh used in religious ceremonies.

meskhen-t, , tablet of destiny.

Meskhen-ti, IV, 227, , the birth stones or tablets (?) In Pap. Anhai one is called Shai and the other Rennit.

meskhen-t, P. 393, M. 56, N. 1167, , Rec. 27, 88, , , birthplace, cradle.

Meskhen, B.D. 110, 16, the birthplace of the City-god in Sekhet-Ḥetep; , B.D. (Saïte) 31, 7, the birth-chamber of Osiris.

meskhen-t, , , Ani Pap. 3, , Westcar 11, 21, , , , , , birth-chamber, birthplace, baby's bed; perhaps also a stone, or pair of stones, upon which a woman sat during childbirth.

meskhenut, the four chief birth goddesses; their names were:— , Meskhen of Āait; , Meskhen of Menkhit; , Meskhen of Nefrit; , Meskhen of Sebqit; , the birthplaces in Abydos.

Meskhenit, P. 397, , M. 566, , N. 1172, the goddess of the birth-chamber.

Meskhenit, , , Rec. 30, 190, , the goddess of the birth-chamber, the goddess of Luck, Fate, or Destiny.

Meskhenit-Āait, B.D. 142, a goddess of childbirth.

Meskhenit-Āait, a hippopotamus-goddess who presided over the 1st epagomenal day (the birthday of Osiris).

Meskhenit-Āait-Nut, Denderah IV, 74, one of the four goddesses who presided over birth.

Meskhenit-Uatchit 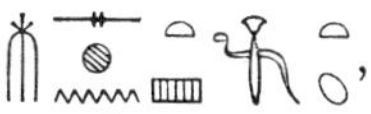, a hippopotamus-goddess who presided over the 5th epagomenal day (the birthday of Nephthys).

Meskhenit-Urit-Tefnut  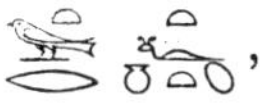, Denderah IV, 74, one of the four goddesses who presided over birth.

Meskhenit-Menkhit 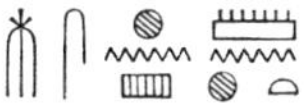 , B.D. 142, a goddess of childbirth.

Meskhenit-Menkhit 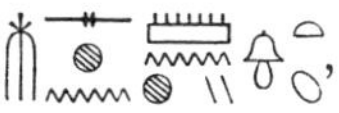, a hippopotamus-goddess who presided over the 4th epagomenal day (the birthday of Isis).

Meskhenit-Menkhit-Neb-t-ḥet 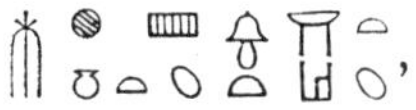, Denderah IV, 74, one of the four goddesses who presided over birth.

Meskhenit-Neferit , B.D. 142, a goddess of childbirth.

Meskhenit Nefertit 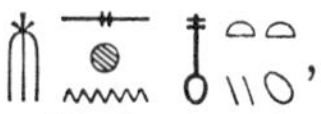, a hippopotamus-goddess who presided over the 2nd epagomenal day (the birthday of Ḥeru (Horus) and Ḥeru-ur).

Meskhenit-nefert-Åst 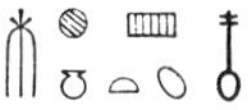  Denderah IV, 74, one of the four goddesses who presided over birth.

Meskhenit-Nekhtit 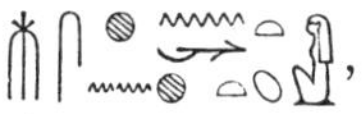, Berg. 73, a goddess of childbirth.

Meskhenit-Sebqit 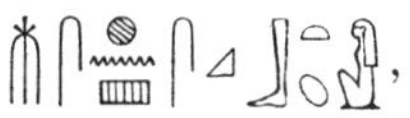, B.D. 142, a goddess of childbirth.

messhen 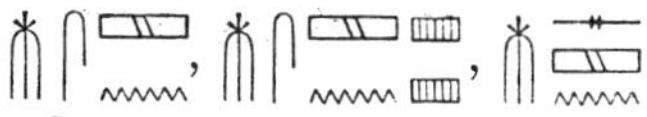 ; see .

messheṭ 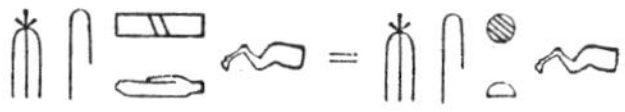, forearm.

Messheṭ , the Great Bear.

mesq , , skin, hide; see 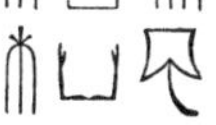.

mesq en Set , the hide of Set.

Mesq-t 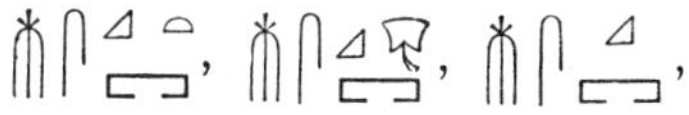, Culte 45, P.S.B. 15, 433, the house of the skin, or the chamber in which the bull's skin was kept.

Mesq-t 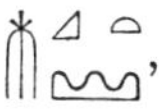, U. 418, 469, T. 220, 239, Metternich Stele 76, , B.D. 17, 122, 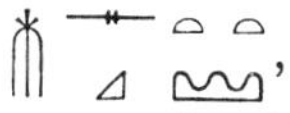, Rec. 31, 163: (1) the place of resurrection in heaven; (2) the place of resurrection on earth; (3) the chamber of the , or bull's skin, which was placed over the dead.

mesq 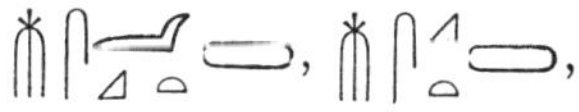, P. 184, N. 897, , Hymn Darius 14, a name of the sky.

Mesq-t seḥṭu 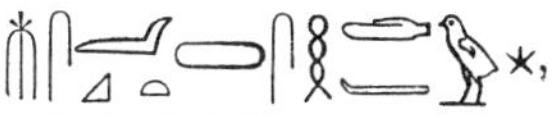, P. 184, 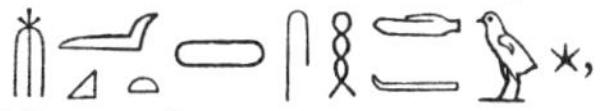, M. 294, 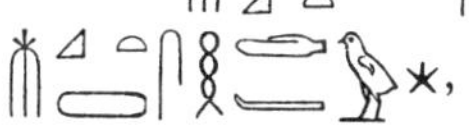, N. 897, a portion of the sky.

mesq , Hearst Pap. 8, 2, a leather tablet used by the sandalmaker,  , Festschrift 5.

mesq , to seize, to drag along.

mesq-t 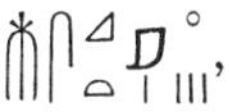, weapons, metal objects.

Mesqatt , Berg. II, 12, the region of resurrection in the Ṭuat.

Mesqen , B.D. 58, 2; see **Mesq-t.**

mesk-t 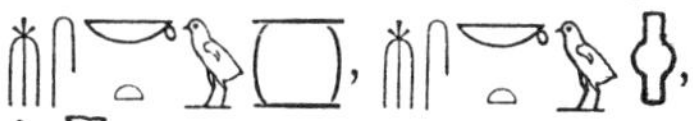, [illegible], IV, 671, armlet.

meska [illegible], N. 976, [illegible], the skin of an animal, the bull's skin in which the dead man was wrapped in order to effect his resurrection; plur. [illegible]; Décrets 29, [illegible], leathern objects, [illegible], P.S.B. 16, 132.

meska-t [illegible], [illegible], a leather tent, the chamber in the tomb, or Other World, in which the deceased was revivified.

meskȧ , Prisse 8, 16, 10, 1, 5, perhaps, a guess (?); Copt. ⲙⲉϣⲁⲕ (?)

meskȧ , Rev. 13, 20, 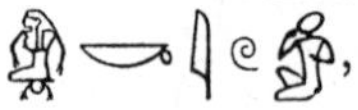, Rev. 14, 11, fault (?) mistake (?)

Mesktt , the boat of the setting sun; see **Semkett**  and **Sektt** 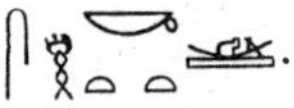.

mesg-t 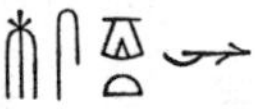, a bull's-skin bier, or the skin of a bull used in funerary ceremonies.

mest 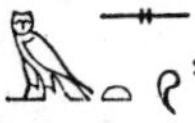, U. 125A, N. 434A, 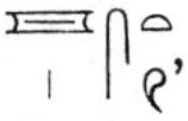, [illegible], liver.

mestti , thighs; see [illegible], T. 335.

mest , Rev. 13, 39, [illegible] , to hate; Copt. ⲙⲟⲥⲧⲉ.

mest 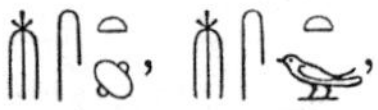, a hateful object, hatred = ; see [illegible].

Mest , son of Horus; see **Mestȧ**.

Mest Ȧsȧr , , Ṭuat II and IV, the name of the crook of Osiris.

Mestet 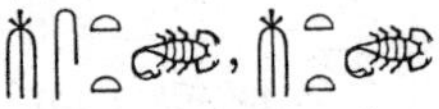, Metternich Stele 51, one of the seven scorpion-goddesses of Isis.

mesta 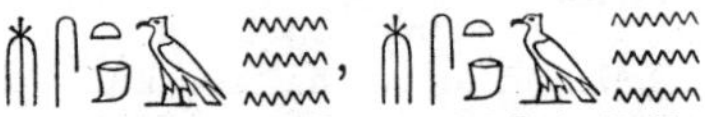 [illegible], Hearst Pap. 16, 12, [illegible], Hearst Pap. 14, 14,  [illegible], a medical solution, a decoction of herbs, a kind of medicated wine.

mesta, mestȧ  , Mar. Karn. 54, 46, a herb used in medicine, a bouquet of flowers (?)

mesta , Rec. 21, 91, [illegible] [illegible], a measure (for fish).

mestȧ 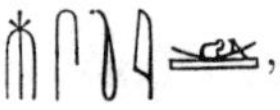, a boat, or part of a boat (?)

mestȧ , palette of a scribe.

mestȧ 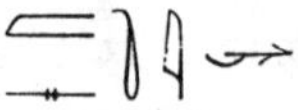, B.D. 175, 8, the writing palette of Thoth; see **gestȧ**.

mestȧ (gestȧ) ṭeb (tcheb) 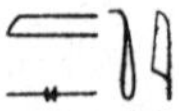 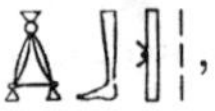, a palette furnished, *i.e.*, fitted with colours and reeds.

Mestȧ (Gestȧ ?)  [illegible], one of the four sons of Horus, god of the cardinal point of the north, and supporter of the northern quarter of heaven; he protected the stomach and large intestine of the dead.

mesti 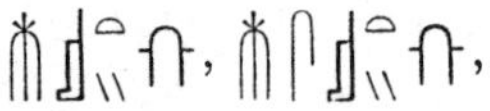, altar table, seat (?) bench (?)

Mesti 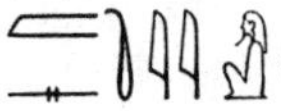, B.D. 99, 22, bolt of a plank in the magical boat.

Mestetf , Metternich Stele 51, one of the seven scorpion-goddesses of Isis.

mestem-t  [illegible], eye-paint, stibium; Copt. ⲥⲧⲏⲙ.

mestem , Love Songs 7, 4, , to smear the eyes with stibium.

mesten , a liquid used in embalming.

mester-t , stuff, cloth.

Mesth , the god of the 12th day of the month; he holds a lizard in each hand.

mesṭ 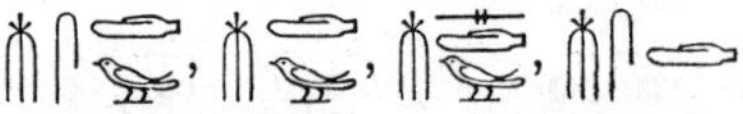 [illegible], to hate, to be at enmity with; Copt. ⲙⲟⲥⲧⲉ.

mesṭ neter , Excom. Stele 5, a person or thing hateful to the god.

mesṭeṭ  [illegible], to hate; Copt. ⲙⲟⲥⲧⲉ.

mesṭ  (Demotic forms), hate, hatred.

mesṭit , IV, 504, hatred, animosity, ill-will.

mesṭ-t 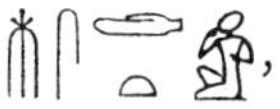, hateful, abominable thing.

mesṭu , Ȧmen. 22, 4, enemy.

mesṭṭ-t 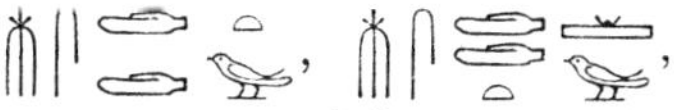, hateful person or thing, rival; 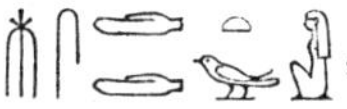, a woman hated or rejected by her husband.

mesṭeṭiu , IV, 480, , haters, enemies, foes, hostile.

mesṭ-t , Rec. 17, 145, a weight for meat.

mesṭti , nostrils; varr. [illegible].

mesṭ-t 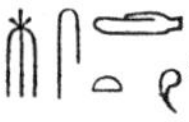 Love Songs 1, 2, breast; Copt. ⲙⲉⲥⲧⲉ.

mesṭ-t 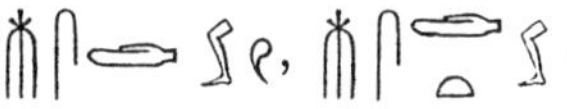, leg, thigh.

Mesṭ-t , B.D. 125, 3, 22, the mystical Leg in Sekhet-Ȧaru.

mesṭ-t , U. 528, garment, apparel.

mesṭ , Rec. 8, 9, a kind of grain, or seed, or stone.

mesṭi , Nȧstasen Stele 36, a kind of vessel.

mesṭem-t , , , eye-paint, stibium; see **mestem-t** and **mestchem-t**; Copt. ⲥⲧⲏⲙ, ⲉⲥⲑⲏⲙ.

mesṭem-t  [illegible], a substance used in medicine?

mesetch 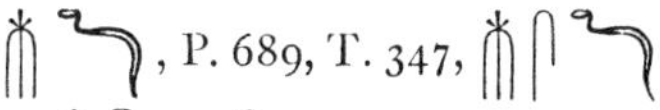, P. 689, T. 347, 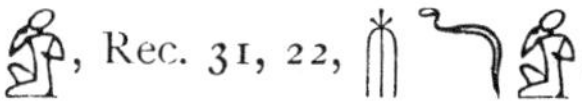, Rec. 31, 22, Hh. 238, to hate; Copt. ⲙⲟⲥⲧⲉ.

mesetchtch 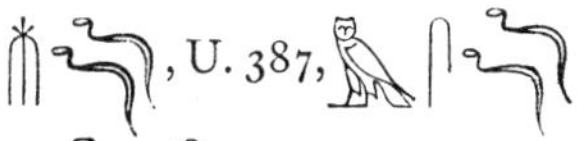, U. 387, , 347; var. U. 1, to hate.

mesetch-t , B.M. 797, hatred.

mesetchtchu , hater, foe, enemy.

Mesetchtch-qeṭ-t , B.D. 174, 5, a god.

mestchem-t , eye-paint, stibium; see **mestem-t** and **mesṭem-t**.

mestcher-t , 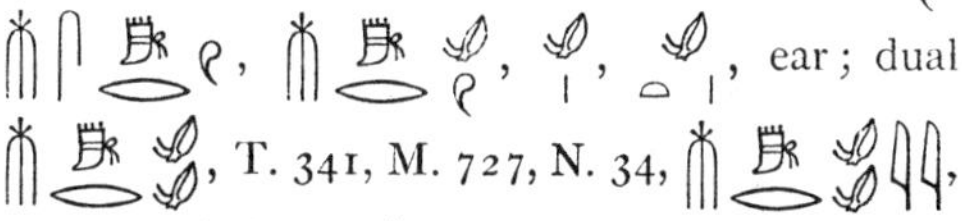, ear; dual, T. 341, M. 727, N. 34, P. 140, , N. 655, M. 214, N. 685, , Rev. 12, 64, , Rev. 12, 65; plur., N. 978; Copt. ⲙⲁⲁϫⲉ, ⲙⲁϣϫ.

Mestcher-ti (?) , a title of the high-priestess of Tanis.

Mestcherui , Ombos I, 1, 186, one of the 14 Kau of Osiris.

Mestcher-Saḥ , Tomb Seti I, one of the 36 Dekans.

mesh , Mar. Karn. 55, 71, to advance, to flow like a waterflood.

meshsh 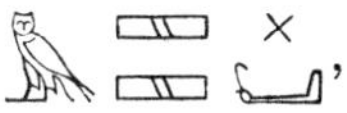, to clean, to polish (?) to rub (?)

meshsh 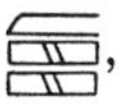, IV, 1121, a log of wood.

mshā, Rev. 11, 143, Rev. 11, 187, to march, to go; Copt. ⲙⲟⲟϣⲉ.

mshā, Chabas Mél. III, 2, 287, soldier, warrior; plur., IV, 323, Rec. 22, 2, 15.

mshā, Pap. 3024, 137, warship.

mshā, a bird.

mshā-t, Rec. 30, 67, cakes, bread.

mshi, Jour. As. 1908, 275, to wound; Copt. ⲙⲉϣ.

mshit, Rev., scales, balance; Copt. ⲙⲁϣⲉ, ⲙⲁϣⲓ.

meshmeshm-t, Hearst Pap. 12, 6, a kind of herb used in medicine.

meshen-t, P. 400, 676; varr., M. 571, N. 1177.

meshnui (?) . . . . . .

meshr, P. 204, N. 165, Rec. 31, 23, Metternich Stele 50, evening.

meshrut, U. 511, evening meal, supper, something hot (?); T. 325, T. 323, T. 287, P. 40.

msheṭ, passage, ford.

meqmeq, Rev. 14, 10, to consider, to ponder, to cogitate; Copt. ⲙⲟⲕⲙⲉⲕ.

meqer-t, A.Z. 1908, 15, an amulet in the form of a serpent's head.

meqeḥ, sorrow, grief, anxiety, mental pain; Copt. ⲙⲕⲁϩ.

Mqeṭqeṭ, the name of a god.

mek, U. 42, 236, 469, P. 97, 402, M. 575, 577 ff., N. 792, 1181, lo! behold!

meku, U. 235, T. 275, N. 67, lo! behold!

mek =, T. 202, protection (?)

meki, U. 457, protector.

mek-t, T. 321, Rec. 30, 198, protection.

meku, A.Z. 1908, 118, protecting, or protected, places.

mekuti (?), Rev. 11, 174, 12, 30, 42, camel cloth; Copt. ⲙⲟⲩⲕⲉ.

meka-t, station, place.

mekȧ, Annales IX, 156, a plant.

mekerr, blue; Copt. ⲙϣⲓⲣ (?)

meker, liar; Copt. ϭⲟⲗ.

mekes, U. 207, P. 701, Rec. 35, 192, sceptre, staff of authority.

mekṭa, Rev. 12, 36, to mix, mixture (?); Copt. ⲙⲟⲩϫⲧ.

mektȧr, tower, Copt. ⲙⲉϭⲧⲟⲗ, Heb. מִגְדֹּל.

mgi, bravery (?)

meg, Hymn to Nile, 2, 13, crier.

mega, crocodile.

Mega, B.M. 32, 91, a fiend who carried away the arm of Rā.

mgaḥu, afflicted; Copt. ⲙⲕⲁϩ.

mgat . . . mi, Ḥerusȧtef Stele, 49, a vessel used in a temple.

meger (?), mortar (?)

megru, things pounded (?)

megerg, the name of a vase or vessel.

met, "de sorte que" (Revillout).

met er, U. 190 = , T. 69, between.

met, ten; Copt. ⲙⲏⲧ; , the ten-day week.

met-ṭua, fifteen; Copt. ⲙⲉⲧⲧⲓⲟⲩ; , Rec. 5, 95, eighteen; , a house of ten at Abydos; , M. 92, P. 123, ten chiefs of Memphis; , M. 92, P. 123, ten chiefs of Heliopolis; , chief of the Ten of the South.

met-nu, tenth; fem. , tenth.

met-ṭua, , , the festival of the 15th day of the month.

Met-sȧs (?), a name or title of Hathor of Lycopolis.

met, death; see **mut.**

met, Ḥerusȧtef Stele 70, male, man; , , , , phallus.

metu, , U. 629, man as a begetter; , N. 812.

met, metut, , U. 260, P. 198, N. 933, , U. 553, , T. 23, , P. 729, , M. 148, N. 650, , P. 690, , P. 216, , T. 297, , Rec. 27, 56, , , , , , , seed, offspring, descendants, posterity.

metut neter, N. 1093, , P. 635, the emission of the god; , Rec. 16, 132.

metut ḥeḥ, seed of eternity; , the generations of men and women.

metmet, a room in a house, sleeping apartment (?)

met en ȧst, I, 102. . . . . . .

met (mut), , , , mother, wife; see **mut**; var.

met ḥent, concubine; plur. , .

met, milch cow.

met, chief, governor, president.

met en sa, , president of an order of priests; var. , A.Z. 1899, 94, Kahun, 11, 17.

met ta, governor of a district.

met, , , , vein, artery; plur. , ,

; Copt. ⲙⲟⲩⲧ; , Rec. 36, 133, , IV, 1219, vessels of the body.

metu-t , , , , , poison, venom; Copt. ⲙⲁⲧⲟⲩ. Late forms: , , Jour. As. 1908, 258.

met , , , inundation, the emission of the Nile-god; var. .

met , Åmen. 7, 2, 18, 22, 26, 18, canal bank.

meti , Rev. 13, 40, abyss; Copt. ⲙⲧⲟ.

met-t , , the middle of anything; Copt. ⲙⲏⲧⲉ.

meti-t , Rev. 13, 41, the middle.

meti , Rev. 11, 137, , Rev. 11, 143, middle; Copt. ⲙⲏⲧⲉ.

met-t , , noon, mid-day; Copt. ⲙⲉⲉⲣⲉ; see

met-t , , , , , , , right, rightly, exact, regular, fittingly, to be right, correct; = .

met-ti , Mar. Karn. 52, 20, Treaty 14, , , Rec. 27, 230, what is right, or usual, or customary, or has always been; = .

metit , , IV, 994, Rec. 31, 147, righteousness, integrity.

metu (metru) , , Åmen. 17, 12, right order, correct arrangement; , IV, 969, right laws.

met-t , Annales III, 110, an obligatory offering.

met-ti åb (?) , Rec. 20, 41, , Gol. 12, 105, right disposition, suitable, conformable.

met-ti er , coinciding with; see **meter.**

met-ti ḥati , true hearts, right dispositions.

met-t (meter-t) , , , , attestation, testimony, declaration, evidence.

metiu (metriu) , Åmen. 20, 11, witnesses.

met-ti (meter-ti) maāt , , IV, 992, testifier to the truth, true witness, agreeing with the truth.

met , Rev. 11, 184, justice; see **meter.**

Metmet (?) , Ṭuat V, a serpent-god.

metmet , IV, 364, , , to pry into (?)

met , IV, 1122, , IV, 1148, , P. 611, a kind of Sûdânî cloth or linen, rope, cord; var. , I, 77.

met , jar.

met , neck (?); Copt. ⲙⲟϯ.

met , unguent, little ball (?)

mett en maā , Rev. 11, 125, true speech; Copt. ϫⲓⲛⲙⲙⲉ.

meta .... (?) , U. 321 ......

meta , U. 111, N. 420, a cake.

Meta-ā (?) , Ṭuat VII, a star-god.

metauḥu 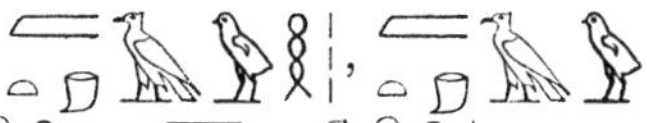, 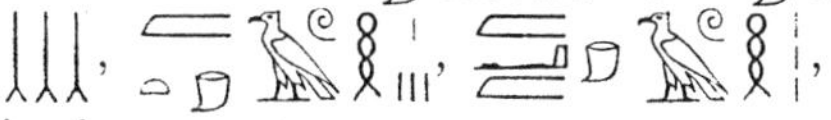, tools, implements, staves.

metȧ , Rev., to be pleased, content; Copt. ⲙⲁϯ.

metȧ , T. 302, , Rec 31, 119, cord, rope.

met-ā (?) 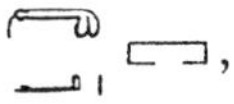, house, abode (?)

meti , Rev. 12, 41, to call; Copt. ⲙⲟⲩⲧⲉ.

meti , Rev. 11, 157, 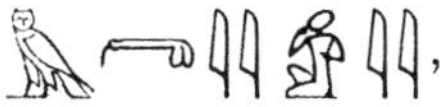, Rev., to be content, satisfied; Copt. ⲙⲁϯ.

meti 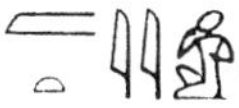, Rev. 13, 67, to occupy, to take possession.

meti , Rev. 12, 30, 31, Nubian guardian, soldier, policeman; Copt. ⲙⲁⲧⲟⲓ.

Meti 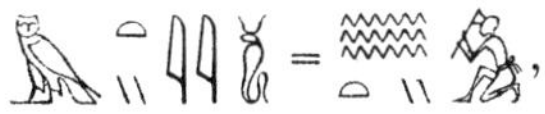, the name of a fiend.

mtu  = Copt. ⲛ̀ⲧⲉ, ⲛ̀ⲧⲁ, with.

mtutu , , the impersonal "one."

mtut , M. 122, N. 646, "one."

metu , scabbard of a sword (?)

metu . . . . , Ḥerusȧtef Stele 103 . . . . . .

mtui , Rev. 12, 31, 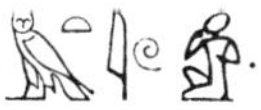.

mtuf , Jour. As. 1908, 267 = Copt. ⲛ̀ⲧⲁϥ.

mtun , Rev. 11, 163 = Copt. ⲛ̀ⲧⲉⲛ, we.

metun (?) , a lassoed ox.

metun , Sallier II, 1, 8, Rec. 36, 16, arena, place where the sacrificial bulls were hunted, or made to fight (?)

mtuten , Rec. 21, 98 = Copt. ⲛ̀ⲧⲉⲧⲛ̄, ye.

metpen-t 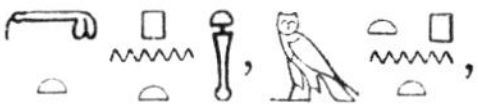, dagger, poignard.

metf-t , poignard, dagger.

metmet , Rec. 32, 67; see **ḥenmemet**.

meten 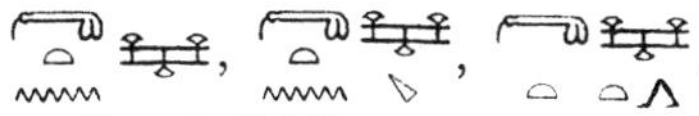, way, road, path; 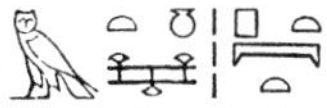, path of heaven, *i.e.*, courses of the heavenly bodies; Copt. ⲙⲱⲓⲧ; var.  , IV, 863.

metenu 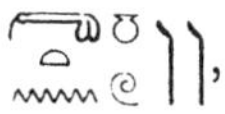, A.Z. 1905, 103, right, correct.

metenu-t 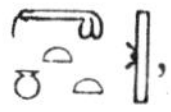, IV, 202, reward.

meten 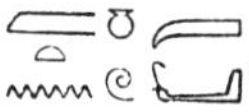, Rec. 24, 185, 186, to decorate a stone with designs.

metnit 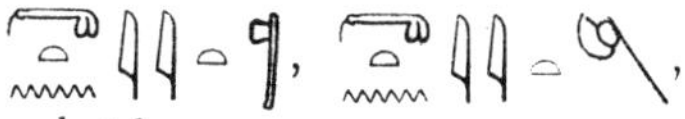, A.Z. 1870, 171, battleaxe.

metenu , knife.

meter-t 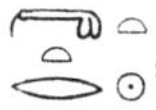, IV, 39, noon, mid-day; , Rev. 6, 26, time of mid-day; Copt. ⲙⲉⲉⲣⲉ.

meter-t 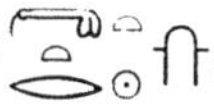, Rev. 8, 171, day-couch.

meter [illegible], presence, the being present or in front of; Copt. ⲙ̄ⲙ̄ⲧⲟ.

meter [illegible], to be right, right, correct, exact, just.

meter [illegible], P. 185, M. 296, [illegible], N. 898, [illegible], U. 454, [illegible], U. 470, [illegible],

, Jour. As. 1908, 253, , Rev. 11, 140, , Rev. 13, 25, to bear testimony, to give evidence; , Anastasi I, 215, "I beg you to inform me"; Copt. ⲙⲉⲑⲣⲉ.

meter , P. 185, , M. 296, , N. 898, , IV, 974, , witness; plur. , Thes. 1297, , A.Z. 1906, 29, many witnesses; Copt. ⲙⲛ̄ⲧⲣⲉ, ⲙⲉⲑⲣⲉ.

metru , Mar. Karn. 52, 11, spies, scouts.

meter , old decisions brought forward as witnesses, old saws quoted; , well-attested integrity; , well-seasoned trees.

Meter — , M. 224, , N. 601 = , U. 190, , T. 69.

meter , bad (false?) testimony, damning evidence.

metrit , integrity, uprightness.

Metrit , a goddess.

Metrui , Ṭuat VIII, one of the bodyguard of Rā.

meter , staff, stick, weapon.

metri-t , Koller Pap. 2, 8, part of a boat's tackle.

meter-t , Koller Pap. 7, 1 . . . .

meter , Rev. 14, 12, , marsh (?) swamp (?)

meteḥ (?) , Rev. 11, 169, , Rev. 11, 173, tied; Copt. ⲙⲟⲩϫϩ, ⲙⲟϫϩ.

metes , knife, weapon.

meteg , bakery; Copt. ⲙⲁⲛⲧⲱϭ (?)

metgi , Rev. 12, 55, part, portion; Copt. ⲙⲟⲩϫⲓ.

meth-t , mother; see **mu-t** .

meth , to die, dead; see **mut** .

metha , Rec. 32, 230, , , IV, 840, to make a claim, to demand a thing insolently, to flout, to insult.

methpen-t , an amulet made of .

methen , , P. 185, way, road, path; plur. .

methni , guide, conductor of a caravan.

Methen , M. 296, , N. 898, the Road-god.

methsu (?) , Rec. 31, 21 . . . . .

meṭu , P. 601, , P. 676, , U. 632, , IV, 968, , , , , , ,

, , , , , to speak, to talk, to say; , U. 632; Copt. ⲙⲟⲩⲧⲉ.

meṭu , P. 365, , N. 1078, , , U. 1, , T. 245, 342, , U. 631 (= , T. 306, , T. 307), , P. 745, M. 754, ; plur. , , , , , , , word, speech, command, order; , a lie.

meṭ-t , , U. 209, , , , , III, 141, , , word, speech, maxim, proverb, decree, verdict, sentence, business, affair, things, talk, opportunity; plur. , , , , , , , , , word, speech; Copt. ⲙⲛ̄ⲧ.

meṭ , Rec. 16, 57, lie, falsehood.

meṭ-t , Rev. 14, 35, , Rev. 11, 178, a foreign speech.

meṭ-ti , a talkative man, chatterer.

meṭut āaiut , high sounding words, boastful words.

meṭ-t bȧn-t , evil word, speech of ill omen, curse.

meṭu pet , P. 304, word of the sky, *i.e.*, thunder.

meṭ-t per nesu , IV, 1031, palace affairs or gossip.

meṭ-t mut , word of death, condemnation, death sentence.

meṭut en per-ā-ȧb , words of pride.

meṭut ent maāt , words of truth or law, legal affairs, or matters, or business.

meṭut en ḥap , , words of hiddenness, *i.e.*, crafty or deceitful words or actions.

meṭut en sa en Ȧṭḥ, etc. , Anastasi I, 28, 6, words of a Delta man with a man of Abu (Elephantine).

meṭut en senmef , Rec 5, 97, last year's words.

meṭ-t nefer-t , , fair speech, smooth words.

meṭut neter , , , , , , hieroglyphs, "words of the god" [Thoth].

meṭu ra en Kam-t , "word of the mouth of Egypt," *i.e.*, the Egyptian language.

meṭ-t khas-t , foul speech, vile words, rebellious words.

meṭut ṭut , evil things or words.

meṭu ṭerf , B.D. 182, 4, word of wisdom (?)

Meṭu-ȧakhut-f , , Litanie 57, a form of the Sun-god.

Meṭu-ȧakhut-f, Tomb Seti I, a ram-headed god, one of the 75 forms of Rā (No. 57).

Meṭ-en-Ȧsȧr, Ṭuat II, a serpent-god.

Meṭ-ḥer, Ṭuat VI, a benevolent god of the dead.

Meṭu-ta-f, B.D. 189, 8, the name of a god.

meṭ, stick, staff; plur., P. 342.

meṭ Ȧnu, "staff of Ȧnu," the name of an amulet.

meṭ, Rec. 30, 66, parts of a boat or ship.

meṭ, A.Z. 1867, 105, to strike.

meṭiu (?) nubu, gold workers (?) tools for working gold.

meṭu, Denderah III, 63: (1) the sceptre of Isis-Hathor; (2) the holy sceptre of Ḥeru-Beḥuṭi; (3) the holy sceptre of Osiris (Ṭuat II).

Meṭi, Ṭuat I, a hawk-headed god with a serpent staff.

meṭ-t, salve, unguent; see .

Meṭ-t-qa-utchebu, the name of the 10th division of the Ṭuat.

mṭa, a preposition = ⲛ̀ⲧⲉ, ⲛ̀ⲧⲁ.

Meṭȧ, P. 695, a god (?)

Meṭiu, Medes; Pers. (the country), Babyl. .

M'ṭiṭi (?), Rougé I.H. 144, 47, the name of a Libyan rebel.

mṭun = Copt. ⲛ̀ⲧⲟⲟⲩⲛ, in any case, at any rate, by all means, certainly, assuredly, undoubtedly; Gr. οὖν.

Meṭni, a hippopotamus-god, a god of evil.

meṭeḥ, the name of a crown.

meṭeḥ, Ȧmen. 13, 19, to tie (?)

meṭeḥ, , , , to work in wood, to cut, to saw wood, to work as a carpenter.

meṭes, U. 510, 553, a knife, something sharp; var. .

Meṭes, Ṭuat XI, a doorkeeper-god.

Meṭes, Hh. 423, a god; plur., U. 420, , T. 240.

Meṭes-ȧb, Berg. I, 10, an ibis-headed god

Meṭes-mau (?), Ṭuat IV, the door of the 3rd section of Rastau.

Meṭes-en-neḥeḥ, Ṭuat IV, the door of the 4th section of Rastau.

Meṭes-neshen, Rec. 16, 132, a god.

Meṭes-ḥer, Ṭuat VII, a lynx-goddess, a defender of Ȧf.

Meṭes-ḥer-ȧri-she, B.D. 144, the herald of the 6th Ārit.

Meṭes-sen (?), the name of the doors of the 7th Ārit.

meṭsu, distinguished.

metch-t, U. 56, , , , , oil, unguent, salve, ointment and pomade, both scented and unscented; var. .

metch , to be deep; , deep; , , Hymn Darius 18, doubly deep.

metchut , , , , , , , , a deep place, deep, pit, cavern extending underground, the subterranean shrine of a god; plur. , ; , U. 418, and see P. 453, two caverns; Copt. ⲙ̅ⲧⲱ.

Metch-t , Ṭuat VI, a gulf in the Other World.

Metch-t-nebt-Ṭuat , the name of the 6th division of the Ṭuat.

Metch-t-qa-utchebu , the name of the 10th division of the Ṭuat.

metch-t , cattle pen, byre; plur. , ; , stalled oxen.

metchut , N. 1386, shelters for cattle in the fields, stalls for cattle.

metch (?) (reading unknown), a measure of capacity = 160 to 165 henu, or 78·78 litres = the old Ptolemaic medimnus.

metchu , I, 77, cord, rope; see , P. 611.

metcha-t , Rev. 14, 49, a measure.

metcha-t , , , chisel, a cutting tool; Copt. ⲙⲁⲭⲓ (?)

metcha , Gol. 13, 113, to destroy, to slay (?)

Metcha , N. 956, the name of a god.

metcha-t , U. 601, book, written roll, decree, writing, manuscript, edict, order, liturgy, document, deed, draft, letter, epistle; plur. ; Copt. ⲭⲱⲱⲙⲉ (?)

metcha-t may be the reading of , , , , ; , Thes. 1295, divine literature; , book of destruction.

metcha-t , , , , , letter, writing, book; plur. , , A.Z. 1908, 114, , , U. 524, T. 331; , Book of the 75 addresses to Rā; , Book of traversing Eternity; , B.D. 162, 13.

metcha-t ent ṭua , Book of Praise.

metcha-t ent ṭua Rā , "Book of the praise of Rā," the title of the great Solar Litany.

metcha-t neter , sacred book or writing; , books of words of the gods, *i.e.*, hieroglyphic papyri.

metcha-t (?) , A.Z. 1899, 72, , Coronation Stele 4, men of books, scribes.

metchau .... , A.Z. 1899, 94, the title of a priest.

metchami (?) , Rev. 14, 16, devourer.

metchab , to restrain, to fetter.

metchab-t , Hh. 479, , , Rec. 30, 67, , vessel used for baling (?)

metchaḥ 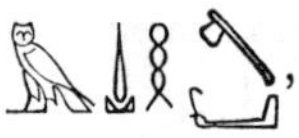, to hew, to chop, to fell a tree.

metcher , U. 607, , , U. 458, 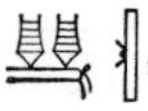, T. 282, Rec. 29, 78, to press, to urge, to be strenuous; , IV, 208, to follow a course of action closely, to be a faithful follower; , E.T. I, 53; , to compel someone to wonder or admire.

metcher-t , Ȧmen. 11, 17, , I, 14, pressure, urgency.

metcher-t , , Décrets 15, 48, impost, tax, charge, burden.

Metcher , the name of a fiend or devil.

Metcher , a walled district; compare Heb. מָצוֹר. The name מִצְרַיִם may have been given to Egypt in respect of its double wall; see Spiegelberg in Rec. 21, 41.

metcherȧ , Mar. Karn. 15, 6, tower, fort.

metcheḥ , to bind; Copt. ⲙⲟϫϩ.

metcheḥ , N. 1217, , P. 428, M. 612, girdle; Copt. ⲙⲟⲩϫϩ.

metcheḥ , P. 428, M. 612, N. 1216, pike, dagger.

metcheḥu 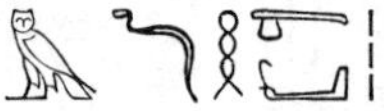, IV, 707, 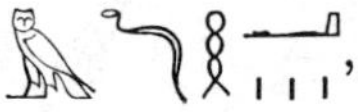, tools or weapons.

metcheṭ , P. 187, M. 348, N. 901, , 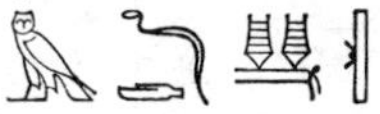 (later form of **metcher**), to press, to urge, to be strenuous, to strike.

metcheṭ-t , 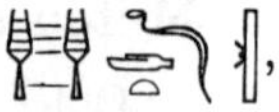, violence, strength, zealous, strenuous.

Metcheṭ-t-ȧt , N. 956, a god.

metcheṭṭef-t , a tool.

N

n, Heb. נ; = ñ in Spanish and Amharic ኘ.

n = , , .

n pers. pron. 1st plur.: we, us, our; Copt. ⲛ.

n , , , , Rec. 27, 83, a mark of the genitive masc. sing.: belonging to; see also , **ni** ; Copt. ⲛ̄.

n-t , , , a mark of the genitive, sing. and plur.

n , often placed before the infinitive: while, as long as, because, since, as, on account of, in respect of.

n , , a conjunctive particle: for, then.

n , , , , a preposition: for, to, on account of, in; Copt. ⲛ̄, ⲛⲁ.

n āb , opposite, facing, along with.

n uaḥ er , in addition to.

n mȧ , like.

n mbaḥ , before, in the presence of.

n men-t , , daily; Copt. ⲙ̄ⲙⲏⲛⲉ.

n meru , , , , Rec. 3, 116, , , so that, in order that.

n neḥeḥ , , for ever.

n ra , Jour. As. 1908, 265, = .

n ḥa , behind, about.

n ḥer , , at, upon; varr. , , .

n khen n benr , inside and outside.

n kher , , with, by.

n tchet , for ever.

n , a particle.

n tuti , Rec. 17, 44 . . . .

n , to turn (?) to come (?)

n (?) , Nȧstasen Stele 36 . . . . . .

n, nn , , , U. 520, , T. 329, P. 315, , , , , T. 623, P. 582, , Rec. 32, 179, no, not; Copt. ⲛ̄; compare Heb. לא.

nn , Peasant 200, no, not so (in answer to a question).

n-t , U. 213, , , , without, destitute of, not possessing; Copt. ⲁⲧ (for **ant**).

ntu , N. 177, , , , a particle of negation.

ntu (for **nti**) , , without, destitute, not possessing.

nti , Ȧmen. 16, 3, 27, 5, , , , , , empty of, destitute of, not possessing, without; Copt. ⲁⲧ.

nti , destitute man, , , a man of nothingness, worthless, poor man.

ntiu (plur. of **nti**) , , N. 960, , Rec. 31, 174,

, Rec. 33, 34, , IV, 1076, , IV, 989, , Dream Stele 38, , , , , , , , (var.), the poor, the destitute, the worthless, the damned.

ntiu , Ṭuat V, the non-existent, a name of the wicked.

nn ȧabu , , ceaselessly.

nn ȧu , faultless.

nn ȧu mȧ , IV, 1073 . . . . . .

n ȧu gert nn ȧri-ntu , most assuredly there cannot be done.

n ȧs, nn ȧs , Rec. 31, 31, , , , unless, except only; , I, 147.

nti ȧsi , imperishable.

nn uā , no one.

nn un, nn unt , , , non-existent; Copt. ⲙⲙⲛ̄; later , ; see Rec. 21, 42.

nn un mṭaf = Copt. ⲉⲙⲛ̄ⲧⲁϥ; see Rec. 21, 42.

nn urṭ , , unresting, unceasing.

n ush , Rev. 14, 16, without; Copt. ⲛⲟⲩⲉϣ.

nti uteb , immutable.

ntt begg , untiring, unresting.

nn paut , A.Z. 1907, 58, never, at no time.

nt per , unseen, invisible.

n petrȧ , unobserved, invisible.

n maa , , , , , , , unseen, invisible, sightless, eyeless, blind, unseeing.

n maā-t , unrighteousness.

n mu , , waterless, arid, desert.

ntt mut , , motherless.

n meḥ , , , , , unplated (?)

nn nu , unseeing, blind.

nn nefu , airless.

nti nen , Rec. 32, 177, unfailing.

n netchnetch-t , incontrovertible, indisputable, not to be gainsaid.

nn re , , numberless, innumerable.

nn ruṭ-f , growthless, barren land.

nn rekh , , , , unknown, unknowing, ignorant; plur. , .

nn erṭat , not allowable.

nti ḥa-ti , Rec. 2, 109, senseless man, fool.

nti khet , , destitute, indigent, possessionless.

nn kheper , uncreate.

n khemu , , U. 322, unknowing.

nti khesef , irresistible; plur. .

nn sep 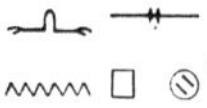, no time, never;   (or ), never before.

nn smȧ , untold, indescribable, unimaginable.

nn smen 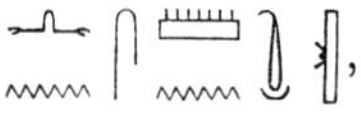, unstable, instability.

nti sen , without second, unique.

nn sekh-t , unseamed, without join.

nti sesh , intransient, impassable.

nti sek 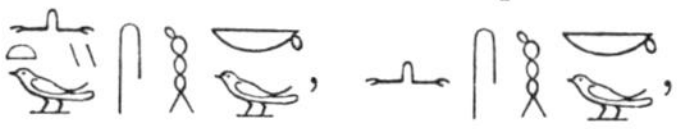, 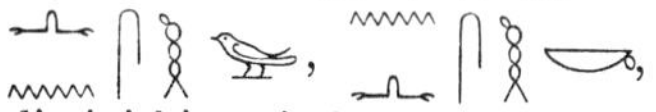, Rec. 2, 30, undiminishing, indestructible, never-failing, incorruptible.

N-sek-f , IV, 366, the name of a star.

nn stut , unusual, unwonted.

n setem , disobedient, deaf (?)

nn seṭ , unslit, unsplit, intact.

nn shenā 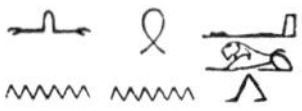, unrepulsed.

nn kat 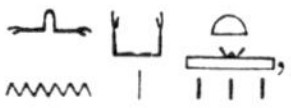, unemployed, idle, workless.

nn ṭenu , without division.

Nna-ruṭf-t ; see **Nruṭf** 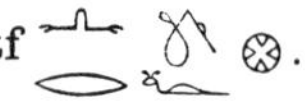.

Nȧa-rruṭf , ; see **Nruṭf** .

N-ȧri-nef Nebȧt-f  , the god of the 11th hour of the day.

N-urṭ-f 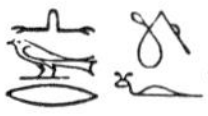, "He who rests not" —a title of Osiris.

N-urtch-nef 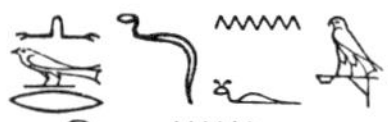, P. 480, N. 7, 1268, 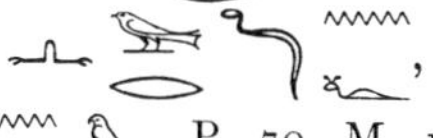, N. 848,  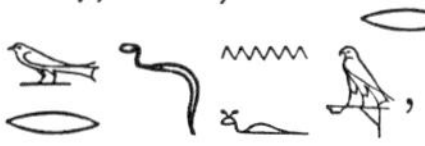, P. 70, M. 101, a title of Osiris.

Nn-rekh 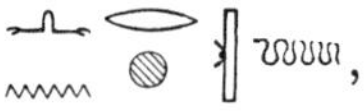, the name of a serpent deity.

N-erṭa-nef-besf-khenti-hehf  , B.D. 17, 103, one of the seven spirits who guarded the body of Osiris.

N-erṭa-nef-nebt , Berg. I, 3, , Edfû I, 10c, one of the eight sharp-eyed custodians of the body of Osiris.

N-ḥeri-rtit-sa 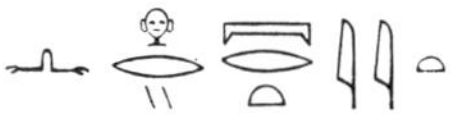 [illegible], B.D. 69, 15, 70, 1, a god.

N-ger-s [illegible], B.D. 149, the god of the 8th Ȧat; varr. [illegible], [illegible], [illegible], [illegible], [illegible], [illegible], [illegible], [illegible].

Nti-she-f [illegible], B.D. 64, 14, a title of a god.

N-tcher-f [illegible], P. 64, [illegible], M. 745, a god, son of Ḥetepi and Urrtȧ.

na [illegible] = [illegible], not.

na [illegible] = Copt. ⲛⲉ.

na [illegible] = Copt. ⲛⲁ, prefixed to words, *e.g.*, [illegible], ⲛⲁⲁ great; [illegible], ⲛⲁⲛⲉ nice, pretty; [illegible], ⲛⲁϣⲉ many, etc.

na [illegible], a demonstrative particle: this, these, [illegible], [illegible], [illegible], [illegible], [illegible], [illegible], IV, 102.

na, U. 196, these = , T. 75, , M. 229, , N. 607.

nau , , T. 75, M. 229, , , these, these who are; , these are they who are behind.

na , wind, air, breeze; plur. ; var. .

naȧ , Rev. 11, 132, 174, their; Copt. ⲛⲉⲩ; , his; Copt. ⲛⲁⲓϥ; , Rev. 11, 149, our; Copt. ⲛⲉⲛ; , Rev. 14, 11, , Rev. 11, 141, , Rev. 11, 134, your; Copt. ⲛⲉⲧⲉⲛ.

naȧt , , Rev. 13, 34 = Copt. ⲛⲉⲧ, those who.

naȧ-t , , Metternich Stele 48, abode, house, prison (?); Heb. נָא, Jeremiah xlvi, 25, Ezekiel xxx, 14.

naȧ ḥerf , Rev. 11, 186, with him; Copt. ⲛⲁϩⲣⲁϥ.

Naȧb , Berg. I, 10, a bird-headed fire-god.

naȧb , Rec. 19, 95, part of a shrine; Copt. ⲛⲁⲃⲓ.

Naȧrik , B.D. 165, 3, a name of a god; var. .

Naȧ-rruṭ , a name of the shrine of Osiris at Ḥensu (Khânês); varr. , ; see **N-ruṭ-f** .

naā , Rev. 11, 185, , Rev. 13, 2, great, greatness; Copt. ⲛⲁⲁⲁ, ⲛⲁⲁ.

naānu , Rev. 11, 185, good, beautiful; Copt. ⲛⲁⲛⲟⲩ, ⲉⲛⲁⲛⲟⲩ; , Rev. 13, 78 = Copt. ⲉⲛⲁⲛⲟⲩⲥ.

naārana , , , young soldier; plur. , , , Anastasi I, 17, 3; compare Heb. נַעַר.

naāsh , , Rev. 13, 29, many; Copt. ⲛⲁϣⲉ, ⲉⲛⲁϣⲉ, ⲉⲛⲁϣⲱⲟⲩ.

naāsha , , , , Rougé I.H., II, 125, to be strong, to be great; the late form is ; Copt. ⲛⲁϣⲉ.

nai = Copt. ⲛⲟⲩ-, ⲛⲉ-.

nai , , Israel Stele 11, this, these; Copt. ⲛⲁⲓ. With suffixes:— , , Rev. 11, 179, , my; , Ȧmen. 5, 9, , , thy; , his; , Ḥerusȧtef Stele 75, , hers; , our; , Rec. 21, 97, , Rec. 21, 97, , , , Israel Stele 23, , Rev. 11, 184, their.

nai , Rev. 13, 28, yet, again.

nai-t , P.S.B. 12, 125, house, abode; plur. , Hymn to Nile, 2, 10, , , , .

naiāru , canals, rivers ; compare Heb. נהר.

nau , gift, present, largesse.

nau, nȧau , , ibex ; plur. , IV, 741.

nau, nu , Koller Pap. 3, 6, , Rec. 4, 30, ostrich ; var. .

nau , Koller Pap. 1, 6, weapon (of Kheta ).

nau-t 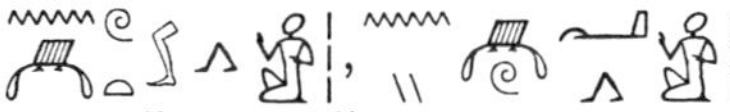, Israel Stele 23, Libyan soldiers.

nau-t , U. 323, plant, leaf, foliage ; plur. , T. 311, herbs, pasture.

nauatha, nauathan 
, Champoll. Mon. 223, 
, Thes. 1204, ,
, to move quickly, to tremble, to shake ; compare נוס.

naur , Rev. 13, 6, great.

nab-t , Litanie 53, lock of hair, tress ; plur. 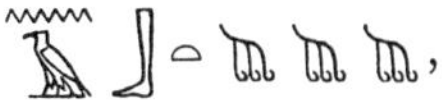, T. 240.

nabenu 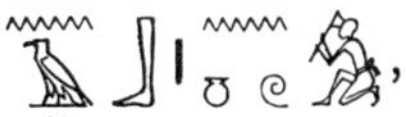, to be bad, evil, wicked, hostile.

Nabkhun 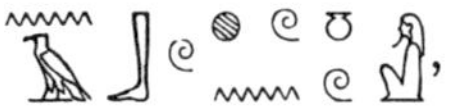, Demot. Cat. 422, the temple of Sebek at Gebelên ; Gr. Νεβχουνις (?)

nabḥnu 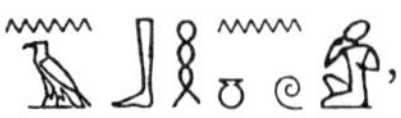, to bark, to bay (of a dog) ; Heb. נָבַח, Arab. نبح.

Nabti  Ṭuat I, a pilot of the boat of the Beetle.

Namart , , Nimrod ; Heb. נִמְרֹד.

namenkh 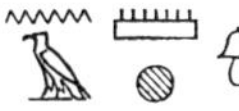, beneficent.

namesmes 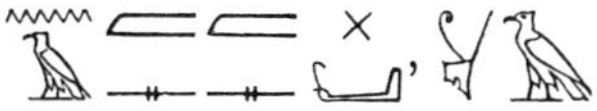
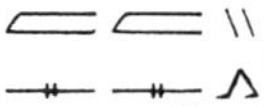, to overflow ; see 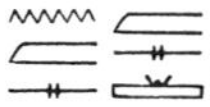 ; the true reading is **ngesges**.

nan , to proclaim ; see [illegible]
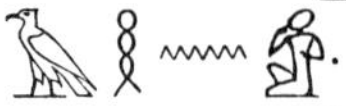.

nanaiu , foreigners.

nani-t 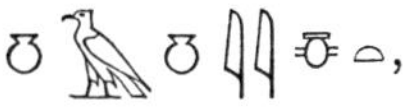, Rev. 13, 21, honeycomb.

nanu , Rev. 14, 10 = , grains.

nanefru , the benevolent.

nanefr-t 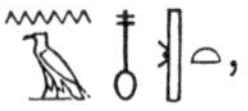, Jour. As. 1908, 308, goodness ; Copt. ⲛⲟⲩϥⲣⲉ.

Na-nefer-ȧri-Sheṭit [illegible]
[illegible], a title (Demotic period).

Nanefrsheṭi [illegible], the name of a goddess.

nar [illegible], B.D. 137, 20, 23 . . . . . .

Narḥ [illegible], Ṭuat II, a god.

nahama [illegible],
[illegible], a plant or twig used in medicine.

nahra [illegible], Thes. 1202, to flow away ; Heb. נהר.

naḥeḥ [illegible], eternal.

naḥa [illegible], Anastasi I, 237,
[illegible], foul, stinking, bad ;
[illegible], Koller Pap. 2, 6, Anastasi IV, 2, 8, [illegible], contrary winds, head winds, stormy winds.

naḥa , Anastasi I, 243, a strong-smelling plant, thorny growth, scrub, bush.

naḥi 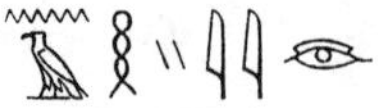, to make a sign with the eye, to wink (?)

naḥn 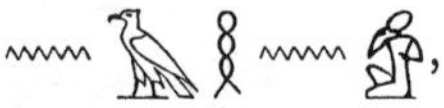, to proclaim, proclamation.

Naḥsu , IV, 716, the Blacks of the Sûdân.

naḥsha 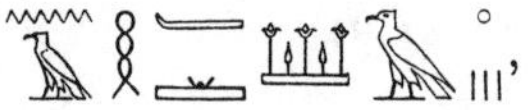, a seed or grain used in medicine.

nasaq , to cut, to stab, to prick, to separate.

Nasaqbu, Nasaqbubu , B.D. 165, 7, a name or title of Åmen.

nask 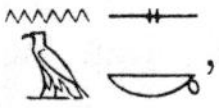, disturbed, distorted.

Nashutnen 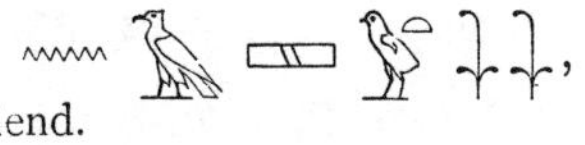, U. 550, a serpent-fiend.

nasht 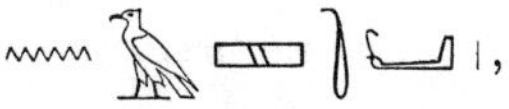, Rev. 13, 13, 22, strength; Copt. ⲛⲁϣⲧⲉ.

naqi , great, exalted; Copt. ⲛⲟϭ.

naaq (?) 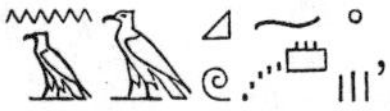, Israel Stele 7, grain.

naqeṭiṭ 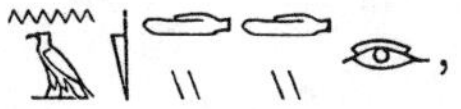, Anastasi I, 25, 7, Sphinx III, 211, sleep; Copt. ⲛ̄ⲕⲟⲧⲕ̄.

nakāiu , stone-cutters.

Natkarti 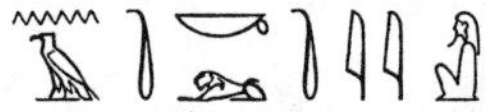, B.D. 165, 1, a Nubian title of Åmen.

nathakhi , castanets, clappers.

naatch , unjust; compare Copt. ⲟϫⲓ.

natchar 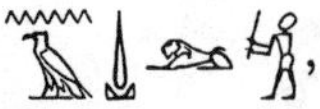, Demot. Cat. 408, to be grown up.

nȧ 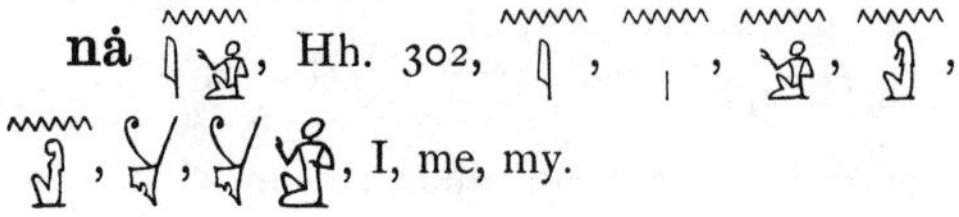, Hh. 302, I, me, my.

nȧ 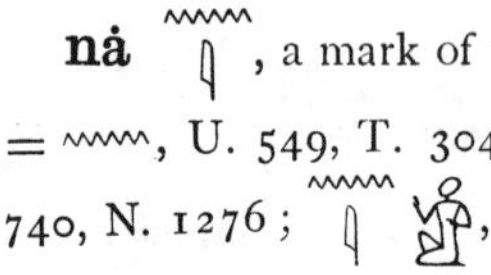, a mark of the genitive masc. sing. =, U. 549, T. 304, P. 421, 672, M. 661, 740, N. 1276; Rec. 27, 54.

nȧ 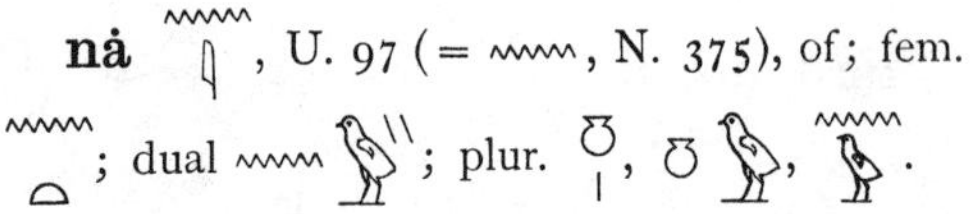, U. 97 (=, N. 375), of; fem.; dual; plur.

nȧ, ni 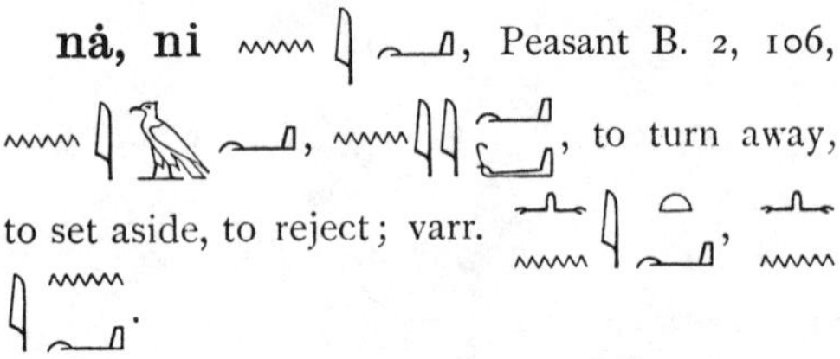, Peasant B. 2, 106, to turn away, to set aside, to reject; varr.

nȧ , a kind of stone or gem.

nȧ, nu , ostriches; var.

Nȧu , U. 576, N. 966, a mythological ostrich.

nȧa , Rec. 31, 180, ibex.

nȧa , a running at the nose.

nȧaȧa , mint of some kind, calamint (?)

Nȧa-rruṭ ; see **N-ruṭ-f**; varr.

nȧasqa , Ebers Pap. 66, 12, to be shaven, baldness; varr.

nȧash-t , an instrument of some kind.

nȧu , to see; Copt. ⲛⲁⲩ.

nȧu 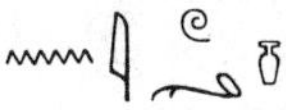, a pot, a vessel.

nȧu 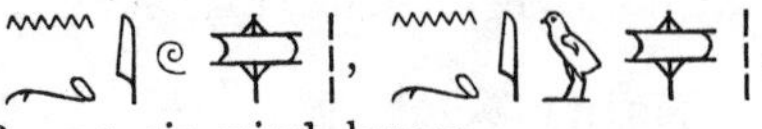, A.Z. 1908, 115, air, wind, breeze.

Nȧu U. 557 = , consort of .

nȧu-t , T. 358, , N. 177, a particle of negation.

nȧuȧu , , , Hearst Pap. 8, 11, , mint, calamint (?)

nȧus (?) , A.Z. 1899, 95, some metal object.

nȧb , flame, fire.

Nȧb-ḥer , Ṭuat III, a god in the Ṭuat.

nȧm , the lowing of cattle.

nȧm (?), Rec. 33, 122......

nȧm[n]ȧm , P. 63, M. 85, to walk, to stride; var. , N. 92.

nȧmtf , Nȧstasen Stele 40 ff. = Copt. ⲛⲉⲙⲟϥ.

nȧnȧ , P. 609, N. 807, , to welcome, to salute joyfully.

nȧrta-t , meaning unknown (Lacau).

nȧh , , injury, harm, evil.

Nȧkh , B.M. 32, 27, a serpent-fiend.

nȧs , to cry out numbers, to tally, to reckon.

nȧs , U. 594, , P. 680, , IV, 1219, , , Ȧmen. 11, 6, 22, 9, , , , , , , IV 953, to cry out to, to call, to invoke, to address, to name, to be named.

nȧs-t , , , Metternich Stele 125, invocation, a calling.

Nȧs , N. 1074, "caller," title of a god.

Nȧs-Rā , B.D. 148, an intercessor with Rā for men.

Nȧs-t-taui-si, etc. , etc., B.D. 145, 146, the 12th Pylon of Sekhet-Ȧaru.

nȧs , Ebers Pap. 94, 2, turtle-meat (?)

nȧsut , ancient [writings], old documents or title deeds.

nȧsbetch (?) , to proclaim (?)

nȧk , to copulate; compare Arab. أَنْكَحَ.

nȧk , , N. 1231, to be injured, to be doomed, damned; , invulnerable.

nȧk-t , a deadly thing; var. .

nȧkiu , cutting weapons or tools, the slain.

nȧkut , knives.

Nȧk , Pap. Nekht 21, , , a serpent-fiend slain by Rā; , B.D. 180, 22, the associates of the same.

nȧki , enemy, foe, devil; plur. , .

Nȧkit , , Ṭuat VII, a goddess.

Nȧkiu-menȧ-t , Tomb Seti I, one of the 75 forms of Rā (No. 8).

nȧtȧt , A.Z. 45, 60, 61, to be kept back = , N. 1159.

nȧtȧt, Shipwreck 17, to stammer.

Nȧṭnȧṭu, Hh. 522, a group of gods.

nȧtchu (?), belly; Copt. ⲛⲉϫⲓ.

nā, Thes. 1322, paint on walls.

nā, nāā, , Ebers Pap. 108, 20, to rub down to a powder, to scour, to clean.

nāā, to draw a coloured design, to paint, to depict in order, to be painted, striped, or variegated; , IV, 690, painted things; , colours on chariots; , IV, 660, variegated stuffs; , , list, catalogue.

nā-t, IV, 717, a painted thing.

nāu (seshu?), Hearst Pap. X, 1, colours used in painting, ink.

nā (n + ā?), P. 596, writing, order, edict.

nāu (?), design, painting, drawing.

nā (n + ā?), , list, catalogue, inventory.

nā neter, A.Z. 1905, 29, painter to the god.

nā-t (?), formulae, liturgy, law, rule, ordinance = (?)

nā, nāi, U. 565, , , , , , , Rec. 21, 96, , P. 641, M. 674, N. 1237, , , , , , , Rev. 13, 39, , T. 336, , , to come, to go, to arrive, to journey, to travel, to sail; Copt. ⲛⲟⲩ, ⲛⲏⲩ.

nāā, A.Z. 45, 124, to sail away.

nā-t, N. 788, a sailing, a journey, a sailing ship; , to sail down stream.

nā-t, the drawing of thread.

nāu, Hh. 447, Rec. 27, 218, 31, 31, worm, serpent, viper, serpent-god; plur. , .

Nā, Ṭuat XII, a serpent-god.

Nāi-t, U. 317, a serpent-goddess, consort of .

nā ur, the festival of the 23rd day of the month.

nāi, the festival of the 22nd day of the month.

nāi, Israel Stele 15, good, benevolent; var. , Thes. 1242.

nā ḥa-t, , Jour. As. 1908, 250, to sympathize with, to be gracious to, to show pity; varr. , , L.D. III, 140B.

nāa, , Rev., to have pity; Copt. ⲛⲁ.

nāa-t, Mar. Aby. I, 7, 56, graciousness.

nāau, wind, air, breeze; see .

nāatch-t, Ebers Pap. 42, 15, some strong-smelling drug (?)

Nāȧu, , B.D. 140, 6, B.D. (Saïte) 32, 3, 4, a benevolent god, a foe to crocodiles.

Nāi, Ṭuat X, Denderah IV, 83, a winged serpent with a pair of human legs.

Nāi, U. 535, T. 294, , Nesi-Ȧmsu 32, 35, B.D. 149, 42, a serpent-fiend in the Ṭuat, a form of Āapep; fem. Nāit.

Nāit, Pap. Mag. 90, a goddess; see **Nāi** and **Neqeb.**

Nāi-ur, Denderah IV, 59, the guardian of a coffer.

Nā-shep, Metternich Stele 85, a blind serpent-fiend.

nāi-t, Rev. 11, 146, , house, abode.

nāit, Rec. 35, 57, , Ȧmen. 3, 16, , stake, pole, post, part of a ship.

Nāutȧ, T. 336, , P. 811, , N. 639, a god.

nām, Anastasi I, 23, 5, pleasant, by your favour or courtesy; compare Heb. √נעם.

nār, Rec. 28, 153, baboon.

nār, , writing reed.

nār-t, , Rec. 15, 102, sycamore tree (Laurier Rose); Copt. ⲛⲏⲣ, Gr. νήριον, Arab. ناريون.

Nār-t, B.D. 15 (Litany), a sycamore tree in the Ṭuat sacred to Osiris.

Nārit, the goddess of the Nār tree.

nār, , cuttle-fish (?) clarias anguillaris (?); plur. , .

Nāri, Tomb Rameses IV, 30, an attendant on the Disk.

Nārit, Rec. 6, 152, 153, a group of goddesses.

nār-t, T. 93, spittle, saliva.

nāru, , Peasant 27, a bird.

Nārti-ānkh-em-sen-nu-f, the name of a mythological serpent.

nāruna, , youth, young soldier; Heb. נַעַר; plur. , Mar. Karn. 54, 45, , L.D. III, 187, , , soldiers; Heb. נְעָרִים.

nākhu; see .

nākh, to tie, to bind together, bundle, bunch.

nākh-t, to strain, strainer.

nāsh[t], , to be strong, mighty, great; Copt. ⲛⲁϣⲧ.

nāshȧ, Ȧmen. 4, 5, strong one.

nāsha, to be strong, able; Copt. ⲛⲁϣⲧ.

nāshati, Thes. 1206, strong man.

nāsht, nāshth, Rec. 13, 80, , Rec. 14, 17, , strong, strength; Copt. ⲛⲁϣⲧ.

Nāq, Ṭuat VII; see **Qān.**

nāg, to break open a door, to force a way, to crush, to reduce to powder.

nāgu, dust, powder; var. (?)

nāgga, to cackle (of geese); see

Nāṭai, Nāṭi, B.D. 125, II, a god; see **Āaṭi.**

ni, belonging to = Copt. ⲚⲀ.

ni, B.D. 113, 2, B.D. 189, 24, Shipwreck 131.

ni, a mark of the genitive masc. sing. =

ni P.S.B.A. 40, 1918, 6, a particle: whereby, thereby, through which.

ni to see; Copt. ⲚⲀⲨ.

ni (neni), a vase, a vessel, leaven, yeast.

ni, neni, N. 860, P. 164, of.

ni, U. 333, serpent's poison.

Ni, Ṭuat XII, Mission 13, 127, a sailor-god with two birds' heads, a supporter of the Disk.

Neni, Nenu, one of the four primeval gods of the company of Thoth.

Nenit, consort of Nenu.

ni, U. 215, P. 390, M. 548, 556, N. 1163, I, 16, a particle of negation: which not, etc.

ni, Ebers Pap. 97, 13, a particle of affirmation: yea, yes.

ni, to pity; Copt. ⲚⲀ.

ni, M. 365, N. 919, to welcome with words of praise or affection; see

niu, professional wailers or mourners.

nini, Rougé I.H. II, 124, Thes. 1205, IV, 567, to greet, to welcome, to do homage to.

ni, ostrich.

ni-t houses, abodes, chambers, halls.

nit Hearst Pap. 12, 15, a seed or plant.

ni-t, Jour. As. 1908, 252, = Copt. ⲚⲈ (in †ⲚⲈ, Revil.).

niu (?) Leyd. Pap. 2, 10, to turn away from.

niut things cast aside, waste, refuse.

nib, IV, 672, Rec. 16, 152, styrax wood staff.

nib, balsam plant, frankincense.

nibun, frankincense; varr. ; Heb. לְבֹנָה.

nif, Stele of Ptolemy I, 11, enemy; plur.

nifi, Jour. As. 1908, 272, breath of serpent, venom.

nifa, Rec. 13, 27, to blow, to breathe; Copt. ⲚⲒϤⲈ.

nifa-t Rec. 14, 21, breath.

nifau, Rec. 4, 31, those.

nim, Berl. 2081, Metternich Stele 175, 204, who? Copt. ⲚⲒⲘ.

nin, crane (?)

Ninárruṭf 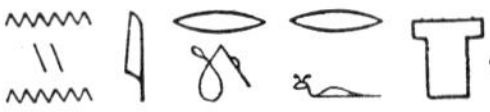, see **N-ruṭ-f** .

nu 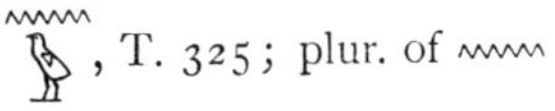, T. 325; plur. of .

nu , a mark of the genitive plur.; the old forms are: **nu** 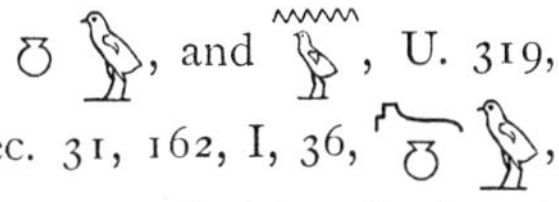, and , U. 319, M. 392, N. 658, Rec. 31, 162, I, 36, , M. 557, 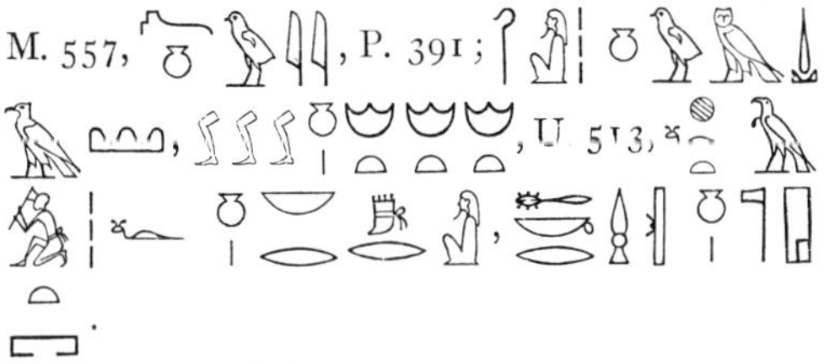, P. 391; , U 513, .

nui , a mark of the genitive (dual).

nu , Ámen. 10, 2, 21, 17, Rev. 11, 134, , they, them, belonging to them.

nu , U. 171, 556, Thes. 1287, Rec. 26, 75, 31, 27, , , a demonstrative particle: this, these; 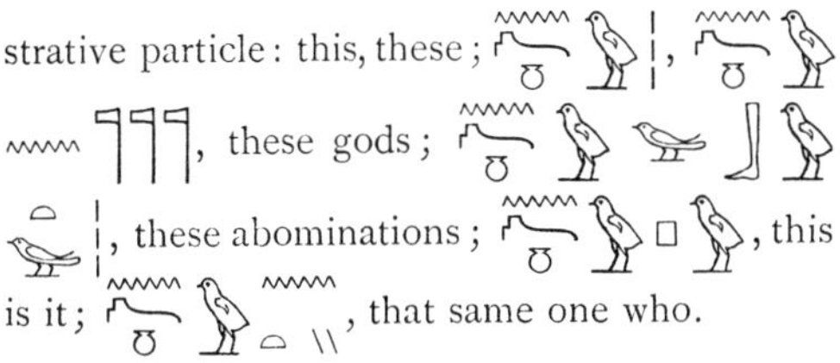, , these gods; , these abominations; , this is it; , that same one who.

nui , P. 392, these two.

nu-t 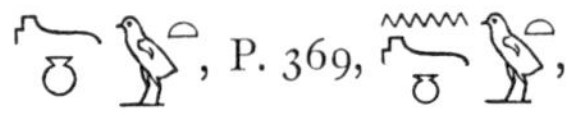, P. 369, , N. 1146, these.

nunu , , , P. 661, 773, M. 770, these..

nu 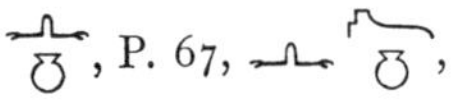, P. 67, , N. 34, a particle of negation.

nut-t 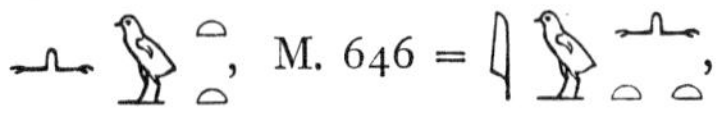, M. 646 = , P. 345, a particle of negation: no, not.

nu 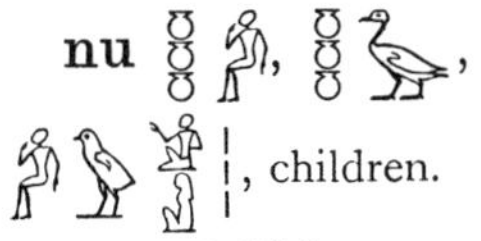, child, son, babe; plur. , children.

nu 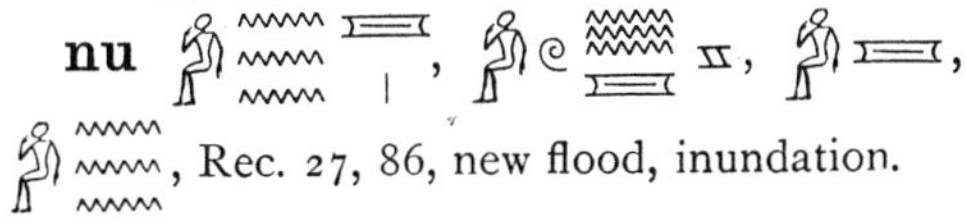, , , , Rec. 27, 86, new flood, inundation.

nu-t , , , , , , , , , Westcar Pap. 12, 13, , , , a mass of water, lake, pool, stream, canal.

nui 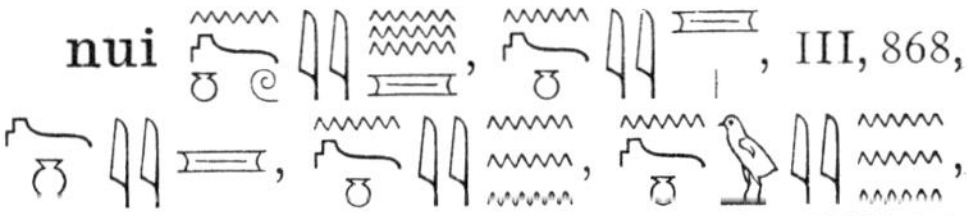, , III, 868, , , , Pap. 3024, 65, , , , , Shipwreck 35, lake, pool, stream, canal.

nui , Thes. 1289, the sacred lake of a temple.

nuit , inundation.

Nu 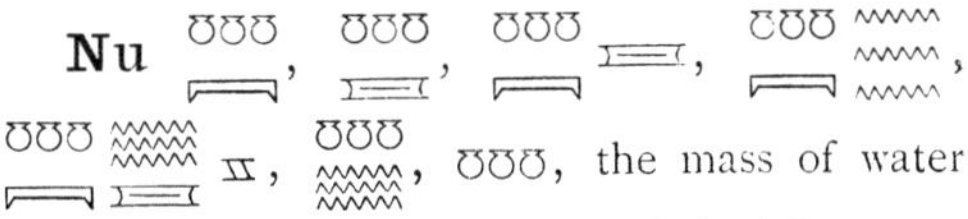, , , , , , , the mass of water which existed in primeval times, Celestial waters; see **Nu, Nenu**; Copt. **ⲛⲟⲩⲛ**.

Nu (Nenu?) 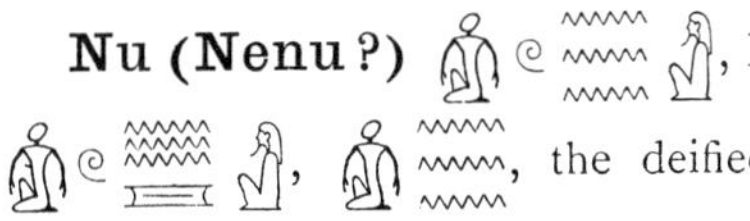, B.D. 27, 2, , , the deified primeval water whence everything came.

Nenu , a name of Áapep.

Nu (Nenu) , T. 258, M. 548, N. 585, 1134, 1229, , T. 77, P. 204, M. 231, 395, 455, 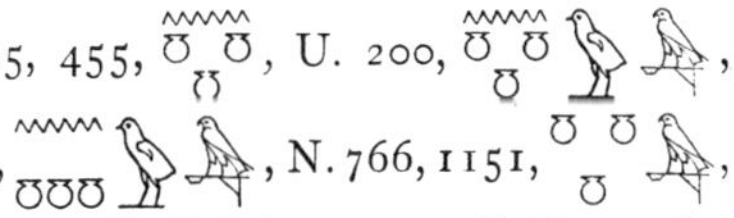, U. 200, , N. 609, 756, , N. 766, 1151, , M. 397, N. 792, , P. 653, , M. 756, , Hh. 472, , 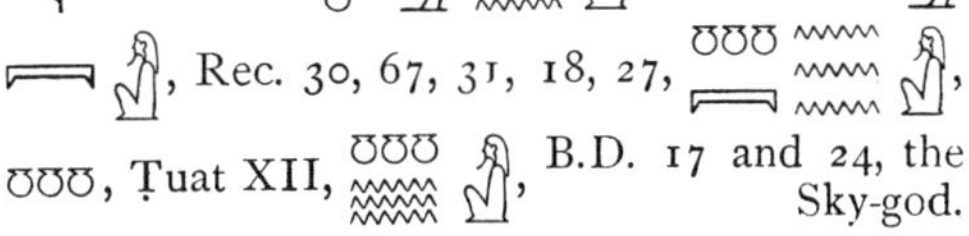, Rec. 30, 67, 31, 18, 27, , , Ṭuat XII, , B.D. 17 and 24, the Sky-god.

Nunu 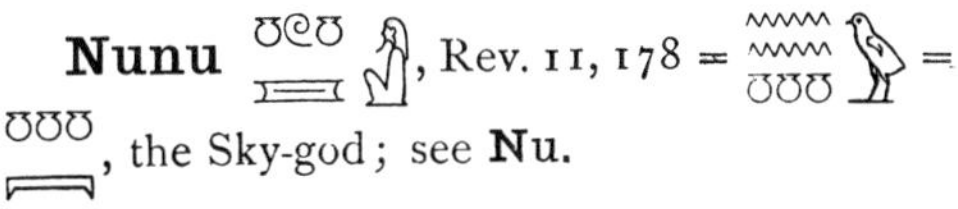, Rev. 11, 178 = = , the Sky-god; see **Nu**.

Nunu [illegible], Berl. 2082, a title (?) (
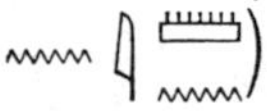).

Nu-t (Nuit) [illegible], U. 244, [illegible], P. 103,
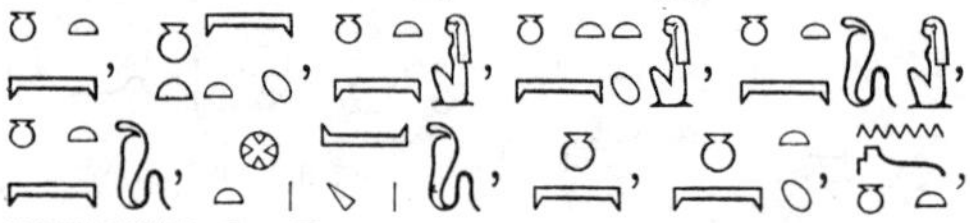
, Berl. 2312, the Sky-goddess.

Nu-t (Nunu-t, Nen-t) [illegible], P. 168, M. 659, N. 72, 951, 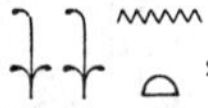, U. 537, 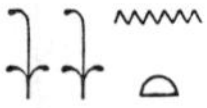
[illegible], U. 239, [illegible], U. 219, , M. 455, , U. 557, 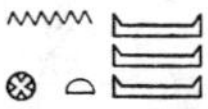, M. 766,

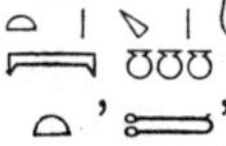, the Sky-goddess.

nuti (nenti) [illegible], A.Z. 1906, 126, , P. 659, 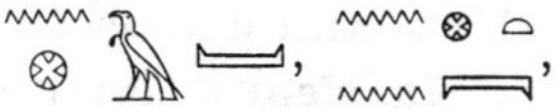, , A.Z. 1908, 117, [illegible], the two halves of the sky, or the day sky and the night sky; , M. 766.

Nu (Nenu) 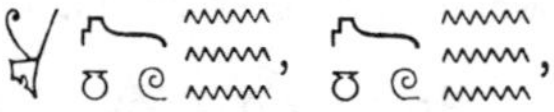, Edfû I, 79, a name of the Nile-god.

Nu , Hymn Darius 31, [illegible], a name of Åmen-Rā.

Nuit-ra ; B.D. 109, 3, "Goose-lake," a lake in the Ṭuat.

Nu [illegible] (later form of Nenu), Ṭuat VIII, the god of an open door in the Ṭuat.

Nu 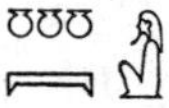, Tomb Seti I, a ram-headed water-god, one of the 75 forms of Rā (No. 20).

Nu [illegible], Ombos I, 62, with the title 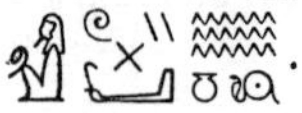.

Nuenrā , Denderah IV, 15, a god who gave water to the dead.

Nu-t [illegible], Berg. I, 19, a goddess who supplied the deceased with water.

Nu-t [illegible], Denderah III. 78, a bandy-legged goddess with hands in the place of feet.

Nu-t [illegible], B.D. 99, 17, the name of the sail in the magical boat.

Nu-t , Tomb Seti I, one of the 75 forms of Rā (No. 16).

Nuit , Mission 13, 127, a goddess.

Nu-t urit , P. 602, the Sky-goddess in woman's form with pendent breasts, 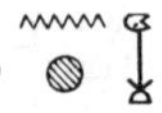
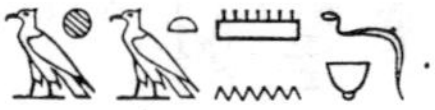.

nuiu (nunuiu) , P. 683, beings of Nu, dwellers in heaven; [illegible], a being appertaining to the sky.

nu , Rec. 16, 57, to drink beer with companions, to swill.

nu , overflowing or brimming pots of beer.

nu-t 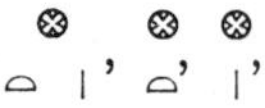, village, hamlet, town, city, community, settlement; plur. [illegible],
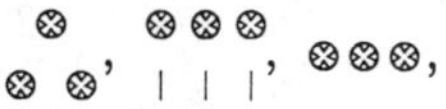, P. 10, M. 12, N. 114, , P. 696, [illegible], Décrets 31, [illegible]
[illegible], Nåstasen Stele 9.

nutiu , Rec. 18, 181,

, IV, 1160, citizens, townsmen, townsfolk, natives.

nutå, nuti , belonging to the town or community, urban; [illegible], the town-god, the local tutelary deity; plur. .

nu-t , towns of the South and North.

Nu-t neter , U. 641, 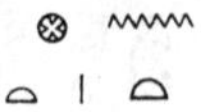
[illegible], the city of the god [Osiris].

Nu-t [illegible], Ṭuat VIII, a god of the Circle Ḥetemit-Khemiu.

Nu-ti , , Ṭuat I, a singing-goddess.

Nu-t urt , , N. 994, a town in the Elysian Fields.

Nu-ti urti , a district in the Ṭuat.

Nu-t ur-[t] , B.D. (Saïte) 110, a lake or settlement in Sekhet-Åaru.

Nu-t-enth-ḥeḥtt , Berg. II, 12, the "Everlasting City" in the Ṭuat.

Nu-t Shesit , , , a goddess.

nu-t , a pyramid town, *i.e.*, the temples, etc., built about a pyramid; dual , A.Z. 1905, 5.

nu , P. 162, , T. 229, , P. 618, 619, N. 1303, , , , , , time, hour; Copt. ⲛⲁⲩ; plur. , P. 697, , Rec. 27, 218; , de bonne heure, early; , Rec. 5, 92.

nuit , , , , a moment of time, interval of rest.

nen (nunu ?) , to rise (of a celestial body), to shine.

Nenit , Thes. 31, the goddess of the first hour of the day.

nen , Thes. 408, Wört. 1621, the winter solstice.

nu , , , Thes. 1201, to tie, to bind together.

nu-t , , , , , Rechnungen 17, 2, 11, 12, cord, thread, rope, material for making cord or twine, bast; plur. , .

Nut hru , B.D. 153A, 22, the cordage of the net used in snaring souls.

nu (nui ?) , , , , , , Amherst Pap. 24, to shake, to rub down into powder, to rend asunder, to grind.

nu ra , to work the mouth, to mouth, to dribble at the mouth.

nui , , , , , , , , , to keep guard over, to watch, to tend, to shepherd, to have a care for, to tend cattle or sheep, to keep together; , cared for.

nu , Rec. 16, 57, will, thought, intention, care for something.

nu , caretaker, guardian.

nui , , , herdsman, shepherd, lassoer, drover.

nuit , Rev. 6, 26, , , P.S.B. 24, 47, Anastasi I, 26, 5, care for someone or something, tending, shepherding, repairing.

nuit , , Rev. 6, 26, shepherds, cattlemen.

nu , Nåstasen Stele 38, stall-fed oxen.

nu , , , , , , to move about, to go about, to walk, to come, to depart; , IV, 1221.

nuu , IV, 966, 1080, , , Thes. 1479, guide, leader, director.

nu , , Åmen. 17, 11, 23, 17, Rec. 21, 81, , , IV,

697, 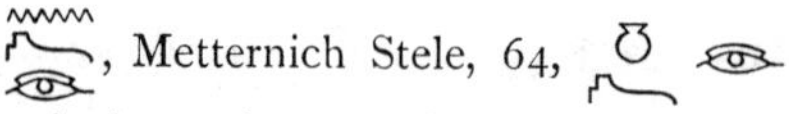, Metternich Stele, 64, to see, to look, to observe; Copt. ⲛⲁⲩ.

nuit (?) , Rev. 14, 10, eyes, glances.

nu 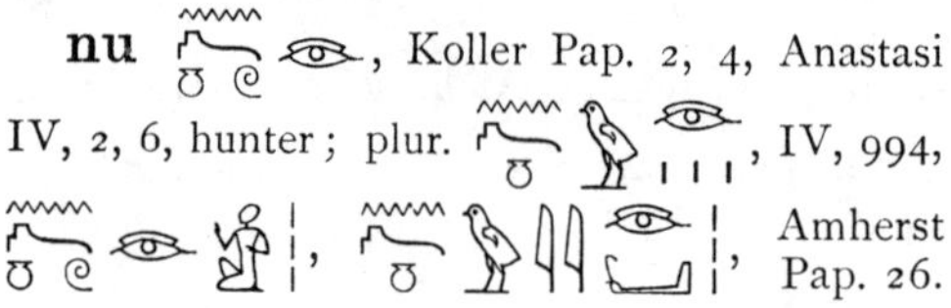, Koller Pap. 2, 4, Anastasi IV, 2, 6, hunter; plur. IV, 994, Amherst Pap. 26.

nu 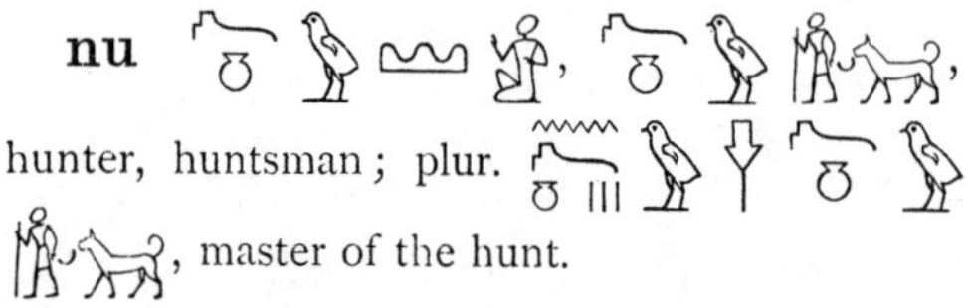, hunter, huntsman; plur. master of the hunt.

nu-t 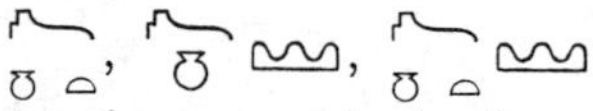, P. 128, N. 101, a hunting ground in the desert or hills.

nu 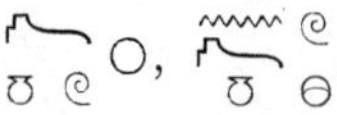, ring, circle, a round or globular object, pill, pastille.

nu-t 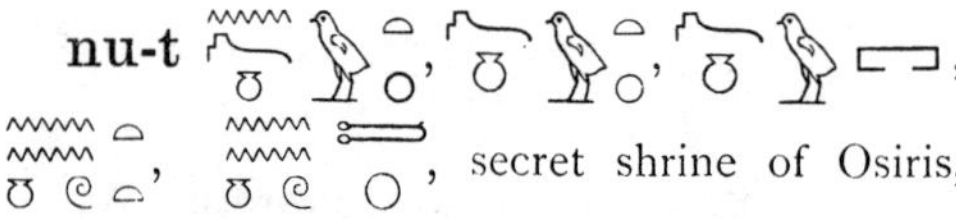, secret shrine of Osiris, crypt, underground chamber or passage.

nu , A.Z. 1865, 112, the post on which a door turns.

nu-t 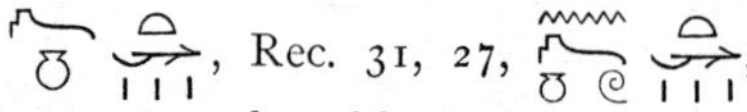, Rec. 31, 27, Leyd. Pap. 3, 11, wooden objects.

nu-t , Ebers Pap. 78, 10, root (?) Copt. ⲛⲟⲩⲛⲓ (?)

nu 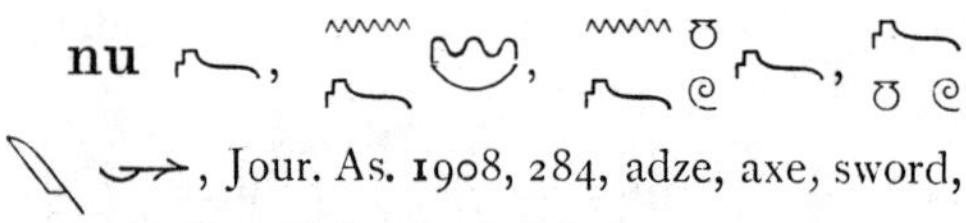, Jour. As. 1908, 284, adze, axe, sword, weapon, any cutting tool or instrument.

nu-t 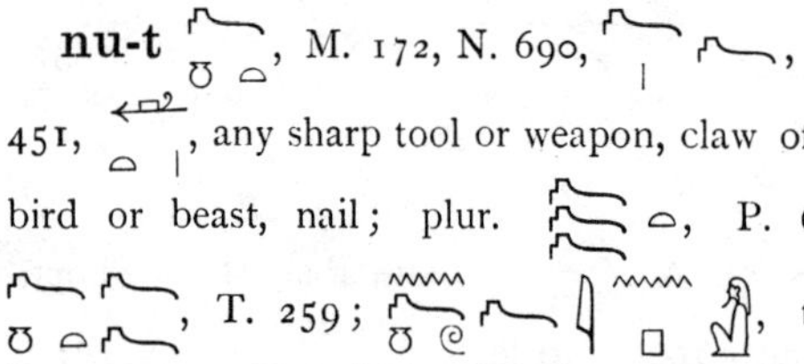, M. 172, N. 690, U. 451, any sharp tool or weapon, claw of a bird or beast, nail; plur. P. 68, T. 259; the instrument with which Anubis "opened the mouth" of the gods.

nui 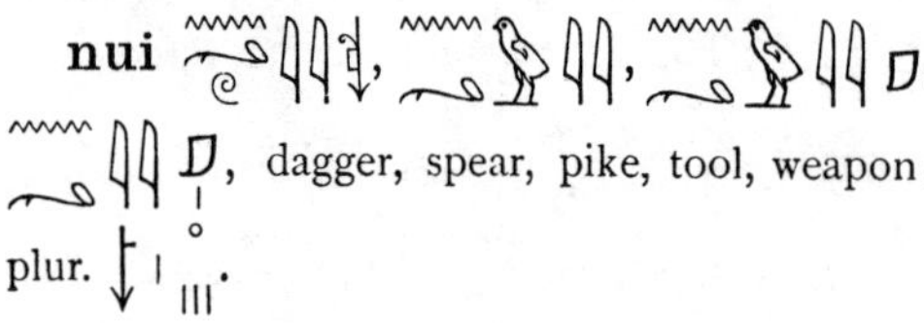, dagger, spear, pike, tool, weapon; plur.

nu 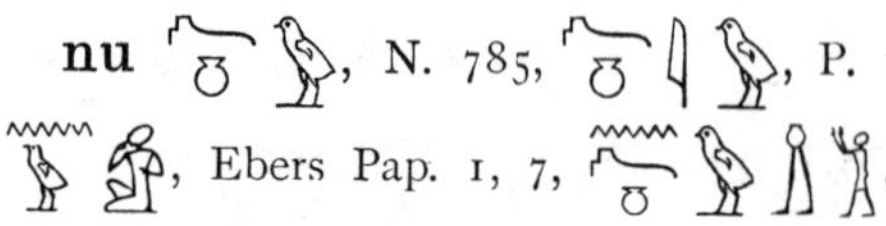, N. 785, P. 154, Ebers Pap. 1, 7, to acclaim, to beseech, to adore.

nu 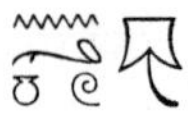, ibex.

nu (nut?) , Annales III, 109, unguent, salve.

nu , crime, wickedness, failure, weakness in judgment, vacillation, hesitation to do right.

nuu , IV, 931, feathers (?)

nu Rā , Lit. 15, solar products; var. Lit. 15.

nua 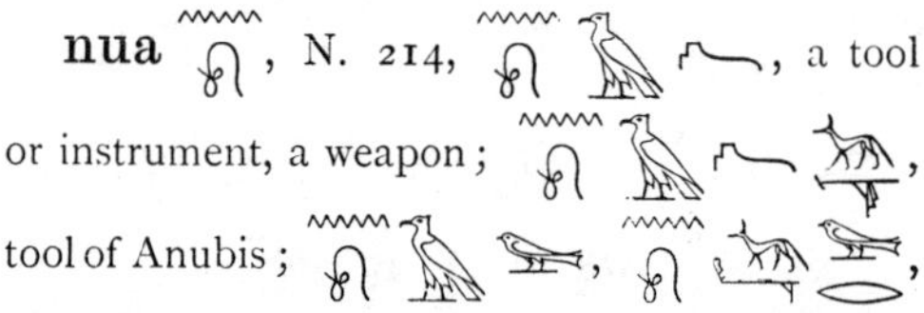, N. 214, a tool or instrument, a weapon; tool of Anubis; M. 824, N. 1316.

Nua , N. 1316, a jackal-god in the Ṭuat.

nua , a herb used in medicine.

nuau , Rec. 30, 196, 36, 217, to be terrified; Rec. 36, 215.

nuaua , T. 178, P. 522, M. 160, N. 651, to tremble, to quake.

nuan 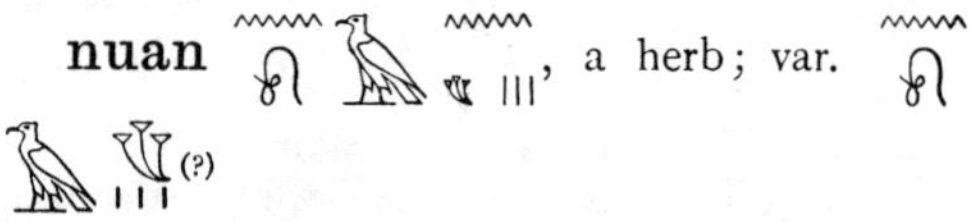, a herb; var.

nuar , L.D. 4, 74B, cord, rope.

n-uȧ , A.Z. 45, 125, I, me.

nuȧ 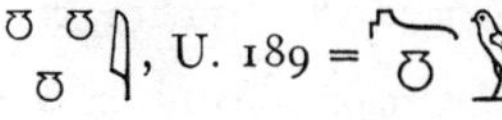, U. 189 = T. 69, this.

nuāba (?) , T. 106 . . . . . .

nub , U. 536, T. 294, P. 164, , P. 471, M. 537, N. 1115, , , , , , gold; , Thes. 1286; , gold of the water, *i.e.*, alluvial gold dust; , gold of the mountain, *i.e.*, gold dug out of a mine; , Nubian gold; , gold of Apollinopolis (Edfû); , gold of Ombos; , gold of Coptos; Copt. ⲛⲟⲩⲃ.

nubu , , T. 39, 200, golden.

nubu , , pieces of gold, gold ingots (?); , golden grain.

nubiu (?) , IV, 1149, gold objects.

nub àāu , gold washed out of the beds of torrents.

nub uatch , , IV, 329, "green gold."

nub en àakhu , gold of light, *i.e.*, shining gold.

nub en ..... , gold of $\frac{1}{1\frac{1}{2}} = \frac{2}{3}$.

nub en ḥesut , IV, 892, , IV, 139, the gold of praise, *i.e.*, the gift of gold given by the king to a subject as a reward for good service or bravery.

nub en sep khemt , "gold of three times," gold thrice refined (?)

nub en qen (?) , IV, 892, the finest gold.

nub en qen-t , gold given by the king as a reward for valour in battle.

nub nefer , , good gold, *i.e.*, fine gold.

nub ḥer ḥetch , gold on silver, *i.e.*, silver-gilt.

nub ḥetch , , white gold, gold alloyed with silver naturally, or silver-gilt (?)

nub senu , IV, 168, 875, gold of an extra fine quality or of medium quality.

nub (per nub) , gold house, *i.e.*, gold foundry, or smelting house; plur. .

Nub , "Golden One," a name of the Sun-god.

Nubit , , , , "Golden Lady," a title of several goddesses.

Nubit , A.Z. 1906, 114, , B.D.G. 102, a title of Hathor as lady of .

Nubit , consort of Àmen and mother of .

Nubit-àith (?) , B.D.G. 1105, , a cow-goddess.

Nubà-nebs-àms , Ombos II, 1, 108, a lion-goddess, one of the 14 forms of Sekhmit.

Nub-neteru , Denderah IV, 84, warder of the 4th Pylon.

Nubit-neterit (?) , Denderah I, 52, a goddess.

Nub-ḥeḥ , "gold of eternity," a title of Osiris.

Nub-ḥetepit , a form of the goddess Tait, .

nub , , , , , , , , , to smelt metals, to work in gold, to form, to fashion, to model, to mould, to plate with metal, to inlay metal.

nubnub 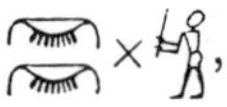, to defend, to protect; var. .

nubi , Rec. 31, 12, , smelter, foundryman, goldworker, goldsmith; plur.  .

nub-t 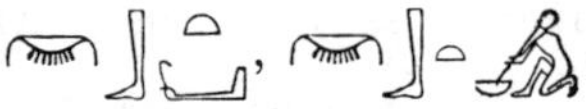, metal working, gold working, to exercise the goldsmith's craft.

nubit 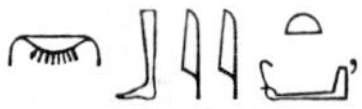, the craft of the goldsmith; var. 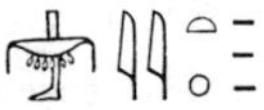 (?)

nub-ti , a metal pot.

nubȧu-ti (?) , goldsmith.

Nub , see **Nebȧperem-khetkhet.**

Nubnub (Nebneb) , Mission 13, 127, a god.

Nubti , B.D., 65, 19, 125, II, , U. 479, Set of Ombos.

nubi , to swim; Copt. ⲛⲉⲉⲃⲉ; var. .

Nubiu , Ṭuat VIII, the "Swimmers" in the Ṭuat.

nubb-t , Rec. 33, 6, basin, quay, shore, coast.

nubut , Hh. 382, baskets.

nubi 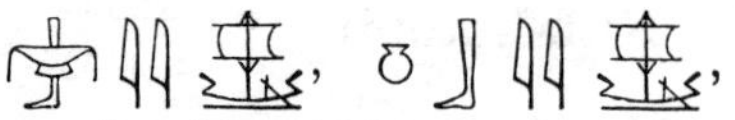, Rec. 33, 6, to sail a ship, a ship.

nubit 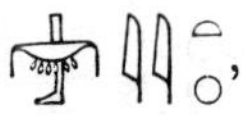, part of a plant, seed, kernel.

nubu , plant.

nub , the stalk of the balsam plant or tree.

nubḥeḥ (?) 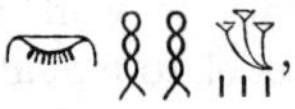, blossom, a kind of flower (?)

nubṭ , see .

nun , Hh. 451, these.

nunu (nen) 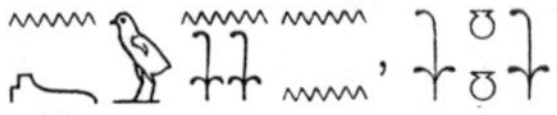, a demonstrative particle: this.

nun , B.D. 68, 35, to do homage to, to greet, to welcome.

Nun , B.D. 179, 3, a god.

Nunu , Rec. 27, 53, a group of gods – functions unknown.

nun 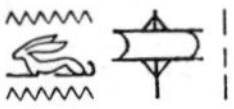, gentle wind, zephyr.

Nun , a god.

Nunun (?) , a form of Ḥeru-ur or Shu.

nun , to roam about.

nun-t (?) , harm, injury.

nunb 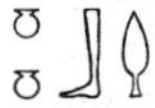, see **nub** , and **nib** 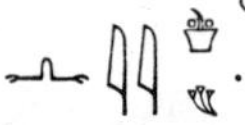.

Nuru [illegible], N. 110, 994, [illegible], T. 175, P. 186, N. 607, [illegible] (*sic*), N. 900, [illegible] [illegible], P. 396, [illegible], M. 565, [illegible] [illegible], N. 1172, a ferry-god in the Ṭuat.

nur [illegible], Hh. 358, [illegible] [illegible], B.D. 149, 8, 4, [illegible], N. 1339, a bird, vulture (?)

nurit [illegible], Rev. 14, 4, 20, vulture; Copt. ⲛⲟⲩⲣⲓ.

nura [illegible], Rev. 13, 10 = [illegible] [illegible], victory.

Nurkhata [illegible], Ṭuat III, a god of spells and guardian of the 3rd Gate of the Ṭuat.

nurta [illegible], T. 175, P. 121, M. 157, N. 110, [illegible], a mythological tool or weapon.

nuh  , A.Z. 1906, 113 =  , to diminish.

nuhȧti  , sycamore tree, or the wood of the same.

nuḥ , , , IV, 612, , to bind, to tie, to tie on, to fasten.

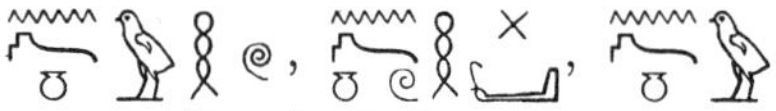

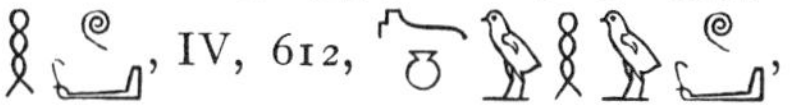

nuḥ , U. 418, , T. 239. , T. 252, , Pap. 3024, 9, , , , , , Rec. 31, 29, , string, cord, rope, cordage, measuring cord, traces, harness; plur. , U. 210, , Rec. 30, 66, , Décrets, 104, , , , , Rev. 14, 21; Copt. ⲛⲟⲩϩ, ⲛⲟϩ.

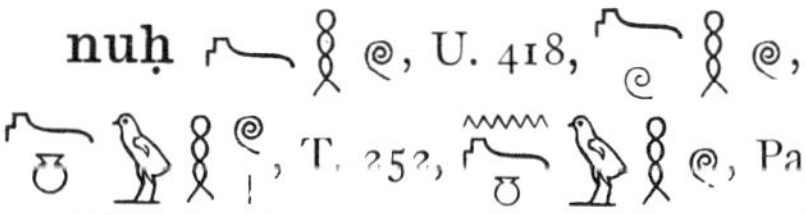

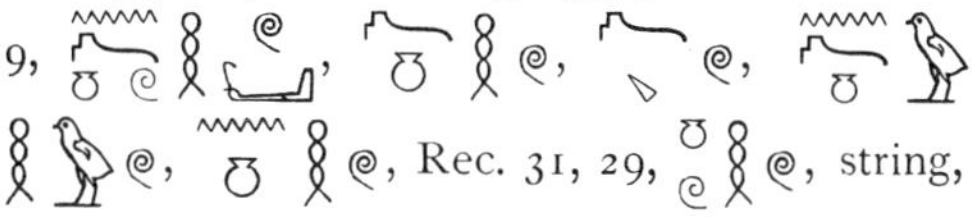

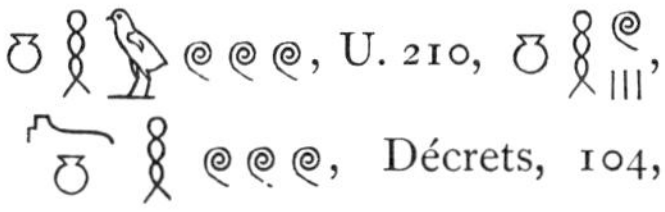

nuḥu   , , bonds, fetters.

nuḥ 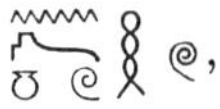 , Ṭuat V, a cord, endowed with reason, used in measuring the estates of the blessed in the Ṭuat.

Nuḥ ḥa-tu 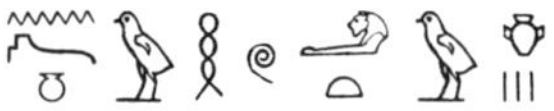 , B.D. 286, a god who fettered hearts.

nuḥ  , A.Z. 1905, 27, a roll or bundle of papyrus.

nuḥ , , , a kind of plant or shrub; plur. , Ȧmen. 7, 13

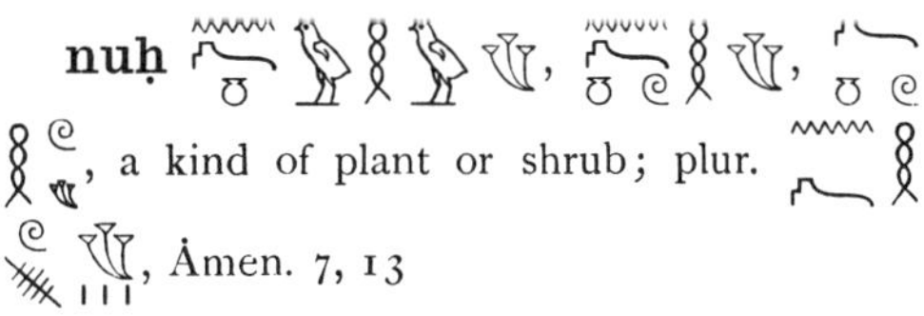

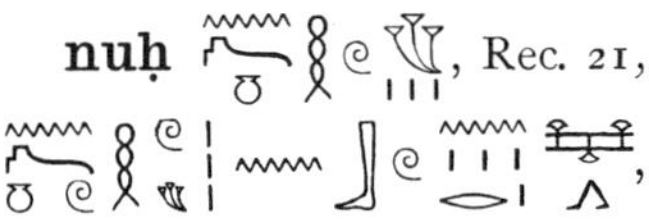

nuḥ , Rec. 21, 91, grass ropes; Koller Pap. 27, outer rope (?)

nuḥ , , Rev. 13, 35, chicory (?)

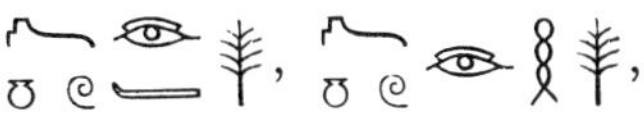

nuḥ 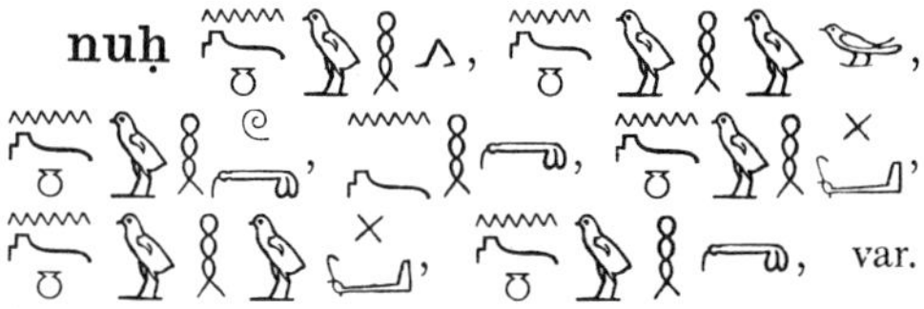 , , , , , , , var.  , to masturbate.

nuḥ , , , , to be drunk with joy or drink.

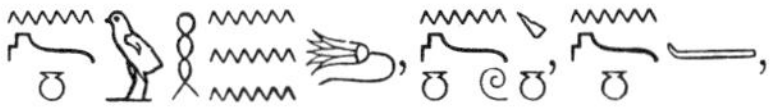

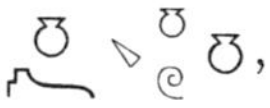

nuḥ  , A.Z. 1906, 125, drunkenness.

nuḥ 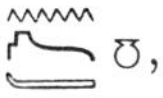 , a drinking pot.

nuḥ-ti , , B.D. 93, 3, 6, pair of horns.

nuḥeḥ  , U. 446, T. 255, eternity; see , .

nuḥeb  , yoke ox; Copt. ⲛⲟϩⲉⲃ, ⲛⲁϩⲃ; plur.  ; see 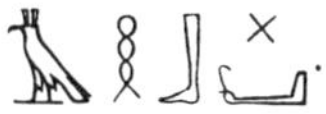 .

nuḥeb-t  , lotus, lily; plur. ; see .

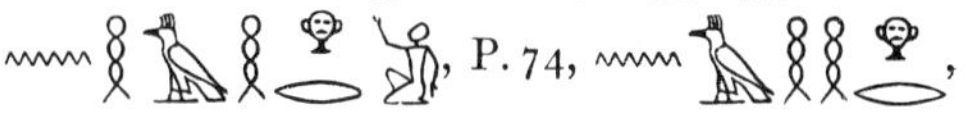

nuḥerḥer 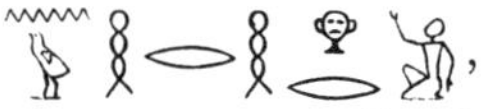 , N. 16, , P. 74, , M. 105, to rejoice.

nuḥes , negro; see .

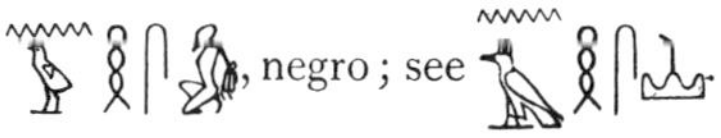

nukh  , L.D. III, 140B,  , to cook, to bake, to roast.

nus , , , Rec. 31, 30, part of a crown.

nus 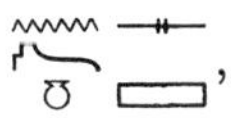 , IV, 708, a block of lead ( ), pig of lead (?)

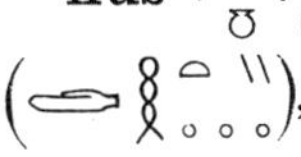

nus , , , Stat. Tab. 48, ring, earring, ring-weight, weight; Copt. λεος (?)

nus (nest) , Rev. 11, 185, in the name , glossed by Copt. πασтoρ.

nusi (nesi ?) , Rev. 14, 40 = Gr. προνησιον.

nusen , curse, evil.

nuqer , to scrape, to polish; Copt. noγкεp.

nuk , , , , , , IV, 807, , , I; , I, this Osiris; , , I, this I; Copt. ανοκ, Heb. אָנֹכִי.

Nukar (Nenkar) , , Asien 316, A.Z. 1906, 97, the Babylonian goddess Ningal.

nut , to boil, to roast, to cook; see .

nuti , , , , cook, messman.

nutȧ , Rev. 11, 180, divine.

nutiu , A.Z. 1900, 67, enemies.

nuti , confectioner, sweetmeat seller.

nuti en Shu , A.Z. 1908, 115, , air, wind.

nuti , Ḥerusȧtef 102, strong; perhaps = .

nutu.... , T. 269, M. 429 ....

Nuth (Nunuth) , Ṭuat XII, the Sky-goddess; see **Nu-t** .

nutha , Greene 2, to shake, to quake, to tremble, to be lame (?)

nuṭ , Peasant 100, 262, , , , , , , , to move out of place, to slip, to yield ground.

nuṭ ḥa-t , wickedness.

nuṭu ḥatu , IV, 1076, rebels.

Nuṭiu , B.D. 78, 8, (Saïte), a group of gods—functions unknown.

nuṭ-t , T. 41, boat.

nuṭ , , to dress, to drape, to clothe.

nuṭ-t , A.Z. 1908, 91, , swaddling band.

nuṭ , A.Z. 1905, 15, to melt.

nuṭ-t , IV, 347, a squeezing, a pressing.

nuṭ-t , , , Thes. 1290, unguent, prepared oil.

nuṭ-t , unguent pot.

nuṭu sheps , a kind of plant.

nutch-t , N. 798, cord, rope.

nutch , M. 72, N. 75, , P. 107 ....

nutch , flour; Copt. noγт.

nutch-t, Ebers Pap. 39, 20. . . . .

Nutchi, , Ṭuat V, a monster-serpent.

neb, , all, any, each, every, everyone, every sort or kind; fem. **neb-t** ; plur. , , , M. 77, N. 79, , , , P. 111; Copt. ⲛⲓⲙ.

nebu, , Rec. 31, 29, everybody, all people.

neb, T. 275, N. 907, , M. 353, , , , Peasant 53, , , , , , , , P. 79, M. 111, A.Z. 1900, 128, , , , , lord, master, owner, possessor; plur. , P. 169, M. 744, , P. 87, , N. 46, , , T. 248, , T. 248, , , , , ; = , lord (late form); Copt. ⲛⲏⲃ.

Nebtả, Nebti, U. 39, P. 65, N. 267, Thes. 1283, Dream Stele 5, Rev. 10, 61, A.Z. 1908, 18, IV, 85, 566, 927, , , , , , , , P.S.B. 20, 200, , B.D.G. 1062, 28, , Ḳubbân Stele 3, , , Rec. 17, 113, lord of the Crowns of the South and North – a royal title = Gr. *κύριος διαδημάτων*.

neb-t, , , , , Rec. 31, 171, , Hh. 404, lady, mistress; plur. , Metternich Stele 53.

nebtaḥemt, Rec. 15, 16, , Rev. 12, 77, the status of a married woman.

neb atpu, IV, 1076, lord of a load, *i.e.*, laden one.

neb ảmakh, , , , "lord of service," *i.e.*, a loyal follower of Osiris; var.

neb ảri khet, the Lord Creator.

neb ảst em Ảmentt, the possessor of a seat in Ảmentt.

Neb-ā, A.Z. 35, 17, P. 1116, 1354, a royal title.

neb āa, overlord, as opposed to , vassal-lord.

neb ānkh, , , , , , , "lord of life," *i.e.*, coffin, sarcophagus.

neb per, N. 708, "lord of the house."

neb-t per, "lady of the house," the chief wife of the master of the house as opposed to a concubine.

Neb peḥtit, the sacred boat of the Nome Metelites.

neb maāt, , , "lord of law," a god or a man whose actions are in accordance with physical or moral law; plur. , , , , .

neb meshma (?), Israel Stele 27, rebel.

neb netches, a vassal lord, as opposed to the overlord, .

neb-t hi , possessor of a husband, married woman.

neb khe-t , possessor of property, a rich man, a spirit provided with sepulchral offerings, a title of a god; fem. ; plur.  .

neb-t khabes , the crown of Upper Egypt.

Neb-t ser (?) 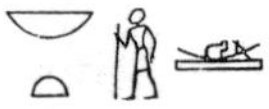, the name of the sacred boat of the Saïte Nome.

neb seshu (?) 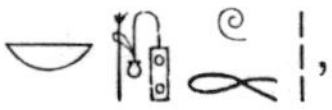, lord of books, author, scribe, librarian.

neb qeṭ 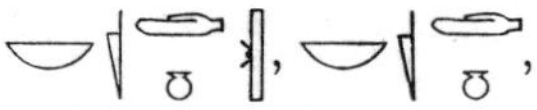, master of design or drawing, draughtsman.

neb kesu , he to whom homage is paid, *i.e.*, Rā, Osiris, the king, etc.

Neb , Thes. 818, Rec. 16, 106, a goose-god, a watcher of Osiris.

Nebti , Ṭuat IX, a god who swathed Osiris.

Nebu, U. 433, , T. 248, the "Lords"—a class of divine beings in the Ṭuat.

Neb-t , Rec. 20, 91 = Nephthys.

Nebti , T. 183,  , N. 766,  , A.Z. 1905, 19, the two goddesses of Upper and Lower Egypt, *i.e.*, Nekhebit and Uatchit.

Neb-[t] Aut , Ombos II, 130, a goddess.

Neb au-t-àb , Ṭuat VI, a god or goddess in the Ṭuat.

Neb-t au-t Khenti Ṭuat 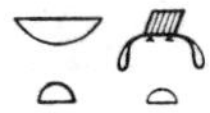 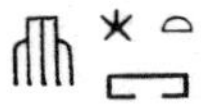, Ṭuat IX, a cow-goddess.

Neb àa , Ṭuat XII, a singing dawn-god.

Neb[t] Àa-t , Ombos II, 132, a goddess.

Neb[t] Àa-t-Then , Ombos II, 130, a goddess.

Neb-t Àamu , a title of Uatchit.

Neb àakhu-t , Metternich Stele, a title of Horus and Rā.

Neb-t àakhu , Ṭuat XI, a serpent dawn-goddess.

Neb àakhu-t , lord of the horizon—Horus or Rā.

Neb Àatit (?) , Ṭuat IX, a god.

Neb-t àaṭ-t , etc., B.D. 145 and 146, the name of the 16th Pylon.

Neb-[t] àāshemit (?)  , Ombos II, 132, a goddess.

Neb[t] àur , Ombos II, 130, the goddess of the river; compare הַיְאוֹר, Isaiah xix, 8, the stream of the Nile.

Neb àbu (ḥatu?) 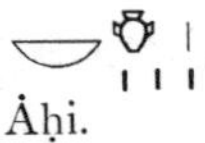, B.D. 149, 4, lord of hearts, a title of Àḥi.

Nebt àm (?) 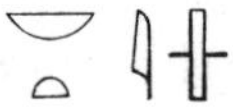, Ṭuat XII, a wind-goddess of dawn who helped to tow Àf through the serpent Ānkh-neteru.

Neb-t ànemit , Ombos I, 61, a goddess of offerings.

Neb àmakh , Ṭuat XII, one of the 12 gods who towed the boat of Àf through the serpent Ānkh-neteru; he was reborn daily.

Neb Àmentt 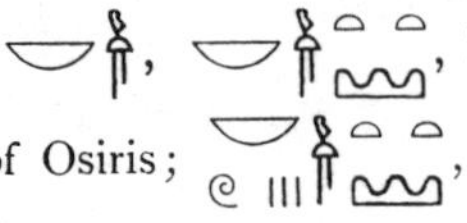, lord of Àmentt—a title of Osiris; the gods with Osiris in Àmentt.

Neb[t] Ȧn, Denderah III, 29, a cow-headed serpent—a form of Hathor.

Neb[t] Ȧnit, Ombos II, 130, a goddess.

Neb[t] ȧri-t-qerr-t, Ombos II, 133, the goddess who made the Nile sources (?)

Neb[t] ȧrit-tchetfiu, Ombos II, 133, the goddess who created reptiles.

Nebui ȧs-t, Cairo Pap. 22, 5, a pair of gods in the Ṭuat.

Neb[t] ȧs-ur, Ombos II, 132, a goddess.

Neb[t] ȧs-t-enti-mu (?), Ombos II, 130, a goddess.

Neb[t] ȧs-ḥatt, Ombos II, 133, a goddess.

Neb[t] ȧkeb, Ombos II, 130, a goddess.

Neb[t] Ȧter-[Meḥ], Ombos II, 131, a goddess.

Neb[t] ȧter-Shemā, Ombos II, 130, a goddess.

Neb-t Ȧṭu, Peasant 120, a goddess.

Neb āui, a title of a god.

Neb[t] āāu, Ombos II, 133, a goddess.

Neb ābui, "lord of the two horns"—a title of Osiris, of Ȧmen, and of Alexander the Great; Arab. ذو القرنين.

Nebt-ābui, Ombos I, 73, a goddess.

Neb ābui, B.D. 125, II, one of the 42 judges in the Hall of Osiris.

Nebt Ānnu, a goddess.

Neb ānkh, "lord of life"—a title of Osiris.

Neb ānkh, Ṭuat XII, a singing dawn-god connected with Sinai.

Neb ānkh ......, Berg. I, 23, a bird-god who revivified the souls of the dead.

Neb-t ānkh, a title of Isis and of other goddesses.

Neb-t ānkh, Ṭuat IV, Ṭuat I, Denderah IV, 60, 84, one of the 12 goddesses who opened the gates of the Ṭuat to Ȧf.

Neb[t] ānkh, Berg. II, 8, the goddess of the 5th hour of the night.

Neb-t ānkhiu, Ṭuat XI, a dawn-goddess (?) with two serpents.

neb, IV, 1105, "lord, life, strength, health [be to him]," *i.e.*, to the king.

Neb ānkh-em pet, P.S.B.A. III, 424, a god of .

Neb ānkh-taui, a title of Osiris.

Neb[t] ārui (?), Ombos II, 130, a goddess.

Neb-t āremuȧa (?), Ṭuat XII, a serpent fire-goddess.

Neb āḥa, Goshen 2, a form of Sepṭ as a war-god, hawk-headed, and hawk-and-lion-tailed.

Neb-t āḥāu , , the name of the 5th Gate in the Ṭuat.

Neb āq-t , Ṭuat X, a jackal-god who destroyed the dead.

Neb-t uauau , Ṭuat IX, a blood-drinking fiery serpent.

Neb Uast , , Ṭuat II and III, a god of the boat of Pakhit.

Neb-t uȧa , a title of each goddess in the boat of Ȧf.

Neb-uā , T. 237, , U. 416, , , Rec. 31, 165, the Lord One.

Neb uāb , title of the high-priest of Sebek.

Neb-t uu-t (?) , , Ombos I, 86, , Ombos II, 130, goddess of the fields and their produce—a form of Hathor and Isis.

Neb-un , Metternich Stele 87, a god.

Neb[t] Un , Ombos II, 130, a goddess.

Neb-t unnut , Pap. Ani 20, 9: (1) a uraeus on the brow of Rā; (2) title of each goddess who piloted the boat of Ȧfu-Rā during the night.

Neb urr-t , M. 708, N. 1324, , possessor of the Urrt Crown—a title of Osiris and of Horus as his successor.

Neb user , Berg. I, 25, a ram-headed god who befriended the dead.

Neb user , "possessor of strength," or "lord of powers"—the name of a god; var. , ,

Neb-t usha , Ṭuat VIII, the goddess of the 8th Division of the Ṭuat.

Neb[t] ugat a title of Hathor.

Neb utchat-ti , B.D. 163, a serpent-god with human legs.

Neb baiu , , Tomb Seti I, one of the 75 forms of Rā (No. 73).

Neb[t] baiu Neb[t] ȧakhu (?) , Ombos II, 132, a goddess.

Neb[t] Bȧa-t , Ombos II, 130, a goddess.

Neb-t Pe , a title of the goddess Uatchit.

Neb-t pet-ḥen-t-taui , etc., B.D. 145 and 146, the name of the 2nd Pylon.

Neb[t] petti , Ombos II, 133, a goddess.

Neb Pai , Rec. 14, 40, a title of Sebek.

Neb pāt , , Ṭuat IX, a god who swathed Osiris.

Neb[t] peru (?) , Ombos II, 131, a goddess.

Neb[t] Per-res , Ombos II, 132, a goddess.

Neb[t] peḥti , Ombos II, 132, a goddess.

Neb peḥti-petpet-sebȧu , B.D. 142, IV, 18, a title of Osiris.

Neb peḥti-thesu-menmen-t , Pap. Ani 29, the name of one half of the door of the Hall of Maāti.

Neb[t] Pesṭ-t (?) 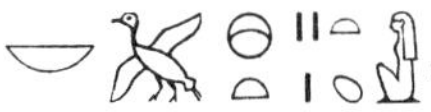, Ombos II, 130, a goddess.

Neb mau  B.D. 151, 2, "lord of eyes"—a title of "Beautiful Face."

Neb Maāt 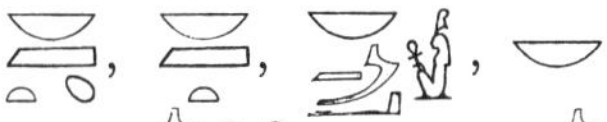

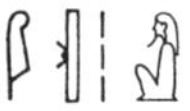, Berg. I, 11, B.D. 125 II, Lanzone, 175, a god of Maāti city, one of the 42 assessors of Osiris.

Neb Maāt-ḥeri-tep-reṭui-f 
, Pap. Ani 29, the name of one half of the door of the Hall of Maāti.

Neb Maq-t 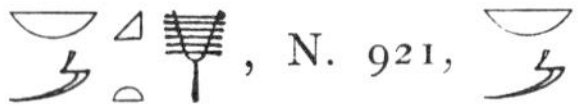
, P. 193, "lord of the ladder"—a title of Horus.

Neb-t måt , Ṭuat IX, a goddess in the Ṭuat.

Neb-t m'k-t , a city in the Ṭuat.

Neb-t m'k-t , Ṭuat I, one of the 12 doorkeeper goddesses of the earth.

Neb[t] mu (?) , Ombos II, 133, a goddess.

Neb[t] em-shen , Ombos II, 132, a goddess.

neb meṭut neter , "lord of sacred words," *i.e.*, of words written in hieroglyphs—a title of Thoth.

Neb[t] Nu-t , Ombos II, 130, the goddess of Ombos.

Neb nebu , B.D. 125, II, one of the 42 assessors of Osiris.

Neb-t neb-t , Ṭuat VII, a star-goddess.

Neb-t nebȧ 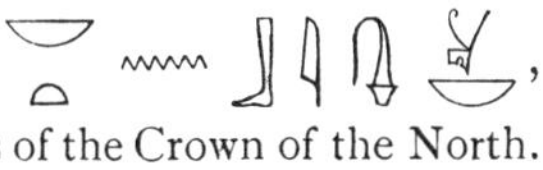, N. 165, a fire-goddess of the Crown of the North.

Neb nefu , B.D. 125, III, 15, a name of the Atfu Crown of Osiris.

Neb nemm-t , lord of the long stride—a title of a god.

Nebu en meḥt , B.D. 110, 20, the "lords of the North," *i.e.*, the inhabitants of the northern sea-coast and islands of the Mediterranean, Greeks; see **Meḥt-nebu.**

Neb[t] nerit , Ombos II, 130, consort of Neb-neru.

Neb neru , B.D. 17, 46, a title of the heart of Osiris.

Neb neru-āsh-kheperu 
, Cairo Pap. 22, 6, a serpent-god with five pairs of human legs from whose body five human heads project.

Neb nerau , Cairo Pap. 22, 3, a gazelle-god of Abydos.

Neb-t Neh-t , Lady of the Sycamore—a title of Nut or Hathor.

Neb[t] Nehemt , Ombos II, 130, a goddess.

Neb-t ent-ḥe-t 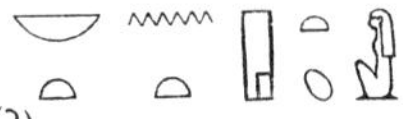, Ombos II, 132, Nephthys (?)

Neb-t en-sheta , Denderah IV, 61, a jackal-goddess.

Neb neḥeḥ , a title of Osiris.

Neb[t] neḥep , Ombos II, 133, a goddess.

Neb[t] Nekhen , Ombos II, 132, the goddess of Nekhen.

Neb nekht-khenen 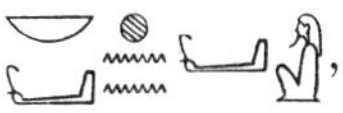, Ombos I, 45, a form of Horus.

Neb[t] neser , Ombos II, 108, a lion-headed goddess, a form of Sekhmit or Bast.

Neb[t] Neshȧ , Ombos II, 133, a goddess.

Neb net, Ṭuat III, a form of Osiris.

Neb-t Netit, Ombos II, 132, goddess of the place near Abydos where Osiris died.

Neb neᵗeru, the g.d of the 10th hour of the night.

Neb[t] Netchemtchem, Ombos II, 133, a goddess.

Neb-er-åri-tcher, Rev. 11, 108 = .

Neb renput, B.D. 85, 10, "lord of years"—a title of Osiris.

Neb rekhit, Ṭuat VIII, a god in the Circle Ḥetepet-neb-pers.

Neb Rasta, a title of Osiris that originally belonged to Seker the Death-god; the beings who lived in Rasta.

Nebt rekeḥ, Ṭuat IX, a blood-drinking fiery serpent-god.

Neb[t] reṭui, Ombos II, 133, a goddess.

Neb-er-tcher, Rec. 31, 17, "the lord to the uttermost limit," *i.e.*, the lord of the universe—a title of the Egyptian god; "his soul shall live in the hand of Neb-er-tcher."

Neb-er-tcher, Ṭuat VIII, one of the nine gods of the bodyguard of Åf in the Ṭuat.

Neb-t-er-tcher-t: (1) consort of Nebertcher; (2) a name of the Eye of Horus.

Neb[t] Ḥen, Ombos II, 131, the goddess of the bier.

Neb-t ḥe-t, U. 220, T. 177, P. 133, 519, M. 159, N. 651, T. 198, Rec. 3, 116, the goddess Nephthys, daughter of Geb and Nut, sister of Isis, Osiris, and Set; Copt. ⲛⲉⲃⲑⲱ. Later forms are :—

Neb-t ḥe-t, Ṭuat I, a singing-goddess.

Neb-t ḥe-t, Ṭuat II, a uraeus in the boat of Åfu.

Neb-t ḥe-t, Denderah IV, 81, an ibis-headed goddess.

Neb-t ḥe-t, Tomb Seti I, one of the 75 forms of Rā (No. 18).

Neb ḥe-t-ā, Cairo Pap. III, 2, a serpent-god.

Neb-t ḥe-t Ānqit, a fusion of the Nubian goddess Ānqit with Nephthys.

Neb[t] ḥa-Rā, Ombos II, 130, a goddess.

Neb[t] ḥuntt, Ombos II, 131, a goddess.

Neb[t] ḥebb, Ombos II, 133, a goddess.

Neb[t] ḥep, Ombos II, 132, a goddess.

Neb[t] ḥep (?), Ombos II, 132, a goddess.

Neb[t] ḥep-neteru (?), Berg. II, 9, warder of the 10th hour of the night.

Neb-t ḥen-t, Ombos I, 91, a goddess of agricultural produce.

Neb-ḥeru, B.D. 125, II, one of the 42 assessors of Osiris.

Neb-t ḥeru, Denderah III, 24, the goddess of the 1st hour of the night.

Neb ḥer-uā, B.D. 71, 3, 5, etc., a form of Horus.

Neb ḥeḥ, , , "possessor of eternity"—a title of Osiris; , the beings who live with Osiris.

Neb[t] ḥekau, Ombos II, 130, the goddess of spells.

Neb-t ḥetep-t, P. 92, M. 191, , N. 699, , , , a title of Hathor.

Neb[t] ḥetep, Cairo Pap. 22, 4, a crocodile-goddess.

Neb khe-t, B.D. 96, 3, "lord of creation"—a title of several great gods.

Neb-t kha-t, , , , B.M. 32, 261, 315, A.Z. 1864, 65, Nephthys.

Neb-t khaut, etc., etc., B.D. 145, 146, the 3rd Pylon of Sekhet Åaru.

nebu khau-t, lords of altars loaded with offerings.

Neb[t] Khasa, Ombos II, 130, a goddess.

Neb khāu, lord of risings, lord of coronations—a title of Rā who ascended his throne daily.

Neb[t] Khebit, , , B.D.G. 571, Ombos II, 131, the goddess of Chemmis.

Neb-t Kheper, Cairo Pap. 22, 3, a serpent-goddess of Heliopolis.

Neb Kheperu, a being who can change his form at will.

Neb Kheper-Khenti-Ṭuat, Cairo Pap. 3, 6, a Maāt-god of the Mesqet.

Neb khepesh, a title of the warrior-gods.

Nebt Kheriu, Ombos II, 108, a goddess, one of the 14 forms of Sekhmit.

Nebu Khert, Ṭuat III, a group of gods who bewitched Āapep and repulsed Åf and Sebȧ.

Neb Khert-ta, Ṭuat VII, a star-god.

Neb[t] Sa, , , Ombos II, 130, 133, a goddess.

Neb Sau, , T. 276, , P. 29, , M. 39, N. 68, Lord of Saïs, *i.e.*, Sebek.

Neb-t Sau, Lady of Saïs, *i.e.*, the goddess Neith.

Neb[t] sau-ta, Ombos II, 130, a goddess.

Neb[t] sam, Ombos II, 130, a goddess.

Neb Sakhb, a form of Horus and Osiris.

Neb[t] Såf (?), Ombos II, 132, a goddess.

Neb seb-t, M. 718, a god.

Neb[t] sebu, , Ombos II, 132, , a goddess.

Neb[t] Septi, Ombos II, 131, a goddess.

Neb senku, Tomb Seti I, a ram-headed god, one of the 75 forms of Rā (No. 75).

Neb-t senk-t, etc., etc. B.D. 145, 146, the 6th Pylon of Sekhet Åaru.

Neb-t senṭ-t , , Berg. II, 9, , , Denderah III, 24, IV, 84, , , Thes. 28: (1) the goddess of the 9th hour of the night; (2) a cat-headed goddess of Ḥet Berber.

Neb[t] s-res , Ombos II, 130, a goddess.

Neb[t] Seher.... , Ombos II, 130, a goddess.

Neb[t] Seḥt..... , Ombos II, 132, a goddess.

Neb sekh-t , T. 83, M. 236, , N. 614, , the master of the Elysian Fields.

Neb sekhut-uatch-t , T. 334, N. 704, lord of the fields of emerald—a title of Horus.

Neb sekhab , Denderah III, 36, a form of Horus and Osiris.

Neb[t] Sekhemu , Ombos II, 133, a goddess.

Neb ses , B.D.G. 1000, a mythological serpent connected with the Inundation.

Neb-t Seshemu-nifu , Ṭuat VIII, the name of a Circle.

Neb-t Seshen-t , the crown of Upper Egypt.

Neb-t sesheshu-ta (?) , Ṭuat XII, a fire-goddess.

Neb-t seshta , the goddess of the 6th hour of the night.

Neb[t] Sekri , Ombos II, 133, a goddess.

Neb[t] Segaui , Ombos II, 132, a goddess.

Neb Seger , Rec. 4, 29, , A.Z. 1908, 118: (1) a title of Osiris; (2) the name of a figure placed in the tomb.

Neb-t Seger , "lady of silence"—the goddess of the necropolis.

neb settut , lord of rays—a title of Rā.

Neb-t seṭau , Ṭuat IX, a singing-goddess.

Neb-t seṭau, etc. , etc., B.D. 145, 146, the 1st Pylon of Sekhet Åaru.

Neb-t setchefu , Ṭuat III, the 3rd Pylon of the Ṭuat.

Neb[t] Shas , Ombos II, 133, a goddess.

Neb-t shāt , Ṭuat IX, a singing-goddess of slaughter.

neb shuti , possessor of plumes—a title of Åmen-Rā.

Neb shefit , B.D.G. 293, a Tanite serpent-god of the Inundation.

Neb-t Shefshefit , Ṭuat IX, a singing-goddess.

Neb[t] shem , Ombos II, 133, a goddess.

Neb[t] shemās-urt , Ombos II, 130, the goddess of the crown of the South.

Neb shesa-t , U. 645, a title of .

Neb shespu , B.D. 21, a light-god.

Neb[t] sheser , Ombos II, 133, a goddess.

Neb[t] shesh-ḥer-âḥit-set  , Rec. 34, 191, one of the 12 forms of Thoueris; she presided over the month [illegible].

Neb qebḥ , Cairo Pap. 22, 4, a stork-headed god in the Ṭuat.

Neb-t qebḥ , consort of the preceding.

Neb[t] qerr-t 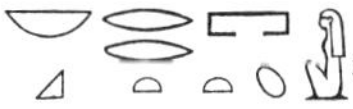, Ombos II, 130, the goddess of the Nile-springs.

Neb qers-t 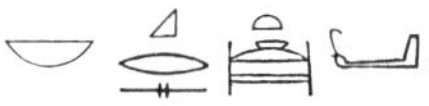, "lord of the coffin"—a title of Osiris.

Neb[t] Qeṭ , Ombos II, 133, a goddess.

nebu kau , P. 788, 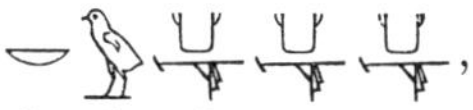, T. 191,  , N. 1288, , P. 429, , M. 614, , N. 1218, [illegible] [illegible], a group of divine beings.

Neb[t] Kepen 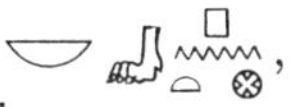, Ombos I, 94, the goddess of Byblos.

Neb[t] gem-âb (?) , Ombos II, 133, a goddess.

Neb[-t] Gerg , Ombos II, 131, a goddess.

neb taui , lord of the Two Lands, *i.e.*, of Upper and Lower Egypt—a common title of kings.

neb taiu , lord of lands, *i.e.*, of the world.

Neb-t taui , a goddess of Buto.

Neb-t taui 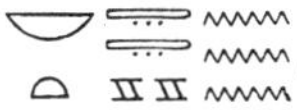, B.D. 110, a lake in Sekhet-Âaru.

Neb[t] Ta-âmen , Ombos II, 132, a goddess.

Neb Ta-ānkhtt 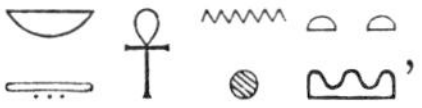, a title of Osiris.

Neb-t taui-em-karâ 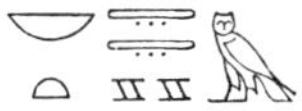 , B.D. 99, 10, the tying-up post of the magical boat.

Neb Ta-ṭesher 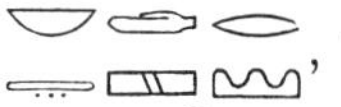, Ṭuat I and II, a singing jackal-god with [illegible] for a phallus.

Neb ta-tcheser-t , "lord of the holy land," *i.e.*, the Other World, a god in the Ṭuat.

Neb tau 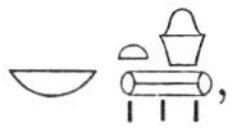, Cairo Pap. 22, 4, a serpent-god of Pa-urt.

Neb-[t] Tep [illegible], B.D.G. 699, [illegible] , a form of Hathor.

Neb-t tep-âḥ , B.D.G. 183, a form of Isis worshipped near Lake Moeris.

Neb[t] Tem 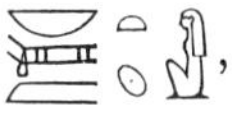, Ombos II, 132, a goddess.

neb temu , "lord of mortals"—a title of Osiris.

Neb-t teḥen , [illegible] , Denderah IV, 84, Berg. II, 8, Thes. 28, Lanzone 20, the goddess of the 1st hour of the night.

Neb tha (?) , "lord of the phallus," *i.e.*, Male—a title of Osiris.

Neb thafui 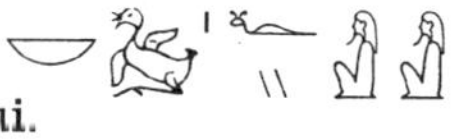, B.D. 71, 11; see **Thafui**.

Neb Ṭuatiu (?) [illegible], Ṭuat XII, a singing-god connected with Sinai.

Neb ṭebui , var. of .

neb ṭema-t , IV, 617, lord of the wing, *i.e.*, hawk.

Nebt ṭemâ-t , Ṭuat IX, a singing-goddess.

Neb[t] Ṭennu , Ombos II, 133, a goddess.

Neb[t] Ṭens 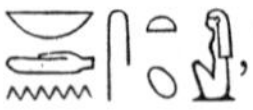, Ombos II, 133, a goddess.

Neb-t Ṭenṭen, etc. 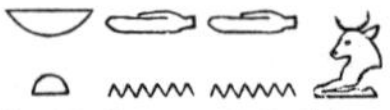, etc., B.D. 145, 146, the 14th Pylon of Sekhet-Åaru.

Neb ṭesher , Berg. I, 18, a crocodile-god who befriended the dead.

Neb ṭesher-t , "lord of blood"—a title of Rā.

Neb ṭesheru , Düm. T.I. 25, , Thes. 818, Rec. 16, 106, a hawk-god, son of Meḥurit, and one of the seven wise lords; see **Tchaåsiu VII.**

Neb tchefa , Lord of celestial food, *i.e.*, Osiris.

Neb tchefau , Pleyte Ét. 261, a serpent-god of offerings.

Neb tcher , , see **Neb-er-tcher.**

Neb-t tcheser 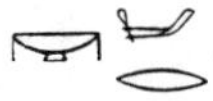, Berg. II, 8, the goddess of the 6th hour of the night.

Neb tcheser-sesheta , Denderah III, 24, the name of the 6th hour of the night.

Neb tchet , "lord of eternity"—a title of Osiris.

nebu tchet , the eternal beings in the Ṭuat.

Neb tchet , Denderah IV, 78, a lion-headed warrior-god.

Neb-t tchet 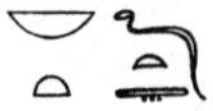, Ṭuat XII, one of the 12 goddesses who towed the boat of Åf through the serpent Ānkh-neteru.

Neb[t] tcheṭ 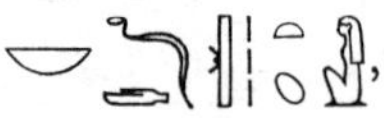, Ombos II, 133, a goddess.

neb , P. 181, M. 282, A.Z. 1906, 118, cup, basin, basket.

neb-t , basket; plur. .

neb , P. 460, , N. 1179, , P. 524, , M. 162, , to swim; Copt. ⲛⲉⲉⲃⲉ.

nebå , T. 180, swimmer.

neb-t , swimming, swim.

nebb  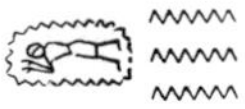, to swim.

nebneb 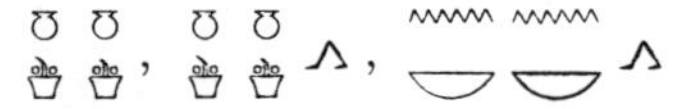, to walk, to journey, to mount up, to overflow.

nebåut , secretions, droppings, emissions.

neb , Rev. 13, 57, to strive, to argue.

neb 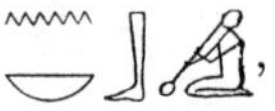, N. 757, to smelt, to work in metals.

nebi , Rev. 6, 42, to form, to fashion.

neb ; var. 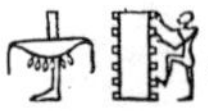, to build.

nebneb , to defend, to protect; var. .

Nebå 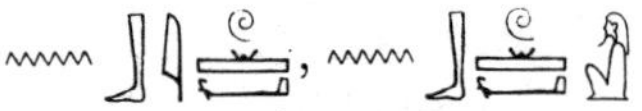, the divine maker of eternity [illegible].

nebi [illegible] [illegible], protector, supporter, friend.

neb-t [illegible], a kind of metal.

neb [illegible], Rec. 4, 29, stick, staff, club, lance.

neb, neb-t [illegible], Metternich Stele 71, [illegible], fire, flame.

nebit [illegible], Rec. 30, 32, [illegible] [illegible], flame, fire.

Nebneb 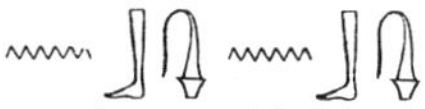, Ombos II, 108, one of the 14 forms of Sekhmit.

Neb , the name of a fiend.

nebi, Rev. 14, 56, fault, sin; Copt. ⲛⲟⲃⲓ.

nebu (ḥu) 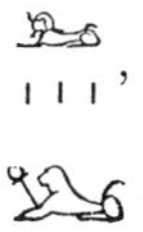, ornaments in the form of lions or sphinxes.

neb ānkh, statue, image (Denderah).

neba , a kind of wig.

neba 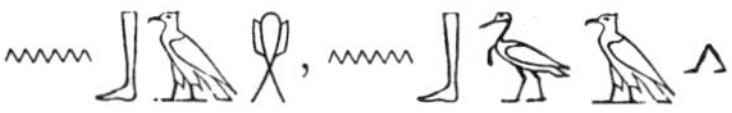, Ebers Pap. 102, 14 . . . .

neba-t  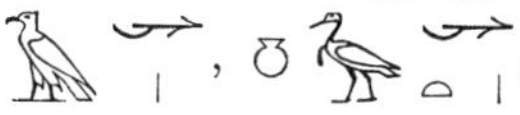, stick, staff, peg, club, implement of slaughter; plur.  .

nebaba , N. 510 . . . .

Neba-t-s-kheper , , Thes. 31, Denderah III, 24, the goddess of the 11th hour of the day.

nebȧ , Rec. 30, 32, N. 969, Hymn Darius 13, to burn, to flame up, flamer, burner.

nebȧ-t , N. 208, , , fire, flame.

nebȧut , T. 26, fire, flame; , IV, 383, flames;  , flame of fire.

Nebȧ , B.D. 125, II, one of the 42 assessors in the Hall of Osiris.

Nebȧ 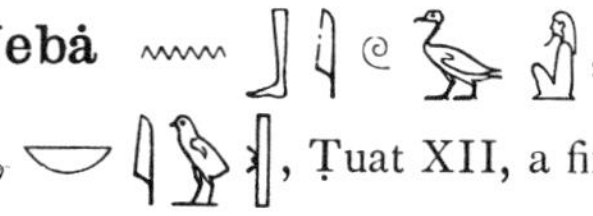, Nesi-Ȧmsu 32, 7, Ṭuat XII, a fire-god.

Nebȧui , Ṭuat II, a double fire-god.

Nebȧ-ȧakhu 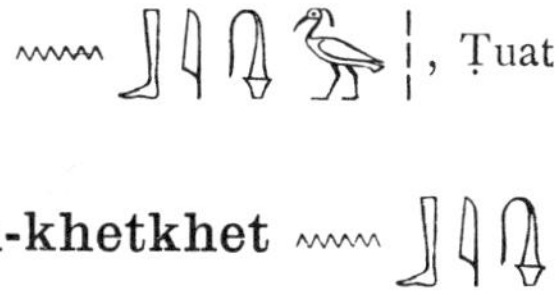, Ṭuat XII, a paddle-god.

Nebȧ-per-em-khetkhet , B.D. 125, II, a god of Sheṭen, one of the 42 assessors of Osiris.

Nebȧ-t-em-reṭui-f 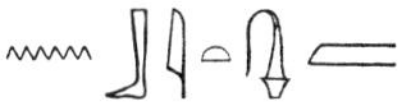 , B.D. (Saïte) 71, 7, a fire-god.

Neb-ḥer, Nebȧ-ḥer , , B.D. 17, Ṭuat III: (1) one of the seven spirit guardians of Osiris; (2) the steersman of the god Penā.

nebȧ 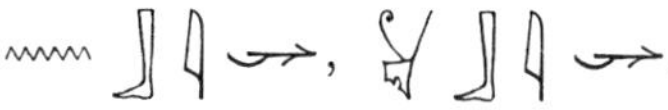, a carrying pole.

nebi , A.Z. 1899, 13, stick, swinging stick, pole, leg of a chair; plur. 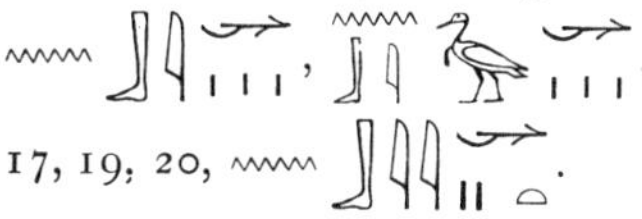, Mar. Karn. 42, 17, 19, 20.

nebȧu , stool, seat, chair.

nebȧ-t 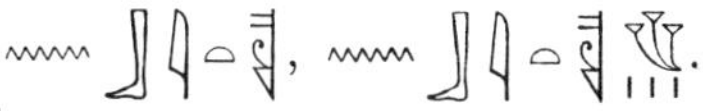. [illegible], a resinous plant.

nebȧu , Rev. 11, 130, lock of hair, tress.

Nebȧu, B.D. 55, 3, a mythological bird (?)

nebȧnȧ , Rec. 19, 95, poles for carrying a shrine.

nebȧnau , flames.

nebit, a seat in a chariot.

nebi, nebibi , , leopard, panther.

Nebeḥ , B.D. 55, 3, a mythological bird.

nebs , M. 336, 720, P.S.B. 13, 496,  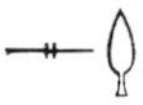, a kind of fruit-bearing tree, mulberry (?); plur. , Rec. 31, 24,  , Koller Pap. 4, 1, zizyphus spina Christi—the lote tree; Arab. نبق.

nebs , U. 160, T. 131, 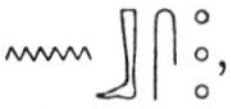,  the fruit of the nebs tree, mulberries (?)

Nebs (?) 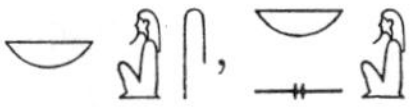, the name of a god (?)

Nebt , a cloud fiend.

nebti 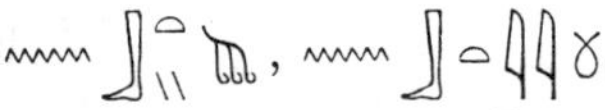, Rev. 11, 109, wig, headdress, tress;  , the hair recently dressed.

nebṭ 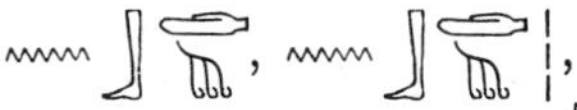, to tie up the hair, to plait the hair, to twist;  , IV, 613, to lead captive by the hair; Copt. ⲛⲟⲩⲃⲧ.

nebṭ-t , 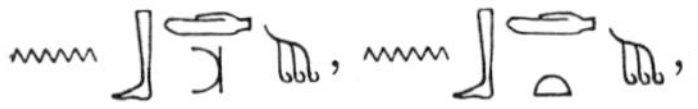, twist, plait, a kind of cloud, tress, lock of hair; Copt. ⲛⲉⲃϯ.

nebṭ 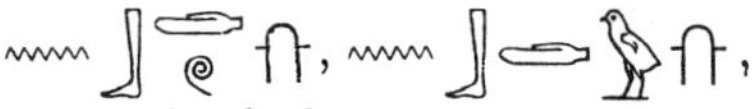, a plaited mat, a string bed.

Nebṭu qeṭ  , Tombos Stele 7,  , 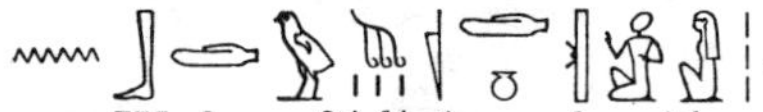, Rec. 22, 107, IV, 84, a Sûdânî people with small round curls all over their heads—“fuzzy-wuzzies.”

Nebṭ 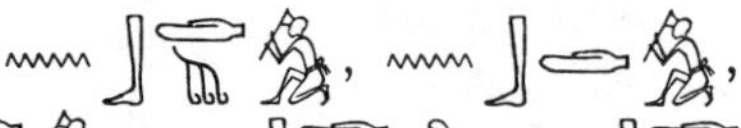, 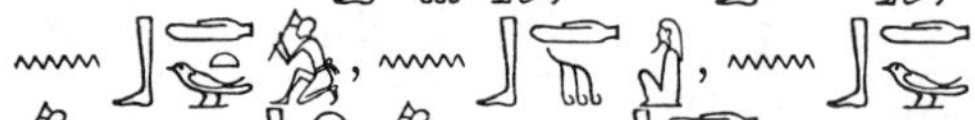, , B.D. 21, 4, 130, 36, Nesi-Åmsu 5, 2, 10, 14, B.M. 32, 106, a storm-fiend.

Nebṭ-åb-f , , B.D. 39, 15, a storm-fiend.

nebṭ 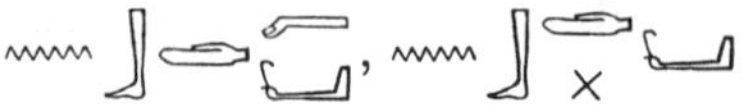, Rec. 16, 94, , to forge, to hammer.

nebṭ , to plate, to overlay with metal, to put bands of metal on something.

nebṭu 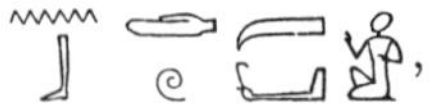, Rec. 19, 92, a plaiter of baskets.

nebṭu 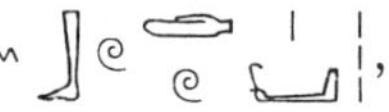, A.Z. 1900, 37 . . . . . .

Nebetch , H. 366, a “hairy” god; plur. , , Rec. 36, 216.

nebetchbetch , P. 194, M. 367, N. 922, to hover (?) to alight.

nep, nep-t , sole of the foot (?) a member of the body, limb.

nepi [illegible], to water, to flood, to pour out water, to overflow.

nepu [illegible], waves (?); [illegible] [illegible], Rec. 5, 97 . . . . . .

nep-t [illegible], land which is regularly watered, corn-land; see [illegible].

nep [illegible], [illegible], grain, corn.

nepi [illegible], [illegible], Rec. 27, 86, grain, corn.

nepit [illegible], grain, corn.

Nep [illegible], Rec. 27, 220, the Grain-god.

Nepit [illegible], Ombos I, 52, [illegible], the goddess of grain.

nepnep [illegible], Amherst Pap. 1, Peasant 50, a kind of cloth.

Nepnep-t, P. 642, , M. 678, , N. 1240, a goddess = .

nepa-t, , U. 137, , , grain, corn.

nepa, Rec. 31, 12, cords.

nepȧ, , , , grain, corn; see .

Nepȧ, the Grain-god.

nepi, , lock of hair.

Nep-meḥ, a god of the Gate Saa-Set; var. , B.D.G. 89.

Nepen, P. 63, M. 86, N. 93: (1) a form of Nut; (2) a corn-god in Ṭuat II; (3) a serpent in Ṭuat I and II.

nepen-t (?), T. 316, food (?)

neper, , , seed, grain, corn; Copt. **ⲛⲁⲡⲣⲉ, ⲛⲁⲫⲣⲓ.**

neper-t, , , Gol. 14, 4, corn land, arable land.

neper-t, corn-bin, corn-store, granary.

Nepr, Neprȧ, P. 219, , Rec. 31, 20, , Rec. 30, 193, 31, 16, (=), Rec. 31, 15, , , Ṭuat II, , Hymn to Nile 1, 5, the Corn-god.

Nepertiu, Ṭuat II, a group of grain-gods or harvest-gods.

neper-t, boss, stud; plur. , Rec. 27, 225, ; , thou washest thy feet on a slab of silver studded with turquoises.

nper = **per**, N. 88, 95, P. 100.

nepeḥ, , , , Rec. 17, 176, , , Rec. 18, 176, udder; , Hearst Pap. 3, 4, , udder and teats.

nept, , to strike, to stab, to slay.

nepṭ, Rec. 30, 69, , , , Hh. 453, to strike, to stab, to shoot down, to slay.

neptchtch, , , T. 389, M. 404, to shoot, to slay.

nef, , , , a demonstrative particle; var. , , , A.Z. 1874, 149, 1877, 34, Mendes Stele 25.

nef, Rec. 26, 12, IV, 1091, Wazîr 12, Shipwreck 149, Pap. 3024, 129, to commit an act of injustice or folly, to do wrong.

nefi (?), to sin (?) Copt. **ⲛⲟⲃⲉ.**

nefi, , , , foe, enemy, evil one, evil-doer, sinner; plur. , .

nefi, , , , , to breathe, to blow at; , A.Z. 1874, 65, to give breath to, *i.e.*, to set free (a prisoner); Copt. **ⲛⲓϥⲉ**, compare Heb. נָפַח, Arab. نفخ, Eth. ነፍኀ :

nef, , , , , , , Rec. 31, 16, , Rec. 33, 36, air, wind, breath;

, gentle breezes; , breath of life; , the dawn wind; Copt. ⲛⲓϥⲉ.

nefu , Israel Stele 3, breath, *i.e.*, freedom.

nefut, nefuit , , Rec. 36, 216, breezes.

nefu , Koller Pap. 3, 7, , Rev. 12, 11, , , , , , A.Z. 1907, 125, , , , sailor; plur. , Rev. 12, 57, , Rev. 11, 173, , chief of the sailors, *i.e.*, captain; Copt. ⲛⲉⲉϥ, ⲛⲉⲉⲃ.

Nef-ur (?) , name of a district (?)

Nef-em-baiu , Tomb Seti I, one of the 75 forms of Rā (No. 7).

Nef-ḥati, etc. , Ombos II, 134, a mythological being.

nefuti (?) , Rec. 30, 67, a part of the sail tackle of a ship.

nef-t , , fan.

nefut , a cook's fans for blowing the fire.

nef , P.S.B. 22, 146, , Koller Pap. 4, 3, the wind plant (cyperus esculentus).

nefa , , , P. 1116B, 30, , , , , , a demonstrative particle: that, those; plur. of , or , or ; , in this and that.

nefafa , , , Rec. 36, 213 . . . . .

nef , U. 609, P.S.B. 20, 325, to drive away (?)

nefā , to glide (?) to slide (?)

nefā , Anastasi IV, 2, 12, Koller Pap. 3, 1, a plant, herb.

nefnef , , , flood, inundation.

Nefnef , Edfû I, 78, a name of the Nile-god.

nfetfet , Sphinx 14, 204, , rising flood.

Nefnef , a serpent deity; var. .

nefer , , , , , to be good, good, pleasant, beautiful, excellent, well-doing, gracious, happy, pretty, to progress favourably in sickness, to recover; Copt. ⲛⲟⲩϥⲉ.

nefer — em neferu , by the favour of; , Israel Stele 6, by the favour of the darkness.

nefer , T. 338, , good, material and immaterial, physical and mental; plur. , T. 338, N. 624, , , , , , ; , , virtues, noble attributes, beauty;

neferui , , , , , , , , , , twice good, doubly good, how beautiful! , very good water; , very good wine.

nefer , fine gold; , very great; , lucky name; ,

happiness, var. 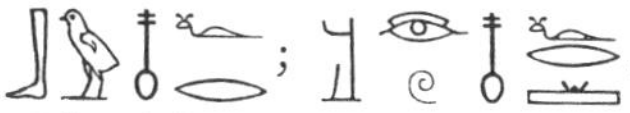 ; , a good look-out;  , good luck.

nefer — , for the best; , I, 102, no one at all plundered; , with the greatest success; 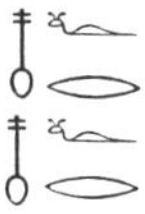  , very, very good; , most beautiful of all.

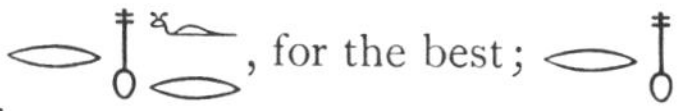

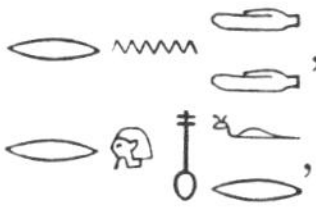

nefer 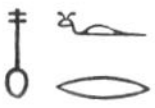 , to succeed, to prosper; Herusâtef Stele 15, it shall not succeed.

neferu 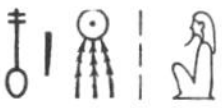 , Rec. 32, 177, splendours.

nefer-t , , , a good or beautiful thing, prosperity, happiness, success; plur. , IV, 967, , ; , all good things.

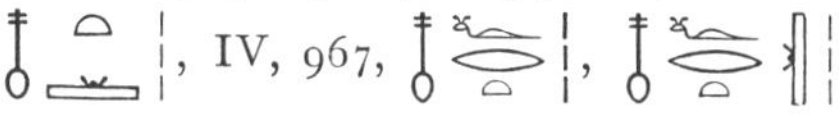

nefer , P. 98, M. 68, , N. 48, assuredly.

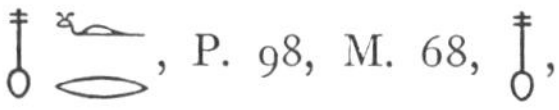

nefer n , , a strong negative.

nefrit er , , , , IV, 1107, up to, until; 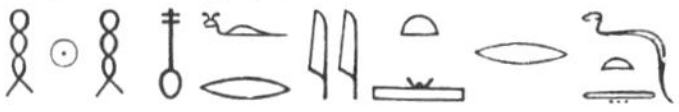 , A.Z. 1905, 31.

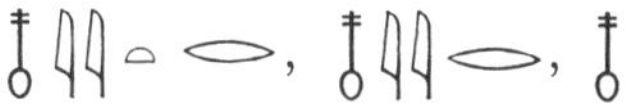

nefer ḥa-t  , to be of a good or kind disposition.

nefer ḥer àb (ḥa-t)  , good to the heart, *i.e.*, good in the opinion of someone.

Nefer-ḥa-t  , a kind of crown.

Nefer-ḥer 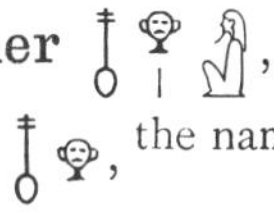 , "beautiful face"—a name of Rā; , the name for the sun at the 4th hour of the day.

nefer-t-ḥer  "pretty face," used of a woman.

Nefer-tut (?)  , the title of the priestess of Memphis.

nefri , , good one, beautiful one.

neferu , , U. 584, T. 42, P. 181, 667, M. 776, 794, those who are good or happy;  , a title of the dead; fem. .

nefer-t , , Rec. 15, 162, door, gate, portal.

nefer 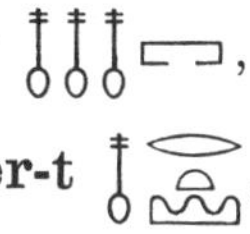 , "house of beauty"—a name for the grave.

Nefer-t , the beautiful, or good, land, a name of Àmentt.

Nefer , (with □), the "good god"—a title of Osiris.

Nefrit 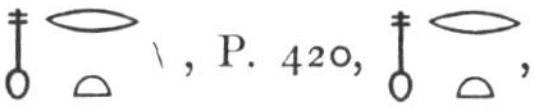 , P. 420, , M. 602,  , N. 1207, a goddess, daughter of the Great God.

Nefrit  , the good, or beautiful, goddess, the virgin-goddess.

Nefrit 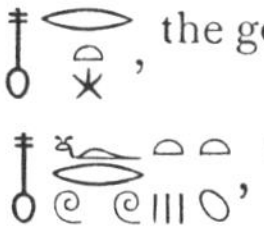 , the goddess of the 11th hour of the day.

Nefrit , Ombos I, 47, a hippopotamus-goddess.

Nefer-àa-t-mek-àr-t , , , Rec. 34, 190, one of the 12 Thoueris goddesses.

Neferàitȧ , a form of Hathor and Nut.

Nefer-usr 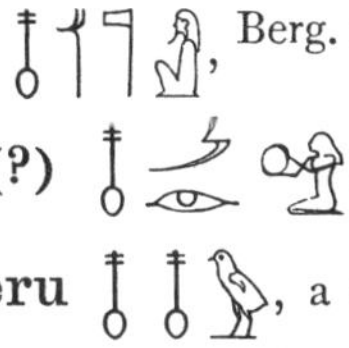 , Berg. 1, 18, a hawk-god.

nefer ma (?) , tambourine girl.

Nefer-neferu , a ram-god, the god of the 4th day of the month.

Nefer-ḥat  , Rec. 4, 28,  , Düm. T.I. 25, Thes. 818, , Rec. 16, 106, a god of learning and one of the seven divine sages, sons of Meḥurit.

Neferit-ḥerit-tchatchat , Ṭuat XII, a fire-goddess.

Nefer-ḥetep 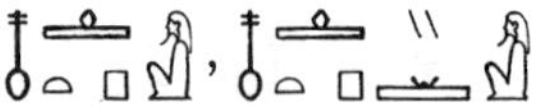, 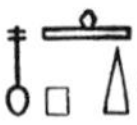, a god of Thebes specially associated with Khensu.

Nefer-ḥetep-pa-āa  , Nefer-ḥetep Major.

Nefer-ḥetep-pa-neterāa 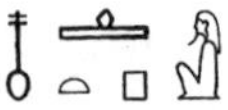 , Nesi-Åmsu 17, 20, Nefer-ḥetep the Great God.

Nefer-ḥetep-pa-khart  , Nesi-Åmsu 17, 20, Nefer-ḥetep Minor.

Neferit-khā 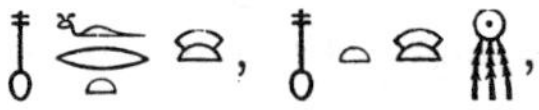, Ṭuat I and II, a fire-goddess and guide of Åfu-Rā.

Nefer-Shuti 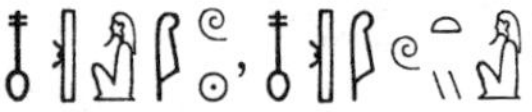, Rev. 14, 40, a form of the Sun-god.

nefer shefi , terribly beautiful one.

neferu kau , a class of divine beings.

Nefer-Tem  , B.D. 125, II, one of the 42 assessors of Osiris.

Nefer-Tem 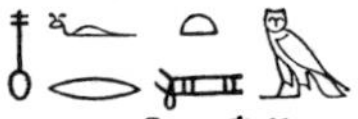, U. 592, , P. 680, 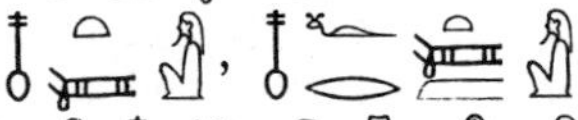, 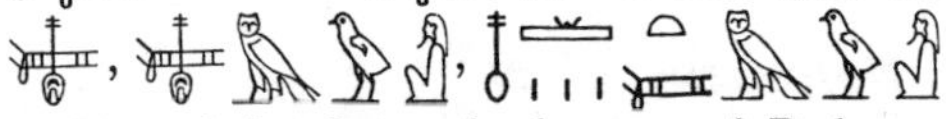, a form of the Sun-god, the son of Ptaḥ and Sekhmit; , is the name of the Sun-god at the 2nd hour of the day.

Nefer-Tem-Rā-Ḥeru-åakhuti 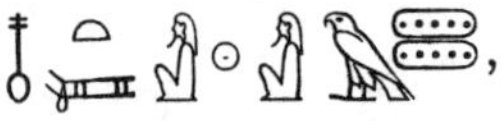, a triad of solar gods.

Nefer-Tem-khu-taui , , a form of Tem.

Nefer-Tem-kau 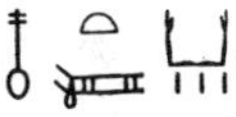, a god worshipped at Abydos.

nefer , seed, phallus; plur.  , Hymn Darius 27.

nefer 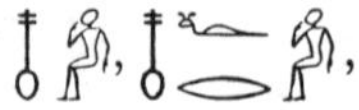, child, youth, young man; , B.D.G. 1064, , IV, 1006, , young soldiers; , young men and maidens.

nefer-t 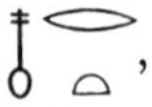, U. 182, 183, 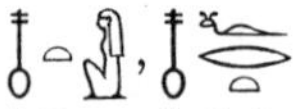 , virgin; plur. , , 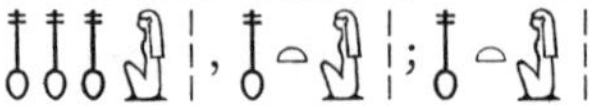; , palace beauties.

nefer 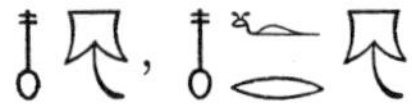, young horse; plur. [illegible] [illegible], Rec. 33, 6, cavalry, [illegible].

nefer-t [illegible], young cow; plur. [illegible] [illegible], IV, 1023, 1161, [illegible].

nefer-t [illegible], Thes. 919, young lioness.

nefer [illegible] [illegible], Rev. 14, 65, grain; Copt. ⲡⲁⲫⲣⲓ.

nefrit [illegible], Rev. 14, 65, grain.

nefer-t [illegible], IV, 688, a kind of bread.

nefer-t [illegible], a plant or tree; [illegible], flowers, blossoms.

nefer, nefer-t [illegible], a name of the White Crown, or crown of the South.

nefer [illegible], a kind of woven stuff; plur. [illegible].

nefer-t [illegible], bandlet, [illegible] [illegible], Peasant 158, cord, rope, tow-line.

neferu [illegible], A.Z. 1908, 88, weavers of nefer cloth.

nefer , a slow fire; , sacred fire.

nefrit , fire.

nefrit  (N. 1043), 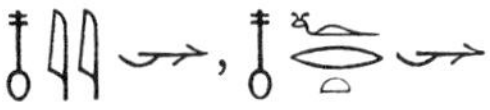, paddle, steering pole.

nefru , B.D. 15, 47, the look-out perch in the boat of Rā.

nefer-t , guitar; Heb. נֵבֶל.

nfekhfekh , to untie.

neft , Famine Stele 21, to bow under oppression, to suffer.

nem , Rev. 12, 8, who? Copt. ⲛⲓⲙ.

nim-t (?)  Rev. 13, 3, who? Copt. ⲛⲓⲙ.

nem , B.D. (Saïte) 101, 5, 163, 15, 164, 10, with; Copt. ⲛⲉⲙ.

nem ,  to do evil, to defraud, mistake, error, mean, abased, contemptible.

nemi , wrong-doer.

nemm , Rev. 14, 14, , to persecute.

nemȧ , destroyer, evil-doer.

nemm-t 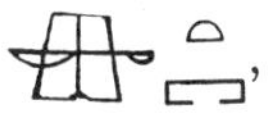, P. 87, T. 332, execution chamber, the block of punishment. Later forms are:—  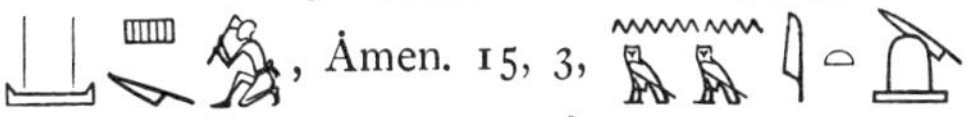 (Åmen. 15, 3)  (Åmen. 21, 20) , Rev. 11, 185.

Nemm-t , P. 87, N. 46, the slaughter-house of Khenti Åmenti.

nemm-t , slaughter-house for cattle.

nemtiu , executioners, headsmen.

nemmȧ , , torture, slaughter.

nemit , torture.

nemit , Rev., a sacrifice.

nem, nemȧ  (T. 37, 395),  (P. 204, Rec. 29, 146, A.Z. 1905, 22), to travel or walk about, to journey hither and thither.

nem-t 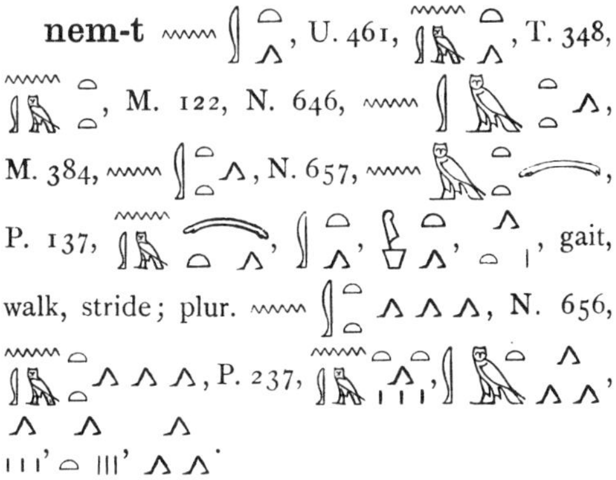 (U. 461, T. 348, M. 122, N. 646, M. 384, N. 657, P. 137), gait, walk, stride; plur. (N. 656, P. 237).

nemti 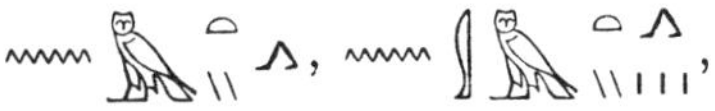, A.Z. 1908, 116, walker, strider.

Nemȧu shā , Thes. 1296,  , those who traverse the sand, *i.e.*, the nomad tribes of the desert; var.  

nemm M. 81, 436, to walk, to stride.

nemm Rev. 12, 72, to escape.

nemmȧ walk, stride.

nemmti to walk, to stride.

nemmti , walker, strider.

nemnem  , P. 688, N. 88, , N. 1032,  , U. 497, T. 27, 346, Rec. 31, 27,  , A.Z. 1901, 45, to run, to hurry one's steps.

nemnemȧ  , wriggler, applied to a reptile, worm, snake, etc.

nem  , star; plur. .

Nemu 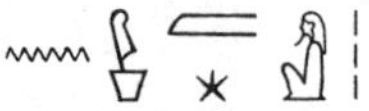 , Leemans Pap. Eg. II, 2, the Dekans (?) a group of star-gods.

Nemu  , Rec. 31, 17, a group of gods, wandering stars (?)

Nem  , U. 545, T. 299, , P. 232, a god, son of Nemȧ-t .

Nemȧt  , U. 544, T. 299, , P. 232, a goddess, the mother of Nem.

Nemit 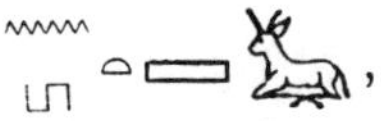 , P. 352, , N. 1068, a cow-goddess in the Ṭuat.

Nem-ur , , B.D. 206, , Rev. 13, 74, a bull-god of Ȧnu (Heliopolis); Gr. Μνηυις. Strabo XVII, 1, 22; Diodorus I, 24, 9; Am. Marcellinus XXII, 14, 6; Aelian, De Nat. Animal. XII, 11.

nemȧ  , P. 306, , P. 613,  , P. 480, , P. 77,  , P. 162, M. 413, to travel by boat, to sail, to float;  , P. 706.

nemȧu  , boats.

nem , P. 440, M. 543, N. 1124, lake.

nemȧ , Rec. 31, 192, lake.

nem  , to bathe, to swim;  , IV, 1031.

nem , , IV, 687, wine press, wine vat.

nem  , cellar, storeroom.

nem (nekhnem?) , , , unguent, perfume, perfume pot.

nemu  , large stone or mud vessels for storing grain; , A.Z. 1904, 91, metal storage pots.

nemt-t  , pot, vessel, vase.

nem , Rev. 13, 22, tamarisk flowers; Copt. ⲛⲁⲙ.

nem  , Rec. 19, 96, part of a shrine.

nem , Metternich Stele 223, , , , , , pygmy, dwarf.

Nemmȧ  , B.D. 164 (Vignette), a man-hawk-god, a form of Menu.

Nem  , B.M. 32, 208, consort of .

nem 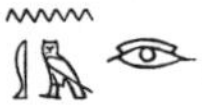 , Thes. 926, to sleep, slumber.

nemnem  , to sleep soundly.

nem  , Rev. 12, 32, 56, to repose, to sleep, to slumber; compare Heb. נוּם, Arab. نام, Syr. ܢܡ, Eth. ኖመ:

nemm  , Rec. 6, 117, to stretch oneself out to sleep.

nemm  , to sit, to dwell.

nemm , , to lie down, to sleep, bed, couch, bier.

nemt-t  , couch, bed, bier.

nemm-t, bedchamber.

nemmȧ-t, , , , Rec. 3, 54, couch, bed, bier, burial.

nemmit, bed, couch, bier.

nem-ti, nostrils.

nemai, Rev. 12, 62, , Demot. Cat. 352, island; Copt. ⲙⲟⲩⲉ.

nemai, Rev. 13, 10, , Rev. 13, 23, , Rev. 14, 36, to be new, to bloom afresh.

nema, , , , , to be new.

nema-t, , a new thing.

nematchu (?), U. 557 . . . .

nemȧ, to bellow, to roar, to low; varr. , .

nemȧ (nemt?), , , Hymn to Nile, to move up and down (of the Nile).

nemȧtạ (?), to stride, to walk.

nemȧti-t, stride, walk.

nemmȧta, , walk, stride.

nemā (nem'), Hh. 431, , Rev. 14, 97 , , , , who; Copt. ⲛⲓⲙ.

nemā, Peasant B. 2, 104, Pap. 3024, 2, 3, to shout down, to overargue.

nemā, Rev. 11, 174, strong (?)

nemā, Rev. 13, 68, destruction.

nemā, Thes. 1482, IV, 971, , , Gol. 10, 43, to destroy, to overthrow, to punish.

nemmāi, destroyer, evildoer.

nemā, Festschrift 117, 12, , Mar. Aby. I, 6, 38, to sleep, to lie down, to rest.

nemmā, , , , , to lie down, to sleep, to rest.

nemmā, , , couch, bedclothes, bier, burial.

nemā, Mar. Aby. I, 6, 4, to build, to construct.

nemmā, , , to build, to construct.

nemer, steering pole, paddle.

nemḥ (?), P. 538, , , P. 539 . . . .

nemḥ, A.Z. 1880, 56, a stone used for making amulets.

nemḥ, , , , to be poor or helpless, to be in need, to be destitute.

nemḥu, , , , Rec. 17, 4, , , , , , Edict 14, poor man, orphan, any destitute person; plur. , Israel Stele 14, , , IV, 972, , , A.Z. 1905, 103, , ; , Rec. 21, 14, fountain for the poor.

nemḥit , an unmarried woman, a woman who is not provided for.

nemḥit , Rec. 17, 160, the poor of the city; 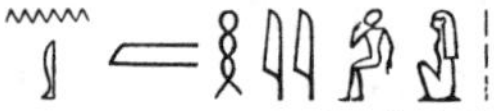 , B.M. 41645, poor women and rich women.

nemmḥu , Åmen. 25, 12, , Åmen. 9, 1, 10, 7,  , poor man, orphan; plur. , .

nems , A.Z. 1908, 16, an amulet; , a golden nemes.

nems-t 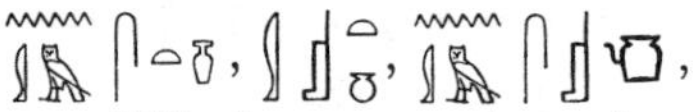,  , a kind of vase or pot in stone or alabaster, used in ceremonies; plur. , P. 551, 610,  .

nems-t — , P. 333, M. 735, , the four vases which were used ceremonially.

nems , to put on a head-cloth, to clothe, to be arrayed, to veil.

nems   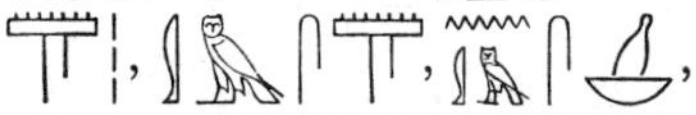, Rec. 31, 172, 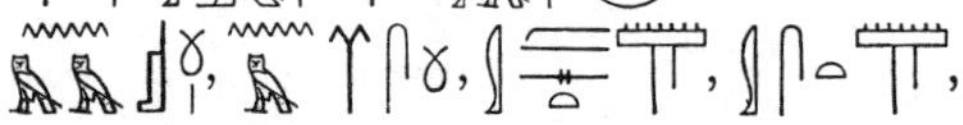, a covering for the head, tiara, fillet, a head-cloth worn by the king ceremonially, veil (?); 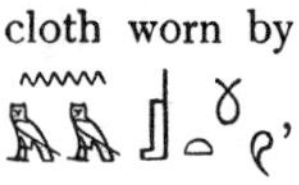, Metternich Stele 159, a covering of flesh.

nems, nemms , to illumine, to enlighten.

nems , to provide with (?)

nemt-t  , a kind of fish.

nemmta (?) , a kind of fish.

nemta 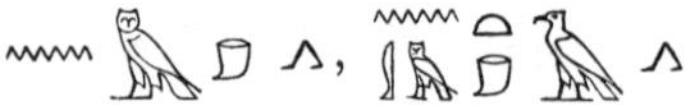, to stride, to walk over, to go about.

nemmta , to stride, to walk.

nemmtita (?) , to walk, to step out.

nemti , Rev. 11, 124 = Copt. ⲙⲙⲁⲧⲉ.

nemti , Rev. 11, 124, 151, , Rev. 11, 160,  , strength; Copt. ⲛⲟⲙϯ.

nemtch-t , B.D. 149, V, 6, place of slaughter.

nn [illegible], not, no.

nn [illegible] = Copt. ⲁⲛⲟⲛ.

nn [illegible], a demonstrative particle; [illegible], B.D. 64, 19, [illegible], Rec. 3, 49, 5, 86, [illegible], this or that; [illegible], Åmen. 5, 18, these things.

Nen [illegible], U. 537, [illegible], B.D. (Saïte) 64, 11, the Sky-god.

Nenit (fem.) [illegible], U. 537, [illegible], B.D.G. 1064.

nen [illegible], to smear, to anoint.

nenu (nu?) , salve, ointment.

nen , to be weary, to be tired, to be helpless, to be inactive, to be inert, to be lazy, to do nothing, to rest, to be sluggish.

nen , Koller Pap. 4, 8, indolence; , Rec. 6, 7.

neni , Rec. 31, 171, , an inert or lazy or helpless man, sluggard, idler; plur. .

Neniu , B.D. 7, 2, "the helpless," *i.e.*, the damned.

Nenut , Rec. 31, 15, , the helpless, inert wicked.

Neni , evil spirit, fiend, devil (masc.).

Nenit , evil spirit, fiend (fem.).

Neniu , the allies of Āapep.

nen-t , , the place where nothing is done, the grave.

nen , the time of inactivity, the night.

nen , likeness, image.

nen , P. 831, 832, to move, to go, to retreat; , Rec. 25, 126, to pass by (of the years).

nenu , U. 450, , T. 258, he who retreats; , N. 774, , N. 662.

Neni , T. 305, a serpent-fiend.

nen , a kind of stuff, a bandlet, thread, = .

nen-t , A.Z. 1906, 118, a kind of plant; , rushes.

nen-t , flame, fire.

nenai , he who tarries or delays.

nenai (?) , air, breath, breeze, wind.

nenȧ , = , to do homage.

nenȧab-t , Rhind Pap. 30 . . . .

Nenā , Ṭuat II, a god in the Ṭuat.

Nenā‘ ; see .

nenā-t , bundle of reeds, book (?) N. 838 = , P. 166, M. 320.

Neniu , B.D. 168, a group of four goddesses who befriended the dead.

neniu (nuiu?) , beings who observe or keep watch over time, the divine timekeepers in the Ṭuat.

nenibu , the frankincense plant.

neniben , frankincense; see **niben** ; Heb. לְבֹנָה?.

nenib, balsam, frankincense; varr.

nenib, Rec. 16, 152, , styrax, frankincense; Copt. λαβω, Heb. לְבֹנָה.

nenu (?), B.D. 1B, 19 . . . .

nenu (?), hours.

nenu, B.D. (Saïte) 125, 4 . . . .

Nenui, B.D. 17, 77, primeval watery matter.

Nenunser, B.D. 177, 7, a black-haired cow-goddess.

nenebnit, styrax.

nenm; see .

nenm-t (nem-t), , bier, coffin chamber.

Nenr, Edfû I, 77, a name of the Nile-god.

Nenḥa, a god of the Gate Saa-Set.

nenḥu (nḥu), to masturbate.

nenser (neser), excitement (?)

nenshem, U. 126, , N. 435, , A.Z. 67, 106, , , , , , , , , spleen, intestines; Copt. ⲛⲟⲉⲓϣ.

nenk, , I = , .

nenk = **nek** .

Nentchā, B.D. 39, 16, a storm-god, a form of Āapep.

nerit, P. 815, , , , Rev. 12, 119, , , , , , vulture; Copt. ⲛⲟⲩⲣⲉ.

ner-ti, , , , P. 302, two vultures.

nerit, A.Z. 1908, 16, the vulture amulet.

Nerit, the name of a serpent of the royal crown.

Nerȧ-t, name of an uraeus of Rā.

Ner, the god of the two Utchats.

Ner-ti, P. 302, two vulture-goddesses (Isis and Nephthys) with long abundant hair and pendent breasts: .

ner, U. 182, N. 133, , U. 441, , U. 69, , N. 330, , T. 267, , , , , , , , Rec. 31, 162, 167, to be strong, to be mighty, to be master, to be victorious, to terrify, to strike awe into people.

nerut, P. 683, , Rec. 26, 230, victory.

nerr, B.D. 181, 23, to rule, to be master of.

nerit, IV, 362, , , Rec. 36, 210, rule, government.

nerȧ, , , , , , conqueror, vanquisher.

nerȧu-t, Ȧmen. 22, 12, victory.

nerui, Amherst Pap. 20, he who vanquishes.

neru, strength, power, victory, valour, mighty one.

neru, IV, 613, B.D. 146, XVI, 42, strength, might, victory.

nerit, victory, victorious one.

Nerit, a goddess of strength.

Neri, B.D. 145 and 146, the doorkeeper of the 1st Pylon.

Nerit-āབui (?), Ṭuat XI, a wind-goddess of the dawn (?)

ner, ner-t, year; opening of the year, *i.e.*, New Year's Day.

ner, P. 396, M. 565, N. 1172, to herd cattle.

neru, herdsman, cow-keeper.

ner, U. 329, cattle (collective); U. 419, T. 239, 300.

nerȧu, bull.

ner-t, IV, 61, Stele of Nekht Menu 11; IV, 888, men and women, mankind.

Nerȧu-ta, a god.

ner, Koller Pap. 4, 1, ostriches (?)

ner, Nȧstasen Stele 33, staff, stick.

Ner-t, A.Z. 1906, 145 = **N-t**; Gr. Νηϊθ.

nerau, Koller Pap. 3, 6, ibex, antelope.

nerau, a kind of medicine (?)

nren, Demot. Cat. 366, to praise; Copt. ⲣⲁⲛ, ⲣⲓⲛ.

Nerta, Ṭuat III and XI, a form of Ȧfu-Rā.

Nertānefnebt, Rec. 4, 28, a god.

nehȧ, U. 468, P. 657, M. 763, P. 761, T. 316, P. 664, T. 219, P. 657, M. 763, to suffer loss, to diminish.

neh, nehu, Rec. 30, 72, Shipwreck 8, Peasant 178, loss, disaster, calamity.

neh sep sen, little by little, by degrees.

nehai, some, a few.

neh-tu, little, diminished, shortened.

nehi, a little of something, a few, a small quantity; Peasant 47, 48, a little natron, a little salt.

nehhu, poor man, needy one.

nehu, those who suffer, the indigent, the destitute.

neh-t, nehȧ-t, P. 174, U. 555, Rec. 3, 50, sycamore-fig tree; P. 646, two sycamore-fig trees; plur. IV, 1064, sycamore-figs; IV, 327, myrrh trees; Copt. ⲛⲟⲩϩⲉ.

nehi, Jour. As. 1908, 266, Rev. 13, 14, sycamore-fig.

neh-t en ṭeb, Rec. 2, 107, fig tree, ficus carica (?)

Nehet, P. 174, M. 440, N. 941, a mythological sycamore tree in the eastern sky; B.D. 59, 1.

Neh-ti, P. 646, B.D. 109, 5, 149, II, 9, the two sycamores from between which Rā appeared each morning.

neh-t, a drink made from syrup of figs.

neh, Rec. 27, 87, protection.

neh-t, an amulet worn to obtain protection.

neh-t U. 456, Rec. 16, 57, defence, protection.

neh-t, IV, 910, 972, Rec. 17, 5, place of protection, refuge, asylum.

neh, Rec. 16, 142, to shake, to shake up medicine.

nehneh, Rec. 16, 143, to be perturbed, to be terrified, to shake, to quake.

nehh, flame, fire.

nehi, T. 292, Rev. 12, 15, Rev. 12, 38, to escape, to separate from; Copt. ⲛⲟⲩϩⲉ, ⲛⲉϩⲉ ⲃⲟⲗ.

neha-t, walls, fence, cover.

nehau, Ṭuat IX, the windings or coils of Āapep.

Neha-ḥer, Ṭuat III, a goose-god.

Neha-kheru, Ṭuat III, a jackal-god in the Ṭuat.

Neha-ta, Ṭuat IX, a god who swathed Osiris.

nehaut sentrȧ, incense trees.

nehap; see .

Nehap, Rec. 32, 176, the god who renews himself.

nehap, to rise (of the Sun-god).

neham, Israel Stele 21, Rec. 2, 116, to rejoice, to cry out through pleasure; see .

nehamu, those who rejoice.

neha-maa, a plant or fruit used in medicine.

nehar ...., Anastasi I, 20, 2, tramps (?) wandering beggars (?)

nehas , to wake up.

nehas-t 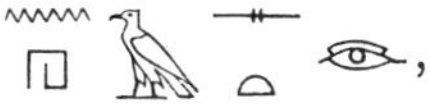, a waking up, resurrection.

nehȧs 
[illegible], B.D. (Saïte) 145, 38, to awake, to wake up.

nehim , Rev. 13, 9, to acclaim.

nehis , outcry (?) uproar (?)

Nehui , Ṭuat XII, a crocodile-god.

nehp , Ḥeruemḥeb 25, [illegible], Metternich Stele 61, 92, to get up very early.

nehp 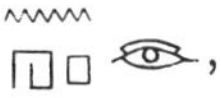, to wake up very early in the morning.

nehp 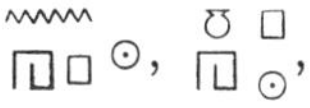, Rec. 16, 110, dawn, morning, morning light, morning work, early day.

nehpu , N. 925, dawn, early light; , morning light.

nehpu , U. 547, 548, yesterday, to-morrow.

nehp , the sky (?)

Nehp , Ṭuat VII, [illegible], Ṭuat IV, a serpent-god with 12 pairs of lion's legs.

nehp 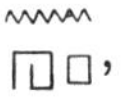, U. 240, [illegible], to copulate; compare נָאַף, to commit adultery.

nehp 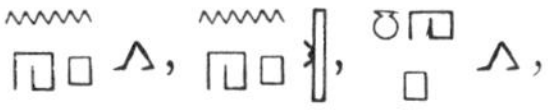, Rec. 16, 140, [illegible], Mar. Karn. 55, 68, to go in front, to lead, to be first, to be master of, to fly through the veins (of poison, Metternich Stele 29), to swell up (of a boil or tumour).

nehp-t , a hard boil, swelling, tumour.

nehp 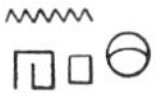, a pastille, tablet.

nehp , Israel Stele 15, [illegible], 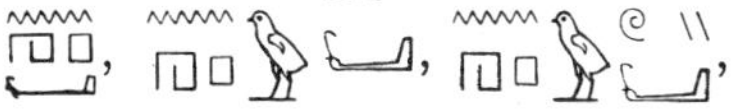, to defend, to protect, to guard, to drive away enemies from someone, to have a care for.

nehpi , to mourn; Copt. пєϩпє.

nehem 

, to rejoice, to praise, to beat a drum or tambourine.

nehemu 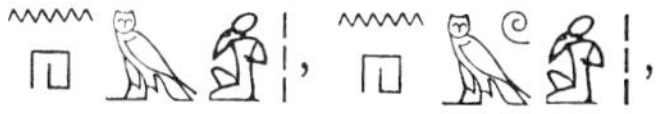, rejoicings, those who rejoice.

nehem trȧ , a bandlet (?)

nehem 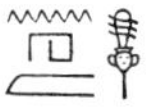, a musical instrument.

nehem , Rev. 13, 7, roar.

nehemhem , U. 235, P. 304, 710, M. 696, [illegible], Rec. 29, 153, to roar like an angry beast, or like thunder, or like a raging flood of water, or a storm.

nehemhemȧ , P. 350, N. 1066, roarer.

nehemnehem 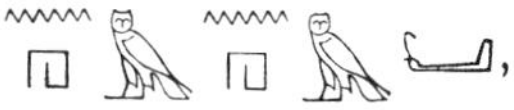, B.D. 39, 6, to roar, to rage.

Nehem-kheru 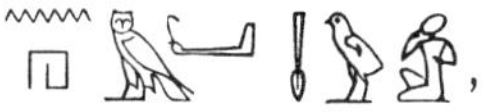, Ṭuat III, a jackal-god.

nehen 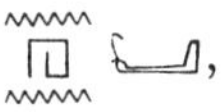, to grip, to grasp a spear, to hold a club firmly.

nehnȧ , U. 473, warrior.

Nehen , Rec. 16, 149, a name of Aapep.

nehen , a kind of tree.

Nehnu (?) , Hh. 564 . . . .

Nehenut 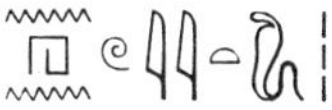, Ṭuat I, a company of singing-goddesses.

Neher , Rec. 16, 108, a name of Āapep.

neher-t , Rec. 16, 110, violence.

nehes, U. 187, P. 165, , T. 65, , Rec. 31, 34, , Rec. 26, 229, , , , , Israel Stele 23, , Rec. 12, 55, , Rec. 11, 187, to wake, to rouse from sleep; Copt. ⲛⲉϩⲥⲉ.

nehsȧ, U. 187, , T. 65, , M. 221, , N. 597, , Rev. 12, 110, watcher; plur. .

nehes, , , , , , (*sic*), to wake, to rouse oneself from sleep.

nehes[ȧ], the look-out man on a boat.

nehsait, , Rev. 14, 11, watch, wakefulness.

nehsit, she who keeps watch.

nehs-iu, the two Utchats which were painted on the two sides of the front of a boat to keep a look-out.

Nehes[ȧ], the god of the 30th day of the month.

Nehes[ȧ], the "look-out" god in the boat of Åf.

Nehes[ȧ], Rec. 31, 171, the name of a god.

Nehesu, , the divine watchers.

Nehesu, B.D. 144, 21, the gods who watched the road for Osiris.

Nehes-ḥer, B.D. 145A, the doorkeeper of the 15th Pylon.

nehes, Tomb of Åmenemḥat, hippopotamus.

Nehes, , , rebel, a name of Set.

nehes, Denderah IV, 82, P.S.B.A. 15, 437, something foul, boil (?) epithet of a panther.

neheq, Ebers Pap. 108, 16 . . . . . .

neheṭ, U. 505, T. 321, , to need, to lack.

neheṭ, to complain (?) to command (?); var. .

neheṭhet, A.Z. 1904, 91, , , Sphinx 14, 206, to be bold, strong, courageous.

neḥ, U. 560, , P. 450, , , , , , to ask, to petition, to request, to pray for, to beseech, to supplicate.

neḥi, , Peasant B 2, 121, , Rec. 4, 135, suppliant.

Neḥi, Tomb of Seti I, one of the 75 forms of Rā (No. 71).

neḥḥ, IV, 972, Thes. 1482, , Rec. 31, 170, , , to beseech.

neḥ-t, , , , U. 601, , , , supplication, request, entreaty, prayer, invocation; , petition.

neḥ-ti, , , Rev. 13, 14, faith, belief; Copt. ⲛⲁϩϯ.

neḥ, B.D. 153B, 13, a kind of bird; , Ebers Pap. 105, 6, the great neḥ.

neḥ-t, , , Rev. 12, 62, oil; Copt. ⲛⲉϩ.

neḥḥ-t 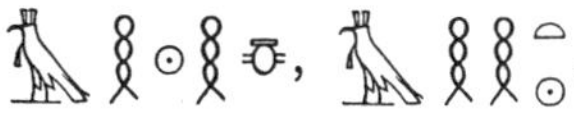, Rev. 14, 74, oil, unguent; Copt. ⲛⲉϩ.

Neḥ , B.D. 153B, 15, the name of a god.

Neḥit 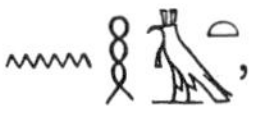, U. 601, , N. 748, the mother of the gods in the boat of Rā.

neḥeḥ , U. 446, T. 255, , , Rev. 14, 33, 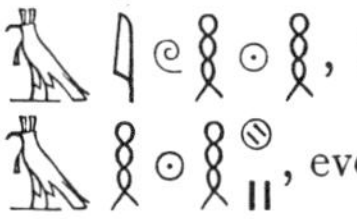, Rev. 12, 72, 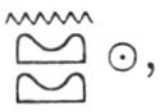, eternity; , ever and ever; Copt. ⲉⲛⲉϩ.

neḥeḥ tchet , Rec. 27, 59, , eternity and everlastingness.

Neḥeḥ , Rec. 27, 220,  , the god of eternity;  Rec. 31, 170.

neḥa , T. 121, a kind of wine.

neḥa , Ebers Pap. 39, 10, a disease (?); var. .

neḥa 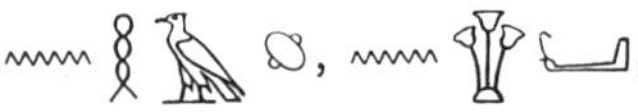, Gol. 14, 3, to stink, to be loathsome or disgusting, to be in a foul condition.

neḥaḥa , 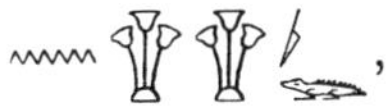, to be foul, diseased, physically or mentally.

neḥa , to take an unfavourable turn (of an illness), to suppurate (of a wound).

neḥa-t , suppuration, rheumy disease of the eye.

neḥa-t ḥa-t , Leyd. Pap. 12, 3, mental loathing, disgust.

Neḥa , a mythological crocodile; see **Neḥa-ḥer.**

Neḥa-ḥa 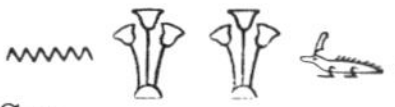, "stinking face"—a title of Set.

Neḥa-ḥāu , B.D. 125, II, a god of Rastau, one of the 42 assessors of Osiris.

Neḥa-ḥer , B.D. 125, II, , , Rec. 34, 179,  , "stinking face"—the name of one of the 42 judges in the Hall of Osiris.

Neḥa-ḥer , Ṭuat VII and X, a serpent-fiend that was strangled by Serqit, and his body pegged to the ground with six knives.

Neḥait-ḥer , Ṭuat II, a serpent-fiend, consort of Neha-ḥer.

Neḥa-ḥer , the name of a canal at Lycopolis.

neḥait 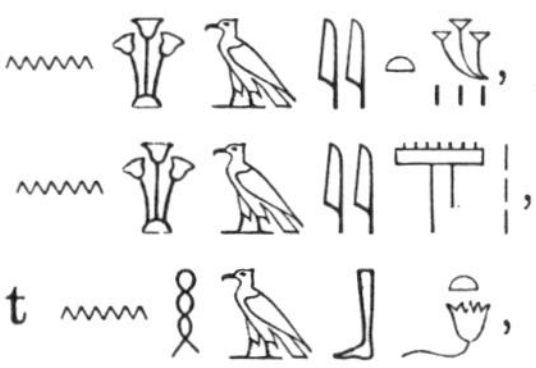, flowers, wreaths.

neḥait , naked things.

neḥab-t , P. 437, lotus, lily; see **neḥeb.**

neḥasāā (?) , Hearst Pap. 111, 7, a seed or plant used in medicine.

Neḥȧ 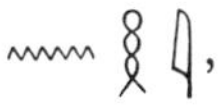, Ṭuat II, a time-god or season-god; var. .

neḥi 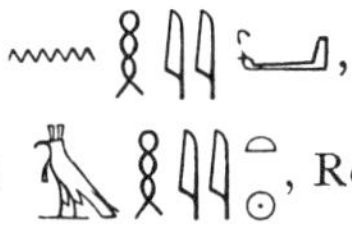, Rev. 11, 169, work, craft.

neḥit , Rec. 32, 178, eternity; see 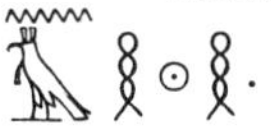.

neḥu , Jour. As. 1908, 36, more; Copt. ⲛ̄ϩⲟⲩⲟ.

neḥb-t , U. 548, 631, 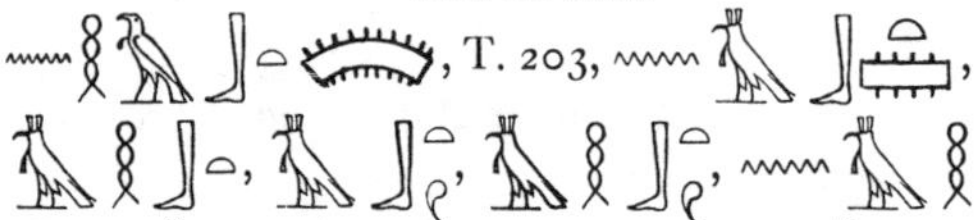 T. 203, 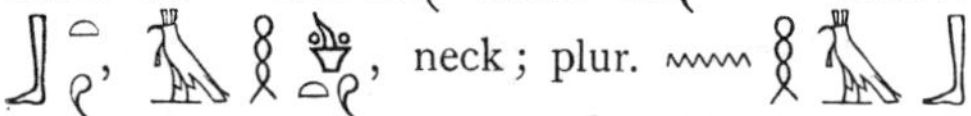 neck; plur. 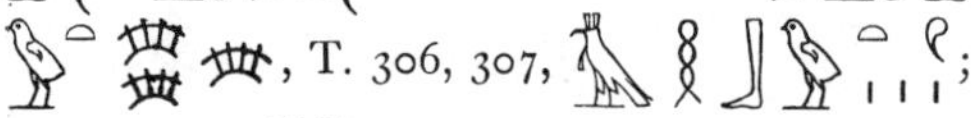 T. 306, 307,  U. 630, his seven necks; Copt. ⲛⲁϩⲃⲉ.

neḥeb 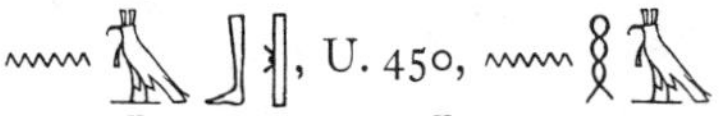 U. 450,  T. 258, 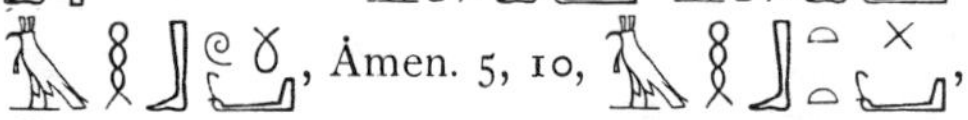 Åmen. 5, 10, , to yoke cattle or horses, to put under the yoke, *i.e.*, conquer, to be entrusted with something; , coupled with fields.

neḥeb ka 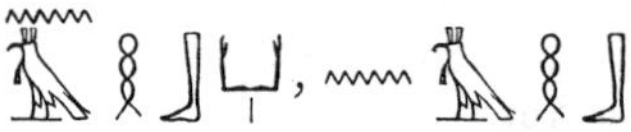 , Rec. 26, 75, to yoke the *ka*, to subjugate the double; , U. 234.

neḥb-t , the act of yoking.

neḥb-t 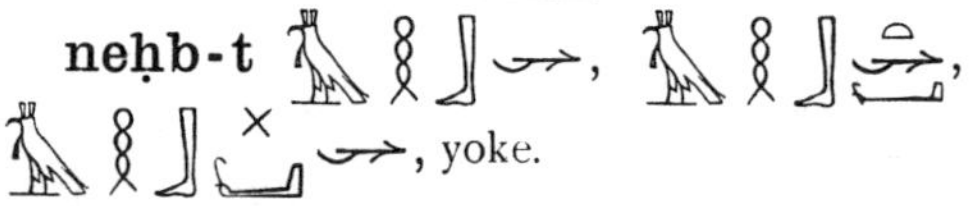, yoke.

neḥeb 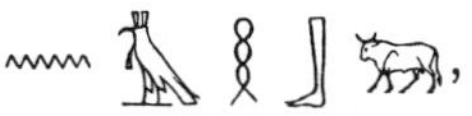, an ox for ploughing.

Neḥeb-ti , Ṭuat IX, the god of the serpent staff.

Neḥeb-nefert , B.D. 125, II, one of the 42 assessors.

Neḥeb-kau  T. 230, M. 690, 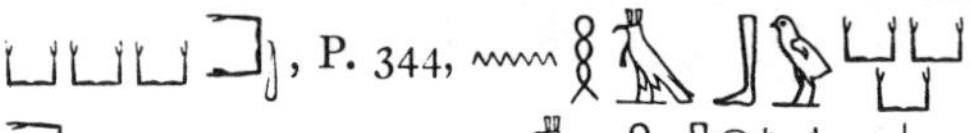 P. 344, 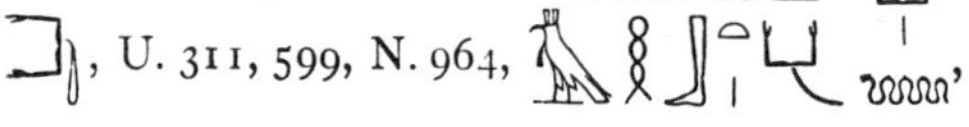 U. 311, 599, N. 964, 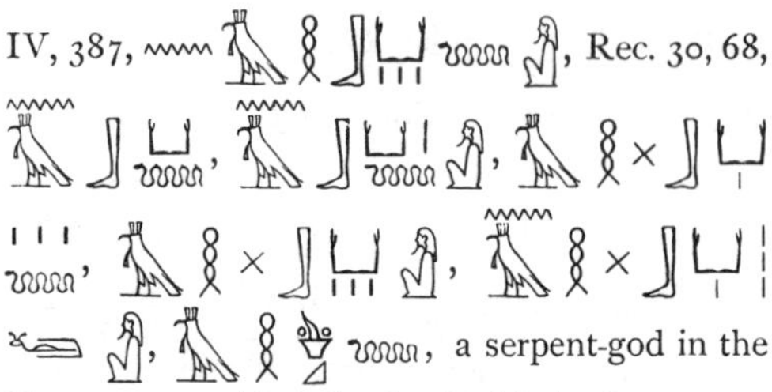 IV, 387, Rec. 30, 68, a serpent-god in the Ṭuat who provided the dead with food.

Neḥeb-kau 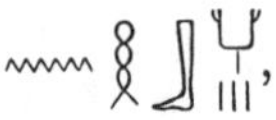, Ṭuat IV, a self-existent serpent, with two heads at one end of his body and one at the other.

Neḥeb-kau em Seshsh  Mar. Aby. I, 44, a form of the preceding.

neḥb-t 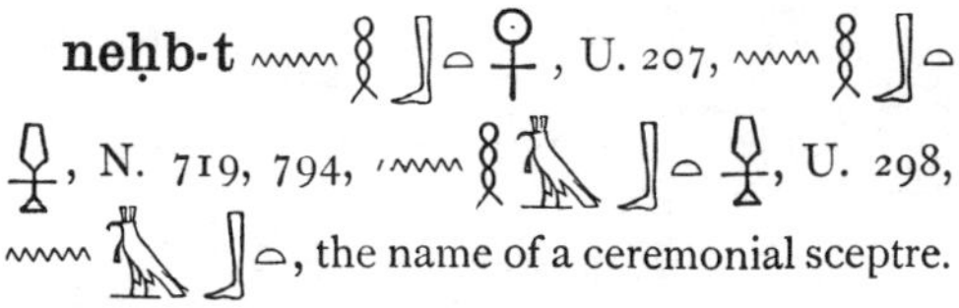 U. 207, N. 719, 794, U. 298, the name of a ceremonial sceptre.

neḥb-t , P. 439, 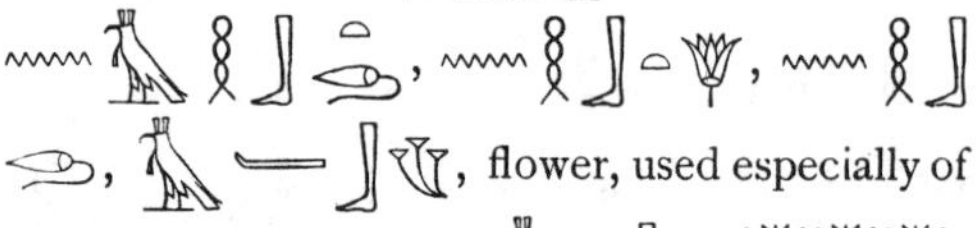 flower, used especially of the lotus; plur. , M. 655, 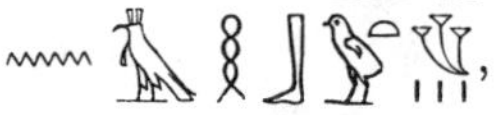, Rec. 29, 148,  IV, 918, flowers in general, blossoms.

neḥeb , title, official description.

neḥb-t 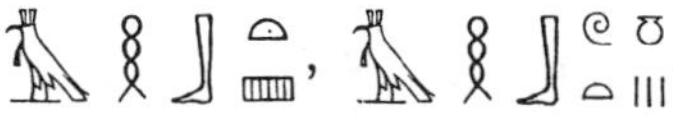, Ebers Pap. 46, 9, a kind of stone used in medicine (?)

Neḥebsa 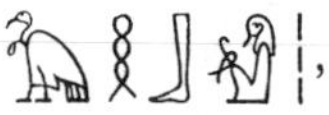, Rec. 16, 108, a proper name.

neḥep , Rec. 27, 88; 30, 217, , to exercise the potter's craft, to fashion a pot, or figure, or man.

neḥpi 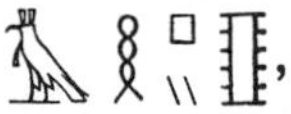, fashioner, modeller, potter.

neḥep  Åmen. 12, 16, the potter's table, the board on which the clay is moulded into form.

Neḥep , Rec. 32, 177, the divine Potter and the table used by him.

Neḥep 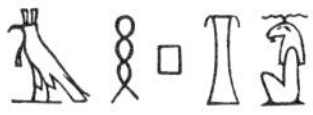, A.Z. 1872, 5, one of the seven forms of Khnemu.

neḥep 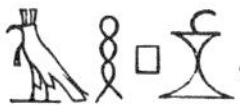, Rec. 27, 83 = .

Neḥep 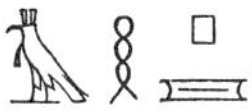, Rec. 16, 56, a title of the Nile-god.

neḥpi 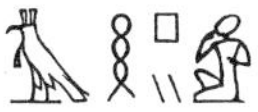, he who prays (?)

neḥpu , Pap. 3024, 16 . . . . .

neḥem 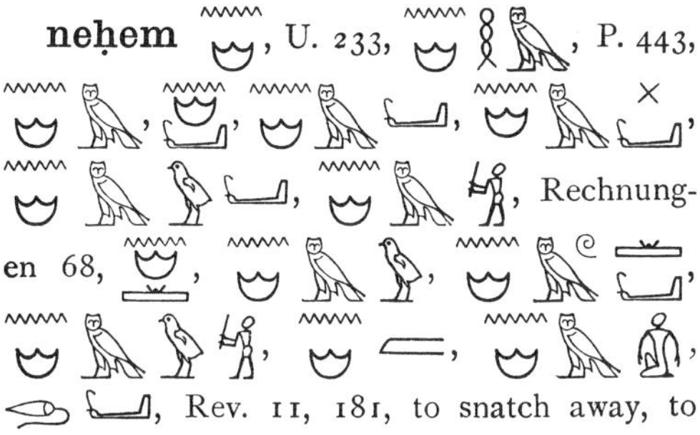, U. 233, P. 443, Rechnungen 68, Rev. 11, 181, to snatch away, to seize, to remit a tax, to deliver, to rescue, to save; Copt. ⲛⲟⲩϩⲙ̄.

neḥmi 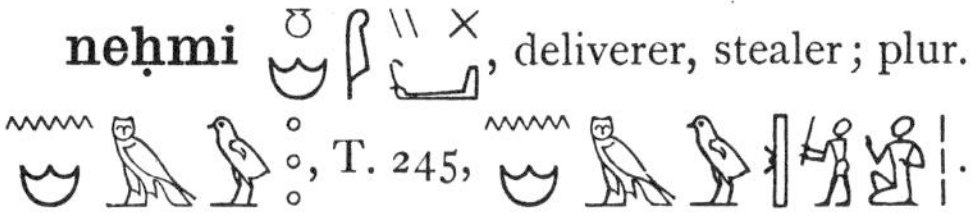, deliverer, stealer; plur. T. 245.

neḥemm , T. 394, M. 407, Hh. 368, to carry off, to seize.

neḥm-t , U. 54, deliverance, rescue.

neḥem-ra , to steal the mouth, *i.e.*, to kill.

neḥem , a "take off" arm of a canal.

Neḥemu , M. 481, N. 1248, the "delivering" god.

Neḥem-t-āuait , IV, 1011, IV, 389, a daughter of Rā and a consort of Thoth; she avenged the oppressed, and was the goddess of Righteousness, *i.e.*, Gr. Δικαιοσύνη, Plutarch, De Iside 3; 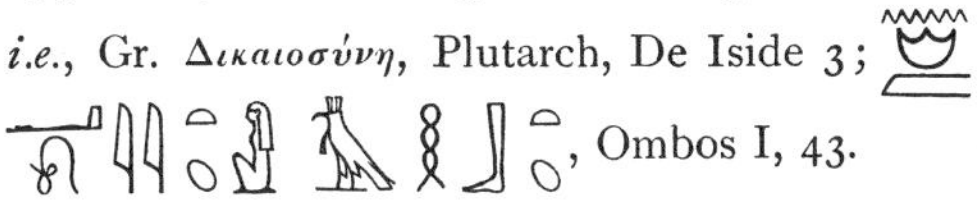, Ombos I, 43.

neḥem , Love Songs 1, 11, 2, 8, bud, flower; plur. lily buds.

neḥem , Rev., to cry out; Copt. ⲥⲗϩⲛⲙ.

neḥem-t , lament, cry.

neḥmȧ , Rev., a kind of bird.

neḥem n , A.Z. 1906, 159, a particle meaning something like "behold."

neḥmu ; see  .

neḥmen 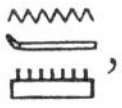, Wört. Suppl. 691, to praise (?)

neḥen-ti , repulser, striker.

neḥer 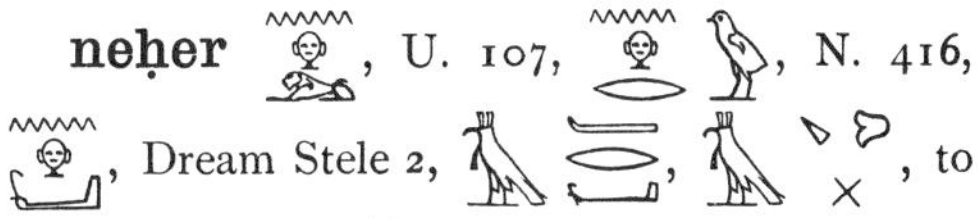, U. 107, N. 416, Dream Stele 2, to resemble, be like (?)

neḥer 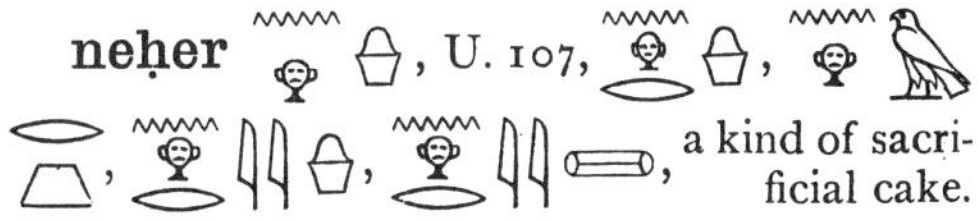, U. 107, a kind of sacrificial cake.

Neḥru , a sacred boat (?)

noḥerneḥer , N. 1325, to rejoice.

nḥerḥer 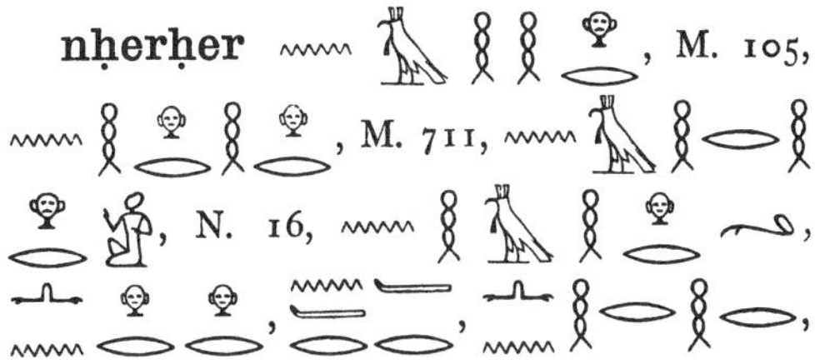, M. 105, M. 711, N. 16, Sphinx 14, 207, to rejoice.

Neḥer-ti , the name of a star, a kind of light.

Neḥer-tchatcha (?) , B.M. 46631, a god, functions unknown.

Neḥsi 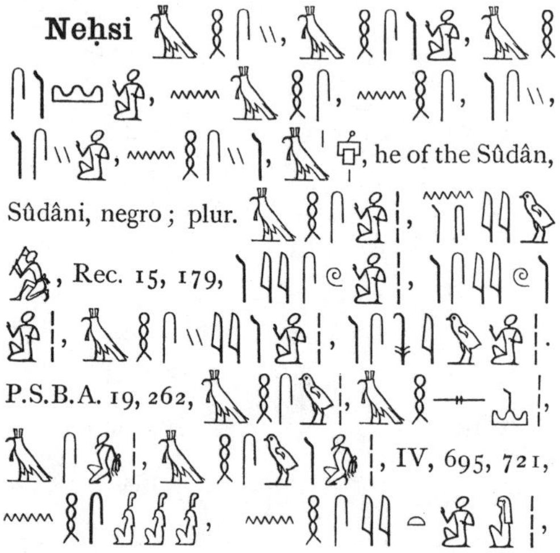, he of the Sûdân, Sûdâni, negro; plur., Rec. 15, 179, P.S.B.A. 19, 262, IV, 695, 721, IV, 743.

Neḥesu 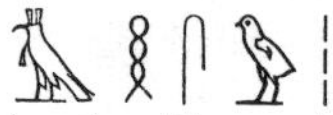, Ṭuat V, the Sûdânî tribes in the Ṭuat, the results of the masturbation of Rā.

Neḥsiu ḥetepu 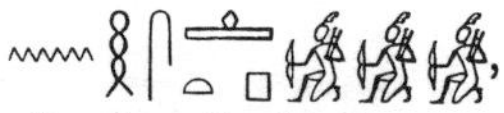, Décrets 104, , A.Z. 1905, 10, the "Friendlies" in the Sûdân, Sûdânî police.

neḥsiu thaiu , IV, 703, male Sûdânî slaves.

neḥsit 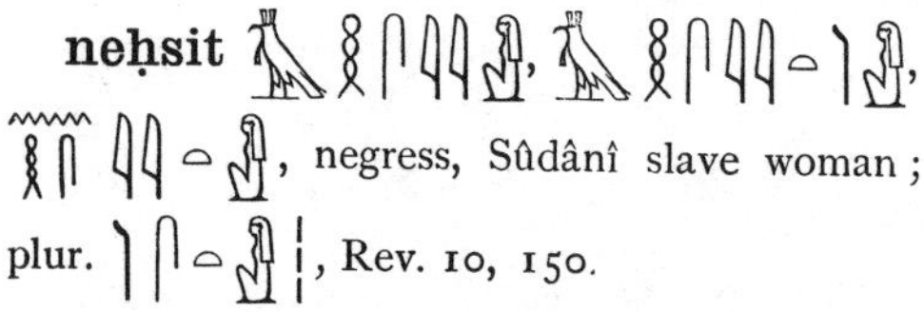, negress, Sûdânî slave woman; plur., Rev. 10, 150.

Neḥsit 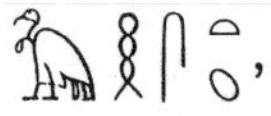, a title of the Sûdânî Hathor.

neḥes , to mutter incantations; compare Heb. נָחַשׁ.

neḥes 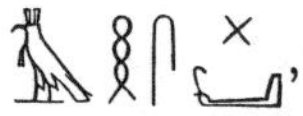, P.S.B.A. 13, 411, to be restless, to kick out with the legs.

neḥsi 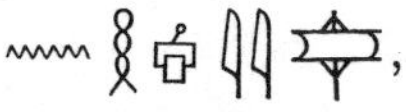, Rev. 12, 114, to wake up, to rouse oneself.

neḥsu , to cover oneself.

neḥṭ-t , tooth; plur. 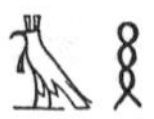 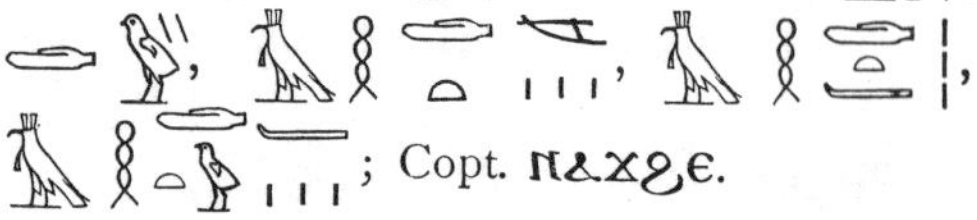; Copt. ⲛⲁϫϩⲉ.

neḥṭ-t 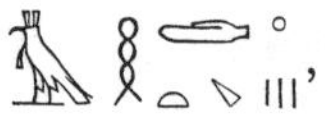, grain or powder (?)

neḥetch-t  , I, 137, tooth, tusk; Copt. ⲛⲁϫϩⲉ.

nekhi , Peasant 117, 204, , Israel Stele 8, Rec. 14, 12, to cry out, to lament, to complain.

nekhu-t , Pap. 3024, 148, 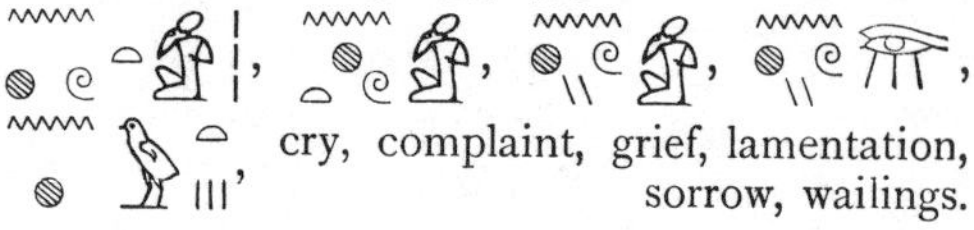, cry, complaint, grief, lamentation, sorrow, wailings.

nekhi  , calamity, lamentation, the death-cry, death.

nekhu , IV, 1045, 1078, , Rec. 2, 30, 6, 116, 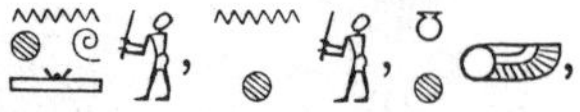, , to protect, to keep guard over, to care for (the widow), to comfort.

nekhȧ 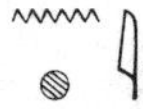, U. 378, T. 184, 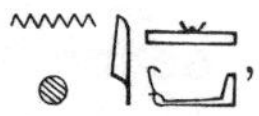, 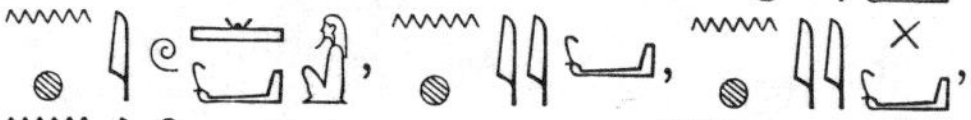, , Rec. 32, 179, , protector, guardian.

nekh , Tombos 7, to attack.

nekhekh 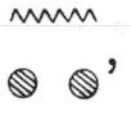, U. 165, T. 136, N. 400, to overpower, to be mighty.

nekhnekh 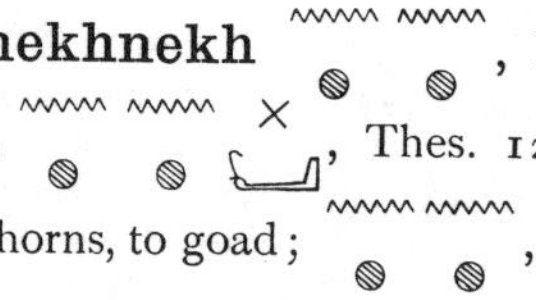, M. 205, N. 664, 665, Thes. 1201, to butt with the horns, to goad; P. 284, to flutter (of the heart).

nekh , to be young; see .

nekhnekh , Rec. 20, 80, to grow young.

nekh 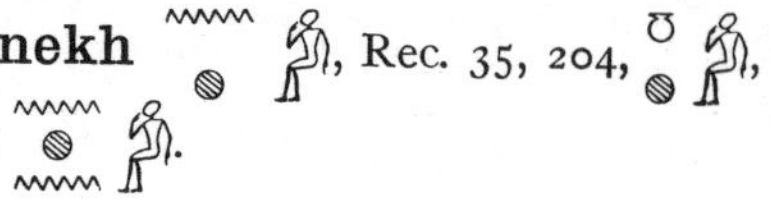, Rec. 35, 204, child; see.

nekhekh , U. 297, P. 631, M. 780, N. 345, 534, 1377, , , , to be old, to grow old, , to reach second childhood.

nekhekh , Metternich Stele 38, old man, aged.

Nekhkhu , P. 170, , T. 364, P. 788, the aged spirits and gods.

Nekhekh , U. 467, , N. 612, , T. 218, , P. 47, , M. 64, 234, N. 33, the "Old God."

Nekhekh , Thes. 430, a form of Rā, the autumn sun.

Nekhekh , the sun as an old man, the winter sun.

Nekhekh ur Ȧtem , the name of the sun at the 12th hour of the day.

nekhekh , , to pour out, flux, emission.

Nekhekh , B.D. (Saïte) 146, 27, title of a goddess.

nekhekh , Rec. 27, 86, to sharpen (arrows or spears), to thrust with the phallus, to fecundate.

nekhekh , , , , a kind of whip or flail.

nekhekh , A.Z. 1908, 19, the amulet of the whip.

nekhakha , N. 1387, , , P. 701, to beat, to strike.

nekha , , a whip.

nekha-t , A.Z. 1873, 90, to sharpen, a cutting tool.

nekha-t , Rec. 16, 110, knife; , slice of flint.

nekha , N. 756, , T. 315, , N. 756, to sprinkle, humours, emissions.

nekhakha-t , something presented as an offering; var. .

nekha-t , N. 802, pendent, hanging (of a woman's breasts).

nekhakha-t , T. 360, , P. 602, pendent (of a woman's breasts).

nekhai , to hang, to descend.

nekhau , a kind of ornament worn on the body.

nekhabit , Rec. 15, 17, deed, document, title, inscription.

nekhan , cataplasm.

nekhȧ , whip.

Nekhȧ , T. 301, a serpent-fiend in the Ṭuat.

nekhi , Rec. 27, 85, 88, to give birth to.

nekhir (?) , Anastasi IV, 15, 7, brook, stream, river; Heb. נַחַל, Babyl. nakhlu, .

nekhu-t , U. 182, flame, fire.

nekheb , , , , , to give a name or title to some person or thing, to be named, to be described; , Hymn Darius 4, "he gave things names from the mountains to the sky"; , , , title, rank, document.

nekhb-t , , , Ḥeruemḥeb 19, title, official title, title of honour, decoration; plur. , , , Rec. 27, 224.

nekheb , A.Z. 1905, 27, flat land cleared for building purposes.

nekheb , pedestal of a statue.

nekheb , to kill, to slay, to dig into.

nekhebkheb 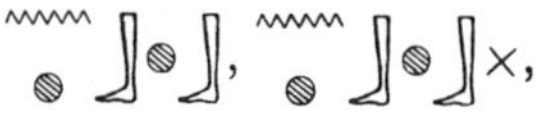, U. 269, P. 609, N. 806, to unbolt a door, to open, to break open.

Nekheb , the South as opposed to , the North.

Nekhbi-t 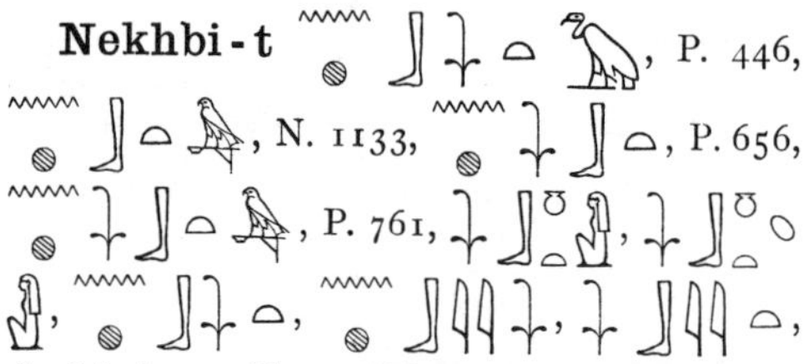, P. 446, N. 1133, P. 656, P. 761, the Mother-goddess of Upper Egypt, having her seat at Nekheb-Nekhen. The Greeks identified her with Eileithyia and Artemis, and the Romans with Lucina.

nekhb-t , plants or flowers of the South.

nekhbu-t , a flower, lotus (?) lily.

Nekhbu-ur , A.Z. 1900, 74, "Great Flower," a name of Rā.

Nekhben , U. 459, a goddess, Nekhebit (?)

nekhebṭ-t , malice, envy, wickedness.

nekhf , to burn, to be burned.

nekhen 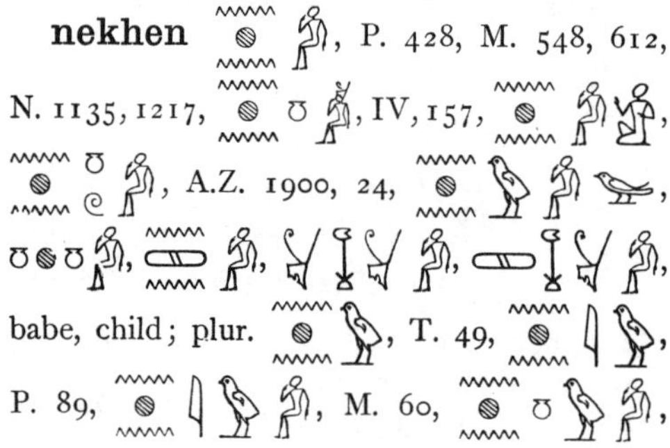, P. 428, M. 548, 612, N. 1135, 1217, IV, 157, A.Z. 1900, 24, babe, child; plur. T. 49, P. 89, M. 60, N. 70, .

nekhen-t , female child, babyhood (?) infancy (?)

nekhen , humility, lowly.

Nekhen , T. 301, the babe "with his finger in his mouth," 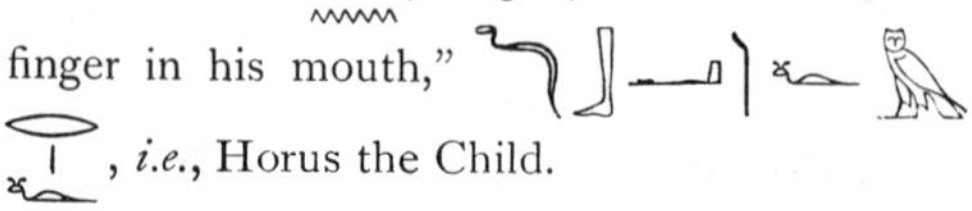, *i.e.*, Horus the Child.

Nekhen , Thes. 420, a form of Rā as the sun of spring; 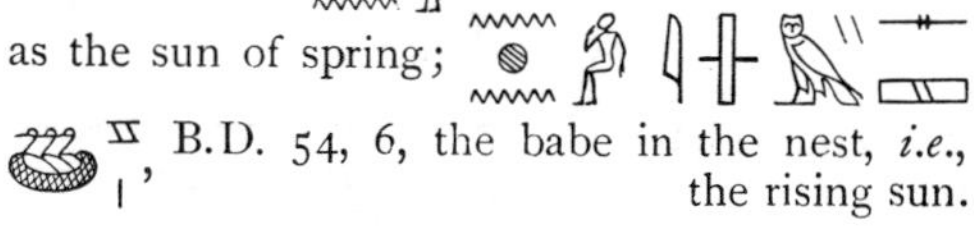, B.D. 54, 6, the babe in the nest, *i.e.*, the rising sun.

Nekhen 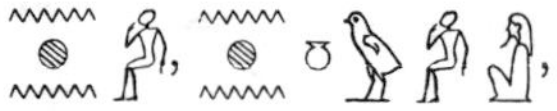, B.D. 125, II, one of the 42 assessors of Osiris.

Nekhenu , B.D. 125, III, 32, name of the doorposts of the hall of Maāti.

nekhenu , young serpents; , the young of uraei.

nekhen , enemy.

Nekhenit , a class of priestesses (?)

nekhnem , a kind of strong-smelling oil; see **neshnem.**

nkherkher , T. 282, N. 132, to be destroyed.

nekht 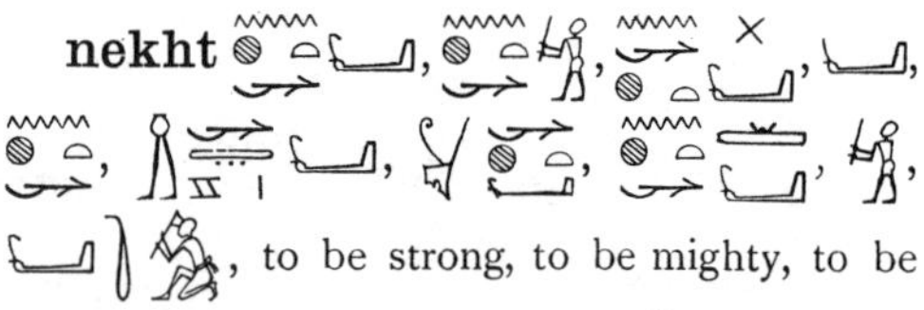, to be strong, to be mighty, to be powerful, strength, might; Copt. ⲛ̀ϣⲟⲧ.

nekht 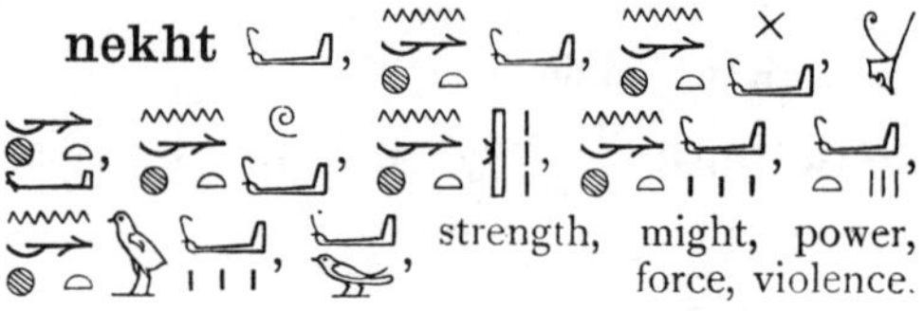, strength, might, power, force, violence.

nekht , Ȧmen. 21, 3, a strong man; plur. , strong men, troops, forces.

nekht-t 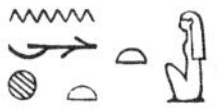, Rec. 31, 168, a strong woman.

nekht, nekhtȧ , giant, mighty man.

nekhti , strong, mighty.

nekht , strong white, *i.e.*, dead white (of colour); , dead black (of colour).

nekht-ā 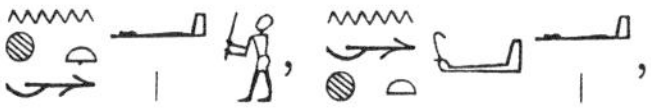, 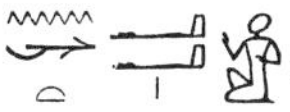, IV, 1078, [illegible], strong of arm, *i.e.*, strong man, warrior; plur. 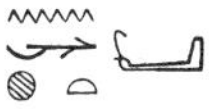 [illegible].

Nekht-ā , a god.

Nekhtut em Uas , Rev. 9, 28, name of a horse of Rameses II.

Nekht khepesh , Dream Stele 1, "strong sword," a royal title.

nekht kheru 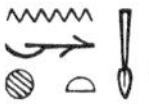, "strong voice," *i.e.*, "crier," a title of an official.

Nekht , Rev. 13, 40, Divine Power.

Nekht 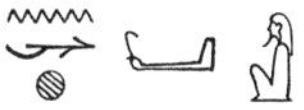, Ombos I, 186, "Strength," one of the 14 kau of Rā.

Nekht[it] 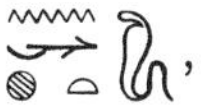, B.D. 140, 7, a goddess.

Nekht, Nekht-ti  [illegible], "Giant," *i.e.*, Orion.

Nekht-tu-nti-setem-nef  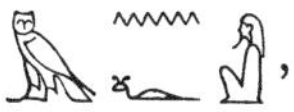, Ombos II, 134, a mythological being.

nekht 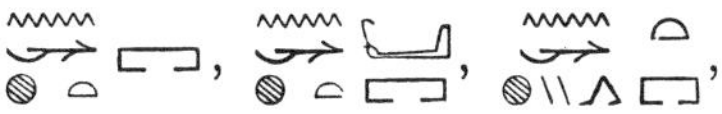, , Ȧmen. 8, 19, fortified place, fortress; plur. , [illegible].

nekht-tiu , Hearst Pap. XII, 4, a kind of plant.

nekhth , strength, strong.

nes 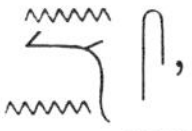, P. 405, 579, [illegible], M. 681, [illegible], [illegible], pronominal suffix: she, it.

nes 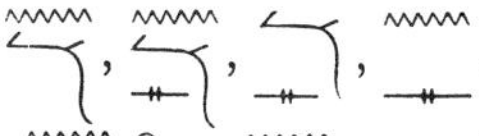, belonging to.

nesi 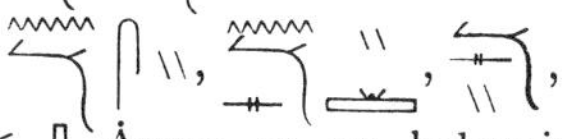, L.D. III, 140C, [illegible], Ȧmen. 19, 20, belonging to, property of (used in proper names).

nes ȧm 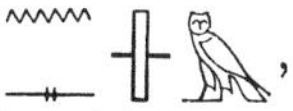, belonging thereto; , A.Z. 1877, 34, belonging to him that is in.

nes-su , Pap. 3024, 148, , T. 77, M. 230, [illegible], U. 199, N. 609, belonging to him.

nes-t 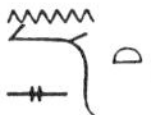, belonging to (used in proper names); [illegible], things belonging to; , attached to the seal, *i.e.*, one in charge of an official seal.

Nesmekhef , Ṭuat XII, a serpent fire-god.

Nesst-naisu , , Methen 15 ......

n sen ȧmi , A.Z. 77, 34, belonging to them.

Nes-N-t [illegible], or [illegible] = Heb. Asenath אָסְנַת, Cr. Ασενέθ.

Nes-neter 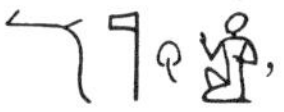, title of the high-priest of Busiris.

nes [illegible], Peasant 166, [illegible], [illegible],  [illegible], tongue; plur. [illegible], [illegible]; [illegible] [illegible], to talk too much; [illegible], IV, 968, Thes. 1480, the speaking tongue; Copt. λⲁⲥ, Heb. לָשׁוֹן.

nes she (?), Ebers Pap. 65, 2, 88, 11, "sea tongues," a seed or plant used in medicine.

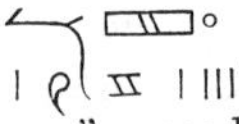

nes, to devour, to consume.

nes, to arrive, to approach.

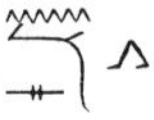

nes-t, Anastasi I, 14, 4, part of an inclined plane.

nes, U. 416, T. 237, Rec. 31, 167, , , to burn, flame, fire.

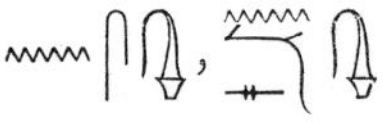

nesu-t, IV, 613, , , flame, fire.

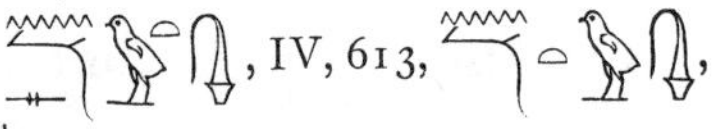

nesnes, to burn.

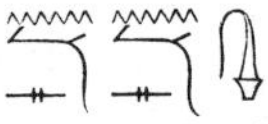

nes-ti, , fiery.

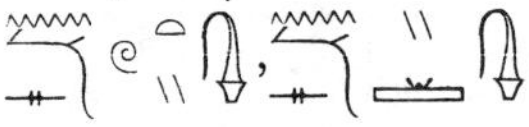

ness, to destroy.

nesnes, Anastasi I, 16, 5, , to chop, to mince, to cut up into small pieces (?)

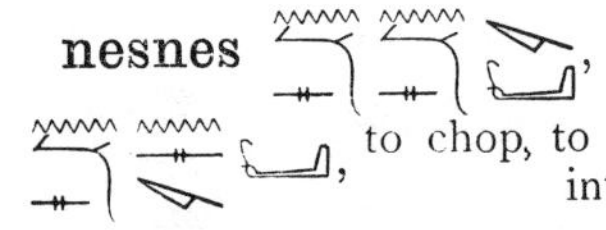

nes, sword, knife, a thin blade.

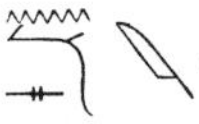

nesut, , weapons, arrow-heads, spears, darts.

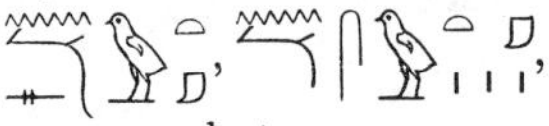

nes-t, place of slaughter, shambles.

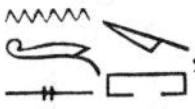

nes-t, U. 440, T. 251, , Hh. 392, , , , , , , , , , , , , , throne, royal seat; plur. , M. 456, U. 454, , , .

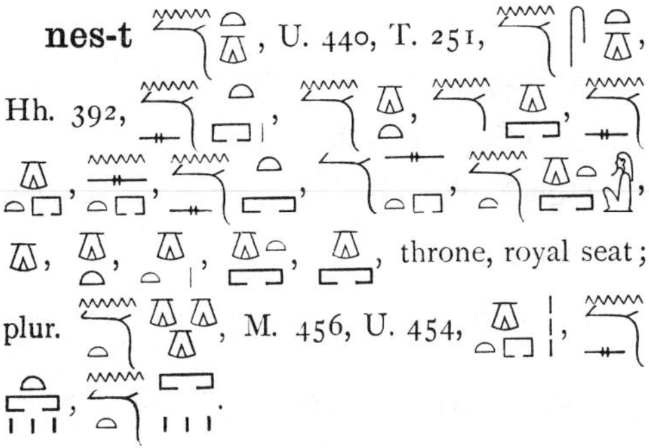

Nes-t taui, "throne of the Two Lands," or 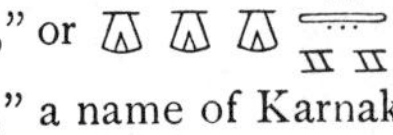 , "thrones of the Two Lands," a name of Karnak.

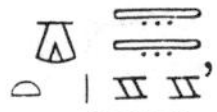

nesti, , , , , the two thrones of Horus and Set;  , **Kherp nesti,** director of the Two Thrones, a title; 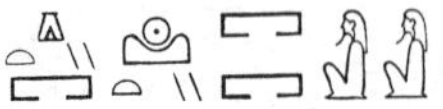 , the two thrones of the two gods of the horizon.

Nestiu, the gods of the throne or thrones.

Nestȧ, Ṭuat VI, a god.

Nesti-khenti-Ṭuat, Ṭuat IX, a ram-god.

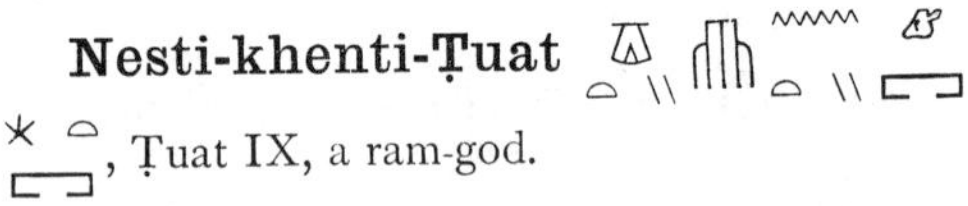

Nesttauit, , a name of Hathor.

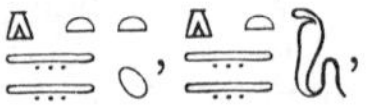

nes-t, a kind of plant; plur. , .

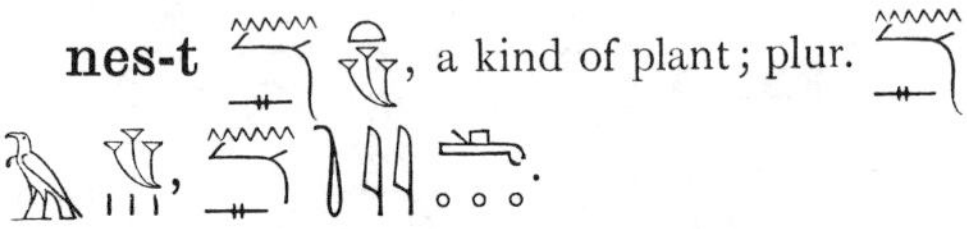

nes-t, , grain, wheat, dhurra, or cakes made of the same.

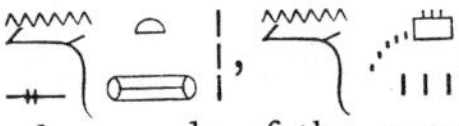

nes-ti, IV, 1157, a kind of bread cake.

nes-t, B.D. (Saïte) 108, 1, a measure.

nes-t, disease, sickness.

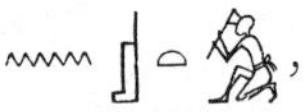

nesit, , a kind of skin disease.

Nesiu, B.M. 32, 144, a group of fiends in the Ṭuat; fem. **Nesiut** .

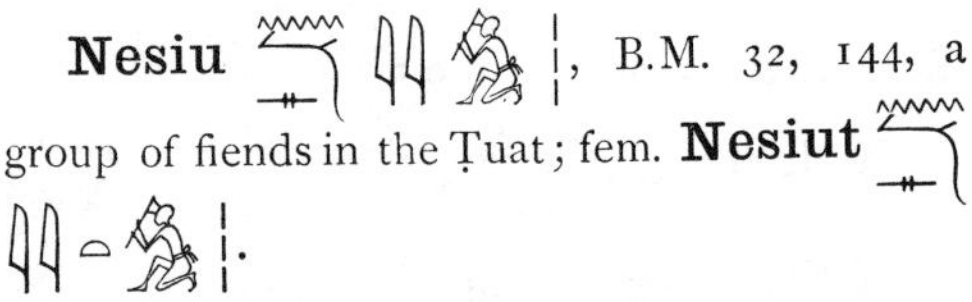

nes-ti, , a man suffering from the nes disease.

nesut, Nesi-Ȧmsu 555, 556, cases to hold spells.

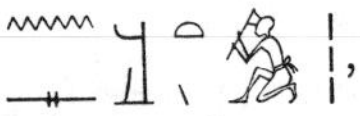

n sa = , Rec. 35, 193 (Maspero).

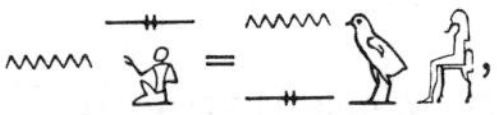

nesa-t, knife, dagger.

Nesa . . . (?), T. 40, a town in the Ṭuat.

nesa, IV, 1120, goat's hide.

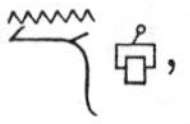

nesaui, Rec. 30, 67, two parts of a boat or ship.

nesȧs , T. 336, P. 812, N. 642; var. , M. 254 . . . .

nsȧsȧ , 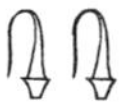,  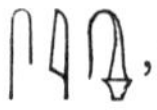, flame, fire = 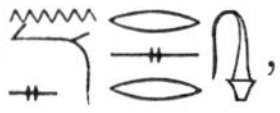, 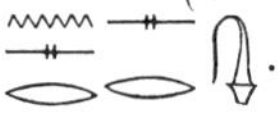.

Nesu , N. 700 = , M. 122, , P. 92,  = 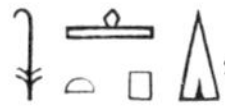, Rec. 35, 228,  = , Rec. 26, 235, , 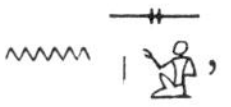, Teachings of Åmenemḥat 4, 3, 17, 5, , B.M. 374, , Thes. 942, 943, king of Upper Egypt; plur. , L.D. III, 140c; , or , is transcribed in cuneiform by in-si, and represents the  of the title . See the discussion in A.Z. 49, 15 ff., and Ranke's article Keilschriftliches Material, in Abhandl. K. P. Akad. Phil. Hist. Classe, 1910. According to Spiegelberg (A.Z. 1912, 125) , Ai-ma-seb = in-si-ib-ja, a cuneiform transcription of , n-su-t-bȧ-t.

Nesu  , N. 131, , N. 1137, 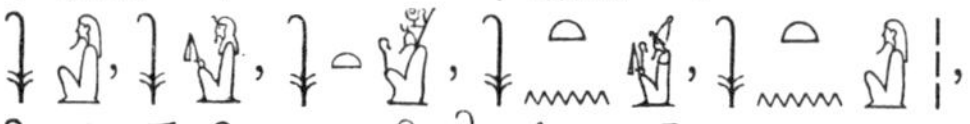 , Rec. 16, 54, king of Upper Egypt, king in general; plur.  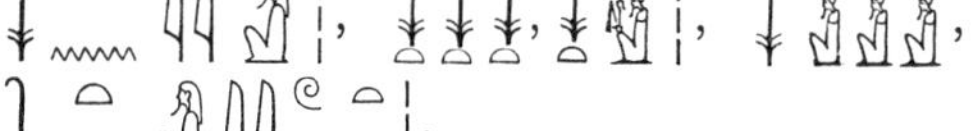 .

Nesuit, nesit  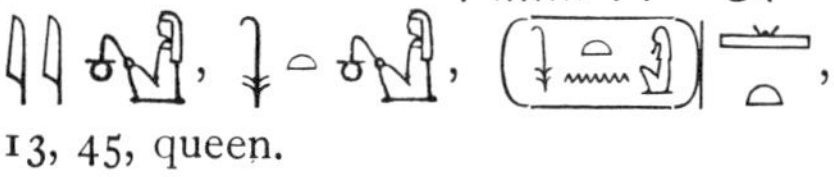, Rev. 13, 45, queen.

Nesu bȧti , P. 61, M. 129, 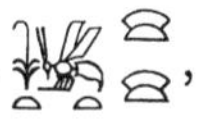, Palermo Stele, [illegible], [illegible], IV, 208, 936, [illegible], king of the South and North, *i.e.*, king of all Egypt; plur. [illegible] .

Nesu [illegible], Palermo Stele, [illegible], palace, king's house; [illegible], [illegible], I, 51, the king's private apartments; [illegible], the ladies of the same; [illegible], the king's axeman, [illegible], Royal Tombs I, 42; [illegible], IV, 1015, [illegible], "the two eyes of the king," title of an official; [illegible], king's butler(?); [illegible], Sphinx II, 132, [illegible], [illegible] [illegible], Décrets 23, [illegible], ibid., king's scribe; [illegible], IV, 1001, veritable royal scribe, *i.e.*, not an honorary king's scribe;  [illegible], king's scribe of the storehouse and palace; [illegible], IV, 1026, king's scribe and registrar of the bread; [illegible] [illegible], the king's barge; [illegible], king's libationer; [illegible], the king's envoy to all lands; [illegible] [illegible], His Majesty's chief herald; [illegible], king's decree, or order; [illegible], king's cup-bearer; [illegible], king's mother; plur. [illegible]; [illegible] [illegible], king's children; , Décrets 19, the king's chancery; , III, 142, king's folk; , king's throne, or throne room; , Mar. Aby. I, 6, 47; , , , king's kinsman; plur. , N. 974; , , real king's kinsman, not an honorary title; , , king's wife, *i.e.*, queen; plur. , ; , king's great wife, *i.e.*, first wife; , king's artificer or workman; , , IV, 1006, king's servants, or royal priests; , U. 42, A.Z. 1876, 101, I, 144, IV, 412, , P. 168, N. 680, with , M. 695, , P. 43, , A.Z. 1907, 45, , , "the king giveth an offering," an offering formula that begins the inscription on funeral stelae of all periods, A.Z. 1907, 45, and 49, 20; , a double offering of the king; , the altar for the king's offering; , Palermo Stele, , , the coronation of the king of the South; , , , , , king's son, prince; , prince of Kash, *i.e.*, viceroy of Nubia; , , , , king's daughter, *i.e.*, princess; , I, 52, king's eldest daughter; , king's brother; , king's sister; , IV, 966, king's confidential noble; plur. ; , IV, 898, king's bodyguard; , royal ancestors; , Methen 5, Décrets 18, king's serfs.

nesu , ...

nesusu , ...

nesut , haste (?)

nesb , U. 519, , T. 329, , U. 310, , , , , , to bite, to eat, to eat up, to devour, to consume.

nesbu , devourers.

nesbit , eater, devourer (fem.).

nesb , , , to burn up, to consume, to destroy by fire.

nesbi , , , consumer, fire, flame.

nesbit , , consumer, fire, flame.

Nesbit , Thes. 31, the goddess of the 5th hour of the day.

Nesb-åmenu (?) , Denderah IV, 62, a warrior-god.

Nesb-kheper-åru (?) , the goddess of the 11th hour of the day.

nesp , , , , , , a piece, a portion, a fragment, limb, member; plur. , Rec. 31, 27, , wounds, slaughterings (?)

Nessf (?), Rec. 30, 193, a god (?)

Nesem (?), N. 51, a divine bull; varr., T. 287, , P. 40.

nesensenu, N. 842, , P. 168, M. 323 . . . . .

nesti, Rev. 11, 185, a kind of grain.

N-senṭ (?), Thes. 818, , Rec. 16, 106: (1) a goose-god; (2) a watcher of Osiris.

neser, to eat (?) to consider, to ponder.

neser, U. 433, , T. 248, , to burn, to blaze, fire, flame.

nesri, flaming one, blazing one.

nserser, to burn, to flame.

neser-t, , , , flame, fire.

nesrit, , , the name of one of the royal crowns.

Neserit, U. 269, , Rec. 32, 82, , , , Ṭuat I, , Ṭuat IV, , : (1) a fire-goddess; (2) a lioness-headed hippopotamus-goddess.

Nesru, , , , Thes. 112, one of the seven stars of Orion.

Nesrit-ānkhit, Ṭuat VIII, a serpent-goddess in the circle Āat-setkau.

Nesrem (?) T. 287, divine bull.

Nesermer, P. 40, a divine bull.

Nesereh, Hh. 367, a god.

neseḥ, a part of the leg.

nesq, to cut, to hack, to dismember.

nessq .

nes-th, throne; see .

nesh, I, 100, a kind of garment.

nesh, Nastasen Stele 10, to be helpless; see , in line 18 (?).

nesh, Rev. 6, 22, , , to frighten away, to drive away, to rush out upon.

Nesh, "Terrifier," a name of Set.

neshi, , , to stand on end (of the hair).

neshu-t, Love Songs, 6, 1, , the hair in its natural state, undressed hair, dishevelled locks.

Neshi-shentiu, , B.D. 58, 4, the oars of a magical boat.

neshu, , , a kind of disease, palsy, ague.

nesh, , , to hover over, to flutter, to tremble.

neshsh, to hurry, to hasten.

neshshu, Ebers Pap. 99, 16, , storm wind.

neshsh, , , to be shaken, agitated, disturbed.

neshnesh-t, Rec. 26, 226, things shaken.

nesh, , , part of a door, or doorway; plur. , .

nesh (?), to sprinkle; perhaps = .

neshesh, A.Z. 1910, 128, , Hh. 158, saliva.

nesh-t, neshut, , , , moisture, saliva, spittle.

neshnesh, U. 286, emission, saliva.

nesh, a plant.

nesh, , , , gravel, pebbles.

Nesh-renpu, N. 355, a divine name.

nesh, neshȧ, , , , metal pot or vessel.

nesha, , , metal weapons of some kind, strips of metal; var. , a metal pot (?)

nesha, Peasant 16, , Ebers Pap. 83, 14, a plant; there were two kinds: and .

nesha, Rec. 16, 69 = Copt. ⲛ̄ⲛ̄ⲡϣⲁ, ⲛ̄ⲛ̄ϣⲁ.

neshua, to threaten, to abuse, to revile.

neshuau, reviler (?)

neshb, lotus, a flower bud.

nshebsheb, U. 98, N. 377, to be fed, satisfied (?); var. .

neshp, , , , , to snuff the air, to breathe, to inhale; , inhaled.

neshpȧ, A.Z. 1900, 27, inhaler.

neshef, U. 312, moisture (?)

nshefshef, N. 187, Sphinx 14, 209, to eject fluid, emission.

Neshmit, , , , , , Rec. 16, 109, , Rev. 11, 183, , , A.Z. 1900, 20, a sacred boat; , IV, 98.

Neshmit, B.D. 40, 3, 123, 125, I, 11, a sacred boat of Rā and Osiris.

Neshem, the god of the Neshem boat.

Neshmit, , , the goddess of the Neshem boat.

neshmit, neshmut, , Rec. 38, 63, , Rec. 38, 64, , B.D. 172, 3, , scales of fish.

neshm-t, a kind of precious stone, mother-of-emerald (?); , , , , , gems in general.

neshem, , , a meat offering.

neshmm, P. 188, M. 352, N. 904, to flourish (a knife), to sharpen.

nshemshem, to sharpen.

neshen, U. 437, , T. 250, , U. 555, , Rec. 31, 21, , IV, 1078, ,

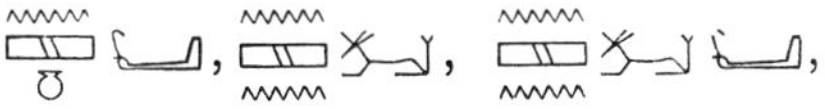, terror, fright, horror, alarm, fury, rage, something horrible or alarming, storm, thunderstorm, calamity, disaster.

neshnn , storm, hurricane, tempest.

neshni 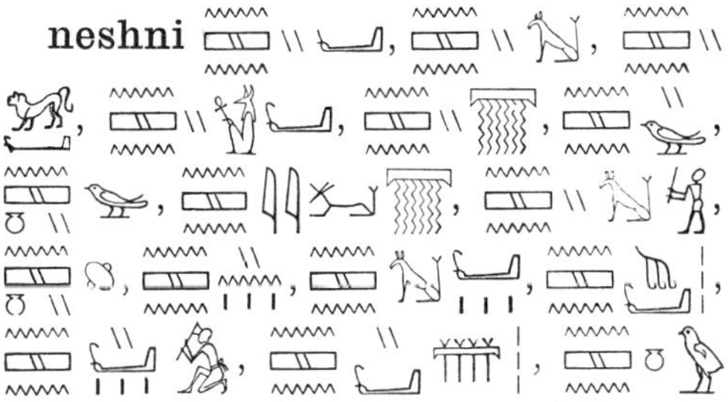 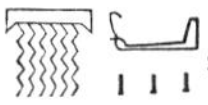, to terrify, to alarm, to frighten, to paralyse with fear,

neshni , a title of Set.

Neshenti , P.S.B.A. 24, 44, 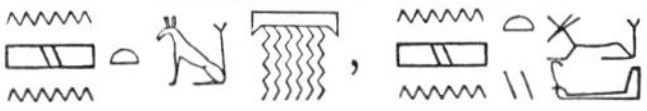, Rev. 11, 69, rage, destructive fury, calamity, disaster, a title of Set.

neshnit 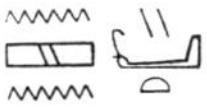, storm, tempest.

neshen 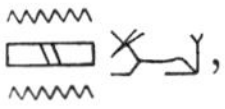, to be eclipsed (of a heavenly body); 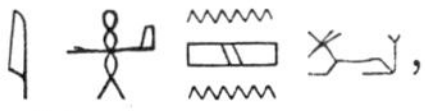, moon eclipsed; , a great eclipse.

neshni , to eat into, to pierce (of fire).

neshen , to pluck a bird.

neshnem , U. 59, a kind of unguent, holy oil; var.

nesher 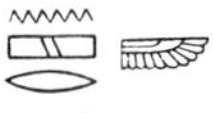, Rev. 12, 65, hawk (?) crane (?); Copt. ⲡⲟϣⲉⲣ.

neshes 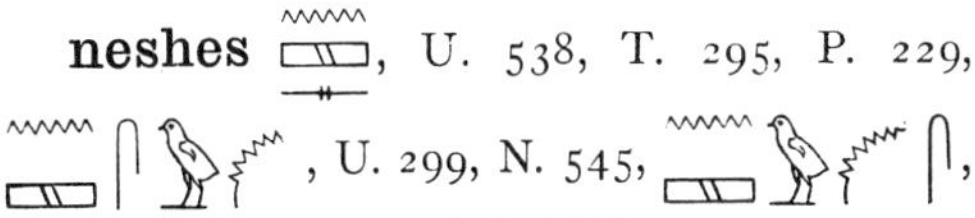, U. 538, T. 295, P. 229, U. 299, N. 545, T. 137, P. 148, to emit fluid (?)

neshes 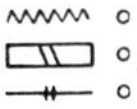, P. 713 . . . . .

neshsesut 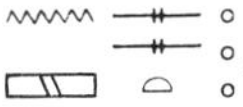, P. 713 . . . . .

nesht 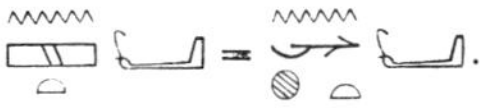.

neshti , cruel, violent.

nesht̩ 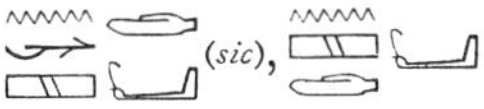 (*sic*), to be strong, strong; Copt. ⲛ̄ϣⲟⲧ.

Nesht̩ , Nesi-Ȧmsu 32, 14, a form of Āapep.

nesht̩ , to cut, to slay.

nesht̩-ti , Amherst Pap. 26, , sculptor, hewer; plur. .

nesht̩ 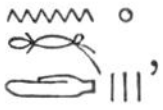, a kind of seed (?)

nesht̩u , N. 954, a girdle (?)

neq , Rev., to commit adultery; Copt. ⲛⲟⲉⲓⲕ.

neq ḥuut , Jour. As. 1908, 302, sodomy.

neq-t , Rev. 13, 53, Jour. As. 1908, 278, Jour. As. 1908, 289, Rev. 13, 7, things, goods, possessions; Copt. ⲛ̄ⲕⲁ.

neqan , to be lacking, or wanting.

neqȧ , Rev. 13, 2, goods, things, stuff.

neqā , to rub down, to grind grain, to polish (?)

neqāut , Ebers Pap. 87, 5, Ebers Pap. 25, 3, Sphinx 14, 225, what is rubbed or ground down to powder, meal, fine flour.

neqāut , B.D. 27, 1, 175, 25, foes crushed or beaten to death.

Neqāiu-ḥatu  , B.D. 27, 1, the fiends who tore up hearts.

nequ-t , something crushed, meal, powder (?)

neq-t 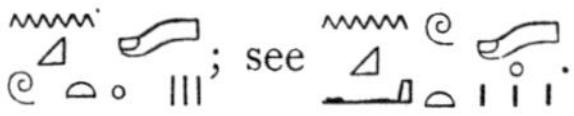 (see).

nequt , Shipwreck 49, some edible plant.

neqeb , Metternich Stele 6, to mourn, to be afflicted.

Neqebit (?) 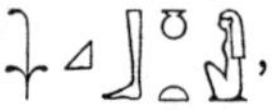, Berg. I, 8, the white vulture-goddess of Nekhen.

neqem  (T. 12, N. 959), Metternich Stele 3, to be afflicted, to mourn, to grieve, to lament.

neqmu , mourners, afflicted ones.

neqma 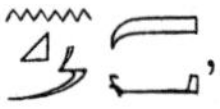, to work in metal.

neqn , to bear in mind, to think, to remember.

neqn-t , injury, affliction.

neqr , Rec. 5, 86, 16, 159, to sift; Copt. ⲛⲟⲕⲉⲣ (?)

neqr 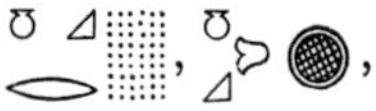, dust, powder, what is sifted.

neqerqer 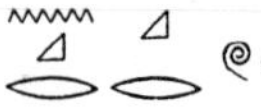, P. 703 . . . . . .

nqeḥqeḥ 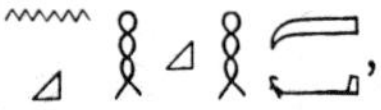, to work in metal, to beat out plates of metal.

neqt (?) 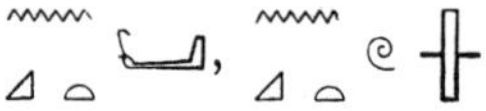, Ebers Pap. 60, 11. . . . .

neqeṭṭ , Israel Stele 23, to sleep.

neqeṭṭ 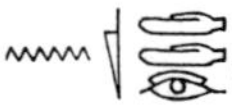, sleep; Copt. ⲛ̀ⲕⲟⲧⲕ̄.

Nqeṭqeṭ 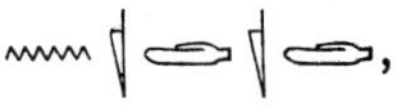, Hh. 101, a god.

nek , pronominal suffix: thou, thee; 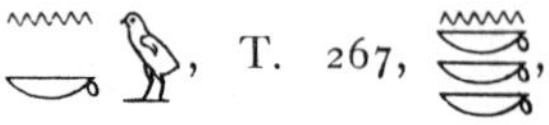 (T. 267), M. 402.

nek 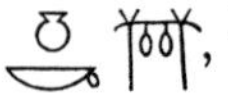, Inscrip. Methen, vineyard, pergola (?)

nek 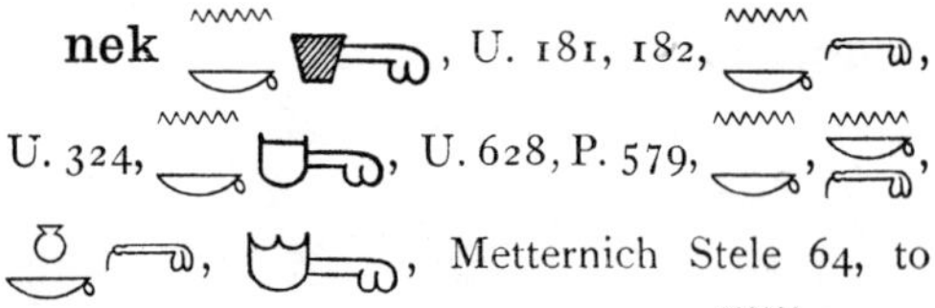 (U. 181, 182, U. 324, U. 628, P. 579), Metternich Stele 64, to copulate, copulation; var. **nenk** 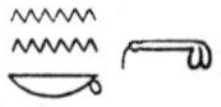; , he copulated with himself (of Rā); Copt. ⲛⲟⲉⲓⲕ.

nekk 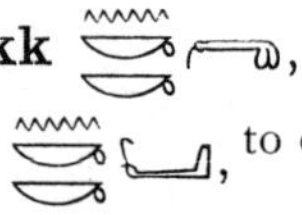, to commit sodomy, sodomite; to copulate with violence, to rape (?)

nekåkå 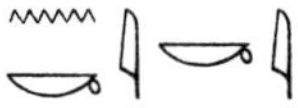, P. 198, M. 373, N. 933, Verbum I, 428, swived, fecundated, pregnant.

nek , Shipwreck 145, ox, bull; plur. .

nek , to smite, to attack, to injure, outrage, crime, murder; see 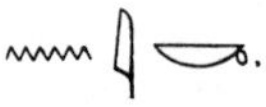.

nekit 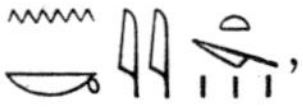, pieces cut off, slashings, hackings.

nekut , Peasant 119, transgression (?)

nek-t , injury, outrage, some wanton act, crime.

nekt 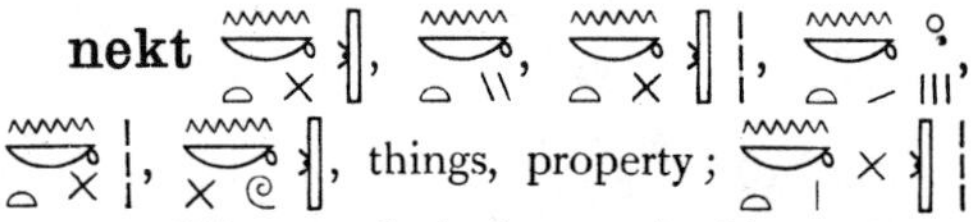, things, property;  Nåstasen Stele 64, certain things; Copt. ⲛ̀ⲕⲁ, ⲛ̄ⲕⲏ.

nekå , things, goods, possessions.

Nekit 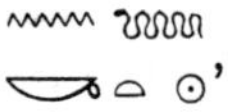, Denderah III, 24, one of seven solar goddesses.

nek-t , cord, rope, string, band.

neka , IV, 46, , to think, to meditate, to cogitate, to devise a plan.

neka-t , thought; plur. .

nekau , bad deeds, offences.

nka .... , Rev. 13, 10, things; Copt. ⲛⲕⲁ.

Nekait, Nekai-t , the goddess of the 7th hour of the day; var. .

nekau , bulls, male animals.

neki , , criminal, malefactor, murderer; plur. , , , .

Nekȧ , , , B.D. 164, 16, Nesi-Ȧmsu, 29, 21, B.M. 32, 421, a serpent-fiend, a form of Set.

nekpatȧ , , , a plant with a gummy juice, a kind of astragalus.

nekpeth , Rec. 4, 21, an aromatic plant.

nekfitȧr , an unguent from Sangar.

neken , U. 214, , , , , , , to make an attack on someone, to commit an outrage, to commit murder, to do evil or harm, to be attacked by an internal pain or disease.

nekenit , T. 249, , , injury, violence, attack, transgression.

nekenu , murderer, malefactor; plur. .

Neknit , the goddess of the 7th hour of the day.

nkens , Rev. 12, 66, injury, violence; Copt. ⲛϭⲟⲛⲥ.

Nekentf , Ṭuat I, a god in the Ṭuat.

nekhi , to grieve, to lament, mourner.

nekt , Jour. As. 1908, 505, a bird.

neg, nega , , , , , , , , , to strike, to smite, to cut off, to cut open, to hew, to slay, to crush.

nega-t , , Peasant 277, a smiting, a blow, a breach in a wall or dyke.

neg-t , Ebers Pap. 39, 7, ...

neg, nega , , , , , , , Ȧmen. 12, 4, to lack, to want, to be short of; , , Rec. 30, 216, 217, to be few in number; , Ḳubbân Stele 11, want of water.

nega-t , L.D. III, 65A, 10 .....

neg , T. 45, , M. 53, P. 441, M. 544, N. 1125, , P. 704, N. 915, 955, , , bull; plur. , T. 45, , P. 87, M. 54, , N. 69, ; , , U. 613, bull of bulls.

nega, P. 704, , , bull.

negau, Rec. 26, 64, , IV, 1124, bull, ox; , A.Z. 1910, 125, cow.

Neg, U. 577, N. 966, the four-horned ( ) bull-god of heaven.

Neg, N. 955, a bull-god who appeared from .

Negau, B.D. 146, the doorkeeper of the 4th Pylon.

Neg-en-kau (?) , T. 45, P. 87, M. 83, N. 69, a bull-god who befriended the dead.

neg, Hh. 541, to cackle.

negg, N. 749, to cackle, to quack.

negaga, , to cackle, to quack.

negȧ, cackler.

Negg-ur, , B.D. 59, 3, the goose-goddess who laid the sun-egg.

Negneg-ur, Berl. 2296; see .

Negaga-ur, B.D. (Saïte) 54, 1, 56, 2, 59, 2; see .

Negit, Denderah IV, 44, one of the eight weeping goddesses.

negagat, , P. 712, N. 1365, pendent (of the breasts of a woman).

negait, A.Z. 1905, 36, semen, essence.

negam, Metternich Stele, 3, to lament, to mourn.

negu pet (?) , Ṭuat X, ...

negeb, , to break, to be destroyed, to come to an end.

negebgeb, , to break.

Ṅegeb, a water-god.

negemgem, Rec. 13, 161, to conspire against, to hatch a plot.

negen, to cut, to slay.

negengen, Hh. 344, to destroy, to break in pieces.

Negnit, Berg. I, 14, a goddess (solar ?) who befriended the dead.

negeḥ, , to be weak, inactive.

neges, to overflow.

ngesges, , , P.S.B.A. 20, 313, to be heaped up full with something, to overflow; varr. ; , IV, 951, overloaded; , IV, 1143, overflowing.

net, , pronominal suffix, fem.: thou, thee.

nt, , who, which; Copt. ⲛ̄ⲧ.

ntȧ, T. 60, P. 185, 310, 641, N. 1238, , M. 295, a relative particle: who, which; Copt. ⲛ̄ⲧ, ⲉⲧ.

nti, , , , N. 1235, , a relative particle: who, which;

, everyone who; , A.Z. 1900, 130: , like that which.

ntt , T. 61, M. 219, N. 294, , that which is; , everything which is; , this which; , N. 1385, the two (fem.) which; , Rev. 13, 81 = = = Copt. ⲚⲦⲈ.

nti = , A.Z. 1908, 120.

nti ȧm , Pap. 3024, 142, , he who is there, *i.e.*, a dead man; plur. , , Berl. 7317; Copt. ⲈⲦ ⳉⲈⲘⲘⲀⲨ.

nti , the thing which is, what is; plur. , , , ; var. .

Ntiu , Ṭuat V, "those who exist," *i.e.*, the righteous.

Ntiu , Rec. 32, 78, , Rec. 32, 79, , , , , , , , , those who are; , the gods who exist as opposed to the dead gods, , , , Rec. 33, 34; varr. , T. 364, .

Nti-em-sert , a title of an official.

Nti-ḥer-f-mm-masti-f , the name of a god.

nt ḥesb , , devoted, or attached, to accounts.

ntt , because; , opens a letter or a narrative.

ntt (?) , , , , to weave, to bind, to tie; var. .

ntt-t , , cord, band, thread, fillet, bandlet; plur. , , cords, ties, bandages, ligatures.

Net , Lanzone 175, a creation-god who stablished the world.

Net , U. 67, , T. 207, , P. 615, , N. 1140, , U. 627, , , Rec. 26, 65, , , , , N. 600, , , , , , , Gr. Νηΐθ, a self-produced perpetually virgin-goddess, who gave birth to the Sun-god; originally she was a goddess of the chase. The centre of her cult was at Saïs where she had the four forms:—

Net Ḥetch-t , Ṭuat XI, Neith of the White Crown.

Net Sher-t , Ṭuat XI, Neith the maiden.

Net tha (?) , Ṭuat XI, Neith of the phallus.

Net Ṭesher-t , Ṭuat XI, Neith of the Red Crown.

Net-tepit-Ȧn-t , Ṭuat II, Neith as lady of the tomb.

Net ḥetut , the great temple of Neith at Saïs.

net , U. 461, T. 351, Hh. 108, Rec. 31, 26, , A.Z. 45, 124, , , , , the Crown of the North, the Red Crown; plur. , U. 540, , Rec. 31, 174.

net , to sprinkle; varr.  .

netnet , to pour out, to flow, to gush out.

netnet , fluid, liquid; plur.  , issues, emissions, secretions.

net , stream, canal; , water of their streams.

net-t , secretion, emission;  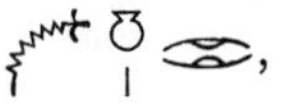, Metternich Stele 170, foam of the lips.

net 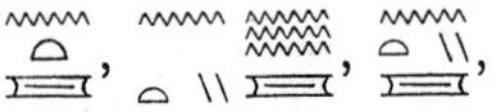, a collection of water, water in general.

netu , stream, canal.

Netit (?) 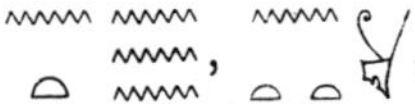, Ṭuat I, a singing-goddess.

Net , Edfû I, 81, a form of the Nile-god.

Netu , Ṭuat V, a river of boiling water, or liquid fire, in the Ṭuat.

Net Ȧs-t 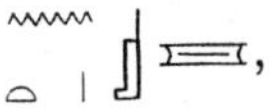, lake of Isis (?)

Net Ȧsȧr 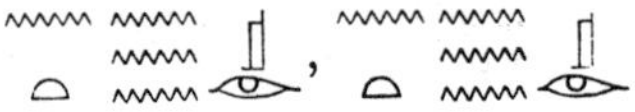 , Ṭuat III, stream of Osiris in the Ṭuat.

Net-neb-uā-kheper-aut  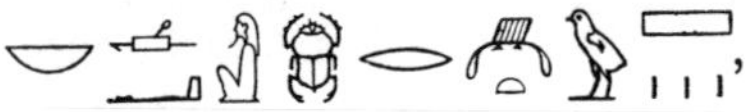, Ṭuat III, a stream in the Ṭuat.

Net-Rā 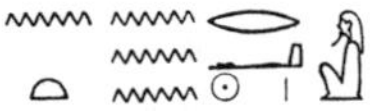, Ṭuat I, a river or canal in the Ṭuat.

net , Israel Stele 3, to be suffocated.

neti , to vanquish, to overcome.

netnet , to cut, to kill, to pour out blood.

netnet , joint, slice of meat.

ntt , bulls for sacrifice.

net , a vase, pot.

nt 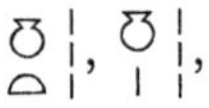, rules, ordinances, regulations.

net-t , skin, hide, pelt.

neta , P. 700, , N. 1159, , P. 41, M. 62, N. 29, to come, to advance.

ntau , ibex; plur.  .

Netȧ , T. 307, the name of a god = , U. 632, , T. 306.

nt-ā [illegible], Ḥeruemḥeb 21, to arrange or codify laws and ordinances, to arrange in proper order the various parts of a religious service, to edit a text.

nt-ā [illegible], rule, order, canon, custom, ordinance, statute, law, formula; plur. [illegible], Thes. 1207, [illegible] [illegible], A.Z. 1908, 122, [illegible], Treaty 5, Rec. 32, 176, stipulations, ordinances, ceremonies; [illegible], Rec. 5, 92, the liturgy for the burial of the dead.

ntu [illegible], Rec. 26, 236, [illegible], [illegible], Rec. 31, 173, those who.

ntu [illegible], N. 607, gods = [illegible], M. 229; [illegible], Stunden 49.

Ntu-ti [illegible], Tomb of Seti I, one of the 75 forms of Rā (No. 25).

ntu-ten [illegible], pronominal suffix, 2nd pers. plur.

neteb [illegible], Rec. 36, 78, [illegible] [illegible], Rhind Pap. 14, [illegible], [illegible] [illegible], to hear, to understand; var. [illegible].

netbit [illegible], Rec. 5, 93, leaves (of the sycamore-fig tree).

ntef [hieroglyphs], pers. pron. 3rd masc. : he, his, him ; Copt. ⲛ̄ⲧⲟϥ.

netf [hieroglyphs], Israel Stele 6, [hieroglyphs], Rev. 13, 4, [hieroglyphs], [hieroglyphs], [hieroglyphs], [hieroglyphs], to untie, to set free, to loosen, to unharness ; [hieroglyphs], Ȧmen. 11, 8, 15, 4 ; Copt. ⲛⲟⲩⲧϥ̄.

netfi [hieroglyphs], Rev. 13, 4, explanation or solution (of a difficulty).

nctf [hieroglyphs], [hieroglyphs], Peasant 144, 263, to sprinkle, to water a garden, to pour out.

nteftef [hieroglyphs] ; see [hieroglyphs].

netm [hieroglyphs], Jour. As. 1908, 291, sweet ; Copt. ⲛⲟⲧⲙ.

neter, nether [hieroglyphs], U. 70, N. 330, [hieroglyphs], T. 237, [hieroglyphs], M. 147, [hieroglyphs], N. 649, [hieroglyphs], [hieroglyphs], [hieroglyphs], [hieroglyphs], [hieroglyphs], [hieroglyphs], ✦, the word in general use in texts of all periods for God and "god" ; Copt. ⲛⲟⲩⲧⲉ, [hieroglyphs] = ⲛⲟⲩⲧⲉ (Rev.)

neteru [hieroglyphs], P. 190, [hieroglyphs], [hieroglyphs], [hieroglyphs], [hieroglyphs], [hieroglyphs], [hieroglyphs], [hieroglyphs], [hieroglyphs], [hieroglyphs], [hieroglyphs], [hieroglyphs], [hieroglyphs], [hieroglyphs], ★★★, [hieroglyphs], [hieroglyphs], Berg. II, 12, [hieroglyphs], Jour. As. 1908, 452, [hieroglyphs], Rec. 27, 83, [hieroglyphs], Rec. 27, 84, gods ; Copt. ⲛ̄ⲧⲏⲣ.

neteru — [hieroglyphs], [hieroglyphs], [hieroglyphs], Rec. 27, 222, [hieroglyphs], [hieroglyphs], gods, male deities ; [hieroglyphs], A.Z., 1906,

124, Rec. 6, 10, [hieroglyphs], [hieroglyphs], [hieroglyphs], T. 197, P. 678, N. 1293, the gods, male and female.

netrit [hieroglyphs], [hieroglyphs], [hieroglyphs], [hieroglyphs], [hieroglyphs], [hieroglyphs], Rec. 30, 67, [hieroglyphs], [hieroglyphs], [hieroglyphs], [hieroglyphs], goddess ; Copt. ⲧⲛⲟⲩⲧⲉ.

netrit [hieroglyphs], U. 209, [hieroglyphs], [hieroglyphs], [hieroglyphs], [hieroglyphs], IV, 565, [hieroglyphs], [hieroglyphs], IV, 838, [hieroglyphs], [hieroglyphs], [hieroglyphs], [hieroglyphs], A.Z. 1906, 126, [hieroglyphs], [hieroglyphs], [hieroglyphs], goddesses.

netr [hieroglyphs], P.S.B.A. 14, 232, strength, force.

netri [hieroglyphs], Rec. 27, 220, [hieroglyphs], [hieroglyphs], [hieroglyphs], [hieroglyphs], [hieroglyphs], [hieroglyphs], Thes. 1284, to be, or to become divine, to deify, divine ; [hieroglyphs], I deify ; [hieroglyphs], [hieroglyphs], more divine than the divine ones ; [hieroglyphs], a divine god ; [hieroglyphs], a divine youth ; [hieroglyphs], a divine Power.

netri [hieroglyphs], divine one.

netrå-t, netrit [hieroglyphs], [hieroglyphs], [hieroglyphs], [hieroglyphs], a divine woman or thing ; plur. [hieroglyphs].

netrå [hieroglyphs], Rev. 14, 33, divine magic or literature.

netri-ti, Israel Stele 14, divine (adj.).

netrer, power, divinity; , IV, 340.

neterteri, divine, strong.

neter àab (àab neter), divine form or image.

neteru àbu, valiant (?); , those who are made valiant.

neter àt (àtf neter), "divine father," or "father of the god," *i.e.*, of the king, the king's father-in-law.

neter àtf (àtf neter), a father who is a god; , two divine fathers; , the father-gods; , the mother-gods.

Neter-uash (Uash-neter) Thes. 112, one of the seven stars of Orion.

Neter uhem (Uhem neter), herald of the god, divine messenger.

neteru peru (peru neteru), gods' houses, temples.

neter feṭ-t (feṭ-t neter), divine sweat.

Neter mut (Mut neter) (1) the mother of the god (*i.e.*, Isis); (2) the title of a priestess.

netrit men (men netrit), the building made for a goddess.

neter meṭut (meṭut neter), , the words of the god [Thoth], any book or inscription written in hieroglyphs.

neter metcha-t (metcha-t neter), U. 396, , , a book of sacred writings.

neter nemmàt (nemmàt neter), Rec. 31, 20, , the god's block of slaughter.

neter ḥe-t (ḥe-t neter), Palermo Stele, , IV, 421, , , , , , , house of the god, temple; plur. , ; , two divine temples; , , IV, 768, , an order of priests who attended in the temple at certain hours of the day and night.

neter ḥāu (ḥāu neter), divine flesh or body, the body of the god.

neter ḥem (ḥem neter), , servant of the god, priest; plur. , ; see **ḥem** , .

neter ḥeteput (ḥeteput neter), , , , , , propitiatory offerings made to a god, sacrifices, the property or possessions in general of the god, the instruments used in making offerings.

Neter Kher-t (Kher-t neter), , , , , , , , , , , , , , the mine of the god, the tomb, the cemetery.

neter kherti (kherti neter), I, 149, quarryman, miner, stonemason, mortuary mason; plur. , , .

neter khe-t (akh-t neter) , , IV, 965, the property of a god, anything sacrosanct; , , sacred book, book of temple services; plur. .

Neter khetmi (khetmi neter) , the keeper of the seal of the god.

neter seḥ-t (seḥ-t neter)  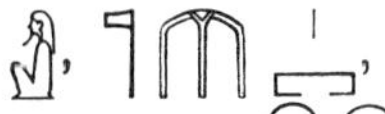, the council-chamber of the god; plur. , T. 398, , M. 400.

Neter Sekh-t (Sekh-t neter)   "the field of the god"—the name of the necropolis of Eileithyiaspolis.

Neter seshu (seshu neter) 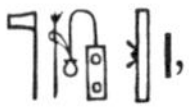, P. 345, 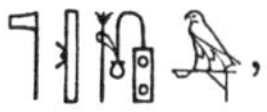, M. 646, the scribe of the god.

Neter seshshit (seshshit neter) , a priestess who carried the god's sistrum.

Neter shemsu (shemsu neter) 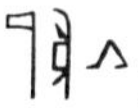, a member of the god's body-guard; plur. .

Neter ta (Ta-neter) , Inscrip. Henu, 14; 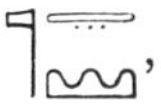, IV. 329, , IV, 615, 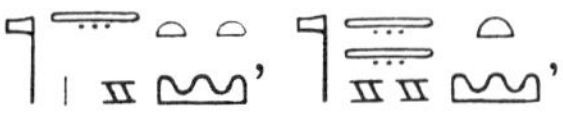, heaven.

Neter-ta 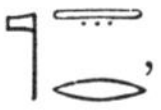, the title of the priestess in Lycopolis.

neter ṭua (ṭua neter)  , Shipwreck 5, , , to adore, to give thanks, to offer thanksgiving.

Neter ṭuait (Ṭuait neter) , , "Adorer of the god," the title of the high-priestess of Thebes; , the house of the high-priestess of Thebes.

Neter ṭuaut (Ṭuaut neter)  , P. 611, star of the morning—Venus; later forms are: , .

Neter ṭep-t (Ṭep-t neter)  , T. 93, N. 629 , the boat of the god Rā.

neter tcheṭ (tcheṭ neter) , speech of the god, hieroglyphs (?)

Neter , Berg. I, 13, a serpent-god who bestowed godhood on the dead.

Neterti (?) , Ṭuat V, a god in the Ṭuat.

neter āa [illegible], U. 416, [illegible], T. 237, , "great god"—a title of many gods; [illegible], the great self-produced god; [illegible], the seats of the great god, N. 764, 800.

Neter āa [illegible], Ṭuat V, a two-headed winged serpent with a tail terminating in a human head.

Neter āa [illegible], Ṭuat IV, a three-headed winged serpent with two pairs of human legs.

Neter uā [illegible], the god One, a title applied to any god and even any goddess, *e.g.*, Neith, who is for some special purpose regarded as the "Great God."

Neter baḥ (?) [illegible], Rec. 4, 28, a god.

Neter peri [illegible], the god who appeareth = Epiphanes.

Netrit fent (?) [illegible], Ṭuat V, an axe-god or goddess.

Neter mut [illegible], a title of Isis = Termuthis.

neter merti [illegible], Mar. Aby. II, 23, 16. . . . .

Neter nuti , N. 859,  [illegible], P. 164, 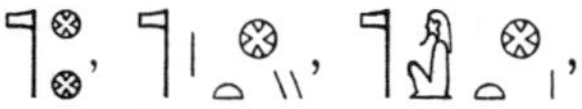, the god of the town, the local god.

Neter neferu [illegible], Ṭuat III, a god.

Neterit-nekhenit-Rā 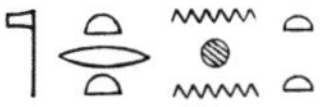 , Ṭuat IX, a singing-goddess in the Ṭuat.

Neter-neteru [illegible] Ṭuat IX, a singing-god.

Neter-ḥāu 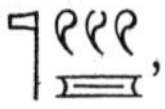, Edfû I, 79, a name of the Nile-god.

Neter-kha 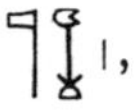, B.D. 137A, I, god of one thousand [years]; compare  , boat of one thousand [years], ibid., l. 3.

Neter Sepṭ-t , Jour. As. 1908, 290, one of the 36 Dekans.

Neter-ka-qetqet , Edfû I, 106, one of the eight gods who guarded Osiris.

Netrit-ta-åakhu (?) 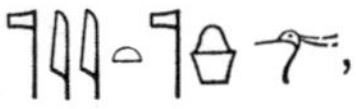, Ṭuat V, an axe-god.

Netrit-ta-meḥ (?) , Ṭuat V, an axe-god.

Neter ṭuau , P. 80; see **Ṭuaut neter** (p. 403).

Neter-tchai-pet , Annales I, 88, the planet Saturn.

Netrit-Then (?) , Ṭuat V, an axe-god.

Neterui , 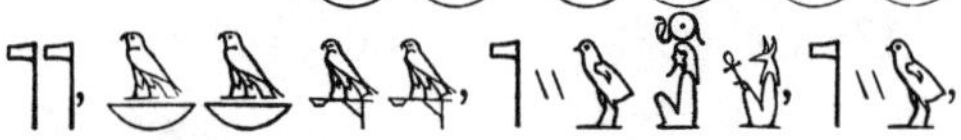, the twin gods.

Neterui [illegible], U. 558, the two lion-gods, Shu and Tefnut, 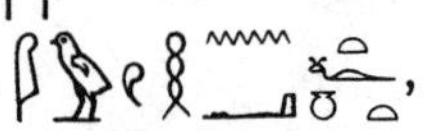, who made their own bodies, 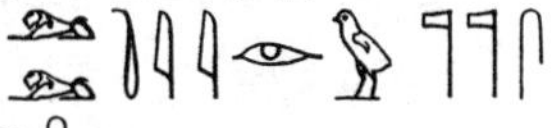 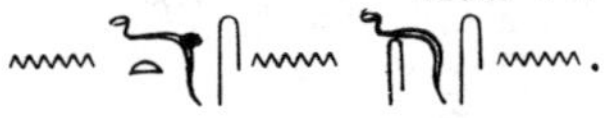.

Neter-ti 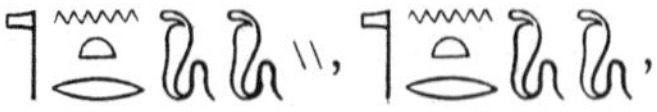, the two goddesses, Isis and Nephthy̆s (?)

Neterui āaui , P. 311, , U. 575, N. 968,  , the two great gods in heaven.

Neterui [illegible], the two very great gods of Sekhet-Åaru,  , M. 454.

Neterui perui , the two gods Epiphanes.

Neterui menkhui [illegible], the two beneficent gods.

Neterui merui åt , the two father-loving gods, *i.e.*, Philopatores.

Neterui merui mu-t 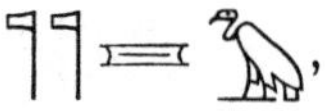, the two mother-loving gods, *i.e.*, Philometores.

Neterui netchui [illegible], the two gods who act as defenders.

Neterui ḥetepui , P. 348, 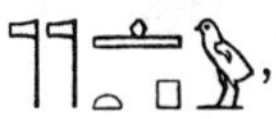, M. 649, the two gods who give peace, or satisfaction, by offerings.

Neterui senui [illegible], the two brother-gods, or Adelphoi.

Neterui sheptui , P. 348, , M. 649, the two devouring gods.

Neteru IV [illegible], B.D. 135, 2, Hymn Darius 28, the four chief gods of heaven; **Neteru VII** 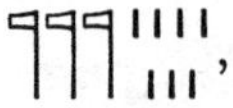, the seven gods who founded the earth; **Neteru VIII** [illegible], the eight gods of the Company of Thoth.

Neteru IX – pestch-t neteru 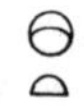 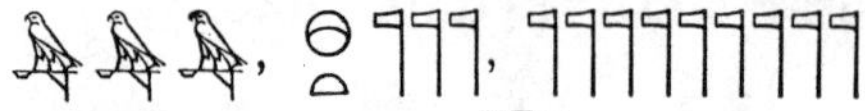, the nine gods, also written 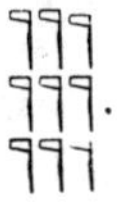.

1. , U. 251, N. 216, 714, the Great Nine Gods.

2. , U. 252, N. 714, the Little Nine Gods.

3. , P. 602, , U. 179, 480, , N. 47, 134, 1267, , N. 198, , P. 97, 479, M. 67, 222, U. 188, T. 66, , P. 217, the two groups of nine gods, *i.e.*, the Great and Little Companies.

4. , U. 418, P. 218, the three groups of nine gods, *i.e.*, the Companies of the Gods of Heaven, Earth, and the Ṭuat.

Neteru XLII , B.D. 125, I, 5, the 42 assessors of Osiris.

Netriu , Thes. 133, the 36 Dekans.

Neteru Áatiu , , B.D. 141, 45, the gods of the Áats.

Neteru áau , Berg. II, 4, a group of gods who re-joined the limbs of the deceased.

Neteru tepiu áa-t-sen Mar. Aby. I, 28, the gods on their pedestals.

Neteru áabtiu , U. 572, , B.D. 141, 40, eastern gods; , gods of the East.

Neteru áakhutiu , B.D. 141, 47, the gods of the horizon.

Neteru ámiu , Nesi-Ámsu 12, 6, the gods who dwell in:—(1) , heaven; (2) , earth; (3) , the Ṭuat; and (4) , the Nile.

Neteru ámiu āqet , a group of six gods of the Gate Saa-Set.

Neteru ámiu Uáa-ta , Ṭuat III, the seven gods of the boat of the Earth.

Neteru ámiu Meḥon , B.D. 168, the gods who dwell in the serpent-goddess Meḥen; var. .

Neteru ámiu-khet Ásár , , B.D. 168, , the gods and goddesses who were in the train of Osiris.

Neteru ámiu she kheb , Ṭuat III, the gods of the lake of Fire.

Neteru ámiu qeb Meḥen , , the gods associated with the serpent-goddess who protected the night sun.

Neteru ámiu karát , B.D. 168, the 14 gods of the shrine of Osiris.

Neteru ámiu ta Ṭuat , the gods in the earth and in the Ṭuat.

Neteru-ámentiu , U. 572, , B.D. 141, 39, western gods; , gods of the West.

Neteru áru pet , U. 586, M. 805, N. 1335, , P. 298, the gods belonging to heaven.

Neteru åru ta , U. 586, M. 805, N. 1335,  , P. 298, the gods belonging to the earth.

Neteru åtfiu , B.D. 168, 12, the father-gods ; fem. .

Neteru uatu , B.D. 141, 50–53, the gods of roads ; southern , northern 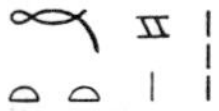, eastern 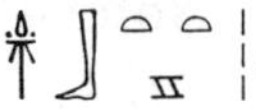, western 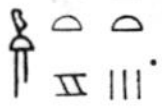.

Neteru Baiu Pu , the gods, the souls of Pu (Buto).

Neteru Baiu Nekhen  , the gods, the Souls of Nekhen (Hieraconpolis).

Neteru pe-t , the gods of heaven ; var. .

Neteru pauttiu , the primeval gods.

Neter —  , B.D. 17 (Nebseni), 39, the god with a face like a dog's.

Neteru Per-ur , 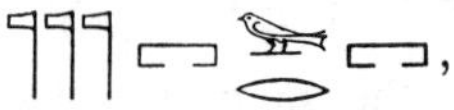, B.D. 141, 43, gods of the "Great House."

Neteru Per-neser 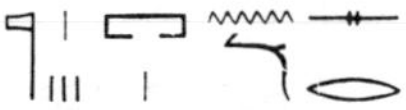 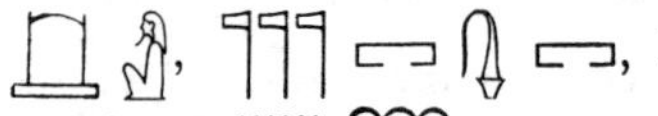, B.D. 141, 44, 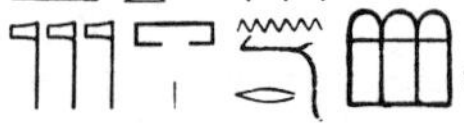, gods of the House of Fire.

Neteru Pertiu , B.D. 141, 48, , the gods of the exits (?)

Neteru mastiu  , B.D. 141, 41, the gods of the Great Bear.

Neteru Mefakitiu  , Ṭuat XII, the gods of the Sinaitic Peninsula.

Neteru meḥtiu , U. 572, , N. 967,  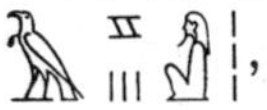, northern gods.

Neteru-nu-Ḥe-t Ba 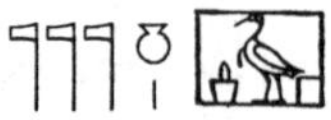 Pap. Ani I, 6, the gods of the Soul-Temple who weigh heaven and earth,  .

Neteru en Ṭuat 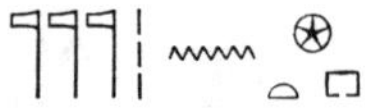, the gods of the Ṭuat.

Neteru nuttiu , the native gods of towns.

Neteru nebu nutiut , P. 696, all the gods of the cities.

Neteru nebu septtiu  [illegible], P. 696, all the gods of the nomes.

Neteru netchestiu (?) [illegible] [illegible], B.D. 141, 49, [illegible], [illegible], "the little gods."

Neteru resu [illegible], U. 572, N. 967, [illegible], B.D. 141, 42, southern gods.

Neteru Ḥettiu [illegible], Ṭuat VII, the eight gods of Ḥe-t Benben in the Ṭuat.

Neteru ḥau kar [illegible] [illegible], Ṭuat IV, the 12 gods of the shrine of Osiris.

Neteru ḥeriu Kheti [illegible] [illegible], Ṭuat VIII, the seven gods who stood on the fire-spitting serpent Kheti.

Neteru Ḥeteptiu, B.D. 141, 42, the gods who are endowed with offerings.

Neteru khetiu Åsår, Ṭuat IV, a group of gods who ministered to Osiris.

Neteru saiu Khas-t, Ṭuat VII, the eight gods who guarded the lake of fire on which Osiris dwelt.

Neteru suu en ka-sen, Ṭuat IV, a group of gods in the Ṭuat.

Neteru semsu, U. 446, T. 255, the senior gods.

Neteru sekhtiu, B.D. 141, 47, the gods who are over the fields of the Ṭuat.

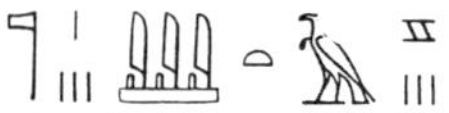

Neteru seshemu Ṭuat, B.D. 142, 137, the guides of the Ṭuat.

Neteru set (semt), Ṭuat I, the gods of the funerary mountain; 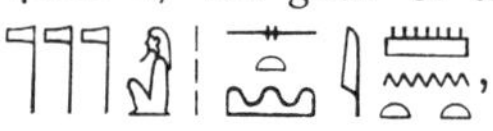 , Ṭuat I.

Neteru qerti, , B.D. 127A, 1, the gods of the two Nile-caverns in the First Cataract.

Neteru Qertiu, B.D. 141, 48, the gods of the Circles in the Ṭuat.

Neteru ta, the gods of earth; var.

Neteru ṭuatiu, the gods of the Ṭuat.

Neteru tchaṭiu, Ṭuat X, 12 gods who held the fetter of Āapep.

Neteru tcheseriu, Ṭuat III, a group of 12 gods protected by Seti.

neterit, Ṭuat II (Gate II), false gods (?)

Netr, Netru,  , , T. 39, P. 334, 499, P. II, 1345, the God-city, or city of Osiris.

Netrå, a name of the necropolis of Coptos.

netrit, , , a name of either eye of Horus.

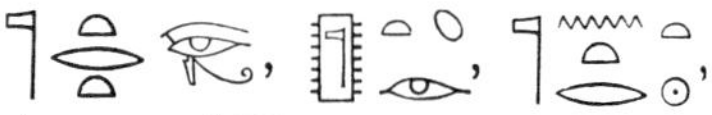

neterti, N. 951, , , , , Rec. 32, 178, the two eyes of Horus or Rā, *i.e.*, the sun and moon.

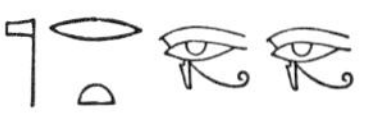

Netrit, , , the name of a festival.

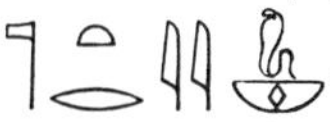

netrå, U. 22, , , Annales III, 110, natron, incense, to cleanse, to purify; Heb. נֶתֶר, Syr. ܢܬܪܐ, Gr. νίτρον, λίτρον, nitrum.

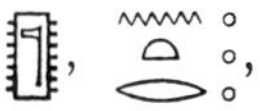

neter, censer; perhaps neter seḥetpi.

neter, N. 289, 290, a kind of garment or stuff; see **nether**.

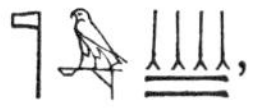

neterut, , a kind of strong-smelling plant or herb.

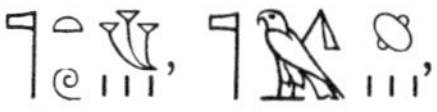

neter, Rev., axe; varr. , ; compare Copt. ⲁⲛⲑⲏⲣ.

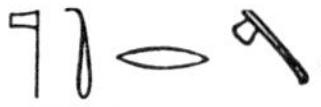

neter-ti (?), a double tool, or a pair of instruments used in "Opening the Mouth."

neter, stream, canal (?)

netrå, water house.

neter, wine, strong beer.

netri (?), a kind of thread or string.

Nteriush Darius; varr. , , , ; Pers. , Babyl. , Heb. דָּרְיָוֶשׁ, Gr. Δαρεῖος.

neth̟, B.D. 110, 13 .....

neth̟ = , , , those who appertain to horses, *i.e.*, cavalry, horsemen.

ntes, pers. pron. 3rd fem.: she, it; Copt. ⲛ̄ⲧⲟⲥ.

nt-sen, , pers. pron. 3rd pl.: they, their, them.

Netqa-ḥer-khesef-aṭu, B.D. 144, the herald of the 4th Ārit; var. .

ntek, U. 544, P. 647, , M. 745, , pers. pron. 2nd masc.: thee, thou; Copt. ⲛ̄ⲧⲟⲕ.

nt-th, pers. pron. 2nd fem. sing.; Copt. ⲛ̄ⲧⲟ.

nt-then = , pronominal suffix 2nd pers. plur.; Copt. ⲛ̄ⲧⲱⲧⲛ̄.

neth, = , of.

nth-ḥetr, , Rec. 8, 134, 136, those who appertain to horses, horsemen, cavalry.

nthu, P. 607, I, 61, , U. 365, P. 606, , P. 63, thee, thou; Copt. ⲛ̄ⲧⲟ.

neth, P. 255, M. 475, N. 1064, = **nest,** seat, throne.

nethu, Mission 13, 61, necklace, collar.

neth̟th, chain, cord, fetter; plur. , T. 234.

Netheth, Ṭuat X, a goddess associated with Seṭfit.

Nethef, title of the ram of Mendes.

nether, T. 24, P. 742, , T. 202, , N. 792, , Rec. 32, 82, god; plur. , ; see **neter.**

netherit, goddess; plur. , T. 206, , Rec. 27, 220, , , .

Nether Rethnu, Ṭuat X, an ape-god with a star.

Netherit, the eye of Rā or Horus.

Netherit Tomb of Seti I, one of the 75 forms of Rā (No. 24).

netherit, eyes.

nether, natron; , , natron of the North; , , natron of the South; Heb. נֶתֶר, Gr. νίτρον.

Nether, , P. 334, M. 637, the Lake of Nether in Nethru.

nether, , cloth, woven stuff. Different kinds and qualities are enumerated, *e.g.*, , , , , , , , , .

Ntheriush, Darius; see **Nteriush.**

nthehtheh, P. 349, N. 1065, Sphinx 14, 213, to blow, to spit (?)

nethes (?), U. 540, T. 296, P. 230 . . . .

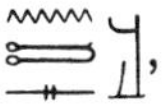

nthk = , thee, thou.

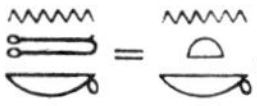

neṭ, P. 97, 684, , to tie, to bind.

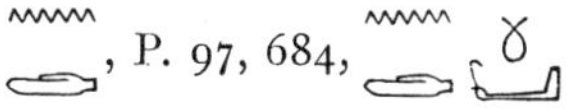

neṭṭ, to tie, to bind.

Neṭneṭit-uḥtes-khakȧbu, Ṭuat X, a pilot-goddess of Ȧf.

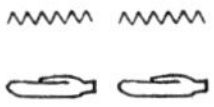

neṭa, to escape.

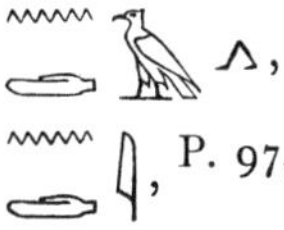

neṭa, P. 97, 186, M. 67, N. 47, to overthrow.

Neṭȧ, U. 279, 291, , N. 719 =  .

nṭā; see **n-tā** .

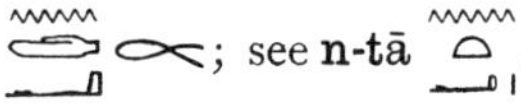

nṭ-ā, ordinance, precept, regulation.

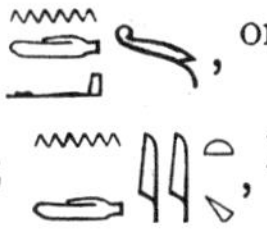

neṭit, Metternich Stele 47, bank of a river or canal.

neṭuȧu, Ebers Pap. 14, 20, 15, 12 . . . .

neṭb, M. 247, N. 638, to drink.

nṭebṭeb, P. 810,  , T. 335, to drink.

neṭbit, Peasant 56, part of a sail.

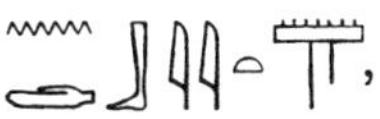

neṭebut, , Tombos Stele 11,  , territories, lands, domains.

neṭbu, Annales III, 109, , , , Thes. 1286, IV, 168, 387, 766, to plate an object with metal, to be plated.

neṭef, , , to sprinkle, to moisten.

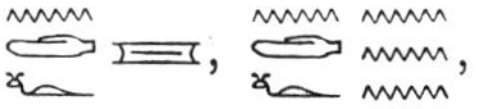

nṭefṭef, U. 201, , T. 78, M. 231, N. 610, to drop water, to distil moisture.

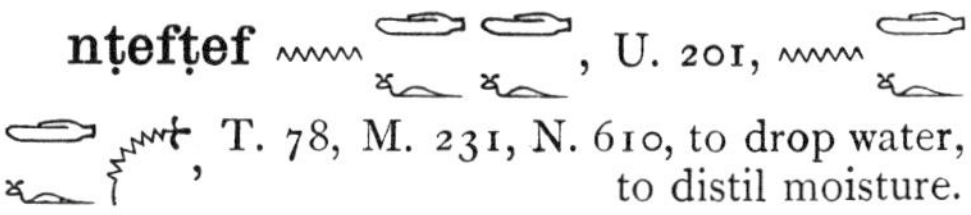

nṭefṭefu, T. 331, N. 621, droppings.

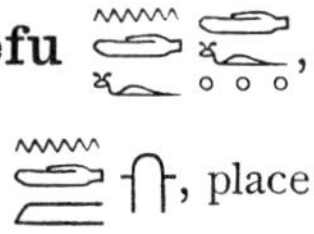

neṭm, place of rest, couch.

neṭnuṭu, IV, 766, unguent of some kind.

neṭr, eye.

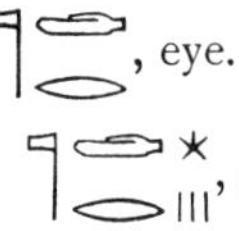

neṭru, gods, Dekans, stars.

Neṭru, Ṭuat XI, one of the 12 gods who carried Meḥen.

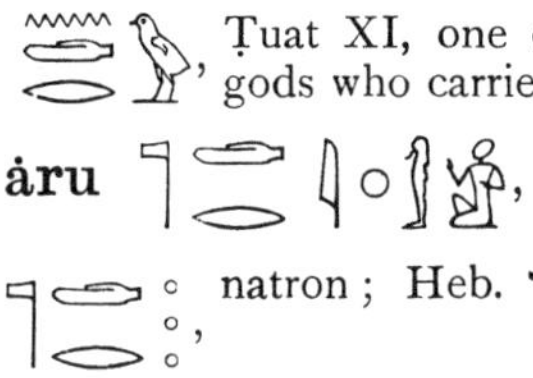

neṭer ȧru, a title of a priest.

neṭer, natron; Heb. נֶתֶר, Gr. *νίτρον*.

Nṭeriush; varr. , , Darius; see **Nteriush.**

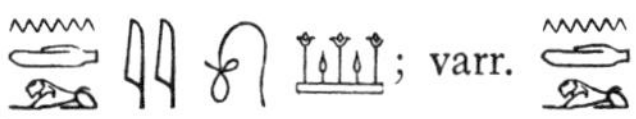

nṭes, she, it; Copt. ⲛ̄ⲧⲟⲥ.

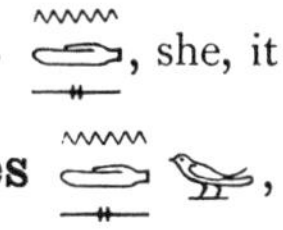

neṭes, little, low (of Nile).

neṭsit, diminution.

nṭesṭesi, N. 1201, , P. 416, M. 596, , N. 298 . . . .

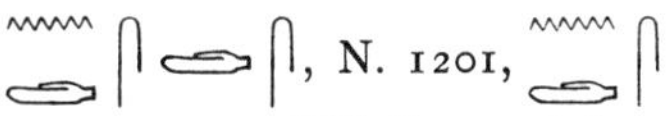

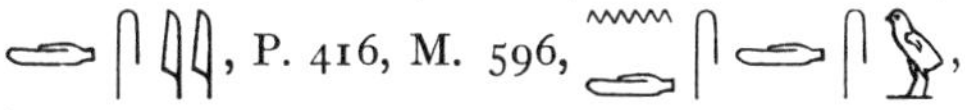

nṭek, thee, thou; Copt. ⲛ̄ⲧⲟⲕ.

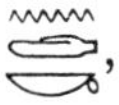

netch, U. 428, P. 204, , U. 296,  , T. 245, , M. 134, , , , , , , , to protect by word or deed, to act as a defender or advocate for some one.

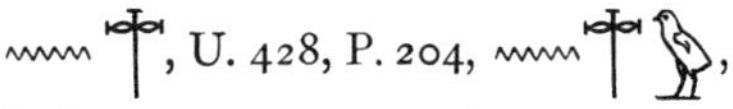

netchnetch , T. 285, , Rec. 30, 194, 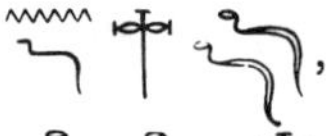, P. 36, , N. 66, , M. 44, to protect, to defend.

netch-ti 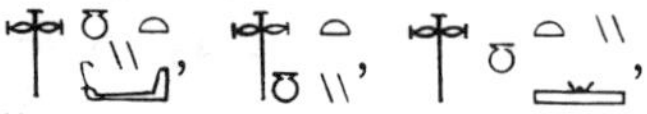, , protector; fem. , protectress; [illegible] [illegible], beings who protect.

netch ḥer , 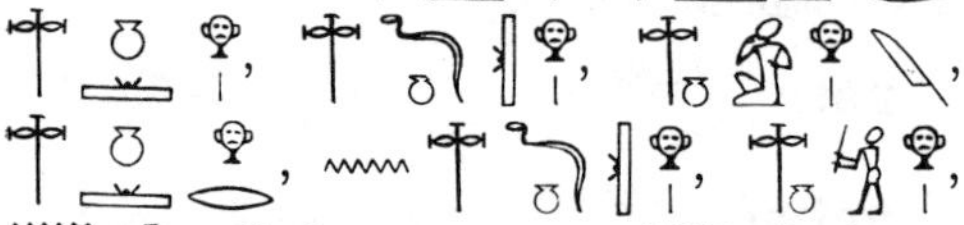, , to protect; [illegible], N. 766, [illegible], Rec. 31, 170.

netch ḥer , or , the opening words of many hymns, meaning something like "homage to thee."

Netch-ḥer-netch-ḥer , god of the 9th hour of the day.

netch khet  , a guardian of property, to take care of something, trustee, councillor; 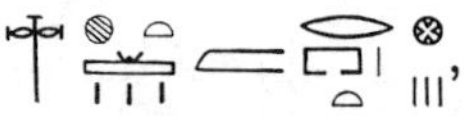, member of council in the temples; 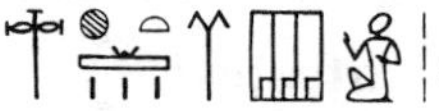, temple councillors.

Netchti , Ṭuat VI, a god who fed the dead.

Netch ȧt-f 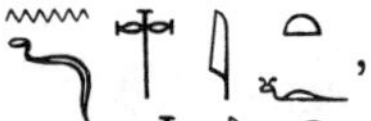, T. 277, [illegible], P. 31, [illegible], N. 69, [illegible], "protector of his father" —a title of Horus.

Netch-ȧt-f , Ṭuat VI, a god who fed the dead.

Netch-ti-ur 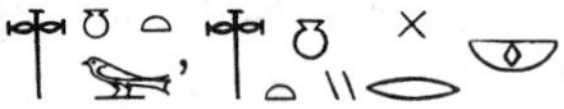, the god of the 11th day of the month.

Netch-baiu , Tomb of Seti I, one of the 75 forms of Rā (No. 25).

Netch Nu  , a title of Rā.

Netchui — neterui netchui 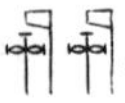, the two protecting gods (Soteres).

netch 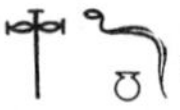, IV, 1105, 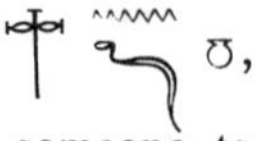, [illegible], to take counsel with someone, to seek advice, to talk a matter over.

netchnetch 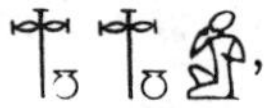, Ȧmen. 11, 9, P. 1116B, 64, 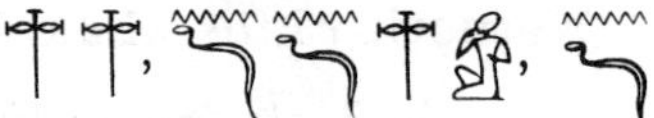 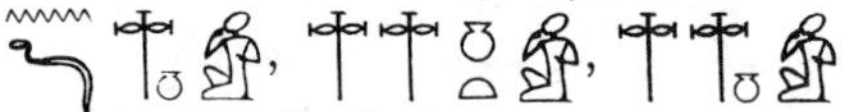, Rec. 15, 178, 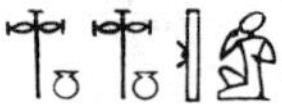, to discuss, to debate, to take counsel about a matter, to argue, to disagree, to contradict, to question a statement; varr. ; , incontrovertible, unquestionable; Copt. ⲛⲟϫⲛⲉϫ, ⲛⲟϭⲛⲉϭ.

netch ȧau-t , to exercise or enjoy a dignity.

netch meṭut  , to converse, to exchange speech.

netch ra , , to consult about a matter, to take counsel, to discuss, to debate a matter, to be eloquent, to play the orator, to make an order after due deliberation, an address, counsel, consultation.

netchnetch ra , [illegible]; see [illegible].

netch ren, to proclaim the name.

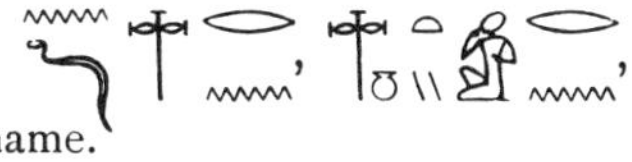

netch khert, to direct affairs, to perform duties.

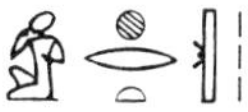

netch, Rec. 31, 170, to laugh.

netch, to pound, to crush, to break up, to smash; crushed; Copt. ⲚⲞⲨⲦ.

netch senāā, Rec. 4, 21, to rub to a fine powder, to rub down drugs for medicine.

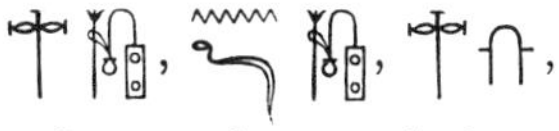

netchit, Rec. 16, 146, something rubbed down, or brayed in a mortar.

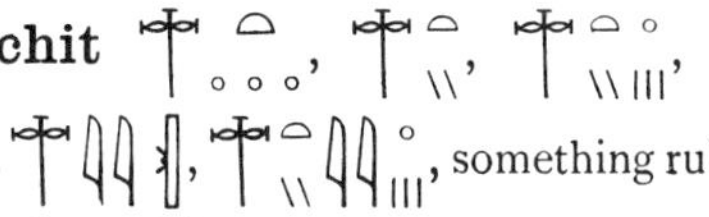

netchit, Rev. 14, 3, paintings in colours; Rec. 15, 16, prayers painted in colours.

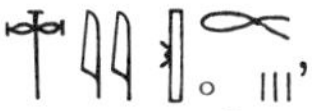

netchit, Nȧstasen Stele 43, crushed grain.

netch, Rechnungen 39, crushed grain, meal; Copt. ⲚⲞⲈⲒⲦ.

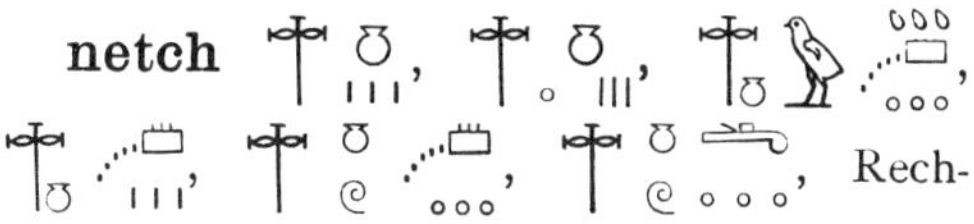

netchnetch, Rec. 1, 48, meal (?) flour (?)

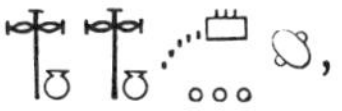

netch, limit, boundary.

netch-t, serf, peasant, vassal, hind; plur.; Rec. 29, 166, women servants, female slaves; var. **netchit**, slave woman.

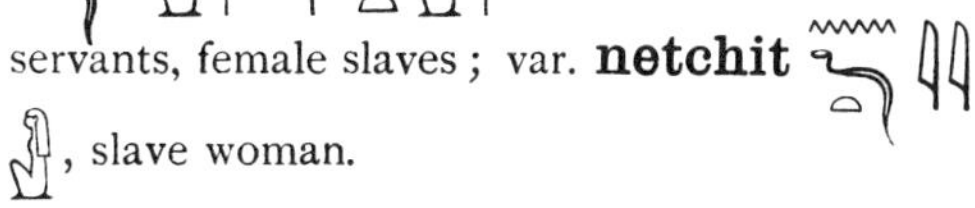

netch, a kind of cloth or woven stuff.

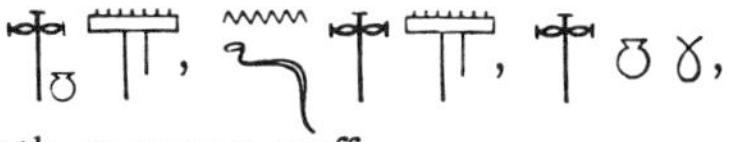

netch, almond (?) tree; Heb. לוז (?)

netch, little, something small.

netchiu, serf, subject, enemy; plur.

netchi-t, littleness, subjection, degradation.

netcha, greedy, hungry, ravenous, death-rattle (?)

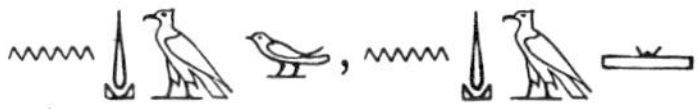

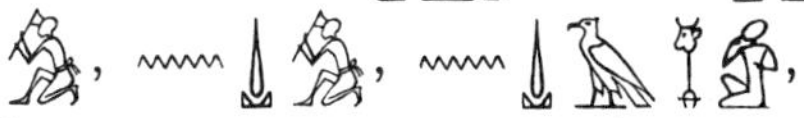

netcha (?), L.D. III, 140B, to be cooled or eased (of the throat).

netcha-t, the deposit left by the inundation of the Nile.

netchatcha, to fill with water (?)

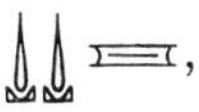

netchatchait, Ebers Pap. 36, 17, Ebers Pap. 10, 8, 30, 4, 32, 12, dregs.

netcha, IV, 171, 754, Thes. 1288, a weight (for dates).

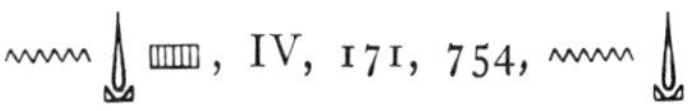

ntch-ā; see **nt-ā**.

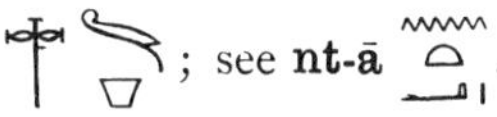

Netcheb-ȧb-f, B.D. 39, 15, a storm-god.

netchoftchef; see

netchf-t, nuts, fruit of a tree.

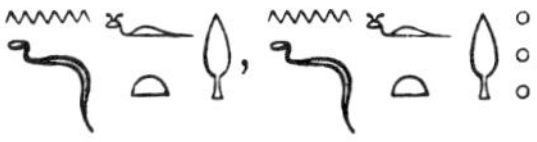

Netchf-t, a town of Osiris.

netchem, Rec. 27, 226,

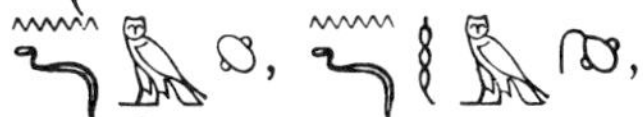

, to be sweet, sweet, pleasant, happy, glad, jolly, mirthful, delighted, delightful, to have relief from pain or anxiety, convalescence; , very glad, very nice, very pleasant; comp. Heb. √נעם, Copt. ⲛⲟⲩⲧⲙ, Arab. نَعِمَ.

netchem-t , , , any sweet thing, sweetness, sweet, love.

netchemu , , things sweet and pleasant; , sweet life; , , sweet-smelling; , happy every day.

netchem ȧb (?) , U. 431, , T. 247, 338, Rec. 27, 219, , Rec. 33, 30, to be happy, glad, to rejoice, to make merry.

netchemnetchem , , , , Rec. 15, 47, to be happy, to make love, sweet, happy.

netchemnetchem ȧb (?) , to rejoice.

netchemit , Rec. 30, 196, sexual pleasures.

netchmemut , P. 466, M. 529, N. 1108, , Rec. 27, 56, , , sexual delights, love pleasures.

netchemnetchemiu , love joys.

netchemnetchemit , concubines, harlots.

Netchem , B.D. 39, 20, a god.

Netchemnetchemit , Lanzone 112, the divine midwife, .

Netchem-ȧb , Ṭuat XII, a singing dawn-god; plur. , Rec. 31, 174.

Netchem-ānkh , Rec. 37, 63, a god.

netchem, netchemnetchem , , , , Rec. 15, 114, , mandragora (?)

netchm'u , U. 338 . . . .

netcher , U. 282, N. 719, P. 309, 607, , T. 278, , T. 308, , Rec. 31, 170, , U. 487, P. 12, , T. 283, M. 670, , Rec. 31, 19, , , , , , , , , , , to seize, to grasp, to hold, to hold fast, to constrain, to restrain; , Thes. 1483, to strike the footsteps of.

netchrer , T. 291, to seize, to grasp.

netcher-t , , place of restraint, prison, captivity, imprisonment.

netchrit , , B.D. 153A, 19, parts of a net.

netcher tep reṭ , to observe laws, to keep ordinances.

Netchertt , a place of restraint in the Ṭuat.

Netcher , a god.

Netcher 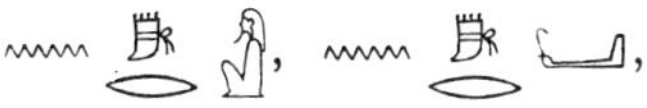, a god, sustainer of heaven and earth.

Netchrit , B.D. 168, the eight goddesses who were armed with hatchets.

netcher 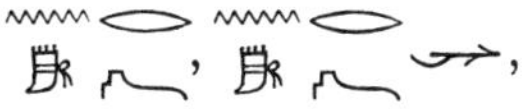, N. 757, to sharpen a tool or the claws.

netchru 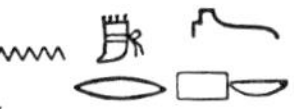, carpenter; compare Arab. نجّار.

netcher-t , N. 975 . . . . .

Netcherf , P. 651,  , P. 729, , M. 783, the limitless god.

netcheḥ-t , B.D. 110, 13, with  . . . .

netcheḥ-t , IV, 708, , a tusk of ivory, a tooth; plur.  , Shipwreck 164, , 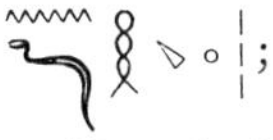; Copt. ⲛⲁⲁϫϩⲉ, ⲛⲁϫϩⲓ.

Netcheḥnetcheḥ 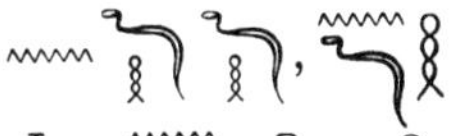, , Edfû I, 10A, Rec. 4, 28, B.D. 17, 102, Berg. I, 3, one of the eight gods who watched over the body of Osiris; var. , Hh. 101.

Netcheḥtcheḥiu  , Hh. 524, a group of gods.

netcheḥtcheḥ , to suffer, to be in pain.

netchḥā 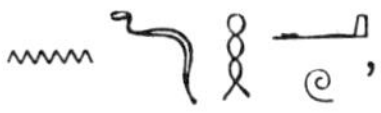, P. 204 + 7 . . . .

netchḥātchḥāt , a kind of grain or seed.

netches , U. 90, , P. 173, N. 939, , P. 590, , Rec. 31, 147, , to be little, to become small, little.

netchesu , P. 1116B, 10, , peasant, poor man, little person, miserable man, child, underling; plur.  , 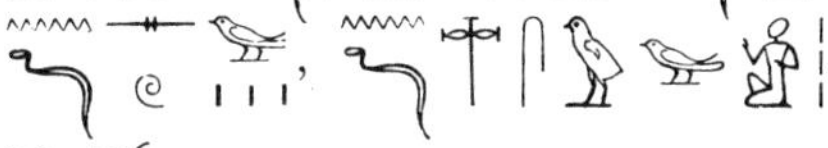, Rec. 32, 216.

netches-t 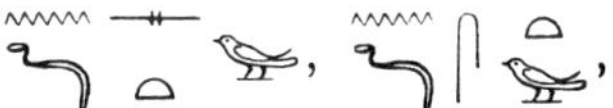, 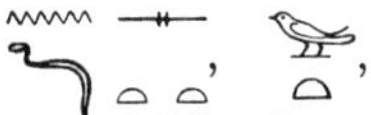, a little thing, small, little; plur. .

netches-ti , little.

netches , a "little" god, as opposed to a great and important god; var. [illegible]; plur. [illegible].

Netchses [illegible], B.D. (Saïte) 146, the doorkeeper of the 9th Pylon.

Netches-ti [illegible], a name of Osiris.

Netches-ti [illegible], Tomb of Seti I, a bearded child-god, one of the 75 forms of Rā (No. 61).

netcheṭtcheṭ [illegible], M. 146, N. 649, Sphinx XIV, 214, to be permanent, to endure.

R

r = Heb. ר and ל, and Coptic ⲣ, ⲣ̄ and ⲗ.

er, at, by, near, to, towards, into, with, among, against, from, every, upon, concerning, up to, until, so that. The old form of the word is **år**; var., upon; Copt. ⲉⲣⲟ.

er au, all, entirely.

er åuṭ, between.

er åm', towards.

er åmi-tu, IV, 365, between, among, IV, 415.

er åsu, in return for.

er åqer, exceedingly, very much.

er āa, greatly.

er āa ur, greatly, exceedingly.

er āq, exactly opposite.

er bunr, outside; Copt. ⲉ ⲃⲟⲗ.

er ber, Metternich Stele 167, outside; Copt. ⲉ ⲃⲟⲗ.

er peḥ, to the uttermost, to the end.

er em, Nåstasen Stele 26, with, near; Copt. ⲛⲙⲙ; III, 142 = Copt. ⲛⲙⲙⲙⲁⲛ, with us; Nåstasen Stele 17, 28 = Copt. ⲛⲙ̀ⲙⲙⲁϥ, with him.

er må, Rev. 11, 147, 13, 68, as, like, according to = Copt. ⲉ ⲑⲉ (Rev.).

er måtet, according to the likeness, likewise.

er men, up to.

er men em, IV, 618, as far as.

er meti, IV, 657, corresponding to.

er n, without, not.

er nuit, straightway, instantly.

er nefer er, successfully.

er neḥeḥ, everlastingly.

er enti, so that, because, inasmuch as, according to that which = Gr. ἐπειδή.

er rā (?), as far as, to the limit of.

er ruti, Rev. 11, 133, at the two doors, *i.e.*, outside; var.

er ruṭi, outside.

er hau, towards.

er hu, over against.

er hen, Rev. 13, 54 = , up to.

er ḥa-t, before, in front of.

er ḥai, exceedingly.

er ḥenā, with.

er ḥer, over and above, in addition to.

er kha-t = , in accordance with.

er kheft , opposite, in face of.

er khent , before.

er kher , with.

er khet , in the following of, in the charge of.

er sa , Peasant 244, at the side of, after.

er shaā , up to, until; , for ever.

er ges , , , , by the side of, near.

er tep , before, in front of.

er tcher , , utterly, entirely, to the utmost limit; var .

er, err , , a sign of the comparative: *e.g.*, , stronger than the gods; , thy voice is shriller than that of the tcheru bird; , thou hast created more than all the gods; , more splendid, more beautiful.

er , a prefix used to mark fractions *e.g.*, = $\frac{1}{3}$, = $\frac{2}{3}$, = $\frac{1}{5}$, = $\frac{1}{10}$ (Copt. ⲣⲉ ⲙⲏⲧ), = $\frac{1}{15}$, = $\frac{1}{20}$, = $\frac{1}{30}$, = $\frac{1}{80}$, = $\frac{1}{100}$, = $\frac{1}{360}$; Copt. ⲣⲉ.

er ā , number; , they were without number; , numberless; , according to the amount of, as far as, as much as; , in proportion to the offerings; **em erā** , , most certainly, assuredly, none the less; , not having effected it in reality.

er pu , , , , , , U. 290, or; , Åmen. 11, 8, good or bad.

er-ru , Rev. 13, 34 = Copt. ⲉⲣⲱⲟⲩ; , Rec. 4, 21, , Rec. 4, 22, the list of them.

er per = **åri per,** belonging to the house [of God]; see Rec. 21, 47.

er = **åri** , *e.g.*, , I, 49, "belonging to Nekhen."

re (ret) = , man.

re , , , a kind of goose; plur. , ; , IV, 745, fattened goose.

reu , bread cakes, loaves of bread.

reu (?) , a kind of precious stone; compare .

er-t = (?) to go about.

er in , U. 538.

er-[t] , magazine, storehouse.

re , , a covered court, portico, entrance to a house.

re , chapter or section of a book; plur. , ; , a single chapter; , P. 463, , , P. 175,

, P. 469, , P. 469, M. 533, N. 1112; , Chapters of Coming forth by day; , Chapters of Divine rites; , Chapters of Praisings; , Chapters of Mysteries, etc.

re , , , , , Rev. 14, 46, mouth, entrance, opening, door, gate, speech, words, deposition, opinion; plur. , , , , Rev. 14, 17; , , mouth of a canal; , door with two leaves; , door of the earth; Copt. ⲣⲟ.

re , mouth:— , Thes. 1480, (at) his words; , L.D. III, 140D, mouth to mouth; , to mince matters; , unanimously; , Rec. 3, 116, wise man; , a man of bold, determined speech; , by hearsay; , by the mouth of every priest's head; , to work the mouth overmuch, *i.e.*, talk too much.

re with **un** , appearance.

re en Kam , speech of Egypt, *i.e.*, the Egyptian language.

re , with to set the mouth in motion, to speak against anyone; with , to speak scornfully of anyone.

re-ā , Rec. 26, 236, canal.

re āti , a member of the body (medical term).

Re-āa-ur , B.D. 64, 16, the city of Osiris.

re — in **re uat, re en uat,** , , , the entrance to a path or road, the portion of the road in front of one.

re up-t , top of the forehead or skull.

Re pān , M. 127, 128, a title of Geb, the Erpā of the gods.

Re Peshnȧ , T. 311, a mythological locality.

Re Peq , Door of Peq, the grave of Osiris at Abydos, "his glorious seat from primitive times," .

Re Peqr-t , a sacred lake of Osiris at Abydos.

re-petch-t , , , , archers, bowmen; compare Copt. ⲣⲉⲙⲡⲓⲧⲉ.

Re nen , B.D. (Saïte) 142, 2, 8, a town of Osiris.

Re en-qerr-t-ȧp-t-khatu , Ṭuat XI, the name of the door of a Circle.

re ḥa-t , , the opening in the diaphragm, the stomach, belly.

reu ḥatu , Thes. 1296, , , the mouths of the Nile in the Delta.

Re Ḥāp , the mouth of the Nile-god or of his river.

Re Ḥep , U. 419, , T. 239, the basin of the Nile.

Re ḥeri, Ḥeruemḥeb 6, Thes. 1296, chief, commander, overseer, director, headman.

Re-ḥes, B.D.G. 197, "Fierce mouth," the Crocodile-god of the Fayyûm.

re ḥetch, treasury; plur., treasure boats.

Re Khemenu, B.D. 28, 5, a part of Hermopolis; varr.

Re sma, Ṭuat XI, a locality in the Ṭuat.

Re sehrer em ta, N. 1030, "Mouth pacifying the land"—title of an official.

Re-Skhait, B.D. 142, V, 16, a goddess.

Re-stau, U. 556, the abode of the dead of Memphis.

Re Qerr t, a name of the tomb or Other World; a title of Anubis was, IV, 1183.

re, serpent, reptile; var. Metternich Stele, 81, B.D. (Saïte) 164, 16.

rai ua-t (rṭa ua-t?), Rosetta 16, to remit, to set aside.

rain, Rev. 12, 26, 14, 21, steel; Copt. λⲁⲉιn.

reȧ, powdered ochre, paint, ink; green ink.

erȧu, Rev. 11, 142 = Copt. ⲉⲣⲉ.

rȧa-t, Anastasi I, 24, 3, side; Copt. ⲣⲁⲧⲏ.

rȧaȧ, Ȧmen. 6, 7, to go about.

rȧau, to go away, to be far off or remote.

rȧu, N. 760, M. 339, N. 865, to drive away, to keep off or away.

rȧi, Rev. 12, 116, to wish, to desire.

rȧm, Ebers Pap. 27, 12, a part of the body.

rȧsha, head, headland, hill; Heb. רֹאשׁ: = Heb. ראשׁ קדשׁ.

rȧuṭ, Mar. Aby. I, 6, 32, steps; var.

reȧt, doorway, entrance chamber; var.

Rȧtȧt (Rȧtit), a goddess worshipped at Philae.

rȧṭ, steps; see

Rā, the sun, the day; day and night; every day, daily; Copt. ⲣⲏ.

Rā ȧs-t ȧb, name of the sun-temple of Saḥurā.

Rā en ḥequ, name of a statue of Ȧmenḥetep III.

Rā Nekhen, name of the sun-temple of Userkaf.

Rā shesp ȧb, name of the sun-temple of Userenrā.

Rā tem ȧb, name of the sun-temple of Kakau.

Rā, U. 305, 748, , Pap. 3024, 60, the Sun-god Rā; , Rā the great; or , Rā the little; Heb. רַע, Copt. ρн.

Rāit, U. 253, the Sun-goddess, the consort of Rā.

Rā-ur, Thes. 429, Rā, the summer sun.

Rā, Ṭuat VI, a jackal-headed standard.

Rā Ȧfu, Denderah III, 78, the night form of Rā.

Rā Ȧsȧr, B.D. 130, 18, Rā-Osiris.

Rā Ȧtni, Tomb of Seti I, a beetle-god, one of the 75 forms of Rā (No. 4).

Rā em-ȧten-f, Denderah III, 66, a form of Rā with a beetle in disk.

Rā em-nu, the name of the Sun-god in the 2nd hour of the day.

Rā em-ḥetep (?), Denderah II, 11, a lunar form of Rā.

Rā em-ta-en-Ȧtem, Denderah III, 35, a form of Rā.

Rā nub (?), the golden Rā.

Rā er-neḥeḥ, B.D. 140, 6, "Everlasting Rā," a form of the Sun-god.

Rā Ḥeru, Rā Horus.

Rā Ḥeru-ȧakhuti, Rā Harmakhis, *i.e.*, Rā + Horus of the two horizons.

Rā Kheper . . ., Denderah III, 78, a bandy-legged god with hands for feet.

Rā khenti-ḥe-t-Mesq, Nesi-Ȧmsu 32, 5, a title of Rā.

Rā sa-em-ȧkhekh, the god of the 12th hour of the day.

Rā sesh (?), B.D. (Saïte) 42, Rā the scribe; var.

Rā sherȧ, the little sun, *i.e.*, the winter sun.

Rāit taui, Rec. 15, 162, consort of Menthu.

Rā Tem, U. 216, M. 449, Rā-Tem.

Rā Tem Kheper, a triad of the solar-gods of Heliopolis.

rā, Tombos Stele 2, ruler.

rā āui, Hymn Darius 43, the action of the two hands and arms; , Thes. 1283.

rā, IV, 82, 912, Ȧmen. 3, 15, work, act, action, to do;

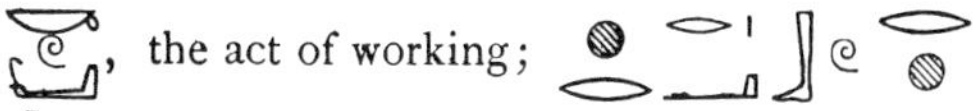, the act of working; , Åmen. 22, 5; Coptic ⲣⲁ.

rā åb (?) 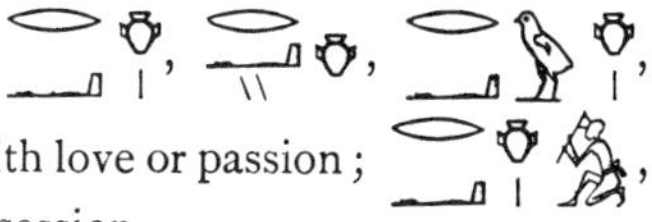, to be excited with love or passion; demoniacal possession.

rā-t , , IV, 657, weapon, tool, working instrument, arms, armour; plur. 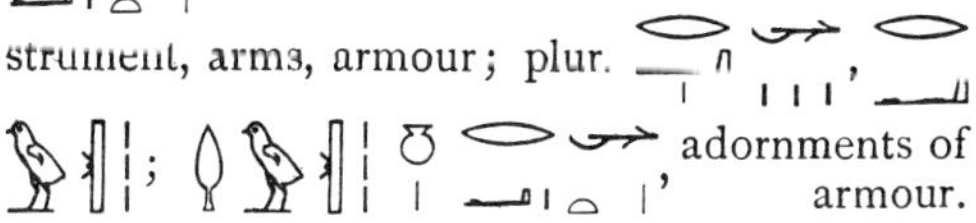, adornments of armour.

rā-t , Rev. 14, 11, an instrument of music.

rā , place (?)

rā 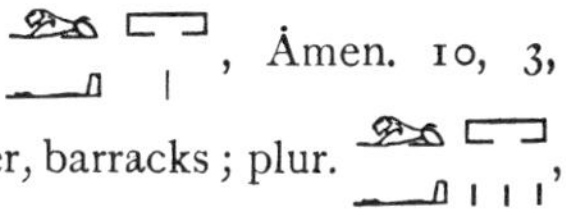, Åmen. 10, 3, storehouse, chamber, barracks; plur. , Thes. 1206.

rā , a kind of fish; Copt. ⲣⲏⲓ.

rā (ra ?) 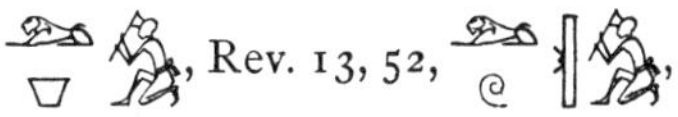, Rev. 13, 52, , malice, calumny; Copt. ⲗⲁ.

rārā (rara) , Rev., to cry out; Copt. ⲗⲟⲩⲗⲁⲓ.

rāi 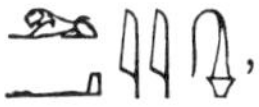, light, flame, fire.

rāppt (lappt) 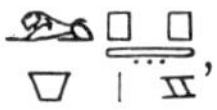, Rev. 11, 180, ...

rāhi , to complain (?)

rāḥā (?) , Rev. 11, 144, station, abode (?); Copt. ⲣⲓ.

rāqiu , Rev. 13, 27, devils, fiends, disaster.

rāges 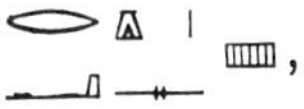, a variegated stone.

ri 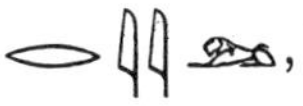, lion.

ri , 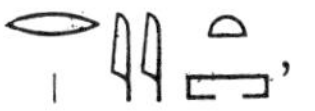, door, doorway, entrance, forecourt of a house or temple.

ri-t (reri-t ?) , De Hymnis 28, 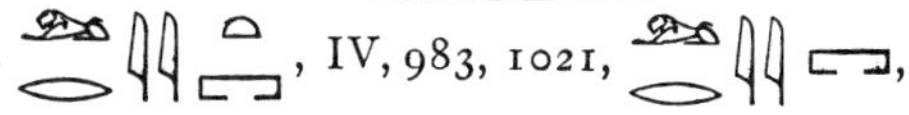, IV, 983, 1021, , gate, abode, den of a lion, cave.

ri , cord, rope, bandage.

ri-t 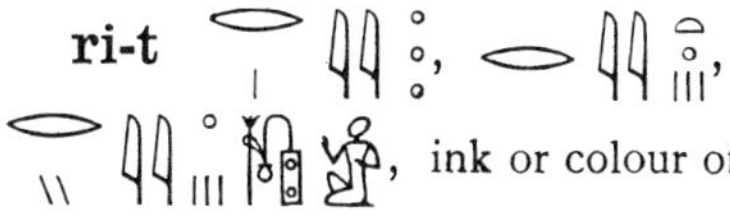, paint, ink; , ink or colour of the scribe.

riu , emanations, effluxes.

rib , Rev. 13, 38, madness, folly, lust, fool; Copt. ⲗⲓⲃⲉ.

ribsh , Rev. 11, 145, 170, armour; Copt. ⲗⲱⲃϣ.

rim , Rev. 12, 11, , Rev. 14, 10, weeping, tears; Copt. ⲣⲓⲙⲉ.

rim , Rev. 13, 2, fish.

rin , Rev. 12, 29, steel; Copt. ⲗⲁⲉⲓⲛ.

rirārå , Rev. 12, 8, joy, merry noise; Copt. ⲗⲟⲩⲗⲁⲓ.

rit , sky, ceiling, roof, a roofed chamber.

Rit (?) 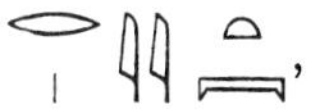, Berg. II, 13, a form of Nut.

rit , Rev. 11, 178, 12, 63, vestment, girdle.

ritch 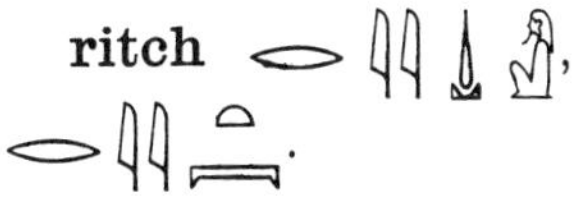, Rev. 11, 185 = .

ru (?) , lion.

Ru (?) 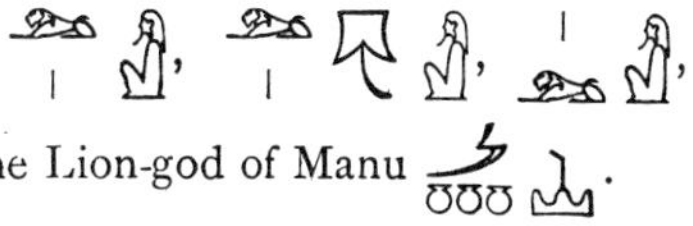, B.D. 28, 2, the Lion-god of Manu .

Ruru (?) , Hh. 337, a god.

Ruru-tȧ 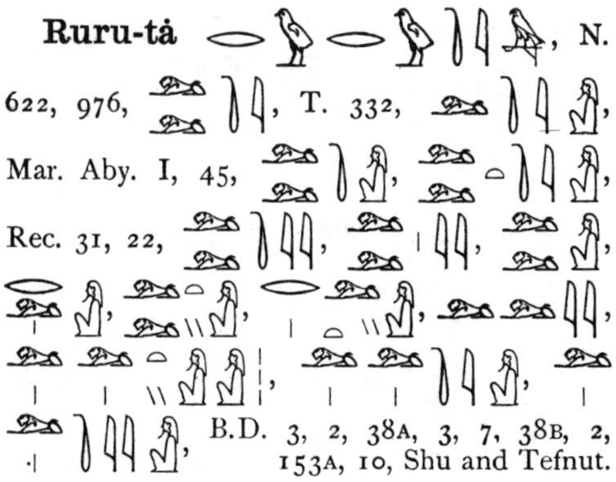, N. 622, 976, [illegible], T. 332, [illegible], Mar. Aby. I, 45, [illegible], [illegible], Rec. 31, 22, [illegible], [illegible], [illegible], [illegible], [illegible], [illegible], [illegible], [illegible], [illegible], [illegible] [illegible], B.D. 3, 2, 38A, 3, 7, 38B, 2, 153A, 10, Shu and Tefnut.

Ruru-ti 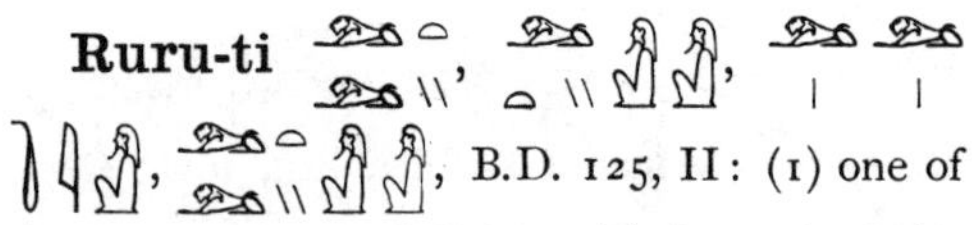, [illegible], [illegible] [illegible], [illegible], B.D. 125, II: (1) one of the 42 assessors of Osiris; (2) the god of the 17th day of the month.

Ru-Iukasa , B.D. 165, 1, a Nubian god (?)

Ru-Rā , B.D. 62, 5, the Lion-god Rā.

ru , Rev. 14, 46, malice, calumny.

ru , M. 380, N. 656 ....

ru , N. 163 ....

ru 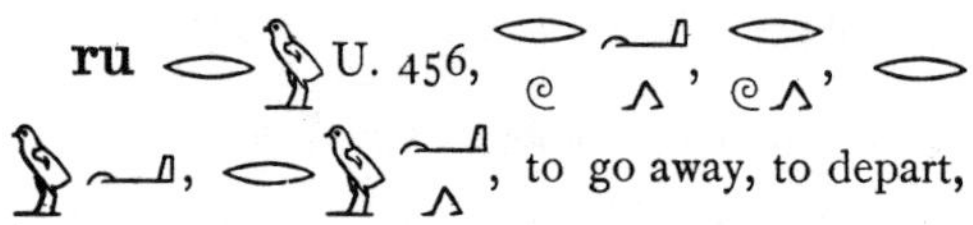 U. 456, [illegible], [illegible], [illegible] [illegible], [illegible], to go away, to depart, to be removed, defaced (of an inscription).

ruu 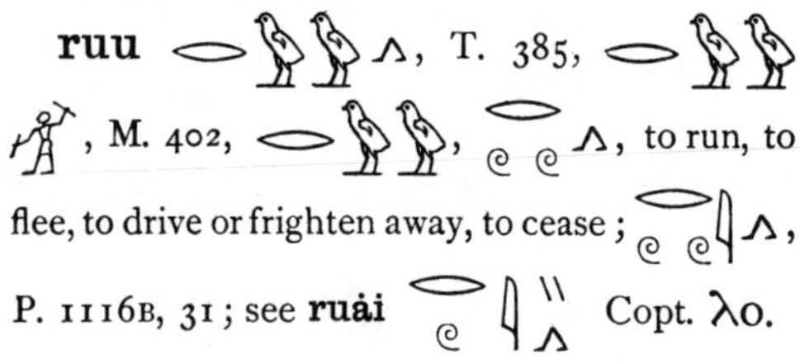, T. 385, [illegible], M. 402, [illegible], [illegible], to run, to flee, to drive or frighten away, to cease; [illegible], P. 1116B, 31; see **ruȧi** [illegible] Copt. λο.

ru-khtt (?) , U. 561 ....

rer , Jour. As. 1908, 274, to turn round.

rui , journey, traveller.

ruti 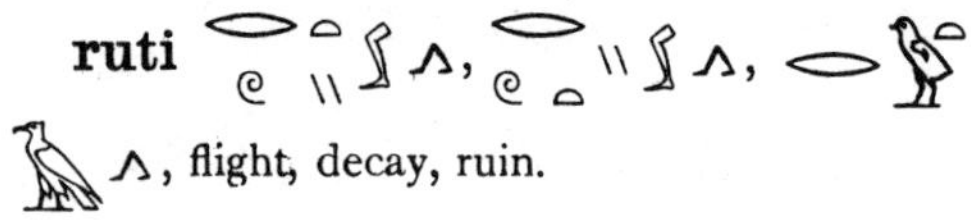, [illegible], [illegible] [illegible], flight, decay, ruin.

ruu-t , Peasant 255, separation; var. [illegible].

ruu 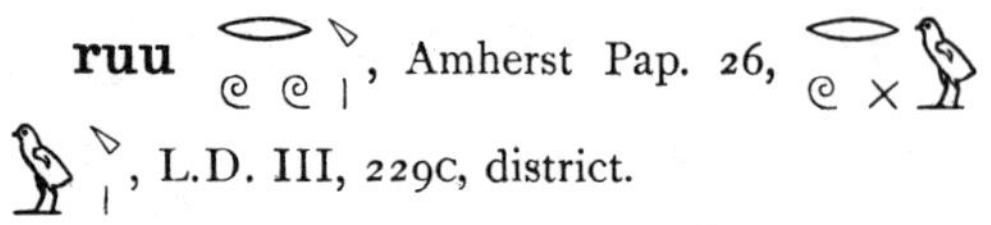, Amherst Pap. 26, [illegible] [illegible], L.D. III, 229C, district.

rui (?) , Rec. 16, 72, evening.

ru-t , T. 201, M. 699, [illegible] [illegible], [illegible], [illegible], [illegible] [illegible], [illegible], [illegible], stele in form of a false door of a tomb and its framework.

ruti , [illegible], [illegible], [illegible], [illegible], [illegible] [illegible], [illegible], [illegible], [illegible], the two leaves of a door, court, portico, porch, entrance to any large building; [illegible], IV, 1105, [illegible].

ruti , P. 1116B, 47, [illegible], foreign, external; [illegible], from outside; [illegible], P.S.B.A. 11, 256, alien country.

Ruti Ȧsȧr 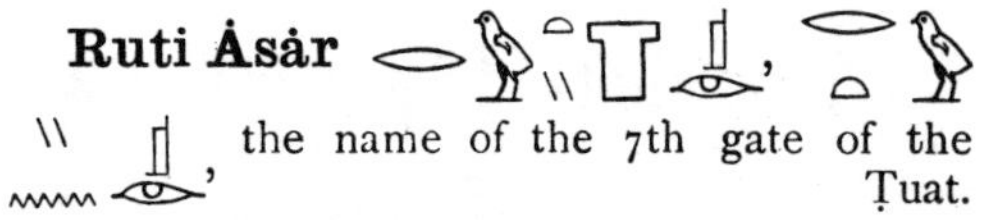, [illegible] [illegible], the name of the 7th gate of the Ṭuat.

rua , [illegible], to drive away, to chase away.

ruru , Rev. 12, 40, to burn.

ruȧi 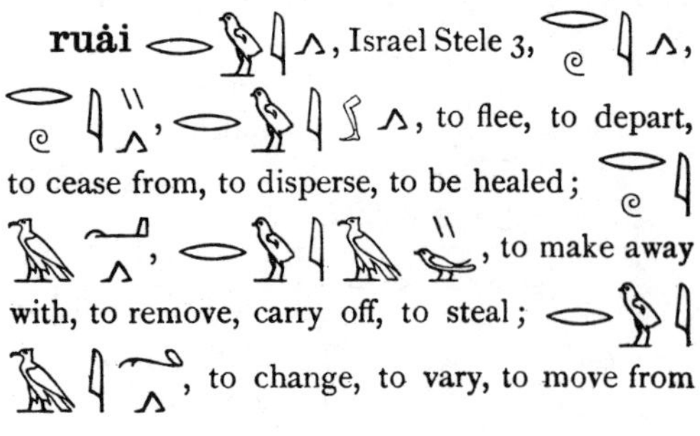, Israel Stele 3, [illegible], [illegible], [illegible], to flee, to depart, to cease from, to disperse, to be healed; [illegible] [illegible], [illegible], to make away with, to remove, carry off, to steal; [illegible] [illegible], to change, to vary, to move from place to place; , Åmen. 19, 6; Copt. λο.

rui-t 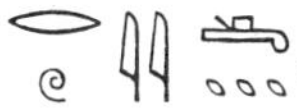, a kind of grain.

rui (reri) 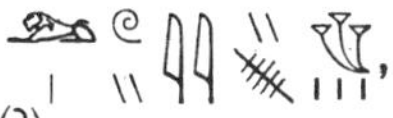, Åmen. 5, 4, reeds (?) grass (?)

rui-t 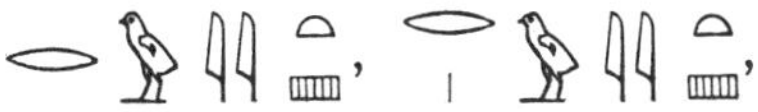, sepulchral stele, the base or frame of a false door of a tomb; plur. 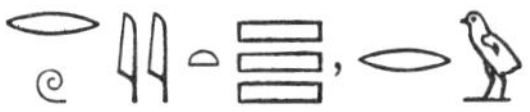 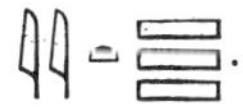.

ruit , a disease of the side.

rur , Rev. 14, 18, pleasantness.

ruh, ruha (?) , , 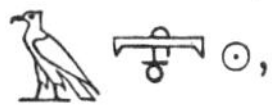, evening; Copt. ρογϩε; compare Heb. רוּחַ הַיּוֹם.

ruḥ 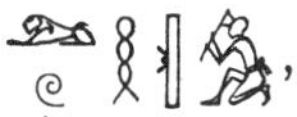, Jour. As. 1908, 308, , Rec. 14, 22, , mud; Copt. λοιϩε.

rush 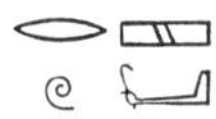, Jour. As. 1908, 293, [illegible] , to take care for or about a thing; Copt. ροογϣ.

rut , to grow; Copt. ρωτ.

rut , inspector; plur. [illegible] .

rutȧri , Rev. 11, 180, basin; Gr. *λουτήριον*.

ruṭ , Peasant 153, , , Rec. 31, 178, , Rec. 26, 67, , IV, 974, [illegible] , , to be strong, to thrive, to succeed, to prosper, to grow, to be sound, to flourish; Copt. ρωτ.

ruṭu 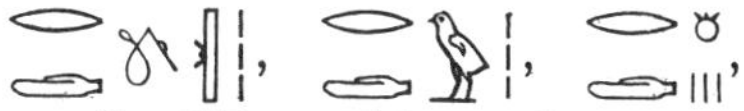, 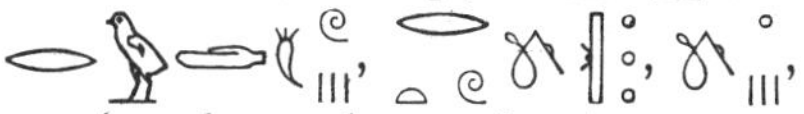, healthy, growing plants, shoots of a plant.

ruṭ-t , a disease of the eye.

ruṭ , Rec. 26, 229, [illegible] 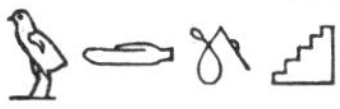, Rec. 30, 69, , , steps, stairway, stairs; plur. .

ruṭ-t , Mar. Karn. 53, 30, 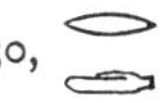 , Rechnungen 44, a kind of ground, bank, shore, terraced ground (?)

ruṭu , T. 239, , U. 418, ground cultivated in terraces.

ruṭ [illegible], [illegible], string, cord, bowstring, tie, bandlet.

ruṭut [illegible], Koller Pap. 1, 5, thongs of a whip.

Ruṭ-en-Ȧst [illegible], B.D. 153B, 4, the fishing line of the Akeru-gods.

Ruṭu-nu-Tem [illegible] [illegible], B.D. 153A, 10, the ropes of the net of the Akeru gods.

Ruṭ-t-neb-rekhit [illegible] [illegible], B.D. 153A, 20, the ropes of the net of the Akeru gods.

ruṭ-t [illegible], [illegible], hard sandstone (quartzite sandstone); plur. [illegible], IV, 505.

ruṭu  , overseer, agent, inspector, superintendent; plur.  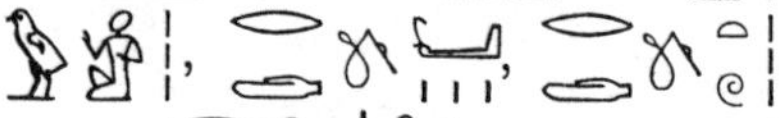, Åmen. 15, 11, , Rec. 31, 15, , P.S.B.A. 10, 47, Shipwreck 132, oppressor.

ruṭu , male and female overseers in a field (?)

ruṭa , Mar. Karn. 55, 70, to march (?) to stand (?)

rutch 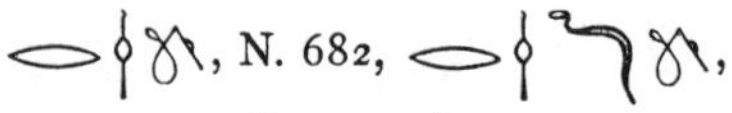, N. 682, 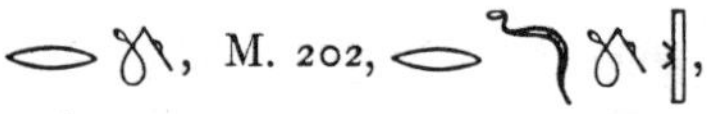, M. 202, Thes. 1290, to be strong, to be healthy, sound, vigorous, permanent, flourishing; see 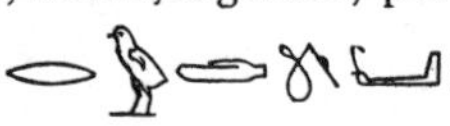; Copt. ⲣⲱⲧ.

rutchu , cord, band, ligament; plur.

rutchu 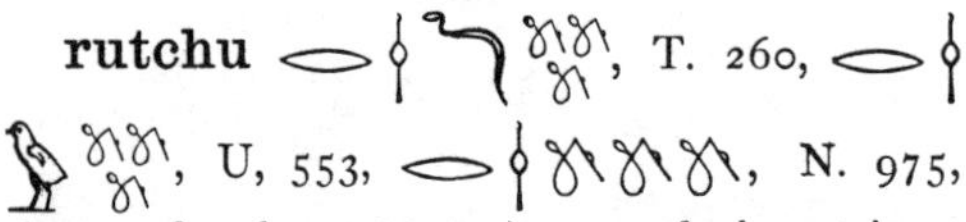, T. 260, U, 553, N. 975, shoots of a plant, strong ones, cords, bowstrings, knotted ropes of a ladder.

rutchu , Rec. 31, 15, overseers, inspectors.

reb 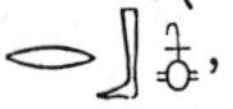, Nȧstasen Stele 38, a milk vessel, pot, bowl.

Rebasunna (?)  , L.D. III, 164B, a Hittite (?) name.

rebasha , to be clothed in armour; compare Heb. לְבַשׁ.

rebashaiu , Koller Pap. 1, 7, leather jerkins, cuirasses, trappings; compare Heb. לְבוּשׁ.

rebaka , cake, loaf.

Rebati , B.D. (Saïte), 162, 4, a god.

rebu , Rec. 12, 22, , Sallier Pap. IV, 18, 3, Rec. 17, 96, lion; , Rec. 12, 22, lioness; Heb. לָבִיא, Copt. ⲗⲁⲃⲟⲓ.

Rebu , Mar. Karn. 54, 57, 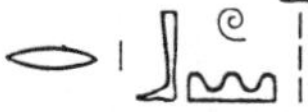, Libyans.

Rebu-inini (?)  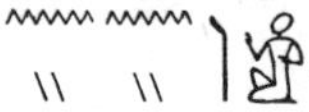, Bibl. Ég. 5, 221, a foreign name.

rebner-khenu 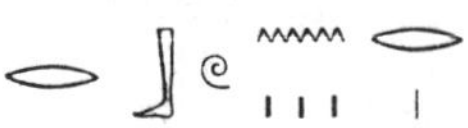 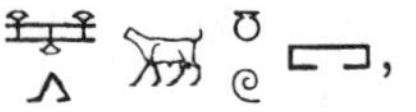, Rev. 11, 130 = Copt. ⲉⲃⲟⲗ ϩⲛ̄.

rep, rep-t 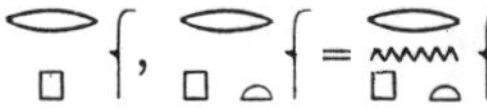, year.

repit, repuit , Hh. 439, 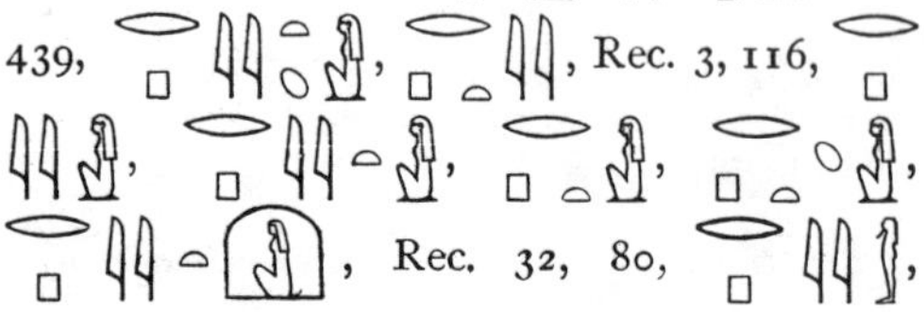, Rec. 3, 116, Rec. 32, 80, Rev. 11, 90, a lady of high rank, noblewoman, princess, statue of a woman, image, likeness; plur. .

Repit  a goddess; Gr. Θριφις (?)

rep-ti , the two Ladies Isis and Nephthys.

rep-t , P. 101, M. 89, N. 95, statue, image (?)

repit ahit , A.Z. 1908, 19, an amulet in the form of the Cow-goddess.

Repit Ȧnu 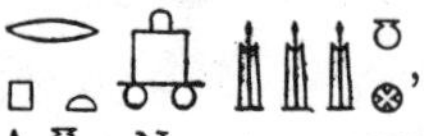, P. 101, M. 89, 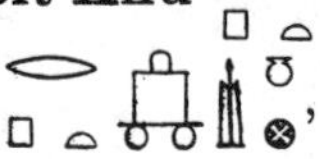, N. 95, a name of the goddess Nut.

repit Ȧst, A.Z. 1908, 20, an amulet made of fine gold in the form of Isis.

repa (reper), temple, temple estate; plur., IV, 1045, IV, 1151, Rec. 31, 24; Copt. ⲣ̄ⲡⲉ, Arab. بربة.

repaȧ, Rev. 11, 123, prince = .

repȧ (renpȧ), to be young, to rejuvenate; see .

repā, prince, hereditary chief.

repā maā, I, 118, a real or true prince, a prince or chief by birth.

repāt, repāti (?), P. 660, 663, 783, M. 769, 775, Rec. 31, 146, IV, 945, chief, heir, hereditary ruler, chieftainess; according to A.Z. 1907, 31, note 13, = , "mouth of the people."

Repā, a title of Geb as the hereditary chief of the gods; P. 124, M. 93, N. 99, chief of the ten great ones of Memphis, chief of the ten great ones of Ȧn.

Repā[t]-t, B.D.G., a consort of Menu of Panopolis.

repi, Jour. As. 1908, 313, to become young, to be young, flourishing.

repit, young herbs and plants, flowers, spring fruits and vegetables; see .

repi, a kind of fish; plur. ; Copt. ⲗⲉⲓϥⲓ.

repi, temple; plur., Rec. 33, 128; Copt. ⲉⲣⲡⲉ, ⲉⲣⲫⲉⲓ.

repu, Koller Pap. 1, 2, groomed (of a horse).

repen-t, Ebers Pap. 75, 10, meadow, some kind of land.

repnen, pitch, bitumen; Copt. ⲁⲣⲡⲟⲛⲟⲛ.

ref, to rest (?)

ref, to swell up, be inflated.

refref, soft, crumby bread; Copt. ⲗⲉϥⲗⲓϥⲓ.

Refref, B.D. (Saïte) 39, a monster serpent in the Ṭuat.

remu, Nȧstasen Stele 9, Nȧstasen Stele 13, people, mankind, men; Rec. 27, 85; Copt. ⲣⲱⲙⲉ; see **remt, remth, reth**.

remmu, people.

rem ā, Jour. As. 1908, 268, Rev. 13, 32, great man, rich man; Copt. ⲣⲙ̄ⲙⲁⲟ.

rem p neter, Rev. 13, 33, man of god.

rem em maā-t, Rev., man of truth; Copt. ⲣⲙ̄ ⲙ̄ ⲙⲉ.

rem , U. 236, N. 710, P. 212, Rec. 29, 157, to weep; Copt. ⲣⲓⲙⲉ.

remm 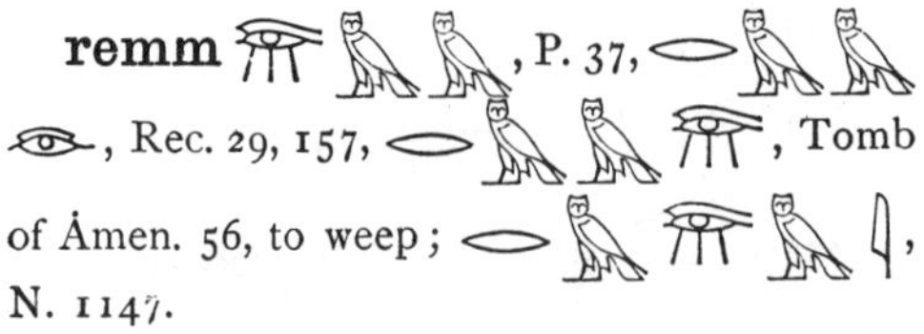, P. 37, Rec. 29, 157, Tomb of Åmen. 56, to weep; N. 1147.

remi , T. 51, P. 160, , Rev. 11, 164, to weep; Copt. ⲣⲓⲙⲉ.

rem-t, remit , P. 371, IV, 1078, Pap 3024, 57, 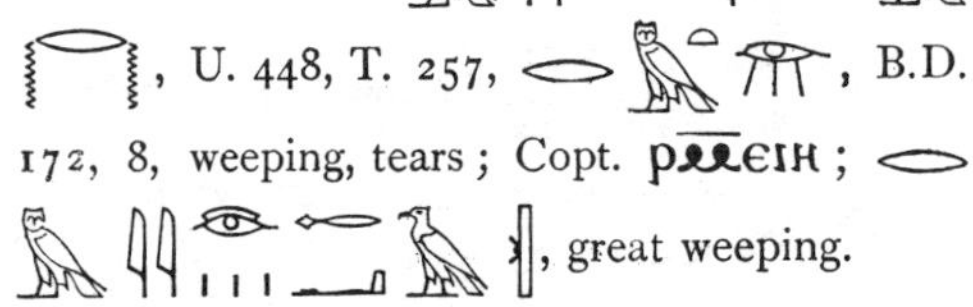, U. 448, T. 257, B.D. 172, 8, weeping, tears; Copt. ⲣⲙⲙⲉⲓⲏ; great weeping.

rem-tu , U. 569, the two weepers.

remiui , A.Z. 1900, 24, tears, crying, weeping.

remith 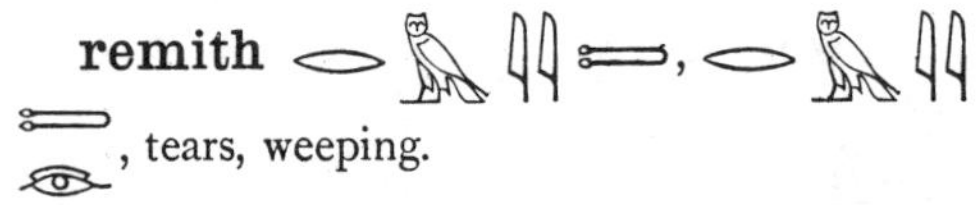, tears, weeping.

remut , Rec. 29, 157, tears, weeping.

remu , IV, 972, weeper, mourner.

Remi 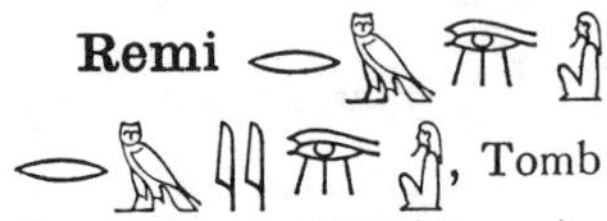, Nesi-Åmsu 29, 3, Tomb of Seti I, one of the 75 forms of Rā (No. 21).

Remit , Ṭuat III, a weeping goddess in the Ṭuat.

Remuiti 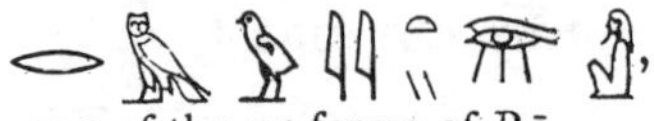, Tomb of Seti I, one of the 75 forms of Rā.

Rem-neteru , Ṭuat VIII, a ram-god in the Ṭuat.

remrem 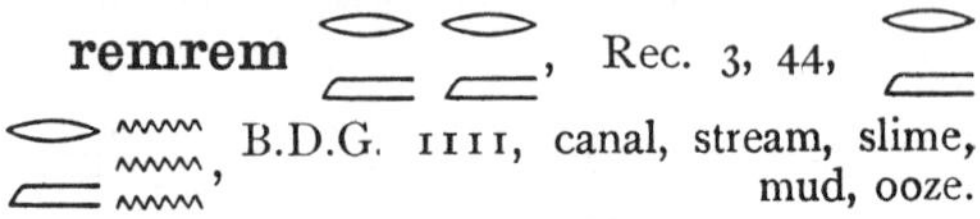, Rec. 3, 44, B.D.G. 1111, canal, stream, slime, mud, ooze.

rem , fish, fishes; plur. 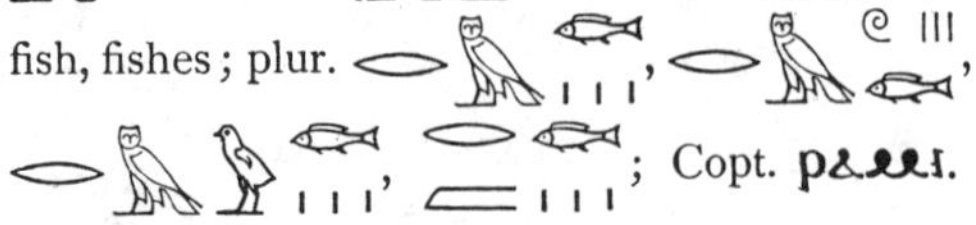; Copt. ⲣⲁⲙⲙⲓ.

Remi , the Fish-god.

Remi-ur-āa 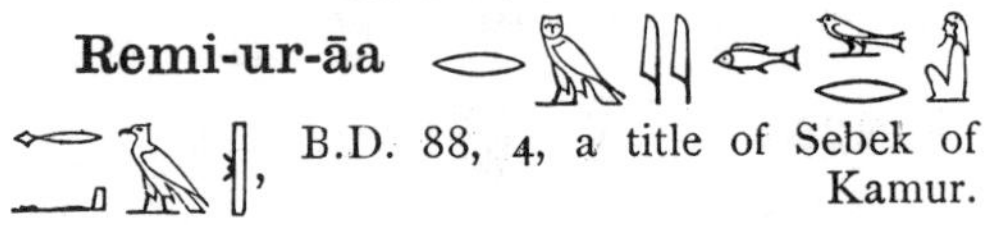, B.D. 88, 4, a title of Sebek of Kamur.

Remu , B.D. 113, 5, the Fish-city.

rem  B.D. 172, 20, studded (with gold).

rem-t 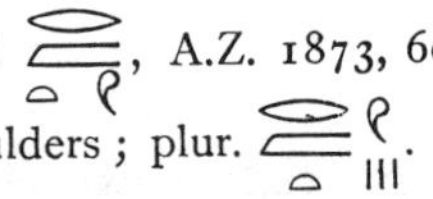, A.Z. 1873, 60, a part of the body, shoulders; plur.

Remit , Lanzone 190, Mission 13, 126, a goddess of offerings. She had four forms with the following titles: 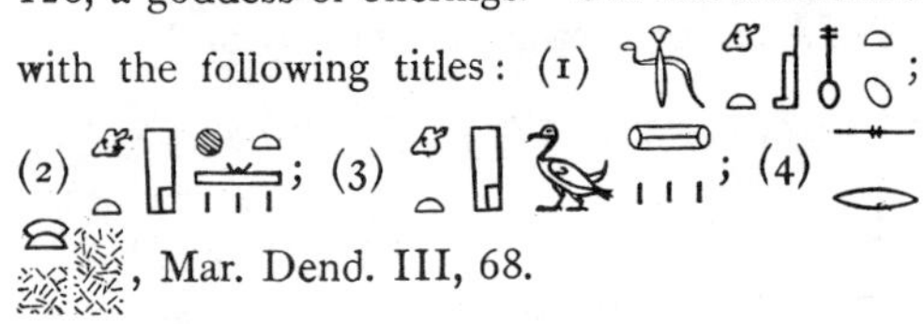 (1); (2); (3); (4), Mar. Dend. III, 68.

remrem , IV, 1076 . . . . .

Remrem 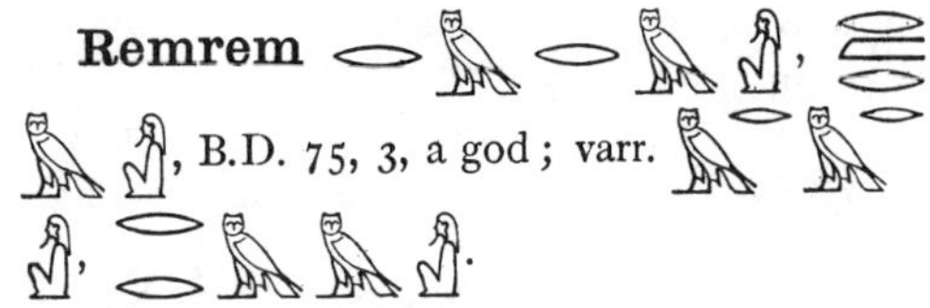, B.D. 75, 3, a god; varr.

rema (?) , P.S.B.A. 13, 419, a plot of ground; the $\frac{1}{32}$ part of an arura.

rema , lion.

rema (?) , Wört. 884, a kind of garment (?)

rem' 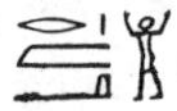, height, elevation, high place; compare Heb. רוּם.

Rem' , [illegible], Alt. K. 618, a Semitic proper name.

Remtit , Rev. 13, 2 = .

remen , marks a new paragraph in a composition.

remen , : (1) a linear measure = 5 palms or 20 fingers; (2) = ½ arura = 5000 sq. cubits.

remen , T. 362, [illegible], IV, 968, [illegible], N. 958, [illegible], [illegible], , arm, shoulder, side; , the one side of a lake; , the crew on one side of a boat; , I, 50, a piece of land on the west side; dual 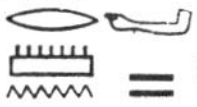, U. 462, [illegible], P. 568, [illegible], P. 710, N. 1353, [illegible], IV, 497, [illegible], [illegible], [illegible], [illegible], [illegible], [illegible] [illegible], the two upper arms, the shoulders, the arms of a tree; [illegible] [illegible], the two sides of a ladder; plur. [illegible] [illegible], [illegible], [illegible], [illegible], [illegible] [illegible], [illegible].

remen , P. 698, [illegible], M. 171, [illegible], N. 656, [illegible], U. 213, [illegible], [illegible], [illegible], [illegible], Anastasi I, 20, 6, to bear, to carry on the shoulders, to carry off or away, to support, to hold up; , P. 142, M. 412, carried, supported.

remen , with **ṭua** , to acclaim, to offer thanksgiving.

remennu , [illegible], [illegible], [illegible], Åmen. 6, 16, 7, 12, 16, 2, 17, 8, 18, [illegible], to carry away, to do away, to carry off (steal), to abrogate.

remenu 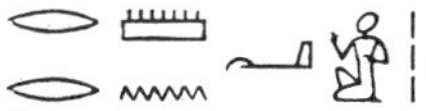, [illegible] [illegible], [illegible], carriers, bearers, porters.

remenu , Peasant 166, the beam, the two arms of a large pair of pillar-scales.

remen-t , a pot carried on the shoulder.

remen-t , , idleness (?) inactivity (?)

Remen pet , title of the high-priest of Upuat of Lycopolis.

Remenu , Ṭuat XII, a god in the Ṭuat.

Remenui , Ṭuat X, a god who had  for a head, and who stripped and broke up the dead.

Remenui-Rā , [illegible], Rec. 26, 233, a god.

Remnu (?) , Ṭuat XI, one of the 12 carriers of Meḥen.

Remnit , Rec. 4, 26, a cow, or cow-goddess.

Remen ḥeru , Denderah II, 10, , one of the 36 Dekans; Gr. Ρεμενυαιρε; , Tomb of Seti I.

Remen kheru , Zod. Dend., , [illegible], Tomb of Seti I, one of the 36 Dekans; Gr. Ρεμ[εν]χ[αρε].

Remen ta 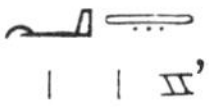, Ṭuat VIII, a warder of the 8th Gate.

remen , Thes. 1322, to fall.

rems , Rev. 11, 157, 173, 12, 9, , Rev. 12, 54, [illegible] [illegible], Rev. 12, 55, [illegible], a kind of boat, ship.

remth , U. 406, 568, T. 203, man; Copt. ⲣⲱⲙⲉ; plur. 

P. 274, T. 358, , M. 675, people, mankind = **reth** , N. 177, 751, 792.

remth neb 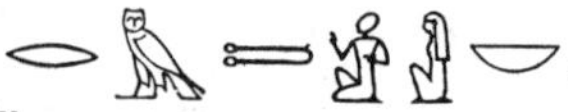, anybody, everybody.

ren , P. 790, [illegible], [illegible], name; plur. [illegible], , [illegible], IV, 943; Copt. pan.

ren , divine name; [illegible], accursed name; , N. 990, imperishable name; 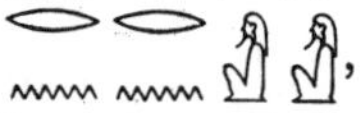, Rec. 30, 201; , IV, 174, 1037, names; , great names; 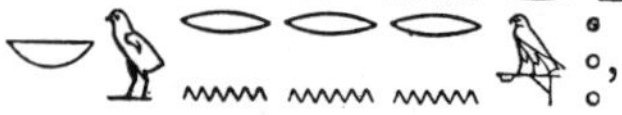, N. 151, lords of names.

Ren ur , L.D. III, 140B, the full official name of the king.

Renu , B.D. 17, 11, the names of the limbs of Rā, which became the gods of his company.

Renniu 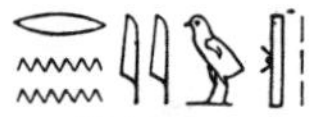, Ṭuat XI, a group of gods who magnified the names of the Sun-god.

Renn-sebu 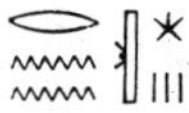, Ṭuat X, a god who named the stars.

ren , Bubast. 51, an altar vessel.

ren, renn , T. 289, M. 66, N. 128, [illegible], L.D. III, 194, to nurse, to dandle.

Rennit 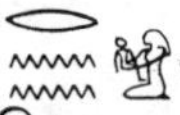, Anhai Pap. 4, the name of the object [illegible].

Rennit 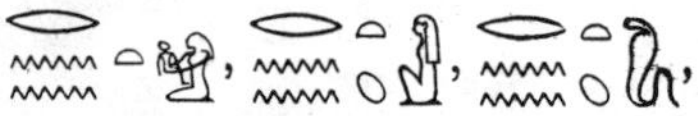, the World Nurse-mother-goddess.

Rennit-neferit 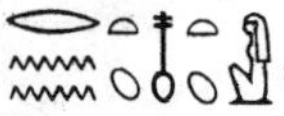, Ombos I, 75, a hippopotamus-goddess.

Renti , B.M. 32, 471, a nurse-goddess (?)

Renenti 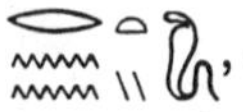, a nurse-goddess (?)

renen-t 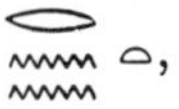, IV, 357, [illegible],

, child, babe, nursling; [illegible], [illegible], Åmen. 9, 11, 21, 16, [illegible], girl, virgin, young woman.

rennu , babe, male child, boy, youth; plur. .

ren, renn , Palermo Stele 22, any young creature not full-grown; [illegible] , P. 82, M. 112, N. 26, young gazelle.

renn , heifer, calf; plur. [illegible] .

rennȧ , young ox.

renn-t , young cow; plur. [illegible].

rennu , L.D. III, 194, 13, harvest, provision.

rennu-t 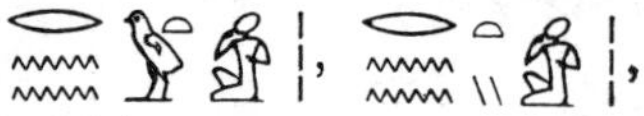, [illegible], joy, rejoicing, gladness.

Renit , T.S.B.A. III, 424, a harvest-goddess of [illegible] and [illegible].

Rennutt , U. 441, 564, T. 251, , IV, 1161, [illegible] [illegible], N. 133, [illegible], IV, 1015, 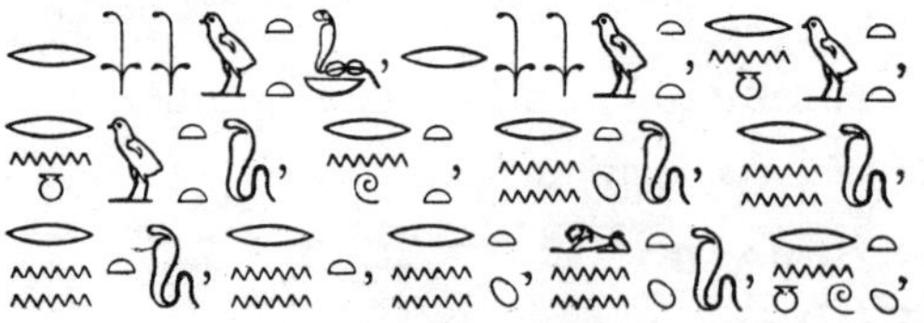, B.M. 1055, 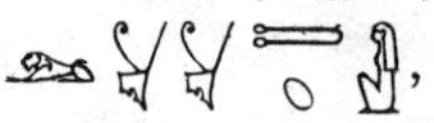, [illegible], 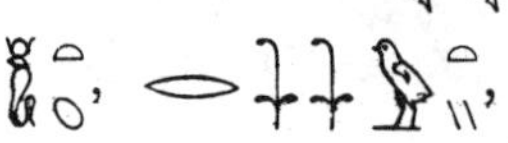, Rev. 24, 161, the goddess of harvest.

Rennutt , the goddess of the 8th month of the Egyptian year; Copt. ⲫⲁⲣⲙⲟⲩⲑⲓ.

Rennutt 
, the name of an uraeus on the royal crown.

Rennutt , B.D. 170, 13, the firstborn of Tem.

renkh , to cook, to roast.

renpi , T. 343, Rec. 1, 51, 

, to become young, to be young, to grow; 
, to rejuvenate; 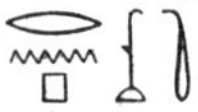, T. 180, 
, P. 525, , U. 270; later forms are: 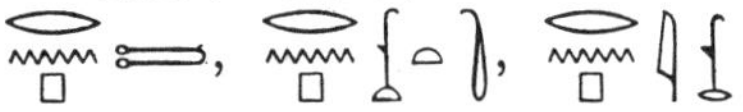
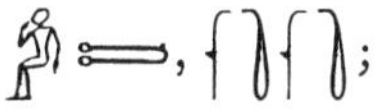; 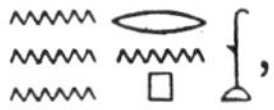, water of youth.

Renpi , title of the high-priest of Libya-Mareotis.

Renpi , young god.

renp 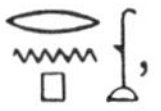, IV, 663, , young horse, young cattle.

renpi , a spring plant or flower; plur. 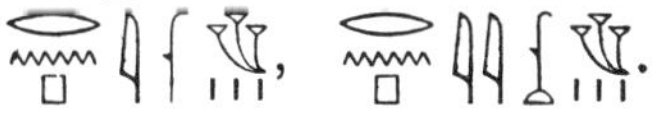.
, IV, 1165.

renput , P. 189, T. 355, , N. 907, , IV, 1165,
, fruit, vegetables; , young trees.

renp-t ,
,
, year; Copt. ⲣⲟⲙⲡⲉ; plur. 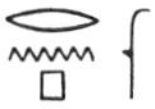
, P. 162, , N. 708, , P. 355, T. 228, , A.Z. 45, 124, 
, T. 335, [illegible] = ḥa-t sep [illegible].

renp-t — tep renp-t [illegible], new year's day; [illegible], festival of new year's day; [illegible], year by year, *i.e.*, each year; [illegible], lean years; [illegible], everlasting years; [illegible], IV, 1160, millions of years; [illegible], the five days over the year, *i.e.*, the five epagomenal days; [illegible], see **snef;** [illegible], N. 977.

renp-t — [illegible], festival of the great year of 365 days (solar year); [illegible], festival of the little year of 360 days (lunar year).

Renpu [illegible], M. 823, N. 1316, the Year-god.

Renpit [illegible], P. 189, [illegible], N. 907, [illegible], the Year-goddess.

Renpiti [illegible], Ṭuat II, a Time-god.

Renp-t ākhemu [illegible], Ombos II, 134, [illegible], Denderah I, 30, a god and goddess (?)

Renfreth [illegible], Ṭuat IV, a god in the Ṭuat.

rensu (?), beads, ornaments.

Rentheth, Ṭuat I, a goddess of the 1st Gate.

rentchpȧu, pitch, bitumen; Copt. λⲁⲙⲙⲭⲁⲡⲧ.

rer, man; plur., ; see **remth.**

rer, to nurse, to dandle a child; , nursed.

rer-t, nurse, foster-mother.

reruti, nurse.

Rerit, Rec. 27, 55, a nurse-goddess.

rer, child, nursling.

rer, young cattle, calf.

Rer, B.D. 112, 5, the Black Pig—a form of Set.

rer, Rec. 31, 18, pig; Copt. **ⲣⲓⲣ.**

rerut, sow.

rerȧ, , = , pig, hippopotamus.

Rerit, , , , B.D.G. 413, L.D. 4, 63, Metternich Stele, 79, a hippopotamus-goddess.

Rerȧ-t, a fire-goddess, the hippopotamus-goddess.

rer (read **pekhar)**, to turn round, to go round; , Rev. 12, 66, , Ȧmen. 22, 13, to answer.

rer (pekhar) nes-t, , successor to the throne.

rer-t, something rolled, a pill, = .

rer-t, Jour. As. 1908, 273, , , medicine; varr. , , Rev. 14, 37.

rerȧ, bracelet; Copt. **ⲗⲏⲗ.**

Reru (Pekharu), Ṭuat XI, , Rec. 29, 158, a serpent-god; var. **pekhari**, .

Reri (Pekhari), , Ṭuat XI, a serpent-god.

Rer (Pekhar) ḥer, name of a fiend or serpent.

reri, Rev. 12, 12, to sail; Copt. **ⲗⲱⲓⲗⲓ.**

rer —, , , , , , Rec. 5, 92, outside.

Rerti Nifu, B.D. 142, § 3, 3, a town of Osiris.

rerf = .

Rerp, Rec. 30, 190, a fiend or devil.

rerem, , to weep, tears; see **remi,** Copt. **ⲣⲓⲙⲉ.**

rerem, fish; plur. , Rec. 21, 91, , Ȧmen. 7, 4, Rev. 14, 12; see **rem** .

rerem, a mineral (?) seed (?)

Rerek, B.D. 33, 2, 149, , Hh. 364, a serpent in the 7th Ȧat with a back seven cubits long; the Saïte Recension has .

reh, care, anxiety; Copt. **ⲗⲉϩ**; compare .

reh, to walk about, to go, to run (?)

rehan, to come to a stop, to stand still, to rest.

rehiu, a mineral substance (?)

rehit, evening; compare ; Copt. ⲣⲟⲩϩⲉ.

rehi Rev., evening; Copt. ⲣⲟⲩϩⲉ.

rehbu, , Rev. 4, 76, , flame, heat, warmth; Heb. לָהַב, Copt. ⲉⲗϩⲱⲃ.

rehb-t Rev. 14, 21, flames, fire.

rehen, Thes. 1296, , Pap. 3024, 121, Metternich Stele 81, , , , , , to lean on something, to support oneself on something, to rest upon, to bend over a stream to make water; , N. 1146 = , P. 369.

rehenu Hearst Pap. I, 4 . . . . .

Rehen, , Lanzone 22, a title of the ram of Åmen.

rehṭ-t, , pot, caldron, kettle, cooking vessel; plur. ; Copt. ⲣⲁϩⲧⲉ.

reḥ, B.D. 38A, 6, to enter.

reḥu, A.Z. 1868, 33, , P. 1116B, 6, , , IV, 327, , IV, 1154, men, mankind, people.

Reḥui, U. 190, , T. 69, , M. 224, , N. 601, , , , , , , , , , , , the Two Men, Horus and Set, the Twin Fighter-gods.

Reḥ-ti, , , , , N. 1385, , Hh. 342, , , B.D. 80, 2, the Two Women, *i.e.*, Isis and Nephthys.

Reḥ-ti-sen-ti, B.D. 37, 1, , the combatant sisters, *i.e.*, the Merti, , , or Isis and Nephthys.

Reḥu (Ruḥu), , B.D. 17, 133, a god identified with the phallus of Osiris.

Reḥu, Rec. 27, 87, a form of Shu.

reḥ (reḥreḥ), Israel Stele 11, to be burnt out.

reḥreḥ, , (?) to burn, to be burned.

reḥ (?), to kill oneself.

reḥab, a vessel, pot.

Reḥar (?), T. 317, the name of a fiend.

reḥen, crocodile.

Reḥen-t, B.D. 68, 4, the entrance to a canal in the Ṭuat.

Reḥnen, the name of a town and of a god (?)

reḥsu-t, , , a kind of cake.

rekh , , , , to be wise, to know, to be acquainted with, to be skilled in an art or craft; , B.D. 153A, 29; , to know carnally; , he knew his reins, *i.e.*, understood his nature; , knowingly, wittingly.

rekh , opinion; , in my opinion; , the opinion of men.

rekh-nef , IV, 971, one known to him, *i.e.*, intimate friend; , a man well known by his master; , a stranger.

rekhit , knowledge, learning.

rekh , science, knowledge.

rekhu , IV, 972, the known characteristics of a person.

rekhā , Jour. As. 1908, 281, wise, understanding.

rekhiu , , , , skilled workmen, craftsmen, trained mechanics; , N. 55, knowers of god.

rekhiu , , IV, 1081, , men, people, mankind, rational beings; see **rekhit.**

Rekhit , Denderah III, 77, a class of human beings in the Ṭuat.

rekh-t , , acquaintance (female); , a woman well known in her town; , Egyptian women.

rekhȧ-t , Rec. 11, 187, wise woman, *i.e.*, Isis.

rekh kh-t , , , sage, learned man; plur. , , Pap. 3024, 146, , , , ; late form, , , P. 1116B, 17, wise men of the East.

rekh , kinsman of.

rekh nesu , , , royal kinsman, a formal title; , a man who was actually a relative of the king.

rekh re , , skilled mouth, *i.e.*, wise in speech.

rekh ṭet , cunning of hand, a skilled workman.

rekh-t , , list, catalogue, statement, summary, account, report, contents of a document.

rekhit , a detailed statement, an account.

Rekh , Ṭuat XI, the god of knowledge in the Ṭuat.

Rekhit , B.D.G. 461, , knowledge personified.

Rekhit , Thes. 99, a title of Isis-Sothis.

rekhit , Palermo Stele, , U. 646, , , Rec. 27, 225, , Rec. 31, 18; , IV, 1026, , , , , , , , men and women, mankind, rational beings.

Rekhit Åpit , Ombos I, 46, a hippopotamus-goddess.

rekh , a scribe's mistake for .

rekh , N. 550, to slay = 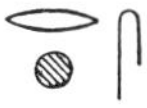.

rekh , affliction.

rekhiu 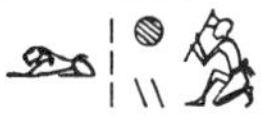, the wicked, foolish.

rekh[t] , Rec. 14, 51, basin, pool, washing-place.

rekh (?) , Rev. 12, 22, birds.

rekher (?) , milk-pot.

rekhes , U. 508, 511, P. 204, T. 343, Rec. 29, 159, , Peasant 177, A.Z. 1905, 37, 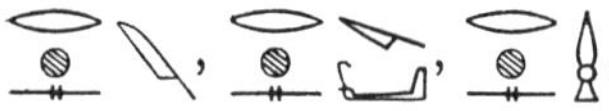, to kill, to slay, to offer up a sacrifice; , T. 144, to slay a sacrificial victim.

rekhses , P. 222, to sacrifice.

Rekhsi , Tomb of Ram. IV, 29, 30, 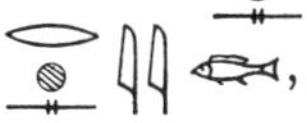, Rec. 6, 152, a fish-god.

rekht , Hh. 459, 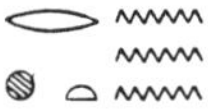, to wash; Heb. רָחַץ, Copt. ⲣⲱϩⲉ.

rekhti 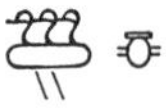, Rec. 12, 93, [illegible] [illegible], Peasant 169, [illegible], , washer-man; plur. [illegible], [illegible]; [illegible], washer of the treasury; Copt. ⲣⲁϩⲧ.

Rekhtti , a pair of goddesses, usually Isis and Nephthys.

Rekhtti Merti neb-ti Maāti  , the two Maāti goddesses (Isis and Nephthys) in the Judgment Hall of Osiris.

res , a decree (?)

resi , Anastasi I, 17, 2, [illegible] [illegible], L.D. III, 194, [illegible], very much, exceedingly; [illegible], he is in very evil case.

Res  , the South, Upper Egypt; , South, North, West, East; **tep res** , the South, *i.e.*, Upper Egypt.

resi , southern; fem. [illegible]; plur. [illegible], [illegible], south, southern; [illegible], N. 1292, [illegible], T. 196; Copt. ⲣⲏⲥ.

Resiu , P. 829, [illegible], N. 772, [illegible], A.Z. 1907, 2, [illegible], southern tribes, peoples in the South.

resi , T. 81, M. 235, N. 613, Rec. 29, 145, [illegible], wind of the South.

resi , precious stone of the South.

resi , corn, grain.

resut , reeds.

res ur , Décrets 18, chief of the South.

res nefer-t , fine linen of the South.

res-s , IV, 266, [illegible], Crown of the South; perhaps to be read **shemā-s**.

res shesu , IV, 1148, garments made in the South.

Resu , Ombos I, 84, the god of the South and its vegetation.

Resit (Shemāit ?) , Denderah II, 66, 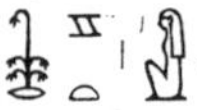, the goddess of the South.

Resu , Ṭuat IV, one of the warders of the serpent Nehep.

Res-åfu (?) , Ṭuat XI, a dawn-god (?)

Resi-åneb-f 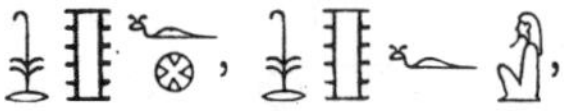, "the southern one of his wall"—a title of Ptaḥ of Memphis.

Resit-neterit-kheper (?) 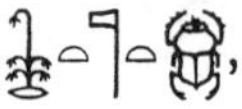, Ṭuat V, a crowned axe-god.

res , U. 66, N. 326,   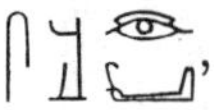, Rec. 27, 232,  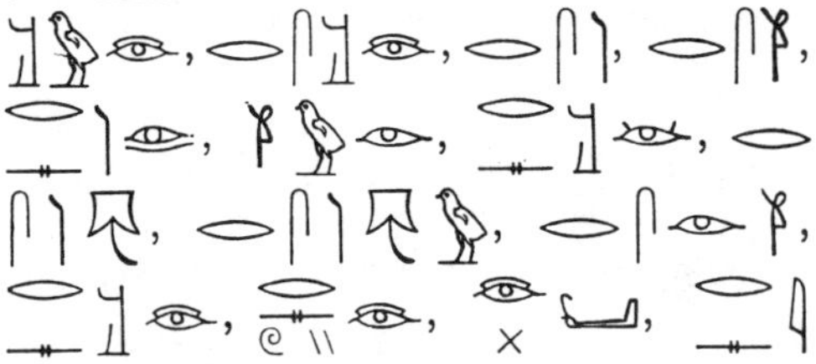 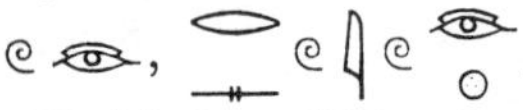, Jour. As. 1908, 293, 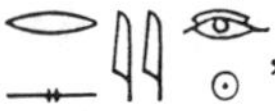, ibid., 285, to wake up, to keep awake, to watch; Copt. ⲣⲟⲉⲓⲥ.

res tchatcha 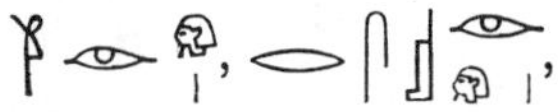 , to keep good watch; , IV, 752.

resu 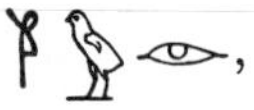, IV, 656, watchman.

Res , title of the priest of the Nome Metelites; priestess, [illegible].

resut 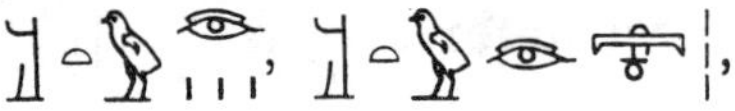, night watches.

res 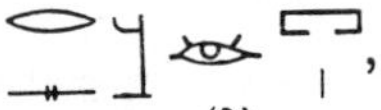, watch-tower, sheepfold; Copt. ⲉⲣⲥⲱ (?)

resu-khā , IV, 927, [illegible], IV, 928, a building at Karnak.

Resu 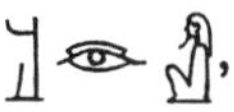, "Watcher"—a name of Rā.

Resit , B.D. 168, IX, the nine watchers.

Res-åb , B.D. 144, 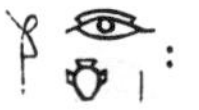: (1) the god of the 1st day of the month; (2) the Watcher of the 4th Ārit.

Res-utcha , Rec. 37, 62, a form of Ptaḥ.

Res-utcha khenti ḥeh  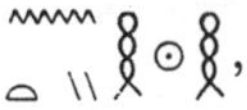, Cairo Pap. III, 7, an ichneumon-god with [illegible] on his head.

Res-pet (?) , Ombos II, 133, a god of offerings.

Res-ḥer , [illegible], B.D. 144, the Watcher of the 3rd Ārit.

Res-tchatcha , B.D. 147, 1, the Watcher of the 4th Ārit.

resi , Rev. 12, 32, [illegible] [illegible], Rev. 12, 110, , Rev. 12, 110, 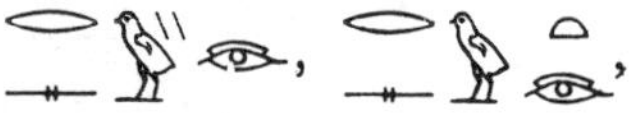, dream; Copt. ⲣⲁⲥⲟⲩⲓ.

resu-t , Peasant 217, , Gol. 14, 137, [illegible], Karnak 53, 28, dream, vision; [illegible] [illegible] Dream Stele 4, 7, two dreams; Copt. ⲣⲁⲥⲟⲩ.

resit 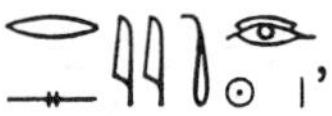, Jour. As. 1908, 302, to-morrow; Copt. ⲣⲁⲥⲧⲉ.

res , Rec. 36, 79, 81, [illegible], tongue; Copt. ⲗⲁⲥ.

resres [illegible], to build (?)

res [illegible], Rev. 11, 174 . . . . .

resef , , , Pap. 3024, 90 , Thes. 1199, , , , , fish, a catch of fish, food, provisions, subsistence.

resm , boat (?)

Resent , , , , the Southern shrine.

Resenit , , a goddess.

resh , = , to know.

reshi , , Rec. 33, 31, 33, , IV, 1160, , , , , , , , , , to rejoice, to be glad; Copt. ⲣⲁϣⲉ.

reshȧ , Ȧmen 10, 6, 24, 19, joy, gladness.

reshresh , N. 1010, , to rejoice.

reshresh-t , Ḥeruemḥeb 14, , , joy, gladness.

resh , Peasant 176, , , , Ḥeruemḥeb 26, joy, gladness; Copt. ⲣⲁϣⲓ.

reshi , Rev. 11, 142, 12, 44, , Rev. 13, 7, joy, gladness.

reshit, reshut , , , , , , , , joy, gladness.

resh , , a disease or ailment of the nose.

resh , , Rev. 13, 8, impudent, bold; Copt. ⲗⲁϭ, ⲗⲁϫⲓ.

reshi , Rev., shameless man.

resha , Rev., to have a care for; Copt. ⲣⲟⲟⲩϣ.

reshȧ (rushaȧ) , , , peak, tip, head, top, summit; , chief, governor; compare Heb. ראשׁ.

reshaā (?) , to suffice (?) be sufficient (?); Copt. ⲣⲱϣⲉ.

reshau , a kind of bird.

Reshitt , Berg. II, 12, a form of Ȧmentt.

reshpȧ , , to insult (?)

Reshpu , Thes. 1200, A.Z. 1906, 97, , B.M. 191, Asien 311, , the Lightning-god (?); compare Heb. √רשׁף.

Reshpiu , lightning-gods.

reshen , kind of speech.

reshnuiu = .

resher-t , scent-pot, pomade.

roshqui (?) , ferocity.

reshti , Westcar Pap. 5, 15 . . . . . .

reqi , Ȧmen. 14, 11, , , Rec. 29, 146, , , , , , , , , A.Z. 1905, 23, to fail, to fall away from, to rebel, to revolt, to cease from.

reqaȧu-t, A.Z. 1899, 145, revolt, defection.

req ḥa-t, IV, 910, evil-hearted.

reqi, evil-doer, rebel, fiend, foe, opponent, enemy; IV, 612, 938.

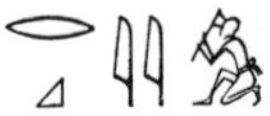

requ, IV, 969, IV, 1075, Åmen. 5, 12, 15, 14, fiend, foe, rebel; plur.

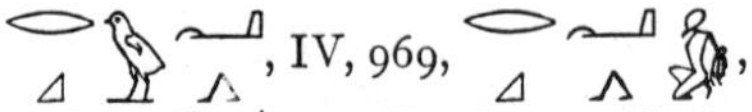

Requ, Rec. 27, 57, a god (?)

requt, a kind of disease.

reqit, Rec. 27, 84, river bank.

reqen, mean, wicked, evil.

reqrreqr, Brugsch, Rec. IV, 86, 3 = Copt. λοϭλεϭ, λοχλεχ.

reqeḥ, flame, heat, fire.

rek, Rev. 11, 190 = Copt. ⲉ ⲣⲟⲕ.

rek, to kindle a fire, to burn = .

Rekit, fire-goddess = .

rek, time, period, age.

rek, Rev. 11, 146, to incline towards; Copt. ⲣⲓⲕⲉ.

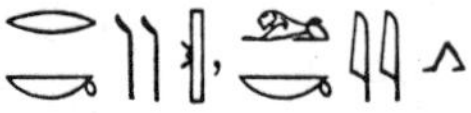

reka, heat, burning.

reka, to bewitch, to work magic on someone.

reki, fiend, foe; plur. ; varr. .

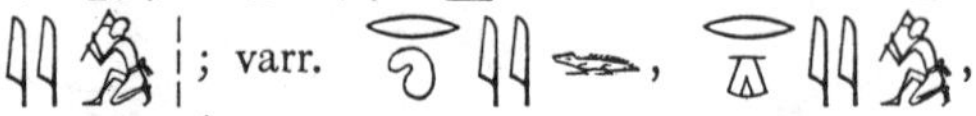

Rekit, Tomb Ram. IV, 28, a shadow-god (?)

Reku, Mar. Karn. 52, 1, a foreign tribe or people.

Rekem, B.D. (Saïte) 99, 30, a god.

rekeḥ, Åmen. 13, 7, to be hot, to burn, to consume by fire; Copt. ⲣⲱⲕϩ.

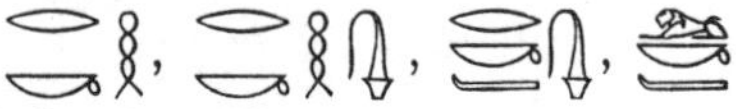

rekḥit, P. 90, M. 119, N. 698, heat, fire, flame.

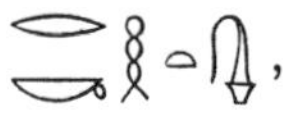

rekḥuit, heat, flame.

Rekḥu, a hot-weather festival.

Rekeḥ āa, festival of the Great Heat.

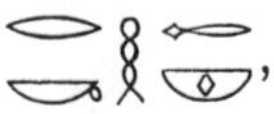

Rekeḥ ur, the festival of the Great Heat.

Rekeḥ netches, festival of the Little Heat.

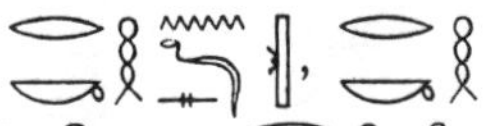

Rekḥi, Tomb of Seti I, one of the 75 forms of Rā (No. 40).

Rekḥit, Ṭuat XI, a fire-goddess.

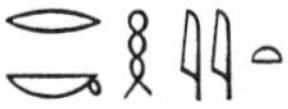

Rekḥiu, B.D. 141, 62, the fire-gods of the Ṭuat.

Rekeḥ ur, the god of the 6th month of the Egyptian year; Copt. ⲙⲉⲭⲓⲣ.

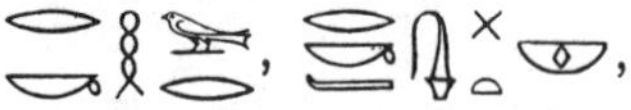

Rekhit-besu, etc.,  [illegible], etc., B.D. 145, 146, the 8th Pylon of Sekhet-Ȧaru.

Rekeḥ netches 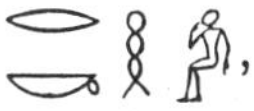, the god of the 7th month of the Egyptian year; Copt. ⲫⲁⲙⲉⲛⲱⲑ.

Rekes , Seker, the Death-god.

Rekes , B.D. 39, 9, a conqueror of Ȧapep.

reksu , Koller Pap. I, 1, a yoke (of horses); compare Heb. רֶכֶשׁ

Rekkt , Rec. 27, 53, a god (?)

rekt (?) , Ḥerusȧtef Stele 103, 107, to destroy.

reg , to destroy, make to cease; Copt. ⲗⲟ.

reg , Rev. 12, 42, to turn aside; Copt. ⲣⲓⲕⲉ.

reg-t , denial (?)

regai , a woven stuff used in burials.

regai , a liquid or unguent (?)

ragatȧ-t  [illegible], Anastasi I, 149, part of a ramp or inclined plane.

regiu , a kind of precious stone.

reges , to slay = .

regth , fuller; Copt. ⲣⲱϩⲉ.

ret , Rev. 13, 32, mode, manner; Copt. ⲣⲏϯ.

ret , Rev. 11, 143, foot; Copt. ⲣⲁⲧ, B. ⲗⲉⲧ.

ret , Rec. 6, 116, men, mankind; see **remth** [illegible]; Copt. ⲣⲱⲙⲉ.

ret nebt , everybody.

ret-ȧf-menu 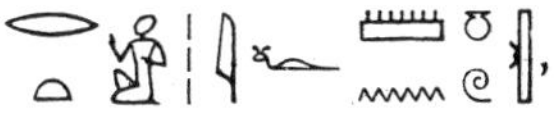, herdsman; Copt. ⲣⲉϥⲙⲟⲟⲛⲉ.

Reti , B.D. (Saïte) 80, 2 = [illegible].

Retui (Ruti)-en-Ȧsȧr  [illegible], Ṭuat VII, name of the 7th Gate.

Ret-t shesit (?) 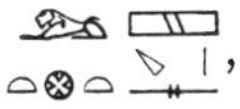, a goddess: attributes unknown.

Retas - shaka 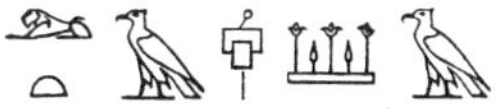 [illegible], B.D. 165, 7, a name of Ȧmen or of Ȧmen-Rā.

reteb 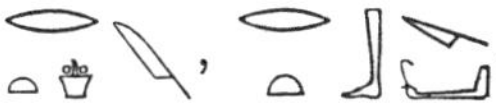, to slay, to kill.

Reteb-mut-f , Thes. 818, Rec. 16, 106, a hawk-god, a watcher of Osiris.

retemu (?) , IV, 1024 . . . .

Retnu 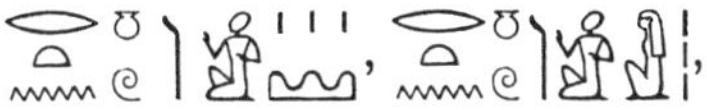 [illegible], a people of Northern Syria.

Retnu — , Eastern Reten (Syria).

reteḥ 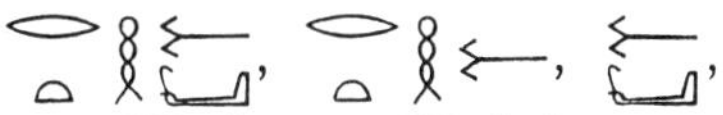 , Tombos Stele 4, to capture, to hook, to shut in, to imprison, a hook; var. .

reteḥ 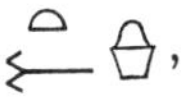, U. 89, N. 366, a kind of sacrificial cake.

Retḥuarekh , Ombos I, 193, a goddess of offerings.

reth 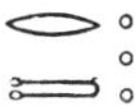, P. 85, 347, [illegible], P. 641, , N. 43, 751, 792, M. 647, [illegible],  [illegible], men, folk, people, mankind = 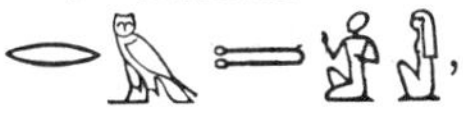, M. 675, Copt. ⲣⲱⲙⲉ.

, everybody; , Amherst Pap. 32, sailor folk; , serfs; , drunken people; , private soldiers; , Rec. 17, 150, servants; , inscribed wax figures of men; , L.D. III, 219E, 17, the servants of Pharaoh's temples.

reth —, , IV, 1075, the three classes of mankind.

Reth , Ṭuat V, "men," *i.e.*, the Egyptians in the Ṭuat. They were formed of the tears, , that fell from the eyes of Rā.

reth āau , great folk, the rich (?); Copt. ρⲉⲙⲙⲁⲟ

reth rekh , Rev. 8, 22, sensible, mild of manner; Copt. ρⲙρⲁϣ (?)

rethp , Rev. 2, 43 = Copt. ρⲟⲧⲡⲉ (?)

Rethnu , , a part of Syria; , Upper Syria; , Lower Syria; var. .

reṭ , , , , leg; dual , T. 385, , M. 402, , , , , , , , , , , , , ; plur. , P. 310, 612, N. 746, , T. 326, , , ; Copt. ρⲁⲧ.

reṭ then , IV, 327, "[mind] your feet"; compare Arab. "huwa riglak," the cry of the porters at the railway stations in Egypt.

reṭ ur , N. 798 . . . . . .

reṭ , , , , , M. 825, , P. 258, , P. 584, , N. 1318, steps, stairs, stairway, terrace; , IV, 497, the Great stairs.

Reṭu , , , , B.D. 136A, 4, the stairs of Sebek.

reṭu-t , places, abodes.

reṭ , , , , to grow, to flourish, to spring up, to spread out; Copt. ρⲉⲧ in ρⲉⲧⲧⲉⲛϩ.

reṭ , , men, people, folk; see .

reṭ , , Rec. 14, 46, agent, officer; plur. .

erṭa (?) , T. 280, P. 61, M. 29, N. 87, , , , to give, to place, to place oneself, to appoint, to establish, to cause, to set; **erṭa** is also used as an auxiliary verb: , Israel Stele 2.

erṭi-t , something given; plur. , IV, 425, things given.

erṭa pa ḥer , Rec. 14, 11, to pray; Copt. ϯϩⲟ.

erṭa em sa , to set oneself by the side of, to protect someone.

erṭa er ȧs-t , to seat oneself on a throne.

erṭa er ta, Pap. 3024, 109, to establish oneself, to arrive at a place, to land; , to set foot on the ground.

erṭa ruti, to cast out at the door, to put outside.

erṭa rekh, to inform.

erṭa ḥer khat, to lay to heart.

erṭa ḥer ges, IV, 411, 971, Peasant 268, to set oneself on one side, *i.e.*, to act with partiality, to show favour unjustly, to judge wrongly.

erṭa sa, to turn the side or back, *i.e.*, to yield, to put a stop to something.

erṭa senter, to put incense on the fire, *i.e.*, to burn incense.

erṭa gerg, to give the lie, *i.e.*, to contradict.

erṭa as a causative: , , , , , etc.

Erṭa nefu, "Giver of winds"—a name of Osiris.

Erṭa-ḥen-reqaiu, B.D. (Saïte) 146, the doorkeeper of the 5th Pylon.

Erṭa Sebanqa, B.D. 146, the guardian of the 3rd Pylon in the Ṭuat.

Reṭ-ā, Ṭuat XI, one of the 12 gods who carried Meḥen.

Reṭau (?), Ṭuat X, a god; var. , Ṭuat XI.

erṭit, Anastasi I, 23, 8.........

erṭu, , P. 608, N. 344, 398, 806, , P. 609, , Rec. 5, 88, , , , humour, liquid emanation, emission; plur. , , , , , ; , emission of the god.

Reṭuk, B.D. (Saïte) 149, 26, a serpent-god (or goddess) = .

reṭm-t, Leyden Pap. 3, 9, a plant or herb growing in the Great Oasis.

reṭeḥ, , , to imprison, to catch in a net or snare; see .

retcha, to steal, to thieve.

retchau, , , thieves, robbers.

retcha, , , a kind of fish.

H

h = generally ה, also א, but rarely; Copt. ϩ.

h in Nubian texts for .

h-[t] , , , hall, habitation, a building (temple or palace), courtyard, roof; see .

ha-t , IV, 429; see .

h-ui (?) , U. 457, , the two halls of the sky.

h[i] , , , , an interjection, O!; , cries, lamentations.

ha, ha-t , , , , an interjection, O; varr. , , .

ha , Leyd. Pap. 105, to cry out, to praise, to shout "Oh!" "Hail!"

h , Naville, Bubas. 51 = (?) an altar vessel.

h, hau , Rev. 13, 48, to spend, gift, expense; plur. , Rechnungen 64, expenditure.

hau , , , , the matters which concern someone; , IV, 1106, all matters, every kind of business.

hai , Rec. 21, 79, a few.

ha , , , a place near at hand, neighbourhood; , in the neighbourhood of this city.

hau — em hau , , , , , close by, near by, near; , round about him.

hau , IV, 1024, , , , , a man's neighbours or contemporaries, family, household; varr. , .

ha, hau , P. 607, , , , Rec. 21, 14, , Rec. 11, 129, , , , , , , , , Nåstasen Stele 19, , Jour. As. 1908, 290, day, time, season; Copt. ϩⲟⲟⲩ.

ha-t , Rev. 11, 138, moment, time; Copt. ϩⲟⲧⲉ.

ha — **pa-ha** , Rec. 21, 14, to-day; Copt. ⲡϩⲟⲟⲩ; , Rev. 11, 187 = Copt. ⲙⲡϩⲟⲟⲩ.

hau — , Nåstasen Stele 42, birthday.

ha nefer , Rec. 25, 191, a day of rejoicing or festival; , to keep a festival.

ha, hai , U. 629, IV, 219, , , ,

husband; plur. ; , to act the part of a husband; , husband, man; Copt. ϩⲁⲓ.

Hai , B.D. 40, 1, , , a name of .

ha , 26, 66, , to beat, to strike, to do hard work of some kind.

ha , , Décrets 27, A.Z. 1905, 6, some kind of forced labour.

ha-t , work, toil, labour.

hai , workman, a mover of stone (?); plur. , Rec. 17, 146, , , , Rec. 17, 158.

ha , Israel Stele 12, to invade a country, to cross the frontier.

ha, haa , P. 99, N. 51, Peasant 307, , M. 68, , Rec. 26, 79, 31, 18, 25, , , , , , , Åmen. 17, 2, , , , Pap. 3024, 107, Rec. 26, 79, 31, 23, P. 650, M. 750, to descend, to go down into a boat, to embark, to travel by sea, to fall down, to enter; Copt. ϩⲉ.

ha-t, hai-t , P. 409, M. 585, N. 1191, , Rec. 8, 136, , arrival, fall, embarcation, entrance; , things laid aside.

hai , , , Rec. 21, 77, , , , he who enters, oncomer, he who embarks in a boat, or sails; plur. , , .

haut , descendant, progeny

ha-ti , Rec. 23, 196, the leaps (of an animal).

ha-t. . . . , Rec. 36, 162, inlaid stuffs (?)

H[a]ḥetep , B.D. (Saïte) 144, 30, a god.

Ha-ḥetep-t , , , B.D. 149, VIII, the name of the shaft or canal at Abydos into which offerings were placed for transmission to the Other World.

Ha-kheru , , B.D. 145, 147, the herald of the 1st Ārit.

Ha-ser , B.D. 149, the 7th Åat.

Ha-t Sett (?) , a name of the Ṭuat.

ha , L.D. III, 140B, , , to fall down, to go to waste and ruin, to be destroyed.

hau , , , things in a state of ruin, things destroyed.

ha , , , Thes. 1209, to burn, to break into flame, heat, fire, warmth.

haha , Rec. 25, 197, to flame, to burn up.

haiu , birds, insects (?); var. .

Hahaiu , Ṭuat VI, the four heads of gazelle in the Hall of Osiris.

haȧnȧu , Gol. 3, 1, , sweetmeat, confectionery (?)

Haȧker , the name of a festival; see **Haker.**

hai , ,  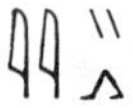, an interjection, O! hail!

haiu , an interjection.

hai , , to rejoice, to utter cries of gladness.

haiu , praises.

haihai , cries of joy, shouts.

hai, hi , , , Rev., to fall; Copt. ϩⲉⲓ.

hai-t , , 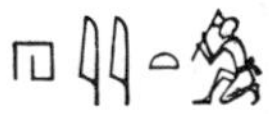, destruction, waste, ruin.

hai , A.Z. 46, 126, an animal of the cat species.

haiu , deed, document, writing; plur. .

hai-t , Rechnungen 44, , , hall, temple, palace, bakehouse.

haina , Rec. 18, 183, abode.

hainu , Rec. 28, 214, , wave, billow; Copt. ϩⲟⲉⲓⲙ.

hau , an interjection.

hau , , hall, temple, palace; plur. , Rec. 31, 25, , ,  , .

haua-t ,  [illegible], Ȧmen. 3, 17, 5, 18, 17, 15, time, period.

haua-t [illegible], Ȧmen. 7, 13, grounds, estate, field.

hauana [illegible], a kind of fish; plur. [illegible].

hauati, hauti [illegible] [illegible], Ȧmen. 27, 1, [illegible], [illegible], workman, toiler.

hauathana [illegible] [illegible], Anastasi III, 2, 8, a fish.

Ha-Bār-ru (?) [illegible] [illegible], Harris Pap. 501, a magical name.

hamen [illegible], [illegible] [illegible], a kind of handwoven cloth or byssus, garment, stuff.

haut (?) [illegible], Rec. 17, 151, a measure.

hautin [illegible], [illegible] [illegible], [illegible], III, 14, ceiling.

hab [illegible], M. 127, [illegible] [illegible], A.Z. 1900, 36, [illegible], [illegible], [illegible], ibis; Copt. ϩⲓⲃⲱⲓ.

Habu [illegible], the Ibis-god.

hab [illegible], Ȧmen. 15, 15, [illegible], [illegible], [illegible], [illegible], [illegible], [illegible], [illegible], [illegible], to send, to send away, to drive away, to send a message, to transmit; [illegible], Ȧmen. 4, 8, 15, 18, despatch, mission.

hab-t [illegible], a journey.

hab , Tombos Stele 6, , Åmen. 7, 16, [illegible], Rec. 27, 86, 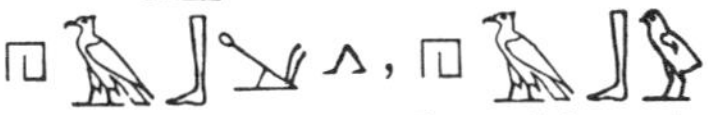, , , to despatch an armed force, to traverse a country, to invade a country, to make a raid.

habit  [illegible], mission, raid.

Hab-em-at (?)  [illegible], B.D. 14, 1, a god (?)

hab , to plough; see [illegible].

habni , Koller Pap. 3, 8, ebony, log of or tree; plur.  ; Heb. הָבְנִי, Ezekiel xxvii, 15; varr. .

habq 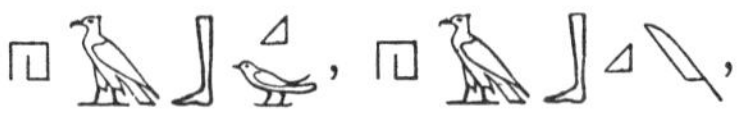, Rec. 37, 21, , [illegible], to pound [drugs], to beat, to crush, to pierce; see [illegible]; Copt. ϩⲱⲃⲕ.

hap 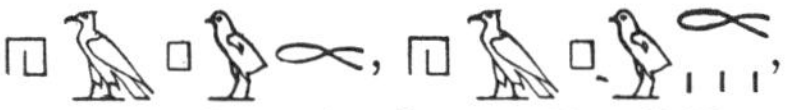, , law, laws, regulations, edicts, restrictions, prohibitions, the Law; see [illegible]; Copt. ϩⲁⲡ.

hapiṭrus , Demot. Cat. 368 . . . . . .

hafi , Verbum I, 434, 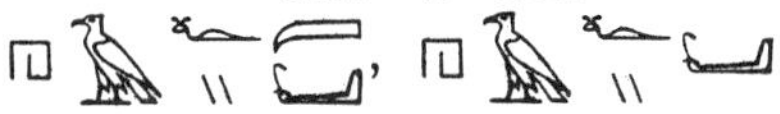, to dry, to parch; [illegible], dryness.

hafi , a hard-baked cake, rusk.

ham , pelican.

hamu 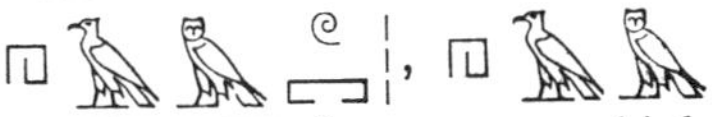 , Åmen. 27, 3, 4, bird-houses, aviaries.

hamu , blemish, defect, sin.

hamemu , P.S.B.A. 10, 77, , men and women (?) a class of spirits; varr. [illegible]  ; see **ḥenmem-t.**

hames , IV, 621, Annales 5, 18, L.D. III, 194, 25, to approach someone with fear; var. [illegible].

han  [illegible], P.S.B.A. 13, 412, Anastasi I, 26, 3, [illegible] , Åmen. 20, 17, P.S.B.A. 10, 43, Anastasi I, 12, 7, , to bow, to submit to, to nod, to assent, to admit, to confess, to incline to something; see [illegible].

hann , to be bowed, *i.e.*, loaded.

Han , B.D. (Saïte), 78, 19, a god.

hann , Rec. 15, 67, stag, gazelle (?)

hana , Anastasi I, 27, 4, Rec. 21, 79, 89, O that! Would that!

hana , Anastasi IV, 2, 8, Koller Pap. 2, 6, the current of a stream (?) wave; Copt. ϩⲟⲉⲓⲙ.

hanu , Rec. 21, 82, Festschrift, 117, 8,  [illegible], wave, billow; see [illegible] and .

hanu-t , Åmen. 7, 2; see .

hanu 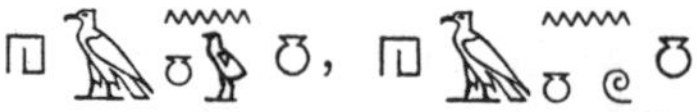, a liquid measure of about one pint; plur.  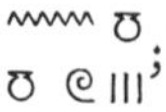; see ; Heb. הִין.

han , to praise, to adore, to rejoice.

hanu , praises, plaudits, men who praise.

hanu , Rec. 16, 56, friends, intimates.

haru , Rec. 21, 15,  , day; see ; Copt. ϩⲟⲟⲩ.

hari , Rev. 12, 98, daily register.

har , Rec. 16, 113, to oppress, to be hard.

haru , a kind of soldier.

har , Åmen. 21, 9, a measure.

har 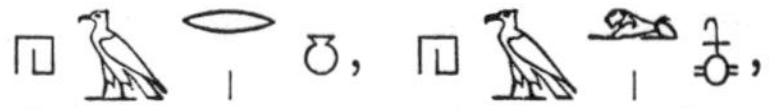, , Ḥerusȧtef Stele 43, Nȧstasen Stele 37, a metal milk-vessel; var. .

har , , a kind of tree.

har 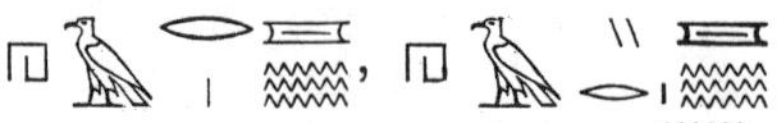 , pond, lake, sheet of water; var. .

har , mountain; Heb. הַר.

hari , with **ḥa-t** ,  , to please, to gratify, to rest the heart.

har-t ḥatu (?) 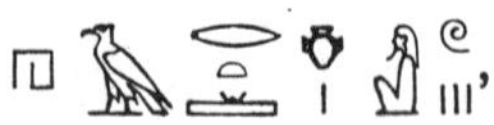, Rec. 32, 181, joy.

har-t , a small fleet animal, gazelle (?); plur. , IV, 697.

harp 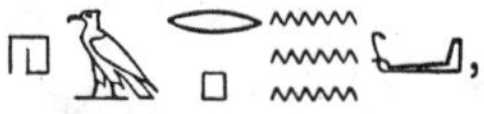, to plunge in water, to be submerged, drowned (?)

harpi , Åmen. 10, 1, drowned man, sunk.

harp  , marsh, lake.

Harmis 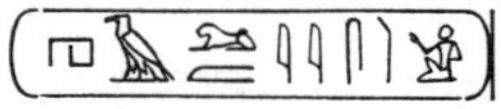 A.Z. 49, 87, the Roman; Greek Ῥωμαῖος.

harnatȧ , spelt.

harthatha , Anastasi I, 16, 4, secretly (?)

Hahuti-ȧm . . . (?) [illegible] [illegible], the name of a fiend.

hahemti [illegible], murmurs, cries; see [illegible]; Copt. ϩⲗⲗϩⲗⲗ.

Hasau [illegible], Harris I, 77, 3, a Libyan tribe.

hastkatȧ [illegible], Anastasi I, 24, 4, to travel with difficulty.

haq [illegible].

Haqa-haga-ḥer [illegible] [illegible], B.D. 162, 4, a Nubian (?) title of Rā.

Haker [illegible], B.D. XVIIIE, a god of Abydos associated with the slaughter of the dead.

Haker ḥeb [illegible], [illegible], the festival of Haker; [illegible], the night festival of Haker.

hatȧ-t [illegible], Anastasi IV, 14, 1, a cake, loaf of bread.

hatȧhatȧ, to trample upon; see .

hatu, B.D. 163, 11, part of the head (?)

hatutu, Stunden 10........

hatr-t, leather band for a bow

Hatestt, Düm. Rec. 50, 14, Hades; Gr. Ἅδης.

hathes, N. 264, 265, a kind of vessel, pot.

hatḥ, , Åmen. 7, 15, 8, 9, , to seize, to attack, to assail, to gore, to pull down a boundary stone or wall.

hatm-t, , footstool; compare Heb. הֲדֹם.

hatmu, Rec. 19, 96, part of a shrine.

hatn, papyrus cord or rope, vine tendril (?); var. .

hatr-t, an arm ornament, bracelet, armlet; see .

hatcha, fever (?) weakness.

hatcher-t, an armlet or bracelet (of gold,).

hȧ, U. 272, N. 662, , N. 704, , an interjection.

hȧhȧ, an interjection, Ha-ha!

hȧ, A.Z. 1905, 36, to copulate.

hȧ, IV, 1078, , IV, 972, husband; varr. , , ; Copt. ϩⲁⲓ.

hȧu (?), Rec. 2, 116, family, progeny, seed, posterity.

hȧ-t, illness, sickness; var. , Pap. 3024, 132.

hȧ, , Jour. As. 1908, 251, Rev. 14, 52, cost, expense, profit; Copt. ϩⲏⲩ.

Hȧu, U. 326, , U. 545, T. 300, , Hh. 560, , Ṭuat II, a serpent-fiend in the Ṭuat.

hȧu, , Rec. 31, 31, an animal of the gazelle class.

Hȧu, U. 332, T. 300........

hȧu-t, Rev. 12, 79, gate, forecourt; Copt. ϩⲁⲉⲓⲧ, Gr. προαύλιον.

hȧu-t, T. 16..........

Hȧri-Ȧu, Rev. 11, 185, a proper name = Copt. ⲩⲉⲣⲓ̈ ⲓ̈ⲟⲩ.

Hȧuk, Devéria, Pap. Tur. 148, Rev. 2, 19, a serpent-fiend in the Ṭuat.

hȧm, Pap. 3024, 49, to lead, to drive, to urge.

hȧmes, with , IV, 704, to approach or walk with reverence; see and .

hȧnnȧ, P. 115, to cry out in joy, to sing praises.

hȧhi, , an interjection, O! Hail!

Hȧtȧtȧbȧtȧ shesaḥȧfg-t, U. 325, name of a mythological serpent.

hāisȧ, Rev. 12, 62, to immerse, to submerge; Copt. ϩⲁⲥⲓⲉ.

hi 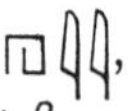, Rec. 32, 82, 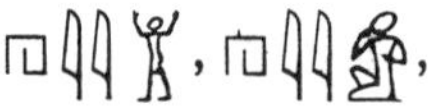,
, an interjection, O! Hail!

hi , , Ḥerusâtef Stele 7, , Rev. 13, 14, 14, 3, , , to descend, to fall down; see ; Copt. ϩⲉⲓ.

hiu 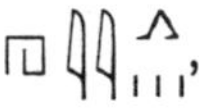, those who descend or fall.

hi-t 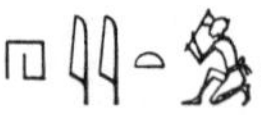, Ebers Pap. 40, 11, 14, sickness, disease; see .

hi 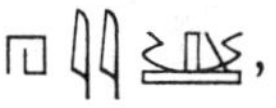, U. 443, , T. 252, to tow a boat.

hi , husband; Copt. ϩⲁⲓ.

hi , Rec. 27, 87, ram.

hi , A.Z. 1906, 123, music, joy, gladness.

Hi 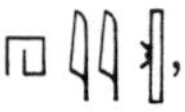, Ṭuat XII, a singing dawn-god.

hiu (?) , birds.

hi , Rev. 12, 11, a kind of officer =  (Revillout).

hi-t , Dream Stele 19, hall, temple, palace; varr. , Dream Stele 22.

hit (?) , IV, 1073, court or palace officials.

hin-t , Rec. 27, 191, 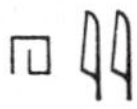
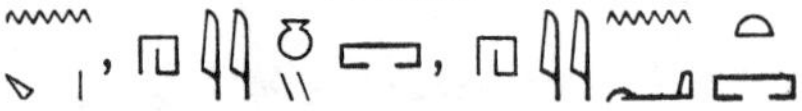, house, abode, habitation.

hin , to be situated (of a house or town).

hini , Rev. 13, 39 = Copt. ϩⲉⲛ, ϩⲁⲛ.

hinu ,
, Rev. 13, 29, Jour. As. 1908, 294, some (?); Copt. ϩⲟⲉⲓⲛⲉ (?)

hinu 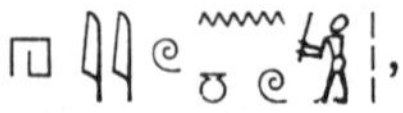, Rec. 33, 120, neighbours.

Hirna-t , Rec. 33, 3, the Greek name "Irene."

hihen (?) , IV, 1075, to praise (?)

Higer , a name for the Nile.

hit , Rev. 12, 68, dog-headed ape; see .

hit , Jour. As. 1908, 277, to prove, to try; Copt. ϩⲓⲧⲉ.

hit-t , proof, trial.

hitȧ , Rev. 13, 29, ditches, pits; Copt. ϩⲓⲉⲓⲧ.

hith [illegible], A.Z. 1878, 49, pit; Copt. ϩⲓⲉⲓⲧ.

hu [illegible], day; see **hru** [illegible]; Copt. ϩⲟⲟⲩ.

hu [illegible], district, place.

hu [illegible], Treaty 14, with [illegible], in the time of.

hu [illegible], IV, 584, with [illegible], over against.

hu [illegible], to go down, to fall; see [illegible].

hu [illegible], belongings, relatives, household; see [illegible].

hui [illegible], a demon animal.

hunnuȧ [illegible], Rev. 13, 24 . . . . .

hur [illegible], Ȧmen. 9, 1, day; see [illegible].

Hurmȧis , A.Z. 49, 80, the Roman; Gr. 'Ρωμαῖος; var.  [illegible]

huhu , light breeze, puff of wind.

Hu-kheru , B.D. 144, the name of the herald of the 1st Ārit.

hushi [illegible], Rev. 12, 107, , Jour. As. 1908, 257, 267, to be in danger, peril, danger; Copt. ϩⲱϣ.

husha 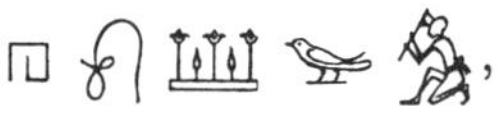, to be in danger; Copt. ϩⲱϣ.

hut (?) , fear, terror (?) Copt. ϩⲟϯ.

hut, hutut , Rec. 30, 187, to burn, flame.

Hutt , B.D. (Saïte) 100, 2.

hutem (?) , Rougé, I.H. II, 114 . . . . .

heb [illegible], Rev., to question (?); Copt. ϩⲓⲟⲓ (?)

heb  , Rev. 11, 188, ibis; Copt. ϩⲓⲃⲱⲓ.

Heb , the Ibis-god.

heb , IV, 938, 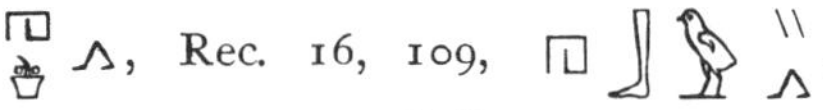, Herusȧtef Stele 89, [illegible], to send out, to despatch a mission; Copt. ϩⲱⲃ.

hebb [illegible], Rougé, I.H. 256, to send.

hebu , a messenger.

heb , IV, 345, ,  [illegible], to make a way through, to traverse.

hebheb , Ȧmen. 8, 15, , Rhind Pap. 16, [illegible], N. 902, , IV, 394, 955, Rec. 15, 179, , IV, 677, [illegible], Rev. 11, 70, 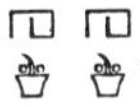, Rec. 16, 109, [illegible] , to force a way through, to march through, to traverse, to trample down; [illegible] , IV, 1026, traverser of mountains and deserts; , passing through ravines and marshes.

hebheb , Ebers Pap. 1031, to drive out pain.

heb , to butt, to gore, to thrust with the horns.

hebi 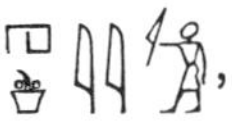, to attack.

hebiu , a group of fiends who attacked the dead.

heb  [illegible], T. 305, , P. 658, 763, , M. 764, to plough, plough; Copt. ϩⲃ̄ⲃⲉ, ϩⲉⲃⲓ.

heb-t , Rec. 16, 108, storehouse, magazine, slaughter-house.

hebā 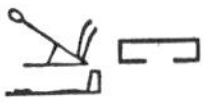, workshop.

heb , south wind.

Hebai (Hebi) [illegible], Dendereh IV, 26, a lion-god of Denderah.

Hebit , Rec. 16, 109, a goddess.

hebin , Rev. 13, 15, ebony; Heb. הָבְנִי.

hebar , Jour. As. 1908, 301, anguish; Copt. ϩⲃⲁ.

hebar , Rev.; Copt. ϩⲃⲟⲣⲃⲣ̄.

hebaq , embrace, to clasp; compare Heb. √חבק.

hebi 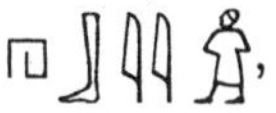, weeper, mourner.

hebin , Rec. 6, 128, ebony.

hebu-t , a kind of wood.

hebni , N. 719, ebony; ebony trees; Heb. הָבְנִי; a coffin of ebony.

heben-t 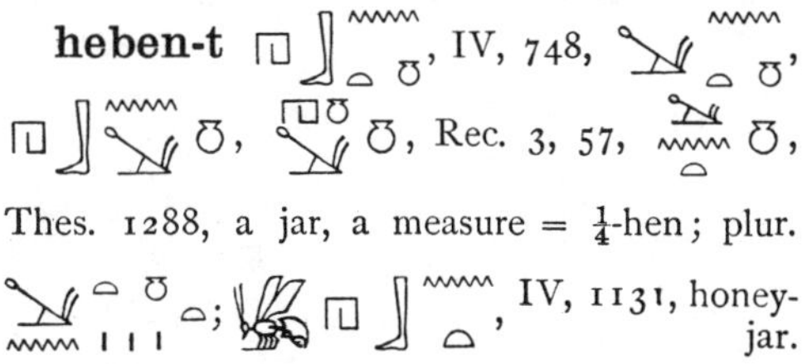, IV, 748, Rec. 3, 57, Thes. 1288, a jar, a measure = ¼-hen; plur. IV, 1131, honey-jar.

heben-t āa-t , the great heben.

heben-t netches-t , the little heben.

hebner , collar, pectoral, neckband.

hebs , Rec. 6, 9, to attack, to slay, to wound.

hebq 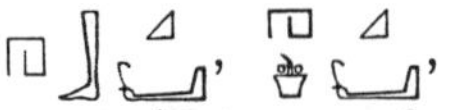, Rec. 37, 21, to pierce, to stab, to pound drugs; Copt. ϩⲱⲃ̄ⲕ.

hebq , a game trap (?)

hebq , to disappear.

hep 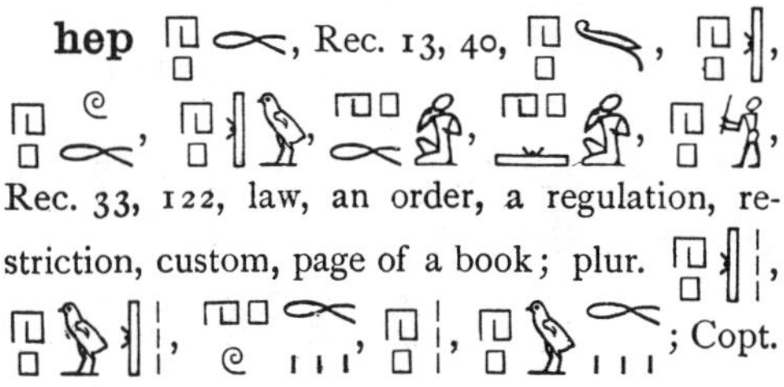, Rec. 13, 40, Rec. 33, 122, law, an order, a regulation, restriction, custom, page of a book; plur.; Copt. ϩⲁⲡ.

hepu 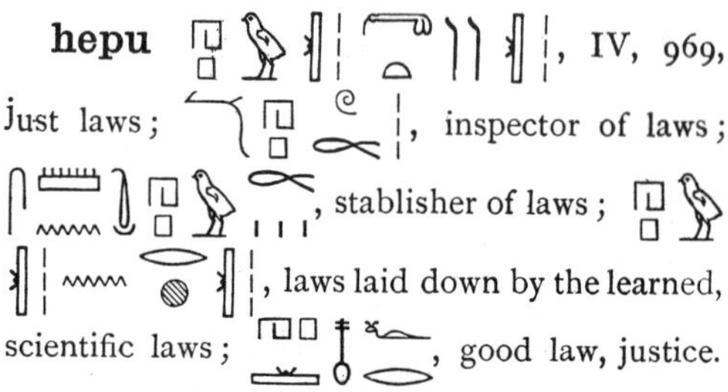, IV, 969, just laws; inspector of laws; stablisher of laws; laws laid down by the learned, scientific laws; good law, justice.

hep , to bind, to regulate.

hep-t 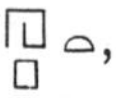, U. 43, something seized or snatched.

hep-tut , N. 148 . . . . .

hep , to walk, to move, to step.

hephep , to run, to travel.

Hepa , N. 1383 . . . .

Hepaf , P. 638 . . . . . .

Hepath 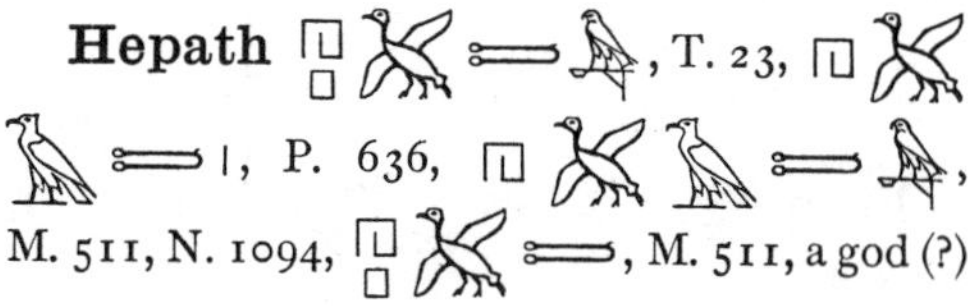, T. 23, P. 636, M. 511, N. 1094, M. 511, a god (?)

Hepȧu , T. 293, a serpent-fiend who devoured the hearts of the gods.

Hepȧuu , N. 801, a proper name.

Hepenu , Ombos II, 233, a god of offerings.

Hepnentȧ , name of a god (?)

Hepṭes , Thes. 112, one of the seven stars of Orion.

hem , Rev. 14, 52, expense, cost.

hem , hire of a boat; Copt. ϩⲉⲙⲙⲉ.

hemi , Rev. 12, 73, a kind of tax.

hem-t , U. 469, T. 220, food for the journey.

hem-t 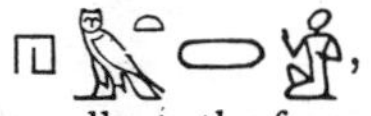, Peasant 172, the ferryman who collects the fares of his passengers.

Hemti 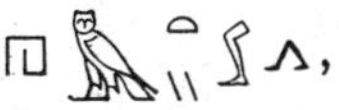, B.D. 64, 35, the god who carried to heaven the shadows and spirits of the dead.

hem , Rougé I.H. II, 125, to fall.

hemhem , to enter into, to fall (?)

hem , fire, heat, hot; Copt. ϩⲙ̄ⲙⲉ, ϩⲙⲟⲙ.

hemem-t , IV, 233,
a class of spirits, men and women, people; see **ḥenmem-t.**

hem , to moan, to utter a cry of pain.

hemhem 
, Rec. 16, 109, 
, to roar, to bellow; Copt. ϩⲙ̄ϩⲙ̄.

hemhem-t , IV, 162, a cry, roar, bellow, battle-cry; plur. .

hemhem-t ānkhiu 
, the noise made by a mass of human beings, the roar of the people.

hemhem-t ḥer-t , the roar of the sky, *i.e.*, thunder.

hemhemut ,
, IV, 1008, peals of thunder.

hemhemut ta ,
"roarings of the earth," earthquake (?)

hemut , beings who cry out, or roar.

Hem , Ṭuat VI, a god of offerings.

Hemhem ,
Ṭuat I and VI, a singing-god.

Hemhem , Nesi Ȧmsu 32, 48, a thunder-god.

Hemhemti , Nesi Ȧmsu 32, 17, a title of Āapep.

hemhem , a kind of triple crown.

hema , to rise, to ascend.

hemȧs , Rec. 30, 72 . . . .

hemi , Jour. As. 1908, 279, government; Copt. ϩⲉⲙⲓ, ϩⲙ̄ⲙⲉ.

hemu , to butt, to gore with horns.

hemen 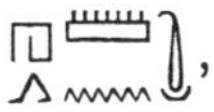, P.S.B.A. 14, 140, to work skilfully.

hemes , Thes. 1204, Thes. 1198, to approach someone in fear; var.

Hemthet 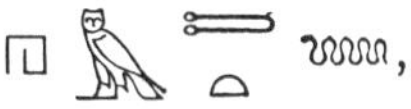, U. 549, T. 304, a serpent-god.

hen , U. 532 . . . .

hen 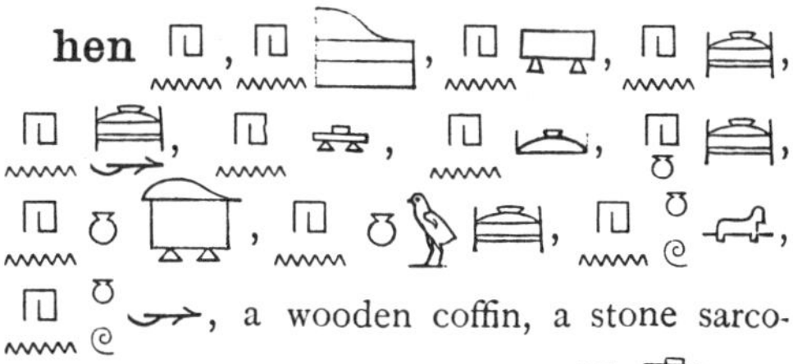, a wooden coffin, a stone sarcophagus, box, coffer, chest; plur. ,
U. 601, 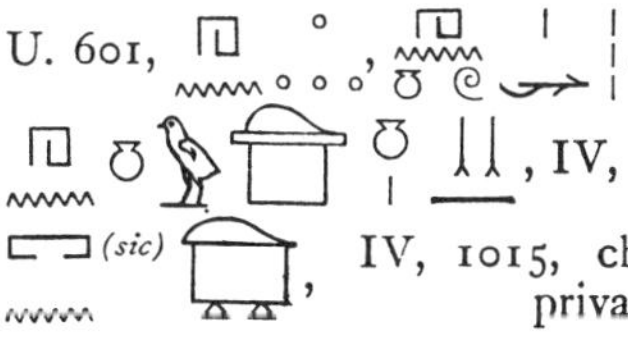, Leyd. Pap. 3, 4, IV, 338, linen chest; (*sic*) IV, 1015, chest for keeping private documents in.

hen , P. 1116B, 15, a scribe's writing box.

hen , a box for holding the skull; plur.

Henu shetatu ,
Ṭuat VII, the coffins of the dead in the Ṭuat.

hen , Rec. 31, 175, to overthrow.

hen, Thes. 1206, , , Love Songs 3, 13, to bow, to nod, to bend, to assent to, to agree, to make a sign of agreement, to incline the head, to lean heavily on someone; Copt. ϩⲉⲛⲉ.

hen, Mar. Karn. 53, 26, to nod.

hen, nod, signal.

hen, skull, brain pan.

hen-t, rest, respose.

henen, Rec. 26, 10 (=), , IV, 1107, , , , IV, 1090, to bow, to bend the head, to agree, to conform to, to assent.

hennhenn, U. 609, bowings.

henhen, Rec. 2, 116, to lull to sleep.

Henen-henen-henen, P. 638, N. 1383, a magical formula (?)

heni, P. 817, , U. 616, , Rec. 26, 224, 36, 211, , Rec. 26, 234, 34, 177, , , Rec. 34, 177, , , , , , , , to praise, to acclaim, to sing to, praise, song.

heniu, , those who praise.

henȧut, N. 834 . . . .

henhen, Nȧstasen Stele 30, to dance, to praise.

henti henti, Nȧstasen Stele 2, dance, praise.

Heniu ȧmiu Ṭuat, Ṭuat V, the choirs of angels in the Ṭuat.

henu, , , Mission 13, 117, , , , friends, neighbours, household.

henu, whip, flail, scourge.

hen, henu, U. 535, , , , , , , , a measure, jar, vase, pot for sweetmeats, unguents, etc.; plur. , , U. 539, T. 296, ; Heb. הִין; Copt. ϩⲓⲛ.

heni, maker of sweets or jam, confectioner.

heni-t, , Hearst Pap. 13, 5, the contents of a hen measure, *i.e.*, about four-fifths of a pint.

henu, De Hymnis 52, Rec. 28, 214, wave; see **henhen**; Copt. ϩⲟⲉⲓⲙ.

henhen, , , a sheet of water with waves on it.

henhenit, the watery abyss of the sky.

henhenu, Rec. 31, 170, , Rec. 29, 154, a kind of boat.

henn, , , , IV, 718, an animal found in Syria, a kind of stag.

henen, to recommend (?)

Henen, T. 24, a god.

Henit, Hennit, M. 691, , N. 797, a goddess.

henn, Rev., phallus =

henhen , Rev., order, command; Copt. ϩⲟⲛϩⲉⲛ.

henȧ , Rev. 11, 179, 187, vase; Copt. ϩⲛⲟ.

henȧu , Rec. 32, 178, praise (?)

henȧhen[ȧ] , to praise.

Hennȧ 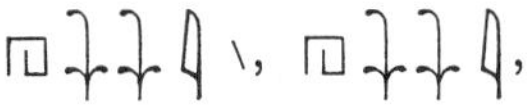, P. 636, , M. 514, N. 1096, 1097, 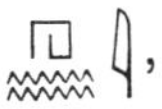, N. 1314, a god.

henȧnȧ 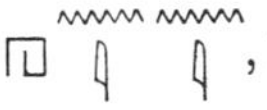, M. 96, , N. 102, to sing, to praise.

henȧnȧu  sweet, gracious, pleasant.

Hennȧthf , a star.

heni 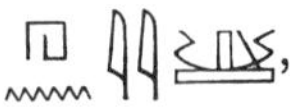, U. 446, T. 255, to sail.

Heni : (1) a god; (2) a title of Rā.

henu 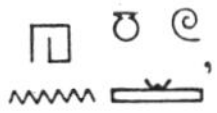, up to (of time), until.

henuḥ , Ebers Pap. 109, 6, a kind of animal.

Hennut , P. 473, N. 1118, P.S.B.A. 20, 308, dual of .

henkheses , the east wind, the god of the east wind; varr. 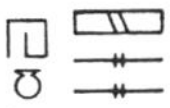 .

hensheses , 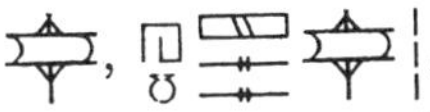, Berg. I, 35, the east wind, the god of the east wind; see above.

henṭ , Israel Stele 2, to charge (of an animal).

heṅtcher 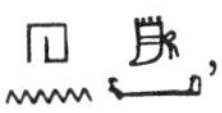, Tomb of Ȧmenemḥat 20, to seize, to capture.

her , Verbum I, 248 = Heb. אֶל.

heru , more, addition; Copt. ϩⲟⲩⲟ.

heri 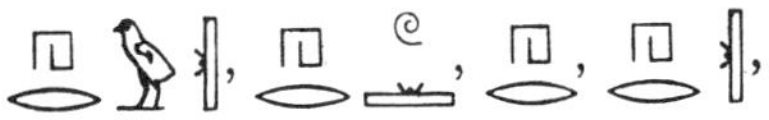, , to be at peace, to be content, to rest, to be satisfied, to sink to rest; , pleasing; , gracious; , take care! go softly; Copt. ϩⲣ̄ⲣⲉ.

heri with 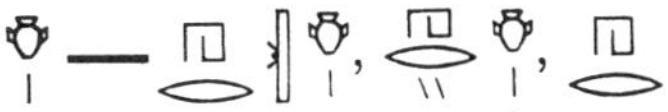,  , to be content, satisfied; Copt. ϩⲉⲣⲓ.

her ȧb (?) , Pap. 3024, 126, a man of a contented disposition.

her-t 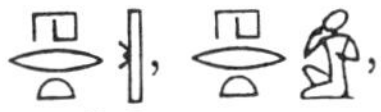, rest, peace, satisfaction; 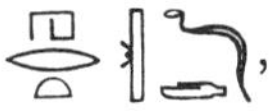, soft speech.

herut , Rev. 14, 15, , Rev. 12, 112, repose, contentment, joy, rejoicing.

hertȧ , feast, festival; Gr. ἑορτή (?)

herr [illegible], [illegible], IV, 938, [illegible], IV, 1156, 1183, to be content.

herr-t [illegible], things that please or satisfy.

Herr [illegible], Ṭuat III, a mythological boat.

Her-ti [illegible], Isis and Nephthys.

her [illegible], to go away; Copt. ϩⲱⲗ.

heri [illegible], Rhind Pap., to go up; Copt. ϩⲱⲗ.

her [illegible], IV, 745, lake, pond, goose-pond.

her [illegible], field, plot of ground, mountain.

her ȧra [illegible], "mountain of god," *i.e.*, a high hill; Heb. הַר־אֵל.

heru [illegible], vegetables (?)

her [illegible], a metal pot.

her , Rev., lofty; Copt. ϩⲱⲗ.

herher , Rev., to extend, to prolong; Copt. ϩⲉⲗϩⲱⲗ.

herr 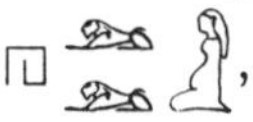, to conceive, to be with child.

her-t  , grief, sorrow, lamentation, calamity, evil hap.

her-t , bandlet, fillet.

hrar , day; see .

herȧ , B.D. 58, 6, a milk vessel.

herȧ , Rev. 11, 180, food; Copt. ϩⲣⲉ; 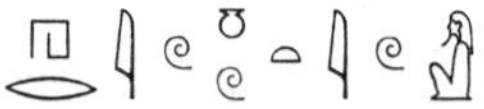 = Copt. ϩⲣⲉⲛⲟⲩⲧⲉ (Rev.).

hrārā , Rev. 12, 111, conception.

hru  , A.Z. 1906, 130, day; Copt. ϩⲟⲟⲩ; plur.  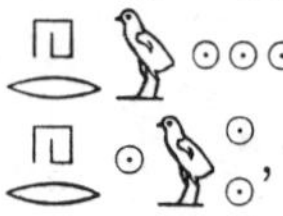, P. 288, 339, M. 570, N. 1176, N. 626; , daily; , to-day; , every day; , mid-day; , Rec. 3, 49, , , day and night = always, for ever.

Hru , day — the 30 Day-gods were: (1) Teḥuti; (2) Ḥerunetchtef; (3) Åsår; (4) Åmset; (5) Ḥāp; (6) Ṭuamutef; (7) Qebḥsenuf; (8) Maati-tef-f; (9) Åritchetef; (10) Årireneftchesef; (11) Netchetur; (12) Netchsnāā (?); (13) Teken; (14) Ḥemba; (15) Årmāuai; (16) Meḥefkheruf; (17) Ḥeruḥeriuatchf; (18) Åḥi; (19) Ånmutef; (20) Upuatu; (21) Ånpu; (22) Nā; (23) Nāur; (24) Nāṭesher; (25) Shema; (26) Maameref; (27) Nut; (28) Khnemu; (29) Utettefef; (30) Nehes.

hrui-t , IV, 693, daily list or register, diary, journal, day-book, ledger = Gr. ἐφημερίδες.

hru up renpi-t , day of the opening of the year, *i.e.*, New Year's Day.

hru utchā meṭu , day of the weighing of words, *i.e.*, the day of judgment.

hru mit , death day.

hru mestu , birthday;  , birthday of Osiris.

hru en Ån-mut-f , the name of the 19th day of the month.

hru en Åḥi 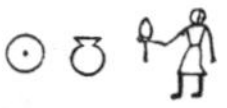, the name of the 18th day of the month.

hru en Åsår , the name of the 3rd day of the month.

hru en Upuatu , the name of the 20th day of the month.

Hru en utchā meṭṭu  , B.D. 1, 7, the day of judgment.

hru en netch snāā , a name of the 12th day of the month.

hru en ḥeb [illegible], day of the festival.

hru en Ḥem ba [illegible], the name of the 14th day of the month.

hru en Khnemu [illegible], the name of the 28th day of the month.

hru en sma-ta [illegible], day of union with earth, *i.e.*, the day of the burial.

hru en sekhenu [illegible], Rec. 33, 4, day of the manifestation of Mnevis.

hru en Shema [illegible], [illegible] [illegible], the name of the 25th day of the month.

hru en tep renpi-t [illegible], New Year's Day.

hru en tekh , A.Z. 1907, 46, "day of drunkenness"—a yearly festival.

hru nefu , Pap. 3024, 134, a windy day.

hru nefer , , a happy day, day of rejoicing, feast-day; 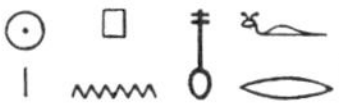, this happy day; , Pap. 3024, 68, "follow the happy day," *i.e.*, always be happy.

hru khennu , day of a water procession.

hru Sheṭ-f meṭu-f 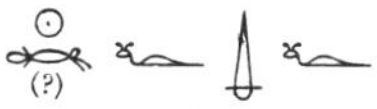, the name of the 16th day of the month.

hru qesen , an unlucky day, day of calamity.

hru Ṭeḥuti , festival day of Thoth, *i.e.*, the 1st day of the month.

hru ṭiu ḥeru renpit , the five days over the year, *i.e.*, the five epagomenal days, or the birthdays of Osiris, Horus, Set, Isis, and Nephthys, , , respectively.

heru .... 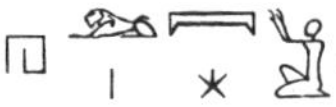, III, 141 ....

herp , , to be submerged, drowned, to sprinkle, to make wet; Copt. ϩωрп̄.

herp with , to let a matter sink deeply into the mind or heart.

herpiu , the submerged, the drowned.

Herpiu , Ṭuat VIII, the spirits of the drowned in the Ṭuat.

hern , Nav. Litanie, 69 ......

hernutȧ , field produce, herbs, vegetables.

hersh , Jour. As. 1908, 304, to be slow, patient; Copt. ϩорϣ̄.

herqaḥ , Alt. K. 662, a correction of Düm. H.I. I, 22, 21A.

herk , Rev. 12, 25, to embrace, to be girded or embraced; Copt. ϩωλϭ̄.

herk 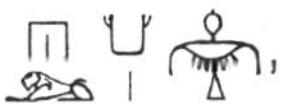, ring, bracelet; Copt. ⲁⲗⲁⲕ, ϩⲁⲗⲁⲕ.

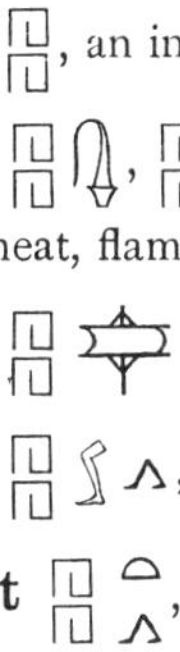

heh, an interjection, O.

heh, 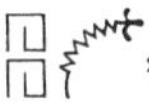, T. 34 = [illegible], M. 115, N. 132, heat, flame, fire.

heh, A.Z. 1905, 39, warm wind, breath, to breathe into.

heh, to go, to march.

heh-t, step; see 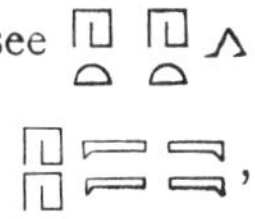

heh-ti (?) 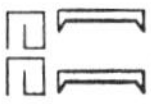, hall (?); see .

hehȧ , Anastasi V, 17, 3–5, to be deaf to good advice, to be inattentive.

hehȧ-t , inattention (?)

hes , Rev. 12, 68 = [illegible], dung.

hes , Rev. 13, 22 = [illegible], to march, to meet.

heshes , Rev. 7, 187, fire, flame.

hesenṭ , praise.

heq , Rev. 12, 18, to oppress, to inflict pain, to diminish.

Heqes , Ṭuat VI, a warder of the 6th Gate

heqes 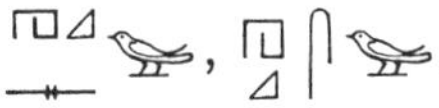, Peasant 251, to defraud.

heqsut-t , Nav. Litanie, 24, disappearance (?)

Hekȧ , U. 541, T. 297, a serpent-fiend in the Ṭuat = ; fem. .

Heker = Gr. Μανέρως (Brugsch).

Heker , the name of a festival; plur. .

Hekru , Rev. 13, 3, people of Heker.

Heker-t , U. 541, , T. 297, a serpent-fiend.

het , fear; Copt. ϩⲟϯ.

hett , , to run, to revolve.

hethet , , , to run, to revolve, to turn about; , "Circler"—a title of the Nile.

het (?) , to drill a hole in wood.

hetȧ , a boring tool, bradawl (?)

Hett , Denderah IV, 79, one of the four ape-gods who slew Āapep.

Hettȧ , Berg. I, 20, a singing ape-god.

hetȧ , a kind of herb.

hetȧ-t , Rev. 12, 66 . . . . . .

hetti-t , chisel, boring tool.

Hetu , an animal in the Ṭuat.

hetutu (?) , Ebers Pap. 102, 1, fire, flame.

hetb , Rec. 27, 86, sky.

hetem , , footstool; compare Heb. הֲדֹם.

heter-t , , a kind of collar, an ornament of dress.

hethen , Nav. Litanie, 69 . . . . .

Hethet , U. 615, the name of a god (?)

Hethti , Ṭuat I, one of the nine singing ape-gods.

heṭ , , IV, 1090, , , IV, 971, to strike, to trample upon, to vanquish, to suppress, to subdue.

heṭheṭ , IV, 710, , , Verbum I, 338, , to batter down, to beat small, to crush.

heṭ-t , Berl. Med. Pap. 21, 7 . . . . .

Heṭṭ , Rec. 30, 189, a god in the Ṭuat.

Heṭṭut , N. 623; see .

heṭṭut , N. 706, apes.

heṭem , Ebers Pap. 92, 9, to break, to shatter.

heṭmu , IV, 666, Rec. 8, 171, footstool; compare Heb. הֲדֹם.

heṭen , T. 332, , N. 623, , a plant used in making incense; var. .

Heṭennut , T. 332, , N. 623, a deity.

heṭer-t , , A.Z. 1908, 16, a pectoral, a pectoral amulet.

Hetchhetch , P. 173, , M. 738, 740, N. 940, a god.

hetchen , incense plant (?)

Ḥ

ḥ, has a sound similar to ח in Heb. פָּתַח = Arab. فتح, Syr. ܦܬܚ, Eth. ፈትሐ.

ḥ, , Rev., self; = ϩⲱⲱϥ.

ḥ, , U. 178, 537; see , to strike.

ḥ, Rev. 13, 52, profit; Copt. ϩⲏⲩ.

ḥe-t, lands, estates; see and ; Copt. ⲉⲓⲱϩⲉ, ⲓⲁϩ, ⲓⲟϩⲓ, ⲓⲱϩⲉ.

ḥe-t, Palermo Stele, , , , , , , , great house, temple; dual , , U. 538, , T. 305, two temples, double temple; plur. , U. 67, , T. 258, , , Rec. 31, 175, , , , , , , ; , U. 609.

ḥe-t, the hall of a tomb, the tomb itself; plur. , Rec. 13, 38.

ḥetu (?), men attached to the temple, temple servants.

Ḥetit (?), Mar. Cat. 452, a form of Ānqit (?)

Ḥe-t åau, "House of the Aged One," a temple of Memphis; , House of the Aged Prince; see **Ḥet-ser.**

Ḥe-t Åuti, a name of a shrine of Osiris.

Ḥe-t Åptt, the temple and town of Ombos.

Ḥe-t Åmen-t, "hidden temple," a name of the tomb and of the Ṭuat in general.

Ḥe-t ånes, , B.D. 17, 105, the house of the Ånes bandlet, the temple of Herakleopolis.

Ḥe-t åḥ-t, a sanctuary of Libya Mareotis containing the right leg of Osiris.

Ḥe-t Åsår, the Serapeum of Mareotis.

Ḥe-t Åsår-ḥemaga-t, a sanctuary of Osiris.

Ḥe-t åt, M. 207, , N. 668 . . . .

Ḥe-t åtu, T. 281, , N. 130 . . . .

ḥe-t āa-t, , , , U. 598, , N. 964, great house, palace, town, a name of the tomb and of the sky.

ḥe-t āa-t, law court; , IV, 1030, director of the Six Courts of Law; , the mansion of the nobles.

Ḥe-t āa-t ent ḥert, the mansion of the sky.

Ḥe-t āa-t Tem, the mansion of Tem of Heliopolis.

Ḥe-t ān : (1) the temple of Hathor at Denderah; (2) a temple-town in the Delta.

Ḥe-t ānkh , U. 550, T. 308, 310, : (1) the abode of ; (2) a temple of Osiris.

Ḥe-t ānkh-t , "house of life"—the college of learned men attached to the temple.

Ḥe-t ākhmiu , , temple of the statues of the gods; var. , B.D. (Nu) 141, 142, 16.

Ḥe-t āshemu , B.D. 142, 26, 148, 9, the chamber containing the statues of the gods.

ḥe-t uāb , "pure house," a name of the sky.

ḥe-t unuiti , chamber of the slaughterer, the sacrificial chamber in a tomb or temple.

ḥe-t ur-t , court of law, judgment hall; 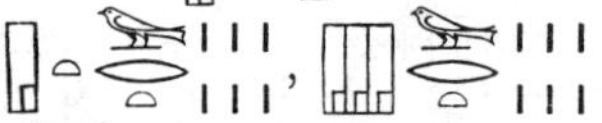, IV, 1036, 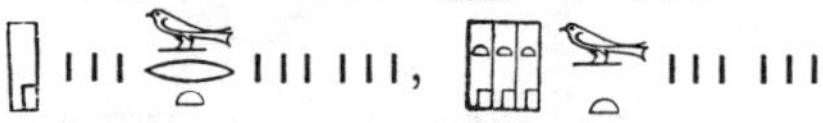, IV, 1039, , IV, 1071,  Rec. 31, 146, 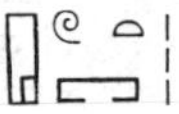 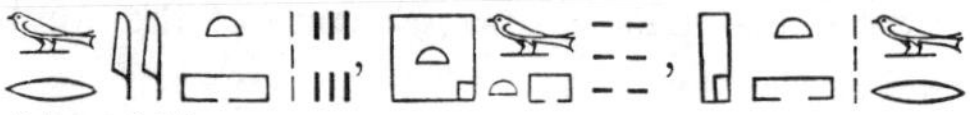 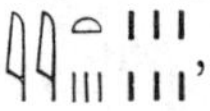, the six courts of justice.

Ḥe-t ur-t , the goddess of the great temple, *i.e.*, heaven or the sky.

Ḥe-t ur-t 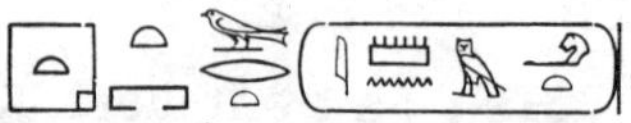, IV, 1130, a temple of Åmenemḥat in Upper Egypt.

Ḥe-t Uhem-ḥer , B.D. 123, the temple of Uhem-ḥer.

Ḥe-t User Menu , the temple of the goddess Åpit at Thebes.

Ḥe-t usekh ḥer 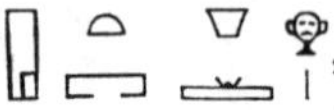, B.D. 28, 5, house of the Broad Face—a temple of Rā.

Ḥe-t utet-t 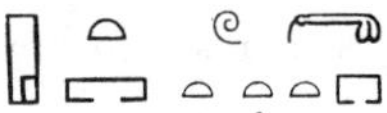, temple of the genetrix, *i.e.*, the goddess Åpit, at Karnak.

ḥe-t utet-t 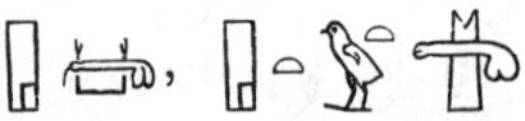, 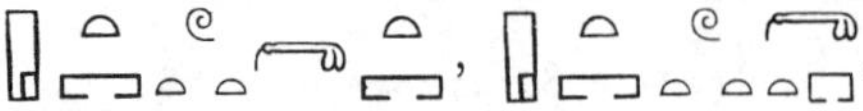, the house wherein one was begotten, the ancestral home.

Ḥe-t Ba 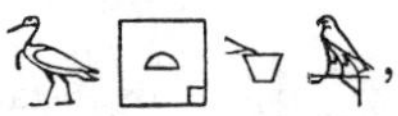, M. 743, "house of the soul," , Ani 1, 6, a name of heaven.

Ḥe-t Baiu  , the temple of souls at Mendes; var. 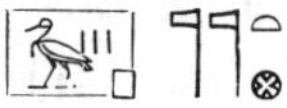, A.Z. 1871, 81.

Ḥe-t Ḥe-t Baiu 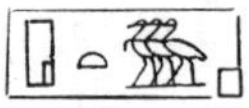, the temple of the temple of souls, *i.e.*, the temple of Apit at Thebes.

Ḥe-t Banban , Buch. 22; see **Ḥe-t Benben.**

Ḥe-t Bast , the temple of Bast at Bubastis.

Ḥe-t Båti , , house of the king of the North, *i.e.*, the Serapeum at Saïs.

Ḥe-t Benben-t  , the sanctuary at Heliopolis in which the Sun-god was worshipped under the form of a stone which resembled in shape a truncated obelisk.

Ḥe-t Benben 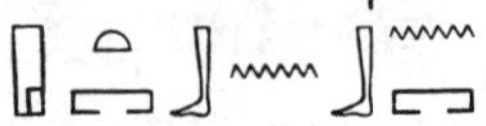, Ṭuat VII, the temple of the blazing body of Rā.

Ḥe-t Benu, , the temple of the Benu-bird at Heliopolis.

Ḥe-t Berber ; see **Ḥe-t Benben.**

ḥe-t betȧ, , the incense chamber.

Ḥe-t Mut ānkh, IV, 935, a temple in Upper Egypt.

Ḥe-t men-t, a sanctuary in Libya Mareotis; var.

ḥe-t menn-t, Buch. 57, incense chamber (?)

ḥe-t menkh, box or chamber for vestments.

Ḥe-t menkh, the Serapeum at Saïs.

Ḥe-t meritit, a temple in the 15th Nome of Lower Egypt.

Ḥe-t mesnekhtit, the chamber of the Meskhenit goddess; var.

ḥe-t nub, P. 589, , , , , "house of gold," a name of the sarcophagus and of the chamber in which it stood.

ḥe-t nub, "house of gold," *i.e.*, a goldsmith's workshop, the goldsmiths' quarter of the city.

ḥetut nub, smelting-houses, gold refineries.

Ḥe-t Nefer-t, a temple (?) in Hermopolis.

Ḥe-t nemm-t, the Serapeum of Letopolis.

ḥe-t nemes, B.D. 78, 20, the chamber of the Nemes crown.

Ḥe-t ent ḥeḥ en renput, the temple of hundreds of thousands of years.

Ḥe-t ent Gemḥeru, B.D. 58, 3, 108, 3, temple of a group of gods.

ḥe-t neter, temple; plur. , , Rec. 26, 236.

Ḥe-t neter en Ȧsȧr Ḥep, the Serapeum of Ṣakkârah.

Ḥe-t neter enti Ḥāp-res, the Serapeum in the Nome Prosopites.

Ḥe-t Renrenui, Rec. 30, 201, a temple of a pair of gods.

ḥe-t rekhes (?), slaughter-house.

Ḥe-t erṭu, temple of the emissions of Osiris.

Ḥe-t sma (?) (Ḥe-t rekhes?), Rec. 31, 12, the kitchen of Horus.

Ḥe-t ḥeb Sept-t, temple of the Sothis festival.

ḥe-t ḥemag-t, Buch. 52, laboratory.

ḥe-t ḥem', the linen closet of the temple or palace.

ḥe-t Ḥenu, , the chamber of the Ḥenu boat of Seker.

Ḥe-t-Ḥer, U. 574, N. 37, 968, T. 43, P. 89, M. 52, , , , , , , , , , the goddess Hathor; , Thes. 801, the seven Hathors; Copt. ϩⲁⲑⲱⲣ, ⲁⲑⲱⲣ.

Ḥe-t-Ḥeru-Sekhmit 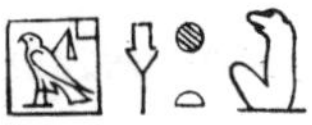, the goddesses Hathor and Sekhmit.

ḥe-t ḥesmen 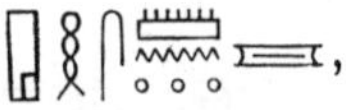, the chamber containing the bath of natron in which the dead to be mummified were immersed.

Ḥe-t ḥetch uru (?) 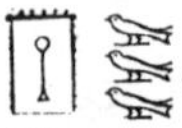, U. 469, T. 220, P. 184, M. 294, , N. 897 . . . . . .

Ḥe-t VI em Åthi-taui  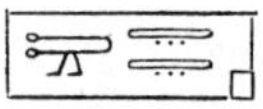, B.M. 255, the court of the Six in Åthi-Taui, south of Memphis.

Ḥe-t Såp 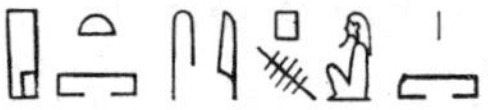, the temple of Såp.

Ḥe-t sutenit en Rā 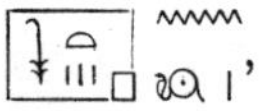, a temple of Rā in the Nome Gynaecopolites.

Ḥe-t ser  U. 296, P. 656, M. 762; 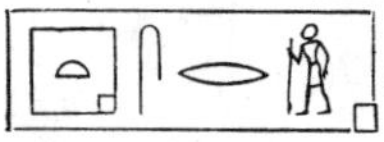, P. 186, 758, M. 124, N. 216, 533, 646; 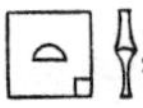, T. 271; , N. 122; , Buch. 50; , B.D. 153A, 17, a famous temple of the Sun-god in Heliopolis.

Ḥe-t Serqit , P. 665, 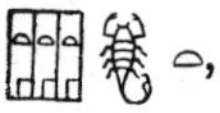, P. 508, a temple of the goddess Serqit.

Ḥe-t sekh-t (?) 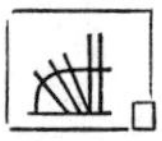 Mar. Kar. 42, 30, the temple of the hunting net.

Ḥe-t Sekha-Ḥeru  , a temple of Apis in Libya Mareotis.

Ḥe-t Sekhun-t , a temple in the Metelite Nome.

Ḥe-t Sekhemu 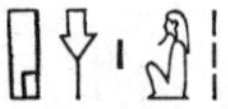, "house of the Powers," the capital of the 7th Nome of Upper Egypt.

Ḥet-t Sekhmit 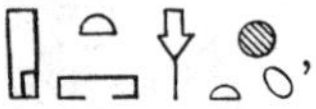, a temple of the goddess Sekhmit in Memphis.

Ḥe-t stau Rā-kher-āḥa 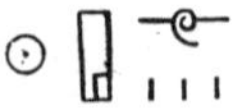 , Ṭuat VI, a chamber containing a symbol of Rā in the form of a wing.

Ḥe-t shāt 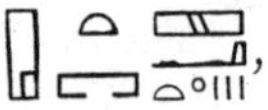, Rec. 19, 19, a fortress of Rameses III.

Ḥe-t shen-t 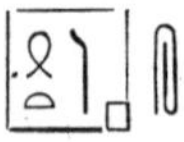, M. 209, N. 672, the name of a temple, the Labyrinth (?)

Ḥe-t qa , Metternich Stele 83 . . . . .

Ḥe-t ka 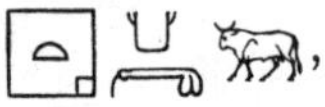, U. 554, T. 303, the abode of a sacred bull.

Ḥe-t Ka 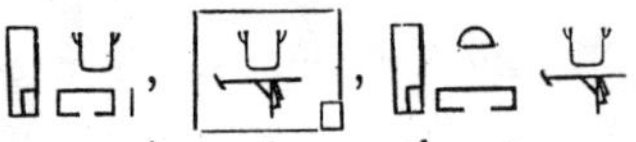, the KA-chapel, or portion of a tomb set apart for the dwelling of the KA.

Ḥe-t ka Seker , the chapel of the KA of the Death-god.

Ḥe-t kau Neb-t ertcher 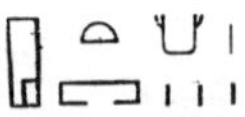 , B.D. 141, 148,  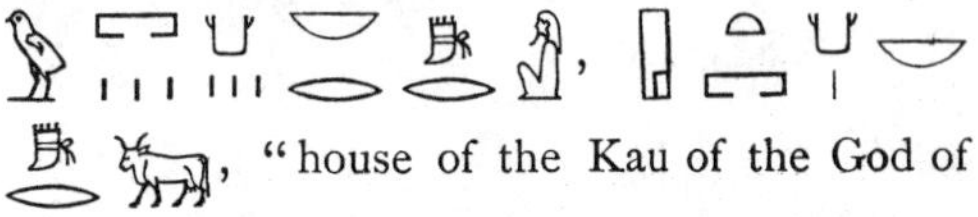, "house of the Kau of the God of the Universe," the name of one of the seven divine Cows.

Ḥe-t ṭa-t ānkh , a temple of Thothmes III at Thebes.

Ḥe-t ṭuau Rā , Ṭuat VI, a temple of the Sun-god in the Ṭuat.

Ḥe-t Ṭebutiu-t 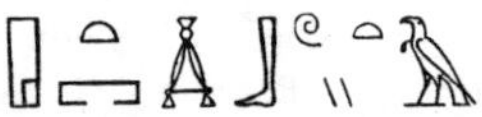 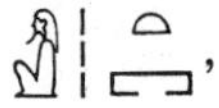, the abode of the gods who embalm.

Ḥe-t ṭemṭ-t Rā 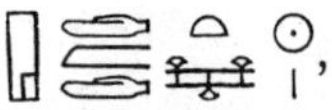, Ṭuat VI, a chamber with an image of Rā in the form of a man.

Ḥe-t Ṭesheru , B.D. 142, 27, 148, 9, the temple of the red devils, followers of Set.

Ḥe-t Ṭeṭ , Rec. 3, 51, the famous chamber of the Ṭeṭ of Osiris at Abydos.

ḥe-t 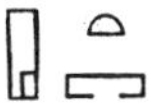, section of a book, chapter, strophe, stanza; plur. , 1st strophe; , B.D. 172, 9th strophe; , 1st chapter; 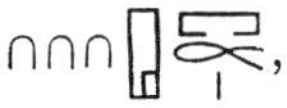, Ȧmen. 27, 7, thirty chapters; compare Syr. ܒܝܬܐ, Arab. بيت.

ḥa , L.D. III, 140c, , IV, 96, 658, Peasant 36, a particle, O that! Would that! , O that it were possible! , Peasant 43, Dream Stele 34, Would that I had! , Metternich Stele 216, a cry of desire; and see Golénischeff, Hammâmât 10, 44.

ḥa, ḥai , T. 51, , P. 160, , T. 387, , Rec. 36, 78, , B.D. 172, 8, , B.D. 172, 13, to rejoice; var. .

ḥau, ḥaiu , N. 996, mourner; plur.  , B.D. 1, 15, men who recite the praises of the dead at funerals, criers, mourners.

ḥa , Palermo Stele, wall.

ḥa-t 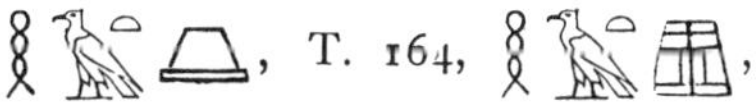 T. 164, P. 607, 609, 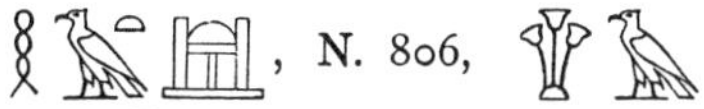 N. 806, 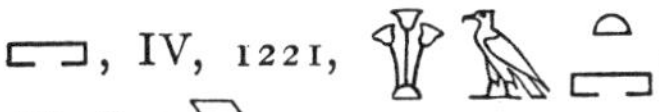 IV, 1221, Rec. 30, 72, 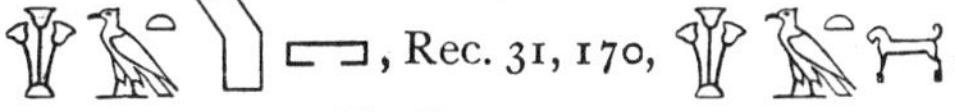 Rec. 31, 170, Pap. 3024, 53, , tomb, grave, bier, funeral bed, tomb buildings, coffin, sarcophagus.

ḥa 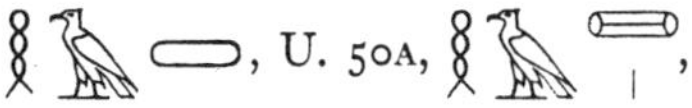 U. 50A, cake, bread-cake.

ḥa-t 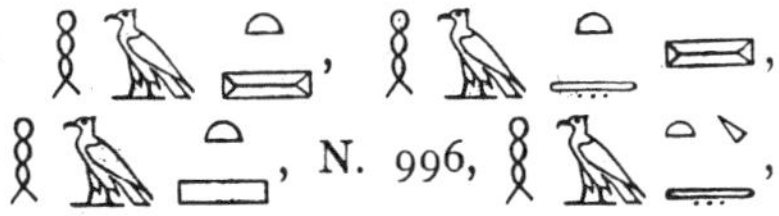 Methen, N. 996, Décrets 73, 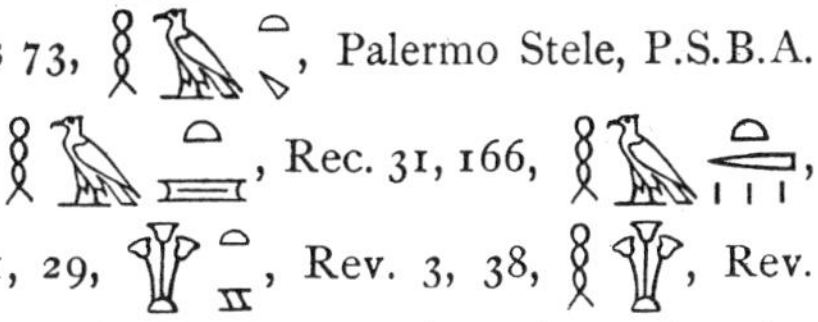 Palermo Stele, P.S.B.A. 12, 87, Rec. 31, 166, Rec. 31, 29, Rev. 3, 38, Rev. 12, 96, land, field, estate, park, territory, domain, farm, an arura of land; Copt. ⲓⲱϩⲓ, ⲓⲟϩⲓ, ⲉⲓⲱϩⲉ.

ḥa, ḥau , a dweller on the irrigated land, especially a peasant, farm-labourer, vassal; plur. 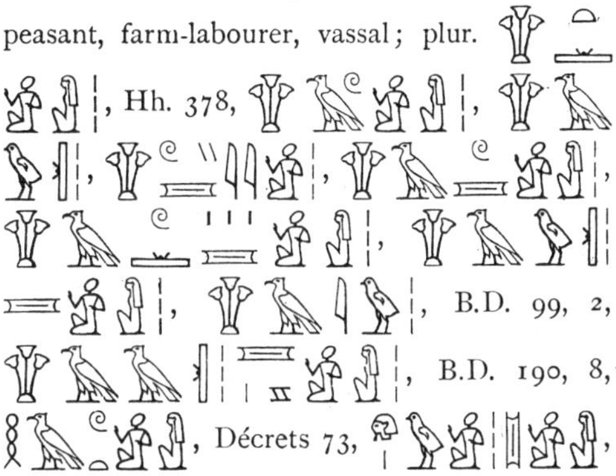 Hh. 378, B.D. 99, 2, B.D. 190, 8, Décrets 73, peasants in general (?)

ḥau, P. 702, followers, servants.

ḥa, to go back, to retreat, to set behind.

ḥaḥa, IV, 994, to go back, to retreat.

ḥa , behind, at the back of; plur. , those who are behind or at the back of anything, apostates, sinners.

ḥaȧ  N. 748 = U. 600, , behind.

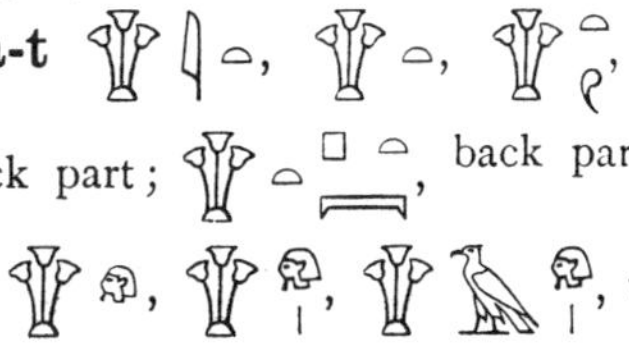

ḥaȧ-t, behind, the back part; back part of the sky.

ḥa, the back of the head, or of the neck.

ḥai , Love Songs 6, 1, the back of the neck.

Ḥa-f-em-ḥa-f , U. 648, T. 279, the god with the back of the neck in front; see 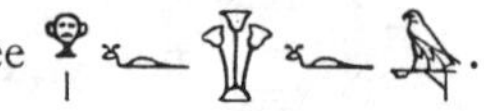.

ḥa, ḥa-t 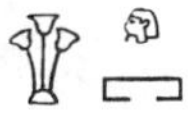, Ḥeruemḥeb 20, IV, 499, 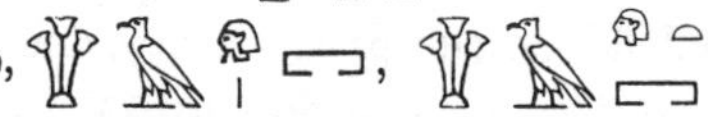, a back hall, a place behind, outside, place to hide behind; 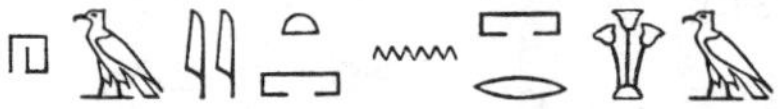 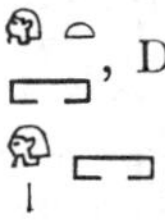, Dream Stele 22; **er ḥa** , outside.

ḥa , B.D. (Saïte) 97, 4, to act as a protector behind someone.

Ḥau-kar , U. 416, 434, , T. 237, 248, the guardian gods of the shrine of Osiris.

ḥa tep re , Ṭuat III . . . .

ḥa 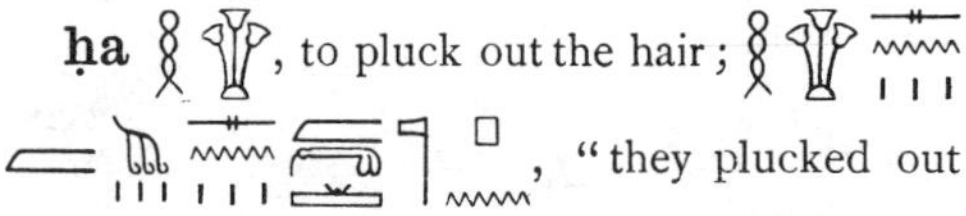, to pluck out the hair; "they plucked out their hair before this god."

ḥau 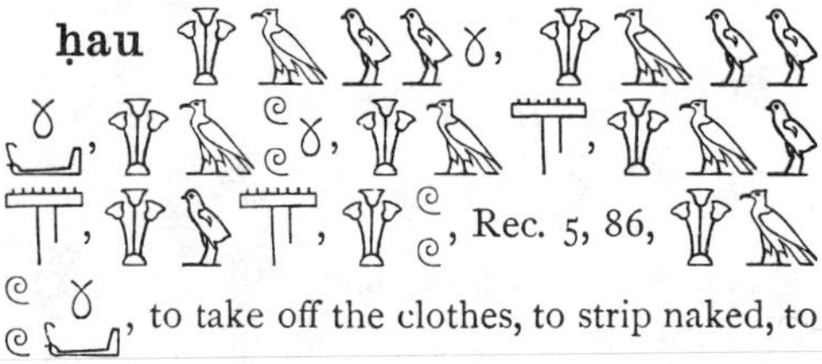, Rec. 5, 86, to take off the clothes, to strip naked, to undress, to be naked; Copt. ϩⲏⲩ in ⲕⲁϩⲏⲩ.

ḥai 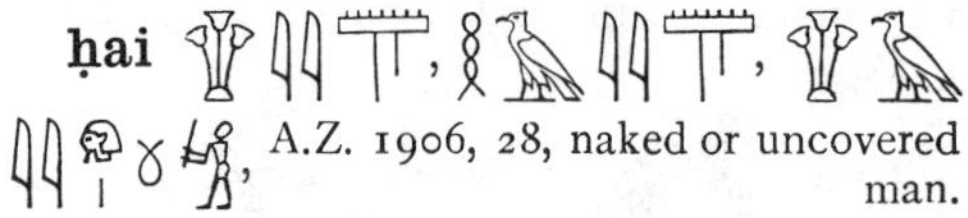, A.Z. 1906, 28, naked or uncovered man.

Ḥai 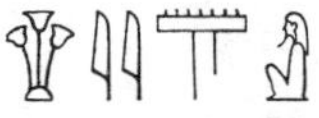, the naked god.

ḥau, ḥaiu 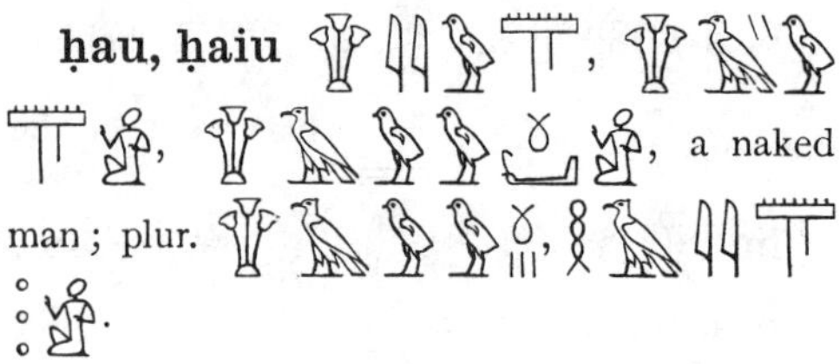, a naked man; plur.

ḥait 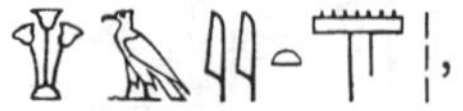, nudity, nakedness.

ḥa-tu (ḥaut?) , Peasant 243, nakedness.

ḥa-ti 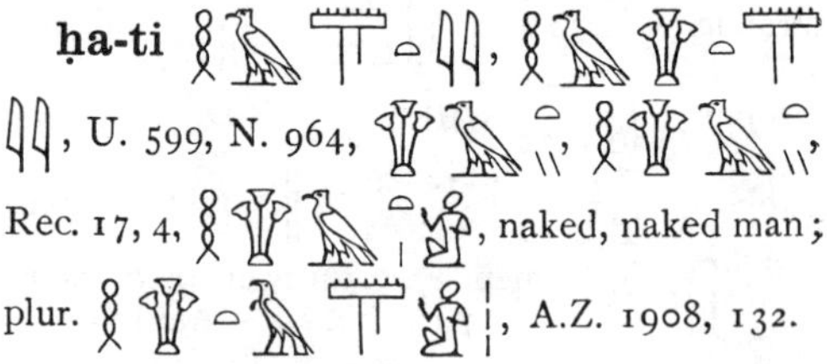, U. 599, N. 964, Rec. 17, 4, naked, naked man; plur. A.Z. 1908, 132.

ḥa-t 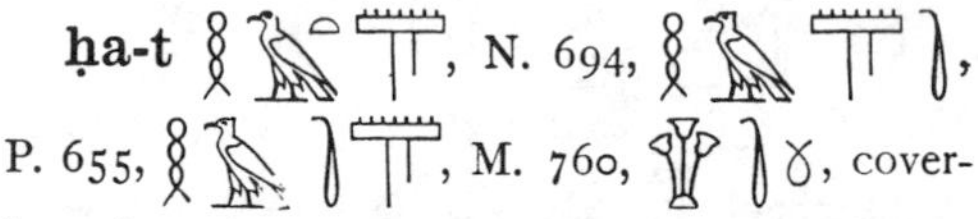, N. 694, P. 655, M. 760, covering, obscurity.

ḥa , P. 437, M. 650, cap, bonnet, head covering.

ḥai[t] , Nav. Lit. 94, head cloth.

ḥau , cloth, a covering.

ḥa-tȧ 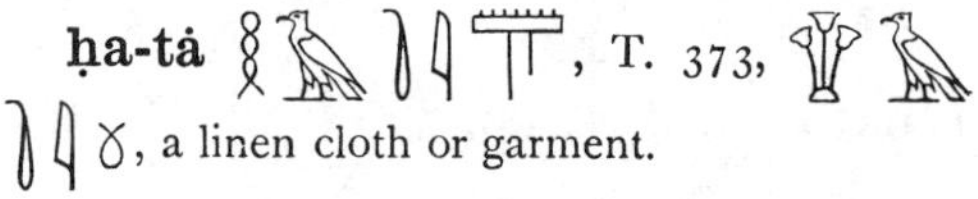, T. 373, a linen cloth or garment.

ḥa-ti 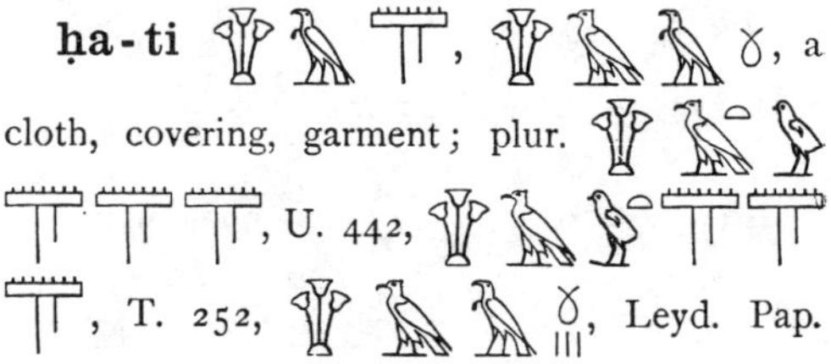, a cloth, covering, garment; plur. U. 442, T. 252, Leyd. Pap. 14, 4, garments; Copt. ϩⲟⲉⲓⲧⲉ.

ḥa-ti 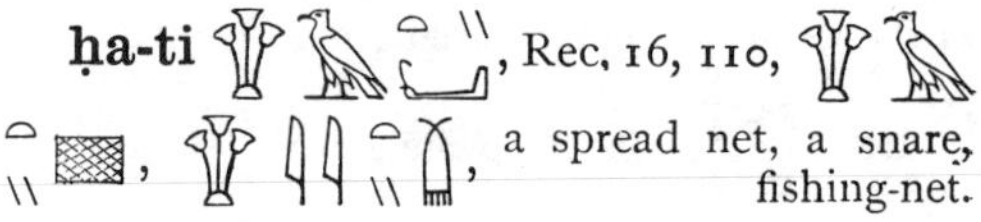, Rec. 16, 110, a spread net, a snare, fishing-net.

ḥa, ḥau 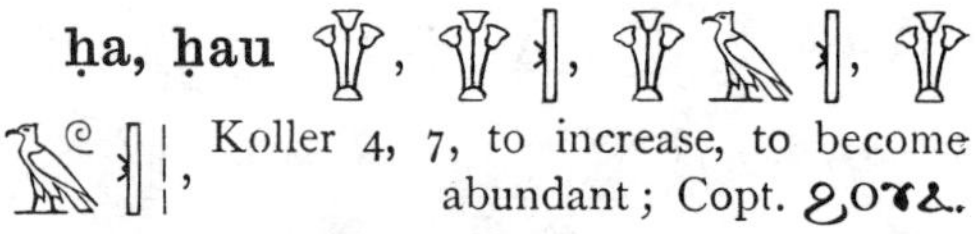, Koller 4, 7, to increase, to become abundant; Copt. ϩⲟⲩⲟ.

ḥau , Åmen. 6, 15, 9, 14, increase, increment, an addition to something, abundance, superfluity, superabundance, something useful or profitable, advantage, benefit ;  , more than this ; Copt. ϩⲏⲩ, ϩⲟⲩⲟ.

ḥau with **m**  [illegible], in addition to ;  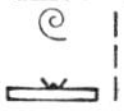, there is nothing superior to [Literature].

Ḥau , Rec. 30, 70, a group of gods.

ḥa , club, mace, battle-axe (?)

ḥa-t , Rec. 16, 110, lance, spear.

ḥaiuti , Tombos Stele 8, cuttings, slaughterings.

ḥa , P.S.B.A. 14, 232, to seize, to strike, to destroy, to fight ; , Nav. Litanie 53, "fighters" (?)

ḥai 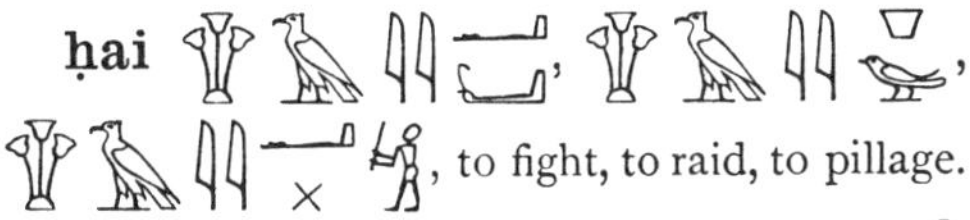, to fight, to raid, to pillage.

ḥai-t , Rec. 27, 228, grasp, seizure, war, fight, feud, strife.

ḥaiu , advantage, benefit, exceedingly.

ḥa , filth, waste, evil thing, evil ; plur. 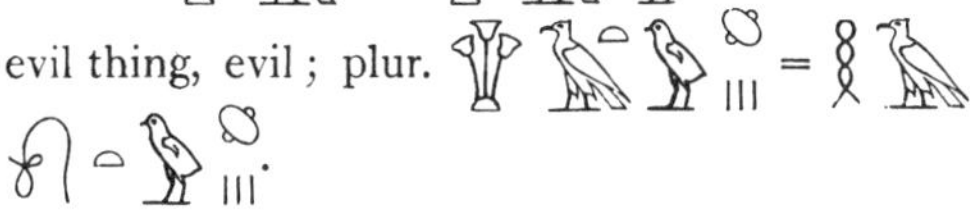.

ḥaa-t , P. 477, filth =  [illegible], N. 1264.

ḥa-it , Ebers Pap. 72, 1, 87, 11, 91, 4, , some foul excretion, pus (?)

ḥaḥa , Ebers Pap. 101, 3, some foul excretion from the body, a kind of disease (?)

ḥa-tt 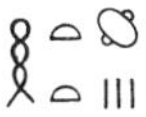, evil or shameful deeds.

ḥa-t ȧb , Pap. 3024, 57, grief, sorrow.

Ḥa-ḥer ; see .

Ḥa-ḥer , Nesi-Ȧmsu 32, 16, B.D. 145, XIX, 72, "Foul-face"—the name of a fiend and also of a form of Āapep.

ḥa-t , a second of time.

ḥa, ḥai 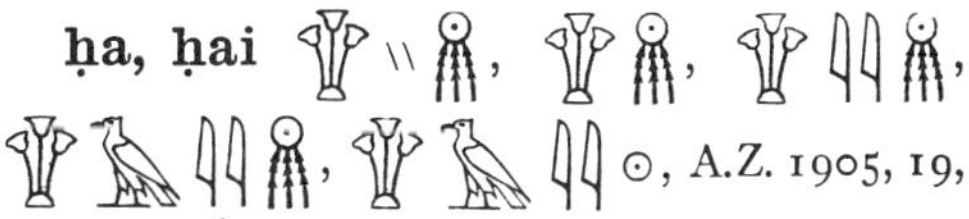, A.Z. 1905, 19, Hymn to Ȧmen 7, 22, luminary, the sun, light-giver.

ḥai-t , light, radiance, brilliance.

Ḥai-ti , the two light-givers, *i.e.*, the Sun and Moon.

ḥa-t 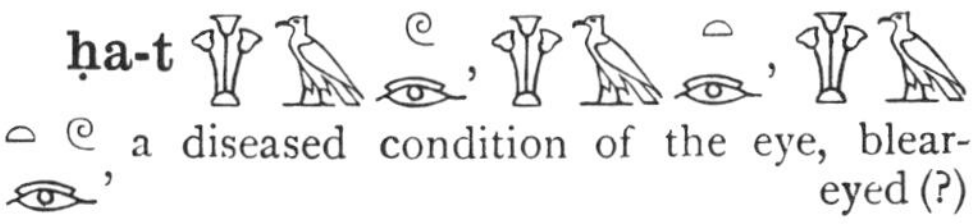, a diseased condition of the eye, blear-eyed (?)

ḥa-ti 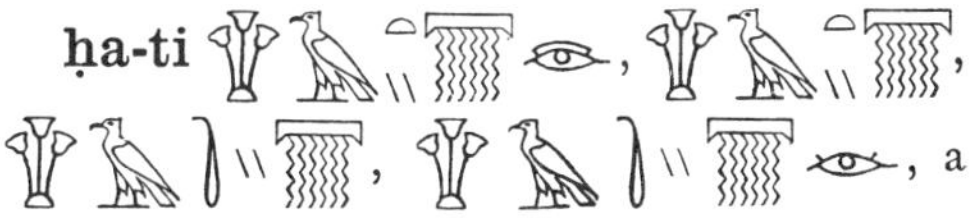, a man suffering from chronic rheum in the eyes.

Ḥati , the tear from the eye of Isis that fell into the Nile and caused the Inundation. The "Night of the Drop," , is the original of the Arabic "Lêlat al-Nuḳṭah," which was observed on the 11th of Paoni (June 17).

ḥaiu , rain, flood, storm ; Copt. ϩⲟⲩ, ϩⲟⲟⲩ, ϩⲱⲟⲩ.

ḥa-t 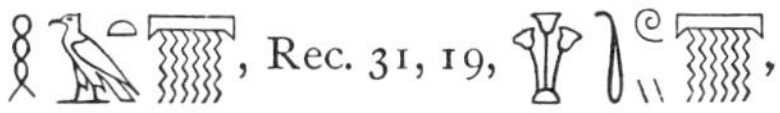, Rec. 31, 19, water from the sky, rain ; see .

ḥa, ḥai , Peasant 158,  [illegible], to sail, to cross over.

ḥa, ḥai , papyrus.

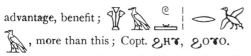

Ḥa , M. 699, 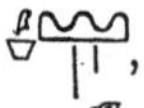, N. 1320, 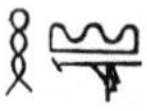, Hymn to Åmen 17; see  .

Ḥa-t , P. 536, a god.

ḥa-t , P. 475, N. 1262, a kind of bird.

ḥa 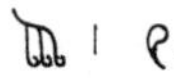, Rev. 12, 39, face; Copt. ϩⲟ.

Ḥait 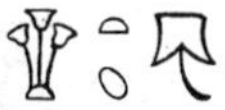, the goddess Tefnut.

ḥa-t 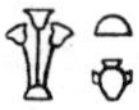, Rec. 33, 32, heart = ; plur. .

ḥati , heart, affliction (?) heart-ache (?)

ḥa-t , IV, 650, the front or forepart of anything, the beginning, the breast, the advance-guard of an army; , U. 128, the forequarter joint; , IV, 1116, first of the boats, head of the navy; , your breasts to the darkness; , path leading to a door; , Rec. 21, 99; Copt. ϩⲏ.

ḥa sep , 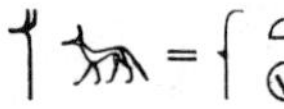, the first year of a king's reign; Copt. ⲁⲥⲫⲟⲩⲓ, ⲁⲥⲫⲱⲟⲩⲓ of Daniel i, 21; see Beiträge (Sethe) III, 94.

ḥa-t  with **m** , in front of;  , IV, 344, those who were in the beginning, ancestors; 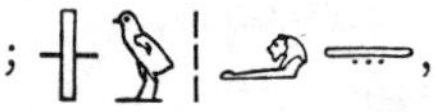, IV, 617, those who live in front of [their] land; , P. 314.

ḥa-t with **r** , before; , from the beginning to the end.

ḥa-t  with **kher** , of olden time, in the beginning.

ḥa ā , the beginning, the first part; , "the first of the chapters of Per-em-hru";  , "the first of the chapters [treating of] divine matters"; , existing in the beginning.

ḥa-ti ā , the first one or thing; 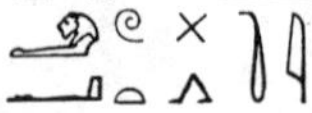, marching in front.

ḥa-ti ā [illegible] [illegible], A.Z. 1906, 98, [illegible], the chief of a Nome, prince, archon (in late times); plur. [illegible], IV, 456, [illegible], IV, 436, [illegible], IV, 973, [illegible].

ḥa-āu [illegible], a man in the advance-guard; plur. [illegible], Thes. 1483.

ḥatt ā [illegible], chieftainess, princess.

Ḥa ā ur [illegible], title of the high-priest of Edfû.

ḥa tep (?) [illegible], Rev. 11, 146 = [illegible], nobles.

ḥati [illegible] [illegible], B.D. 28, 7, [illegible] [illegible] (late form), heart, mind, will, disposition; plur. [illegible], U. 430, T. 246, P. 20, [illegible], A.Z. 1873, 62, [illegible], Israel Stele 4, [illegible], B.D. 124, 10; see also [illegible]; Copt. ϩⲏⲧ.

ḥati, heartless, timid, without sense, stupid; , Mar. Karn. 53, 29, despairing, timid; , Ȧmen. 9, 7, a sweet disposition.

ḥatu, breast of an animal.

ḥa-ti, what is in front, the best, the finest, the forepart.

ḥa-ti, the foremost man.

ḥau-ti, Ȧmen. 17, 2, , IV, 875, , the first one, the foremost one, the finest or best thing of a class; , the chief captain; plur. , leaders, chiefs, captains.

ḥau-ti, A.Z. 1873, 75, 1905, 27, , Rec. 1, 77, 83, 32, 177, Culte Divin 109, , the two dominant aspects of Rā or Ȧmen.

Ḥat-meḥit, the consort of of Mendes; , B.D. 110, 1.

Ḥa-khau (?), Annales I, 84, one of the 36 Dekans; Copt. ϩⲧϩⲧ.

Ḥa-tchat, Tomb Seti I, Ram. IV, Denderah II, 10, one of the 36 Dekans; Copt. ϩⲧϩⲧ.

ḥa, a kind of bread.

ḥa [ ], Nȧstasen Stele 38, a full-grown ox.

ḥa, a kind of very fine linen.

ḥa-t, an amulet (Lacau).

ḥa-t, Ȧmen. 12, 2, canal.

ḥa-t, P. 604, , Rec. 30, 68, Shipwreck 4, Rec. 20, 40, , IV, 1077, B.D. 99, 12, the towing rope of a boat, as opposed to , the stern rope; plur. , Rec. 31, 31, (?), , IV, 60, "tow-rope of the South," a title.

ḥa-t, Rec. 20, 42, the forepart of a boat.

ḥatt, T. 382, , oil of the finest quality; plur. , Ebers Pap. 92, 6, , finest ānti oil; , finest cedar oil; , finest oil of Manu; , finest Libyan oil.

ḥaȧ, enmity, war, fight.

ḥaȧu, calamity.

ḥaȧu, back of the neck.

Ḥaȧs, B.D. 40, 2, 3, a title of Āapep.

ḥaā-t, U. 441, , T. 252, fighting, raid, seizure; , pillaging, raiding.

ḥaāit, Rec. 27, 228, , Rec. 36, 210, , Leyd. Pap. 3, 11, , fighting, war, quarrel, enmity, fighters.

ḥaā-ut, Rec. 27, 228, fight, fighters.

ḥaāā , Peasant 58 = .

ḥaāā (?) , to examine into, enquire into, spy into.

ḥai-t 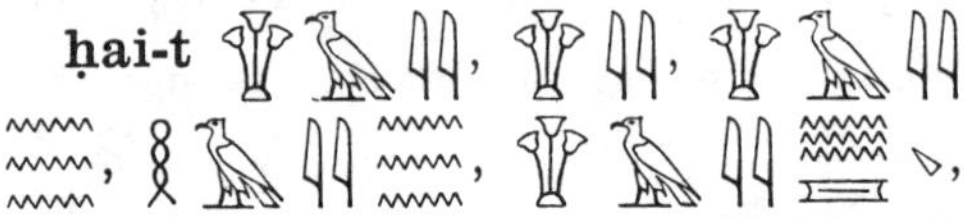, Rec. 21, 14, Åmen. 4, 13, 10, 10, , the Nile-flood, Inundation ; var. 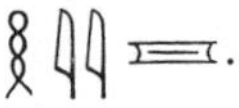.

Ḥai 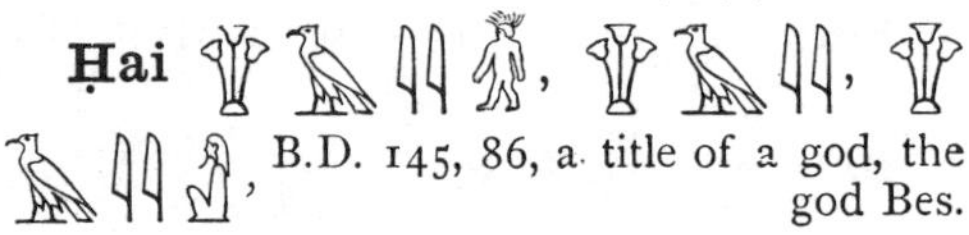, B.D. 145, 86, a title of a god, the god Bes.

Ḥait , A.Z. 1873, 75, 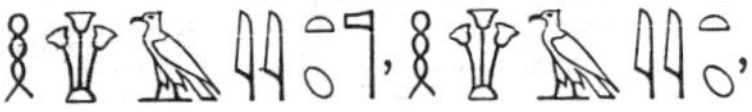, a goddess.

Ḥai 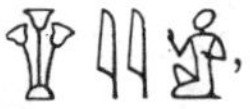, A.Z. 1906, 130, a title of a priest.

ḥai , to weep, to sorrow, to mourn, to lament, grief, sorrow, crying.

ḥai-ti , professional mourner, crying man or woman ; plur. 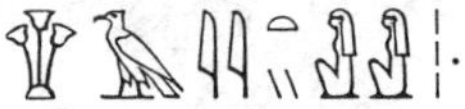.

Ḥait , Ṭuat III, one of four weeping-goddesses.

Ḥait 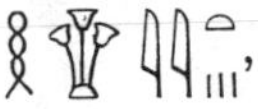, Ṭuat XI, a group of four weeping-goddesses.

Ḥai- (ui or **ti)** , B.D. (Saïte) 1, 5, a pair of weeping-gods (or goddesses).

Ḥai-ti , , the two weepers, *i.e.*, Isis and Nephthys.

ḥai-t , Hearst Pap. 11, 5, a kind of disease.

ḥai , to fly (of sand, dust, etc.).

ḥai-t 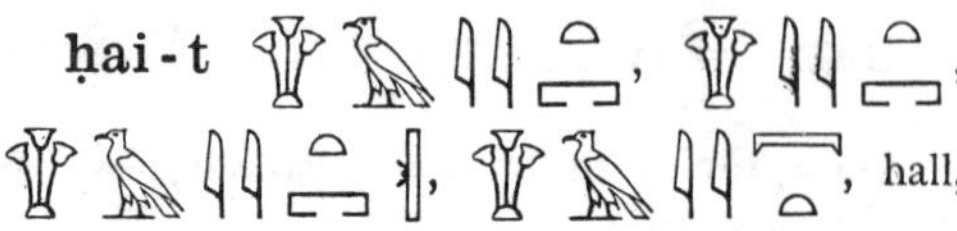, hall, vaulted chamber, sky, the vault of heaven.

Ḥai-t-enth-Åāḥ 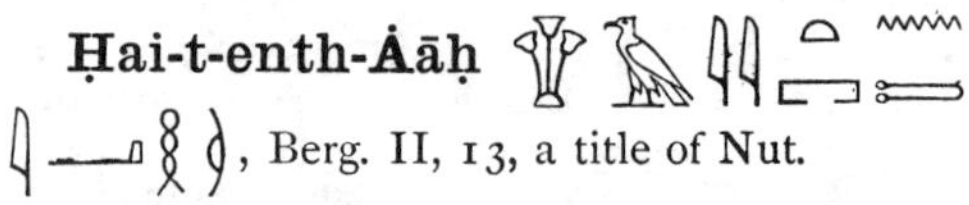, Berg. II, 13, a title of Nut.

Ḥaika , a god, form of Rā (?)

ḥau (?) 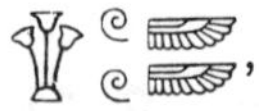, to fly, wings.

ḥatt 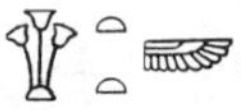, flight of birds.

ḥau , Anastasi I, 26, 6, part of a chariot, or a bit of its furniture.

Ḥau , generator, a title of the Sun-god.

ḥaukh-t , 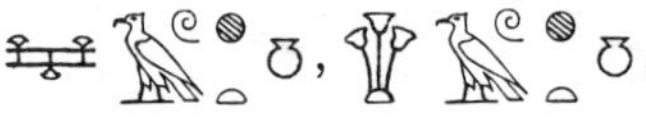, a wine bowl, flask, wine (?)

Ḥauq 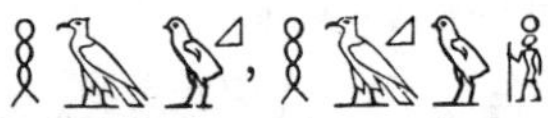, the god of the 9th day of the month.

ḥab , a fish destined for a feast.

ḥab , T. 82, , M. 236, N. 614, a goose destined for a feast.

ḥabi 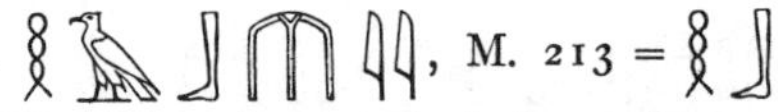, M. 213 = , N. 684, to keep a festival, to observe a day of rejoicing.

ḥabi-t , Rec. 3, 54, cupboard, recess.

ḥabāti (?) , evil doer, a harmful being or thing.

ḥabs , a festival.

ḥap , Rec. 31, 16, 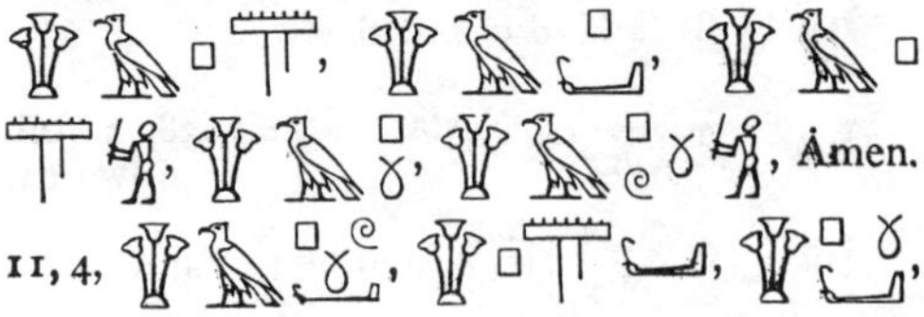, Åmen. 11, 4,

, to cover over, to hide, to conceal, to envelop, to shroud; Copt. ϩⲱⲡ.

ḥap-t, cover, covering; plur., things hidden, or covered, or concealed.

ḥapu, IV, 834, decaying walls.

Ḥapu-àutitt, Berg. II, 12, the goddess who hid the excrementa of the dead in the Ṭuat.

Ḥap-seshemu-s, Ṭuat VIII, the name of a Circle.

Ḥap-tcheser, Denderah III, 24, one of seven divine disks.

Ḥap-tchesert-s, Thes. 31, the goddess of the 12th hour of the day.

Ḥap-tchet-f, "hider of his body," the name of a god.

ḥapt, to embrace; see .

ḥap-ti, Rec. 8, 133, , spy.

Ḥapṭre, B.D. 125, III, 13, the god in whose temple the Sāḥu and Cat talked; var. .

ḥam, to snare fish or birds, to fish, to act as a fowler; see also .

ḥamu, Pap. 3024, 94, fisherman, fowler, hunter; plur., Rec. 27, 220.

ḥami, to shine.

ḥan-t, mistress, lady = .

Ḥanā-àru-ḥer-ḥer, Nesi-Àmsu 32, 50, the name of a devil and of a crocodile-headed serpent.

Ḥa-nebu, T. 275, P. 28, M. 38, 142, L.D. III, 16A, Rec. 32, 68, N. 68, IV, 930, Rec. 22, 2, N. 648, Rec. 6, 117, N. 98, Reise, 24, Thes. 943, A.Z. 1910, 117, A.Z. 1865, 26, Rec. 13, 127, Tombos Stele 4, Stele of Ptolemy I, a very ancient name of the inhabitants of the islands of the Mediterranean, later the Ionians (Ἰάονες); the Ionian Sea; Heb. יָוָן, Babyl. , Assyr. , Pers. , Sus. (Behist. I, 15, I, 11), Copt. ⲟⲩⲉⲓⲛⲓⲛ.

Ḥa-neb (?), Rec. 19, 22, a Greek of Naucratis.

ḥanr , Love Songs 2, 12, Hymn to Nile 4, 7, 16, 5–8, , Fest. 117, 13, 14, , Rec. 30, 216, to have a care about something, to be troubled or anxious or disturbed about a matter, to wish for something, a wish, O that! Would that!

ḥanr , to grieve, to be sorrowful, to care, anxiety.

ḥanrr , A.Z. 1905, 29, squint (?)

ḥanreg , Rec. 36, 6, to rejoice; Copt. ϩⲗⲟϭ.

ḥanrega , Anastasi I, 13, 8, to be dismayed.

ḥar , Rev. 12, 31, head.

Ḥar , Berg. I, 7, one of the four grandsons of Horus.

ḥarr-t , Mission 13, 50, flowers, bloom; see 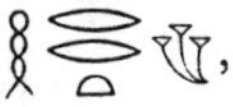, 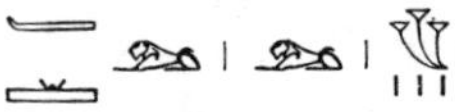; Copt. ϩⲣⲏⲣⲉ.

ḥaruru , Hearst Pap. 13, 4 . . . .

Ḥarpugakasharshabaiu   , B.D. 164, 5, a Nubian title of Rā (?)

Ḥarti , B.D. 163, 2, a god of .

ḥaḥaṭu 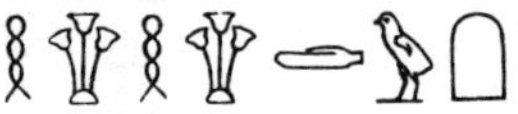, pits, caverns, furnaces, ovens.

ḥas , Rec. 6, 151; see  .

ḥasit , a kind of plant.

ḥasmen , natron; Copt. ϩⲟⲥⲙ̄.

ḥaq , Gol. 12, 96, , , Rec. 4, 130, , , , Rev. 12, 18, to rob, to plunder, to take spoil or prisoners, to capture, to seize.

ḥaq ḥaq-t , to seize spoil.

ḥaqa ḥati , to oppress, to afflict; Copt. ϩⲱϫ.

ḥaq-t , IV, 659, , IV, 1094, , Rec. 20, 40, , , plunder, spoil, booty.

ḥaqu , , Mar. Karn. 53, 37, captured prisoners; 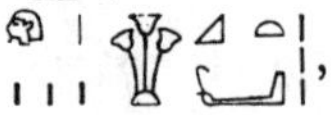, Thes. 1296, best of the captives.

ḥaqu [illegible], thief, robber, plunderer; plur. [illegible].

Ḥaqau [illegible], B.D. 99, 23, [illegible] (Saïte), a bolt-peg in the magical boat.

ḥaqar-t [illegible], stone; compare Arab. حَجَر.

ḥaqr [illegible], hungry man; see heqr [illegible]; Copt. ϩⲟⲕⲉⲣ.

ḥak [illegible], T. 309 = [illegible], to enchant, to cast a spell on, to bewitch.

ḥak-t [illegible], A.Z. 1875, 29, a word used in geometry, segment of a field.

ḥag [illegible]; see [illegible] [illegible]; Copt. ϩⲗⲟϭ.

ḥagg ,
Culte 241, to complain (?) make a petition (?)

ḥagag-t , petition (?)

ḥag , Peasant 58 . . . .

ḥatȧ 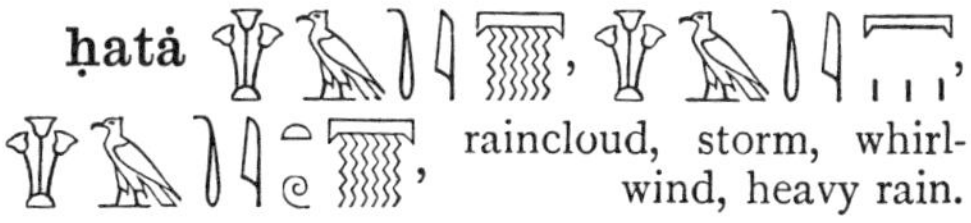, raincloud, storm, whirlwind, heavy rain.

ḥatuit , rain.

Ḥatȧba (?) , Rec. 21, 98, a queen of Cyprus.

Ḥat-ti , L.D. IV, 85, a form of Bes.

ḥatef (?) 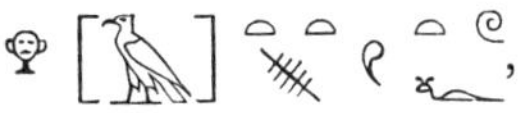, Rev. 14, 33 = Copt. ϩⲓⲱⲧϥ.

ḥatsh 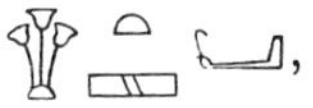, to cast a net.

ḥathi 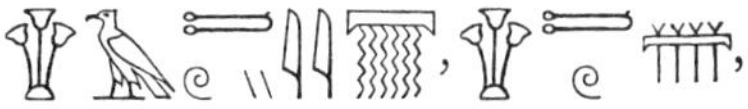, rainstorm.

ḥaṭ , to fish, fishing net.

ḥaṭ 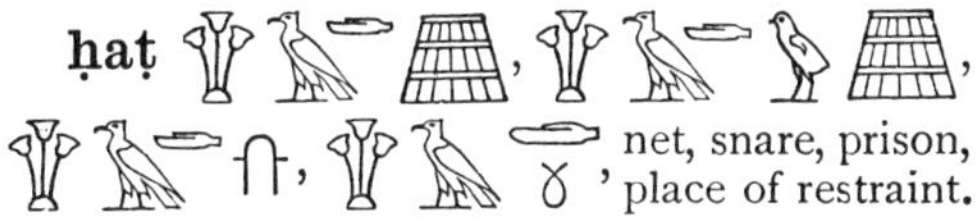 net, snare, prison, place of restraint.

ḥaṭ 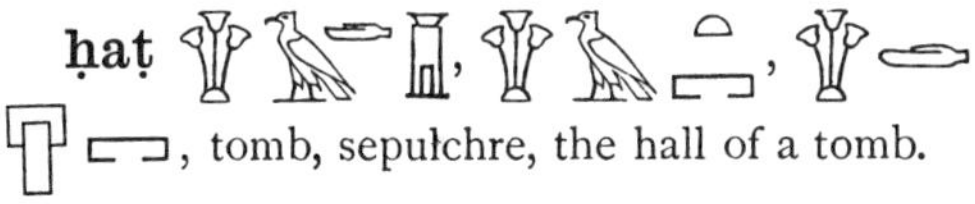, tomb, sepulchre, the hall of a tomb.

Ḥaṭ-t , a pit of fire in the Ṭuat. The names of the five pits (Division XI) were: Ketits, Ḥanṭus, Neknit-s, Nemtit-set, Sefu-s, 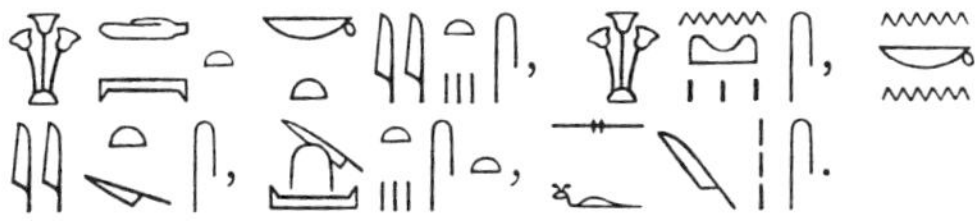.

ḥaṭu , Ṭuat IV, , ovens, furnaces; Copt. ϩⲓⲉⲓⲧ.

Ḥaṭ-t-nemmtit-set , Ṭuat XI, a fiery furnace in which the shadows were destroyed.

Ḥaṭ-t-Neknit-s , Ṭuat XI, a fiery furnace in which the spirit-souls were destroyed.

Ḥaṭ-t-ḥanṭu-s , Ṭuat XI, a fiery furnace in which the enemies of Rā were consumed.

Ḥaṭ-t-sefu-s 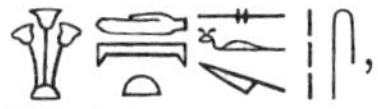, Ṭuat XI, a fiery furnace in which the heads of the damned were consumed.

Ḥaṭ-t-ketit-s , Ṭuat XI, a fiery furnace in which the foes of Rā were consumed.

ḥaṭ , Rec. 31, 172, cake, bread.

ḥaṭ , to spread out the wings, to fly.

ḥaṭṭ , a flight (of birds).

ḥaṭ , IV, 219, to copulate.

ḥaṭ-t , folk, people.

ḥaṭ-t , sickness, pain.

ḥaṭu 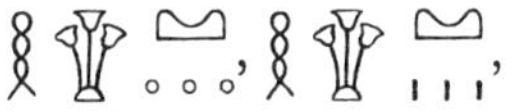, caverns in the mountains (?)

ḥaṭsh , to spread a net.

ḥaṭeg, to cut in pieces.

ḥȧ 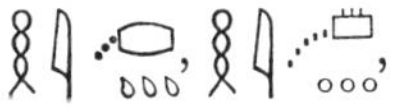, grain; see .

ḥȧ-t , P. 156, flame, fire = , N. 786.

Ḥȧit, Metternich Stele 79, a form of Bes.

ḥȧā-t, members of the body, limbs; see 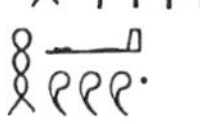.

ḥȧb-t , P. 68, reckoning, counting, summation = , M. 196, N. 36.

ḥȧp , P. 242, 243, to go forth.

ḥȧm , a kind of plant used in making incense.

ḥȧm , T. 121, to catch fish, to snare birds = , U. 150, N. 458.

ḥā , , , Rec. 6, 6, 13; for **ḥenā** , and, with.

ḥā, ḥā-t , , , , , a member of the body, a limb; plur. , , , , , , , , the flesh of the body, the body, person, self; , Rev. 6, 39, in bodily form; , , B.D. 133, 20, 137A, 31, thyself; , Rec. 21, 93, mine own self; Copt. ϩⲱⲱ.

ḥā ānkh , progeny.

ḥā-uā , one body.

ḥā neter , IV, 1031, , a god's body, *i.e.*, statue.

ḥā-Sar , the limbs, or members, of Sar, *i.e.*, grain, wheat.

ḥāu , IV, 1073, human bodies, persons, people.

ḥā-t , female pudenda, woman.

Ḥāuau (Ȧfuau?) , B.D.G. 1259, a serpent in the Ṭuat.

Ḥāu-em-nubit , Ombos II, 132, a goddess.

ḥāu (?) , children, youths.

ḥāau , , , , child, boy; plur. , Rec. 31, 173, , Rec. 3, 2, Hh. 446.

ḥā , U. 127, a joint of meat, a meat offering.

ḥā, ḥāi , , , N. 127, 948, , , , , , , , , , , Rec. 20, 43, , to rejoice, to be glad; , glad.

ḥāiu , T. 288, N. 1070, , M. 66, , P. 356, , P. 279, , M. 523, those who rejoice.

ḥāā , , Hh. 198, , , , , , , , , , T. 276, M. 41, , P. 30 = , N. 69, to rejoice, to exult, to be glad.

ḥāāut , , Rec. 26, 232, , , Rec. 27, 218, , , , , , , , rejoicings, gladness.

ḥāa-t ḥa-t , , joy of heart.

ḥāā-t , Rec. 19, 22 . . . . . .

Ḥāi , Tomb of Seti I, one of the 75 forms of Rā (No. 46).

Ḥāā-ȧakhu , Ombos I, 186–188, a god or goddess.

Ḥāā-ȧb-Rā = Heb. חָפְרַע, Jeremiah xliv, 30; Gr. Οὐαφρῆ, Οὔαφρις, Ἀπρίης, Hophra.

Ḥāā-t-em-sepu-s , Ṭuat XII, a fire-god of dawn.

Ḥāt-em-tauis , Ṭuat XII, a fire-goddess of dawn.

ḥā 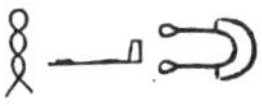, land as property, estate.

ḥā , stake, staff, pole, cudgel; plur. 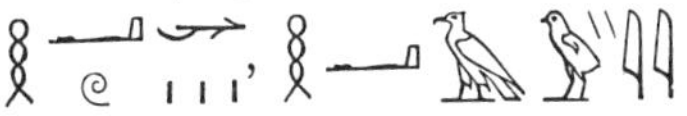 [illegible], Koller Pap. 1, 6.

ḥā , flowers, bloom.

ḥā-t , Nȧstasen Stele 37, a vessel or pot for milk or beer; , Ḥeru-sȧtef Stele 49, a temple vessel.

ḥāāu (?)  (?), IV, 1121, a vessel (?)

ḥāir , Rev. 13, 20, dung, filth; Copt. ϩⲟⲉⲓⲣⲉ.

ḥāu , boat, ship; plur. 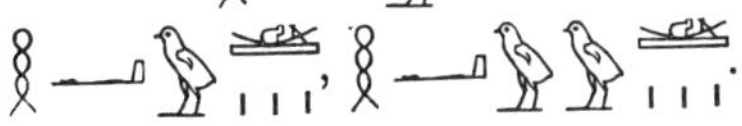.

ḥāutcha ; see  [illegible], IV, 648, to attack, to rob, to strive.

ḥāb ; var. 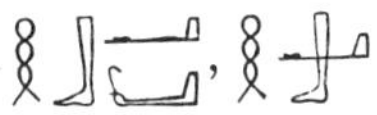 [illegible], Rev. 6, 22, collected, assembled.

ḥābu , staves.

Ḥāp, Ḥāpi 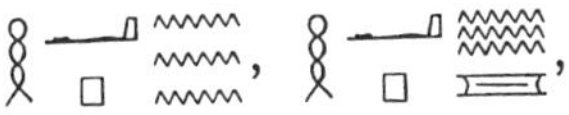, , [illegible], the river Nile, the Nile-flood; [illegible] [illegible], Rec. 20, 40, a high Nile; 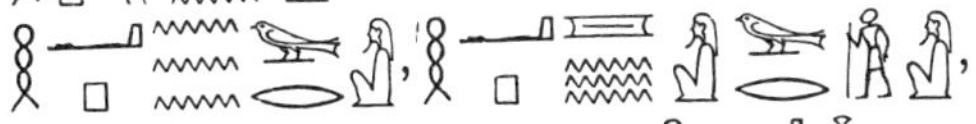, the Nile of the Other World; , the Nile of Lower Egypt; 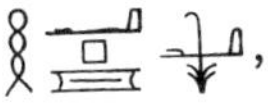, the Nile of Upper Egypt; , P.S.B.A. 18, 196, Niles, rivers; 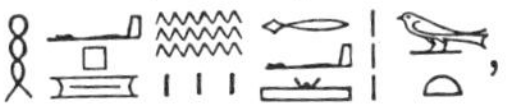, IV, 217, very high Niles.

Ḥāp, Ḥāpi 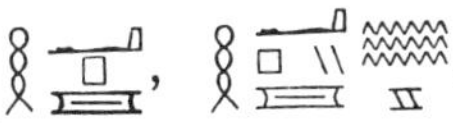, the Nile-god; see [illegible].

Ḥāpr 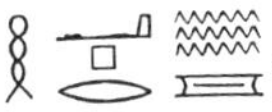, A.Z. 45, 140, Beni Hasan I, 8, 21, Niles, inundations.

Ḥām , Ṭuat XII, a singing dawn-god.

ḥān  = **ḥenā** , with.

ḥānsek 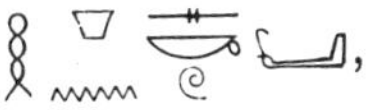, Tombos Stele 5 . . . .

ḥāru , filled, swollen (?)

ḥātȧ , Rec. 15, 141, seat, bed, bedstead, angarêb; [illegible], part of a shrine.

ḥātcha , Pap. 3024, 112, Peasant 193, 275, [illegible], IV, 648, to rob, to plunder, to fight, to attack; Copt. ϩⲏϫ.

ḥātcha , wickedness, depravity, violence.

ḥātchaut , Rec. 36, 210, theft, plunder.

Ḥātcha , Berg. I, 35, the god of the West Wind.

ḥi , B.M. 447, to smite, to strike.

ḥi (ḥui) 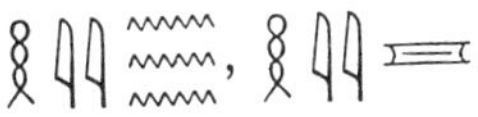, Metternich Stele 55, to rain; Copt. ϩⲱⲟⲩ.

ḥi-t (ḥui-t) , Rec. 33, 6, [illegible], water-flood, rain, a rise of the Nile, the Inundation.

Ḥi , T. 338, P. 344, M. 645, [illegible], N. 625, the Water-god of the Mediterranean, [illegible]; [illegible], Ḥi, the lord of years.

Ḥi , B.D. 125, II, one of the 42 assessors of Osiris.

ḥi 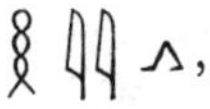, Rec. 27, 86, to rise up, to ascend, to rear (of animals and serpents).

ḥiu 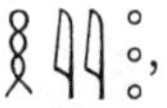, T. 340, , N. 628, those who rise.

ḥi , Rec. 33, 6, grain, wheat, barley, etc.

ḥi 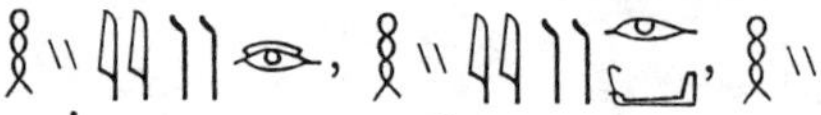 , Åmen. 14, 19, to discover, to inspect, watcher, overseer, inspector, spy.

ḥi-t , throat, food (?); see 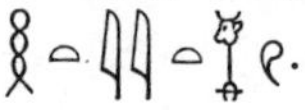.

ḥi-t 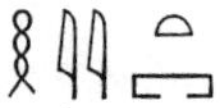, hall, room, chamber.

Ḥi-t 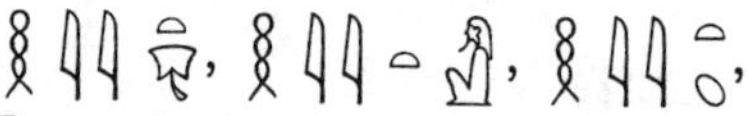, , a goddess, the female counterpart of Bes.

Ḥitiu 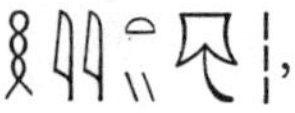, A.Z. 1906, 126, the Bes gods.

Ḥi-åakhu .... , Ṭuat VII, a star-god.

Ḥiāt (?) 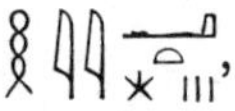, Ṭuat VII, a star-god, a constellation.

ḥiua(?) , sceptre.

ḥiq , Jour. As. 1908, 289, domination, rule.

ḥiq 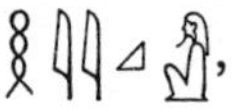, Rev. 12, 32, demon; Copt. ϩⲓⲕ.

ḥu 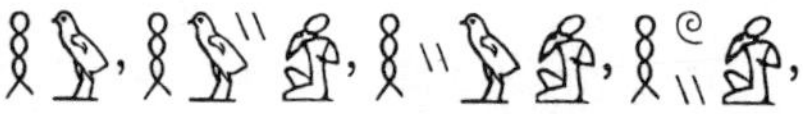, P. 1116, B. 11, a particle: Would that! (with  added for emphasis, ); , IV, 1074, I beg thee to do; , I, 38, Would that thy ka would give the order!

ḥu , to entreat.

ḥu, ḥui , U. 572, , U. 520, , Rec. 31, 30, , Rec. 26, 231, , Rec. 32, 85, , Shipwreck 4, , Nåstasen Stele 39,   , to beat, to strike, to crush, to slay, to kill, to hammer metal, to thresh, to tread grapes, to strike (a harp), to work a plough; Copt. ϩⲓ.

ḥuiu , IV, 1076, blows, smiters, , U. 602, 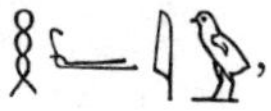, P. 204.

ḥuiu 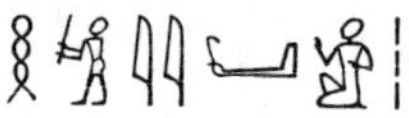, men who have been beaten or bastinadoed.

ḥui-ni 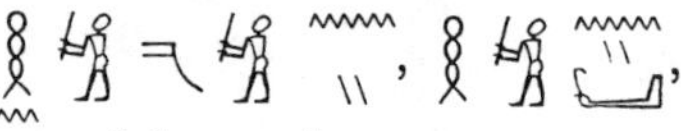, [illegible], a fighter or beater.

ḥui-re-ni [illegible], [illegible], L.D. III, 65A, 7; [illegible], they clapped their hands; [illegible], to thrust aside the right.

ḥui [illegible], P. 707, [illegible], [illegible], to rise like the Nile, to dash water on someone; [illegible], to break out into a sweat; [illegible], rising like the Nile; [illegible], IV, 1116, high Nile.

ḥuit [illegible], IV, 1107, [illegible], Hh. 204, a beating, bastinado, a striking; [illegible], Rec. 30, 185.

ḥuit āsh [illegible], A.Z. 34, 17, to preach, to announce, to proclaim; Copt. ϩⲓⲱⲓϣ.

ḥuit stcheṭut 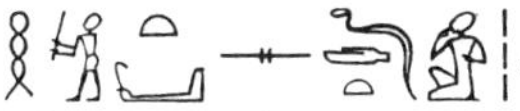, Israel Stele 9, 10, to coin a proverb.

ḥuut  cry, outcries; a death-cry.

Ḥuit Ȧntiu , a title of Sekhmit.

Ḥu-ȧḥuāȧ , Rec. 30, 67, a magical name.

Ḥui-Nu 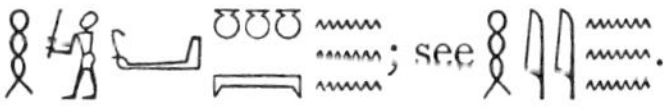 (; see).

Ḥu-nesmit (?) 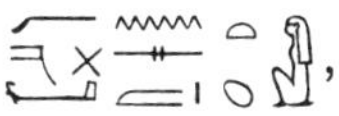, Ombos II, 133, a goddess.

Ḥuit-Rā (?) , B.D. 168, a group of four goddesses of offerings.

Ḥu-tepa , B.D. 146, the doorkeeper of the 4th Pylon.

ḥu 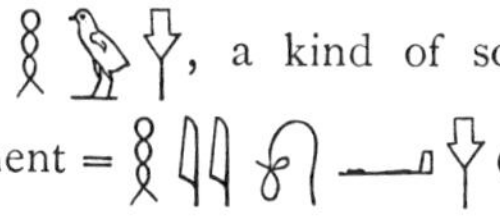, a kind of sceptre, tool, or instrument = (?)

ḥu 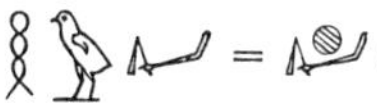 (?)

ḥuit , dust, powder.

ḥu 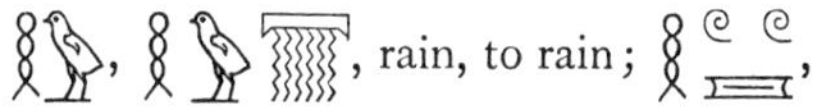 rain, to rain; inundation; Copt. ϩⲱⲟⲩ.

ḥuit  Pap. 3024, 137, rain; Copt. ϩⲟⲩ.

Ḥu 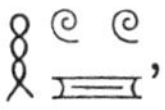, Edfû I, 78, a title of the Nile-god.

Ḥuḥu , B.D. 175, 18, the primeval watery mass whence came everything.

ḥu-t 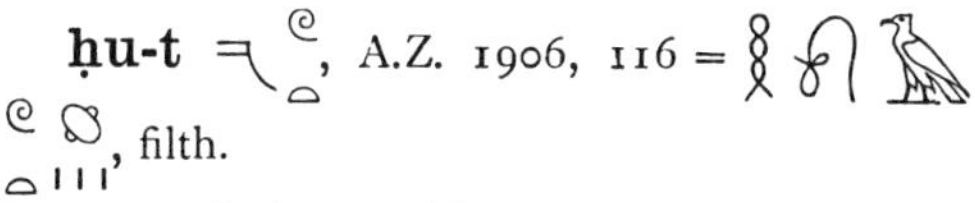 A.Z. 1906, 116 = filth.

ḥuit , a disease.

ḥu 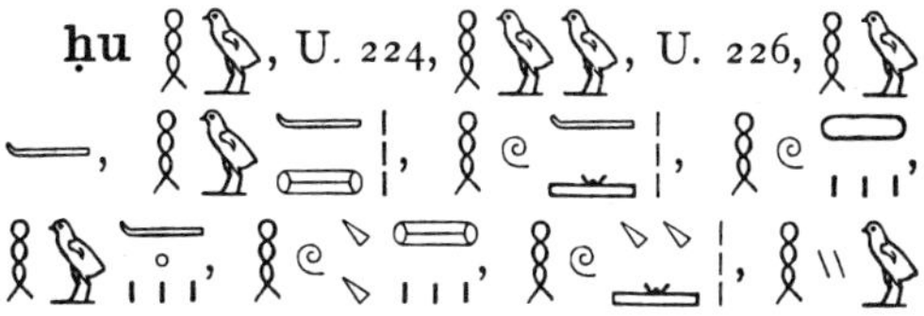 U. 224, U. 226,  food, meat and drink; divine food.

ḥut 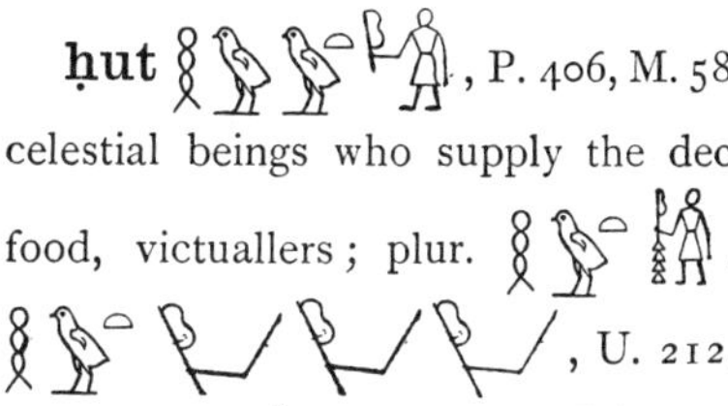 P. 406, M. 580, N. 1186, celestial beings who supply the deceased with food, victuallers; plur. M. 251, U. 212.

ḥu 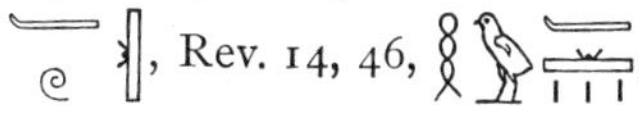 Rev. 14, 46, surplus, plenty; Copt. ϩⲟⲩⲟ.

Ḥu 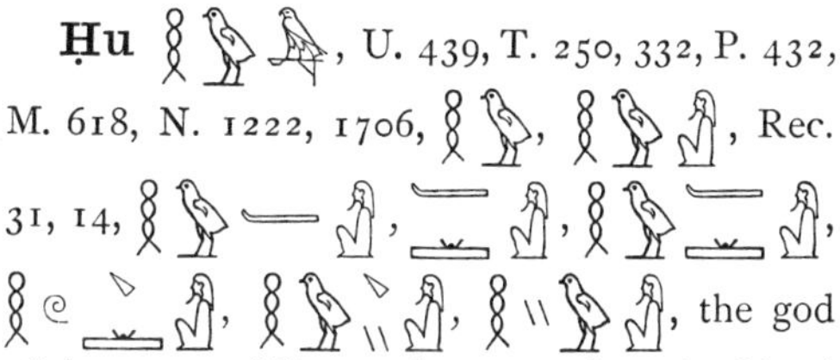 U. 439, T. 250, 332, P. 432, M. 618, N. 1222, 1706, Rec. 31, 14, the god of the sense of Taste; he sprang from the blood of the phallus of Rā.

Ḥu , Ombos I, 186–188, one of the 14 kau of Rā.

Ḥu 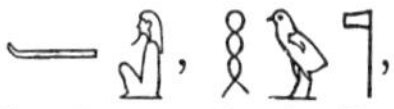, Ombos I, 84, Denderah III, 78, a god of offerings.

Ḥu , the god of the 2nd hour of the day.

Ḥu  the Sphinx at Gîzah;

ḥu , to lack, be in want.

ḥu  A.Z. 1907, 46, naked; var.

ḥu ȧb , Peasant 271, lamentation, sorrowful man.

ḥu , Rec. 27, 57, to grieve, to tear the hair.

ḥu , parts of a ship, planks, ribs (?)

ḥu 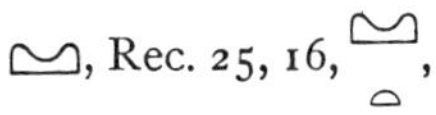 Rec. 25, 16, bad, wicked; Copt. ϩⲟⲟⲩ.

ḥua 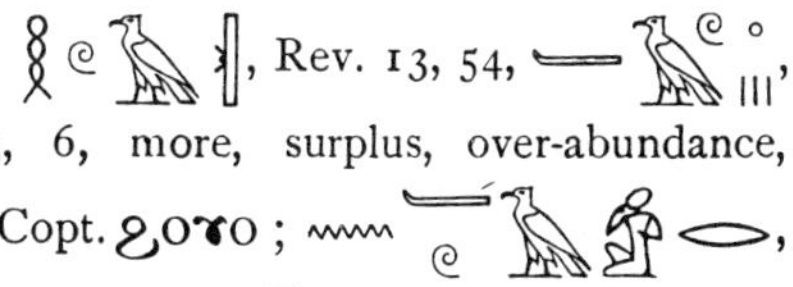 Rev. 13, 54, Rev. 13, 6, more, surplus, over-abundance, plenty; Copt. ϩⲟⲩⲟ; Rev. 13, 21 = Copt. ⲡ̄ϩⲟⲩⲟⲉ.

ḥua 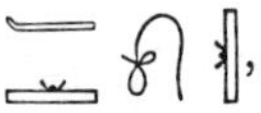, excess, greatly; Copt. ϩⲟⲩⲟ, ϩⲏⲩ.

ḥua , , to decree, to order, to command.

ḥua , A.Z. 34, 15,  , Rec. 21, 98, , Rec. 21, 99, to throw, to drive.

ḥuai, ḥiu ,  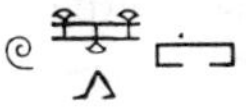, to throw, to cast; Copt. ϩⲓⲟⲩⲉ.

ḥua-t , T. 347, , , , , , ,  , , P. 505,  , P. 608, N. 33, , T. 348, , P. 66, , Rec. 29, 157, 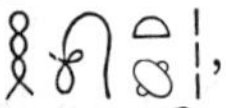, ,  , ,  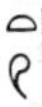, , , 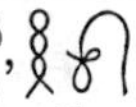 , ,  [illegible], Rec. 6, 157, filth, offal, decay, stink, stinking, dirt, corruption, putrid, putrefaction, falling into decay, musty (of wine); [illegible] [illegible], B.D. 33, 3, filthy cat.

ḥua [illegible] (late form), foul, beastly.

Ḥuau [illegible], a class of foul devils.

ḥuati [illegible], Litanie 63, filth.

ḥua [illegible], moisture, damp, water; Copt. ϩⲟⲩ.

Ḥuaiti [illegible], Tomb of Seti I, one of the 75 forms of Rā (No. 22).

Ḥuaur [illegible], Rec. 29, 157, a god.

ḥuā [illegible], [illegible], Rec. 32, 83, [illegible], Rec. 16, 118, [illegible], club, staff, stick, cudgel, pole.

ḥuā [illegible], U. 162, a kind of grain or fruit.

ḥuā [illegible], Rec. 15, 122, [illegible], Rec. 15, 107, dried carob (Loret); varr. [illegible], [illegible], [illegible], [illegible], etc.

ḥuā [illegible], P. 609, to work a boat.

ḥuāu [illegible], Rec. 22, 3, [illegible] [illegible], boats.

ḥuā [illegible], dwarf, cripple.

ḥutcha (ḥuātcha?) [illegible], [illegible] [illegible], dirty, filthy; var. [illegible].

ḥui [illegible], Rev. 11, 157, self; Copt. ϩⲱ.

ḥui (ḥi) [illegible], Israel Stele 6, [illegible] [illegible], Rev. 11, 140, [illegible], Rec. 30, 155, [illegible], Rev. 14, 12, to throw, to cast, to project, to reject, to shoot venom, Jour. As. 1908, 258.

Ḥuit-Rā [illegible], a class of divine beings.

ḥui [illegible], illumination, light.

ḥui [illegible], apex of an obelisk.

Ḥuit [illegible], Ṭuat I, a doorkeeper-goddess.

Ḥuiti [illegible], Tomb of Seti I, one of the 75 forms of Rā (No. 74).

Ḥuiti [illegible], the gods of the company of Bes.

ḥubs [illegible], Rev. 14, 40, to cover over, to hide; Copt. ϩⲱⲃⲥ̄.

ḥup (ḥep) [illegible], Rev. 13, 2, to hide, to conceal, to be mysterious.

ḥup [illegible], to embrace.

Ḥup [illegible], [illegible], [illegible], the Nile.

ḥuf [illegible], Rev. 13, 25 = Copt. ϩⲱⲱϥ.

huf, serpent, worm; Copt. ϩⲟϥ.

ḥufḥuf, to eavesdrop, to spy out.

ḥuft (ḥutf), Rec. 33, 68, to spoil, to rob; Copt. ϩⲱϥⲧ.

ḥufṭ, to faint, to collapse.

ḥuftcha, to hasten, to move with trepidation; compare Heb. √חָפַז.

ḥumm, Rev. 13, 5, heat, fever; var. Rev. 13, 4; Copt. ϧⲙⲟⲙ.

ḥuma (ḥumama?), a kind of plant.

ḥumaka-t, carnelians from the Sûdân.

ḥumāqa (ḥum'qa) Koller 4, 2, a precious stone, amethyst(?) carnelian (?)

ḥum'tcha, vinegar; compare Heb. חָמֵץ, Copt. ϩⲙⲁϫ.

Ḥumen (Ḥemen), a god of Letopolis.

ḥun, IV, 1032, IV, 939, 1207, to be or become young, to refresh oneself.

ḥunu, P. 78, M. 108, N. 21, Metternich Stele 198, boy, youth, young man; U. 287, N. 719, young, youthful.

ḥun-t, P. 683, N. 801, IV, 218, A.Z. 79, 53, girl, maiden.

ḥunu, ḥunut, youths; the young of both sexes; P. 85, N. 43, the women of Rā.

ḥunu neferu, young soldiers.

ḥun, pupil of the eye.

ḥun-t, U. 149, T. 120, pupil of the eye; girl in the eye of Horus; compare Heb. אִישׁוֹן, the little man in the eye, Deut. xxxii, 10, Prov. vii, 2, בַּת־עַיִן, daughter of the eye, Psalm xvii, 8, Arab. بنت العين, Eth. ብንት: ዐይን:, Gr. κόρη, Deut. xxxii, 10, Psalm xvi, 9, Prov. vii, 2.

Ḥun, Ḥunu, a youthful god; plur.

ḥunu: (1) the name of the sun at the 3rd hour of the day; (2) the name of the spring sun.

Ḥun, Ṭuat XII, B.D. (Saïte) 46, 1, a singing-god of dawn.

Ḥun, Ṭuat II, a god.

Ḥunit, Ṭuat I, a doorkeeper-goddess.

Ḥunit Denderah I, 6, a serpent-goddess of the North.

Ḥunit, L.D. 3, 276H, a lioness-goddess who rejuvenated the dead.

Ḥunit, the goddess of the 21st day of the month.

Ḥunut, P. 85, , N. 43 . . . .

Ḥunit urit, T. 313, 357, a goddess of Heliopolis.

Ḥunit Pe, B.D. (Nefer-uben-f) 99, 55, a goddess of Buto.

Ḥunn-em-nu-t, etc., B.D. 85, 15, "child in the town, youth in the country"—a title of Rā.

Ḥun-sāḥu, Ṭuat III, one of a group of four gods.

Ḥunnu-Shu, B.D. 46, 2, the children of Shu, *i.e.*, Geb, Nut, Osiris, Isis, Set, Nephthys, and Anubis.

Ḥun-shemā, P. 78, , M. 108, N. 22, "boy of the South"—a title of Ṭeṭun.

ḥun-t, to castrate.

ḥun-t, Rev. 2, 86; see , lizard, crocodile, evil.

ḥun-ta, , a kind of plant.

ḥunu; see **ḥen**, to escape from, be free from.

ḥunugeg-t, throat.

Ḥunb, B.D.G. 1364, a serpent-god of Ḥensu.

ḥunkhekh; see , , to make an offering.

ḥuntȧ, lizard, crocodile; Copt. ⲁⲛⲑⲟⲩⲥ (?)

ḥuntes, Rev. 14, 9, lizard; Copt. ⲁⲛⲑⲟⲩⲥ.

Ḥuntheth, Ṭuat X, a lioness-goddess.

ḥur (ḥer), and, together with.

ḥur, Rev. 14, 9 = .

ḥur, Ȧmen. 15, 17, , A.Z. 1899, 72, to be poor, miserable, weak, wretched, to beg.

ḥuri, Rev. 12, 116, fraud, wrong.

ḥuru, Peasant 169, , IV, 510, 1199, , , , , , , , , , beggar, poor man, destitute; plur. , Peasant 175.

ḥuru ḥa-t, poor-spirited, cowardly, timid.

Ḥurit urit, N. 1387, a goddess.

ḥur-t, seed, grains.

ḥur, Harris I, 7, 12, a flowering plant.

ḥurr-t, , , , , , , bloom, flowers; , Turin Pap. 67, 12, blue flowers; Copt. ϩⲣⲏⲣⲉ.

ḥurḥur, to cry out with gladness; see .

ḥurr, Thes. 1200, , to utter cries, to roar; see .

ḥur, a mass of water.

ḥurr, scorpion.

ḥura, Rev. 13, 2, to fly; Copt. ϩⲱⲗ.

ḥuraq, Rev. 13, 13, to be at rest (in a bad sense); Copt. ϩⲟⲣⲕ.

ḥurā, Mar. Karn. 52, 18, , , Thes. 1205, , Ȧmen. 4, 4, , Ȧmen. 9, 16, 10, 6, , to rob, to plunder, to defraud; late forms are: , ; Copt. ϩⲟⲩⲣⲱ.

Ḥurā, "Robber"—the name of a devil.

ḥurpu, Koller 1, 5, , , sword; plur. (?) , A.Z. 1880, 94; Heb. חֶרֶב, Arab. حَرْبَة.

ḥurḥ, , , Rev. 13, 6, to protect, to keep watch over; Copt. ϩⲁⲣⲉϩ.

ḥursh, Rev. 14, 45, heaviness; Copt. ϩⲣⲏϣⲉ, ϩⲣⲟⲟⲩϣ.

ḥurk, Rev. 14, 19, sweetness; Copt. ϩⲟⲗϭ.

ḥurtȧ, vision, phantom; Copt. ϩⲟⲣⲧϥ.

ḥukhas, some strong-smelling substance.

ḥus, Ebers Pap. 39, 13, to swell.

ḥus, vine prop.

ḥus, , a kind of stone, alabaster (?)

ḥus-t (?), a kind of stone.

ḥus, Rev. 13, 12, dung, filth.

ḥus, Rougé I.H. II, 125, to be destroyed, to be scattered.

ḥuspi, Rec. 3, 45, basin, hollow vessel, receptacle.

ḥuq, to capture spoil.

ḥuq = , to hunger; Copt. ϩⲕⲟ, ϩⲟⲕⲉⲣ.

ḥuq, A.Z. 1906, 113, hunger.

ḥuqq, , , , Koller 4, 2, , , , , the fruit of the dûm palm (?)

ḥuqamamu, a kind of precious stone.

ḥuken, oil.

ḥuken, a door bolt.

ḥut, Rev. 11, 185, , Rev. 15, 17, male, masculine; plur. , Rev. 14, 16; Copt. ϩⲟⲟⲩⲧ.

ḥut, first, foremost; Copt. ϩⲟⲩⲓⲧ.

ḥutȧ, to sail up the river; Copt. ϩⲱⲧ.

ḥuta-t, , , Hh. 447, sail.

ḥutȧr, a kind of animal (?)

ḥuti, Rev. 13, 5, fear; var. , , Rev. 14, 12, 22; Copt. ϩⲟⲧⲉ.

ḥuti, Anastasi I, 12, 5, officer, chief; plur. , , .

ḥutf, L.D. III, 65A; see **ḥuft**.

ḥutem, garlic (?) onions.

ḥutr, late word, meaning doubtful.

ḥutha, Dream Stele 19, Rec. 2, 116,

, Amherst Pap. 22, , to inlay, to plate, to overlay, to make children look well and healthy.

ḥuṭ , throne.

ḥuṭ-t , winged disk; see **Beḥt, Beḥuṭ-t.**

ḥuṭf , to steal.

ḥutch-t , to bestow (?)

ḥutchai , , Rev. 13, 4, 5, cold; Copt. ϩωϫ.

Ḥutchai , , , Lanzone 558, the god of the west wind.

ḥeb , N. 684, , , , , , M. 213, , , , feast, festival, panegyric; plur. , , , , , Rec. 13, 89.

ḥebi , N. 684, , M. 213, , , to keep the feast.

ḥeb , , , to triumph.

ḥeb , , festivity, rejoicing.

ḥeb , T. 36, , P. 387, unguent used on festal occasions.

ḥeb-t , N. 754, , a festal offering.

ḥebit , , , , festal offerings; , P. 608.

ḥeb-t , N. 513, a kind of drink offering (?) beer (?)

ḥebu , festival revellers.

Ḥeb , T. 312, a god, the son of .

Ḥebit , , Berg. I, 23, an air-goddess.

ḥebit , , , , , , , , , the book of the festival, the roll of papyrus containing a copy of the service recited.

ḥeb-t em aḥ-t , estates roll.

ḥeb Åpt the Karnak festival.

ḥeb en ån-t , Rec. 19, 16, , Rec. 20, 40, the festival of the valley.

ḥeb āḳh pe-t , festival of suspending the sky.

ḥeb ur , , the great festival.

ḥeb em mit , P. 609, festival of the dead.

ḥeb Nu , the festival of Nu.

ḥeb nu pet , the festival of the 30th day of the month.

ḥeb ent sås , festival of the 6th day.

Ḥeb nefer en pet ta , the good festival of heaven and earth, the festival of the 4th epagomenal day.

ḥeb nefer tepi ṭu , the good festival of him that is on the mountain, *i.e.*, Anubis.

ḥeb Ḥennu , the festival of the god of the Ḥennu boat of Seker.

ḥeb Ḥensit , the festival of the goddess Ḥensit.

ḥeb khen , a festival procession of boats.

ḥeb kheru , a festival of the beings on earth.

ḥeb Seker , Palermo Stele, festival of the boat of Seker.

ḥeb Seṭ  , Thes. 1124, the "festival of the tail"; the chief object of this festival was to renew the life of the king; varr. , Rec. 15, 68, .

ḥeb tep-t 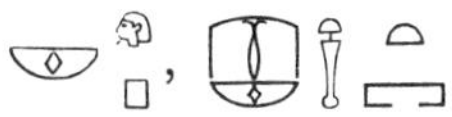, the festival of the 1st of the five epagomenal days.

ḥeb tekh år-t Rā , the festival of drunkenness of the Eye of Rā, *i.e.*, Hathor.

ḥeb 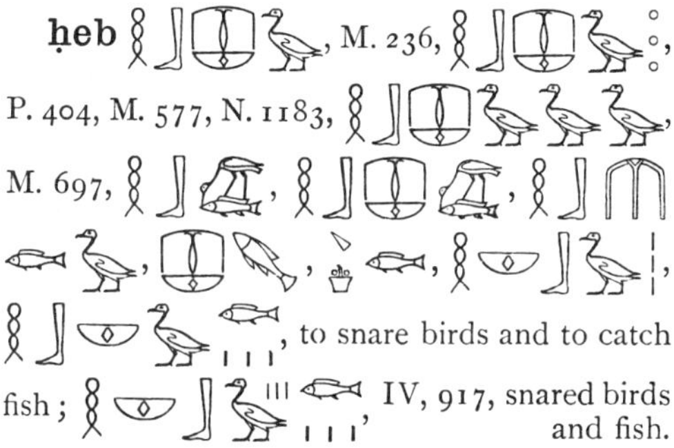, M. 236, P. 404, M. 577, N. 1183, M. 697, to snare birds and to catch fish; IV, 917, snared birds and fish.

ḥebi , fowler, bird-catcher, hunter.

ḥebi āa , chief fowler.

Ḥebi , the god of fowling and fishing, the Hunt-god.

ḥeb 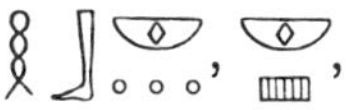, a precious stone, turquoise (?)

ḥeb , a hall, garden-tent, booth, tabernacle.

ḥebit 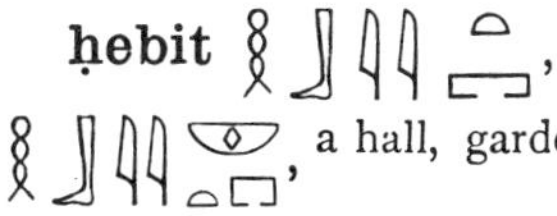, L.D. III, 65A, 14, a hall, garden-tent, booth, tabernacle.

ḥebit en ḥebsu 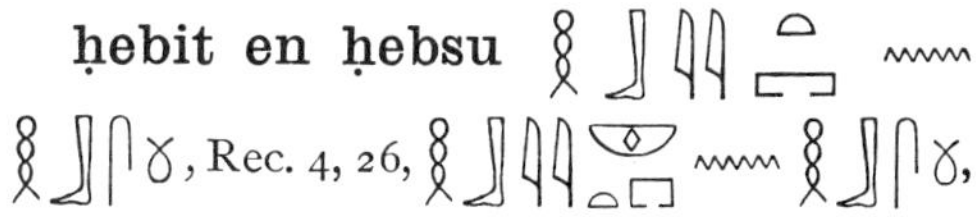, Rec. 4, 26, Rec. 5, 91, linen-chest, cupboard for clothes.

ḥeb 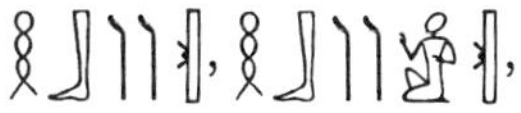, to play a game, player.

ḥeb-t , Rec. 12, 84, a kind of land, grounds for recreation; plur. , .

ḥeb 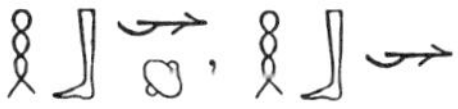, Rec. 12, 84, staff, sceptre, stick, rod.

ḥeb-t , a kind of shrub or plant.

ḥebit 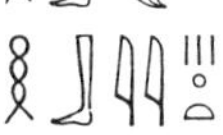 Leyden Pap. 3, 9, the seed of a plant.

ḥeb 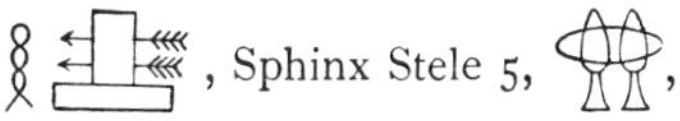, Sphinx Stele 5, Mar. Karn. 35, 63, target, a mark for shooting at.

ḥeb , Mar. Karn. 42, 12 . . . . . .

ḥeb , to grieve, to mourn, to lament; Copt. ϩⲏⲃⲉ.

ḥeb-t , lamentation, grief.

ḥeb 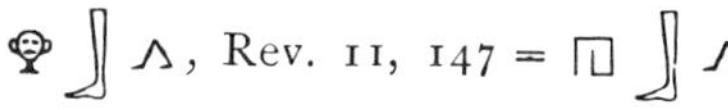, Rev. 11, 147 = , to send.

ḥeb neb-t 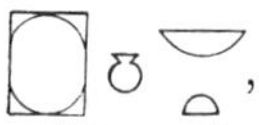, Nåstasen Stele 31, every matter, everything; Copt. ϩⲱⲃ ⲛⲓⲙ.

ḥeb-t , stream, flood.

ḥebb-t , deep water, flood, the deep, source of a spring.

Ḥebb-t 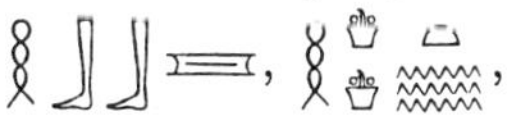, Edfû I, 78, a title of the Nile-god.

ḥeb-t , fish.

Ḥeba 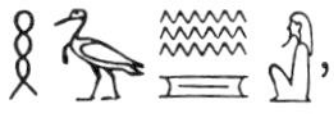, Rev. 14, 17, Inundation-god.

ḥeba , P. 64, M. 87, N. 94, a kind of boat.

ḥeba , Rev., obscurity, shadow; var. , Rev. 14, 20; Copt. ϧⲏⲓⲃⲓ.

ḥeba , Jour. As. 1908, 299, grief, misery; Copt. ϩⲏⲃⲉ.

ḥebau , Nåstasen Stele 19, miserable man, wretched; with , "poor folk."

ḥeba , Hearst Pap. XIV, 11 .....

ḥebaba , Verbum I, 336, to waddle (of a goose).

ḥebbȧ , Hymn to Åmen 41, to bubble up (of a spring).

ḥebāi , A.Z. 1868, 10, 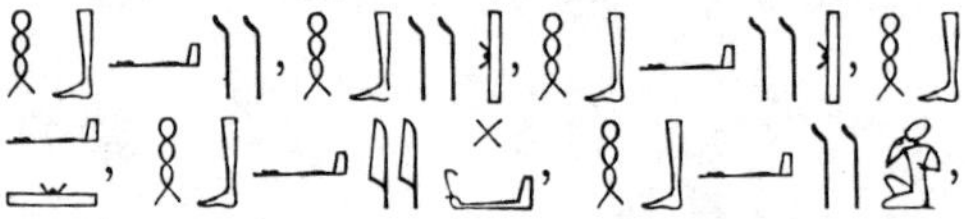, to play, to jest, to play a game of draughts; 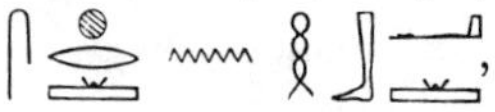 in a jesting manner, playfully.

ḥebāi , to injure.

ḥeben-t , humility, low estate.

ḥebenben , Mar. Aby. I, 6, 36, to be cast down, to grovel on the ground.

ḥeben , Rougé I.H. II, 115, one who is dejected or cast down.

ḥebnen-t , a ring, a round cake, a circular object; plur. 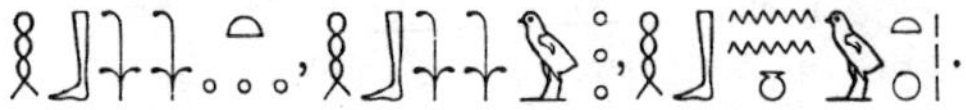.

ḥebnen-t 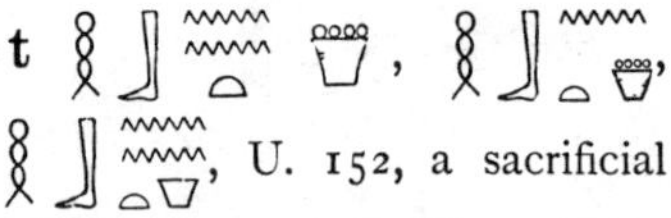, U. 113, 422, U. 152, a sacrificial cake, a vessel full of grapes or wine (?)

ḥeber-t 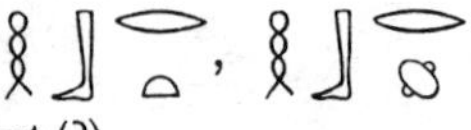, dirt (?) filth (?) excrement (?)

ḥeberber , to bow, to do homage, to grovel; see 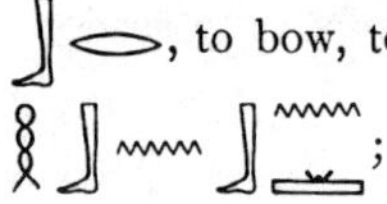; Copt. ϩⲃⲟⲣⲃⲣ̄.

ḥebs , 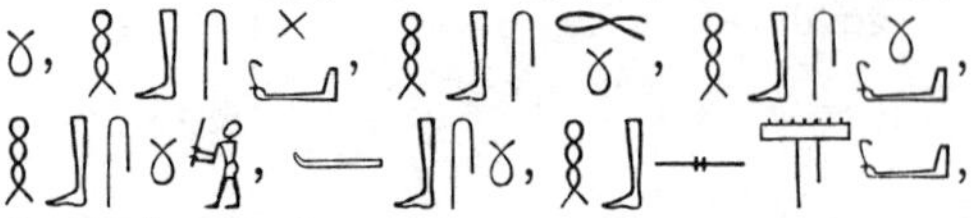, 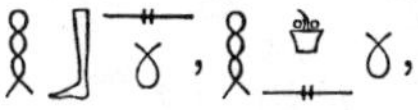, to put on clothes, to clothe, to dress, to cover over;  , T. 144; Copt. ϩⲱⲃⲥ̄, compare Heb. חָבַשׁ, Arab. حبّس; , P. 239, clothed in very best clothes; 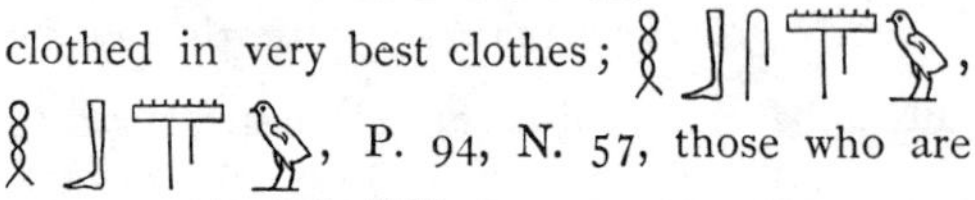, P. 94, N. 57, those who are clothed; , IV, 944, with covered head.

ḥebs 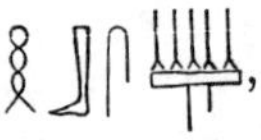, T. 339, N. 743, clothing, apparel, raiment, cloth, coverings, drapings, 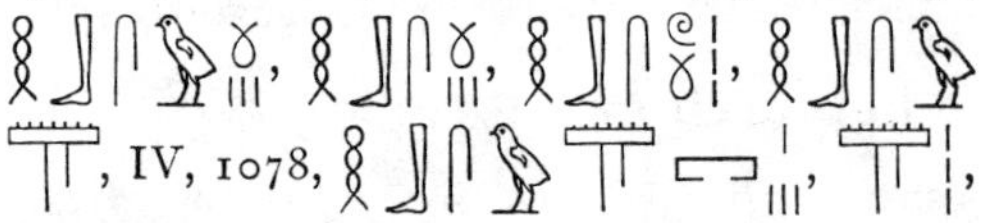, IV, 1078, 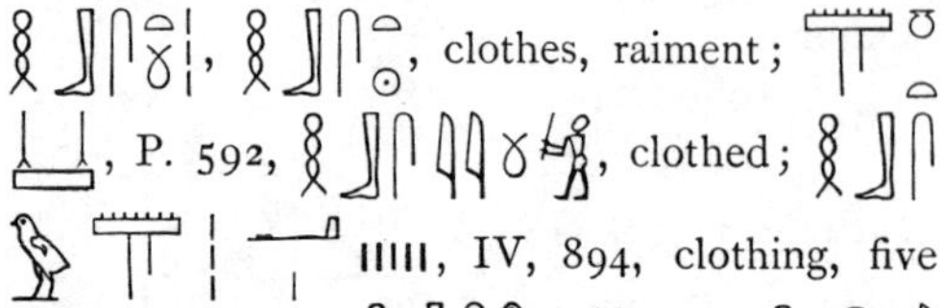, clothes, raiment; P. 592, clothed; IV, 894, clothing, five changes or suits; 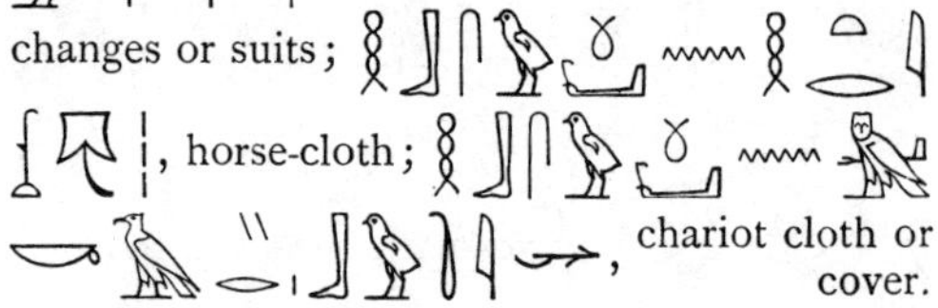, horse-cloth; chariot cloth or cover.

ḥebs-t 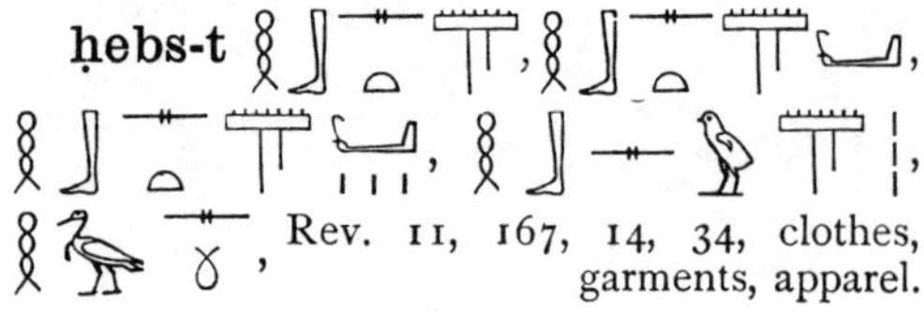, Rev. 11, 167, 14, 34, clothes, garments, apparel.

ḥebs-t 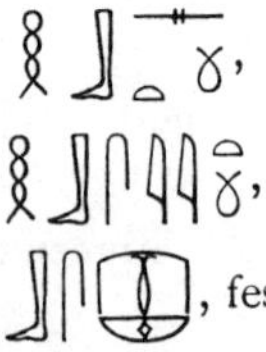, Rec. 4, 21, a linen strainer.

ḥebsit, linen (raiment).

ḥebs, festival apparel.

ḥebs 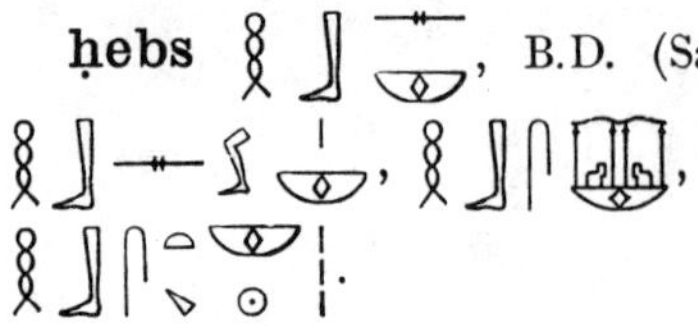, B.D. (Saïte) 19, 13, festival; plur.

ḥebs, Rec. 25, 197, clothing, *i.e.*, a wife.

ḥebsit, A.Z. 1873, 39, , Amherst Pap. 30, sewing-woman.

ḥebs, IV, 847, to face a building with stone.

ḥebs nu åner, Rec. 3, 49, a stone covering.

ḥebs, , cover of a vessel.

ḥebs, , to cast up mounds about a city, to encircle a city with walls.

ḥebs behen, to screen, to protect.

Ḥebs, Ṭuat IX, god of raiment and funerary swathings.

Ḥebsit, Ṭuat VIII, a goddess in the Circle Ḥep-seshemu-s.

ḥebs, a title of the priest of the Nome Athribites.

Ḥebs-ån, Rec. 16, 106, a watcher of Osiris.

ḥebs beg-t, Thes. 1252, , , what covers the dead, the Underworld.

Ḥebs-neb-s-em-shesp-s, Ombos II, 108, a lioness-goddess, a form of Sekhmit.

ḥebs neter, the apparel in which a god was arrayed.

ḥebs.kheperu, a title of the priest of Up-uat of Lycopolis.

ḥebs, Rec. 21, 14, a kind of well in the Great Oasis.

ḥebs, , = , to reckon, to count.

ḥebs = , calf.

ḥebti, Rec. 12, 84 = , nome, province.

ḥebtḅåt, Rev. 6, 111, the slain, dead bodies, the dead on a battlefield.

Ḥebṭre, , see , the god of the hidden mouth (?)

Ḥebṭ-re-f, Denderah IV, 83, B.D. 149, § B, a hippopotamus-goddess of the 13th Åat.

ḥebtch, Rec. 29, 155, a serpent-god.

ḥep, , , , Rev. 12, 49, to hide, to be hidden, to disappear; see ; Copt. ϩωπ.

ḥepḥep, Rev., to hide; Copt. ϩωπ.

ḥep-t, a hidden or secret place; see .

ḥepu (?), caves, caverns, hidden places, hiding-places.

Ḥep, U. 187, N. 955, A.Z. 45, 141, , Rec. 27, 217, the Nile-god; see , . For his nine forms see Denderah III, 25, 26.

Ḥep-ur, U. 431, , T. 217, the great Nile-god; see , B.D. 57, 1, 145, 13, 48.

Ḥep-em-ḥep-f, Ombos I, 86, a god of offerings.

Ḥep, U. 219, , T. 60, M. 218, , N. 592, , P. 262, , M. 482, 495, N. 1279, , P. 269, 593, 600,

700, , P. 673, 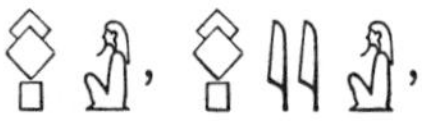,
 : (1) one of the four sons of Horus; (2) god of the northern cardinal point; (3) protector of the small intestines of the dead.

Ḥep , U. 424, , Palermo Stele 23, 24, , T. 243, , P. 571, , Rec. 33, 5, ,  (of Saïs), the Apis Bull of Memphis; Copt. ϩⲁⲡ. For accounts of him see Herodotus III, 28, 38, 41, Pliny VIII, 72, Strabo XVII, 31, Diodorus I, 85, Aelian XI, 10, Plutarch, De Iside, 56.

Ḥep peḥrer , Palermo Stele, the circuiting of Apis.

Ḥep 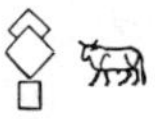, Denderah IV, 7, a bull-god of offerings.

Ḥep[it] , B.D. 69, 7, a cow-goddess who yielded milk in the Ṭuat.

Ḥepti , Ṭuat VIII, a god of the 7th Gate.

Ḥepti-ta-f 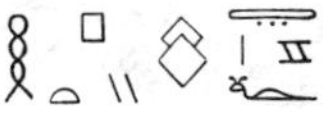, Ṭuat IX, a singing-god who gave drink to the dead.

ḥep 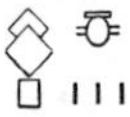, B.M. 448, unguent.

ḥep-t , a square.

ḥep , a kind of goose.

ḥep 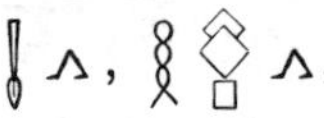, to move onward, to advance, to paddle a boat.

ḥep 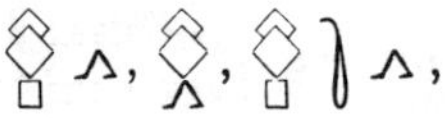, to move slowly, to slink along, to advance cautiously.

ḥepp 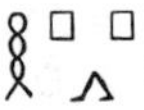, to advance, to travel, to go about.

ḥep-t 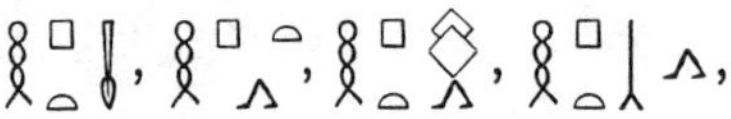, advance, progress.

ḥep-t , a course.

ḥeputi , IV, 617, , A.Z. 1905, 17, runner, traveller, he who slinks along like a wolf or a jackal.

ḥep 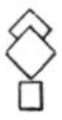 — **åkhmiu ḥepu** 
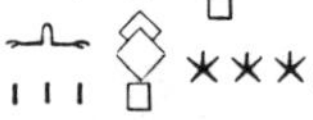, fixed stars.

ḥep åten 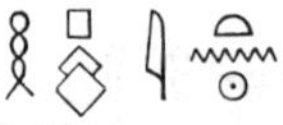, the dropping of the disk, *i.e.*, sunset.

ḥept kheru 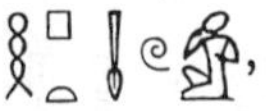, A.Z. 1907, 123, the gossip.

ḥepḥep 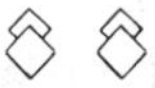, Hh. 331, to paddle.

ḥep-t [illegible], U. 422, [illegible], T. 241, [illegible], P. 603, N. 1158, [illegible],

guiding pole of a boat, paddle, oar; plur. [illegible]
[illegible].

ḥeptiu , Rev. 6, 41, paddlers, sailors.

ḥep-t [illegible], M. 399, [illegible], N. 949, boat.

Ḥep 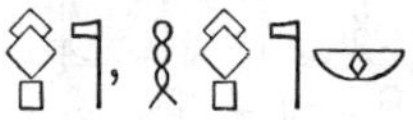, the god of the 2nd hour of the night and of the 5th day of the month.

Ḥep-ti 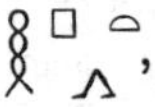, Hunefer 1, 17, a title of Rā.

Ḥepi 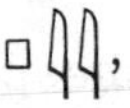, the god of the 13th day of the month.

Ḥepi 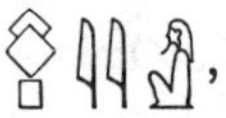, B.D. 99, 22, a bolt-peg in the magical boat.

Ḥep-t tep , Ṭuat XII, a deity in the Ṭuat.

Ḥep-tcheserit (?) 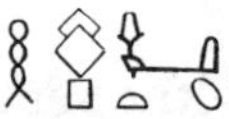, the goddess of the 12th hour of the day.

ḥepḥep [illegible], to turn round, to retrace a path.

ḥep [illegible], turn, turning, solstice; dual [illegible],

, Southern Solstice , Northern Solstice , together ; plur. , the limits or ends of the earth.

Ḥepḥep (Ḥepti) , , , Suppl. 812, , Buch 71, the god of the Ecliptic (?)

Ḥep-ti , the god of the 20th day of the month.

Ḥepḥep , the name of a sanctuary.

ḥep , rope, fetter, tie, band.

ḥep , U. 187 = , T. 66, M. 221, N. 598, nome.

Ḥep-ā , Ṭuat XI, a form of Åfu-Rā.

ḥepā , a hard stone.

ḥepāpā-t , , a plant used in medicine.

Ḥeper , Amamu 15, 1, 3, , A.Z. 45, 151, the Nile-god; see **Ḥep** and **Ḥāpi.**

ḥeprer = **peḥrer** .

ḥepeq , place, region.

ḥepeq , , , to praise.

ḥept , L.D. III, 194, , , , , , , , , to embrace, to hug, to take to the breast.

Ḥepit , a monster serpent in the Ṭuat.

Ḥept khet , , B.D. 125, II, one of the 42 assessors of Osiris.

Ḥepit-Ḥeru , , Lanzone 211, a goddess of resurrection.

ḥept , , , the side posts of a door, part of a ship.

Ḥepṭur ; see .

ḥepṭ-ra , B.D. 38B, 5, to shut the mouth (in chewing?).

ḥef , a plot of ground.

ḥefi (?) , , , , , , to fear, to pay reverence to, to be timid.

ḥefiu , , , adorers, worshippers.

ḥefit , , a timid step.

Ḥefa .... , Ṭuat III, a god bowed to the earth.

Ḥefaiu, Ḥefait , , B.D. 168, a group of four gods of the boat of Rā.

ḥefa-t , , , , , , Mission 13, 225, Shipwreck 61, , Dream Stele 4, asp, viper, adder; Copt. ϩⲃⲱ, ϩϥⲱ; plur. , , , Rec. 26, 224, 31, 30, 162, , , ; , snake with two legs; , Shipwreck 128, 75, serpents.

ḥefau , U. 305, 335, 552, , T. 312, M. 645, , serpent, snake; plur. , ; Copt. ϩⲟϥ.

Ḥefau , Ṭuat VII, the great Worm, or serpent of evil, called Āapep, Seba, etc.

Ḥefau enti em Restau  , B.D. 1B, 4, the Nine Worms of Restau. Their names are :—
(1), (2) ; (3) 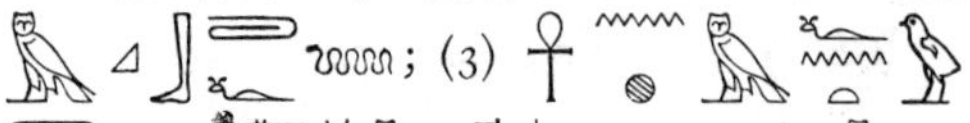; (4), (5) ; (6) ; (7) 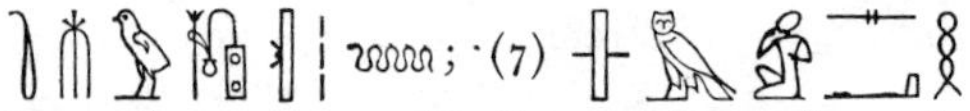; (8) ; (9)  .

ḥef tchet 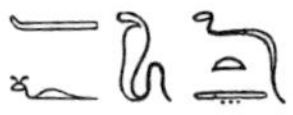, Rev. 13, 41, 42, the everlasting serpent.

ḥefā , a tool or instrument.

ḥefn  , the number 100,000; plur. , IV, 612, .

ḥefen 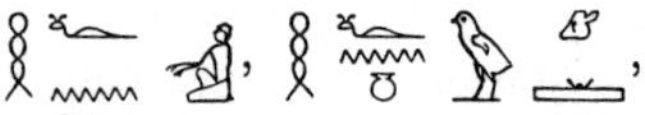, to fear, to be humble.

Ḥefnu , T. 309, a mythological serpent.

Ḥefnen-t 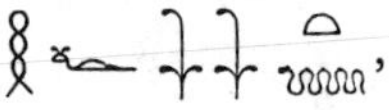, T. 309, a mythological serpent.

ḥefren , leech (?) tadpole (?); plur. , Ebers Pap. 65, 15; Copt. ϩⲁϥⲗⲉⲉⲗⲉ (?)

ḥeft , Rec. 12, 45, to overthrow.

ḥeft , to fly down, to alight.

Ḥeft-ent ...... , P. 636, 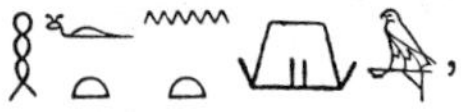, M. 512, N. 1095, the "mother of the gods."

ḥeftenu 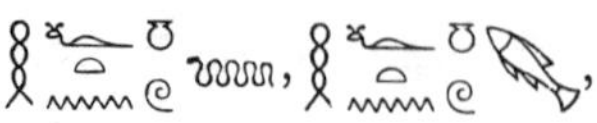, eel.

ḥefṭ , Metternich Stele 229, to hover, to alight (of birds).

ḥefṭ , T. 399, Rec. 29, 156, [illegible], M. 409, [illegible], U. 486, [illegible], P. 201, 640, M. 670, N. 937, [illegible], A.Z. 1908, 120, [illegible], to sink down, to subside, to come to rest, to faint, to swoon.

ḥefṭ , a swoon, fainting during a religious ecstasy.

ḥefṭ , to cleave, to cut, to force a way or passage.

ḥem , A.Z. 1905, 24, forty; Copt. ϩⲙⲉ.

ḥem ; see [illegible].

ḥem , U. 492, [illegible], U. 503, [illegible], T. 320, [illegible], I, 78, [illegible], Rec. 30, 185, [illegible], Décrets 105, [illegible], Leyd. Pap. 13, 9, [illegible], Rec. 18, 98, [illegible], Culte 105, [illegible], a particle meaning something like but, however, certainly, assuredly; 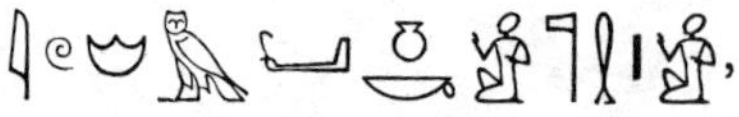, but indeed I am a priest;  , but certainly Egypt is happy.

Ḥem , P. 618, [illegible], N. 1299, a god (?)

ḥem , P. 1116B, 30, [illegible], to rub down, to pound, to tread out.

ḥemḥem , Rec. 16, 153, [illegible], Rev. 12, 22, to bray in a mortar, to pound, to crush.

ḥem , U. 323, , P. 64, 303, 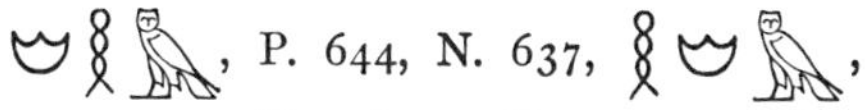, P. 644, N. 637, M. 173, , , Rev. 27, 188, to flee, to escape, to run off, to hasten away, to shun, to avoid, to retreat; , P. 605, , U. 617, 618, , T. 293, N. 234, get back!

ḥemi , retreater.

ḥem-t , N. 107, repulse.

Ḥemit , Ṭuat VI, a goddess.

ḥemm , U. 520, , N. 873, , to retreat, to get out of the way, to withdraw.

ḥemḥem , to retreat, to withdraw.

ḥemu  — **åkhmiu ḥemu** , stars that do not go back.

ḥem-t , sole of the foot.

ḥem-t 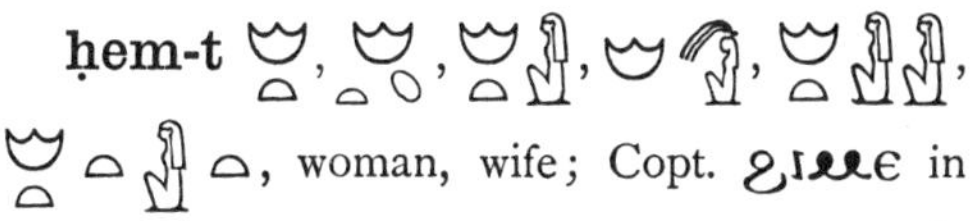, woman, wife; Copt. ϩιⲙⲉ in ⲥϩιⲙⲉ; plur. 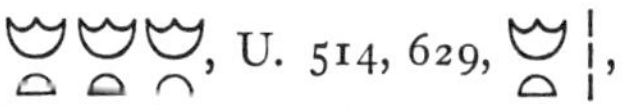, U. 514, 629, T. 326, 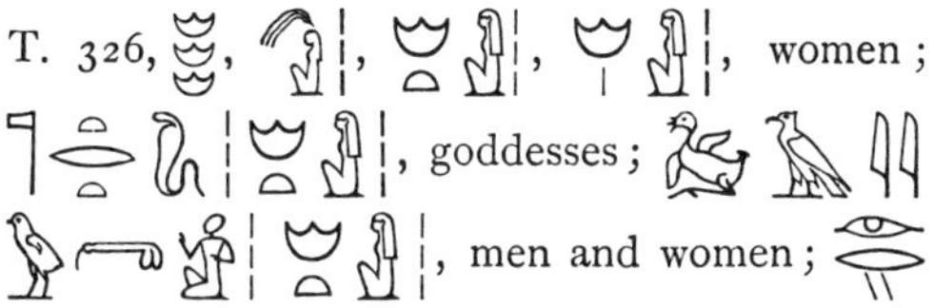, women; goddesses; men and women; , to live with a wife; , woman of a man, *i.e.*, wife.

ḥem-t peḥ-t , Rec. 12, 100, a divorced wife (?)

ḥem-t nesu , king's woman, *i.e.*, queen.

Ḥem-nenu (?) 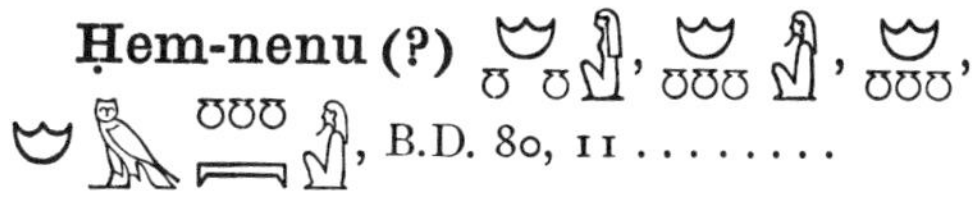, B.D. 80, 11 . . . .

ḥem-t neter , the wife of the god, a title of the high-priestess of Åmen.

ḥem 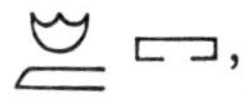, the apartments of the women in a house.

ḥem-t (åtå?) 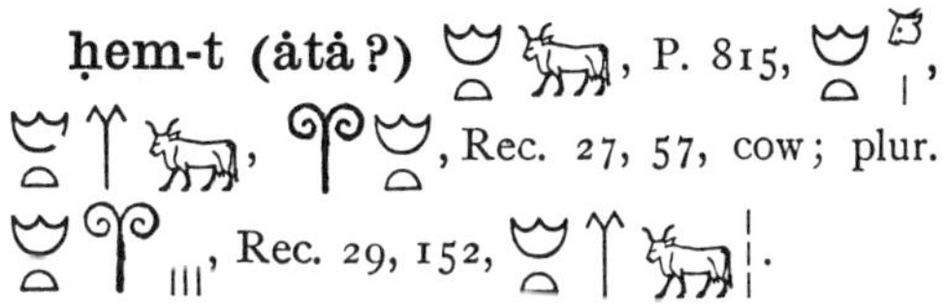, P. 815, Rec. 27, 57, cow; plur. Rec. 29, 152.

Ḥemit , cow-goddess.

Ḥem-ti , T. 23, P. 739, the two black cow-goddesses.

ḥem-t (åtå?) 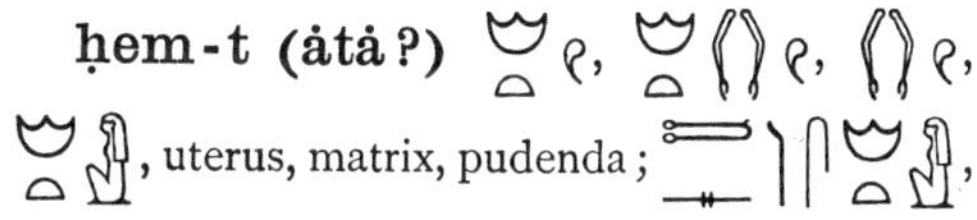, uterus, matrix, pudenda; Rec. 27, 56, she raised her genitals. If the reading be **åtå** compare Copt. ⲟⲧⲓ, vulva, uterus.

ḥem , little ball, pupil of the eye, testicle; dual , the two testicles.

ḥem-ti 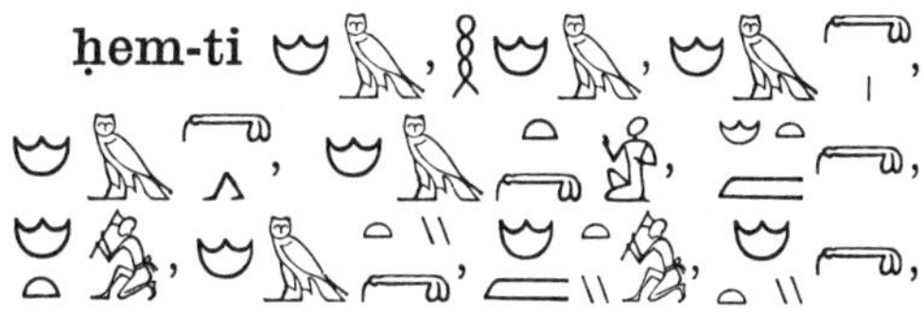, eunuch, a castrated man or animal, a coward, poltroon; plur. , Teach. Åmenemḥat 2, 10, T. 320, U. 503, 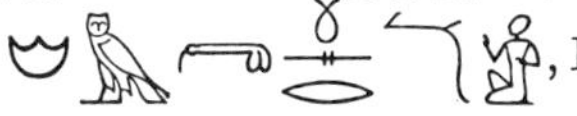, Rec. 16, 56.

ḥemut , Rec. 10, 116, cowardice.

ḥemi [illegible], Rev. = Copt. ϩⲱⲱⲙⲉ.

ḥem-t [illegible], hyena.

ḥem [illegible], Åmen. 5, 1, 15, 6, 20, 5, to steer,

to direct the course of someone or something; , director of hearts; Copt. ϩⲙ̄ⲙⲉ.

ḥemi , , , , , Peasant 126, 221, steersman, rower; plur. , P. 263.

ḥemit , , , , , , , , A.Z. 1880, 94, rudder, steering-pole; **àri ḥemit** , steersman.

ḥemu , P. 174, N. 941, , Peasant 127, , Rec. 30, 67, , , , rudder, the steering oar or paddle; Copt. ϩⲙ̄ⲙⲉ; , rudder of heaven; dual ; plur. , , Rec. 27, 224, 225, , , , T. 340, 341, , to work a paddle.

ḥemu , Rec. 30, 67, the rudder of the magical boat.

Ḥemu àabti , B.D. 64, the two-faced rudder of the East.

Ḥemu IV [ ], B.D. 141 and 148, the four rudders of heaven.

ḥem , to cut to pieces, to chop up; Copt. ϩⲱⲙⲓ.

ḥem , , , , A.Z. 1900, 33, to catch fish.

ḥemi āiu , IV, 968, skilled hands.

ḥemm , Ebers Pap. 90, 12; see .

ḥemu , Hearst Pap. 4, 12, , , Ebers Pap. 74, 2, a plant used in medicine.

ḥemu , a decoction of the same.

ḥemiu (?) , a kind of grain or seed (flax seed?).

ḥemm , , , Ebers Pap. 106, 7, 13, 17, metal-worker.

ḥemit , Anastasi I, 25, 7, , Koller Pap. I, 4, a metal weapon.

ḥemit , A.Z. 1880, 94, copper fittings of a chariot.

ḥemut , Ebers Pap. 55, 3, 11, a preparation of copper.

ḥem = in , servant of Menu, Rec. 32, 46; see also **Pa-ḥem-neter,** "servant of the God," , A.Z. 46, 109.

ḥem , , , , , slave, servant; plur. , , , , , , , , Nàstasen Stele 13, servants; , , male and female slaves; Copt. ϩⲙ in ϩⲙϩⲁⲗ.

ḥem-t , , , IV, 346, female slave, handmaiden; plur. , .

ḥem ānkhiu , Rec. 24, 160, "servant of the living"—a priestly title.

ḥem neter , , , , servant of the god, *i.e.*, priest; plur. , , , , .

ḥem neter tepi , high-priest, priest; , office of priest, priesthood;  , title of the high-priest of Letopolis.

ḥem-t neter , priestess.

ḥem ka , IV, 1205, , Rec. 29, 77, priest of the Ka; plur. 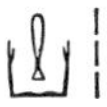, IV, 1032.

Ḥem pestchet , U. 305, 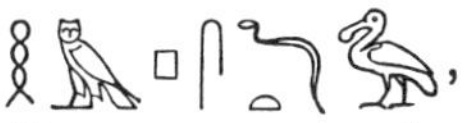, U. 545,  , T. 300, P. 232, , T. 312, a god (?)

Ḥem nu ba , the god of the 14th day of the month.

Ḥem-Ḥeru , Ṭuat II, a god.

ḥem  , majesty, especially the king's majesty, the king; plur. .

ḥem 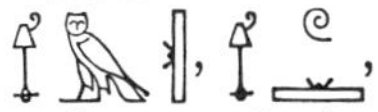, to be skilled in the work of a trade or profession.

ḥemu-t  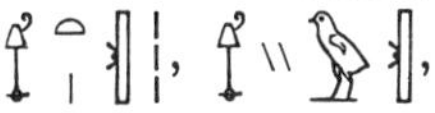, any kind of handicraft, craftsmanship, trade, the profession of artist or physician, a man's speciality.

ḥemu , P.S.B. 10, 46, 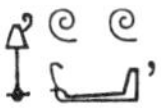, Berl. 6909,  , Rec. 11, 148,  , IV, 970,   , a handicraftsman, a skilled labourer, workman; plur.  ; Copt. ϩⲁⲙ in ϩⲁⲙϣⲉ.

ḥemut , artificer, artisan, workman; plur.   (*sic*),  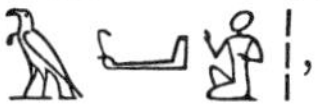, IV, 421;  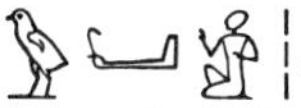, chief workmen or artists; 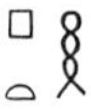 [illegible], Rec. 27, 189, Ptaḥ, creator of skilled workmen.

ḥem-khet (?) [illegible], [illegible] [illegible], [illegible], Rec. 11, 169, carpenter; plur. [illegible]; Copt. ϩⲁⲙϣⲉ.

ḥemu ḥat [illegible], Rec. 20, 40, [illegible], skilled or trained mind.

Ḥem-f-ṭes-f (?) [illegible], Ṭuat V, a serpent doorkeeper.

Ḥem-taiu [illegible], one of the names of Āapep.

ḥem-t (?) [illegible], workshop, factory; plur. [illegible].

ḥem [illegible], a tool for working in metal, hammer (?); **Ur-kherp-ḥem** [illegible], "chief director of the ḥem tool"—a title of the high-priest of Memphis.

ḥemit [illegible], a stone (?) tool.

ḥem-t [illegible], B.D. 100, 10, mineral, a precious stone.

ḥem-t [illegible], coward, outcast (?) (a late form); see **ḥem-ti.**

ḥem-t re [illegible], [illegible]; plur. [illegible], et cetera, and so forth; see Piehl, Sphinx 3, 83, Goodwin, A.Z. 1868, 89.

ḥem khert (?) [illegible], Rec. 21, 91, a kind of garment.

ḥem-t sa (?) , a disease.

Ḥemmit , Denderah III, 77; see **Ḥenmemit.**

ḥema , to fish, to hunt; see .

ḥema , Nav. Lit. 70......

ḥema , ball, testicle (?) a circular object.

ḥema-t , salt land, the shore of a salt lagoon.

ḥema , Jour. As. 1908, 275, salt; Copt. ϩⲙⲟⲩ.

ḥemai-t , , salt; salt of the North, *i.e.*, sea salt; Copt. ϩⲙⲟⲩ; compare Heb. חָמִיץ, Arab. حَمَض.

ḥemau 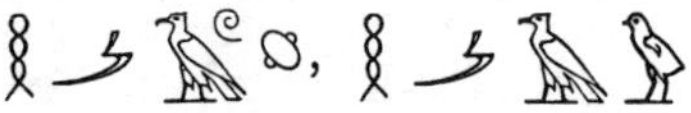, , an illness or disease.

ḥemau , De Hymnis 28, forge, shop in which fire is used.

ḥemamu , Rec. 19, 92, 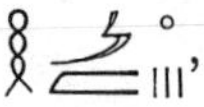, Rec. 30, 217, plants, herbs of some kind, lentils (?)

ḥemami-t , 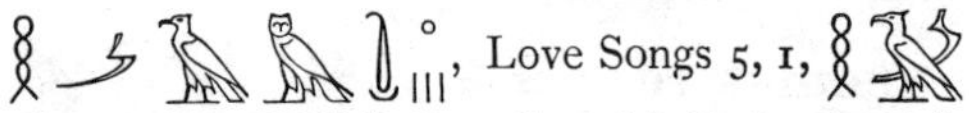, Love Songs 5, 1, , 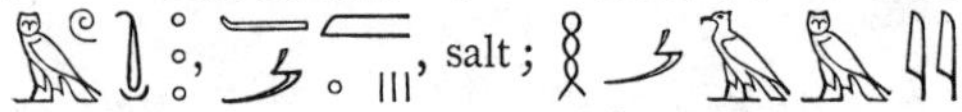, salt; 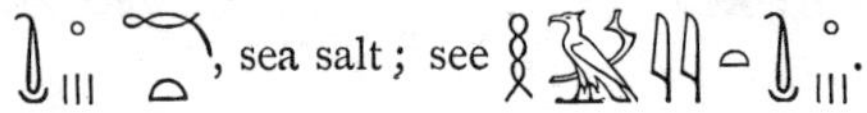, sea salt; see.

ḥemamu , , a disease or illness.

ḥemar-t , Hearst Pap. 111, 15, a kind of seed or grain used in medicine.

ḥemak-t , hall, chamber.

ḥemaka, Rec. 5, 92, sack, bag.

ḥemag 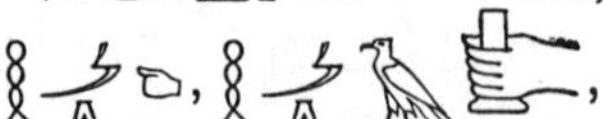, Rec. 4, 22, 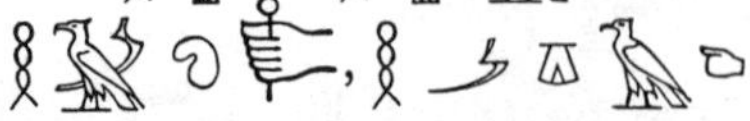, to grasp, to clasp tightly, sack, bag.

ḥemag-t , , Rec. 37, 70, a shrine or workshop of Osiris; var. 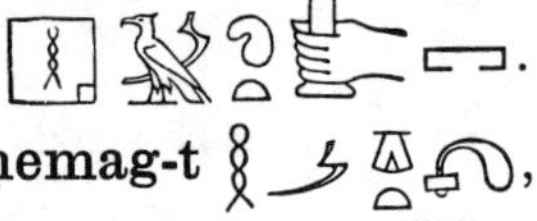.

ḥemag-t, a neck ornament —the equivalent of the 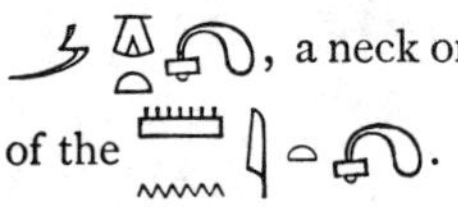.

Ḥemag , the god of the city of Ḥemag, *i.e.*, Osiris.

Ḥemag, Berg. 52, a form of Osiris.

ḥemaga, Libro dei Fun. 365, the name of a ceremony.

ḥemaga-t , Rec. 4, 21, 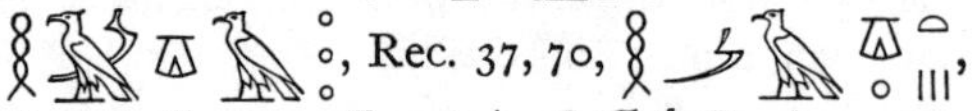, Rec. 37, 70, , Leyd. Pap. 3, 2, amethyst (?)

ḥemati 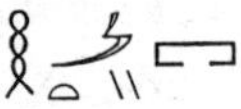, B.D. 78, 38......; varr. 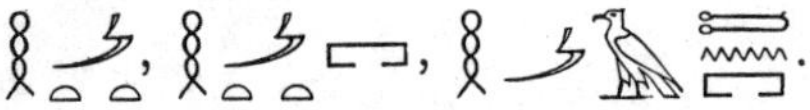.

ḥematheth , U. 482, 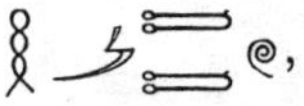, N. 146, cord, rope.

ḥemā 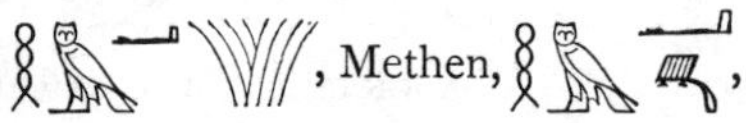, Methen, flax.

ḥemāu , Rec. 36, 78......

ḥemi, Rev. 12, 52, anxiety, care. Copt. ϩⲉⲙⲓ.

ḥemit , , , a disease.

ḥemi , a kind of wine from , in the Delta.

ḥemen , , eighty; Copt. ϧⲉⲙⲙⲛⲉ.

ḥemen , B.D. 146, 58 . . . .

ḥemen , , to praise (?) to heap up (?)

ḥemen , a vessel, bowl, bottle.

ḥemen = , natron.

Ḥemen , N. 849, P. 204, , Hh. 447, B.D. 99, 18, , B.D.G. 547, 1255, , A.Z. 1881, 19, , Rec. 3, 116, a god; , U. 321; compare Heb. חַמָּן.

Ḥemnit , Rec. 11, 79, a goddess.

ḥemer , , , a raised seat with steps, throne.

ḥemsi , M. 120, , U. 192, , U. 70, , , , , , , P. 91, , , , , to sit, to seat oneself, to besiege a city, to inhabit a place, to be at home in a place, to dwell; , to sit dressing the hair; , P. 309, , P. 211, , N. 698, , M. 451, , P. 264, , P. 281, , N. 1239, , P. 642, , M. 677; Copt. ϩⲉⲙⲙⲥⲓ, ϩⲙⲙⲟⲟⲥ.

ḥemsi , , Rev. 13, 31, , Rev. 13, 11, to dwell; Copt. ϩⲉⲙⲙⲥⲓ, ϩⲙⲙⲟⲟⲥ.

ḥemsit , U. 192, , T. 71, , Pap. 3024, 133, , , IV, 349, 1103, a sitting down, enthronement, session.

ḥemsi , , , dweller, inhabitant; plur. , , , .

ḥems-ti , Hh. 342, the two sitters.

Ḥems-beqsu-ȧrit-f , B.D. 31, 4, a god (?)

ḥemsi , T. 277, P. 30, M. 41, phallus.

ḥems , , to castrate.

ḥems , drink.

ḥems , Rec. 25, 158, crocodile; fem. , , ; varr. , , ; Gr. χάμψαι.

ḥemsut , B.M. 797, attributes, qualities.

ḥems , P. 642, N. 679 = , N. 1240, to make to sit.

ḥemg-t , IV, 1099, carnelians from the Sûdân.

ḥemt , , , , , , , , copper; Copt. ϩⲟⲙⲛ̄ⲧ, ϩⲟⲙⲧ; , furnaces for smelting copper; , ingots of copper; , weapons of copper; , , copper javelin.

ḥemt āḥā (?) ...... (?)

ḥemt ḥer-set-f, IV, 692, "rock copper," *i.e.*, copper ore.

ḥemt seft, Mar. Karn. 54, 58, copper swords.

ḥemt setfu, IV, 708, smelted copper.

ḥemt Sett, IV, 817, 1150, Asiatic copper.

ḥemt kam, Thes. 1286, , , black copper.

ḥemti , , , , Rec. 16, 70, , , , coppersmith; plur. .

ḥem ......, Åmen. 21, 10 ...... (?)

Ḥemt, B.D.G. 820, a title of Set.

ḥen, IV, 862, , and, with, together with; see .

ḥen-t , , , , , , , , , , , , , , Ebers Pap. 95, 3, , Rev. 13, 26, , Rev. 14, 16, lady, mistress, queen, goddess; , queen of the gods; , , queen of the South and North, queen of the Two Lands, *i.e.*, Egypt.

ḥen-t ta, A.Z. 45, 125, queen.

Ḥenit-netit (?), a goddess of Sma-Beḥt.

Ḥenit-ḥeteput, Cairo Pap. III, 7, a goddess of the Mesqet.

Ḥenit-ṭesher-t, Rec. 34, 192, a hippopotamus-goddess and regent of the 3rd epagomenal day (the birthday of Set). She was one of the five Meskhenit goddesses.

ḥen, N. 709, a scent (?) from Osiris.

ḥen, A.Z. 1908, 20, an amulet.

ḥen, band, tie, cord, rope.

ḥenu, N. 660, measure (?)

ḥenu , , A.Z. 1866, 99, , , , , , , , , pot, vessel, a measure, like the Heb. הִין; plur. , , IV, 665, , IV, 1023, , , Rec. 30, 217; Copt. ϩⲛⲁⲁⲩ.

ḥen-t, U. 54, 55, , , , pot, vase, vessel; , IV, 1046, pots of silver, gold, and copper.

ḥenut , , Ebers Pap. 59, 19, a kind of metal.

ḥen-t, purification (?)

ḥen , , , , , , , , , , , , , , , Rev. 11, 144, to command, to direct, to admonish, to rule, to administer, to arrange, to keep in order; Copt. ϩⲱⲛ.

ḥen-t , , affairs, business, functions.

ḥen-t, IV, 1148, a command, order, law, ordinance, regulation, a rubrical direction, anything prescribed by authority, legal function.

ḥenu, Rec. 21, 83, a business mission.

ḥenu, cries of joy, praises.

ḥenu, B.M. 657, commanders, directors.

ḥentiu (?), officers.

ḥenuti, Ȧmen. 19, 4, labourers.

ḥen, to provide, to endow, to supply with, to bestow.

ḥenu (?), gift, tribute, offerings, presents.

ḥen-t, work, what is produced by toil, products.

ḥen-t ḥemut, IV, 933, work of the handicraftsmen.

ḥenu, products both natural and artificial, things, property, goods, possessions, tools (?) fabrics.

ḥenn-t, M. 301, P. 186, revenues, income, supplies, equipment, stock, store.

ḥenu, Rec. 5, 87, 31, 50, bread, cakes.

ḥen, Edict 18, A.Z. 1908, 118, to run, to make haste, to rush forward, to travel; Love Songs 4, 10; Copt. ϩⲱⲛ.

ḥenn, Treaty 10, to advance quickly, to hasten.

ḥen-t, a journey, an advance.

ḥen, to turn back, to retreat, to withdraw.

ḥenḥen, Rec. 31, 32, to shake (of the body in sickness), to totter, to tremble (of the legs).

ḥenḥen, IV, 498, to impede, to obstruct, to drive back, to turn away.

ḥenḥen-t, a turning back.

ḥenḥen-t, ulcer, sore.

ḥenu-t, Ebers 39, 4 ....

ḥen, Thes. 1285, to be, or become, or be made, young.

ḥenu, boy, youth, young man; young soldiers.

ḥen, T. 100, P. 814, flower, plant, branch, seed; Copt. ϩⲛⲁⲩ.

ḥen ānkh, "plant of life" (?)

Ḥenui-Shu (?), B.D. (Saïte) 46, 1, the offspring of Shu (?)

ḥenu Shu, B.D. 64, 41, blossoms of Shu, *i.e.*, light.

ḥen ta, grain, seed.

ḥen-t, , P.S.B. 14, 409, border, boundary, end, limit, frontier; , A.Z. 1865, 26, the eight boundaries of Egypt; , the two ends of heaven; , IV, 362, the two ends of the river.

ḥenti, P.S.B. 14, 264, a period of 120 years, at the end of which one whole month was intercalated in the calendar; , , Thes. 1297, endless.

ḥenti renput, years as long as ḥenti periods.

Ḥen-t, U. 417, , T. 238, a mythological locality.

ḥen-t, M. 395 (var. , N. 948), lake, sea (?)

ḥent-tȧ, N. 1031, 1158 ......

ḥen-t, P. 377, , N. 1151, , , , , , , , , , , Rec. 31, 174, , , , Rev. 13, 14, , , , , , , , canal, stream.

Ḥen-t-she, B.D. 67, 5, the lake in the Ṭuat from which Rā appeared; var. .

ḥen-t, U. 401, horn; dual

ḥenti, ḥenuti, , , , , , , , , , .

ḥen, , , , , to be evil, to do evil, to behave in a beast-like manner, to harm, to injure.

ḥen-t, , , Peasant 291, , evil, greed, avarice, hostility.

henuit, , , , , , , evil, wickedness, fraud, deceit.

ḥenti, ḥenuti, , , greedy man, bestial person.

Ḥen-t, B.D. 67B, 4, a district in the Ṭuat.

Ḥent, the crocodile of Set.

Ḥenti, , : (1) a name of Osiris; (2) a crocodile-headed god in the Ṭuat; (3) , crocodile-gods.

ḥenn, M. 696, , , , , to plough, to break up the ground, to chop.

ḥennu, ploughs, tools for tillage.

ḥennui-t , , plough, hoe.

ḥennti, ḥennuti , , , , , ploughman, field labourer, farmer; plur. , , , , , , fellaḥîn.

Ḥent-nut-s , Ṭuat IX, a singing-goddess.

ḥenn , P. 466, M. 529, N. 969, 1107, Metternich Stele 153, , U. 628, , P. 216, , T. 312, , , , , , , phallus, penis; , phallus of Baba; , phallus of Rā; , Mar. Karn. 54, 50, 51, phalli in skin cases.

ḥenut , pudenda.

Ḥennu-Neferit , a name of Hathor, any beautiful woman.

Ḥennu-en-Rā , B.D. 17, 60–63, the phallus of Rā which the god himself cut off: Ḥu and Sȧa sprang from the blood. Of Rā it is said , B.D. 93, 2.

Ḥenn-Shu , N. 969, the phallus of Shu.

ḥenḥen , , , , , , Osiris 32, Berg. I, 26, destruction, calamity, stroke, blow, death-blow.

ḥenḥentiu , stripes, blows.

Ḥenḥenu , B.M. 32, 134, the butcher-gods in the Ṭuat.

Ḥenḥenith , Ṭuat VI, a goddess (?)

ḥenȧ , Rec. 29, 148, , , Jour. As. 1908, 290, a plant.

Ḥen-ȧh-t , title of the priest of the Nome Prosopites.

ḥenā , , , , , with, and; varr. , ; , along with; , acquitted with you.

ḥenā , , , to be full (?) a title of Rā (?)

ḥenāu , a disease.

Ḥenātiu (?) , Ṭuat X, a group of gods who slew Āapep with knives and staves.

ḥenit , , IV, 719, , spear; plur. , , IV, 719; Copt. ϩⲛⲁⲁⲩ, Heb. חֲנִית.

ḥeni-t Rev. 13, 14, , , Rec. 35, 204, coffer, coffin.

Ḥenu , Ṭuat III, the hawk-god Seker.

Ḥenu , T. 270, , N. 759, , , , , , B.D. 145c, 153A, 6, Nesi-Ȧmsu 8, 16, the god of the Ḥenu boat of Seker and the Seker boat itself.

Ḥenuit , T. 89, , N. 619, M. 241, a goddess (?)

Ḥenu, Ṭuat VI, the name of a standard in the Ṭuat.

Ḥenu, U. 211, , M. 435, , the sacred boat of Seker, the Death-god of Memphis. For the oldest picture of the boat, see B.M. 32650.

ḥenu (?), the sanctuary of the Ḥenu boat (?)

ḥenu (?), IV, 503, barn (?)

ḥennu, , to fill, to be filled.

ḥenu-t, a kind of bird.

ḥenḥ, , Rev. 4, 86, terror, evil.

ḥennusu; see .

ḥenb, , IV, 746, , A.Z. 1905, 27, , A.Z. 1905, 21, , to measure land, to delimit, to make a frontier boundary, to allot land by measure, to tie, to bestow.

ḥenb-t, , land, field, arable land in general; plur. , Tombos Stele 3, .

ḥenbit, arable land, estate, domain.

ḥenbu (?), , produce of tilled lands, provisions (?)

Ḥenb-t, Ṭuat I, the god of corn-land.

Ḥenb, B.D.G. 1364, , Nesi-Åmsu 27, 24: (1) a serpent-god of Ḥensu; (2) a serpent-god in the Ṭuat.

Ḥenbi, B.D. 180, 29, a god who measured out estates for the blessed in the Ṭuat; plur. .

Ḥenbiu, Ṭuat V, a group of four gods who measured land in the Ṭuat.

Ḥenb-requ, B.D. 145A (Nav. II, 156), a jackal-god who guarded the 7th Pylon of Sekhet-Åaru.

ḥenb, ball, pill, bolus, a ball of unguent.

ḥenb-t, Ebers Pap. 75, 8, chick-pea, pulse (?); Copt. ϩⲟⲩϥ.

ḥenbab, to curse, to anathematize, to exorcise.

ḥenbaba-t, , Ebers Pap. 107, 11, 15, 108, 4 . . . . .

ḥenbi, fountain, well, spring.

Ḥenbu, P. 603, a kind of boat.

ḥenbu, U. 461, , P. 425, M. 608, N. 1213, darts, weapons.

Ḥenbethm, Ṭuat VI, a goddess (?)

ḥenp, to cast a net, to drag a stream.

ḥenf, T. 179, P. 523, M. 161, N. 652, to seize (?) to curb (?)

ḥenf, Rev. 12, 29, to fear; Copt. ϩⲉⲛϥ.

Ḥenemit, a goddess.

ḥenmemit, U. 211,

, P. 155, 312, 711, T. 221, N. 785, 1260, 1361, , M. 449, , Rec. 26, 234, varr. , , , , men and women of a bygone age.

ḥenemnem , to creep, to crawl, to slink away.

ḥenemnemu , B.D. 149, X, 3, those who slink away, cowards.

ḥenemi , to creep away (?)

ḥenemu-t , Rec. 2, 129 = , cistern, well.

Ḥenkherth , Ṭuat IV, a lioness-goddess.

ḥens , Peasant 45, Amherst Pap. I, , , IV, 649, to be narrow (of a road), restricted, blocked (of a vein or artery).

ḥens-t , , obstruction, soot (?) charcoal (?)

ḥensek , IV, 83, knotted, tied.

ḥensek-t , T. 352, , N. 174, , , lock of hair, tress; plur. , , P. 710, , ; , P. 436, , M. 649, , U. 473, locks of Horus; , Rec. 30, 67, lock of the Lynx (?)

ḥensekti , , , , hairy one, a boy or man with side-locks; , a woman with side-locks; , a god with side-locks; plur. , , , , , Isis and Nephthys.

Ḥensektit , Ombos II, 130, a goddess with abundant hair.

Ḥensektiu , the gods with long hair and beards.

Ḥensek-t-menȧ-t, etc. , etc., B.D. 99, 12, the rope of the magical boat.

Ḥensektit Ḥeru , U. 473, , M. 649, P. 436, the tresses of Horus; the "four spirits," , who dwelt in them were the four sons of Horus.

ḥenq , U. 46, , , Thes. 1204, to squeeze, to press out, to seize.

ḥenq , , , , drink, juice, beer; Copt. ϩⲛ̄ⲕⲉ.

Ḥenq , Hh. 382, a god.

ḥenk , P. 18, M. 136, IV, 342, , N. 647, , Metternich Stele 246, , , , , , , to make an offering.

ḥenk-t , U. 576, , gift, offering; plur. , U. 165, , , , N. 771, , , , , Rec. 3, 53, , IV, 1165, , IV, 954.

ḥenkit 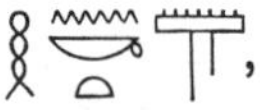, Rec. 31, 163, 

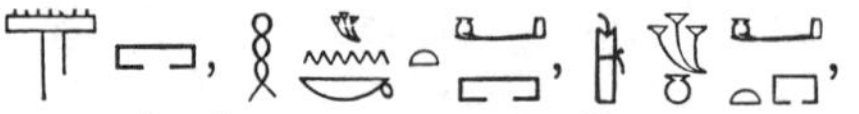 Rec. 3, 53, 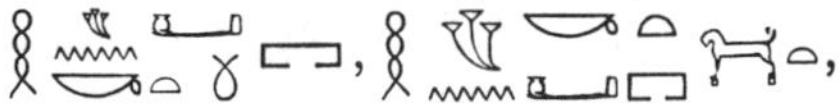
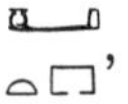, IV, 955, , bed, couch, bed coverlet; plur. 
, Rec. 26, 230, 

Love Songs V, 7, .

Ḥenktt , the Other World.

ḥenkit ānkh , IV, 1020, the name of a chamber.

Ḥenku-en-årp  , B.D. 125, III, 30, left lintel of the hall of Maāti.

Ḥenku-en-fat-maāt  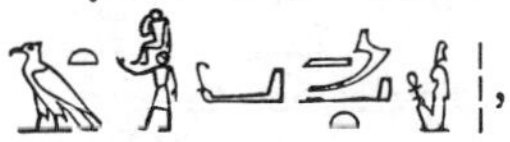, B.D. 131, 3, 29, the right lintel of the hall of Maāti.

ḥenk  , pan of scales; plur.  , Peasant 323.

ḥenk , to cut or pluck fruit and flowers.

ḥenku , mattocks (?) hoes (?)

ḥeng 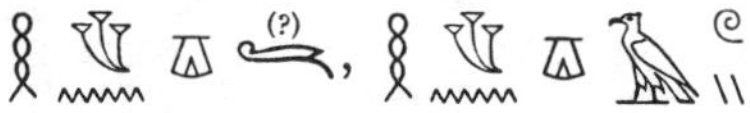 , to be narrow, constricted; , N. 213, to press or squeeze the mouth.

Ḥeng , Berg. II, 6, a crocodile-god.

Ḥeng-re , the god of the 20th day of the month.

ḥengeg 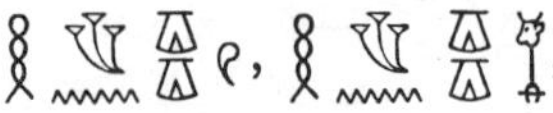, Rec. 35, 56, Metternich Stele 41, throat, gullet.

ḥengeg , , to rejoice.

ḥengegtiu , those who rejoice (?)

ḥengu , Rec. 30, 67 . . . .

ḥenta , to fall into ruin, oblivion.

ḥenta (?) ; see following word:

ḥentasu , lizard; Copt. ⲁⲛⲑⲟⲩⲥ.

ḥenti , smiter, fighter.

Ḥenti , the Smiter-god.

Ḥenti-neken-f , Denderah III, 9, 28, a serpent-god.

Ḥenti-requ [illegible], B.D. 146, a god of the 5th Pylon.

ḥentui [illegible], A.Z. 17, 57 . . . .

ḥenth [illegible], P. 189, N. 908, [illegible], M. 357 . . . . . .

ḥer [illegible], a mark of the infinitive.

ḥer [illegible] [illegible], a conjunction, for, because, with, and, therefore, moreover, [illegible], gold and silver; [illegible], Anubis and Usert.

ḥer [illegible], T. 312, 361 (with suffixes [illegible]), a preposition: on, upon, at, by, by way of, with, by means of, through, in respect of, on account of, besides, away from, in addition to, over; Copt. ϩⲓ.

ḥeru  Thes. 1296, with **r**, besides, except, with the exception of.

ḥer —em ḥer , opposite, facing.

ḥer enti , because of.

ḥer enti sa , because, through.

ḥer ḥer , because of, on behalf of.

ḥer 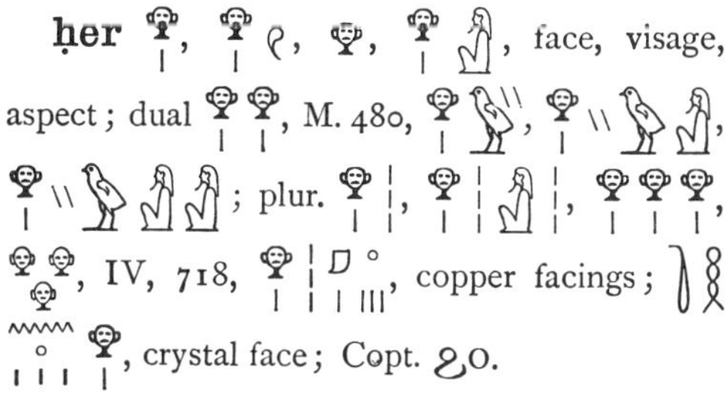 face, visage, aspect; dual, M. 480; plur., IV, 718, copper facings; crystal face; Copt. ϩⲟ.

ḥer , Rev. 13, 42 . . . .

ḥer ānt , pointed face (of cattle), cattle without horns.

ḥeru (?) bȧku , a kind of seed used in medicine.

ḥer — 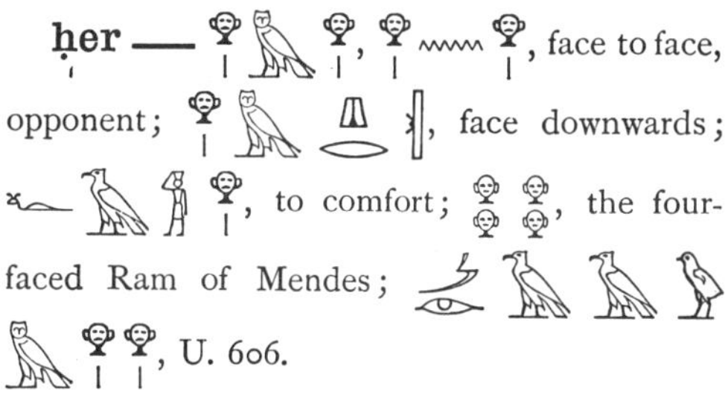 face to face, opponent; face downwards; to comfort; the four-faced Ram of Mendes; U. 606.

ḥer neb  Åmen. 10, 18, everybody, all mankind.

ḥer en pāt 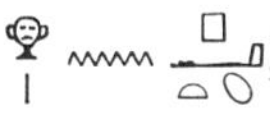, an amulet.

Ḥer-Åten , Ṭuat X, the face of the Sun-god.

Ḥer-uā 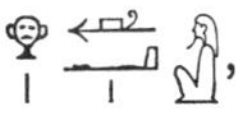, "One Face"—a title of the Sun-god.

Ḥerui-fi (?) , Ṭuat IX, the god of two faces, *i.e.*, Horus-Set.

Ḥer-f-āui-f (?) , Ṭuat II, a two-headed man-god.

Ḥer-f-mm-ḥa-f  U. 604, P. 204, N. 1002, "his face behind him"—the name of a god.

Ḥer-f-em-khent-f 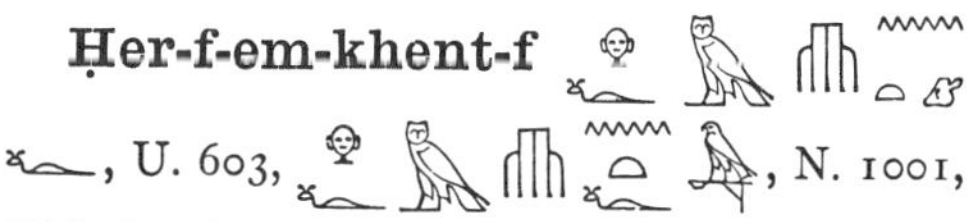 U. 603, N. 1001, "his face in front of him"—the name of a god.

Ḥer-f-em-she-t, etc. 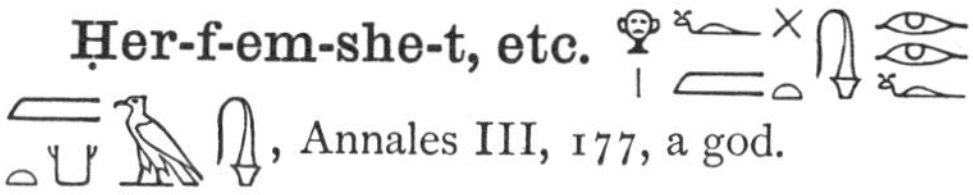, Annales III, 177, a god.

Ḥer-f-em-qeb-f , the name of a mythological serpent.

Ḥer-f-ḥa-f  N. 913, N. 1129, M. 589, 752, P. 411, N. 1194, one of the 42 assessors of Osiris; Rec. 31, 22, "he loveth righteousness, he hateth sin."

Ḥer-f-ḥa-f 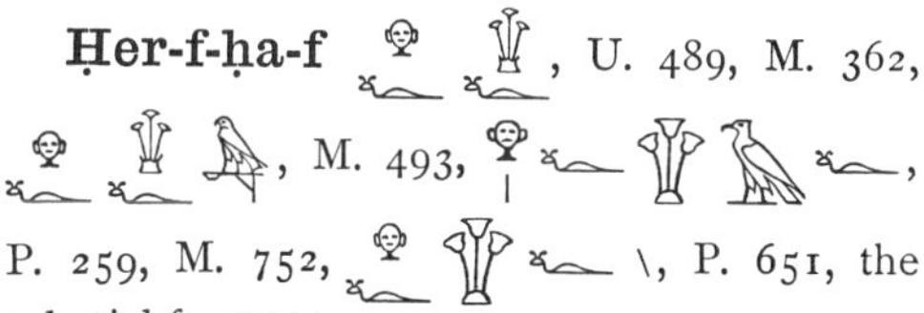 U. 489, M. 362, M. 493, P. 259, M. 752, P. 651, the celestial ferryman.

Ḥer-en-ba , Lanzone 689, a god with three serpents in the place of a head.

Ḥer-nefer 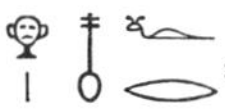, B.D. 151, 2, a title of Rā.

Ḥer-ḥer-ḥer (?) , U. 542, T. 298, a serpent-fiend in the Ṭuat.

Ḥeru IV ḥer neḥeb-uā, Goshen 2, a god with four rams' heads and a pair of hawk's wings.

ḥerui senu, P. 267, , M. 480, , N. 1248, "two-faced," a title of the cow-goddess **Bat**, .

Ḥer-sen (?), , Ṭuat I, a singing-goddess.

Ḥer-k-en-Maāt, , B.D. 31, 3, an opponent of the Crocodile-god Sui.

ḥer, Rev. 12, 95, a term of relationship; fem. .

ḥeri, Tombos Stele 2, , P. 396, M. 566, N. 1172, , , , , , , , , , chief, chieftain, master, captain, president, governor, overseer, superior, he who has chief charge, control, or authority, a celestial being, he who is over; , chief of the two heavens; dual , P. 402, M. 575, N. 1181; plur. , U. 174, , T. 335, , M. 246, , Rec. 31, 172, , IV, 83, , , , , , , , , , , , , , Rev. 11, 173.

ḥeri-t, , , , Åmen. 18, , Rec. 13, 5, , mistress, chieftainess, goddess; , P. 182, , N. 895, upper, superior (fem. plur); , Thes. 1199, which is in heaven.

ḥeri åb, , , , , , , the middle of anything, the intestines, what is inside, interior; plur. , , U. 512, N. 781, ; , T. 308, P. 29, , the goddess dwelling in a temple; , Rec. 31, 28, the gods inside a temple; , in their midst.

ḥeri-åb-t, , , , the sanctuary of a temple, the middle room of a palace.

ḥeri åb hru, , mid-day.

ḥeri åb gerḥ, midnight.

ḥeri åb, , image, statue, bust.

ḥeri baḥ, before, in the presence of.

ḥeri ruti, outside, at the door.

ḥeri khenti, to the front, in front.

ḥeri kher, beneath, under.

ḥeri sa, , after, in addition to; , P. 704.

ḥeri sa åri, thereafter.

ḥeri-ā, L.D. III, 6594, 5, , at once, immediately, straightway, instantly; , Ebers Pap. 40, 21, a medicine to be taken at once, speedy remedy.

ḥeri-ā (?), Anastasi 1, 1, 7, a medicine which is a speedy remedy.

ḥeri-ā, , , arrears;  , arrears of taxes due on the land.

ḥeri uat  , he who is on the road, traveller.

ḥeri usekh-t 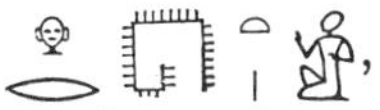 , keeper of the great hall of a temple or palace.

ḥeri per 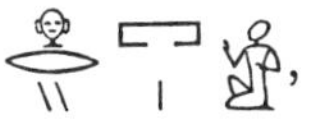 , house master.

ḥeriu petchetiu  , chiefs of the foreign mercenaries.

ḥeri em ā , , straightway, forthwith.

ḥeriu m's  , chiefs of the transport.

ḥeri m'tchaiu  , chief of the Nubians employed as police in Egypt; plur. , .

ḥeri mensh 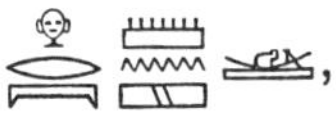 , Rec. 21, 77, captain of a boat.

ḥeri meràt  , corvée ganger.

Ḥeri-nes-t , , the title of a priest or priestess in Apollinopolis.

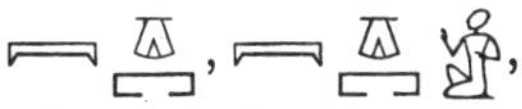

Ḥeri-sa  , a title of the priest of Hibiu.

Ḥeri-sa-ur  , U. 396, master of great knowledge.

Ḥeriti senti 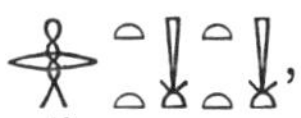 , a title of the two priests of Heroopolites.

Ḥeri sesh 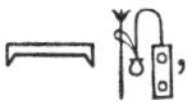 , chief scribe;   , Rec. 16, 57, chief librarian of the temple;  , chief scribe of the altar of all the gods.

Ḥeri seshta , , , , , , , , , confidential adviser or secretary, trusted councillor;  , men learned in the most sacred mysteries;  , P.S.B. 13, 568,  , a title.

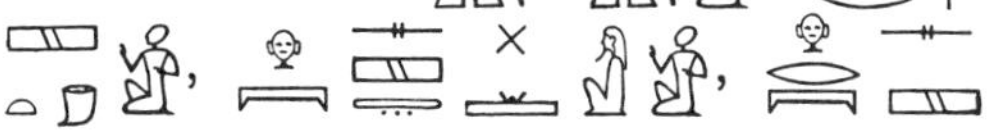

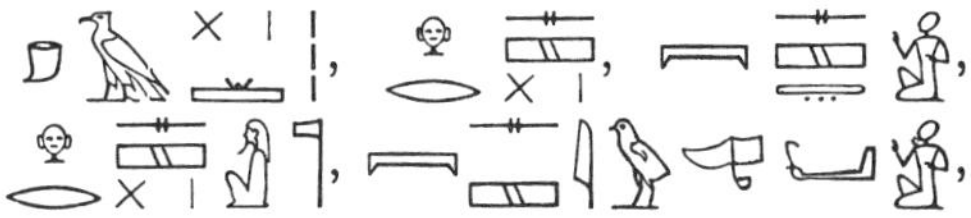

Ḥeri seqer , Methen, , Rec. 26, 236, a title in the IVth dynasty.

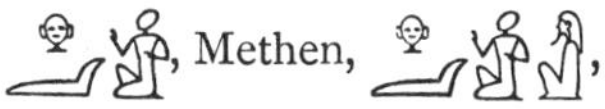

Ḥeriu-shā  , Tombos Stele 3, , , , , , , , , "[dwellers] on the sand," *i.e.*, the tribes who live in the deserts.

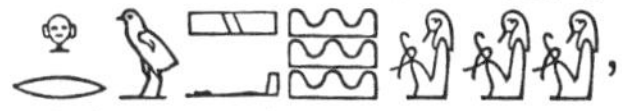

Ḥeri (ānkh utcha senb) shi  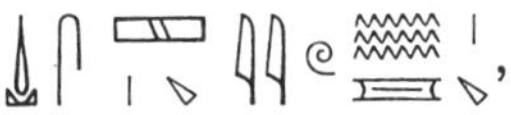 , "chief (life, strength, health!) of the Lake," title of the priests of the Crocodile-god Šebek in the Fayyûm.

Ḥeri ka-t 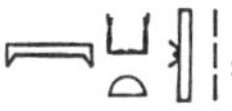 , inspector of works.

ḥeri ges  , at the side of.

ḥeri ta  , Pap. 3024, 41, an earthly being, *i.e.*, a man; plur. 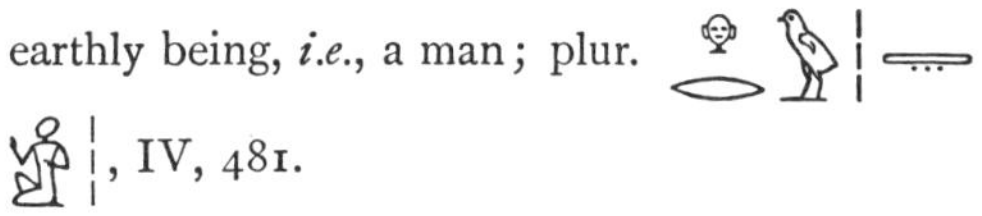 , IV, 481.

ḥeri tchatcha , , , , , , , , , , chief governor, commander-in-chief; plur. , , , the great chief governors, , U. 592, chief of gods, chief of men.

ḥerit tchatcha, chieftainess, dominion; , a goddess; , the name of a crown or diadem.

ḥerit, skull, top of the head.

Ḥeri, B.D. (Saïte) 133, 9, 145, 42, 147, 21, a god, God.

Ḥerit, Berg. II, 12, goddess of heaven, a form of Nut.

Ḥerit, a goddess of Red Mountain .

Ḥeri-Agbȧ-f, B.D. 64, 15, a title of Nu or Rā.

Ḥeri-ȧa-t-Ṭeṭ-t, Mythe, 20, a sacred tree.

Ḥeri-ȧau, B.D. 125, II, one of the 42 assessors of Osiris.

Ḥeri-ȧb-ȧr-t-f, B.D. 96, 1, a light-god in the Ṭuat.

Ḥeri-ȧb-uȧa, Zod. Dend., Denderah II, 10, Tomb Seti I, one of the 36 Dekans; Gr. Ρηουω.

Ḥeri-ȧb-uȧa-f, B.D. 134, 2, a title of Kheperȧ.

Ḥeri-ȧbt-uȧa-set, Ṭuat I, one of the 12 goddess-guides of Rā.

Ḥeri-ȧb-uu, Berg. I, 13, 19, a light-god.

Ḥeri-ȧbt-nut-s, Mar. Aby. I, 44, a goddess.

Ḥeri-ȧb-khentu (?), Tomb of Seti I, one of the 36 Dekans.

Ḥeri-ȧbt-Shai-t, a name of a serpent on the royal crown.

Ḥeri-ȧb-Karȧ-f, B.D. 134, 1, a title of the Sun-god.

Ḥeri-ȧriu-āa en Ṭuat, Cairo Pap. III, 7, a lion-god.

Ḥerit-ȧst, Ombos II, 130, a goddess.

Ḥeri-ȧst-f-ur-t, "chief of his great seat"—a title.

Ḥeri-ā-f, Berg. I, 11, , Rec. 4, 28, the name of a lion-god.

Ḥeriu-āmāmti, Ṭuat IX, the masters of nets (?) in the Ṭuat.

Ḥeri-ānkhiu, Chief of men—a title of Rā.

Ḥeriu-ārit, the chiefs of the Divisions of the Ṭuat.

Ḥeri-ākhu-t, chief of an altar, *i.e.*, a god or divine being at whose altar offerings are made; plur. .

Ḥeriu-ākhu-sen, B.D. 17 (Nebseni), 38, a title of the Eyes of Rā and Horus.

Ḥerit-āshm (?), Ombos II, 132, a goddess.

Ḥeri-uaref, Ṭuat IV, a god who towed the boat of Ȧf.

Ḥeri-uatch-t-f, B.D. 112, 12, a title of Horus; fem. .

Ḥeri-uā, B.D. 71, 3, a title of Horus.

Ḥeri-uā-f, U. 450, , T. 258, a divine title.

Ḥeriu-unut , U. 399, the hour-gods.

Ḥeri-uru , one of the 42 assessors of Osiris.

Ḥeri-utu-f (?) , Ṭuat XI, a god who lived on the sounds made by the shadows and souls of the enemies of Rā.

Ḥeri-ba-f , Tomb of Seti I, one of the 75 forms of Rā (No. 58).

Ḥeri-beḥ , B.D. (Saïte) 39, 6, a god.

Ḥeri-maāt , Berg. I, 11, a god.

Ḥeri-meḥt 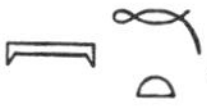, Ṭuat IX, the god of the North.

Ḥeriu-meṭut-ḥekaiu 
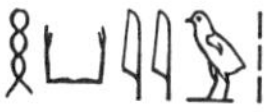, Ṭuat IX, the gods who cast spells.

Ḥerit-neferu-en-neb-s 
, Berg. II, 9, the goddess of the 12th hour of the night.

Ḥerit-nemmtit-s , Ṭuat XI, a goddess.

Ḥerit-nest 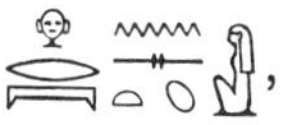, Ombos II, 133, a goddess.

Ḥeri-nest-f 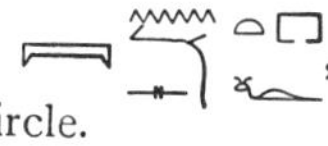, Ṭuat X, the doorkeeper of a Circle.

Ḥerit-neqef , a title of Sekh-mit.

Ḥerit-neteru 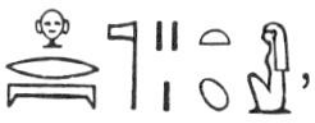, Ombos II, 132, a goddess.

Ḥeri-remen , Rec. 37, 67, a god.

Ḥerit-remen (?) , Ṭuat X, a goddess of the South.

Ḥeri-retitsa (?) 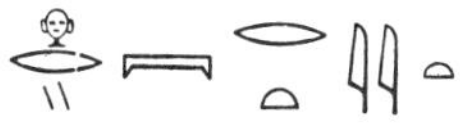
, B.D. 69, 14, 70, 1, a god.

Ḥeri-reṭ-f , T. 261, the "eldest of the gods."

Ḥeriu-ḥaṭu , Ṭuat IV, the gods of the fiery furnaces.

Ḥerit-ḥaṭus , Ṭuat XI, a goddess of the fire-pits in the Ṭuat.

Ḥeri-ḥerit , , B.D. 39, 9, a god or goddess who chained Āapep; var. (Saïte), .

Ḥeri-ḥetemtiu 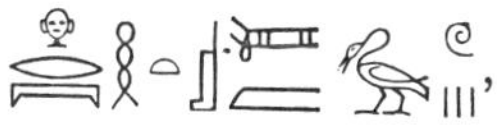, the god of destruction.

Ḥeri-khat-f , "he who is on his belly," *i.e.*, worm, serpent; plur. .

Ḥeri-khu , Ṭuat V, a god.

Ḥeri-khent , Ṭuat X, a god in the Ṭuat = the Dekan Χουτάρ.

Ḥeri-khenṭu-f , Ṭuat III, a form of Osiris in the Ṭuat.

Ḥeri-sau (?) , Ṭuat IV, the overseer of the furnaces in which the wicked were consumed.

Ḥeri-sep-f , B.D. (Nebseni) 17, 44, a title of Āmḥeḥ.

Ḥerit-sefu-s 
, Ṭuat XI, a goddess in the Ṭuat.

Ḥeriu-senemu 
 (var. ), T. 335, P. 1810, gods who gave food.

Ḥeri-serser 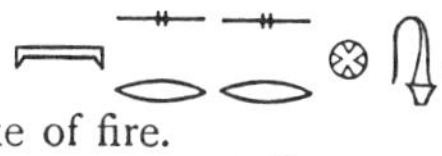, Ṭuat VIII, chief of a lake of fire.

Ḥeriu-set [illegible], U. 174, [illegible], T. 335, P. 808, gods of food.

Ḥeri-shā-f [illegible]
[illegible], a title of Osiris.

Ḥeri-shā-f , Ṭuat III, an ape-god.

Ḥerit-shā-s 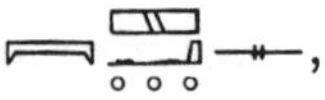, Ṭuat XI, a goddess of the desert.

Ḥeri-shefit 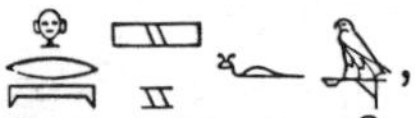, Peasant 195, 
, Ahnas 2, Lanzone 552, , Rec. 35, 138, a ram-god of Ḥensu (Herakleopolis); , Mar. Aby. I, 45.

Ḥeri-shefit Ba-neb-Ṭeṭ-t  , a god of the Fayyûm.

Ḥeri-shemā (?) , Ṭuat IX, the god of the South.

Ḥeri-sheta-taui , Ṭuat X, a destroyer of the bodies of the dead.

Ḥeri-qat-f , U. 422, , T. 241, a god who worked a paddle.

Ḥeri-qenb-t-f 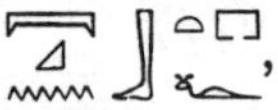, Ṭuat V, a chief of the Hall of Judgment.

Ḥeri-ka , the son of Shu and Tefnut, *i.e.*, Geb.

Ḥeri-kau , U. 396, the chief of Kau.

Ḥerit-ketut-s  , Ṭuat XI, a goddess in the Ṭuat.

Ḥeri-ta 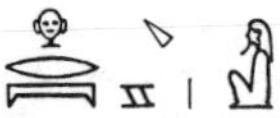, B.D. 168 (Circle XII), the Earth-god who allotted estates to the blessed.

Ḥeri-thertu 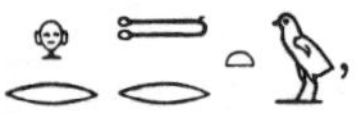, U. 510, , T. 323, the god of the lasso.

Ḥeri-ṭeba-t-f , Ṭuat IV, a god with two curved objects, , in the place of a head.

Ḥeri-ṭesu-f , Ṭuat VII, a fetterer of Neḥa-ḥer.

Ḥerit-tchatcha-åḥ , the goddess of the 7th hour of the night.

Ḥerit-tchatcha-āḥa-ḥer-neb-set  , Thes. 28, Denderah IV, 84, Berg. II, 9, the goddess of the 7th hour of the night.

Ḥerit-tchatcha-neb-s 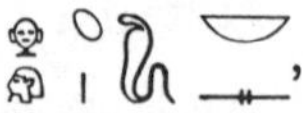, Ombos II, 108, one of the 14 forms of Sekhmit.

Ḥeri-tchatcha-senu-f 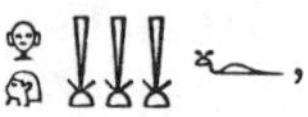, Rec. 37, 70, a god.

Ḥeri-tchatcha-taui 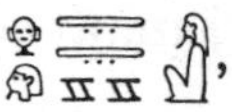, Mythe 2: (1) a dog-headed warrior-god; (2) a name of the heart of Osiris.

Ḥerit-tchatcha-ṭuatiu  , Ṭuat II, the chieftainess of the gods of the Ṭuat.

ḥerit , U. 223, P. 64, [illegible], N. 95, [illegible], IV, 843, [illegible], the sky, heaven, celestial region; [illegible], celestial mansions; [illegible], the sky, heaven.

ḥeriti , belonging to the upper regions.

ḥeriu 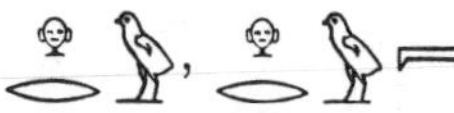, the upper part, what is above; Copt. ϩⲣⲁⲓ.

ḥeriu  [illegible], upper, *i.e.*, high-lying land or estates.

ḥeritt , a tomb in the hills, a hill cemetery, the hill side in which tombs were hewn; 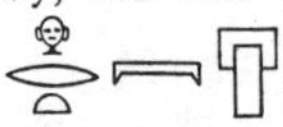, the hall of a hill tomb; , the everlasting or eternal tomb.

ḥeri , to fly, to ascend in the air; Copt. ϩⲏⲗ.

ḥer, P. 64, M. 88, N. 95, N. 105, T. 179, Pap. 3027, 8, 7, to be far from, to be remote, to move away from, *i.e.*, to avoid, to depart from; Peasant 306, remote; Culte Divin 132, coming forth, withdrawing from within his egg; ( ) "away with this drunkard."

ḥerti, a caravan march.

ḥer-t, U. 462, U. 390, P. 161, 381, way, path, road; Copt. ϩⲓⲏ.

ḥerḥer, Lib. Fun. 244, to rejoice, to be glad.

ḥer, Thes. 1205, to arrange, to set in order, to array; IV, 325, to pitch a tent.

ḥer, to terrify, to frighten, to be afraid; Åmen. 8, 10, 13, 9, 19, 11, someone or something fierce, terrible, terrifying, *e.g.*, a lion, IV, 184.

ḥeriu, Rev. 11, 181, to attack; Copt. ⲟⲩⲟⲓ (?)

ḥeri-t, IV, 908, Rec. 15, 179, IV, 887, 1081, Leyd. Pap. 2, 12, fear, awe, reverence, terror, fright; Copt. ϩⲉⲗⲓ.

ḥeri-t en im', Rec. 21, 93, fear of the sea.

ḥeru, Rec. 4, 134, threats, threatenings.

ḥerḥer, Love Songs 3, 2, to abash, to put to shame, to confound.

ḥerḥer, to demolish, to pull down; Copt. ϧⲉⲣϧⲱⲣ, ϣⲟⲣϣⲣ̄.

ḥerr, to linger, to delay, to hesitate; Copt. ϩⲣⲟⲩⲣ (?)

ḥer, house, abode, dwelling.

ḥer, furnace; see .

ḥer-t, Rec. 6, 7, prison, place of restraint (?)

ḥer-t, IV, 171, Thes. 1288, garden.

ḥer-t, watercourse, canal, aqueduct.

ḥer-t, Nile deposit.

ḥeriu, A.Z. 1905, 5, a kind of boat.

ḥer, pot, vase, vessel; plur. .

ḥer, Rev. 12, 101 = , register, day book.

ḥer-t, worm; Copt. ϩⲟⲗⲓ.

ḥerr-t, worm (intestinal), locust (?) serpent; plur. ; Copt. ⲁⲗⲟⲩⲗⲁ.

Ḥerrit 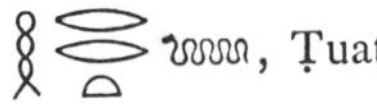, Ṭuat IV, a monster serpent that spawned 12 serpents.

Ḥerrit 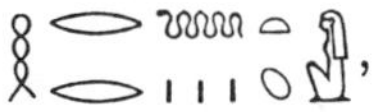, Ombos II, 133, a goddess.

ḥerr-t 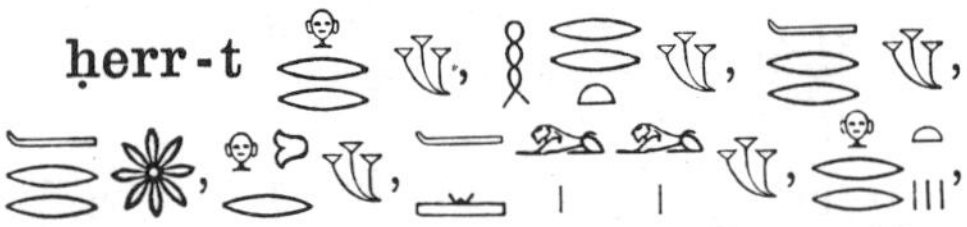, Rec. 20, 14, 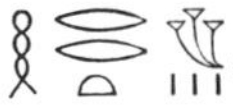, IV, 915, flower, blossom; Copt. ϩⲣⲏⲣⲏ.

Ḥer, Ḥeru , U. 83, U. 443, T. 253, M. 454, , , an ancient Sky-god, his right eye was the sun and his left eye the moon; Copt. ϩⲱⲣ, Heb. חור (in חורנופי = ).

Ḥerit 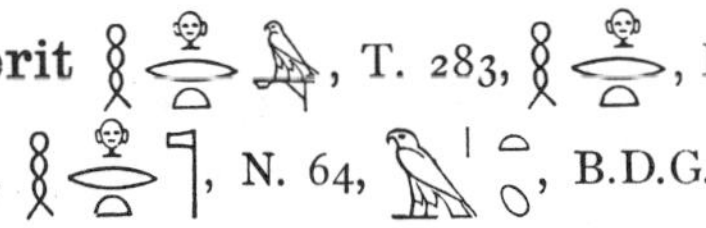, T. 283, P. 49, M. 31, N. 64, B.D.G. 385, 386, , the female counterpart of Horus; , a goddess (Ṭuat XI).

Ḥeru , Tomb of Seti I: (1) one of the 75 forms of Rā (No. 19); (2) an air-god, Berg. I, 23; (3) a god who hacked the dead in pieces (Ṭuat VI).

Ḥeru , Ṭuat XI: (1) the name of the sceptre 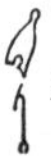; (2) Ṭuat VI, the name of a jackal-headed standard to which the damned were tied.

Ḥer-ȧt 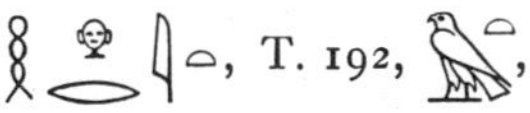, T. 192, P. 677, N. 1289, appertaining to Horus, the opposite of , Set-ȧt, appertaining to Set.

Ḥerui , U. 16, B.D. 172, 17, 183, 11, the two brother Hawk-gods, Horus and Set.

Ḥeru-ȧa 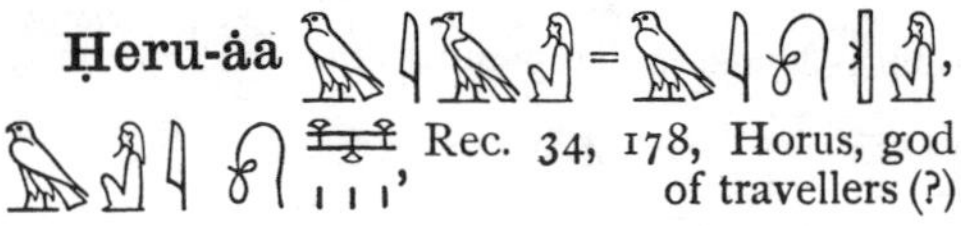, Rec. 34, 178, Horus, god of travellers (?)

Ḥeru-ȧabtȧ 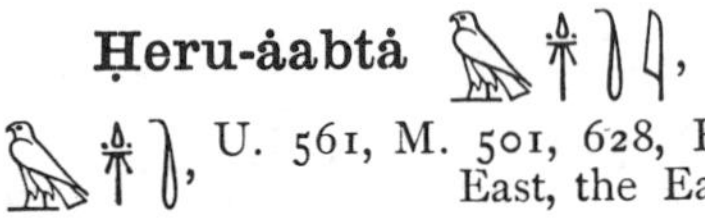, P. 322, 632, U. 561, M. 501, 628, Horus of the East, the Eastern Horus.

Ḥeru-ȧakhuti , P. 138, 670, , M. 274, N. 889, M. 390, M. 457, N. 1272, , Horus, the god who dwells in the horizon.

Ḥeru-ȧakhuti , the god of the 12th month of the Egyptian year; Copt. ⲙⲉⲥⲱⲣⲏ.

Ḥeru-ȧakhuti-Kheperȧ  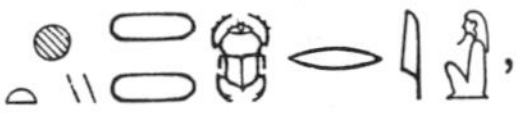, a double form of the Sun-god.

Ḥeru-ȧakhuti-Temu-Ḥeru-Kheperȧ  , a tetrad of Sun-gods.

Ḥeru-ȧmi-ȧbu , B.D. 29A, 3, Horus, dweller in hearts.

Ḥeru-ȧm[*i.e.*, unem'i]-ȧfu  , Rec. 3, 54, a form of Horus.

Ḥeru-ȧmi-ȧthen-f  , B.D. 125, I, 5, Horus of his Disk.

Ḥeru-ȧmi-u (?) , a hawk-headed crocodile with a tail terminating in a dog's head.

Ḥeru-ȧmi-Uatchur , P. 690, the Mediterranean Horus.

Ḥeru-ȧmi-uȧa 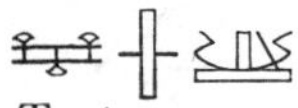, Ṭuat IX, a form of Horus in the Ṭuat.

Ḥeru-ȧmi-Ḥenu , U. 202, 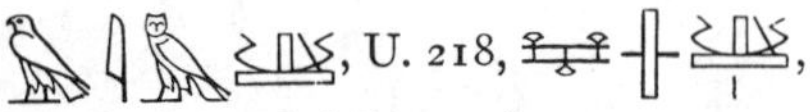, U. 218, Ṭuat IX, a hawk-headed lion-god.

Ḥeru-ȧmi-Khent-n-ȧr-ti  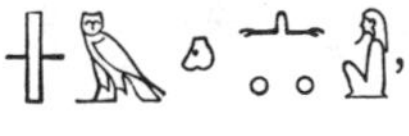, the Blind Horus.

Ḥeru-åmi-Sepṭ-t, T. 277, , P. 31, M. 41, , M. 149, N. 69, 650, Horus of Sothis.

Ḥeru-Ånmut-f, Rec. 17, 119, a form of Horus worshipped at Edfû.

Ḥeru-åntch-f-åt-f Åsår, P. 630; see **Ḥeru-netch-åtf**, N. 1374.

Ḥeru åtem . . . ka-t-f, M. 129, a form of Horus.

Ḥeru-åṭebui, Horus of Upper and Lower Egypt.

Ḥeru-āa-åbu, Ḳersher Pap. II, 7, the Bold Horus.

Ḥeru-ānkh-ḥeri-serekh (?), Edfû I, 12, 20, Horus, lord of the serekh.

Ḥeru-āḥai-sebåu, Tomb of Seti I, Horus, destroyer of rebels.

Ḥeru-āḥāi, B.D. 99, 24, Horus the Stander (or Pillar).

Ḥeru-uāt-t, IV, 390, a title of Queen Ḥatshepset.

Ḥeru-up-shet, , , the planet Jupiter.

Ḥeru-Un-nefer, Horus, god of all Egypt.

Ḥeru-ur, , , , , , U. 358, B.D. 107 and 136B, 12, Sinsin (Pellegrini) 19, Nesi-Åmsu 26, 1, Horus the Great, or Horus the Ancestor; Gr. Ἀρωῆρις, Ἀρουηρις.

Ḥeru-uru, Denderah IV, 60, a warrior-god.

Ḥeru-ur-khenti-år-ti, , Horus as master of his eyes (sun and moon).

Ḥeru-ur-shefit, Denderah IV, 78, a jackal guardian-god of Denderah.

Ḥeru-ukhakhat-tå, Rec. 30, 67, a form of Horus.

Ḥeru-Usāsit, Denderah III, 58, Horus and the Heliopolitan goddess Usāsit.

Ḥeru-Baåt, P. 34, N. 40, Horus of the sepulchral monument.

Ḥeru-Ba-Ṭaṭa, Berg. II, 4, Horus, Soul of Ṭeṭ.

Ḥeru-Beḥuṭ, , Horus of Edfû. His wars and conquests are related in Naville, Mythe, Geneva, 1870.

Ḥeru-Beḥti-ti, Rec. 12, 211, Horus of the two thrones.

Ḥeru-p-Rā, Nesi-Åmsu 17, 13, the great first-born son of Åmen.

Ḥeru-p-Rā, the son of Menthu and Rāit-taui.

Ḥeru-pa-kharṭ, Harpokrates, son of Osiris and Isis; Gr. Ἁρποκράτης.

Ḥeru-p-kharṭ, Horus, the Child; Gr. Ἁρποκράτης.

Ḥeru-p-kharṭ-ḥeri-åb-Ṭeṭ, B.D.G. 348, Harpokrates of Busiris.

Ḥeru-p-ka, Horus the Bull, a name of the planet Saturn.

Ḥeru-em-åakhuti, Rec. 3, 38, Harmakhis.

Ḥeru-em-åakhuti-Kheperå-Rā-Tem, a tetrad of sun-gods.

Ḥeru-em-àakhuti 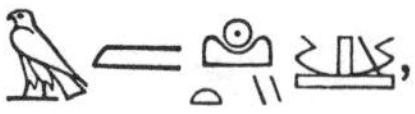, the name of the sacred boat of Athribis.

Ḥerit-em-Ḥetepit 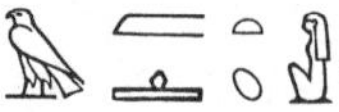, Ombos I, 46, a goddess.

Ḥeru-em-Khebit , Horus of the Delta swamps.

Ḥeru-em-Khent-n-àr-ti (?)  , the Blind Horus.

Ḥeru-em-sau-àb 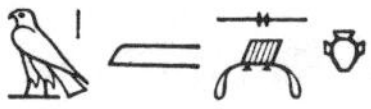, 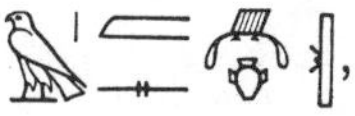, the god of the 7th hour of the day.

Ḥeru-em-Saḥ-t (or **Beḥ-t ?**)  [illegible], Ombos I, 64.

Ḥeru-em-tchatchaui  [illegible], B.D. (Nebseni) 17, 28, the two-headed Horus.

Ḥeru-m'thenu 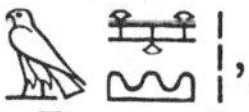, a form of Horus worshipped in the Eastern Delta.

Ḥeru-merti  , Sinsin (Pellegrini) 20, Quelques Pap. 46, Nesi-Åmsu 25, 24, 26, 7, Denderah IV, 63, the two-eyed Horus, his eyes, , being the sun and moon.

Ḥeru-meriti ; see **Ḥeru-merti** .

Ḥeru-meri-tef , Horus, the lover of his father.

Ḥeru-nub , Br. Relig. 664, Horus of Hierakonpolis.

Ḥeru-nub , the Horus of gold, which was worshipped at Antaeopolis in the form of a hawk standing on a bull, .

Ḥeru-nub (?) , the third title of the king of Egypt, commonly rendered "Golden Horus"; early forms are:— , Pepi I; , Merenrā; , Pepi II.

Ḥeru-neb-àabtiu , Nesi-Åmsu 25, 24, the Eastern Horus.

Ḥeru-neb-àakhut , Denderah IV, 63, Horus, lord of the horizon.

Ḥeru-neb-au-àb , Denderah IV, 78, an ape-god.

Ḥerit-nebt-uu , Ombos I, 334, a goddess (?)

Ḥeru-neb-urr-t  [illegible], B.D. 141, 9, Horus as possessor of the supreme crown.

Ḥeru-neb-Behen , a form of Horus worshipped at Βοῶν (Wâdî Ḥalfah).

Ḥeru-neb-pāt 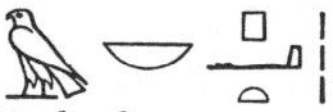, P. 478, N. 216, 1265, Horus, lord of men.

Ḥeru-neb-taui , P. 478, N. 1266, Horus, lord of the Two Lands.

Ḥeru-nefer , Ombos I, 47,  , Horus, the young man.

Ḥeru-nefer-renpi-ta (?)  [illegible], Denderah IV, 65, Horus as rejuvenator of the earth.

Ḥeru en mābiu , Rec. 2, 118, a form of Horus.

Ḥeru en meḥiu 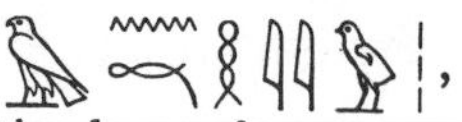, Ṭuat X, Horus as god of the drowned.

Ḥeru-nekhni , U. 433, , T. 248, Horus of Hierakonpolis.

Ḥeru-netch (netchti)-àt-f [illegible] 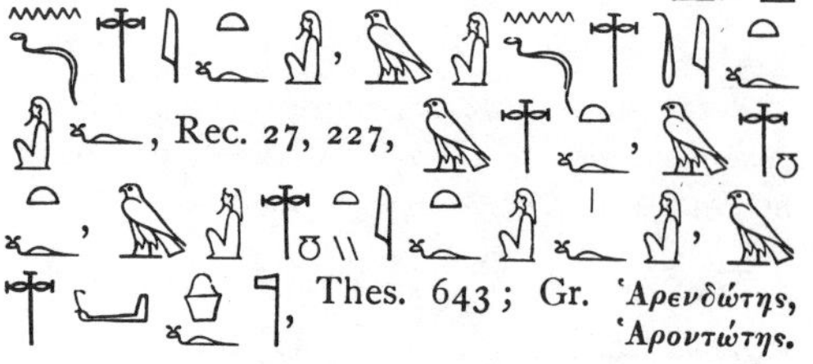, Rec. 27, 227, Thes. 643; Gr. 'Αρενδώτης, 'Αροντώτης.

Ḥeru-netch-ḥer-tef-f , , , ; see **Ḥeru-netch-àt-f.**

Ḥeru-netch-tef-f , , , the god of the 2nd and 30th days of the month.

Ḥeru-netch-s-Àmen , Reise 18, a form of Horus worshipped in the Oases.

Ḥeru-Rā-p-khart̤ , B.D.G. 348, Harpokrates of Hermonthis.

Ḥeru-renpti (?) , P. 33, N. 40, , N. 355, Horus of the two years.

Ḥeru (?) ḥa , P. 204, M. 331, , N. 850; see **Aḥa.**

Ḥeru-ḥu-sti-pest̤ (?) , Denderah IV, 79, an ass-god.

Ḥeru-Ḥennu , B.D.G. 348, one of the seven forms of Harpokrates.

Ḥeru-ḥenb , Ombos I, 93, a god of offerings.

Ḥer-Ḥer- . . . . . . , , the god of the 12th day of the month.

[Ḥeru]-ḥeri-àb-àmi-khat , B.D. 29A, 3, the unborn Horus.

Ḥeru-ḥeri-àb-ḥemui , Ombos I, 185, Horus between the steering oars.

Ḥeru-ḥeri-ā-f , Berg. I, 35, a hawk-god.

Ḥeru-ḥeri-uatch-f , , , B.D. 12, 12, Denderah IV, 84, , Rec. 37, 66, Horus, master of his sceptre of feldspar.

Ḥeru-ḥeri-uatch-f (*sic*), , , , the god of the 5th hour of the night and of the 17th day of the month.

Ḥeru-ḥeri-masti, etc. , Edfû I, 12, 24, Horus of Edfû.

Ḥeru-ḥeri-neferu , B.D. 15 (Ani 20), Horus on the pilot's place.

Ḥeru-ḥeri-khent̤-f , , Ṭuat VII, Horus, master of the stars and hours.

Ḥeru-ḥeri-khet (?) , Berg. II, 8, a hawk-god.

Ḥeru-ḥeri-she-ṭuatiu , Ṭuat IX, Horus, master of the lakes in the Ṭuat.

Ḥeru-ḥeri-qenb-t-res (?) , Rec. 37, 71, a god.

Ḥeru-ḥeri-tchatcha-m'kha[it] , Berg. II, 5, Horus, master of the scales of judgment.

Ḥeru-ḥeri-tchatcha-Tchestches , Ombos 2, 195, Horus of the Oasis of Dâkhlah.

Ḥeru-ḥequi (?) , Ṭuat V, Horus of the two sceptres.

Ḥeru-Ḥekenu , , B.D.G. 1229, a singing-god in the boat of Àf.

Ḥeru-kheper-merti , Rec. 11, 129, a form of Horus.

Ḥeru-khenti , Ṭuat X: (1) Horus, master of the serpent Thes-ḥeru; (2) one of the 36 Dekans; Gr. *χονταρ.*

Ḥeru-khenti-åakhu , P. 75, , M. 106, N. 18, , P. 690, Horus, master of spirit-souls.

Ḥeru-khenti-år-ti , B.D. 17, 100, Horus with his two eyes, the sun and moon.

Ḥeru-khenti-åḥ-t-f , Ṭuat VI, Horus, master of his field.

Ḥeru-khenti-peru , U. 202, , T. 79, M. 232, N. 611, Horus, master of temples.

Ḥerui-khentui-peru , T. 331, , N. 621, the two Horus-gods, masters of temples.

Ḥeru-khenti-per-ḥeḥ , B.D. 42, 26, the Eternal Horus.

Ḥeru-khenti-menå-t-f , M. 709, Horus, master of his bandlet.

Ḥeru-khenti menut-f , P. 79, , M. 109, , P. 204, , N. 23, Horus, master of his thighs (?)

Ḥeru-khenti-n-år-ti (?) , , , , B.D. (Nebseni) 17, 16, 18c, 1, 42, 4, 5, Horus without eyes, *i.e.*, the night sky without sun or moon.

Ḥeru-khenti-khatti , Horus in the belly, the unborn Horus.

Ḥeru-khenti-khat-th ; see , Horus in the belly.

Ḥeru-khenti-khaṭi , , , B.D. 142, 114, Nesi-Åmsu 25, 22, the unborn Horus.

Ḥeru-khenti-khaṭi , the god of the 10th month (ⲡⲁⲱⲛⲓ).

Ḥeru-khenti-sekhem , P. 85, , U. 532, , N. 44, , B.D. 18B, 2, Horus of Letopolis.

Ḥeru-khenṭi-ḥeḥ , B.D. 42, 15, Horus, traverser of hundreds of thousands of years.

Ḥeru-khesbetch-år-ti , U. 370, , B.D. 177, 7, the blue-eyed Horus.

Ḥeru-kheti , Ṭuat III, Horus as a fire-god.

Ḥeru-kharṭ , Tetå 301, Horus the Child with his finger in his mouth, .

Ḥeru-khattå , N. 1265, the unborn Horus; var. , P. 477.

Ḥeru-sa-Åst , , , , Horus, son of Isis; , Rev. 11, 125; Gr. Ἁρσιῆσις, Copt. ϢⲢⲤⲒⲎⲤⲈ.

Ḥeru-sa-Åsår , Horus, son of Osiris; , Horus, son of Isis, son of Osiris.

Ḥeru-sa-Ḥe-t Ḥer , Horus, son of Hathor.

Ḥeru-sba-res , Horus, star of the South, *i.e.*, Jupiter.

Ḥeru-Sepṭ , U. 465, T. 277, P. 31, N. 650, M. 149, N. 41, Horus-Sothis, Horus the Dog-star.

Ḥeru-smai-en-nub (?) 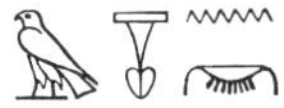 , Denderah III, 36, a Horus-god of Upper Egypt.

Ḥeru-smai-taui 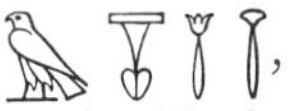, Denderah III, 9, 28, a serpent-god with the titles .

Ḥeru-smai-taui  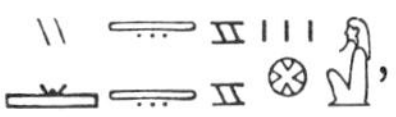, Horus, uniter of the Two Lands, *i.e.*, of the two Egypts.

Ḥeru-smai-taui-p-khart 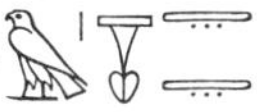 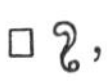, Denderah I, 75, , ibid. 1, 6, Harpokrates, uniter of Egypt.

Ḥeru-smai-taui-neb-Khaṭṭ  , Nesi-Ȧmsu 26, Horus, uniter of the Two Lands, lord of Khaṭṭ.

Ḥeru-Skhait 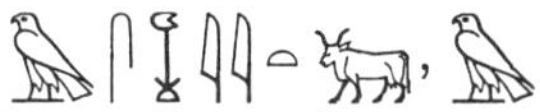, 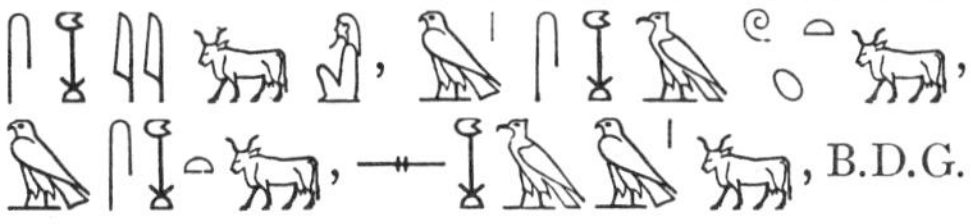, B.D.G. 526, B.D. 142, 113, B.M. 32, 206, L.D. III, 194, a cow-goddess who protected Isis and Horus.

Ḥeru-seqi-ḥāu , Denderah IV, 59, a warrior-god.

Ḥeru-Set , 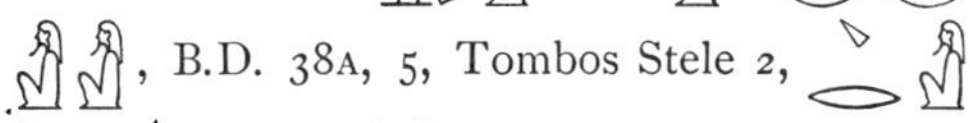, B.D. 38A, 5, Tombos Stele 2, 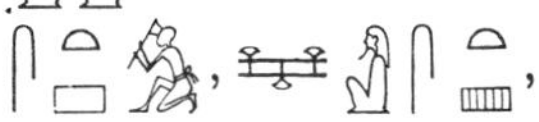, Horus + Set.

Ḥeru-sethen-ḥer 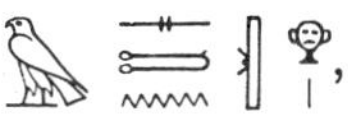, Ṭuat VII, a god.

Ḥeru-shāu , T. 287, , P. 39, M. 49, Horus the slaughterer.

Ḥeru-Shu-p-khart-p-āa  , B.D.G. 348, one of the seven forms of Harpokrates, son of 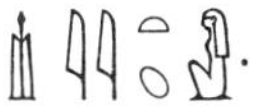.

Ḥeru-shemsu , , U. 17, N. 241, P. 166, M. 319, N. 832, a group of mythological beings of the last divine king of Egypt, with whom later were identified the blacksmiths of Edfû and the beings who assisted in the embalming and burial of Osiris.

Ḥeru-shest-tȧ 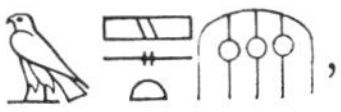, U. 561, 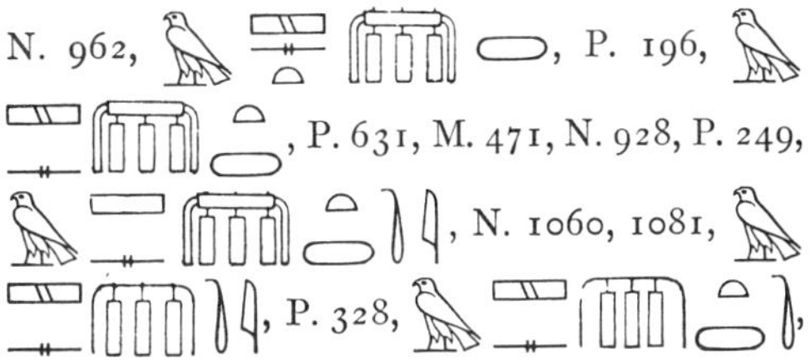, N. 962, P. 196, P. 631, M. 471, N. 928, P. 249, N. 1060, 1081, P. 328, M. 632, a form of Horus.

Ḥeru-Sheta , U. 561, P. 477; var. , N. 1265.

Ḥeru-Sheta-taui 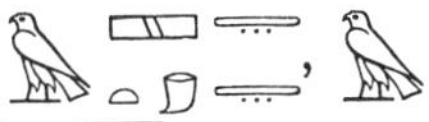, 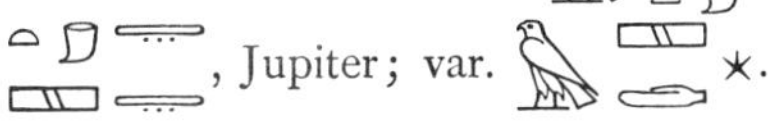, Jupiter; var.

Ḥeru-Sheṭti , B.M. 32, 409, a form of Horus.

Ḥeru-Sheṭ-ḥer , Sinsin II, a form of Horus.

Ḥeru-Qebḥ , IV, 808, Horus of the First Cataract (?)

Ḥeru-ka-pet (?) 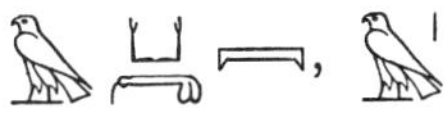 , a bull-god, the planet Saturn.

Ḥeru-ka-nekht , Denderah IV, 81, Horus the mighty Bull.

Ḥeru-Keftȧ , Mar. Aby. II, 3, 17, a form of Horus.

Ḥeru-ta-useru , a form of Horus.

Ḥeru-tema-ā , Tombos Stele 9, Horus the mighty-armed.

Ḥeru-Teḥuti (Tcheḥuti) , B.D. 142, 5, 11, Horus-Thoth.

Ḥeru-thema-ā 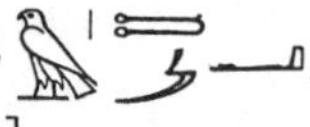, IV, 1160, Horus, stabber [of Set].

Ḥeru-theḥen 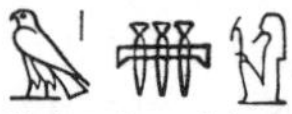, Denderah III, 35, Horus the lightning (?), Horus "the Sparkler."

Ḥeru-Ṭuat , P. 325, M. 630, , P. 158, N. 1266, , N. 787, 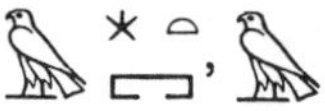 [illegible], Denderah IV, 84, Horus of the infernal regions; var. .

Ḥeru-Ṭuati , Ṭuat IX, the god of the serpent Khepri.

Ḥeru-Ṭuati  [illegible], Horus, god of the 7th hour of the night.

Ḥeru-ṭemam  [illegible], Nesi-Ȧmsu 25, 34, Horus, father of 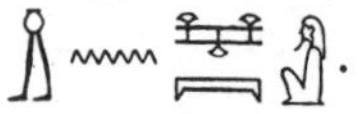.

Ḥeru-ṭesh[r] 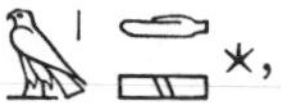, Desc. de l'Ég. 20, , the Red Horus, *i.e.*, the planet Mars; varr. , 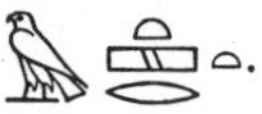.

Ḥeru-ṭesher ȧr-ti , U. 370, N. 719 + 17, 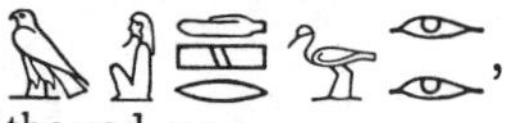, B.D. 177, 7, Horus of the red eyes.

Ḥeru-tchatcha(?)-nefer , Denderah II, 11, a lion-god, one of the 36 Dekans.

Ḥeru-tcham-ā-ā (?)  [illegible], Hh. 195, a form of Horus.

Ḥeru ren (?) , Palermo Stele, the name of a temple.

Ḥeru taiu 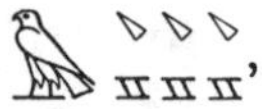, the Horus-lands, *i.e.*, temple estates.

Ḥeru-ṭaṭa-f  [illegible], B.D. 30B, 64 (Rubrics), a prince, the son of King Khufu (Cheops), who was famed for his learning and wisdom, and was reputed to have "edited" certain of the Chapters of the Book of the Dead.

ḥerȧ-t 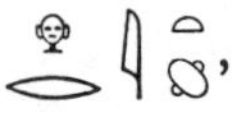, some strong-smelling substance.

Ḥerrȧtf , U. 323, the name of a malicious mythological serpent.

ḥerā 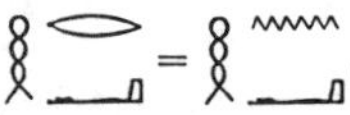, with, and.

ḥerātcha (ḥātcha) , the west wind; see 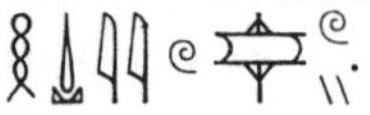.

ḥeri-t , a beam of a boat; plur. 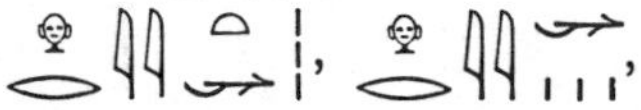, the planks of a boat.

ḥerit 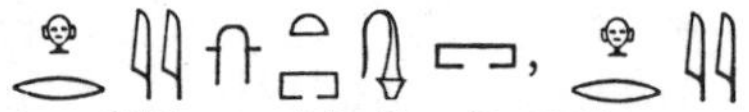 [illegible], furnace; 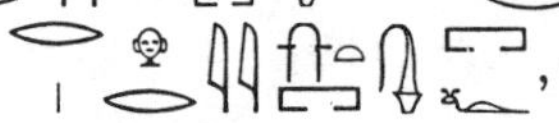, door of his furnace.

ḥerur , A.Z. 1880, 97, to be weak, helpless.

Ḥerp , A.Z. Bd. 45, 141, the Nile, the Nile-god; see **Ḥepr** [illegible], Āmamu, 15, 1, 3.

ḥeref (ḥef) , bread cake, offering.

ḥereḥ , Rev. 11, 164, [illegible] [illegible], to guard, to watch over; Copt. ϩⲁⲣⲉϩ.

ḥers (?) , T. 363, N. 179, a sceptre .

ḥers-t, necklace of beads, beads.

ḥerset, Rec. 26, 75, , Rec. 4, 21, , a kind of precious stone; , Rec. 4, 21.

ḥers, , to be heavy, burdensome, grievous.

ḥers-t, something hard, or heavy, or unpleasant.

ḥersa, IV, 1126, , , hornless ox.

ḥersh, , Rev. 12, 15, 49, to be heavy, burdensome; Copt. ϩⲣⲟϣ, ϩⲟⲣϣ.

ḥertt, IV, 668, a kind of stone.

ḥerṭ = , child.

ḥerṭi-[t], fear.

ḥerṭes (ḥeṭes), a kind of stone.

ḥerṭes, , a precious stone.

ḥeha, T. 182, N. 653, , P. 529 = , P. 135, M. 165.

ḥeḥ, , a great but indefinite number; Copt. ϩⲁϩ.

= one million years in Ptolemaic times.

= one hundred thousand millions of years.

= ten millions of millions of years.

= ten million hundred thousand millions of years.

ḥeḥ-en-sep, , Metternich Stele 188, a million times; dual , , B.D. 131, 9; plur. , millions of years.

ḥeḥ, , , , , A.Z. 1908, 122, , , , , , , a long indefinite period of time, eternity, the Eternal; , endless or limitless eternity; , for ever and ever; , city of eternity, the tomb.

Ḥeḥ, B.D. 17, 45, 48, the god of hundreds of thousands of years.

Ḥeḥ, Rec. 13, 29, the "eternal land," the necropolis.

Ḥeḥ-tt the "eternal land," the necropolis.

ḥeḥ (?), a kind of land; plur. , .

Ḥeḥu, , , , , , eternity, one of the four elemental gods of the company of Thoth.

Ḥeḥit, , , the consort of .

Ḥeḥu, Ṭuat XII, a dawn-god; his consort was .

ḥeḥ, ḥeḥi, , Rec. 18, 165, the Nile-flood, Inundation.

Ḥeḥ, Edfû I, 78, a form of the Nile-god.

ḥeḥ, M. 692, to rejoice.

ḥeḥ, , , , oil, unguent.

ḥeḥi, M. 365, , N. 919, , P. 459, , , , to seek, to search for, to seek after, , searching the heart or mind.

Ḥeḥ-neb-Ḥeḥ-ta, B.D. 64, 38, a god.

ḥeḥ, Shipwreck, 36, to strike; , to cut, to smite off, sword.

ḥeḥui (?), , the two ears; var. .

ḥeḥes, a kind of bird.

ḥes, , , , Sinsin II, 20, , , , , , , , , , , , , , , , to praise, to commend, to honour, to do honour to, to reward, to recompense, to remunerate, to requite, to show favour to; , to sing or recite laudatory writings, praises, etc.; Copt. ϩⲱⲥ.

ḥess, IV, 972, , to praise, to ascribe merit to, to applaud.

ḥessu, praises, hymns of praise, songs.

ḥessu, one who is praised.

ḥes-t, ḥesu-t, Rec. 31, 166, , , , , , , , , P. 655, M. 760, , IV, 944, , , , , , , , , , , , , praise, approval, approbation, commendation, favour, reward, gift, act of grace, gratification.

ḥess-t, , , , IV, 1154, , , favour, an act of grace, something that pleases, a reward, pleasure.

ḥesi, ḥesu, , , , , , , one to whom grace and favour have been shown [by Osiris], *i.e.*, a dead person, one who is approved of by a god; plur. , , , , , , , , , , , , , the blessed dead.

ḥesi, he who is praised, he who praises; , the praised one who praises those who are to be praised; , IV, 967, the praises of those who are praised.

ḥesit, I, 139, a personal decoration or mark of favour.

ḥesutȧ, P. 424, N. 1212, , praised, renowned, famous; said of a weapon, "thou seizest thy famous javelin."

ḥestȧ, Tombos Stele 10, will.

ḥes, ḥesi, , , , , , , to sing, to chant, to repeat laudatory compositions; Copt. ϩⲱⲥ.

ḥesi, , , , A.Z. 1906, 123, , to sing to the accompaniment of an instrument.

ḥes, Rev. 12, 32, song; Copt. ϩⲱⲥ.

ḥes-t, chant.

ḥesu, chant, song, any rhythmical composition; (var.), the 70 chants or songs of Rā.

ḥesi em ben-t, , , to sing to the harp, harper.

ḥesi em ṭe-t, to sing to the hand, *i.e.*, to sing whilst playing a musical instrument.

ḥesiu, , Rec. 21, 97, , , , singers, musicians, musical entertainers, professional mourners; , male singers; , female singers, wailing women.

ḥesi-àb, to sing to the heart (?)

ḥesi-t, Love Songs 4, 1, a song of love.

ḥesi, , a spell to be recited against evil creatures in the water.

Ḥes-ā, Ṭuat I, a singing-god.

ḥesi, IV, 971, , IV, 1105, , , IV, 85, 613, 945, , Sphinx Stele 11, to run or rush against, to attack, to advance with hostility, to show himself (of the enemy), to come on against, to encroach (of the sand about the Sphinx); , Tombos Stele 12.

ḥes-t, an attack.

ḥesi ḥer, , , , , , to thrust forward the face in a threatening manner.

ḥesiu ḥer, fierce-looking or savage beings.

ḥesi, , to fascinate.

ḥesi, , , , , , to pierce with a glance of the eye, to look savagely at someone, to look fierce, to cast a malicious look, to terrify with the eye.

ḥesi, to repel with a look.

ḥesiu, , fierce-looking creatures, uncouth, savage.

Ḥes-ḥer, B.D. 153, 4, , a god who devoured souls.

Ḥes-tchefetch, B.D. 163, 10, the god of the fierce eye.

ḥes, , calf; see **beḥes.**

Ḥesit (?), Denderah IV, 80, a scorpion-goddess.

Ḥesit, P. 267, , M. 480, N. 1247, a cow-goddess, the mother of .

ḥes, to submerge, to be submerged; Copt. ϨⲀⲤⲒⲈ.

ḥes, U. 95, N. 372, , U. 551, N. 600, , M. 223, , T. 344, , Rec. 29, 150, 30, 193, , , , , , , , , , dung, filth.

ḥess, Rev. 15, 47, river spume (?) froth (?)

ḥes-t, , a seat, stool; var. .

ḥess, seat, stool; see .

ḥes-t , Thes. 1289, 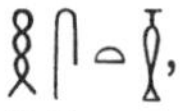, vase, vessel, pot, libation vessel; plur. 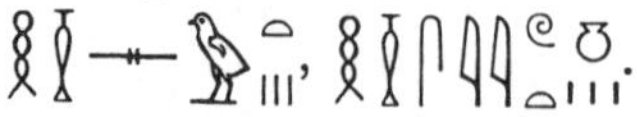.

ḥess-t 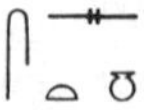, pot, vessel.

ḥesḥes , to be hot, to burn, fire, flame.

ḥess , heat, flame, fire.

ḥes-t 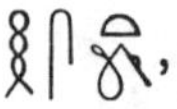, Rec. 32, 66, to sprout.

ḥesti (?) , U. 337, two sceptres (?)

ḥesa 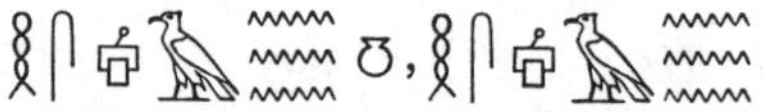, 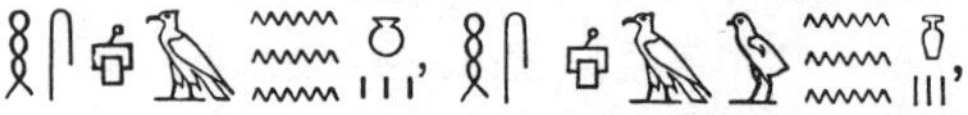, Hearst Pap. 3, 2, , Love Songs 1, 7, 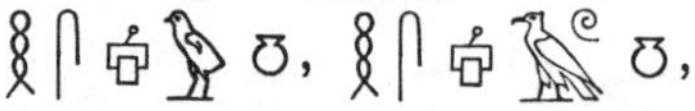, 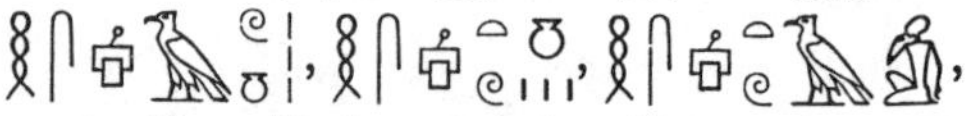, new milk, milk in general, milk supply, milk vessels full or empty.

Ḥesait , P. 204 + 10, , N. 976, , Rec. 26, 224, , A.Z. 1906, 130, 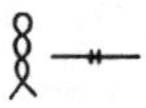 , the Cow-goddess of heaven who supplied the blessed with milk.

ḥesau , P. 306, the Milky Way (?)

Ḥesa 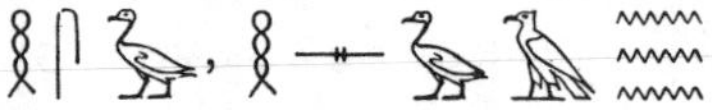, Rec. 37, 64, the god of the drowned.

ḥesa , Rev. 12, 25, cord, rope, string, thread, string of a seal; , the loops of a pectoral; plur. .

ḥesai , Israel Stele 7, fierce; see **ḥesi**.

Ḥesa , A.Z. 1905, 37, a "fierce-eyed" god.

Ḥesamut (?) , Tomb of Seti I, the goddess of a constellation in the northern sky who appears in the form of a hippopotamus.

ḥesaru , Hearst Pap. I, 6, a medicine.

Ḥesȧt , L.D. III, 194, , , a cow-goddess.

ḥesi 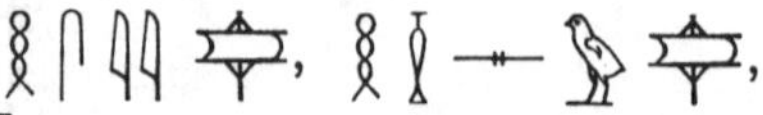, , Pap. 3024, 46, a person who is trembling or shivering with cold or fear; plur. , 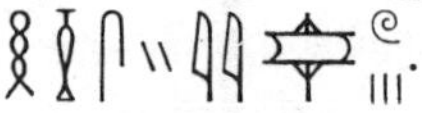.

ḥesu , a kind of wine or beer.

ḥesb-t , vine land, vineyard; 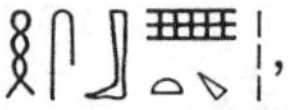, estates.

ḥesb , U. 517, T. 328, [illegible], Ȧmen. 16, 3, [illegible], P. 341, M. 643, [illegible], Rec. 32, 79, [illegible], [illegible], to compute, to calculate, to reckon, to assess, to tax, to count, to estimate, to settle accounts; [illegible], the best of reckoning, most accurate counting; [illegible], the very best examples of fine language; compare Heb. חָשַׁב, Arab. حَسَبَ.

ḥesb-t 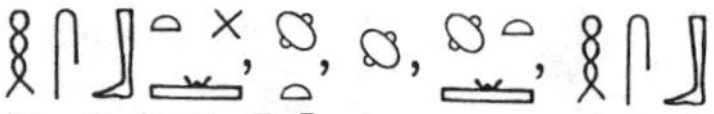, [illegible], Rec. 6, 7, [illegible], Rec. 32, 66, an account, a reckoning, a calculation, estimate, the total, scheme, plan, design, a measuring stick or cord, a result arrived at by thinking, the right, or true, or correct measure; **per ḥesb-t** [illegible], house of counting, *i.e.*, office, bureau.

ḥesb-t 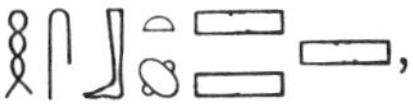, M. 196, N. 36, , P. 68, tablets on which calculations were written.

ḥesbi , B.M. 828, accountant, controller, registrar; , registrar of cattle; , registrar of the wheat of the North; , registrar of holy offerings; , IV, 968, registrar of amounts due or received; 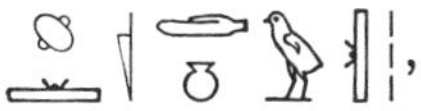, assessor of qualities, or dispositions, of men.

ḥesb-t , Rev. 14, 4, accountant's office.

ḥesbu (?) , Rec. 16, 57, L.D. III, 140E, , people registered for the corvée.

ḥesbu , assessments, dues, taxes, things taxed.

Ḥesbi ȧnu (?) , Thes. 818, a jackal-god.

Ḥesbi ȧnu , Berg. I, 12, a protector of the dead.

Ḥesbi āḥā , "he who computes the period of a man's life"—a title of Khensu.

ḥesb , B.D. 133, 17, an earthy paste (?) of which the boat of four cubits was made.

ḥesb-t , a plaque or tile of the same; plur. .

ḥesb-t 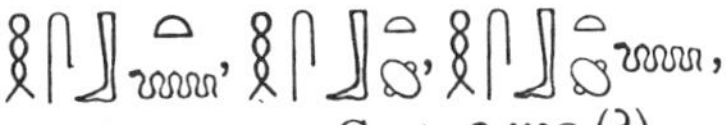, a kind of worm, tapeworm; Copt. ϩⲱⲥ (?)

ḥesb 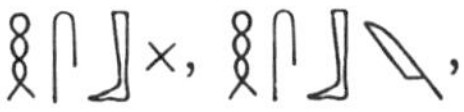, to separate, to cut, to bark a tree, to strip.

ḥesb , two-crossed bands (Lacau), tallies, sticks used in counting.

ḥesb-t , B.D. 153A, 9, and 153B, 7, knife, the instrument used for severing the  or umbilical cord.

Ḥesb-t-ent-Ȧst , B.D. 153B, 7, the knife of the net of the Akeru-gods.

ḥesbi ..... , B.D. (Saïte) 145, 31; var. .

ḥesbu ; see  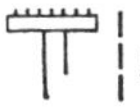; Copt. ϩⲉⲃⲥⲱ.

ḥesp, ḥesp-t 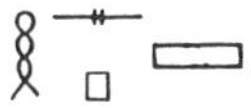, T. 66, M. 221, 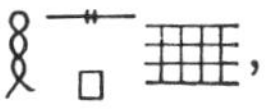, N. 598, 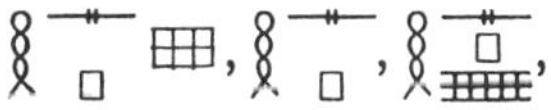, 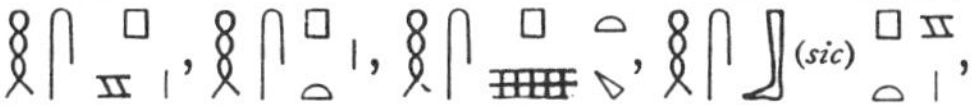, a district, a division of Egypt, the Nome of the Greeks; plur. 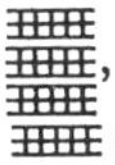, Palermo Stele, , 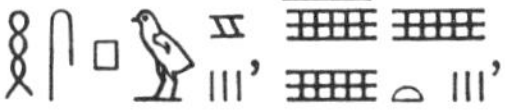, Metternich Stele 63.

ḥesput (?) , the inhabitants of a Nome.

ḥesp ent tchett , the Nome of eternity, *i.e.*, the cemetery, the Other World.

ḥesp , a measure of land = ¼ arura (?) or 2,500 square cubits.

ḥesp nu ȧḥit , Rec. 33, 4, a district of trees, the wooded part of an estate.

ḥesp [illegible], portion of the precincts of a temple.

ḥesp, ḥespit [illegible], [illegible], [illegible], vine land.

ḥosp-t [illegible], booth in a vineyard, summer house.

ḥesp-t [illegible], Rec. 3, 48, [illegible], Rec. 3, 46, basin, trough, vat, tub.

ḥesp [illegible], a wreath of flowers.

ḥesem [illegible], a kind of animal.

ḥesma [illegible], Jour. As. 1908, 275, nitre; Copt. ϩⲟⲥⲉⲙ.

ḥesma, Rev. 12, 109, , Rev. 12, 110, , to have monthly courses, to be after the manner of women.

ḥesmen, Rec. 16, 56, to use nàtron ceremonially or in embalming, to salt or season one's discourse.

ḥesmen, U. 17, P. 612, N. 692, P. 145, natron; , Annales IX, 156; Copt. ϩⲟⲥⲙ.

ḥesmen ṭesher, red natron; Copt. ϩⲟⲥⲉⲙ ⲉϥⲧⲣⲟϣⲣⲉϣ.

ḥesmen, a nitre purge.

Ḥesmen, P. 669, M. 656, , N. 1271, the Natron-god.

ḥesmen, Leyd. Pap. 3, 2, , IV, 425, , IV, 891, amber-coloured plated bronze; compare Heb. חַשְׁמַל, Ezek. i, 4, 27, viii, 2.

ḥesmeni, a vase, vessel (of gold, , or silver,).

ḥeser, a part of the body, one of the intestines (?)

Ḥeser, B.D. 142, III, 13, a temple-town of Thoth in Hermopolis; see .

ḥesq, T. 278, , P. 59, , M. 26, , N. 904, , P. 188, M. 352, , A.Z. 1900, 128, , to cut off, to sever, to slay, to separate, to set apart; , Peasant 289, men who can tie on a head that has been cut off.

ḥesqiu, the slain.

ḥesqeq, T. 387, , M. 404, to slay, to kill.

ḥesq-t, a cutting off, mutilation, a cutting instrument.

Ḥesq, T. 278, N. 84, , P. 59, a god (?)

Ḥesq-t-ent-Seshmu, B.D. 153A, 32, the knife of the net of the Akeru-gods.

Ḥesqit-kheftiu-set, Ṭuat I, a fiery serpent-goddess.

ḥesk, A.Z. 1907, 57, to cut, to sever; with , to dismember.

ḥeski, a title (?)

ḥeseg, IV, 641, an ointment pot.

ḥeq, Nàstasen Stele 39, 44, to capture, booty; see .

ḥeq, Ḥerusàtef Stele 69, captive.

ḥeq, ḥeqa, M. 252, , Rec. 32, 86, , to rule, to govern, to direct, to guide, to reign.

ḥeq, ḥeqi, Rev. 11, 138, (Demotic forms), rule, power.

ḥeq-t, rule, authority, sovereignty, dominion, government.

ḥeq-t, the crook, , emblem of rule.

ḥeq-t, A.Z. 1908, 19, an amulet.

Ḥeq, Rec. 36, 67, ruler, governor, director, prince; plur., IV, 975, A.Z. 45, 125; ruler of rulers, a title of Osiris.

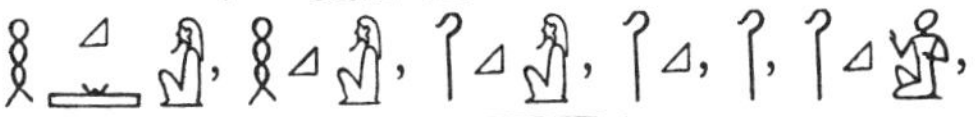

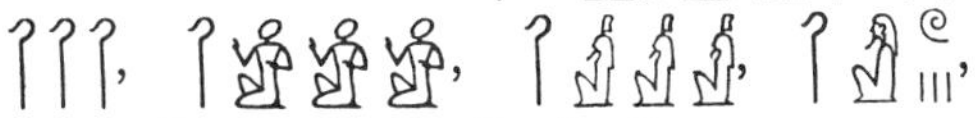

ḥeq-t, princess, chieftainess, queen.

ḥeqit, A.Z. 1905, 16, princess.

Ḥeq Åmam, chief of Åmam (in the Sûdân).

Ḥeq Åment, chief of Åmenti, a title of Osiris.

Ḥeq ārq, title of the priest of Ḥeru-shef in Herakleopolis.

Ḥeq metcha (?), governor of books, a title of Thoth.

ḥeq taui, governor of Egypt; governor of the world.

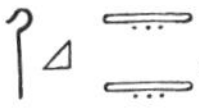

Ḥeq tchet, governor of eternity, a title of Osiris.

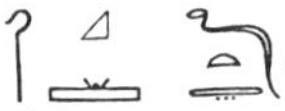

ḥeq ḥe-t, Peasant 190, governor of a town or towns; plur., IV, 973, 1108; governor of cities; plur.; governor of a district, mudîr; plur.

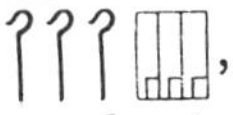

Ḥeq, the god of the 5th hour of the night.

Ḥeq-t, Rec. 31, 161, a god (?)

Ḥeqit, P. 570, Rec. 26, 224, a goddess who presided over the buttocks.

Ḥeqit, Ombos I, 26, II, 133, a goddess of Ombos; Mar. Mon. D. 1, 6.

Ḥeqtit (Ḥeqit), B.D. (Saïte) 142, 18, B.D.G. 153, a form of Hathor.

Ḥeq-år-ti-tef-f, Rec. 37, 15, a god.

Ḥeq-nek-mu (?), Ṭuat XII, one of the 12 gods who drew the boat of Åf through Ānkh-neteru; he was reborn daily.

Ḥeq-neteru-f, Ṭuat IX, a god.

Ḥeq-ḥesi, B.D. 17, 34, a title of .

Ḥeq-sa-neter, U. 562, a title of Horus.

ḥeq-t, IV, 367, 1136, a measure of capacity equal to ten, P.S.B. 14, 424; = the artabe; the double ḥeqt; the quadruple ḥeqt.

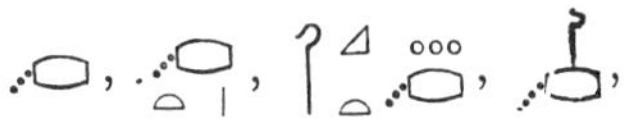

ḥeq-t, fractions of the ḥeqt are: = $\frac{1}{2}$, = $\frac{1}{4}$, = $\frac{1}{8}$, = $\frac{1}{16}$, = $\frac{1}{32}$, or = $\frac{1}{64}$; see P.S.B. 14, 424.

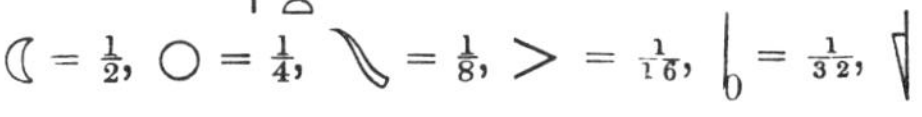

ḥequ, to measure grain.

ḥeq-t, N. 636, beer; beerhouse; plur.; N. 285A, beer of iron; sweet beer; U. 145, beer of Sti (*i.e.*, Nubia).

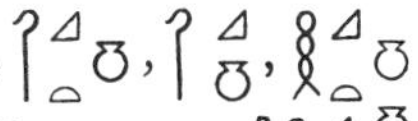

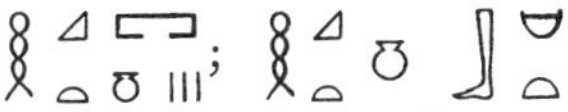

ḥeq-t-ȧkhem-t-āma, T. 288, M. 65, N. 126, divine beer which did not go sour.

ḥeq-t-enth-Maāt, "beer of truth"—a kind of divine beer drunk by the 12 gods who guarded the shrine of Osiris.

ḥeq-t-ent-neḥeḥ, P. 391, M. 557, N. 1164, divine beer of everlastingness, *i.e.*, inexhaustible beer.

Ḥeqit, Lanzone 853, Rec. 3, 65, IV, 224, the Frog-goddess, a goddess of reproduction and resurrection. On a Christian lamp in the form of a frog is the inscription Ἐγώ εἴμι ἀνάστασις.

ḥeqq, box, chest, safe, safe place.

ḥeq-t, misery, want; compare Copt. ϩⲏⲕⲉ.

ḥeqa, Jour. As. 1908, 254, 301, Rev. 14, 19, Jour. As. 1908, 308, Rev. 13, 25, hunger; Copt. ϩⲕⲟ.

ḥeqā (?), hunger; Copt. ϩⲕⲟ.

ḥeknu, want, hunger; see

Ḥeqenbit (?), Ombos II, 133, a goddess.

ḥeqr, U. 172, U. 173, Rec. 26, 78, to be hungry, hunger; hunger years, *i.e.*, years of famine.

ḥeqr, Rev., hunger; Copt. ϩⲕⲟ.

ḥeqr, hungry man; = Copt. ϩⲕⲟⲉⲓⲧ.

Ḥeqrit, a famine-goddess (?)

ḥeqr-t, Rec. 35, 58, an earthen pot.

Ḥeqrer, P. 438, M. 652, a god who, with , worked the celestial ferry-boat.

ḥeqes, wild goat; Copt. ϭⲁϩ, ϭϩⲟⲥ, ϭⲁϩⲥⲓ, ϭⲟϩⲥⲉ.

ḥekes, net, cage, a place where birds are kept, aviary.

ḥeqes, a birdcatcher, a fisherman.

Ḥeqes, Rec. 4, 28, B.D.G. 479, P.S.B. 8, 193, the god of fishermen, fowlers, and hunters.

Ḥeqsi, P.S.B. 8, 193, "the fisher"—a title of Menu.

Ḥeqes, the god of the 19th day of the month.

ḥeqes, Mar. Karn. 53, 29, timid.

ḥekḥek (keḥkeḥ), old age, old man, aged.

ḥeka, Rec. 25, 191, 192, gift, dedication.

ḥeka, to utter charms, or spells, or incantations, to recite words of power, to bewitch.

ḥekai, enchanter, magician, sorcerer; plur.

ḥekait, sorceress.

ḥeka, M. 316, , P. 176, N. 874, , Rec. 31, 166, , , , , , magic, the power of working magic, sorcery, spell, incantation, charm, word of power; plur. , U. 363, 584, , T. 321, , P. 176, , N. 917, , P. 667, M. 777, , , , , , , , , , , beneficent spells; Copt. ϩⲓⲕ.

ḥekaut , , , , , the spells and magical formulae produced by the god Ḥeka.

ḥekau metchau (?) , U. 455, books of spells (?)

ḥekau , the name of a diadem or crown.

Ḥekau , P. 176, , M. 316, , N. 917, , B.D.G. 537, , a god—the author of spells, incantations, words of bewitchment, etc.; his shrine was .

Ḥeka , Ombos I, 186–188, , , one of the 14 Kau of Rā.

Ḥekaui , Berg. 13.....

Ḥeka-ur , Ṭuat VII, the magician of Åfu-Rā who cast spells on the foes of the god as he sailed through the Ṭuat.

Ḥekau-ur , , the god of the 10th hour of the day.

Ḥeka-p-kharṭ , B.D.G. 348, a form of Harpokrates, the son of Sekhmit of Temeḥ, .

Ḥeka-ka-en-Rā , Nesi-Åmsu 32, 1, a form of Rā.

Ḥekab-p-neb-taui , Ombos I, 48, a form of Horus.

Ḥekkȧ , a name of .

ḥeki , throat, gullet.

ḥeki , Rev. 12, 15, to fight; Copt. ϩⲱⲕ.

ḥeken , U. 563, , A.Z. 45, 124, , to praise, to adore, to sing, to acclaim.

ḥeknu , , , , , , , hymn of praise, song of praise, praise of any kind; plur. , .

ḥekniu , , , singers.

Ḥeknit , , Ṭuat I, a singing hour-goddess (?)

Ḥeknit , , Ṭuat IV, a serpent-guardian of the Aḥeth chamber.

Ḥeknit , U. 323, a serpent-fiend (?) with two faces, .

Ḥeknutt , T. 243, Rec. 31, 169, , U. 425, a goddess.

Ḥekniu , B.D. 168, a group of singing-gods.

Ḥeken-em-ānkh , Denderah III, 12, a Horus-god.

Ḥeknit-em-ba (?)-s, Ṭuat I, a goddess of the Gates in the earth.

Ḥeken-em-benf, Ṭuat I, a singing ape-god.

Ḥeknit-em-tep-Ḥeru, Ombos I, 46, a vulture-headed hippopotamus-goddess.

Ḥeken-Rā, Ṭuat I, a singing-god.

Ḥeken-Kheperȧ, Ṭuat XII, a singing-god.

Ḥeknith, Ṭuat VII, a lioness-goddess.

Ḥeknithth, Ṭuat VII, a star-goddess.

ḥeken-t, , , , the bolt of a door, staple, fastening.

ḥeken, a cake, a loaf of bread.

ḥeken, Ebers Pap. 35, 19, , to anoint (?) to be pleasant, easy.

Ḥeknu, Hh. 499, a god.

ḥeknu, U. 57, , N. 309A, , , , , , , , unguent, pomade; plur. , U. 536, , U. 543, , T. 298, , T. 294.

ḥeknu, , , a kind of precious stone found in the Sûdân.

ḥegargar, Rechnungen T. 1, 3 . . . . . .

ḥegi, Rev. 12, 9, to arm oneself; Copt. ϩⲱⲕ.

ḥegi, Rev. 11, 171, place for fighting; Copt. ϩⲱⲕ.

ḥegb, Pap. 9610 . . . .

ḥegen, , to praise, hymn; see .

ḥet, Rev. 13, 64, customs, taxes, imposts, levies; Copt. ϩⲱϯ.

ḥet, N. 369A, a drink offering.

ḥet, pot, vessel; plur. , IV, 871.

ḥet, canal, stream of water; var. , Rec. 31, 166; Copt. ϩⲁⲧⲉ.

Ḥet (?), Metternich Stele 83, a primitive water-god.

ḥet, N. 786, U. 476, , vapour, fumes, smoke; , N. 958, the fumes of incense.

ḥet, , Rec. 30, 188 . . . .

ḥet (?), oxen; see .

ḥet, Rev. 11, 168, tunic, shirt; Copt. ϩⲟⲓⲧⲉ.

ḥet, ḥeta, Westcar 5, 15, , rag.

ḥet-t, scorpion.

Ḥet, N. 1140, the scorpion-god; see .

ḥetit, , , weapon, cudgel, lance, dart, goad, bow.

ḥet-ā (?), IV, 667, a long stick, staff.

ḥet-ākh, IV, 870, vessels or implements for the altar.

ḥetḥet, to cut = .

ḥet, ḥeti, A.Z. 1908, 116, , , , U. 539, heart, breast; Copt. ϩⲏⲧ.

ḥett, quarry.

ḥet-t 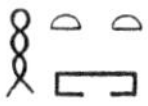, shaft of a mine; plur. [illegible] [illegible], workings in a mine.

Ḥett 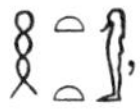, a name or title of Osiris (?)

ḥeta , U. 457, an animal.

ḥeta , Rev. 11, 153, horse (?); plur. , Rev. 11, 151; Copt. ϩⲧⲟ.

ḥeta 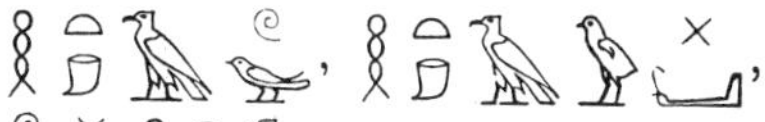, , to break, to tear up, wrinkled (of the face) (?)

ḥeta , Rec. 2, 116, dirty rags.

ḥetai[t] , Åmen. 21, 2, rag (?) bandage.

ḥeta , Pap. 3024, 133, [illegible], Peasant 56, [illegible], 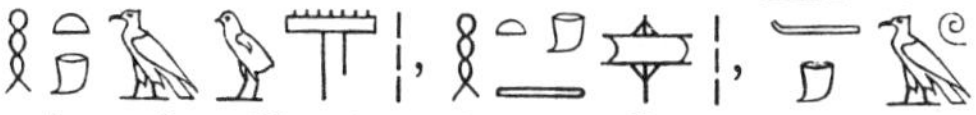, [illegible], Rec. 21, 87, sail, sailcloth, rigging, masts with sails.

ḥeta , to burn, fire, burning incense.

ḥetā 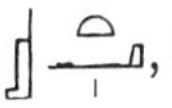, fever, sickness; Copt. ϩⲁϫ.

ḥeti-t , [illegible], IV, 482, [illegible], [illegible], [illegible], Rec. 29, 155, [illegible], Rec. 26, 236, throat, gullet; plur. [illegible], U. 562, [illegible]; var. [illegible].

Ḥeti[t] , a goddess.

ḥeti 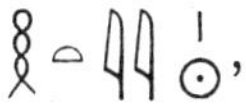, Rec. 11, 128, moment; Copt. ϩⲟⲧⲉ.

Ḥeti[t] , one of 12 goddesses who drew the boat of Åf through the serpent Ānkh-neteru; she was reborn daily.

ḥeti , Rev. 13, 49, 14, 60, to exercise a right.

Ḥetu , B.D. (Saïte) 78, 38, a god.

ḥeteb , to come, to arrive.

ḥetep 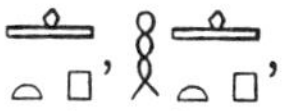, Pap. 3024, 23, , 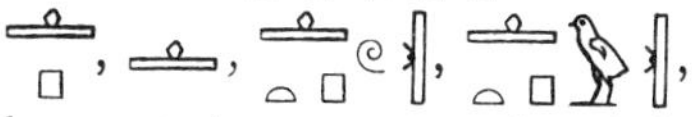, to rest, to be happy, to be content, to be glad, to do good to someone, to repose, to be at rest or to go to rest, to set (of the sun), to rely upon, to be at peace with; Copt. ϩⲱⲧⲡ.

ḥetepu , 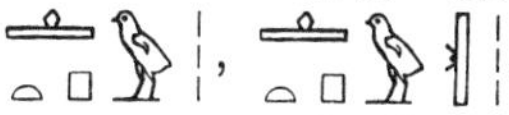, peace, joy, content, satisfaction; , soft or gentle winds.

ḥetepu , he who sits at home in peace.

ḥetep-t , U. 648, peaceful, gracious, applied to the .

ḥetepi 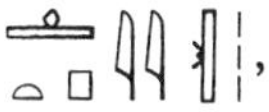, Rec. 4, 135, benevolent.

ḥetepiu 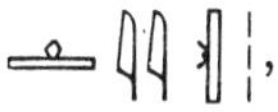, IV, 665, [illegible], IV, 704, [illegible], non-combatants in a campaign.

ḥetep, with **åb** (or **ḥat**) 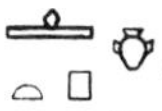, IV, 971, contented in mind, satisfied; , their hearts were satisfied.

ḥetep 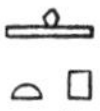 with , N. 948, , P. 176, [illegible], Rec. 2, 110, literally, "in peace," *i.e.*, happily, successfully; ; , it (*i.e.*, the book) hath gone out in peace, *i.e.*, is finished successfully.

ḥetep ḥer , Pap. 3024, 108, "peaceful of face."

ḥetep ḥer maāt , "resting on law"—a royal title.

ḥetep ḥer mu 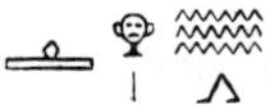, to be of the same mind as someone else, to follow the same course of action, to be of the same kidney.

Ḥeteputiu , U. 584 (=  , M. 796), P. 667, M. 776, 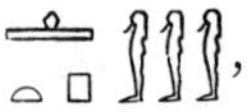  , those who are at rest, the blessed dead, beings in the Other World to whom offerings are made.

Ḥeteptiu 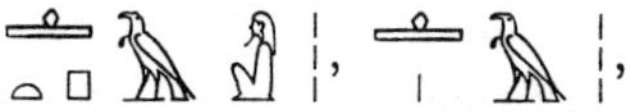, , Ṭuat VI, a group of gods in the Ṭuat.

ḥetepu 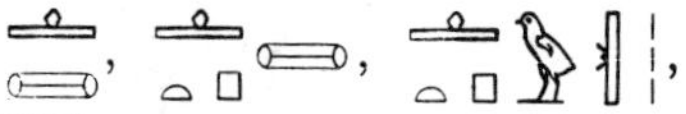, 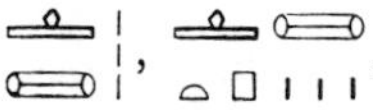, offerings, gifts, alms, oblations, endowments; , the offerings prescribed by law or custom;  , geese for offerings; , a two-fold offering.

ḥeteptiu , peace-cakes, offerings; 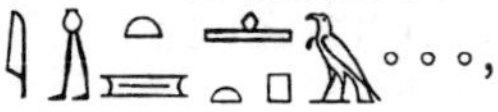, P. 172,  , N. 939, the valley of offerings.

ḥetep-t , U. 39, 508, 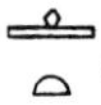, 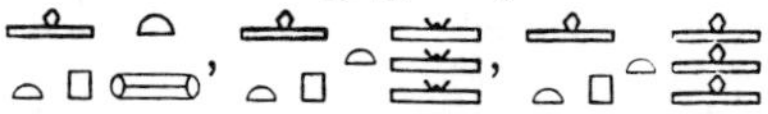, N. 940, 952, 1075, , M. 203, N. 683, 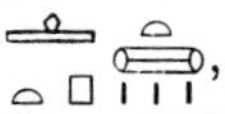, , 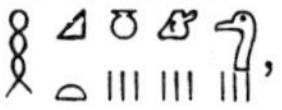, sepulchral meals, the offerings made to the dead.

ḥetep-t , , an offering of flowers or vegetables, a funerary bouquet.

ḥetep nesu , N. 353A, U. 84, , U. 83A, the offering which the king in very early times sent to the tomb of a favourite noble. The formula , "the king has given an offering," was used from the earliest to the latest period. Old forms are: 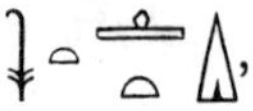, T. 150, 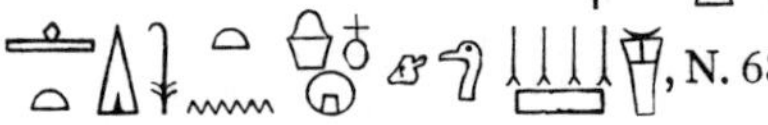, N. 683. Sometimes Geb, or Osiris, or Tem is asked to give the offering: , T. 150, , N. 501, , T. 140, , P. 517, 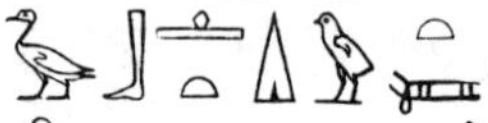, P. 513,  [illegible], Rec. 36, 212, , IV, 485.

ḥetepu neter [illegible], [illegible], [illegible], offerings of every kind made to the god, the property of the gods and the temples; [illegible], temple estate.

Ḥetep [illegible], B.D. 110, the god of the Sekhet-ḥetepet, or Elysian Fields.

Ḥetep [illegible], Ṭuat IV, a god with a boomerang.

Ḥetepit [illegible], P. 646, [illegible], P. 715, [illegible], M. 744, [illegible], Berg. I, 14, a goddess of offerings and a friend of the dead.

Ḥetepi [illegible], [illegible], Rec. 6, 157, 18, 182, a god who gave offerings.

Ḥetepit [illegible], [illegible], Ṭuat I, a serpent-goddess in the Ṭuat.

Ḥetepui (?) [illegible], Ṭuat VI, one of the nine spirits who destroyed the bodies of the dead.

Ḥeteptiu [illegible], [illegible], [illegible], Ṭuat VI, Ombos I, 85, the gods who provided offerings.

Ḥetep [illegible], B.D. 110, a city in the Elysian Fields.

Ḥetep [illegible], [illegible], B.D. 110, a lake in Sekhet-Åaru.

Ḥetepit-àb-neb ....., Ombos II, 132, a goddess.

Ḥetep-uȧa, Ṭuat IX, a water-god.

Ḥetepit-em-ȧakhu-t-s, Ṭuat XII, one of the 12 wind-goddesses of the dawn.

Ḥetepi, B.D. 180, 30, the chief of the Ṭuat of Ȧn.

Ḥetep-mes, B.D. 145, a god of the 21st Pylon.

Ḥetepiṭ-neb-t-per-s, Ṭuat VIII, the name of a Circle.

Ḥetep-neteru, Ṭuat V, one of the eight gods who burned the bodies of the damned.

Ḥetep-ḥem-t, a goddess.

ḥetep-Ḥeru, etc., etc., B.D. 153A, 15, part of the net of the Akeru-gods.

Ḥetepu - ḥeteput - neter - neteru, Ṭuat IX, a god who supplied the gods with food.

Ḥeteptiu-kheperu, Ṭuat VI, gods of offerings.

Ḥetep-khenti-Ṭuat, Ṭuat VI, a god of meat and drink.

Ḥeteptiu-kherui-auut, Ṭuat VI, a group of gods with their offerings.

Ḥetep-sekhu-s, B.D. 17, 84, 93, 94, a fire-goddess who had the form of the Eye of Rā and burned up the souls of the enemies of Osiris.

Ḥetep-ka, B.D. 65, 2, a god of offerings.

Ḥetep-ta, Ṭuat VIII, one of the nine gods of the bodyguard of Rā.

Ḥetep-taui, B.D. 38A, 8, a god.

Ḥeteptiu - ṭuaiu - Rā, a group of gods in the Gate of Saa-Set—they represent the orthodox righteous.

Ḥetep-ṭe-t, Rec. 37, 63, a god.

Ḥetep-tches, B.D. (Saïte) 110, a lake in Sekhet-Ȧaru.

ḥetep-t, , , , , , , IV, 667, , , a slab of stone or metal, or a wooden tablet, which was used as a table for offerings, an altar; plur., T. 339, N. 627, , IV, 705; , N. 85, the altar of the hall of the tomb.

ḥetep, , place of peace or propitiation, shrine of a god.

ḥetep, the sum total.

ḥetep, , Rec. 19, 93, a basket, a crate, a measure of 160 henu.

Ḥetep (?), the name of a god (?)

ḥetep, a roll, bundle.

ḥetep, to cut, to wound.

ḥetep (?), , , a graving tool, stylus, chisel.

ḥetep, Rev. 12, 52, to flee, to escape.

ḥetepāiu, Rev. 12, 16, chiefs.

ḥetem, U. 9, N. 342, , U. 25, , U. 99, , N. 395, , ,

, to be provided with, supplied with, to be full, filled with.

ḥetem , U. 447, , T. 256, , to disappear, to die out, to perish, to be destroyed, to render weak or helpless.

ḥetmiu , destroyers.

ḥetem-t , destruction, doom, decay, perdition.

ḥetemti , destroyer, destroyed; plur. , the damned.

ḥetemit , place of destruction, the abode of the damned; , P. 606, house of destruction.

Ḥetemit , Ṭuat VII, , the goddess of destruction.

Ḥetemit , Ṭuat X, , Ombos I, 61, B.D. 110, 31, Denderah IV, 6: (1) a cow-goddess; (2) a serpent fire-goddess; (3) a goddess of Sekhet-Åaru; , B.D. 168.

Ḥetemith , Ṭuat VII; see .

Ḥetemit-àakhu , Ṭuat IX, a destroyer of spirit-souls.

Ḥetem-àb (or **ḥat**) , one of nine singing-gods.

Ḥetem-ur , B.D. 19, 14, a god.

Ḥetemit-baiu , B.D. 149, a destroyer of heart-souls.

Ḥetemit-ḥer , B.D. 168 a deity of the 11th Circle.

Ḥetemit-khemiu , Ṭuat VIII, the name of a Circle.

ḥetem-t , hyena; plur. , Anastasi I, 23, 7.

ḥetem-t , Rechnungen 64, a piece of wood.

ḥetem-t , Hearst Pap. 8, 8, , Annales IX, 156, a mineral used in medicine.

ḥeter , Rec. 27, 190, to join together, to yoke, to unite, to be friends or allies, to be twins, to marry (?); Copt. ϩⲟⲧⲣⲉ, ϩⲱⲧⲣ̄.

ḥeter , twins; Copt. ϩⲁⲧⲣⲉ, ϩⲁⲧⲣⲉⲩ, ⲁⲑⲣⲏⲩ.

ḥeterti , Rec. 26, 80, twin pools, a pair of lakes.

ḥetru , doorposts.

ḥetru , N. 975,  , Rec. 31, 26, , Rec. 31, 18, cords, bonds, ligatures.

ḥeter , I, 144, , a pair of oxen for ploughing, cattle suitable for yoking together.

ḥetru 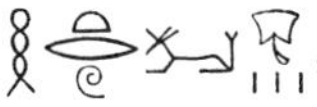, P. 1116B, 19, cattle.

ḥeter , Nȧstasen Stele 12, , , Ḥerusȧtef Stele 110, , ibid. 81, ,  , horse; Copt. ϩⲧⲟ; plur.  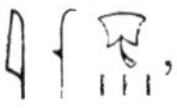, , , , , IV, 710; , pair of horses; , cavalry.

ḥetrȧu , cavalrymen.

ḥeter , , stable, stall, cage (?)

ḥeter , Rev. 14, 40, to compel, to force.

ḥeter , , , , , 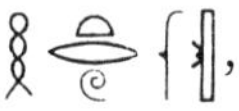,  , , to levy taxes, to put under tax or tribute, to be liable to tax or tribute;  , IV, 1114, to levy a tax; Copt. ϩⲱⲧⲉ, ϩⲱϯ.

ḥeter, ḥetrȧ , Rec. 31, 24, [illegible], Rec. 33, 5, IV, 700, [illegible], Rechnungen 51, [illegible], [illegible], [illegible], [illegible], [illegible] [illegible], tax, tribute, something levied or assessed, a forced payment, dues; [illegible] [illegible], New Year's tax; [illegible] [illegible], annual tribute; [illegible] [illegible], IV, 745, a tax fixed for ever, perpetual tax or tribute.

ḥetrut [illegible], [illegible], [illegible] [illegible], [illegible], gifts, tribute, taxes, revenues, income.

ḥetrȧ [illegible], socket of a leaf of a door; plur. [illegible], sockets of doors.

ḥeterr [illegible], Rev. 11, 180, will, wish; Copt. ϩⲧⲟⲣ.

ḥetes [illegible], [illegible], Rec. 4, 31, [illegible], [illegible], to be perfect, to make perfect or complete.

ḥetes [illegible], N. 171, [illegible], B.D. 110, 14, to be lord of, to rule.

ḥetes [illegible], a kind of Nubian stone or gem.

ḥetgȧt [illegible], door, opening.

ḥeth [illegible], U. 106A, [illegible], [illegible], [illegible], [illegible], [illegible], [illegible], [illegible], [illegible], IV, 1157, a kind of loaf or cake, an offering; plur. [illegible], B.D. 172, 35.

ḥethet [illegible], [illegible], hyena; Copt. ϩⲟⲉⲓⲧⲉ.

ḥetheth [illegible], N. 1155, to bear up on the shoulders.

ḥetheth-t [illegible], shoulder; plur. [illegible]; [illegible], Rec. 30, 67.

ḥetha [illegible], [illegible], [illegible], [illegible], [illegible], [illegible] [illegible], to engrave a design, to inlay with gold or precious stones, to exert pressure.

ḥethit [illegible], throat, gullet.

ḥether, to levy a tax; see .

ḥether, pair of wings, pinions, shoulders.

ḥethes, , weasel, shrewmouse.

Ḥethes, weasel-god (?), shrewmouse-god (?). For figures see B.M. 41562, 11588, 29602, etc.

ḥeṭṭ, scorpion.

Ḥeṭṭit, B.D. 39, 10, a scorpion-goddess.

Ḥeṭi, the flying, winged sun-disk.

ḥeṭi, to be weary, exhausted.

ḥeṭeb, , A.Z. 45, 132, to arrive at, to drop into a chair or seat.

ḥeṭeb, Annales V, 34, , Rec. 8, 136, , Ȧmen. 22, 8, 23, 11, , , , , to overthrow, to upset, to slay; see .

ḥeṭbit, Thes. 1201, overthrow.

ḥeṭeb, , a disease.

ḥeṭen, an unguent.

ḥeṭes, , to be complete, perfect; see **ḥetes.**

ḥetgȧ-t, door, the leaves of a door.

ḥetch, , , , , , , to become bright, to become light, to shine, to illumine.

ḥetchḥetch, , to become bright, to become light

ḥetchut (ḥetchtchut), , , , , , , , , , , light, radiance, splendour, brilliance; var. .

ḥetch-t, , dawn, daybreak.

ḥetch-t ta, N. 492, , U. 493, , Rec. 26, 229, , Rec. 27, 229, , , , "the lighting up of the land," the dawn, daybreak; , , the earliest dawn; Copt. ϩⲧⲟⲟⲩⲉ, Amharic ነግሀ : ብሐር : Oriental 661, fol. 61B, 3, as opposed to መሸየ : ብሐር : ibid. fol. 76A, 3.

ḥetch-t, , , , , , white, anything bright and shining; , U. 488, P. 640, M. 672, , , P. 428, , U. 41.

Ḥetchit, , , , , the "white goddess," *i.e.*, Nekhebit, the Vulture-goddess of Nekhebet, or Eileithyiaspolis.

Ḥetch-t, the name of a serpent on the royal crown.

ḥetchtch, scorpion.

Ḥetchtch; see , B.D. 39, 10, a scorpion-goddess.

Ḥetchḥetch, B.D. (Saïte) 17, 39, a god.

ḥetchi, , light-giver.

Ḥetchuti, , , Tomb of Seti I, a beetle-god, one of the 75 forms of Rā (No. 50).

Ḥetchtchut , Ṭuat II, , Ṭuat VI, a god holding ānkh inverted.

Ḥetch-àbḥu 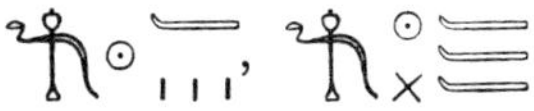, , B.D. 125, II, one of the 42 assessors of Osiris.

Ḥetch-t-àṭi (?) 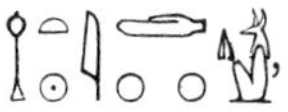, the name of a god or goddess.

Ḥetch-ā , Ṭuat I and II: (1) a singing-god; (2) a grain-god.

Ḥetch-ua , B.D. 145A, the doorkeeper of the 13th Pylon.

Ḥetch-ur , M. 723, , N. 1328, a god.

Ḥetch-nāu (?) , Ṭuat X, a serpent-god.

Ḥetch-ḥetep 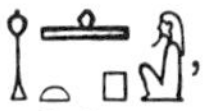, Düm. Dend. 47A, , N. 326, 971, a god of clothing.

Ḥetch-re-pesṭ-tchatcha  , B.D. 17, 133, a name of the phallus of Osiris.

Ḥetch-tchatchau-em-per-khet , Ombos II, 134, a god.

ḥetch-t , T. 359, P. 167, 614, M. 781, N. 802, 1138, , , Rec. 27, 222, , Rec. 31, 11, , the White Crown of the South, *i.e.*, of Upper Egypt; , Rec. 31, 26.

Ḥetch-t , the country of the White Crown, *i.e.*, Upper Egypt.

ḥetch 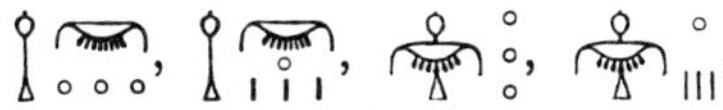, white metal, silver; 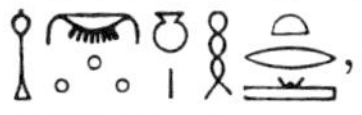, Rec. 33, 3, tax paid in silver; , Rec. 2, 125, silver ore.

ḥetch-t , milk; , vessels of milk.

ḥetch , a white goose.

ḥetch , Rec. 29, 148, white oxen.

ḥetch 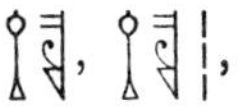, the nails of the fingers and toes.

ḥetch , IV, 754, white bread, a kind of cake.

ḥetch-t , a plant with white leaves or flowers; , white buds or seeds; , IV, 548, white grain, wheat.

ḥetchu , onion; plur. , N. 270, onion; plur. .

ḥetch-t 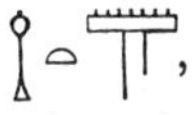, IV, 742, , IV, 1148, , Annales III, 109, white linen or cloth, flags (?)

ḥetch-ti [illegible], a pair of white sandals.

ḥetch [illegible], shrine, chapel.

ḥetch-t [illegible], IV, 72, house.

ḥetch-t [illegible], white stone, white alabaster.

ḥetchit [illegible], N. 803, [illegible], [illegible], Rec. 16, 110, club, mace.

ḥetch-t [illegible], spear (?)

ḥetchiu (?) [illegible], Rec. 30, 66.....

ḥetch [illegible], Thes. 1297, [illegible], to destroy, to do harm to, to injure, to filch from, to steal; Copt. ϩⲓⲧⲉ; [illegible], injurious, harmful.

ḥetch-t , , , harm, injury, destruction, affliction; , blocked (of a road).

ḥetch åb (or **ḥat**) , Åmen. 13, 13, to be of small courage, dismayed, disheartened.

ḥetch re , Åmen. 17, 19, ...

Ḥetchi ḥeru , Rec. 31, 30, a god who destroyed faces (?)

Ḥetchu kau , , Rec. 31, 30, a god who destroyed doubles in the Ṭuat; var. , ibid.

ḥetcha , bad, wicked, dirty, evil.

ḥetchai , the west wind.

ḥetchas , B.D. 99, 24 . . . .

ḥetchtchiti , Mission 13, 227, a pair of sacred birds (?)

Ḥetchfu , Ṭuat VI, a naked god.

ḥetchenu , , , , Rec. 21, 82, , Rec. 21, 92, , Anastasi I, 28, 5, P.S.B. 10, 44, to be overweighted, oppressed, disheartened, vexed, angry.

ḥetchenu , mental discomfort, wretchedness.

ḥetchentchen , Love Songs 2, 13, to be vexed, miserable.

ḥetcher-t , an animal, ichneumon (?); plur. , Rec. 36, 81.

ḥetcherr , an animal.

KH

kh = usually Heb. ח, and, rarely, ע and שׁ; in later times **sh** often takes the place of .

kh[i] , , to be high, to rise (of the Nile).

khi , , , , , boy, child, babe, youth; Copt. ϣⲉ.

Khi , B.D. 64, 19, "Babe," *i.e.*, the rising sun.

khe-t , , , thing, object, subject, matter, affair, business, fact, point, concern, cause, case; plur. , , things, belongings, clothes, goods, furniture, possessions, property, chattels, wealth, riches; see .

khe-t , U. 183, , food, meat and drink offerings.

khe-t , people, folk.

khe-t , learning, literature, literary matters; , books dealing with eternity, *i.e.*, the future life.

khe-t , , products of; , products of Egypt; , products of the Sûdân; , products of Arabia and Punt.

khe-t àtf , paternal property.

khe-tt per , , handmaiden, maidservant.

khe-t men-t , , , , things of earth, *i.e.*, the world.

khe-t meshu , the members of crocodiles.

khe-t neb-t , everything; , every bad thing; , every good thing.

khe-t nenu , inert matter, things without motion.

khe-t neter , IV, 1044, , , , temple property, the god's possessions; , sacred books.

khe-t haat-n , Rec. 36, 136 . . . . .

khe-t ḥa-t , T. 363, N. 179, a kind of crown or headdress; var. , coiffure.

khe-t ḥa Àsàr , B.D. 18, I, 4, things about Osiris.

khe-t ḥer khau , , , , , "things on the altar": (1) the name of a festival; (2) the name of the 5th day of the moon.

khe-t Ḥeru , , "things of Horus," *i.e.*, salt.

khe-t khau , , , Thes. 232, the name of a festival.

khe-t kha-t-sen , their personal affairs or dress.

khe-t gerg neter , cemetery property.

Khet, the god of things that exist.

Khe-t-ānkh-uȧa-f, Ṭuat XII, a goddess in the Ṭuat.

Khe-t-ua-t-en-Rā, Ṭuat XII, a goddess in the Ṭuat.

Khe-t-Kheperȧ, Ṭuat XII, a goddess in the Ṭuat.

khe-t, , Rec. 31, 167, Ȧmen. 5, 14, fire, flame, heat, to burn up; , , burning incense.

Khe-ti, , , Ṭuat VII, VIII, a fire-spitting serpent in the Ṭuat.

Khe-t-ānkh-ȧm-f(?), Ṭuat XII, a fiery serpent-goddess.

Khe-t-uat-en-Rā, Ṭuat XII, a fire-goddess.

Khe-t-em-Ȧmentiu, B.D. 141, the fire in the gods of Ȧment.

Khe-tt-neb-t-rekhu, etc., etc., B.D., 145 and 149, the 5th Pylon of Sekhet-Ȧaru.

khe-t, N. 925, , IV, 175, hall, chamber; , citadel, fort.

kha, , P. 711, N. 1361, one thousand; plur. , , U. 516, T. 388, , ; Copt. ϣo; , Ḥerusȧtef Stele 57, a thousand years; , a thousand of every kind of offering; , U. 582, , IV, 966.

Kha, , B.D.G. 554, T.S.B.A. III, 424, the god of .

Kha, a god; , Litanie 79, a group of gods.

kha, , , , , , , , IV, 1087, office, chamber, bureau, dîwân; plur. ; , general office; , muniment room, record chamber, library; , the mayor's office; , estate office; , chamber by the door.

kha, Rev. 12, 29, column; , P.S.B. 10, 42, hall of columns.

kha ur-t, hall, large room.

kha en ḥi, Ȧmen. 24, 17 . . . . . .

Kha, P. 369, , U. 475, N. 1146, , M. 684, , , , , Rec. 27, 223, a lake in the Ṭuat.

kha-t, marsh, swamp.

khait, canal, stream.

kha-en-ta, Love Songs 7, 7, , , field (applied to a woman), acre.

kha ta, Rechnungen 34, farm-land; , Rev. 6, 26, Pharaoh's farms.

kha, to measure a road.

kha, to measure; , measured; Copt. ϣι, ϣιⲁⲓ, ϣⲟⲓ, ϣⲏⲩ.

khai , Rec. 15, 165, Åmen. 18, 19, 19, 2, 19, 6, , Rev. 13, 31, , Rec. 5, 86, 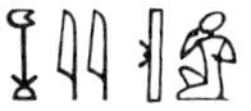 (late forms), to measure; Copt. ϣⲓ.

khai , U. 509, , T. 323, N. 1386, , IV, 1206,  , , IV, 660,  , , to weigh with the balance or scales; , IV, 669, unweighable; Copt. ϣⲓ.

kha , Rec. 16, 144, account, measure.

khau , M. 883, 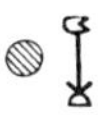 , N. 1188, , Rec. 31, 22, , ibid. 31, 21, , ibid. 31, 22, , ibid. 31, 22, IV, 1076, , a measuring cord; plur. , P. 306, cords, nets; , ropes, fetters.

khai , the measuring tape; see .

khait 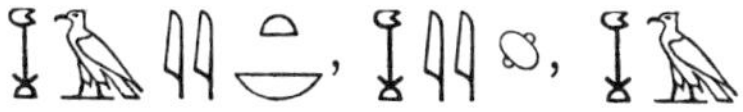 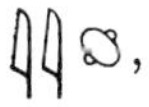, a measured quantity.

khait , a bowl for milk; , a copper bowl.

kha-t , a standard weight.

kha-t , a place for weighing things in.

kha , to touch, to feel, to seek to find out, to examine a patient by the touch.

kha , to winnow, to scatter.

khakha , to winnow, to scatter.

khau , winnower, reaper (?)

khakha-t 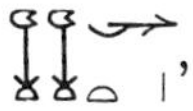, Tanis Pap. 19, 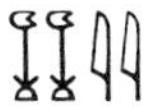 , a winnowing tool or instrument.

kha [illegible], [illegible], [illegible], plant, herb, flowering plant (?), plur. [illegible], [illegible], [illegible], [illegible], [illegible], [illegible], Love Songs 7, 8, [illegible], IV, 329, [illegible], IV, 524, [illegible], sweet herbs.

kha [illegible], [illegible], to cut, to engrave, to carve; [illegible], [illegible], cut, engraved, carved, inscribed.

khaiu [illegible], Hh. 234, slayers, conquerors (?)

khaiu [illegible], P. 494, [illegible], P. 509, slaughtering knives, slayers (?)

kha-t [illegible], [illegible], [illegible], Rev. 12, 40, [illegible], Jour. As. 1908, 285, stroke, blow, calamity, overthrow.

kha-t [illegible], [illegible], Westcar Pap. 7, 19, sorrow, pain, misfortune.

Khaut [illegible], [illegible] [illegible], [illegible], Rec. 26, 235, the divine dead.

kha [illegible], the last; Copt. ϩⲁⲉ, ϧⲁⲉ.

kha [illegible], [illegible], to adjure (?) to cry out; [illegible], T. 393, [illegible], M. 407.

kha-t 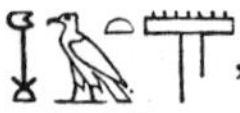, III, 139, Aelt. Texte 35,  , head cloth (kafîyyah), tiara, diadem, crown, head attire in general, the feathers of a headdress.

kha 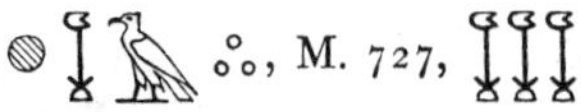, M. 727, T. 304, substance of the body.

khakha 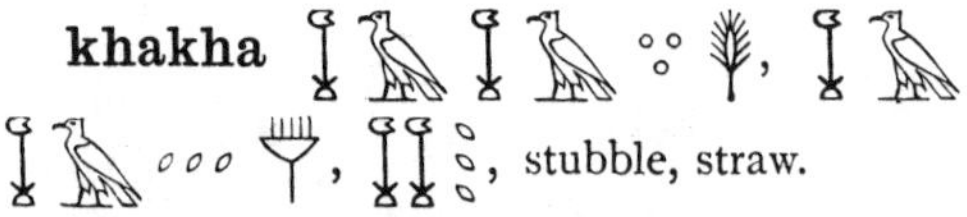, stubble, straw.

khakha 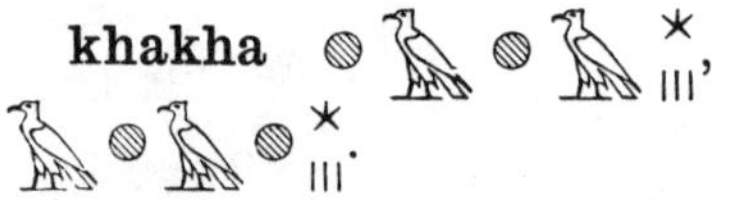, stars; see.

Khau 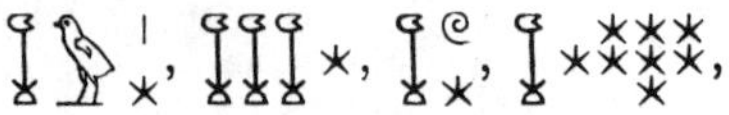, Denderah II, 10, Tombs Seti I, Ram. IV, 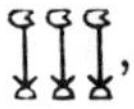, Annales I, 86, one of the 36 Dekans; Gr. χωου.

khaa 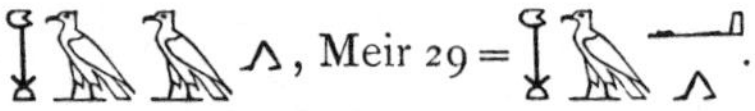, Meir 29 =.

khaȧ , to leave, to forsake; Copt. ⲕⲱ, ϫⲱ.

khaȧ , unguent (?); 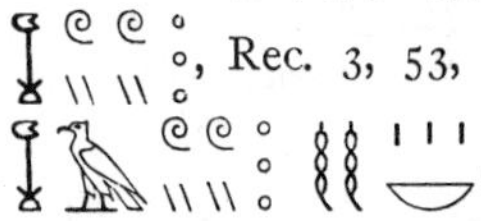, Rec. 3, 53, 5, 90, incense, spices; Rec. 3, 48, all kinds of aromatic gums and spices; Copt. ϣⲟⲟⲩⲉ.

khaȧnȧ  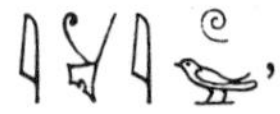, Israel Stele 12, stupid, silly, unwise, fool.

khaȧnȧ , Thes. 1203, grace, favour; compare Heb. חֵן (?)

khaā 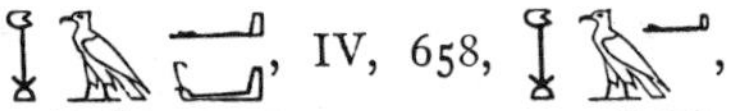, IV, 658, 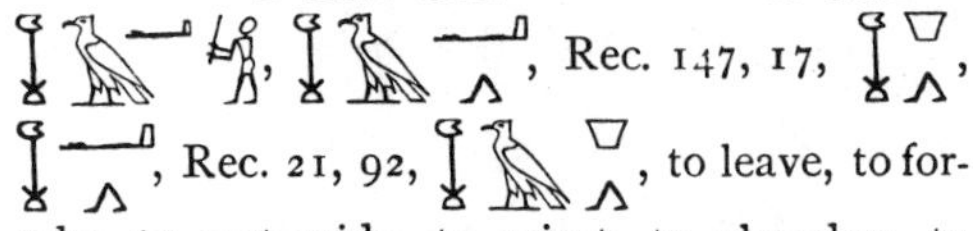, Rec. 147, 17, Rec. 21, 92, to leave, to forsake, to cast aside, to reject, to abandon, to cast away, to release, to slip away from, to yield, to throw; , rejected, forsaken; Copt. ϫⲱ, ⲕⲱ.

khaā ḥa , to turn the back.

khaā , Peasant 206, to knock over (a hippopotamus).

khaā 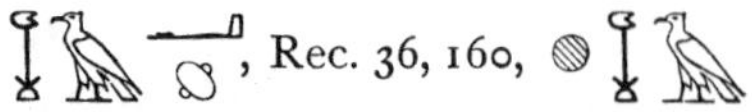, Rec. 36, 160, , Rec. 27, 223, Wört. 1026, Suppl. 888, spear-thrower, slinger.

khāā 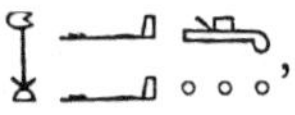, seed reserved for sowing.

khaā , to make water, a diuretic, aperient, or ekbolic.

khaā-t 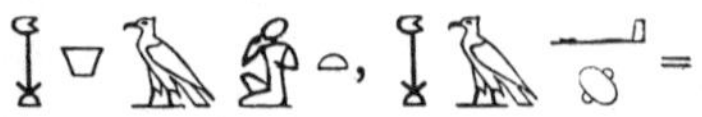 , dead body.

khāā , sling, catapult; plur.

khaā , a leather bag to hold tools or weapons.

khaāi (?) , a tool or weapon.

khaāir , Rev. 13, 21, excrement.

khaāu-ti , T. 144, N. 540, a pair of sandals.

khaām , to attack, to force, to injure, to break down.

khaāra, khaārȧ  , food, edible seeds or fruit; Copt. ϧⲣⲉ.

khai , to descend, to go down.

khai , Nȧstasen Stele 39, Ḥerusȧtef Stele 82, to slay, to defeat, to overthrow.

khai-t  , slaughter, massacre, ruin.

khai-ti 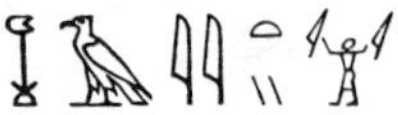, Thes. 1202, , slain, slayer (?)

Khaitiu , , the gods who slaughter the enemies of Rā and Osiris.

khait , , , sickness, a kind of disease; plur.  .

khai , to be high, to lift up = .

Khai , Rev. 13, 25, "Exalted one"—a title of Rā.

Khait , Ombos II, 130, a title of Uatchit of Ombos.

khai[t] , leather bag, sling.

khai 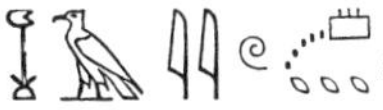, grain, wheat.

khai-t , altar, table for offerings.

khaib-t , , A.Z. 1905, 21, 27, , , Rev. 14, 37, shade, shadow; , U. 523, T. 330, , shadows, good and bad, in the other World; Copt. ϩⲁⲓⲃⲉⲥ, ϧⲏⲓⲃⲓ.

khaib-t neter , IV, 56, divine shadow.

khaib-t Rā 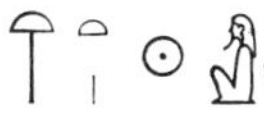, IV, 498, the shadow of Rā; 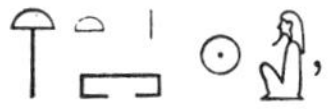, Rec. 17, 149, the shadow-house of Rā.

Khaibittiu (?) , Tomb Ram. IV, 28, a group of shadow gods.

khair , street, quarter; , Rev. 14, 41, the king's highway; Copt. ϧⲓⲣ.

khaiṭ , garden, courtyard; Copt. ϩⲁⲉⲓⲧ.

khau 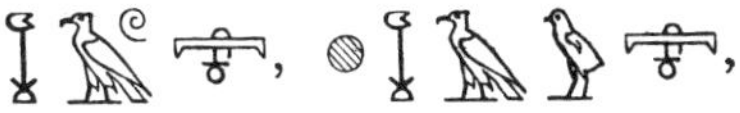, , , Rec. 29, 147,  , evening, twilight, darkness, early night; Copt. ⲉⲩϣⲏ, ⲟⲩϣⲏ.

khaui 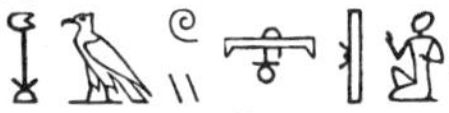, Leyd. Pap. 5, 11, a benighted traveller.

khau , P. 581,  , Rec. 27, 225, , IV, 753, , pot, altar-vessel, milk-bowl, , Nav. Bubas. 51; plur. , P. 707, [illegible], [illegible].

khau-t [illegible], pan of the scales.

khau-t [illegible], U. 82, [illegible], N. 361, [illegible], [illegible], altar, table for offerings; plur. [illegible], [illegible], [illegible]; Copt. ϣⲏⲩⲉ.

kha , I, 77, carcase of a sheep or goat; plur. , Rec. 29, 148, .

khau-t , Peasant 15, skins, hides.

khau , A.Z. 35, 17, the gunwale of a boat.

khau (?) , Rec. 21, 81, to fall into an ecstasy, to prophesy during a frenzy.

khab , Åmen. 5, 12, , to bend, to bow, to do homage, to be bowed.

khab remen 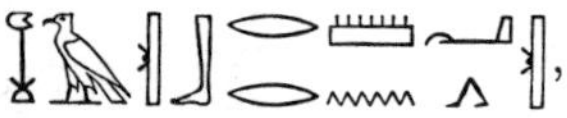, to bend the shoulders in homage.

khabb , Thes. 1202, to bow oneself; , Peasant 107, to wreathe (?) to decorate (?)

khab-t 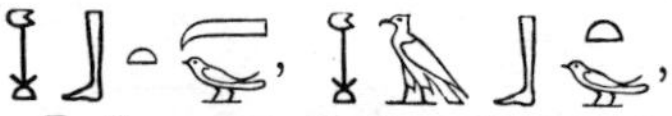, , moral obliquity, fraud, guile, deceit.

khabu , Rec. 21, 92, shadow, warped, bent, or twisted (of wood) by the heat.

khab-t , the neck, shoulder.

khab-t , , part of a crown.

khab 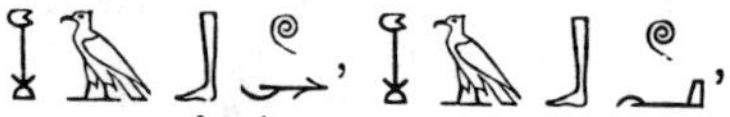, part of a waggon or chariot.

khab , Åmen. 6, 11, ...

khab , a crescent, a crescent-shaped object.

khabit , the vulture amulet (Lacau).

khabu , U. 302, 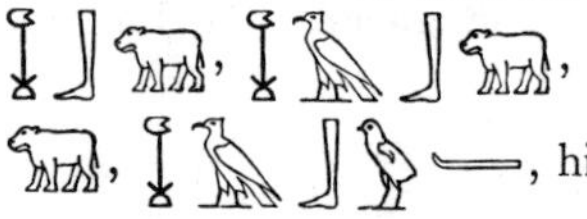, Rec. 30, 60, , hippopotamus.

khabȧr , Rev. 14, 137, Jour. As. 1908, 303, companion, confederate; compare Heb. חָבֵר, Copt. ϣⲃⲏⲣ.

khabru , Rev. 13, 24, Rev. 13, 13, image, transformations.

khabs 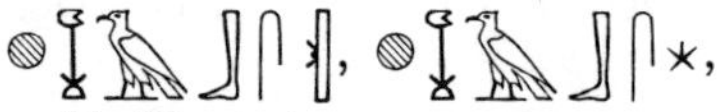, to shine or sparkle like a star.

khabs , P. 64, 538, 565, M. 87, N. 94, 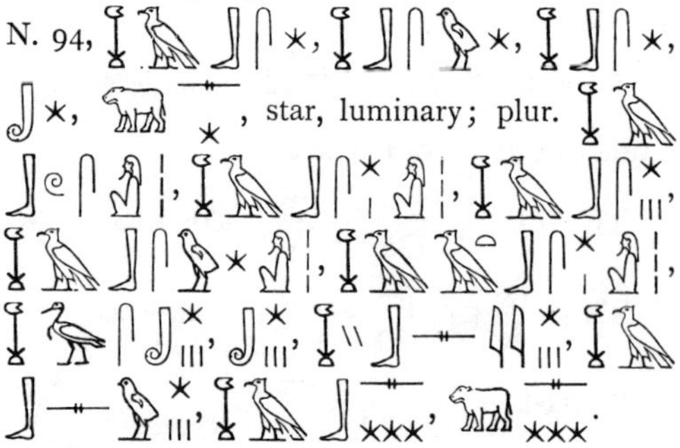, star, luminary; plur.

Khabsu 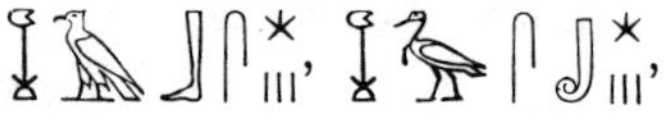, 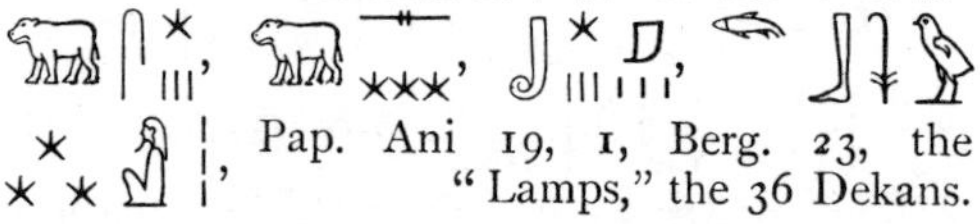, Pap. Ani 19, 1, Berg. 23, the "Lamps," the 36 Dekans.

khabs , , , Jour. As. 1908, 278, Rev. 14, 74, 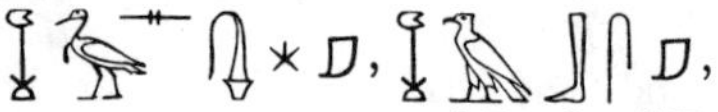, Rec. 13, 25, lamp, light; Copt. ϩⲃ̄ⲥ̄, ϧⲏⲃ̄ⲥ̄, ϩⲏⲃⲉⲥ, ϩⲏⲃ̄ⲥ̄.

Khabsit , 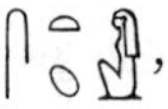, the goddess who lighted up the Elysian Fields.

khabs-t 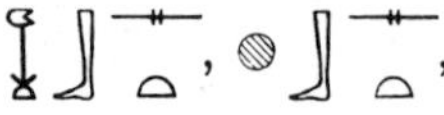, an amulet, A.Z. 1908, 17.

khabs , pavilion of a ship.

khabs , a kind of goose.

khabs , , Rec. 3, 53, beard; , long-bearded.

khabsi , hippopotamus (?)

khabsit 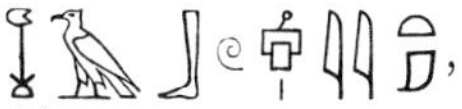, a part of the body, chin (?)

khabsti , "digger," "rooter up,"—the name of a dog.

khafā , to seize, to grasp; see .

kham , IV, 1073, Rec. 2, 15, 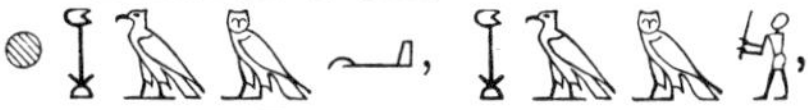, Shipwreck 87, 161, , IV, 927, 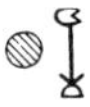  , Mar. Karn. 52, 4, , , Rev. 13, 89, , Ḥeremḥeb 3, 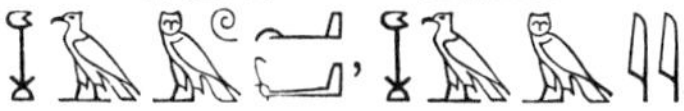 , Israel Stele 16, to bend, to bow, to submit, to bend away (of a ship), to be burdened, occupied, to have influence over someone, to gain the mastery.

khamiu , I, 149, , 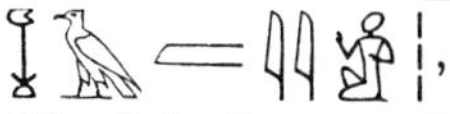, Thes. 1251,  , Rev. 9, 28, silent (?) helpless, men bowing in homage.

khamiu , enemies; see .

kham , Rec. 32, 81, to embrace.

kham , burning hot; Copt. ϧⲉⲙ, ϧⲙⲟⲙ.

khamm , Rev. 11, 141, heat, fire, hot, fever; Copt. ϧⲙⲟⲙ.

khamm , P. 474, , M. 540, N. 1119,  , Book of Honouring Osiris 24, to hasten, swift.

kham , Leyd. Pap. 10, 12 = , offices.

khamḥ 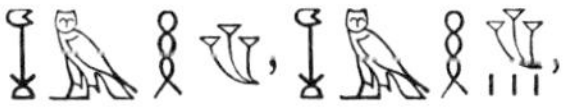, plant, flower.

khams 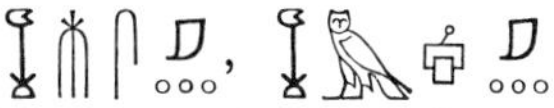, Rev. 11, 169, a substance used for cleaning purposes.

khann , haven, harbour.

khann-t [illegible], Rec. 2, 24, core, kernel; plur. [illegible].

khann reṭui [illegible], A.Z. 1868, 12, anklet.

khanakh [illegible], a wooden tool, a winnowing instrument, mill; var. [illegible], Rev. 13, 123.

khanin [illegible], Rev. 13, 27, [illegible], Rev. 11, 129, [illegible], Rev. 14, 16, fight, struggle, rebellion.

khanf [illegible], U. 112, N. 421, sacrificial cakes.

khanr [illegible], [illegible], Mar. Karn. 55, 74, [illegible], to drive or chase away, to carry away, to seize.

khanr [illegible] [illegible], to be out of one's mind through fright or terror, to be struck speechless with fear; [illegible], a name of Āapep.

Khanr . . . . āa, Nesi-Åmsu 32, 34, a form of Āapep.

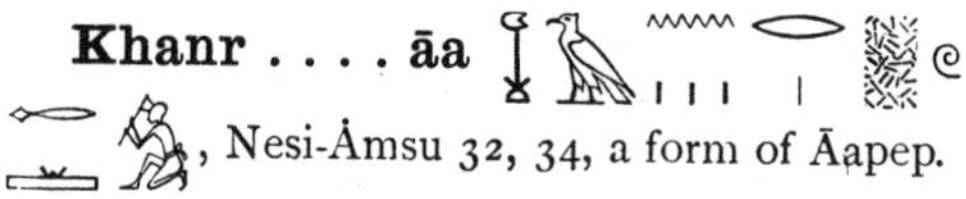

khanr, , IV, 669, a corselet.

khanre, , Chabas Mél. 3, 1, 182, a weapon, harness (?)

khanref, Anastasi I, 11, 3 . . . .

khansnȧ, wrathful man, angry.

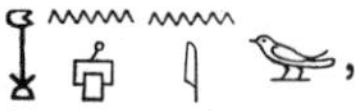

khar, , , , Rev. 13, 3, 4, 14, 65, food, fodder; Copt. ϩⲣⲉ, ϧⲣⲉ.

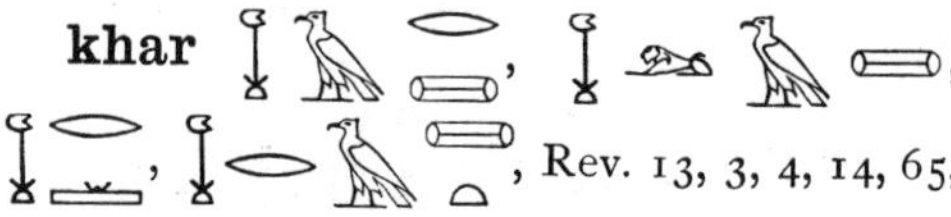

khar, Hymn to Nile, 4, 8, 9, to remove.

khar, Rev. 14, 21, to fly; Copt. ϩⲱⲗ.

khar, , , , , village, a quarter of a town or city, street; Copt. ϩⲓⲣ, ϩⲉⲓⲣ, ϧⲓⲣ.

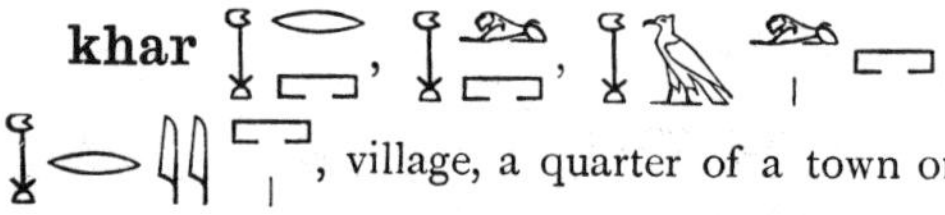

kharȧ, , , , , lower, downwards.

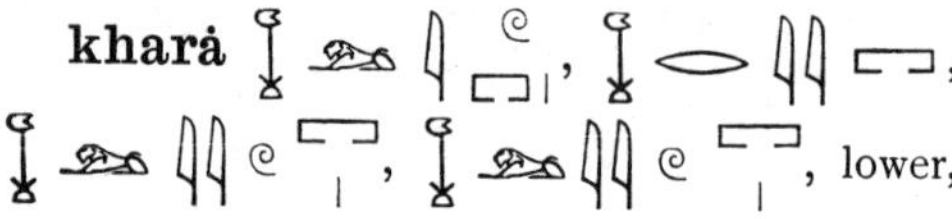

kharr-t, open space, waste ground, desert; plur.  , L.D. III, 229c, 16.

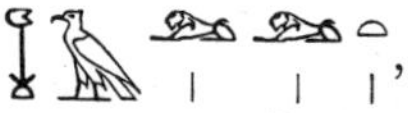

khar, child, youth, servant; Copt. ϩⲁⲗ in ϩⲙ̅ϩⲁⲗ;  = ϧⲉⲗϣⲏⲣⲓ (?)

khar-āa, old man; Copt. ϩⲗ̅ⲗⲟ, ϧⲉⲗⲗⲟ.

khar, Rev. 13, 37, , , , , Rev. 14, 12, to destroy, to spoil; Copt. ϣⲱⲗ, ϣⲁⲣ, ϣⲁⲁⲣ.

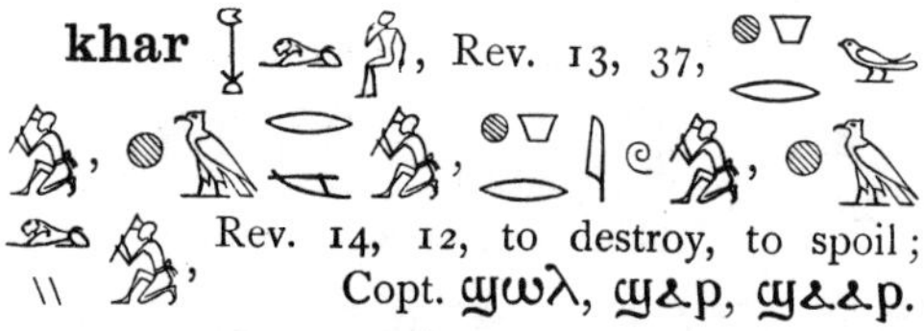

khari, widower.

khar-t, Israel Stele 27, , , , , , IV, 1045, widow; , the two widows, *i.e.*, Isis and Nephthys.

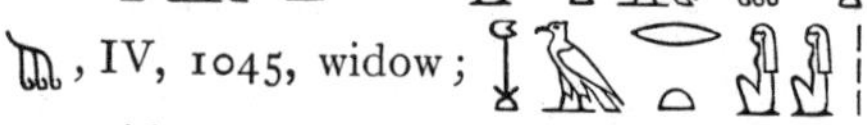

khar-t, B.D. 169, 26, a kind of goose (?); plur.  , B.D. 109, 3,  , B.D. 149, 6.

kharr (for **khaprr**), Jour. As. 1908, 498, scarab.

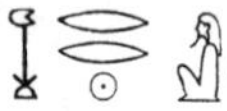

Kharu, IV, 743, , , , , , , , , a native of Palestine or Syria; Heb. חֹרִי; plur. 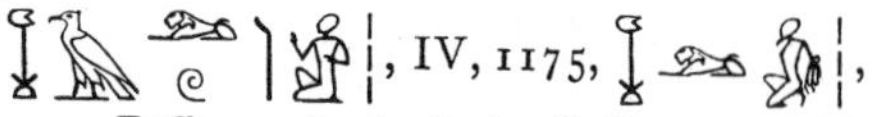 , IV, 1175, , IV, 649, , , .

Kharibt, , , , a woman of Palestine or Syria; Heb. חֹרִית.

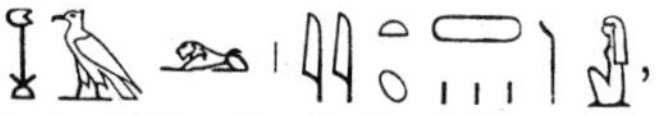

khara, Rev. 12, 25,  , Rev. 11, 167, to weave, stuff, garment; Copt. ϩⲱⲗⲕ.

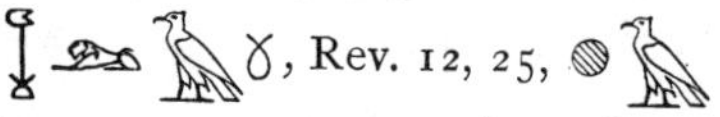

kharā (?), thong, strap.

khari, Rev. 12, 26, workman, weaver; Copt. ϧⲉⲗϧⲉⲗ.

khari, Rev. 12, 41, to descend.

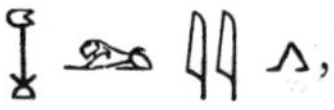

kharb = ; Copt. ⲭⲉⲣⲉⲃ.

Kharbṭu (?), Nesi-Åmsu 32, 40, a form of Āapep.

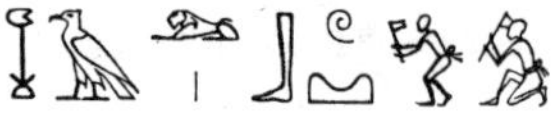

kharpi , Rev. 11, 167, navel; Copt. ϩⲗ̄ⲡⲉ.

kharpsa , a kind of cake, a loaf.

kharf , Jour. As. 1908, 260, to contradict; Copt. ϭⲱⲣϥ.

kharn 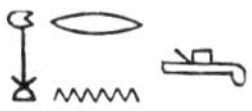, grain.

kharkhes , P. 461, N. 1098, , M. 517, be fettered (?)

Kharstȧ 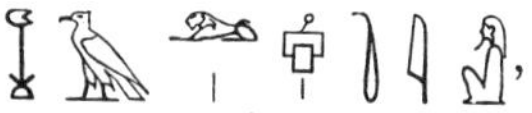, B.D. 162, 5, a form of Rā or of Ȧmen.

khargenn , P.S.B. 28, 179 = Gr. χαλκιον, χαλκια.

khart̩ 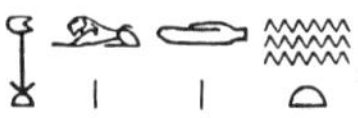, ravine, canal.

khakh , Israel Stele 20,  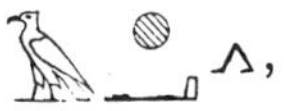, Hh. 505, , Rec. 29, 145, 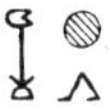, IV, 893, , , Peasant 229, to make haste, to be speedy, to be quick, swift; see 

khakhiu 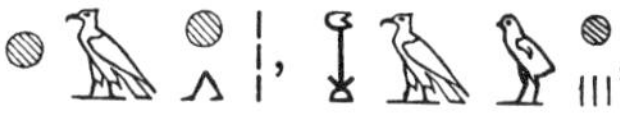, , swift, speedy, rapid runners.

khakh ȧb , Peasant 213, a man of ready mind, willing.

khakh re 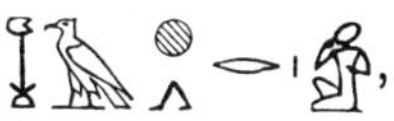, Peasant 208, "hasty of mouth," a man who speaks without much thought, glib.

khakha 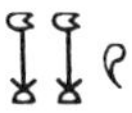, neck; see , and ; Copt. ϧⲁϧ.

khakhai , beak (?) of a bird.

khakha , A.Z. 45, 131, to cut, to shave.

khas , Sphinx Stele 6, , IV, 658, to make haste, swift;  . . . . .

khas , Sphinx Stele 7 . . . . . .

khasu 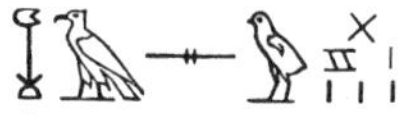, Pap. 3024, 95, swampy districts, marshes.

khasi , Jour. As. 1908, 293, 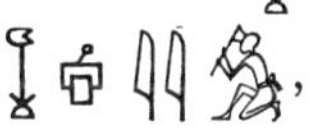, to suffer, to be tired; Copt. ϩⲓⲥⲉ, ϩⲓⲥⲓ.

khas , lamp wicks.

khasit , a kind of resinous plant, cassia (?)

khasb , Nȧstasen Stele 44, lamp; see [illegible].

khasf , Ebers Pap. 99, 22, to swell, tumour.

khaser , P. 350, [illegible] [illegible], N. 1041, to drive away, to scatter a storm.

khaskhet , P. 204 + 11, A.Z. 45, 140, foreign countries, lands.

khast [illegible], U. 536, [illegible], T. 294, [illegible], IV, 339, [illegible], Hearst Pap. 5, 2, [illegible], district, a kind of land, desert (?) foreign land (?); plur. [illegible]; [illegible], IV, 343, 645, all foreign lands; [illegible], necropolis in the hills; [illegible], IV, 480, the nine foreign lands.

khasti [illegible], a dweller on [illegible] land; plur. [illegible], , foreigners barbarians.

Khastiu , the four great tribes of the Sûdân.

khasti (?) 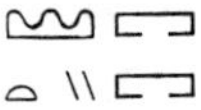, IV, 1180 . . . .

khast(th) 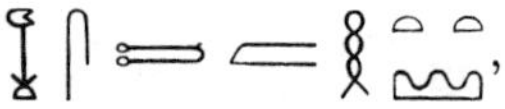, A.Z. 1907, 46, northern foreign land; 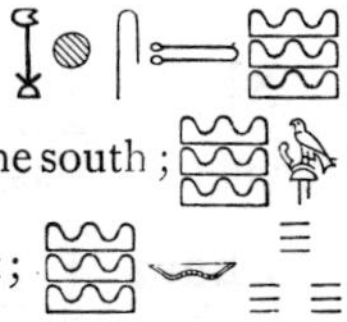 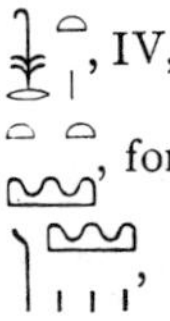, IV, 334, foreign lands of the south; foreign lands of the west; III, 138, the countries of the nine great peoples who fight with the bow.

Khashairsha , L.D. III, 283, , Xerxes; Persian , Heb. אֲחַשְׁוֵרוֹשׁ, Chald. חשישרש, Babyl. [illegible] 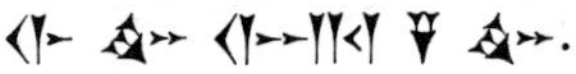.

khaqu , barber.

khaqu , Mar. Karn. 55, 61, razors, hair-cutting knives.

khaqȧ 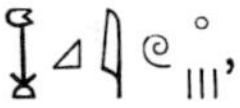, Rev. 12, 69, powder.

khat , dough, bread; var. .

khati , exhaustion, weariness.

Khati , B.D. (Saïte) 145, 82, 86, 149 (Saïte) 24, gods hostile to the wicked; var. , B.D. 149, 24.

Khatt-Satt , Mar. Aby. I, 44, the goddess of 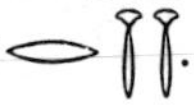.

khata , N. 942,  [illegible], P. 174, the two halves of heaven.

Khatȧthana.... , Annales IV, 131, the name of a nation or tribe.

khateb , T. 278, P. 59, M. 26 (= , N. 84), to kill, to slay; Copt. ϩⲱⲧⲃ, ϧⲱⲧⲉⲃ; compare Heb. חָטַב, Arab. حطب.

khatru , P.S.B. 7, 194, ichneumon; Copt. ϣⲁⲑⲟⲩⲗ.

khatha , IV, 781, a refuge (?) place of protection; compare Heb. חָסָה, 1 Chron. xvi, 38.

khathakhatha 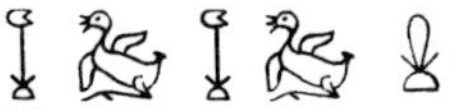, dough (?) bread of some kind.

khaṭ  (var. ), exhausted, tired.

khaṭ-ȧb , weak-hearted, timid, coward, a term of abuse applied to an enemy.

khaṭ 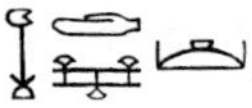, the necropolis of Denderah.

khatch , P. 204, [illegible] [illegible], [illegible], , bread, loaves of bread.

khȧp 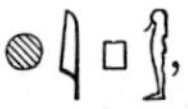, form, image, similitude.

khā, khāi [illegible], U. 552, M. 634, [illegible], U. 547, [illegible], P. 331, [illegible], [illegible], [illegible], [illegible], [illegible], [illegible], [illegible], [illegible], [illegible], [illegible], [illegible], [illegible] (in Nubian texts, *e.g.*, III, 140), to rise like the sun, or like a king on his throne, to ascend, to shine, to appear (of a god or king in a festal procession); , crowned; Copt. ϣⲁ.

Khā khā , U. 524, T. 330 . . . . . .

khāt-tȧ 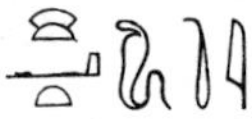, Rec. 32, 79, [illegible], 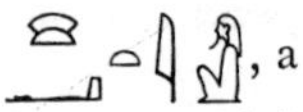, a rising, a manifestation; [illegible], IV, 361, shining with crowns.

khāut , Tombos Stele 3, [illegible] [illegible], [illegible], , Hh. 494, [illegible], Rec. 27, 218, [illegible], Rec. 27, 222, [illegible], [illegible], [illegible], [illegible], rising or appearance of a god or king, the ascending of the throne by the king, splendour, radiance, brilliance, a king's ornaments, *i.e.*, crown, rings, sceptre, necklace, etc.; Copt. ϣⲁ.

khā neter 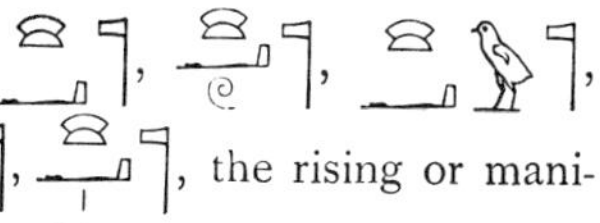, the rising or manifestation of a god or king, a procession in which a god or king is shown to the people.

khāit , the chamber in which a god or king appears.

khāu 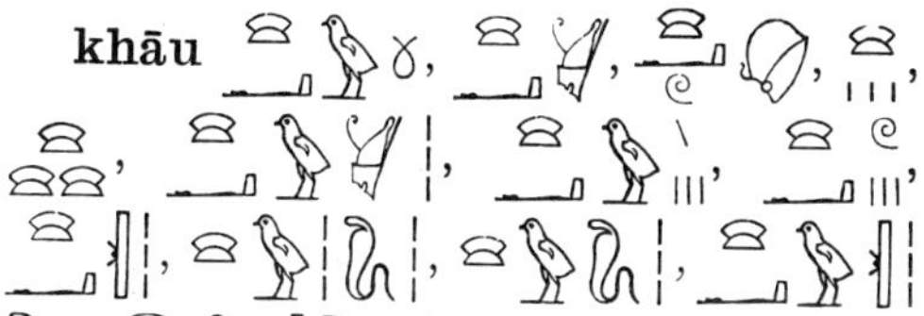 , the crown of the king of Egypt.

khā , coronation, coronation festival; , a happy coronation; , IV, 648, the festival of the king's coronation.

khāi[t] 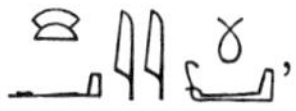, a tie or bandlet of a crown.

Khā-åakhu-t , IV, 422, the name of a shrine of Åmen.

Khā-em-Men-nefer 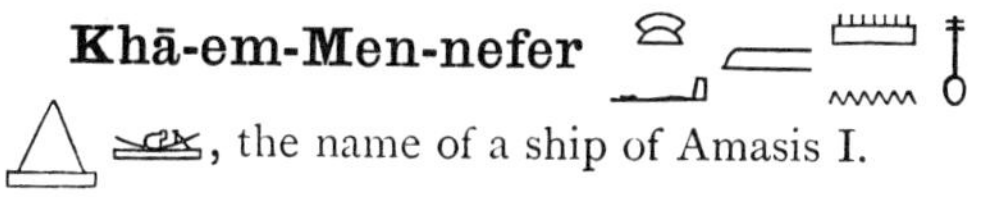, the name of a ship of Amasis I.

Khā-nefer Mer-en-Rā 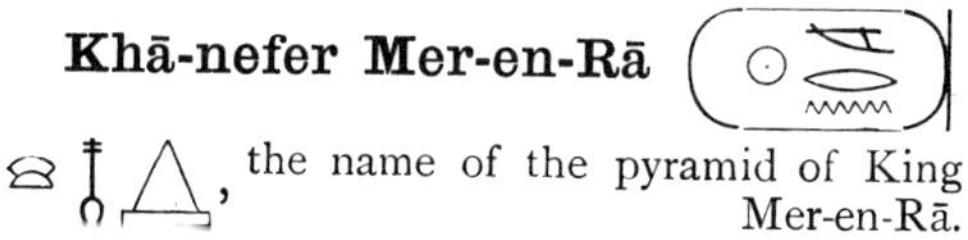, the name of the pyramid of King Mer-en-Rā.

khā-khenti , a title of an official.

khā Sti-t 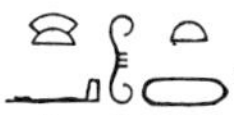, Mar. Aby. II, 23, 17, the crown of the land of the Bow (Nubia).

Khāit , B.D. (Saïte) 11, 3, a goddess.

Khāå-tau 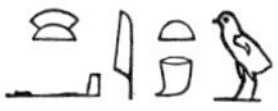, U. 536,  , T. 294, a god (?)

Khā-ā 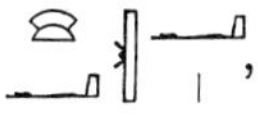, Ṭuat X, a divine bowman.

Khā-urit , the name of a uraeus-goddess.

Khā-em-Maāt , P.S.B. 21, 156, the name of a sacred barge of Osiris.

Khā-mut-f , Culte 20, a name or title of Åmen.

Khā-neferu-en-Rā , Thes. 31, the goddess of the 1st hour of the day.

khā 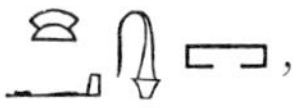, furnace, fire-place, cauldron.

khā, khāu 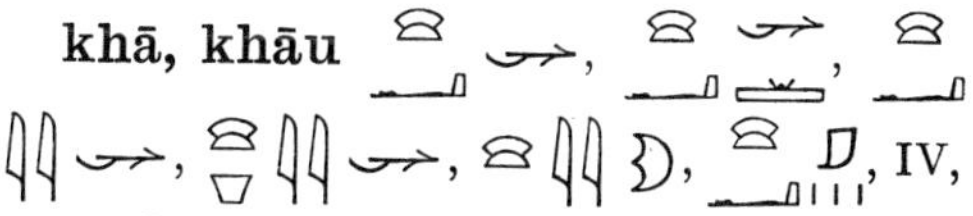, IV, 656, , Anastasi I, 26, 1, 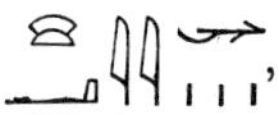, 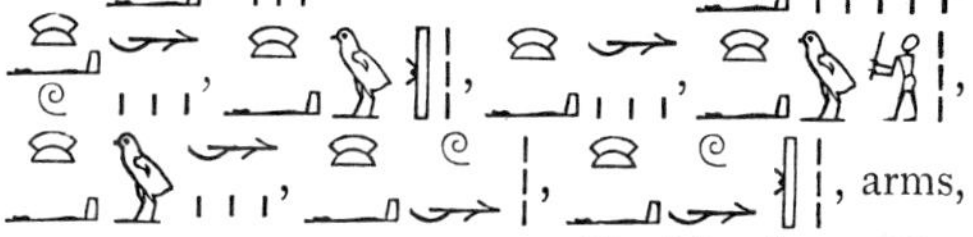, arms, armour, tools, implements; 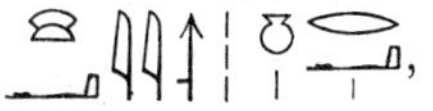, 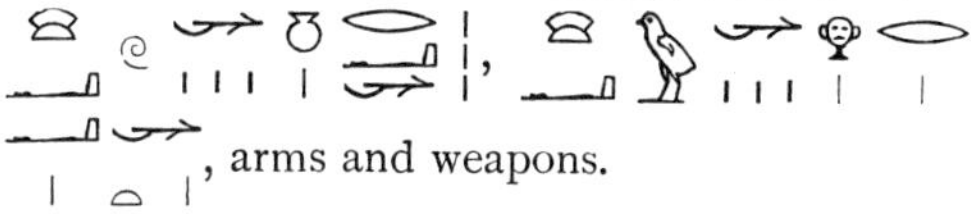, arms and weapons.

khāi 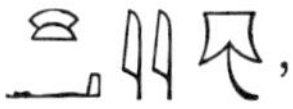, leather war tunic (?); Copt. ϣⲁϯ (?)

khāt (?) 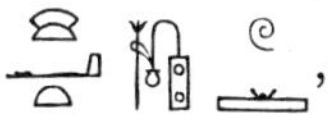, engraved, inscribed (?)

khāi , Rev. 13, 4, to kill, to slay; Copt. ϣⲁⲣⲓ.

khāikh , Rev. 14, 11, players on an instrument.

khāu (?) , disgraceful, shameful, inferior.

khāur (?) , a worker in stone, miner (?)

khāus  (*sic*), Pap. 3024, 61, to build, builder.

khāuṭ (?) , Peasant 227, a kind of fisherman; var. .

khām 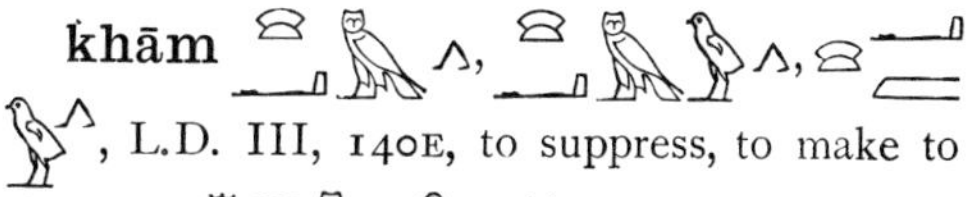, L.D. III, 140E, to suppress, to make to bow; see .

khām, neck, throat.

khār, , unguent, incense.

khār, A.Z. 1878, 49, skin, hide.

khār, , , , , , Rec. 16, 108, to be angry, to rage.

khārt, Rev. 14, 21, slaughtering knife; Copt. ϭορτε.

khāsu = **khus**, to build.

khi (?), T. 312 ....

khi, as, so, , L.D. III, 140c, for, because.

khi, Festschrift 117, 11, to cry out loudly.

khi, , , , , , , = , Rev. 11, 186, to lift, to raise up, to support, to be high, to rise (of the Nile); Copt. ϣωι.

khi, Rev. 12, 8, high-pitched voice.

khi, high ground.

khi, Ȧmen. 4, 16, high place, heaven, sky.

Khi, one of the four supporters of the sky.

Khi, the Exalted One, *i.e.*, God.

Khi, Rec. 27, 87, winged disk.

khi-t, , , the sky, heaven.

Khit, Denderah II, 55, , Rec. 27, 189, a goddess of the East.

khi uaut (?), a kind of Nubian (?) perfume = .

khibarr (?), a kind of cake.

khipenpenu, a fish; see .

khipṭ pennu, a kind of fish.

khim'tha, violence, evil, bitterness; compare Heb. חָמָס, Genesis vi, 11.

khinuȧ, a kind of beer.

khinr, to be lost, or destroyed, to be robbed.

khinru, harness, trappings.

Khirpasar, L.D. III, 160, 165, a Hittite name.

khirḥu (?), teeth.

khirrteb, Nȧstasen Stele 38, a vessel.

khirsh, Demot. Cat.......

khirqatȧtȧ, Anastasi I, 25, 9, slippery ground; compare Heb. חֲלַקְלַקּוֹת, Psalm xxxv, 6.

khireṭ, a kind of worked cloth or stuff.

khikhi, , , to swoop down like a bird of prey; , a man of hurried steps.

khikhi (?), , A.Z. 1913, 125, dust; Copt. ϣοειϣ, ϣωειϣ, ϣωιϣ, ϣιϣ.

Khisharsha, Xerxes; see .

khitȧ, wrath, rage, fury (?)

khithana, , wine, grapes.

khu , U. 512, T. 325, , P. 432, M. 618, , N. 1222, , M. 172, N. 690, evening, night.

khu 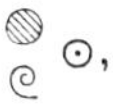, Rev. 12, 12 = , high.

khu , A.Z. 1907, 134, the "steps," *i.e.*, terraces, of the Lebanon mountains.

khu-t , house, palace.

khu 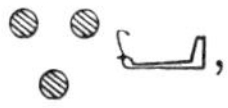, Décrets 14, to make an exception, to reserve.

khu-t , Décrets 105, , ibid. 31, , M. 728, N. 1329, 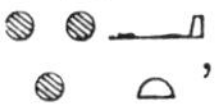, I, 15, 131, an exception, a withholding, a reservation; 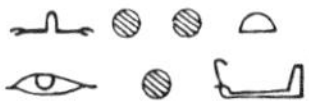, ibid. 31, making no exception; 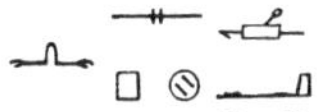 , Shipwreck 108;  , A.Z. 1908, 65, with the exception of myself; , A.Z. 45, 135.

khu uā ntu senu-f  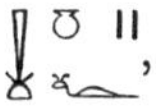, "a unique and unrivalled exception," said of a highly valued official.

khui , P. 656, 663, 758, 784, M. 136, 170, 729, 761, 775, N. 647, 1330, 1368, , N. 344, , P. 701, 712, Rec. 30, 200, , T. 340, , Rec. 30, 200, 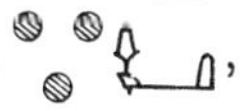, P. 700, , Rec. 31, 19, , , 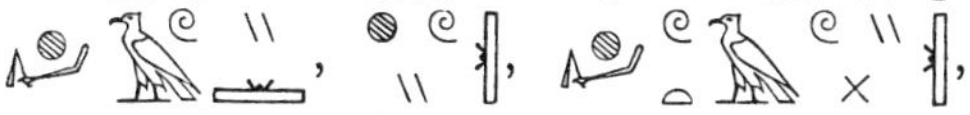, , to protect.

khui , Ḳubbân Stele 2, protector.

kh̬ui , Rev. 11, 174, protection.

khu-t , , protection, power, rule, charm, amulet, talisman.

khui , Ebers Pap. 63, 4, spirit; plur. .

Khuit , title of the priestess of Athribis.

Khutt , N. 995, a serpent-goddess (?)

Khuit-mu (?) [illegible], Ṭuat I, a fire-goddess.

Khu-Ḥeru [illegible], the title of the priest of the 10th Nome of Upper Egypt.

Khut-Ṭuat [illegible], Ṭuat IX, a fiery, blood-drinking serpent.

Khu-tchet-f [illegible], B.D. 146, a doorkeeper of the 8th Pylon.

khu-tchet-f [illegible], "his body shines," a kind of metal.

khu-t [illegible], [illegible], Rec. 17, 4, fan, fly-flapper.

khu [illegible], Rec. 27, 86, cattle for sacrifice.

khu [illegible], fish.

khu [illegible], [illegible], IV, 1077, dirt, what is nasty or foul.

khuti [illegible], helpless one.

khu [illegible], to dress.

khu [illegible], vases, pots.

khui [illegible], to weep, to cry; see [illegible].

khui (khi) [illegible], ground, earth, estate.

khui (khi) 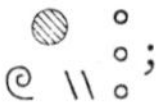; var. , vegetable paste, unguent (?)

khua (?) , to abound, to be abundant.

khuau , food.

khu , fire, flame.

Khuait (?) , Nesi-Åmsu 25, 23, , R.G. 66, a goddess, a form of Hathor.

khuas , to build; see **khus**.

khui 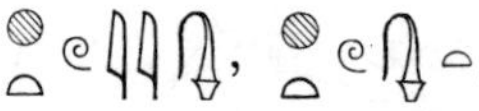, Rev. 14, 34, 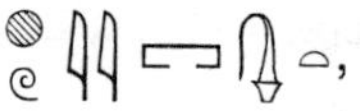, Rec. 36, 173, altar; Copt. ϣнтє, ϣнотı.

khumen-t 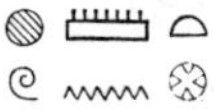 = οἰκουμένη (?)

khun , Metternich Stele 189, to sting (of a scorpion).

khunn , to bite.

khun-t 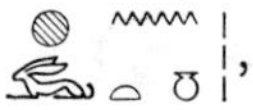, drink offerings.

khunnu , IV, 1080, animals for sacrifice (?)

khunnu 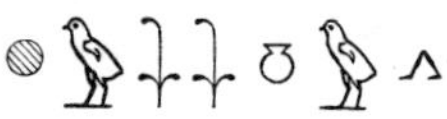, P. 459, messenger.

Khuràb (?) , Berg. I, 10, a bird-goddess.

khukha , Rev. 14, 137, seeds; Copt. ϣоєıϣ.

khus , to slay, to kill.

khus , L.D. III, 140B, , Thes. 1297, IV, 807, , Edfû II, 61, , , Mar. Karn. 42, 13, to build.

khus-t 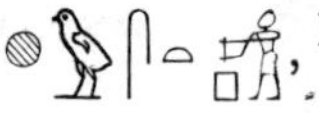, IV, 1141, the crushing of grain.

khuskhus , Thes. 1323, to build carefully and well.

khus ṭeb-t , IV, 1152, bricklayer, brickmaker.

khuṭ , , to be rich, opulent;  , Leyd. Pap. 8, 2; 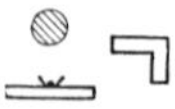, rich man, gentleman.

khuṭ , Rec. 35, 138, evil.

khuṭ-t , I, 43, steps of a tomb.

khuṭu , a fisher for kheṭ fish; var. 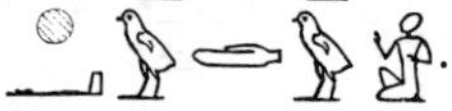.

khutch[u] , a fisher for kheṭ (khetch) fish.

kheb 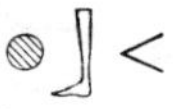, N. 1231, , , [illegible], Ḥeruemḥeb 25, [illegible], [illegible], [illegible], Rev. 13, 68, to diminish, to subtract (in arithmetic), to carry away, to withdraw, to transfer, to pilfer, to cut down, to destroy, to lay waste, to deceive, to defraud; Copt. ϣıϐє, ϣıϐı, ϣωϐ, ϣωϥ.

kheb-t [illegible], IV, 1114, [illegible], [illegible], distribution, apportioning, cut, division, a hurt, mean, little (as opposed to [illegible]), weak; Copt. ϣıϐϯ.

khebit [illegible], destruction.

khebti [illegible], waster, destroyer, sinner, damned; plur. [illegible].

kheb-t [illegible], Rec. 26, 231, [illegible], Rec. 31, 29, place of destruction, den, cave, torture-chamber, slaughter-house; plur. [illegible],

, L.D. III, 140c, prison at the gate; var. .

khebkheb , , Rec. 6, 9, , 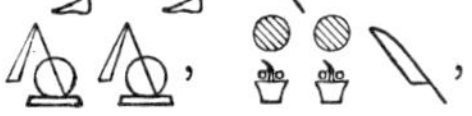, to break, to break or force open, to kill, to destroy.

khebkheb , a cutting-board, carpenter's bench, trap, snare.

khebkheb-t , destruction.

Khebit-ḥeri-snef, etc.  , B.D. 145 and 146, the 17th Pylon of Sekhet-Åaru.

kheb  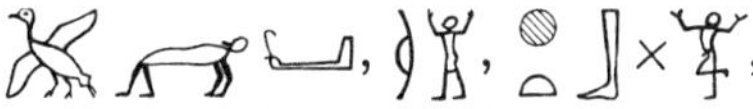, IV, 1162, to dance, to do gymnastic feats.

kheb-t , IV, 1162, , dance.

khebb , A.Z. 45, 125, IV, 386, to dance.

khebb-ti , dancer, acrobat.

khebu , acrobats, gymnasts.

kheb , IV, 1062,  , IV, 453, , hippopotamus.

kheb , flame, fire; , boiling lake.

kheb , Rec. 32, 51, wasp; Gr. σφήξ.

kheb , Dream Stele 6, , Metternich Stele 187,  , marsh, swamp.

kheb , Ebers Pap. 90, 9, "honey plant" or flower.

kheb , lotus.

Khebitt-sāḥ-t-neter  , B.D. 141, 148, one of the seven divine Cows.

khebkheb , plants, bushes.

kheb , B.D. 155, (Rubric), to steep in water, be immersed.

khebb 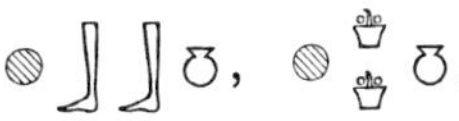, Rec. 16, 142, , pot, vessel; plur. , jars.

khebkheb 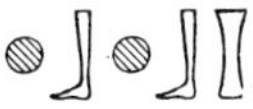, vase, vessel, pot.

kheba , to bow, to bend, to make to bend.

kheba , to dance; see [illegible].

khebait [illegible], Rec. 29, 166, tumbling girls, dancing women.

kheba [illegible], Peasant 112, Hymn to Nile 1, 9, [illegible], Peasant 230, [illegible], Leyd. Pap. 2, 11, [illegible], [illegible], [illegible] [illegible], A.Z. 1905, 28, [illegible] [illegible], [illegible], [illegible] [illegible], [illegible], to diminish, to cut off, to shorten, to make to cease, to destroy, to exhaust, lack, loss.

kheba-t [illegible], Peasant 143, diminution, lack, loss.

kheba [illegible], Peasant 286, faces lacking [intelligence].

khebai-t (= kheb-t) [illegible], cave, hole, den, cavern.

khebar [illegible], to be associated with, to be a friend, neighbour, or ally; compare Heb. חָבַר.

khebar , Rec. 21, 84, friend, associate, ally; Heb. חָבֵר, Copt. ϣⲃⲏⲣ; , to make a league with.

khebaru , boats, ships.

khebasi , a plough, hoe.

khebaṭi , A.Z. 1912, 56, to abuse, to disapprove.

kheben 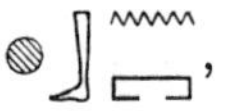, IV, 1164, chamber, office, house (?)

kheben-t , a girdle, belt.

Khebnit , B.D. 75, 4, a goddess (?)

kheben-t , U. 570, , Rec. 32, 78, [illegible], [illegible], [illegible], , moral obliquity, deceit, fraud, lie, defect, sin, evil, wickedness.

khebenti , , [illegible], [illegible], IV, 1107, [illegible], IV, 1081, offender, sinner, criminal; plur. [illegible], IV, 969, Thes. 1481, [illegible].

khebekh , U. 308, T. 310, to strike, to destroy (?)

khebekh 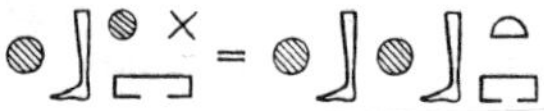; see [illegible].

khebs , U. 525, [illegible], T. 331, 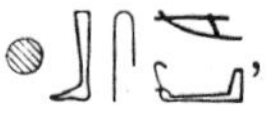, [illegible], [illegible], [illegible], Rec. 33, 5, 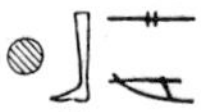, [illegible], to plough, to dig up, , A.Z. 1894, 119.

khebsu , a plough.

khebsti , digger, plough-man; , , Wört. 1067.

khebsu , 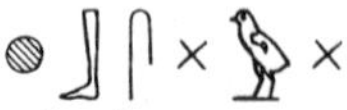, ploughed land; plur. , IV, 746, [illegible], [illegible], Wazir 16, [illegible], IV, 1051, ploughed fields.

khebs-ta 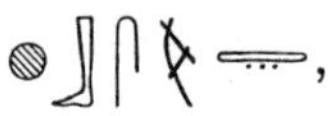, M. 696, P. 305, 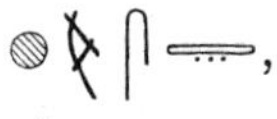, [illegible], T. 318, [illegible], P. 95, [illegible], Rec. 29, 147, [illegible], , [illegible], [illegible], [illegible], [illegible], [illegible], [illegible], B.D. 18, [illegible], Rec. 3, 50, 5, 86, the ceremony of digging up the earth at the festival of commemoration of ancestors. Other forms are:—

khebss-ta , P. 581, [illegible], P. 331, [illegible], N. 925.

Khebsi-ta , Ṭuat VIII, a god of the Circle Seḥerit-baiu-s.

khebs , , , lamp, star, luminary; plur. , [illegible].

Khebsit 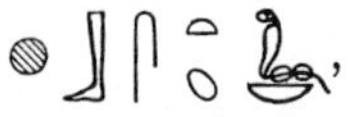, a goddess of Ḥetep-ḥemt.

khebsit 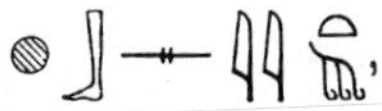, Rec. 30, 68, Hh. 437, [illegible], ibid. 27, 217, [illegible], ibid. 31, 10, [illegible], beard.

khebs-t 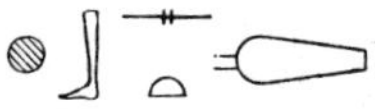, T. 166, [illegible], U. 622, M. 176, N. 688, [illegible], Shipwreck 63, [illegible], tail; [illegible], the lower hairy part of the body.

Khebestiu (?) , IV, 345, the name of a people in the South.

khebsti , part of a crown or diadem

khebs-t, an amulet.

khebs, a diving bird.

khebstȧ, a grass mat or pillow (?) a piece of furniture.

khebseth, A.Z. 1907, 46 = .

khebt, M. 695 . . . .

khebṭ, Ȧmen. 15, 5, to dislike, to loathe, evil-doer, horror.

khebṭ-t, , horrible, disgraceful, or terrible things.

khebetch, U. 434, T. 249, to bend in two, to force together.

Khebetch, U. 434, , T. 249, a sky-god.

Khebetchtch, Rec. 30, 200, a sky-god.

khep = , , ; , Rec. 27, 88, he creates what is; Copt. ϣωπε.

khep-t = .

khepiu, those who are = .

khep, , (?), , palm of the hand as a measure, grasp, fist; plur. , Rev. 11, 182.

khepi, , , N. 856, , IV, 220, , to go, to travel, to march, to sail (of a boat), to fly away (of birds), to flow (of water).

khepȧ, M. 519, , N. 1100, flower, flowing.

khep-t, step, advance.

khepp, to move; see .

khepp-t, step, advance.

Khepi, "traveller," a name of Rā.

khep, , , to pour out, to vomit, vomit.

Khep, Edfû I, 80, a title of the Nile-god.

khep, , , , , , shame, disgrace; , Leyd. Pap. 16, 2, death (?); Copt. ϣιπε.

khepp, to be strange, alien.

kheppu, , , , strangers, foreigners, strange or uncouth words.

khepput, strange things.

kheput, Rec. 10, 62, foreigners; var. , Hh. 536.

khep (?)-t, scalpel, knife.

khep-t, a kind of goose, bird.

khep-t, Rec. 24, 160, lion.

khepp, Love Songs, 5, 12, to play a musical instrument.

khepp, Rec. 16, 150, "tears of gum."

khep-tchesef-ānta, a kind of incense made of ānti.

khepanen, waterfowl.

Khepȧ = , .

khepȧ-t, Koller, 4, 5 . . . . . .

khepȧrer, Rec. 2, 30, 6, 116 = .

khepi, beetle = ; , Thes. 420, a name of the spring sun = .

Khepi (Khepri) , Tomb of Seti I, one of the 75 forms of Rā (No. 49).

khepi 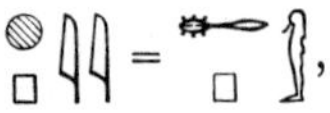, a figure, similitude.

khepu , a wooden object.

khepush  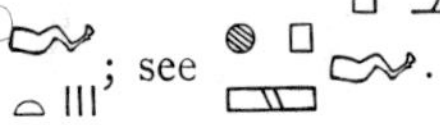; see .

khepen , to be fat.

khepenu 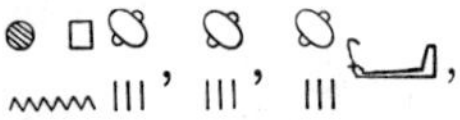, fat birds or other creatures.

khepnen 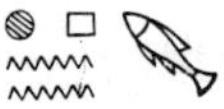, a kind of fish, fatted fish (?)

khepen 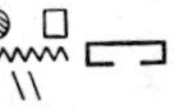, a measure (?)

kheper 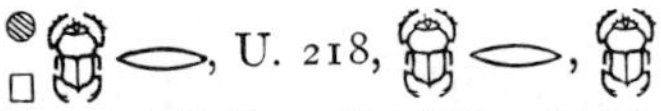 U. 218, 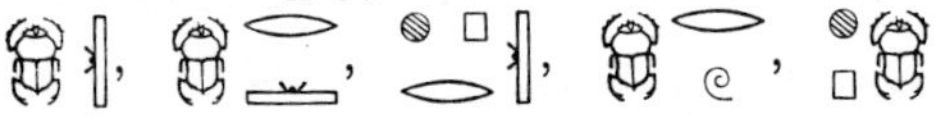 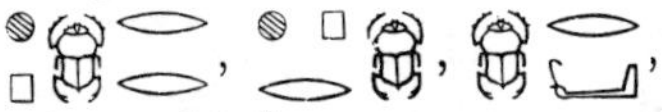 Rec. 32, 181, , to be, to exist, to have being, to subsist, to come into being, to happen, to fashion, to form, to create, to make, to bring into being, to take the form of someone or something, to transform oneself; 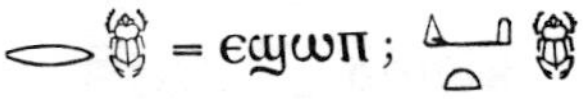 = ⲉϣⲱⲡ; = ϯϣⲱⲡⲉ; Copt. ϣⲱⲡⲉ; , non-existent; , P. 662, M. 773, N. 1229, there was not; , IV, 967, to happen at once; 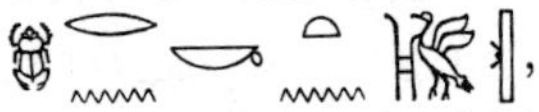, is thy name what?; , IV, 1014, making them to do everything according to the wish of his heart in everything he pleaseth; 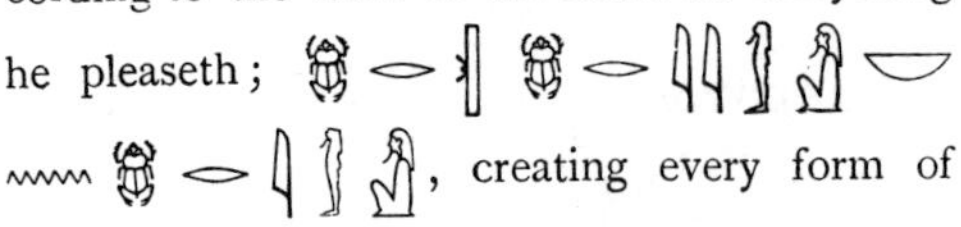, creating every form of Khepera: 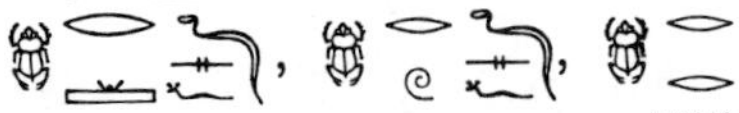, 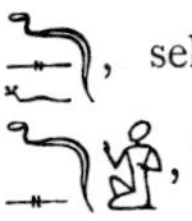, self-made, self-produced; , I made myself.

kheperu 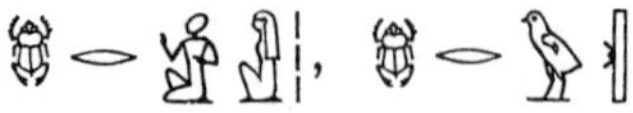, , living men and women as opposed to posterity, .

khepriu en ḥenti 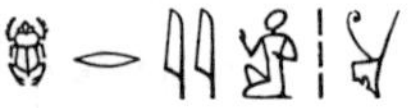 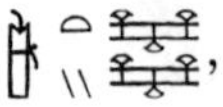, Rec. 16, 56, posterity.

kheper-t 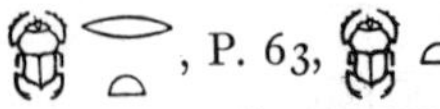, P. 63, M. 85, 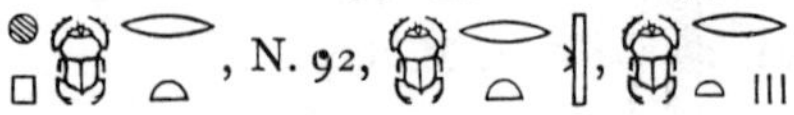, N. 92, what is, what exists, things that are.

kheprit 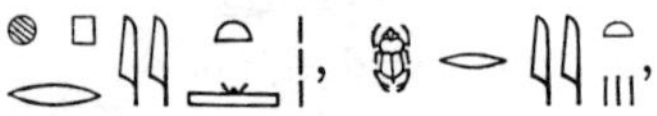, beings or things that exist, events, occurrences; , beings who create the things that are.

Kheper-keku-khā-mesut  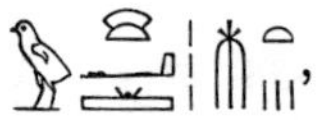, Ṭuat XII, the 12th Division of the Ṭuat.

kheperu 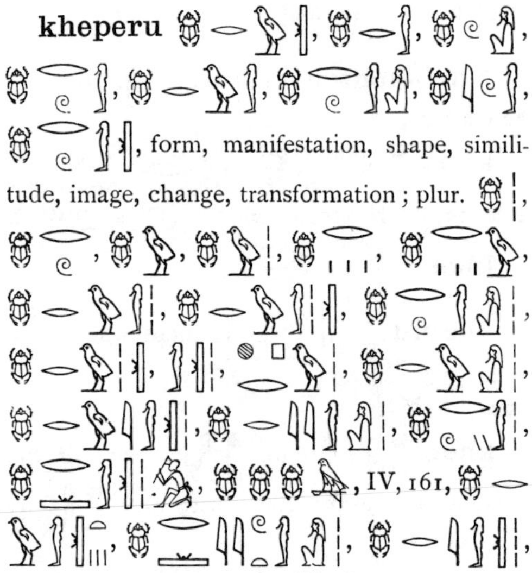, form, manifestation, shape, similitude, image, change, transformation; plur. , IV, 161, Rec. 36, 156; , 1st form of Ta-tanen; 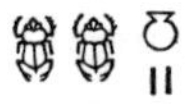, 2nd form of Ta-tanen; 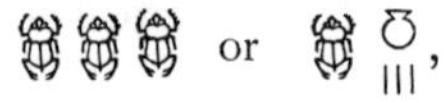 or , 3rd form of Ta-tanen; 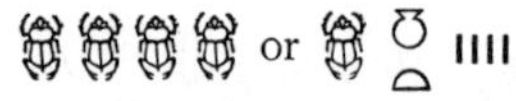 or , 4th form of Ta-tanen.

Kheperu 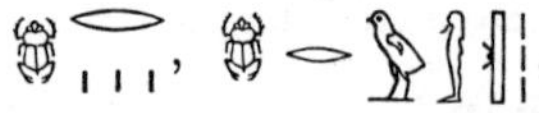, the transformations which the deceased might make in the Ṭuat; see B.D. Chapters LXXIX–LXXXVIII.

kheper  = (1) Cancer, the sign of the Zodiac; (2)  , the rising sun; (3)  , Thes. 412, the spring equinox and the spring itself.

khepher, kheprerȧ  , U. 476, M. 460,  , N. 747, , , , , , , a beetle (scarabaeus sacer).

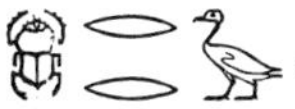

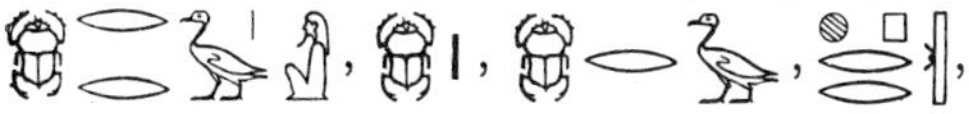

Kheprer , U. 277,  , U. 477,  , N. 619, 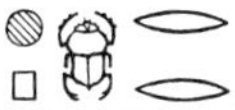 , N. 747,  , N. 856,  , N. 975, , , the beetle-god and the sacred beetle itself; the Creator of the world.

Kheper, Kheprer , N. 137,  , Rec. 31, 163,  , ibid. 31, 25,  , T. 254, , , T. 105, N. 719, P. 653, M. 755,  , P. 820, 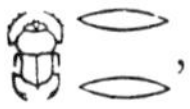 , N. 702, 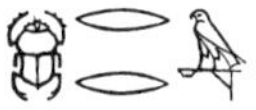 , M. 605, N. 856,  , N. 1210, the self-produced Beetle-god (who was later identified with Rā), *i.e.*,  , N. 767.

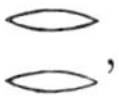

Kheper  , Ṭuat VI, one of the nine spirits who destroy the damned.

Kheper  , Ṭuat XI, a staff, with human head, guarding the 11th Gate.

Kheper  , Ṭuat VI, a jackal-headed standard to which the damned are tied.

Kheprer , Tomb Seti I, one of the 75 forms of Rā (No. 32).

Kheprit  , Ṭuat XII, a wind-goddess of dawn.

Kheperȧ , ; see **Kheper, Kheprer**; , Kheperȧ who produces every form of his being.

Kheperȧ  , Tomb of Seti I, one of the 75 forms of Rā (No. 11).

Kheperȧ , , Ṭuat IV,  , J.K.S. II, 9, Denderah IV, 84: (1) a winged solar-disk; (2) a guardian of the 12th Pylon.

Kheperȧ , , the god of the 12th hour of the night.

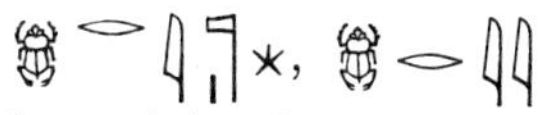

Khepri 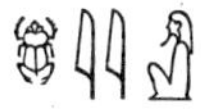 , Tomb of Seti I, one of the 75 forms of Rā (No. 2).

Khepri , , Ṭuat IX, a magical serpent-boat with human heads and wings.

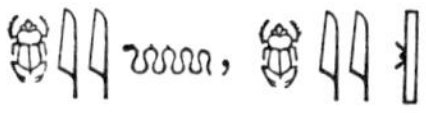

Khepri , Rec. 27, 217; see **Kheperȧ**.

Khepru , Rec. 27, 220, Khepru self-created.

Kheprit , , Denderah III, 24, Thes. 36, the goddess of the 8th hour of the day.

Kheper-ānkh , Ṭuat X, a beetle-god.

Kheper-Khenti-Ȧmentt , Cairo Pap. III, 1, a beetle-god, chief of the mesqet (bull's skin).

Kheper-tchesef , Rec. 31, 175, the great god who created himself.

Kheper-tchesef , B.D. 17, 9 = Gr. *αὐτογενής*, a title of several gods.

kheper , a medicine in which a beetle is an ingredient.

kheprȧ , , a drink or medicine.

kheperu , Rechnungen 17, 1, 10, a pot.

khepprer , socket; plur. 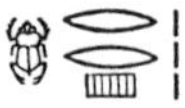.

khepri , Jour. As. 1908, 285, 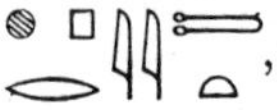, Jour. As. 1908, 248, , wonder, miracle; Copt. ϣпнрє, ϣпєєрє, ϣфнрı.

kheprur , Peasant 19, a plant (medicinal?).

khepersh , a crown, helmet.

khepekh 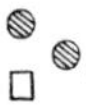, N. 213, U. 119, N. 428 = , fore-leg of a beast, arm and shoulder of a man; fem. 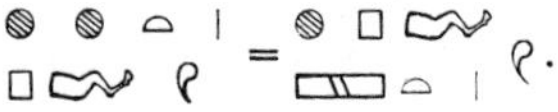.

khepesh 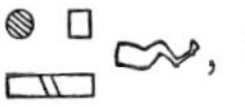, U. 119A, III, 141, , fore-leg of an animal, the arm and shoulder; dual 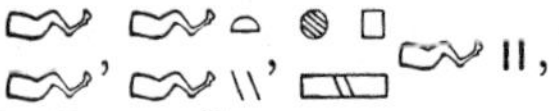, Nåstasen Stele 45, 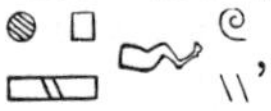, Ḥerusȧtef Stele 75, the two arms of a man; plur. 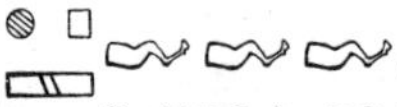, T. 326, , U. 513, ; Copt. ϣωπϣ.

khepesh , IV, 1082, strength, power, valour; 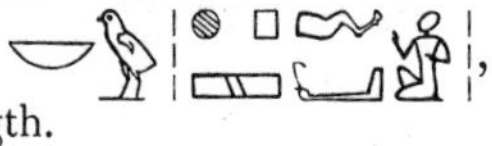, IV, 974, lords of strength.

khepesh 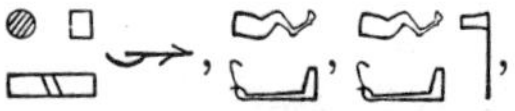, sword, scimitar, any weapon; plur. , IV, 726, swords.

khepesh , Anastasi I, 26, 4; A.Z. 1907, 125, 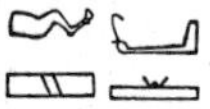, blacksmith's forge, foundry, forge, armoury, place in which weapons are stored.

Khepesh 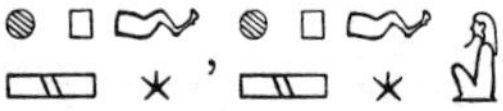, B.D. 17, 92, 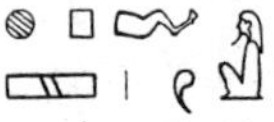, the constellation of the Great Bear.

khepesh 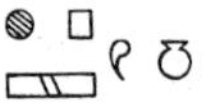, gift, dowry (?)

khepshȧ 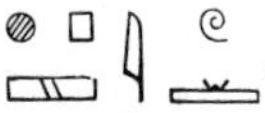, Rec. 14, 50, a measure (?); Copt. ϭⲁпıⲭн (?)

khept 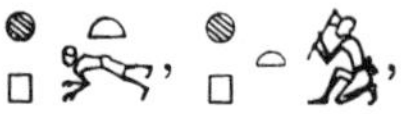, Rev. 11, 83, 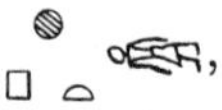, Rec. 3, 116; var. , Leyd. Pap. 16, 2, to overthrow, to destroy, dead, death.

khepti , , a shameful person or thing, disgrace.

Khepau (Kheptiu ?) , Ṭuat VIII, a group of drowned beings in the Ṭuat.

khepṭ, khepṭ-ti 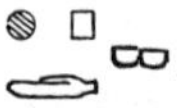, P. 570, 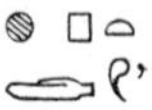, , , the buttocks, thighs, loins, the shame; plur. , the genital organs, male and female.

khepṭ-t 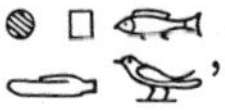, shame, disgrace.

khepṭ [illegible], [illegible], to overthrow.

khef [illegible], to bow down.

khef [illegible], Israel Stele 11, [illegible], Rev. 11, 62, [illegible], to be undone, to be laid waste, destroyed.

khefiu [illegible], Rec. 21, 15, things proved by documentary evidence; Copt. ϣωϥ.

khefi [illegible], [illegible], to see, to look upon.

khefi-t [illegible], [illegible], A.Z. 1908, 118, quay, shore, bank, landing-stage.

khefkhef [illegible], to heap up, to collect.

khefkhef [illegible], to flood.

khefkhef-t [illegible], U. 434, T. 248, flood, deluge.

khefkhefu [illegible], dust storms (?) dust.

khefa, to be over full, swollen, puffed up.

khefa-t, fullness, abundance.

khefa-t, T. 93, N. 629, M. 415, P. 162, Hh. 460, offerings. Late forms are :—

khefā, T. 363, IV, 892, Rec. 30, 69, 31, 17, to seize, to grasp, to capture, to plunder; varr.

khefā, Rec. 30, 196, Rec. 3, 56, fist, clenched hand.

khefā-t, grasp, fistful.

khefā, IV, 1120, a substance.

khefā, a packet or bundle of arrows.

Khefā-t, the name of a serpent on the royal crown.

khefā-am, a plant.

khefen, bread-cake, loaf.

kheft, with, together with, in front of, inasmuch as, according as, corresponding to, at what time, for, on behalf of. Late forms are :—

kheft-åmi, B.D. 101, 10, in, into.

kheft-ḥer, (Nåstasen Stele 20); varr. the front, what is in front, before, face, countenance.

kheftu, likeness, image.

kheft-ḥer, Rev. 12, 79, the dromos of a temple.

Kheft-ḥer-neb-st, A.Z. 1905, 21, IV, 312, a fortress of Thebes on the west bank.

kheft-ḥer-s, Rec. 30, 67, a rope in the magical boat.

Kheft-ta, P. 405, M. 579, N. 1186, a goddess.

khefti, T. 267, M. 423, Peasant B. 2, 113, Åmen. 8, 3, foe, enemy, opponent; female enemy; plur. Hh. 728, Rec. 16, 116; Copt. ϣⲁϥⲧ.

Kheftiu Åsår, Ṭuat VII, the foes of Osiris.

Kheftiu Åsår butchiu, Ṭuat VIII, the burnt foes of Osiris.

kheft[i], child, boy, girl.

Kheftes-håu-ḥesqit-Neḥa-ḥer, the hour-goddess of the 7th Division of the Ṭuat.

khem, khemi, U. 330 (= T. 300), P. 172, N. 938, Peasant 287,

, , , Israel Stele 12, , to bring to an end, to cease, to make an end of, to be ignorant of, to have no knowledge of, to disregard, to feign ignorance, to play the fool; , P. 646, M. 744, not unknown, nothing is unknown.

khemm, khemmi , U. 416, , T. 237, Pap. 3024, 124, Leyd. Pap. 7, 4, , to be ignorant, unlearned, inactive.

khem —— , he whose name is unknown, *i.e.*, God; , IV, 971, he who is not known, *i.e.*, a stranger; , he felt not his body, *i.e.*, he felt dead; , Peasant 219, the ignorant man; , Leyd. Pap. 7, 3; , IV, 324, unknown to men, *i.e.*, to the Egyptians.

khem — em khem , , , without, destitute of; **em khemt** , A.Z. 1900, 28, , , without, destitute of, exclusive of; , the number remaining when one number is subtracted from another.

khem , A.Z. 970, , , , Åmen. 27, 10, 11, an ignorant man, fool, dolt, stupid, untrained (of an animal); plur. , .

khem , stranger, alien.

khem , , A.Z. 1878, 48, Rev. 11, 126, 148, , , Rev. 11, 172, little, small, slight; Copt. ϣⲏⲙ.

khem khar = Copt. ϩⲙϩⲁⲗ (Rev.), slave, servant.

khem-ni (?) , , Pap. 3024, 57, ignorant.

khemi , , foe, enemy, fiend, worthless person; plur. , , , ; , Rev. 13, 112, men of nothing.

khemiu-urṭu , , , Rec. 26, 234, , Rev. 14, 7, the stars that rest not.

Khemiu-ḥepu , J.K.S. II, 13, a class of stars; , they come out of her womb and go into her mouth daily.

Khemiu-ḥemu , J.K.S. II, 13, a class of stars, planets (?)

khemiu-seku , Rec. 26, 234, , , , Rev. 14, 7, the stars that are always above the horizon, the circumpolar stars.

khem , P. 332, , IV, 157, , IV, 157, , , , shrine, holy of holies, sanctuary; plur. , , .

Khem , god of procreation and generative power; see **Menu**.

khem, khemm 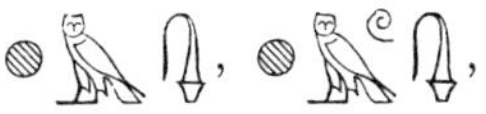, , to be hot, to be dry, to burn; varr. ; Copt. ϩⲙⲟⲙ.

khem-t , fire, heat; var.  .

khemu-t 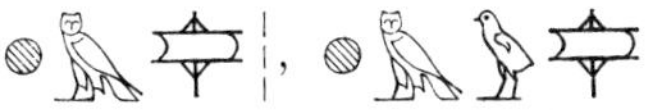 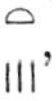, IV, 837, hot parching winds, the khamâsîn, or khamsin, *i.e.*, winds of the "fifty" hot days.

khem-nef(?) , , asthma, breathlessness, difficulty in breathing.

khem , P. 609, , T. 371, P. 536, N. 806, , T. 392,  Rec. 16, 142, aromatic herbs; compare Arab. سمّ.

khemkhem , Koller 4, 1, a fruit.

khemi , Thes. 1251,  , Rec. 36, 210,  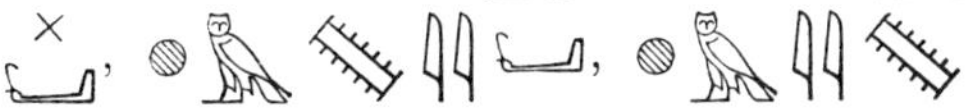 , to push over, to overthrow, to destroy, to attack;  , destroyers.

khemut , Rec. 26, 232, overthrow.

khemkhem  , to break, to overthrow; Copt. ϩⲉⲙϩⲱⲙ.

Khemkhem, etc. 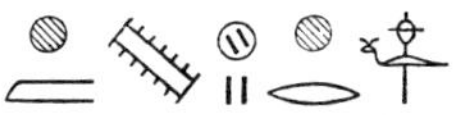 , Ombos II, 134, a name.

Khemi 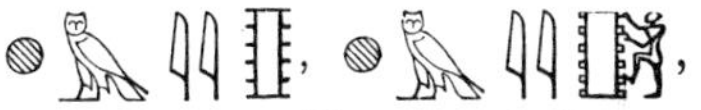 , B.D. 125, II, one of the 42 assessors of Osiris.

Khemit , Denderah IV, 44, a weeping-goddess.

Khemit , Ṭuat V, a goddess of destruction.

Khememit , Mar. Aby. I, 6, 36 = .

khema , Rec. 32, 81, , child at the breast, child, youthful, graceful, slender.

khema   ......; Copt. ϣⲙⲙⲁ, ϣⲟⲟⲙⲉ (?)

khemā , T. 46, , P. 87, [illegible], P. 33, [illegible], [illegible], [illegible], Rev. 11, 90, to grasp, to seize, to lay hold upon, to hold, to possess, to contain.

khemāu (?) [illegible], [illegible], [illegible], a class of workmen, labourers in general.

khemā-t [illegible], a part of a boat.

khemi [illegible], P.S.B. 13, 411, Sallier II, 5, 6, Anastasi IV, 12, 9, [illegible], a kind of water-bird, pelican; plur. [illegible], Rec. 18, 181; Copt. ϩⲏⲙⲓ.

khemen [illegible], A.Z. 1908, 38, [illegible], [illegible], eight; [illegible], eighth; [illegible], T. 391, [illegible], M. 405; Copt. ϣⲙⲟⲩⲛ, Heb. שְׁמֹנָה.

khemen-t [illegible], a period of eight days (?)

khemen-t [illegible], a kind of stuff, eight-thread cloth.

khemen-ti 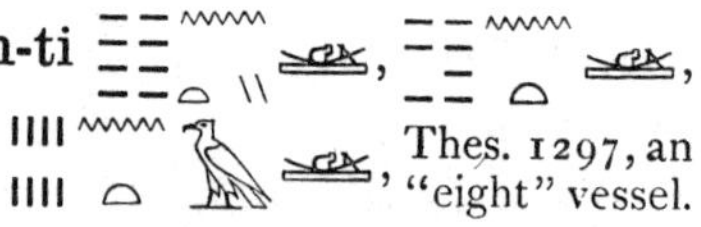, Rec. 29, 149, Thes. 1297, an "eight" vessel.

Khemenu 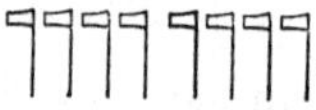, Mar. Karn. 42, 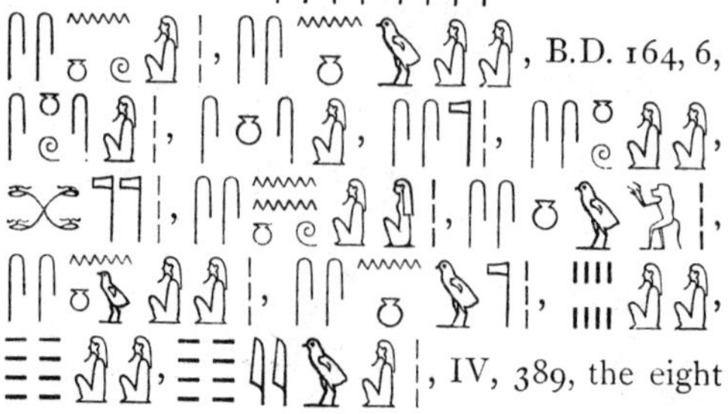, B.D. 164, 6, IV, 389, the eight elemental deities of the Company of Thoth: they were Nu, Nut, Ḥeḥ, Ḥeḥit, Kek, Kekit, Nen, Nenit.

khemni (?) , eighty; Copt. ϩⲙⲉⲛⲉ, ϧⲁⲙⲛⲉ.

khemen-t 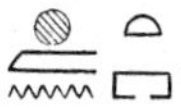, Rev. 13, 104, shrine.

khemes 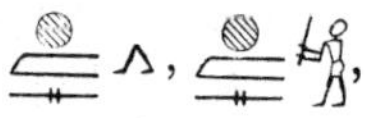, a post on a boat or ship (?)

khemes ; see, friend, companion.

khemes , ear of corn; plur. ; see ; Copt. ϩⲙⲥ̄, ϧⲉⲙⲥ̄.

khemsau (?) , Annales II, 238 . . . .

khemt (khem) , Pap. 3024, 140, 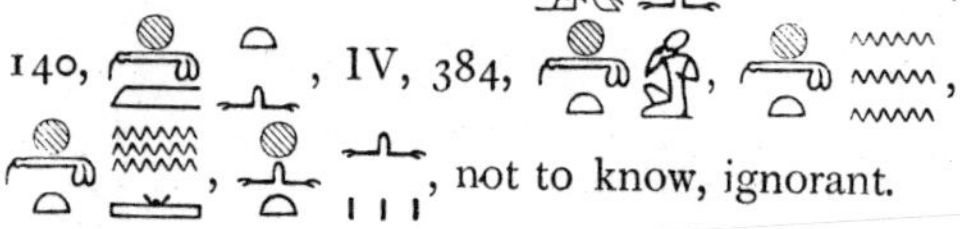, IV, 384, not to know, ignorant.

khemt (khem) , coward, poltróon.

khemt (khem) , IV, 344, without =.

khemt-ni 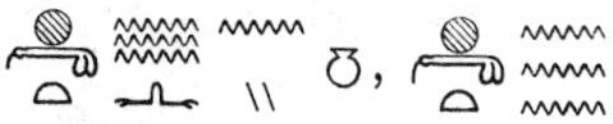 , yeast; Copt. ϣⲉⲙⲏⲣ.

khemt 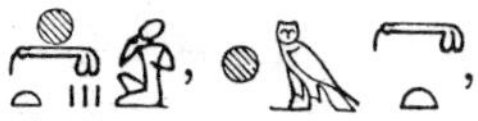, to observe, to think, to think out a matter.

khemt 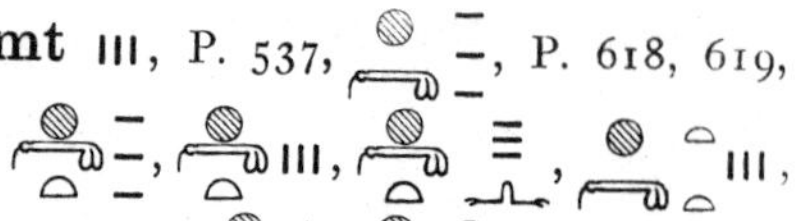, P. 537, P. 618, 619, N. 1304, U. 179, N. 1040, 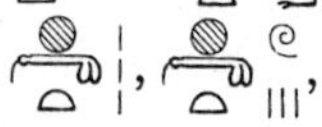, three; Copt. ϣⲉⲙⲧ, ϣⲟⲙⲧ̄, ϣⲁⲙⲉⲧ; 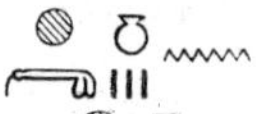 , A.Z. 45, 125, third of three; 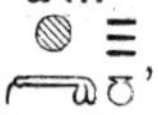, P. 641, 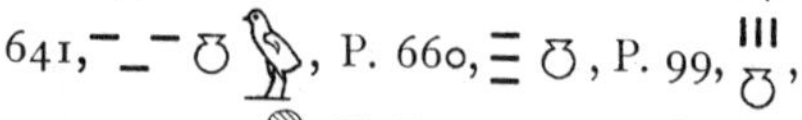, P. 660, P. 99, N. 970, third; fem. 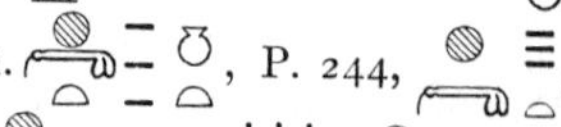, P. 244, M. 675, N. 1238, , M. 68, third time; 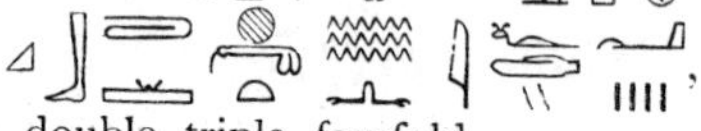, Rec. 29, 165, double, triple, fourfold.

khemt 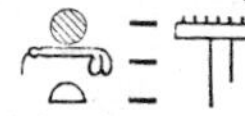, Rec. 26, 230, threefold or three-ply linen or stuff.

khemt 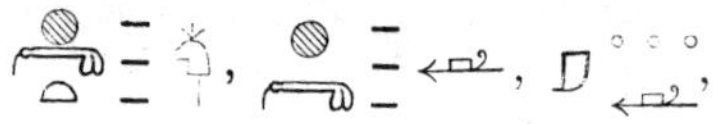, trident.

khemt , Rec. 30, 67, part of a ship.

khen , Rev. 13, 2, 11, well then; perhaps = Copt. ϣⲁⲛ.

khen, Rev. 14, 33, to ask, to enquire; Copt. ϣⲓⲛⲉ.

khen 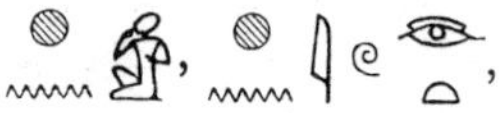, to embrace, to kiss, to marry.

khen , L.D. III, 194, 23, event, hap.

khen , A.Z. 1906, 109, to cry out for joy.

khenu 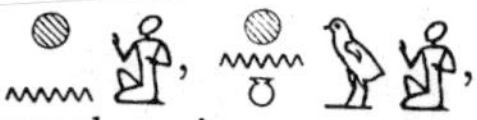, an officiating priest, a prophet, singer, one who announces or proclaims; plur. 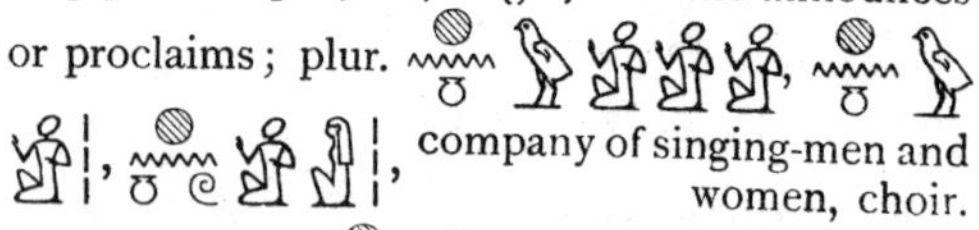, company of singing-men and women, choir.

khen-t , singing-woman; plur. .

Khen-t , title of the priestess of Cusae.

khenu 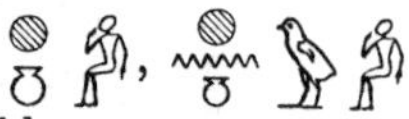, the "crier," *i.e.*, baby, child.

khenu, Rec. 2, 116, cradle-songs, invocations, cries.

khen, Peasant 280, IV, 968, , , , IV, 751, speech, word, report; also ; , a good report, a good thing; , an evil report; , antiphon; , speech, discourse, talk, oration; compare .

khenu (?) , , , Åmen. 12, 4, 22, 21, utterances, speech, words.

khen-t, L.D. III, 65A, 11 . . . . . .

khen , , , , A.Z. 1906, 107, to dance, to perform gymnastics.

khenit, dancing girl; , , a company of dancers, male and female.

kheni , , , N. 759, , Tombos Stele 10, , , , , , A.Z. 1905, 21, , A.Z. 1908, 116, , Love Songs 4, 4, to flutter, to hover, to alight (of a bird), to drop down, to halt.

khenn, U. 477, M. 693, P.S.B. 17, 262, , , , to alight, to rest (of the sky on a mountain), to flutter, to hover.

khen-t, P. 693, an alighting bird; , birds hovering in the air.

khen , , Rev., to visit; Copt. ϣⲓⲛⲉ.

khen , , to advance, to approach.

khen, khenu, Rechnungen 59 ff., , L.D. III, 140B, market-place, bazaar; Arab. سوق, a khân in the desert, karwânsarai.

khenuit, Mar. Aby. I, 8, 75, halls (?) warehouses.

khen, A.Z. 1905, 17, , the most private part of a building, cabin of a boat.

khen, to stir up trouble, to disturb.

khenu, Thes. 1480, rebel.

khen, to lament, to bewail.

khen , , , Rec. 32, 182, calamity, an event that causes sorrow, misfortune.

khenn , , , , , to disturb, to cause a commotion, to revolt, to rebel; , Rec. 32, 178, those who make opposition.

kheni, disturbance, disturber.

khenn, to stab, to wound.

khen, Rev. 13, 112, storm, tempest, war.

khen, M, 239, N. 616 (var. in T. 85,), basket (?)

kheni, a kind of fish.

khenn, Rec. 18, 182, fish.

Khen, Rec. 31, 27, a god.

Khen-remenu, Ṭuat XII, a singing-god.

khen-t (?), Ḥeruemḥeb 8, gratified, pleased.

khen-t, Thes. 1111, red egg-shaped objects.

khenȧ  IV, 1081, to be shut up, kept captive, to seclude, to restrain, buried in oblivion; see 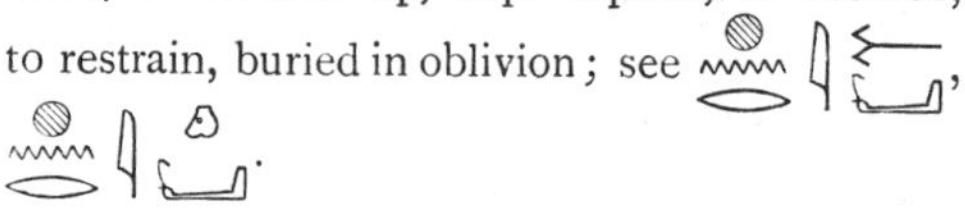.

khenȧ 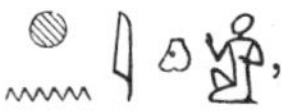, for , prisoner.

khenȧ-t (for **khenrȧ-t**) 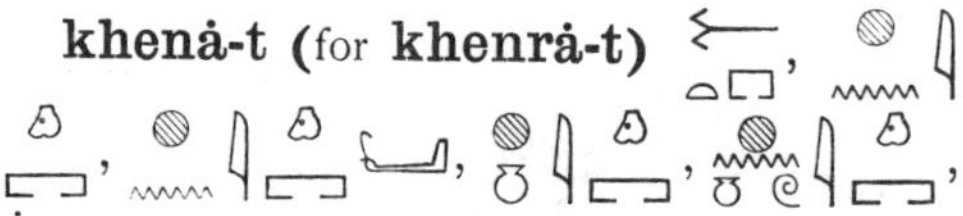, Ȧmen. 3, 7, ḥarîm, house of restraint, prison.

khenȧr , to be shut in, secluded.

khenār , Canopus Stele, miserable; Copt. ϣⲱⲛⲉ.

Kheniu , the four pillars of heaven.

khenu  in Dream Stele 14, a particle.

Khenub , the god Khnemu (a late form).

khenup , fat (applied to birds), well-favoured (of oxen).

khenup 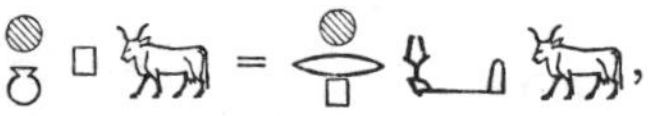 = , a stalled ox.

khenup (khenp) , an animal (?)

Khenup (Khenp)  Edfû I, 80, a title of the Nile-god.

khenup , private parts.

Khenuf (Khenf) , Berg. I, 15, a fire-god who gave light to the righteous, and cast darkness on the wicked.

khnum , unguent.

khenus , gnat (?) midge (?)

khenus 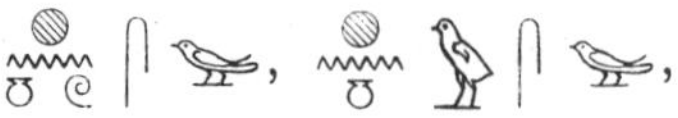, Ebers Pap. 102, 2, disease, languor; see .

khenut (khenutesh ?) , see **khent (khentesh ?)**

khenb , to prostrate oneself.

khenp , Peasant 99, 123, , 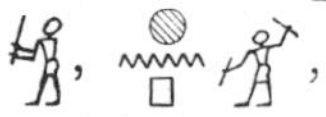, Rec. 31, 12, 30, , , to steal, to rob, to plunder, to seize, to carry off, to pluck out, to offer, to present.

khenpiu , robbers.

khenp , to inhale, to suck out the essence, .

khenpit 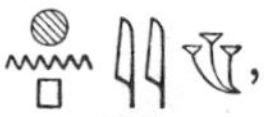, Rec. 4, 27, rush, a kind of grass; var. 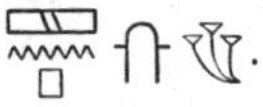.

Khenp shānu , the name of a festival.

khenfu 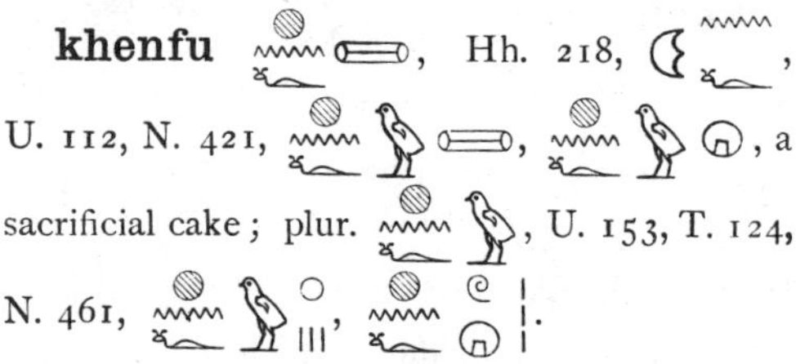 Hh. 218, U. 112, N. 421, a sacrificial cake; plur. U. 153, T. 124, N. 461.

khenfut , Hearst Pap. 11, 15, medicinal cakes or tablets.

Khenf , the god of the 11th day of the month; he has a lizard in each hand.

khenfa , arrogance, anger.

khenfi 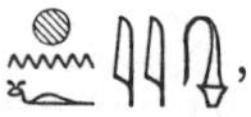, to burn up, to frizzle, to fry.

khenfi , a fish.

khnem 

, to sniff at, to smell, to breathe an odour, to give out a smell; , Leyd. Pap. 5, 12, to smell the blow of a stick, *i.e.*, to suffer a beating; Copt. ϣⲱⲗⲉⲙ.

khnemm  , Rev. 13, 15, , to sniff, to smell.

khnem 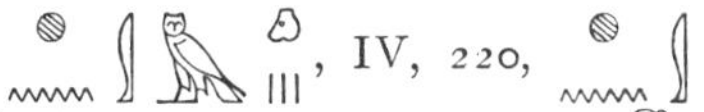, IV, 220, 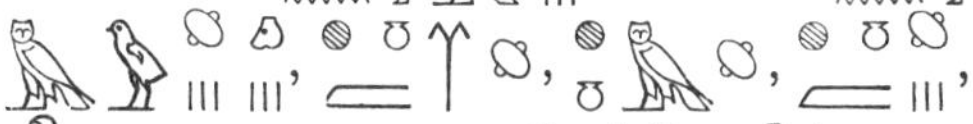 , smell, odour; Love Songs 5, 2, breath.

khnem-t  nostrils.

khnem , to nurse.

khnem-t 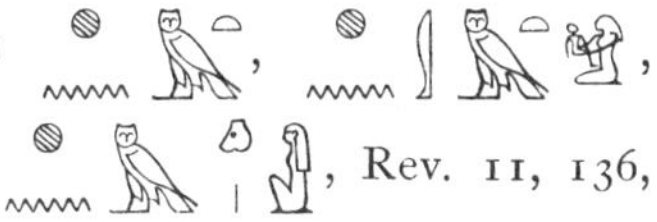, Rec. 27, 230, Rev. 11, 136,  , nurse, companion, friend; plur.  .

khnem-ti  a nursing woman, a professional nurse.

khnem-t , a man's mistress.

khnemiu  , varr. friends, acquaintances.

Khnemtit 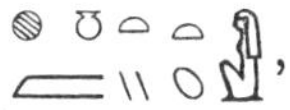, Ombos I, 61, a goddess of offerings.

Khnemit , Lanzone 112, a divine nurse of the kings and queens of Egypt.

Khnem[it] , Ombos I, 46, a hippopotamus-goddess.

Khnem-ti , U. 197, T. 76, , M. 229, N. 608, , T. 261, 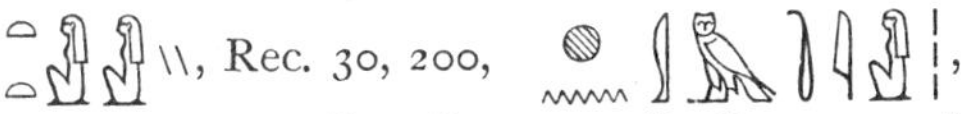 \\, Rec. 30, 200, ibid. 116,  , Rec. 30, 199, the two nursing-goddesses, Isis and Nephthys.

Khnem-nefer , B.D. 182, 23, "Good friend"—title of a god.

khnem-t , a kind of bread or cake.

khnem-t , Koller Pap. 4, 2, Turin Pap. 67, 11,   , a red stone used in jewellery; compare Heb. אַחְלָמָה (Exodus xxviii, 19, xxxix, 12) which the LXX rendered by ἀμέθυστος, *i.e.*, "amethyst."

khnemes , a kind of beer, .

khnemes , IV, 874, to smell; var. .

khnemes , Rec. 4, 121, , to behave as a friend, to be on good terms or associated with someone, friendship.

khnemes , Ȧmen. 25, 4, friend, protector ; plur. , Pap. 3024, 103, 104, Rec. 31, 12,  , protectors, men of rank and dignity.

khnemes , , Anastasi IV, 12, 9, Sallier II, 5, 6, a fly, gnat, mosquito, midge, any flying insect ; Copt. ϣⲟⲗⲙⲥ̄.

khenr , Statistical Tablet 41, 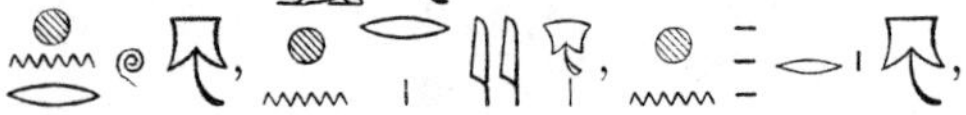, 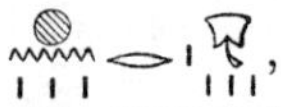, Anastasi I, 25, 8, , , the bridle and reins, harness (?) corselet ; , IV, 711.

khenr, khenrȧ 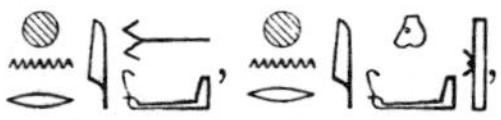, , 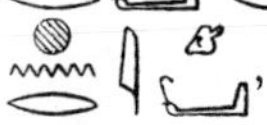, to shut up, to shut in, to seclude, to keep in restraint.

khenrr 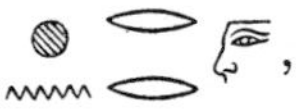, Rec. 27, 219, to shut in.

khenr, khenrȧ  , Pap. 3024, 35, , 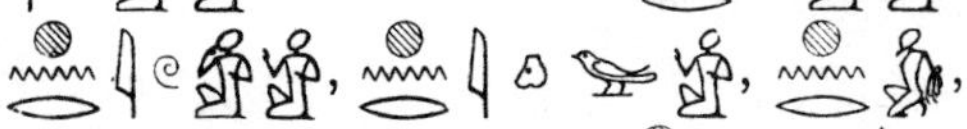, captive, beggar, prisoner ; plur. 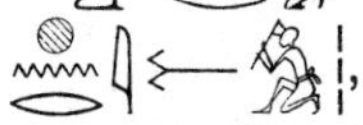, fiends, captives.

khenru , recluses.

khenrȧ 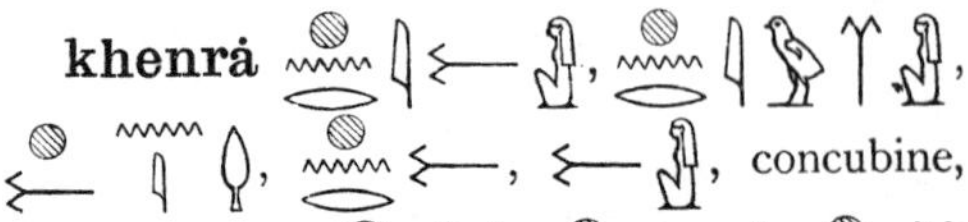, concubine, ḥarîm woman ;  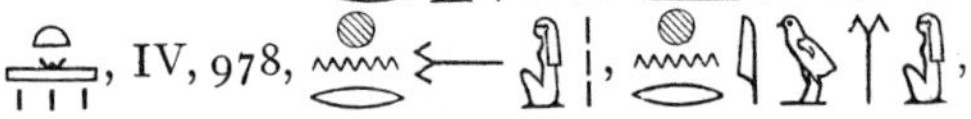, IV, 978, Mar. Aby. I, 6, 47, , the ladies of the ḥarîm ; 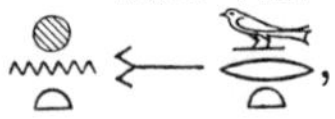, the chief concubine.

khenrit , the apartments of the secluded women.

khenr , tooth, tusk (?)

khenr , Thes. 1198, 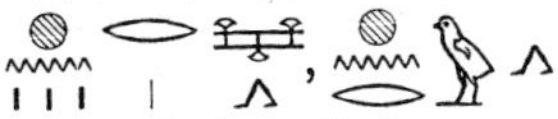, to take away, lost, destroyed, despoiled.

khens 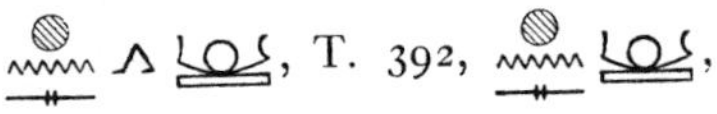, T. 392, U. 195, M. 766, 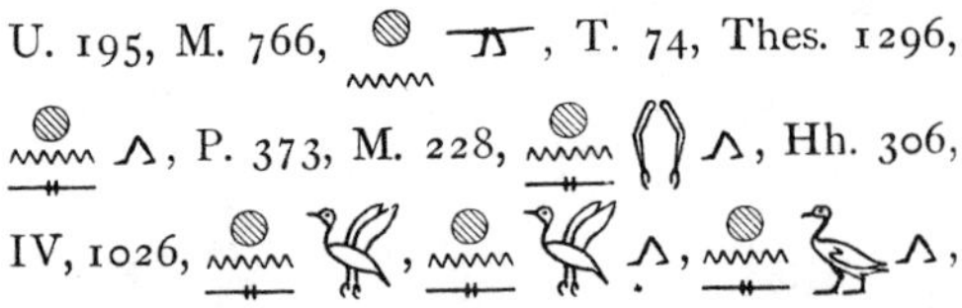, T. 74, Thes. 1296, P. 373, M. 228, Hh. 306, IV, 1026, to traverse, to travel over, to stride over, to fly over, to sail over.

khensȧu , P. 691, travellers.

khens 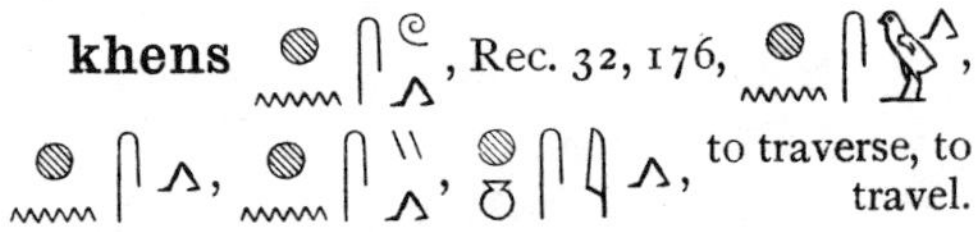, Rec. 32, 176, to traverse, to travel.

Khens[ui] 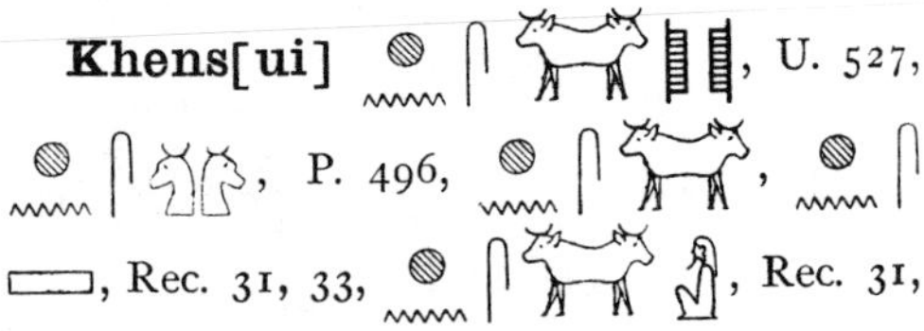, U. 527, P. 496, Rec. 31, 33, Rec. 31, 164, the two portals of heaven.

Khens-ur 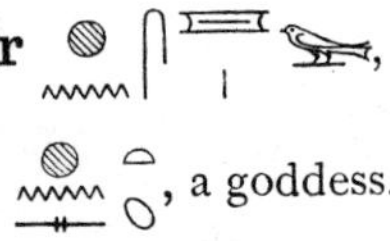, P. 566 . . . . . .

Khensit, a goddess.

khensait 

, a plant or herb used in medicine ; see 

khensit 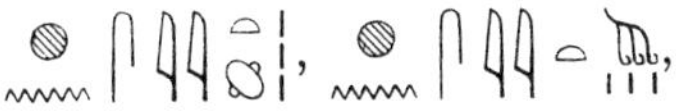, a disease, illness, languor.

khensu , pus, foetid matter, putrefaction, stink ; Copt. ϫⲱⲛⲥ.

Khensu , U. 510, , T. 323, , 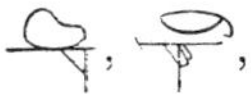, P. 200, 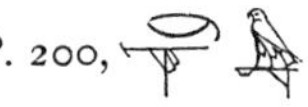, N. 936,  , the Moon-god as the "traveller"; Copt. ϣⲟⲛⲥ ; , Khensu of the two names.

Khensu , the god of the 9th month (Pakhons);  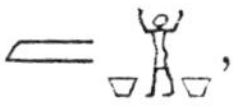, the god of the 8th hour of the day.

Khensu , Denderah I, 22, the name of the standard .

Khensu-ur , Lanzone 341, a god with two hawks' heads and two pairs of wings, who stands on the heads of two crocodiles.

Khensu-Beḥeṭ [illegible], the Moon-god of Edfû.

Khensu-pa-ȧri-sekher-em-Uas-t , Bekhten Stele, , Rec. 28, 181, Khensu of Thebes, the arranger of men's destinies.

Khensu-pa-khraṭ , , Mar. Karn. 42, 7, god of the crescent moon and of conception.

Khensu-em-Uas-t 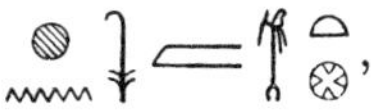, Religion, 360, a local Theban form of the Moon-god.

Khensu-Nefer-ḥetep  , Bekhten Stele, a god of all learning, a skilled magician and conqueror of evil spirits.

Khensu-Nefer-ḥetep-em Uas-t , see the preceding.

Khensu-Nefer-ḥetep-Ḥeru 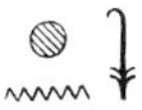 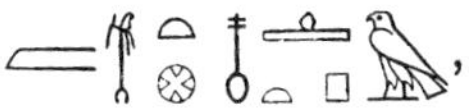, the Theban god Khensu-Horus.

Khensu-Nefer-ḥetep-Ṭeḥuti  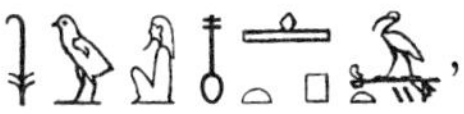, the Theban god Khensu-Thoth.

Khensu-Rā , Lanzone 343, a form of Khensu.

Khensu-ḥunu , the Moon-god at the 1st quarter.

Khensu-ḥeri-ȧb-Benn-t  , Nesi-Âmsu 17, 14, a form of Khensu.

Khensu-sa-Tekhit , Denderah IV, 78, an ape-god, a form of Thoth.

Khensu-Sepṭ , U. 588, M. 819, Khensu + Sothis, the Moon-god of the Eastern Delta.

Khensu-Shu , the Moon-god of Edfû.

Khensu-Ṭeḥuti , a form of the Moon god of Edfû. With the title [illegible], "twice great," this god was worshipped at Hermopolis.

khensem , U. 91, 92, N. 368, a kind of beer ; see **khnemes**.

khensh , a plant used in medicine.

khensh [illegible] [illegible]

, Rev. 12, 113, to stink, putridity, stinkingness; Copt. ϣⲛⲟϣ.

khenshit , Rev., putridity, stink, a disgusting or stinking thing.

khent, khenti , , , , the nose, the face; Copt. ϣⲁⲛⲧ.

khenti , , , , , , , , , , , , the first, he who is at the head, chief, in the first rank, forerunner, leader; old forms, , ; dual , P. 589; plur. , P. 437, M. 655, , U. 569, , P. 436, M. 649; , the snout (of Āapep), , forehead.

khentiu , those who go forward.

khenti āḥa , leader of the fight.

khent , , , , , , , in the front, in the fore part, before, aforetime, formerly, previously, in advance, the beginning, the land south of Egypt; , before him; , U. 37, before thee.

khentu , an intimate or chief friend.

khentu , with , outside, in the open air; , Pap. 3024, 82, he went outside.

khentu , pre-eminence, exalted condition.

khenti , , , IV, 902, the South land, any prominent place, point, tip, limit, , IV, 988.

Khentiu , , dwellers in the South, *i.e.*, Nubians; , Rec. 35, 128, the people of the Tanite Nome.

Khentiu Ḥen-nefer , , the peoples or tribes of Nubia and the Egyptian Sûdân.

Khenti Theḥenu , U. 565, chief of Libya.

Khenti , the god of the month Paone.

Khentu , T. 355, , N. 175, the dwellers in the most sacred part of heaven.

Khenti-ȧaut-f , Palermo Stele, , Rec. 37, 62, a form of Ptaḥ.

Khenti-Ȧabtt , , , Denderah I, 23, , A.Z. 1913, 124, a form of Hathor, and mother of Menu.

Khenti-ȧakhut-taui , B.D.G. 564, a form of Hathor.

Khenti-Ȧmenti, Khenti-Ȧmentt , U. 202, M. 232, , , N. 610; later forms: , , , , chief of Ȧmentt, a title of Osiris; Copt. ⲉⲙⲛⲧ.

Khenti-Ȧmentiu , U. 70, , N. 796, , N. 118, 963, , U. 582, , T. 183, , N. 654, , P. 86,

, N. 44, , Rec. 31, 173, , , 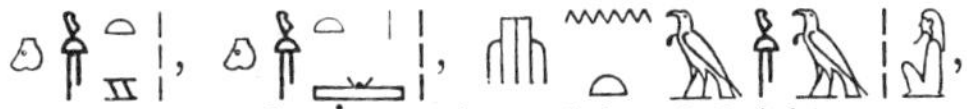, first of those in Åmenti—a title of Osiris.

Khenti-Åmenti  , Tomb of Seti I, one of the 75 forms of Rā (No. 31)

Khenti-Ån 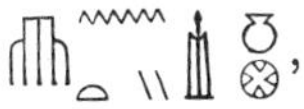, a gazelle-god, associated with the Mesqet.

Khentt-ȧn-t-s 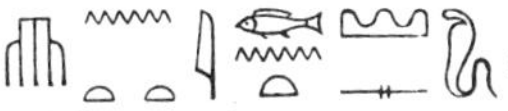, the name of a serpent of the royal crown.

Khenti-ȧr-ti , U. 6, , U. 73, P. 104, N. 72, , P. 611, N. 334, 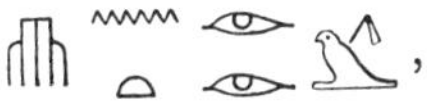, M. 63, N. 31, 660, 1211, , M. 70, , U. 352, P. 423, 697, 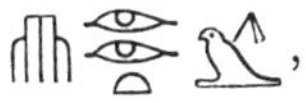, N. 980, 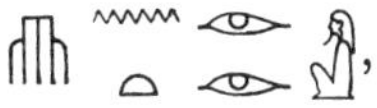, a form of Horus.

Khenti - Återti  , T. 369,  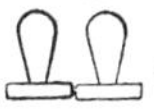, P. 363, N. 179, 1077, Master of all Egypt.

Khenti-ā-t-Åment 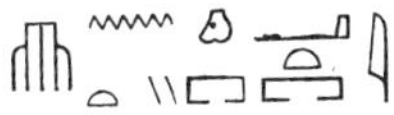 , B.D. 127A, 11, a title of Osiris.

Khenti-āat , Quelques Pap. 37, a god of embalmment.

Khenti-ānkhiu , P. 17, , M. 19, , N. 119, 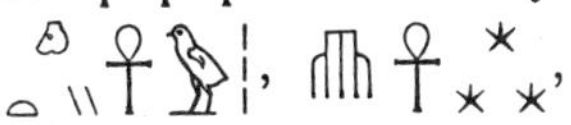, "Master of the living"—a title of Osiris and of his sarcophagus.

Khenti-uar-f , Berg. I, 23, a wind-god.

Khenti-un , B.D. 142, 6, a title of Osiris.

khentui — in the title  , A.Z. 1910, 126, "Horus and Set, the two great ones, the two chiefs of the land of the South."

Khenti-petchu , U. 557,  M. 699, a title of Seker.

Khenti-men 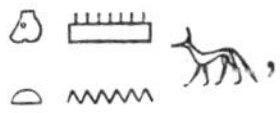, Berg. I, 17, a form of Anubis.

Khenti-men-t-f 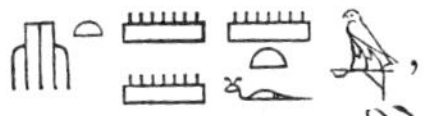, T. 288, 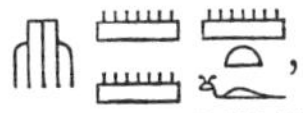, M. 65,  , P. 79, , M. 109, [illegible], N. 23, a god who carried the souls of the dead to heaven. Later forms are :—[illegible], B.D. 67, 3, [illegible], Ṭuat X.

Khenti-menȧ-t-f [illegible], U. 422, [illegible] N. 850, a title of Horus.

Khenti-Menṭ [illegible], the name of a goddess; var. [illegible].

Khenti-mentchet-ti [illegible], Mar. Aby. I, 45, the god of [illegible].

Khenti meḥt agbȧ [illegible] [illegible], U. 620, "of the green skin"—a title of the god Sebek.

Khenti em ṭeft [illegible], [illegible], Rec. 37, 61, ...

Khenti-Naȧruṭef [illegible] [illegible] "chief of the place where nothing groweth," *i.e.*, the tomb—a title of Osiris.

Khenti-n-år-ti , T. 198, , Rec. 31, 162, , 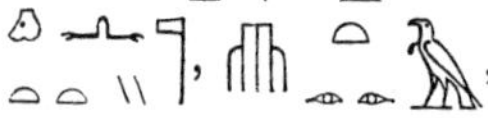, "Horus without eyes," the Sky-god when neither the sun nor moon was visible.

Khenti-nu-t-f , "chief of his town"—a title of Osiris.

Khenti-Nunu-t , N. 952, a title of Osiris.

Khenti-en-Sa-t 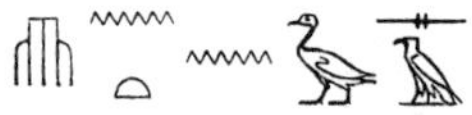 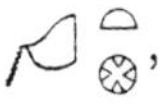, T. 40, a star-god.

Khenti - neper , master of grain—a title of Osiris.

Khenti - nefer (?) 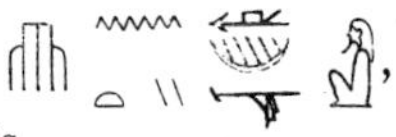, B.D. 142, 69, a title of Osiris.

Khenti-Rastau 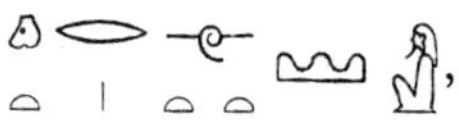, , chief of the Other World of Memphis—a title of Osiris.

Khenti-hut-f , , Hh. 101; see **Khenti-heh-f.**

Khenti-heh-f , , Edfû I, 10, Berg. I, 3, Rec. 4, 28, one of the eight knife-eyed gods who guarded the tomb of Osiris.

Khenti-Ḥet Ånes , Rev. 4, 28, a god.

Khenti-Ḥe-t res-utcha-t  [illegible], Rec. 37, 62, a form of Neith.

Khenti-ḥensekt-t 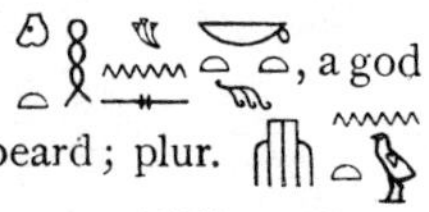, a god with long hair and a long beard; plur. 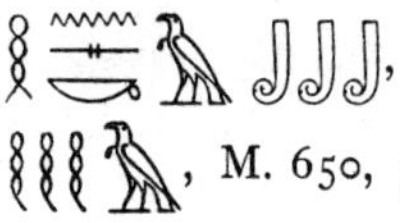, P. 436, , M. 650,

B.D. 30A, 4, the gods of the four cardinal points—the sons of Horus. 

Khenti-ḥenthau 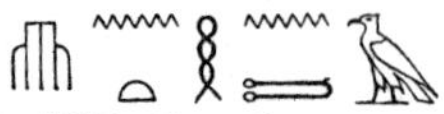 [illegible], P. 189, , M. 358, 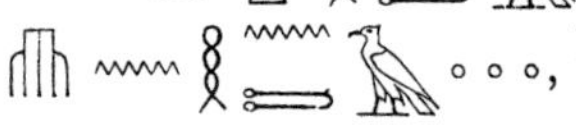, N. 908, a god.

Khenti-ḥeri-t , , Tombs Seti I and Ram. II, Denderah II, 10, one of the 36 Dekans; Gr. Χονταρε.

Khenti - ḥeri - åb - ḥe - t - ṭesheru 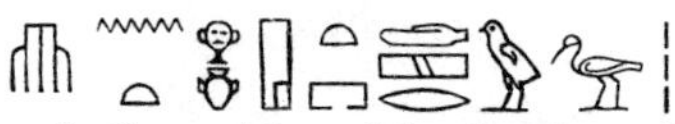, B.D. 141 and 148, the rudder of the Southern heaven.

Khenti-ḥeḥ 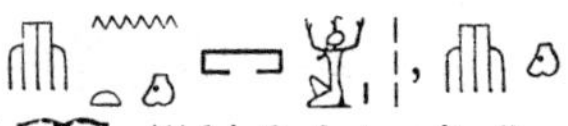, 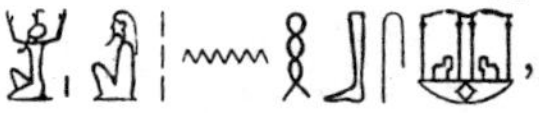, "chief of eternity"—a title of Osiris.

Khenti-ḥespu , B.D. 99, 23, the prow of the magical boat.

Khenti-Ḥeser-t 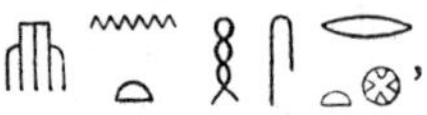, IV, 161, a title of Thoth.

Khenti-Ḥeq-āntch 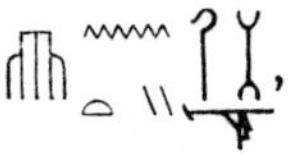, B.D. 99, 9, a title of Osiris.

Khenti - Khas , B.D. 42, 7, 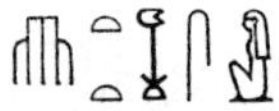, Mar. Aby. I, 45, a god who protected the nose of the deceased.

Khenti-khati , , "chief of the belly," *i.e.*, Horus in the womb; Greek form Κεντεχθαι.

Khenti-kha-t-ånes 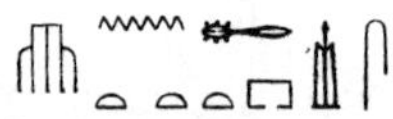 [illegible], Berg. I, 3, one of the eight knife-eyed gods who guarded Osiris.

Khenti-kheri , ,

Tombs of Seti I and Ram. II, Denderah II, 10, one of the 36 Dekans; Gr. Χονταχρε.

Khentt-sebkhet  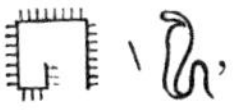, the name of a serpent of the royal crown.

Khentt-senut-s , P. 433, M. 619, N. 1224, a god.

Khenti-seḥ-neter 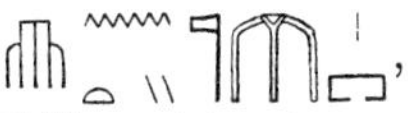, 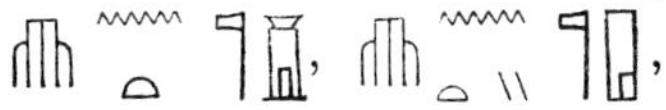, a title of Anubis.

Khentit-seḥ-neter 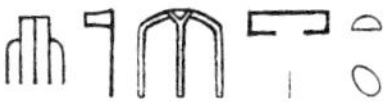 [illegible], Ombos II, 130, a goddess.

Khenti-seḥ-kaut-f 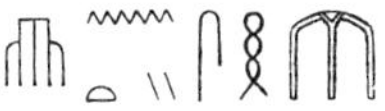 [illegible], B.D. 141, 110, , a title of Osiris.

Khentt-sekhet-s 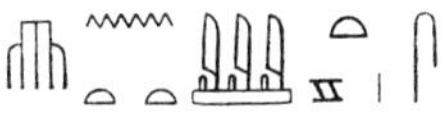 [illegible], a name of the uraeus on the royal crown.

Khenti-Sekhem 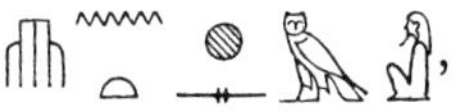, 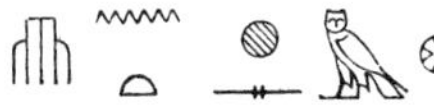, Rec. 31, 12,  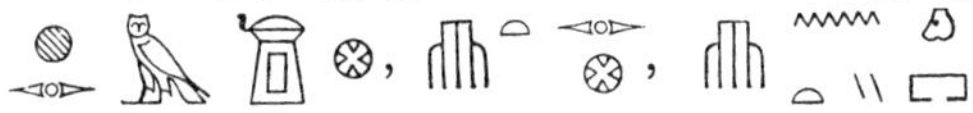, , B.D. 83, 6, a title of Horus and of Menu.

Khenti-she-t-āa-perti 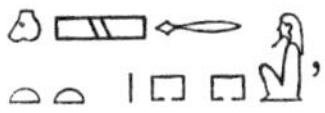, B.D. 142, IV 3, a title of Osiris.

Khenti-she-f (?) , Ṭuat I, an ape-god.

Khentt-Shepsit , Ombos I, 111, a serpent-goddess.

Khenti-shenen (?) 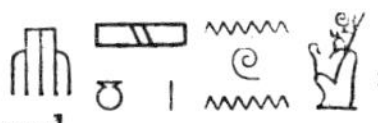, Denderah IV, 61, a warrior-god.

Khenti-Qerr , Tomb of Seti I, one of the 75 forms of Rā (No. 6).

Khentiu kau , P. 436, M. 622, N. 1227, beings in heaven who are masters of their Kau.

Khentt-ta-shemā  [illegible], the name of a serpent of the royal crown.

Khenti-Tenn-t 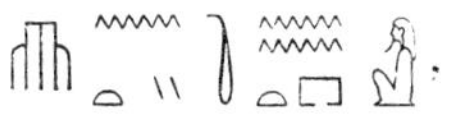, 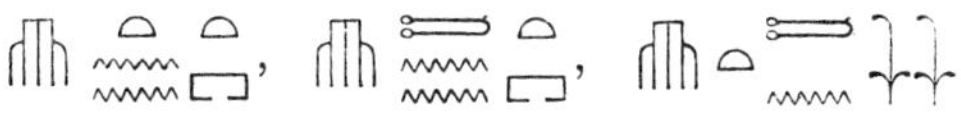 [illegible], Rec. 37, 58: (1) a title of Osiris; (2) a form of Ptaḥ.

Khentt-thes 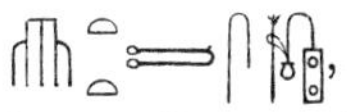, Annales I, 85, one of the 36 Dekans; Gr. Σεσμέ.

Khenti-thethef 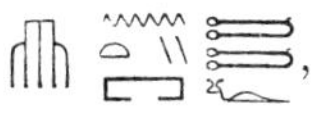, Ṭuat XII, a paddle-god in the boat of Àf.

Khenti-Ṭesher-t , Methen 5, a title (?)

khent , to be shut up, enclosed, confined, imprisoned.

khent , P. 672, M. 663, N. 1278, 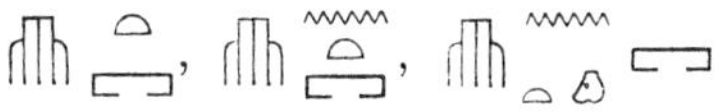, [illegible], a place of seclusion, ḥarîm, prison-house, the part of the temple not generally accessible to the public.

khenti , Rev. 14, 76, office, court; 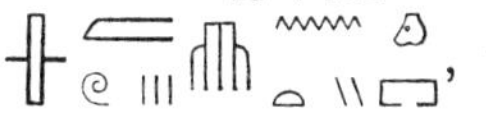, Mar. Aby. I, 6, 46, courtiers.

khenti , P.S.B. 10, 42, the hall of a temple.

khent , IV, 966, high or prominent positions.

khent, khenti , Àmen. 6, 2, , shrine, sanctuary; plur. 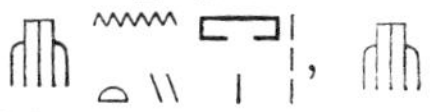 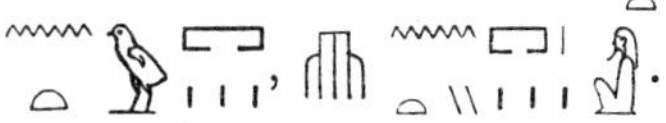.

khent , garrisons, forts.

khentȧ , sepulchres.

khenti , Mar. Aby. II, 37, image, statue, figure.

khent , , for , a lady in a ḥarîm, a concubine; plur. ; , Thes. 943, a ḥarîm of beautiful women.

khent — ȧmi khent , the title of a funerary priest.

khenti , IV, 84, defenceless.

Khentu , Ṭuat VII, a class of helpless fiends in the Ṭuat.

khent , Rev. 15, 152, to ascend.

khent , , throne with steps.

khent , to rise (of the Nile).

khenti , A.Z. 45, 134, , , , , to advance, to bring forward, to promote a man to high rank, to march southwards.

khenti , Peasant 36, , Dream Stele 26, , , , , , , , , , , to sail upstream, to sail southwards; Copt. ϩⲱⲛⲧ, ϧⲱⲛⲧ.

khenti, khenṭi , Pap. 3024, 79, , A.Z. 1905, 28, , , , , , crocodile.

Khenti , Peasant 119, , the Crocodile-god.

Khenti-ȧst-f , Ṭuat X, a god who destroyed the souls and bodies of the damned.

khent , pot, vase, vessel.

khentu , IV, 666, dishes, bowls.

khenti , , , , , , IV, 638, , IV, 1096, red earth, red ochre, red paint.

khent , IV, 990, 1219, , , A.Z. 1905, 24, , , L.D. III, 194, Festschrift 117, 11, , Rev. 11, 60, 92, to enjoy oneself, to be happy; , A.Z. 1908, 129, to walk about at pleasure; , with , IV, 1064; , Metternich Stele 250. The sign is that for "lake" and not the letter *sh*, as de Rougé proved.

khent , IV, 746, garden land, plantation; , , grove, shrubbery.

khenti , , , , a kind of workman, irrigator.

khenti sha (?) , Décrets 106, , , , A.Z. 45, 129, , IV, 407, , IV, 169, , , Rec. 29, 64, , ibid. , ibid. 31, 20, , A.Z. 45, 129, , , , , , , a large garden with a lake in it and many trees, grove, orchard, pleasure ground; Copt. ϣⲏⲛ.

khenti sha (?) 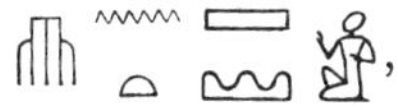, an official or person employed on garden land or in irrigation; fem. , A.Z. 1905, 4; plur. 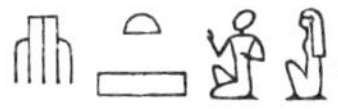, Décrets, 106, 
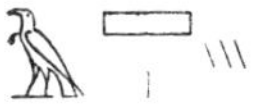, P. 604.

khenti tatȧ , Anastasi IV, 2, 9, Koller 2, 7, a rope of a boat.

khentu 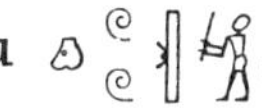, baker.

khentuf , Rev. 13, 21 = Copt. ϣⲁⲛⲧⲉϥ.

khenth 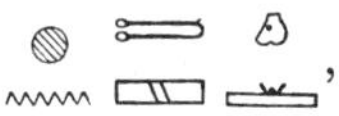, Mar. Karn. 35, 69, to rejoice.

khenṭ , to sail upstream.

khenṭ , Ḥeruemḥeb 9, 
, Pap. 3024, 21, ,
, to walk, to traverse, to march, to travel; var. .

khenṭu , stridings.

khenṭut , Hearst Pap. 14, 6, , priestesses of Neith, dancing women.

khenṭ 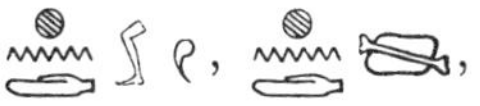, an offering of a haunch of beef or a leg of some animal.

Khenṭ , B.D. 125, III, 22, the "thigh" in Sekhet-Ȧaru.

Khenṭ-Ḥepui (?) 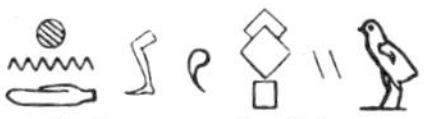
, B.D. 99, 11, the rudder of the magical boat.

Khenṭ[it]-ḥer , Berg. I, 17, a form of Bes, a goddess of perfume, unguents and spices.

khenṭ 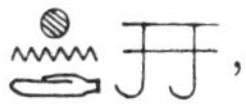, U. 206, [illegible],
T. 371, [illegible], P. 76, [illegible],
P. 148, 610, M. 451, [illegible], N. 719,
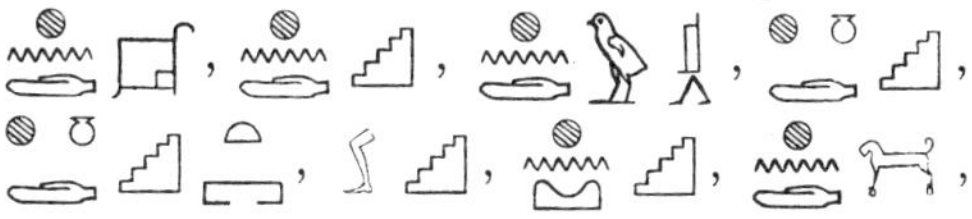
throne, chair of state, royal couch; varr. [illegible],
[illegible].

khenṭ , U. 330, T. 35, 300, M. 116, N. 133, to plough.

khenṭ , wheat; Heb. חִטָּה, Targ. חִנְטָא, Arab. حِنْطَة.

khenṭ , Rec. 17, 54; , garden, orchard; see [illegible].

khenṭu , Rec. 30, 67, a part or parts of a ship.

khenṭi , A.Z. 1872, 97, [illegible], crocodile.

khentch , Rec. 30, 188, [illegible]
[illegible], Hh. 396, , A.Z. 1908, 118,
[illegible], to travel, to march, to stride.

khentch 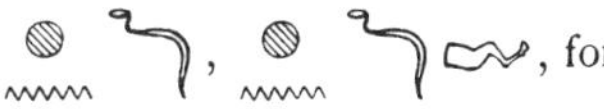, fore-leg, thigh of an animal.

khentchu , Rec. 26, 78, rising ground, terraces.

khentch , to slay a sacrificial victim.

khentchui , P. 705, parts of a bull.

khentch , Hh. 338, bad smell, evil odour (?)

khentchem , P.S.B. 13, 411, sleep (?); Copt. ϩⲓⲛⲓⲙ, ϩⲓⲛⲏⲃ (?)

kher , (*sic*), Nåstasen Stele 60, , Book of Breathings 1, 23, a preposition, by, with, from, towards, before; , with thee; , with, or before, thyself; , under the majesty of; , for ever; , they eat their forms, *i.e.*, they disappear; , by a man who is with himself (*i.e.*, alone); Copt. ϣⲁⲣ-.

kher re-ā , Åmen. 23, 8, assuredly; , Åmen. 22, 5.

kher , , a conjunction; var. .

kher , Israel Stele 8, to speak, to say; , Rec. 21, 43, , , it is said, it is related that.

kher, kheru , U. 571, , U. 263, P. 72, , U. 13, 599, P. 289, 779, , P. 204, 662, , Rec. 29, 148, , Shipwreck 57, , , , , , , , , , , , Jour. As. 1908, 262, voice, word; plur. , , , , ; Copt. ϩⲣⲱⲟⲩ.

kheru em pe-t , sound from heaven, Copt. ϩⲣⲟⲩⲙⲡⲉ, thunder; **kheru remm** , N. 760, the sound of weeping; **kheru ḥeri shemāit** , singing voices; **kheru qa** , , highly pitched voice; **kheru qerå** , the roar of thunder; **kheru ta** , Rec. 31, 15, the roar of the earth; **kheru tau** , the whistling of the wind.

Kheru , P. 662, M. 773, , P. 779, voice personified.

kher , Rec. 21, 87, to thunder.

Kheru-qerå , B.D. 39, 6, voice of Qerå, *i.e.*, thunder.

kher , Rec. 36, 212, to seize.

Kher , B.D. (Saïte) 20, 4, a god.

kher , U. 305, 542, , T. 297, , P. 226, , , , , , , , , , to fall, to fall down, to light upon, to meet, to throw down, to overthrow.

kherkher , T. 282, N. 132, , , to root up, to destroy, to be destroyed; Copt. ϣⲟⲣϣⲣ̄.

kherit , defeat, overthrow, fall; plur. ,

kheru , IV, 648, , , , a vanquished chief, a defeated foe, a slain man; plur. .

kherit , , , , the dead, the damned, creatures slain for sacrifice.

kherit , , , , , , Rec.

32, 85, , ibid. 31, 27, 
, Hh. 541, victims, animal or animals for sacrifice.

kherit , wounds, gashes, slaughter.

kheru , Israel Stele 19, 

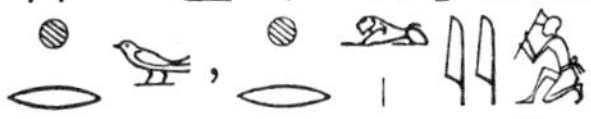, Rec. 25, 195, foe, enemy, criminal; plur. , IV, 651,
, IV, 711, , IV, 658,
, IV, 650, 
.

Kher [illegible], Nesi-Åmsu 32, 14–42, a form of Āapep.

Kheriu-Uamti-Neḥaḥer 
, Nesi-Åmsu 33, 12, a triad of forms of Āapep.

kheru ,
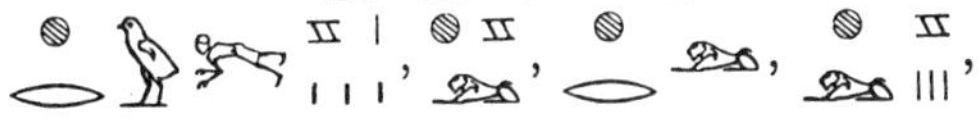, low-lying land, swamp.

kher sha-t (?) , a kind of incense (?); , the wood from which it is made.

kher [illegible], a mistake for [illegible], to know.

kher-t , that which belongs to someone, possessions, property, goods, substance, nature, what is destined for a man, things required for daily needs, things which concern someone, affairs, state, condition, need, wish, desire; 
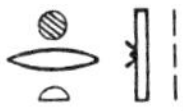, lords of destiny; , yearly event; , products of every land;
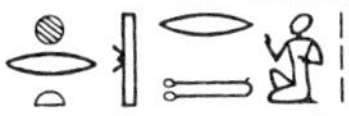, the concerns of men; 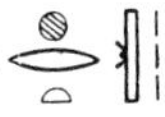
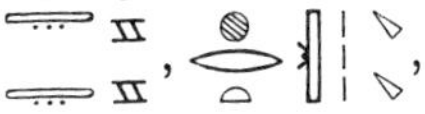, IV, 966, the affairs of the Two Lands (*i.e.*, Egypt); , in one state.

kheru [illegible], P. 688, [illegible], possessions, property.

kher-t åb , the heart's desire, dearest, favourite.

Kheru-åb [illegible], Berg. I, 10, a bird-god.

kher 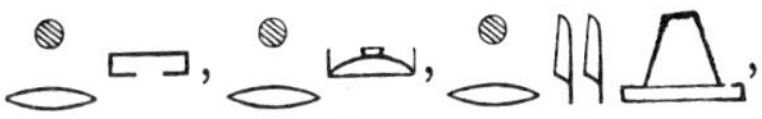,
, grave, tomb, necropolis, cemetery.

kher en āḥåut , storehouse.

kher [illegible], to pour out, to eject fluid.

kher [illegible], boat, ship.

kher [illegible], Rev. 11, 173 = Copt. ϭωλ (Revillout).

kher 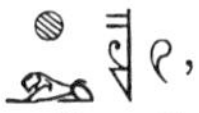, Rev. 14, 137, [illegible], Rev. 11, 168, bundle; Copt. ϣολ.

khera [illegible], Rev. 11, 169, to intertwine, to tie up; Copt. ϣολ.

kher , Annales 9, 155, Rec. 5, 93, [illegible], Rev. 14, 34, 37, spice, myrrh; Copt. ϣⲁλ.

Kherå , B.D. 109, 9, a goddess, mother of the calf ; varr. [illegible]
.

kheråu , Nåstasen Stele 26, a weapon.

kherrå , (late form), destruction, overthrow.

Kherru, Khurr-ti  , B.D. 109, 9, father of the calf.

kherp , M. 641, , IV, 746, , Ȧmen. 10, 8, 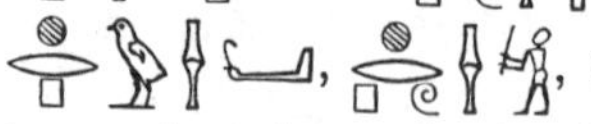, to lead, to direct, to superintend, to rule, to lay under tribute, to be master, to excel, to be in front, to present, to offer, to give, to bring gifts; Copt. ϣωρπ.

kherp ȧb (or **ḥat)** , to be superior, haughty (?)

kherp , Rec. 11, 156, 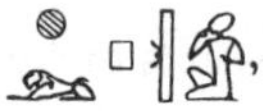, Rev. 11, 122, first; Copt. ϣορπ.

kherpu 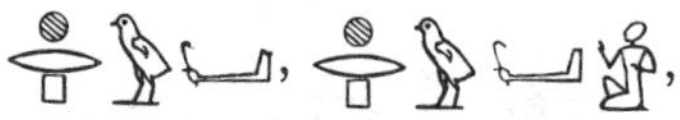, , IV, 966, director, governor, overseer, leader, chief, master, president; , divine chief; , landlord; , , , , chiefs, foremen, bailiffs, wardens, superiors; , IV, 1105, overseer of the landlords.

kherp 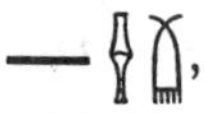, chief of the crew; , Rec. 3, 150, chief huntsman, Gr. ἀρχικυνηγός; 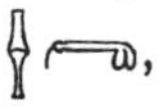, title of the priestess of Herakleopolis; , Rec. 33, 6, chief of the cavalry; , IV, 1051, vigilant overseer; , director of the throne, a title of Anubis; 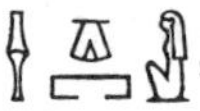, A.Z. 1908, 120, title of a priestess; , director of the two thrones, a title of Thoth and of Horus; , title of the high-priest of Saïs; , title of the high-priest of Neith; var. 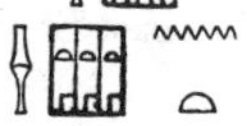; , , Rec. 2, 128, title of a priest; 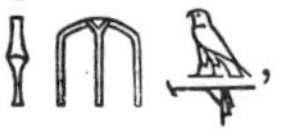, N. 618, title of a priest; 

, IV, 1056, director of works; , steersman, captain.

kherp-t , title of the chief priestess in Cynopolis, Xoïs, and Gynaecopolites.

kherp , a fine ox for sacrifice.

kherpit , IV, 1007, Rec. 20, 41, offerings, tribute.

Kherp , the steersman of the boat of Åf.

Kherp neteru , Ṭuat III, a form of Osiris.

Kherp Ḥeru-em-ḥetep [illegible] [illegible], the name of the sacred boat of the Nome Letopolites.

Kherp seḥ [illegible], T. 87, M. 240, [illegible], N. 618, the master of the council-hall of Rā.

kherp ṭua [illegible], III, 143, to prevent the dawn, *i.e.*, to get up early; Copt. ϣωρπ.

kherp [illegible] [illegible], Rec. 30, 68, part of a boat, or some object used in working it.

Kherefu [illegible], B.D. 136B, 4, [illegible] (Nebseni), a group of lion-gods, identified by some with the Heb. כְּרוּבִים.

kherem [illegible], Rev. 12, 16, to hasten; Copt. ϫωλεⲙ.

Kherm'u [illegible], a mythological crocodile.

Khermuti [illegible], Nesi-Åmsu 32, 24, a form of Āapep.

kheres, khersek [illegible] [illegible], [illegible] [illegible], to destroy; var. [illegible].

Kherserȧu [illegible], B.D. (Saïte) 162, 5, a Nubian (?) title of the Sun-god.

Khersek-Shu , B.D. 125, the name of the door of Usekht-Maāti.

Khersek-kek , Thes. 31, the goddess of the 2nd hour of the day.

khersh , to tie up things in a bundle.

khershu , Hearst Pap. IV, 11, bundles of seeds used in medicine.

khersh , Rec. 17, 156, Rechnungen 78, , bundle.

khersh 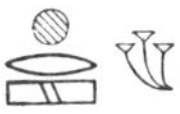, IV, 171, Thes. 1288, 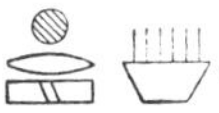, bundle of vegetables, bouquet; , Annales IX, 156, bundles of papyrus.

khersh 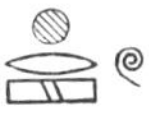, a rope to which rows of vegetables were tied; compare a "string of onions"; plur. , Rec. 15, 2.

khersh-t , a bundle of arrows.

khekh , 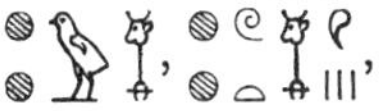, neck, throat; var. ; Copt. ϧⲁϧ.

khekh , to hasten, swift, quick.

Khekh , Düm. Temp. Inschr. 25, a god of learning and letters, one of the seven sons of Meḥurit.

Khekh nemm-t , A.Z. 1905, 22, "swift-foot"—a name of Rā.

khekh (khakha?) 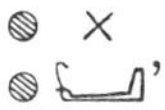, A.Z. 45, 135, to make level, to measure, to weigh.

khekh , a level, what is equal to something else.

khekhu , darkness, night.

khekhth (?) , to fight, to struggle.

khekhṭ , Hh. 215, to invert, to turn upside down.

khesu , rite, ritual, liturgy, service book.

khes , Rec. 36, 78, prescriptions.

khes , IV, 919, a hollow in the ground, well (?)

khes , Rec. 2, 127, , to build, builder.

khesut , building.

khes , spindle.

khesi , Ebers Pap. 47, 10, 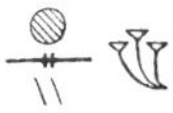, IV, 1079, , Hearst Pap. IV, 13, a fruit or plant used in medicine.

kheskhes , a kind of ānti, or incense.

khess 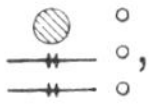, a kind of ānti, or incense.

khess 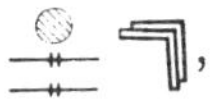, Rec. 4, 30, bolt, fastening, angle, corner.

khesa , A.Z. 1899, 96, a kind of tree, tamarisk (?); , , the fruit of the tamarisk (?)

khesait , IV, 548, Hearst Pap. 9, 1, cassia (?) parts of a plant used in medicine; [illegible]; compare Heb. קְצִיעָה, Gr. *κασσία*.

khesa [illegible], leather strap, thong.

khesas [illegible], [illegible], to hasten.

Khessi [illegible], Tomb Ram. IV, 29, 30, [illegible], Rec. 6, 153, a god who assists [illegible].

kheseb [illegible], U. 559, to repulse, to drive out of one's course.

khesbeb , U. 603, , P. 204, M. 304, N. 1001, to drive out of one's course ().

khesbau , to drive a furrow, to plough.

khesbet 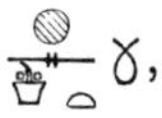, blue cloth.

khesbet , lapis lazuli.

khesbeṭ 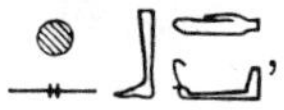, to be blue, to shine like heaven.

khesbeṭ 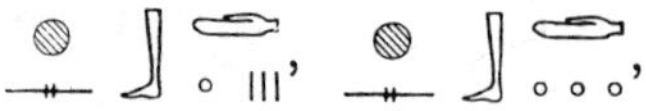, 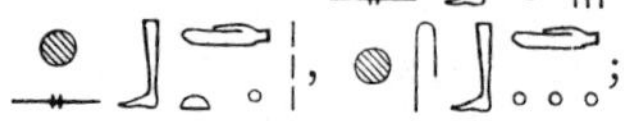; var. , lapis lazuli; 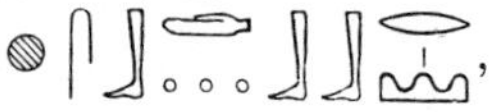, IV, 701, lapis lazuli of Babylon.

khesbeṭ maāit 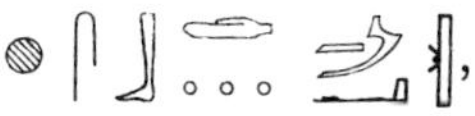, 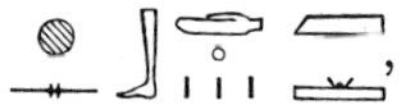, real lapis lazuli.

khesbeṭ årit 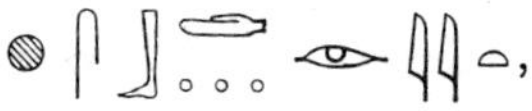, artificial lapis lazuli.

khesbeṭ-ti 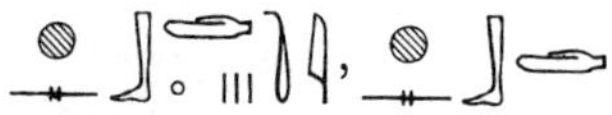 , bluish.

khesbetch , U. 639,  , , Rec. 27, 57, 31, 28, , lapis lazuli; , real lapis lazuli, not the artificial blue paste.

Khesbetch 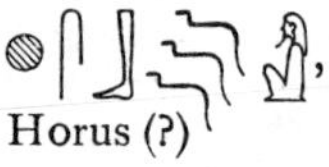, Rec. 30, 200, the blue god, *i.e.*, Horus (?)

Khesbetch år-ti (?) , the blue-eyed god, *i.e.*, Horus (?); var. 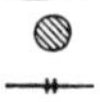 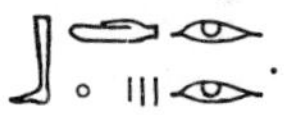.

khesper , Mission 227, a bird or insect.

khesef , U. 510, , T. 323, , Pap. 3024, 29,  , , Israel Stele 8, , Pap. 3024, 24, , Peasant 47, to repulse, to drive a herd of cattle, to oppose, to resist, to punish, to be punished, beaten or conquered; 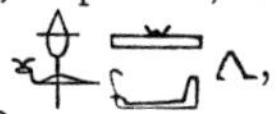, , to drive away; , to treat with contempt; , to send back an answer to a letter, to abate or remit a tax; 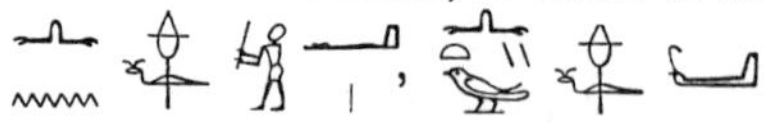, unopposed, resistless; Copt. ⲥⲱϣϥ̄.

khesefu [illegible], Rev., dishonoured, shame, ignominy; Copt. ϣⲱⲥϥ̄, ⲥⲱϣϥ̄.

khesf-t [illegible], repulse, obstacle; plur. [illegible].

Khesef Åntiu [illegible], L.D. III, 55A, IV, 195, "repulse of the Åntiu"—the name of the festival that commemorated a great defeat of the enemies of Egypt in predynastic times.

Khesef-neteru [illegible], Palermo Stele, the name of a building.

khesfu [illegible], P. 93, M. 117, N. 54, [illegible], opponents, adversaries.

Khesfu [illegible], Ṭuat X, a light-god.

Khesef-aṭ [illegible], the herald of the 4th Ārit.

Khesfu-āu-s [illegible], P. 93, [illegible], M. 117, N. 54, a group of gods of doors.

Khesef-nerit [illegible], Edfû I, 13, [illegible], Berg. I, 35, a lion-god.

Khesef-ḥer [illegible], Nesi-Åmsu 32, 31, Berg. I, 34, a crocodile-god, a form of Āapep; [illegible], a company of fiends.

Khesef-ḥer-āsh-kheru [illegible] [illegible], B.D. 144 the doorkeeper of the 4th Ārit.

Khesef-ḥer-khemiu 

, B.D. 144, the herald of the 7th Ārit.

Khesef-khemiu 
, the herald of the 7th Ārit.

Khesef-khemit 
, D.E. 20, Thes. 28, ,
, Denderah III, 24,
IV, 84; , Berg. II, 9,
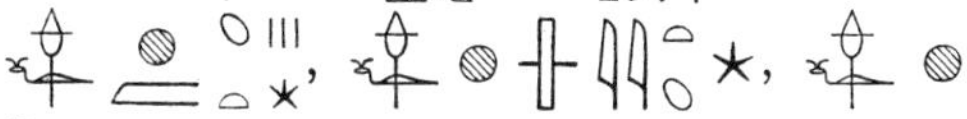
, the goddess of the 11th hour of the night,
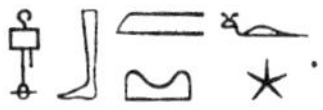

Khesfit-smait-set ,
Ṭuat I, one of the 12 guides of Rā.

khesef , N. 1325, 
, M. 712, , to approach, to meet, to draw near to a person or thing.

khesefu 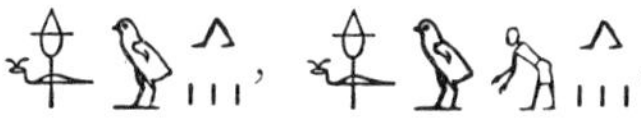,
homage.

khesef , Hh. 437, peg, picket (?)

Khesfit-sebȧ-em-perit-f 
, Ṭuat XI, the goddess of the 11th hour of the night.

Khesef-hai-ḥesq-neḥa-ḥer 

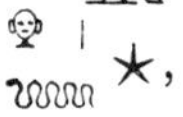, the goddess of the 7th hour of the night.

khesef , T. 354, ,
N. 175, , to sail up the river.

khesfut ,
a sailing, a journey upstream.

khesfit , Hh. 460,
, a kind of boat.

khesfut 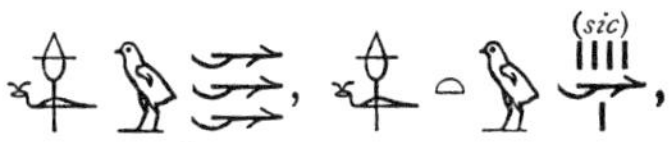,
Rec. 30, 66, parts of a boat.

khesem , IV, 1071, 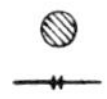
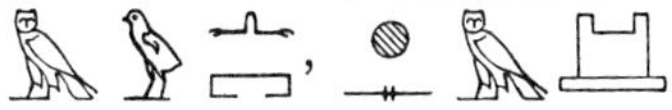, Thes. 1286,
shrine, sanctuary; plur. ,
; see .

kheser , U. 609, P. 170,
N. 1065, , M. 601, [illegible],
M. 760, [illegible], [illegible], Thes. 1199,
[illegible], to break, to rub down, to destroy, to drive away; var. [illegible], P. 350.

kheser [illegible], [illegible], [illegible]
[illegible], [illegible], [illegible], [illegible],
to destroy = khersek.

Kheser kek [illegible], the goddess of the 2nd hour of the day.

khesteb [illegible], [illegible], [illegible],
[illegible], [illegible], [illegible], lapis lazuli.

khesṭ [illegible], N. 879, [illegible], [illegible]
[illegible], stink, boil, blain, ulcer, decay, dry rot, rust (?)

khesṭṭ [illegible], Rec. 30, 191, [illegible]
[illegible], Hh. 221, to perish.

khesṭeb [illegible], [illegible],
[illegible], [illegible], [illegible], [illegible],
[illegible], IV, 875, lapis lazuli.

khesṭetch [illegible], T. 144, N. 539, a pair of short drawers, loin-cloth.

khestch [illegible], T. 288, [illegible],
N. 126, [illegible], N. 885, [illegible], P. 442,

M. 546, N. 1125, to go mouldy, to decay, dry rot, rust (?)

khestcheb maāt, real lapis lazuli; see **khesbeṭ, khesbetch, khesteb**, and **khesṭeb.**

khesh, to dance, to perform gymnastics.

kheshkhesh, Amherst Pap. 24, slabs of stone, pavement blocks.

Khshairsh, L.D. 230, Xerxes = Ahasuerus; Pers., Median, Babyl., Aram. חשיארש, Heb. אֲחַשְׁוֵרוֹשׁ, Esther i, 16.

kheshb, to cut off, to slit open.

Kheshrish, Xerxes.

Kheshṭerp, Stele of Ptol. I, 13, II, 19, satrap; Gr. ἐξατράπης, σατράπης, Pers. Khshatrapâvâ, "protector of the realm," Heb. אֲחַשְׁדַּרְפְּנִים; see Spiegel, Altpersische Keilinschriften, 215, and Behist. III, 14, 56. For the forms:, and, see Jour. As. May–June, 1917, 395; Clay, Business Documents, XI, 21.

kheqir, Rev., to sail a boat or ship; Copt. ϣϭⲏⲣ.

khekrek, a plant used in medicine.

khet, U. 555 (, T. 303), , , , Rev. 12, 30, wood, tree, branch of a tree, twig, staff, sceptre, stick, board, tablet, canon, timber, plank, pole; Copt. ϣⲉ; plur., Shipwreck 59, , N. 975, , , , of the best planks; , trees of every kind.

khet, impaling pole; , impaled.

khet-...., , , a kind of tree or shrub; , the berries or fruit or seed of the same.

khet ȧakh-t (?), N. 296, 297A, a staff or club made of a special kind of wood.

khet āatcher, balsam tree (?)

khet āua, a kind of berry used in medicine.

khet ut-t, , coffin, sarcophagus.

khet en ānkh, P. 431, M. 616, , A.Z. 1900, 30, , Rec. 27, 87, , , "staff of life," wheat, grain, foodstuff.

khet en shen, the hair tree, cotton plant (?)

khet ḥetch-t, , , white wood.

khet kher ȧakh-t (?), a kind of spice or balsam tree.

khet shem, , , Rec. 17, 145, firewood, kindling wood.

khet kam, IV, 705, black wood,

khet tau (?), , , , "wind pole," *i.e.*, mast; plur., , , , Rec. 30, 67.

khet thagu, IV, 705, planks of thagu wood.

khet ṭesher, red wood planks or beams.

khet, grain.

khetit 
, a place where grain is stored for sale, the barn floor, the ground in a village where the corn-chandlers heap up their grain.

kheti , Stat. Tab. 5, heap of grain; plur. , IV, 687, 
, Rec. 27, 219, 
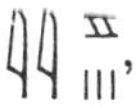, Anastasi I, 14, 8.

khet , I, 56, , I, 113,
, IV, 98, 765,
, Annales III, 109, the terraces on the sides of hills planted with trees; , stairs; 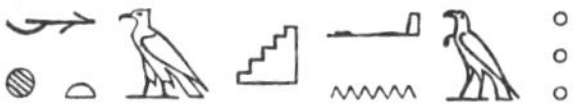, IV, 325,
 myrrh tree terraces.

Khet 
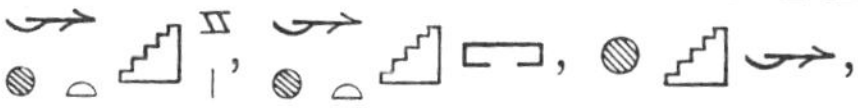, B.D. 22, 7, B.M. 1202, the steps or stairs which held up the judgment seat of Osiris.

Khet āa  the great throne on which Osiris sat.

khet , Rec. 30, 192, a land measure of 40 and also of 100 cubits (the cubit = 20·65 inches); plur. 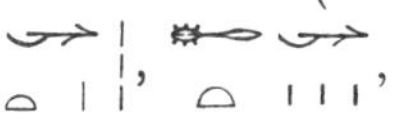
P.S.B. 14, 410; 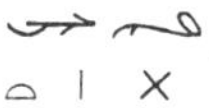 = ¼ khet; 
P.S.B. 13, 420, the square cubit; , a measure of land.

khet en nuḥ , P.S.B. 10, 77, , Rec. 4, 24, 
Rec. 16, 98,  = 40 Egyptian cubits, or 21·31 metres, and the Gr. σχοινίον of 400 cubits; Copt. ϣⲉⲛⲛⲟϩ.

khet nuḥ 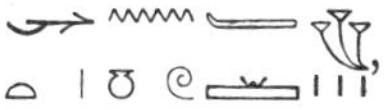, carpenter (?); Copt. ϣⲉⲛⲛⲟϩ.

kheti 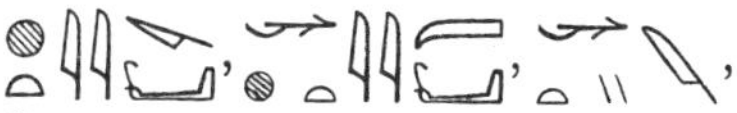

, to engrave, to cut into, something carved or inscribed or engraved; 
, an engraver of letters;
, Thes. 1323, sculptures on a wall.

khetiu , Rev. 6, 26, reapers.

khetkhet 
, to break, to cut into pieces, to destroy, to break a command, to engrave; Copt. ϣⲟⲧϣⲉⲧ.

khet-t , a writing cut in stone or wood.

kheti , A.Z. 1905, 103, an engraved seal.

khet , Rev. 13, 116 = [illegible], decree.

khet [illegible], Thothmes III Stele, to pierce, to penetrate; [illegible]
[illegible], "thy roaring penetrateth every country."

khet [illegible]
[illegible], to be behind someone or something, to follow, to march back, to turn back, to retreat, the hinder part; [illegible], to go through countries, throughout the lands;
[illegible], followers; [illegible], all under my direction; **em khet** [illegible]
[illegible]
[illegible]; plur. [illegible], those who come after, posterity, descendants.

khetkhet [illegible], U. 336, P. 227,
[illegible]

, to follow, to march after, to pass away, to slip behind, to drop out (of soldiers on the march), to drop (of the jaws), alienation (of property).

khet per (?) , servant, domestic.

Khet Ḥeru , U. 606 . . . .

khet-ta , Mar. Karn. 53, 22, to wander about the earth.

Khetiu Geb , the followers of the Earth-god Geb.

Khetiu-ta , , B.D. 153A, 5, 27, a class of fiends.

khet , , , , , to sail down the Nile, to go to the North; see .

Khet-t , a canal in Memphis.

khet āa , a kind of goose; , IV, 756, a goose kept for breeding purposes; , IV, 754, a fattened khet āa goose.

khet , Pap. Hunefer I, 17 . . . . . .

Khetasar , , , the name of a Hittite king.

khetȧ , a rectangular plot of land.

Kheti , Ṭuat VII, a form of the serpent Māmu.

kheteb , , Rev., to destroy, to punish, punishment.

khetem , , , U. 601, , , , , , , , , to seal, to seal up, to close, to shut up, to imprison, to end, to finish; Copt. ϣⲱⲧⲙ̄; , IV, 68, sealing [with] seals; , IV, 1105, sealing the strong rooms; , IV, 421, sealing up valuables; Heb. חָתַם.

khetemi , P.S.B. 27, 287, seal-maker.

khetemti (?) , , , treasurer, chancellor, the official who had charge of the seal; plur. , , , Coronation Stele 4, ; , the god's seal-bearer.

khetemt , valuable objects under seal; , the treasures of the god.

khetem , , , , , a seal, a seal in a ring; , ring for ring; , P. 697, seal of the gods; , A.Z. 1908, Taf. III, 22, two seal rings; Heb. חוֹתָם.

khetem-t , , , , a sealed document, contract, agreement, treaty; , Rec. 31, 171, a secret contract.

khetem , Rechnungen 69, contract, agreement.

khetem , cake, stamped bread.

khetem , , A.Z. 1908, 47, ring money: 12 of these = 1 ṭeben.

khetem , P.S.B. 13, 438, a unit of value:— , .

khetemu , the ornaments of a crown.

khetem , leather bag, leather bottle, wine-skin.

khetem , IV, 661, , , , ,

, fort, fortress, blockhouse; plur.  ,  ,  ;   , governor of the fort.

khetemiu  ,   , prison, closed chambers.

khetemit 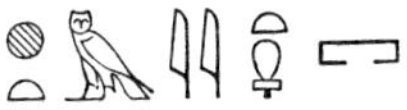 , B.D. 64, 11, a sealed place.

khetem-t  , a piece of unfruitful ground.

khetem  , 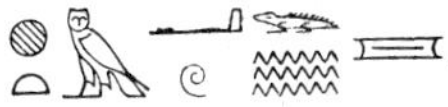 , tank, pool.

Khetrȧ  , Ṭuat III, the keeper of the 3rd Division of the Ṭuat.

kheṭ, kheṭṭ  ,  , 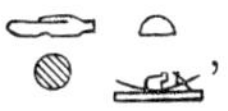 , I, 129, 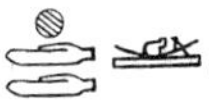 , 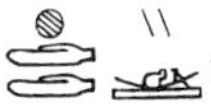 , to sail down stream, to sail to the North.

kheṭ , stream, running water.

kheṭ 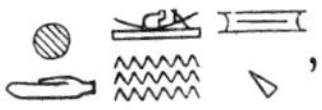 , ford, passage.

kheṭṭ  , IV, 687, stream, running water.

kheṭṭ 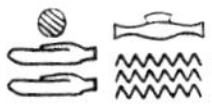 , Rec. 11, 120, water-skin; var. 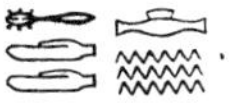 .

kheṭ  , to go back, retreat.

kheṭ  , pain, misery, anguish.

kheṭṭu  , jar, vase.

kheṭu  ,  , birds, fish.

kheṭeb  for  , blue, bluish.

kheṭem 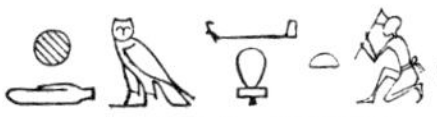 , Rev. 13, 2, to close up; compare Heb. חָתַם.

kheṭemu 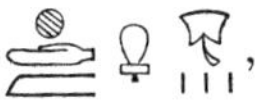 , branded cattle, cattle marked for sacrifice.

kheṭer 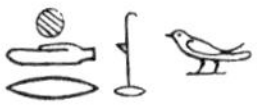 , shame, shyness.

Khetchtch  , Ombos I, 50, a god of marshes and waterfowl.

khetcha-ā 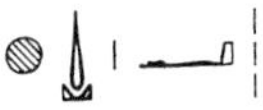 , needy (?)

[illegible] KH, KHA   KH, KHA [illegible]

kha [illegible] = Copt. ϩ and ϧ indifferently and Heb. ח. It appears sometimes as a variant of [illegible], and seems to have been in some words the equivalent of an older [illegible].

kha-t , M. 338, N. 864 (= [illegible]
, P. 204 + 1), , N. 70, ,
N. 963, , M. 59, , Rec. 32, 79 (var. of ), 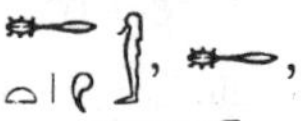,
[illegible], body, belly, womb; plur. 
[illegible], T. 48, 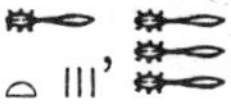, IV, 201, 807; [illegible]
[illegible], at one birth; ,
his belly is evil, *i.e.*, he is wicked; 
[illegible], cool, calm; 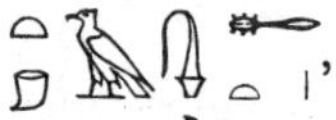, heated, excited; Copt. ϩⲏ, ϩⲏⲧ, ϧⲏ.

kha-t , a man; plur. , people, mankind.

kha-t , Ḥeruemḥeb 4, assembly, council; [illegible], Rec. 8, 136, corps of soldiers;
, first generation; 
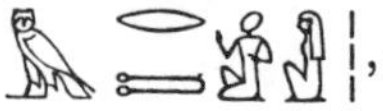, generations of men; 
[illegible], intestines, Copt. ⲙⲁϧⲧ; 
[illegible], to place oneself on the belly, *i.e.*, to lie prostrate; , secretive disposition; , people told him their affairs.

kha-t , the body, *i.e.*, heart, of the sycamore; [illegible], P. 172, "belly of heaven"—a part of the sky very full of stars; , T. 284, P. 83, M. 32, N. 65, "of the body," *i.e.*, issue, children;
, P. 468, M. 452, 533, N. 111, the body of the company of gods;
, son of his body, *i.e.*, his own son.

kha-ti [illegible], exhausted, used up.

Kha[-t]-Kheprer 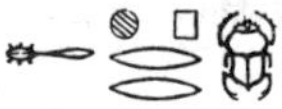, Berg. I, 35, a form of Isis.

kha-t [illegible], Ḥerusȧtef Stele 26, house, temple; [illegible], body (of a temple).

kha-t [illegible], A.Z. 45, 125, 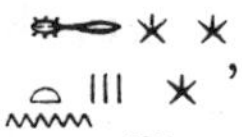, IV, 869, houses of the stars; [illegible], Thes. 160, a wet mass; 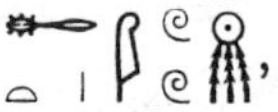, a dry mass;
, or , house of 8 or 13 stars; [illegible], Copt. Cat. 378.

kha-t neter sheps-t ,
= [illegible]

kha-t 

[illegible], IV, 484, ,
Hymn Darius 9, a dead body, corpse, a mummified body; 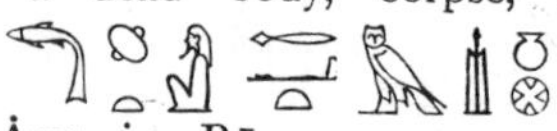, the Great Body in Ȧnu, *i.e.*, Rā.

Kha-[t]-āa-t [illegible], B.D. 163, 1, "Great Body" (Rā and Osiris).

kha-tiu 
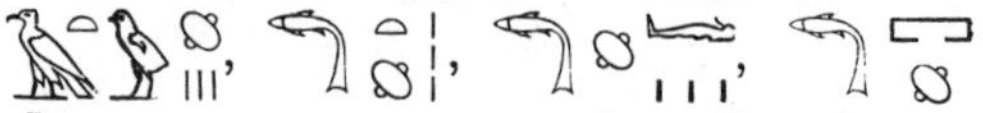
[illegible], Jour. As. 1908, 292, 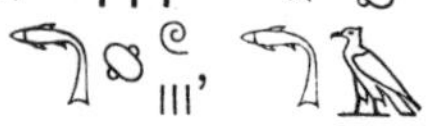

, Shipwreck 132, the dead in general, the damned, the slain; , the bodies of Sekri.

khaut , , general slaughter, massacre.

kha-t , Jour. As. 1908, 292, sepulchre.

khatt 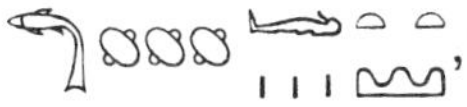, the land of the dead, the grave.

kha-t , dirt, disease, filth, sickness.

kha-t , Kubbân Stele 30,  , P. 1116B, 29, , swamp, marsh; plur. ; , IV, 1184, the swamps of Egypt.

khaut , skins, hides.

kha nu ḥemt , rust, verdigris.

kha-t 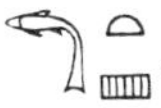, Rec. 30, 217, , , Rec. 10, 136, quarry, mine; plur. .

kha , , to cut, to rub down (of substances used in medicine), to pound, to crush, to mix together by rubbing.

khakha , Rec. 27, 218, to crush, to bruise, to pound, to mix by pounding.

kha , Hearst Pap. XVIII, 2, , crushed or pounded drugs (?)

kha-t , , , shower, rain, rainstorm, tempest.

khakha-t , , storm, tempest; var. ; compare Copt. ϧⲁⲣⲁⲃⲁⲓ.

kha , Pap. 3024, 148 wooden object (?)

kha , T. 180, P. 525, M. 162, N. 652, to attack, to injure; , T. 286 = , P. 38, M. 47.

khaȧ-t , body, belly; Copt. ϩⲏⲧ.

khaȧ-t 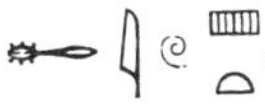, quarry, mine.

khaā 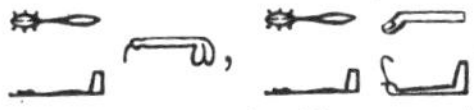, to force a woman, to cut or carve hollow-work patterns.

khaā , Ȧmen. 7, 6, 18, 20, 22, 9, crush (?)

khaā [illegible], to mix.

khaāut [illegible], refuse, dung, filth; [illegible], emissions.

khaā [illegible], dust (?)

khaāit [illegible], house, dwelling.

khaām [illegible]; var. [illegible], [illegible], to suppress, to make to bend, to split, to force down, to break open.

khaāmu [illegible], men paying homage.

khaāq [illegible], [illegible], to cut, to shave.

khaāqu [illegible], [illegible], barber; [illegible], shaving his customers.

khaāq , razor.

khaāqe-t 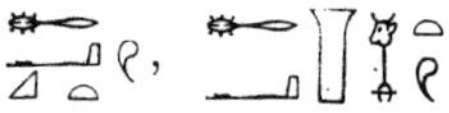, neck, throat.

khait , Rec. 3, 118, altar.

khab 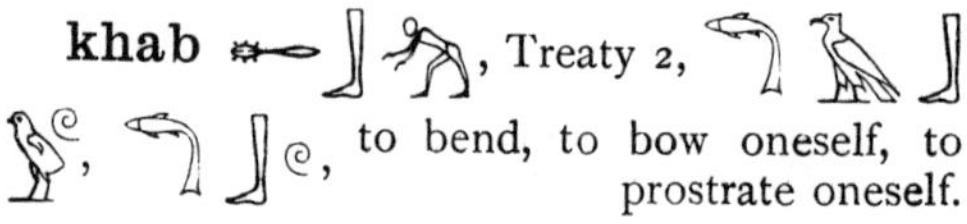, Treaty 2, to bend, to bow oneself, to prostrate oneself.

khab-t 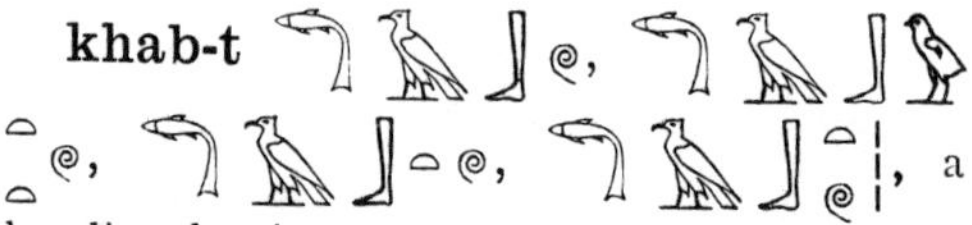, a bending, bowing.

khabut , IV, 200, a part of a crown.

khab-t , moral obliquity, guile, deceit, fraud, wickedness.

khabuit , Love Songs, 2, 4. bent staves.

khab-t , scythe, sickle; plur. , Hh. 457; Copt. ϫⲣⲟⲃⲓ.

Khabiu , Ṭuat VI, the divine Reapers of Osiris.

khabb , to wreathe (?) to decorate (?)

khabsu , the gods of the 36 Dekans, star-gods in general.

khap 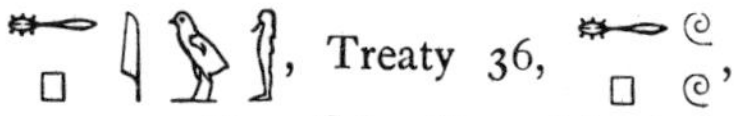, Treaty 36, figure, design; plur. 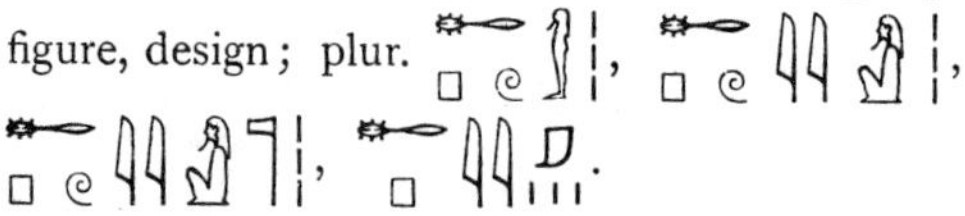.

khapi , N. 186 =  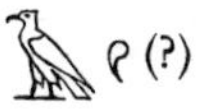 (?)

khapa 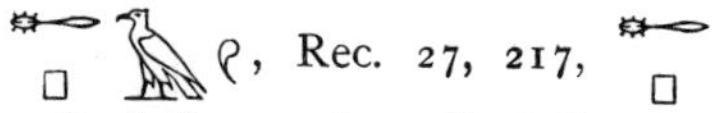, Rec. 27, 217, , , Gol. Ham. 12, 99, navel string, umbilicus; plur. 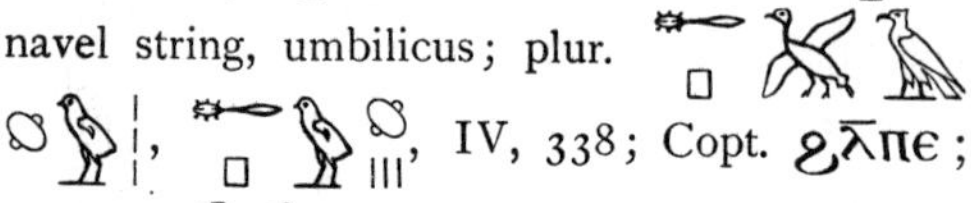, IV, 338; Copt. ϩⲗ̄ⲡⲉ; var. , U. 171.

khapā , Ebers Pap. 72, 16, to eat, to chew.

khapā , medicated tablets, pastilles.

khapā-t , bead.

khapnen en nub 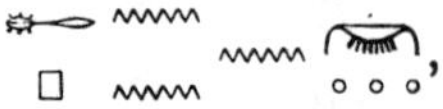, pierced beads of gold.

Khapri , the god of the 12th hour of the night.

khaf , to seize, to grasp.

khafṭ , to steal, to plunder; Copt. ϩⲱϥⲧ̄.

kham 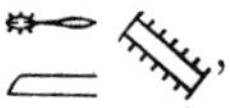, to fall down (of a wall).

khamu 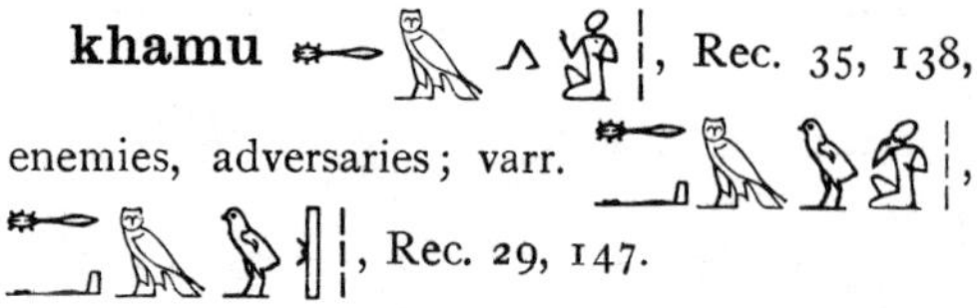, Rec. 35, 138, enemies, adversaries; varr. Rec. 29, 147.

kham-t , Rec. 3, 118, a kind of drink (?)

khamm , to smell.

khamm-ti 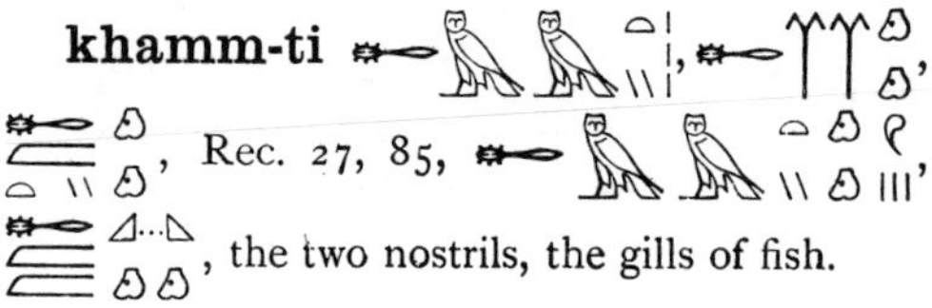, Rec. 27, 85, the two nostrils, the gills of fish.

khamm , to be hot, to blaze; Copt. ϩⲙ̄ⲙⲉ, ϩⲙⲟⲙ, ϧⲙⲟⲙ, Heb. חָמַם, Arabic حَمَّ; see  .

khamā 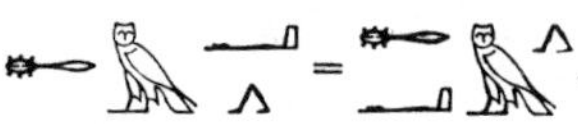.

khames 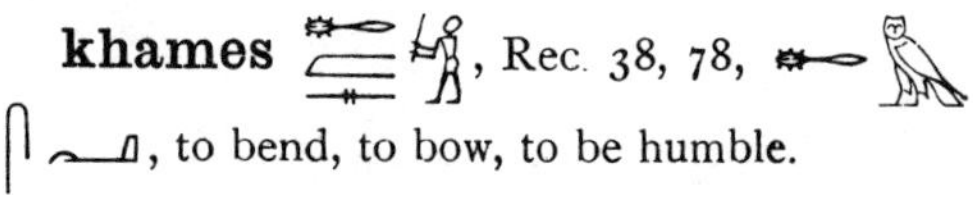, Rec. 38, 78, to bend, to bow, to be humble.

khames 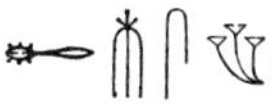, ear of corn; plur. , 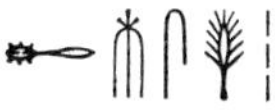; var. ; Copt. ϩⲙ̅ⲙ̅ⲥ, ϩⲙ̅ⲙ̅ⲯ, ϧⲉⲙⲙ̅ⲥ.

khames , 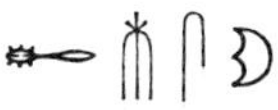, , spear, lance, javelin.

khames , poultry, fowls.

khamṭ , Rec. 14, 108, to smell, to sniff.

khamṭ , nostrils.

khan , he who is in, dweller in:  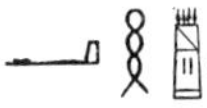, P. 521, , N. 651, "Dweller of the palace" = , T. 178 and M. 160.

khanu  with , P. 610, , P. 3, 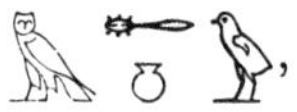, P. 122, 521, 613, within.

khanutt , N. 754 ......

khanu , T. 250, N. 648, private part of a building, most sacred part of a temple, cabin of a boat.

khan-t , , Ebers Pap. 42, 17, a part of the body, skin (?)

khan , P. 160, veil = 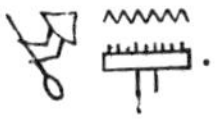.

khanm 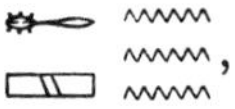, Rec. 27, 83; see .

khann , storm, violence.

khanu , to destroy.

khanuḥ 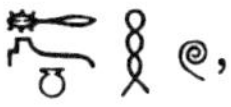, , a measure of land; Copt. ϣⲉⲛⲛⲟϩ, Gr. σχοινίον; see .

khanp uṭen , $\frac{1}{5}$th of an uṭen or 292 grains; , $\frac{1}{20}$th of an uṭen or 73 grains, P.S.B. 15, 310.

khank , to strike, to smite.

khar , with.

khar , Rec. 3, 50; see .

khar , A.Z. 35, 18, [illegible], P.S.B. 14, 4, 21, [illegible], [illegible], [illegible], [illegible], Koller 1, 3, a corn-sack, a corn measure = 21 gallons, or $2\frac{1}{2}$ bushels, or 97 litres; plur. [illegible], [illegible] [illegible], [illegible], Mar. Karn. 54, 46.

khar-t [illegible], Rec. 30, 68, a part of a ship.

khar-t [illegible], fibre of a tree (?)

khar-t [illegible], [illegible] [illegible], Rec. 17, 4, widow.

kharkhar [illegible], Annales I, 85, one of the 36 Dekans.

kharkhar [illegible], thunderstorm, hurricane, tempest.

kharb [illegible], [illegible], A.Z. 1879, 19, to pound, to mix together by crushing.

kharṭ [illegible], [illegible], M. 612, N. 1217, [illegible], [illegible], boy, child; [illegible], maiden, girl; plur. [illegible], Treaty 12, [illegible] [illegible], Rec. 21, 15, [illegible], [illegible] [illegible], [illegible], Åmen. 25, 9, [illegible], [illegible], [illegible], Rev. 14, 74, [illegible], [illegible], Rev. 12, 15; [illegible], B.D. 151, 6, [illegible], B.D. 64, 43; Copt. ϧⲣⲟϯ.

kharṭ [illegible], Rec. 29, 148, the young of an animal.

khakha [illegible], neck, throat; see [illegible] [illegible]; Copt. ϧⲁϧ.

khas-t , B.D. 67, 3, , territory (?) valley (?)

khas-t , basin, lake, pool, well.

Khas-t , Ṭuat VII, a lake of fire, guarded by light-gods, wherein Osiris lived.

Khas-t-shemu-ruṭ (?)  , Ṭuat VII, the gods who guarded Khast, the lake of fire.

khass 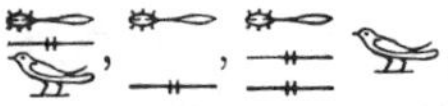, to be feeble, sick, weak, helpless; Copt. ϩⲓⲥⲉ, ϭⲓⲥⲓ.

khas-t , IV, 720, weakness, timidity, cowardice, feebleness.

khas-t , defect of body, a helpless person.

khasit , IV, 507,  [illegible], laxness, tiredness, effeminacy.

khasi , U. 539, T. 295, , Israel Stele 5, , a wretched, miserable, exhausted, or weary man; late forms are:— 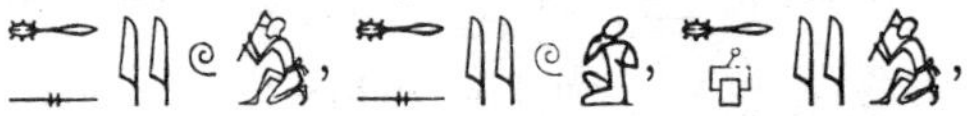, Rev. 11, 164; , coward, .

khas , to be inactive, inert.

khasi-t 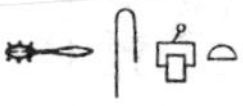, A.Z. 45, 135, 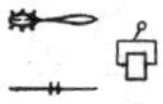 [illegible], an offering of scented unguent.

khasit 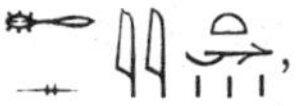, IV, 329,  [illegible], Shipwreck 141, [illegible], Rec. 16, 111, [illegible], [illegible], [illegible] [illegible], Leyd. Pap. 6, 3, [illegible], [illegible], Shipwreck 141, a sweet-smelling plant or wood, cassia (?)

Khasi, Khasti 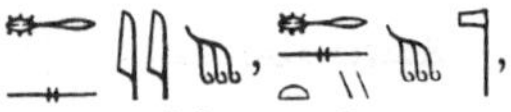, Wört. 1015, , , Rev. 3, 46, , Hh. 233, a lock of the hair of Osiris preserved at [illegible].

khass 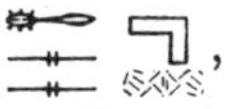, Rec. 33, 6, angle of a building; plur. [illegible].

khas , B.D. 172, 15, parts of the face (?) eyelids (?)

khasbet 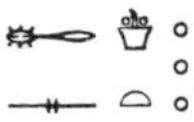, lapis lazuli; see [illegible] [illegible].

khasru , Peasant 288, exiles, banished ones.

khaqses , P.S.B. 28, 124 . . . .

khak , , to enclose, to gird; var. [illegible].

khaku , "despicable," a term of abuse; plur. [illegible].

khak-ȧb , 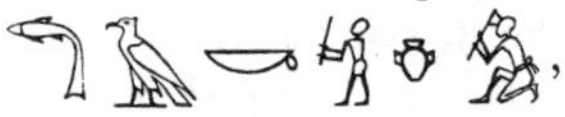, "despicable" and accursed being, foe, enemy, rebel; plur. .

Khak-ȧb , Nesi-Ȧmsu 32, 33, a form of Āapep.

khaker 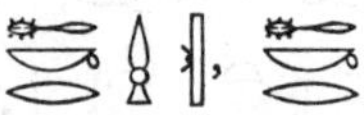, to adorn, to decorate, to put on armour; var. ; Copt. ϩⲱⲱⲕⲉ, ϭⲱⲕ.

khakeru, ornaments, decorations, jewellery, armour.

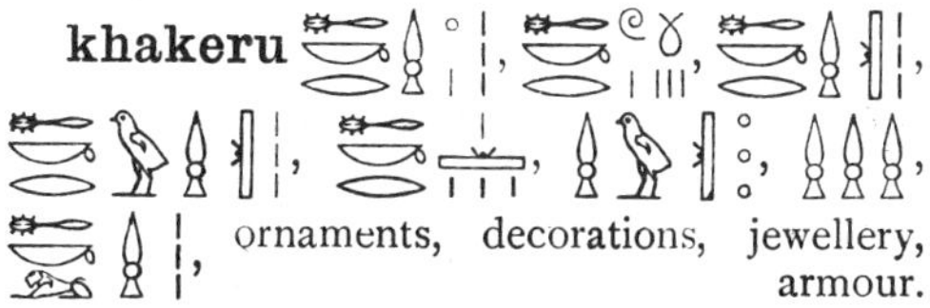

khakerit, ornaments, collar, pectoral, head-attire.

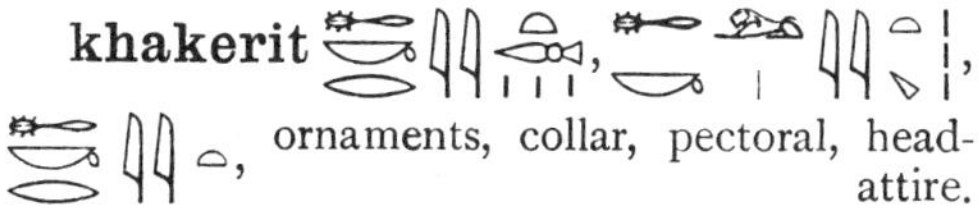

khakerit, a name of the Eye of Horus.

Khakeritha-t, Ombos II, 130, a goddess.

khatt, to cut reeds, to gather.

khatkhat, to seek for; Copt. ϩⲟⲧϩⲉⲧ, ϧⲉⲧϧⲉⲧ.

khati, Rev. 12, 19, Rev. 11, 158, to sail downstream; Copt. ϧⲁϯ.

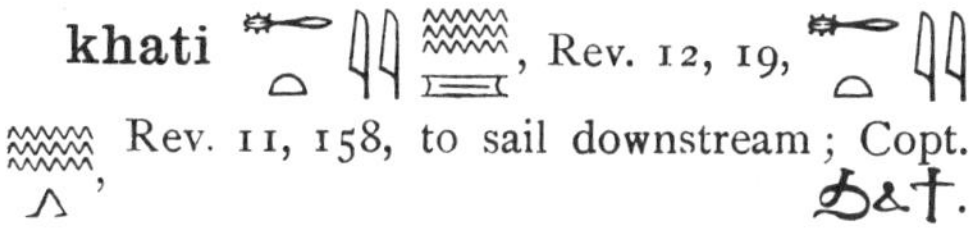

Khati, B.D. (Saïte) 112, 1, the god of .

Khatu, B.D. 112, 1, the gods of .

khateb, Rev. 12, 29, to slay, to kill; see ; Copt. ϩⲱⲧⲃ̄.

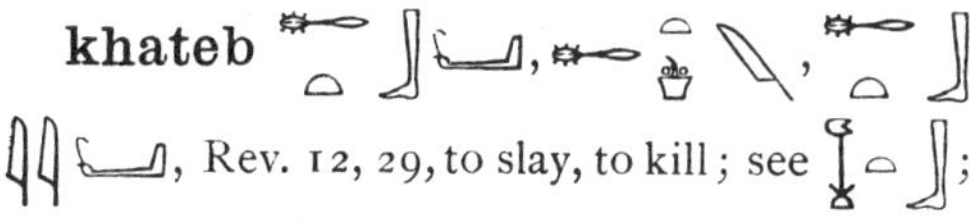

Khateb-mut-f, Berg. I, 15, a serpent-god.

khatr, to destroy, to overthrow; Copt. ϩⲧⲁⲣ in ϩⲧⲁⲣⲧⲣⲉ, ϣⲧⲟⲣ in ϣⲧⲟⲣⲧⲣ.

Khatri, Ṭuat VIII, the Ichneumon-god in the Ṭuat.

khatheb, L.D. III, 140c, to slay, to kill.

khaṭ, I, 51, child, for .

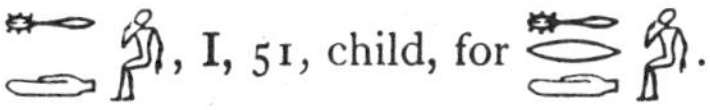

khaṭ 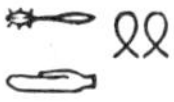 ....

khaṭ-áb =, timid, coward, a term of abuse applied to an enemy.

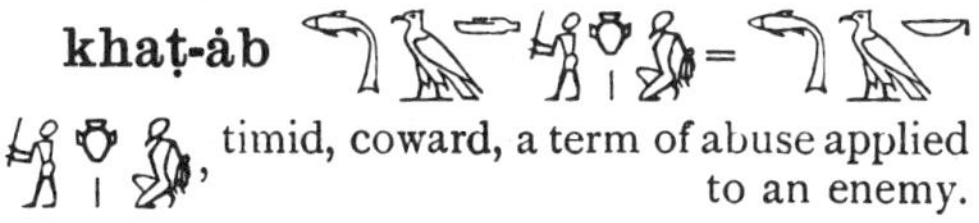

khaṭi, to sail down the river; Copt. ϧⲁϯ.

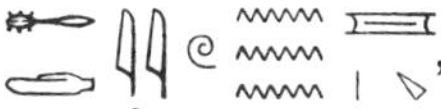

khaṭeb, to kill, to slay; Copt. ϩⲱⲧⲃ̄, ϧⲱⲧⲉⲃ.

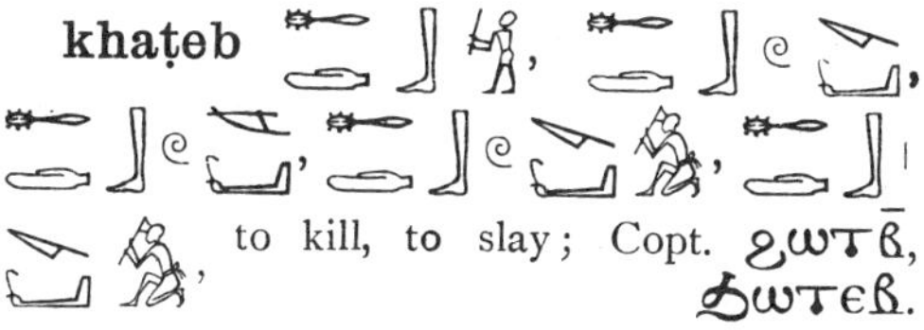

khaṭbu, butchers, executioners.

khaṭeb, Rev. 11, 160, butcher's knife, sacrificial knife.

khaṭer, Peasant 138, Prisse Pap. 4, 3, to drop, to keep quiet, to be helpless.

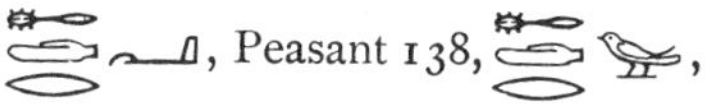

khen, khenu, U. 213, 438, M. 142, 589 (var., N. 648, T. 250), T. 178, Rec. 36, 210, the most private part of a building, the most sacred part of a temple, dwelling, cabin of a boat, house, palace; T. 178, he who is inside the palace, *i.e.*, the king; varr. 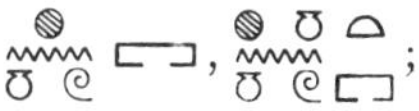 ; Copt. ϩⲟⲩⲛ, ϧⲟⲩⲛ.

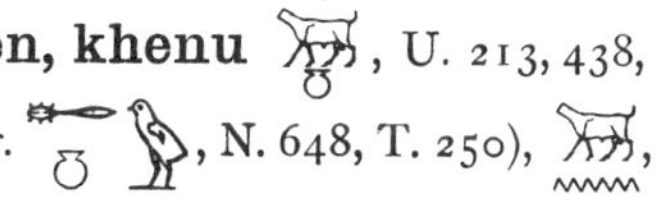

khenu, Leyd. Pap. 7, 6, Dream Stele 40, the Court, the capital, the town in which the king lives; L.D. III, 194, 16.

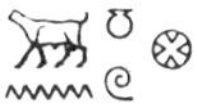

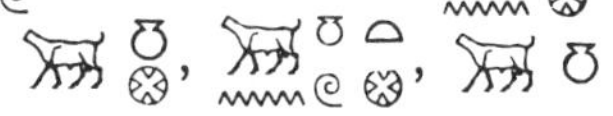

khenu, Rec. 29, 144, the innermost part of the body.

khenu with **m**, Rec. 27, 219, within.

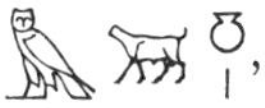

khen, Methen 10, walled enclosure.

Khen, the front land, the South; Middle Egypt (?)

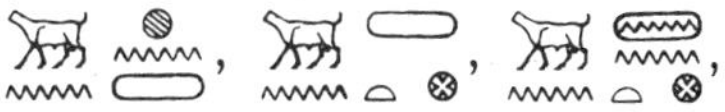

Khenutiu (?) , , Tombos Stele 5, inland folk, peoples or tribes from the interior.

khen unṭu (?) , the waist of a ship.

Khen-pet (?) , Ṭuat IV, a god.

Khen-ḥer[t] , Denderah III, 12, a Horus god.

khen , T. 208, 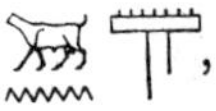, I, 130, to cover over, cover, covering, awning on a boat, tent; var. , P. 160.

khen-t 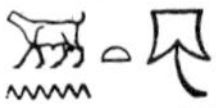, Rec. 1, 48, 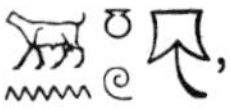, Rechnungen 69, 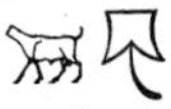, hide, skin, water-skin, leather bottle; plur. 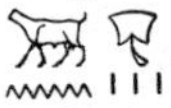, Mar. Karn. 55, 62, 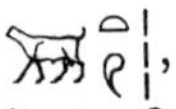, Israel Stele 5, , A.Z. 1905, 9, , Peasant 14.

khen 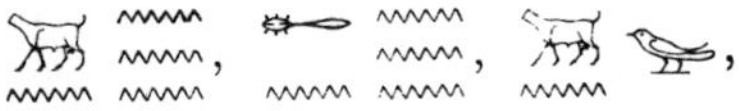, , less, what is cut off.

khen , , L.D. III, 140B, . IV, 655, brook, well, pool, lake, a water-station in the desert.

khennn 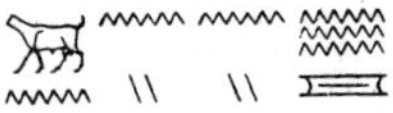, water-course, stream.

kheni 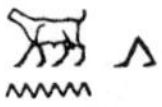, IV, 984, , Love Songs 7, 5, 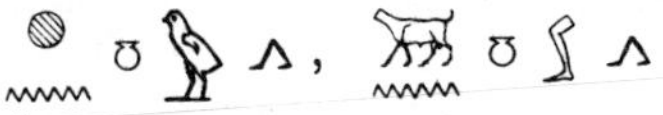, 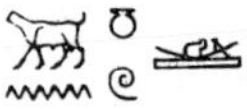, Åmen. 26, 17, to go in, to come to or go near, to approach, to come by boat; Copt. ϩⲱⲛ.

khenu , visitor, incomer.

khen-t , an entrance, an approach.

khenkheni 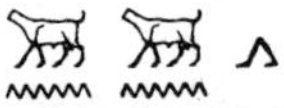, L.D. III, 219E, 9, Rev. 6, 40, 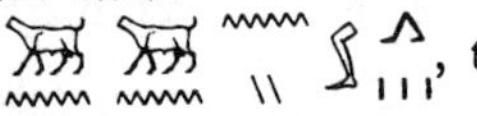, to run towards something, to go in, to enter; , Åmen. 11, 13.

kheni , T. 252, , 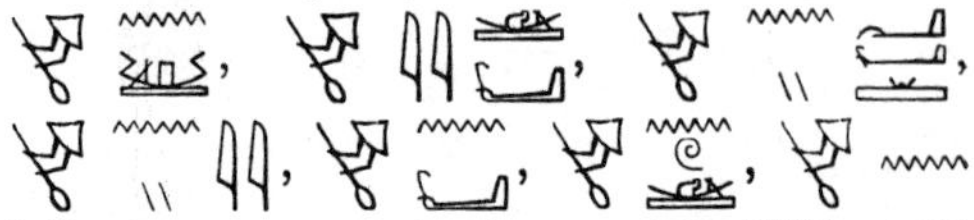, , Rev. 14, 34, , , to travel by boat, to sail, to row, to ferry over, to transport.

khenn 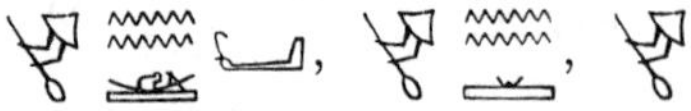, , P. 578, to navigate, to sail a boat, to row, to paddle.

khenit , , ferryman; plur. [illegible], IV, 1006, [illegible], Meïr 2, 6, [illegible].

khennu [illegible], M. 550, [illegible], [illegible], sailor, rower, paddler; plur. [illegible], T. 340, [illegible], U. 409, [illegible], IV, 1192, [illegible], [illegible], Rev. 14, 8.

khenn-t [illegible], transport.

khen-t [illegible], M. 395, [illegible], [illegible], transportation, a ferry-boat, transport.

khenn-t [illegible], T. 344, boat, skiff, ferry-boat.

khen-t åḥu [illegible], [illegible], Koller 3, 6, cattle-boat.

khen-t [illegible], IV, 1008, [illegible], IV, 753, [illegible], a procession of boats, periplus, panegyric; [illegible], festival of the periplus; [illegible], the great periplus; [illegible], periplus of Osiris.

Khennu , Ṭuat IX, a singing-god.

Khennu 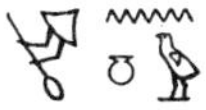, Ṭuat III, the steersman of the boat Pakhet.

Khen-unnut-f , Ṭuat IX, a singing-god.

Khen-n-urṭ-f , Ṭuat III, a rower in the boat Heres.

Khenn-set 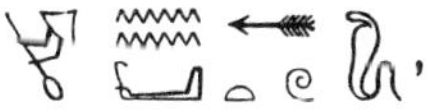, Denderah III, 29, a serpent-god.

khenti (?) , A.Z. 1905, 33,  IV, 1185, image, statue, likeness, portrait, figure; plur. , divine form.

khen, khenn , Rec. 30, 191, 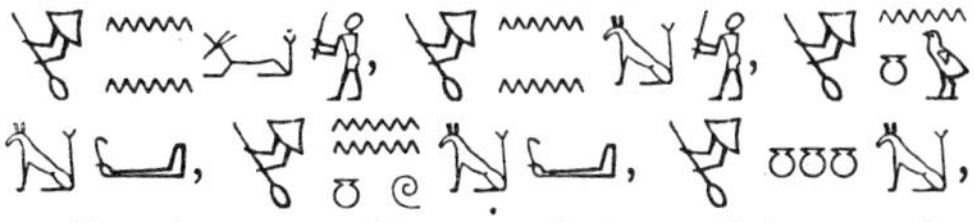, to disturb, to trouble, to rebel, to violate, to be disturbed internally, to be sick;  , calamity (?) misfortune (?); 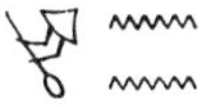 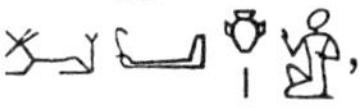, IV, 969, Thes. 1481, restless or unquiet man; , N. 948, disturbers of the peace.

khenkhen , to disturb, to scare, to terrify, to frighten away.

khenu , U. 311,  , T. 253, N. 1229,  disturbance, trouble, revolt, rebellion, strife, opposition.

khennu , , disorder, confusion, disturbance, disaster, calamity, storm, commotion among the elements; 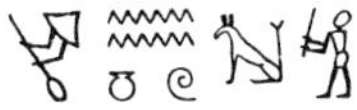 , Rec. 32, 178, rebels, rioters.

khenn-t , disturbance, destruction.

khenu-nn 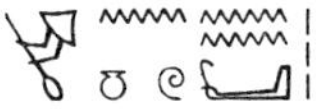, Åmen. 19, 19, disturbers (?)

khenn-tȧ , T. 269, M. 428, disturbed, disarranged.

Khennu , U. 445, T. 254, M. 773, P. 662, 780, a fighting-god.

khenui , U. 427, , T. 245, the two fighters, *i.e.*, Horus and Set.

khenn 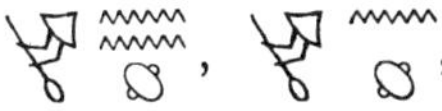, nausea, indigestion.

khen-t , internal disturbance of the body, nausea, upset of the stomach.

khen-ā (?) , embrace (?)

khen , to beg, to beseech, to demand.

khnem 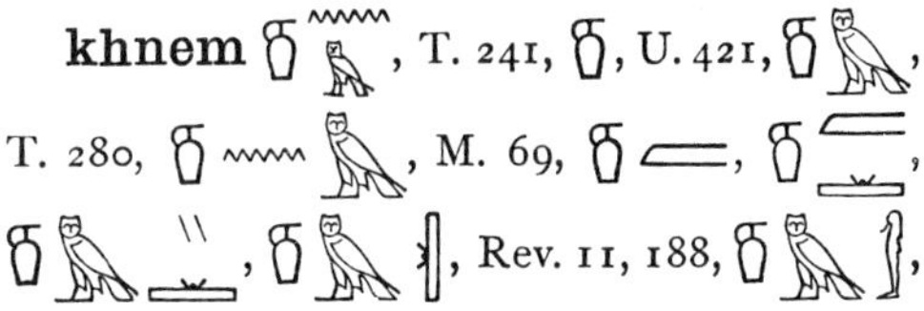, T. 241, U. 421, T. 280, M. 69, Rev. 11, 188, Rev. 11, 181, to unite with, to join, to join together, to reach or attain, to associate with; var. , U. 558; Copt. ϣⲟⲛⲃ̄.

khnem-t , N. 311, M. 69, 78, IV, 221, etc., associate, confidant, friend, a title of certain queens of Egypt.

khnemu 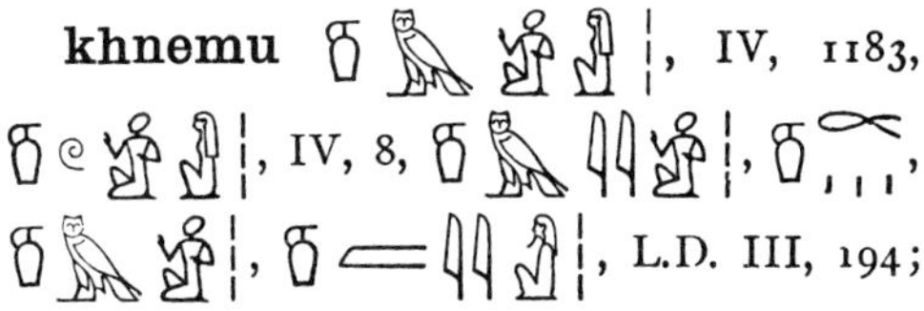, IV, 1183, IV, 8, L.D. III, 194; var. , associates, companions, friends.

khnem , to build, to put together.

khnemu 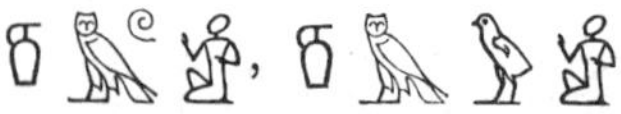, P.S.B. 10, 45, builder, mason, cook.

khnem åten 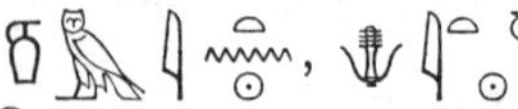, , Thes. 434, conjunction of the sun; 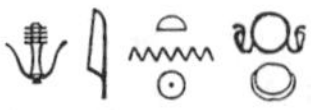, Rec. 3, 49, a conjunction of the disk morning and evening.

Khnem ānkhtt 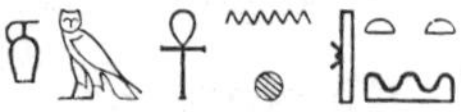, a title of the necropolis.

Khnem , U. 556, , , , the flat-horned Ram-god, creator of the universe; later forms of the god's name are :— 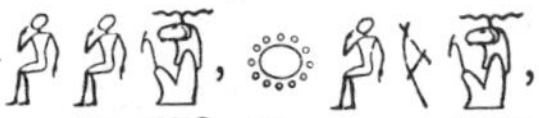, , A.Z. 1869, 25; compare Heb. חנום in the name תחנום = , Aram. Pap. 22; Gnostic χνουμις, χνουφις, χνουβις.

Khnem 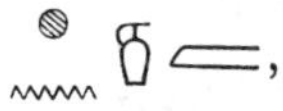, the god of the 28th day of the month.

Khnem , Ṭuat XI, a god who supplied offerings.

Khnemit 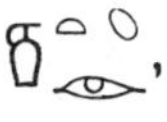, the left eye of Horus, *i.e.*, the moon.

Khnemit 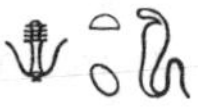, consort of Khnem.

Khnemit , P. 682, a goddess.

Khnemiu , Ṭuat XI, a group of gods who counted time.

Khnemut 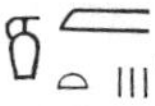, Ṭuat XI, a group of goddesses of time and years.

Khnemit-ur-t , P. 62, 116, N. 103, , M. 69, 97, , B.D. 178, 33, "Great Creatrix"—a title of Nut.

Khnemit-em-ānkh-ånnuit  , B.D. 141 and 148, one of the seven divine cows; var.  .

Khnem Neb , one of the seven forms of Khnemu.

Khnem Neb-Uāb-t , Denderah IV, 83, Khnemu, lord of Elephantine and Philae.

Khnem Neb-per-Meḥti 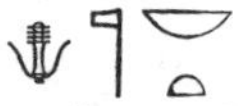 , Denderah IV, 83, a form of Khnemu.

Khnem Neb-Peshnu  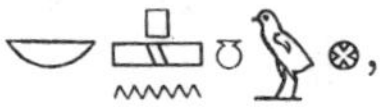, B.D. (Saïte) 36, 2, a form of Khnemu.

Khnem Neb-Smen , Denderah IV, 83, a form of Khnemu.

Khnem Neb-ta-ānkhtt  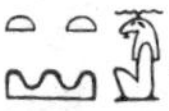, Khnemu as lord of the Other World.

Khnem Neb-Tcherur  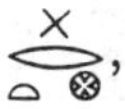, Denderah IV, 83, a form of Khnemu.

Khnem-neḥep , Khnemu the potter.

Khnem-Rā , [illegible], Khnemu-Rā.

Khnem-renit (?) [illegible], Ṭuat XI, a ram-god.

Khnem-Ḥeru-Ḥetep [illegible] [illegible], B.D. 142, V, 8, a form of Khnemu.

Khnem-khenti-åneb-f [illegible], [illegible], a form of Khnemu.

Khnem-khenti-uar-f [illegible], Ombos I, 93, [illegible], a god of offerings.

Khnem-khenti-per-ānkh  , Khnemu, master of the house of life.

Khnem-khenti-netchem-tchem-ānkh-t , Khnemu, master of the marriage-chamber.

Khnem-khenti-taui-neteru  , Khnemu, master of the lands of the gods.

Khnem-sekhet-ȧsh . . . . f 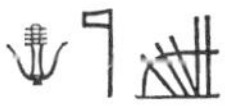 , one of the seven forms of Khnemu.

Khnem-qenbti , , Ṭuat II, a ram-god with a knife-shaped phallus.

Khnem-qeṭ-ḥeru-nebu  , B.M. 32, 202, Khnemu, maker of mankind.

khnemit , Rec. 21, 14, IV, 1064, , Metternich Stele 171, , spring, well, fountain, cistern; plur., Ḳubbân Stele, Israel Stele 23; Copt. ϩⲟⲛⲃⲉ

khnemit   B.D. 163, 16, the "western well of Egypt."

khnemit ḥer , the "upper pool"; site unknown.

khnemit ur-t , the name of an object painted on coffins.

khnemit 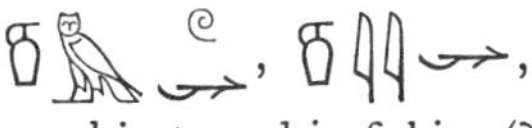, Rev. 11, 172, a wooden object used in fishing (?)

khnemiu , birds, waterfowl.

khnemes-ti 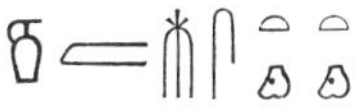, nostrils.

khenseṭ , a tiara or crown.

khenk , a kind of stuff, a garment.

kher , later, under, having or possessing something; Copt. ϩⲁ, ϧⲁ.

kheri 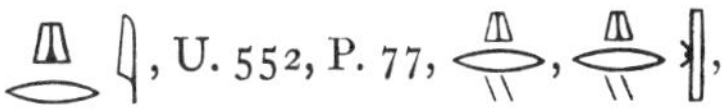, U. 552, P. 77, , under, subservient to, a person or thing under something, lower, the lower part; Copt. ϩⲁⲉ, ϧⲁⲉ; , face downwards; downwards; under the favour of.

kherȧ, kheri , subject, serf, vassal, servant; fem. ; plur. 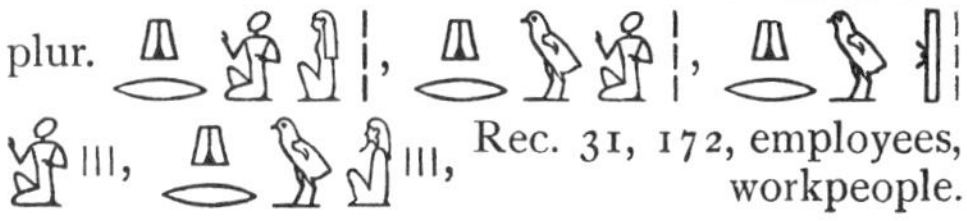, Rec. 31, 172, employees, workpeople.

kherit 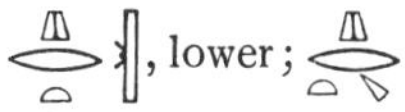, lower; IV, 919, estate.

kheriu , the lower, or last, as opposed to , the upper or first.

kheru  = Copt. ϩⲣⲁⲓ, ϧⲣⲏⲓ.

Kheriu , beings of earth, beings and things terrestrial, those who are below; Copt. ϩⲣⲁⲓ, ϧⲣⲏⲓ.

kheri ȧst re 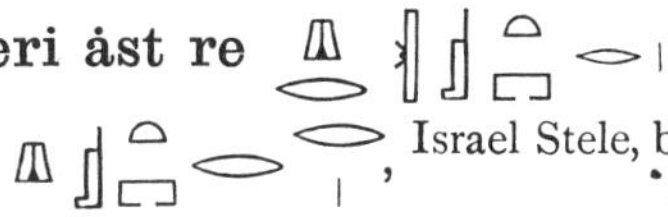, Rec. 21, 43, Israel Stele, because of.

kheri ā , "under the hand of," *i.e.*, assistant, deputy; 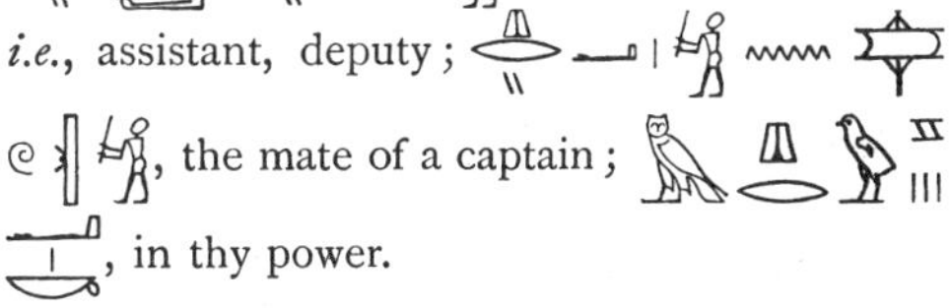, the mate of a captain; in thy power.

kheri peḥ-t 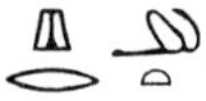, Metternich Stele 51, behind, "under the back of"; 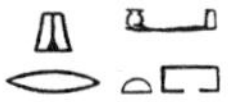, ibid. 51.

kheri meṭu (?) 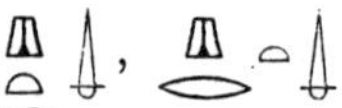, subordinate, deputy of the .

kheri er ḥeri , P. 1116B, 55, bottom side uppermost.

kheri ḥa-t , before, formerly, originally.

kheri khait , he who is suffering from sickness, the patient.

kheri khetem 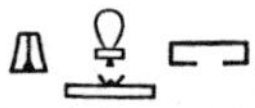, Décrets 19, "under the seal," said specially of orders sealed with the palace seal.

kheri ta ḥa-t , Rev. 12, 39, at the front; Copt. ϩⲁⲧϩⲏ.

kheri ṭem-t 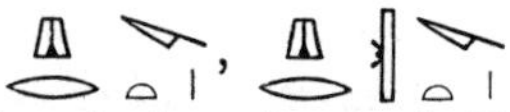, 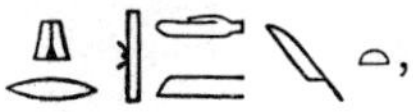, he who is under the knife, a sufferer from a disease.

kheri tchatcha , Thes. 1295, deputy, he who is under the chief.

kheri , U. 214, scrotum; **kherui** , P. 662, 780, M. 773, , U. 532, T. 27, , P. 183, , , , the testicles.

Khert (?) , L.D. III, 277A, a god, the Mole-god; compare Heb. חֹלֶד.

Kherit , P. 705, a goddess mentioned with .

Khert-neter 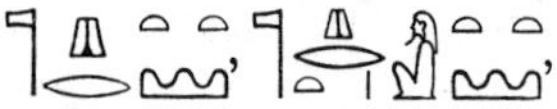, 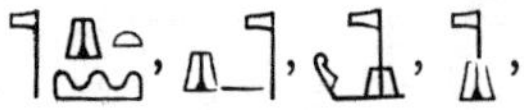, the cemetery, necropolis.

Khertt-neter , Berg. II, 12, the necropolis personified.

kher 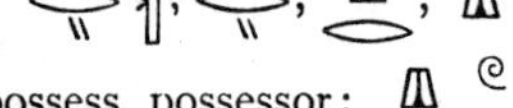, to have, to hold, to possess, possessor; , possessors.

khert, kherit , IV, 968, , IV, 656, 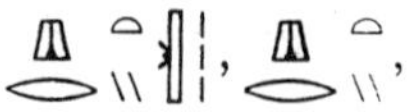, 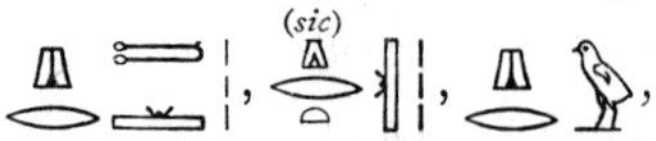, goods, objects, possessions, property, wants, needs, share, portion, the things which belong to someone, events, circumstances, matters, affairs, course of events; Copt. ϩⲣⲉ, ϭⲣⲉ;  , everybody's business or affairs; , the affairs of the gods; 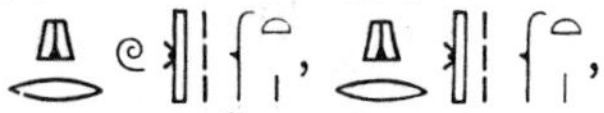, annual produce; 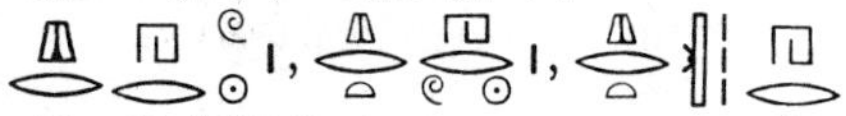 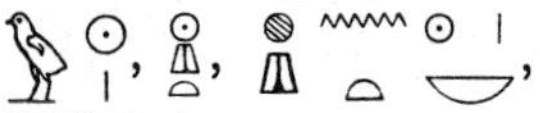, IV, 482, 992, [illegible] [illegible], IV, 743, [illegible], [illegible], [illegible], the thing of the day, the business or matter of every day, the daily round or course; , the matters or affairs of to-day.

kherit [illegible] [illegible], what one needs, *i.e.*, provisions, means of subsistence; Copt. ϩⲣⲉ, ϭⲣⲉ.

kheri-ā [illegible], Rec. 6, 9, dues, revenues, impost, tax.

kheri ḥeb [illegible], I, 138, [illegible] [illegible], Rec. 27, 230, [illegible],  [illegible], a priest or magician, the reader of the holy books in the temple or at funerals; [illegible], Rec. 11, 131; Gr. Ταριχευτής.

kheri ḥeb āshau , A.Z. 99, 95, the priest of the people.